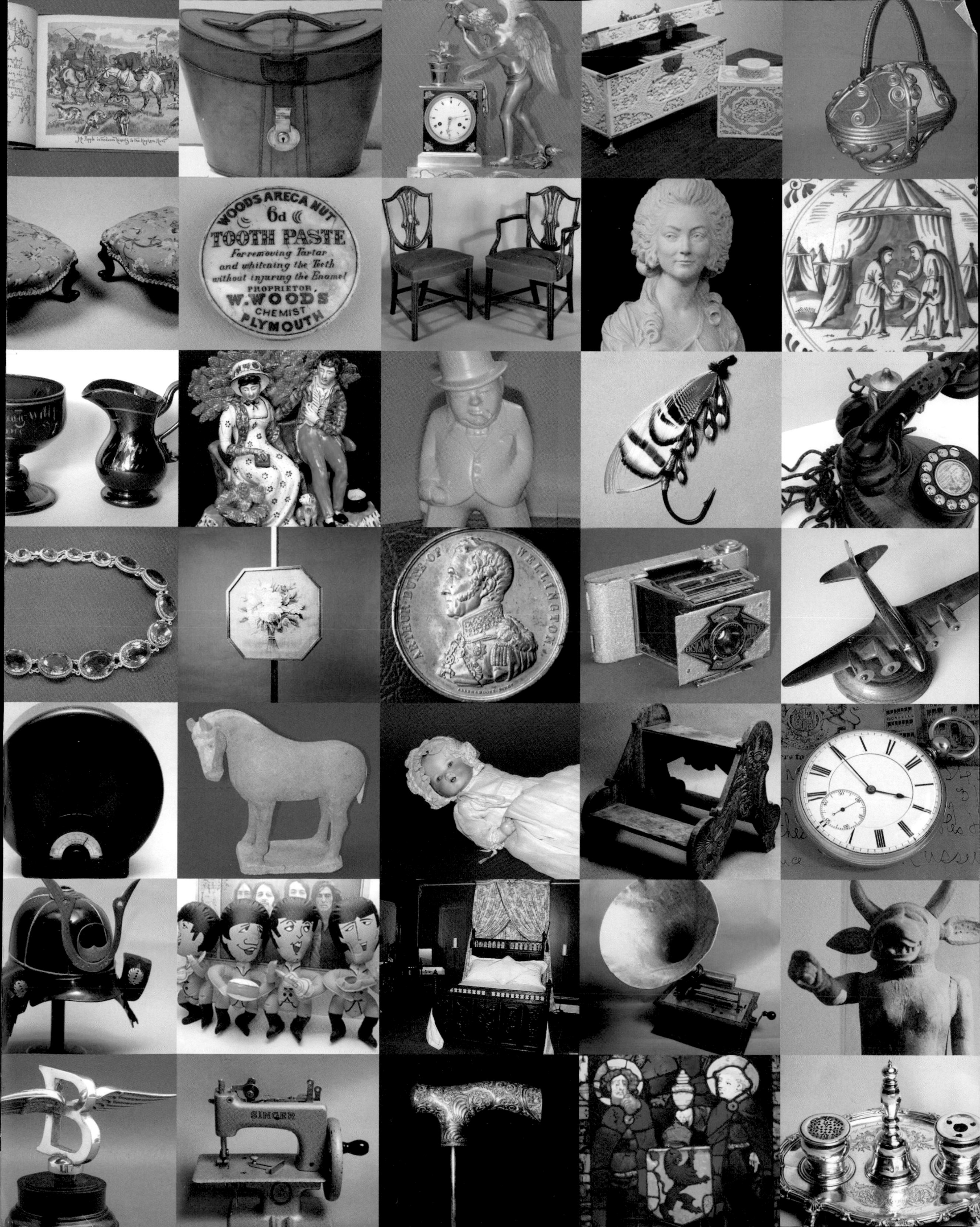
WOODS ARECA NUT
6d
TOOTH PASTE
For removing Tartar
and whitening the Teeth
without injuring the Enamel
PROPRIETOR
W. WOODS
CHEMIST
PLYMOUTH
ARTHUR DUKE OF WELLINGTON
ENSIGN
SINGER

CARLTON BOOKS

THIS IS A CARLTON BOOK

This edition published in 2003 by Carlton Books Ltd
A Division of the Carlton Publishing Group
20 Mortimer Street
London W1T 3JW

A CIP catalogue for this book is available from the British Library.

ISBN 1 84222 931 1

Printed in Dubai

Martin Miller

THE COMPLETE GUIDE TO ANTIQUES

CONTENTS

ACKNOWLEDGEMENTS

GENERAL EDITOR
Martin Miller

EDITORS
Marianne Blake
Peter Blake
Simon Blake
Richard Bundy
Abigail Zoe Martin
Michael Spilling
Charlotte Stock

PHOTOGRAPHERS
Neil Fox
Anders Gramer
Ryan Green
Carmen Klammer
Anna Malni
Abigail Zoe Martin
Chris Smailes
James Beam Van Etten
Lee Walsh

DESIGN
Michelle Pickering

HOW TO USE THIS BOOK

I started publishing antiques guides in 1969 – and they have always been very successful – but one criticism that I have heard is from people saying, rather wistfully, 'I loved the book, but what a pity that so many of the items were already sold.' And it was perfectly true. *The Complete Guide to Antiques* was designed more as a compilation of information from auction sales that had already taken place than as immediate guide – as a reference book rather than a handbook.

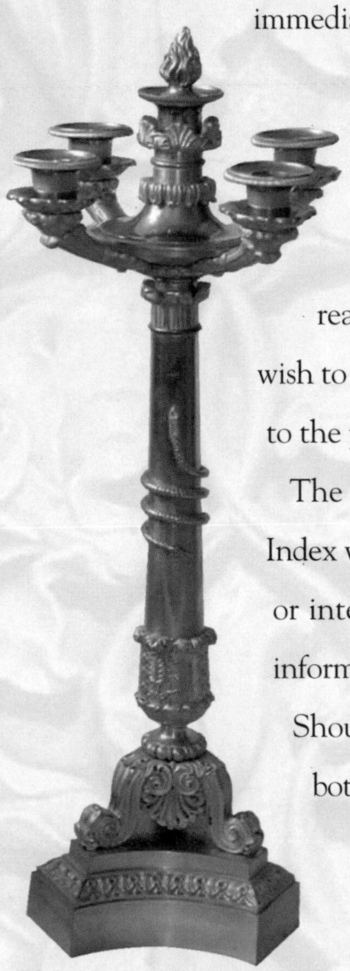

The difference between this book and other antiques guides is that here we have used retailers, rather than auction houses, as our sources of information. A reputable and experienced dealer's assessment of the price of an antique is at least as reliable – and usually a great deal more reasoned – than a price achieved at auction, and so even when an item you wish to purchase from the book turns out to have been sold, you have a reliable guide to the price you should pay when you happen upon another.

The book is designed for maximum visual interest and appeal. The Contents and Index will tell you in which area to find items that you are specifically seeking, but the collector, enthusiast or interior designer will profit most from reading through a section or several sections and gathering information and inspiration as they go.

Should you happen upon something that you wish to purchase, simply note the dealer reference to the bottom right of the entry and look up the dealer's full name and details in the Directory of Dealers section towards the back of the book. You can telephone, fax and, in many cases, visit the dealer's website. All the dealers who have helped us with the book will be happy to assist you, and if the piece you wish to buy has already been sold, they will almost certainly be able to help you find another. The price shown against an entry is per individual item, unless the heading and description refer to more than one item, a set, or pair. Should you wish to sell an item, the relevant section and dealer reference will again be of help, but do not expect to be offered the same price at which the delaer is selling.

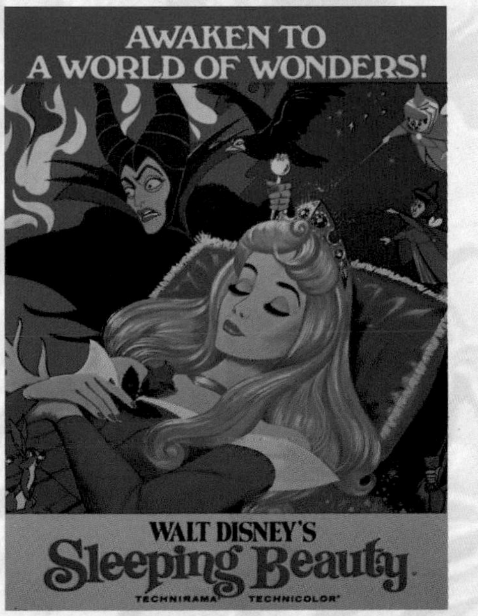

We hope you find these instructions easy to follow. Good luck and enjoy your journey into the world of antiques.

INTRODUCTION

The world of antiques is probably one of the most fascinating, challenging and, to the newcomer, one of the most confusing and impenetrable. *The Complete Guide to Antiques* is an invaluable part of your arsenal if you are starting out in the world of antiques or are a serious collector already.

The Complete Guide to Antiques contains a vast array of items from the main countries of Europe and the Orient. Unlike many publications, I have selected antiques, collectables and works of art that have recently been for sale in antique shops or markets in Great Britain. All the illustrations have been photographed and selected by our team to bring the reader a comprehensive cross section of items that can be purchased in the market place and not just admired in a museum or gallery.

The Complete Antiques Guide covers all the essential categories of interest, such as furniture, porcelain and pottery, glass, clocks, textiles and silver, but we have also included many items which, although not strictly antiques, are a massive part of the antiques trade: comics, telephones, car mascots, photographs and stuffed parrots among other collectable items.

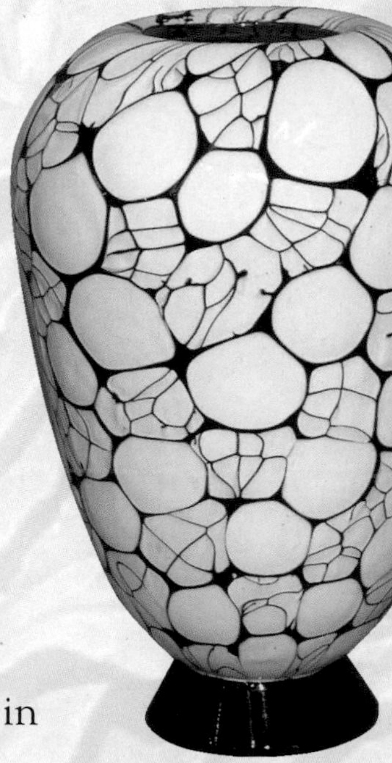

The Complete Guide to Antiques is a definitive compilation of many styles from many periods and countries, and aims to give newcomers and keen collectors an extensive understanding of what is collectable and how to identify and compare.

When collecting antiques, the importance of comparison cannot be overemphasised and it is only with experience that small differences and variations in

style and quality can be recognised. One question I am frequently asked is, 'how do I know if an item is genuine?'. The answer comes with time, experience and by absorbing books such as this. When you have the answer to this question, your enjoyment will really begin. It is much like mastering the clutch-control on a car or learning to ride a bike – from that point on, it's pure pleasure. Any publication in isolation has a limit to its resources and must, therefore, be used in conjunction with getting out and handling antiques and collectables, picking the brains of specialists and making friends with dealers – these relationships can save you a fortune.

One of the difficulties for the newcomer to antiques is valuing an item. Once you have satisfied yourself that the items you are looking to acquire are indeed what you want and what they purport to be, then the problem is determining their worth. *The Complete Guide to Antiques* is an invaluable resource. It offers the retail value on over 6,000 fully-illustrated items and information about where a similar item may be purchased. By providing a price list, *The Complete Guide to Antiques* offers a starting point from which to assess the value of an item you wish to purchase. People are generally unsure about whether the asking price of the item they wish to purchase is fair and they get nothing short of paranoid if the treasure they are interested in has no price or a code displayed. Codes are for the trade and if you know the keyword, you can tell the price. Reputable dealers and members of the British Antique Dealers Association have a code to uphold and if you have any complaints about any of its members, the association are only too happy to help you out.

The Complete Guide to Antiques is a must-have for all antiques enthusiasts and will prove to be an invaluable source of information for years to come.

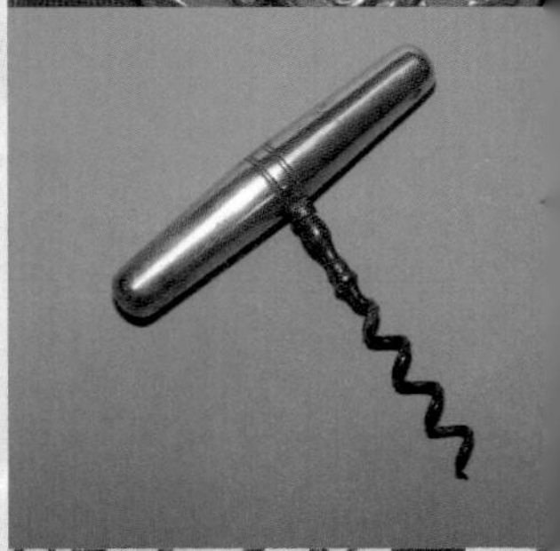

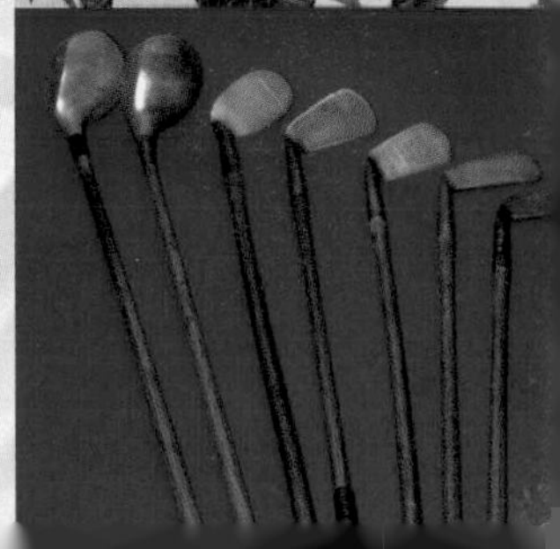

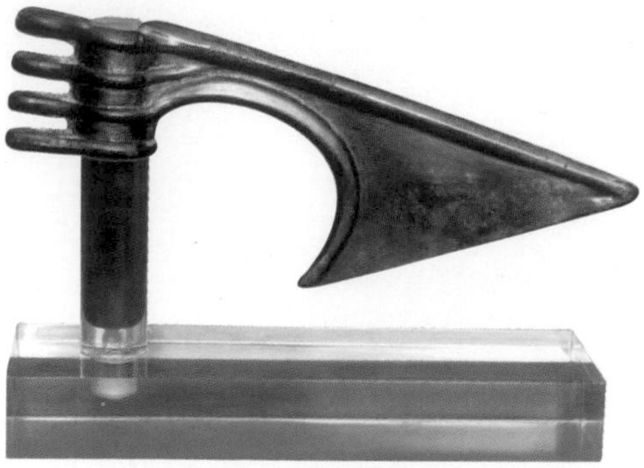

ANTIQUITIES

Most people don't even realise that an antiquity that seems to many to be something reserved for the shelves of the finest museum can also find a place in your home. Museums have far more material than can be displayed; for example, the Museum of Mexico has a million pieces of pre-Columbian artefacts in its basement, such as coins, jewellery and everyday utensils, that increasingly have become part of the collector's world. Rock star Mick Jagger has been collecting them for 30 years, while country legend Johnny Cash specialises in coins from biblical times. Not only are ancient coins items of incredible beauty, they have also become an investment, with yearly returns often exceeding 25 per cent.

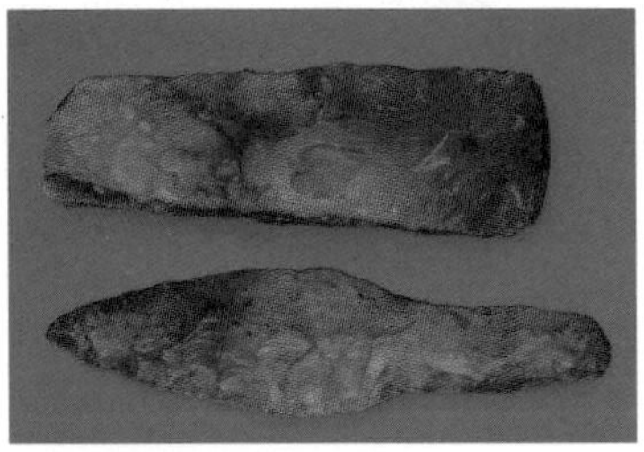

△ Neolithic Stone Flint

- *3600–2500 BC*

A large flint arrow head from Denmark, 18cm long and a large polished flint axe.

- *length 16cm/axe*
- £750 • Pars

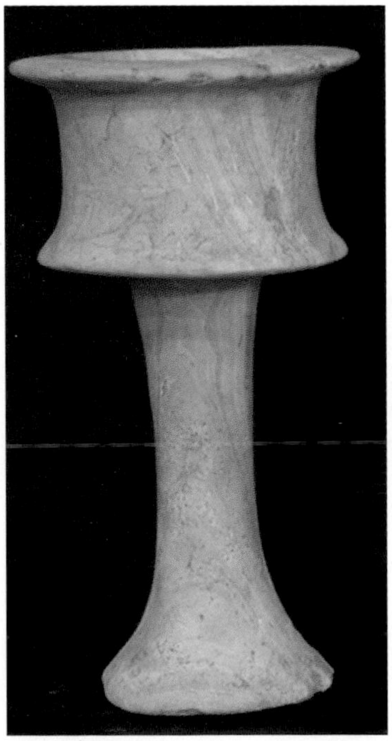

◁ Alabaster Cup

- *3000 BC*

Alabaster cup from Afghanistan, carved from one piece of stone, with a concave body, and an extended stem, raised on a splayed foot.

- *height 24cm*
- £1,500 • Sultani

◁ Bactrian Idol

- *3rd millennium BC*

A Bactrian idol from Central Asia, with granite base inscribed with geometric patterns.

- *height 8.5cm*
- £1,900 • Shahdad

△ Clay Cylinder

- *circa 2200 BC*

Royal cylinder bearing inscription of the King of Larsa.

- *height 33cm*
- £220 • Pars

◁ Tablet

- *circa 3000 BC*

A well-preserved and well-written fragment of a Mesopotamian pictographic tablet on clay.

- *length 10cm*
- £1,200 • Pars

△ Cuneiform Tablet

- *2500–1500 BC*

One of a group of Sumerian and Babylonian cuneiform tablets with administrative texts recording lists of produce, livestock and named persons.

- *length 10cm*
- £250 • Pars

△ Samarian Clay Cylinder

- *2300–2200 BC*

A clay cylinder bearing a royal inscription of Sin-Illinam, King of Larsa. Text refers to royal life.

- *height 15cm*
- £4,000 • Pars

▽ Camel Oil Burner

• *circa 2000 BC*
Stylised two-headed camel oil burner with raised pillar to its back. Kerman, Southern Iran.
• *height 19cm*
• £400 • Shiraz

▽ Foundation Cone

• *circa 2100 BC*
Foundation cone from Gudea, Sumaria, for Ningirso, warrior of Enil, ruler of Lagash.
• *length 14cm*
• £300 • Pars

▽ Terracotta Vase

• 2200–*1800BC*
Harra Pan civilisation terracotta vase of baluster form, from the Indus Valley, with black banding and three geometric panels.
• *height 23cm*
• £650 • Rasoul Gallery

△ Harra Pan Vase

• 2200–*1800 BC*
Small terracotta vase of ovoid form with a deep truncated neck and geometric design applied to the body, from the Harra Pan civilisation.
• *height 9cm*
• £250 • Rasoul Gallery

△ Terracotta Wine Strainer

• 2200–*1800 BC*
Terracotta wine strainer of cylindrical form, with uniform perforations within the body.
• *height 15cm*
• £600 • Rasoul Gallery

△ Pilgrim's Flask

• *1st millennium BC*
An Egyptian, terracotta circular pilgrim's flask with spiral detail.
• *height 43cm*
• £250 • Pars

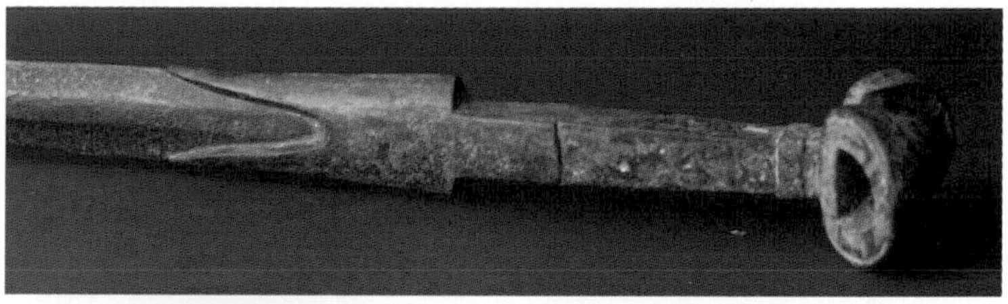

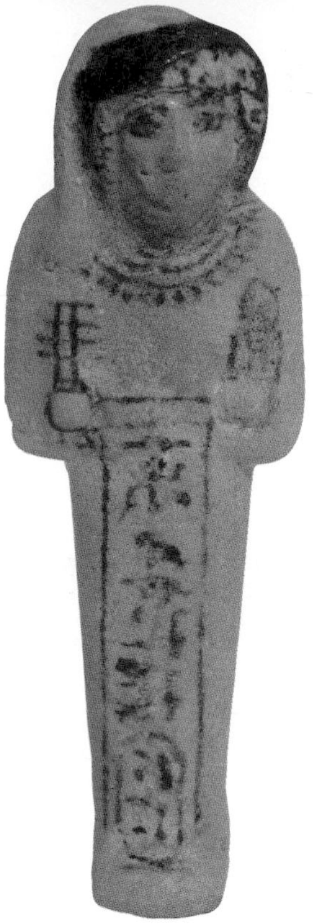

△ Bronze Sword

• *circa 1200 BC*
Bronze Persian sword with engraved hilt and scrolled pommel. From Luristan.
• *length 98cm*
• £2,500 • Pars

△ Bull Oil Vessel

• *circa 1000 BC*
Amlash Persian pottery bull oil vessel, on four legs with head upright and pronounced horns and hump.
• *height 22cm*
• £3,000 • Shiraz

△ Ushabti

• *1000–900 BC*
An Egyptian Ushabti of the third intermediate period, with green faïence and a column of hieroglyphic text including a Royal Cartouche. Dates from the 22nd dynasty.
• *height 17.5cm*
• £2,800 • Pars

▽ Fertility Goddesses

• *1st millennium BC*
Two carved ivory Bactrian fertility goddesses of bulbous proportions accentuating their femininity.
• *height 7cm*
• £6,500 • Yazdani

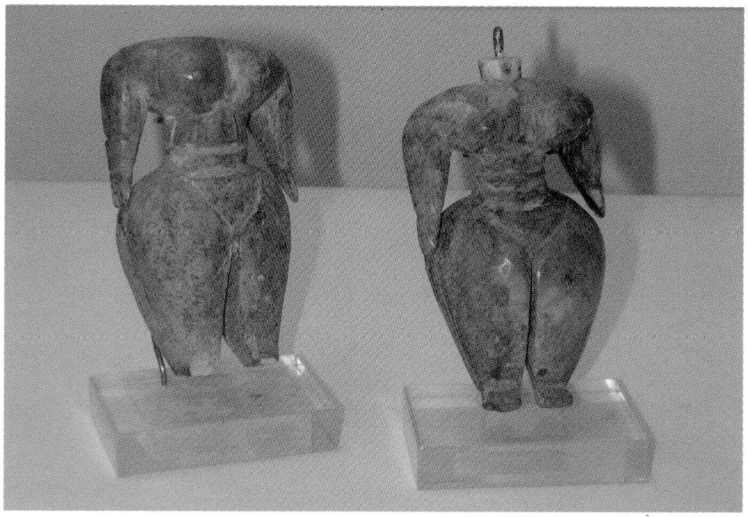

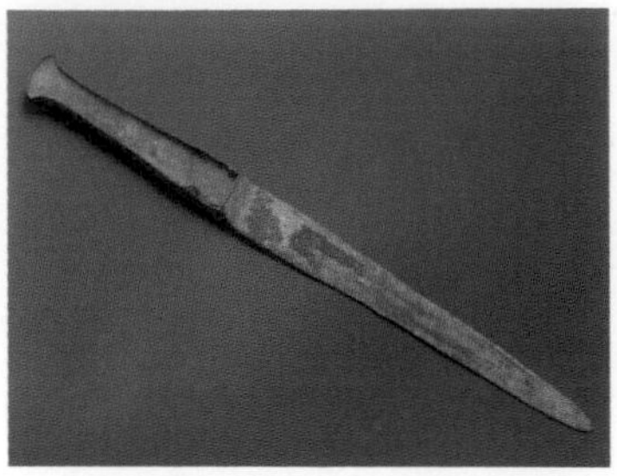

△ Dagger

- *circa 1000 BC*

A Persian, sand-cast bronze dagger from Luristan.

- *length 33cm*
- £220 • Pars

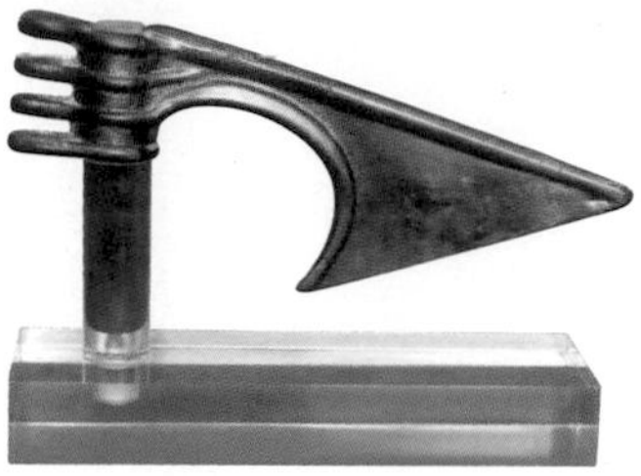

△ Axe Head

- *circa 8th century BC*

An axe head from Luristan, Western Iran, showing good patination.

- *length 18cm*
- £450 • Pars

△ Master of Animals

- *8th century BC*

A bronze icon showing the master of animals god. Persian, from Luristan in Western Iran.

- *height 12cm*
- £800 • Pars

▽ Marble Tablet

- *8th–7th century BC*

Large fragment of Assyrian royal inscription pictographic tablet in marble, with script.

- *length 30cm*
- £3,000 • Pars

▽ Lion Paw

- *8th–7th century BC*

An Assyrian lion's paw with royal inscriptions and projection for slot in wall.

- *length 18cm*
- £2,500 • Pars

▽ Amphoriskos

- *5th century BC*

Amphoriskos with yellow and white feathering and turquoise glass handles.

- *height 14cm*
- £3,000 • Pars

▽ Amphoriskos

- *9th–6th century BC*

An amphora fashioned on a cone, with band combed into a zigzag.

- *height 12cm*
- £2,200 • Pars

△ Bridle

- *8th century BC*

A bit from a decorative bridle, fashioned in bronze in the shape of two horses.

- *length 10cm*
- £1,500 • Pars

◁ Amphoriskos

- *5th century BC*

Feather-patterned amphoriskos with an ochre background with black and white feathering and clear glass handles.

- *height 12cm*
- £2,500 • Pars

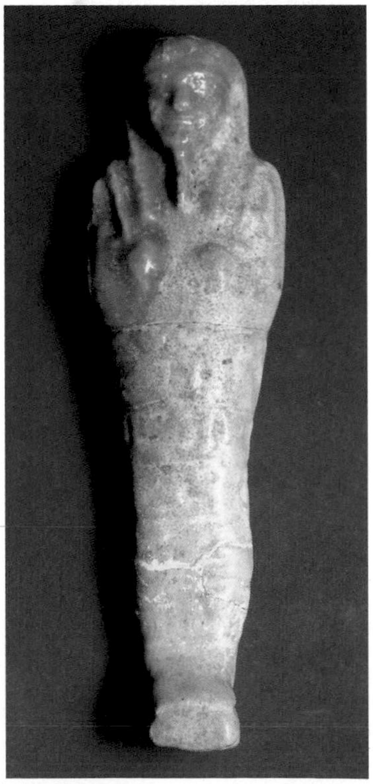

△ Shabti

- *5th century BC*

A large Egyptian Shabti in turquoise glaze with iridescence, with faded inscriptions.

- *height 19cm*
- £800 • Pars

△ Lekanis

- *circa 350–320 BC*

Lekanis drinking vessel made in Greek South Italy, hand-painted with white floral decoration on a black ground. With two large handles all on a pedestal base.

- *height 11cm*
- £500 • Pars

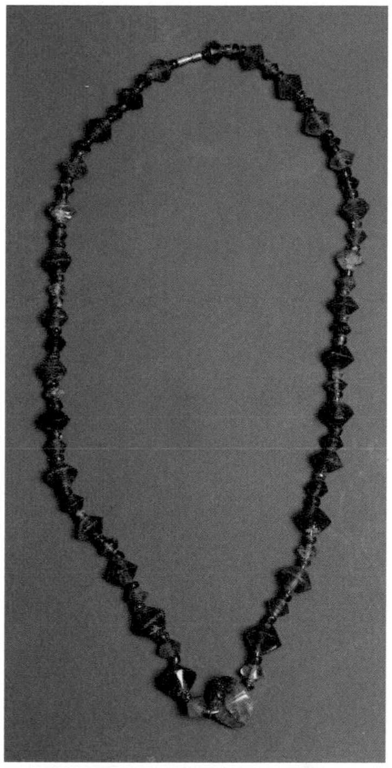

△ Amethyst Necklace

- *3rd–1st century BC*

Roman amethyst necklace with blue glass spacers.

- *length 52cm*
- £2,500 • Pars

▷ Kantharos

- *circa 320–300 BC*

A pair of South Italian, Greek kantharoi, urn-shaped with large, elegant handles, hand-painted with red figures.

- *height 25cm*
- £4,500 • Pars

△ Roman Glass Flask

- *2nd century BC*

Roman glass flask of ovoid form with fluted neck and spiral decoration with good iridescence.

- *height 10cm*
- £7,500 • Yacobs

△ Cup and Cover

- *350–320 BC*

South Italian Lekanis cup and cover with female and leaf decorations.

- *height 11cm*
- £500 • Pars

▽ Bactrian Pot

- *circa 2nd century BC*

Bactrian alabaster pot, with concave sides and splayed lip.

- *height 12cm*
- £3,200 • Yacobs

△ Marble Head

- *2nd–1st century BC*

Marble head of a Syrian prince of the Palmyran period, with strong features showing wreath with gem at centre of forehead.

- *height 20cm*
- £3,000 • Shiraz

△ Oil Lamp

- *100 BC–100 AD*

Fine Roman, bronze oil lamp with dolphin finials and stylised bird adornments and fantail scrolled handle.

- *length 15cm*
- £2,800 • Pars

▽ Glass Amphorae

- *100 BC–300 AD*

Pair of Roman amphorae of amber-coloured glass, with applied blue ribbon handles and banding around neck.

- *height 12cm*
- £5,000 • Pars

◁ Pair of Roman Beakers

- *3rd–1st century BC*

A pair of Roman beakers with a green iridescence.

- *height 9.5cm*
- £800 • Shahdad

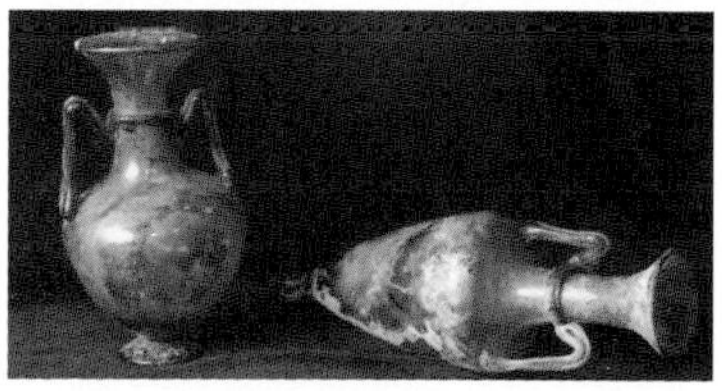

▽ Glass Bowl

- *1st century AD*

A glass bowl which has been cast and lathe-cut into a deep, rounded form and decorated with 32 diagonal ribs tapering from the base, with good iridescence.

- *diameter 12.5cm*
- £2,500 • Pars

▽ Roman Flask

- *1st century AD*

Roman blue glass flask, the body encircled with spiral threads.

- *height 9.4cm*
- £1,500 • Pars

▽ Blue Ink Well

- *1st century AD*

Royal blue and white marbled ink well; this container has been shaped into a cylinder and the top opening is quite small. The large flat base and small hole would make this a practical inkwell.

- *height 7.5cm*
- £7,000 • Pars

△ Cat Head

- *1st Century AD*

An Egyptian mummified cat head with polychrome painted features mounted on a metal shaft.

- *length 14cm*
- £5,500 • Pars

△ Face Mask

- *1st century AD*

A Romano-Egyptian face mask, with handle at back for holding in front of the face.

- *diameter 12cm*
- £200 • Pars

△ Flask

- *circa 1st century AD*

A mould-blown flask from Sidonia, of the Roman period, with floral designs.

- *height 13cm*
- £2,500 • Pars

▽ Bronze Zeus

- *1–200 AD*

A Roman statue of Zeus, cast in bronze. Mounted on a modern, wooden plinth.

- *height 15cm*
- £2,200 • Pars

▽ Roman Bottle

- *1st–3rd century AD*

Roman, ribbed-body tear bottle with handle and splayed lip. With good iridescence.

- *height 12cm*
- £680 • Shahdad

△ Egyptian Pot

- *1st–3rd century AD*

Romano-Egyptian terracotta pot modelled in the shape of the face of Bes, the dwarf god.

- *height 6cm, diameter 7cm*
- £400 • Pars

△ Roman Cameo Ring

- *circa 1st century AD*

Roman gold cameo ring decorated with a hand squeezing an ear inscribed 'Remember me and always be mine'.

- *width 2cm*
- £5,000 • Pars

△ Bronze of Selinus

- *1st–3rd century AD*

Romano-Egyptian bronze casting of the dwarf god, Selinus, shown with wings which would perhaps have formed part of the base of a table.

- *height 10.5cm*
- £600 • Pars

◁ Tear Bottle

- *1st–3rd century AD*

Roman tear bottle with spiral decoration running from base to neck. Robert Maxwell Collection.

- *height 10cm*
- £1,200 • Shahdad

▽ Necklace

- *1st–3rd century AD*

Roman necklace with iridescent beads of tubular, twisted form, with ancient gold spacers.

- *length 39cm*
- £3,000 • Pars

△ Roman Jars/Vessels

- *2nd century AD*

One jar is made of aubergine glass, decorated with iridescent glaze, the other with an interesting patina.

- *height 22cm and 23cm*
- £1,500 each • Shiraz

△ Glass and Flask

- *1st–2nd century AD*

Roman green glass cup with pad foot and pronounced banding around body. Bottle-shaped flask. Both with iridescence.

- £600 • Pars

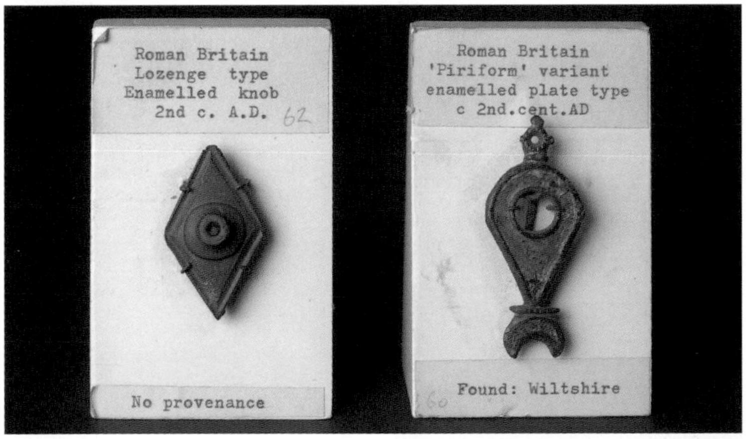

△ Bust of Woman

- *2nd century AD*

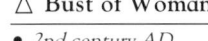

Roman terracotta bust of a woman with good definition to hair, dress and face.

- *height 10cm*
- £300 • Shahdad

△ British Brooches

- *2nd century AD*

Romano-British brooches. Lozenge-shaped with enamelled knob and 'piriform' type, with pin, the latter found in Wiltshire.

- £80/£130 • Pars

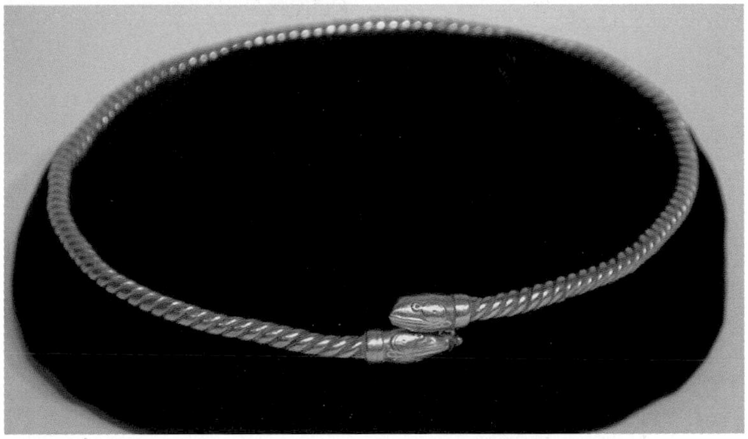

◁ Roman Mirror

- *1st–3rd century AD*

Bronze Roman mirror with two handles from grotesque masks. Circular and folding.

- *diameter 4.5cm*
- £2,200 • Pars

△ Gold Bracelet

- *3rd century AD*

A Roman gold bracelet, with the terminals styled as serpents' heads mounted on a coiled hoop.

- *diameter 10cm*
- £2,800 • Pars

▽ Green Glass Flask

- *3rd–4th century AD*

Bottle-shaped green glass flask, with globular body and cylindrical neck wound with clear spiral threads, four applied handles, flared foot and surface encrustation.

- *height 11cm*
- £6,500 • Pars

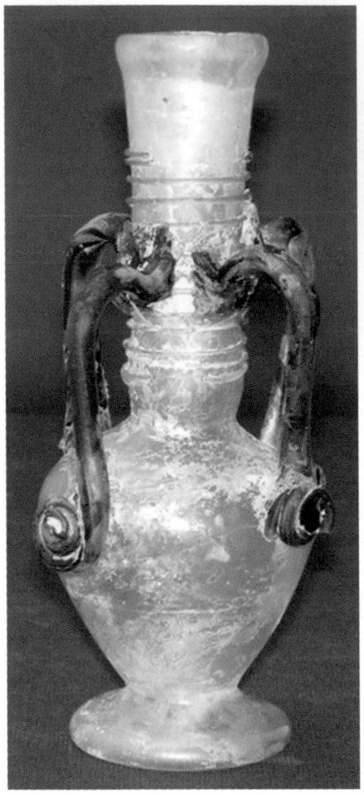

▽ Judaica Relief

- *6th century AD*

A carved basalt relief showing a Jewish temple light with six branches and a master light to the centre. The image also shows a six-petalled flower on the right of the light, balanced by Judaic script on the left. The whole is set within a border.

- *60cm x 37cm*
- £25,000 • Pars

▽ Stele

- *5th century AD*

Late Egyptian Coptic funerary stele with reclining lady in Greek dress and Greek pediment above. Inscription in Greek.

- *height 29cm*
- £3,500 • Pars

◁ Perfume Bottle

- *3rd–5th century AD*

Roman double phial balsamarium with iridescence.

- *length 11cm*
- £600 • Pars

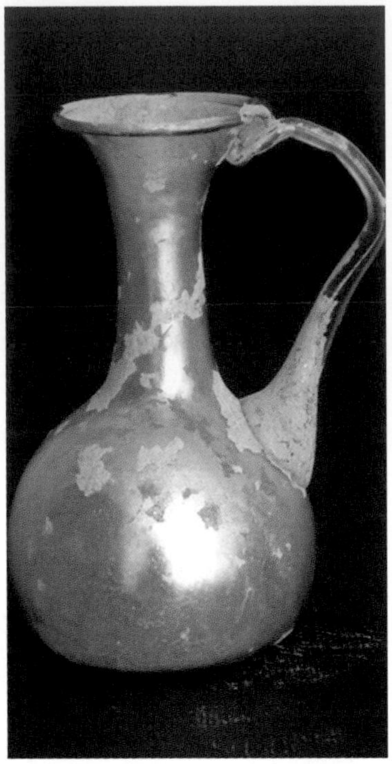

△ Roman Iridescent Flask

- *4th century AD*

Iridescent green flask with silver and gold decoration.

- *height 12cm*
- £1,000 • Pars

△ Green Glass Flask

- *4th–6th century AD*

Green glass flask with bulbous body, indented sides and double handles.

- *height 13.5cm*
- £1,000 • Pars

△ Green Glass Balsamarium

- *4th century AD*

A translucent green glass double balsamarium cosmetic container with twin fused tubes and loop handles.

- *height 17cm*
- £900 • Pars

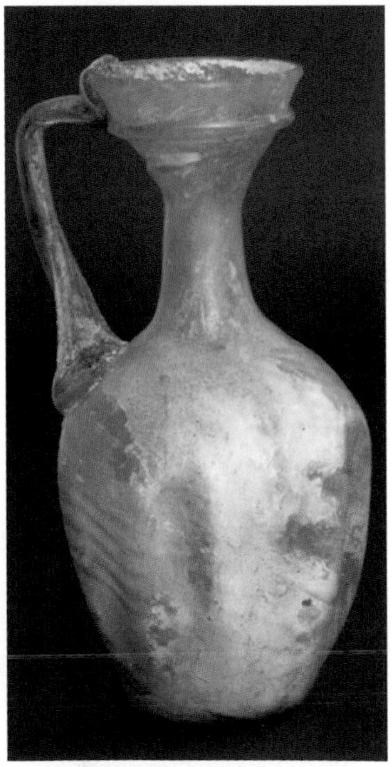

△ Indented Glass Flask

- *4–6th century AD*

Green glass flask, with applied handle and six-sided body, with indented sides.

- *height 15cm*
- £1,000 • Pars

◁ Glass Flask

- *6th century AD*

Pale green translucent glass flask. The globular body with six handles attached to the shoulder and collared rim.

- *height 7.5cm*
- £1,000 • Pars

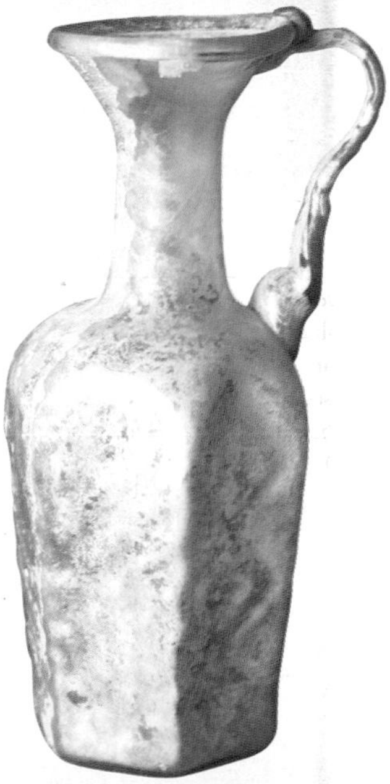

△ Pilgrim Flask

- *6th–7th century AD*

A terracotta pilgrim flask with spiral decoration to the body and double handles to the shoulders.

- *height 17cm*
- £600 • Pars

◁ Roman Flask

- *7th century AD*

A Byzantine Roman five-sided glass flask with designs around body and ribbon handle.

- *height 18cm*
- £3,000 • Pars

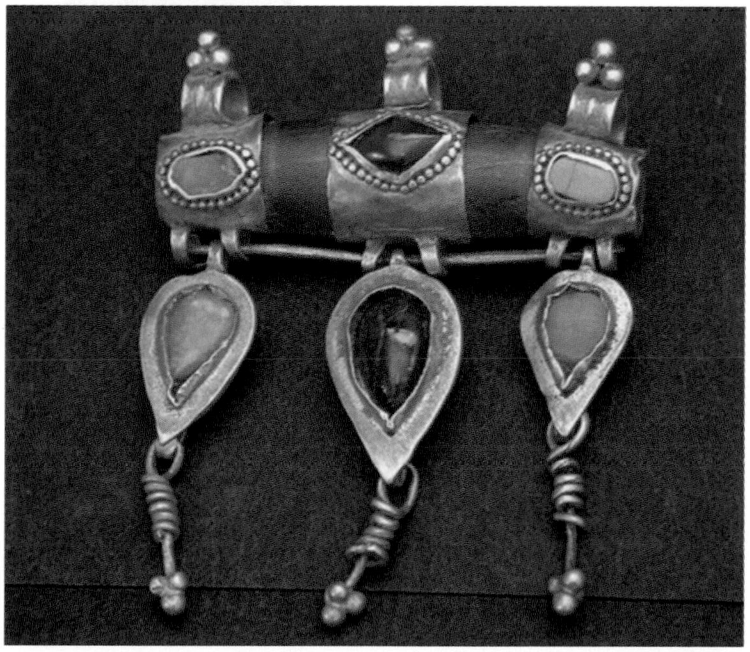

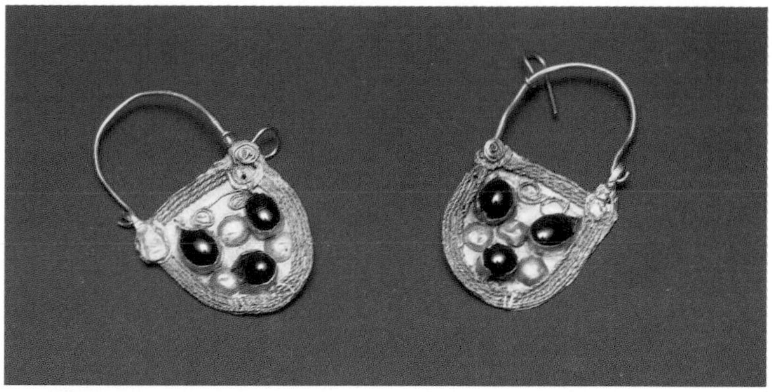

△ Earrings

- *7th century AD*

Late Roman, Sassanian earrings in the form of flat, semicircular bases with three garnets, the whole in solid gold.

- £1,500 • Pars

▽ Bronze Reliquary

- *7th century AD*

Bronze cross with hinge showing Jesus and the Apostles.

- *height 25cm*
- £4,500 • Pars

▽ Byzantine Flask

- *7th century AD*

Light green Byzantine hexagonal flask with iridescence, mould-blown. Each side decorated with early Christian iconography.

- *height 22cm*
- £6,000 • Pars

△ Aubergine Glass Jar

- *7th century AD*

Small ovoid aubergine glass jar, with moulded rim and extensive iridescence.

- *height 7cm*
- £800 • Pars

◁ Islamic Pendant

- *7–8th century AD*

Early Islamic pendant with rubies and turquoise stones set in gold, with a further three lozenge-shaped droplets.

- *length 3cm*
- £4,000 • Pars

ARCHITECTURAL & GARDEN FURNITURE

The boom in television gardening programmes has led to an increase in demand for garden furniture and garden design. The garden designers of the United Kingdom are currently leading the way with their innovative designs, as they once did in the past. Not since the time of Capability Brown, the greatest eighteenth-century landscape designer, and Edwin Lutyens, the house and garden architect, has there been so much excitement about the 'outdoor room'. The home owner increasingly sees his or her garden as a space to be considered with as much thought and care as any room in the house. Most antique garden furniture is made from wrought or cast iron and was produced in the Victorian era. Although age is important, it is not an essential, as decorative appeal and size also play an important part in the choosing of an item.

△ Fire Surround

- *1650*

A fine statuary marble fire surround from Warwick Castle depicting a classical allegorical frieze with a chorus of sea horses and mermaids playing with musical instruments.

- *180cm x 200cm*
- **£585,000** • **Drummonds**

▽ Stone Lions

- *17th century*

A pair of English standard holders in the form of stone lions, with forefeet clasped as receptacles for standard staffs.

- *height 94cm*
- **£5,700** • **Andrew Bewick**

◁ Cistern

- *circa 1660*

17th-century Italian marble cistern, with lobed decoration.

- *height 62cm*
- **£580** • **Riverbank**

△ Georgian Columns

- *circa 1730s*

Three early Georgian square stone columns with reeded capitals and chamfered corners.

- *height 195cm*
- **£785 each** • **Drummonds**

▽ Pair of Urns

- *circa 1720*

One of a pair of Istrian Rosso di Verona urns of semi-lobed campano form.

- *height 89cm*
- **£15,000** • **Westland & Co.**

◁ Marble Fireplace

- *circa 1750*

An Irish George III statuary marble Palladian chimneypiece.

- *height 2.21m*
- **£200,000** • **Westland & Co.**

△ Panelled Door

- *18th century*

A superb panelled door with imagery embracing hunting and mythology with wild and fantasy beasts.

- *1.65m x 95cm*
- £2,600 • Gordon Reece

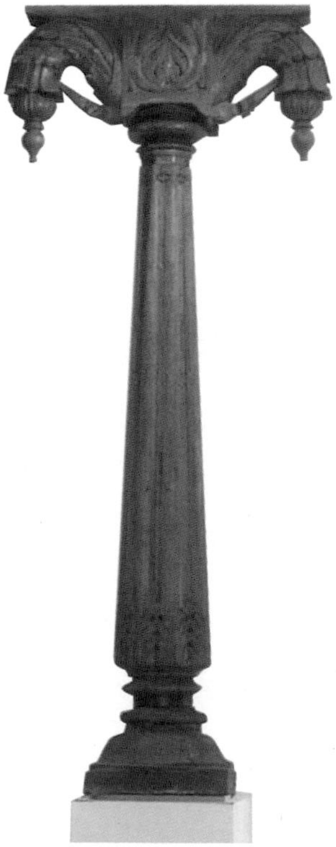

△ Teak Pillars

- *circa 18th century*

One of a pair of teak columns from the Kanara province of India, with fluted stem on a pedestal base surmounted by a heavily carved capital, modelled on the banana flower.

- *height 2.14m*
- £3,800 • Gordon Reece

▽ Indian Rosewood Doors

- *18th century*

A pair of rosewood doors from Kerala, South India. Includes a splendid ornate ironwork lock.

- *167cm x 64cm*
- £920 • Gordon Reece

▽ Marble Columns

- *circa 1760*

One of a set of six Solomonaic Istrian marble columns.

- *height 2.82m*
- £25,000 • Westland & Co.

△ Palladian Chimneypiece

- *circa 1730*

An English Palladian statuary marble chimneypiece, after a design by William Kent. The projecting inverted breakfront shelf with moulded edge above a band of lotus moulding and a boldly carved egg and dart moulding, the frieze centred by a rectangular panel carved with a bacchante mask, the hair intertwined with berried vines, and a border of Siena marble.

- *1.66m x 2.31m*
- £315,000 • Anthony Outred

△ Mughal Panel

- *18th century*

An 18th-century Indian sandstone Mughal panel, carved in relief with a flower at the centre and numerous sprays emanating from rocks. Set within a rope twist border.

- *66cm x 85cm*
- £9,200 • Gordon Reece

▷ Fire Grate

- *circa 1727–1820*

Cast-iron Georgian fire grate, with architectural and stylised leaf designs.

- *height 97cm*
- £4,200 • Drummonds

△ Stone Sundial

- *mid-18th century*

Important English Portland stone sundial, the triangular waisted pedestal with moulded top and canted corners, carved with rams' heads flanked by their lower legs linked with drapery. The sides with ribbon ties, and wreaths around the central panel. The base is carved with shells and raised on C-scrolled feet.

- *35cm x 24cm*
- £14,500 • Crowthers

△ Louis Philippe Fireplace

• *early 19th century*
French Louis Philippe black marble, monopodia chimneypiece. The breakfront frieze is carved with acanthus leaves and supported by scrolled legs terminating in lion's paws.
• *1.09m x 88cm*
• £11,500 • Crowthers

△ Acorn Finials

• *circa 1810*
One of a pair of late Georgian stone acorn finials with good patination.
• *55cm x 24cm*
• £600 • Drummonds

△ Regency Chimneypiece

• *circa 1820*
A fine English Regency chimneypiece of statuary marble with two architectural pilasters with recessed panels tapering to the top and moulded capitals.
• *height 1.22m*
• £3,750 • Westland & Co.

△ Stone Trough

• *circa 1820*
A stone trough with attractive weathering of lichen and moss.
• *40cm x 78cm*
• £260 • Drummonds

△ Brass Fire Dogs

• *circa 1800*
A pair of decorative French brass fire dogs with shield motifs surmounted by flame finial designs, raised on acanthus scrolled feet.
• *height 54cm*
• £780 • Drummonds

▽ Fire Grate

• *1805*
A fine George III cast-iron fire grate of the Regency period. Includes pierced and moulded decoration.
• *125cm x 130 cm*
• £4,600 • Drummonds

▽ Stone Trough

• *circa 1820*
A rectangular stone trough with good patination.
• *38cm x 89cm*
• £250 • Drummonds

▷ Heraldic Beasts

• *circa 1820*
A magnificent pair of Regency statuary marble heraldic beasts, supporting the arms of the Dukes of Beaufort, in the form of a panther and a wyvern.
• *height 1.65m*
• £38,000 • Westland & Co.

◁ Petite Palace Shutters

• *early 19th century*
Pair of shutters from the Petite Palace, Hyderabad, India, of eight panels.
• *1.82m x 1.11m*
• £1,600 • Gordon Reece

△ Wall-Masque

• *19th century*
Stone-carved wall-masque.
• *height 38cm*
• £1,550 • Drummonds

△ Marble-Topped Table

• *19th century*
Serpentine, marble-topped table with ornate ironwork base.
• *height 72cm*
• £1,050 • Drummonds

△ Regency Fender

• *1800*
A Regency steel fender standing on claw feet.
• *22cm x 1.24m x 26cm*
• £600 • Old World

△ English Stoneware Urns

- *19th century*

One of a pair of large English stoneware urns with loop handles terminating in patriarch masks; the campana form bodies with everted lip over Greek key frieze and gadrooning. Set on turned socles over square bases. Attributed to the workshops of John Marriott Blashfield.

- *height 1.09m*
- £23,500 the pair • Crowthers

△ Pair of Urns

- *19th century*

One of a pair of statuary marble classical urns in the Campano shape.

- *height 93.5cm*
- £6,500 • Westland & Co.

▷ Fire Basket

- *1810*

A George III serpentine basket grate with urn finials on tapered legs with an apron.

- *82cm x 88cm x 38cm*
- £5,500 • Old World

△ Cupboard Doors

- *circa 1860*

A mid-19th-century pair of glazed and gesso cupboard doors with fanlight.

- *height 1.9cm*
- £875 • Drummonds

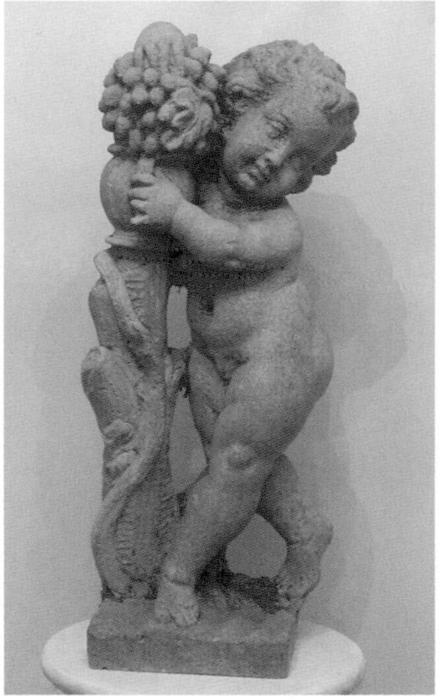

△ Stone Angel

- *19th century*

Italian statue of a cherub embracing a pillar.

- £495 • Rainbow

◁ Elmwood Planter

- *1850*

Elmwood planter with brass inlay.

- *length 30cm*
- £1,950 • Dial Post House

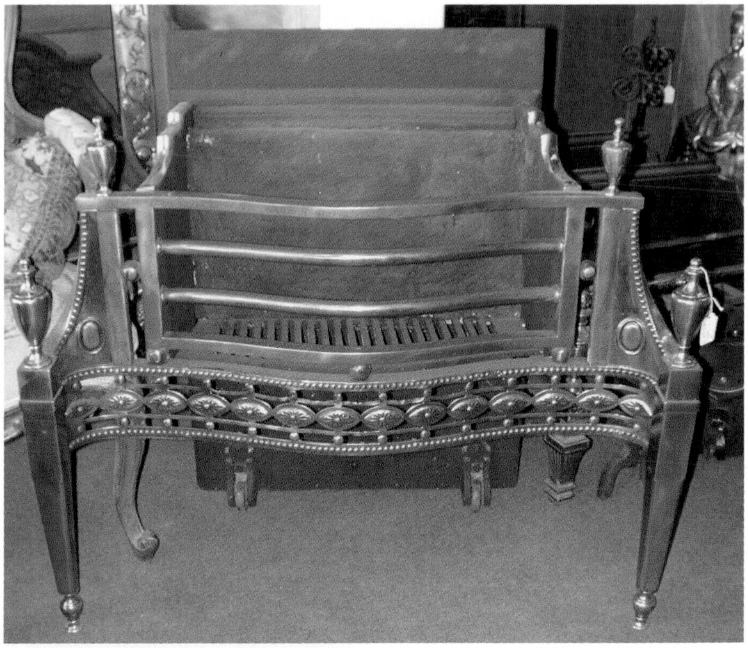

△ Stone Bench

- *1860*

Stone bench with lead frieze, including allegorical figures of above average size. Formerly belonged to Lloyd George.

- *1.21m x 1.85m x 61cm*
- £9,598 • Drummonds

△ Gothic Windows

- *circa 1860*

A stone, Gothic, mullioned double window with quoining, gothic tracery and quarter-lights.

- *height 1.98m*
- £1,750 • Drummonds

▽ Ram's Head

- *circa1850*

One of a pair of fine limestone Victorian wall masks, naturalistically carved, depicting a ram's head with resplendent horns. Both shown with good patina and weathering.

- *height 38cm*
- £3,950 • Drummonds

▽ Garden Bench

- *circa 1850*

A finely carved, French, marble garden bench with elaborate frieze to backrest and scrolled armrests supporting statues.

- *width 2.26m*
- £24,000 • Westland & Co.

▽ Second Empire Spiral Flight

- *1863*

A romantic French Second Empire spiral flight, floor-to-floor walnut with fine cast-iron spindles.

- *height 6.2m*
- £25,750 • Drummonds

▽ French Well Head

- *circa 1870*

Limestone well head with a wooden winch and handle within a steel housing, the limestone with good patination.

- *diameter 1.32m*
- £3,400 • Drummonds

◁ Garden Borders

- *circa 1870*

Glazed terracotta garden borders with barley-twist top.

- *height 18cm*
- £6 • Curios

△ Classical Urn

- *circa 1870*

An important 19th-century classical urn, decorated with swags and rosettes, mounted on a pedestal with figurative relief.

- *height 1.67m*
- £13,800 • Ranby Hall

▽ Shanks Cistern

- *circa 1870*

Polished and lacquered cast iron 3-gallon cistern with original brass fittings.

- *height 35cm*
- £875 • Drummonds

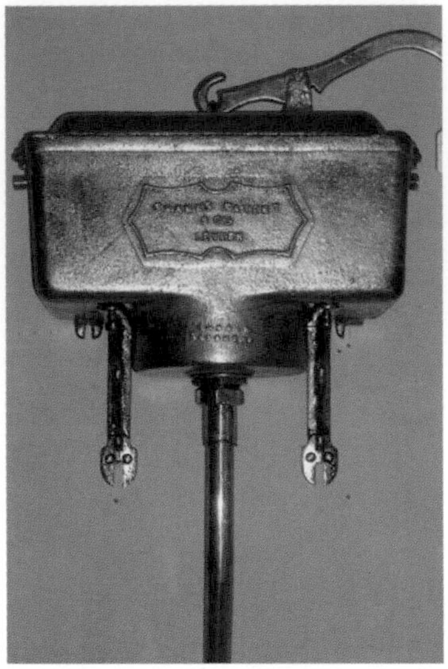

▽ Teak Planter

- *circa 1870*

A carved Burmese teak planter.

- *height 95cm*
- £685 • Tredantiques

▷ Cast-Iron Garden Roller

- *circa 1870*

Cast-iron garden roller with turned wooden handle and cast-iron medallion with maker's logo.

- *height 1.2m*
- £225 • Drummonds

△ Cast-Iron Garden Seat

- *circa 1870*

An unusually attractive Victorian double-sided cast-iron seat. Painted white with a floral design. In original condition.

- *length 2m*
- £1,690 • Drummonds

△ Pair of Gates

- *circa 1870*

A pair of fine-quality, 19th-century wrought-iron gates, each with a central oval panel and with profuse applied scrolling.

- *height 2.14m*
- £1,750 • Riverbank

△ Grangemouth Terracotta Urn

- *circa 1870*

A Victorian urn in biscuit terracotta from the Grangemouth Pottery in Scotland. Carved in relief with flowers and leaves.

- *height 1.5m*
- £2,950 • Drummonds

△ Register Grate

- *circa 1870*

Arched cast-iron register grate with a polished metal finish and decorated with a peacock design.

- *height 97cm*
- £920 • Drummonds

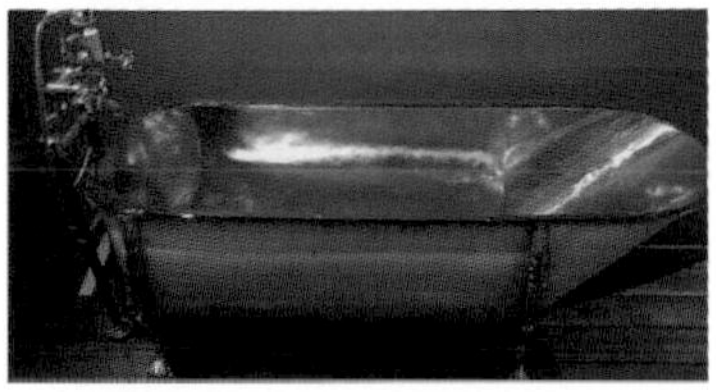

△ French Copper Bath

- *circa 1880*

French double-skinned bath with copper lining, on cast-iron claw feet.

- *length 1.67m*
- £7,950 • Drummonds

▽ Roof Finial

- *circa 1870*

A Victorian fleur-de-lys finial terracotta rooftile with heavily moulded decoration.

- *height 1.1m*
- £450 • Drummonds

▽ Lead Water Feature

- *circa 1880*

A very fine quality Victorian lead water feature of a child holding a goose.

- *height 60cm*
- £2,350 • Drummonds

△ Brass Sundial

- *circa 1880*

A Victorian rustic sandstone sundial with a brass dial.

- *height 88cm*
- £285 • Tredantiques

△ Gothic Revival Niches

- *1880*

One of a pair of Victorian niches, of heavily carved Bathstone, with foliate design and leaf decoration terminating in fleur de lys finials.

- *height 1.4m*
- £1,450 • Drummonds

▽ Classical Urn

- *circa 1880*

Large classical urn with handles rising from masks, on a plinth with wreath.

- *height 1.5m*
- £2,800 • Drummonds

▽ Victorian Terracotta Urn

- *circa 1880*

A fine Victorian terracotta urn with heavily carved floral swags.

- *height 2.4m*
- £1,880 • Drummonds

△ Vase and Cover

- *circa 1880*

A late 19th-century baluster iron urn in the Roman manner, representing 'Tempus Fugit', with the winged hour-glass as a central feature and profuse acanthus-leaf decoration above a circular, pedestal base.

- *height 59cm*
- £750 • **Westland & Co.**

△ Deck Chair

- *circa 1885*

A 19th-century rustic deck chair-style garden chair with slatted seat and backrest and scrolling to both.

- *height 88cm*
- £130 • **Myriad**

▽ Marble Statue

- *circa 1880*

Victorian marble statue of a young boy naturalistically posed on a circular base. In excellent condition.

- *height 1.02m*
- £5,400 • **Drummonds**

▽ Garden Set

- *circa 1890*

The chair from a late 19th-century three-piece garden set in wrought iron and teak, with oval back-splat.

- £3,000 • **North West 8**

◁ Marble Chimneypiece

- *circa 1880*

A very large, carved Carrara marble fireplace, with frieze with acanthus, arabesques and foliate scrolling and armorial tablet.

- *height 2.54m*
- £123,000 • **Westland & Co.**

△ Bronze Statue

- *1880*

A very fine 19th-century bronze statue of a boy.

- *height 1.4m*
- £14,250 • **Drummonds**

▽ Terracotta Urns

- *circa 1880*

One of a pair of large Victorian terracotta urns with carved floral swags set on a square base.

- *height 1.8m*
- £3,800 • **Drummonds**

▽ Carved Head

- *circa 1880*

Victorian ecclesiastical-style carved stone corbel. Designed to support roof trusses.

- £750 • **Drummonds**

▽ **Pair of Urns**

- *1880*

One of an ornate pair of urns with floral garland carved out of stone.

- *height 1.5m*
- £3,400 • Drummonds

▽ **French Planter**

- *circa 1880*

A French dual-laquered planter with drawer to front.

- *80cm x 50cm*
- £850 • Tredantiques

△ **Classical Urn**

- *circa 1880*

Large classical urn with double handles from mask decoration, mounted on a plinth with wreath decoration.

- *height 1.5m*
- £2,800 • Drummonds

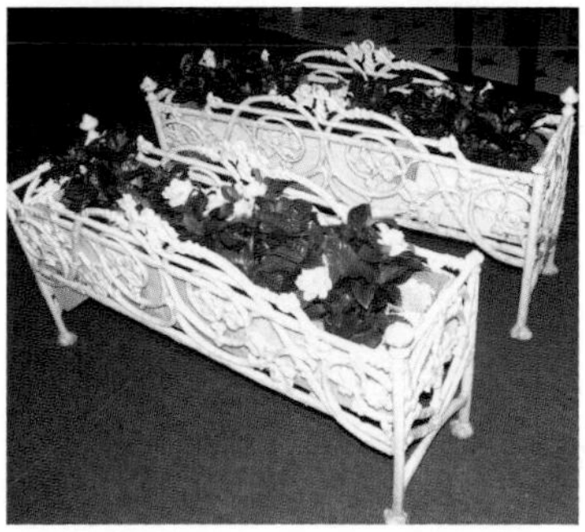

◁ **Copper and Nickel Bath**

- *circa 1880*

A deep, late 19th-century nickel and copper bath of kidney shape, with a scrolled rim and central taps.

- *length 1.78m*
- £12,800 • Drummonds

△ **French Chairs**

- *circa 1890*

One of a pair of metal chairs with curved seats with scrolled terminations and tassels and heart-shaped back-splat.

- *height 61cm*
- £475 • R. Conquest

▽ **Garden Chair**

- *late 19th century*

A French metal garden chair, white-painted with pierced decoration to back and seat and scrolling to frame.

- *height 79cm*
- £210 • Myriad

◁ **Planters**

- *circa 1890*

A pair of late 19th-century cast alloy planters with leaf motif.

- *length 1.1m*
- £1,950 • French Country

△ **Marble Fire Surround**

- *1890*

A Victorian English fire surround from white statuary marble with supporting classical figures on each side.

- *1.6m x 1.5m*
- £30,000 • Drummonds

△ **Pair of Urns**

- *19th century*

One of a pair of cast-iron urns, of fluted melon shape, with egg and dart moulding.

- *height 49cm*
- £620 • Myriad

△ **Neptune Fountain**

- *circa 1890*

Cast-iron wall fountain showing Neptune wrestling with a carp.

- *height 1.55m*
- £1,775 • Drummonds

◁ Chimney-Piece

- *circa 1890*

Unique Catalonian Art Nouveau modernista chimney-piece with mosaic and burnished wrought-iron work, by Lluis Domenech i Montaner, an associate of Gaudi.

- *height 3.5m*
- £215,000 • Westland & Co.

△ Iron Gong

- *circa 1890*

Iron gong with a hand-beaten finish supported by chains within a mahogany frame with turned decoration.

- *1.14m x 75cm*
- £885 • Drummonds

▽ Waywiser

- *1890*

Late nineteenth century iron-spoked waywiser for measuring distance.

- *height 1.08m*
- £11,000 • Langfords Marine

▽ Regency Fireplace

- *circa 1890*

White marble Regency fireplace, with reeded columns and black marble insert, surmounted by a carved frieze with urn decoration.

- *height 1.45m*
- £18,950 • Drummonds

▽ Pair of Heraldic Beasts

- *circa 1890*

One of a large Lion and Unicorn carved in Portland stone.

- *height 1.78m*
- £18,000 • Westland & Co.

▷ Cast-Iron Lamp Stands

- *circa 1890*

Pair of Victorian cast-iron ornamental lamp posts. With pierced and moulded leaf decoration, the whole surmounted by moulded glass shades.

- *height 1.95m*
- £3,725 • Drummonds

▽ Wall Fountain

- *circa 1890*

A late 19th-century carved stone water fountain in the shape of a man's face with facial hair and distended cheeks.

- *height 41cm*
- £1,150 • Drummonds

▷ Victorian Stone Frieze

- *circa 1890*

Victorian carved stone frieze surround, depicting cherubs with allegorical animals.

- *length 3.2m*
- £5,800 • Drummonds

▽ Glazed Terracotta Urns

• *late 19th century*
English glazed terracotta conservatory urns, one of a pair, stamped Doulton Lambeth and incised with the numbers 8496 and 0088 and the letter M. The ovoid bodies are decorated with bold swags of fruit and flowers hung from central wreaths with a bronze glaze.
• *height 62cm*
• £11,750 • Crowthers

▽ Roofing Finial

• *circa 1890*
Victorian terracotta roofing finial, with trademark 'RCR'.
• *height 18cm*
• £220 • Drummonds

△ Garden Borders

• *circa 1890*
Terracotta garden borders with relief decoration and glazing to the upper portion, unglazed and arched to the buried portion.
• *width 31cm*
• £12 each • Curios

△ Victorian Radiator Cover

• *circa 1900*
One of a pair of Victorian cast-iron radiator covers with pierced panels and moulded column supports.
• *93cm x 49cm x 1.03m*
• £1,400 • Drummonds

▽ Fire Bellows

• *circa 1900*
Large cast-iron fire bellows with original leather membrane.
• *length 1.6m*
• £980 • Drummonds

▽ Terracotta Finial

• *circa 1890s*
One of a pair of red terracotta finials with acanthus leaf designs, raised on a plinth base.
• *height 1.7m*
• £3,870 • Drummonds

◁ Lead Mask

• *early 20th century*
Lead mask copied from an original 18th-century original, depicting a Bacchanalian head.
• *width 40cm*
• £300 • Crowther

△ Japanese Lantern

• *circa 1890*
A Victorian carved granite decorative Japanese-style lantern. Free standing.
• *height 1.8m*
• £3,950 • Drummonds

△ Pair of Victorian Lions

• *circa 1890*
One of a fine pair of Victorian fire clay lions from the Nurford fire clay works of Kilmarnock. Produced by A. & G. Craig of Hillhead, Kilmarnock, from a design by J. Neil of rare black fire clay.
• *74cm x 1m*
• £8,250 • Drummonds

ARMS & ARMOUR

Interest in arms and armour has never been greater and there is still a wealth of material to choose from at all price ranges. There are many different avenues for the collector of militaria to pursue, including weapons, pictures, prints, postcards and medals. A fine weapon should be as beautiful as it is deadly, and therein lies its charm. Traditionally, at the top end of the market, the price leaders such as pistols in their original cases and military headdresses continue to rise in value, although these must be in their original condition. Most swords available today date from the period after 1796 when British military patterns were standardised. Swords come in two types, those for action and those for dress wear. Court swords with decorative hilts and slender blades often have a good provenance and can also be highly decorative. Without the precise details of the weapons used, and by whom, history would be lacking in material and it is often research by collectors that can unearth episodes in history.

△ **Tibetan Helmet**

- *circa 1500*

Very rare Sino-Tibetan helmet with pierced Derge work and gilded Tibetan characters.

- *height 28cm*
- £9,000 • Robert Hales

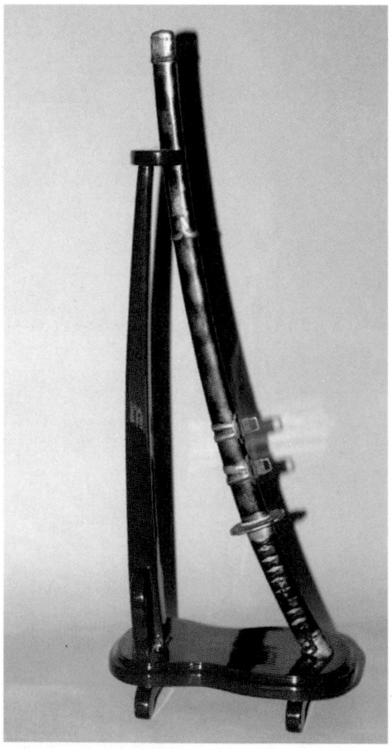

◁ **Venetian Rapier**

- *circa 1580–1622*

Venetian rapier with traditional swept hilt iron guard. Acorn-shape pommel with chiselled ornament grip. Wooden bound with iron wire. Blade with two fullers.

- *length 1.12m*
- £900 • C.F. Seidler

◁ **Japanese Ko Bizan Blade**

- *early 16th century*

Early 16th-century Ko Bizan blade. A single-handed court tachi nobleman's sword. With nashiji lacquer and silver wash mounts with gold brocade.

- *length 59cm*
- £4,500 • Don Bayney

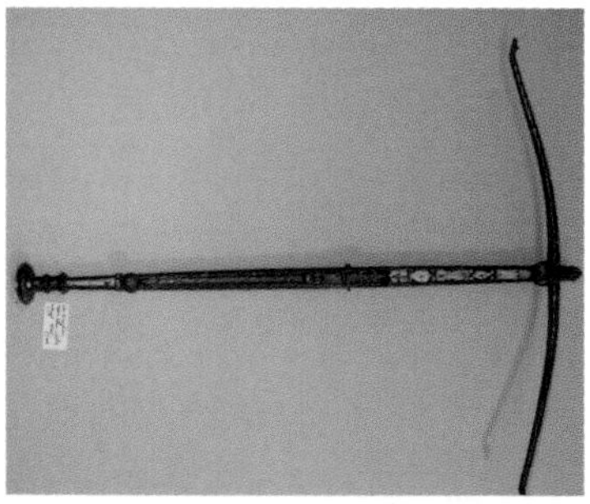

△ **Inlaid Crossbow**

- *17th century*

English crossbow with bone inlay.

- *62cm x 52cm*
- £1800 • Peter Bunting

▷ **Wheel-Lock Pistol**

- *circa 1620*

German holster pistol with fish tail butt and steel mounts.

- *length 62cm*
- £5,800 • Michael German

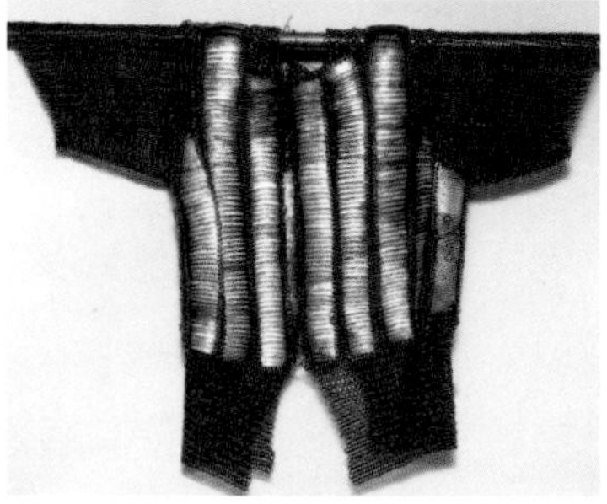

△ **Mail and Plate Shirt**

- *17th century*

A rare officer's mail and plate shirt with Islamic inscriptions. Previously preserved in the Bikaner Fortress, Rajasthan, and in recent times worn by the palace camel corps at the coronation durbar for Edward VII in Delhi.

- *height 83cm*
- £1,600 • Robert Hales

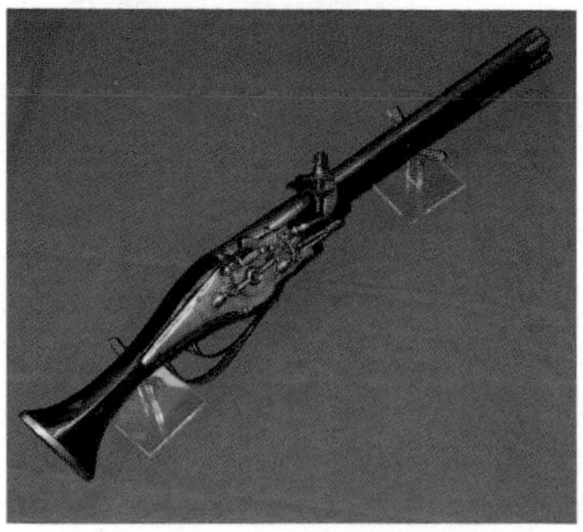

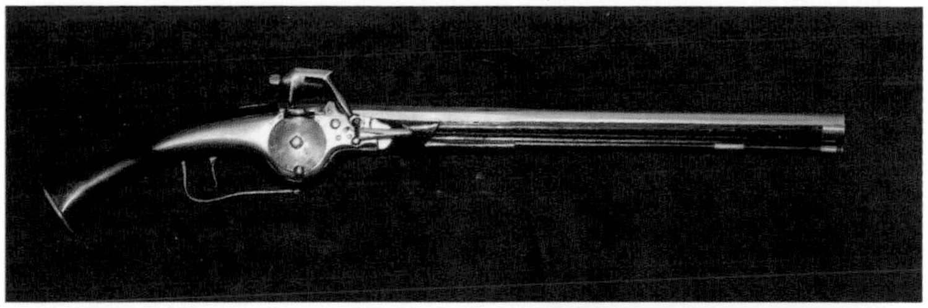

△ Holster Pistol

- *1630*

Rare 17th-century wheel-lock holster pistol. Ebony stock, external wheel and sliding pan cover. With steel fittings. English or Dutch.

- *length 60cm*
- £4,200 • Michael German

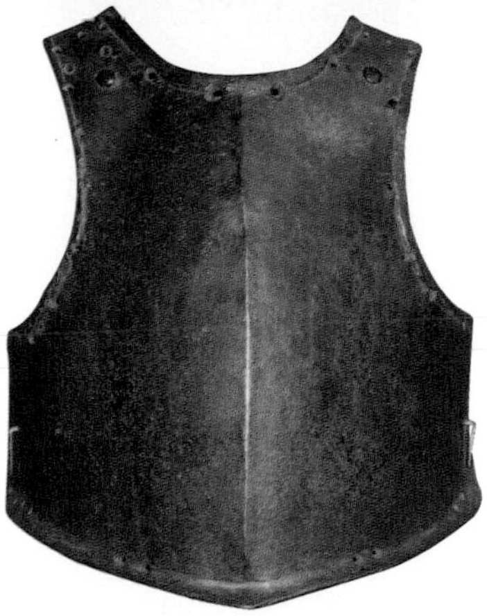

△ Civil War Breast Plate

- *1640*

English Civil War reinforced breast plate forged in one piece by local armourers with original black finish.

- *height 36cm*
- £950 • Michael German

△ Japanese Facemask

- *circa 18th century*

Late 18th-century Japanese mempo facemask of iron and lacquer. With neck guard, original cord and badger-hair moustache. Fine quality.

- £950 • Don Mayney

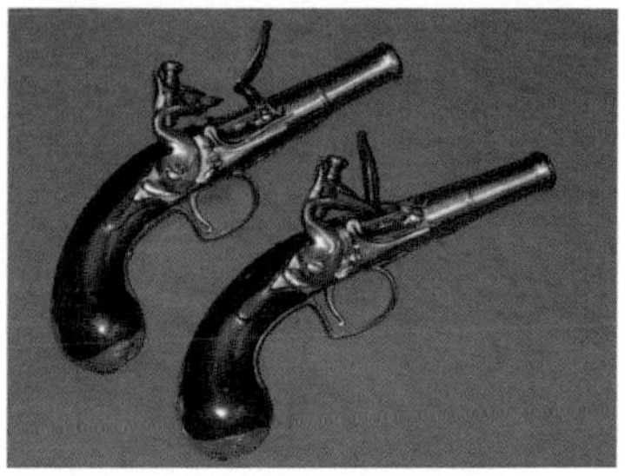

△ Pocket Flintlock Pistols

- *circa 1720*

Pair of English Queen Anne pocket flintlock pistols, with cannon barrels and silver lion mask butt caps, signed John Segelas. Hammers fitted with dog catches.

- *length 18cm*
- £3,400 • Michael German

△ Cup Hilt Rapier

- *1630*

A fine 17th-century cup hilt rapier with signed blade. Pierced cup guard with leaf designs. Wire bound wood handle and twist pattern quillions.

- *length 1.17m*
- £3,900 • Michael German

▽ Holster Pistol

- *circa 1680*

English holster pistol by John Dafte, London, with strawberry-leaf engraving and steel mounts. Fully stocked.

- *length 47cm*
- £4,600 • Michael German

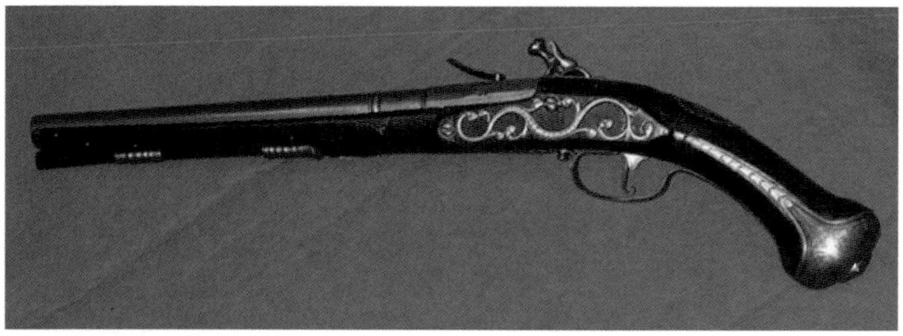

△ Japanese Kabuto

- *circa 18th century*

Sixty-two plate 18th-century Japanese kabuto with mempi face mask, maidate crest of a demon and gilded lacquer neck band.

- *height 51cm*
- £3,500 • Don Bayney

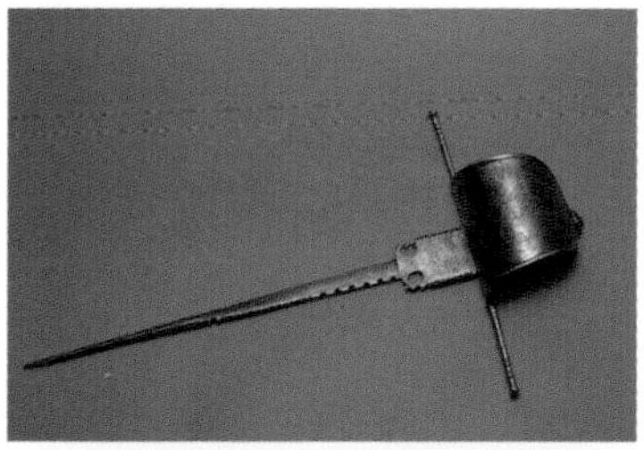

◁ Left-Handed Dagger

- *1620*

A fine Main Gauche (left-handed) dagger with engraved steel guard. Long twisted quillions. Thick blade with chiselled decoration thumb indentation.

- *length 51cm*
- £2,300 • Michael German

▽ Flintlock Pistol

- *circa 1770*

Cannon-barrelled flintlock pistol with rifled barrel. The stock with silver wired inlay designs, with maker's mark.

- *length 24cm*
- £1,250 • Michael German

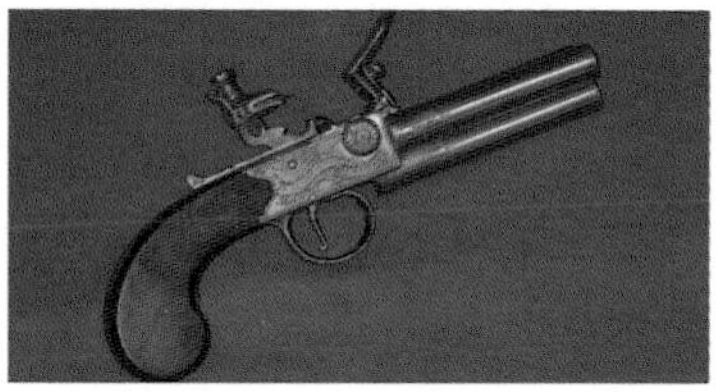

◁ Flintlock Blunderbuss

- *circa 1700*

English flintlock blunderbuss of early type, maker Savage.

- *length 68cm*
- £3,200 • Michael German

△ Horn Powder Flask

- *circa 1770*

Very simple 18th-century horn powder flask with screw top. Good condition.

- £30 • Ian Spencer

△ Flintlock Pistol

• *circa 1770*
Box-lock .30-bore flintlock travelling pistol. Walnut slab butt.
• £400 • Ian Spencer

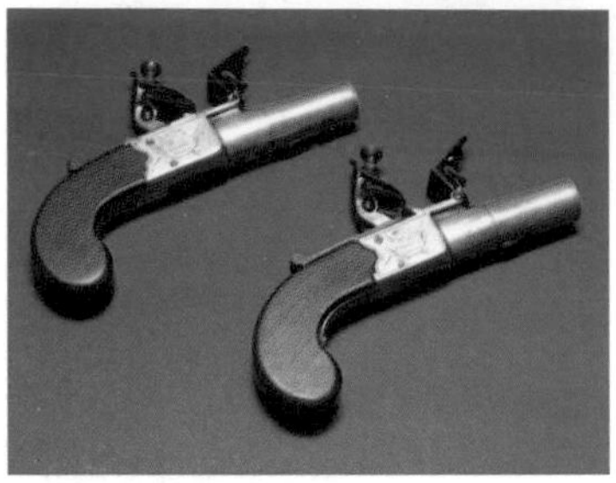

△ Nicholsen Pocket Pistols

• *1790*
Pair of .50-calibre flint box lock pocket pistols by Nicholsen, Cornhill, London. Brass barrels, walnut grip with safety catch.
• *length 15cm*
• £750 • C.F. Seidler

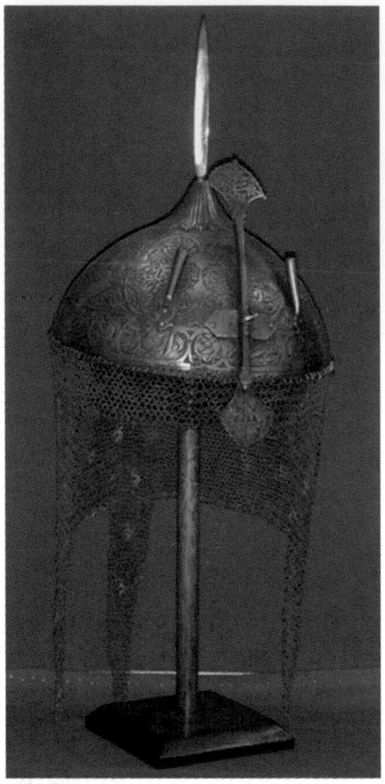

▽ Indo Persian Khula-Khad

• *circa 1780*
Indo Persian Khula-Khad steel helmet, chiselled with foliate designs, sliding nose guard and top spike, with chain mail neck guard.
• *height 30cm*
• £1,400 • Michael German

◁ Two-Cornered Hat

• *circa 1800*
Metal trunk with 'Andrew Blair' inscribed on the lid, made to house a Naval Admiral's hat. The original hat is included, with original sash and lapels decorated with gold braiding.
• *width 42cm*
• £1,200 • Julian Smith

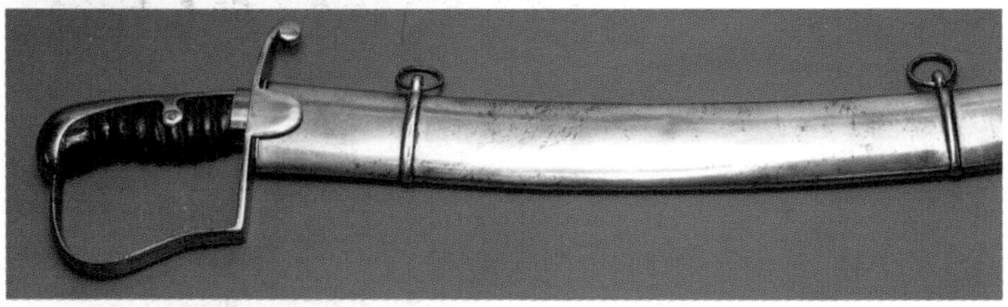

△ Military Sabre

• *1800*
British cavalry sabre 1796 pattern complete with steel scabbard.
• *length 99cm*
• £680 • Michael German

▽ Turkish Rifle

• *circa 1800*
Turkish rifle with fine Damascus twist barrel. Inlaid with silver and brass.
• *length 1.07m*
• £2,500 • Robert Hales

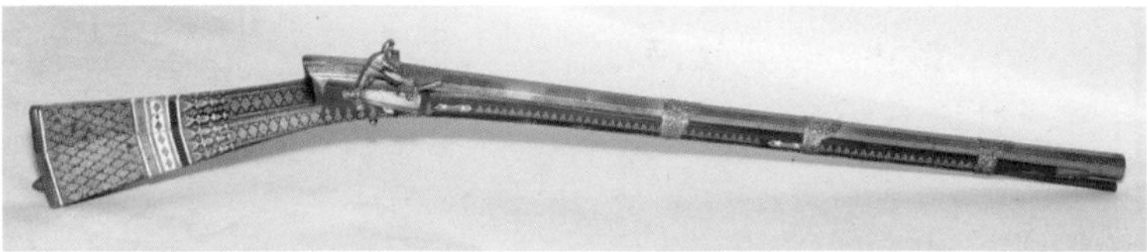

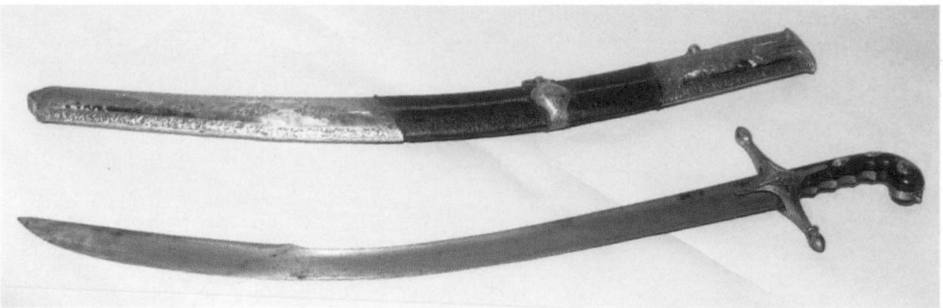

△ Turkish Killig

• *1780*
Turkish killig with patterned, welded steel blade, silver gilt mounts, ass skin scabbard and horn hilt.
• *length 84.5cm*
• £2,200 • Robert Hales

▽ Indian Katar Dagger

• *1780*
Large Indian katar dagger. The thick blade has an armour-piercing point. Partly inlaid with silver floral decoration.
• *length 58cm*
• £1,200 • Michael German

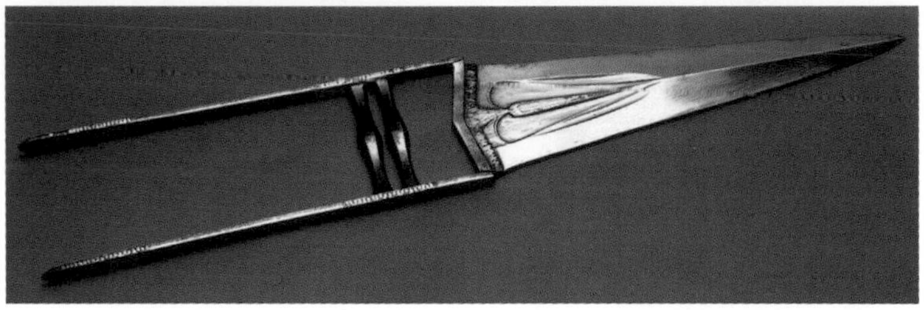

△ Japanese Facemask

• *circa late 18th century*
Mempo face mask made from iron and lacquer. Is in the form of a grimace with neck guard and badger-hair moustache.
• £900 • Don Mayney

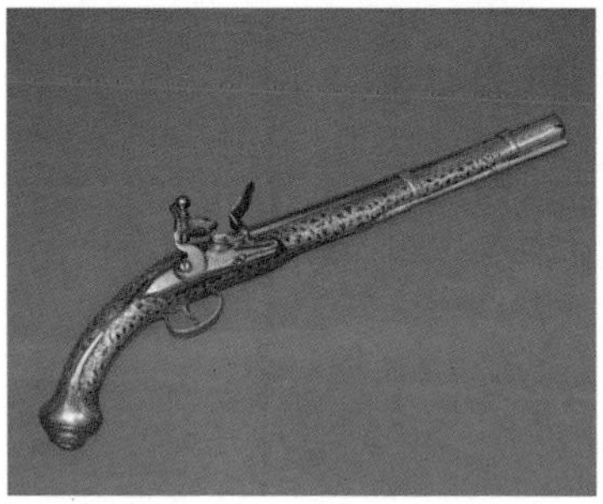

▽ Indo-Persian Dagger

• *1800*
With curved steel blade and original scabbard. Iron hilt inlaid with gold floral designs and two semi-precious stones.
• *length 37cm*
• £800 • Michael German

▽ Henry Noch Pistol

• *1800*
A pocket flintlock English pistol made by Henry Noch of London.
• *length 24cm*
• £600 • Michael German

◁ Turkish Holster Pistol

• *circa 1800*
Fine Turkish flintlock holster pistol with silver mounts.
• *length 51cm*
• £1,700 • Michael German

▽ Coconut Powder Flask

- *circa 1810*

A coconut powder flask, carved and polished by a French POW in the West Indies. The carving depicts the Battle of Austerlitz, 1805.

- *length 14cm*
- **£1,000** • **C.F. Seidler**

▽ French Belt Pistol

- *1813*

French cavalryman's belt pistol with flintlock action, brass mounts and walnut furniture.

- *length 21.5cm*
- **£1,000** • **C.F. Seidler**

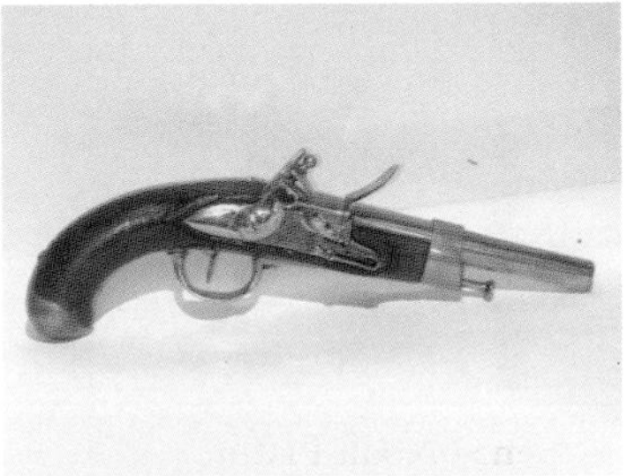

▽ W & J Rigby Service Pistol

- *1820*

Rigby service pistol used by Irish Police, Customs and Inland Revenue. Unusual .16 bore. By W & J Rigby with typical Irish fishtail grip. Converted to percussion 1840.

- *length 37cm*
- **£700** • **C.F. Seidler**

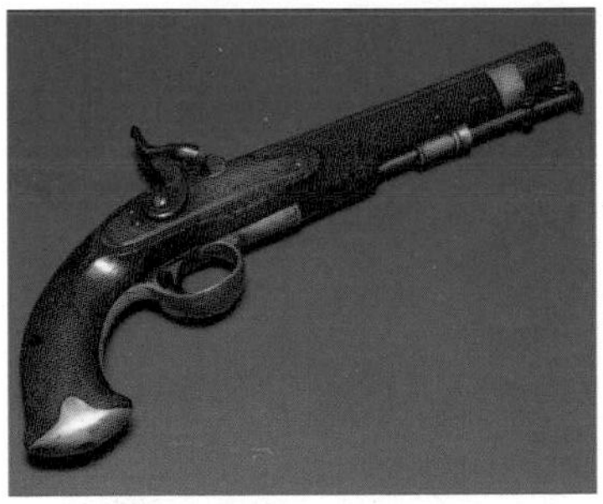

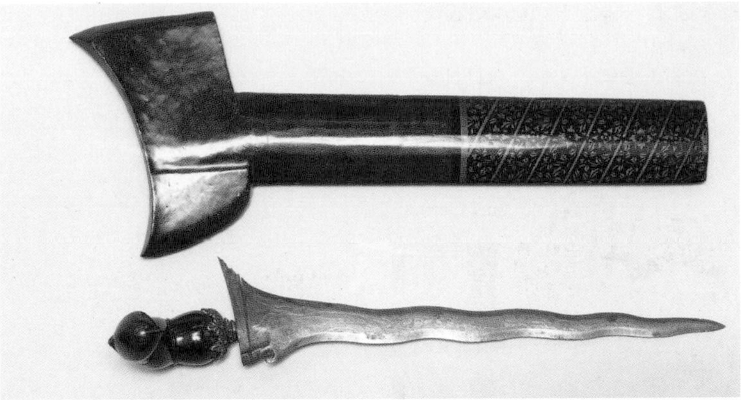

▷ English Copper Powder Flask

- *circa 1800*

An English copper powder flask, used for the storage of powder for guns.

- *length 12cm*
- **£180** • **H. & H.**

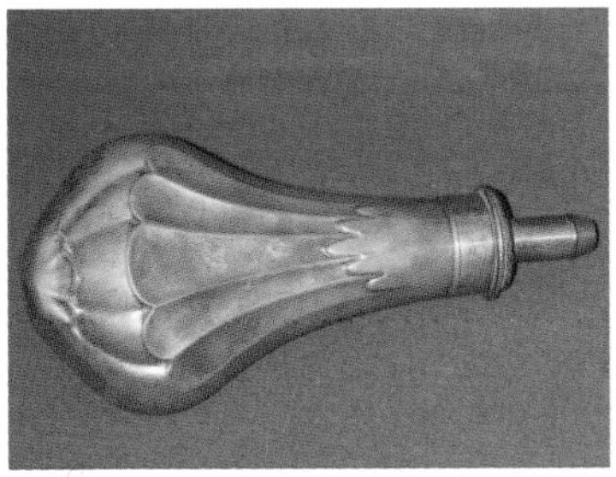

▽ Kulah Khad Helmet

- *1820*

Fine Indian kulah khad helmet. The shallow bowl inlaid overall with gold decoration and three plume holders with moving nosebar and chain mail camial.

- **£1,600** • **Michael German**

◁ Scottish Powder Flask

- *circa 1800*

A Scottish powder flask, embossed with a shell pattern.

- *length 20cm*
- **£180** • **H. & H.**

△ Indian Steel Shield

- *1820*

A fine Indian circular shield. Steel inlaid overall with gold designs including four metal bosses. Complete with original padded velvet lining and handles.

- *diameter 39cm*
- **£1,400** • **Michael German**

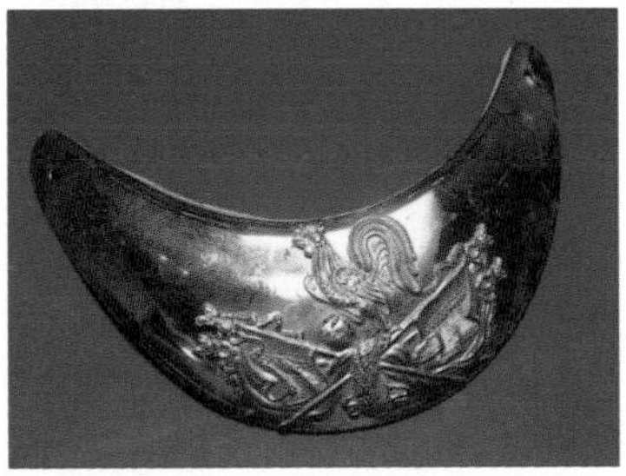

◁ Indonesian Dagger

- *19th century*

Indonesian keris dagger from Celebes with burr wood and gold and black lacquer ed sheath. Silver mendak and nine-lock pattern welded blade.

- *length 43cm*
- **£280** • **Robert Hales**

△ Japanese Kabuto

- *early 19th century*

Eight-plate Japanese kabuto (helmet) with maidate. Lacquered and gilded, with a four lame shikoro lace neck guard.

- **£2,700** • **Don Bayney**

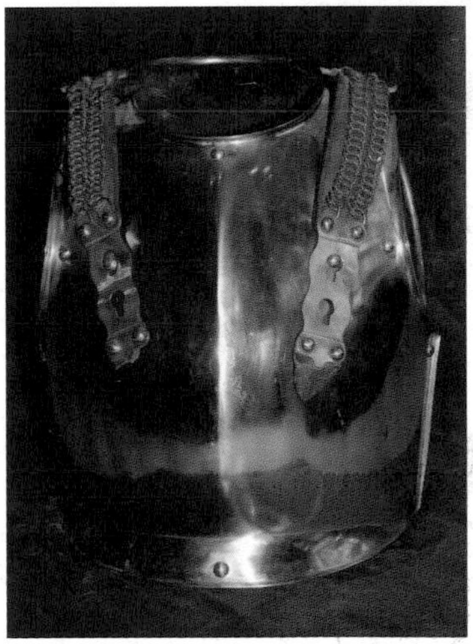

△ French Cavalry Cuirass

- *1833*

French heavy cavalry cuirass comprising breastplate and backplate with straps. Brass fittings with interlaced linkages. Signed with arsenal of manufacture, 'Klingenthal' dated and numbered.

- **£900** • **Michael German**

◁ Officer's Gorget

- *circa 1830–1848*

Officer's gorget – Garde National de Paris. With original leather liner. Shield showing Bourbon cockerel over French flags with wreath choker.

- *height 14cm*
- **£280** • **C.F. Seidler**

▷ Flintlock Pistols

• *1840*
A pair of flintlock pistols heavily inlaid. Made in France in the mid-nineteenth century, specifically for export to the Middle East.
• £750 • **Chelsea (OMRS)**

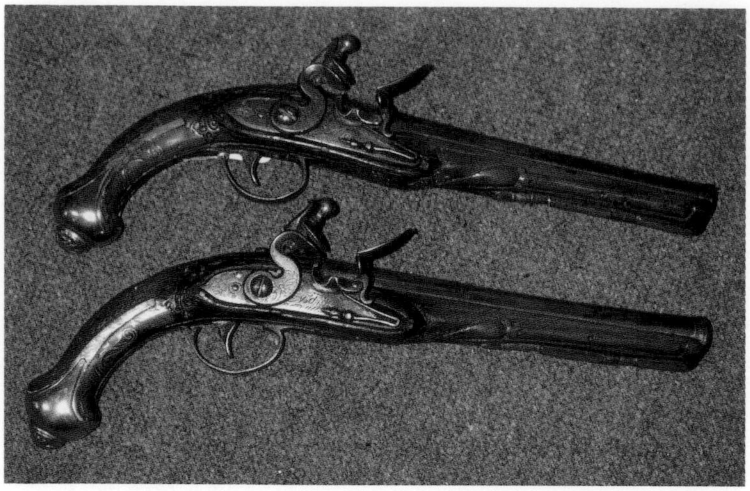

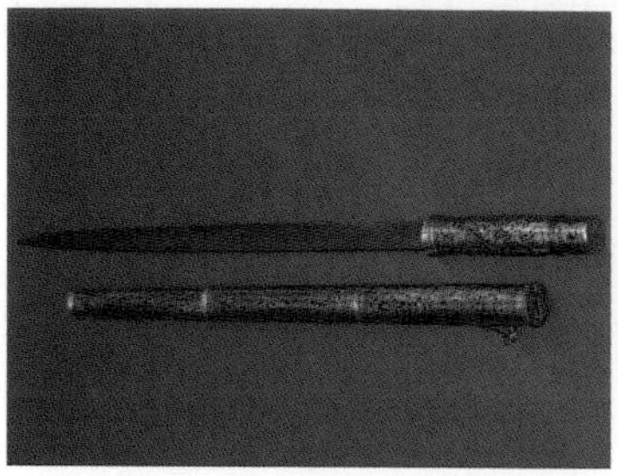

△ Burmese Dagger

• *circa 1830*
Burmese Dhar dagger with ornate silver handle and scabbard inlaid with niello foliate design.
• *length 54cm*
• £620 • **Michael German**

△ Patterned Plaid Brooch

• *circa 1836–71*
Patterned plaid brooch of 93rd Highlanders (Sutherland) decorated with thistles and inscribed in solid silver. Not hallmarked; as worn by the 'thin red line' in the Crimea.
• *diameter 10cm*
• £550 • **C.F. Seidler**

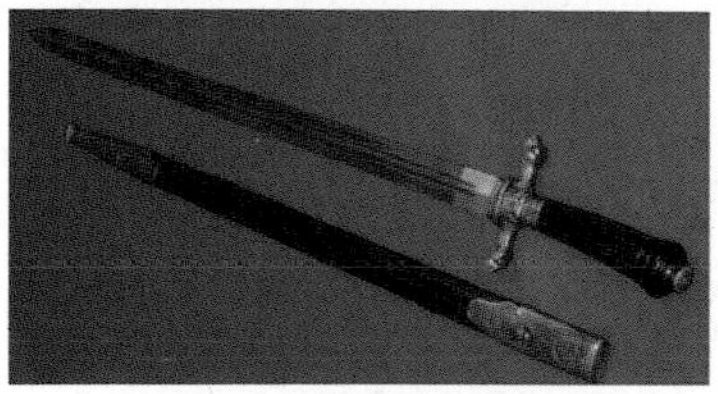

△ Hunting Sword

• *circa 1850*
With grooved blade, fluted ebony handle and plated mounts with dog head cross guard.
• *length 70cm*
• £750 • **Michael German**

▽ Brass Powder Flask

• *circa 1840*
A larger than most brass powder flask, with brass nozzle for fowling or hunting.
• *length 25cm*
• £60 • **C.F. Seidler**

▷ Persian Helmet

• *circa mid-19th century*
Oversized Persian parade helmet etched with figures and silver decoration. Brass and steel chain mail. Large nose guard, two plume holders and helmet spike.
• £2,800 • **Robert Hales**

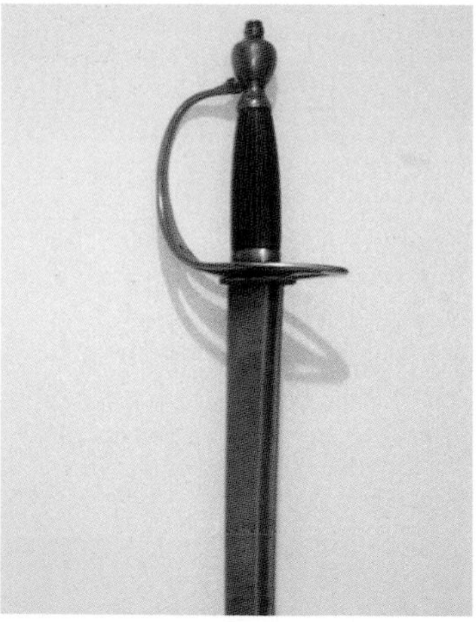

△ Midshipman's Hanger

• *circa 1850*
Navy Midshipman's Hanger, with brass guard, steel blade with original washer still present, without scabbard.
• *length 86cm*
• £275 • **C.F. Seidler**

▽ Deane Harding Percussion Pistol

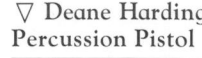

• *circa 1840*
Deane Harding .54-calibre officer's percussion cap and ball pistol, with hexagonal barrel and original grip and varnish. London proof marks.
• *length 30cm*
• £750 • **C.F. Seidler**

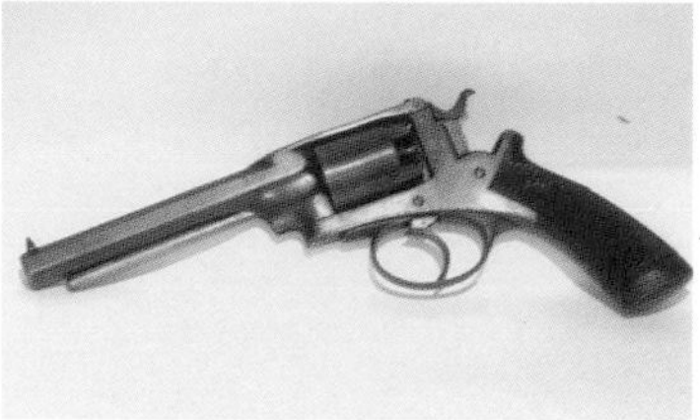

▽ Percussion Pistol

• *1840*
An English .50-calibre cap and ball Turnover pistol with turn off barrels. Retailed by Tipping Lorden, made in Birmingham.
• *length 21.5cm*
• £350 • **C.F. Seidler**

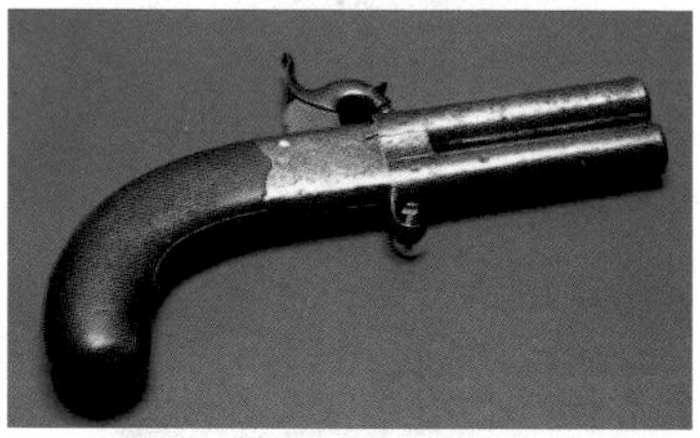

▽ Percussion Revolver

• *circa 1854*
English Tranter patent, double-action, percussion revolver, overlaid in gold, retailer B. Cogswell 224 Strand, London, in original fitted case,with accessories.
• *length 32cm*
• £3,800 • **Michael German**

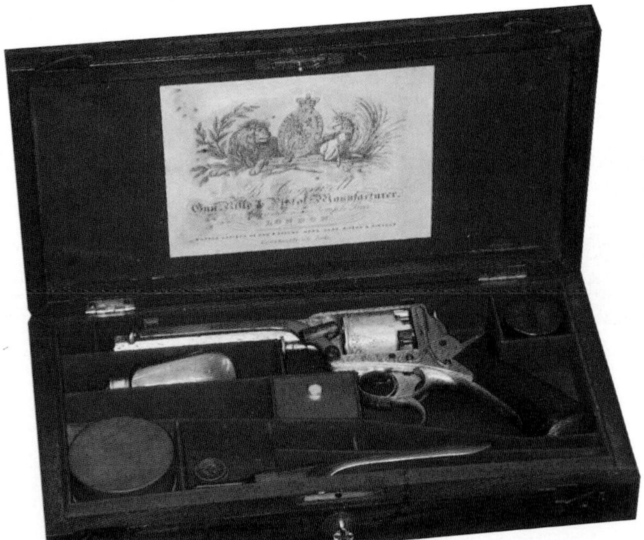

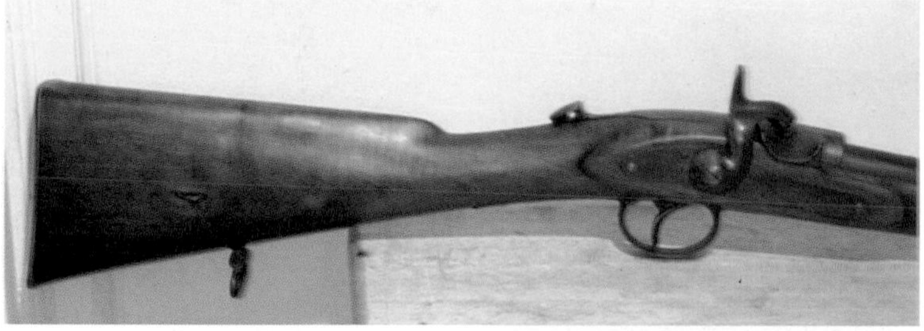

△ Percussion Carbine

- *circa 1850*

Percussion carbine in working order with original mould for the making of ammunition and walnut funiture, made by the Westley & Richards & Co., with a Whitworth patent, complete with strap holders and ram rod.

- *length 1.03m*
- £600 • C.F. Seidler

△ Belt Buckle

- *1860*

Belt buckle for the St Martin in the Fields Rifle Volunteers (Patent unit of Queens Westminster).

- *width 7.5cm*
- £275 • C.F. Seidler

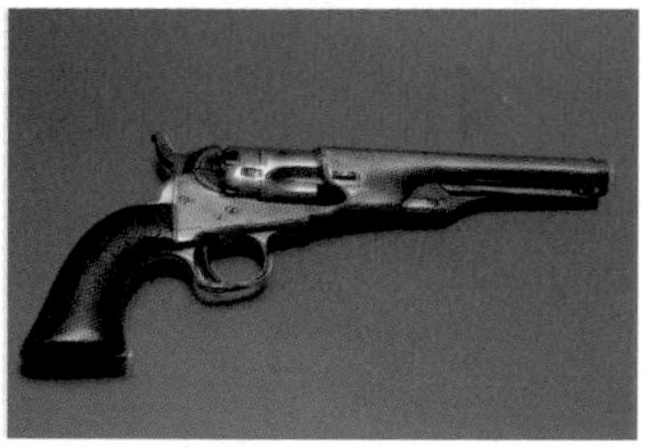

△ Colt Police .36-Calibre Pistol

- *1862*

Colt police .36-calibre smooth barrel pistol, including barrel wedge for civil use or military back up.

- *length 27.5cm*
- £675 • C.F. Seidler

△ Cheshire Regiment Belt Clasp

- *1855*

Belt clasp of the 22nd Cheshire Regiment with crown over regimental number and silver and gilt belt loops.

- *width 13cm*
- £135 • C.F. Seidler

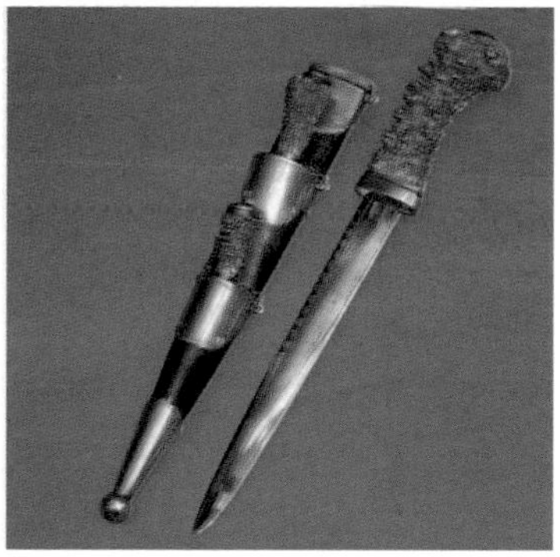

△ Scottish Dirk

- *circa 1860*

Scottish silver-mounted highland dirk, complete with knife and fork, the handles carved from stag horn.

- *length 38cm*
- £1,600 • Michael German

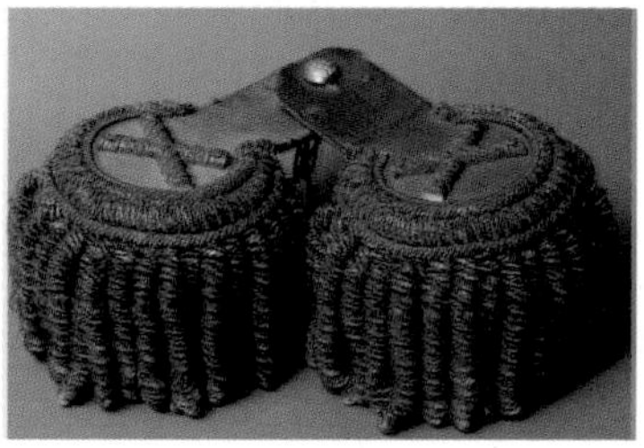

△ Imperial Russian Epaulettes

- *1870*

Imperial Russian Field Marshal's epaulettes. Reputedly those of Emperor Wilhelm 1st of Prussia. Of twisted and spun gold wire.

- £6,500 • The Armoury

▽ Danish Cavalry Sword

- *1860*

Danish cavalry sword with original polished steel scabbard with maker's mark 17 S & K.

- *length 85cm*
- £220 • C.F. Seidler

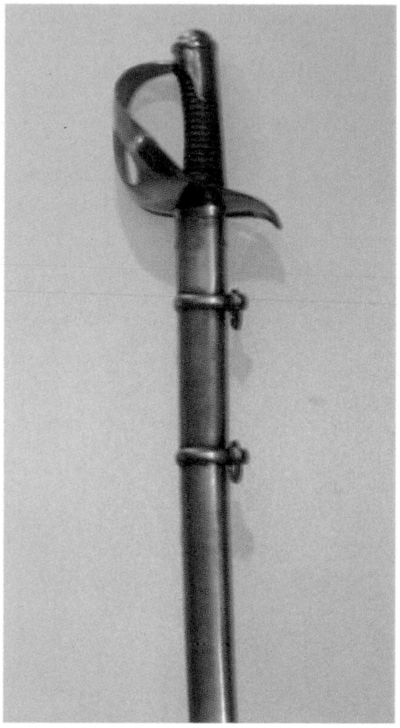

▽ American Trapdoor Trowel Bayonet

- *1873*

Springfield trowel bayonet as used by plainsmen as a trenching tool.

- *length 36cm*
- £230 • C.F. Seidler

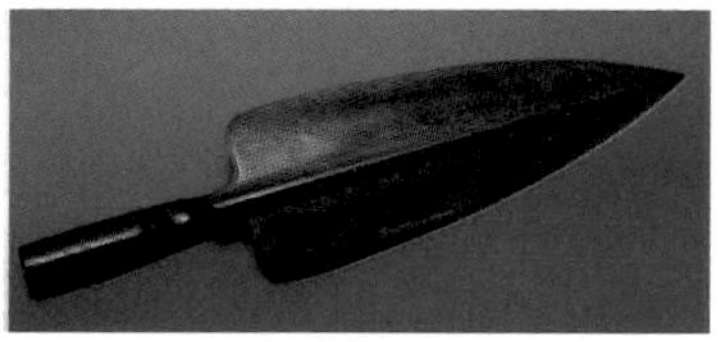

▽ Russian Dagger

- *circa 1880*

Russian Kinjal dagger with ornate silver hilt and scabbard, the blade with long grooves and foliate design.

- *length 51cm*
- £1,400 • Michael German

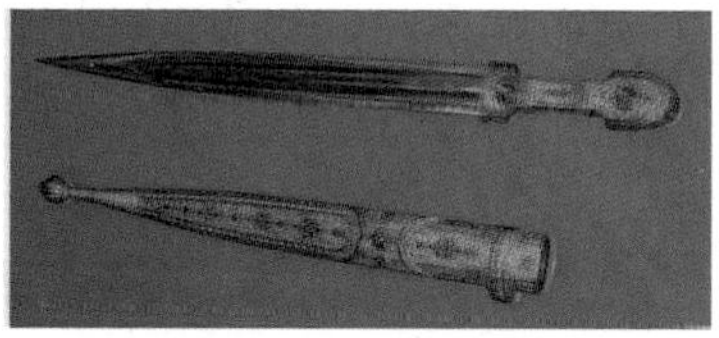

▷ French Cuirassier's Helmet

- *1890*

With Medusa head, horsehair plume, steel skull with ostrich feathers side plume and original scaled chin strap.

- £1,100 • Michael German

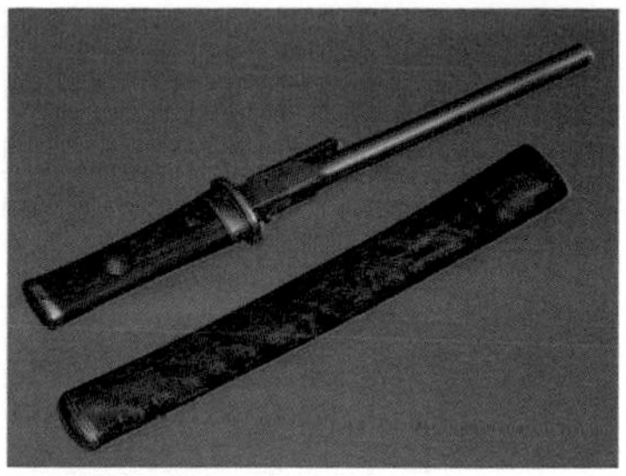

△ Japanese Tanto

- *circa 1860*

Japanese Tanto concealing a percussion pistol, with copper and brass fittings and burr-wood furniture.

- *length 48cm*
- £3,250 • Michael German

△ Remington Pistol

- *1862*

Remington New Model Army .44 percussion cap and ball pistol. Original varnish and inspector's stamp in the grip. Hexagonal barrel. Military weapon.

- *length 36cm*
- £795 • C.F. Seidler

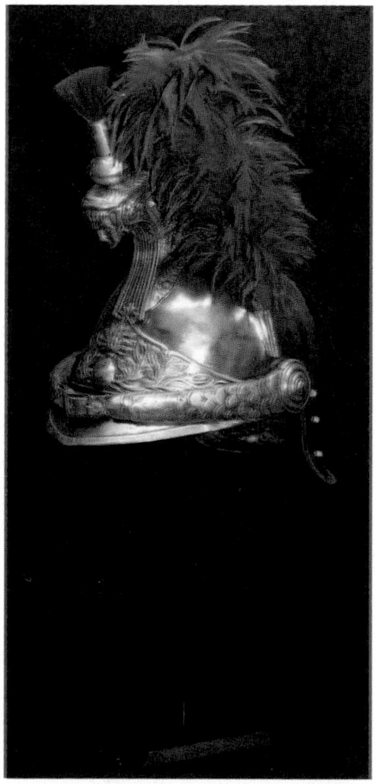

△ Boer War Two-Pound Shell Case

- *1900*

A Boer War two-pound 'Pom Pom' artillery shell case, in brass with projectile head in place but powder and percussion cap removed.

- *length 20cm*
- £15 • Chelsea (OMRS)

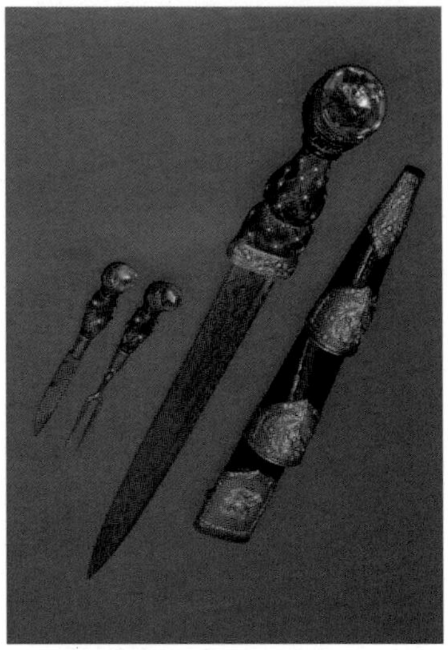

△ Scottish Full Dirk

- *circa 1905*

Scottish military full-dress dirk blade etched with battle honours for the Highland Light Infantry, coloured stones, regimental crest.

- *length 46cm*
- £1,800 • Michael German

△ Lancer Chape Plate

- *circa 1900*

Lancer chape plate with royal coat of arms and battle honours showing the Death Head of 17th Lancers.

- *height 12cm*
- £90 • C.F. Seidler

▽ Trooper's Sabre

- *circa 1908*

British trooper's sabre, pattern dated and inscribed W.W.I. Paint.

- *length 1.1m*
- £275 • C.F. Seidler

▽ Dress Busby

- *1916*

A dress Busby with white plume and brass fittings and chin strap, showing insignia of the Royal Engineers and dating from World War I.

- *height 33cm*
- 275 • Chelsea (OMRS)

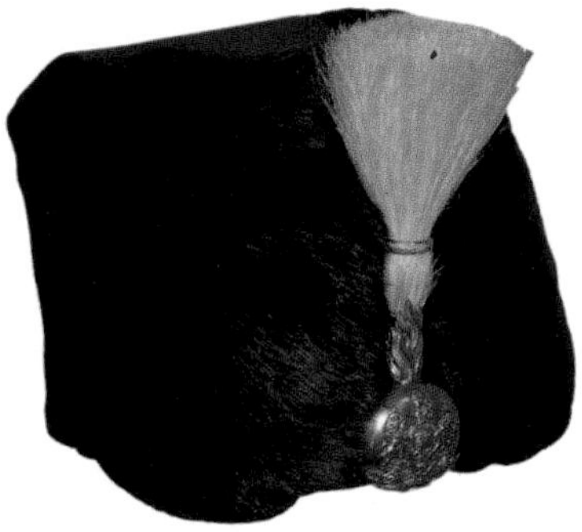

▽ Officer's Helmet Plate

- *1900*

Officer's helmet plate of East Surrey. Showing the coat of arms of Guildford with the Queen's crown device. 95 per cent original gilt finish.

- *height 12.5cm*
- £200 • C.F. Seidler

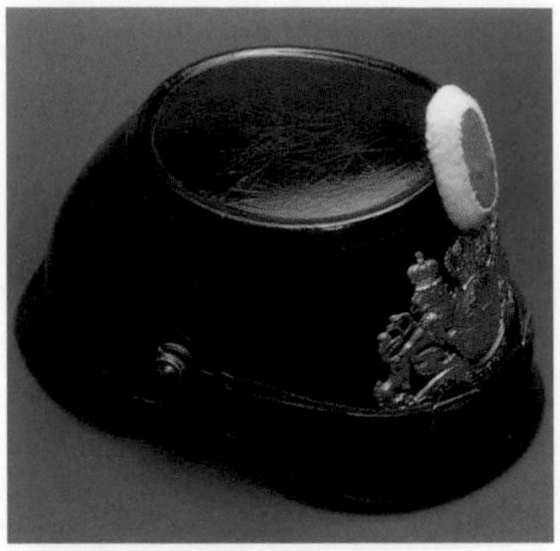

△ Bavarian Helment

- *1913*

Patent leather Bavarian helmet of the Royal Bavarian airship flying section. With original blue and white woollen cockade, helmet plate and chin strap.

- *height 23cm*
- £590 • C.F. Seidler

△ World War I Sniper's Helmet

- *1916*

Sniper's helmet with sniper's plate in the 1916 model. Matching camouflage colours and paint. Stamped with Krupp logo of three concentric circles. Leather line slightly worn. No chin strap.

- *height 20cm*
- £450 • C.F. Seidler

△ Tin of Boer War Chocolate

- *1900*

A hinged metal tin from the Boer War, originally containing chocolate and showing the royal crest, the profile of Queen Victoria, the inscription 'South Africa 1900' and a signed message in the Queen's handwriting wishing the recipient 'A happy new year'.

- *19cm x 11cm*
- £145 • Chelsea (OMRS)

▽ Beer Stein

- *circa 1900–10*

Beer stein from the Cavalry Division. Five-litre stein. Maker is Mettlach. Nice piece. Lid of the stein is decorated with a model of an eagle.

- £950 • Gordon's

▽ World War I 'Brodie' Helmet

- *1917*

A British army second type 'Brodie' steel helmet, from the latter part of World War I, complete with adjustable leather strap.

- £75 • Chelsea (OMRS)

▽ World War I Dagger

- *World War I*

A World War I German fighting knife by 'Ern'. Has a studded wooden handle and is complete with a leather and steel sheath.

- *length 70cm*
- £70 • Chelsea (OMRS)

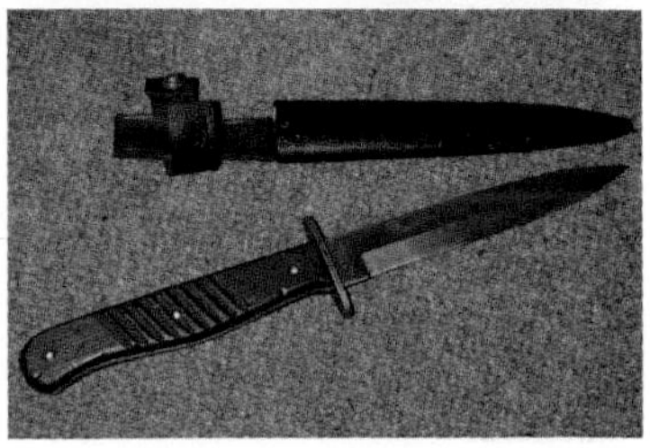

△ **Royal Engineers Officer's Tunic**

• *1914*
An officer's full dress tunic of the Royal Engineers, in scarlet, dating from the beginning of World War I.
• £185 • Chelsea (OMRS)

△ **World War I Binoculars**

• *1917*
Pair of military binoculars dated 1917, with leather carrying case inscribed with the name of a soldier serving with the Highland Light Infantry.
• *length 18cm*
• £115 • Chelsea (OMRS)

▽ **S.A. Dagger**

• *1933*
NSKK-type with black enamel finish to scabbard. S.A. dagger etched blade with 'Alles für Deutschland'. Wood handle with Nazi insignia.
• *length 37cm*
• £245 • C.F. Seidler

▽ **Miniature Cavalry Helmet**

• *1920*
A one third-sized cavalry helmet of the 2nd County of London Yeomanry, with purple horse-hair plume. Possibly made as an officer's desk ornament.
• £450 • Chelsea (OMRS)

▽ **Old Bill Mascot**

• *1920*
A bronze car mascot mounted on a wooden base of Bruce Bairnsfather's 'Old Bill' character.
• £200 • Chelsea (OMRS)

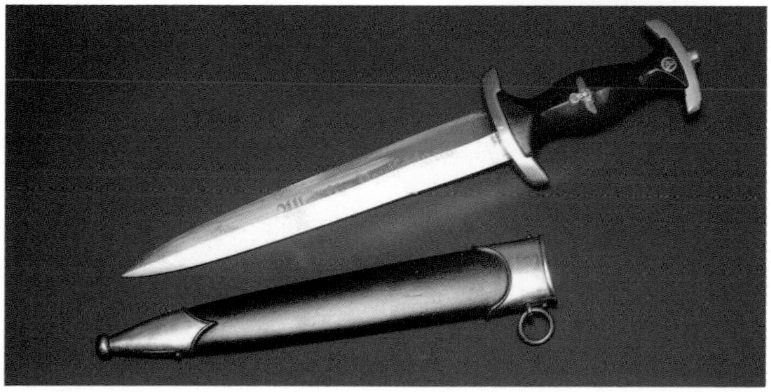

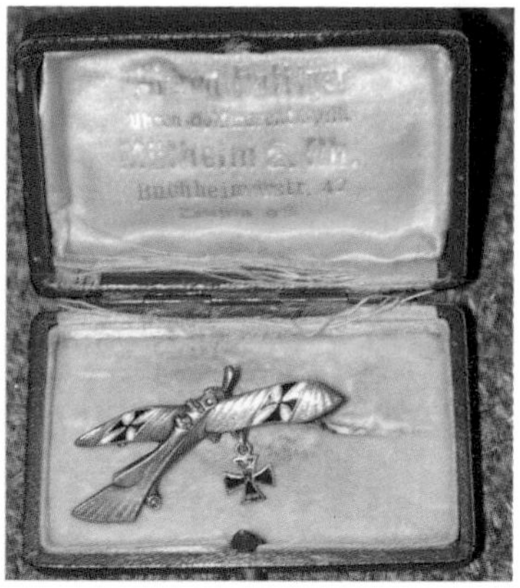

△ **World War I German Sweetheart Brooch**

• *1917*
A World War I German Eindekker sweetheart's brooch in the shape of a monoplane, with a German cross insignia attached by a chain. In original box with inscription in gold print.
• *length 3.8cm*
• £1,917 • Chelsea (OMRS)

△ **Silver Regimental Spoon**

• *World War I*
A silver regimental teaspoon showing the ornate crest of the London Rifle Brigade, topped with a crown.
• *length 9cm*
• £25 • Chelsea (OMRS)

△ **Luftwaffe Nachrichten Signals Tunic**

• *1940*
With four pockets, NCO shoulder boards with silver braid, one pip, tan piping and number 11, with piping and silver braid collar.
• £395 • Gordon's

▽ **Luftschutz Dagger**

• *1939*
Luftschutz dagger, lst pattern rankers issue, complete with single strap hanger, with the maker's mark 'Kroneck Ernst Erich Witte Solingen' on blade and 'RZM M5/71 OLC' on the hanger clip.
• *length 40cm*
• £825 • Gordon's

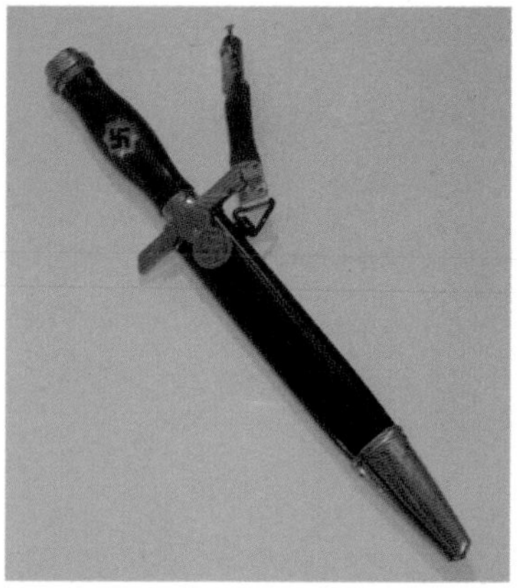

▽ **Luftwaffe Dagger**

• *1937*
German Luftwaffe dagger, second type, with yellow bakelite grip and original maker's mark 'Eickhorn Solingen', hanger straps and porte-épée.
• *length 37cm*
• £325 • Gordon's

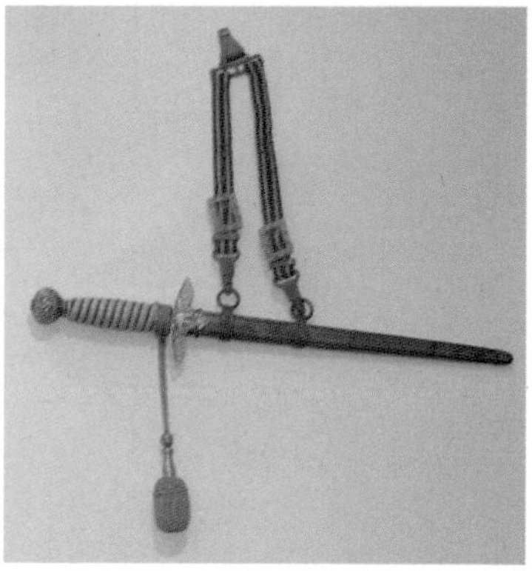

▽ **German Dagger**

• *1937*
A pre-war Third Reich Brownshirt's dress dagger, made by Friedrich Geigis. Complete with scabbard and nickel fittings; showing insignia.
• *length 30cm*
• £225 • Chelsea (OMRS)

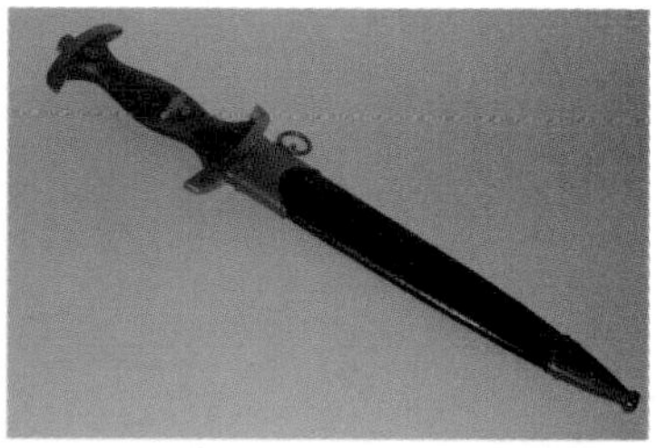

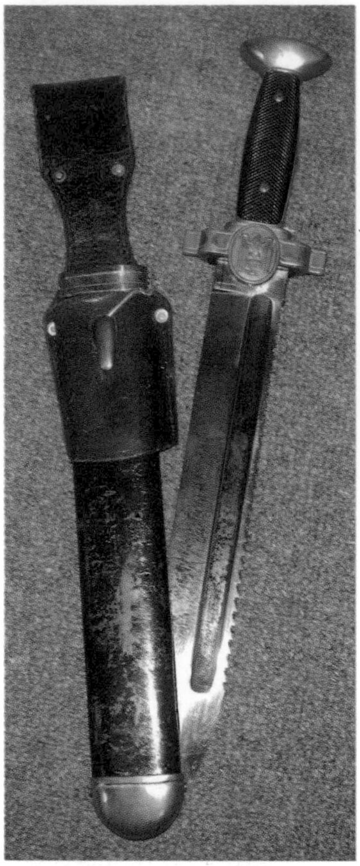

△ World War II German Red Cross Dagger

• *World War II*
A World War II German red cross man's 'heuer' dress dagger, with serrated edge and blood gutter.
• *length 30cm*
• £375 • Chelsea (OMRS)

△ German Peaked Cap

• *1940*
German WWII peaked cap of the Luftwaffe Artillery. Blue with red piping, in good condition, badges and cockade. Makers mark 'Deutsche Wert Arbeit' inside.
• *size 8*
• £285 • Gordon's

▽ SS Kepi Cap

• *1940*
Early SS Kepi with skull and leather strap.
• *size 8*
• £975 • Gordon's

▽ Schutzenschnur Silver Luftwaffe

• *1940*
Pilot officer's silver braid of the Luftwaffe with an eagle and National Insignia.
• *length 14cm*
• £100 • Gordon's

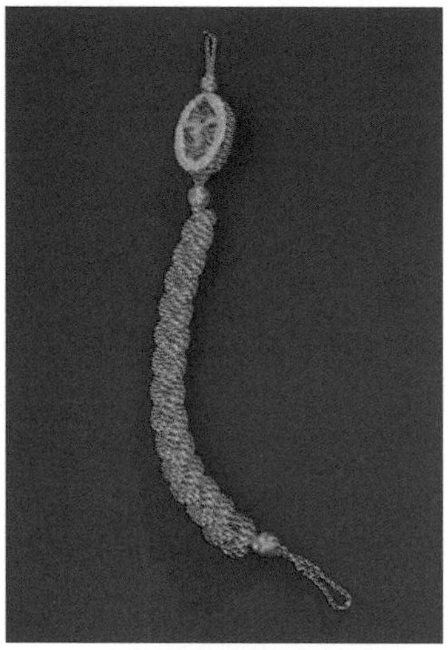

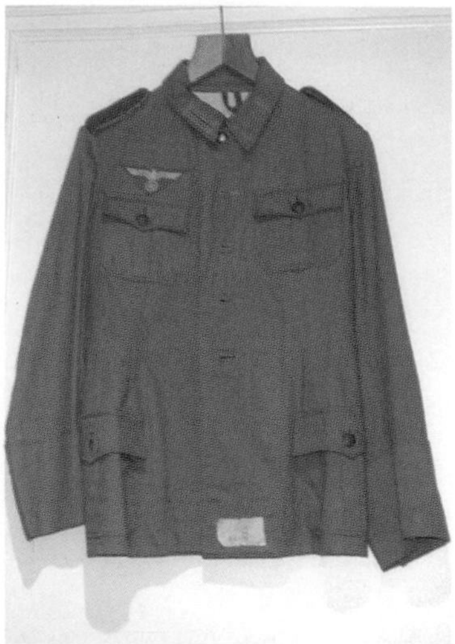

△ Infantry Tunic

• *1941*
Africa Corps infantry tunic with four pockets complete with all insignia and buttons. In excellent condition.
• *large*
• £375 • Gordon's

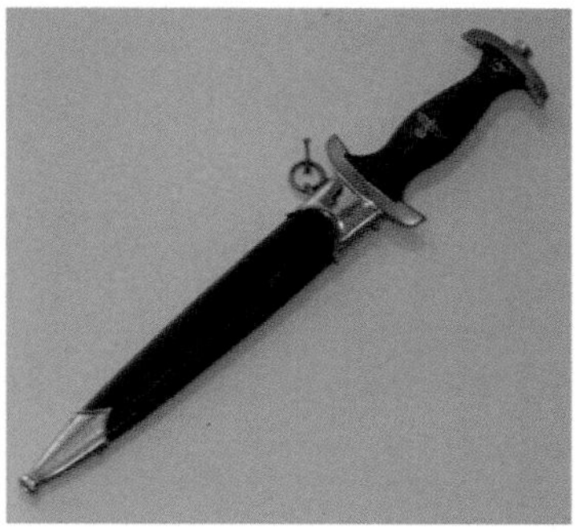

△ SA Dagger

• *circa 1932*
SA honour dagger Rohm Widmung with partly erased inscription. The Ernst Rohm has been neatly erased from the blade but the rest remains. Some light wear on the scabbard, otherwise dagger in very good condition.
• *length 39cm*
• £695 • Gordon's

▽ World War II Flying Helmet

• *1944*
A World War II RAF 'C' type flying helmet with intrinsic radio earpieces and MK VIII goggles with webbing strap and H-type oxygen mask for high altitude.
• £185 • Chelsea (OMRS)

▽ German Naval Artillery Forage Cap

• *1942*
A German Naval Coastal Artillery soldier's forage cap in field grey wool, from World War II. With badge and insignia.
• £140 • Chelsea (OMRS)

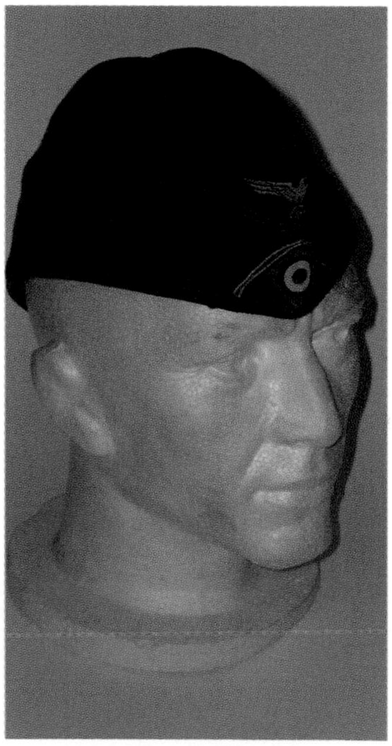

◁ World War II RAF Cap

• *1940*
A Royal Air Force warrant officer's uniform cap dating from the beginning of World War II.
• £85 • Chelsea (OMRS)

▷ RAD Dagger

- *World World II*

Rad Hauer honour dirk. Has marker's mark and is numbered. Reasonably scarce.

- £375 • Gordon's Medals

▽ World War II Commando Knife

- *1944*

A World War II British Commando fighting knife in steel and brass, complete with scabbard.

- *length 30cm*
- £85 • Chelsea (OMRS)

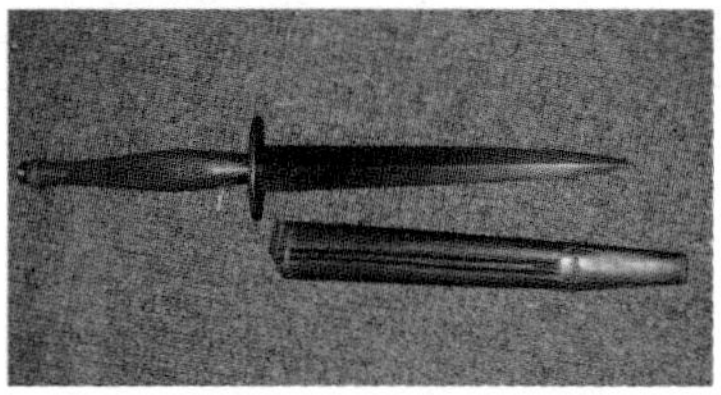

▽ Gebirgsjäeger NCO's Peaked Cap

- *1940*

Gebirgsjäeger NCO's peaked cap. Maker's diamond on the inside. Uniform Krungshaus Karl Petrasch Klagenfurt. All outside emblems attached, complete and in good condition.

- *size 8*
- £495 • Gordon's

▷ Luftwaffe Paratrooper Helmet

- *1940*

Luftwaffe paratrooper's helmet. Rare double decal version, with both Luftwaffe eagle and national shield. The chinstrap and liner are complete showing makers mark: Baumuster: Heisler Berlin C2 Hersteller F. W. Muller JR and sizes; Koptwelte GR 61 Stahlhaube Nr. 71, all clearly readable. Helmet stamped on the inside, 'ET71', paintwork and overall finish excellent.

- *size 8*
- £3,500 • Gordon's

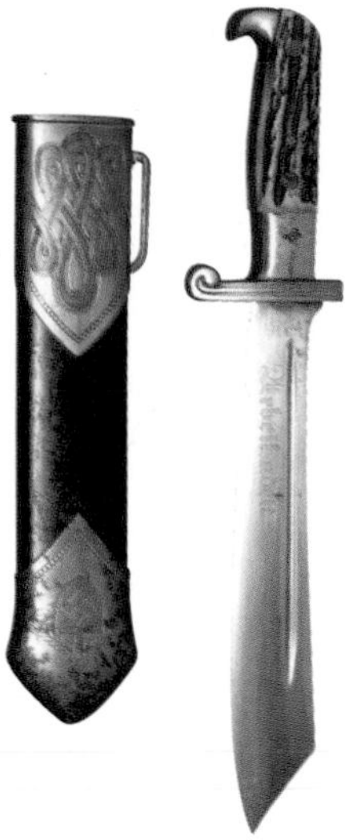

▽ Paper Rack

- *1940*

A paper rack from World War II, hand-crafted and scrolled in wrought iron and mounted on a splay-footed stand constructed of pieces of collected shrapnel.

- *height 46cm*
- £100 • Chelsea (OMRS)

▷ World War II Tunic

- *World War II*

An NCO Artillery dress tunic of the 79th Artillery Regiment. Complete with ribbons bar, breast eagle, shoulder boards, two pips and number 79. In very good condition.

- £325 • Gordon's

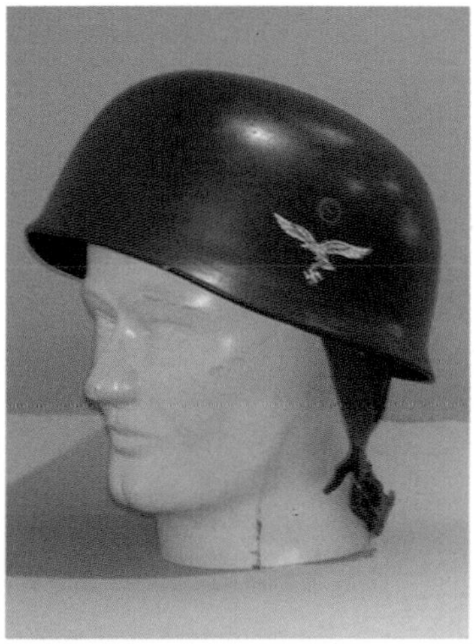

▽ Luftwaffe Flying Helmet

- *1940*

Luftwaffe flying helmet. Summer issue version, with canvas hood, straps, leads and sockets still present. Stamped inside earpiece. Ln 26602.

- *height 19cm*
- £245 • Gordon's

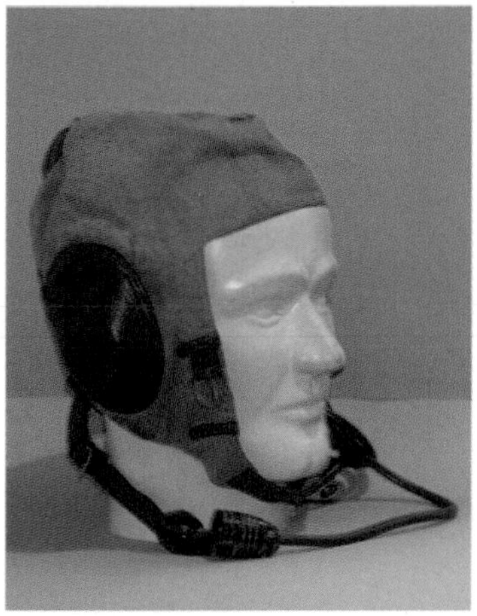

▷ Korean War Pilot's Helmet

- *1950*

A fighter pilot's helmet, Soviet-made for a MiG fighter, used by a North Korean pilot in the Korean War.

- £150 • Chelsea (OMRS)

▽ Grenadier Guards Cap

- *circa 1940*

A World War II-period Grenadier Guards peaked dress cap, with regimental cap badge insignia.

- £40 • Chelsea (OMRS)

△ Kriegsmarine Colani Jacket

- *1940*

A rare Kriegsmarine Colani Jacket-Haupt Feldwebel, Coxwain rank, complete with breast eagle, shoulder boards and all original buttons.

- *medium*
- £315 • Gordon's

▽ German Officer's Ski Cap

- *1942*

German officer's ski cap (mountain troops). Fine quality quilted lining and Edelweiss cockade. With ear flaps, in blue-green.

- *height 16cm*
- £300 • C.F. Seidler

AUTOMOBILIA

Motor racing and rallies are as popular today as they have ever been, along with the collecting of automobile memorabilia. The collection of automobilia is based predominantly around clubs, racetracks and personalities; for example, any memorabilia relating to the Brooklands and Monte Carlo racetracks or the the Morgan, Aston Martin and MG car clubs is regarded as highly collectable. They provide items of interest to the collector, who is prepared to pay large sums of money for a certain badge or mascot to add to their collection. A huge industry has sprung up around the classic car and, for thc avid collector of automobilia, the auto sales that take place across the country provide an opportunity to purchase anything from racing programmes, garage signs and car parts to archival photography. While a vintage car may be too expensive, memorabilia is affordable. To be auctioned shortly is the Bugatti Royal, which is estimated to fetch more than £7 million. What greater respect for its craftmanship can we bestow on the motor car?

△ **Spirit of Ecstasy**

- *circa 1915*

A nickel-plated Rolls Royce mascot, designed by Charles Sykes, on a trophy base. Would have adorned a Silver Ghost.

- £1,500 • C.A.R.S.

▽ **Pedal Fire Truck**

- *early 1920s*

An American-made fire truck with fine detailing. Wooden ladder with mascot on bonnet.

- *1.05m x 52cm*
- £3,500 • C.A.R.S.

▽ **Bentley Flying B**

- *circa 1920*

Bentley flying-winged B radiator-mounted mascot by Charles Sykes.

- *height 17cm*
- £300 • C.A.R.S.

▽ **Motor Club Mascot**

- *circa 1915*

A Brighton & Hove Motor Club dolphin in nickel-plated bronze on a marble base.

- £150 • C.A.R.S.

▷ **Brighton & Hove Motor Club Badge**

- *circa 1920s*

Brighton and Hove Motor Club membership badge of the inter-war period. Die-struck brass, chrome-plated with vitreous enamel.

- *diameter 6cm*
- £200 • C.A.R.S.

▽ B.A.R.C. Badge

- *from 1907*

Brooklands Automobile Racing Club member's and guests brooches. Every year on joining a member would be issued with a pin brooch tag in gilt brass with vitreous coloured enamel centre and two smaller versions on coloured string for the guests. These were sent to the member in an official box with the matching year date shown. The dates issued were from the opening of the circuit in 1910.

- *height 14cm*
- **boxed sets £200** • **C.A.R.S.**

▽ Bentley Mascot

- *circa 1920s*

Bentley flying-winged B radiator-mounted mascot designed by Charles Sykes. This example is from the 1920s roadster sports model and is a large brass casting used for a short period.

- *wing span 22cm*
- **£400** • **C.A.R.S.**

△ Bugatti Pedal Car

- *late 1920s*

A Bugatti Eureka made in France. Two-seater replica of the type 35 Grand Prix Sports with very fine chrome and leather detailing.

- *1.65m x 56cm*
- **£3,500** • **C.A.R.S.**

▷ Jaguar Mascot

- *circa 1925–30*

Jaguar leaping-cat car mascot by Desmo, after a design by Frederick Gordon Crosby, cast brass, chrome plated and mounted on a radiator cap. An after-sales accessory mascot popular during the inter-war period.

- *length 20cm*
- **£300** • **C.A.R.S.**

▽ R.A.C. Badge

- *circa 1930s*

Royal Automobile Club associate badge affiliated to the Junior Car Club (J.C.C.) Inter-war period. Chromed brass and vitreous enamel collars.

- *height 13cm*
- **£150** • **C.A.R.S.**

◁ Brooklands Badge

- *1920*

A Brooklands B.A.R.C 120mph speed award badge.

- *height 13cm*
- **£3,000** • **C.A.R.S.**

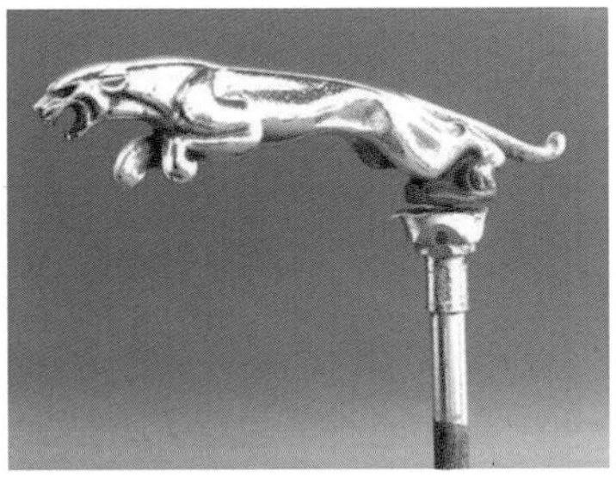

▽ Club Badge

- *circa 1935*

A Junior Car Club radiator badge in pressed steel with enamel in black, red and white with chromium-plated wings.

- **£250** • **C.A.R.S.**

△ J.C.C. Ashtray

- *circa 1920s*

Ashtray of the J.C.C. Junior Car Club produced in epns, with the club badge positioned in the centre.

- *diameter 14cm*
- **£75** • **C.A.R.S.**

△ Kneeling Spirit

- *circa 1920–1940*

A kneeling Sprit of Ecstasy, designed for the ergonomics of the bonnets of the Phantom III and the Silver Wraith.

- **£450** • **C.A.R.S.**

△ Jaguar Mascot

- *circa 1936*

A Jaguar SS 100 leaping-cat mascot, mounted on a Panther J72 radiator cap.

- **£300** • **C.A.R.S.**

△ Measuring Cans

• *circa 1930*
Two- and five-gallon measuring vessels with copper bodies and brass banding. Funnel tops and brass spouts, positioned to prevent over-filling. The five-gallon vessel with hinged carrying-handle.
• £195/£180 • Castlegate

△ Club Badge

• *circa 1935*
Radiator badge for the Junior Car Club, of circular form with wheel design on reverse, standing on a marble base.
• *height 7cm*
• £150 • C.A.R.S.

△ Fire Truck Pedal Car

• *1940s*
An American fire truck replica from the 1940s period. A pedal-powered car with very fine chrome detailing.
• *96cm x 38cm*
• £200 •C.A.R.S.

▷ Bentley B

• *circa 1940s*
Bentley flying-winged B radiator-mounted mascot, designed by Charles Sykes. This example is shown to be leaning backward.
• *wing span 17cm*
• £300 • C.A.R.S.

△ MG Pedal Car

• *1950s*
An MG TD pedal-powered car with a fibreglass body and chrome detailing.
• *1.22m x 51cm*
• £650 • C.A.R.S.

△ Mercedes Radiator Grill

• *circa 1950*
Radiator shell with grill and star mascot, pressed steel chromium plated.
• *width 65cm*
• £100 • C.A.R.S.

△ Club Badge

• *1950s–70s*
British Racing and Sports Car Club badge in die-struck brass, chrome-plated with coloured vitreous enamels.
• *height 10cm*
• £75 • C.A.R.S.

△ Zephyr/Zodiac Pedal Car

• *mid-1950s*
A Tri-Ang Zephyr/Zodiac with a pressed-steel body and chrome detailing.
• *1.15m x 42cm*
• £650 • C.A.R.S.

△ Club Badge

• *circa 1957*
A British Motor Racing Marshals' Club badge, in steel and polychrome enamel.
• £150 • C.A.R.S.

▽ Wolseley Pedal Car

• *late 1950s*
A Tri-Ang pressed-steel bodied model of a Wolseley with chrome detailing and working headlights.
• *1.05m x 43cm*
• £450 • C.A.R.S.

▽ Bentley Drivers Club Badge

• *1950s*
Bentley Drivers Club wheel spinner style club membership badge in chrome and painted enamel.
• *diameter 8cm*
• £45 • C.A.R.S.

◁ Japanese Cadillac

• *1950*
A tin-plate Japanese 50s Marysan Cadillac, cream and green with working lights. Forward and reverse, very rare, in original box.
• *length 30cm*
• £250 • Langfords Marine

▽ Jaguar Badge

- *circa 1950*

Jaguar Drivers' Club member's badge in the form of a steering wheel. In die-struck brass chrome-plated with central cat's head in brass and red vitreous enamel legend on scroll beneath. Made by Pinches, London, with member's name engraved on reverse.

- *diameter 8cm*
- £75 • C.A.R.S.

▽ Jaguar Pedal Car

- *1950s–mid-1960s*

A Jaguar XK-120 open Roadster. Fibreglass body with chrome detailing, pedal-powered car.

- *length 1.5m, width 53cm*
- £950 • C.A.R.S.

▽ Ford Pedal Car

- *early 1960s*

A Tri-Ang Ford Zephyr-style police car with working siren and chrome detailing.

- *84cm x 36cm*
- £300 • C.A.R.S.

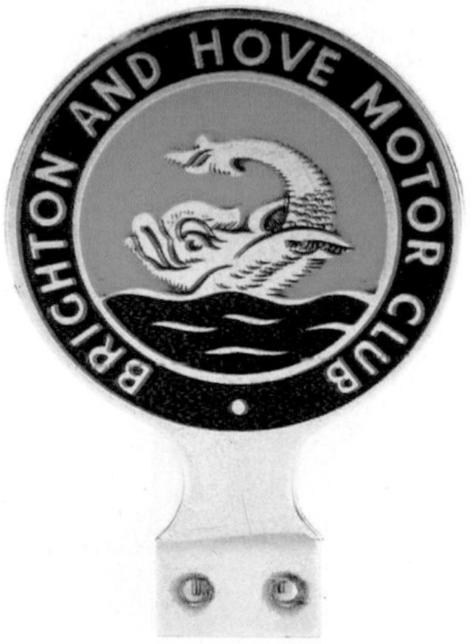

△ Club Badge

- *circa 1958*

A radiator membership badge of the Brighton & Hove Motor Club, in navy blue and sea blue chrome and enamel.

- £30 • C.A.R.S.

△ Tri-Ang Convertible

- *mid-1960s*

A plastic Rolls Royce convertible with chrome detailing, made by Tri-Ang.

- *1.22m x 46cm*
- £650 • C.A.R.S.

△ Brooklands Society Badge

- *circa 1960s–1980s*

B.S. (Brooklands Society) membership badge in die-struck brass, chrome-plated with vitreous coloured enamels.

- *height 14.5cm*
- £100 • C.A.R.S.

▽ Bentley Pedal Car

- *mid-1960s*

A Tri-Ang Bentley continental convertible. Plastic body with chrome detailing.

- *1.22m x 46cm*
- £950 • C.A.R.S.

▽ F3 Racing Pedal Car

- *early 1970s*

A Tri-Ang plastic-bodied F3 racing car with dummy rear engine.

- *1.22m x 63cm*
- £150 • C.A.R.S.

▽ RAC Silver Jubilee Badge

- *1977*

RAC Queen's Silver Jubilee 1977 specially produced limited edition commemorative badge sold with certificate. Die-struck brass chrome-plated with plastic based enamel colours.

- *diameter 10cm*
- £200 • C.A.R.S.

Steering Wheel Ashtray

- *circa 1950s*

Ashtray in the form of a steering wheel in moulded porcelain produced by Beswick, England, for Les Leston (Motoring Suppliers).

- *diameter 19cm*
- £55 • C.A.R.S.

△ Club Badge

- *circa 1985*

Brighton Morgan Sports Car Club. Perspex front on steel, chrome-plated badge.

- £35 • C.A.R.S.

△ Morgan Pedal Car

- *1980*

A Morgan 4/4 Roadster with a fibreglass body and chrome detailing, and has working headlights and horn.

- *1.22m x 50cm*
- £950 • C.A.R.S.

BOOKS, MAPS & ATLASES

The current collector's market is saturated with books so it is important to know how to determine a book's value before you start to invest. Look out for first editions as these can add considerable value to your purchase, along with whether the book is by a collectable author or illustrator. A book can be collectable in later editions if the first tends to have a high price that places it out of reach for most collectors. The binding of a book can considerably add to its appearance and in some cases can be more fascinating than the words contained within. The lure of collecting old maps lies not only in their historical value, but also in their decorative appeal. It is thought that the first printed atlas dates back to around 1477, using maps drawn by the Greek geographer, Claudius Ptolemy. It is now rare to find a complete atlas as the majority have been broken up over the years. The value of an atlas not only depends on colour and condition but also the area depicted.

▽ Print of Conil

• *1580*
A print of the views of Conil. J. Gerez De la Frontera. The author is the publisher, Braun Hogenburg. Showing allegorical views of costume and trades of the 16th century.
• £220 • Paul Orssich

◁ Kufic Page

• *9th century*
Kufic page from the Koran on vellum, with illuminated sura heading. Middle East.
• £900 • Oasis

△ Prayer Book

• *1607*
The Book of Common Prayer translated according to Hebrew and Greek, and conferred with the best translations in Diuers languages. London: Robert Barker Crown, 4to. Contemporary panelled calf, with brass corners and centre-pieces.
• £500 • Ash Books

△ A Display of Heraldrie

• *1611*
A first edition of a single volume from the 17th century, written by John Guillim. Illustrated and hand-coloured throughout with associated family history.
• *30cm x 20cm*
• £1,000 • Chelsea Gallery

▽ Gerard Mercator Atlas

• *1632*
Gerardi Mercatoris Atlas sive Cosmographicae Meditatones. Amsterdam, Johann Cloppenburg, with fine hand-coloured copperplate 'architectural' title and 179 fine, recent hand-coloured, copperplate maps.
• *22cm x 28cm*
• £27,500 • Peter Harrington

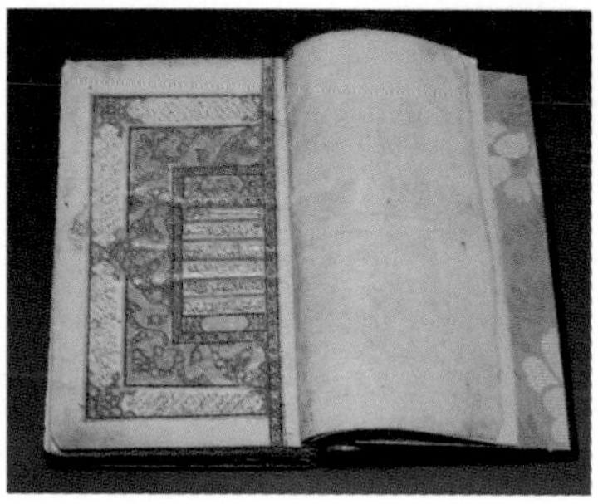

◁ Persian Koran

• *17th century*
Illuminated double page with divider of sura heading illumination, lacquer binding and stamped leather.
• *31cm x 19cm*
• £700 • Oasis

△ Académie de L'Epée-Fencing

• *1680*
Various engraved and hand-coloured plates by Thebauld depicting the sport of fencing.
• *height 43cm*
• £1,100 • **Chelsea Gallery**

△ Virgil

• *1680*
Virgil (Publius Virgilius Maro): Leiden: Jacob Hack / Amsterdam: Abraham Wolfgang. Three volumes of The Eclogues, the Georgics and the Aeneid in a fine scholarly variorum edition, with notes, edited by Jacobus Emmenessius, with plates by Leiden.
• £450 • **Ash Books**

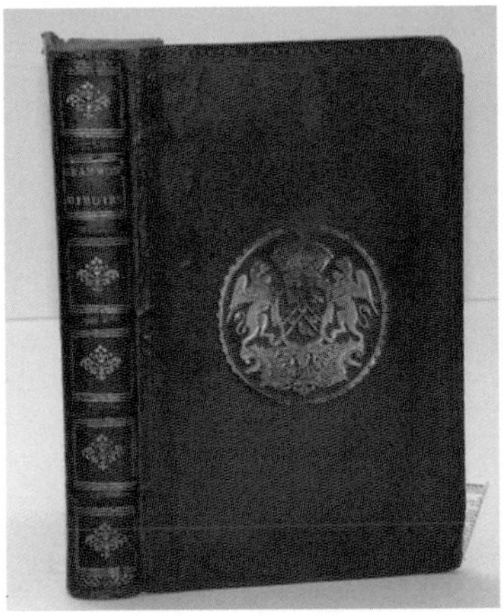

▷ Green's Voyages and Travels

• *1745–47*
Four-volume set of the first edition of *Green's Voyages and Travels*. Illustrated throughout with maps and views.
• *27cm x 22cm*
• £4,000 • **Chelsea Gallery**

▽ Clarendon

• *1712*
The History of the Rebellion and Civil Wars in England, begun in the year 1641. Oxford: printed at the Theatre. A very good early edition of Clarendon. Clarendon was Chancellor to both Charles I and Charles II. Panelled calf, banded and ruled in gilt.
• £495 • **Ash Books**

▽ Antiquities of Surrey

• *1736*
Antiquities of Surrey by Nathanaël Salmon. London: for the Author. First edition; mottled calf expertly re-backed and refurnished, banded and gilt.
• £300 • **Ash Books**

◁ Memoirs of the Life of Grammont

• *18th century*
Memoirs of the Life of Count de Grammont, containing, in particular, the amorous intrigues of the court of England in the reign of King Charles II. Printed: London and sold by J. Round.W. Taylor. J. Brown. 1714.
• £350 • **Ash Books**

△ Bibliothèque des Prédicateurs

• *1716*
Four volumes bound in 18th-century calf.
• £375 • **Mark Ransom**

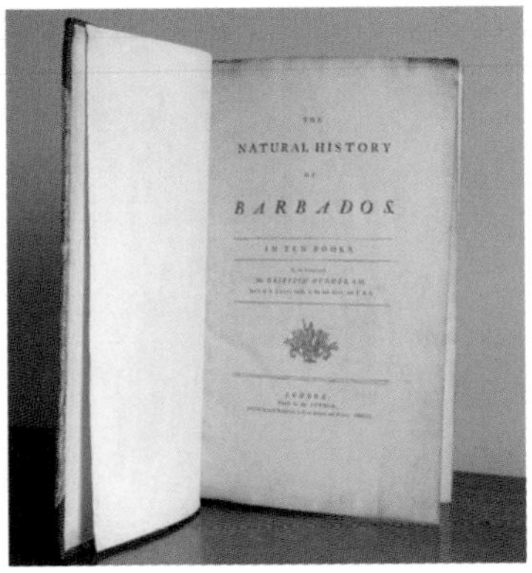

▽ Illmo D. D. Rogerio Duplesseis

• *1729*
By François Perrier. Half calf over marbled boards. Written in Paris 1638 but not printed until 1729. Pictorial title, index of plates and 98 (of 100) plates on 49 sheets of classical statues.
• *43cm x 30cm*
• £900 • **Russell Rare Books**

▽ Don Quixote

• *1742*
By Cervantes. This book contains 18th-century plates engraved by Vander Gucht, London. Of fine quality.
• *25cm x 16cm*
• £800 • **Paul Orssich**

◁ The Natural History of Barbados

• *1750*
First edition and subscribers large-paper copy of *The Natural History of Barbados*. In ten books by Griffith Hughes. Printed in London for the author. Bound in half brown calf and gilt lettered with burgundy.
• *height 43cm*
• £6,500 • **Peter Harrington**

▽ Maitland's History of London

• *1756*
Maitland's History of London, Vol I & II. London: for T. Osborn & J. Shipton and J. Hodges. Second edition. Originally published in one volume in 1739. Five general maps (two folding), nineteen maps of wards and parishes (five folding); views of over sixty principal buildings on forty-two plates (three folding), and over eighty churches.
• £2,950 • **Ash Books**

△ Blackstone Commentaries

• *1765–1769*

Blackstone Commentaries by Sir William Blackstone. A rare first edition. With the engraved 'Table of Consanguinity' and the 'Table of Descents' in Vol II. The date is stamped in black at the base of each spine.

• *28cm x 22cm*

• **£9,750** • **Peter Harrington**

△ Sallustius; Et L Annaeus Florus

• *1773*

By C. Crispus. Birmingham, Baskerville. Latin text printed at the Baskerville Press. In full mottled calf, gilt floral decoration, morocco label, marbled endpapers, all edges gilt.

• **£120–140** • **Adrian Harrington**

▷ Captain Cook Voyages

• *1773–1784*

A complete set of first editions of Cook's Southern Hemisphere, Pacific and Polar voyages. Eight volumes with Atlas. Bound in full antique panelled calf.

• **£15,000** • **Adrian Harrington**

▽ Complete English Traveller

• *1771–1773*

The Complete English Traveller by Robert Sanders and Nathaniel Spencer. London: J. Cooke. First edition. A well illustrated folio containing sixty plates that offer a general survey of the whole of Great Britain.

• **£950** • **Ash Books**

▽ Decline and Fall of the Roman Empire

• *1777*

Six volumes of *The History of the Decline and Fall of the Roman Empire*, by Edward Gibbon, published London, printed for W. Strahan and T. Cadell. 6 volumes, of which 4, 5 and 6 are first editions. With author's frontis portrait in vol.1, and 2 folding maps.

• *height 29cm*

• **£3,500** • **Peter Harrington**

◁ The British Sportsman

• *circa 1790*

A book of British sports by William Augustin Osbaldiston, containing 44 copper-engraved plates depicting scenes of recreation and amusement associated with riding, racing, hunting and shooting. Published by J. Stead.

• *22cm x 27cm*

• **£550** • **Chelsea Gallery**

▷ Letters by Mary Wollstonecraft

• *1796*

The first account of a business trip made by a woman, Mary Wollstonecraft, written during her short residence in Sweden, Norway and Denmark. Published by J.J. Johnston, London. First edition bound in full tan calf, with gilt lettering and a burgundy label.

• *height 21.5cm*

• **£1,250** • **Peter Harrington**

▷ Encyclopaedia Londinensis

• *1808*

A collection of British heraldry containing 105 hand-coloured plates, from King George III and Queen Charlotte down to the esquires and gentleman (patrons of the work). Published by J. Wilks.

• *28cm x 22cm*

• **£2,800** • **Chelsea Gallery**

◁ The Triumph of Maximilian

• *1778*

A book of woodcuts featuring the triumphs of the Holy Roman Emperor Maximilian I. This is one of the greatest series of woodcuts ever cut by Hans Burgmair.

• *56cm x 69cm*

• **£18,000** • **Chelsea Gallery**

◁ Travels in Turkey

• *1803*

By William Wittman. Richard Phillips, London. First edition, 4to. Illustrated with 15 hand-coloured costume plates, five engraved plates (one folding)and two folding maps (one coloured). Speckled calf leather, skilfully rebacked to match.

• **£1,500** • **Bernard Shapero**

△ Works of Shakespeare

• *1811*
Miniature set of eight volumes, all in excellent condition, with binding and gilding by Hayday.
• *12.5cm x 8cm*
• £750 • **Chelsea Gallery**

▽ Annals of Sporting

• *1822–23*
A 13-volume bound and gilded set entitled *The Annals of Sporting*, with 155 plates, 50 of which are hand-coloured. Published by Sherwood, Neely & Jones.
• *23cm x 15cm*
• £3,800 • **Chelsea Gallery**

△ Cooke's Views of the Thames

• *circa 1811*
Views of the Thames, from the Source to the Sea by Samuel Owen and William Bernard Cooke. London: by W. B. Cooke. Eighty-four tissue-guarded etched plates. Contemporary full morocco, all edges gilt.
• £750 • **Ash Books**

▽ Journal of a Residence in Chile

• *1824*
Journal of residence in 19th-century Chile. In English, including 14 aquatint plates. Published by John Murray. Of fine quality.
• £1,200 • **Paul Orssich**

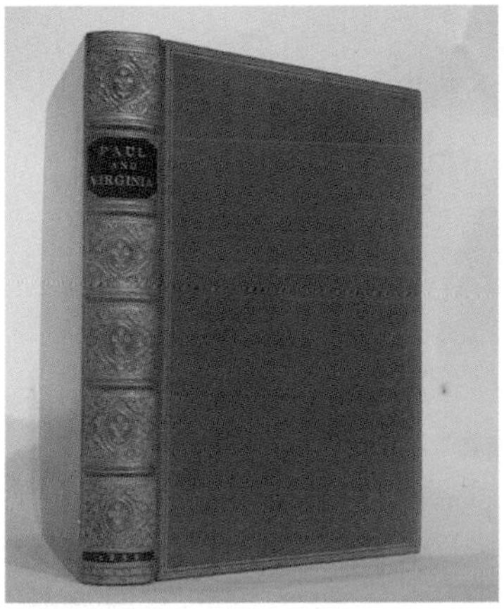

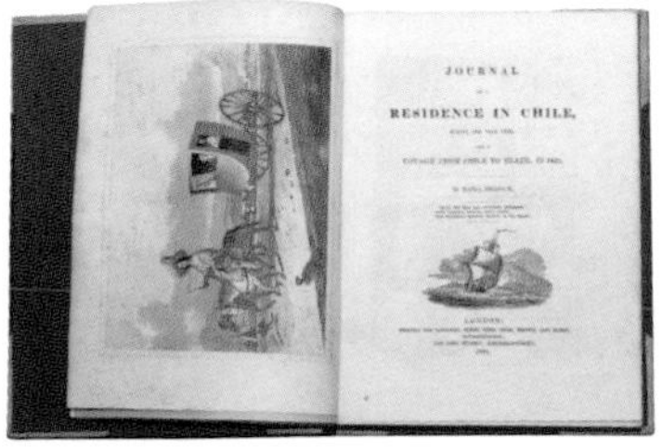

◁ Paul and Virginia

• *1839*
Book by Bernardin de St Pierre with an original memoir of the author. Illustrated throughout, leather-bound and gilded.
• *height 45cm*
• £550 • **Chelsea Gallery**

▽ The Spirit of the East

• *1839*
By David Urquhart. Colburn, London. Second edition. Lithographed folding map and one plan. In 1830 Urquhart was sent on a tour of the northern territory and the frontier and this work is a study of the Greeks and the Turks, and highlights his admiration for the Turks.
• £575 • **Bernard Shapero**

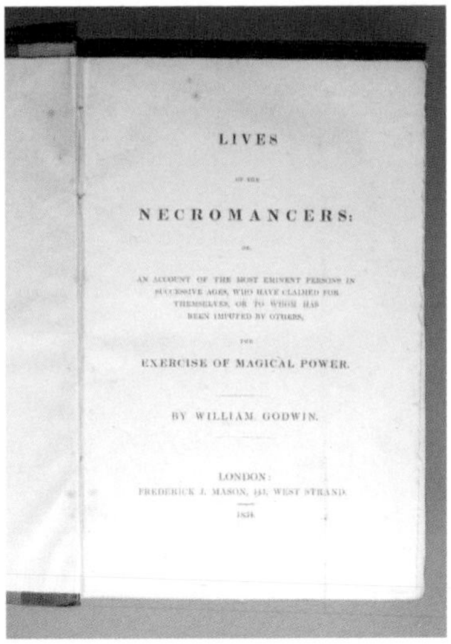

△ Lives of the Necromancers

• *1834*
By William Godwin. Published by Frederick J. Mason, London. First edition. The final literary endeavours of the ageing Godwin (1756–1836), summoning all his powers to attack people's credulity. Original linen-backed. Paper label. A little worn at the foot of the spine.
• *15cm x 24cm*
• £750 • **Ash Books**

▷ Lithographs of Architecture

• *1836–1837*
By Joseph Philibert Girault de Prangey. Hauser, Paris. Lithographs of Moorish architecture. Both volumes housed together in a slipcase.
• £ 8,500 • **Bernard Shapero**

▽ Pyrus Malus

• *1831*
By Hugh Ronalds on selected apples. Old green cloth recently rebacked with green morocco. London. 42 fine hand-coloured lithograph plates; drawn by author's daughter, Elizabeth Ronalds.
• *33cm x 25cm*
• £2,400 • **Russell Rare Books**

△ Four Landscape Annuals

• *1836–1838*
Four volumes by Jennings; landscape annuals of Spain, produced each year. 20 steel engravings in each volume.
• £850 • **Paul Orssich**

△ The Ladies' Flower Garden

• *1843–44*
'The Ladies' Flower Garden of Ornamental Perennials'. Published by Smith, 113 Fleet St, London.
• *23cm x 30cm*
• £3,500 • **Russell Rare Books**

▽ Large Landscape Folio

• *1839*
By Heinrich von Mayr. A very rare coloured copy. This is a collection of Mayr's engravings of Egypt, Syria and Palestine. Hand-coloured lithograph title and 60 hand-coloured plates. Contemporary morocco-backed boards. A fine copy.
• £20,000 • **Bernard Shapero**

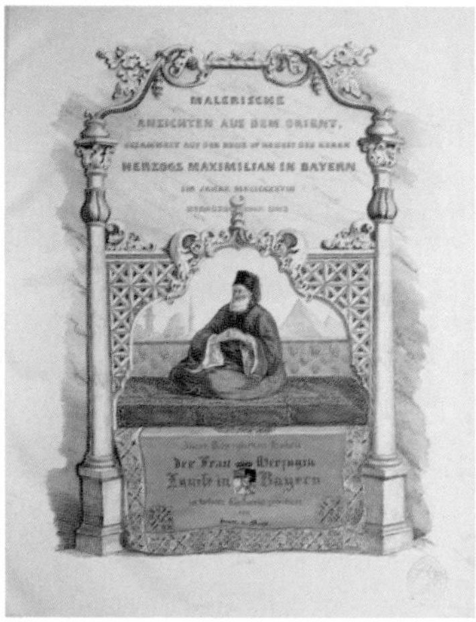

◁ Uncle Tom's Cabin

• *1852*
Uncle Tom's Cabin, or *Life Among the Lowly* by Harriet Beecher Stowe. Boston, John P. Jewett & Company. First edition. Two volumes finely bound by Bayntun-Riviere.
• *height 18cm*
• £3,500 • **Peter Harrington**

▷ Prehistoric Man

• *1862*
Prehistoric Man by Sir Daniel Wilston. Cambridge: Macmillan & Co. First edition. Extensive researches into the origin of civilisation in the old and the new world. Colour frontispiece. Map bound without half-titles, in a handsome half roan.
• £250 • **Ash Books**

▽ Conquest of Mexico

• *1843*
History of the Conquest of Mexico with a preliminary view of the ancient Mexican civilisation, and the life of the Conqueror, Fernando Cortes, by William Hickling Prescott. London. Richard Bentley. First edition. Engraved frontispiece portraits, facsimile, and two folding maps. Bound in polished calf with gilt and marbled edges by Clarke and Bedford.
• £500 • **Ash Books**

▷ Mogg's London

• *1854*
Mogg's travel guide to London. The leading London guide of its day – very comprehensive with accurate, pull-out map.
• *18cm x 13cm*
• £250 • **Bernard Shapero**

△ Monograph of Ramphastidae

• *1854*
Ornithological work on the toucan family by John Gould, London. Fine quality.
• £55,000 • **Bernard Shapero**

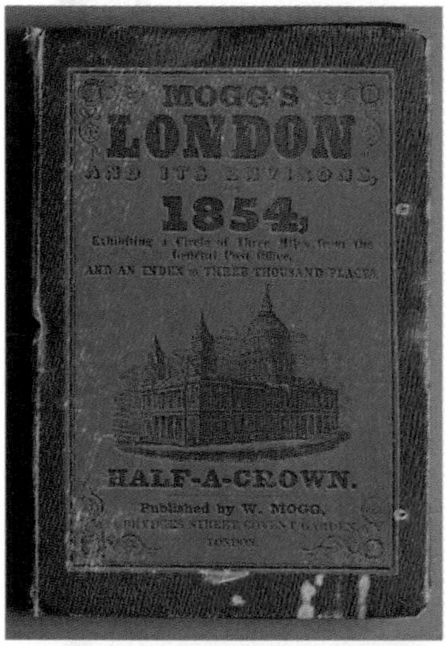

▽ Journeys Through London

• *1870*

By James Greenwood (1832–1929). A book concerning a journalist and social explorer, investigating aspects of contemporary life and fleshing out the facts with domestic incident and anecdote.

• £125 • Ash Books

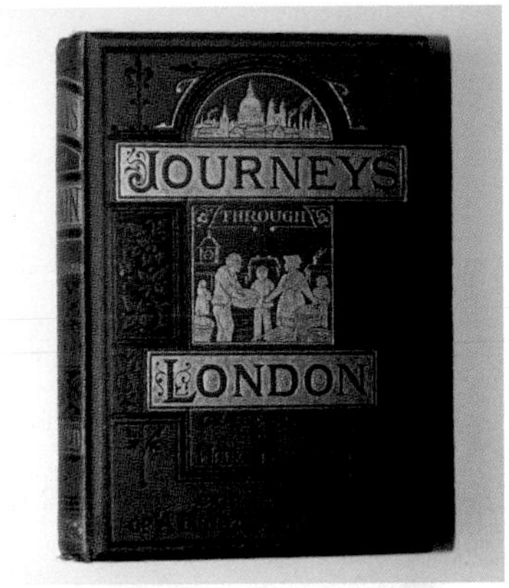

▽ Through the Looking Glass

• *1872*

By Lewis Carroll. Macmillan, London. First edition, 8vo. Illustrations by Tenniel throughout. Modern full red morocco gilt, all edges gilt.

• £350 • Bernard Shapero

▷ Tennyson's Works

• *1882*

Tennyson's Works published in London by Kegan Paul. Finely bound by Sangorski & Sutcliffe in full green morocco, spine faded to antique brown, gilt title and decoration to spine. With a fore-edge painting showing 'The Lady of Shalott' after William Holman Hunt, and a portrait of Tennyson.

• *18cm x 13cm*

• £350 • Peter Harrington

△ Holy Bible

• *1872*

Holy Bible. Philadelphia. With illustrated maps and full-page steel engravings. Coloured map of Palestine. Bound in full black morocco, ornate gilt.

• £90–120 • Adrian Harrington

△ French Fashion

• *circa 1881*

'La Mode'. Contemporary half black cloth. Four volumes, 91 attractive hand-coloured, engraved fashion plates. 'La Mode Illustrée' was one of the most important publications to appear in the mid-19th century.

• *38cm x 27cm*

• £1,000 • Russell Rare Books

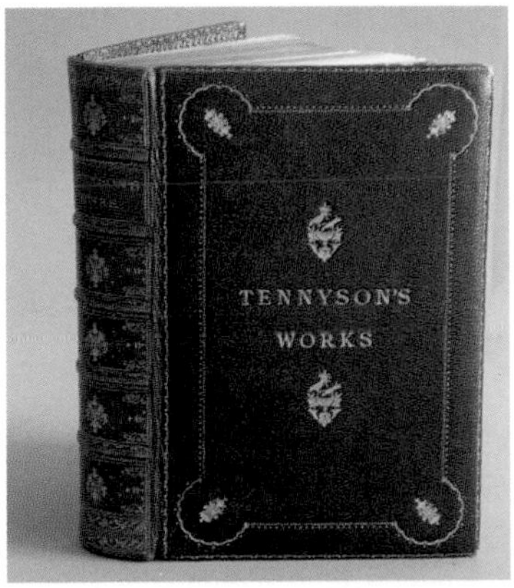

▽ Moses and Geology

• *1882*

'The Bible in Harmony with Science', by Samuel Kinns, London. Tinted frontispiece, with 110 illustrations. Near fine copy in superb presentation style. Binding of full polished calf.

• £200–250 • Adrian Harrington

▽ Greater London

• *circa 1884*

Greater London: A Narrative of its History, its People, and its Places by Edward Walford. London: Cassell & Co. Heavily illustrated with 400 wood engravings. Two volumes. Crown 4to. Original decorative cloth gilt.

• £195 • Ash Books

▷ Australian Pictures

• *1886*

Hand-drawn pen and pencil sketches, landscapes and portraits by Howard Willoughby.

• *34cm x 25cm*

• £125 • Bernard Shapero

△ The Rubaiyat of Omar Khayyam

• *1884*

Signed first edition. The astronomer-poet of Persia rendered into English verse by Edward Fitzgerald. Drawings by Elihu Vedder. Japanese tinted paper. A superb first edition. Signed by the artist.

• *45cm x 38cm*

• £700–900 • Adrian Harrington

△ The Congo

• *1885*

'The Congo and the Founding of its Free State'. This is a late 19th-century publication by Henry M. Stanley. Published by Sampson Low, London.

• £650 • Bernard Shapero

▽ Washington Square

• *1881*

By Henry James. Illustrated by George du Maurier.

• £200–250 • Adrian Harrington

▷ The Happy Prince

• *1888*

The Happy Prince and Other Tales by Oscar Wilde. Publishers: David Nutt, London. First edition, only 1,000 copies were printed. Illustrations by Walter Crane and Jacob Hood. Plates and illustrations. Bound in an elegant later half morocco by Riviere & Son.

• £1,000 • Ash Books

△ Climbing in the Himalayas

• *1894*

By William Martin Conway. Fisher Unwin, London. First edition. Large 8vo. Map and 300 illustrations, original pictorial cloth, top edge gilt. A fine copy.

• £525 • Bernard Shapero

△ Book of Sport

• *1885*

A book of sport written by W. Bromley Davenport and illustrated throughout with various plates. Exquisitely bound and gilded by Zaehnsdorf.

• *29cm x 22cm*

• £950 • Chelsea Gallery

▽ Early Adventures

• *1887*

Early Adventures in Persia, Susiana and Babylonia including A Residence among the Bakhtiyari and other wild tribes before the discovery of Nineveh, by the archaeologist Sir Henry Layard. John Murray, London. First Edition. Two volumes with plates and maps.

• £575 • Bernard Shapero

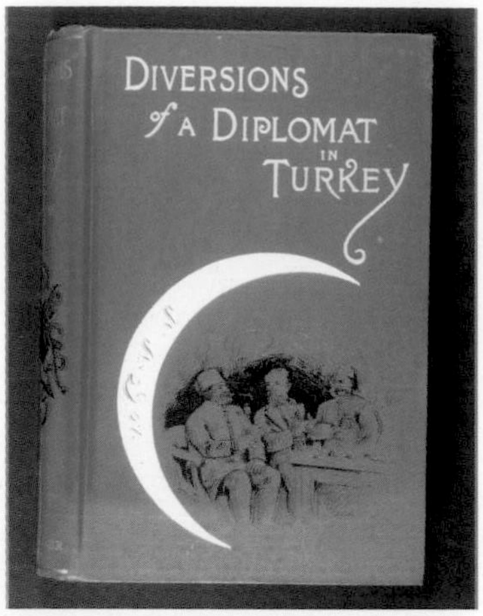

△ Magic

• *1897*

By Albert A. Hopkins. Stage illusions and scientific diversions including trick photography. Publisher's cloth.

• £120–150 • Adrian Harrington

◁ Diversions of a Diplomat in Turkey

• *1893*

By Samuel S. Cox, published by Webster, New York. Contains observations by U.S. Ambassador to Turkey from 1885–1887. Portrait frontispiece, 2 coloured lithographs, wood-engraved illustrations throughout.

• £220 • Bernard Shapero

△ Malay Sketches

• *1896*

Malay Sketches by Sir Frank Athelstane Swettenham, the distinguished colonial administrator and linguist. London: John Lane. Second edition (i.e. impression) of the original 1895 publication.

• £50 • Ash Books

△ Dream Days

• *1899*

Dream Days by Kenneth Grahame, pub. John Lane, New York & London.

• £100 • Ash Books

△ The First Men in the Moon

• *1901*
Early 19th-century novel by H.G. Wells. Illustrated with 12 monochrome plates. Publisher's blue cloth. A very good copy with bright boards. This is the first edition.
• £100–£180 • **Adrian Harrington**

△ Farewell Nikola

• *1901*
Farewell Nikola by Guy Boothby. First edition. The final adventures of one of the world's first fictional super-villains. Plates by Harold Piffard. Crown 8vo. Original bevelled cloth with pictorial onlay; white enamel on spine. Publishers: Ward, Lock & Co, London.
• £75 • **Ash Books**

▷ The Sporting Adventures of Mr Popple

• *1907*
By G.H. Jalland. Bodley Head, London. Landscape folio. Illustrated title page. Ten full-page captioned colour plates. each with facing illustrated textleaf in sepia. Original linen-backed colour pictorial boards. A very good copy.
• £250 • **Bernard Shapero**

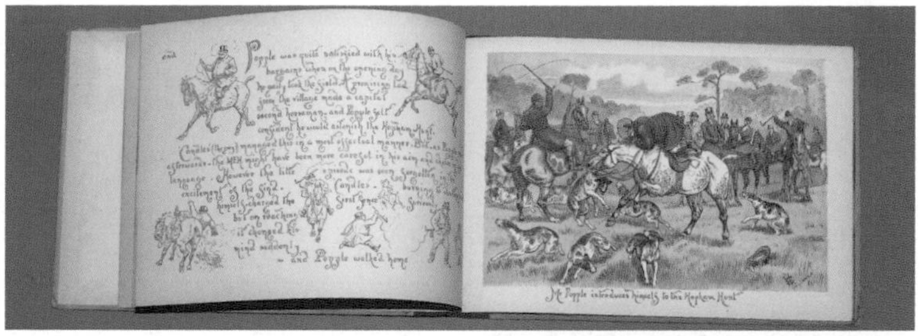

▽ The Hound of the Baskervillles

• *1902*
First edition of *The Hound of the Baskervilles* by Arthur Conan Doyle. Published by George Newnes Limited, London. Bound in recent full burgundy morocco, gilt lettering and decoration to spine.
• *19cm x 12cm*
• £1,200 • **Peter Harrington**

◁ Mirages

• *1906*
A book of various Arab stories compiled by Sliman Ben Ibrahim Bamer. It contains hand-painted illustrations throughout by E. Dinet. Decorative French binding by René Kieffer.
• *23cm x 17cm*
• £1,400 • **Chelsea Gallery**

△ Orange Fairy Book

• *1906*
First edition of the *Orange Fairy Book* by Andrew Lang. Published in 1906.
• £300 • **Ash Books**

▽ Gulliver's Travels

• *1909*
By Jonathan Swift. 'Journey Into Several Remote Nations of the World'. Illustrated by Arthur Rackham. Published by J.M. Dent & Co., London. A fine quality book.
• £150–180 • **Adrian Harrington**

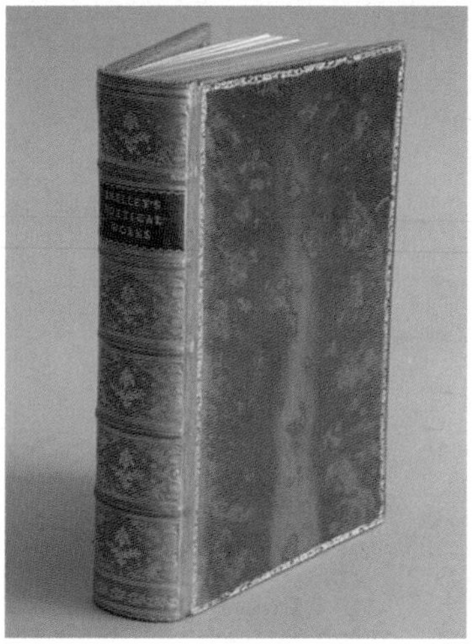

△ The Poetical Works of Percy Bysshe Shelley

• *1908*
The Poetical Works of Percy Bysshe Shelley. Macmillan and Co., Limited London. Bound by Riviere in full tree calf, and gilt-lettered green morocco label and gilt decoration to spine with marbled end papers, all edges gilded.
• *18cm x 12cm*
• £475 • **Peter Harrington**

△ Viala Paul V. Vermod

• *1910*
Traité Gérard de Viticulture: Amplography. 6 volume folio, Paris: Marsonet Cie. 500 chromolithograph plates of grapes. Publisher's maroon cloth. Blind-stamped art nouveau.
• *35cm x 26cm*
• £7,500 • **Russell Rare Books**

△ La Reine des Neiges

- *1911*

Hans Christian Andersen, *La Reine des Neiges et Quelques Autres Contes*. Illustration by Edmund Dulac. Publishers decorated vellum, with 29 full-colour illustrations by Edmund Dulac. Published by H. Piazza Paris.

- *20.5cm x 24cm*
- £850 • **Peter Harrington**

△ Hans Andersen's Fairy Tales

- *1913*

Signed limited edition of *Hans Andersen's Fairy Tales*. Constable and Company Ltd, London. Limited to 100 copies, this one being numbered 59 and signed on the limitation page by the illustrator W. Heath Robinson.

- *height 29.5cm*
- £3,950 • **Peter Harrington**

▽ The Book of the Dead

- *1913*

'The Papyrus of Ani' by Sir Ernest Alfred Wallis Budge. Phillip Lee Warner, London and G.P. Putnam Sons, New York. A reproduction in facsimile. Two volumes, 8vo. 37 folding colour plates and numerous illustrations in the text. Signature on endpapers, original gilt blindstamped red cloth, gilt lettering to spines. A fine and scarce copy.

- £450 • **Bernard Shapiro**

▽ A Midsummer Night's Dream

- *1914*

Illustrations by W. Heath Robinson. Constable & Co Ltd.

- £200–250 • **Adrian Harrington**

▷ Oscar Wilde

- *1925*

A set of twelve limited-edition books by Oscar Wilde, numbered from 482 to 575. Each book is bound with leather and has a marble insert.

- *height 21cm*
- £1,900 • **Chelsea Gallery**

◁ British Birds

- *1915*

A book of the birds of Britain by Thorburn comprising four volumes, which contain 80 hand-coloured plates. Published by Longmans, Green & Co.

- *32cm x 27cm*
- £680 • **Chelsea Gallery**

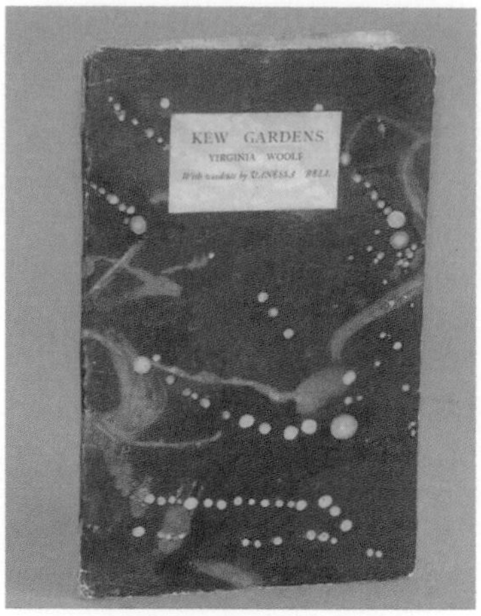

△ Kew Gardens

- *1919*

Kew Gardens by Virginia Woolf with woodcuts by Vanessa Bell. There were only 150 copies made and Virginia Woolf set the type.

- *23cm x 14cm*
- £18,000 • **Peter Harrington**

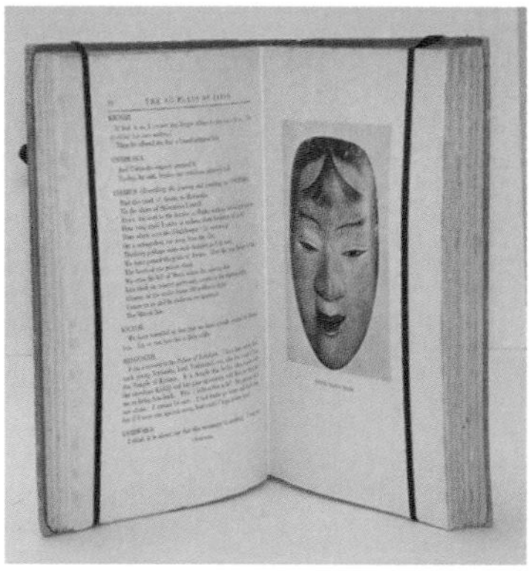

△ The Noh Plays of Japan

- *1922*

The Noh Plays of Japan by Arthur Waley. New York: Alfred A. Knopf. First American edition. Translations of the most celebrated Noh plays. Eight plates of masks. Original linen-backed boards.

- £125 • **Ash Books**

▽ Tales of Mystery and Imagination

- *1919*

By Edgar Allan Poe. First edition, 4to. Original blindstamped limp suede. Rebacked preserving original covers.

- £150 • **Berbard Shapero**

▽ Winnie the Pooh

- *1926*

Limited edition of 350 of *Winnie the Pooh* by A.A. Milne, with wonderful onlaid binding, and decorations by Ernest H. Shephard. Methuen & Co. London, numbered copies, signed by Milne and Shephard.

- *23cm x 17cm*
- £8,500 • **Peter Harrington**

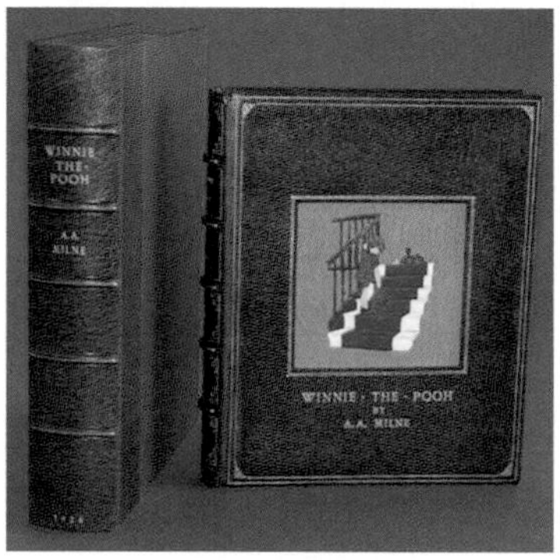

▽ The Tempest

- *1926*

Deluxe edition of Shakespeare's *The Tempest*, illustrated by Arthur Rackham. Published by William Heinemann Ltd. London. Signed by Rackham.

- *32cm x 26cm*
- £3,250 • **Peter Harrington**

▷ Asle Maps

- *1579*

Titled Angliae, Scotlae, et Hiberniae. By Abraham Ortelius in the late 16th century. Copper line engraving on laid paper. Engraved 'Theatrum Orbis Terrarum' of Abraham Ortelius, Antwerp 1570. Latin text on reverse.

- £750 • Ash Books

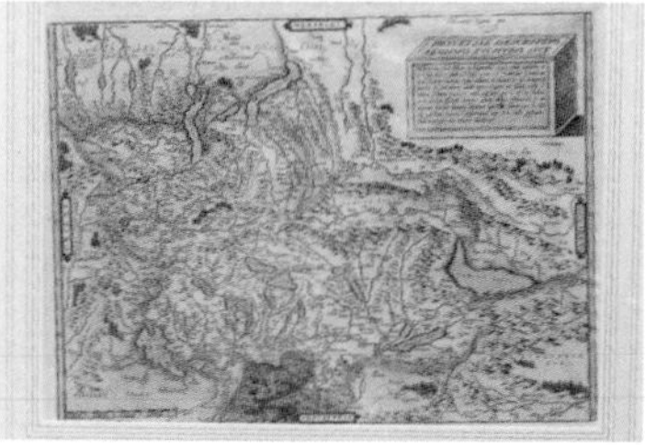

△ Tschudi Helvetiae

- *1579*

Tschudi (Aegedicus) Helvetiae. Copper line engraving on laid paper. Originally engraved for the 'Theatrum Orbis Terrarum' 1529.

- *45cm x 34cm*
- £750 • Ash Books

△ Graeciae Universae

- *1584*

By Giacomo Gastaldi. Copper line engraving. Based on the work of Gastaldi and originally engraved for the 'Theatrum Orbis Terrarum' of Abraham Ortelius in Antwerp.

- *51cm x 38cm*
- £500 • Ash Books

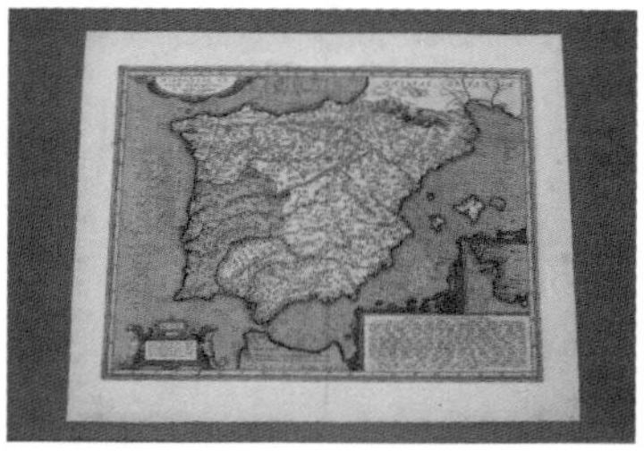

△ Map by Ortelius

- *1586*

Ortelius was the first person to publish an atlas. Shows Iberian peninsula in full contemporary colour. The language text, page number and pagination signature are the key to dating the copper engraving on paper.

- *38cm x 50cm*
- £250 • Paul Orssich

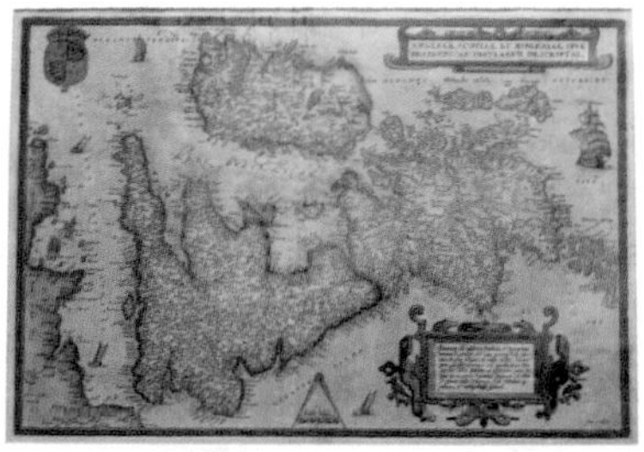

▽ Map of London

- *1598*

One of the earliest maps of London. A 16th-century wood engraving published in Switzerland, based on the famous Braun & Hogenberg map of 1572.

- *39cm x 23.5cm*
- £950 • Ash Books

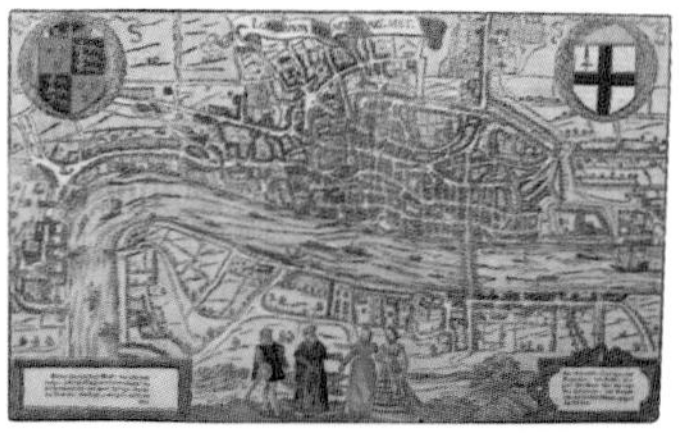

▽ Map of Lothian

- *circa 1500s*

A map depicting the area of Lothian in Scotland, by the Dutch cartographer Joannes Janssonius, 1646, Amsterdam. A fine example of this well-known map of the Edinburgh region.

- *36.5cm 54cm*
- £400 • Ash Books

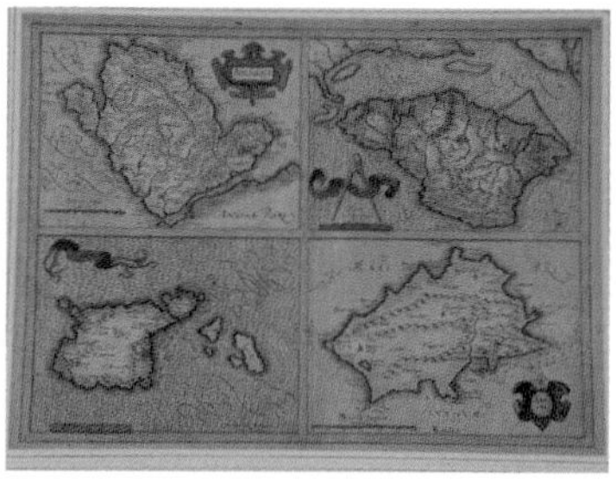

▽ Bertius of America

- *1616*

Engraving on paper. Originally produced for the 1616 edition of the Bertius 'Tabularum Geographicarum Contractarum Libri Septem'. Published by the younger Hadius at Amsterdam.

- *15cm x 11cm*
- £350 • Ash Books

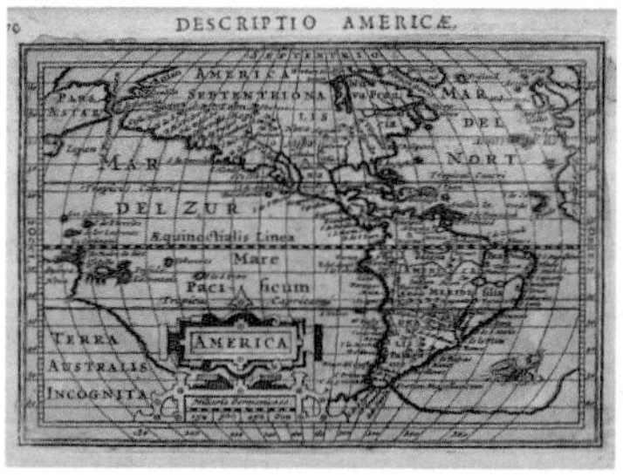

▽ Map by J. Mettullus

- *1601*

Very rare. Includes the Canary Islands. Showing galleons with sight lines and inset of Madeira.

- £220 • Paul Orssich

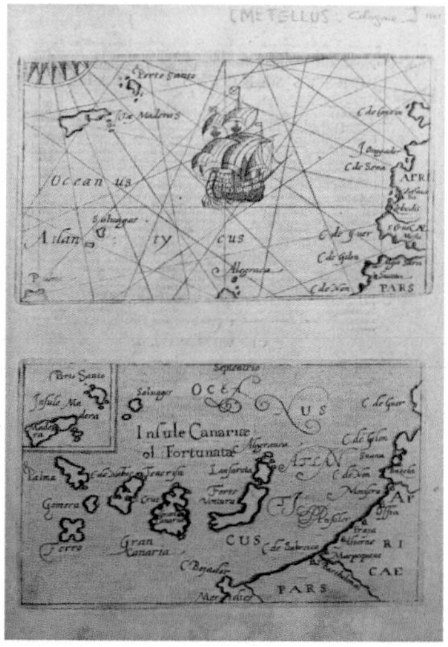

▽ Le Relatiani Universali di Giovanni Botero Bienes

- *1605*

By Giovanni Botero,Venice. Renaissance geographical and anthropological 'relatives' of Giovanni Botero. With maps and illustrations.

- *14.5cm x 20cm*
- £1,450 • Ash Books

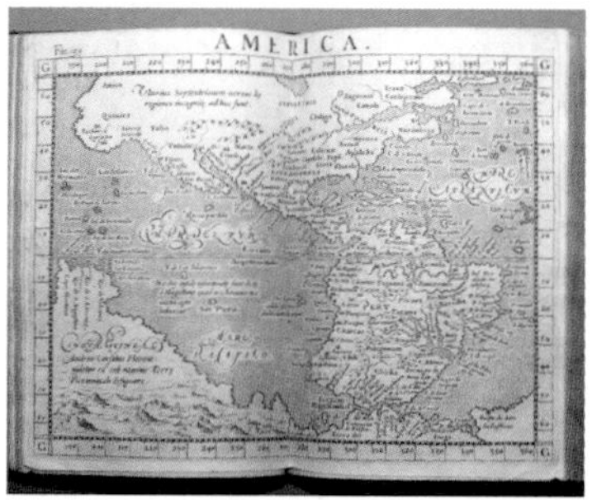

▽ The Panorama. A Traveller's Instructive Guide

- *1620*

17th-century book, 'A Traveller's Instructive Guide'. Published in London by J. Wallis & W.H. Reid. Original cover. 40 English county maps, 12 Welsh county maps.

- *12cm x 9cm*
- £250 • Russell Rare Books

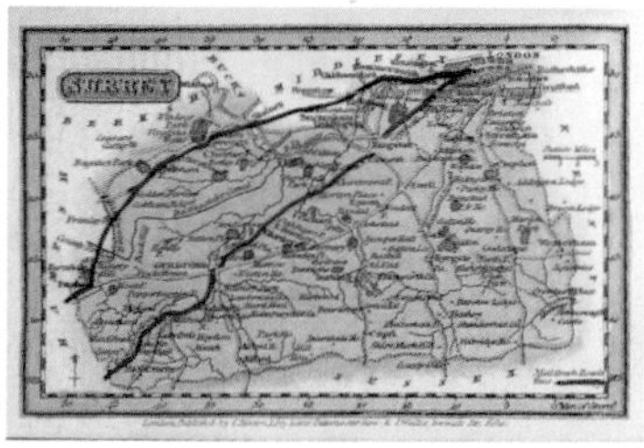

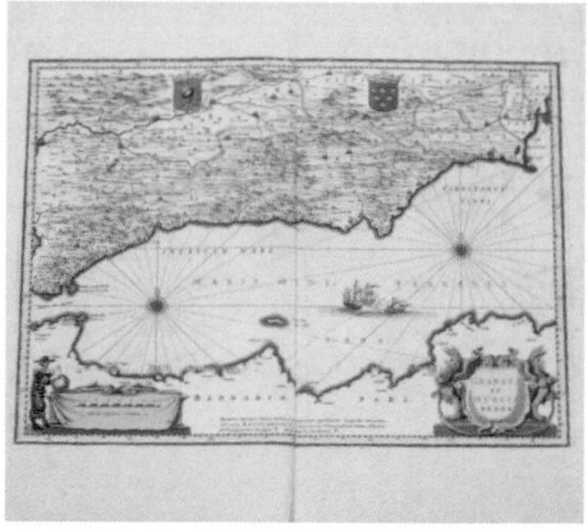

△ Map by Van Santer

- *1640*

Hand-coloured map of Granada and Murcia, with superb high-lighting in gold, by Van Santer. The publisher is Johann Blaeu.

- *49.5cm x 38cm*
- £600 • Paul Orssich

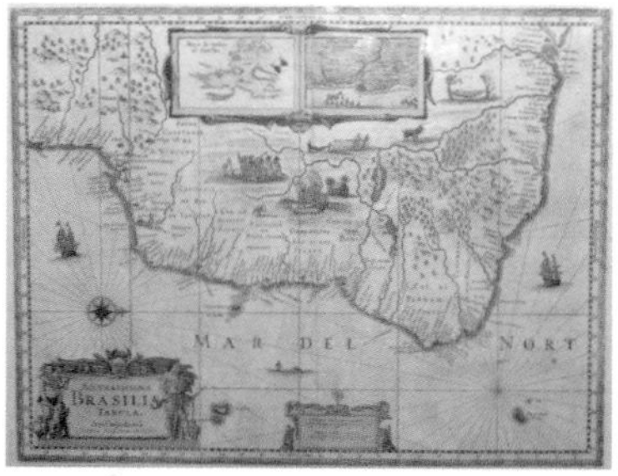

△ Map of Brazil

- *1649*

By J. Janssonius. Copper line engraving on paper with original hand-colouring. Originally produced for the Hondius-Janssonius. The present version is dated 1649. Amsterdam. Showing figures cannabalising one another.

- *49cm x 58cm*
- £595 • Ash Books

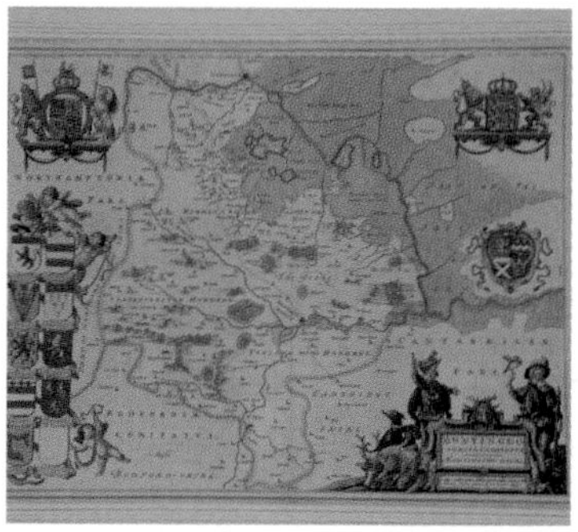

△ Map of Huntingdonshire

- *1645*

Map of Huntingdonshire by J. Willem Blaeu with the inscription, 'Hvntingdo-Nensis Comitatvs, Huntington-shire'. Published in Amsterdam. Decorated with a ribanded display of coats or arms, the Stuart Royal Arms, and a hunters and hounds title-piece, with stags, falcon, boar, hare and rabbit. Originally produced by Blaeu in 1645.

- £350 • Ash Books

△ A Map of Portugal

• *1635*

Map maker Willem and Johann Blaeu of Holland. Copper line engraving on laid paper. Hand-colouring. Based on the 16th-century map maker Fenazlo Averez Secco, 1560.

• £450 • Ash Books

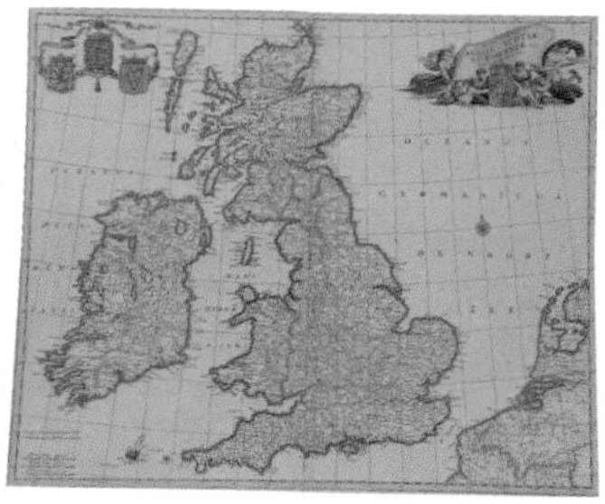

△ Frederick de Wit

• *17th century*

Fine map of the British Isles from the engraver and mapseller Frederick de Wit (1630–1706). Decorated with the arms of England, Ireland and Scotland and an attractive title-piece of frolicking nymphs. Original hand-colouring.

• £600 • Ash Books

▷ Map of Africa

• *1674*

By Herbert Jaillot showing the Mediterranean and Africa.

• £450 • Paul Orssich

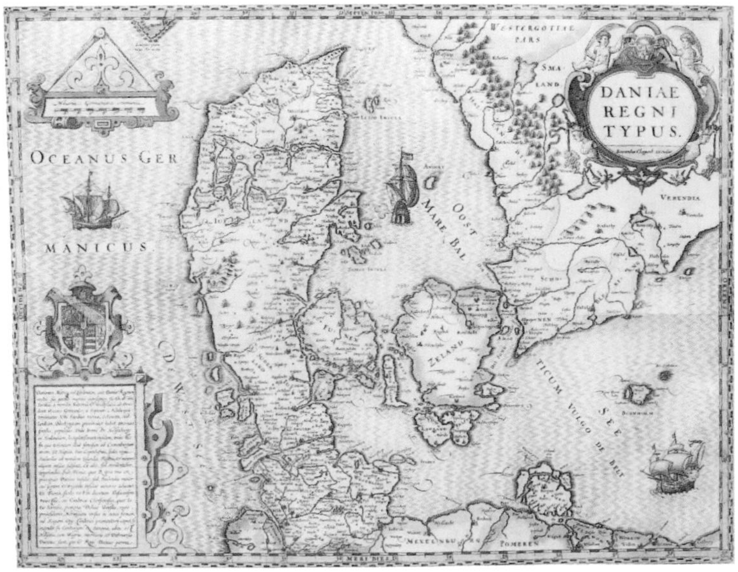

▷ World Map

• *1662*

Double hemisphere world map. Published by Johann Blaeu of Amsterdam. Hand-coloured and copper engraved. At the top, outside the twin hemispheres are celestial figures seated amid clouds.

• £9,850 • The Map House

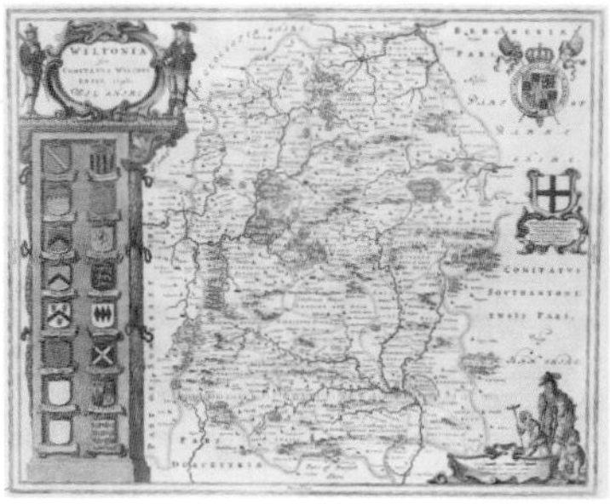

△ Armorial Map

• *1659*

By J. Willem Blaeu. A fine armorial map of the county of Wiltshire, decorated with an attractive scale bar, depicting a surveyor at work. Amsterdam. Blaeu produced the finest maps of the 17th century. Hand-coloured.

• *49cm x 41cm*

• £350 • Ash Books

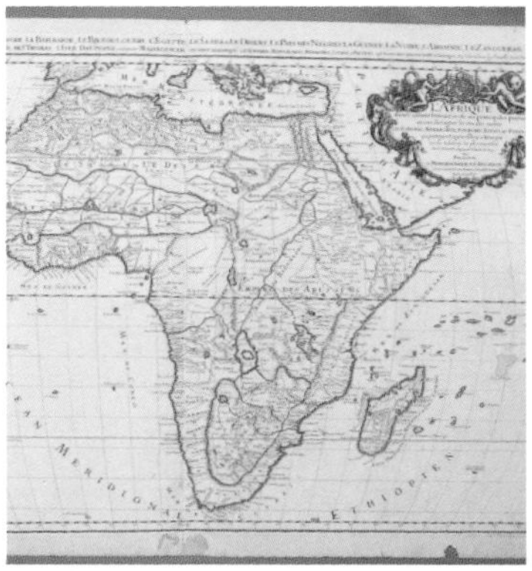

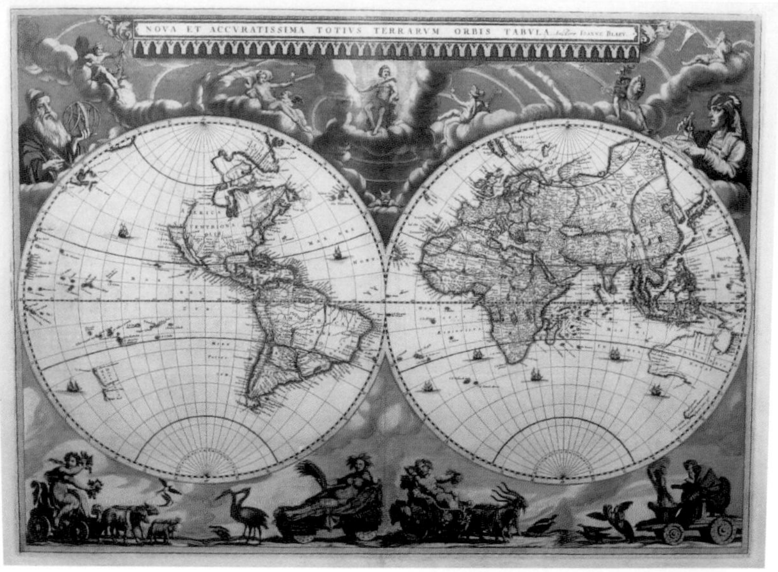

▽ Map of the Orkney & Shetland Isles

• *1654*

Map of the Orkney and Shetland Isles by Willem Janszoon Blaeu, Amsterdam, 1645. With the inscription, 'Orcadvm et Schetlandiæ Insvlarvm accuratissima descriptio'. Finely decorated.

• *40.5cm x 53cm*

• £350 • Ash Books

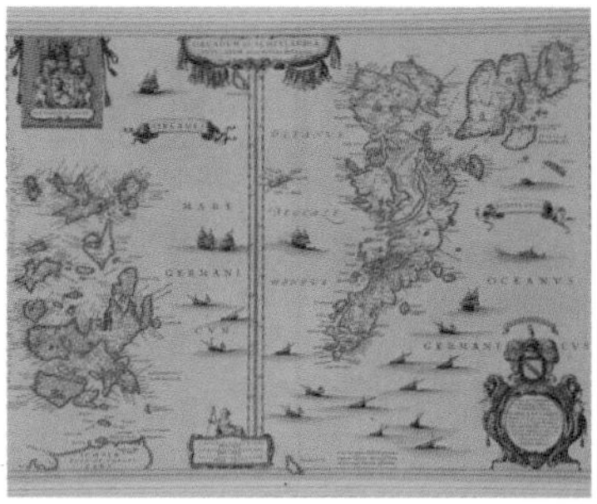

▷ Merian Map of the British Isles

• *mid-17th century*

Map of the British Isles from Mathaus Merian the Elder (1593–1650). With a baroque title piece draped in cornucopia, the Royal Arms, sailing ships etc. Originally produced for the 'Neuwe Archontolgia Cosmica' (Frankfurt 1638) and here in a later issue, with Merian's name removed.

• £400 • Ash Books

◁ Daniae Regni Typus

• *17th century*

A copper line engraving on kid paper bearing the imprint of Everard Cloppenburgh, Dutch school. Early 17th century. The engraving work has been attributed to Jodocas Hondius.

• *49cm x 38cm*

• £650 • Ash Books

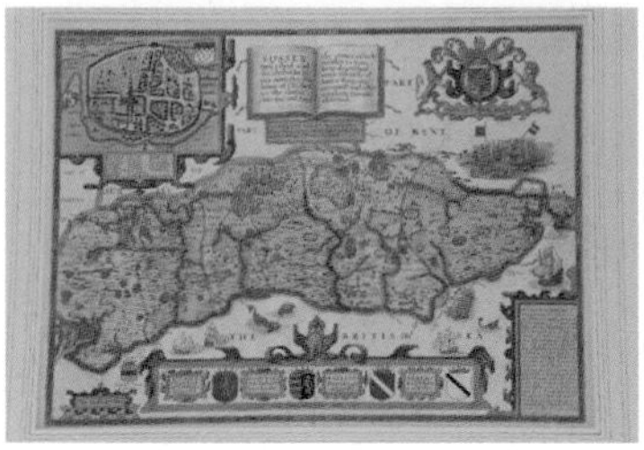

△ Chichester

• *1676*

Sussex described and divided into rapes with the situation of Chichester by John Speed. Copper line engraving on paper by Jodocus Hondius.

• £750 • Ash Books

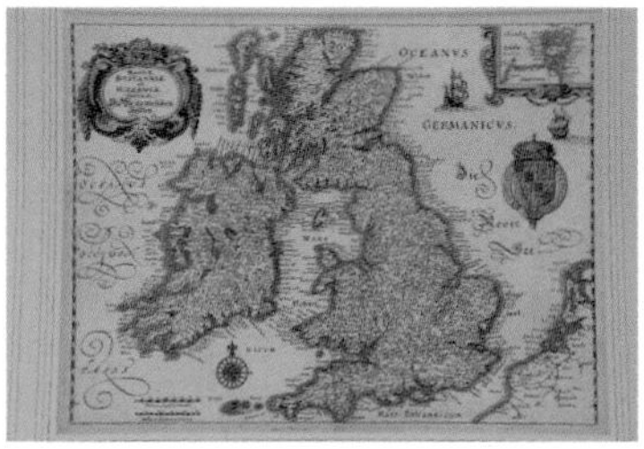

▽ London

• *1673*

An early map of London by Wenceslas Hollar, with the coat of arms of the City of London, fifteen of the great Livery and Merchant Companies and those of Sir Robert Vyner of Viner.

• £400 • Ash Books

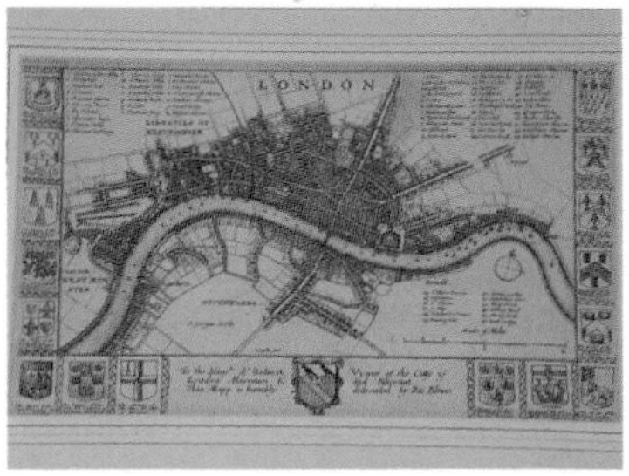

▷ Sea Chart of West Morocco

- *circa 1700*

By Pierre Mortimer. Sea chart showing the west coast of Morocco. Published in Holland. 32- and 16-point compasses. Raised lines.

- £280 • Paul Orssich

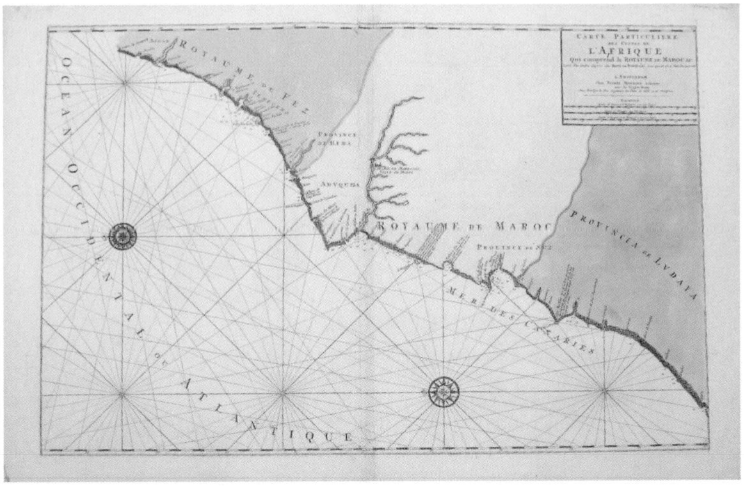

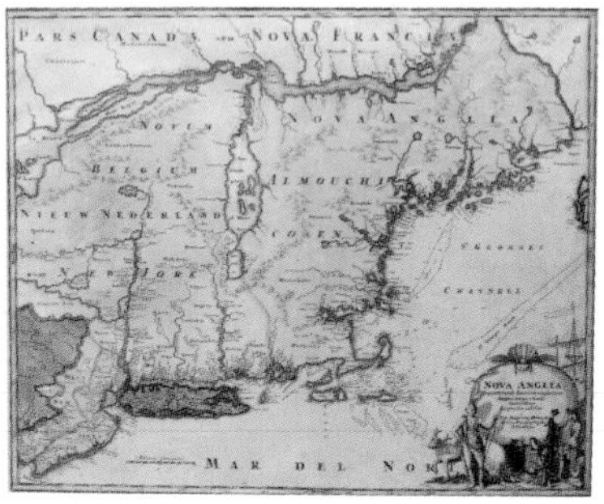

△ Map of New York

- *1720*

By Johann Baptist Homann. Striking map of New York, New Jersey and New England, up to Maine. J.B. Homann was the geographer to the Holy Roman Empire. Full original hand-colouring. Of good quality.

- *48.5cm x 57cm*
- £995 • Ash Books

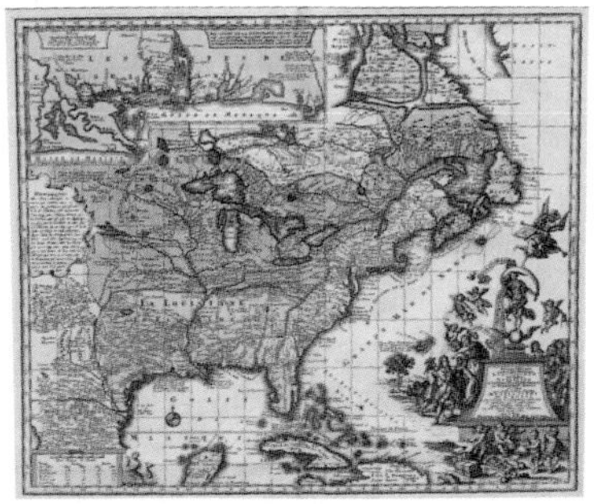

△ Seutter (Matthaeus)

- *late 18th century*

A line engraving of north-east America on paper, with original hand-colouring. Published by Seutter at Augsberg. The cartouche by Rogg and engraved by Rhein.

- *57.5cm x 49cm*
- £1,750 • Ash Books

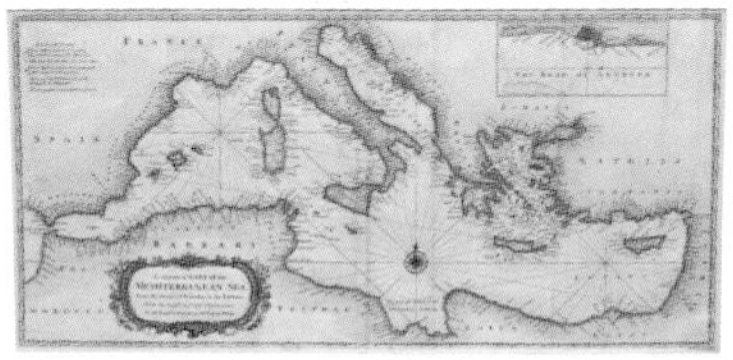

△ Chart of Mediterranean Sea

- *1747*

'A Correct Chart of the Mediterranean Sea' by Richard William Sene. Copper line engraving on laid paper. Originally produced for an English edition of Paul Rapin de Thoyzes (1661–1721).

- *71cm x 35cm*
- £400 • Ash Books

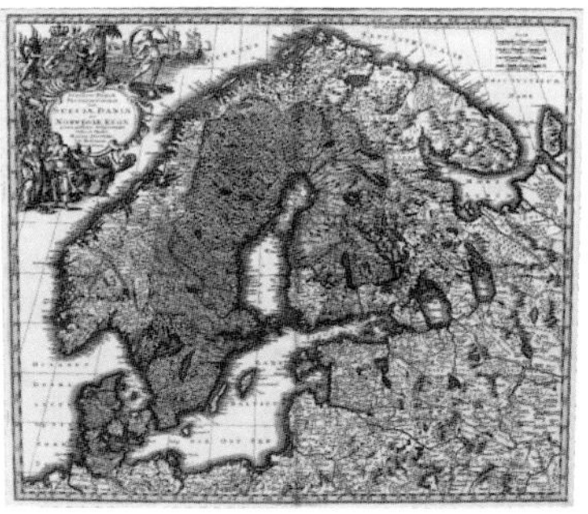

△ Synopsis Plagae Septemtrion alis Duecia Daniae

- *1740*

By Matthaeus Seutter. Copper line engraving on paper with original hand colour. Produced by the Augsberg geographer Matthaeus Seutter.

- *56cm x 49cm*
- £450 • Ash Books

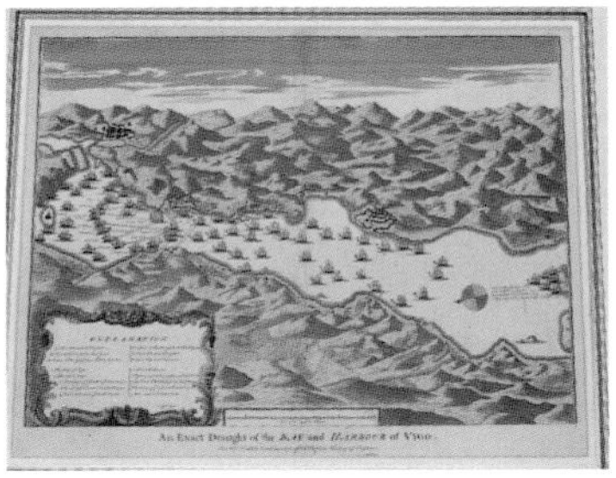

△ Map of Vigo Harbour

- *1750*

18th-century map of the harbour of Vigo. Shows naval engagement in the Bay of Vigo, northwestern Spain.

- *47cm x 35.5cm*
- £120 • Paul Orssich

▷ Celestial Chart

- *1742*

A celestial map by Doppelmayr of the northern hemisphere. Hand-coloured and engraved by Honann, and shows celestial sky and heroes of mythology.

- *64cm x 55cm*
- £1,400 • Chelsea Gallery

▽ Spanish Sea Chart

- *1799*

Published by the Spanish Hydrographic Office. Attributed to Vincent Tolfino of Cartagena. Fine copper engraving with minute detail and various depth readings. Good detail of the town.

- *52cm x 37cm*
- £140 • Paul Orssich

▽ Map of Europe

- *circa 1836*

Early 19th-century map of Europe by Thomas Bowen. A new and accurate map, with engravings on paper. Thomas Bowen was the son of noted English map maker, Emmanuel Thomas Bowen. Colours remain vivid.

- £ 8,500 • Ash Books

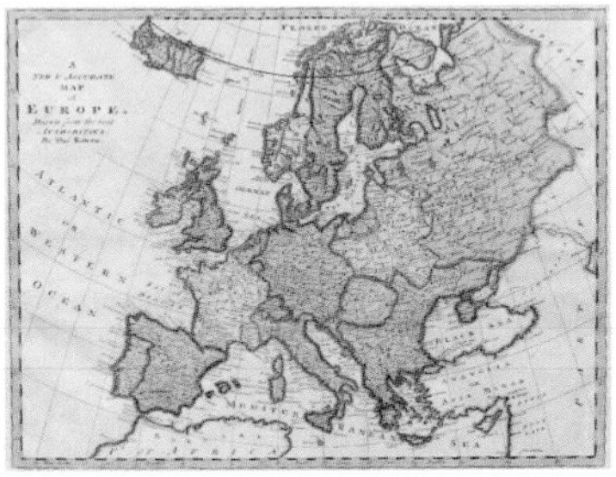

▽ The British Colonies

- *1870*

Late 19th-century book by R. Montgomery Martin. The London Printing and Publishing Company. 12 volumes with 40 double-page hand-coloured Tallis maps plus 33 engraved plates and portraits. Publisher's cloth with slight rubbing.

- £1,500–1,800 • Adrian Harrington

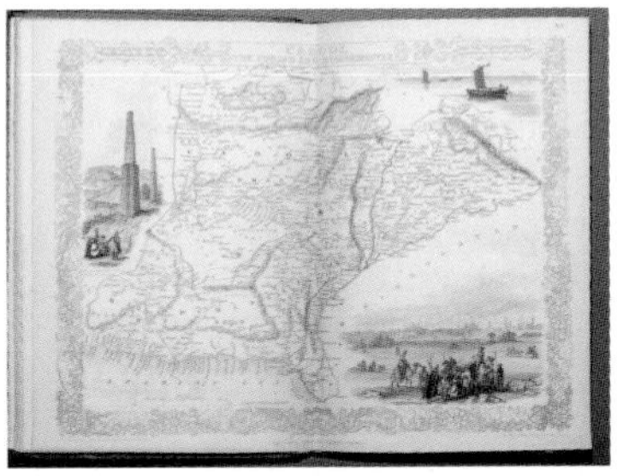

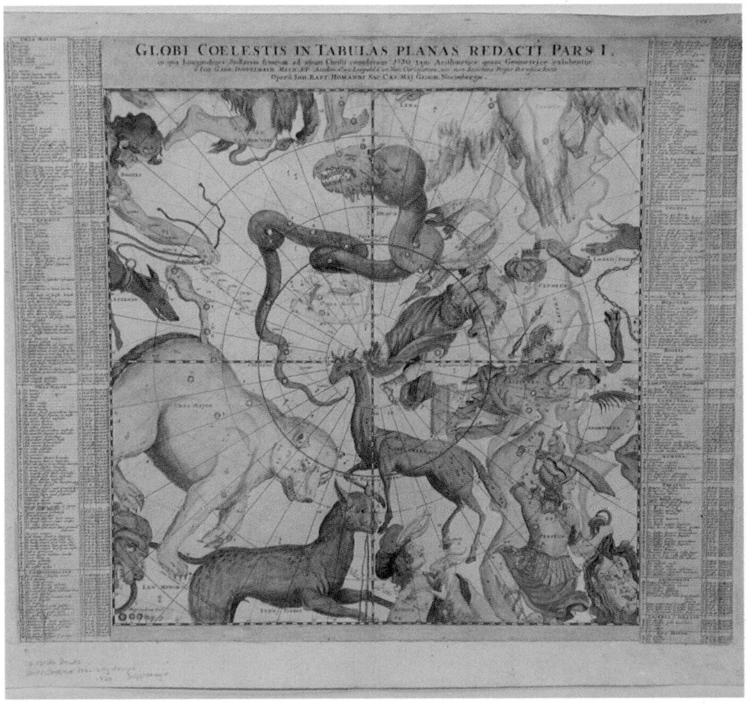

CARPETS & RUGS

Carpets and rugs were initially made by nomadic tribes, with the Persians being amongst the first carpet weavers of the ancient civilisations. Through centuries of creativity they achieved a unique degree of excellence in their craft. The element of luxury with which the Persian carpet is associated today provides a marked contrast with its humble beginnings as a necessity to protect the nomadic tribes from the cold, as well as a form of writing for the illiterate. Their bright colours and magical designs brought relief to these people's hardy lives. Out of necessity was born art and their beauty found them new homes throughout the ancient and modern world. European needlework carpets of the nineteenth century have also become an interesting area for the collector.

△ Tibetan Saddlebag

- *1500*

A Tibetan wool saddlebag, with central red panel with floral design and a cobalt border.

- *68cm x 58cm*
- £1,500 • A. Rezai Persian

△ French Panel

- *circa 1760–1780*

French needlepoint panel with central figured cartouche in petit point.

- *51cm square*
- £1,950 • Classic Fabrics

▽ Nomadic Rug

- *19th century*

Nomadic tent decoration. From Azari, Southern Caucusus, with a Soumak weave.

- *length 1.1m, width 65cm*
- £680 • Gordon Reece

▽ Russian Rug

- *1820*

A unique Russian wool rug, being part of a cradle. The design is an old Suman brocade design.

- *1.09m x 42cm*
- £1,000 • A. Rezai Persian

▷ Kilim Cushion

- *1870*

Fragment of a kilim from Turkey used as a cushion cover.

- *47cm x 38cm*
- £150 • David Black

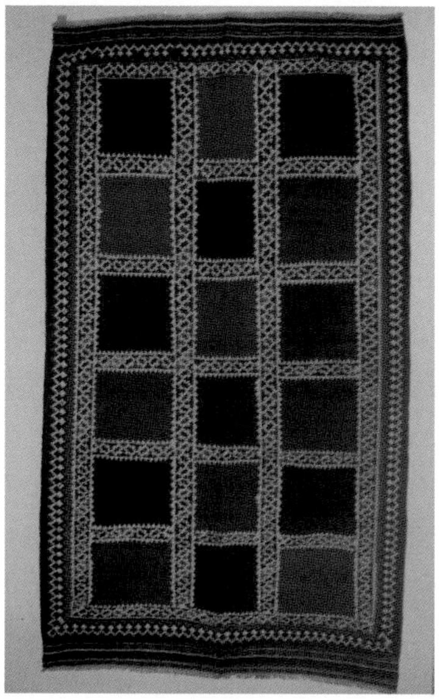

△ Early Antique Kilim

- *early 19th century*

With stunning panels in vibrant colours. By the Quashqui tribe from the Zagros mountains. Natural dyes.

- *length 2.86m, width 1.56m*
- £2,999 • Gordon Reece

▽ Shirvan Kilim Runner

- *19th century*

Caucasus runner. Slit-woven wool on a cotton warp, one selvedge wiped, the other turned.

- *length 2.6m, width 1m*
- £950 • Gordon Reece

△ Ning Xia Province Carpet

• *1850*
Section of a Chinese carpet with dragon designs from Ning Xia Province.
• *68cm square*
• £800 • David Black

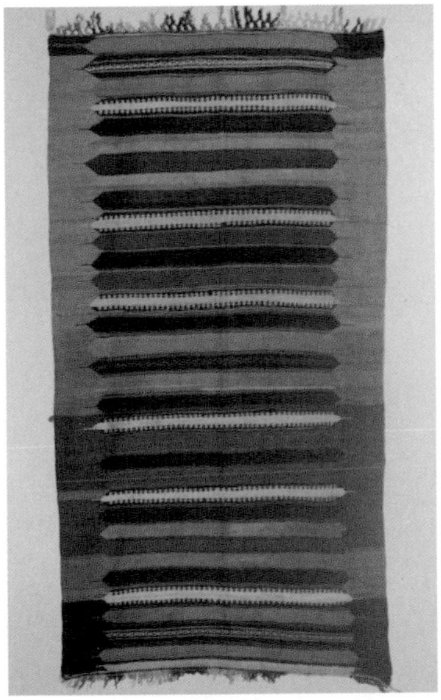

△ Kilim Prayer Rug

• *19th century*
A most unusual kilim form with a multiple mirhab layout in two directions with striking colours.
• *length 2.56m, width 1.35m*
• £1,700 • Gordon Reece

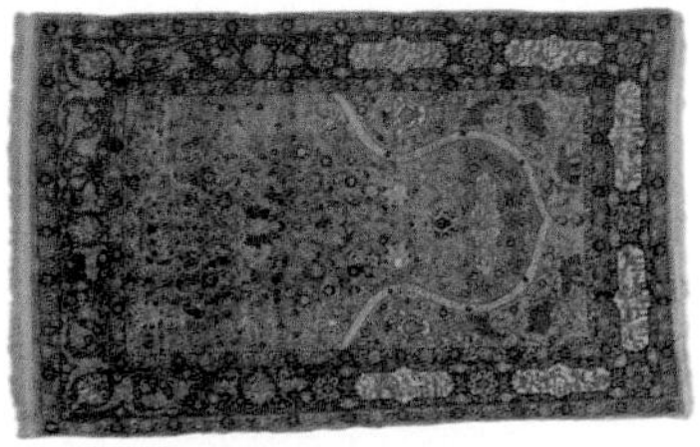

△ Ottoman Prayer Rug

• *circa 1880*
A pure silk Mihrab Ottoman design prayer rug with gold silk woven throughout. The design script are verses from the Qu'ran.
• *1.8m x 1.2m*
• £5,500 • A. Rezai Persian

▽ Bazouch Nimruz Kilim

• *19th century*
Bazouch Nimruz kilim from Afghanistan. Weft faze patterning.
• *length 2.07m, width 97cm*
• £1,400 • Gordon Reece

▽ Thracean Rug

• *circa 1870*
Thracean kilim from Turkey with geometric pattern.
• *1.19m x 1.07m*
• £1,500 • David Black

▷ Baluchi Carpet

• *1860*
Section of a hand-woven carpet from Baluchistan.
• *length 2.8m*
• £2,800 • David Black

△ Melas Rug

• *1880*
Melas prayer mat from Turkey, with a central design of a red mosque bordered with rosettes and stars.
• *length 1.25m*
• £1,250 • David Black

△ Persian Kilim

• *circa 1880*
Kilim made by the nomads of Persia and dyed with rose madder from the Luti Tribe.
• *length 2.25m*
• £1,200 • Gordon Reece

▽ Indian Durrie

• *circa 1880*
Indian cotton durrie made by prisoners in the North Indian gaols. Dyed with indigo and turmeric.
• *length 2.03m*
• £740 • Gordon Reece

▽ North Persian Runner

• *circa 1890*
Runner from northern Persia.
• *2.5m x 91cm*
• £2,500 • David Black

▽ Luri Gabbeh Rug

• *circa 1880*
Exceptional Luri Gabbeh banded design rug from south-west Persia with incredible use of natural dyes contrasted with woven bands of cotton pile.
• *length 1.48m*
• £3,250 • Gordon Reece

△ Malayer Runner

• *circa 1880*
Malayer runner made by the Malayers who live sixty miles south of Hamadan in West Central Persia. The rug is decorated with blue, red, ochre and burnt orange vegetable dyes.
• *1m x 4.9m*
• £2,950 • Oriental Rug

△ Persian Jozan Rug

• *circa 1890*
A rare Persian Jozan rug in perfect condition decorated with deer and an angular floral design in ochre, red, blue, green and black.
• *1.37m x 2.04m*
• £4,500 • Oriental Rug

▽ Baluchi Rug

• *1880*
Prayer rug from Baluchistan with a central cream panel depicting navy blue stars, with red and white squares bordered by a navy, cream, red and white geometric design.
• *length 2.4m*
• £850 • David Black

▽ Plain Weave Kilim

• *late 19th century*
An Azari or Shahsavan kilim with natural dyes.
• *length 2.6m, width 1.8m*
• £1,400 • Gordon Reece

△ Dragon and Phoenix Seat Rug

• *circa 19th century*
Embroided seat cover with a stylised dragon and phoenix within floral and vine decoration set against a yellow background.
• *63cm x 84cm*
• £810 • Gordon Reece

△ Tabriz Carpet

• *circa 1890*
An antique rug from Tabriz, in East Azerbaijan, in Northern Iran. The rug shows scrolling, foliate designs in red, blue and brown.
• *length 1.98m, width 1.42m*
• £2,900 • Oriental Rug

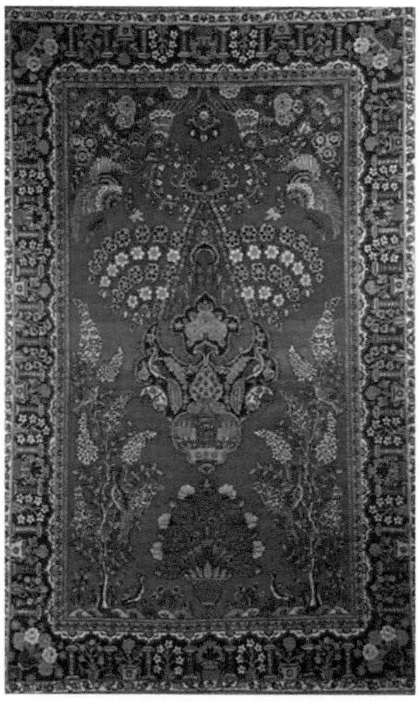

▽ Tekke Rug

• *circa 1920*
Acha-Tekke are woven by the famous tribesmen from the Tekke tribe who are noted for their fine work. In geometric design in reds, cream and black.
• *20cm x 2m*
• £1,400 • Oriental Rug

▽ Kashan Medallion Rug

• *circa 1920*
Kashan rug with classical elongated medallion designs in coral and dark blue and corner decorations. Extremely good example of a curvilinear Persian floral rug.
• *1.37m x 2.07m*
• £4,500 • Oriental Rug

◁ Kashan Rug

• *circa 1920*
Kashan pictorial rug with peacocks in red, blue and green design surrounding a central vase.
• *137cm x 207cm*
• £4,500 • Oriental Rug

△ Western Anatolian Kilim Cushion

- *1920*

Western Anatolian kilim converted into a cushion cover.

- *35cm square*
- £45 • **Oriental Rug**

△ Kurdish Rug

- *early 20th century*

A central field of interlocking diamonds, wool on wool warp. From Eastern Iran.

- *length 1.4m, width 90cm*
- £1,800 • **Gordon Reece**

△ Western Anatolian Kilim Cushion

- *1920*

Western Anatolian kilim converted to a cushion cover.

- *35cm square*
- £45 • **Oriental Rug**

▽ Anatolian Kilim

- *1920*

Western Anatolian kilim covering a beechwood chest.

- *50cm x 90cm*
- £750 • **Oriental Rug**

▽ Sharshavan Cushion

- *1920*

Cushion made from a Sharshavan rug, which was originally part of a cradle.

- *35cm square*
- £65 • **Oriental Rug**

▽ Bibibaff Quajquoli

- *circa 1940*

An unusual and fine example of a Bibibaff Quajquoli.

- *80cm x 118cm*
- £1,100 • **Oriental Rug**

△ Karabagh Cushion

- *circa 1920*

Karabagh kilim converted into a cushion cover.

- *width 48cm*
- £60 • **Oriental Rug**

△ Tent Trappings

- *1920*

In red, purple, orange and cream with red, yellow and brown tassels.

- *height 50cm*
- £65 • **Oriental Rug**

△ Luri Jijim Rug

- *20th century*

Luri Jijim rug with brown, navy, blue and cream, woven striped design, and navy, blue and red binding on the edge.

- *length 2.83m*
- £990 • **Gordon Reece**

▽ Persian Rug

- *circa 1940*

A Persian Baku rug, from the Caucasus, showing a typical quincunxial medallion arrangement with floral border.

- *length 1.6m, width 1.07m*
- £550 • **Oriental Rug**

▽ Bakhtiari Rug

- *circa 1940*

Bakhtiari rugs were woven by nomads and villagers of Luri, Kurdish and other ethnic origins from the Chahar Mahal region of Iran. With medallion design.

- *1.4m x 2.28m*
- £2,300 • **Oriental Rug**

▷ Shuli Gabbeth Rug

- *circa early 20th century*

Shuli Gabbeh wool rug.

- *length 1.63m*
- £620 • **Gordon Reece**

CERAMICS

The golden age of European porcelain is the eighteenth century, the era of Meissen in Germany, Sèvres in France, Capodimonte in Italy and Bow, Chelsea and Worcester in England. The everyday domestic pottery of this century has steadily risen in value and is now very collectable. The nineteenth century also offers immense scope to the collector; at one end there are the superb Empire-style cabinet wares, such as vases and urns with fine painting and gilding, made by Worcester, and at the other end are Staffordshire figures, which present a fascinating tableau of the social and political history of the Victorian era. Chinese porcelain continues to exert a magnetic pull over the west, which began in the seventeenth century, when the European nobility began to compete for the finest pieces. Condition is a major factor in estimating the value of a ceramic as it is very easy for a piece to become damaged.

ENGLISH CERAMICS

◁ **Water Jug**

- *circa 1270–1350*

Lead-glazed water jug probably from Hill Green, Essex. Potter's marks on handle.

- *height 22cm*
- £4,450 • Jonathan Horne

▷ **Saltglazed Jug**

- *13th century*

Saltglazed jug of bulbous form. Strap handle and turned decoration on neck.

- *height 22cm*
- £1,300 • Jonathan Horne

▷ **Earthenware Jug**

- *12th century*

English earthenware vessel with a dark green glaze and circular design around the neck found at Sible Hedingham, Essex.

- *height 29cm*
- £5,500 • Jonathan Horne

▷ **Earthenware Vessel**

- *1270–1350*

Elongated vessel with a light green glaze and thumb prints around the base and top of handle, from Hill Green, Essex.

- *height 30cm*
- £4,400 • Jonathan Horne

▷ **English Tile**

- *circa 14th century*

English tile with panther-head design made at Penn, Buckinghamshire.

- £250 • Garry Atkins

△ English Earthenware Jug
- *13th century*

English earthenware jug of bulbous form with handle, in good condition.
- *height 28cm*
- £2,200 • Jonathan Horne

△ Earthenware Vessel
- *circa 14th century*

Earthenware vessel with a green glaze, found in the foundations of a house in Gracechurch Street, London, in 1873.
- *height 21.5cm*
- £1,950 • Jonathan Horne

△ Terracotta Tile
- *circa 14th century*

English terracotta tile with grotesque design.
- *11cm x 11cm*
- £435 • Jonathan Horne

▽ English Jug
- *circa 14th century*

An early English jug with bib in green lead glaze. Of bulbous form with handle.
- *height 19.5cm*
- £950 • Garry Atkins

▽ Delftware Fuddling Cup
- *1650*

Delftware fuddling cup consisting of three small interlaced containers. Each container is filled with a different alcoholic beverage, before being passed amongst friends.
- *height 7.5cm*
- £6,600 • Jonathan Horne

▽ Earthenware Jug
- *circa 15th century*

15th-century earthenware glazed jug, with lip, probably from North Wales. Maker's mark on neck; around the belly is a distinct groove.
- £4,400 • Jonathan Horne

△ Earthenware Jug
- *13th century*

English earthenware jug of bulbous form with incised banding and a burnt orange glaze.
- *height 20cm*
- £2,950 • Jonathan Horne

△ Earthenware Jug
- *16th century*

Small earthenware jug of bulbous proportions, with moulded handle, splayed lip and a green glaze.
- *height 14cm*
- £780 • Jonathan Horne

△ Chamber Pot
- *circa 17th century*

Early lead-glazed chamber pot with handle.
- *height 13cm*
- £1,350 • Jonathan Horne

▽ Olive Green Jug
- *circa 14th–15th century*

A very early lead-glazed jug, turned with rich olive-green glaze, heavily restored. The item was discovered at Watton Priory, Humberside, in 1923.
- *height 27cm*
- £3,300 • Jonathan Horne

▽ Chamber Pot
- *circa 1680*

Chamber pot. Found in Devonshire among waste from disused kiln.
- *height 16cm*
- £1,250 • Garry Atkins

▽ Chamber Pot
- *circa 17th century*

Early chamber pot with glazed interior and unglazed exterior, with handle.
- *height 19cm*
- £1,650 • Jonathan Horne

△ Delftware Tile

- *circa 1720–30*

Delftware tile depicting the biblical scene of Judith with the head of Holofernes.

- *height 14cm*
- £95 • Jonathan Horne

△ Bristol Vase

- *circa 1715*

A polychrome Bristol vase of bulbous proportions raised on a splayed base with scrolled and floral decoration.

- *height 19cm*
- £6,800 • Jonathan Horne

△ Drinking Cup

- *circa 18th century*

An English lead-glazed drinking cup with handle.

- *height 10cm*
- £220 • Jonathan Horne

▽ Flower Brick

- *1730–40*

One of a pair of very rare flower bricks, with twenty-one receptacles and a sepia and yellow fern design, with houses in the background.

- *10cm x 15cm*
- £7,500 • Jonathan Horne

▽ Staffordshire Lion

- *circa 1740*

Staffordshire lion, recumbent on base with claw raised. From the Rous Lench collection.

- *height 17cm*
- £1,950 • Jonathan Horne

▽ Pair of Plates

- *circa 18th century*

One of a pair of plates, possibly Staffordshire or Yorkshire, showing oriental garden scenes.

- £125 pair • Jonathan Horne

△ Worcester Teapot

- *circa 1723–92*

Of the first period. Blue and white, with the Mansfield pattern. Decorated similarly to the lid.

- *height 13cm*
- £455 • London Antique

△ Bristol Tile

- *circa 1740–60*

Bristol tile depicting a European scene of an 18th-century lady in a pretty landscape.

- *height 14cm*
- £70 • Garry Atkins

△ Terracotta Tile

- *1720–30*

English terracotta tile, with pattern showing musicians.

- *height 14cm*
- £95 • Jonathan Horne

▽ Worcester Plate

- *circa 18th century*

Worcester plate with mixed oriental influence, showing kakiemon-style birds of paradise with oriental floral decoration.

- *diameter 16cm*
- £585 • London Antique

▽ Tea Canister

- *circa 1735*

An octagonal Staffordshire bottle with moulded decoration showing figures in a Chinoiserie setting.

- *height 10cm*
- £1,455 • Jonathan Horne

▽ Staffordshire Sauceboat

- *circa 1745*

Staffordshire sauceboat with a scrolled handle, decorated with a pink house and clouds, with shaped rim and foot.

- *height 8cm*
- £1,850 • Jonathan Horne

◁ Prattware Cow

- *circa 18th century*

Prattware, probably Staffordshire, showing cow and calf. There is some restoration to the horns.

- *height 5.5cm*
- £660 • Jonathan Horne

△ Polychrome Tile

- *1750–75*

A polychrome tile from Liverpool. The tile shows a floral design and some restoration.

- *height 14cm*
- £135 • Garry Atkins

△ Agate Teapot

- *1755*

Staffordshire blue and brown agate teapot in pecten shell design with a recumbent dog finial.

- *height 14cm*
- £4,950 • Jonathan Horne

△ Chelsea Dish

- *circa 1753*

A Chelsea famille rose dish, painted in the famille rose style, showing songbird and flower heads on a lattice border.

- *height 16cm*
- £4,000 • E. & H. Manners

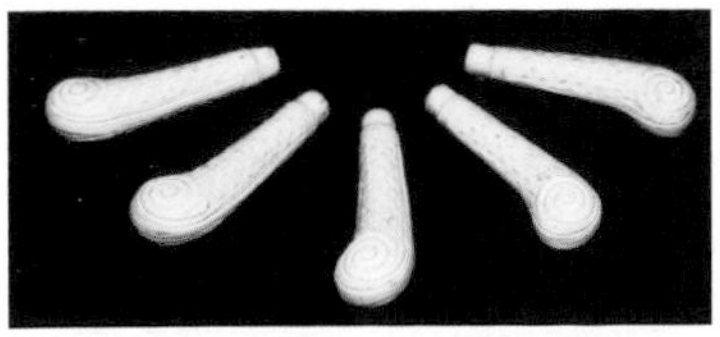

▽ Saltglazed Bottle

- *circa 1750*

Restored, Staffordshire saltglazed bottle with floral relief and crown and rose detailing.

- *height 25cm*
- £1,650 • Garry Atkins

▽ Delftware Bowl

- *circa 1750*

A mint-condition Delftware bowl, showing oriental designs of landscapes. The designs are inside, outside and around the lip of the bowl.

- *diameter 30cm*
- £1,750 • Garry Atkins

▽ Chelsea Dish

- *circa 1750*

Chelsea lozenge-shaped dish with floral sprays of pink roses, a scalloped edge with gilt trim and scrolling.

- *diameter 25cm*
- £1,450 • Stockspring

◁ Knife Handle Set

- *circa 1755*

A set of Staffordshire knife handles with leaf scroll design.

- *height 7cm*
- £3,850 • Jonathan Horne

△ Figure of Ceres

- *circa 1756*

Modelled by Joseph Williams, the figure is shown in classical pose, wearing a wreath and holding a wheat sheaf and blue cornflowers. She is strategically swathed in purple. Wheat sheaves and flowers also at her feet.

- *height 33cm*
- £7,500 • E. & H. Manners

△ Fluted Cup and Saucer

- *1755–90*

A Worcester cup and saucer with fluted design, interlaced floral decoration around the rim in gilt and blue, with gilt floral sprays.

- *height of cup 6cm*
- £195 • London Antique

△ Bristol Tile

- *circa 1750–70*

A European river scene of a man fishing on central panel, with floral decoration.

- *height 14cm*
- £60 • Garry Atkins

▽ Worcester Sauceboat

- *1756*

Worcester cos lettuce moulded sauceboat, painted with scattered floral sprays, and a twig-moulded handle. Unmarked.

- *length 8.75cm*
- £1,250 • Dando

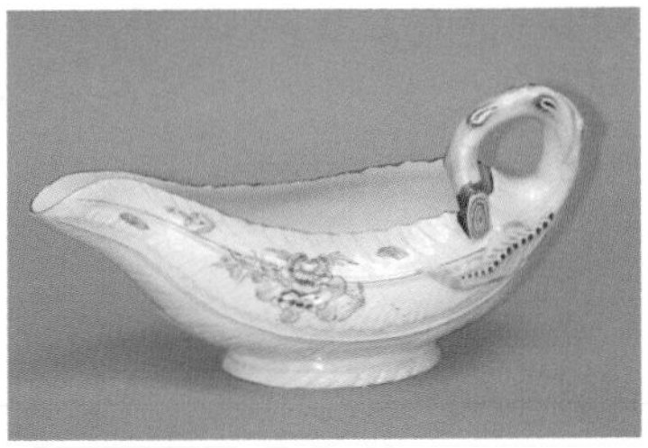

▽ Delftware Tile

- *circa 1720–60*

An English Delftware tile, London, slightly damaged. The design depicts an urn and floral arrangement.

- *height 14cm*
- £30 • Garry Atkins

▽ Dish & Cover

- *circa 1750*

Staffordshire dish and cover with cow in relief on cover, and floral decoration throughout.

- *height 7cm*
- £1,750 • Jonathan Horne

△ Worcester Tea Bowl

- *1760*

Small Worcester tea bowl decorated with a courting couple in a classical setting, a small dog and garden roller in the foreground.

- *height of bowl 5cm*
- £560 • Stockspring

△ Staffordshire Teapot

- *1765*

Staffordshire underglazed oxide teapot with floral decoration and a finial lid.

- *height 11cm*
- £1,355 • Jonathan Horne

△ Flower Brick

- *circa 1760*

A rare blue and white flower brick, with twenty-one receptacles and painted panels of water lilies, chrysanthemums and a bird within a dark blue border.

- *10cm x 15cm*
- £1,450 • Jonathan Horne

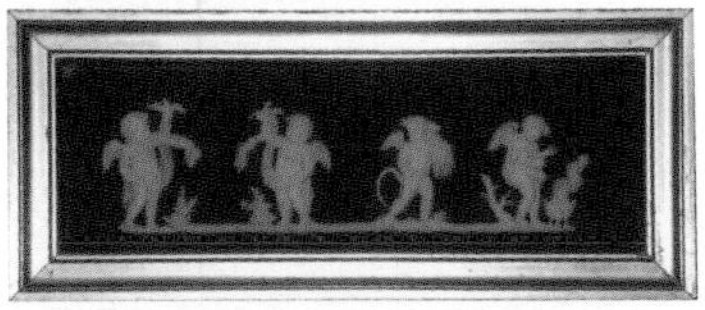

△ Wedgwood Plaque

- *1768–80*

A Wedgwood cameo plaque dipped in black and white, showing four mischievous putti, mounted in a gilt frame.

- *20cm x 8cm*
- £200 • London Antique

▽ Chelsea Sugar Bowl

- *circa 1760–65*

A Chelsea sugar bowl of the Gold Anchor period. Decorated with floral sprays and a graduated cell pattern with border in purple and gilding. Gilding is also shown on the lip and base. The lid shows similar decoration and gilding, with a finial top.

- *height 8cm*
- £3,200 • E. & H. Manners

▽ Bow Grape-sellers

- *circa 1760*

Pair of Bow figures, of a young girl wearing a pink hat with finely painted dress of pink flowers and boy seated with matching breeches, and outstretched arm holding grapes.

- *height 16.5cm*
- £3,800 pair • Stockspring

▽ English Tile

- *circa 1760*

An English blue and white tile, made in Liverpool. The tile depicts a scene of a windmill amongst a diaper design.

- *height 14cm*
- £55 • Garry Atkins

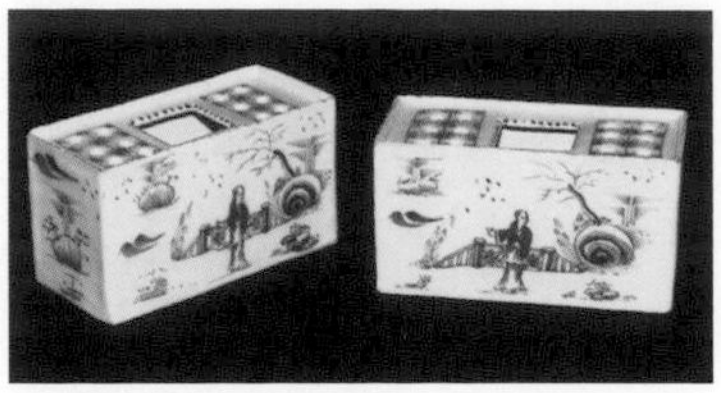

△ Flower Bricks

- *1760*

A very unusual pair of English Delftware flower bricks. The bricks have oriental designs. Probably from Liverpool.

- *height 8.5cm*
- £1,650 • Garry Atkins

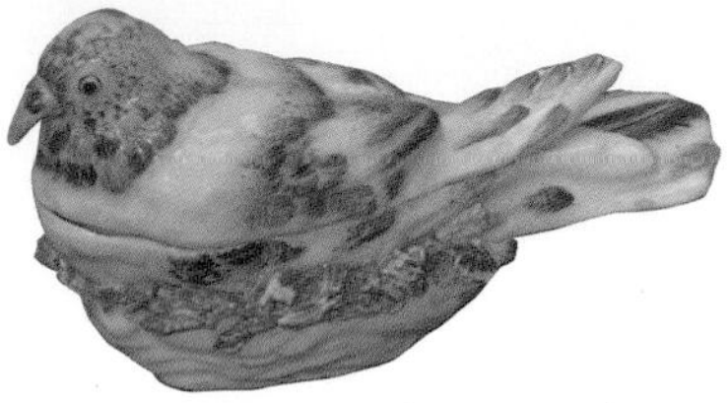

△ Derby Squab Tureen

- *circa 1760*

Finely painted Derby Squab tureen, naturalistically styled as a bird, with floral encrustation.

- *height 10cm*
- £3,400 • Stockspring

△ Blackware Teapot

- *circa 1765*

Small blackware teapot, with ear-shaped handle and a raised floral design, on pad feet, with a bird finial lid.

- *height 8cm*
- £475 • Jonathan Horne

▽ Saltglazed Teapot

- *circa 1760*

Staffordshire teapot, with damaged neck and base which has been reconstructed. Interesting detailing, with serpentine handle.

- *height 15cm*
- £850 • Garry Atkins

▽ Worcester Dish

- *circa 1768*

Worcester oval Imari-pattern dish with a central cartouche of a pagoda and an orange-blossom tree with clouds to the side, and twig orange handles.

- *length 28cm*
- £11,500 • Stockspring

▽ Staffordshire Plate

- *circa 1765*

Staffordshire saltglazed plate, with polychrome floral decoration to central panel and raised basket design to lip.

- *diameter 19cm*
- £995 • Jonathan Horne

◁ Staffordshire Jug

- *circa 1765*

Rare little blue Staffordshire saltglazed jug.

- *height 19cm*
- £990 • Jonathan Horne

△ Staffordshire Creamware Teapot

- *circa 1770*

A Staffordshire creamware teapot with moulded decoration, crossover strap handle and finial lid. Painted with a chinoiserie-style design.

- *height 5.5cm*
- £ 1,450 • Jonathan Horne

△ Bow Candleholder

- *circa 1760*

Bow candleholder encrusted with yellow and pink flowers around the trunk of a tree with two pheasants perched on the top and a central flower candleholder.

- *height 23cm*
- £1,850 • Stockspring

△ Tile

- *circa 1760–80*

A polychrome tile from Bristol with floral arrangement.

- *height 14cm*
- £280 • Garry Atkins

▽ Glazed Teapot

- *1760*

A Staffordshire octagonal green glazed teapot with moulded decoration depicting chinoiserie scenes. Scrolled handle and finial lid.

- *height 16cm*
- £3,950 • Jonathan Horne

▽ Worcester Jug

- *circa 1765*

Small Worcester jug decorated with a spray of pink flowers, with an orange line and scalloping on the inside of the rim.

- *height 8.5cm*
- £980 • Stockspring

▽ Blackware Bowl

- *circa 1765*

Blackware bowl decorated with a raised design of gilt fruit and trailing foliage.

- *diameter 14cm*
- £660 • Jonathan Horne

△ Jelly Mould

- *circa 1760*

A saltglazed jelly mould.

- *height 3.5cm*
- £325 • Garry Atkins

△ Chelsea Dish

- *circa 1760*

Chelsea dish in the shape of a peony encircled by a green leaf, with a turquoise handle in the shape of a branch with a bud.

- *diameter 19cm*
- £2,700 • Stockspring

△ Staffordshire Vase

- *circa 1765*

Staffordshire vase with oriental floral decorations in pink and green. Small chips to body.

- *height 17cm*
- £3,300 • Jonathan Horne

▽ Sauceboat

- *circa 1760*

An 18th-century creamware sauceboat with underglazed oxide, probably Wedgwood. Slightly damaged.

- *height 7cm*
- £850 • Garry Atkins

▽ Blackware Coffee Pot

- *circa 1765*

Blackware coffee pot, raised on three feet with a pinched lip, moulded handle and a bird finial cover.

- *height 15cm*
- £550 • Jonathan Horne

▽ Derby Figures

- *1765*

Pair of Derby figures of a young girl holding a basket and her companion holding a lamb under his arm, standing on a scrolled base scattered with flowers.

- *height 24cm*
- £3,600 the pair • Stockspring

△ Tea Kettle

- *1770*

A Leeds tea kettle with a crossover strap handle and moulded spout with female decoration and black and white geometric design.

- *height 16cm*
- £3,650 • Jonathan Horne

△ Porcelain Set

- *1773*

A Worcester porcelain cup and saucer decorated with pink roses and gilding to the rim and handle.

- *height of cup 5.5cm*
- £295 • London Antique

△ Worcester Mug

- *1780*

Cylindrical Worcester porcelain tankard decorated with a painted urn in purple enamel, with garlands and sprays of polychrome flowers between underglaze blue and gilt bands. Crescent mark.

- *height 13.5cm*
- £1,050 • Dando

▽ Creamware Teapot

- *1760*

A Staffordshire creamware teapot with a cabbage spout design, scrolled handle and painted designs of flowers.

- *height 7cm*
- £880 • Jonathan Horne

▽ Tea Canister

- *circa 1770–80*

A creamware tea canister with chinoiserie design. Probably made in Leeds.

- *height 8.5cm*
- £295 • Garry Atkins

▽ Staffordshire Plate

- *circa 1770*

An 18th-century creamware underglazed oxide Staffordshire plate.

- *diameter 23cm*
- £375 • Garry Atkins

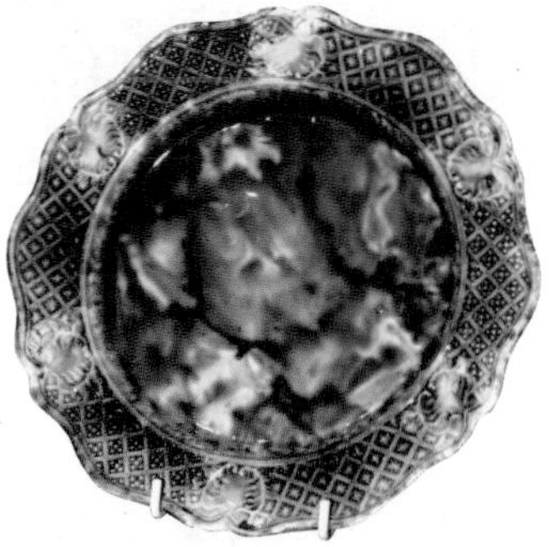

△ Terracotta Teapot

- *circa 1770*

Terracotta teapot decorated with oriental designs in relief. Flower finish on lid.

- *height 9cm*
- £550 • Jonathan Horne

△ Printed Tile

- *circa 1770*

Late 18th-century tile, printed and overprinted in enamel. The painting shows an urn in green with green enamel foliate designs to the edge, the whole on a white enamel ground.

- *height 14cm*
- £150 • Garry Atkins

△ Barber's Bowl

- *circa 1780*

A creamware matching barber's bowl and jug from Leeds pottery. The jug has a crossover strap handle with acanthus terminals.

- *height of jug 33.5cm*
- £1,850 • Garry Atkins

▽ Chelsea Derby Mug

- *1770*

Chelsea Derby white mug delicately painted in a soft palette with a spray of pink roses, with scrolled handle and gilt rim.

- *height 10cm*
- £1,100 • Stockspring

▽ Derby Figure

- *circa 1770*

Derby figure of a young maiden wearing a white dress and bonnet holding a basket of green and red grapes under her arm, on a circular base with gilt banding.

- *height 14cm*
- £1,180 • Stockspring

▽ Copeland Cup and Saucer

- *circa 1770–82*

Copeland cup and saucer produced for Thos. Goode and Co., gilded and jewelled on royal-blue base.

- *height 13.5cm*
- £1,950 • London Antique

△ Pepperette

- *circa 1780*

A creamware pepperette, slightly damaged.

- *height 11cm*
- **£75** • **Garry Atkins**

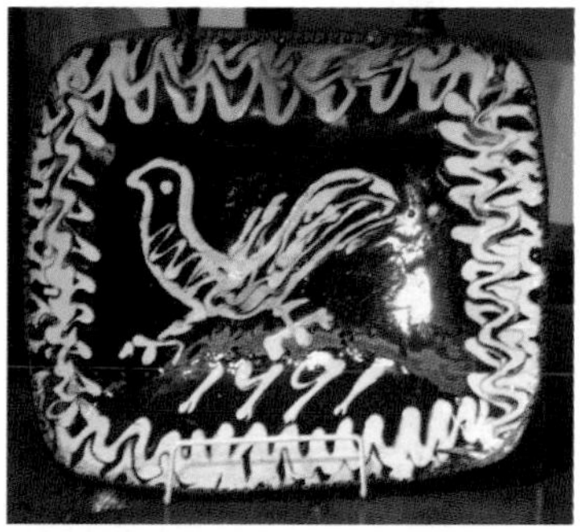

△ Slipware Dishes

- *1791*

One of three Derbyshire slipware dishes dated 1791. Decorated with a cockerel.

- *length 40cm*
- **£400** • **Peter Bunting**

△ Prattware Tea Caddy

- *late 18th century*

Prattware tea caddy with a brass cover, depicting a comical scene in relief of two ladies.

- *height 13cm*
- **£550** • **Jonathan Horne**

▽ Caughley Plates

- *circa 1785–90*

One of a pair of Caughley plates with scalloped edges and underglaze blue border, probably painted and gilded at Worcester. 'S' mark in underglaze blue.

- *diameter 23cm*
- **£650** • **Dando**

▽ Toby Jug

- *circa 1790*

A Staffordshire Prattware Toby jug showing an old lady sitting, entitled 'Martha Gunn'. With painted decoration.

- *height 25cm*
- **£1,680** • **Jonathan Horne**

▽ Deer with Bocage

- *circa 1790*

Pair of Prattware deer with bocage, reclining on grass base.

- *height 14cm*
- **£2,500** • **J. Oosthuizen**

△ Creamware Plate

- *circa 1780–90*

A creamware plate, in excellent condition, with pierced rim.

- *diameter 24cm*
- **£165** • **Garry Atkins**

△ Ralph Wood Spill Vase

- *1790*

A Ralph Wood spill vase showing a recumbent stag with bocage in which a squirrel is perched. Painted in a green and iron red glaze.

- *height 12.5cm*
- **£1,680** • **Jonathan Horne**

△ Urn and Covers

- *circa 1790*

Very rare Wedgwood basalt urns and covers, decorated in gold and bronze. Typical Wedgwood ivy borders, with acanthus-leaf finials and floral swags from satyr masks.

- *length 19.5cm*
- **£3,500** • **R.A. Barnes**

▽ Slipware

- *circa 1780*

Buckley or Staffordshire oval dish with decoration of lines and circles.

- *height 44cm*
- **£1,750** • **Garry Atkins**

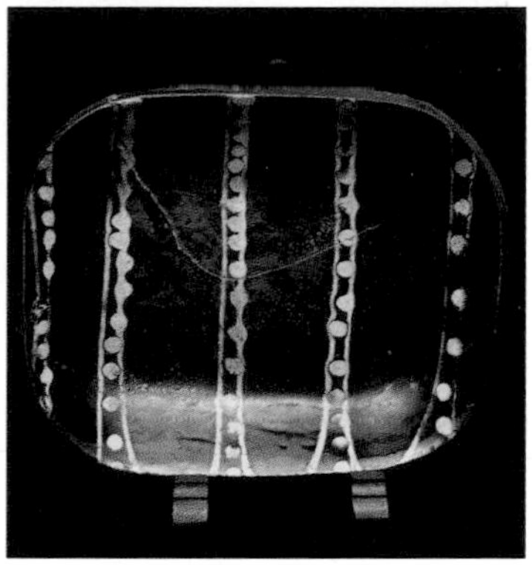

▽ Staffordshire Teapot

- *circa 1795*

Staffordshire teapot with fleur-de-lys design on lid and grotesque design on pot.

- *height 8cm*
- **£1,990** • **Jonathan Horne**

▽ Liverpool Cream Jug

- *1790*

Liverpool cream jug depicting pastoral scenes representing summer, and winter the reverse.

- *height 19cm*
- **£550** • **Jonathan Horne**

△ Staffordshire Mug

- *early 19th century*

Rare commemorative mug celebrating Vauxhall Gardens. Picture shows pipe-organ band stand, decorated with ivy. Probably Staffordshire.

- *height 15cm*
- £660 • Jonathan Horne

△ Tulip Holder

- *circa 1800*

Staffordshire tulip holder with a central panel depicting a pastoral scene, flanked by putti, with mask and leaf decoration to the scalloped rim, raised on three glazed bun feet.

- *height 13cm*
- £1,850 • Jonathan Horne

▽ Staffordshire Group

- *early 19th century*

A Staffordshire Prattware figure of a young woman and a small boy holding a baby chicken in his hat entitled 'Spring'. Both standing on a rectangular base .

- *height 23cm*
- £780 • Jonathan Horne

▽ Tulip Vase

- *circa 1800*

Rare Staffordshire fluted vase, finished in pink lustre with green dolphins. Interlaced flutes, after the Ralph Wood design.

- *height 20cm*
- £850 • Constance Stobo

◁ Staffordshire Jug

- *circa 1800*

Staffordshire jug showing four horses and a coach with a driver and two other figures. On the side of the carriage are the words the 'Liverpool Fly' the initials J.R. under the lip, and a cartouche of flowers with the following poem: 'The Ale is good, Then pray pour out, The Glafs is full, Come Drink a bout'.

- *height 18cm*
- £1,650 • Jonathan Horne

△ Staffordshire Plate

- *early 19th century*

Probably Staffordshire Prattware, incorporating rural scene, with decorative rim.

- *diameter 16cm*
- £235 • Jonathan Horne

△ Worcester Jug

- *1805*

Worcester jug with terracotta, dark blue and white floral and scroll design, with gold trim on rim and handle.

- *height 18cm*
- £1,280 • Stockspring

△ Prattware Jug

- *circa 1800*

Showing Toby Philpot holding a tankard and a man smoking a pipe on reverse. There is a leaf design around base and neck.

- *height 12cm*
- £395 • Constance Stobo

▽ Staffordshire Hound

- *circa 1800*

A Staffordshire figure of a hound, finely modelled shown standing on a naturalistically styled base.

- *height 14cm*
- £2,200 • Jonathan Horne

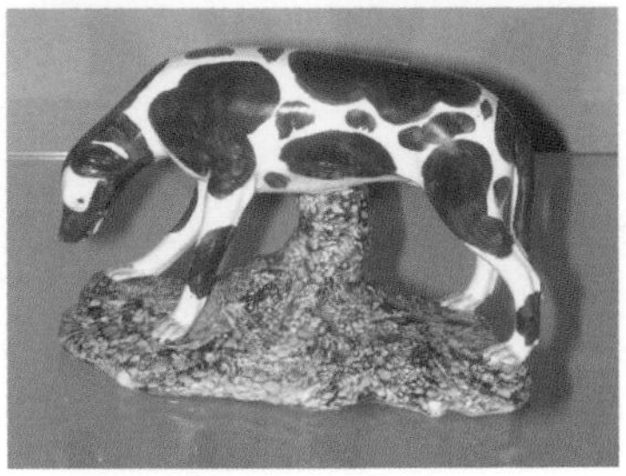

▽ Staffordshire Platter

- *1800*

Small Staffordshire plate with dark blue, scalloped border, with a raised design of a lobster in the centre.

- *length 11.5cm*
- £750 • Jonathan Horne

▽ Derby Vase

- *circa 1800*

Derby vase, painted in a soft palette, with foliage, grass and scattered sprigs of leaves on a white ground. Pattern primarily depicting red-legged grouse. There is some inexpert restoration to the rim.

- *height 16cm*
- £480 • Ian Spencer

△ Prattware Horse

- *circa 1800*

Prattware dapple-grey horse, with head erect, a long black tail and blue saddle, standing on a plinth base.

- *height 16cm*
- £4,550 • Jonathan Horne

△ Bear Figure

- *circa 1800*

Staffordshire figure of chained and muzzled bear in sitting position on a green base.

- *height 9cm*
- £780 • Jonathan Horne

△ Wedgwood Candle Holders

- *circa 1800*

A pair of rare Wedgwood candle holders mounted on gilt bronze. Bases show classical cameos with frieze motifs.

- *height 26cm*
- £2,500 • R.A. Barnes

▽ Chestnut Horse

- *circa 1800*

Chestnut horse with tail raised and head bowed, with a white saddle and yellow girth, a fine example of Prattware.

- *height 16cm*
- £4,400 • Jonathan Horne

▽ Musician with Horn

- *circa 1800*

Musician with hunting horn, wearing theatrical dress.

- *height 24cm*
- £895 • J. Oosthuizen

▽ Staffordshire Fox

- *circa 1800*

Staffordshire English scene depicting fox with prey upon base of a grassy knoll.

- *height 14.5cm*
- £1,450 • Jonathan Horne

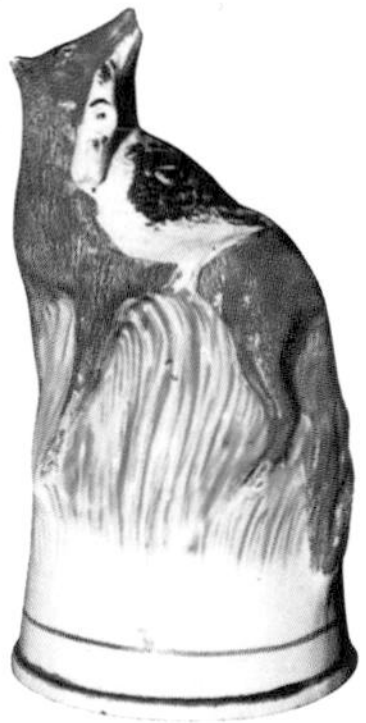

△ Prattware Skewbald Horse

- *circa 1800*

Prattware skewbald horse with a blue glazed saddle, on a plinth base.

- *height 16cm*
- £4,400 • Jonathan Horne

△ Classical Figure

- *circa 1800*

A rare classical figure of Mars, possibly Yorkshire, in armour, with hand resting on sword hilt.

- *height 19cm*
- £750 • Jonathan Horne

△ Tea Canister

- *circa 1800*

Tea canister showing rather comical scene of two ladies. Two gentlemen on reverse.

- *height 13cm*
- £215 • Jonathan Horne

▽ Cow Creamer

- *circa 1800*

Speckled brown naturalistic cow on a green base.

- *height 15cm*
- £800 • J. Oosthuizen

▽ Staffordshire Figure

- *circa 1800*

One of a pair of Staffordshire groups depicting friendship and tenderness. Figures shown embracing. Minor repairs.

- *height 18cm*
- £1,350 pair • Jonathan Horne

▽ Hip Flask

- *circa 1800*

A hip flask decorated with floral design on front and reverse, Staffordshire or Yorkshire.

- *height 18cm*
- £660 • Jonathan Horne

△ Blue and White Jug

• *1817*

Large blue and white jug decorated with an Indian hunting scene with elephants and hounds giving chase to a tiger.

• *height 28cm*

• £1,700 • Libra

△ Brickmaker's Staffordshire Jug

• *circa 1815*

Staffordshire jug with the words 'Succefs to all Jolly Brickmakers 1815', under the lip and a cartouche on each side depicting artisans at work.

• *height 19cm*

• £1,750 • Jonathan Horne

△ Cow Creamer

• *circa 1810*

A Staffordshire cow creamer with yellow spots.

• *height 13cm*

• £630 • J. Oosthuizen

▽ Staffordshire Teapot

• *1813*

Rare black Staffordshire teapot and cover, inscribed, 'India, Portugal, Spain, Victoria 21st June 1813', with a laurel wreath.

• *height 24cm*

• £990 • Jonathan Horne

▽ Bear Teapot

• *1815*

Staffordshire teapot modelled as a bear wearing a muzzle and collar.

• *height 17cm*

• £2,850 • Jonathan Horne

△ Clock with Figures

• *1815*

Staffordshire group depicting a long-case clock flanked by two figures leaning against a pillar. The man holding a scroll, and a lady leaning against a pillar with her hand raised.

• *height 27cm*

• £1,250 • Jonathan Horne

△ Staffordshire Figure

• *circa 1810*

A rare Staffordshire female figure leaning in classical pose against an obelisk.

• *height 20cm*

• £780 • Jonathan Horne

◁ Staffordshire Spill Vase

• *1815*

Staffordshire pottery 'Game Spill' vase of unusual and fine quality in the form of a hollow tree, hung with various game and a hunter's satchel. Pearlware with overglaze enamel colours.

• *height 22cm*

• £400 • Dando

▽ Derbyshire Bowl

• *1810*

Derbyshire double-handled sugar bowl, decorated with a pink heart-shaped pattern and gilt foliate designs and banding.

• *height 9cm*

• £360 • Stockspring

▽ Chimney Sweep

• *circa 1810*

Early Staffordshire pottery figure of a chimney sweep decorated in overglaze colours.

• *height 18cm*

• £445 • Dando

▽ Newhalls Walberton Teapot

• *1810*

Newhalls Walberton patent teapot and cover, with a gilt finial lid and foliate designs. The body is profusely gilded and decorated with a painted landscape, with a blue enamelled band at the base of the spout.

• *height 16cm*

• £1,290 • Stockspring

△ Scene from Persuasion

• *circa 1820*
A scene from Jane Austen's *Persuasion*, made by Sharrat. An eager male and a coy female on a garden seat with dog; spreading pineapple bocage behind.
• *height 20cm*
• £6,200 • Constance Stobo

▽ Staffordshire Dandies

• *circa 1820*
A Staffordshire couple, the lady wearing a large yellow hat with blue feathers, a pink jacket and yellow skirt, the gentleman wearing black morning coat with top hat and yellow trousers.
• *height 21cm*
• £1,780 • Jonathan Horne

▽ Mounted Staffordshire Figure

• *circa 1820*
Mounted cavalry officer wearing a blue uniform with gold braiding, at full charge brandishing his sabre.
• *height 28cm*
• £2,950 • Jonathan Horne

▽ Winchester Measure Jug

• *1815*
Winchester measure jug with scrolled handle and pinched lip, with moulded leaf design around neck and blue banded decoration.
• *height 14cm*
• £290 • Libra

◁ Derby Cup and Saucer

• *circa 1820*
Derby cup and saucer, the inside of the cup and the plate boldly decorated with orange blossom and leaf designs.
• *height 5cm*
• £95 • A. Piotrowski

△ Lustre Ware Mug

• *1820*
A double-handled lustre ware mug, with floral decoration, on a pedestal base.
• *height 12cm*
• £66 • Cekay

△ Seated Shepherdess

• *circa 1820*
A Staffordshire figure of a shepherdess seated on a flower-encrusted base with a goat.
• *height 13.5cm*
• £135 • Cekay

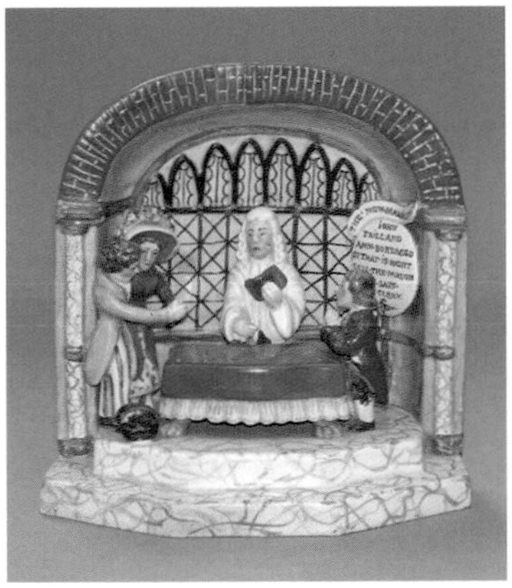

△ The Marriage Act

• *circa 1820*
Staffordshire group entitled, 'The Marriage Act'.
• *17cm x 17cm*
• £4,450 • Jonathan Horne

△ Pink Lustre Mug

• *circa 1820*
The mug shows scenes of Remembrance of Home with domestic scenes by river setting. Reverse with children and The Verse of Love. Pink lustre rim.
• *height 7.5cm*
• £195 • Constance Stobo

▽ Charles Bourne Vase

• *circa 1820*
Charles Bourne vase with a band of finely painted flowers, between gilded floral borders on a blue ground.
• *height 15cm*
• £480 • Stockspring

▽ Sunderland Plaque

• *circa 1825*
Transfer with coloured wash. Pink lustre showing sailing ships and anecdote of peace and plenty. With copper lustre.
• *height 23cm*
• £295 • Constance Stobo

▽ Sugar Bowl

• *1825*
Dawson Squire and Lackey blue and white sugar bowl, with cover and finial lid, decorated with a scene depicting a castle in a parkland setting.
• *height 10cm*
• £245 • Libra

▽ Yates Egg Cups

- *circa 1820*

An early and rare set of six egg cups with stand by Yates, with finely painted flowers between scrolled cartouches, centred with birds.

- *height 5cm*
- £750 • Stockspring

▽ English Sauce Tureen

- *circa 1820*

English blue and white sauce tureen and cover on fitted base with a landscape depicting grazing rabbits within a country setting.

- *height 17cm*
- £375 • Libra

▽ Staffordshire Groups

- *1830*

Unusual Staffordshire groups depicting a dog with puppies and a cat with kittens.

- *height 11cm*
- £2,500 • J. Oosthuizen

▷ Miniature Ewer and Stand

- *circa 1835*

English ceramic miniature ewer and stand with original porcelain stopper, with a painted floral panel set within gilded borders.

- *height 11cm*
- £420 • Dando

△ Staffordshire Turkeys

- *circa 1820*

A rare and unusual pair of Staffordshire turkeys. The male with his plumes displayed, both on a naturalistically formed green-glazed base.

- *height to head 9cm*
- £4,450 • Jonathan Horne

△ Staffordshire Model

- *circa 1820*

Staffordshire model depicting Romulus and Remus, with their adoptive mother, in wilderness.

- *height 20cm*
- £3,950 • J. Oosthuizen

▽ Staffordshire Lion

- *circa 1820*

Staffordshire lion in red glaze on base, with silvered mane, eyes and nose and a protruding tongue. One paw is raised, resting on a single rock. Small amount of restoration.

- *height 13cm*
- £1,780 • Jonathan Horne

▽ Staffordshire Castle

- *circa 1830*

A cream Staffordshire castle with four turrets standing on a bushy base.

- *15cm x 18cm*
- £880 • Jonathan Horne

▽ Wine Jug

- *1820*

Large blue and white wine jug, with a scene depicting wine makers at the press, with vine and fruit decoration.

- *height 24cm*
- £1,150 • Libra

△ Chamberlain Worcester Plate

- *circa 1820*

An armorial plate with gilded and floral decoration, on a green background.

- *diameter 26cm*
- £350 • London Antique

△ Coalport Cream Jug

- *circa 1835*

Coalport cream jug with gilded floral designs on a blue ground with small hand-painted panels of birds.

- *height 12.5cm*
- £165 • Dando

△ Porcelain Turk

- *1830*

A porcelain figure of a Turk, seated on a pink cushion.

- *height 12cm*
- £89 • Cekay

△ Elephant Spill Vases
• *1830*
Pair of grey elephant spill vases with pink saddles.
• *15cm x 10cm*
• £2,700 • J. Oosthuizen

△ Pair of Staffordshire Poodles
• *circa 1835*
One of a pair of Staffordshire poodles with flower-basket, on a cushion base.
• *height 12cm*
• £695 • J. Oosthuizen

△ Theatrical Figures
• *1845*
A Staffordshire group showing a man and a woman in theatrical costume.
• *height 22cm*
• £165 • Cekay

▽ Staffordshire Jug
• *circa 1830*
Metallic glaze with panels showing flower arrangement, with acanthus-leaf handle and acanthus-leaf spout.
• £250 • Constance Stobo

▽ Copper Lustre Goblet
• *1840*
An English copper lustre goblet, decorated with a floral design around the body with turned decoration.
• *height 12cm*
• £45 • Cekay

▽ English Lustre Jug
• *1845*
An English copper lustre jug, with a scrolled handle and decorated with a rose and leaf pattern.
• *height 11cm*
• £88 • Cekay

△ Series of Plates
• *circa 1830*
One of a series of ten plates showing scenes from 'The Sacred History of Joseph and his Brothers'. Daisy pattern to rim with pink lustre dots.
• *diameter 20cm*
• £600 the set • Constance Stobo

△ Staffordshire Greyhounds
• *circa 1845*
Pair of Staffordshire greyhounds reclining on blue base. Pen holders.
• *diameter 8cm*
• £545 • J. Oosthuizen

△ Staffordshire Archer
• *1840*
Staffordshire figure of a lady archer wearing a plumed hat and green coat, holding a bow and arrow, standing on a plinth base.
• *height 17cm*
• £295 • P. Oosthuizen

▽ Floral Cottage
• *1830*
A Staffordshire cottage encrusted with flowers.
• *height 11cm*
• £135 • Cekay

▽ Wedgwood Teapot
• *1830*
A Wedgwood white stoneware teapot of compressed form with moulded relief to the body, spout and handle, and a finial formed as a hound on the cover.
• *height 11cm*
• £275 • London Antique

▽ Pastille Burner
• *circa 1845*
Staffordshire pastille burner depicting Windsor lodge.
• *height 14cm*
• £185 • J. Oosthuizen

△ Pair of Field Spaniels

- *circa 1850*

Pair of eager field spaniels on an ornate base.

- *height 16cm*
- **£800 pair** • **J. Oosthuizen**

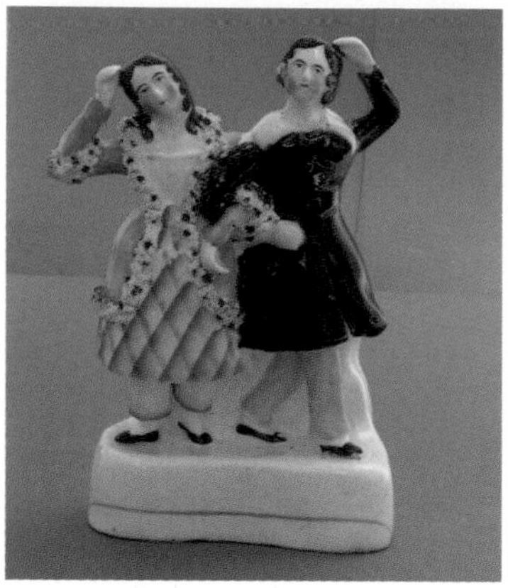

△ Theatrical Dancers

- *1850*

Staffordshire group of theatrical dancers depicting Miss Glover and Mrs Vining as Yourawkee and Peter Wilkins.

- *height 20cm*
- **£295** • **Dando**

△ Wedgwood Plaque

- *circa 1850*

Wedgwood cameo plaque, dipped black and white, showing 'Six Dancing Hours'. Originally modelled by Floxam in the 18th century. Extremely popular mantel in a black laquer frame with gilded mounting.

- *length 56cm*
- **£1,250** • **R.A. Barnes**

▽ Sunderland Mug

- *circa 1850*

Fine-quality mug, with the mariner's arms showing success and commerce. With name and anecdote on reverse. The whole with pink lustre finish.

- *height 9cm*
- **£315** • **Constance Stobo**

▽ Staffordshire House

- *circa 1855*

Commemorative piece – scene of a murder committed by the owner of Pot Ash Farm against the owner of Stansfield Hall.

- *height 20cm*
- **£495** • **J. Oosthuizen**

▽ Dog-head Window Rests

- *circa 1850*

Mid-19th-century Staffordshire dog-head window rests. Yellow ochre glaze showing spaniel dogs with collars.

- *height 13cm*
- **£220** • **Constance Stobo**

◁ Coalport Cup and Saucer

- *circa 1850*

Coalport cup and saucer profusely gilded with floral and swag designs between six roundels.

- *height 7cm*
- **£79** • **A. Piotrowski**

△ House with Bower

- *circa 1850*

Flower-encrusted house with bower and various doors and windows.

- *height 13cm*
- **£250** • **J. Oosthuizen**

△ Painted Cup and Saucer

- *circa 1850*

English cup and saucer centred with a landscape showing a classical ruin, within a gilded floral border.

- *height 6cm*
- **£98** • **A. Piotrowski**

△ Staffordshire Leopard on Base

- *circa 1855*

Very rare stylised leopard.

- *height 18cm*
- **£1,895** • **J. Oosthuizen**

▽ Pastille Burner

- *circa 1850*

Flower-encrusted pastille burner with pagoda roof.

- *height 14cm*
- **£950** • **J. Oosthuizen**

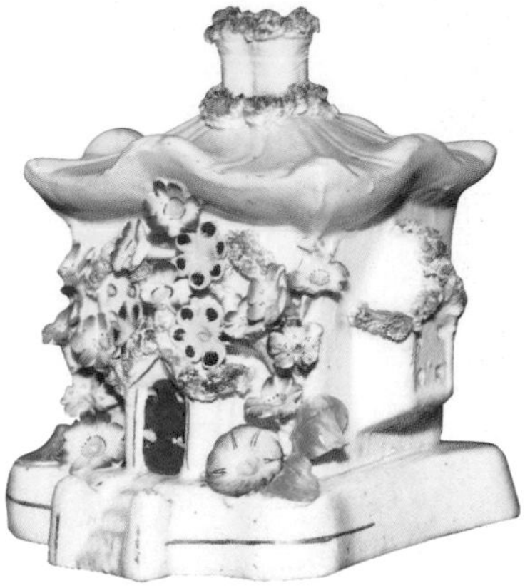

▽ Mayer Jug

- *1850*

T.J. & J. Mayer blue and white jug with pewter mounts and moulded decoration around the body and handle.

- *height 21cm*
- **£175** • **A.D. Antiques**

▽ Minton Trio

- *circa 1856*

Minton trio with Empire gilded design and pink bands. The trio comprises tea cup, coffee cup and saucer.

- *height 7cm*
- **£95** • **London Antique**

△ Toby Jug

• *mid-19th century*
A lady snuff-taker in green coat with candy-striped underdress, holding a snuff bag and taking a pinch to her nose.
• *height 19cm*
• £260 • Constance Stobo

△ Pair of Dalmatian Dogs

• *1875*
An unusual pair of seated Staffordshire Dalmatians with alert expressions, painted with gilt collars on oval cobalt blue bases.
• *height 13cm*
• £795 • Jesse Davis

▽ Stoneware Jug

• *circa 1850*
A good English stoneware jug with embossed rural scene decoration, including windmills, dogs and bucolic characters. The tin-glazed jug has a pewter cover with a highly unusual, open, chair-back thumbpiece.
• *height 9.5cm*
• £150 • Jane Stewart

▽ Staffordshire Jar

• *19th century*
A Staffordshire jar of bulbous form with banding and floral decoration and two applied handles.
• *height 17cm*
• £650 • Jonathan Horne

▷ Chamber Pot

• *circa 1860*
A Victorian chamber pot, decorated with a floral design of roses, inscribed 'Ridgways'.
• *height 14cm*
• £56 • Cekay

◁ Basalt Vase

• *19th century*
A Wedgwood Basalt vase of cylindrical form with trees and figurative relief, below a band of floral swags.
• *height 28cm*
• £115 • London Antique

△ Staffordshire Zebras

• *circa 1850*
Staffordshire zebras with bridles.
• *height 22cm*
• £1,500 pair • J. Oosthuizen

△ Staffordshire Model of 'The Lion Slayer'

• *circa 1850*
Mid-19th-century Staffordshire figure depicting 'The Lion Slayer'.
• *height 40cm*
• £265 • J. Oosthuizen

▽ Staffordshire Soldier Returning

• *circa 1855*
Staffordshire 'Soldier's Return' depicting couple on a base embracing after Crimean War.
• *height 21cm*
• £270 • J. Oosthuizen

▽ Stoneware Mug

• *circa 1860*
Mid-19th-century stoneware mug in baluster shape. Tin-glazed with curved handle and lip.
• *height 5cm*
• £65 • Jane Stewart

▽ Bird with Chicks

- *1860*

A Staffordshire inkwell showing a bird with chicks on a nest, encrusted with flowers.

- *height 4cm*
- £68 • Cekay

▽ Pair of Spaniels

- *circa 1860*

A pair of spaniels, in alert, seated pose, with rounded shape.

- *height 16cm*
- £400 • J. Oosthuizen

▽ Uncle Tom's Cabin

- *circa 1860*

Uncle Tom and Eva from the novel by Harriet Beecher-Stowe. Staffordshire.

- *height 24cm*
- £465 • J. Oosthuizen

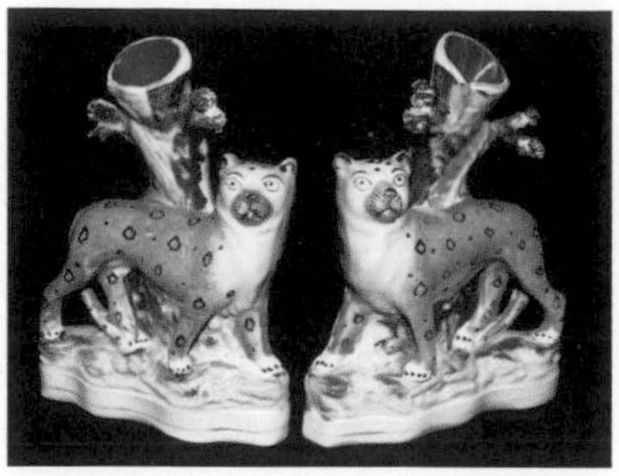

△ Staffordshire Spill Holders

- *circa 1860*

A pair of Staffordshire leopard spill holders. Very rare.

- *height 16cm*
- £3,995 • J. Oosthuizen

△ Staffordshire Gardeners

- *circa 1860–70*

Staffordshire spill vase group of two figures, probably gardeners. The man is holding a basket of flowers and there is a potted plant behind the seated girl.

- *height 21cm*
- £185 • Dando

△ Staffordshire Lion

- *circa 1860*

Staffordshire lion with bocage.

- *height 18cm*
- £1,395 • J. Oosthuizen

▽ English Painted Plate

- *circa 1860*

English plate with a hand-painted scene of boats at harbour, within a raised ribbon border with gilt jewelling and banding.

- *diameter 23.5cm*
- £115 • A. Piotrowski

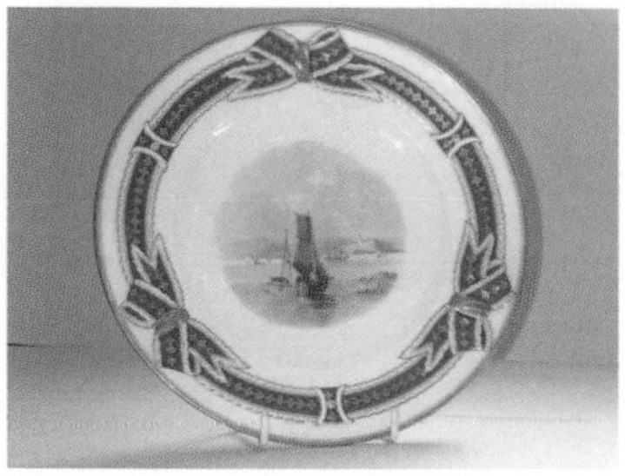

▽ Staffordshire Elephant

- *circa 1860*

Staffordshire elephant, with bocage, on plinth.

- *height 18cm*
- £1,195 • J. Oosthuizen

▽ Minton Cake Stand

- *1863*

A Minton cake stand, which is part of a dessert service comprising ten plates.

- *diameter 24cm*
- £125 • London Antique

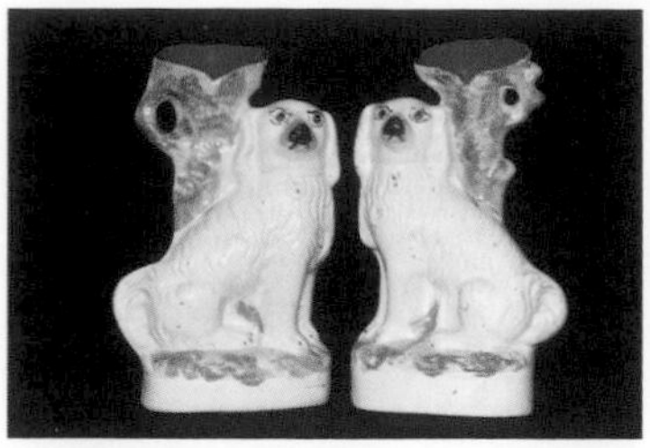

△ Dog Vases

- *circa 1860*

Pair of vases used for spills.

- *height 53cm*
- £295 • J. Oosthuizen

△ Tapered Vase

- *19th century*

English Worcester square tapered vase with gilt decoration. Frog and branch design.

- *height 9cm*
- £475 • David Brower

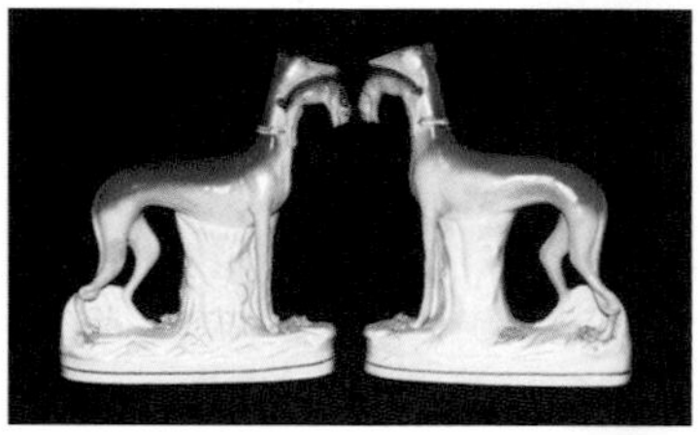

△ Staffordshire Greyhounds

- *circa 1860*

Pair of Staffordshire greyhounds with their catch.

- *height 28cm*
- £995 • J. Oosthuizen

△ Staffordshire Lions

- *1860*

Pair of Staffordshire lions with lambs resting at their sides, reclining on oval moulded bases, with gilding.

- *27cm x 17cm*
- £6,500 • J. Oosthuizen

▽ Sweet Dish

• *circa 1870*

Hand-painted English sweet dish with corn, ferns, insects, a ladybird and a butterfly on a cornflower-blue ground, raised on a splayed foot.

• *diameter 21cm*

• £98 • A. Piotrowski

▽ Swansea Mug

• *1870*

Blue and white Swansea mug with chinoiserie decoration and a bamboo moulded handle.

• *height 18cm*

• £340 • Libra

▽ Staffordshire Windmill

• *circa 1870*

Brightly coloured windmill with adjoining house.

• *height 21cm*

• £170 • J. Oosthuizen

△ Sunderland Jug

• *circa 1870*

A Sunderland lustre jug with scenes of the coal trade and a comical sailor farewell scene.

• *height 19cm*

• £850 • Garry Atkins

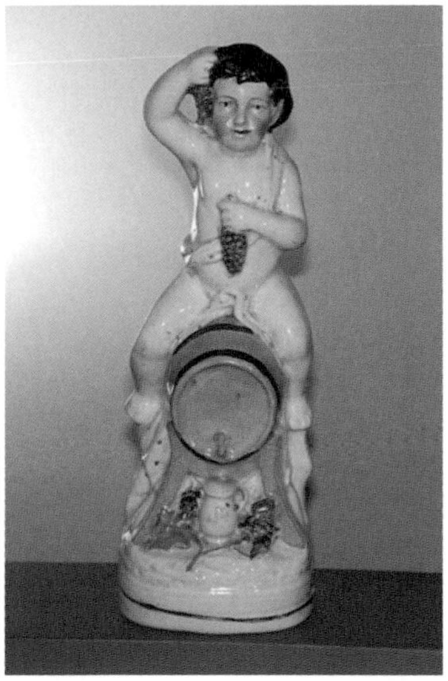

△ Bacchus

• *1870*

Staffordshire figure of Bacchus astride a pink wine barrel holding a bunch of grapes.

• *height 34cm*

• £245 • J. Oosthuizen

▷ Davenport Trio

• *circa 1870–86*

Davenport ceramic trio of cup, saucer and plate, with Imari pattern.

• *diameter 16cm, height 6cm*

• £75 each • London Antique

▽ Doulton Jug

• *1876*

Royal Doulton Lambeth jug designed by Frank Butler with a silver lid and thumb piece, the body decorated with a stylised leaf pattern, with jewelling.

• *height 17cm*

• £235 • Lynda Brine

▽ Staffordshire Cats

• *circa 1870*

A pair of Staffordshire cats, painted black and white, with yellow ribbon collars.

• *height 8cm*

• £475 • Dando

△ Staffordshire Dog Jugs

• *circa 1870*

Mid to late 19th-century Staffordshire. With scrolling handles, painted faces with gilt flecks. The spouts of the jugs are hat-shaped.

• *height 20cm*

• £495 • Constance Stobo

△ Staffordshire Country Gentleman

• *1870*

Staffordshire figure of a country gentleman, presenting a basket of trout, while standing on a naturalistically styled base.

• *height 25.5cm*

• £295 • Dando

△ Royal Doulton Pepper Pot
• *1884*
Royal Doulton pepper pot with blue glazed neck decorated with a raised, repetitive design, above a turned body, raised on a moulded foot.
• *height 8cm*
• £65 • Lynda Brine

△ Pepper Pot
• *1884*
Royal Doulton pepper caster of bulbous form, with pewter cover and finial top, the neck and body decorated with a stylised leaf design, with jewelling.
• *height 10cm*
• £95 • Lynda Brine

▽ Sailor with Parrot
• *1880*
Staffordshire figure of a man in theatrical dress with a plumed hat, holding a parrot.
• *height 20cm*
• £175 • Bellum

▽ Derby Soup Tureen
• *1885*
Late 19th-century large Crown Derby soup tureen, being part of a dinner service consisting of one hundred and six pieces. Heavily patterned on the body and lid of the tureen.
• £7,500 • Judy Fox

▷ Wedgwood Jasper Vase
• *circa 1860*
Wedgwood solid blue jasperware vase, pilastered to head and foot with floral design, with panels between. Ribbons and ivy accentuating lip and base.
• *height 19cm*
• £575 • R.A. Barnes

◁ Royal Worcester Tureen
• *1888*
Part of a Royal Worcester dinner service comprising 18 dinner plates and 3 soup tureens of oval form, with blue and white floral decoration and gilding.
• *35cm x 11cm*
• £2,500 • A.D. Antiques

△ Staffordshire Inkwell
• *1880*
Staffordshire inkwell showing a boy and his sister seated on an orange base.
• *height 11.5cm*
• £175 • Bellum

△ King Charles Spaniel
• *1880*
A Victorian Staffordshire King Charles spaniel painted white with green markings.
• *height 24cm*
• £115 • Cekay

▽ Staffordshire Soldier
• *1880*
Staffordshire figure of an officer in a blue uniform with gilt buttons and a floral sash, within a bocage.
• *height 15cm*
• £175 • Bellum

▽ Victorian Spaniel Group
• *1880*
A Cream Victorian Staffordshire King Charles spaniel and two puppies.
• *height 20cm*
• £115 • Cekay

▽ English Dessert Plate
• *circa 1880*
Painted plate with Red Admiral butterfly and wild flowers on a white ground, within a salmon-pink border with scalloped rim and gilding.
• *diameter 22cm*
• £115 • A. Piotrowski

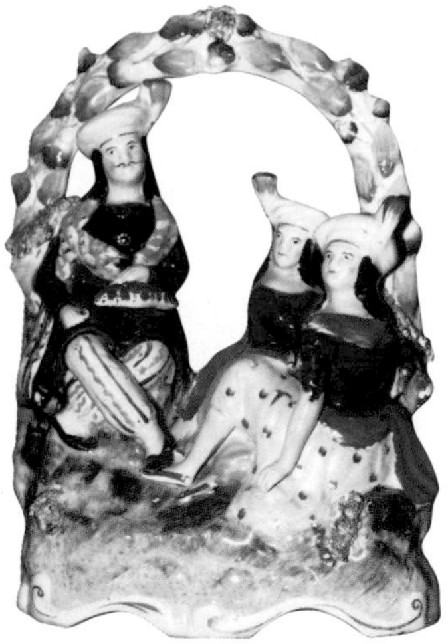

△ Siamese-Twin Circus Act

- *circa 1860*

Chang and Eng, the famous Siamese-twin circus act, shown under bower.

- *height 28cm*
- £595 • J. Oosthuizen

△ Copeland Teapot

- *1895*

Copeland teapot decorated with Burns' quotation and chinoiserie scenes, with finial lid.

- *height 21cm*
- £75 • A.D. Antiques

△ Royal Doulton Vase

- *1890*

One of a pair of 19th-century Royal Doulton vases with enamelled floral decoration.

- *height 24cm*
- £165 • A.D. Antiques

▽ Delftware Posset Pot

- *1885*

Posset pot with painted oriental figures and a pagoda in the background. Blue striped design on the handles and spout.

- *12cm x 12.5cm*
- £1,750 • Jonathan Horne

▽ Pair of Vases

- *circa 1890*

A pair of English baluster vases with floral gilding and gilding to inside and outside of lip. With polychrome panels of flowers all on a powder-blue ground.

- *height 15cm*
- £450 • Ian Spencer

▽ Cream Jug

- *1891*

A Wedgwood blue jasper cream jug decorated with classical figures in relief.

- *height 7cm*
- £758 • A.D. Antiques

▽ Coalport Cup & Saucer

- *late 19th century*

Coalport demi-tasse octagonal cup and saucer, gilded and jewelled on red background.

- *height 5.5cm*
- £180 • London Antique

△ Portland Vases

- *circa 1885–90*

Wedgwood Portland vases in various colours – bleeding green, dark blue and black – with Victorian draping.

- *height 10cm*
- £350 • R.A. Barnes

△ Victorian Pail

- *1890*

A Victorian Staffordshire pail and cover, with floral transfer decoration and two scrolled handles.

- *height 37cm*
- £275 • A.D. Antiques

△ Quatral Cup and Saucer

- *circa late 19th century*

Coalport demi-tasse quatral cup and saucer. Polychrome, gilded and jewelled.

- *height 5.5cm*
- £175 • London Antique

▽ Coalport Quatrolobe Set

- *1890*

A Coalport Quatrolobe cup and saucer, heavily gilded on a green base.

- *height 2.5cm*
- £185 • London Antique

▽ English Coalport Plate

- *1893*

English Coalport plate heavily gilded, with scene of Rothwell Castle. Signed by the artist.

- *diameter 24cm*
- £450 • David Brower

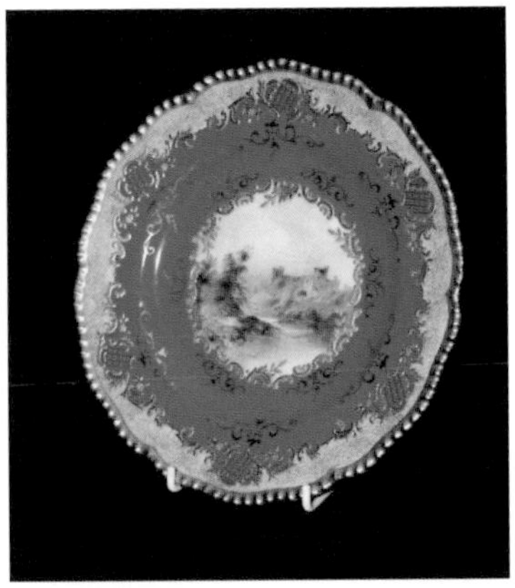

▽ Wemyss Pig

- *circa 1890*

Early Wemyss Pig from the late 19th century, with pressed mark, 'Made in Scotland, RH&S'. Black, white and pink glaze with wrinkles to snout.

- *length 46cm*
- £3,300 • Constance Stobo

◁ Davenport Stilton Dish and Cover

- *1860*

Davenport blue and white Stilton dish and cover decorated with a chinoiserie harbour scene.

- *height 35cm*
- £2,600 • Libra

EUROPEAN CERAMICS

△ Stoneware Jug

- *15th century*

Seidborg Kanne stoneware drinking vessel with handle and turned decoration.

- *height 28cm*
- £650 • **P. Boyd-Carpenter**

△ Albarello Vase

- *circa 1500*

Montelupo Albarello, decorated with stylised feathers.

- *height 20cm*
- £2,000–3,000 • **Bazaart**

▽ Italian Albarello Faenza Jar

- *16th century*

Painted in yellow, green, blue and white, with an oval medallion portrait of a woman in profile at the centre, against a blue and white ground of stylised flowerheads and foliate scrolls. All above a basal frieze in the form of a scroll of paper, with the inscription 'FILONIUM R.S.M.'

- *height 18cm*
- £4,200 • **A. & S. Gray**

▽ Sicilian Wet Drug Bottle

- *1599*

Workshop of Geronimo Lazzario, Palermo. Majolica with 'A Tropei' decoration.

- *height 26cm*
- £4,000–6,000 • **Bazaart**

◁ Fruit Plate

- *circa 1570*

Extremely rare Urbino fruit plate. Majolica.

- *diameter 27cm*
- £10,000–15,000 • **Bazaart**

△ Early Italian Tin-glazed Dish

- *16th century*

Scene painted to the centre of Roman soldiers dividing up the spoils of war. The rim with a narrow yellow band, the reverse decorated with similar yellow lines around the rim and base.

- *height 13.5cm*
- £4,500 • **A. & S. Gray**

△ Hispano-Moresque Dish

- *16th century*

An unusual and highly collectable Spanish Hispano-Moresque dish from Catalunia, probably Valencia. In a lustre glaze. The dish is of silver form and it has a raised central boss and is elaborately decorated with oak leaves and geometric patterns.

- *diameter 45cm*
- £2,500 • **E. & H. Manners**

▽ Trapani Albarello Jar

- *16th century*

Apothecary jar, slightly cracked, with panel showing figure.

- *height 28cm*
- £2,600 • **Bazaart**

▽ Ponte Negro Dish

- *circa 1560*

Castel Durante Crespina. With Susanna and the Elders. Three crosses in foreground are a hallmark of his work.

- *diameter 24.5cm*
- £18,000 • **Guest & Gray**

◁ Ceramic Jug

- *16th century*

Ceramic jug with handle and a central panel, showing the portrait of Cardinal Bellarmine.

- *height 24.5cm*
- £2,500 • **Peter Bunting**

△ Drug Jar

- *17th century*

Rare Sicilian Caltagirone ovoid drug jar with painted, scrolling foliage, in green, orange and manganese.

- *height 30cm*
- £2,200 • Guest & Gray

△ Rhineland Jug

- *17th century*

Rhineland Westerwald saltglazed stoneware vessel of bulbous form with strap handle, turned neck and a floral pattern on a blue-glazed ground.

- *height 26cm*
- £850 • Jonathan Horne

▽ Oil Lamp

- *circa mid-17th century*

Dutch oil lamp with handle on pedestal base. The piece shows irregularities caused through the firing process.

- *height 12cm*
- £375 • Garry Atkins

▽ Wet Drug Jar

- *1600–20*

Montelupo, majolica vase with sea-horse handles.

- *height 36cm*
- £4,000–6,000 • Bazzart

▽ Pipkin

- *17th century*

Low Countries pipkin showing a turned, two-handled pot in lead glaze.

- *height 18cm*
- £150 • Garry Atkins

◁ Bell-Shaped Jug

- *circa mid-17th century*

Dutch bell-shaped jug in a green glaze, with a pinched handle. Jug on a tripod base.

- *height 9cm*
- £150 • Garry Atkins

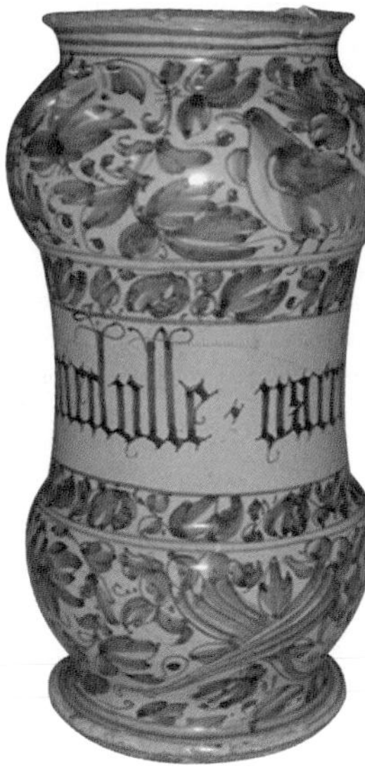

△ Albarello

- *late 17th century*

Italian blue and white apothecary jar of baluster form with central name band.

- *height 35cm*
- £1,100 • Dial Post House

▷ Westerwald Ewer

- *1630*

Westerwald blue and white ewer with pewter cover, a central cartouche of Jesus on the cross with two figures either side, ten angels each side of the handle and lion mask decoration on lip.

- *height 23cm*
- £3,300 • Jonathan Horne

▽ Albarello Vase

- *circa 1670*

Probably Bassano. Of dumbbell form with floral swags from mask decoration.

- *height 27cm*
- £1,200–1,500 • Bazaart

◁ Delft Dish

- *17th century*

Late 17th-century Dutch Delft lobed dish.

- *diameter 33cm*
- £700 • Guest & Gray

◁ Lead-glazed Jug

- *17th century*

Low Countries jug with lead glaze and scroll design to body with pinched handle.

- *height 16.5cm*
- £575 • Garry Atkins

△ Albarelli

- *circa 1700*

Pair of albarelli from Sciacca, Sicily. Predominantly blue with cartouches showing maritime scene framed with leaf design.

- *height 22cm*
- £3,000–4,000 • Bazaart

△ Meissen Teabowl and Saucer

- *circa 1735*

Meissen teabowl and saucer painted with a continuous scene of a merchant's encampment beside an estuary and the interior with a quayside scene.

- *height of bowl 5cm*
- £2,450 • London Antique

△ Slipware Dish

- *1738*

Low Countries pottery slipware dish with date. Banded with interlacing wavy pattern in lead glaze.

- *diameter 35cm*
- £850 • Garry Atkins

▽ Flemish Tile

- *18th century*

Flemish tile with geometric patterns and stylised floral designs with rearing lion.

- *height 15cm*
- £75 • Garry Atkins

▽ Pear-Shaped Bottle

- *1730*

A Meissen bottle of square section. Shown with kakiemon panels of flowers and bamboo on a sea-green/blue base.

- *height 32cm*
- £15,000 • David Brower

▽ Meissen Teabowl and Saucer

- *circa 1745*

Meissen teabowl and saucer, each decorated with landscape scenes within gilt quatralobe cartouches with dark brown edges, painted with flowers and insects in the manner of J.G. Klinger.

- *height of bowl 5cm*
- £2,800 • London Antique

△ Meissen Teapot

- *circa 1735*

Meissen teapot and cover with a painted cartouche on each side, within a purple lustre and gilt scrollwork, encircling a Kauffahrtei scene of merchants and their wares.

- *height 10cm*
- £6,500 • London Antique

△ Orvieto Jug

- *18th century*

Orvieto, lattice and panel, strap handle.

- *height 11cm*
- £500–700 • Bazaart

△ Meissen Tureen

- *1745*

Bombé form, decorated in deep purple with figures on horseback hunting boar and deer through wooded landscapes, alternating with flower sprays. The cover decorated with a boar's head as finial, with gilding.

- *height 25.5cm*
- £6,500 • A. & S. Gray

▽ Meissen Cup and Saucer

- *1736*

Small Meissen cup and saucer, with panels depicting romantic landscapes set within gilt borders.

- *height 2.5cm*
- £486 • London Antique

▽ Chantilly Mug

- *1735*

Chantilly white porcelain mug decorated with a hand-painted chinoiserie design of bamboo and flowers.

- *height 9cm*
- £1,680 • Stockspring

▽ Meissen Coffee Pot

- *circa 1745*

Meissen pear-shaped coffee pot with a scrolled handle and satyr mask to the base of the spout, finely painted with floral sprays, with crossed swords. Mark 'Z' incised on the rim of the foot.

- *height 20cm*
- £3,350 • London Antique

△ Meissen Lattice-Work Plate

- *circa 1750–75*

Meissen plate with sprays of flowers, and insects and a butterfly, within a lattice-work border marked with blue crossed swords.

- *diameter 23cm*
- £245 • London Antique

△ Cup and Saucer

- *1766*

Sèvres cup and saucer with textile-based design, with floral meanderings, gilt foliage with *oeil-de-perdrix* decoration to both cup and saucer. Interlaced 'L' with date mark 'N'. Painter's mark 'Mereaud'.

- *height 8cm*
- £6,500 • E. & H. Manners

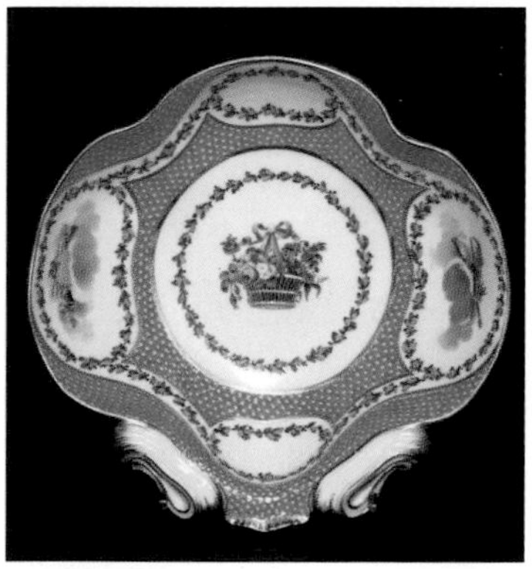

△ Sèvres Compotière

- *1772*

From the Sefton service, part of a dessert service. With leafy garlands on *oeil-de-perdrix* base.

- *width 23cm*
- £6,800 • E. & H. Manners

▽ Meissen Tea Bowl and Saucer

- *circa 1750*

Meissen tea bowl and saucer painted with a central cartouche of merchants' boats, with a yellow background and purple flowers.

- *height 5cm*
- £1,950 • London Antique

▽ Pair of Inscribed Vases

- *1760*

Rare pair of vases inscribed 'PB 1760'. One painted with a leopard, the other with a horse.

- *height 25cm*
- £4,950 • Dial Post House

▽ Porcelain Group

- *circa 1772*

A Sèvres biscuit porcelain group, showing Cupid, with a broken bow, igniting a fire, with a female figure, holding a heart in the flames.

- *height 31cm*
- £3,800 • E. & H. Manners

△ Meissen Salts

- *circa 1750*

Pair of Meissen salts of a lady and gentleman with tri-cornered hats seated on a pair of baskets.

- *height 15.5cm*
- £780 • London Antique

△ Meissen Tea Set

- *1765*

Meissen tea set comprising sugar bowl, tea cup, saucer and milk jug, with gilded and painted decoration.

- £3,550 • London Antique

△ Model of Cat & Dog

- *circa 1770*

Brussels faience models of a cat and dog naturally modelled with paleblue-green and black glaze. Both animals are on a green base.

- *height 20cm*
- £8,500 • E. & H. Manners

▽ Vincennes Sucrier

- *1754*

Early Vincennes sucrier painted with birds on cartouches against a blue lapis ground and chrysanthemum finial gilt decoration. With interlaced 'L' and the date letter 'B'.

- *height 10cm*
- £5,000 • E. & H. Manners

▽ Model of Harvester

- *1785–90*

Model of harvester reclining on a wheatsheaf, made by the Gera factory, Germany. The figure rests on a base with Omega mark.

- *height 23cm*
- £1,250 • E. & H. Manners

▽ Maricolini Cup and Saucer

- *circa 1780*

Meissen Maricolini cup and saucer with floral design.

- *height 6cm*
- £295 • London Antique

◁ Cup and Saucer Set

- *1788*

Sèvres-style cylindrical cup and saucer with floral and red and white banding as decoration. The cup carries an elaborate monogram in a white oval panel.

- *height 6cm*
- £355 • London Antique

△ Dessert Plate

- *1780*

White dessert plate with blue and gold ribboning and floral design.

- *diameter 14cm*
- £100 • London Antique

△ Nymphenburg Group

- *1800*

Nymphenburg group in monochrome, showing a mounted huntsman directing his eager hounds on a moulded rock.

- *height 17.5cm*
- £275 • London Antique

△ Tazzie Plates

- *circa 1820*

Pair of Etruscan-style 'Tazzie' plates on pedestal foot. Giusiniani factory, Naples.

- *diameter 22cm*
- £1,500–2,500 • Bazaart

▽ Dresden Coffee Pot

- *circa 1800*

Dresden white coffee pot with yellow and lilac floral swags and gilt scrolling around the base, handle and spout. With Crown and Dresden on the base.

- *height 19cm*
- £180 • London Antique

▽ Gilded Cup and Saucer

- *19th century*

Sèvres-style cup and saucer with profuse gilding on a blue ground and a painted panel on the side of the cup.

- *height 5.5cm*
- £365 • London Antique

▽ Cabaret Set

- *19th century*

French cabaret set in Sèvres style with original fitted case.

- *box 29cm x 14cm*
- £650 • David Brower

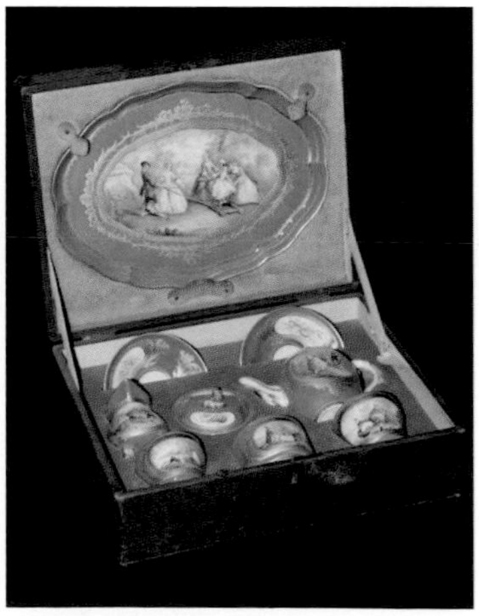

△ Tobacco Jar

- *1800*

Dutch Delft blue and white tobacco jar from the De Bloempot factory. Inscribed 'Spaanse'.

- £800 • Dial Post House

△ Cantagalli Vase

- *19th century*

A baluster-form vase in 15th-century Faenza style.

- *height 35cm*
- £800–1,200 • Bazaart

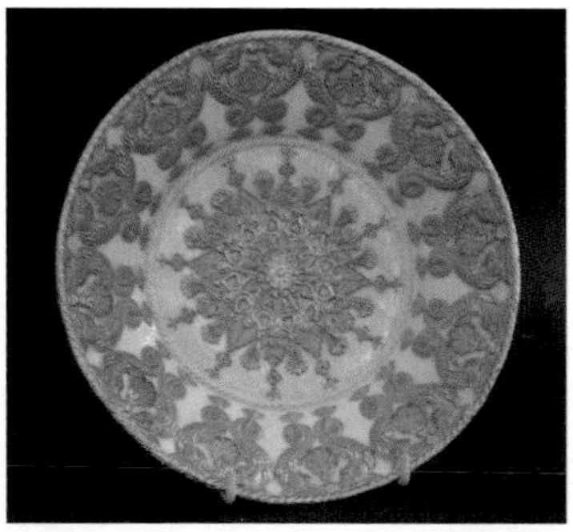

△ Gilded Plate

- *circa 1814–60*

Meissen plate with heavily gilded water serpents with shells, and a central flower, within a gilt rope border. Blue crossed swords.

- *diameter 22cm*
- £165 • London Antique

▽ Tea Cup and Saucer

- *1805*

Meissen tea cup and saucer painted in grisaille. Depicting the Rhine within a gilt roundel below pendant.

- *height 6cm*
- £295 • London Antique

▽ Majolica Teapot

- *1820*

Majolica teapot with a monkey astride a coconut with his tail coiled around the twig handle, with leaf decoration.

- *height 18.5cm*
- £1,695 • Jesse Davis

▽ Berlin Cup and Saucer

- *1840–60*

Berlin cup and saucer heavily gilded around the rim and the foot of the cup.

- £145 • London Antique

▽ Dresden Teapot

- *circa 1843*

Dresden miniature square teapot of bulbous form, with a central cartouche of a courting couple. Marked A.R. Helena Wolfsohn Dresden.

- *height 9cm*
- £145 • London Antique

△ Vienna Tray

- *circa 1850*

Heavily gilded. Scene of the 'Shepherds of Arcadia' after Nicholas Poussin.

- *height 31cm*
- £2,750 • David Brower

△ Majolica Oyster Plate

- *1865*

Circular polychrome Majolica oyster plate, with six concave receptacles centred around a cobalt-blue boss.

- *diameter 27cm*
- £450 • Jesse Davis

△ Italian Majolica Vase

- *19th century*

Urn shape with snake handles emerging from lion masks. Painted with battle scenes, cherubs and a castle.

- *height 49cm*
- £750 • Shahdad

▽ Model of Red Squirrel

- *1856*

A Vienna model of a red squirrel holding a walnut. The figure is perched on an acorn-encrusted tree stump base.

- *height 26cm*
- £720 • David Brower

▽ Hollandaise Vases

- *1860*

A pair of Sèvres-style Hollandaise vases with under dishes, painted with 'jewelled' panels of maidens with instruments, music and flowers.

- *height 19cm*
- £3,250 • David Brower

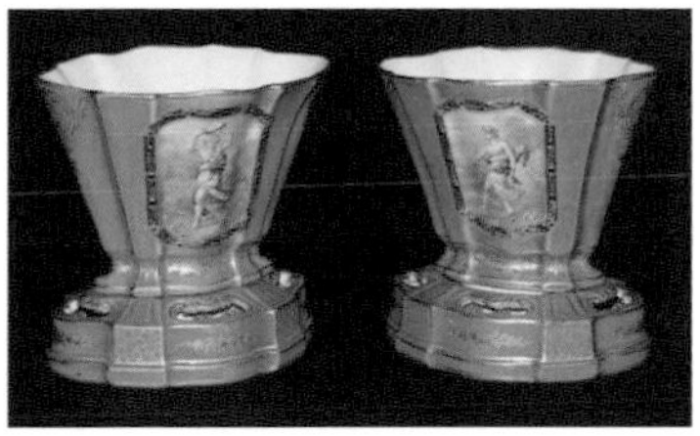

▽ Vase and Cover

- *circa 1860*

A Meissen flower-encrusted vase and cover with cherub adornment, decorated with a Watteau pastoral scene.

- *height 61cm*
- £3,500 • David Brower

△ Meissen Candelabra

- *1860*

One of a pair of Meissen candelabra, encrusted with flowers and fruit decoration and figures depicting a shepherd and shepherdess.

- *height 43cm*
- £3,500 • London Antique

△ Dresden Tea Bowl

- *1866*

Dresden tea bowl with two floral displays painted on the sides by Adolph Hamann. Inscribed with 'P223' marks.

- *height 3.5cm*
- £45 • London Antique

△ French Bisque Figures

- *circa 1860*

French Bisque courting couple in 18th-century costume in a romantic pose.

- *height 38cm*
- £375 • Gloria Sinclair

▽ Small Cup and Saucer

- *1860–1924*

Small Meissen cup and saucer encrusted with flowers.

- *height 3cm*
- £435 • London Antique

▽ Porcelain Plaques

- *circa 1860*

Pair of finely painted porcelain plaques by Thevenot.

- *81cm x 59cm*
- £26,000 • Sinai

▽ Volkstand Romantic Group

- *circa 1860*

Volkstand romantic couple, the young girl with blonde hair and outstretched arm wearing a pale green dress with pink flowers while a youth wearing a floral tunic has his arm around her waist.

- *height 24cm*
- £475 • Gloria Sinclair

△ Royal Vienna Plate

- *circa 1870*

Royal Vienna plate hand-painted with a scene of lovers in a boat, with one cherub holding a basket and the other with his arm around the lady. To the side is a man pulling up the anchor.

- *diameter 24cm*
- £375 • Gloria Sinclair

▽ Gallé Salt

- *1875*

Showing two women in one dress. Signed 'Gallé'.

- *height 20cm*
- £1,200 • Cameo Gallery

▽ Gallé Coffee Pot

- *circa 1870*

Coffee pot with twisted and fluted design. Leaf lid, vine handle, swan neck spout. Lion mask to lip.

- *height 26cm*
- £1,800 • Cameo Gallery

◁ Majolica Jug

- *1870*

Majolica wine jug with Bacchanal figures dispersed around the body, standing on a drum base.

- *height 35cm*
- £395 • Jesse Davis

△ Gallé Pot

- *circa 1870*

Reputedly from the house of Gallé with full signature 'Emile Gallé'. Decorated with geometric designs and moths with partial gilding.

- *height 21cm*
- £6,000 • Cameo Gallery

△ Sèvres Cup and Saucer

- *1870*

Sèvres-style cup and saucer with gilding to the inside of the cup and the centre of the saucer, with gilt ribbons and swags on a dark cobalt-blue base.

- *height of cup 5.5cm*
- £235 • London Antique

△ Swan Centrepiece

- *circa 1870*

Three bowls in the form of swans with interlaced necks. With gilding and floral decoration.

- *height 18cm*
- £2,800 • Cameo Gallery

◁ Strawberry Plate

- *1876*

Polychrome French Surrequenine strawberry plate with moulded strawberry decorations about the border, with gilding and jewelling on a light-blue base.

- *diameter 21cm*
- £245 • Jesse Davis

▽ Dresden Groups

- *circa 1870*

A pair of Dresden groups showing amorous courting couples.

- *height 22cm*
- £500 • Gloria Sinclair

▽ Gallé Rooster

- *circa 1870*

A Gallé model of rooster with unusual mark. Signed Gallé. Hand-painted and glazed.

- *height 19cm*
- £150 • Cameo Gallery

◁ Water Jug

- *circa 1870*

Gallé. Musician on a drum with scrolling leaf design and gilding and goat painted on the drum.

- *height 40cm*
- £4,800 • Cameo Gallery

△ Meissen Group

- *circa 1870*

A romantic arrangement of two figures and a dog upon a sofa with musical instruments.

- *height 14cm*
- £2,900 • David Brower

△ Meissen Figurative Group

- *circa 1880*

Meissen figurative group with two children seated around a central column encrusted with flowers, a central cartouche of gilt scrolling, and blue and pink flowers on a circular moulded base with a conversion for an electric light.

- *height 26cm*
- £485 • London Antique

△ Berlin Campagna

- *circa 1880*

Urn-shaped vase, heavily gilded, deep blue background decorated with a floral band. Featured on the 'Antiques Roadshow'.

- *height 32cm*
- £5,500 • David Brower

▽ Dresden Trembleuse

- *circa 1880*

Dresden 'trembleuse' cup and saucer decorated with pink, yellow and orange flowers. The saucer has a lattice container to hold the cup in place for trembling hands. Blue crown and 'D' on the base, by Helena Wolfsohn.

- *height 11.5cm*
- £2,325 • London Antique

▽ Meissen Figure

- *circa 1880*

A Meissen figure of cherub with broken heart. Part of a series of 26.

- *height 22cm*
- £1,750 • David Brower

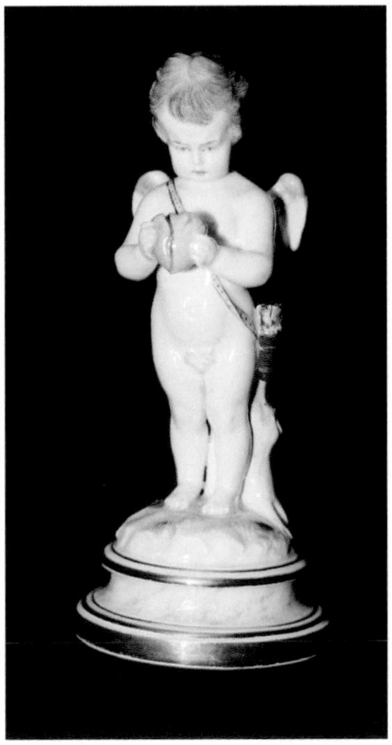

◁ Sweetmeat Dish

- *1880*

Meissen sweetmeat dish showing a central figure between two scalloped dishes.

- *17cm x 24cm*
- £165 • London Antique

△ Stirrup Cup

- *circa 1880*

A Meissen stirrup cup, modelled and painted as a fox's head.

- *height 13cm*
- £595 • David Brower

△ Meissen Figure

- *circa 1880*

A cherub in a classical pose, piercing two hearts with an arrow.

- *height 27cm*
- £2,850 • David Brower

△ Dresden Cup and Saucer

- *1880*

Dresden flower-encrusted cup, cover and saucer, with a yellow bird finial and applied yellow and pink flower decoration.

- *height 18cm*
- £885 • London Antique

▽ Meissen Figure

- *circa 1880*

Meissen figure of cherub in costume of 'St George', standing upon a dragon coiled about the base. One of a series of 26.

- *height 23cm*
- £1,750 • David Brower

▽ Majolica Vase

- *circa 1880*

One of a pair of majolica vases by W. Shiller & Son. With dolphin-shaped blue-glazed handles, rosette decoration.

- *height 37cm*
- £1,250 • David Brower

▽ Meissen Cup and Saucer

- *circa 1880*

Meissen cup and saucer, with flower detailing underneath saucer and insects inside cup.

- *8cm x 13cm*
- £650 • David Brower

△ Cherub Figure

- *1880*

Meissen figure of a cherub sharpening his arrow on a grindstone. Heavily scrolled and gilded.

- *height 12cm*
- £895 • London Antique

△ Helena Wolfsohn Set

- *1880*

Helena Wolfsohn cup and saucer of quatra-lobed form, with lobed rims. Shepherd and shepherdess are shown within gilt cartouches and floral arrangements.

- *height 5cm/cup*
- £255 • London Antique

△ Cup and Saucer

- *circa 1880*

Dresden cup and saucer with cover, by Helena Wolfsohn.

- *height 12cm*
- £650 • David Brower

▽ Viennese Jug

- *19th century*

With mythological representations on the inner and outer sides of the vessel, and fine silver mounts.

- *height 5cm*
- £1,200 • P. Boyd-Carpenter

▽ Meissen Figurine

- *1880*

Meissen figure of a cherub digging, on a heavily scrolled and gilded base.

- *height 12cm*
- £885 • London Antique

▽ Miniature Cup and Saucer

- *circa 1880*

Miniature cup, saucer and cover with painted panels of figures and flowers on a yellow ground, by Helena Wolfsohn.

- *height 4cm*
- £148 • London Antique

△ Rinfrescatoio Bowl

- *circa 1880*

Italian 'Rinfrescatoio'. Le nove majolica with flowers and birds.

- *height 25cm*
- £2,500–3,500 • Bazaart

△ Vienna Tea Caddy

- *19th century*

A tea caddy with painted panels depicting coastal scenes of woman and child with ship in background, on a burgundy ground.

- *height 16cm*
- £1,100 • David Brower

▽ Berlin Cup and Saucer

- *circa 1850*

Berlin cup and saucer, with gilt foliate medallions on a pale salmon-pink ground.

- *height 6cm*
- £235 • London Antique

▽ Meissen Sweetmeat Dish

- *circa 1880*

One of a pair of Meissen sweetmeat dishes. Modelled as a reclining shepherd and shepherdess with dishes with scrolled border.

- *20cm x 31cm*
- £1,950 • London Antique

▽ Charger

- *circa 1880*

Ginai factory majolica. Bacchanal scene in romantic setting with grotesques.

- *height 47cm*
- £2,000–£3,000 • Bazaart

◁ KPM Porcelain

- *19th century*

Tall porcelain vase decorated with scenes of the German royal family. Handcrafted by KPM, the royal porcelain manufacturers of Germany.

- *height 1.9m*
- £85,000 • Sinai Antiques

△ Berlin Plaque

- *circa 1880*

Plaque depicting a Renaissance lady printed on porcelain in a heavily gilded frame.

- *24cm x 16cm*
- £4,200 • David Brower

△ Meissen Teapot

- *1860–1924*

Large Meissen teapot and stand encrusted with flowers, with scrolled brass mounts. The scrolled base has pierced decoration and flower encrustation.

- *height 31cm*
- £6,650 • London Antique

▽ Two-Handled Urn

- *1893*

Rozenburg, the Hague. Urn-shaped vase with mask handles. By W.P. Hartgring.

- *height 42cm*
- £1,755 • P. Oosthuizen

▽ Chocolate Cup and Saucer

- *1890*

Dresden chocolate cup and saucer with lobed rim and scrolled double gilt handles. Decorated with cartouches showing figures in a garden setting within gilt and jewelled borders, and floral arrangements on a primrose yellow ground.

- *height 7cm*
- £285 • London Antique

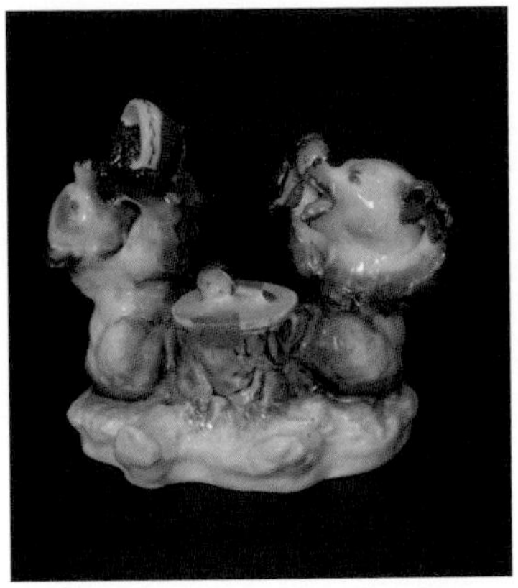

△ Bear Inkwell

- *circa 1890*

Russian group with two bears eating strawberry jam from bowls, and a log in the centre. On the lid is a large ladle covering an inkwell, set on a moulded white base.

- *height 15cm*
- £280 • Gloria Sinclair

△ Sèvres-Style Vase

- *1890*

One of a pair of Sèvres-style vases with ormolu mounts, gilt banding and panels showing profiles of maidens with pineapple gilt finial.

- *height 31cm*
- £1,550 • London Antique

◁ Lady's Writing Set with Candle Holders

- *1880*

Lady's glazed desktop writing set with ink well and candle holders designed with an oriental theme.

- *height 15cm*
- £3,500 • London Antique

▽ Sèvres Vase

- *circa 1890*

Single Sèvres vase, ormolu mounts, showing courtly scenes.

- *height 73cm*
- £2,800 • Judy Fox

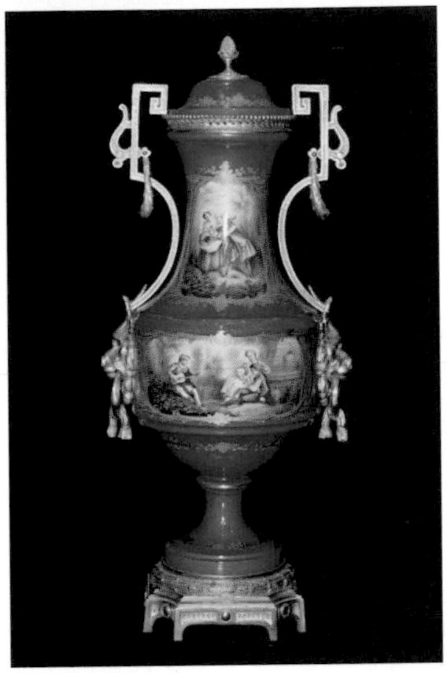

▽ Portrait Cup and Saucer Set

- *1890*

Sèvres cup and saucer with a portrait set within gilded borders on a dark ground with panels decorated with floral designs.

- *height 4cm*
- £355 • London Antique

▽ Dresden Coffee Cup and Saucer

- *1880*

The cup has a barley twist handle and stands on three paw feet. Decorated with a central lobed cartouche showing a romantic setting.

- *height 8cm*
- £285 • London Antique

△ Porcelain Dog

- *1894*

French bisque porcelain model showing an attentive bitch. Original artist Charlotte Bertrand from the factory of Richard Eckert & Co.

- *height 18cm*
- **£700** • **Elizabeth Bradwin**

△ Limoges Plate

- *1895*

Limoges plate enamelled with a floral spray of chrysanthemums on a cream ground within a heavily gilded border.

- *diameter 23cm*
- **£115** • **A. Piotrowski**

△ Writing Set and Ink Stand

- *1890*

Dresden writing set and ink stand with scallop-shell base and urn-shaped inkwell, decorated and gilded with floral sprays.

- *height 10cm*
- **£255** • **London Antique**

▽ Fabergé Cup and Saucer

- *1894*

Fabergé cup and saucer with stylised leaf decoration to the saucer, the cup heavily gilded with lattice design on green base.

- *height 8cm*
- **£85** • **London Antique**

▽ Chocolate Cup

- *1890*

Augustus chocolate cup and saucer with double-scroll handles and pierced basketholder. Decorated with two large panels showing two figures in a garden setting framed by a gilded border.

- *height 9cm*
- **£265** • **London Antique**

▽ Royal Vienna Huntsman

- *circa 1890*

Royal Vienna prancing white horse with a huntsman and hounds on a white base.

- *height 20cm*
- **£320** • **Gloria Sinclair**

△ Miniature Cup and Saucer

- *circa 1899*

Miniature Dresden coffee cup and saucer encrusted with pale lilac flowers, raised on six straight cylindrical legs.

- *height 4cm*
- **£185** • **London Antique**

△ Cabinet Cup and Saucer

- *1890*

Luisentasse cabinet cup and saucer with a grey ground. Cup carries a biscuit profile bust of Queen Luise of Prussia on a vermiculated gilt oval medallion.

- *height 15cm*
- **£9,995** • **London Antique**

△ French Chinoiserie Vase

- *1890*

French copy of a Chinese baluster vase with gilded chinoiserie designs on a blue ground.

- *height 48cm*
- **£425** • **Mousa**

▽ Meissen Coffee Pot

- *1890*

Meissen coffee pot and cover with painted panels depicting harbour scenes set within enamelled and gilt decoration, with scrolled handle and finial lid.

- *height 22cm*
- **£795** • **London Antique**

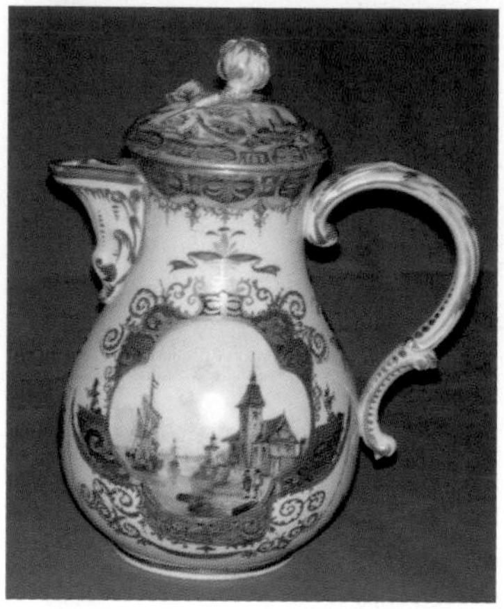

▽ Fluted Cup and Saucer

- *1890*

Meissen cup and saucer with fluted body, with floral decoration and gilding.

- *height 8.5cm*
- **£88** • **London Antique**

▽ Lion and Hare

- *circa 1890*

Russian lion seated and holding a white hare by the neck.

- *height 15cm*
- **£240** • **Gloria Sinclair**

▽ Carlsbad Cup and Saucer

- *late 19th century*

Decorated with flower and leaf design with gilding to the interior of the cup.

- *height 6cm*
- £350 • David Brower

▽ Terracotta Dog

- *late 19th century*

Austrian painted terracotta model of a puggish dog, lying in an alert position, with glass eyes, collar and curling tail.

- *height 20cm*
- £1,450 • Elizabeth Bradwin

◁ Gallé Cat

- *circa 1890*

Highly decorated model of a cat with painted gems and scrolled design. Russian crest on hindquarters. Glass eyes, Gallé marked.

- *height 34cm*
- £4,000 • Constance Stobo

△ Bisque Group

- *late 19th century*

After a French bronze showing two dogs fighting over a duck in flight.

- *height 20cm*
- £1,100 • Elizabeth Bradwin

△ Terracotta Bull Terrier

- *late 19th century*

Recumbent on a stylised fur rug. Black marble base. French.

- *height 17cm*
- £600 • Elizabeth Bradwin

△ Porcelain Busts

- *20th century*

Pair of German porcelain busts of Royal children, after models by Kaendler.

- *height 15.5cm*
- £635 • London Antique

▷ Dresden Figurines

- *20th century*

Dresden group of porcelain figures, modelled as a monkey band.

- *height 17cm*
- £255 • London Antique

▽ Dresden Cup and Saucer

- *circa 1900*

Dresden cup and saucer standing on three paw feet decorated with pink panels of courting couples and flowers divided by gilt scrolling design.

- *height 4cm*
- £235 • London Antique

△ Porcelain Comport

- *1900–20*

Continental porcelain comport by Schashelf, embellished with flying cupids, fruit and flowers. The bowl pierced and embellished with swags.

- *height 57cm*
- £585 • A.D. Antiques

◁ Gilded Cup and Saucer

- *1890*

Porcelain cup and saucer by Sampson. Decorated with a chinoiserie-influenced design. Both the cup and saucer have gilded rims.

- *height 8cm*
- £45 • London Antique

△ Sauce Boat

- *circa 1890*

Sèvres sauce boat, in the form of a swan with white bisque feathers and parcel gilt interior.

- *height 9cm*
- £295 • London Antique

△ Miniature Flower Pot

- *circa 1900*

Miniature flower pot decorated with flowers, a bird, insects and a butterfly. Made in Paris, France.

- *height 11cm*
- £48 • London Antique

△ Cup and Saucer

- *1940–50*

Royal Copenhagen blue and white cup and saucer, decorated with interlaced banding and floral arrangements.

- *height 8cm*
- £45 • London Antique

ISLAMIC CERAMICS

△ Persian Water Vessel

• *circa 800 BC*
Persian water vessel in the form of a duck with an elongated beak with a turquoise glaze.
• *height 15cm*
• £8,000 • Sultani

△ Bamiyan Water Vessel

• *10th century*
Afghanistan water vessel of globular form with strap handle, short neck and dark-green glaze.
• *height 16.6cm*
• £500 • Sultani

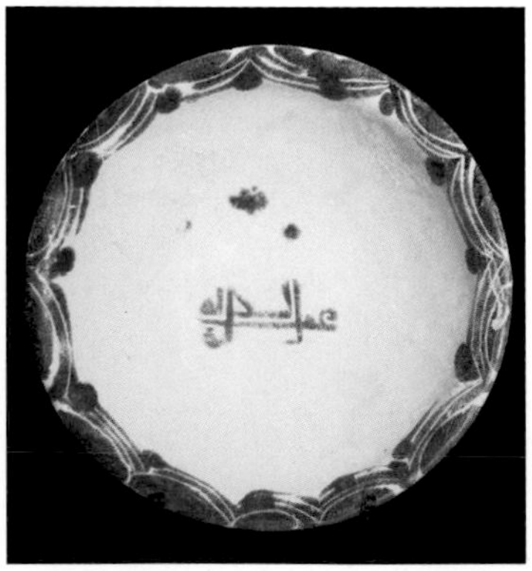

△ Ceramic Bowl

• *circa 9th century*
A blue and white, tin-glazed ceramic bowl of the Abbasid period, the rim with blue swags.
• *diameter 21cm*
• £15,000 • Axia

▽ Nishapur Bowl

• *circa 9th–10th century*
Nishapur, Persian buffware pottery bowl, of deep rounded form with slightly inverted rim decorated in manganese brown and yellow, with a bold seated female figure wearing a shirt with floral designs and spotted trousers, holding a flower and looking into a mirror. Bowl surround with Kufic inscriptions and small arabesque motifs.
• *diameter 21.6cm*
• £1,500 • Rasoul Gallery

▽ Pre-Ottoman Vase

• *circa 10th century*
Monochrome vessel of baluster form with two moulded handles and open-work decoration to the body.
• *height 35.5cm*
• £800 • Pars

▷ Chrome Bowl

• *10th–11th century*
Hand-painted earthenware polychrome bowl with stylised palm-leaf design, from Nishapur, northwestern Iran.
• *diameter 19cm*
• £4,000 • Yacobs

△ Early Saljuq Vessel

• *9th–10th century*
Early Saljuq Islamic pottery vessel of bulbous form with strap handle and panels of pierced designs, raised on a pedestal foot.
• *height 15cm*
• £450 • Pars

△ Persian Dish

• *circa 10th century*
A Persian bowl with three panels with Kufic inscriptions in blue and yellow ochre.
• *diameter 29cm*
• £3,000 • Sultani

▽ Polychrome Islamic Bowl

• *circa 10th century*
A Minai polychrome Islamic bowl with four figures on horseback within cartouches on a cream ground.
• *diameter 22cm*
• £3,500 • Solamani Gallery

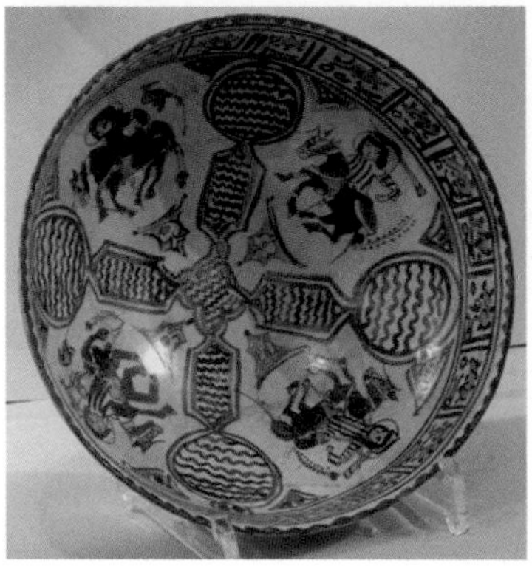

▽ Early Ewer

• *8th century*
Green-glazed ewer with iridescence, tapered neck and strap handle, raised on a small foot.
• *height 20cm*
• £700 • Pars

▽ Painted Nishapur Bowl

• *10th–11th century*
Nishapur earthenware bowl with polychrome lozenge decoration.
• *diameter 19cm*
• £250 • Pars

▽ Central Asian Bowl

• *11th century*
Leaf pattern bowl from central Asia with brown arabesque design inside.
• *diameter 18.5cm*
• £550 • Rasoul Gallery

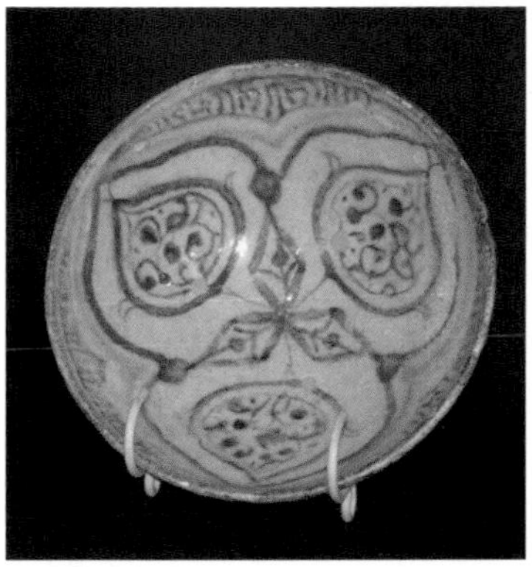

▽ Kashan Water Jug

• *11th–12th century*
Cockerel-headed water jug with lajvar glaze and strap handle.
• *height 29cm*
• £5,500 • Yacobs

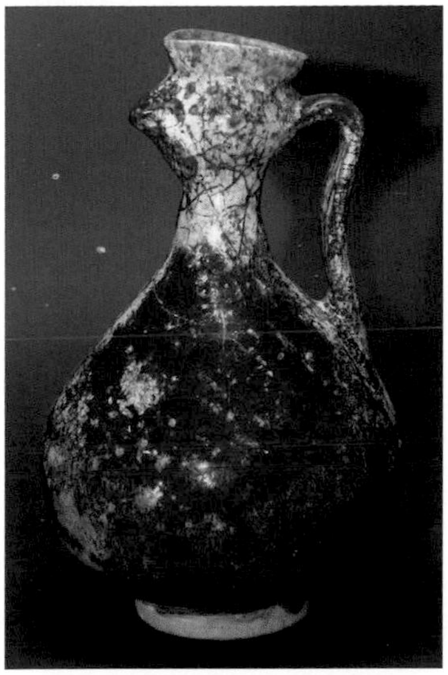

△ Water Jugs and Bowl

• *10th–11th century*
Two water jugs and one bowl with Kufic inscription 'Blessing to the owner', from Central Asia.
• £60,000 • Yacobs

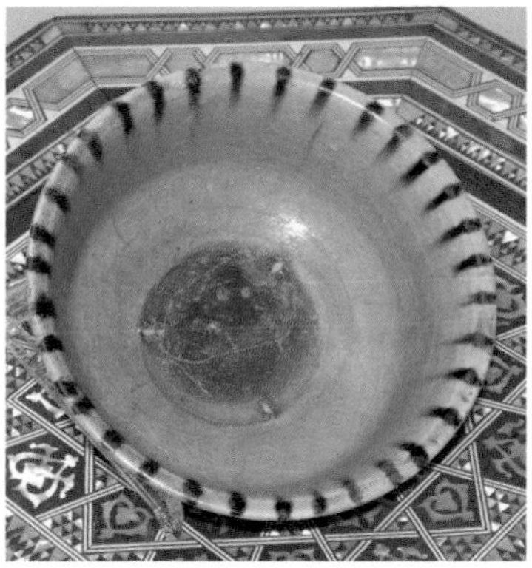

△ Bamiyan Pottery Bowl

• *11th–12th century*
A fine Bamiyan pottery bowl with slightly convex flaring sides decorated with a series of dashes along the rim and covered with a turquoise glaze.
• *diameter 22cm*
• £950 • Yazdani

△ Kashan Bowl

• *11th–13th century*
A Kashan turquoise-glazed conical bowl from central Persia.
• *10cm x 17.5cm*
• £1,800 • Pars

△ Nestorian Bowl

• *10th–11th century*
A bowl from Central Asia, with green, brown and black glaze, with image of cross and scrolling decorations.
• *diameter 13.5cm*
• £2,250 • Axia

△ Nishapur Bowl

• *10th–11th century*
A Nishapur bowl with slip-painted decoration. The bowl is in earthenware, with boldly painted designs. From northwestern Iran.
• *diameter 19cm*
• £250 • Pars

△ Nishapur Dish

• *11th–13th century*
Iranian Nishapur dish with stylised bird and signature.
• *diameter 23cm*
• £800 • Pars

▽ Samakan Bowl

• *circa 11th century*
Central Asian bowl, probably Samakan, with a floral pattern and Kufic inscriptions, translated as, 'Prosperity and Health to the owner of the bowl'.
• *diameter 19cm*
• £1,200 • Rasoul Gallery

▽ Seljuk Tray

• *11th–12th century*
A turquoise-glazed Seljuk tray with iridescence.
• *diameter 15cm*
• £250 • Pars

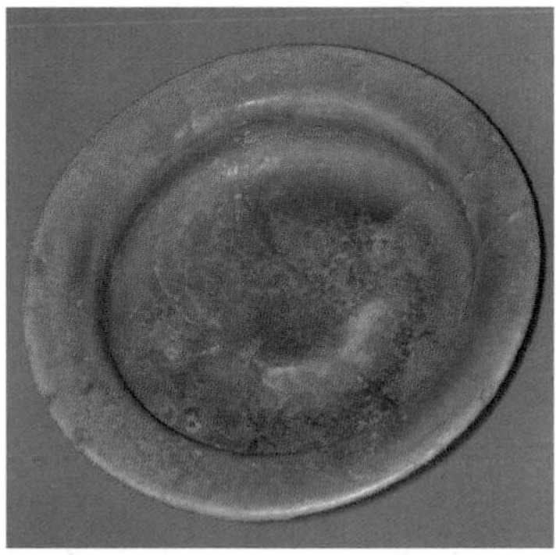

▽ Persian Model

• *11th–13th century*
Persian model of a stable with a turquoise glaze and fine iridescence, with numerous models of animals applied to the surface.
• *8cm x 14cm*
• £10,000 • Pars

▽ Kashan Vase

- *circa 12th century*

12th century Kashan vase of baluster form, with a blue linear design on a white ground.

- *height 10cm*
- £3,500 • Yacobs

▽ Syrian Drug Jar

- *12th century*

Syrian drug jar with black and blue glaze and geometric designs to body, and inscriptions around base and neck.

- *height 28cm*
- £2,300 • Samiramis

◁ Turquoise Bamiyan Ewer

- *11th–13th century*

Turquoise Bamiyan earthenware ewer, with strap handle, the spout in the form of a cows' head, with an unusual rim and a turquoise glaze.

- *height 22.5cm*
- £4,000 • Pars

△ Kashan Sprinkler

- *11th–13th century*

Turquoise monochrome-glazed sprinkler with bosses to neck.

- *height 11cm*
- £550 • Pars

△ Harat Bowl

- *circa 12th century*

Turquoise Harat bowl with a raised lip with black banding and Arabic writing running round the body, raised on a pedestal foot.

- *height 12cm*
- £1,200 • Sultani

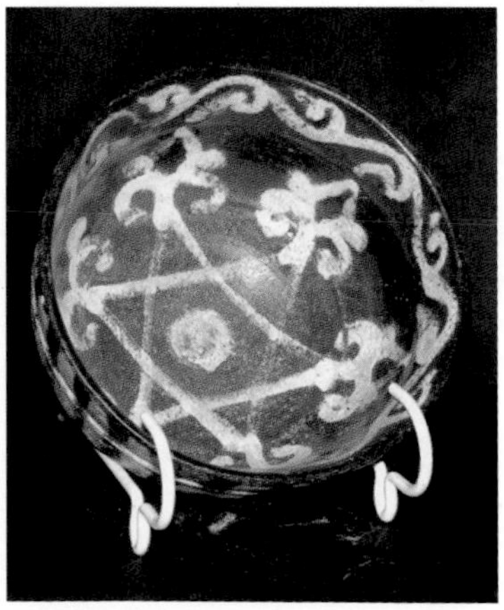

△ Monochrome Pottery Jug

- *circa 12th century*

Monochrome pottery jug with strap handle and thumb piece with a pierced transparent floral design, raised on a pedestal base.

- *height 18cm*
- £1,500 • Sultani

△ Nishapur Bowl

- *12th century*

Nishapur serving bowl with Kufic calligraphic inscriptions.

- *diameter 27cm*
- £6,500 • Aaron

△ Islamic Tiles

- *12th century*

A group of Islamic tiles in original condition with a cobalt-blue and gold glaze showing a repeating geometric pattern.

- *diameter 11cm*
- £800 • Ghaznavid

◁ Star Bowl

- *circa 12th century*

Small brown-glazed bowl with a six-sided star in a cream glaze inside, with scrolling round the inside of the rim.

- *diameter 14cm*
- £800 • Sultani

▽ Persian Bowl

- *circa 12th century*

Persian bowl with a black and blue circular design.

- *diameter 20cm*
- £1,200 • Sultani

▽ Ghaznavi Herat Water Jug

- *circa 12th century*

Ghaznavi Herat water jug of bulbous form with a turquoise glaze with horizontal black stripes, raised on a splayed foot.

- *height 15cm*
- £700 • Sultani

▽ Gold Lustre Bowl

- *circa 12th century*

Small Persian gold lustre bowl with a scrolled design running around the rim and a band of Kufic writing below.

- *diameter 7.5cm*
- £4,000 • Sultani

△ Water Jug

- *circa 12th century*

Small Persian water vessel, of conical form with strap handle, brown circular designs, and raised on a circular foot.

- *height 14.4cm*
- £250 • Rasoul Gallery

△ Persian Ceramic Bowl

- *circa 12th century*

Medium-sized Persian bowl with Arabic inscriptions on the inside of the rim and a peacock and three Persian ladies, with a gold lustre finish.

- *height 10cm*
- £2,700 • Sultani

△ Persian Vessel

- *circa 12th century*

Small Persian vessel of bulbous form, with four moulded handles, raised on a pedestal foot with stops to the base.

- *height 7.5cm*
- £350 • Rasoul Gallery

▽ Shallow Saljuq Dish

- *12th century*

Splayed lip on four globular feet with iridescence.

- *diameter 15cm*
- £100 • Pars

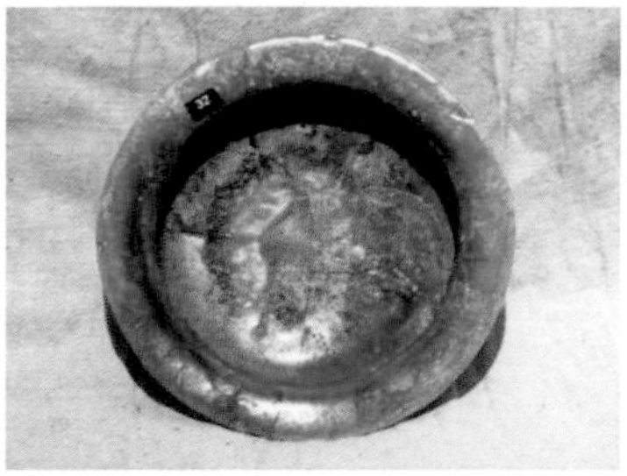

▽ Guazin Water Jug

- *circa 12th century*

Pottery water jug from Guazin with unusual brown, black and sandstone glaze.

- *height 21cm*
- £1,200 • Sultani

▽ Persian Lustre Bowl

- *circa 12th century*

Turquoise bowl decorated with a raised design of two intertwined lions.

- *diameter 15cm*
- £600 • Sultani

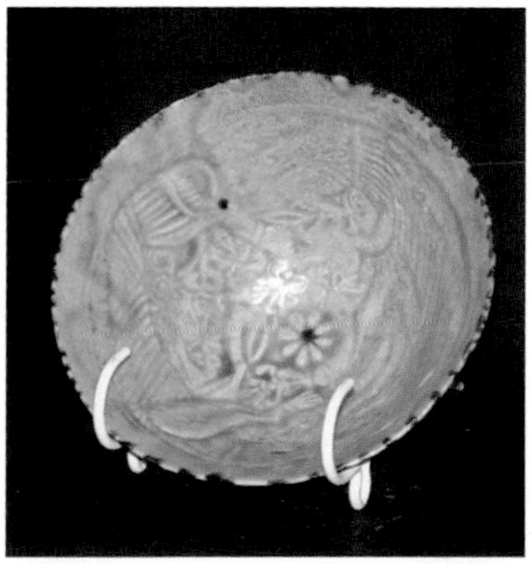

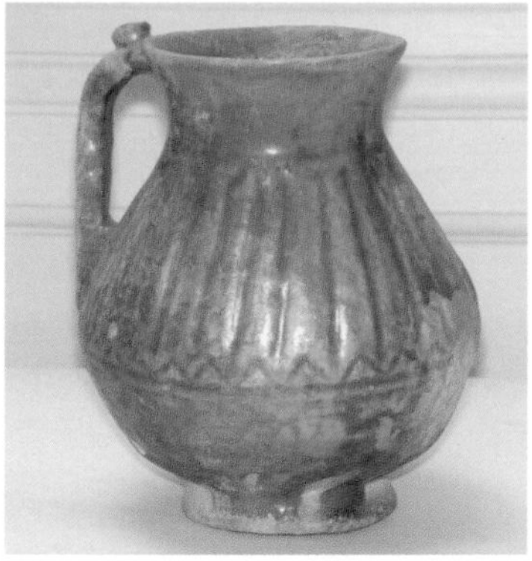

△ Jug with Splayed Lip

- *12th century*

A water vessel with a strap handle and splayed lip with geometric designs under a turquoise glaze. The vessel has an iridescent finish and stops to base.

- *height 20cm*
- £2,800 • Yazdani

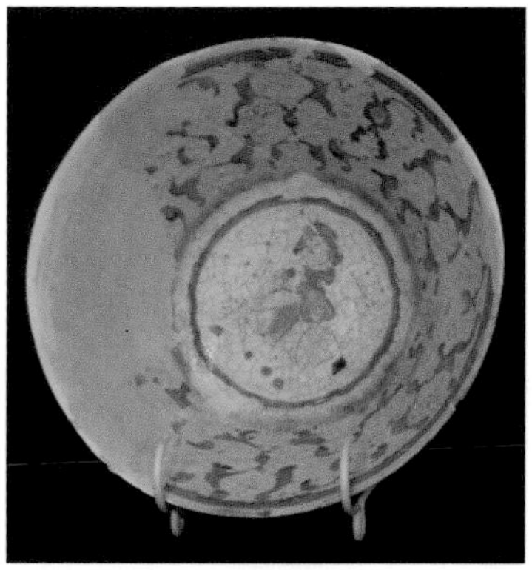

△ Minai Bowl

- *12th century*

Minoae bowl with black and blue banding and a central design.

- *diameter 21.5cm*
- £1,500 • Sultani

△ Bamiyan Dish

- *12th century*

An Islamic Bamiyan plate with concentric designs surrounding the outline of a bird in the centre of the dish under a green glaze.

- *diameter 23cm*
- £3,800 • Yazdani

▽ Afghanistan Stands

- *12th century*

A pair of green glazed Afghanistan stands with organic designs depicting animals.

- *length 23cm*
- £1,500 • Samiramis

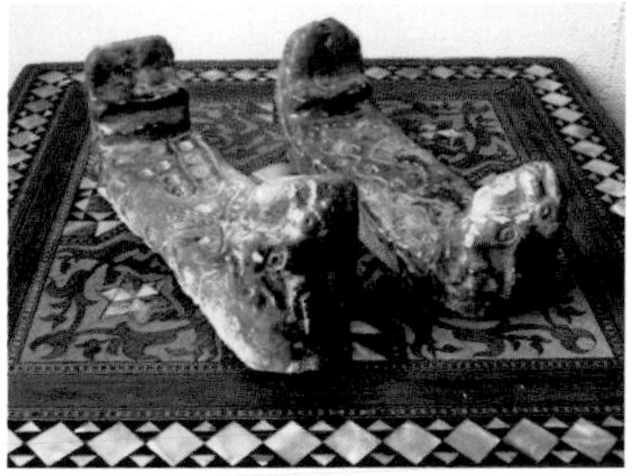

▽ Bamiyan Bowl

- *12th century*

A bright turquoise bowl with Kufic calligraphic inscriptions to the rim.

- *diameter 17cm*
- £1,000 • Pars

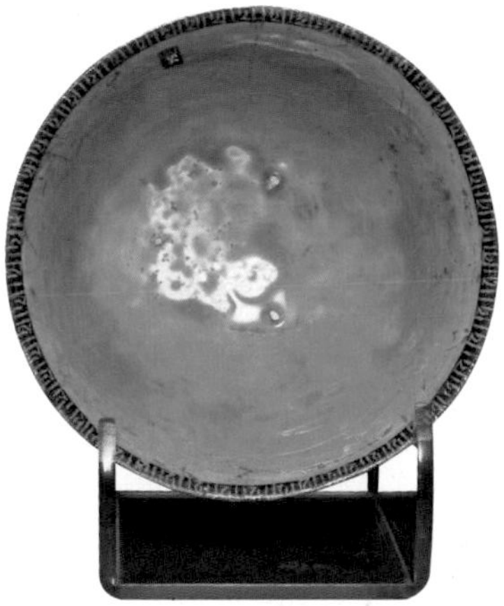

▽ Bamiyan Pottery Bowl

- *12th century*

Bamiyan pottery bowl decorated with a green and brown star pattern with a cream underglaze.

- *diameter 19cm*
- £1,000 • Rasoul Gallery

△ Terracotta Ewer

- *circa 12th century*

Small terracotta ewer of baluster form, with a long upturned spout and strap handle, with a chevron design running around the middle of the body, raised on a circular foot.

- *height 19.5cm*
- £400 • Rasoul Gallery

△ Kashan Water Jug

- *12th–13th century*

Earthenware bulbous form with splayed neck and strap handle.

- *height 20cm*
- £1,000 • Pars

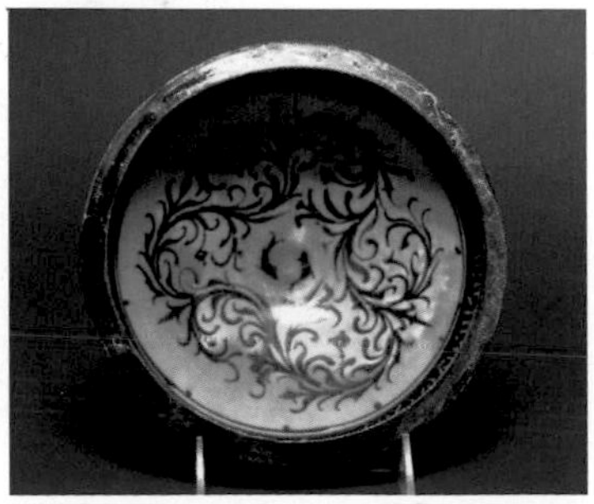

△ Kashan Bowl

- *12th–13th century*

Islamic inscriptions on rim with centred fish and floral design.

- *diameter 19cm*
- £7,000 • Yacobs

▽ Ceramic Ewer

- *12th–13th century*

A Persian Gorgon ewer with original glaze and inscriptions. With pronounced iridescence.

- *height 17cm*
- £18,000 • Aaron

▽ Gold Lustre Bowl

- *circa 12th century*

With ten panels decorated with a floral design, and a lady seated in the centre.

- *diameter 17cm*
- £4,500 • Sultani

▽ Persian Water Vessel

- *circa 12th–13th century*

Persian water vessel of baluster form with strap handle and thumb piece, decorated with birds and circular designs, with Kufic and Arabic inscriptions with a pink lustre glaze.

- *height 21cm*
- £6,500 • Sultani

△ Kashan Vase

- *circa 12th century*

An Islamic vase of bulbous proportions with thumb piece. The body with circular bands of writing and floral designs, raised on a pedestal foot, with stops to the base.

- *height 13cm*
- £1,200 • Solamani Gallery

△ Kashan Jug

- *12th–13th century*

A Kashan jug of bulbous form with a splayed neck and strap handle in a turquoise and black glaze with stops to the base.

- *height 22cm*
- £1,000 • Pars

△ Monochrome Bowl

- *12th–13th century*

A Bamiyan pottery bowl with relief surface decoration and further dot and cross decoration in black on the inside and rim.

- *diameter 25cm*
- £1,100 • Yazdani

▽ Drug Jar

- *12th century*

Persian drug jar with floral design on black and blue glaze.

- *height 23cm*
- £3,200 • Samiramis

▽ Islamic Ceramic Jug

- *12th–13th century*

Jug of globular form, glazed in turquoise and black with stops to base and two handles to the lip.

- *height 18cm*
- £2,500 • Aaron

▽ Kashan Tile

- *13th century*

Eight-pointed star with phoenix and floral decoration.

- *height 21cm*
- £700 • Samiramis

▽ Minai Pottery Bowl

• *circa 1200*
A fine polychrome Minai pottery bowl showing a courtly scene depicting a seated figure in the centre flanked by two attendants. Both the interior and exterior of the rim is decorated with a continuous band of inscriptions.
• *diameter 18cm*
• £5,500 • Yazdani

▽ Persian Jar

• *13th century*
Small Kashan jar with bulbous body and cobalt-blue glaze with splayed footing and strap handle.
• *height 13cm*
• £800 • Pars

▽ Kashan Bottle

• *13th century*
Balloon body with long neck and cup-shaped lip. Turquoise glaze with Kufic writing.
• *height 28cm*
• £3,405 • Samiramis

△ Persian Vessel

• *13th century*
Persian olive-green-glazed pottery vessel with four small moulded handles with an incised design on the body with stops to the base.
• *19.5cm x 11cm*
• £700 • Pars

△ Lustre Tile

• *13th century*
A lustre tile from Kashan, Iran, with Islamic inscription and floral and animal designs.
• *width 30cm*
• £3,000 • Shiraz

△ Kufic Tile

• *13th century*
A turquoise-glazed tile with Kufic inscription.
• *height 25cm*
• £1,750 • Pars

▽ Geometric Wall Tile

• *13th century*
A polychrome Islamic wall tile with repeating geometric pattern.
• *width 12cm*
• £290 • Ghaznavid

▽ Persian Bowl

• *13th century*
A polychrome Persian bowl with a geometric design of seven panels surrounding a central leaf pattern.
• *diameter 18cm*
• £100 • Pars

▽ Islamic Ceramics

• *13th century*
Islamic mouse-head water jug and cockeral-head jug with vertical striped glaze. Both from Nishapur.
• *height 14–18cm*
• £1,000 & £2,200 • Shiraz

△ Nishapur Bowl

• *13th century*
A Nishapur bowl with the Kufic calligraphic inscription 'healthy and long life'.
• *diameter 30cm*
• £2,000 • Shiraz

△ Kashan Vase

• *13th century*
A small Kashan vase with balloon body and long neck with fine iridescence and stops to base.
• *height 14cm*
• £950 • Yazdani

△ Afghanistan Cup

- *13th century*

Small Afghanistan cup with turquoise and black glaze.

- *height 11cm*
- £7,000 • Samiramis

△ Kashan Ewer

- *13th century*

An earthenware Kashan ewer with a strap handle and banding in turquoise glaze with stops to base.

- *height 34cm*
- £1,800 • Yazdani

△ Kashan Tile

- *13th century*

One of a pair of tiles with inscriptions from the Koran among birds and floral meanderings. Blue and turquoise glaze.

- *height 31cm*
- £2,300 • Samiramis

▽ Ewer

- *13th century*

Ewer of bulbous form with rooster neck, strap handle, and turquoise glaze, with iridescence.

- *height 33cm*
- £4,000 • Samiramis

▽ Safaviv Box

- *circa 14th century*

Safaviv cosmetic box decorated with a deer in a cobalt-blue glaze in a romantic setting.

- *11cm x 15cm*
- £900 • Rasoul Gallery

▽ Turquoise Glazed Bowl

- *16th century*

Large bowl with banding and geometric chevron designs and floral medallions under a turquoise glaze.

- *diameter 38cm*
- £2,800 • Yazdani

△ Persian Earthenware Jar

- *13th century*

A moulded, green-glaze jar with stops halfway to base.

- *height 19cm*
- £700 • Aaron

△ Rose-Water Bottle

- *circa 14th century*

Rose-water bottle from Herat, in the west of Afghanistan. Tiamurid Dynasty, in a style imitating Chinese porcelain in the city of Heraz and decorated with an Islamic pattern, with a floral leaf design on the base.

- *height 10cm*
- £800 • Rasoul Gallery

△ Mamluk Bowl

- *16th century*

A Mamluk bowl from Egypt/Syria, with central panel with Islamic inscriptions and blue and black glaze.

- *diameter 20cm*
- £1,000 • Samiramis

▽ Mamluk Bowl

- *13th–14th century*

Ayyoubid Mamluk measuring bowl. Syria or Egypt, with black, blue and white glaze, splayed lip with handle and iridescence.

- *height 11cm*
- £3,000 • Samiramis

▽ Timori Bowl

- *circa 15th–16th century*

Timori bowl decorated with a blue hexagonal design around the inside of the rim, and a central blue and white flower design, with a central turquoise circle with a black cross.

- *diameter 19cm*
- £900 • Rasoul Gallery

▽ Damascus Pottery Tile

- *17th century*

Pottery tile decorated with arabesque and iris motif.

- *20cm x 22cm*
- £400 • Arthur Millner

△ Islamic Fluted-Neck Vase

• *17th century*
Vase with stylised pheasant among cherry blossoms, within arched border, with an unusual off-centre fluted neck.
• *33cm x 16cm*
• £1,500 • **Pars**

△ Large Pottery Tile

• *mid-19th century*
The glazed decoration on this large tile depicts a lady listening to musicians.
• *33cm x 43cm*
• £2,500 • **Arthur Millner**

△ Signed Vase

• *19th century*
A very finely patterned Islamic vase signed by 'T.D.'.
• *34cm x 23cm*
• £5,500 • **Sinai**

▽ Tiled Panel

• *circa 1760*
A North African, hand-painted, tiled panel showing an urn with floral and leaf meanderings.
• *height 88cm*
• £2,000 • **Sinai**

▽ Terracotta Pipe

• *circa 1850*
Terracotta Tophane pipe from Morocco with gold and silver floral gilt design.
• *height 5cm*
• £550 • **Sinai**

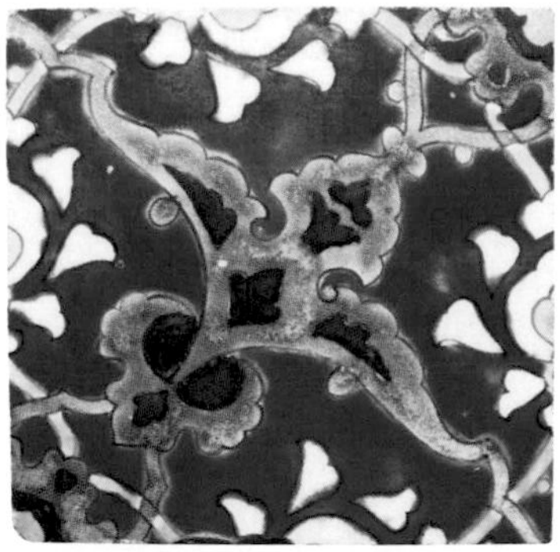

△ Turkish Kutahya Tiles

• *18th century*
One of a pair of blue and white tiles with stylised leaf motif.
• *length 7.5cm*
• £700 • **Shahdad**

△ Vase

• *circa 1860*
A copy of an Iznik ceramic vase, of baluster form, with calligraphic inscriptions and floral design.
• *height 35cm*
• £2,600 • **Sinai**

▽ Tiled Panel

• *circa 1765*
An 18th-century polychrome tiled panel with a mixture of Turkish and Islamic representations, showing mosque with floral decoration. Of North African origin.
• *height 88cm*
• £2,000 • **Sinai**

▽ Turkish Wine Jug

• *1900*
A ceramic Turkish wine ewer with strap handle in a green glaze.
• *height 33cm*
• £300 • **Sinai**

◁ Persian Vases

• *19th century*
Baluster-form vases decorated with flora, birds and animals in a blue glaze.
• *height 27cm*
• £800 • **Shahdad**

△ **Incense Burner**

• *5th century*
Green circular incense burner of two tiers with a dog on the upper section, the whole resting on three feet.
• *height 7cm*
• £150 • Ormonde

△ **Glazed Jug**

• *11th century*
Globular-shaped jug with strap handle, wide splayed neck, lobed body and spout, raised on a circular foot with stops to the base.
• *height 24cm*
• £950 • Ormonde

▽ **Jar and Cover**

• *circa 618–906*
T'ang dynasty jar and cover in baluster form. The jar is in a white glaze which falls short of the base, a sign of hand-dipping and thus authenticity.
• *height 30cm*
• £1,800 • David Baker

▽ **Sung Dynasty Bowl**

• *11th–12th century*
Sung dynasty bowl with an incised repetitive design of stylised flowers, under a green glaze.
• *diameter 20.4cm*
• £400 • Ormonde

◁ **Sung Dynasty Inkwell**

• *11th–12th century*
Inkwell from the Sung dynasty of compressed globular form with a stylised flower pattern in relief, under a green glaze.
• *height 10cm*
• £350 • Ormonde

△ **Stoneware Jar**

• *T'ang 618–906*
Stoneware jar of globular form, with a flared neck and an uneven straw-coloured glaze around the middle from the T'ang dynasty, raised on a circular foot.
• *height 12cm*
• £352 • Ormonde

△ **Rare Junyao Tripod Censer**

• *960–1280*
Junyao tripod censer, Sung dynasty, of compressed globular form.
• *diameter 8.75cm*
• £4,800 • Guest & Gray

▽ **Celadon Vase**

• *circa 12th century*
Chinese Sung Lung Ch'uan celadon vase. Perfect mallet-shape with double handles and incised banding.
• *height 14cm*
• £4,500 • J.A.N. Fine Art

▽ **Koryo Ewer**

• *13th century*
Korean celadon Koryo ewer, with twisted rope handle, slip decoration in black and white and floral panels to front and reverse.
• *height 31cm*
• £8,500 • J.A.N. Fine Art

◁ **Yuan Dynasty Vase**

• *1279–1368*
Yuan dynasty vase, with damage sustained in kiln, in underglazed copper red with scrolling floral decoration and banding.
• *height 24cm*
• £7,500 • J.A.N. Fine Art

△ Glazed Jar

- *14th century*

Thai Sawankhalok celadon glazed squat jar with short inverted neck and twin jug handles. Incised with scrolling motifs above a comb pattern foot.

- *height 16.5cm*
- £585 • Japanese Gallery

△ Oriental Cup

- *16th century*

Blue and white cup with a wide splayed rim, with a blue lattice design running around the exterior, above a song bird with prunus blossom.

- *height 5cm*
- £450 • Ormonde

▽ Pottery Figure

- *1368–1643*

Fine pottery model of a horse and rider of unusual quality, made in the Shanxi province during the Ming dynasty.

- *height 35cm*
- £2,600 • Little River

▽ Swatow Dish

- *early 17th century*

Painted in the centre with a circular panel of two Kylins playing with a brocaded ball, surrounded by symbolic objects and scrollwork.

- *diameter 37cm*
- £1,600 • A. & S. Gray

◁ Porcelain Tureen

- *17th century*

Japanese Imari porcelain tureen and underdish, featuring a bird, fruit and flower decoration.

- £12,000 • Gerard Hawthorn

▽ Anamese Dish

- *15th century*

Anamese dish, from South China, with underglaze blue and leaf and floral decoration to the central panel.

- *diameter 37cm*
- £2,900 • J.A.N. Fine Art

▽ Oriental Jar

- *circa 16th century*

Small blue and white jar with inverted rim and tapered body, decorated with a repeated design of pine trees.

- *height 5cm*
- £240 • Ormonde

▽ Swatow Dish

- *early 17th century*

Decorated at centre with circular panel of two Kylins playing with a brocaded ball. Sides decorated with flowering plants. Has serrated edges.

- *diameter 37cm*
- £1,600 • A. & S. Gray

◁ Pair of Dishes

- *mid-17th century*

A pair of Chinese export sweetmeat dishes, with Chenghua marks of the Chongzhen period, of chrysanthemum flowerhead form, painted with bands of waves. Rim dressed in brown.

- *diameter 15cm*
- £2,600 • Cohen & Cohen

△ Kraak Dish

- *circa 1580*

Large dish of Ming Dynasty, Wan Li period. Deep-cobalt underglaze with scenes of scholars, fans and scrolls.

- *diameter 50cm*
- £5,500 • Cohen & Cohen

△ Kraakware Saucer Dish

- *early 17th century*

Centre painted with an eight-pointed star-shaped panel. With moulded serrated rim.

- *diameter 14.5cm*
- £380 • A. & S. Gray

△ Storage Jar

- *1640*

Blue and white storage jar of bulbous proportions decorated with a repetitive pattern of blue flowers on white ground.

- *height 35cm*
- £550 • Ormonde

△ Chinese Transitional Blue and White Jar

- *Transitional period 1650–1660*

Of ovoid form. Decorated in underglaze blue with a scene of three figures dressed in flowing robes. The rim with a series of single-pointed lappets.

- *height 27.9cm*
- £2,600 • A. & S. Gray

△ Famille Verte Vase

- *1662–1672*

Fine famille verte vase of octagonal baluster form, decorated with panels of flowers, landscapes and precious objects. Floral border showing flowers reserved on fish roe ground.

- *height 92cm*
- £5,500 • Cohen & Cohen

▽ Blue and White Tankard

- *Transitional period*

Tankard of cylindrical form painted with an unusual scene of a man and horse. The beast is standing facing his master in front of a well beneath the sun, as an insect hovers above.

- *height 20cm*
- £3,800 • A. & S. Gray

▽ Blue and White Jar

- *K'ang Hsi period 1662–1722*

Chinese jar, decorated in brilliant underglaze blue with peacocks upon blossoming branches and stylised rockwork. Narrow, triangle-work border at the shoulder and double-line at the foot. Later pierced wood cover.

- *height 20cm*
- £1,400 • A. & S. Gray

◁ Joss-Stick Holders

- *circa 1662–1722*

A pair of Chinese egg and spinach biscuit joss-stick holders, modelled in the shape of the Dogs of Fo Buddhist lions.

- *height 8.5cm*
- £2,300 • Guest & Gray

△ Blue and White Mustard Pot

- *K'ang Hsi period 1662–1722*

The moulded body decorated with alternating panels of maidens and baskets of flowers, between borders of stylised flowerheads. The base with an artemisia leaf.

- *height 10cm*
- £850 • A. & S. Gray

△ Large Chinese Figure

- *K'ang Hsi period 1662–1722*

Guanyin, the Goddess of Mercy, standing on a moulded base, draped in layered robes beneath elaborate headdress.

- *height 64cm*
- £2,800 • A. & S. Gray

▽ Chinese Caddy

- *circa 1662–1722*

Famille verte caddy with alternating panels of ladies in fenced garden and flowers growing from rock work. Kangxi period. Of hexagonal form.

- *height 18.5cm*
- £1,250 • Guest & Gray

▽ Pair of K'ang Hsi Vases

- *1662–1722*

One of a pair of blue and white vases of baluster form, from the K'ang Hsi period. Bodies are painted in bright-blue underglaze with a repeated pattern of meandering floral scrolls.

- *diameter 31cm*
- £1,800 • A. & S. Gray

◁ Famille Verte Bowl

- *K'ang Hsi period 1662–1622*

A Chinese export bowl decorated on the exterior with overglaze enamels in the famille verte palette with birds flying amid prunus plants, issuing from stylised rockwork.

- *diameter 22cm*
- £980 • A. & S. Gray

▽ K'ang Hsi Vase

- *circa 1700*

Vase with three panels depicting insects and river scene on a blue background.

- *length 24cm*
- £1,200 • J.A.N. Fine Art

▽ Pair of Soup Plates

- *1735*

One of a pair of soup plates of famille rose style, painted with the arms of Rose of Kilvarock within a border of flowers and inner rim diaper of *trellis en grisaille*.

- *diameter 23cm*
- £2,600 • Cohen & Cohen

▽ Chinese Candlesticks

- *18th century*

Pair of Chinese export candlesticks of early eighteenth-century European silver form, brightly enamelled in famille rose of dead-leaf brown.

- *height 21cm*
- £16,000 • Cohen & Cohen

△ K'ang Hsi Teapot

- *1700*

K'ang Hsi-period blue and white teapot and cover decorated with peony branches below a Ruyi-head border with floral sprays.

- *height 12cm*
- £1,000 • Cohen & Cohen

△ Chinese Export Basin

- *circa 1725*

Yung Cheng period Chinese export basin, richly decorated in rouge de fer and gilt, with the arms of Mertins impaling Peck. The border is decorated with famille rose flower heads.

- *diameter 39.5cm*
- £8,500 • Cohen & Cohen

△ Japanese Arita

- *circa 1700*

Pair of chicken water droppers used for calligraphy, with red-painted faces. Some restoration.

- *height 14cm*
- £2,600 • J.A.N. Fine Art

▽ Teabowl and Saucer

- *circa 18th century*

European figures fishing for spider, painted on bowl and saucer. Ch'ieng Lung period.

- *height 5cm*
- £600 • Cohen & Cohen

▽ Chinese Cloisonné Vase

- *early 18th century*

Cloisonné enamel vase of yan yan form, from the Ch'ing dynasty period. High-shouldered tapering body with two gilt monster mask and lotus leaf handles, standing on a flared foot. Decorated in colourful enamels on a turquoise and lapis blue ground filled with scrolling lotus, dragon designs, bats, and flower heads, with gilt trim on base and rim.

- *height 67.3cm*
- £18,000 • Gerard Hawthorn

▷ Salt Trencher

- *1715*

Rare Chinese export salt trencher decorated in coloured enamels. The centre is painted with the arms of Louis XV of France.

- *3.5cm x 7cm*
- £3,850 • Cohen & Cohen

△ Fluted Bowls

- *circa 1700*

One of a pair of K'ang Hsi fluted bowls, decorated with panels of flowers and mythological beasts.

- *diameter 18.5cm*
- £2,500 • Guest & Gray

△ Imari Jar & Cover

- *early 18th century*

Of octagonal section, painted in underglaze blue, iron-red, green and gilding with two main lobed cartouches on either side, one depicting a kylin leaping over stylised rockwork, also with peonies, cranes and chicks.

- *height 13cm*
- £3,200 • A. & S. Gray

△ Ch'ieng Lung Vase

• *1736–1796*
Ch'ieng Lung Chinese vase with a coral monochrome glaze. Globular body with a narrow flared neck and splayed foot.
• *height 19cm*
• £1,250 • **Guest & Gray**

△ Chinese Bowl

• *circa 1736–95*
Rare salesman's bowl showing different patterns available to customers ordering from China. Ch'ieng Lung Period.
• *diameter 11cm*
• £3,000 • **Cohen & Cohen**

▽ Nankin Tureen

• *1736–1795*
Elongated, octagonal blue-and-white Nankin tureen. Decorated with tiny figures among pagodas and bridges over waterways. Well-modelled fruit as knob and handles.
• *length 35cm*
• £1,200 • **A. & S. Gray**

▽ Tea Caddy

• *circa 1745*
Ch'ieng Lung, baluster-shaped tea caddy and cover with famille rose pattern. For the Swedish market, with the arms of Gyllenhok, decorated with a moulded base.
• *height 13cm*
• £2,000 • **Cohen & Cohen**

◁ Pair of Baluster Jars

• *1740*
One of a pair of baluster jars and covers of famille rose, painted with three medallions of scenes from a romance on an elaborate floral ground.
• *height 62cm*
• £55,000 • **Cohen & Cohen**

△ Chinese En Grisaille Coffee Pot

• *Ch'ieng Lung period 1736–95*
Squat, moulded ribbed body on flaring foot ring. Decorated with turquoise enamel and gilt. Each side decorated with flowers and leaves beneath a border of diaper cartouches. Rim of spout and handle edged in gold. Gilded knob.
• *height 27.9cm*
• £2600 • **A. & S. Gray**

△ Pair of Canton Vases

• *Ch'ieng Lung Period 1736–95*
Of flattened pear-shaped form with applied 'C'-scroll handles, each decorated with two large moulded oval panels on the bodies.
• *height 23cm*
• £750 • **A. & S. Gray**

△ Chinese Plates

• *circa 1740*
One of a set of 14 Ch'ieng Lung, famille rose enamelled plates, showing two mandarin ducks in dead-leaf brown, within elaborate border.
• *height 22cm*
• £5,800 • **Cohen & Cohen**

▽ Chinese Nankin Vase and Cover

• *1736–95*
Vase and cover of the Ch'ieng Lung period. Of baluster form, painted in underglaze blue with a continuous scene of two pavilions beside a lake. With a domed cover and flaring rim.
• *height 39cm*
• £1,600 • **A. & S. Gray**

▽ Nankin Butter Tub Cover and Stand

• *Ch'ieng Lung period 1736–95*
Oval form. Cover and stand decorated with ogival petal panels radiating from a central oval panel of pomegranates. Surmounted by fruit finial.
• *length 15cm*
• £950 • **A. & S. Gray**

▽ Meiping Vase

• *circa 1745*
Famille rose Meiping vase of globular form, boldly painted with a phoenix among branches of prunus blossom. From the Ch'ieng Lung period.
• *height 34cm*
• £9,100 • **Cohen & Cohen**

△ Bojoab Pattern Bowl

• *1750*

Milk style bowl. Found in the 1990s. Shows the Bojoab pattern. Landscape scenes are shown on the body in blue glaze.

• *height 10cm*

• £850 • Cohen & Cohen

△ Vegetable Tureen

• *1760*

Fine famille rose vegetable tureen decorated with flowers and a fence. The cover features a pomegranate-shaped knob.

• *14cm x 24cm*

• £5,650 • Cohen & Cohen

△ Famille Rose Bowl

• *1760*

Famille rose punchbowl with two large panels of pagodas by a lake and surrounded by mountains on a blue and gilt ground.

• *diameter 39cm*

• £5,000 • Cohen & Cohen

▽ Christening Bowl

• *1750*

Massive and exceptionally rare christening bowl painted with four bands of lotus petals in green, purple, blue and rose, with four floral reserves.

• *24.5cm x 55cm*

• £43,000 • Cohen & Cohen

▽ Famille Rose Ewer and Basin

• *circa 1760*

Famille rose ewer and cover with C-shape handle and matching basin all painted with flowering chrysanthemum growing from rockwork. Ch'ieng Lung period.

• *height of ewer 22cm*

• £5,000 • Cohen & Cohen

▽ Snuff Box

• *1760*

Snuff box unusually handpainted. Famille rose and floral spray decorations.

• *height 4cm*

• £1,760 • Cohen & Cohen

◁ Chinese Sauce Tureen

• *circa 1760*

Very rare Chinese export sauce tureen and cover, modelled as a sitting quail on its nest and painted in iron red, black and green. Ch'ieng Lung period.

• *height 9cm*

• £6,700 • Cohen & Cohen

△ Teabowl and Saucer

• *1756*

Mythological teabowl and saucer in famille rose, depicting the story of Leda and the Swan.

• £4,500 • Cohen & Cohen

△ Famille Rose Plates

• *circa 1760*

One of a pair of Chinese export plates, painted with elaborate scenes within borders in famille rose enamel.

• *diameter 22cm*

• £750 • Dando

△ Octagonal Meat Dish

• *circa 1760*

Famille rose octagonal meat dish, brightly enamelled with butterflies feeding from fruit and flowers within a motttled border of pale green and brown. From the Ch'ieng Lung period.

• *length 33cm*

• £1,300 • Cohen & Cohen

▽ Desk Set

• *circa 1760*

Rare famille rose desk set from the Ch'ieng Lung period. Comprising five quill holders, two inkwells with pewter liners and a covered box.

• *height 6cm*

• £4,800 • Cohen & Cohen

▽ Chinese Coffee Cup

• *circa 1760*

Chinese export coffee cup of unusual size with ear shaped handle and a famille rose pattern.

• *height 8cm*

• £95 • Dando

▽ Sauce Tureen

• *circa 1765*

Armorial tureen with cover, bearing the arms of Countess Macclesfield (Parker impaling Nesbitt). Following a Leeds creamware form with grisaille trellis dipper and rouge de fer rim.

• *width 18cm*

• £15,000 • Cohen & Cohen

△ Chinese Vase

- *circa 1770*

Fine Chinese export porcelain, two-handled vase, with a turquoise chicken-skin ground and bright 'Mandarin' panels. Ch'ieng Lung period.

- *height 24cm*
- £420 • Dando

△ Lattice-Work Basket

- *1780*

Unusual Chinese export basket and stand, with moulded ring handles. Decorated with underglazed blue borders.

- *diameter 14cm*
- £2,200 • Cohen & Cohen

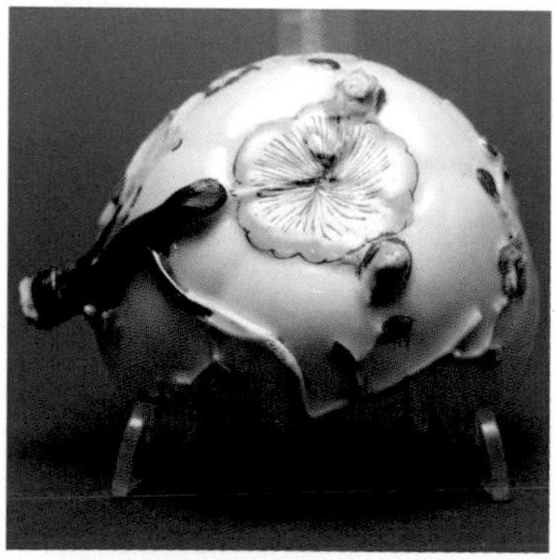

△ Libation Cup

- *18th century*

Ch'ieng Lung dynasty libation cup moulded as open flower with foliate rim, stalk as handle. The applied work painted in famille rose enamels.

- *diameter 8cm*
- £650 • A. & S. Gray

▽ Chinese Tankard

- *circa 1770*

Export Chinese porcelain tankard with 'Mandarin'-style panel depicting a courtly scene.

- *height 24cm*
- £235 • Dando

▽ Chinese Export Vases

- *circa 1780*

A pair of Chinese export vases and stands in Mandarin palette on turquoise ground, each with a tapering square section and butterfly handles. Ch'ieng Lung period.

- *height 24cm*
- £24,000 • Cohen & Cohen

▽ Nankin Bowl and Saucer

- *1790*

Blue and white bowl and saucer with pagoda scenes and later English gilding.

- *diameter of saucer 13cm*
- £125 • Dando

△ Chinese Chocolate Pot

- *circa 1775*

Unusual Chinese export bulbous chocolate pot.

- *height 19.5cm*
- £9,000 • Cohen & Cohen

△ Chinese Soup Plate

- *1775*

Octagonal Chinese export soft paste porcelain soup plate.

- *diameter 23cm*
- £150 • Andrew Dando

△ Floral Coffee Pot

- *circa 1780*

Coffee pot and cover of famille rose, in a conical form, with an S-shaped handle and tall spout decorated with floral sprays.

- *height 20cm*
- £2,300 • Cohen & Cohen

▽ Lemonade Jug

- *circa 1780–1820*

Very rare (so far only one known) Canton enamel lemonade jug decorated with a pastoral scene and figures. The yellow background is decorated with foliate designs and pink blossom, with a lip incorporating a blue foliate design, with a chrysanthemum to the centre.

- *height 18cm*
- £1,200 • Ormonde

▽ Armorial Dinner Service

- *circa 1785*

Ch'ieng Lung dinner service, exported for Swedish market, showing pair of wine coolers, salts, an oval meat dish and charger. Total 62 pieces, each with arms of Colonel Tranefelt.

- £66,000 • Cohen & Cohen

▽ Soup Plate

- *1795*

Polychrome soup plate decorated with tree-shrews and pheasants. Tobacco leaf pattern with blue underglaze.

- *diameter 23cm*
- £2,200 • Cohen & Cohen

△ Okimono of a Tiger

- *19th century*

Porcelain okimono of a tiger with unusual expression. Tail is raised.

- *height 13cm*
- £850 • Gregg Baker

△ Yi Dynasty Vase

- *circa 1800*

Korean blue and white Yi or Chosun dynasty vase. Decorated with a dragon chasing a flaming pearl.

- *length 29cm*
- £1,200 • David Baker

△ Rococo Tureen and Cover

- *1808*

Very rare Chinese export tureen and cover and stand of bold rococo form, with vivid colouring.

- *height 25cm*
- £60,000 • Cohen & Cohen

△ Hirado Incense Burner

- *19th century*

Hirado incense burner with pierced lid and body. Two animal heads showing on the body. Blue flower decorations.

- £480 • J.A.N. Fine Art

△ Satsuma Koro

- *19th century*

Japanese satsuma koro with silver cover decorated with gilt.

- *height 13cm*
- £3,600 • Gregg Baker

▷ Arita Ware Puppy

- *19th century*

Arita ware okimono of a porcelain puppy scratching his ears. Decorated with painted polychrome ruff around its neck, and painted eyes.

- *height 12.5cm*
- £2,000 • Gregg Baker

▽ Fine Japanese Satsuma Box and Cover

- *19th century*

Box is of squat barrel form with moulded mock loop handles and rivet-like border to rim and foot. Finely painted with graduating scene of procession. Base with a gold seal mark.

- *diameter 8cm*
- £1,500 • A. & S. Gray

▽ Blue Glazed Vase

- *19th century*

A 19th-century vase with cylindrical ears on a Mazarin-blue ground, with a flared lip.

- *height 32cm*
- £240 • Namdar

△ Ornamental Duck

- *19th century*

A nicely modelled famille verte model of a duck in recumbent pose. The duck is naturalistically styled with excellent detail.

- *length 30cm*
- £500 • Guest & Gray

△ Double Gourd

- *circa 19th century*

Japanese Kutani double gourd bottle vase, with original cover, decorated with a frieze of lions, peonies and foliage. The upper sections have panels showing pagodas, birds and flowers. The whole profusely gilded.

- *height 46cm*
- £560 • Namdar

▽ Cantonese Bowl

• *circa 1860*
Enamelled with figures, flowers and butterflies, with profuse gilding.
• *diameter 31cm*
• £400 • **Namdar**

▽ Amari Bowl

• *1880*
Amari fluted bowl with famille vert floral decoration and lattice border, set in ormolu mounts.
• *height 20cm*
• £2,885 • **Japanese Gallery**

▽ Incense Burner

• *1890*
Satsuma Koro incense burner decorated with gold figures.
• £385 • **Japanese Gallery**

▷ Kutani Bijin Entertainers

• *late 19th century*
Three Kutani Bijin entertainers wearing kimono and obi. Made in Japan. One is holding a drum and another a fan.
• £3,200 • **J.A.N. Fine Art**

△ Decorated Bronze Vase

• *1860*
Bronze and cloisonné vase.
• *height 50cm*
• £250 • **Tredantiques**

△ Cantonese Vases

• *1870*
One of a pair of Cantonese vases. Decorated with rose medallions.
• *height 37cm*
• £1,600 • **Judy Fox**

▽ Pottery Jar and Cover

• *circa 1880*
Covered jar, probably made at the Bombay School of Arts, with green and yellow glazed floral decoration.
• *23cm x 12cm*
• £200 • **Arthur Millner**

▽ Kutani Vase

• *1880*
Japanese Kutani vase of oval form, decorated with scholarly figures in garden setting.
• *height 11cm*
• £585 • **Japanese Gallery**

△ Satsuma Vases

• *circa 1870*
A pair of gold Satsuma vases of baluster form, painted with holy men and a dragon who keeps away the evil spirits and brings prosperity to the family.
• *height 23cm*
• £450 • **Barrett Towning**

△ Imari Bowl

• *1880*
Imari bowl raised on a padouk wood stand. Decorated with gold rim and floral-pattern exterior.
• *diameter 9cm*
• £2,885 • **Japanese Gallery**

△ Arita-Ware Vase

• *1890*
Arita-ware vase in famille verte, with a baluster form and decorated with stylised floral sprays on a wide splayed base.
• *height 19.5cm*
• £1,350 • **Japanese Gallery**

△ Sake Bottle
- *late 19th century*

Hirado Japanese porcelain sake bottle with polychrome painted dragon chasing its tail, and gilding.
- *height 20 cm*
- £850 • J.A.N. Fine Art

△ Pair of Satsuma Vases
- *1890*

Pair of Satsuma bottle vases in shape of double gourds. Each vase is decorated with two figures at the base of the neck embellished with profuse gilding.
- *height 24cm*
- £2,980 • Japanese Gallery

△ Japanese Group
- *circa 19th century*

Figure of a lohan, in shell boat, talking to a caricatured octopus, the whole on a carved and painted wooden base representing the sea.
- *length 36cm*
- £850 • Gregg Baker

△ Satsuma Teapot
- *1890*

Satsuma teapot, decorated with scholarly figures in a garden setting with rocks and foliage.
- *height 11cm*
- £155 • Japanese Gallery

△ Two Hares
- *20th century*

Figure of two hares, one with red eyes. A fine piece.
- *height 22cm*
- £1,850 • David Brower

▽ Earthenware Bowl
- *19th century*

Japanese Satsuma ware. Earthenware painted with goldfish interior.
- *height 9cm*
- £1,700 • J.A.N. Fine Art

▽ Japanese Bowl
- *1890*

Japanese bowl decorated in gold with painted figures.
- *height 8cm*
- £1,250 • Japanese Gallery

▽ Gilded Vase
- *1910*

Satsuma vase of baluster form, showing figures in a garden setting, and with gilded and stylised floral patterns.
- *height 21cm*
- £355 • Japanese Gallery

▷ Quenti Pot
- *mid-20th century*

Large, impressively constructed Quenti pot, with diagrammatic decoration.
- *65cm x 45cm*
- £1,800 • Gordon Reece

△ Octagonal Vase
- *1890*

Octagonal Satsuma vase of famille verte, with alternating panels of stylised floral decoration and gilding
- *height 24cm*
- £2,980 • Japanese Gallery

△ Kutani Jar and Cover
- *circa 19th century*

Two panels with river setting. Dragon decoration on base and finial.
- *height 20cm*
- £490 • J.A.N. Fine Art

CLOCKS, WATCHES & SCIENTIFIC INSTRUMENTS

This category includes all forms of clock from carriage to longcases, fine watches to the antiques of the future and all scientific artefacts. Einstein once said, 'Space and time are modes by which we think, not conditions under which we live.' The time that we know through clocks and calendars was invented. The measurement of time is an ancient science, though many of its discoveries are relatively recent. The Cro-Magnons recorded the phases of the moon some 30,000 years ago, but the first minutes were counted accurately only 400 years ago. From the mysteries of our past come the wonders of Newgrange in Ireland and Stonehenge in England. These Neolithic peoples' industry and minds laid out the foundation of understanding time. Timekeeping is a mirror reflecting the progress of science and civilisation. Today, a clock is one of the most personal of antiques. For many years it was one of the few items, besides the home and the bed, to be mentioned in a will. In the last few years there has also been increased interest in wrist and pocket watches as well as scientific instruments.

CLOCKS

◁ **Gilt Table Clock**

- *17th century*

Rare continental gilt metal tabernacle clock with engraved side panels.

- *height 22cm*
- £4,500 • Raffety Walwyn

▷ **English Longcase Clock**

- *circa 1710*

Lacquered clock by Peter Wise, London. Chinoiserie style with gilt mouldings and finials. Silver chapter ring, date aperture, engraved and matted centre with crown and cherub spandrels. The trunk has a bullseye window and pendulum movement.

- *height 2.45m*
- £12,000 • Aubrey Brocklehurst

◁ **Basket-Top Bracket Clock**

- *late 17th century*

Ebony basket-top bracket clock with eight-day, hour striking movement and strike silent.

- *height 37cm*
- £15,500 • Raffety Walwyn

△ Queen Anne Longcase Clock

- *1710*

A rare Queen Anne arabesque longcase clock by John Culliford of Bristol, with excellent colour and patination. Eight-day, five-pillar movement with inside count wheel strike. Features 12-inch dial decorated with double cherub and crown spandrels. Typical example of clocks of the period.

- *height 264cm*
- £25,000 • Freshfords

▽ Ebonised Bracket Clock

- *circa 1730*

Fine quarter-chiming clock, brass dial, eight-day movement, hour strike and three subsidiary dials.

- *height 47cm*
- £18,500 • Raffety Walwyn

▽ George III Bracket Clock

- *circa 1760*

Fine brass-moulded and ebonised bracket clock. Eight-day hour striking movement, strike silent.

- *height 48.5cm*
- £9,850 • Raffety Walwyn

◁ George II Clock

- *circa 1760*

George II English lacquer longcase clock with pagoda hood. Painted religious scenes to front door and base depicting scenes from the Bible. The five-pillar, London-made eight-day movement bears an inscription plate engraved 'Andrew Moran, London'. With subsidiary date and seconds ring chiming hours on a bell with strike/silent in break arch.

- *236cm x 35cm x 16.5cm*
- £9,500 • Gütlin Clocks

△ Grand Sonnerie Bracket Clock

- *circa 1750*

Oak-cased original verge escapement Austrian Grand Sonnerie bracket clock. The triple-fusee Austrian movement of short duration (30-hour) with original verge escapement. Maker's name plaque signed 'Augustin Heckel'.

- *53.5cm x 25.5cm*
- £3,900 • Gütlin Clocks

△ Brass Dial Clock

- *1730*

Eighteenth-century oak 30-hour brass dial longcase clock. Made by Savage of Salop.

- *height 195cm*
- £8,750 • Paul Hopwell

▽ Mahogany Longcase Clock

- *circa 1770*

A George III mahogany five-pillar brass dial longcase clock with 8-day brass dial movement with silver chapter ring. Subsidiary seconds and date with separate engraved maker's name plaque. Chimes the hours on a bell.

- *224cm x 56cm*
- £9,500 • Gütlin Clocks

△ Armorial Clock

- *circa 1770*

George III, giltwood, by James Scofield, London. Showing arms of Hewitt impaling Stanhope.

- *height 1.17m*
- £32–42,000 • Norman Adams

△ Wooden Mantel Clock

- *late 18th century*

First Empire, French, birds-eye maple and ebony strung with silk suspension movement.

- *height 36cm*
- £2,500 • Gütlin Clocks

▽ George III Bracket Clock

- *circa 1780*

A George III London-made bracket clock in figured mahogany case with pagoda top. Eight-day movement with fully engraved backplate and original verge escapement. Unusually for an eighteenth-century English clock, it strikes on the hour and half hour. Dial with centre calendar, strike/silent in the arch and signed by the maker.

- *height 58cm*
- £8,900 • Clock Clinic

▽ Striking Bracket Clock

- *circa 1790*

Mahogany bell top. Eight-days duration, silvered dial signed Andrews, Dover.

- *height 51cm*
- £9,200 • Clock Workshop

◁ Oak Longcase Clock

- *1790*

Four-pillar movement with calendar dial and pendulum. Made by Taylor of Manchester. The hood is decorated in two columns with Corinthian capitals.

- *height 2.25m*
- £7,000 • Aubrey Brocklehurst

△ Bracket Clock

- *circa 1780*

By Alex Wilson, London. A bell-top mahogany bracket clock with eight-day striking movement.

- *height 54cm*
- £10,950 • Raffety Walwyn

△ Mahogany Balloon Clock

- *circa 1790*

Late 18th-century mahogany balloon clock by Davis, London. With ormolu handles and white enamel dial.

- *height 61.5cm*
- £16,000 • Norman Adams

▽ English Bracket Clock

- *late 18th century*

Mahogany case with gilt brass feet, side frets and gilt finials. Made by Rivers & Son, Cornhill, London.

- *height 45cm*
- £10,000 • Aubrey Brocklehurst

▽ English Longcase Clock

- *circa 1790*

George III, black lacquer pagoda-hooded eight-day longcase clock. Chinoiserie-decorated case with original hood housing a brass dial and four-pillar movement.

- *height 2.39m*
- £8,500 • Gütlin Clocks

▽ French Mantel Clock

- *1795*

A fine French 18th-century skeletonised ormolu and white marble mantel clock. Original gilding and beautiful case. Eight-day escapement and bells strike.

- *height 47cm*
- £5,750 • **Gavin Douglas**

▽ Signed Bracket Clock

- *19th century*

A fine English bracket clock, the bronzed case with gilded mounts. Engraved dial with matching steel hands, signed by the maker and numbered. Twin fusée movement striking on a bell.

- *height 35cm*
- £7,500 • **Clock Clinic**

▷ French Empire Clock

- *circa 1805*

Gôut d' Egypt. Superb casting, female figures supporting gallery and movement on an oval base.

- *height 44cm*
- £4,250 • **Gavin Douglas**

△ French Directoire Clock

- *circa 1800*

Patinated bronze and ormolu clock. Gôut d' Egypt by Thonissen of Paris.

- *height 45cm*
- £6,750 • **Gavin Douglas**

△ French Clock Set

- *1800*

French slate mantle clock set, with eight-day movement and inlaid with brass. With two side urns, the base of each urn decorated in brass with a scene of children playing within a forest setting with animals.

- *height 46cm*
- £375 • **Julian Smith**

▽ French Mantel Clock

- *1806*

French patinated bronze and ormolu, respresenting astronomy and learning with two busts in double base, on acorn feet.

- *height 53cm*
- £6,150 • **Gavin Douglas**

▽ Cupid Watering a Rose

- *circa 1810*

Patinated bronze and ormolu clock showing Cupid with rose of love. Attributed to Thomire.

- *height 45cm*
- £8,500 • **Gavin Douglas**

▷ Musical Mantel Clock

- *circa 1810*

A First Empire musical gilt ormolu French mantel clock by Alibert of Paris. The timepiece movement has original verge escapement, decorated back cock signed 'Alibert'. The figural case features a boy carrying a bale of hay with original mercury gilding. The clock sits on a rosewood base strung with boxwood, housing a fine music box.

- *38cm x 28cm x 14cm*
- £2,200 • **Gütlin Clocks**

▽ Striking Mantel Clock

- *circa 1810*

English marble with silver-plated dial and double fusée movement. Signed Huntley & Edwards, London. On bun feet.

- *height 41cm*
- £5,750 • **Raffety Walwyn**

▽ French Mantel Clock

- *circa 1810*

Patinated bronze and ormolu clock showing an allegory of horticulture. Made by Lesieur of Paris. The whole on machined bun feet.

- *height 35cm*
- £3,750 • **Gavin Douglas**

△ Empire Clock

- *circa 1815*

A French patinated bronze and Siena marble empire clock.

- *65cm x 40cm x 13cm*
- £2,600 • Tredantiques

△ Charles X Clock

- *circa 1820*

A Charles X patinated bronze and ormolu mantel clock depicting Caeser burning a scroll. Fine military trophies and floral swags.

- *height 52cm*
- £3,750 • Gavin Douglas

△ Egyptian Revival Clock

- *circa 1815*

Patinated bronze and ormolu temple-shaped clock. Movement by Hemon of Paris with sacred bull in alcove below dial. Panel showing Egyptian figure with floral decoration.

- *height 38cm*
- £3,750 • Gavin Douglas

△ French Mantel Clock

- *circa 1820*

French patinated bronze and original ormolu mantel clock showing a child seated by an oil lamp.

- *height 93cm*
- £3,250 • Gavin Douglas

◁ Doulton Mantel Clock

- *circa 1830*

An original silk suspension gilt-ormolu French Louis Philippe mantel clock by Doulton. Original mercury gilding, the case with a maiden resting her arm on a lyre. Watersilked silvered dial with black Roman numerals and fine counterpoised moon hands.

- *56cm x 38cm x 14cm*
- £2,900 • Gütlin Clocks

▽ Charles X Mantel Clock

- *1824–1830*

A French gilded bronze mantel clock. To the left of the clock stands a bronze figure of a male musician playing an instrument while gazing at his music sheet, which rests on a music stand to the top of the dial. To the right is a lyre placed on a small table. To the base is a raised relief depicting a classical scene with cherubs, resting on square legs.

- *height 50cm*
- £1,750 • North West 8

▽ Flame Mahogany Clock

- *circa 1823*

Charles X flame-mahogany and ormolu tombstone-shaped clock. Acanthus moulding with turned bun feet.

- *height 43cm*
- £3,750 • Gavin Douglas

▷ Grandfather Clock

- *circa 1820*

Biedermeier-style grandfather clock. Swedish, birchwood. Signed 'Beurling, Stockholm'.

- *height 2.19m*
- £6,900 • R. Cavendish

△ French Bronze Clock

- *circa 1820*

A French fire-gilded bronze clock commemorating the birth of the Duke of Bordeaux in 1820. With figures of the Duchess of Berry nursing her son with her older daughter Louise kneeling. A very similar example is illustrated and described in *French Bronze Clocks* by Elke Niehuser.

- *height 50cm*
- £6,200 • Clock Clinic

▷ Walnut Mantel Clock

- *1830*

An early 19th-century walnut mantel clock. With anchor escapement movement, pendulum and separately mounted numerals on the dial plate.

- *height 54cm*
- £3,500 • **Aubrey Brocklehurst**

△ Bell Strike Clock

- *circa 1830*

Patinated bronze, ormolu and marble clock by Causard, Horologer du Roy. Bronze designed by Druz of Austria.

- *height 55cm*
- £6,250 • **Gavin Douglas**

△ Charles X Mantel Clock

- *circa 1830*

French patinated bronze and ormolu clock showing Puck descending from the trees, with relief showing Titania, Queen of the Fairies, a scene from 'A Midsummer Night's Dream'.

- *height 44cm*
- £3,150 • **Gavin Douglas**

▽ French Mantel Clock

- *circa 1830*

Ormolu and bronze Cupid and Psyche clock by Gaulin à Paris. Eight-day silk suspension movement with engine-turned watersilk gilt dial. Hour and half-hour striking on a bell.

- *height 59cm*
- £5,900 • **Gütlin Clocks**

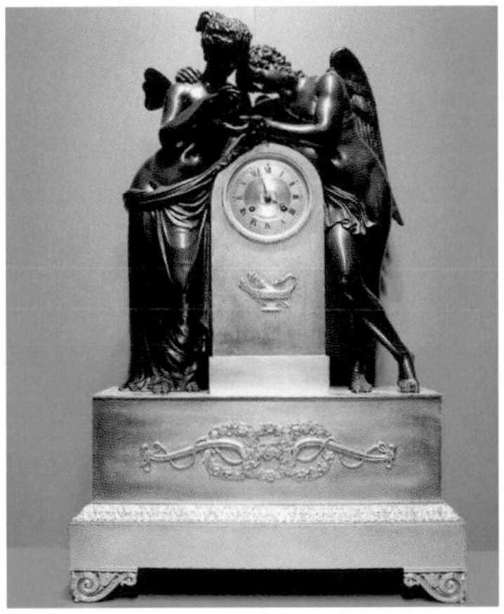

▽ Palais Royal Clock

- *circa 1830*

Fine and rare Palais Royal mother-of-pearl and gilt-brass table clock, with a musical box playing two airs. Records the time, the day and the date.

- *height 21cm*
- £16,500 • **T. Phillips**

▽ French Mantel Clock

- *circa 1830*

Gilt bronze, mounted with soldier and poet. Eight-day silk suspension movement with hour and half-hour strike on bell. With a white enamel dial and black Roman numerals. Made by Gaulin.

- *height 41cm*
- £3,500 • **Gütlin Clocks**

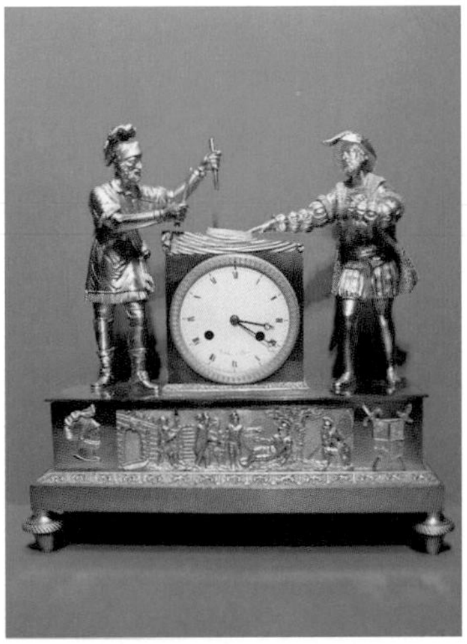

▽ Drumhead Timepiece

- *circa 1830*

Regency clock on ormolu and porphyry marble. By Tupman.

- *height 19.5cm*
- £4,850 • **Raffety Walwyn**

▷ Reims Cathedral Clock

- *circa 1830*

Mercury-gilded mantel clock, eight-day movement, hour and half-hour strike on gong, in rosewood and boxwood-strung case.

- *height 59cm*
- £6,500 • **Gütlin Clocks**

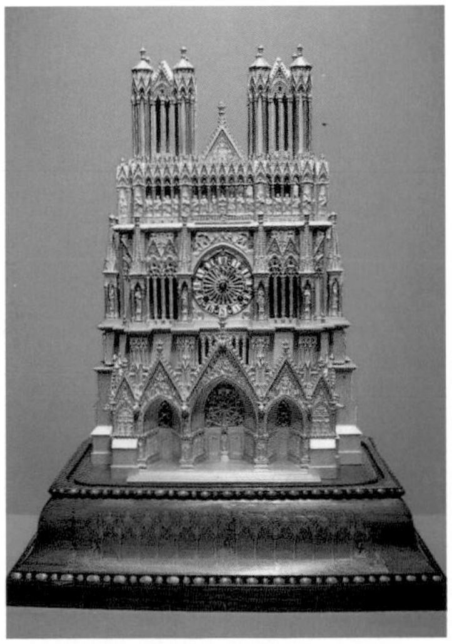

△ French Mantel Clock

- *circa 1830*

A gilt ormolu mantel clock by Lagrange of Paris. Features a finely chiselled gilt bronze case with a maiden and cupid and a laurel wreath to the bottom of the case.

- *42cm x 32cm x 10cm*
- £2,300 • **Gütlin Clocks**

△ Regency Timepiece

- *circa 1830*

Gilt and bronze mantel timepiece with single fusée movement.

- *height 19.5cm*
- £2,950 • **Raffety Walwyn**

△ Louis Philippe Clock

• *circa 1830*
Gilt ormolu and bronze French mantel clock by Douillon. The gilt ormolu and bronze case includes two cherubs holding the face with gilt swag mounts in the center.
• *46cm x 20cm x 12.5cm*
• £2,400 • **Gütlin Clocks**

△ Drop-Dial Wall Clock

• *circa 1835*
Regency mahogany. Brass inlaid with convex dial.
• *height 58cm*
• £2,300 • **Pendulum of Mayfair**

▽ Scottish Longcase Clock

• *circa 1830*
Flame-mahogany trunk with eight-day breakarch dial. By Christie and Barrie of Arbroath.
• *height 2.06m*
• £6,500 • **Gütlin Clocks**

▽ French Wooden Mantel Clock

• *circa 1830*
A bird's-eye maple and ebony-strung French wooden mantel clock. The fine quality silk suspension movement is marked 'Le Paute et Fils. Hrs du Roi' (Horologer to the King). Signed silvered dial. Strikes hours and half hours on a bell.
• *35.5cm x 15cm x 13cm*
• £2,500 • **Gütlin Clocks**

◁ Timepiece Clock

• *circa 1830–35*
Victorian flame-mahogany unnamed single fusee timepiece clock, the single gut fusee eight-day English movement with original pendulum holdfast.
• *29cm x 17.5cm*
• £1,800 • **Gütlin Clocks**

△ Gothic Bracket Clock

• *circa 1839*
An early English flame-mahogany silvered dial gothic bracket clock. The eight-day two-train gut fusee movement with hour and half hour strike on a large nickeled bell signed and dated 'D. Shaw', Leicester 1839.
• *71cm x 46cm*
• £3,900 • **Gütlin Clocks**

△ Mahogany Portico Clock

• *circa 1840*
French flame-mahogany and gilt ormolu-mounted portico clock, with 14-day French movement with hour and half hour strike on a bell supporting a finely chased ormolu regulator type gridiron pendulum.
• *50.5cm x 25.5cm*
• £3,000 • **Gütlin Clocks**

▽ West Country Longcase Clock

• *circa 1830*
An English West Country longcase clock with very good faded colour and ebonised Corinthian columns to trunk and hood. Carved fluting to the curved top. Painted dial signed by the maker, 'G. Stephenson'. Eight-day movement striking on a bell. Overhauled and guaranteed.
• *height 2.13m*
• £4,950 • **Clock Clinic**

▽ Library Four-Glass Clock

• *circa 1840*
A black ebonised Scottish library four-glass clock by 'J. & W. Mitchell', 119 New Cannon Street, Glasgow. The eight-day double-chain fusee movement with hour and half hour strike on a large original nickeled bell and pendulum holdfast.
• *23cm x 15cm*
• £4,800 • **Gütlin Clocks**

△ English Bracket Clock

- *circa 1840*

Mahogany English bracket clock by Taylor of Bristol. The twin gut fusee movement with shoulder plates and hour strike on a bell. White-painted convex dial signed Taylor of Bristol with black spade hands.

- *53.5cm x 30cm x 18cm*
- £3,500 • Gütlin Clocks

△ Rosewood Mantel Clock

- *circa 1840*

Very good four-glass rosewood mantel clock with eight-day movement and hour strike.

- *height 22cm*
- £7,800 • Raffety Walwyn

▽ French Mantel Clock

- *circa 1840*

A fine gilt ormolu and bronze clock with a bronze figure of Napoleon resting his arm on a rock. The bottom section is engraved with his victories. Eight-day movement with hour and half-hour strike on a bell.

- *height 55cm*
- £3,500 • Gütlin Clocks

▽ Bracket Clock

- *circa 1850*

Burr-walnut double-fusee English bracket clock by 'Payne & Co', 163 New Bond Street, London. Numbered clock No. 3234. The double chain fusee 8-day numbered and signed English movement.

- *43.5cm x 30.5cm*
- £6,500 • Gütlin Clocks

◁ 3-Piece Garniture

- *circa 1860*

Capodimonte porcelain three-piece garniture, the finely painted pale blue case with figure of maiden and two cherubs. With eight-day French movement and hour and a half hour strike on a bell.

- *43cm x 22.5cm*
- £5,500 • Gütlin Clocks

△ Mahogany Wall Clock

- *1840*

Mahogany, eight-day duration wall clock. The six-pillar movement is jewelled on the first three pillars. A mercury-compensated pendulum is attached to the back board. Silver dial enclosed in a dome-shaped face.

- *height 1.85m*
- £30,000 • Pendulum of Mayfair

△ Bracket Clock

- *circa 1850*

An English three-train quarter-striking ebonised and gilt ormolu mounted bracket clock standing on its original bracket. The movement chiming on nine bells with hour strike on a large nickeled bell.

- *56cm x 22cm*
- £4,500 • Gütlin Clocks

▽ Skeleton Clock

- *circa 1845*

Double fusee movement. By French Royal Exchange, London. Hour strike on bell. Lancet shape, brass pendulum. Baluster pillars.

- *height 37cm*
- £7,000 • Pendulum of Mayfair

▽ French Striking Clock

- *circa 1860*

Clock with anchor and pendulum escapement. White marble and ormolu mounted with pillars and floral swags on six bun feet.

- *diameter 18cm*
- £750 • Aubrey Brocklehurst

◁ Marble Clock Set

- *circa 1860*

Gilt bronze and rouge marble French figural three-piece drummer boy timepiece clock set. eight-day movement with original cylinder escapement, gilt ormolu hands and two-branch matching candlesticks.

- *33cm x 12.5cm*
- £3,500 • Gütlin Clocks

△ French Clock Set

- *circa 1860*

French ormolu and white marble clock set. Two nymphs holding aloft time. Repeated floral wreath.

- *height 56cm*
- £8,750 • Gavin Douglas

△ French Lyre Clock

- *circa 1860*

Gilt bronze with bronze figural side pieces. Painted porcelain panels depicting lovers in the park. Eight-day French movement chiming hours and half hours on a bell.

- *height 51cm*
- £3,800 • Gütlin Clocks

△ French Mantel Clock

- *circa 1860*

Black mantel clock with a gilt bronze figure of a maiden reading a book resting on a column with a lyre beside her. Eight-day French movement with hour and half hour strikes on a bell.

- *61cm x 56cm x 18cm*
- £3,500 • Gütlin Clocks

△ Wine Barrel Clock

- *circa 1860*

Gilt ormolu French mantel clock with eight day movement chiming hours and half hours on a bell. The case in the form of a wine barrel with cherubs sitting on the barrel, supported by male figures. Twelve-piece white enamel cartouche dial with fleur-de-lys hands and black Roman numerals.

- *50cm x 35.5cm x 16.5cm*
- £2,800 • Gütlin Clocks

△ Skeleton Clock

- *circa 1860*

English cathedral two-train skeleton clock modelled as a cathedral encased in dome-shaped glass case on a moulded marble base.

- *height 65cm*
- £4,000 • Vincent Freeman

▽ English Bracket Clock

- *circa 1860*

A solid mahogany and brass inlaid English bracket clock with quarter striking triple fusee. Retailed by 'Dixon' of Norwich and chiming every quarter on four bells. With eight-day triple fusee movement.

- *68.5cm x 41cm*
- £5,500 • Gütlin Clocks

▽ Pink Porcelain Clock

- *circa 1860*

A gilt bronze and pink porcelain French three-piece clock garniture. Features gilt-bronze case with porcelain panels surmounted by a porcelain urn with gilt-bronze mounts. Eight-day French movement chiming hours and half hours on the bell. Jewelled porcelain dial with black Roman numerals.

- *43cm x 30.5cm x 10cm*
- £5,500 • Gütlin Clocks

▷ Three-Piece Clock

- *circa 1870*

A fine quality gilt ormolu and bronze French mantel clock in the figure of a column with a ball. Gilt bronze arrow hands striking hours and half hours on a bell with two-branch rouge-marble and ormolu cherub candlesticks.

- *38cm x 15cm x 15cm*
- £5,500 • Gütlin Clocks

△ Porcelain Mantel Clock

- *circa 1860*

Gilt bronze and blue jewelled porcelain French mantel clock, the finely chiselled case with original mercury gilding with three blue porcelain urns. eight-day French movement striking hours and half hours on a bell.

- *41cm x 30.5cm*
- £2,700 • Gütlin Clocks

△ Skeleton Clock

- *circa 1860*

A Victorian English striking skeleton clock depicting the Scott Memorial in Edinburgh, with figures of the author and his dog. Two-train movement with lever escapement above the silvered dial, rather than the more usual pendulum, with hour strike and repeat cord. Original rosewood base with mother-of-pearl inlay to the front.

- *height 37cm*
- £5,500 • Clock Clinic

▽ Musical Carriage Clock

- *1870*

Striking and repeating carriage clock with musical alarm. Leroy and fils no. 5324. Musical movement with two airs.

- *height 18.5cm*
- £4,500 • Pendulum of Mayfair

▷ Victorian Bracket Clock

- *circa 1870*

An English triple-fusee black ebonised quarter-chiming Victorian bracket clock. The three-train movement striking the quarters on eight bells with the hour strike on a gong. The brass dial with silvered and engraved chapter ring, silvered strike/silent ring and finely chisselled brass spandrels. The black ebonised case with gilt-ormolu mounts sitting on gilt ormolu lion's paw feet and side carrying handles.

- *38cm x 30.5cm x 20cm*
- £5,500 • Gütlin Clocks

△ Gilt Bronze Clock

- *circa 1870*

Large gilt bronze French clock. The finely chisselled case with maidens to sides surmounted by an urn with draping ormolu swags. The back door is engraved 'Antony Bailly à Lyon'.

- *63.5cm x 38cm 18cm*
- £4,500 • Gütlin Clocks

△ Steamhammer Clock

- *1870*

French 'steamhammer' industrial automation, bronze and ormolu.

- *height 45cm*
- £2,750 • Old Father Time

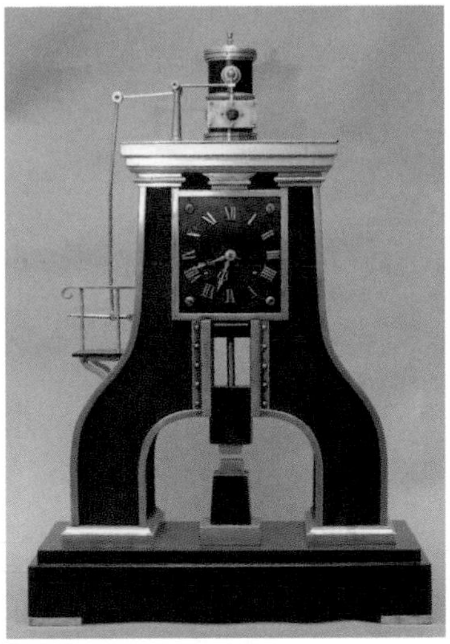

▽ Bronze Mantel Clock

- *circa 1870*

French gilt ormolu and bronze in the form of an oil lamp with a figure of an angel in offering. Eight-day movement and enamel dial.

- *height 35cm*
- £2,800 • Gütlin Clocks

▽ French Mantel Clock

- *1870*

Fine French gilded and silvered mantel clock with original giltwood base. The porcelain dial and side panels with well-painted subjects of various battle scenes. Eight-day movement striking on a bell. Porcelain panels dated 1870. Overhauled and guaranteed.

- *height 38cm*
- £4,200 • Clock Clinic

▽ French Four-Glass Clock

- *circa 1880*

A gilt brass French four-glass clock with signed miniature ivory portrait of a maiden. Eight-day movement by Mougin. Features gilt dial with black Gothic Arabic numerals within a diamante paste stone bezel.

- *30.5cm x 19cm x 14cm*
- £1,500 • Gütlin Clocks

▷ Chariot Clock

- *19th century*

A good late-nineteenth-century chariot clock with bronze cherub driving a rather docile lion. Deep-green veined marble base with gilded classical mounts. Eight-day movement striking the hours and half hours on a bell.

- *32cm x 34cm*
- £4,900 • Clock Clinic

△ English Bracket Clock

- *circa 1870*

Black ebonised and gilt ormolu mounted three-train quarter striking triple-fusee English bracket clock, chiming on eight bells with hour strike on a gong.

- *81cm x 42cm*
- £3,900 • Gütlin Clocks

△ Carriage Clock

- *circa 1880*

A striking French gilded cornice-cased French carriage clock. The eight-day French movement chiming hours and half hours on a gong with original silvered English lever escapement. Features white enamel dial with black Roman numerals.

- *19cm x 9cm x 7.5cm*
- £1,300 • Gütlin Clocks

△ French Lyre Clock

- *1880*

French ormolu-mounted bird's eye maple lyre clock with foliate ormolu mounts.

- *height 44cm*
- £2,000 • **Vincent Freeman**

△ Mahogany Bracket Clock

- *circa 1880*

English mahogany and heavily inlaid bracket clock with columns. The numbered and signed French eight-day movement chiming the hours and half hours on a gong by 'Mougin'.

- *259cm x 20cm*
- £1,800 • **Gütlin Clocks**

△ Perpetual Calendar Clock

- *circa 1880*

A large French black slate and malachite mantel clock. Two-week movement with visible escapement and mercury pendulum. Chimes hours and half-hours on bell.

- *height 56cm*
- £5,500 • **Gütlin Clocks**

▽ Boulle Clock

- *circa 1880*

Ormolu-mounted tortoiseshell, in Renaissance style. Eight-day French square plate movement.

- *height 59cm*
- £750 • **Gütlin Clocks**

▽ Swinging Cherub Clock

- *1880*

Made in Paris by Farcot with scroll-shaped alabaster case.

- *height 22cm*
- £450 • **Old Father Time**

▽ Religious Table Clock

- *1880*

A fine French religious table clock, the case with pewter and brass inlay and with gilt metal mounts. Velvet dial, movement striking the hours on a bell.

- *height 48cm*
- £2,800 • **Clock Clinic**

△ Mahogany Bracket Clock

- *circa 1880*

An English/French flame mahogany arched topped small-sized chiming bracket clock. Eight-day French movement chiming the hours and half hours on a gong by a listed maker, the convex white-enamel dial with black Roman numerals and spade hands. Solid mahogany case with a flame mahogany front and boxwood stringing.

- *25cm x 18cm*
- £1,200 • **Gütlin Clocks**

▽ Porcelain Clock

- *circa 1880*

A fine quality Delft porcelain clock. The eight-day, two-train French movement chimes the hours and half hours on a bell by a listed maker. Blue and white porcelain case surrounded by four cherubs depicting the four seasons, the white convex dial with blue roman numerals and unusually small spade hands.

- *48cm x 30cm x 18cm*
- £2,900 • **Gütlin Clocks**

◁ French Clock

- *1880*

A windmill automaton clock and barometer/thermometer in brass with revolving windmill sails.

- *height 45cm*
- £2,750 • **Old Father Time**

▽ German Porcelain Clock

- *circa 1880*

German porcelain clock modelled as a cherub sitting in a chariot drawn by two lions, raised on a painted rectangular base with a painted panel of a landscape.

- *51cm x 46cm*
- £3,500 • **Vincent Freeman**

△ French Pendule d'Officier

- *circa 1880*

Gilt bronze clock with French eight-day movement and English lever escapement. Engine-turned silvered dial with black arabic numerals. Showing wreath, floral decoration and a carrying handle with snake eating its tail.

- *height 18cm*
- £1,900 • Gütlin Clocks

△ French Carriage Clock

- *1880*

Enamelled porcelain sonnerie carriage clock by Drocourt, Paris. On original stand. Repeats at five-minute intervals, with an alarm.

- *height 22cm*
- £11,975 • Pendulum of Mayfair

▽ Viennese Clock

- *1880*

Vienna clock with porcelain cartouches of celestial scenes with blue-enamelled architectural pillars and gilding, raised on gilt ball feet.

- *height 40cm*
- £4,000 • Vincent Freeman

▽ Third Republic Clock

- *circa 1880*

A French ormulu and turquoise porcelain-mounted mantel clock. Finely chiselled case with original mercury gilding and adorned with an urn. Below the dial is a central plaque depicting storks in a natural foliate setting.

- *53cm x 28cm x 17cm*
- £5,500 • Butchoff

◁ Brass Carriage Clock

- *circa 1880–1890*

French polished brass cornice-cased carriage clock timepiece. The eight-day French timepiece movement with original silvered English lever platform escapement, with brass cornice-style case with solid cast scroll-shaped carrying handle.

- *11cm x 7.5cm*
- £550 • Gütlin Clocks

△ English Bracket Clock

- *circa 1880*

English mahogany cased pad-top bracket clock with eight-day French numbered and signed movement, chiming the hours and half hours on a gong.

- *33cm x 22.5cm*
- £5,500 • Gütlin Clocks

△ Third Republic Clock

- *1880*

A French Third Republic lyre-shaped ormulu and gilt clock, with a Champs-Levée platform movement by G. Jamieson. Seated at the base are two gilt cherubs holding lyres.

- *height 40cm*
- £1,400 • Barham Antiques

▽ Carved Musical Clock

- *circa 1880*

A carved walnut musical automaton Swiss chalet with clock. Eight-day French movement with hour and half hour strike on a bell and music box sitting in the base of the clock. Two doors opening on the hour revealing male and female musicians. The case is in carved walnut and is in a very original undamaged state.

- *48cm x 61cm x 30cm*
- £3,500 • Gütlin Clocks

▽ French Zodiac Clock

- *1885*

French clock made for the Spanish market with barometer, thermometers and revolving signs of the zodiac. The clock is encased within a globe of the world with a silver cloud formation running through the centre of the piece.

- *height 43cm*
- £3,000 • Vincent Freeman

◁ Four Glass Mantel Clock

- *circa 1890*

A gilt-brass mounted green onyx striking four glass mantel clock and garniture, the oval case with moulded top and base on bun feet. The lanceolate-leaf bezel containing a white enamel dial with Arabic numerals decorated with painted floral swags and pierced gilt-metal hands.

- *30.5cm x 20cm*
- £2,900 • Gütlin Clocks

△ Paris Bisque Clock

- *circa 1890*

A white Paris Bisque French timepiece mantel clock with small French eight-day timepiece movement. Features white convex enamel dial with Roman numerals and counterpoised moon hands. The white bisque case with a figure of a maiden.

- *25cm x 16.5cm x 11cm*
- £750 • Gütlin Clocks

△ Gothic Bracket Clock

- *circa 1890*

A very pretty mahogany gothic English bracket clock by Webster of Cornhill, London. Fine quality double fusee English movement chiming hours and half hours on a gong with pendulum holdfast. The mahogany case with pierced wooden side frets, and a one piece silver dial with Hallibrad hands and foliate engravings.

- *25cm x 20cm*
- £2,900 • Gütlin Clocks

▽ Sheraton-Style Bracket Clock

- *circa 1890–1900*

A small, late Victorian mahogany balloon-shaped Sheraton-style English bracket clock. Includes a boxwood inlaid front panel and stringing, and flat white enamel dial with Arabic numerals within thick-cut bevelled glass.

- *28cm x 18cm*
- £1,200 • Gütlin Clocks

▽ Marti et Cie Clock

- *circa 1890*

French mantel clock of the Third Republic in a gilded and champlevé enamel case with brilliant paste around the dial. Eight-day movement, striking the hours and half hours on a gong with matching enamel pendulum. Bearing the maker's stamp of Marti et Cie.

- *height 38cm*
- £3,900 • Clock Clinic

◁ Gilt-Bronze and Silvered Mantel Clock

- *circa 1890*

Gilt-bronze and silvered French mantel clock. Eight-day French movement with half hour chime on a bell. The case with silver mounts depicts Bacchus, ancient Greek god of wine. Includes engraved slate dial with gilt Roman numerals.

- *39cm x 24cm x 18cm*
- £1,700 • Gütlin Clocks

△ Miniature Carriage Clock

- *circa 1890–1900*

French miniature satin-gilded 8-day carriage clock timepiece with original leather travelling box. The small sized 8-day movement with silvered cylinder platform escapement.

- *7.5cm x 5cm*
- £1,200 • Gütlin Clocks

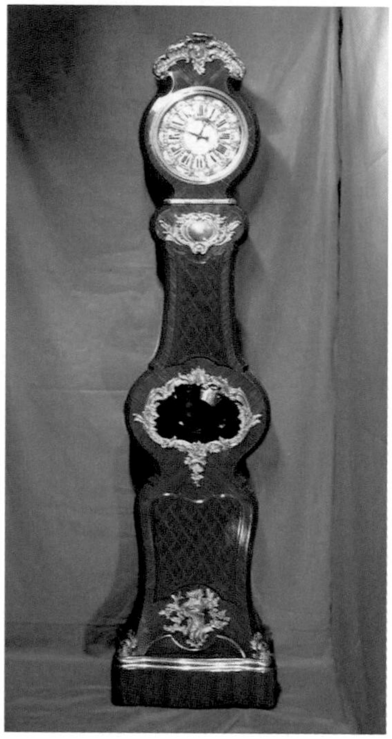

△ French Chiming Regulator

- *circa 1880–90*

Kingwood and parquetry. By Bing of Paris. 25-piece dial. Central second sweep hand of three-week duration.

- *height 2.26m*
- £17,500 • Gütlin Clocks

▽ Maiden on a Horse Clock

- *circa 1890*

Large French clock. A romantic figure on winged horse. Eight-day movement. Striking hours and half hours on a bell.

- *height 79cm*
- £1,900 • Gütlin Clocks

▽ French Comptoise Clock

- *late 19th century*

Wall clock with eight-day movement, anchor escapement, stamped sheet brass and enamelled face. By B. Cadillan of Bazas.

- *height 47cm*
- £2,000 • Aubrey Brocklehurst

◁ English Mantel Clock

- *circa 1890*

Flame mahogany and boxwood strung, lancet shape and sitting on brass ogee feet. Eight-day French movement.

- *height 29cm*
- £1,300 • Gütlin Clocks

▽ Propeller Blade Clock

- *circa 1900*

Industrial timepiece with ships, capstan with a compass, gilded lifebelt, apothec, anchor and eight-day cylinder escapement.

- *height 35cm*
- £1,600 • Gütlin Clocks

▽ Boudoir Balloon Clock

- *circa 1903*

Silver and enamel, French and English hallmarked, Birmingham. Signed L. Leroy & Cie of Paris.

- *height 16cm*
- £1,600 • Gütlin Clocks

▽ 'Moving Eye' Clock

- *1930*

Novelty dogs by Oswold, Germany. One eye is on the hour, the other on the minute.

- *height 14cm*
- £350 • Old Father Time

△ Cast Bronze Clock

- *circa 1900*

A solidly cast gilt-bronze four-glass clock by Maple & Co Ltd, Paris. Beautiful convex white-enamel dial with hand-painted swags of roses around blue Arabic numerals. Movement signed 'Maple & Co'.

- *37cm x 23cm x 18cm*
- £2,200 • Gütlin Clocks

△ Small Travelling Clock

- *1903*

English silver-cased clock with hallmark and French eight-day movement. Original English lever platform escapement. Signed on the movement.

- *height 10cm*
- £1,100 • Gütlin Clocks

△ German Novelty Clock

- *1900*

By Junghans. In papier mâché, original glass dome. The head and tail move as clock ticks.

- *height 30cm*
- £1,250 • Old Father Time

▽ French Carriage Timepiece

- *1900*

A French carriage timepiece combined with barometer, thermometer and compass with gilt brass, glass panels and carrying handle.

- *height 16cm*
- £1,750 • Aubrey Brocklehurst

▽ English Gravity Clock

- *1910*

Made by Eleison, London. With mahogany pillared frame and clock in serpentine-marble case. The weight of the clock powers the movement.

- *height 30cm*
- £1,200 • Old Father Time

▽ French Pendulum

- *1930*

Designed by ATO. First battery-operated French pendulum clock. Spider's web design to dial. Aztec Gothic numerals.

- *height 17cm*
- £350 • Decodence

△ Brass Carriage Clock

- *circa 1900*

Small pediment-topped polished brass carriage clock timepiece. Eight-day movement with platform escapement.

- *height 18cm*
- £1,900 • Gütlin Clocks

△ 'Reason' Electric Clock

- *1910*

English, powered by 1.5 volt battery. Invented by Murday.

- *height 32cm*
- £3,800 • Old Father Time

△ French Art Deco

- *1939*

Clock by JAZ. Typical of French Art Deco style. Maroon and black case with chromium embellishments. Embossed with stylised face.

- *height 18cm*
- £300 • Decodence

WATCHES

△ Verge Watch

• *circa 1710*
Silver pair-cased verge-escapement watch with silver champlevé dial. By John Ogden, Bowbridge.
• £3,450 • C. Frodsham

▽ Hunter Fob

• *circa 1860*
A lady's enamelled and diamond-mounted key-wound hunter fob in 18ct gold, with pierced cover on matching bar brooch in fitted case. Produced by Mellerio Meller, 1 Quai d'Orsay, Paris.
• £4,600 • Anthony Green

▽ Half Hunter

• *18th century*
Half-hunter gold fob watch with blue Roman numerals on the outer casing of the watch surrounding an inset white dial.
• *diameter 4cm*
• £975 • Bellum

◁ Gold and Enamel Watch

• *1801*
A rare 18ct gold and polychrome enamel watch, Peto-cross-detent escapement with scene of children feeding chickens. By Ilbery, London.
• *diameter 6cm*
• £42,500 • C. Frodsham

△ Silver Pocket Watch

• *circa 1878*
English, large silver chronograph, with key wind and key set. White-enamel face with black numerals and gold hands.
• £195 • Sugar

▷ Gentleman's Pocket Watch

• *circa 1870*
Austrian gentleman's pocket watch with a cover engraved with a cartouche depicting a parrot on a swing.
• *diameter 1.5cm*
• £400 • Bellum

△ Verge Watch

• *circa 1800*
An 18ct gold and enamel verge watch, by Vauchez of Geneva, showing a pastoral scene, with jewelling.
• £6,500 • Somlo

△ Cylinder Watch

• *circa 1800*
An 18ct gold, open-face, keyless lever, minute-repeating, split seconds chronograph watch with original box and certificate, by Patek Philippe of Geneva; retailed by Spaulding & Co of Chicago.
• *diameter 45mm*
• £14,750 • C. Frodsham

▽ Cylinder Watch

• *circa 1800*
A Swiss-made, gold and enamel double-dialled watch with visible diamond-set escapement and calendar.
• *diameter 43mm*
• £8,000 • C. Frodsham

▽ Open-Face Pocket Watch

• *circa 1830*
A fine quality open-face pocket watch, the cylindrical case with turned sides. The engine-turned dial with Roman chapter ring and signed 'Simmons Finsbury London'. English lever movement with fusée signed and numbered '778'. The balance has a diamond endstone.
• £1,500 • Anthony Green

▽ Victorian Gentleman's Pocketwatch

• *circa 1866*
Chester hallmarked, gold watch with white-enamel dial and subsidiary seconds. By Thos Russell and Son.
• £1,650 • Anthony Green

▽ Fob Watch

• *circa 1890*
A small, silver, Swiss fob watch with enamel dial and red numerals and gold floral pattern to centre, with incised floral decoration to covers.
• £125 • Sugar

▽ Repeating Watch

• *circa 1891*
Keyless half-hunter in 18ct gold, with lever minute repeating movement.
• *diameter 53mm*
• £6,750 • C. Frodsham

◁ Deck Watch

• *1883*
Shows hours left to run in the main spring and chronograph stop mechanism to synchronise the watch to the main ship's chronometer. Shows little wear. Signed 'Thos. Russell Chronometer Makers to The Queen'.
• £2,300 • Anthony Green

△ Gold Pocket Watch

• *circa 1880*
Gold gentleman's pocket watch. Black Roman numerals, gold seconds on a white enamel face, with a foliate engraved design on the back of the case.
• *diameter 3cm*
• £400 • Bellum

△ Small Silver Fob Watch

• *circa 1890*
Silver hunter with enamelled dial with red numerals. Incised floral decoration to the cover.
• £125 • Sugar

▷ Victorian Lady's Dress Watch

• *circa 1900*
A Victorian 15ct gold lady's dress watch with rubies and diamonds on a gate-type sprung bracelet with numerals in blue and red. With gold decoration on a white porcelain dial.
• *diameter 2.5cm*
• £1,700 • Westminster

△ Open-face Keyless Fusée

• *circa 1895*
An 18ct gold, open-face keyless fusée, free-sprung pocket chronometer with spring detent escapement, enamel dial with up and down indicator, and thief-proof swivel bow. By Charles Frodsham, London.
• *diameter 58mm*
• £9,500 • C. Frodsham

△ Gentleman's Pocket Watch

• *circa 1890*
Gold gentleman's pocket by Balbi, Buenos Aires. With black Roman numerals on a white face with a subsidiary second dial. The front of the case is engraved with a house with mountains in the background, surrounded by a floral design, with diamonds.
• *2.5cm*
• £950 • Bellum

▽ Open-face Pocketwatch

• *circa 1884*
A late 19th-century, 18ct gold, minute repeating pocket watch by Dent of London, with white-enamel face with Arabic numerals and subsidiary seconds.
• £5,900 • Somlo

▽ Omega Fob Watch

• *circa 1900*
Gold Omega pocket watch with Arabic numerals on a white face, with gold hands and a subsidiary seconds dial. Swiss made.
• *diameter 1.5cm*
• £345 • Bellum

▽ Fob Watch

• *1910*
Large gold fob watch by Vetex Revue, with black Roman numerals on a white face with a subsidiary seconds dial.
• *diameter 5cm*
• £223 • Bellum

△ Double-Dialled Watch

• *circa 1910*

A silver, keyless, lever double-dialled calendar watch with moon phases, time and subsidiaries on an enamel dial with Roman numerals on the obverse, and world time indications for seven cities on the reverse dial. The watch, which is unsigned, was made in Switzerland.

• £2,750 • Anthony Green

△ Keyless Lever Watch

• *circa 1908*

An 18ct gold open-face watch with split seconds chronograph and register. By Dent of London.

• *diameter 54mm*

• £4,750 • C. Frodsham

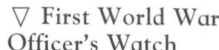

▽ First World War Officer's Watch

• *circa 1913*

Original, enamelled dial with Roman numerals and traditional red twelve. Subsidiary second dial and minute recording. Fabulous example of one of the earliest wristwatch chronographs.

• £2,650 • Anthony Green

▽ Pin-set Wrist Watch

• *circa 1915*

A rare gentleman's pin-set wrist watch by H.Y. Moser & Cie in 14ct pink gold with high-grade lever movement and engraved and enamelled dial. Features a tonneau-shaped case with hinged lugs. The case is signed 'H.Y. Moser & Cie No. 635235', with Russian hallmarks.

• £2,750 • Anthony Green

▽ Lady's Rolex

• *1914*

Lady's silver Rolex watch, of circular form, with original expanding bracelet and early example metal dial with Roman numerals in black, 'XII' in red.

• £675 • Sugar

△ Demi-Hunter Pocket Watch

• *1905*

A 9ct gold demi-hunter pocket watch by Wilson and Sharp of Edinburgh. With three-quarter plate movement.

• *diameter 4cm*

• £495 • Sugar

△ Pocket Watch

• *circa 1910*

A 14ct gold-filled pocket watch, with top-wind button set, by Thomas Russell.

• £800 • Sugar

▷ Gentleman's Rolex

• *circa 1915*

9ct gold precision watch, by Rolex, with subsidiary seconds and a white-metal dial.

• £950 • Sugar

▽ Hunting Chronograph

• *1907*

Swiss-made hunting split seconds chronograph with subsidiary minute recording and sweep second dials. Case ~ 130519. The white enamel dial signed S. Smith & Son 9. The Strand London Maker to the Admiralty. # 142B 68 Non-magnetisable.

• £2,950 • Anthony Green

▽ Vintage Lady's Watch

• *circa 1910*

An 18ct gold lady's watch set with demantoid garnets and diamonds around the bezel. White porcelain face with black numerals and red number 12, decorated with gold pips with an 18ct. expandable bracelet.

• *diameter 2.2cm*

• £1,275 • Westminster

◁ Dress Pocketwatch

• *circa 1915*

An 18ct gold, Swiss pocketwatch with gold-washed dial and subsidiary seconds.

• £395 • Sugar

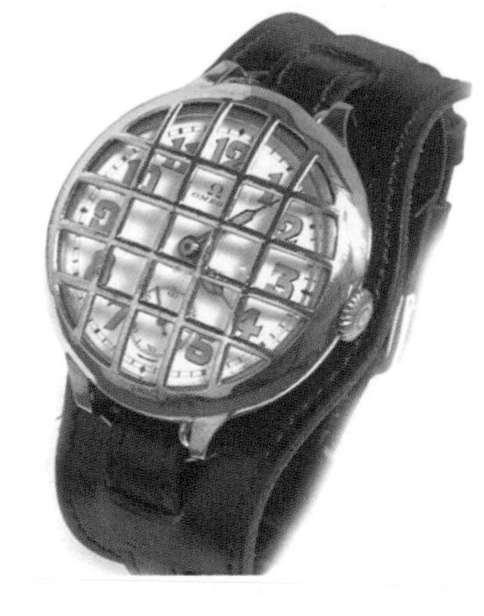

△ Omega Watch

• *circa 1915*
A First World War officer's large wristwatch with original mesh 'Trench Guard'. The white enamel dial with subsidiary seconds, signed Omega. The case struck Omega Depose No. 9846. Case # 5425073. The movement with Swan Neck Micro Reg. Signed Omega # 211504.
• *diameter 4.2cm*
• £2,250 • Anthony Green

△ Rolex Officer's Wristwatch

• *circa 1916*
An early First World War 'Officer's' wristwatch. The silvered dial signed Rolex & Swiss Made. The movement # 4636 and signed Rolex Swiss 15 Jls. Case signed with 'W & D' for Wilsdorf & Davis, the original founders of the Rolex empire. Case # 769936.
• £2,500 • Anthony Green

▽ Lady's Gold Watch

• *1915*
Rolex 9ct gold watch with red numeral 12, enamel dial and expanding bracelet.
• £700 • Sugar

▽ Asprey Watch

• *circa 1916*
Silver Asprey rectangular curved watch with white metal dial and Roman numerals.
• £260 • Sugar

▽ Gold Pocket Watch

• *1920*
A gentleman's gold pocket watch with top-wind button set by Thomas Russell.
• *diameter 4cm*
• £250 • The Swan

◁ Sterling Silver Watch

• *circa 1918*
A Longines sterling silver, early pin-set one-button chronograph with minute recording dial and subsidiary second dial. The sweep centre seconds chronograph operating through the winding stem. The hinged lug case is marked '#2974806 Mvt#2974806'. Eighteen jewels and five adjustment case dial and movement signed 'Longines'.
• £2,950 • Anthony Green

▷ Rolex Wristwatch

• *1918*
Lady's Rolex wristwatch with white enamelled dial set in 9ct gold. Black Arabic numerals.
• *diameter 2cm*
• £580 • AM-PM

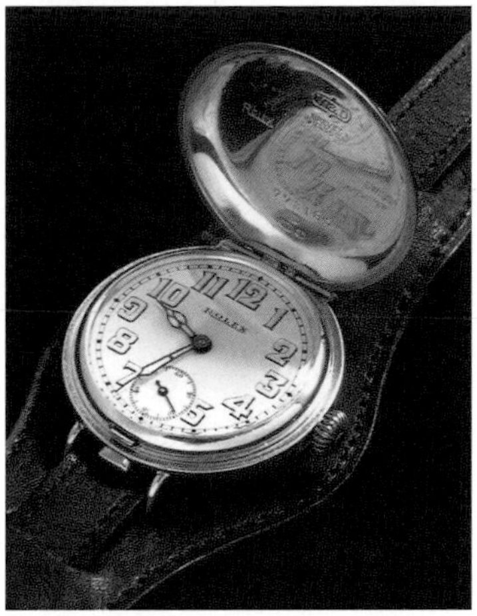

△ First World War Wristwatch

• *circa 1916*
A very rare officer's First World War 'Hunting' cased wristwatch, with waterproof screw-back. The movement is signed by Rolex and the case is marked 'Rolex' with 'W&D', standing for Wilsdorf & Davis, the original founders of the Rolex company. The case is numbered 773185 and the enamel face shows luminous numerals and subsidiary seconds.
• £3,450 • Anthony Green

△ Octagonal Rolex Watch

• *1920*
A octagonal 9ct gold lady's Rolex watch with Arabic figures on a gold dial.
• *diameter 2.5 cm*
• £550 • AM-PM

▽ Rolex Cushion Watch

• *1920s*
Gentleman's Rolex cushion wristwatch set in 9ct gold. With white enamel dial, auxiliary sweep seconds and a red number 12. Rolex signature underneath the dial.
• *diameter 2.5cm*
• £950 • AM-PM

▽ Lady's Swiss Watch

• *1920s*
Lady's Swiss-made wristwatch in 18ct rose gold with enamel dial with old cut diamonds on the bezel, on an expandable 18ct rose gold bracelet.
• *diameter 1.7cm.*
• £500 • AM-PM

△ Rolex Lady's Watch

- *1920*

Rolex lady's sprung bracelet 9ct gold watch with a Rolex-named movement and back plate. Features a white porcelain face with a red number 12, and a secondary minute dial.

- *diameter 3cm*
- £750 • Westminster

△ Gold Cartier Watch

- *circa 1920*

An 18ct gold and platinum Cartier tank wrist watch with square face and enamelled dial with black, Arabic figures.

- £22,000 • Anthony Green

▷ Golf Ball Watch

- *circa 1920*

Swiss watch with silver case modelled as a golf ball. With subsidiary seconds.

- £550 • Sugar

▽ Lady's Oyster Watch

- *1920s*

Lady's Rolex Oyster wristwatch set in 14ct gold with mechanical movement, a sunburst dial, auxiliary sweep seconds and a white face with gold numbers.

- *diameter 2cm*
- £1,500 • AM-PM

▽ Octagonal Watch

- *1920s*

Lady's silver octagonal wristwatch with white enamel dial, auxiliary sweep seconds and a red number twelve.

- *diameter 2cm*
- £250 • AM-PM

△ Rolex Watch

- *circa 1920s*

Silver tonneau-shaped gentleman's wristwatch. The white enamel dial signed Rolex, with luminous numerals and hands and subsidiary seconds. The 3pc case signed Rolex 7 Worlds Records Gold Medal Geneva Suisse (RWC Ltd) #64948. The lever movement signed Rolex Swiss made. 15 Rubies.

- £2,550 • Anthony Green

△ Rolex Oyster Watch

- *1920s*

Rolex Oyster precision auxiliary sweep seconds white dial. 2, 4, 8, 10, and 12 in Arabic numerals, set in stainless steel.

- *diameter 1.6cm*
- £650 • AM-PM

▽ Lady's Swiss Watch

- *1920s*

Lady's Swiss-made 18ct gold watch with a white enamelled dial with Roman numerals.

- *diameter 2.7cm*
- £400 • AM-PM

▽ Tiffany & Co. Watch

- *1920s*

Lady's Tiffany & Co. Set in 9ct rose gold white enamelled dial with Arabic numerals with a red number 12.

- *diameter 2cm*
- £500 • AM-PM

△ Rolex Watch

• *circa 1923*
A medium-sized Rolex gentleman's watch in sterling silver, with 'Sunray' dial, hinged lugs and subsidiary seconds.
• £1,800 • Anthony Green

△ Rolex Prince Watch

• *circa 1929*
Rare Prince chronometer gent's watch. Dial features original, enamelled numerals and tracks.
• £6,650 • Anthony Green

△ Vintage Lady's Watch

• *circa 1925*
An octagonal lady's 9ct gold watch with a 9ct gold expandable bracelet. Arabic figures on a white porcelain face, and a second minute dial.
• *diameter 2.5cm*
• £275 • Westminster

▽ Rolex Pocket Watch

• *circa 1920*
A gold-plated Rolex pocket watch with luminous Arabic numerals and hands and subsidiary seconds.
• *diameter 4.2cm*
• £600 • Sugar

▽ Lady's Cartier

• *circa 1925*
Cocktail watch of 18ct gold, platinum and diamonds set with matching deployant buckle.
• £16,000 • Somlo

▽ Rolex Silver Pocket Watch

• *circa 1920*
A silver Rolex pocket watch with a circular blue enamel insert to the outer casing of the watch.
• *diameter 4cm*
• £700 • Sugar

△ IWC Octagonal Watch

• *circa 1923*
An octagonal IWC 18ct wrist watch with Arabic numerals on a silver face.
• *width 3cm*
• £1,000 • Sugar

△ Gentleman's Manual-Wind Wrist Watch

• *1925*
A gentleman's gold, manual-wind wrist watch by J.W. Benson, featuring a white enamel face with Arabic numerals and subsidiary seconds.
• *diameter 3cm*
• £250 • The Swan

▽ Hermetique Waterproof

• *circa 1923*
Rare, hermaetically sealed 'Waterproof' wristwatch, in double case with hinged lugs. Swiss-made, by Hermetique, in 9ct gold.
• £2,750 • Anthony Green

▽ Lady's Oyster Watch

• *1930s*
Rolex Oyster precision lady's stainless steel wristwatch with a white dial and triangular digits.
• *diameter 1.8cm*
• £650 • AM-PM

◁ Art Deco-Style Bulova Watch

• *1930*
A gold-plated gentleman's manual-wind Bulova wrist watch in the Art Deco-style. With subsidiary seconds on a white enamel dial.
• *3.2cm x 2.2cm*
• £295 • The Swan

△ Gentleman's Longines Watch

• *1930s*
Gentleman's Longines oblong design set in 14ct rose gold, with white dial set with gold Arabic numerals and auxiliary sweep seconds.
• *diameter 1.8cm*
• £950 • AM-PM

△ Open-face Karrusel Watch

• *circa 1930*
An 18ct gold, keyless lever chronograph watch with register and vari-coloured tracking for the tachometer. Swiss, unsigned.
• *diameter 50mm*
• £850 • C. Frodsham

▽ Platinum Watch

• *circa 1930*
A platinum and diamond wrist watch with a sprung platinum bracelet. A light silvered face with five numerals in black and a red number 12 with an outer chapter ring.
• *1.5cm x 1cm*
• £1,275 • Westminster

▽ Peerless Lady's Watch

• *circa 1930s*
An octagonal, Peerless lady's watch in platinum with a light silvered dial, black Arabic numerals and hands, and an expandable gold bracelet. Swiss movement with an English case.
• *diameter 2cm*
• £1,875 • Westminster

△ Rolex Prince 'Brancarde'

• *circa 1930*
A Rolex Prince 'Brancarde' wrist watch in sterling silver, case number '0559 Ref #971', movement number '#72147'. This magnificent chronometer is in its original box with the original two-part chronometer rating certificate dated 1930, the original strap and Rolex sterling silver buckle.
• £12,500 • Anthony Green

△ Rolex Pocket Watch

• *circa 1930*
A Rolex sterling silver pocket watch with white enamel dial with subsidiary seconds. The 17-jewelled movement signed 'Rolex'. Swiss-made British import marks for the year 1930.
• £2,250 • Anthony Green

◁ Omega Chronograph

• *circa 1932*
Rare, steel-cased Omega single button chronograph wristwatch with enamel dial in red and black and sweep second hand.
• £7,000 • Somlo

▽ Longines Watch

• *1930*
A rectangular Longines, stainless steel mechanical watch, with luminous green Arabic numbers on a white face.
• *2cm x 1.5cm*
• £350 • AM-PM

▽ Cartier Pocketwatch

• *circa 1930*
18ct gold and onyx. With European Watch and Clock Co movement.
• £9,200 • Somlo

▽ Peerless Wristwatch

• *1934*
A gentleman's wristwatch, the movement jewelled to the centre signed 'Peerless' Swiss Made # 332257 with S & Co Logo. The case # 331618-2 & FB for Francis Baumgartner Borgelle, the case designer. Enamel dial, subsidiary seconds.
• *diameter 3.3cm*
• £2,750 • Anthony Green

△ Cocktail Watch

- *circa 1930s*

A lady's platinum cocktail watch with diamonds set around the face and Arabic numerals on the dial, with a white expandable platinum bracelet.

- *diameter 3cm*
- £1,150 • Westminster

△ Bucherer Lady's Cocktail Watch

- *circa 1940*

An exquisite lady's 18ct platinum and diamond cocktail watch designed by Bucherer, with a white dial and an original 9ct gold flexi-strap.

- *diameter 2cm*
- £2,100 • Westminster

▽ Art Deco Rolex

- *circa 1937*

A gentleman's Art Deco-period Rolex wristwatch in 9ct gold, with stepped sides and high-grade movement timed to two positions. British import marks for the year 1937.

- £3,650 • Anthony Green

▽ Omega Watch

- *circa 1938*

An 18ct gold wrist chronograph with subsidiary seconds and 30-minute register dial. The main dial with outer tachometer scale. Inner pulsations scale and base 1000 scale. The case signed Omega, with Swiss control marks. CS #9174757. The movement signed Omega Watch Company. 17 Jls #9388131.C333.

- £6,500 • Anthony Green

◁ German Aviator's Watch

- *circa 1942*

A very rare aviator's wrist watch by A. Lange & Sohne Glashutte I Sa. model No. FI23883. German military ordinance marks to inside of case back: 'Mvt #213092 Case #213092 Gerrat #127-560A-1 Werk #213092 Anforderz #FI23883'.

- *diameter 5.5cm*
- £3,500 • Anthony Green

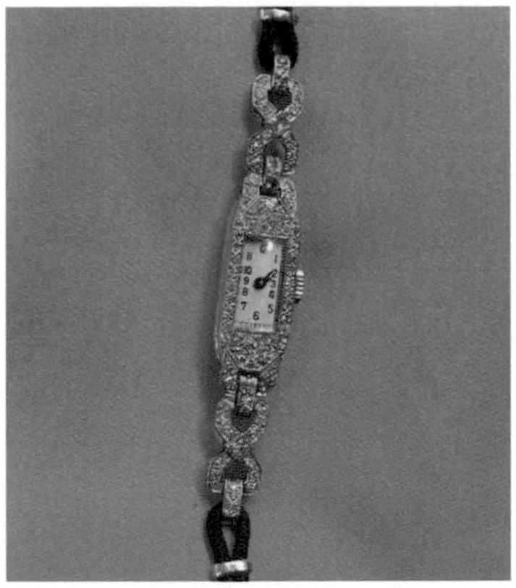

△ Lady's Dress Watch

- *circa 1930s*

Delicate lady's dress watch in platinum with diamonds on a silk strap. Swiss movement with an English case.

- *1.5cm x 1cm*
- £1,100 • Westminster

△ Benson Watch

- *1940s*

J.W. Benson lady's wristwatch set in 9ct gold with fancy lugs and white dial.

- *diameter 1.7cm*
- £250 • AM-PM

△ Chronograph

- *circa 1945*

Chronograph by Eberhard & Co, showing hour/minute registers.

- £3,500 • Anthony Green

▽ Military Pocket Watch

- *circa 1939*

A rare British military issue Rolex pocket watch. The dial signed 'Rolex A9172', has sub seconds and luminous numerals and hands. The nickel case signed inside 'Rolex', with ordinance marks 'A9172 G.S.M.K.II' on the back of the outside case and 'A9172' on the outside band.

- £975 • Anthony Green

▽ Vintage Lady's Watch

- *circa 1930s*

Lady's 18ct gold watch with leather strap. White porcelain dial with Roman numerals and a red number 12, with black cathedral hands. Swiss lever movement and a black leather bracelet.

- *width 3cm*
- £275 • Westminster

▽ Bulova Gold-Plated Wrist Watch

- *1940*

A gold-plated gentleman's wrist watch by Mercheaz Bulova, with a white dial and gold baton numerals.

- *3.5cm square*
- £150 • The Swan

△ Art Deco Watch

- *circa 1940*

A lady's curved heavy 18ct gold bracelet cocktail watch with an Art Deco design. Swiss movement.

- *width 2cm*
- £875 • Westminster

△ Longines Watch

- *1940*

Longines wristwatch set in stainless steel with 3, 6, 9 Arabic numerals. Screw back, for original waterproofing.

- *diameter 1.9cm*
- £340 • AM-PM

△ Omega Seamaster Wristwatch

- *1940s*

Gentleman's Omega Seamaster wristwatch set in stainless steel automatic movement, two-tone dial with gold digits.

- *diameter 2.9cm*
- £300 • AM-PM

▷ Swiss Chronograph

- *circa 1950*

A high grade Swiss-made sterling silver, hunting case 'Split Seconds' chronograph with subsidiary minute recording and sweep second dials. Case number 130519. The white enamel dial signed 'S.Smith & Son, 9 The Strand, London, Maker to the Admiralty, No. 142B 68, Non Magnetisable Swiss Made'.

- £2,950 • Anthony Green

△ Lady's Rolex Wristwatch

- *1940*

Lady's 18ct rose gold Rolex wristwatch with original expanding strap with the Rolex symbol on the buckle, square face with scalloped lugs. Gold digits on a white face.

- *diameter 2cm*
- £1,800 • AM-PM

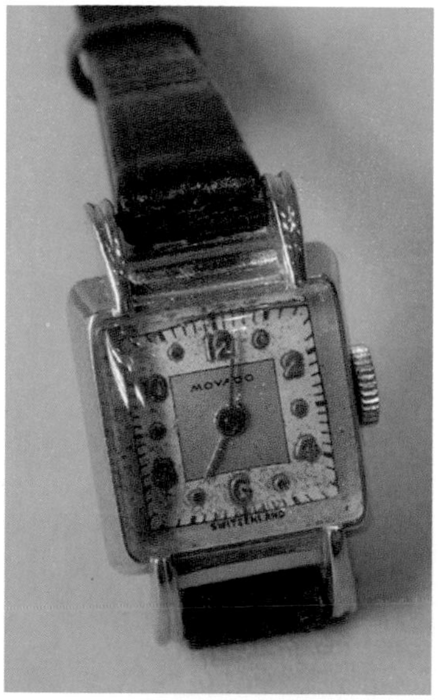

△ Lady's Movado Watch

- *1940s*

Lady's Movado Swiss-made 8ct rose gold wristwatch with a square face and two-tone dial with Arabic numerals.

- *diameter 1.9cm*
- £450 • AM-PM

△ Oyster Wrist Watch

- *1950s*

Gentleman's Rolex Oyster Royal watch set in stainless steel with a white mottled dial with 3, 6, 9 Arabic numerals, Mercedes hands and mechanical movement.

- *diameter 2.6cm*
- £800 • AM-PM

▽ Chronometer

- *circa 1945*

Gentleman's Chronometer wristwatch. The centre seconds dial signed Rolex Chronometer. Swiss-made.

- £3,650 • Anthony Green

▽ Oyster Speedking Watch

- *1950s*

Boy's size Rolex Oyster Speedking. Stainless steel mechanical movement with silver digits and expandable Rolex Oyster bracelet.

- *diameter 2.8cm*
- £950 • AM-PM

◁ Omega Lady's Watch

- *circa 1950*

18ct covered gold Omega lady's watch with a gold linked bracelet strap which, together with the lid, is encrusted with diamonds and Burma rubies.

- *diameter 3cm*
- £2,750 • Westminster

△ Lady's Cartier

• *circa 1950*
An 18ct gold and sapphire set bracelet watch with backwind movement.
• £9,500 • Somlo

△ Gentleman's Incaflex Wrist Watch

• *1950*
A gentleman's manual-wind Incaflex wrist watch by Wyler with gold batons and Arabic numerals.
• *3.2cm x 2.8cm*
• £140 • The Swan

△ Pilot's Wristwatch

• *circa 1951*
An RAF-issue, pilot's wristwatch with centre 'hacking' seconds hand and screw-back case with anti-magnetic inner case. Made by the International Watch Company with case, dial and movement signed and showing the Ministry of Defence arrow insignia. With factory guarantee.
• £2,850 • Anthony Green

▷ Rolex Oyster Perpetual

• *circa 1952*
18ct gold Rolex Perpetual wristwatch with moonphase calendar.
• £35,000 • Somlo

△ Omega Watch

• *1950s*
Swiss-made man's Omega 18ct gold mechanical movement watch with auxiliary sweep seconds and a gold dial with gold hands and gold digits.
• *diameter 3.1cm*
• £650 • AM-PM

△ Longines Cocktail Watch

• *circa 1960s*
A delicate Longines lady's platinum and diamond manual-wind cocktail watch, with a diamond-encrusted strap. Swiss movement with an English case.
• *diameter 1.5cm*
• £3,250 • Westminster

▽ 'Eiffel Tower'

• *circa 1953*
An 18ct gold, rectangular dialled Patek Philippe wristwatch with enamel and gold face and subsidiary seconds.
• £29,000 • Somlo

△ Jaeger Le Coultre Watch

• *circa 1960*
Jaeger Le Coultre Memovox (alarm) stainless steel wrist watch with silver digits on a silver face and automatic movement.
• *diameter 4cm*
• £1,500 • AM-PM

△ Oyster Submariner Diving Watch

• *circa 1964*
Oyster Perpetual Submariner automatic diver's wrist watch, on a Rolex steel 'flip-lock' bracelet.
• £2,950 • Anthony Green

▽ Gentleman's Rolex Watch

• *1960*
Gentleman's Rolex Oyster perpetual explorer wristwatch on a Rolex Oyster expandable bracelet.
• *diameter 3cm*
• £2,400 • AM-PM

▽ SpacemanWatch

• *circa 1970*
Swiss-made watch with stainless steel body and bracelet. Manual and water resistant.
• £220 • Themes

△ **Boxwood Quadrant**

- *18th century*

English boxwood quadrant incorporating 5 star positions.

- *height 12.5cm*
- **£6,500** • **T. Phillips**

△ **Japanned Barometer**

- *circa 1720*

A rare black japanned stick barometer in the manner of Isaac Robelou, London.

- *height 93.5cm*
- **£9,000** • **Norman Adams**

▽ **Telescope**

- *18th century*

Single-draw two-inch diameter telescope, signed by Spencer Browning & Reist of London. A large telescope for use in the field, it has a substantial tripod of a later date.

- *height 1.75m*
- **£879** • **Ocean Leisure**

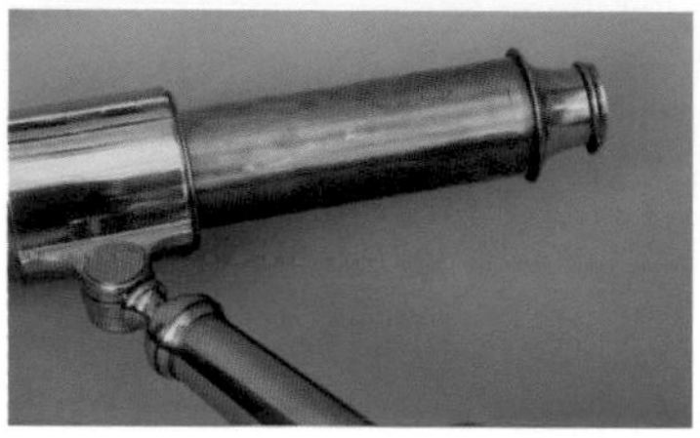

▽ **Terrestrial Telescope**

- *circa 1790*

Reflecting terrestrial telescope. Interchangeable eye pieces on tripod base and fitted mahogany box. By Dudley Adams.

- *length 71cm*
- **£6,000** • **Talbot**

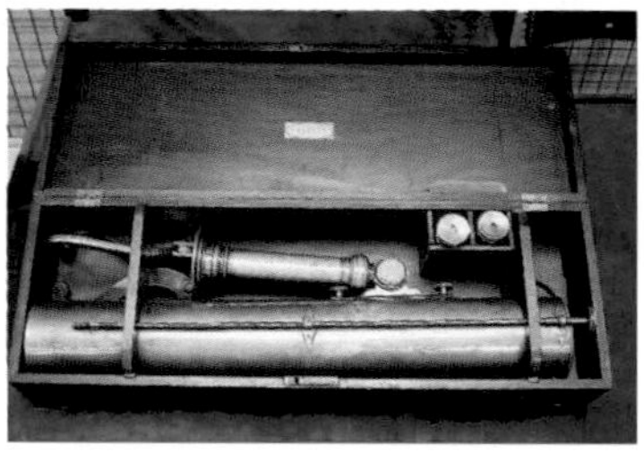

▽ **Sand Glasses**

- *mid-17th century–early 19th century*

One of a group of 3 sand glasses. Made from glass, brass and wood, each glass has a different time duration and would have been employed for marine, business, legal and ecclesiastical uses.

- *height 27cm*
- **£3,000** • **T. Phillips**

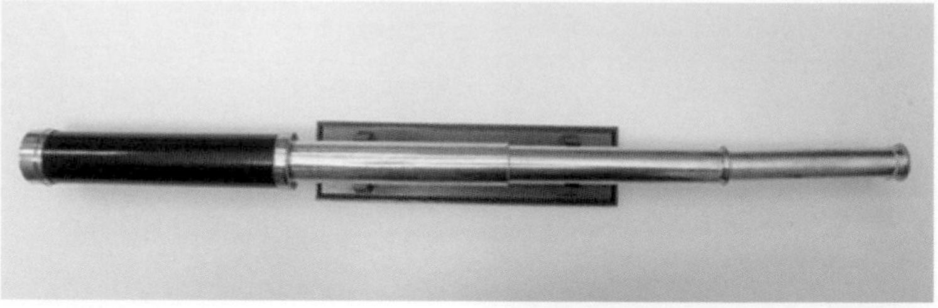

△ **Three-Draw Telescope**

- *1750–1817*

A three-draw telescope signed 'Dolland, London' on the first draw. Polished and lacquered brass with mahogany barrel, lens slide, crisp optics.

- *73cm x 5cm*
- **£329** • **Langfords Marine**

△ **Wheel Barometer**

- *circa 1760*

A rare early George III mahogany wheel barometer in a case of clock form.

- *height 1.13m*
- **£60,000** • **Norman Adams**

▷ **Horizontal Brass Sundial**

- *circa 1780*

Brass sundial with octagonal base engraved with hororary table. Gnomon with filigree decoration.

- *length 18cm*
- **£380** • **Talbot**

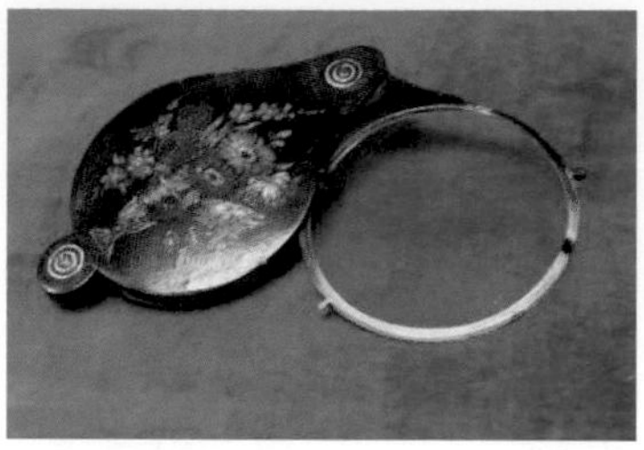

△ **Reading Glass**

- *circa 1760*

Glass with hand-painted horn cover, floral arrangement to front with putti and books on reverse.

- *length 12cm*
- **£450** • **Talbot**

△ **Aquatic Microscope**

- *circa 1780*

An Ellis design, botanist's aquatic microscope. In brass, with original sharkskin fitted box.

- *height 16.5cm*
- **£750** • **Talbot**

▽ Stick Barometer

- *circa 1790*

A George III mahogany stick barometer, by William Watkins, St James's Street, London.

- *height 1.08m*
- £6,000 • **Norman Adams**

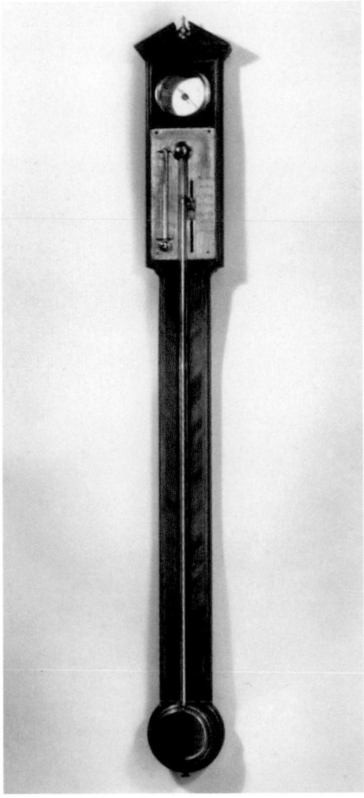

▽ Miniature Microscope

- *mid-19th century*

An exceptionally fine mid-19th century miniature microscope by Ross. Incorporating a highly unusual device for a mechanical stage and further unusual procedures for focusing the instrument and has a hand-held simple microscope and other accessories.

- *height 20cm*
- £4,750 • **T. Phillips**

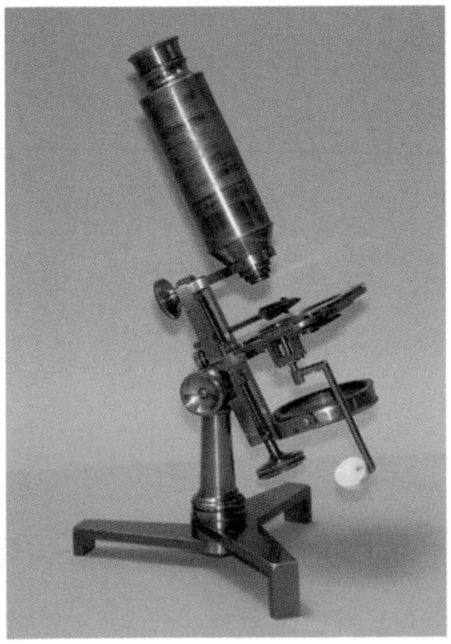

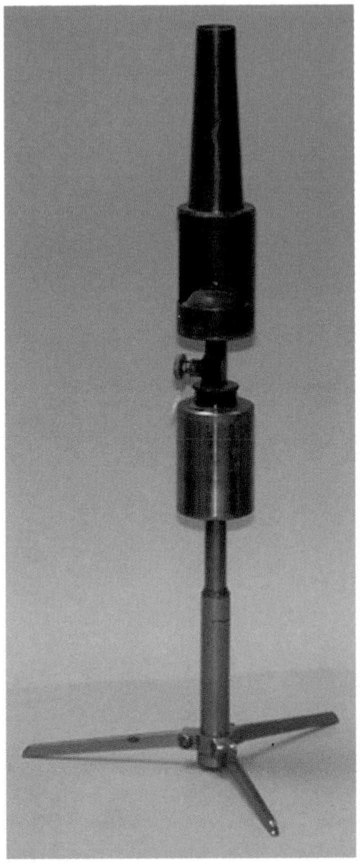

△ Portable Microscope

- *19th century*

Portable microscope illuminating lamp. Housed in its original black japanned tin travelling box.

- *height 33cm*
- £1,400 • **T. Phillips**

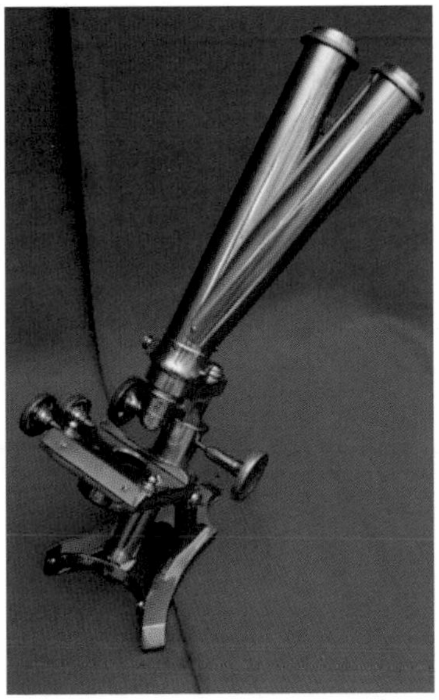

△ Decorative Microscope

- *Victorian*

A polished lacquered brass binocular microscope which is purely decorative.

- *36cm x 15cm*
- £79 • **Langfords Marine**

▽ Library Telescope

- *early 19th century*

Single-draw, 6cm diameter, polished and lacquered brass library telescope. Signed around the eyepiece and end of the barrel "I. Bradford & Sons 136 Minories, London". The long body tube with rack-and-pinion focusing and lens cap, the whole mounted on a turned column with three folding cabriole legs. Original fitted mahogany box with trade label inside the lid.

- *80cm x 46cm*
- £1,795 • **Langfords Marine**

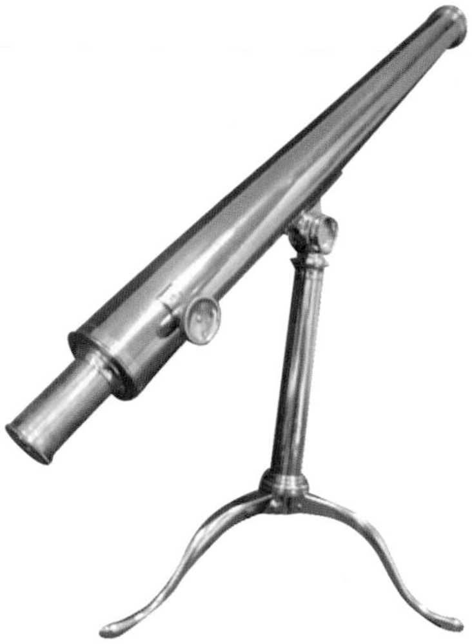

▷ Microscope Oil Lamp

- *circa 19th century*

Microscope illuminating oil lamp incorporating an adjustable bullseye condenser. By R & J Beck of London and retailed by Walmsley of Philadelphia, sole American agents.

- *height 32cm*
- £1,500 • **T. Phillips**

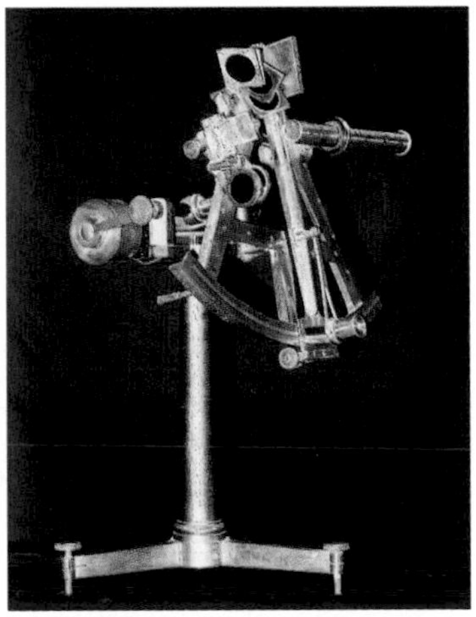

△ Explorer's Sextant

- *circa 1800*

Gimballed explorer's sextant on stand, by Cary of London.

- *height 49cm*
- £4,000 • **Talbot**

△ French Barograph

- *19th century*

A French barograph in unusual moulded glazed brass case on turned feet. With centigrade thermometer and retailer's ivory plate, marked 'S. Block, Strasbourg and Mulhouse'. Overhauled and guaranteed.

- *height 24cm*
- £1,600 • **Clock Clinic**

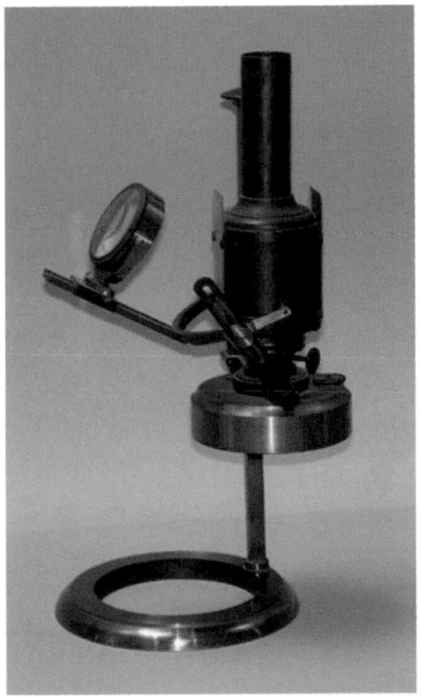

▽ Hour Glass

- *mid-19th century*

Turned mahogany framed hour glass of hand-blown glass.

- *height 18cm*
- £750 • **Talbot**

▽ Cuff-Type Microscope

- *19th century*

Fine and very rare miniature microscope by Cuff. In its original mahogany box, which doubles as a stand for the microscope. The accessories include fish plate, ivory slides, a series of objectives, live stage and nose cone.

- *height 22cm*
- £6,000 • T. Phillips

▽ Pocket Globe

- *circa 1834*

Fine 3-inch pocket globe by Newton Son & Berry, 66 Chancery Lane, London. Housed in its original simulated fish-skin case. The interior with celestial gores for the northern and southern celestial poles.

- *height 7.5cm*
- £6,500 • T. Phillips

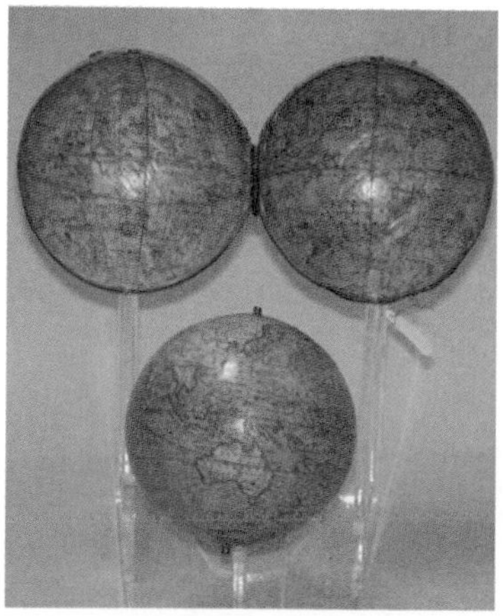

▷ Portable Microscope

- *1830*

Portable microscope by Carpenter, 24, Regent Street, London, housed in its original mahogany box.

- *height 32cm*
- £1,500 • T. Phillips

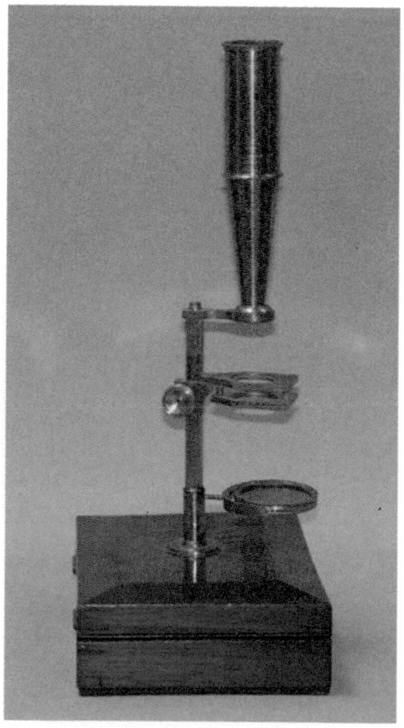

△ Miniature Telescope

- *circa 1820*

One-inch miniature reflecting telescope – probably Scottish – with brass body on tripod base.

- *diameter 3cm*
- £1,500 • Talbot

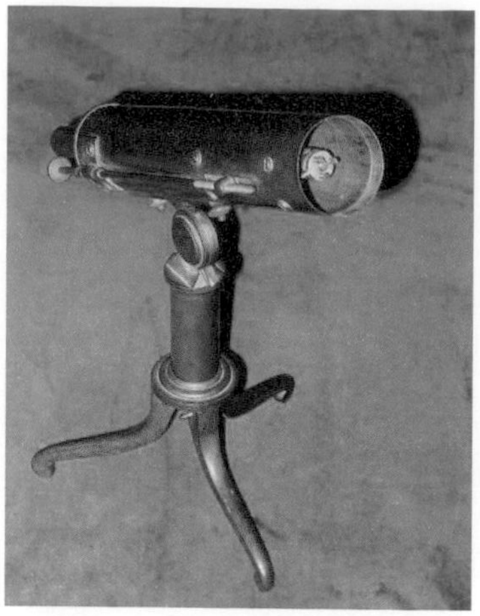

△ Mariner's Compass

- *1860*

Drum, gimble-mounted, mariner's compass with wind-rose and degree scale.

- *diameter 7.5cm*
- £1,500 • T. Phillips

▽ Specimen Cabinet

- *circa 1830*

A William IV specimen cabinet, in mahogany, with gadrooned decoration, the whole on claw feet. Has two locking doors to front and one on each side, protecting six slide drawers to the front and test-tube holders at the sides.

- *height 41cm*
- £1,250 • Gerald Mathias

▽ Oscillating Engine

- *1850*

A vertical two-column oscillating engine on vertical pot boiler with safety valve. Built by Newton & Co, London.

- *height 22cm*
- £1,150 • Langfords Marine

▷ Monocular Microscope

- *1850*

Fine binocular and monocular microscope by Ross of London. No 336 in its original brassbound box with numerous accessories.

- *height 50cm*
- £6,500 • T. Phillips

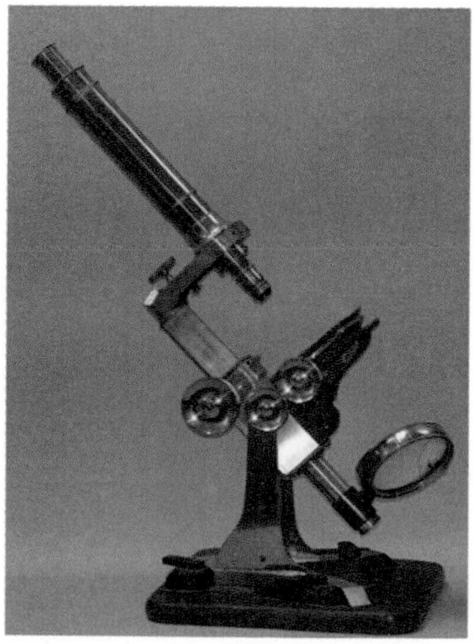

△ Equinoctical Instrument

- *circa 1830*

Newman & Co Calcutta compass with Roman numeral dial.

- *diameter 14cm*
- £1,605 • H. & H.

△ Six-Draw Telescope

- *1854*

Miniature travelling 6-draw telescope signed: Baker, 244 High Holborn, London. Housed in its original leather case with extra eye-piece and folding stand.

- *height 9cm*
- £1,550 • T. Phillips

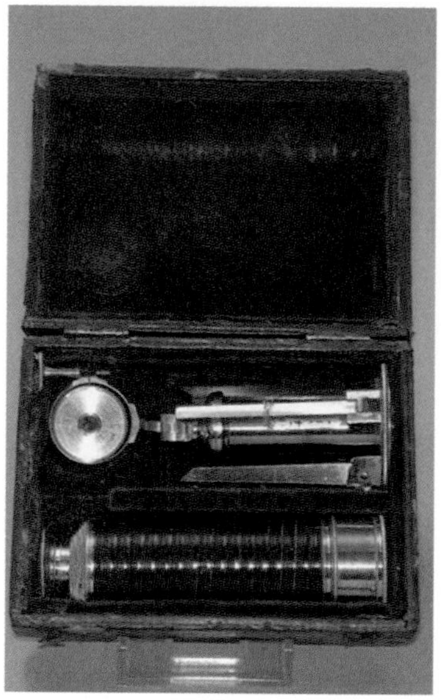

▽ Victorian Steam Crane Engine

- *1860*

A Victorian steam crane engine, Stevens model.

- *height 12cm*
- £600 • Langfords Marine

▽ Deviatometer

- *circa 1880*

Ship's deviatometer by Mugnes, London. Fully gimballed and weighted in mahogany box.

- £650 • H. & H.

▽ Table Telescope

- *circa 1880*

Brass table telescope by W. Ladd, Chancery Lane, London, in original wood box.

- *96cm x 41cm*
- £2,900 • Langfords Marine

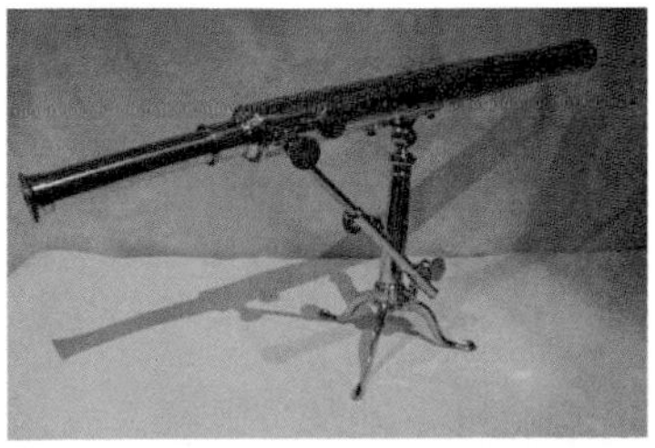

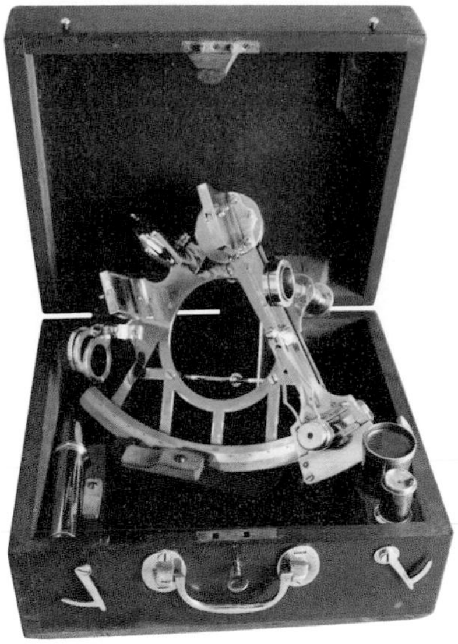

△ Sextant

- *19th century*

Brass sextant in good condition with original brass and mahogany compartmentalised case, with all filters and lenses.

- *height 25cm*
- £680 • H. & H.

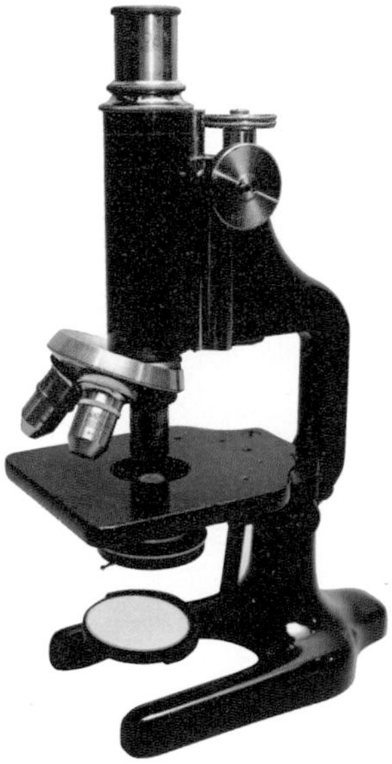

△ Zeiss Microscope

- *circa 1910*

A brass and steel Zeiss monocular microscope with lenses of three different magnifications on a steel rotating nosepiece.

- *height 28cm*
- £250 • Finchley

▷ Rolling Rule

- *circa 1940*

An English polished and lacquered brass parallel rolling rule with original box.

- *length 45cm*
- £79 • Ocean Leisure

▽ Military Marching Compass

- *early 20th century*

A World War I hand-held prismatic military marching compass, in original anodised brass case. Dry card with mother-of-pearl dial, glass port, brass thumb ring, rotating brass bezel with clamp and two-way stopping mechanisms. Government issue, denoted by the chevron.

- *6cm x 9cm*
- £169 • Langfords Marine

▽ French Barometer

- *1880*

French holosteric barometer with leather case.

- *diameter 8cm*
- £320 • Langfords Marine

△ French Armillary Sphere

- *late 19th century*

French armillary sphere signed on the enamel charter ring Grivolat Horloger, Paris. The dial is constructed of steel and brass.

- *height 61cm*
- £5,750 • T. Phillips

△ Pocket Barometer

- *circa 1900*

A brass pocket aneroid barometer with silvered dial. The barometer is contained in its original hinged leather case. Compensated.

- *diameter 6.5cm*
- £160 • H. & H.

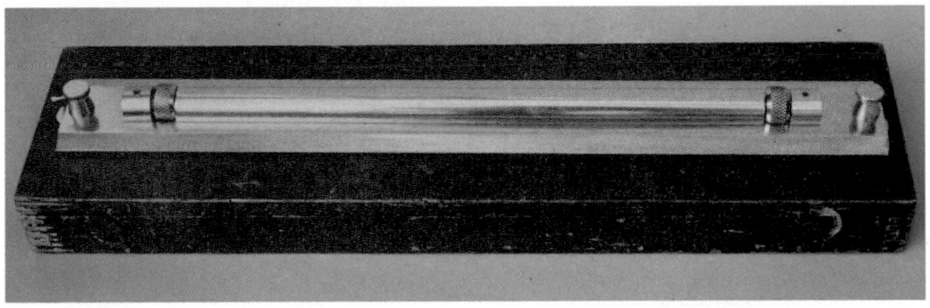

COINS & MEDALS

Since the dawn of time man has been involved with war and a collector's market has sprung up from the paraphernalia associated with conflict and order. Medals are probably the most popular collecting area of all militaria, and the more documentation available to denote provenance, for example, title, rank, and regiment, the more valuable the medal becomes. The two main types of medals are Campaign and those awarded for Bravery in Action, such as the Distinguished Conduct Medal, first issued after the Crimean War. Most cherished of all is the Victoria Cross, always highly priced, although the value depends on the action and the deed. The Napoleonic wars are a popular period for collectors, along with medals from the Crimean War, Indian Mutiny and other Victorian wars. Medals from the Boer War are plentiful and popular. Coins, from their earliest beginnings, around 1000 BC, and up to the present day, bestow history on us in a way that is both fascinating and accurate.

▽ George II Crown

- *1743*

Rare example of George II crown with fine enamels representing England, Scotland and Ireland.

- £400 • James Vanstone

◁ Gold Sovereign Coin

- *1553*

Queen Mary fine sovereign coin of thirty shillings. With Queen enthroned and Tudor Rose on reverse.

- *diameter 44mm*
- £5,000 • Malcolm Bord

△ Gold Guinea Coin

- *1794*

A gold George III guinea coin. This issue is known as the 'Spade Guinea'.

- *diameter 19mm*
- £200 • Malcolm Bord

▷ Prize Medal

- *1760*

Silver Wilhelmus de Wykeham medal from Winchester School.

- *diameter 33mm*
- £100 • Malcolm Bord

△ Copper Medal

- *1799*

A copper William Pitt the Younger medal by Hancock, struck at a time when Pitt was enjoying great popularity due to victories over Napoleon in Egypt, notably the Battle of the Nile.

- *diameter 52mm*
- £40 • Malcolm Bord

▽ George III Coin

- *1798*

A silver George III emergency-issue dollar coin, minted during the War of Independence, with oval countermark.

- *diameter 39mm*
- £600 • Malcolm Bord

▽ Edward VII Florin

- *1902*

Edward VII florin. A scarce example in enamel, centred with Britannia.

- £150 • James Vanstone

▷ Garter Breast Star

- *circa 1810*

A fine Georgian Order of the Garter breast star. An articulated example, with facet-cut silver, gold and enamel.

- £15,000 • The Armoury

△ George IV Shilling

- *1826*

A George IV shilling. Unusual because both sides are enamelled.

- £250 • James Vanstone

△ Victoria Crown

- *1845*

1845 crown with the head of the young Queen Victoria, centred with enamel bearing the Royal Standard.

- £100 • James Vanstone

△ Half-Sovereign Coin

- *1817*

A gold King George III half-sovereign coin.

- *diameter 19mm*
- £250 • Malcolm Bord

▽ Grand Master Jewel

- *1850*

A jewel of the Grand Master's Masonic Lodge, with a face with rays of light radiating behind, within an enamel blue circle.

- £50 • James Vanstone

▽ Naval General Service Medal

- *1847*

A Naval General Service Medal, 1847, with clasps 'Martinique' and 'Guadeloupe'. Awarded to Private Robert Lock of the Royal Marines.

- £1,000 • Chelsea (OMRS)

◁ Belt Buckle

- *1880*

A Victorian Royal Military College belt buckle in brass and silver.

- £1,880 • Chelsea (OMRS)

▽ Military General Service Medal

- *1848*

A Military General Service medal, 1848, with four clasps. Awarded to James Knowles, 5th Foot, Northumberland Fusiliers.

- £850 • Chelsea (OMRS)

▷ Crimea War Medal

- *1854–56*

A Crimea war medal from 1854, with three clasps, 'Alma' 'Inkermann' and 'Sebastopol'. Awarded to G. Bartlett of the 63rd Regiment.

- £350 • Chelsea (OMRS)

△ Naval General Service Medal

- *1861*

General Service medal, with Algiers bar, awarded to Midshipman F.H. Le Mesurier.

- £825 • Gordon's

△ White-Metal Medal

- *1852*

A white-metal medal by Allen & Moore, commemorating the death of the Duke of Wellington.

- *diameter 50mm*
- £30 • Malcolm Bord

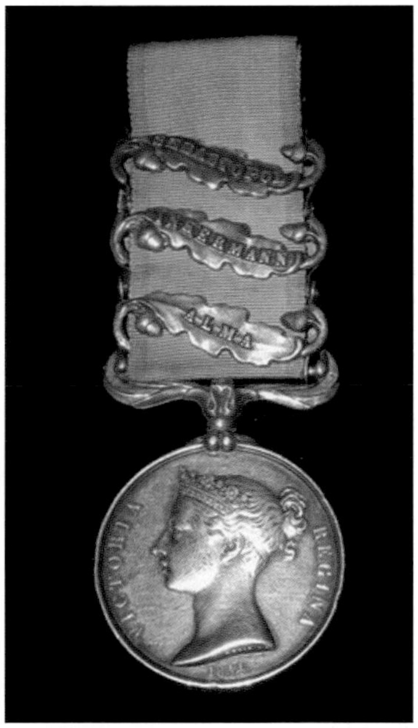

▽ Khedive's Star

- *circa 1890*

Khedive's star dated 1882. Unnamed as issued.

- *diameter 4cm*
- £55 • Gordon's

▷ Regimental Brooches

• *19th–20th century*

A selection of brooches representing regiments of the British Army, the Royal Navy and the Royal Air Force, in gold, enamel and diamonds.

• £200–2,000 • The Armoury

△ Boer War Medal

• *1893–1902*

A Boer War Queen's South Africa medal with seven clasps. Awarded to 2688 Private G. Francis of the Welsh Regiment.

• £325 • Chelsea (OMRS)

△ DSO Miniature Medal Group

• *1895–1902*

An unattributable contemporary group of three miniatures comprising: Distinguished Service Order, VR Gold Type, Delhi Durbar medal 1902, and India General Service medal with 3 clasps, Punjab Frontier 1897–98, Samana 1897, Tirah 1897–98. Medals mounted for wear with attachment pin by Spink & Son, London.

• *diameter 6cm*

• £145 • Gordon's

▽ South African Medal

• *1899–1902*

QSA (Queen's South African) Medal from the Boer War, with bars for Orange Free State and Transvaal. Showing Queen Victoria and Britannia on reverse.

• £65 • Gordon's

▽ Order of the Indian Empire

• *1900*

Order of the Indian Empire Cie breast badge in case of award.

• £450 • Chelsea (OMRS)

▽ Rose Cross

• *1900*

15ct-gold exceptionally rare Rose Cross with coloured jewel and a swan within degrees and dividers surmounted by a hinged crown with seven stars.

• £350 • James Vanstone

▽ Russian Order of St Stanislaus

• *1900*

A Russian order of St Stanislaus, civil type 4th class. 18ct gold.

• £275 • Chelsea(OMRS)

▽ 100-Franc Coin

• *1904*

Gold Monaco 100-franc coin. Showing the head of Prince Albert I of Monaco.

• *diameter 34mm*

• £250 • Malcolm Bord

△ Five-Pound Coin

• *1902*

A very rare gold Edward VII five-pound coin.

• *diameter 35mm*

• £700 • Malcolm Bord

△ India General Service Medal

• *1908*

1908 India General Service medal with clasp, 'North West Frontier'. Awarded to 65 Barghir Daroska of the 51st Camel Corps.

• £60 • Chelsea (OMRS)

△ Good Conduct Medal

• *1909*

Volunteer Long Service Good Conduct medal with Edward VII bust, awarded to: 1538 Sgt I. Harrison. 2nd V.B. Notts & Derby R. With *Daily Mail* Empire Day rifle competition. Silver award medal, named to recipient, dated 1909.

• *diameter 4cm*

• £65 • C.F. Seidler

▽ War Service Cross

• *1912*
War Service Cross of Imperial Austria. Gold with enamelling and official mint maker's mark. Hallmarked 1912.
• *diameter 3cm*
• £280 • C.F. Seidler

▽ Royal Air Force Brooches

• *circa 1918*
Pair of Royal Air Force sweetheart brooches made from 15ct gold, with original box.
• £200 • James Vanstone

▽ Imperial Iron Cross

• *1914*
A World War I Imperial Iron Cross, Second Class with crown, 'W' mark, dated and with Friedrich Wilhelm crest.
• £20 • Gordon's

△ Military Cross

• *1914–19*
Military Cross, GVR, unofficially named on reverse: A. Melville Kennedy. 8th BN. Royal Scots Fusiliers June 1917.
• *diameter 4cm*
• £395 • Gordon's

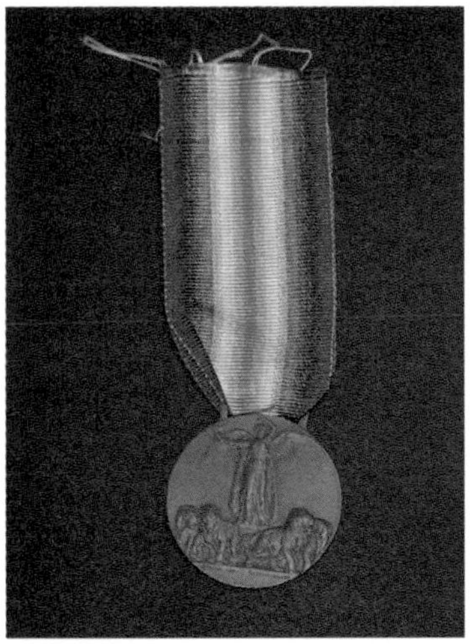

△ Inter-Allied Victory Medal

• *1914–19*
Inter-allied Victory medal for the Great War, this is the Italian version, with maker's mark: 'Sacchimi – Milano'.
• *diameter 4cm*
• £14 • Gordon's

▽ Medal Group

• *1914–18*
A medal group consisting of the NBE, the Military Cross, 1914 Star Trio, Defence medal, War medal and Special Constabulary medal. Awarded to Lieutenant Colonel T.L. Wall of the Fifth Lancers.
• £1,550 • Chelsea (OMRS)

▽ Miniature Medals

• *1918*
Ten KCMG, CB(Gold) miniatures attributed to Major General Sir Andrew Mitchell Stuart. Royal Engineers.
• £385 • Chelsea (OMRS)

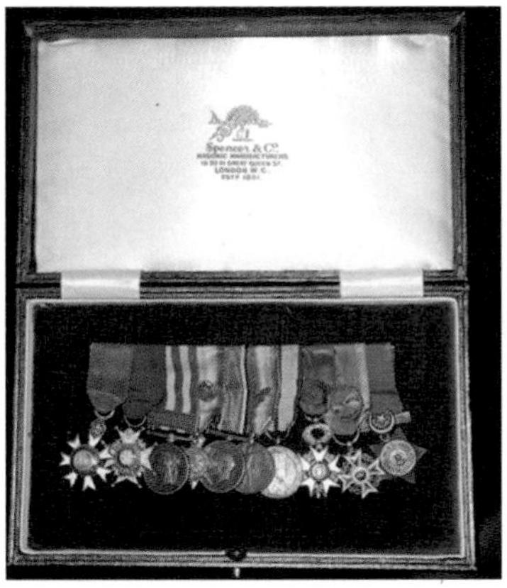

◁ World War I Medal Group

• *World War I and later*
Five medals, consisting of 1914–1915 Star Trio, 1935 Jubilee medal and RAF Long Service Good Conduct medal. Awarded to Corporal L. Thornton RAF.
• £250 • Chelsea (OMRS)

▷ Anna-Luisen Order

• *1918*
Medal commemorating the Anna-Luisen (Schwarzburg-Rudelstadt).
• *diameter 3cm*
• £395 • C.F. Seidler

△ Great War Medal

• *1911–37*
A distinguished service order (George V) in Garrard & Co, in case of award.
• £450 • Chelsea (OMRS)

◁ Military Cross

• *1918*
In original case of issue and inscribed on reverse '2nd Lieut. S.G. Williams 1st Battalion, Devonshire Regiment'.
• £325 • Gordon's

△ Russian Medal

• *1915*
Imperial Russian Cross of St George IV class.
• £45 • Chelsea (OMRS)

▽ German Imperial Group

• *1900–18*

Iron Cross 2nd Cl., 1914; Prussia, German Service Cross 1900–1918; Officer's Long Service Cross for 25 yrs; Friedrich Wilhelm 3rd Civil Service medal, 2nd Cl., 1847–1918, in silver; Army Lower Ranks Long Service medal for 15 yrs; Wilhelm 1st Centenary medal 1897; Braunschweig: Military Service Cross 2nd Cl., 1914–1918 and Service Cross 1st Cl., in gold. All mounted court style for wear.

• *diameter 18.5cm*

• £475 • Gordon's

▽ Masonic Collar Jewel

• *1920*

30th degree Masonic collar jewel with hinged crown above a double-headed phoenix clutching a double-edged sword.

• £60 • James Vanstone

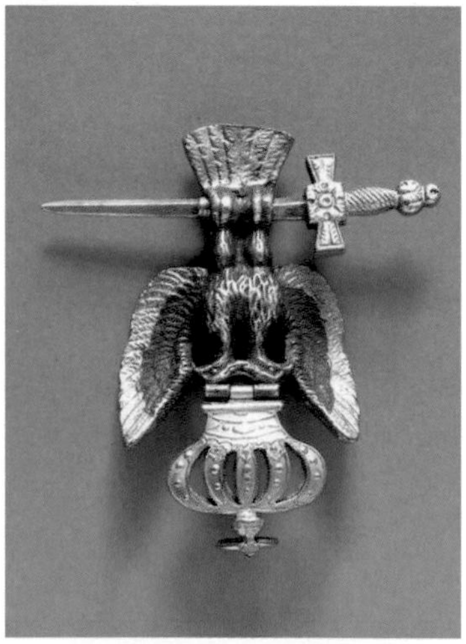

△ Cap Badge

• *1914–18*

Royal Sussex Regiment silver and enamel officer's cap badge.

• £100 • Chelsea (OMRS)

△ Iron Cross

• *1914*

An Iron Cross 2nd Class, awarded to a German soldier at the beginning of World War I.

• £20 • Chelsea (OMRS)

▽ Naval Service Medal

• *1914–19*

Naval Distinguished Service medal with GVR bust, as awarded to: A8654. J. Corkoran. Sea. R.N.R. Mediterranean Service, 23 March, 1918. This award was mentioned in the *London Gazette* on 7.8.1918, and was approved for services in action with enemy submarines.

• *diameter 4cm*

• £395 • Gordon's

▽ Officer's Cap Badge

• *1914*

Irish Guards Officer's silver and enamel Great War cap badge. Attributed to Captain M. Gore-Langton MC.

• £195 • Chelsea (OMRS)

▷ Masonic Jewel

• *1930*

St John's Lodge whole Masonic jewel. This hallmarked jewel bears a good quality enamel of St John the Martyr.

• £70 • James Vanstone

◁ Medal Group

• *1914–45*

WWI and WWII group of eight medals to Master at Arms P. McArthur 'H.M.S. Tamar'.

• £225 • Chelsea (OMRS)

△ Cap Badge

• *1914–18*

Leicestershire Regiment Other Ranks cap badge.

• £10 • Chelsea (OMRS)

△ WWI Military Medal

• *1914–18*

A Great War Military medal for gallantry. Awarded to Private L. Goldthorpe, 10th Battalion, Worcester Regiment. Killed in action 13/07/17.

• £225 • Chelsea (OMRS)

△ Luftwaffe Retired Pilot's Badge

- *1935–45*

Luftwaffe retired pilot's badge with maker's mark: C.E. Junker Berlin SW66.

- *diameter 4cm*
- **£925** • **Gordon's**

△ Purple Heart Award

- *1932–present*

Purple Heart medal of the Vietnam period. This is awarded for gallantry, the wounded or those killed in action in the service of the military forces of the United States of America.

- *diameter 4cm*
- **£24** • **Gordon's**

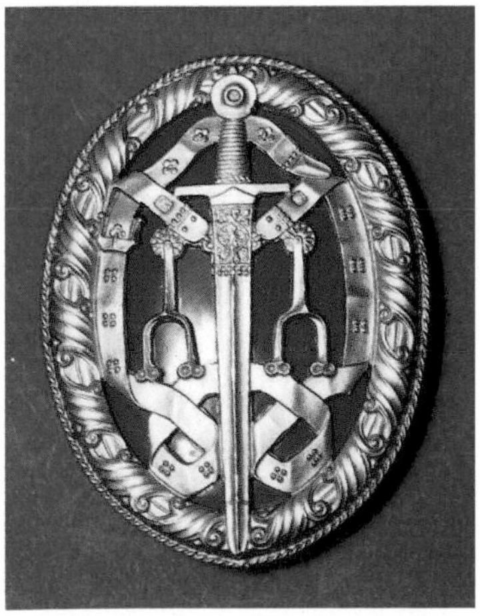

△ Commemorative Coin

- *1935*

A gold coin commemorating the Silver Jubilee of King George V. The coin shows the King and Queen Mary with Windsor Castle on reverse.

- *diameter 31mm*
- **£250** • **Malcolm Bord**

△ German Pilot's Badge

- *1940*

WWII German air force pilot's badge in silver by Bruder Schneider, Vienna.

- **£350** • **Chelsea (OMRS)**

◁ Breast Badge

- *1933*

Knights Bachelor breast badge, silver gilt with red enamel background. From the Royal Mint with original box. Sword shown between two spurs.

- **£220** • **Gordon's**

△ Soviet Military Medal

- *1945*

World War II USSR Order of the Red Banner Military medal awarded for valour to members of the Soviet army.

- **£30** • **Chelsea (OMRS)**

◁ DFC Medal

- *1943*

Distinguished George VI Flying Cross, reverse dated 1943, in case of award.

- **£450** • **Chelsea (OMRS)**

▽ RAF Flying Medal

- *1939–45*

World War II RAF distinguished flying medal. For gallantry. Awarded to Sgt. G. Jones.

- **£950** • **Chelsea (OMRS)**

◁ Military Medal

- *1962 onwards*

Campaign Service medal with three clasps awarded to Bombardier A.J. Williams of 2/9 Commando Royal Artillery.

- **£125** • **Chelsea (OMRS)**

▽ Iron Cross

- *1939*

A Second World War German Iron Cross Second Class, awarded for bravery and/or leadership. Ring stamped with swastika and with red and white ribbon.

- **£38** • **Gordon's**

COLLECTOR'S ITEMS

Elvis and Hendrix may be dead and the Beatles disbanded, but they're all still making record sales. Whether it's instruments, records, concert posters or autographs – even a rocker's underwear – memorabilia of these and other pop musicians is shooting up in value. Internet sites have sprung up to trade on signed photographs of celebrities, but watch out, as not all of these are genuine. Cinema posters are also steadily rising in value, from 'Breakfast at Tiffany's' to 'Goldfinger', and all have a place in the collector's market. The pioneer of French poster advertising was Jules Cheret, and, like Henri de Toulouse-Lautrec, he transformed the Parisian boulevards into an enormous art gallery. Poster enthusiasts would emerge at night to sponge off new creations from the hoardings! Keep a space in your collection for photographs, as some are proving to be a highly lucrative investment, no longer being seen as a mass-produced image, but as art.

ADVERTISING & PACKAGING

▷ **Toothpaste Lid**

- *circa 1900*

A Woods Areca Nut toothpaste lid by W. Woods, Plymouth.

- £20 • Magpies

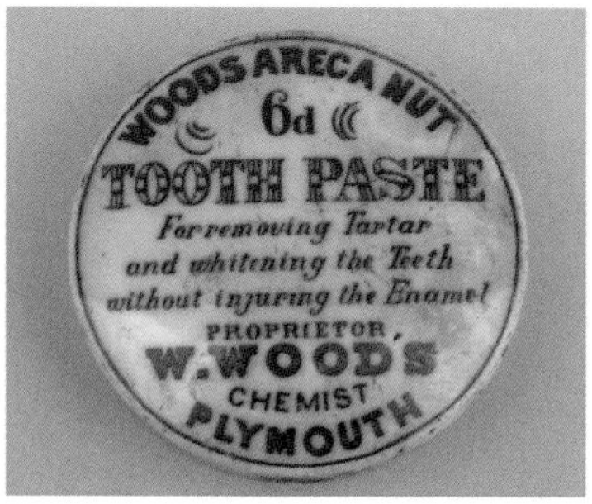

△ **Biscuit Tin**

- *circa 1910*

A biscuit tin in the shape of a book, made by Hoffman Suisse.

- *height 36cm*
- £90 • Huxtable's

▽ **Collecting Box**

- *1914*

Alexandra Day collecting box.

- *height 13cm*
- £16 • Michael Laws

▷ **McVitie Biscuit Box**

- *circa 1910*

A 'Billie Bird' biscuit box made by McVitie.

- *height 32cm*
- £120 • Huxtable's

▽ **Gray Dunn's Biscuits**

- *1915*

Yellow-ochre bus with red roof and wheels with figures looking out of the window and a bus conductor. With the letters 'Gray Dunn's Biscuits' in red and 'Lands End to John o' Groats'.

- *height 9.5cm*
- £1,500 • Huxtable's

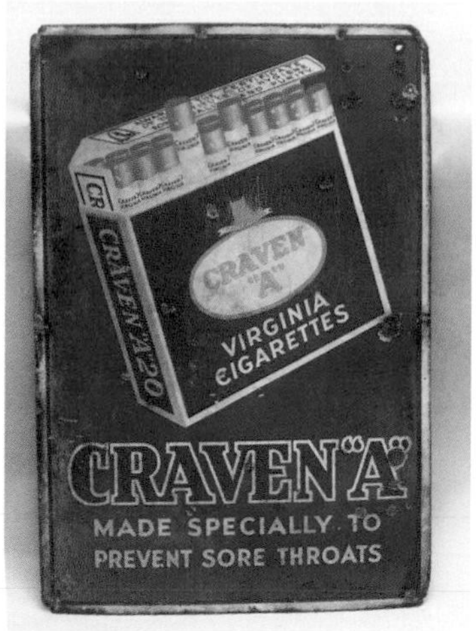

△ Cigarette Sign

- *circa 1920*

A Craven 'A' advertising sign in blue, white and red, including one of advertising's great lies.

- *height 92cm*
- £28 • **Magpies**

△ Queen of Hearts Box

- *circa 1920*

A sweet box from *Alice in Wonderland* in the shape of Tenniel's Queen of Hearts.

- *height 20cm*
- £75 • **Huxtable's**

△ Orlox Beef Suet

- *circa 1930*

Cardboard box of Orlox Beef Suet with the picture of a red bull. In excellent condition.

- *height 9cm*
- £5 • **Michael Laws**

▽ Cocoa Tin

- *circa 1920*

A Dutch cocoa tin from Bensdorp's Cocoa, Amsterdam.

- *height 9cm*
- £20 • **Huxtable's**

▽ Thorne's Creme Toffee

- *1924*

Royal-blue tin with gold scrolling and the words, 'Thorne's Extra Super Creme Toffee and British Empire Exhibition Souvenir'.

- *height 5.5.cm*
- £30 • **Huxtable's**

▽ Toffee Tin

- *1930*

A 'Felix the Cat' toffee tin. With Felix the cat on one side and a cartoon of Felix on the other side.

- *16cm x 16cm x 10cm*
- £500 • **Huxtable's**

△ Wills's Star Cigarettes

- *circa 1920*

An enamelled point-of-sale sign in brown and orange.

- *height 28cm*
- £42 • **Magpies**

△ Huntley and Palmers Biscuits

- *1927*

A British toy tank containing Huntley & Palmers biscuits.

- *height 9.5cm*
- £800 • **Huxtable's**

▽ Boat Biscuit Box

- *circa 1935*

A French biscuit box in the shape of the ill-fated liner, *Normandie*.

- *length 62cm*
- £350 • **Huxtable's**

△ Ink Bottle

- *1930s*

A bottle of blue black Swan ink.

- *height 8cm*
- £6 • **Huxtable's**

▽ Lyons Pure Ground Coffee

- *1930*

Green tin of Lyons pure ground coffee.

- *height 10.5cm*
- £17 • **Huxtable's**

△ Bonzo the Dog Jug

- *1930*

A water jug in the shape of Bonzo the Dog.

- *height 13cm*
- £250 • **Huxtable's**

△ Manufacturer's Sign

- *1930s*

A sign cut from hardwood of the figure of John Bull, advertising John Bull Tyres.

- *height 65cm*
- £120 • **Huxtable's**

△ Volga Caviar

- *1930*

Turquoise tin of Caviar Volga Malossol from Russia.

- *diameter 10.5cm*
- £28 • **Huxtable's**

▽ Saturday Night Lotion

- *1930*

Saturday Night Lotion in a clear glass bottle decorated with a man in a top hat and a lady in evening dress.

- *height 14cm*
- £15 • **Huxtable's**

▽ Ideal Home Cleanser

- *1930*

Unopened cardboard packet of soap with a metal lid and a picture of a house and garden. Inscribed in dark blue and bordered in white with the words 'Ideal Home Cleanser' and below in yellow 'contains Pure Palm & Olive Oil Soap.'

- *height 25cm*
- £44 • **Huxtable's**

▽ Jester Towel Soap

- *1930*

Orange and red box of Jester towel soap with a picture of a jester and the words 'for economy and cleanliness' printed on the side.

- *length 15.5.cm*
- £15 • **Huxtable's**

△ Robin Starch

- *1930*

Box of Robin Starch, which can also be used as a dry shampoo. Decorated with green and white stripes and a robin on a branch with a yellow sunburst background. Inscribed 'Robin The New Starch', on the lid and 'Nursery & Dusting Powder'.

- *height 9cm*
- £14 • **Huxtable's**

△ Castle Polish

- *1930*

Red tin of Castle Ballroom floor polish with a picture of a castle.

- *height 11cm*
- £13 • **Huxtable's**

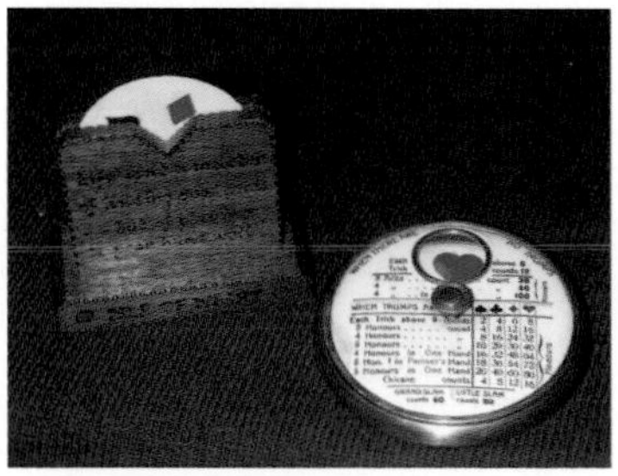

△ Trumps Markers

- *1930s*

Two trumps markers for use in card games.

- £20 • **Huxtable's**

▽ Mustard Tins

- *1930s*

An assortment of Colman's mustard tins. Decorated with red writing and the Union Jack on a yellow background.

- *height 12cm*
- £7 • **Huxtable's**

▽ William Lawson's Figure

- *1930*

Figure of a boxer in fighting pose, with brown hair and moustache, blue eyes, red breeches, a gold sash and black boots, standing on a yellow ochre and black base with the inscription 'William Lawson's Rare Scotch Whisky'.

- *height 36cm*
- £160 • **Huxtable's**

▽ Aero Chocolate

- *circa 1930*

Unused bar of Aero chocolate by Rowntrees in a brown wrapper with cream writing.

- *width 11cm*
- £20 • **Huxtable's**

△ Sam's Own Tobacco

- *1930*

Yellow-ochre tin with a brown Labrador and black writing stating 'Sam's Own mixture blended from the finest Virginia and Oriental Tobaccos' by Samuel Gawith and Co. Ltd., Kendal, est 1792.

- *width 11cm*
- £19 • Huxtable's

△ Lifebuoy Soap

- *1938*

Lifebuoy soap in a red box showing a lifeguard throwing a life-ring with a cartoon bubble above with the words 'More than a good soap – a good habit!' written on it.

- *height 15.5cm*
- £18 • Huxtable's

△ Johnnie Walker

- *1940*

Striding jovial figure of a gentleman in a gold top hat with a brown bow, red jacket with tails, cream breeches, black boots with gold trim and tassels, carrying a black cane and standing on a dark green base with 'Johnnie Walker' in gold writing.

- *height 37cm*
- £120 • Huxtable's

▽ Ipso Washing Powder

- *circa 1930*

Red cardboard box with the inscription 'The Wonder Worker IPSO washes by itself' displayed on a sheet and basket.

- *height 13cm*
- £10 • Michael Laws

▽ Palmolive Soap

- *1930*

Unused Palmolive soap in green paper wrapping with a black band and the word 'Palmolive' in yellow.

- *length 8cm*
- £5 • Huxtable's

▽ Oxo Cubes

- *circa 1930*

Metal tin with red and black geometric design with the inscription 'Oxo Cubes' in cream writing on the top of the lid.

- *width 10cm*
- £12 • Michael Laws

△ Chillexine for the Udder

- *circa 1930*

Bell & Sons in white writing with 'Chillexine' in yellow writing on a brown background and 'For the Udder' in white writing with a picture of a cow's udder.

- *height 20.5cm*
- £26 • Huxtable's

△ V.D. Matches

- *circa 1940*

An assortment of V.D. matches from World War II.

- *5cm x 3cm*
- £5 • Huxtable's

△ Reeves Colour Box

- *circa 1940*

Light and dark blue cardboard box with the inscription 'Reeves Students Colour Box', decorated with a seated dalmatian.

- *width 20cm*
- £20 • Michael Laws

▽ Sandwich Tin

- *1930*

French yellow sandwich tin with a red handle and trim, and Mickey Mouse offering Pluto some sweets on the lid.

- *8cm x 18cm*
- £150 • Huxtable's

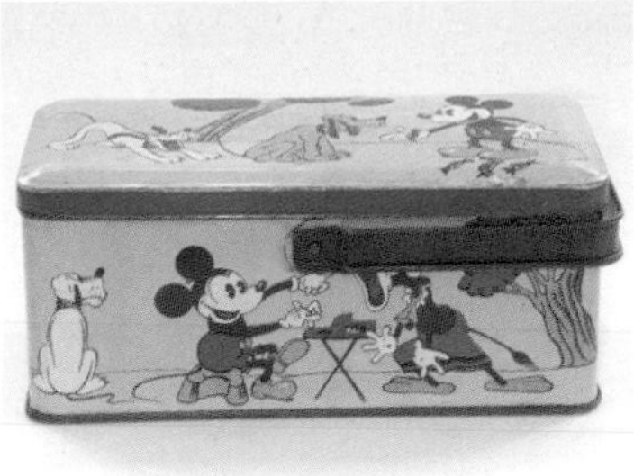

▽ Chipso Soap Flakes

- *circa 1930*

White cardboard box for Chipso soap flakes with a blue and yellow design and inscribed with the words, 'Fine for fine things'.

- *height 15cm*
- £10 • Michael Laws

▽ Michelin Ashtray

- *1940s*

A premium give-away Bakelite ashtray with a seated figure in the form of the Michelin Man.

- *height 18cm*
- £150 • Decodence

▽ Shop Sign

- *1940s*

A wrought-iron shop sign, with scrolled decoration surrounding a clover-leaf emblem with the hand-painted letters 'Sunshine Bakery'. In original condition.

- *102cm x 65cm*
- £220 • Old School

▽ Bournvita Mug

- *1950s*

A white Bournvita mug in the shape of a face with a blue nightcap and a red pom-pom. With large handle.

- *height 14cm*
- £40 • Huxtable's

▽ Guinness Print

- *circa 1950*

Showing a pint glass and smiling face with the famous slogan: 'Guinness Is Good For You'.

- *78cm x 50cm*
- £14 • Magpies

△ Horlicks Mug

- *circa 1940*

A white porcelain Horlicks mug with blue lettering with solid handle.

- *height 11cm*
- £18 • After Noah

△ Salt Cellar

- *circa 1950*

A Sifta glass salt cellar with a bakelite top.

- *height 9cm*
- £4.50 • Magpies

△ Evening in Paris Hair Cream

- *1940*

Evening in Paris hair cream by Bourjois, in a dark-blue glass bottle with dark-blue writing on a pale-blue background.

- *height 15cm*
- £13 • Huxtable's

▽ Peter's Ideal Chocolate

- *1950*

Peter's ideal milk chocolate shop dummy in a brown wrapper with gold writing.

- *width 11cm*
- £15 • Huxtable's

▽ Talcum Powder

- *circa 1950*

A 'Jolly Baby' talcum powder container, with voluptuous cover.

- *height 15cm*
- £40 • Huxtable's

▽ Packet of Condoms

- *1950s*

An assortment of 1950s condoms.

- *16cm x 5cm (packet)*
- £10 • Huxtable's

▷ Pottery Figure

- *1950*

A painted pottery figure of a shoemaker holding a shoe, advertising Phillips Soles and Heels.

- *height 30cm*
- £200 • Huxtable's

△ Dried Eggs U.S.A.

- *circa 1940*

Gold tin inscribed with the words 'Pure dried whole Eggs U.S.A. 5 Ounces net weight equal to 12 eggs' in black writing.

- *height 11cm*
- £16 • Huxtable's

△ Ketchup Bottle

- *1950s*

A bottle of 'Kraft' ketchup.

- *height 19cm*
- £15 • Huxtable's

▽ Sanitary Products

• *1950s*
An assortment of female sanitary towel and tampon boxes.
• *8cm x 4cm (packet)*
• £5 • **Huxtable's**

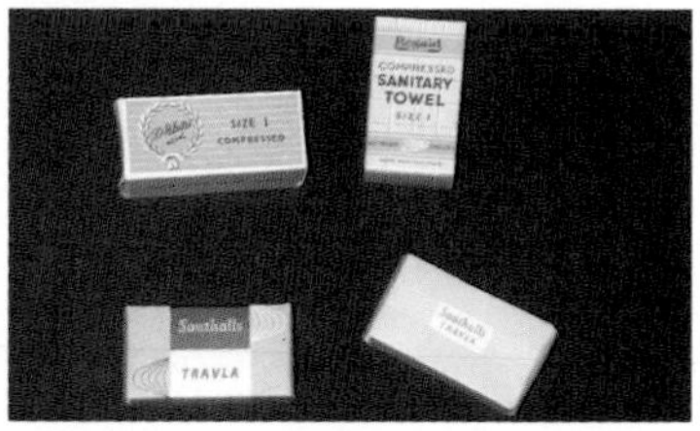

▽ Camay Soap

• *1950*
Unused Camay soap with a turquoise and yellow wrapper showing a cartouche of a lady and inscribed in black 'Camay the soap of beautiful women'.
• *length 8cm*
• £6 • **Huxtable's**

▽ Dog Food Sign

• *1950*
A Spratt's wooden sign advertising dog food with the picture of a Highland terrier in the form of the word 'Spratts'.
• *50cm x 80cm*
• £100 • **Huxtable's**

▷ Pearce Duff's Custard Powder

• *1950*
Tin of Pearce Duff's custard powder with a picture of a bowl of custard and pineapple, plums and pears on each side.
• *height 11.5cm*
• £13 • **Huxtable's**

△ Horlicks Mixer

• *circa 1950*
A Horlicks promotional glass jug with a metal mixer.
• *height 15cm*
• £10 • **Magpies**

△ Tide Washing Powder

• *1950*
Yellow packet of Tide with orange circles and the words 'Tide' and 'Gives clothes a whiteness bonus' in dark blue.
• *height 17cm*
• £19 • **Huxtable's**

▽ Persil Soap Powder

• *1950*
Persil in a green box with a red circle the words 'Persil washes whiter Yes it does!' in white.
• *height 18cm*
• £15 • **Huxtable's**

▽ Tape Measure

• *circa 1950*
A promotional tape measure with the inscription, 'With compliments of A.H. Manning'. Includes original box.
• *10cm x 9cm*
• £14 • **After Noah**

▽ Guinness Toucan

• *1955*
A toucan with a glass of Guinness on a stand advertising the beer with the slogan 'My goodness – my Guinness'.
• *height 7cm*
• £250 • **Huxtable's**

△ Ty-Phoo Tea

• *circa 1950–1960*
Ty-Phoo Tea in a red box with white writing and the words 'Ty-Phoo Tea' in white, surrounded with a foliate wreath and 'Authorised 1/9 price'.
• *height 12.5cm*
• £7 • **Huxtable's**

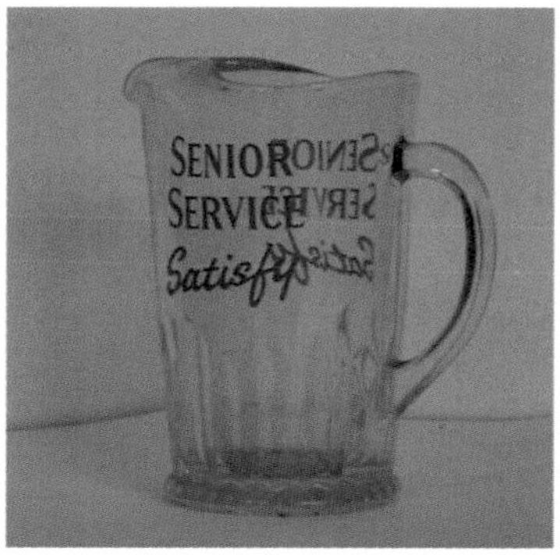

△ Glass Jug

• *1950*
Glass water jug inscribed in blue with the words 'Senior Service Satisfy'.
• *height 21cm*
• £15 • **Michael Laws**

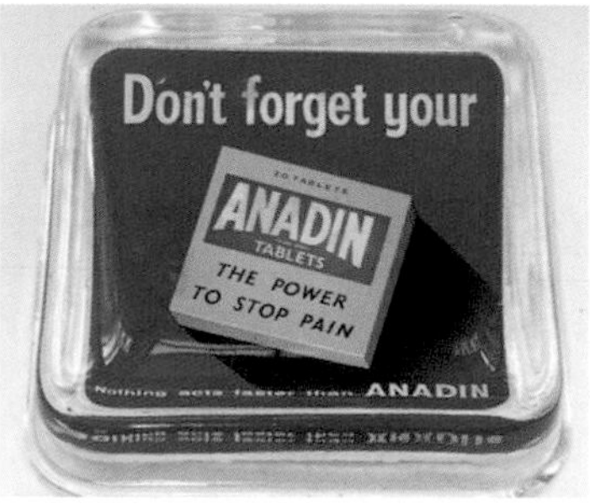

△ Ashtray

• *1955*
Ashtray with 'Don't forget your Anadin' in white writing on a red background and decorated with a two-tone green Anadin packet.
• *15cm square*
• £12 • **Huxtable's**

△ Cue Hair Dressing

- *1955*

Glass bottle of Cue Hair dressing, a Colgate Product.

- *height 14cm*
- £10 • **Huxtable's**

△ Walter's Palm Toffee Tin

- *1950*

'Walter's Palm Toffee' tin with a lady in a red and white striped bikini with matching sunshade, towel and holding a bottle of orange juice on the beach.

- *24cm x 24cm*
- £25 • **Alfie's Antique Market**

△ Battery Advertisement

- *circa 1960*

An Oldham Batteries metal advertising sign, incorporating the 'I told 'em – Oldham' slogan.

- *height 37cm*
- £28 • **Magpies**

▽ Guinness Tray

- *circa 1950*

A circular metal drinks tray advertising glasses of Guinness.

- £50 • **Huxtable's**

▽ Guinness Mug

- *1955*

Large plastic mug of Guinness inscribed on black with white writing 'Guinness is good for you'.

- *height 32cm*
- £120 • **Huxtable's**

▽ Lux Soap Flakes

- *circa 1960*

An unopened box of Lever Brothers' Lux soap flakes.

- *height 28cm*
- £10 • **Huxtable's**

△ Guinness Tray

- *circa 1950*

A metal drinks tray with a toucan holding the advertisement for Guinness.

- *diameter 16cm*
- £50 • **Huxtable's**

△ Oxydol

- *1950*

Yellow box of Oxydol with dark-blue circles and the words 'Oxydol' in white with a white star.

- *height 13.5cm*
- £11 • **Huxtable's**

△ Kay-Tee

- *1958*

Plastic bottle of Kay-Tee golden washing-up liquid by Kearley and Tonge Ltd, London.

- *height 20cm*
- £9 • **Huxtable's**

▽ Everyman's Hair Cream

- *1950*

Everyman's brilliantine hair cream in a glass bottle with a pink rose beneath the words, 'Kenrosa, Made in England'.

- *height 13cm*
- £12 • **Huxtable's**

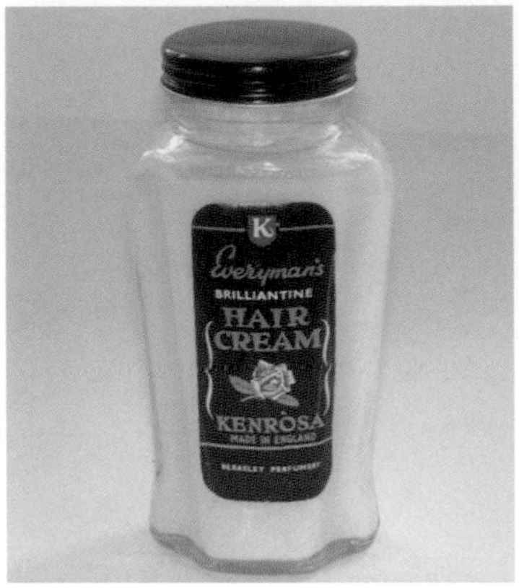

▽ Bisto Tin

- *1960*

Tin of Bisto with a girl with a green hat and a boy with a red hat, both sniffing the aroma from a gravy boat.

- *height 19cm*
- £14 • **Huxtable's**

▽ Rinso Box

- *1950*

Green box of Rinso showing a clothes line with two dresses and sheets blowing in the wind.

- *height 14.5cm*
- £12 • **Huxtable's**

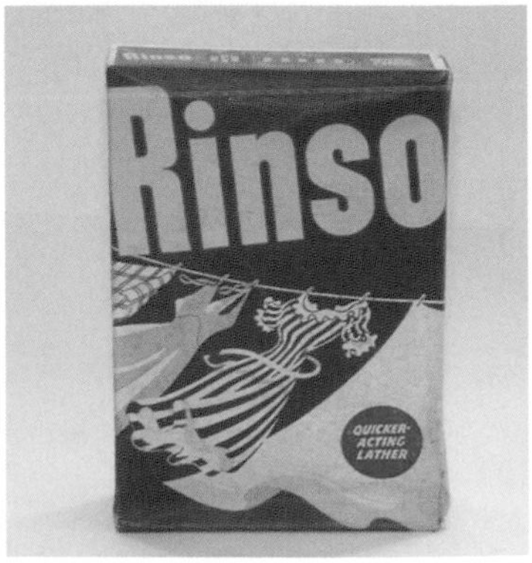

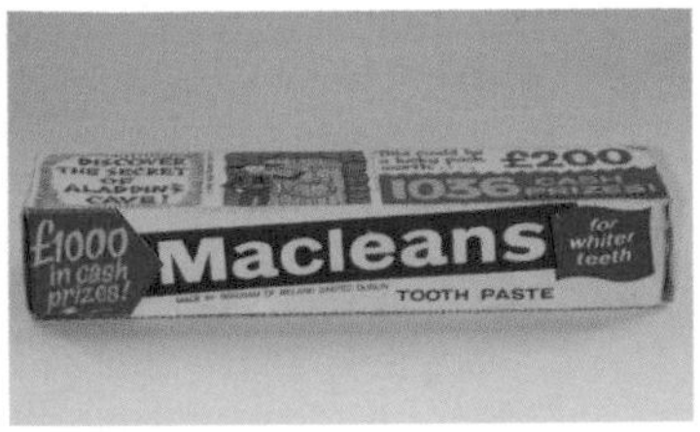

△ Macleans Toothpaste

- *1960*

Macleans toothpaste in a white box with a dark blue line, by Beecham of Ireland Limited, Dublin.

- *width 19cm*
- £8 • Huxtable's

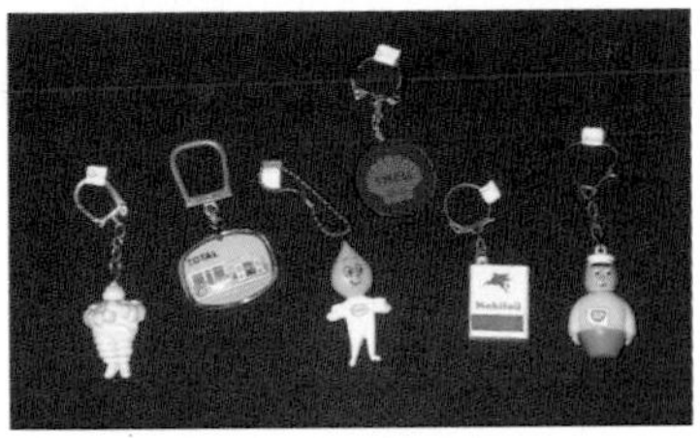

△ Motoring Key Rings

- *1960s*

Assortment of motoring key rings.

- £10 • Huxtable's

△ Cure-C-Cure

- *1960*

Yellow tin of tube repair outfit with a red car and the words 'Cure-C-Cure by Romac', made in England.

- *length 13cm*
- £12 • Huxtable's

△ Oxo Sign

- *20th century*

A red metal double-sided sign advertising Oxo cubes.

- *35cm x 35cm*
- £60 • Huxtable's

▽ BP Anti-Frost

- *1962*

Green oil can with BP in yellow writing on a green shield with the words 'Anti–Frost' in red on a white background.

- *height 14cm*
- £20 • Huxtable's

▽ Black & White Scotch Whisky

- *1960*

Burleigh Ware white pottery jug, made in Great Britain, with two small terrier dogs, one black and one white, and the words 'Black & White Scotch Whisky Buchanan's', decorated on the side with the Royal Crest.

- *height 12cm*
- £30 • Huxtable's

▽ Babycham Glass

- *circa 1960*

Babycham promotional champagne glass.

- *height 12cm*
- £14 • After Noah

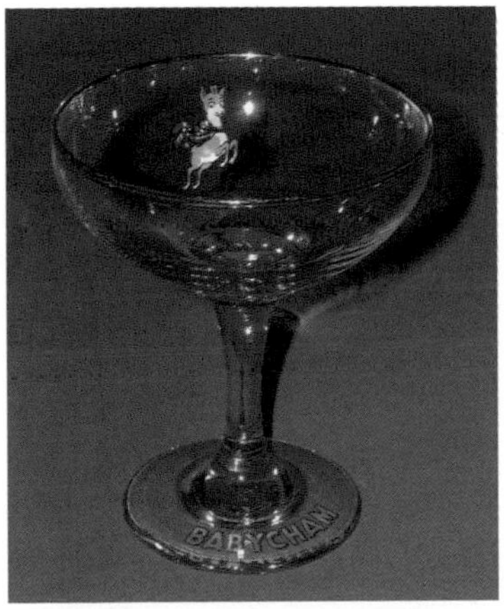

△ My Fair Lady Talc

- *1960*

Cusson's My Fair Lady talc showing a photograph of a blonde-haired lady.

- *height 14cm*
- £14 • Huxtable's

△ Brasso

- *1960*

With 'Brasso' written in white letters on a red ground with a blue and white striped sun design in the background.

- *height 13cm*
- £7 • Huxtable's

△ Michelin Man

- *1966*

A bakelite Michelin Man used for advertising in petrol stations and shops.

- *height 150cm*
- £85 • Huxtable's

▽ Lollipop Man

- *1960s*

A porcelain figure of a Robertson's Golly Lollipop Man.

- *height 12cm*
- £12 • Huxtable's

▽ Rennies Indigestion Tablets

- *1960*

Yellow box of Rennies Indigestion tablets containing 24 boxes, inscribed with the words, 'Just the right size for pocket or handbag'.

- *width 9cm*
- £16 • Huxtable's

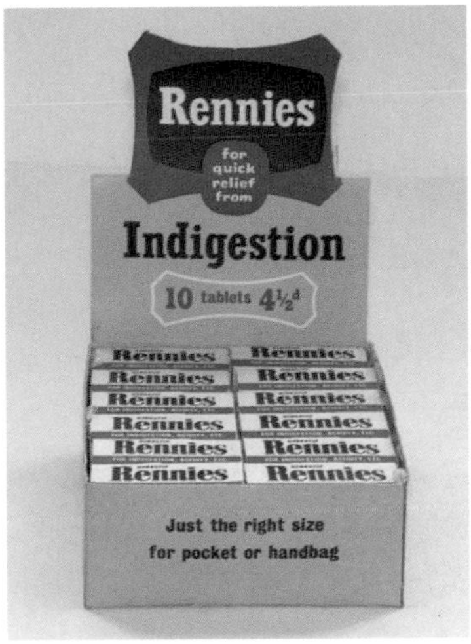

▽ Carton of Cigarettes

- *1960s*

A carton of Senior Service cigarettes. In original white paper wrapping with navy-blue lettering, unopened.

- *13cm x 5cm*
- £40 • Huxtable's

AERONAUTICA

▽ Promotional Magazine

- *circa 1917*

Whitehead aircraft company promotional magazine. In good condition with black and white and colour prints.

- *19cm x 12cm*
- £30 • **Cobwebs**

▽ Spanish Airline Leaflet

- *circa 1922*

In good condition, but with a folding crease down the centre.

- *15.5cm x 12cm*
- £25 • **Cobwebs**

▽ Brooklands Flying Club

- *circa 1920*

A Brooklands trophy, in pressed steel with an alloy finish.

- *height 11.5cm*
- £1,500 • **C.A.R.S.**

△ Aero Club Badge

- *circa 1920*

Brooklands club badge in pressed steel with coloured enamels.The club was established in the 1920s.

- *height 10cm*
- £600 • **C.A.R.S.**

△ Aircraft Propellor

- *circa 1920*

A four-bladed wooden coarse-pitched, wind-generator propellor, in mahogany with lamination and holes in the centre intact.

- *length 61cm*
- £165 • **Cobwebs**

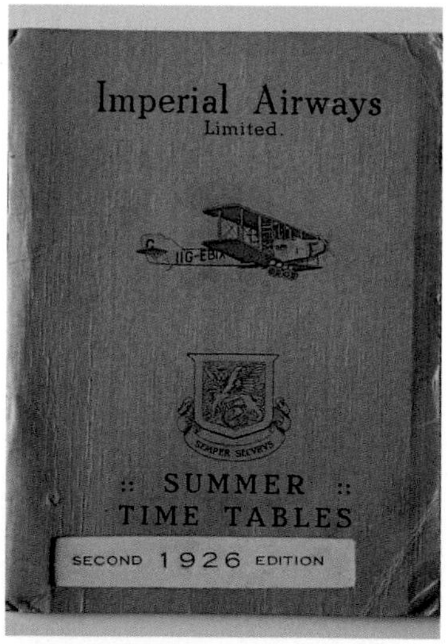

△ Aircraft Timetable

- *1926*

An Imperial Airways Ltd summer timetable, second edition, in good condition.

- *15cm x 11cm*
- £40 • **Cobwebs**

△ Aerial Time Table

- *1927*

'International Aerial Time Table' in good condition and in colour print, with a fascinating cover picture of unlikely flyers.

- *21.5cm x 14cm*
- £50 • **Cobwebs**

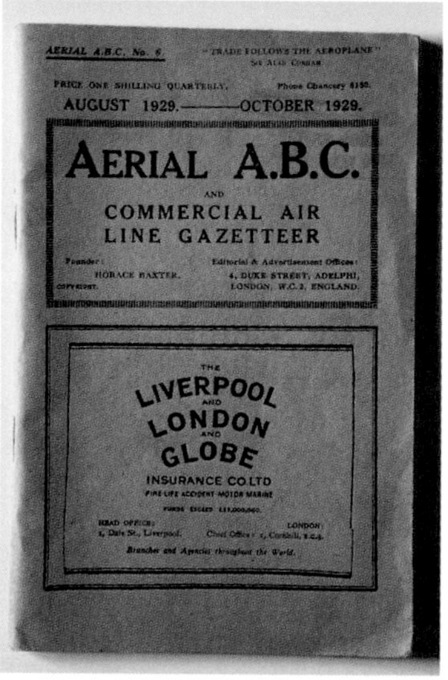

△ Aerial ABC Gazetteer

- *August 1929*

Light-brown in colour with black and white print. In mint condition.

- *22cm x 14.5cm*
- £40 • **Cobwebs**

▽ Souvenir Programme

- *1930*

Illustrated souvenir programme from the British Hospitals' Air Pageant, 1930. In good condition.

- *21.5cm x 14cm*
- £40 • **Cobwebs**

▽ Route Map

- *circa 1930*

Imperial Airways route map from Southampton to Alexandria.

- *22cm x 14cm*
- £50 • **Cobwebs**

◁ German Flying Boat

- *circa 1929*

A black and white photograph of the six-engined German Dorrier Dox flying boat, off Calshot Spit, in Southampton Water.

- *21.5cm x 15cm*
- £15–20 • **Cobwebs**

△ Qantas Empire Airways

- *circa 1930*

A Qantas flying-boat map of the Sydney to Singapore route. Good condition.

- *length 24.5cm, width 12cm*
- £50 • **Cobwebs**

△ Model Airplane

- *circa 1940*

Chrome model, twin-engined unidentified American plane.

- *height 10cm*
- £65 • **Cobwebs**

▽ Route Map

- *circa 1937*

Empire flying-boat route map from England to Egypt. Mint condition.

- *21.5cm x 12.5cm*
- £30 • **Cobwebs**

▽ Model Kit

- *circa 1940*

'Robot Bomb' balsa-wood model of a jet-propelled bomb used against England by the Germans in France during World War II.

- £10 • **Cobwebs**

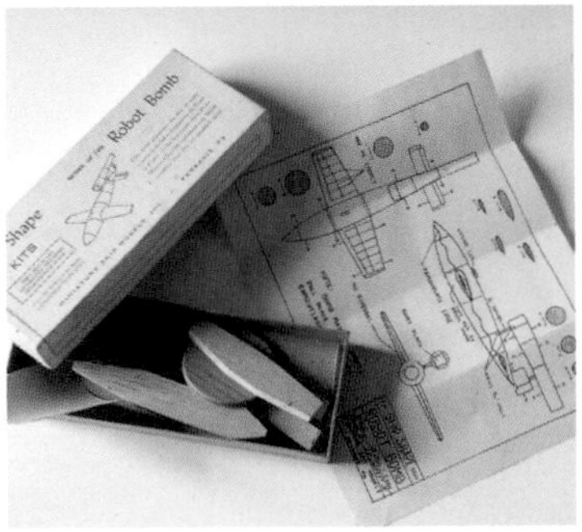

▷ Pan-Am Ticket

- *1949*

Pan-American Clipper ticket, sponsored by the Bulova watch company, in half green and half white with black and white print.

- *diameter 11cm*
- £20 • **Cobwebs**

◁ Four Cannon Shells

- *circa 1942*

Four fighter-plane cannon shells, converted into a desk pen-holder and mounted on oak and brass. The result of a dogfight between British and German fighter planes.

- *15cm x 15cm*
- £45 • **Cobwebs**

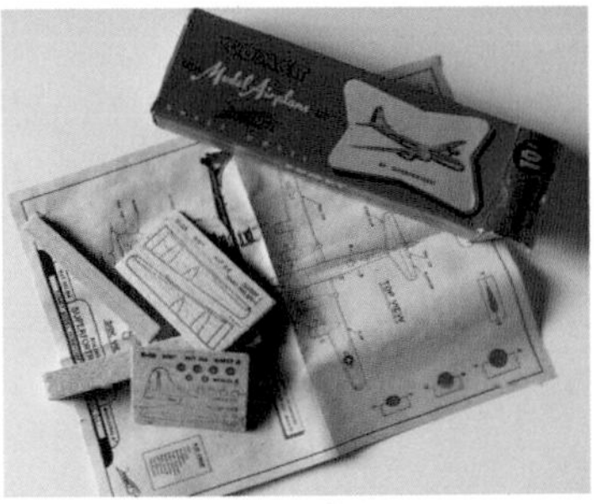

△ Comet Model Plane

- *circa 1940*

A balsa-wood model kit of the B-4 Superfortress. Made by the Comet model factory, Chicago, Illinois. In mint condition.

- £10 • **Cobwebs**

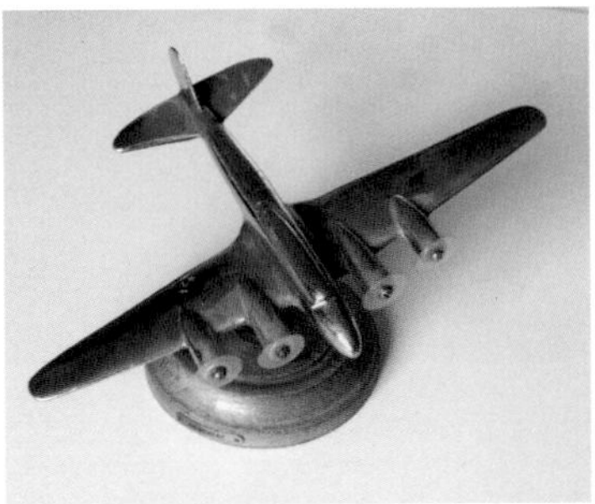

△ Brass Model Plane

- *circa 1940*

Chrome-plated brass model of a four-engined plane set on a beechwood base with brass plate.

- *height 10cm*
- £70 • **Cobwebs**

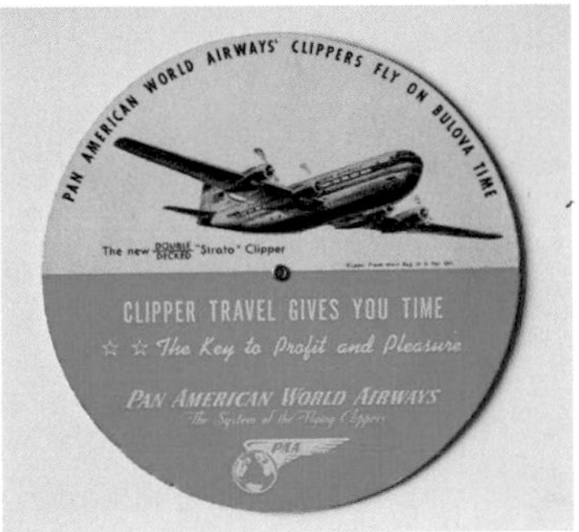

▽ Concorde Postal Cover

- *circa 1978*

Commemorating the first flight from London to New York, with colour print showing an early Concorde in blue sky.

- *19cm x 11.5cm*
- £15 • **Cobwebs**

▽ Model Messerschmitt

- *circa 1940*

Hand-made model of a Messerschmitt ME110 fighter plane on perspex and beaten-steel base, with Nazi insignia modelled into base of stem.

- *wingspan 31.5cm*
- £350 • **Sean Arnold**

▽ Aviation Safety Award

- *circa 1959*

An American 'Aviation Safety Award' with brass engraving set in a plaque of beechwood.

- *16cm x 13cm*
- £25–30 • **Cobwebs**

▽ Fighter Plane Model

- *circa 1980*

Model of a battle-camouflaged Tornado fighter plane. On a steel frame with rubber feet.

- *height 10cm*
- £30 • **Cobwebs**

BICYCLES

▽ Unique French Bike

• *circa 1930*
Independently made. Consists of one lady's frame welded on top of a man's frame. Steel and painted red with Frexel brakes.
• *height 1.4m*
• £500 • Bike Park

▽ Humber Gent's

• *circa 1940*
Gent's bike with enclosed chain, three-speed hub, rod brake.
• *156cm frame, 71cm wheel*
• £150 • Bridge Bikes

▽ Lady's GPO Bike

• *circa 1960*
Rare post-office bike fitted with 35cc petrol engine, yellow finish, hub brakes. Post-office carrier attached to the front.
• *66cm wheel*
• £750 • Bridge Bikes

△ Rival of Norwich

• *circa 1930*
Lady's roadster. Unusual make and very collectable.
• *155cm seat tube, 63cm wheel*
• £50 • G Whizz

△ Lady's Single Speed

• *circa 1930*
Rudge Whitworth black single-speed. With lap frame dynamo. For restoration.
• *138cm frame, 69cm wheel*
• £100 • Bridge Bikes

△ BSA Lady's Junior

• *circa 1950*
Single-speed, cable brake. Original wicker basket attached to the front of the bike.
• *61cm wheel*
• £200 • Bridge Bikes

△ Italian Legnano

• *circa 1940*
Lady's cycle, single-speed, unique rod brakes running through handlebars, full chain cover.
• *66cm wheel*
• £100 • Bridge Bikes

△ Raleigh Roadster

• *circa 1950*
Single-speed post-war bike. Good rideable condition, with Westwood rims and rod brakes.
• *66cm wheel*
• £50 • G Whizz

△ Arnold Schwinn Packard

• *circa 1930*
American lady's bicycle, with pedal back brake, maroon finish, single-speed.
• *66cm wheel*
• £550 • Bridge Bikes

△ Dutch Torpedo

• *circa 1946*
Classic old Dutch bike, probably post war, with torpedo coaster brake. All original.
• *158cm frame, 69cm wheel*
• £80 • G Whizz

△ Triumph Lady's Roadster

• *circa 1977*
Unusual fork crown. Black enamel finish with some pitting. In good order.
• *153cm frame, 66cm wheel*
• £40 • G Whizz

◁ Raleigh Rocky II

• *1986*
With fifteen Shimano gears.
• *153cm frame, 66cm wheel*
• £200 • G Whizz

▽ Stoneware Bottle

- *circa 1647*

Whit stoneware bottle of bulbous proportions with handle, on a splayed base, inscribed 'WHIT, 1647'.

- *height 6cm*
- N/A • Jonathan Horne

▽ Smoky Quartz Snuff Bottle

- *circa 19th century*

Smoky quartz shield-shaped snuff bottle with lion's heads on the sides.

- *7cm x 5cm*
- £250 • Ormonde

▽ Glass Snuff Bottle

- *19th century*

Glass snuff bottle with red overlay carved relief of a water dragon chasing the flaming pearl. Green jade stopper.

- *height 6.5cm*
- £220 • Ormonde

△ Georgian Scent Bottle

- *1727–1820*

Georgian scent bottle in purple glass with a silver stopper.

- *length 6cm*
- £240 • Trio

△ Snuff Bottle

- *19th century*

Smoky quartz snuff bottle.

- *height 2.5cm*
- £250 • Ormonde

△ Opaque Glass Bottle

- *19th century*

French scent bottle of opaque glass with a cameo of a lady on the top.

- *height 11cm*
- £238 • Trio

▽ Green Porcelain Bottle

- *19th century*

Chinese moulded green porcelain snuff bottle with moulded lattice design.

- *6cm x 5cm*
- £300 • Ormonde

▽ Porcelain Bottle

- *19th century*

Porcelain bulbous moulded relief snuff bottle with a cartouche on each side showing the immortals.

- *6.5cm x 5.2cm*
- £350 • Ormonde

▽ Turquoise Bottle

- *19th century*

Turquoise porcelain snuff bottle.

- *7cm x 5cm*
- £220 • Ormonde

△ Crystal Snuff Bottle

- *19th century*

Quartz rock crystal snuff bottle with engraved foliate design with chrysanthemum.

- *height 2.5cm*
- £220 • Ormonde

△ Candy-Striped Bottle

- *circa 1850*

Candy-striped pink glass perfume bottle with a rose gold stopper.

- *height 6cm*
- £288 • Trio

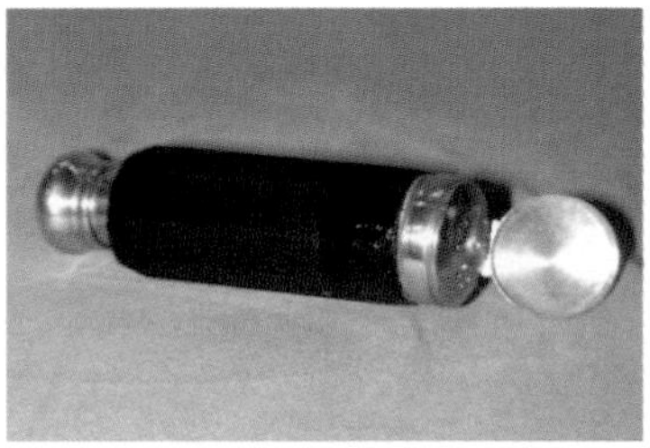

△ Victorian Scent Bottle

- *circa 1860*

Victorian double-ended ruby scent bottle in silver with gilt stoppers, with one side for perfume and the other for smelling salts.

- *length 10cm*
- £358 • Trio

△ French Glass Perfume

- *1860*

Mazarin-blue glass perfume bottle with floral gilding and a large octagonal stopper.

- *height 16cm*
- £145 • Trio

△ Glass Perfume Bottle

- *1870*

Cranberry glass perfume bottle with gilt overlay.

- *height 10cm*
- £420 • Lynda Brine

△ Clear Glass Bottle

- *circa 1870*

Scent bottle decorated with ornate pinchbeck. The stopper is painted with a scene of Church Street, Magdalene.

- *height 7.5cm*
- £188 • Trio

▽ Oval Scent Bottle

- *1870*

A French green oval glass bottle with an elaborate foliate and bird design and a gold stopper.

- *length 6cm*
- £230 • Trio

▽ Turquoise Scent Bottles

- *1880*

Pair of turquoise scent bottles with gold banding and stoppers.

- *height 18cm*
- £368 • Trio

▽ Ruby Scent Bottles

- *1880*

Pair of scent bottles in ruby glass, with slender necks and floral gilt decoration.

- *height 26cm*
- £420 • Trio

△ Scent Bottles with Portraits

- *circa 1870*

Pair of Czechoslovakian opaque and clear-glass scent bottles with oval portraits of young girls, circled with grey and gold to stopper base and rim.

- *height 20cm*
- £590 • Trio

△ Victorian Scent Bottle

- *circa 1880*

Victorian scent bottle in green glass, decorated with gold banding around the base, neck and stopper.

- *height 13.5cm*
- £110 • Trio

△ Mercury Bottle

- *1880*

Very rare perfume bottle in red cut glass with a moulded silver hinged stopper.

- £310 • Trio

▽ Chinese Bottle

- *circa 19th century*

Chinese bulbous-shaped porcelain snuff bottle with a design showing dragons circling each other.

- *height 9cm*
- £220 • Ormonde

▽ European Perfume Bottle

- *1880*

Perfume bottle of latticinio glass with engraved silver cover with a glass stopper inside.

- £190 • Trio

▽ Victorian Scent Bottles

- *1880*

Two Victorian cranberry and vaseline coloured scent bottles, together with their original leather carrying case.

- *height 14cm*
- £245 • Trio

△ Pair of Scent Bottles

- *circa 1880*

A pair of French scent bottles in blue glass with conical-shaped stoppers. All carrying a gold filigree design.

- *height 21cm*
- £345 • Trio

△ Victorian Perfume Bottle

- *1880*

Victorian bulbous-shaped faceted glass perfume bottle with silver stopper decorated with foliate design.

- *height 6.5cm*
- £128 • Trio

△ Cut Glass Bottle

- *1893*

Cut glass cylindrical perfume bottle with ornate foliate designed stopper.

- *height 8cm*
- £140 • Bellum Antiques

▽ Chinese Bottle

- *19th century*

Fossiliferous stone snuff bottle known as pudding stone with a tiger eye stone stopper.

- *7.5cm x 5.5cm*
- £185 • Ormonde

▽ Ruby Flashed Bottles

- *circa 1880*

A pair of ruby flashed Bohemian glass scent bottles with floral decoration.

- *height 12cm*
- £245 • Trio

▽ Chinese Opaque Glass Bottle

- *circa 1900*

An opaque glass Chinese snuff bottle decorated with a rocky landscape and a semi-precious stone stopper set in silver.

- *height 8cm*
- £125 • Bellum

△ Bohemian Scent Bottles

- *circa 1880*

A pair of ruby Bohemian bottles with foliage design with cusp and angle rims.

- *height 18cm*
- £548 • Trio

△ Silver Scent Bottle

- *circa 1886*

English decorative silver scent bottle with scrolls and a cut-glass stopper.

- *height 5.5cm*
- £250 • John Clay

△ Scent Bottle and Vases

- *circa 1910*

A turquoise scent bottle with gold foliage design and ruby glass droplets, together with a pair of decorative vases carrying a complementary design.

- *height 12cm*
- £110 • Trio

▽ Green Scent Bottle

- *circa 1890*

Green simulated vaseline glass scent bottle decorated with red and gold filigree with opaque glass stopper.

- *height 12cm*
- £110 • Trio

▽ Oval Scent Bottle

- *circa 1890*

An oval Victorian scent bottle in white porcelain, with a silver stopper. Decorated with a red butterfly, pink flowers and foliage.

- *height 6cm*
- £158 • Trio

▽ Ceramic Bottle

- *circa 1900*

Ceramic Chinese snuff bottle in the shape of a cabbage leaf, with a stopper encrusted with semi-precious stones.

- *height 9cm*
- £165 • Bellum

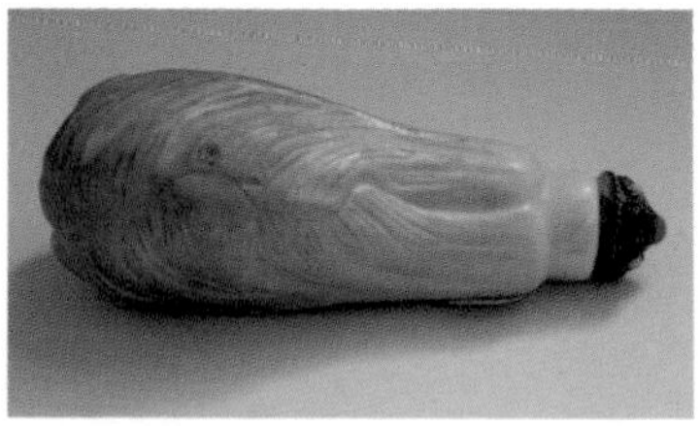

△ Glass Perfume Bottle

• *circa 1903*
Cut-glass perfume bottle with a silver rim and glass lozenge-shaped stopper.
• *height 8cm*
• £85 • Bellum

△ Spherical Wooden Bottle

• *circa 1900*
Unusual spherical wooden Chinese snuff bottle, with a semi-precious stone stopper and the body decorated with a dragon and lotus flower.
• *diameter 10cm*
• £225 • Bellum

△ Pagoda Snuff Bottle

• *circa 1900*
Chinese white snuff bottle decorated with crimson fish underneath a pagoda roof. Green stone stopper set in silver.
• *height 7cm*
• £175 • Bellum

▽ Blue Glass Bottle

• *circa 1900*
A blue glass Chinese snuff bottle with an orange flame effect, silver stone.
• *height 7cm*
• £70 • Bellum

▽ Chinese Bottle

• *circa 1900*
Opaque glass Chinese snuff bottle decorated with butterflies, a bat and cherry blossom, with a silver stopper.
• *height 7cm*
• £145 • Bellum

▽ Cut Glass Perfume Bottle

• *circa 1910*
Glass perfume bottle with lattice design around the middle and a silver stopper.
• *height 11.5cm*
• £150 • Bellum

△ Opaque Bottle

• *circa 1900*
Chinese opaque glass snuff bottle decorated with emerald-green flowers and an oriental bird. With a cornelian stopper set within a silver rim.
• *height 7.5cm*
• £175 • Bellum

△ Circular Scent Bottle

• *1902*
Painted with two Japanese ladies in traditional dress embracing each other, against a background of green foliage.
• *diameter 7cm*
• £155 • Trio

△ Art Deco Scent Bottles

• *1920*
A pair of English Art Deco perfume bottles in clear glass with black geometric designs.
• *height 18cm*
• £268 • Trio

▽ Clear Glass Bottle

• *circa 1900*
Clear glass perfume bottle with a mother-of-pearl stopper set in silver.
• *height 6.5cm*
• £150 • Bellum

▽ Art Deco Perfume Bottle

• *circa 1920*
Art Deco perfume bottle with stopper set in a silver plated base with blue stone set in the centre.
• *14cm x 12cm*
• £155 • Trio

▽ Glass Perfume Bottle

• *circa 1920*
Cut-glass perfume bottle with a generous silver stopper encrusted with flowers and decorated with a foliate design.
• *height 14.5cm*
• £445 • Bellum

△ Jacinthe De Coty

- *circa 1920*

Bottle with metallic plaque and beaded decoration; the stopper has floral designs.
- £150 • Linda Bee

△ Art Deco Scent Bottle

- *1920*

Art Deco bottle in turquoise and silver, with stopper. Decorated with geometric design and inscribed 'R.M.S. Homeric'.
- *height 6cm*
- £68 • Trio

△ Schiaparelli Bottle

- *circa 1938*

A Schiaparelli perfume bottle of twisted and fluted design with red finial top and beaded base.
- £180 • Linda Bee

▽ Cylindrical Bottle

- *circa 1920*

Cylindrical perfume bottle with a silver stopper inset with green stone.
- *height 8cm*
- £110 • Bellum

▽ Czechoslovakian Scent Bottle

- *1920*

An Art Deco smoky glass perfume bottle from the former Czechoslovakia, with a large pink silk tassel attached.
- *height 12cm*
- £58 • Trio

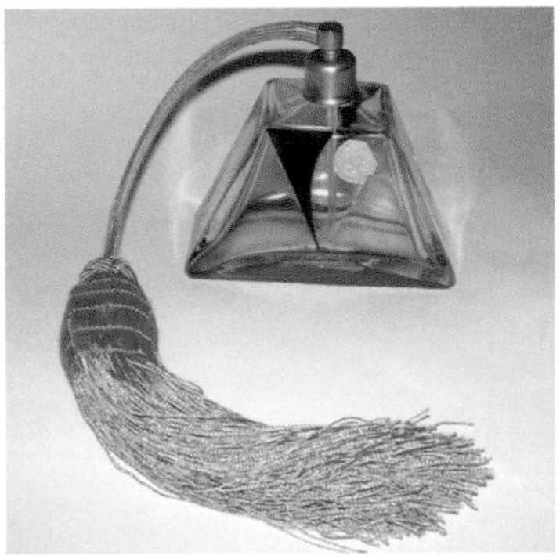

▽ Saville London 'June'

- *circa 1930*

A novelty perfume bottle in the form of a sundial.
- £125 • Linda Bee

△ Pump-Action Perfume Bottle

- *circa 1920*

Red glass perfume bottle with silver screw-top lid with a pump-action spray and a hand-painted butterfly.
- *height 13cm*
- £250 • Bellum

△ Bourjois Kobako

- *circa 1925*

A fashionable oriental-style perfume bottle, designed by Bourjois of Paris, with bakelite cover and carved stand.
- £390 • Linda Bee

△ Glass Bottle

- *circa 1930s*

Glass perfume bottle with moulded base, and a lozenge-shaped stopper.
- *height 20cm*
- £145 • Trio

▽ English Scent Bottles

- *1920*

Three English Art Deco scent bottles, in red, pink and blue glass, each carrying a long silk tassel.
- *height 9cm*
- £125 • Trio

▽ English Scent Bottle

- *1920*

English salmon-pink Art Deco perfume bottle, styled in the shape of a sailing boat with sail.
- *height 14cm*
- £150 • Trio

▽ Wedgwood Bottle

- *circa 1930*

Wedgwood blue bottle with a silver plate stopper.
- *height 4cm*
- £85 • Trio

CAMERAS

△ Half-Plate Camera

• *circa 1900*
Sands and Hunter tail board 5 x 4 half-plate camera of mahogany and brass construction.
• £400 • Jessop Classic

△ Newman & Guardia

• *1913*
The new ideal Sybil camera by Newman & Guardia with an unusual Ross Express 136mm F4.5 Lens. The camera takes 3¼ x 4¼-inch film.
• *height 23.5cm*
• £249 • Jessop Classic

△ Kodak Roll Film Camera

• *circa 1920*
Kodak VPK series 3 camera using 127 roll film.
• £300 • Jessop Classic

▽ Magic Lantern

• *circa 1900*
Lancaster magic lantern used for projective hand-painted glass slides.
• £300 • Jessop Classic

▽ Kodak Eastman

• *circa 1920*
No.2 Hawkette brown tortoiseshell-effect bakelite folding camera by Kodak.
• *height 18cm*
• £69 • Jessop Classic

▽ Autographic Camera

• *circa 1920*
A Kodak vest pocket Autographic camera. Made in Rochester NY, USA.
• £30 • Mac's Cameras

△ Thornton Pickard Camera

• *circa 1909*
Triple extension, Thornton Pickard camera which uses half-plate-sized negatives (glass plates used, not films). Made of wood with leather bellows.
• *21cm x 25.5cm*
• £300 • Jessop Classic

△ Stereo Plate Camera

• *circa 1926*
Rollei Heidoskop camera. It takes two parallel pictures to create a 3D image.
• £700 • Jessop Classic

△ 16mm Cine Camera

• *1928*
Bell and Howell 16mm cine camera with a 20mm F3.5 lens with 100ft spool, and a clockwork motor. The model is covered with grey tooled leather and is quite rare, especially outside the USA.
• *20.5cm x 3.7cm*
• £150 • Jessop Classic

▽ Ensign Cupid Camera

• *1922*
Ensign Cupid simple metal-bodied camera. 4 x 6cm exposures on 120 film. The design is based on a 1921 prototype for a stereo camera which was never produced. Meniscus achromatic F11 lens. Available in black, blue, grey and some other colours.
• *height 8cm*
• £89 • Jessop Classic

▽ Rajar Bakelite Camera

• *1929*
Rajar black bakelite No. 6 folding camera. With 120-roll film, with 6cm x 9cm negative size.
• *height 17cm*
• £49 • Jessop Classic

▽ Purma Roll Camera

• *circa 1932*
Purma 'Special' bakelite 127 roll camera with telescoping lens.
• £30 • Jessop Classic

△ Press Camera

- *circa 1930*

A 9x12 VN press camera with sports finder, ground-glass screen.

- £250 • Finchley

△ Roll Film Camera

- *circa 1935*

Coronet Midget 16mm camera made in five colours, blue being the rarest. Made in Birmingham.

- £350 • Jessop Classic

△ Robot Camera

- *circa 1940*

Luftwaffen Eigentum German Airforce robot camera. With built-in clockwork spring motor.

- £300 • Jessop Classic

▽ Field Camera

- *circa 1930*

Deardorff 10 x 8in camera made of mahogany with nickel-plated fittings. Schneider and Symmar 300mm lens.

- £2,000 • Jessop Classic

▽ Quarter-Plate Camera

- *circa 1935*

Baby speed graphic quarter-plate camera. Made in America. With original leather straps.

- £400 • Jessop Classic

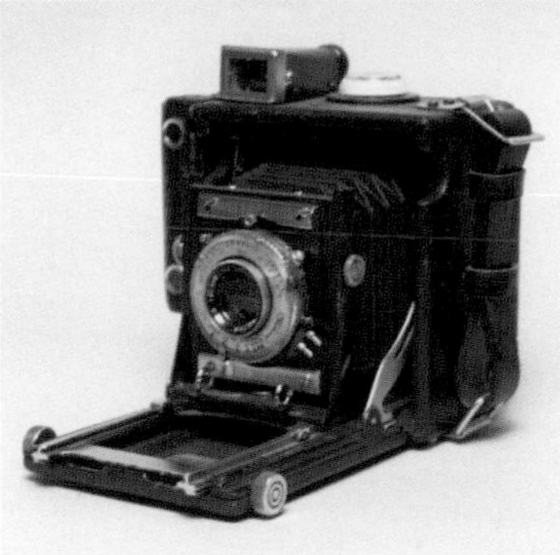

▽ Kodak Medallist II Rangefinder Camera

- *1946–53*

Rare Kodak Medallist II rangefinder camera, fitted with an F3.5 100mm Ektar lens.

- *20cm x 13cm*
- £349 • Jessop Classic

▷ Flash-Bulb Holder

- *circa 1949*

Leica Chico flash-bulb holder for Leica cameras.

- £20 • Jessop Classic

△ Ensign Silver Midget Camera

- *1935*

Ensign Silver Midget Jubilee model camera, made by Houghton, model number 22. Fitted with an Ensarlens F6.3 lens and uses E10 film which is now discontinued.

- *9cm x 4cm*
- £175 • Jessop Classic

△ Leica with 40cm f5 lens

- *circa 1936*

Leica with a 40cm f5 Telyt lens. This lens was used in the 1936 Berlin Olympic Games.

- £4,000 • Jessop Classic

△ Weston Lightometer

- *1940*

Weston lightometer 703 Weston Electrical Instrument Corp, Newark, NJ, USA.

- *width 12cm*
- £50 • Jessop Classic

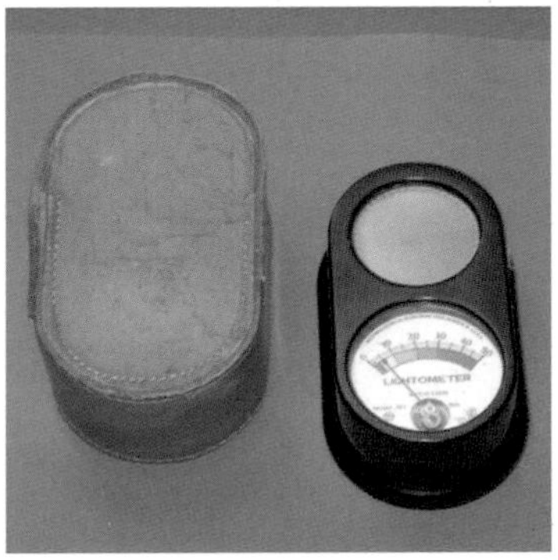

▽ Ensign Auto-speed Camera

- *1932*

Ensign auto-speed camera inscribed on the side, 100 mm F4.5 lens, with focal plane shutter speed of 15-500 sec.

- *height 20cm*
- £199 • Jessop Classic

▽ Balda Jubilette Camera

- *1938*

German Balda Jubilette camera commemorating the 30th anniversary of Balda Werk. Folding 35mm similar to the Baldina. F2.9 50mm lens. Baltar, Trioplan, or Corygon. Compur shutter.

- *height 13cm*
- £69 • Jessop Classic

▽ Kodak Field Camera

- *circa 1950*

Kodak No.1 Autographic 120mm film field camera with folding case.

- £70 • Mac's Cameras

△ Teleca Bino Camera

- *1950*

Relatively rare, subminiature 16mm Teleca Bino camera, which is built into a pair of binoculars. Fitted with standard 10mm x 14mm lenses and supplied with a brown leather case.

- *10cm x 9cm*
- £299 • Photo. Gallery

△ Plate Camera

- *circa 1950*

Plate camera by Aldiss-Butcher with an F4.5 lens with six-inch focus.

- *height 18cm*
- £70 • Mac's Cameras

△ Coronet 3 D Camera

- *1953*

Coronet 3-D marbelised bakelite stereo camera. Takes 127 film. Single speed shutter. Twin F11 meniscus fixed-focus lenses.

- *height 8cm*
- £79 • Jessop Classic

▽ Revere Stereo 33

- *1950*

Revere Stereo 33 made in the USA 35mm F3.5 Amaton. Complete with its original leather case.

- *width 19cm*
- £249 • Jessop Classic

▽ Eastman Kodak Camera

- *circa 1950*

Eastman Kodak camera. The shutter is made in Rochester, N.Y. with an F7.3 10mm lens.

- *height 16.5cm*
- £70 • Mac's Cameras

▽ Kodak Stereo Camera

- *1954–59*

Kodak stereo 35mm camera with Kodak Anaston F3.5 35mm lens, Kodak flash 200, shutter 25-200 with stereo viewer. With original box.

- *width 17cm*
- £249 • Jessop Classic

▷ Miniature Spy Camera

- *circa 1958*

Minox B subminiature spy camera, which takes 8 x 11mm negatives. With brushed aluminium body.

- £180 • Jessop Classic

△ Kodak Suprema Camera

- *circa 1950s*

Kodak Suprema camera fitted with an 8cm Xenar lens. Uses 120 standard film.

- *15cm x 10cm*
- £349 • Jessop Classic

△ No. 4 Ensign Camera

- *circa 1950*

No.4 Ensign carbine camera made in England with a Trichro shutter F77 lens anaston.

- *height 15cm*
- £40 • Mac's Cameras

△ Rolleiflex Camera

- *circa 1955–65*

Rolleiflex camera with a Tessar 1.3.8. F7.5mm lens.

- *height 19cm*
- £70 • Mac's Cameras

▽ Wrayflex

- *1950*

English Wrayflex 1 with outfit lens. Only approximately 1600 ever made. With original leather camera and lens case. Lens 50mm F2. Unilite.

- *height 9cm*
- £799 • Jessop Classic

▽ C8 Cine Camera

- *1954*

Bolex Standard 8 cine camera with a clockwork windup and single interchangeable lens.

- *12.5cm x 6cm*
- £50 • Jessop Classic

▽ Leica M3 35mm Camera

- *circa 1954*

Leica M3 with 50mm f2 standard lens. One of the most highly regarded cameras ever made. Used by many photographers.

- £1,000 • Jessop Classic

△ Exacta Varex Camera

• *circa 1950*
A sought-after first model Exacta Varex, f/2 Biotar.
• £70 • Mac's Cameras

△ 35mm Field Camera

• *circa 1950*
A Thagee 35mm field camera made in München, Germany. All-metal body.
• £50 • Mac's Cameras

△ Light Meter

• *circa 1950–60*
Sixtus light meter with folding bakelite case. No batteries required.
• £30 • Mac's Cameras

▽ Rolleiflex Camera

• *circa 1950*
German Rolleiflex camera with flip-top view-finder and Carl Zeiss twin lenses. 120 film.
• £70 • Mac's Cameras

▽ Field Camera

• *circa 1954*
MPP micro precision 5 x 4 press camera. Made in Kingston-upon-Thames, Surrey.
• £300 • Jessop Classic

▽ Voigtlander Camera

• *1958–60*
Rare Voigtlander Prominent II camera with an Ultron 50mm F2 lens. The camera has a 35mm rangefinder with interchangeable lenses and a clear viewfinder.
• *14cm x 8.5cm*
• £699 • Jessop Classic

△ Square Roll Film Camera

• *circa 1953*
First six V 120 6 x 6cm square roll film camera. One of the first to be made in Japan, inspired by earlier German designs.
• £100 • Jessop Classic

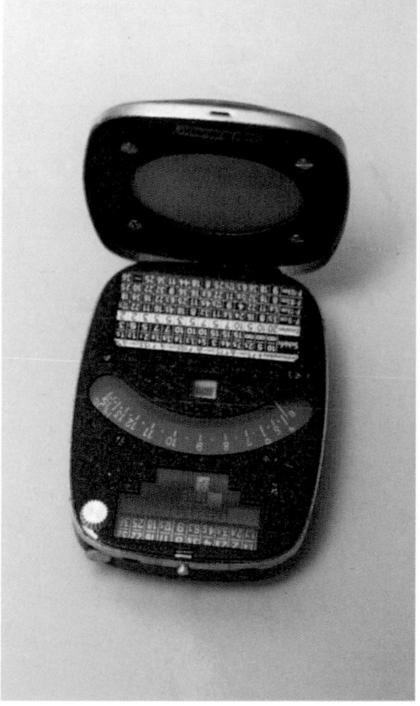

△ Light Meter

• *circa 1950–60*
An electro BEWI light meter in a metal case.
• £30 • Mac's Cameras

△ Kodak Camera

• *circa 1960*
Kodak 35 camera with an F4.5 51mm lens.
• *height 6cm*
• £50 • Mac's Cameras

▽ Meopta Cine Camera

• *circa 1958–65*
A standard 8 Meopta Admira 8mm cine camera with full metal case.
• £30 • Mac's Cameras

▽ 35mm Range Finder

• *circa 1957*
Minolta super A 35mm range finder interchangeable lens camera with standard lens.
• £200 • Jessop Classic

▽ Nikon SLR Camera

• *circa 1959*
Nikon F 35mm single lens reflex camera. This is a landmark camera for the 35mm Japanese camera industry.
• £550 • Jessop Classic

▽ Light Meter

• *circa 1960*
A pocket-sized Weston Master V Selenium light meter with all-metal body construction. In good condition.
• £40 • Jessop Classic

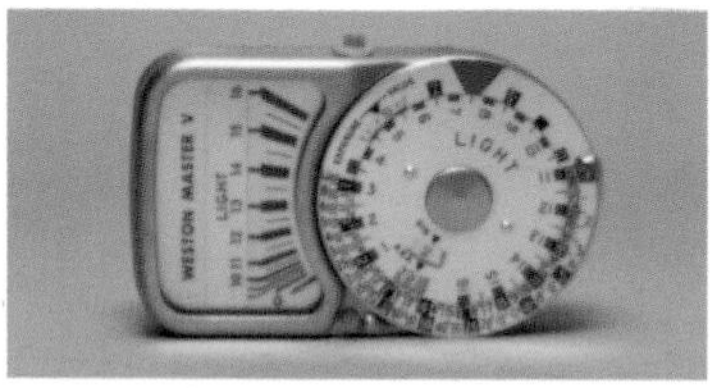

△ Magazine Camera

• *circa 1960*
A Bell & Howell 'Speedster' 16mm magazine camera with film auto load.
• £90 • Mac's Cameras

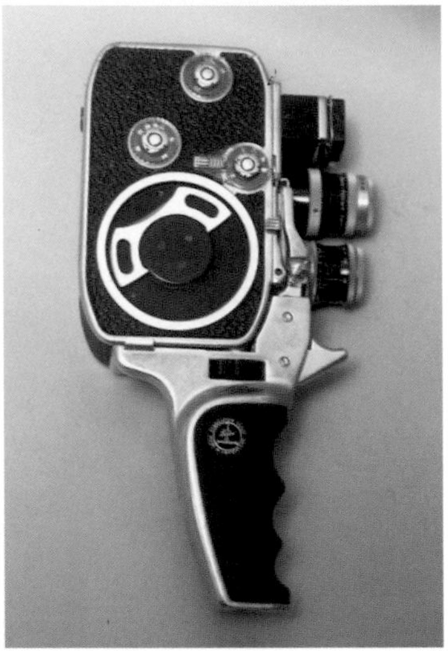

△ Cine Camera

• *circa 1960*
A standard eight-film Bolex 8mm cine camera and a selection of Kern lenses with leather cases and original instructions.
• £100 • Mac's Cameras

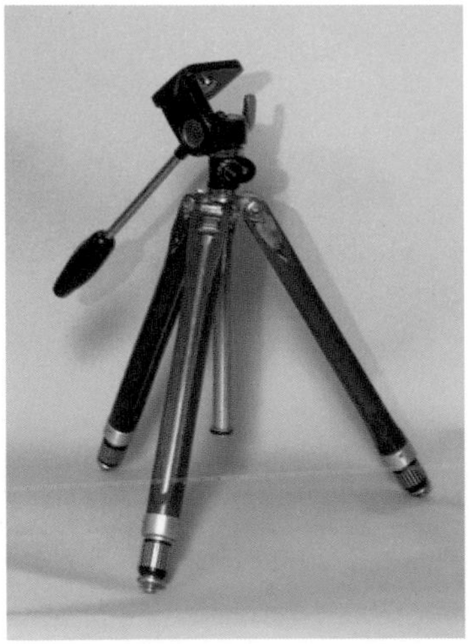

△ Pyramid Tripod

• *circa 1960*
Camera base with wooden legs and adjustable tubular metal stands.
• £15 • Mac's Cameras

▽ Polaroid Camera

• *circa 1960*
The first Polaroid instant film camera – the 900 Electric Eye Land Camera.
• £90 • Mac's Cameras

▽ 16mm Cine Camera

• *circa 1960*
AGFA 16mm cine camera and telephoto lens with 100ft spool. All metal body.
• £90 • Mac's Cameras

△ Colorflex SLR

• *circa 1960*
Agfa SLR with built-in light meter and interchangeable prism.
• £90 • Mac's Cameras

△ Brownie Box Camera

• *circa 1960*
Brownie box camera flash model 'B', with filters.
• £30 • Mac's Cameras

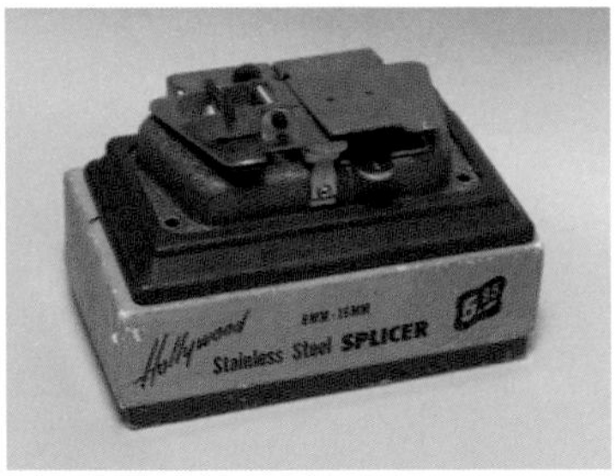

△ Hollywood Splicer

• *circa 1960*
Hollywood stainless-steel splicer. 8mm x 16mm, in original box.
• £30 • Mac's Cameras

▽ M.P.P. Plate Holder

• *circa 1960*
M.P.P. plate holder for 5x4 plate camera used by large format cameras.
• £10 • Mac's Cameras

▽ Slide Projector

• *circa 1960*
Aldis 35mm slide projector with original box.
• £30 • Mac's Cameras

▽ Cine Camera

• *circa 1960*
Standard 8 Bolex cine camera with a fixed zoom lens. All-metal body with a detachable pistol grip.
• £100 • Mac's Cameras

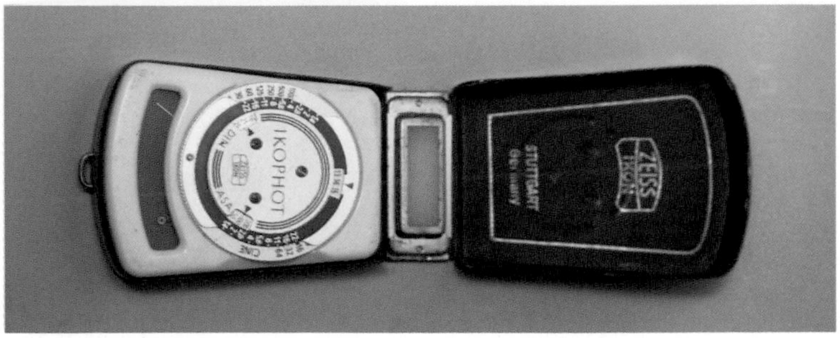

◁ Light Exposure Meter

• *circa 1960*
Kophot light exposure meter by Zeiss in a folding burgundy leather case.
• £30 • Mac's Cameras

△ **Zenit B Camera**

- *circa 1960*

Zenit B camera with 300mm lens.

- *height 8cm*
- £69 • Mac's Cameras

△ **L35 Concava Camera**

- *circa 1960s*

Rare miniature Tessina L35 Concava camera, designed to fit on the wrist in the style of a watch, and comes with a leather strap. It has a 25mm Tessinon lens and is supplied with 35mm film in special cassettes.

- *6.5cm x 6.5cm*
- £899 • Jessop Classic

△ **Brownie Six-20 Camera**

- *circa 1960*

A model 'C' Brownie Six-20 camera. Made in England by Kodak Ltd.

- £30 • Mac's Cameras

▽ **Rolleiflex TLR Camera**

- *1960s*

Rolleiflex 2.8F twin-lens camera (TLR), which uses standard 120 roll film.

- *15cm x 10cm*
- £649 Jessop Classic

▽ **Bolex Projector**

- *circa 1960*

An M.A. Bolex projector.

- *height 50cm*
- £150 • Mac's Cameras

▽ **Rollei Camera**

- *circa 1975*

Rollei 35S gold 35mm camera. A specially finished precision compact camera. Limited edition of 1500, gold-plated.

- £900 • Jessop Classic

△ **Bolex 16mm Cine Camera**

- *circa 1960s*

Bolex 16mm cine camera, model number H16m, with a Swiss-made body and Som Berthiot 17–85mm zoom lens.

- *33cm x 21.5cm*
- £500 • Jessop Classic

△ **35mm SLR Camera**

- *circa 1965*

Leicaflex 35mm SLR with f/2 semi-micron lens.

- £400 • Mac's Cameras

△ **6x7cm Roll Film Camera**

- *circa 1965*

Koni Omega rapid 6 x 7cm roll film camera with interchangeable lenses of Japanese origin.

- £300 • Jessop Classic

△ **Cartridge System Camera**

- *circa 1975*

A 110 cartridge system camera modelled as a caricature of a British Airways Aeroplane. In good condition.

- £60 • Jessop Classic

▽ **Cine Camera**

- *circa 1960*

Bell & Howell 'Sportster Standard 8' 8mm cine camera.

- £30 • Mac's Cameras

▽ **Pentax Roll Film Camera**

- *circa 1969*

Pentax 6 x 7 roll film camera. This has been a very popular professional camera for the last thirty-one years.

- £900 • Jessop Classic

▽ **Mickey Mouse Camera**

- *circa 1980*

A 110 cartridge system camera with a plastic body in the form of Mickey Mouse. With viewfinder placed on the forehead.

- £50 • Jessop Classic

CHESS SETS

△ **Ivory Chess Set**

- *1790*

North German ivory chess set of Selenus design with white and black pieces.

- *height 8cm (king)*
- £2,650 • G.D. Coleman

△ **Ivory Calvert-Style Chess Set**

- *early 19th century*

Carved and turned in natural and red-stained ivory.

- *height 7.5cm (king)*
- £950 • G.D. Coleman

△ **Ivory Rooks**

- *circa 1820*

A pair of early 19th-century ivory rooks, with flag-bearing sentries, from a John Company chess set.

- £350 (pair) • G.D. Coleman

▽ **Spanish 'Pulpit' Bone Chess Set**

- *early 19th century*

Rare set. One side natural colour, the other stained dark brown.

- *height 12cm (king)*
- £8,500 • G.D. Coleman

▽ **Selenus Chess Set**

- *circa 1800*

German carved bone red and white Kings and Queens topped by Maltese crosses.

- £2,850 • G.D. Coleman

▽ **French Ivory Chess Set**

- *1800*

French ivory chess set, with one side in natural ivory and one side coloured in faded Shagreen green.

- *height 9cm (king)*
- £1,750 • G.D. Coleman

◁ **Ivory Chess Set**

- *circa 1825*

With red and white pieces. Kings with Maltese cross and queens with leaf on ball-shaped head.

- *height 13cm (king)*
- £2,350 • G.D. Coleman

△ **East Prussian Chess Set**

- *circa 1795*

Very rare. Made of Baltic amber and wood.

- *height 10cm (king)*
- £7,950 • G.D. Coleman

△ **Inlaid Chess Table**

- *1825*

Fine ebony and ivory inlaid penwork chess table attributed to George Merrifield of London.

- £1,825 • Freshfords

△ **Indian 'Pepys' Chess Set**

- *19th century*

Ivory. Design known as 'Pepys' after famous English diarist.

- *height 18cm (king)*
- £2,350 • G.D. Coleman

△ **Ivory Monobloc Set**

- *circa 1835*

Finely carved. One side in rare stained green, the other natural.

- *height 10.5cm (king)*
- £2,850 • G.D. Coleman

△ **Staunton Chess Set**

- *19th century*

Ebony and boxwood chess set made by Staunton, presented in original box, by Jacques of London.

- *height 9cm (king)*
- £480 • G.D. Coleman

△ Bone Chess Set

- *1840*

English chess set in carved bone, with figures in red and white.

- *height 8cm (king)*
- £1,250 • G.D. Coleman

△ Quartz Chess Set

- *19th century*

An Indian rock crystal (quartz) export chess set with red and white colours.

- £1,250 • G.D. Coleman

△ Wooden Chess Set

- *19th century*

Very rare. All pieces are in the form of 'The Bears of Berne'. Made of Swiss natural wood, some stained darker.

- £2,850 • G.D. Coleman

△ Russian Ivory Chess Set

- *19th century*

Carved and turned in mammoth ivory. One side natural, the other side with unusual pewter effect.

- *height 8.2cm (king)*
- £850 • G.D. Coleman

▽ Indian Folding Chess and Backgammon Set

- *circa 1840*

Fine Indian ivory and horn inlaid sandalwood board, with chess inlaid on the outside and backgammon on the inside.

- *45cm x 50cm x 5cm*
- £4,500 • G.D. Coleman

▽ Staunton Ivory Set

- *circa 1865*

Magnificent rare set by Jacques of London. With gold and red leather case and board.

- *height 14cm (king)*
- £16,500 • G.D. Coleman

▽ Coromandel Games Compendium

- *circa 1880*

Coromandel games box in wood, containing chess, backgammon, checkers, cribbage, dominoes and draughts.

- *33cm x 20cm x 22cm*
- £1,900 • Langfords Marine

△ Backgammon and Chess Set

- *1840*

Indian ivory chess and backgammon set, with black and natural ivory figures. Presented in folding ivory chessboard box.

- *45cm x 50cm x 5cm*
- £4,500 • G.D. Coleman

△ Morphy Chess Set

- *circa 1880*

Late 19th-century metal figural 'Morphy' chess set.

- £1,850 • G.D. Coleman

△ Ivory Chess Set

- *circa 1880*

Late 19th-century Indian ivory export chess set with exquisitely carved figures.

- *height 7.5cm (king)*
- £680 • G.D. Coleman

△ Pottery Chess Set

- *1890*

German chess set in pottery, styled with a figurative theme including kneeling pawns. Figures in black and tan.

- *height 11cm (king)*
- £950 • G.D. Coleman

▽ Folding Game Board

- *19th century*

A Victorian papier mâché folding chess and backgammon board in the form of a two-volume book, with backgammon board on the inside and chess outside.

- £750 • G.D. Coleman

▽ Ceramic Chess Set

- *circa 1880*

Late 19th-century Wedgwood-style ceramic chess set made after a Flaxman design.

- £2,750 • G.D. Coleman

▽ Victorian Travelling Chess Set

- *1895*

Victorian travelling chess set. with red and white pieces, made by Jacques of London. Supplied with its own original leather carrying case.

- *18cm x 18cm*
- £680 • G.D. Coleman

COMMEMORATIVE WARE

▽ Heraldic Plates

- *circa 1780*

One of four heraldic plates by J. Edmondson in handmade, gilded frames.

- *58cm x 40cm*
- £2,800 • Chelsea Gallery

▽ Accession Jug

- *1837*

Blue and white Accession jug inscribed 'Hail Victoria'. Showing a portrait of the young Queen Victoria.

- *height 29cm*
- £1,275 • Hope & Glory

▽ Prince of Wales Plate

- *1847*

Child's plate showing the young Edward, Prince of Wales, on a pony. Entitled 'England's Hope'.

- *diameter 16.5cm*
- £340 • Hope & Glory

△ Child's Plate

- *1821*

Very unusual child's plate depicting Queen Caroline.

- £325 • Hope & Glory

△ Bust of Wellington

- *circa 1835*

Parian bust of Wellington in Felspar porcelain. Issued by Copeland and Garrett.

- *height 20cm*
- £290 • Hope & Glory

△ Bronze Gilt

- *circa 1840*

Bronze gilt of Napoleon crossing the Alps. After Jacques-Louis David.

- £475 • The Armoury

▽ Bronze Plaque

- *circa 1820*

An oval bronze plaque showing the Duke of Wellington.

- *length 26cm*
- £450 • The Armoury

▽ Queen Victoria Mug

- *1838*

Staffordshire Queen Victoria coronation mug with an unusual black and white depiction of the young Queen Victoria.

- *height 10cm*
- £1,250 • Hope & Glory

▽ Pair of Perfume Flasks

- *circa 1840*

Hand-decorated porcelain perfume flasks by Jacob Petit, commemorating the marriage of Queeen Victoria and Prince Albert.

- *height 31cm*
- £3,750 • Hope & Glory

△ Gilt Bronze

- *circa 1837*

Bronze of the young Queen Victoria, on armorial bronze acanthus-leaf base.

- *height 32cm*
- £1,500 • The Armoury

△ Small Children's Plate

- *circa 1838*

Made at the time of Queen Victoria's coronation. Staffordshire earthenware with transfer printing.

- *diameter 12cm*
- £290 • Hope & Glory

△ Moulded Jug

- *circa 1863*

Jug with fixed, hinged silverplate cover, commemorating the wedding of Edward, Prince of Wales to Princess Alexandra.

- *height 18cm*
- £175 • Hope & Glory

△ **Imperial Beer Stein**

- *1870*

Imperial half-litre-size beer stein with attractive painted enamelled panel of Ulanen, of the Imperial Lancers, hunting in a mountainous landscape. Inscribed with the following undamaged lettering: 'Zur Erinnerung an meine Dienstzeit'.

- *height 24cm*
- **£495** • **Gordon's**

△ **Queen Victoria Plate**

- *1887*

Bone china plate depicting Queen Victoria's Golden Jubilee with Queen Victoria in the centre with a crown above her head, flanked by flags with a wreath border.

- *diameter 21.3cm*
- **£95** • **Hope & Glory**

▽ **Victorian Mug**

- *circa 1878*

Mug commemorating the visit of Edward, Prince of Wales, to India on the occasion of Queen Victoria being made Empress.

- *height 10.5cm*
- **£150** • **Hope & Glory**

▽ **German Bronze Statue**

- *circa 1886*

Bronze statue of a German guards officer in uniform, standing with his left hand on hip and grasping sword in his right. Excellent patina and finely detailed modelling. Mounted on heavy granite base, with inset presentation plaque: 'to Hptm. Heinrich Esenbeck from the Officers of k.b.1 Inf Regt. Konig. 4.12.1886 to 11.12.1901'.

- *height 32cm*
- **£725** • **Gordon's**

◁ **Bone China Jug**

- *1888*

Continental bone china jug commemorating the silver wedding anniversary of Prince Edward and Princess Alexandra.

- *height 12.5cm*
- **£85** • **Hope & Glory**

△ **Jubilee Tile**

- *1887*

A tile commemorating Queen Victoria's Golden Jubilee with fragmented Coat of Arms.

- *15.5cm x 15.5cm*
- **£75** • **Hope & Glory**

△ **Scottish Ceramic Jug**

- *circa 1887*

To commemorate the Golden Jubilee of Queen Victoria.

- *height 21cm*
- **£195** • **Hope & Glory**

△ **Gordon Highlanders**

- *1890*

One of a pair of Gordon Highlander commemorative plates. Decorated with a picture of a soldier standing guard, with the words 'Gordon Highlander' inscribed around the figure.

- *height 21cm*
- **£75** • **Gordon's**

▽ **Golden Jubilee Mug**

- *1887*

Small cream and blue mug, commemorating the golden jubilee of Queen Victoria. Sold in the Isle of Wight.

- *height 6cm*
- **£125** • **Hope & Glory**

▽ **Golden Jubilee Beaker**

- *1887*

Beaker commemorating the golden jubilee of Queen Victoria, showing young and old portraits. Issued as a gift to school children in Hyde Park.

- *height 10.5cm*
- **£125** • **Hope & Glory**

▽ **Teapot**

- *circa 1897*

Commemorating the Diamond Jubilee of Queen Victoria. Copeland bone china with gold decoration. Portrait of Victoria in relief.

- *height 14cm*
- **£525** • **Hope & Glory**

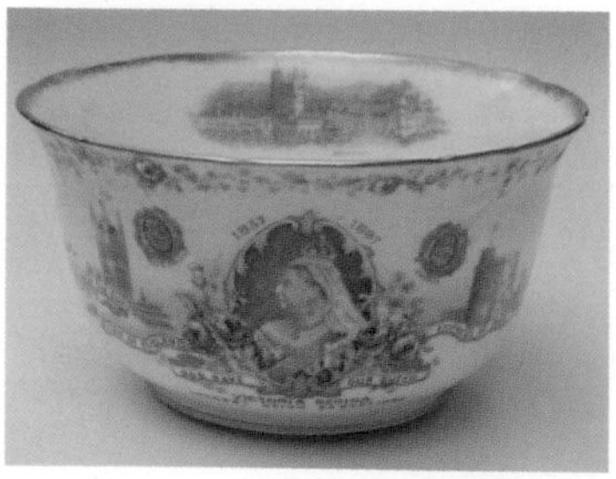

△ Diamond Jubilee Bowl

- *1897*

Bowl commemorating the diamond jubilee of Queen Victoria. Made by Aynsley for W. Whiteley.

- *height 8cm*
- **£140** • **Hope & Glory**

△ Glass Soldier

- *19th century*

Glass figure of a soldier standing holding a rifle.

- *height 20cm*
- **£78** • **P. Oosthuizen**

△ Coronation Cup and Saucer

- *1902*

Bone china cup and saucer commemorating the coronation of Edward VII. Made by Foley.

- *height 5.5cm*
- **£58** • **Hope & Glory**

▽ Blue and White Plaque

- *1898*

Blue and white plaque of William Gladstone to commemorate his death. Maker Burgess and Lee.

- *39cm x 25.8cm*
- **£230** • **Hope & Glory**

▽ Boer War Egg Cups

- *1900*

Continental bone-china egg cups depicting generals from the Boer War.

- *height 6.5cm*
- **£60 each** • **Hope & Glory**

▽ Boer War Mug

- *circa 1902*

Mug commemorating the end of the Boer War on the front, with the back celebrating the coronation of King Edward VII.

- *height 8cm*
- **£125** • **Hope & Glory**

▷ Three Egg Cups

- *1911*

Three bone-china egg cups commemorating the coronation of King George V.

- *height 6.5cm*
- **£33 (each)** • **Hope & Glory**

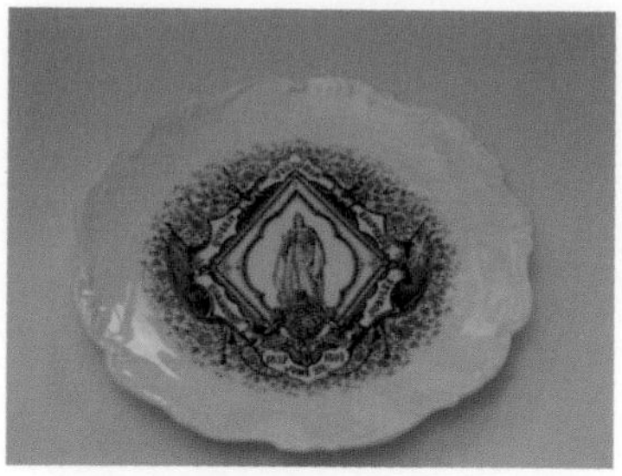

△ Coalport Plate

- *1897*

Bone-china plate issued by Coalport to commemorate Queen Victoria's diamond jubilee.

- *diameter 22cm*
- **£140** • **Hope & Glory**

△ Commemorative Cup

- *circa 1900*

A commemorative cup with three handles. With W.H. Goss on the base, depicting The Dominion of Canada, South Africa 1900 with a soldier and a flag and 'H.M. Queen Victoria' beneath the coat of arms.

- *height 8.5cm*
- **£125** • **P. Oosthuizen**

△ Bone-China Plate

- *circa 1900*

By Royal Worcester to commemorate the relief of Mafeking. Transfer shows Baden-Powell.

- *diameter 23.5cm*
- **£140** • **Hope & Glory**

▽ Brass Shield Plaque

- *1897*

Brass plaque of Queen Victoria in the shape of a shield to commemorate the Diamond Jubilee of Queen Victoria.

- *43cm x 32cm*
- **£175** • **Hope & Glory**

▽ Four Castles Plate

- *1901*

Black transfer on earthenware plate to commemorate the death of Queen Victoria, such items are quite scarce.

- *diameter 24.5cm*
- **£240** • **Hope & Glory**

▽ Coronation Mug

- *1902*

Copeland mug for the coronation of King Edward VII and Queen Alexandra, showing the correct date of August 9, 1902. Most items give the date as June 26, 1902, which was postponed because of the king's appendicitis.

- *height 7.5cm*
- **£160** • **Hope & Glory**

△ **Cup & Saucer**

- *circa 1910*

Cup and saucer with letter attesting to the fact that they were used by King Edward VII at 4.45pm on the afternoon of his death.

- £1,200 • The Armoury

△ **Officer on Horseback**

- *circa 1910*

German officer on horseback. Napoleonic period. Probably Dresden.

- *height 38cm*
- £2,500 • The Armoury

△ **Commemorative Plaque**

- *1914–15*

Bone china plaque commemorating the alliance between Germany and Austria, Kaiser Wilhelm II and Franz Joseph.

- *diameter 23.5cm*
- £170 • Hope & Glory

▽ **Shaving Mug**

- *1911*

Shaving mug, probably continental, commemorating the coronation of King George V and Queen Mary.

- *height 10.5cm*
- £80 • Hope & Glory

▽ **Kitchener Figure**

- *circa 1915*

Staffordshire figure of Kitchener standing with his hand on his belt and a sword by his side on an oval base with the word 'Kitchener' on it.

- *height 35cm*
- £220 • P. Oosthuizen

▽ **Jigsaw Puzzle**

- *circa 1934*

With original box showing the young Princess Elizabeth and Princess Margaret in front of Windsor Castle.

- *28cm x 34cm*
- £75 • Hope & Glory

△ **Porcelain Roundel**

- *1914*

German domed porcelain roundel, decorated with a coloured portrait of General Field Marshal Hindenburg shown in uniform.

- *diameter 7cm*
- £70 • Gordon's

△ **Ink Well**

- *circa 1915*

Hand grenade casing used as an ink well to commemorate the First World War.

- *height 10.5cm*
- £80 • Hope & Glory

△ **Silver Jubilee Ashtray**

- *1935*

King George V and Queen Mary silver jubilee ashtray in Burleigh ware.

- *diameter 22cm*
- £55 • Chelsea (OMRS)

▽ **Royal Horse Guard**

- *1915*

'The Blues' made by Copeland to commemorate the centenary of the Battle of Waterloo.

- *height 39cm*
- £1,700 • The Armoury

▽ **German Knight**

- *1918*

German bronzed spelter figure of a knight in armour on a stained wood plinth, with a dedication plate on the side to Major Niemann from his brother officers of the 39 Field Artillery Regiment, 22 March to 16 November 1918.

- *height 45.5cm*
- £325 • Gordon's

◁ **Jubilee Mug**

- *1935*

Ceramic mug commemorating the Silver Jubilee of King George V and Queen Mary.

- *height 7cm*
- £24 • Magpies

△ Jubilee Mug

- *1935*

Armorial mug commemorating the Silver Jubilee of King George V and Queen Mary.

- *height 7cm*
- £24 • Magpies

△ Royal Albert Commemorative Mug

- *1935*

Bone-china Royal Albert commemorative mug of the Silver Jubilee of King George V and Queen Mary.

- *height 7cm*
- £58 • Hope & Glory

△ Coronation Mug

- *1936*

Bone china mug made for the proposed coronation of Edward VIII.

- *height 9cm*
- £40 • Hope & Glory

▽ Masons Jug

- *1935*

Masons ironstone jug commemorating King George and Queen Mary, a limited edition of 1000. With King George and Queen Mary in profile within a wreath border.

- *height 19cm*
- £275 • Hope & Glory

▽ Bone-China Mug

- *1936*

Bone-china mug made for the proposed coronation of Edward VIII with abdication details on the reverse.

- *height 9cm*
- £170 • Hope & Glory

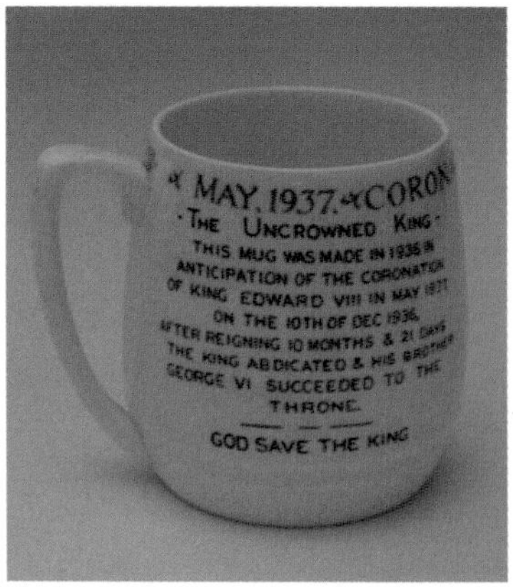

▽ Wall Plaque

- *1938*

German black ash wall plaque with metal relief of artillery crew serving their gun, and metal label reading: 'Res. battr. Opel 39.8.38. 11 10.38'.

- *23cm x 32.5cm*
- £115 • Gordon's Medals

△ Copeland Mug

- *1936–37*

Earthenware mug for the proposed Coronation of Edward VIII, made by Copeland for Thomas Goode of London.

- *height 9.8cm*
- £95 • Hope & Glory

△ Loving Cup

- *1936–37*

Loving cup to commemorate the proposed Coronation of Edward VIII.

- *height 25.3cm*
- £135 • Hope & Glory

△ Crown Devon Jug

- *1937*

Crown Devon jug musical 'Super Jug' to commemorate the coronation of King George V1 and Queen Elizabeth. Limited edition. With a lion handle.

- *height 30.5cm*
- £2,250 • Hope & Glory

▽ Vase

- *1937*

Single-handled vase to commemorate the coronation of King George VI and Queen Elizabeth. Designed and signed by Charlotte Rhead.

- *height 18.5cm*
- £325 • Hope & Glory

▽ Commemorative Plate

- *circa 1937*

For the proposed coronation of Edward VIII. Made by Paragon with the Royal Coat of Arms.

- *diameter 27cm*
- £450 • The Armoury

▽ Wedgwood Mug

- *1939*

Wedgwood mug to commemorate the visit of King George and Queen Elizabeth to America with the inscription 'Friendship makes Peace'.

- *height 10cm*
- £165 • Hope & Glory

△ War Effort Teapot

- *1939*

A teapot commemorating War against Hitlerism, Liberty and Freedom, given in exchange for aluminium utensils. Made by Crown Ducal.

- *height 14cm*
- £140 • Hope & Glory

△ Winston Churchill Figure

- *circa 1943*

Ceramic figure of Winston Churchill, with the inscriptions 'Our Gang Copyright The Boss' on the base of his right foot and 'The Bovey Pottery England' on the base of his left foot.

- *height 12cm*
- £150 • P. Oosthuizen

△ Caricature Mug

- *1991*

A caricature mug of the former Prime Minister Margaret Thatcher and her husband.

- *height 9cm*
- £33 • Hope & Glory

▽ The Queen's Vesta Box

- *1939*

The Queen's regiment vesta box with 'The Queen's' in relief.

- *width 5cm*
- £35 • Gordon's

▽ Queen Elizabeth II Bust

- *1953*

Bust of Queen Elizabeth II to commemorate her coronation in 1953, by Staffordshire Morloy.

- *height 18cm*
- £80 • Hope & Glory

△ Chocolate Tin

- *circa 1953*

Royal-blue enamelled tin with fleur-de-lys motif, commemorating the coronation of Queen Elizabeth II.

- *height 7cm*
- £5 • Magpies

▷ Birthday Mug

- *1991*

Bone china mug by Aynsley to commemorate the thirtieth birthday of Princess Diana.

- *height 9.5cm*
- £70 • Hope & Glory

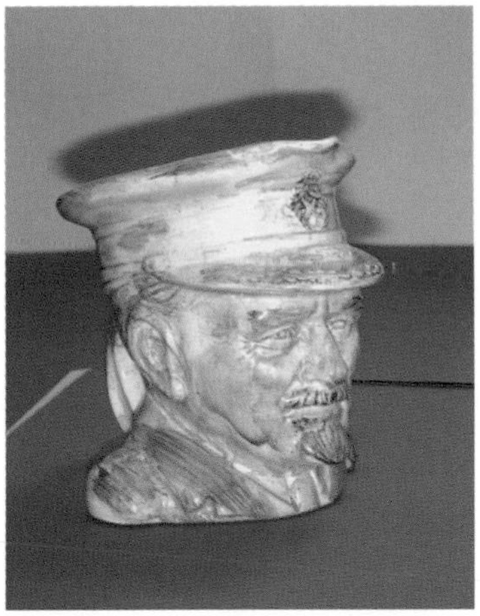

△ Prime Minister

- *circa 1941*

Pottery jug modelled as the Prime Minister of South Africa by J.C. Smutts.

- *height 13cm*
- £98 • P. Oosthuizen

△ Pottery Folly

- *1969*

Caernarvon castle folly in Keystone pottery, issued to commemorate the investiture of Prince Charles in July 1969,

- *height 21cm*
- £65 • Hope & Glory

▽ Dutch Delft Plaque

- *circa 1945*

Delft plaque to commemorate the liberation of Holland. Showing mother, child and aeroplane.

- *height 20cm*
- £150 • Hope & Glory

▽ Curtseying Cup

- *1977*

Carlton Ware porcelain cup in a curtseying pose, commemorating the silver jubilee of Queen Elizabeth II.

- *height 11cm*
- £50 • Hope & Glory

▽ Wedgwood Mug

- *2000*

Black basalt mug issued by Wedgwood in commemoration of the Millennium. Designed by Richard Guyatt in a limited edition of 500.

- *height 10cm*
- £190 • Hope & Glory

△ **Cricket Series**

• *circa 1896*
Wills's first set of 50 cricketing cigarette cards. Illustration shows Dr W.G. Grace of Gloucestershire.
• £3,250 • Murray Cards

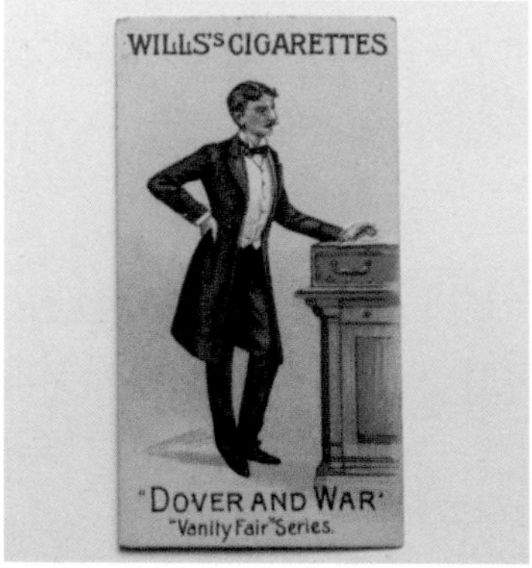

△ **Vanity Fair Series**

• *circa 1902*
Set of 50 cigarette cards of *Vanity Fair* caricatures from Wills. Illustration shows George Wyndham, MP.
• £225 • Murray Cards

△ **Highland Clan Series**

• *1907*
Set of 25 cigarette cards from Players. Illustration shows a representative of the Murray clan.
• £80 • Murray Cards

▽ **National Costumes Series**

• *1895*
Wills's cigarette cards set of 25. This card shows a Venetian beauty.
• £4,125 • Murray Cards

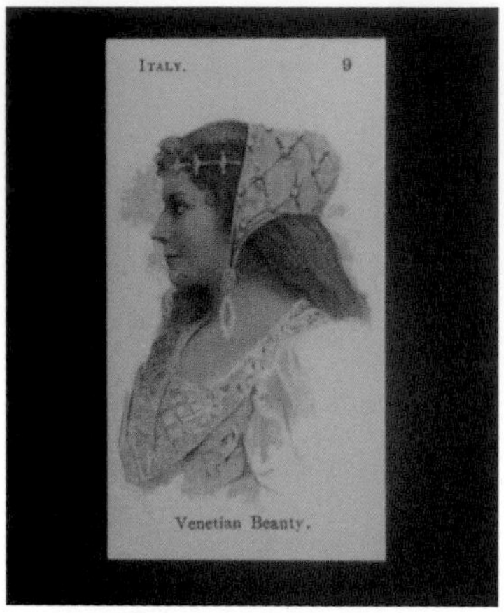

▽ **Opera Series**

• *1895*
Set of six opera cards, collected with products of The Liebig Extract Meat Co, France.
• £80 • Murray Cards

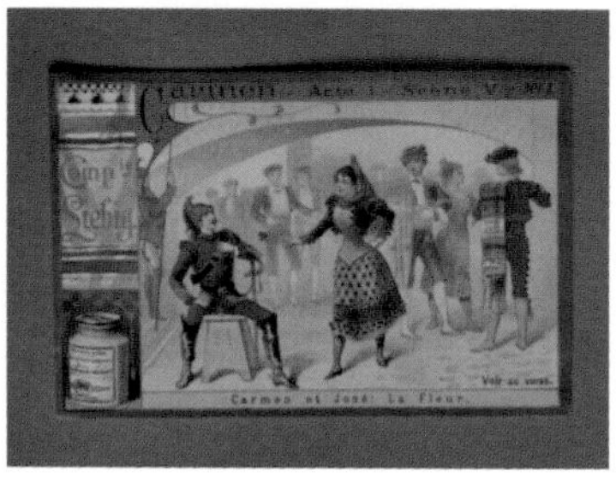

▽ **Waterloo Series**

• *circa 1914*
Set of 50 cigarette cards from Wills, never issued because of fear of offending French during First World War.
• £4,750 • Murray Cards

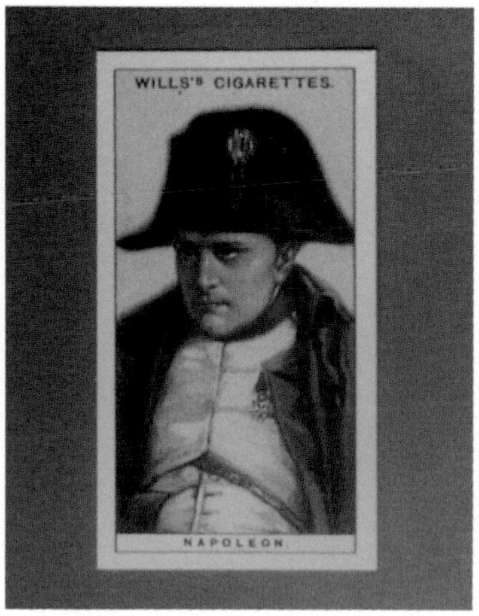

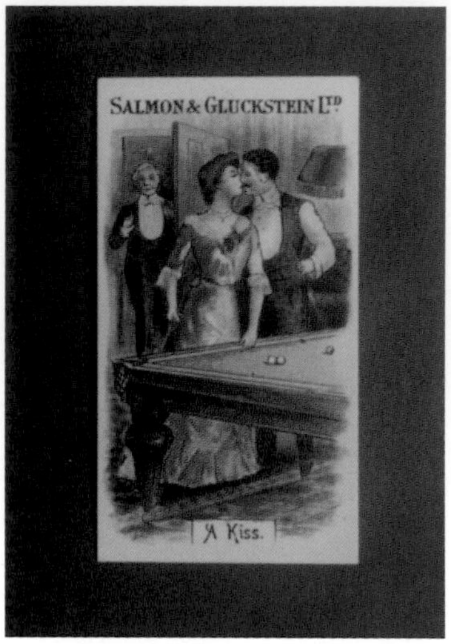

△ **Billiard Series**

• *circa 1905*
Set of 15 cards of *double entendre* billiard terms, from Salmon & Gluckstein.
• £825 • Murray Cards

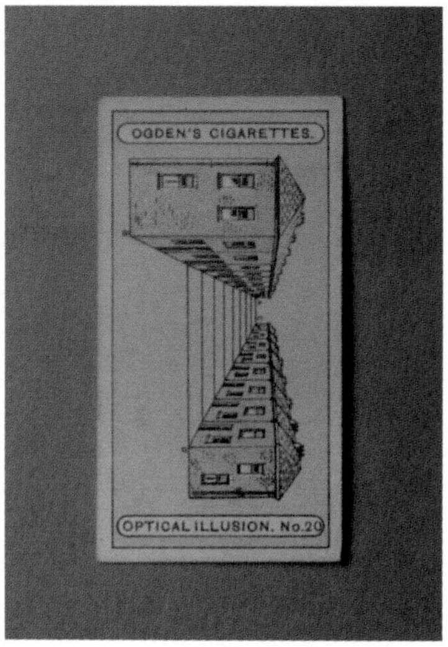

△ **Optical Illusions Series**

• *1923*
Set of 25 cigarette cards from Ogdens.
• £65 • Murray Cards

▽ **Taddy's Clown Series**

• *1920*
One of 20 known sets of Taddy's 'Clowns' – the most prized of British cigarette cards, with completely blank backs.
• £13,000 • Murray Cards

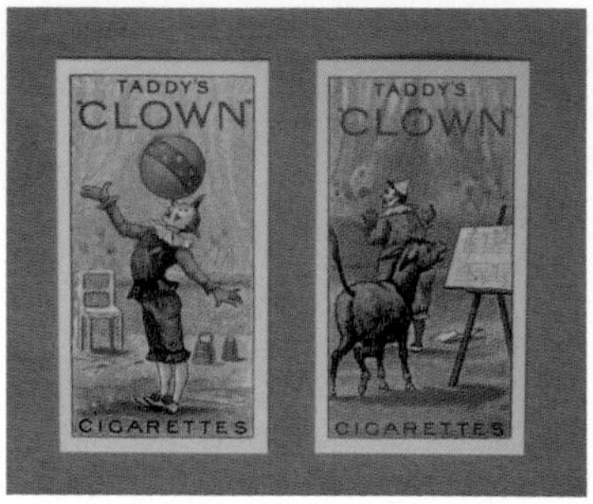

▽ **Curious Beaks Series**

• *1929*
Set of 50 cigarette cards from John Player & Sons. Illustration shows Australian Jacana.
• £40 • Murray Cards

▽ **Builders of the British Empire Series**

• *circa 1929*
Set of 50 cards by J A Pattreiouex. Illustration shows General Gordon.
• £135 • Murray Cards

◁ **Kensitas Flower Series**

• *1933*
Unusual series of 60 cigarette collecting items with silk flowers enclosed in envelopes. By J. Wix & Sons.
• £168 • Murray Cards

△ Famous Film Scene Series

• *1935*

Set of 48 cigarette cards, by Gallaher Ltd. Shows Laurel & Hardy from 'Babes in Toyland.'

• £36 • Murray Cards

△ True Romances

• *November 1938*

November 1938 issue of women's magazine *True Romances*.

• £4 • Book & Comic

△ Bulletman

• *1941*

Bulletman, a Fawcett Publication No.3.

• £160 • 30th Century Comics

▽ Famous Crowns Series

• *1938*

Set of 25 cards, by Godfrey Phillips Ltd. Illustration shows an Italian crown.

• £8 • Murray Cards

▽ Special Edition Comics

• *1940*

Special Edition Comics featuring Captain Marvel, No.1. A Fawcett Publication.

• £400 • 30th Century Comics

▽ Batman

• *May 1942*

Very early Batman magazine – issue No.10, by D.C. Comics.

• £220 • Gosh

△ Types of Horses

• *1939*

Set of 25 large cigarette cards from John Player & Sons. Illustration shows a Cob horse.

• £85 • Murray Cards

△ Bulletman

• *1941*

Bulletman featuring Bulletman and Bulletgirl 'Be an American', No.1. Published by Fawcett.

• £475 • 30th Century Comics

△ Star Spangled Comics

• *May 1942*

Star Spangled Comics issue No.8 published by D.C. Comics.

• £185 • Gosh

▽ Racing Yachts Series

• *1938*

Set of 25 cards, from paintings by Charles Pears. Illustration shows 'X' One Design class.

• £80 • Murray Cards

▽ All Winners

• *1941*

All Winners starring The Human Torch, Captain America No.3, Winter Issue Timely.

• £650 • 30th Century Comics

▽ Superman

• *1943*

Superman issue No.20. Published by D.C. Comics.

• £230 • 30th Century Comics

△ Vogue

• *November 1946*
A November 1946 copy of *Vogue* by Condé Nast.
• £10 • Radio Days

△ Wonder Woman

• *1947*
Wonder Woman No.22. 'Wonder Woman and the Color Thief!' published by D.C. Comics.
• £135 • 30th Century Comics

△ The Hotspur

• *1950*
The Hotspur No.699.
• £3 • 30th Century Comics

▽ Sun

• *1947*
The Sun No.1. Published by J.B. Allen.
• £20 • 30th Century Comics

▽ Vogue

• *July 1949*
A July 1949 edition of *Vogue* magazine by Condé Nast.
• £10 • Radio Days

▽ Eagle Annual

• *1951*
Eagle Annual No.1. Published by Hulton.
• £15 • 30th Century Comics

△ Star Spangled Comics

• *1947*
Star Spangled Comics – Batman's famed partner-in-peril Robin – the boy wonder in Solo Action! No.65.
• £160 • Gosh

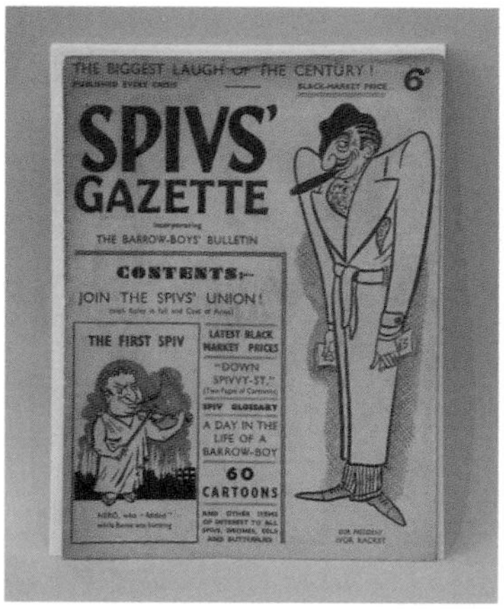

△ Spivs' Gazette

• *circa 1950*
Spivs' Gazette published by Clare & Son Ltd.
• £3 • 30th Century Comics

△ Comic Cuts

• *1955*
Comic Cuts No.2983. Published by Amalgamated Press.
• £4 • 30th Century Comics

▽ The Champion

• *1949*
'Johnny Fleetfoot gets 'em guessing'. *The Champion.* No.1428 Vol.55.
• £4 • 30th Century Comics

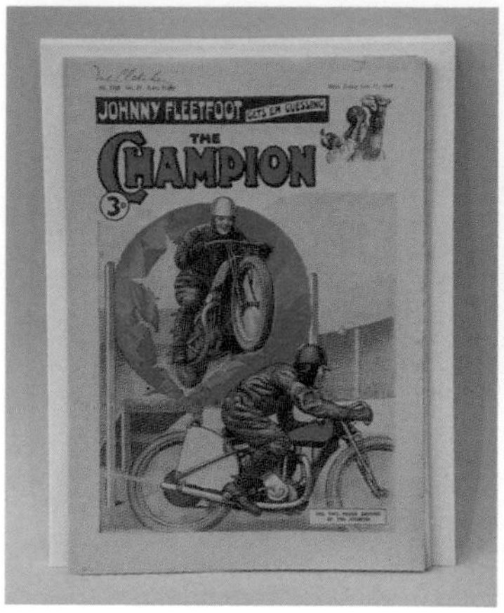

▽ Monte Hale

• *1952*
Monte Hale Western comic. Issue No.76, price 10 cents.
• £15 • Book & Comic

▽ Rupert Adventure Book

• *1955*
Rupert Adventure Book, published by Express Newspapers Ltd.
• £10 • 30th Century Comics

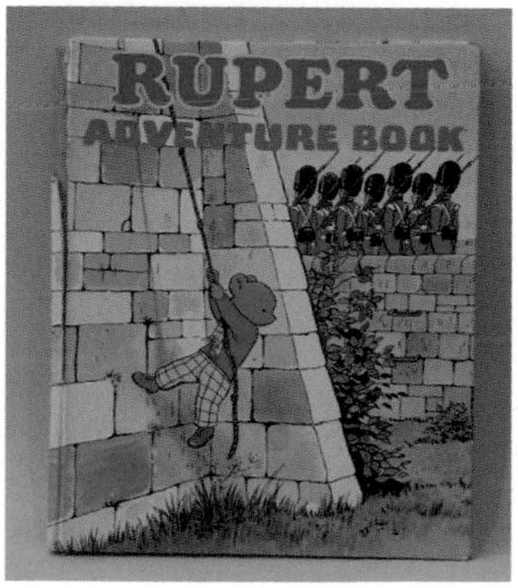

△ Amazing Stories

• *1954*
Issue No.5, Volume 1 of sci-fi magazine featuring a story by Philip K. Dick.
• £5 • Book & Comic

△ Film Fun

• *1957*
Issue No.1971. Published by The Amalgamated Press.
• £1.50 • Gosh

△ Romantic Story

• *September 1958*
No.40 – *Love's Tender Moments* – published by Charlton.
• £17.50 • Gosh

▽ Rupert

• *1955*
Rupert The Daily Express Annual. No.20.
• £40 • 30th Century Comics

▽ Dennis the Menace

• *1958*
Dennis the Menace, published by D.C. Thompson.
• £15 • 30th Century Comics

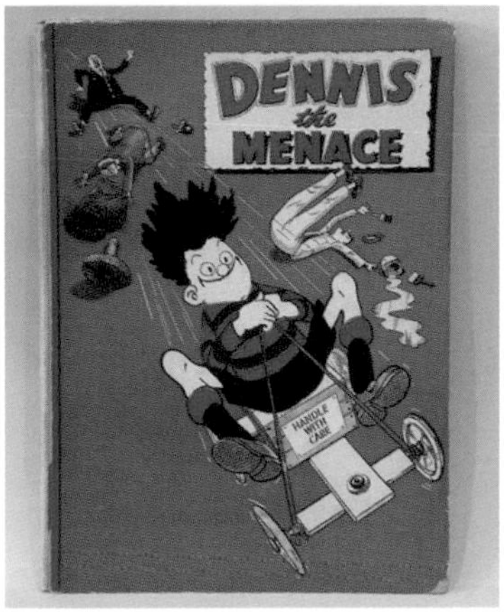

▽ Beano

• *1959*
The Beano Book. Published by D.C. Thompson.
• £70 • 30th Century Comics

△ Knockout

• *1954*
Issue No.806 of Knockout comic, by The Algamated Press.
• £1 • Gosh

△ Esquire Magazine

• *1959*
A publication of *Esquire* magazine for March 1959.
• £8 • Book & Comic

△ Konga

• *1960*
An issue of Konga magazine, published by Charlton Comics.
• £15 • Gosh

▽ The Lone Ranger

• *1958*
The Lone Ranger comic book published by Gold Key.
• £6 • Book & Comic

▽ Green Lantern

• *1959*
Showcase presents *Green Lantern* published by D.C. No.23.
• £280 • Gosh

▽ Searle Lithograph

• *circa 1960*
A Ronald Searle lithograph from 'Those Magnificent Men in Their Flying Machines'.
• £420 • Gosh

△ Cheyenne

• *1960*
Cheyenne, Exciting Adventure. Published by Dell.
• £10 • Gosh

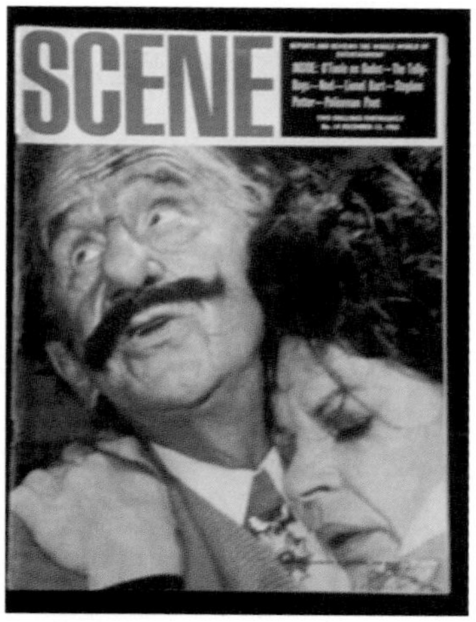

△ Scene

• *1962*
Issue No.14 of *Scene*, a theatre review magazine.
• £4 • Book & Comic

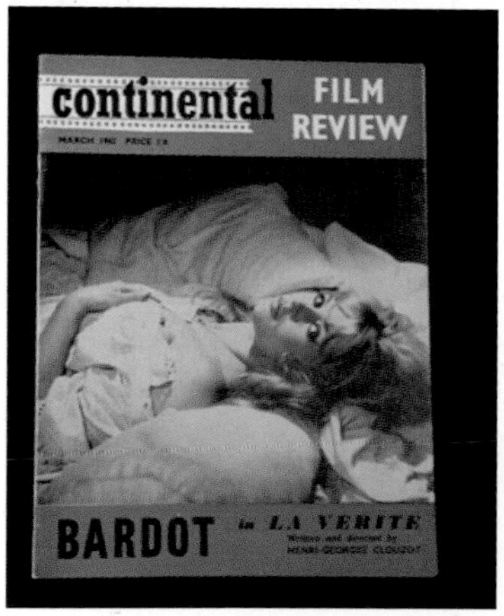

△ Continental Film Review

• *March 1962*
March 1962 issue of *Continental Film Review*, featuring Brigitte Bardot.
• £4 • Book & Comic

▽ Buster

• *1960*
Buster No.1, published by Fleetway.
• £30 • 30th Century Comics

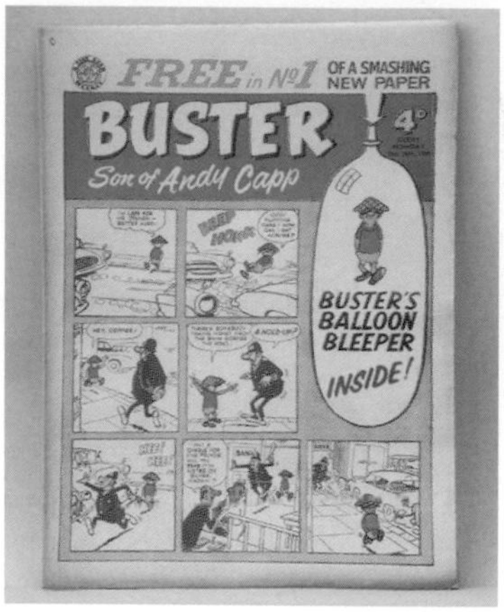

▽ Mystery in Space

• *1962*
Mystery in Space – featuring The Robot-Wraith of Rann! Published by D.C.
• £17 • Gosh

▽ Metal Men

• *1962*
Issue No.39 of *Metal Men* comic, featuring a special appearance by 'The Thanker'. Published by D.C. Comics.
• £20 • Book & Comic

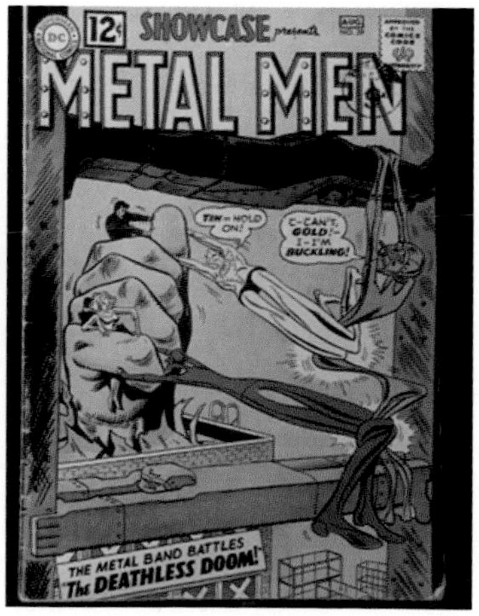

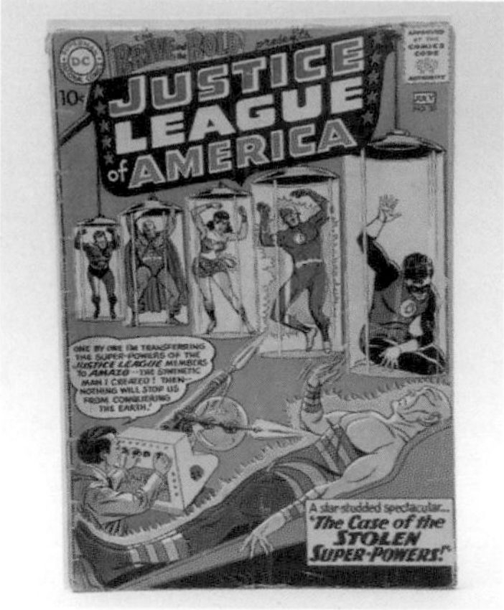

△ Justice League of America

• *1960*
Justice League of America – published by D.C. No.23.
• £50 • Gosh

△ Strange Sports Stories

• *1963*
The Brave and the Bold presents *Strange Sports Stories*. No.48, published by D.C.
• £10 • Gosh

△ Aquaman

• *1963*
Aquaman featuring Aqualad and The War of the Water Sprites! Published by D.C. No.10.
• £7.50 • Gosh

▽ Hawkman

• *July 1961*
Hawkman issue No.36 – *The Brave and the Bold* – published by D.C. Comics.
• £90 • Gosh

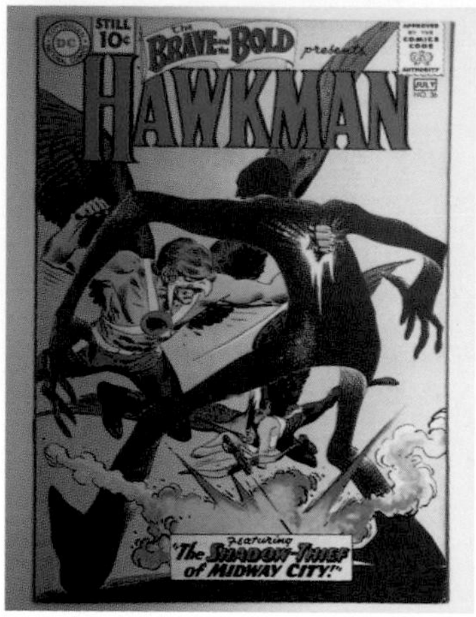

▽ X-Men

• *1963*
The X-Men published by Marvel Comics Group.
• £175 • Gosh

▽ Tales of Suspense

• *1963*
Tales of Suspense approved by the Comics code – No.37.
• £50 • Gosh

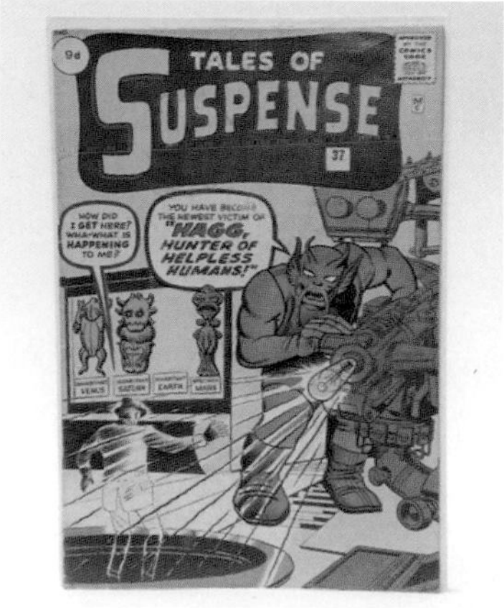

△ X-Men

• *1963*

The X-Men published by Marvel Comics Group. No.1.

• £250 • 30th Century Comics

△ Fantastic Four

• *July 1964*

Fantastic Four issue No.28 – *The Coming of Galactcus* – published by Marvel Comics.

• £55 • Gosh

△ Herbie

• *January 1965*

Herbie issue No.13 – *Pirate Gold* and *Mom's New Coat* – by ACG Comics.

• £15 • Gosh

▽ Giant Superman Annual

• *1963*

Edition No.7 of the *Giant Superman* annual.

• £20 • Book & Comic

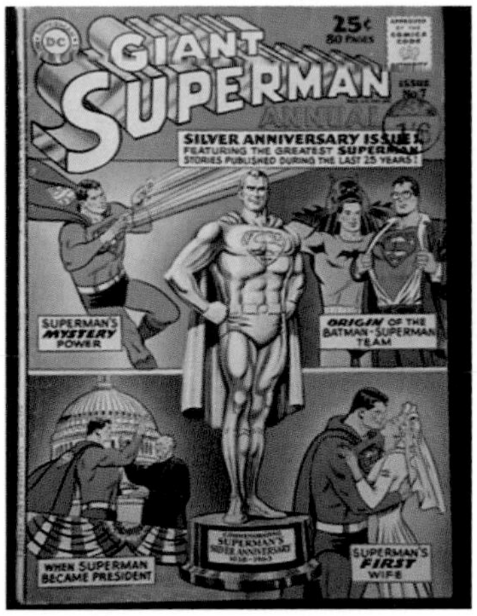

▽ Here Comes Daredevil

• *1964*

Daredevil the Man Without Fear! Published by Marvel.

• £45 • Gosh

▽ Modeling with Millie

• *December 1964*

Modeling with Millie magazine, No.36 – *The Greatest Love Story!* Marvel.

• £10 • Gosh

△ Strange Tales

• *March 1964*

Strange Tales issue No.118 – *The Human Torch* – by Marvel Comics.

• £17 • Gosh

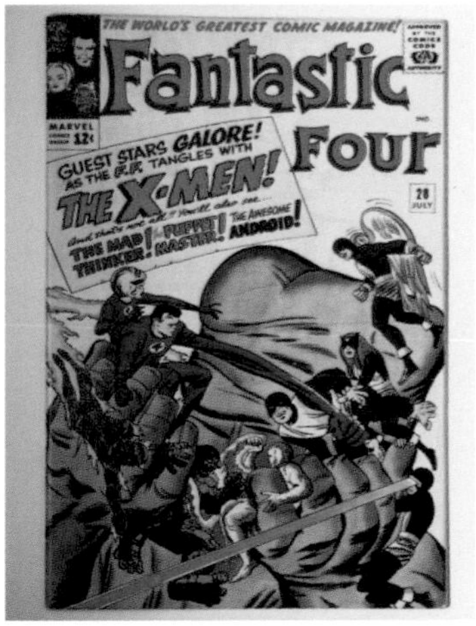

△ Fantastic Four

• *March 1966*

Issue No.48 – *The X-Men!* – published by Marvel Comics.

• £225 • Gosh

△ Diana

• *1968*

Diana No.305, an English comic published by D.C. Thompson.

• £1 • 30th Century Comics

▽ Daredevil

• *June 1964*

Daredevil issue No.2, published by Marvel Comics.

• £135 • Gosh

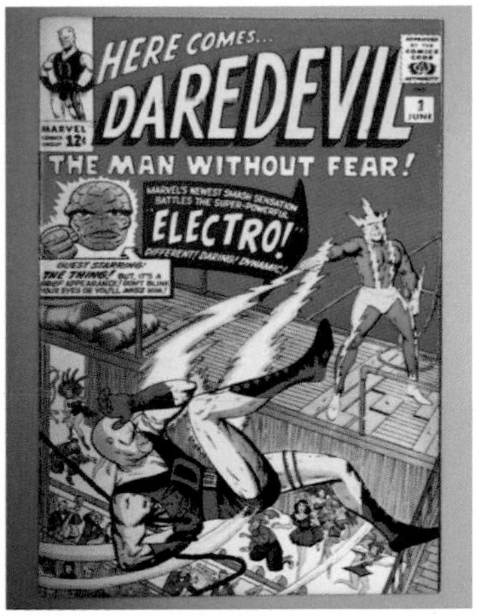

▽ Amazing Spiderman

• *February 1966*

Amazing Spiderman No.333 – *The Final Chapter!* – published by Marvel Comics.

• £50 • Gosh

▽ Man's World

• *1967*

Man's World Volume 13. No.1.

• £3–5 • Book & Comic

▽ Vogue

• *March 1967*
Volume 124, No.4 of Condé Nast's *Vogue* magazine.
• £15 • **Book & Comic.**

▽ Teen Titans

• *1967*
Teen Titans No.12 – published by D.C.
• £7 • **Gosh**

▽ Playboy

• *November 1968*
A 1968 issue of *Playboy* magazine with election cover.
• £8 • **Radio Times**

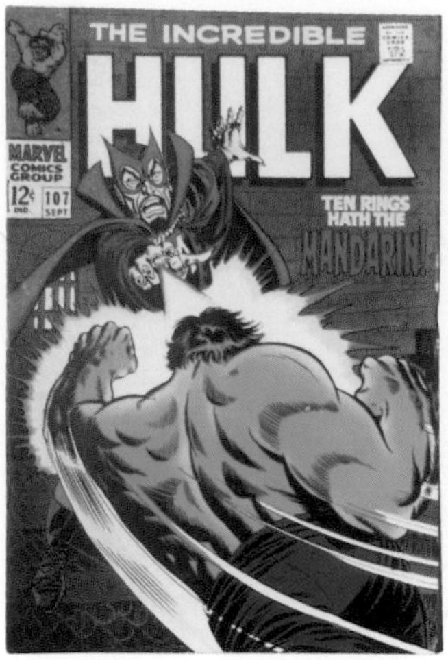

△ The Incredible Hulk

• *September 1968*
The Incredible Hulk, issue No.107, by Marvel Comics.
• £13.50 • **Gosh**

△ The Invincible Iron Man

• *June 1968*
Issue No.2 of *The Invincible Iron Man – Enter the Demolisher!* – by Marvel.
• £24 • **Gosh**

▽ Famous Monsters No.46

• *1967*
Famous Monsters of Filmland. Issue No.46.
• £5–10 • **Book & Comic**

▽ X-Men

• *January 1969*
X-Men magazine, issue No.52 – *Armageddon Now!* – published by Marvel Comics.
• £20 • **Gosh**

▷ Incredible Hulk

• *1969*
Incredible Hulk, issue No.112 – *The Brute Battles On!* – published by Marvel Comics.
• £12 • **Book & Comic**

◁ Superman Series

• *1968*
Set of cards, issued as series 950 by Primrose Confectionery Co, with sweet cigarettes. Illustration shows 'Space Nightmare'.
• £15 • **Murray Cards**

△ Strange Tales

• *1967*
Strange Tales No.161 – *Doctor Strange – The Second Doom.* Published by Marvel Comics.
• £15 • **Book & Comic**

△ The Dandy

• *1969*
The Dandy Book published by D.C. Thompson.
• £30 • **30th Century Comics**

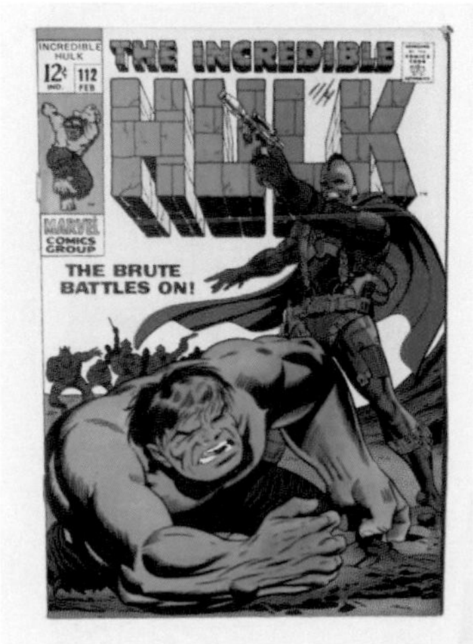

△ Playboy

• *May 1969*
May 1969 issue of *Playboy* magazine, in good condition.
• £6 • Radio Days

△ Thor

• *January 1970*
The Mighty Thor, No.172, original price one shilling, from Marvel Comics.
• £10 • Gosh

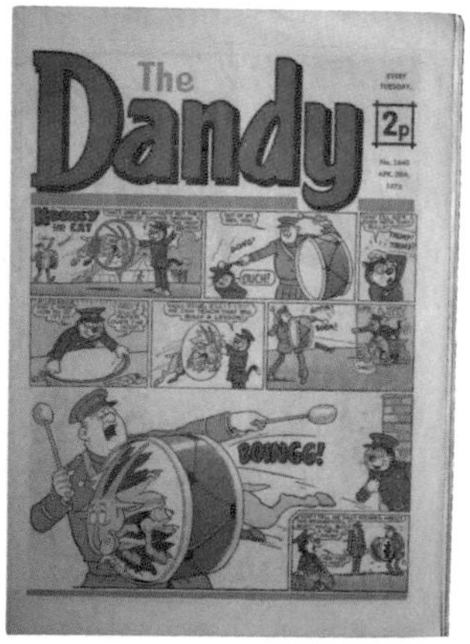

▽ Playboy

• *1969*
August 1969 issue of adult magazine, *Playboy*, featuring Penny Spinster and the living theatre.
• £12 • Book & Comic

▽ Star Trek

• *1970*
Star Trek No.7 March 1970. Published by Gold Key.
• £50 • Book & Comic

▷ Whitbread Inn Signs Series

• *1974*
Set of 25 cards of Isle of Wight public houses. This one shows The Railway Inn, Ryde.
• £80 • Murray Cards

◁ The Dandy

• *April 1973*
The Dandy, issue No.1640, published by D.C. Thompson.
• £1 • Gosh

△ Mayfair Magazine

• *1970*
Volume 3, No.1. British edition.
• £20 • Book & Comic

△ Legion of Super-Heroes

• *1973*
Legion of Super-Heroes- The lad who wrecked the Legion. No.1.
• £7.50 • Gosh

▽ Soho International

• *1971*
Volume 1, No.1.
• £10 • Book & Comic

▽ The House of Secrets

• *1971*
The House of Secrets No.92, published by D.C. Artist: Wrighton.
• £60 • Gosh

▽ Music Star

• *February 1974*
February 1974 issue of teenager's pop magazine, *Music Star*.
• £3 • Book & Comic

△ International Times

• *1974*
Issue No.2, Volume 2, of UK underground newspaper, *International Times*.
• £1.50 • Book & Comic

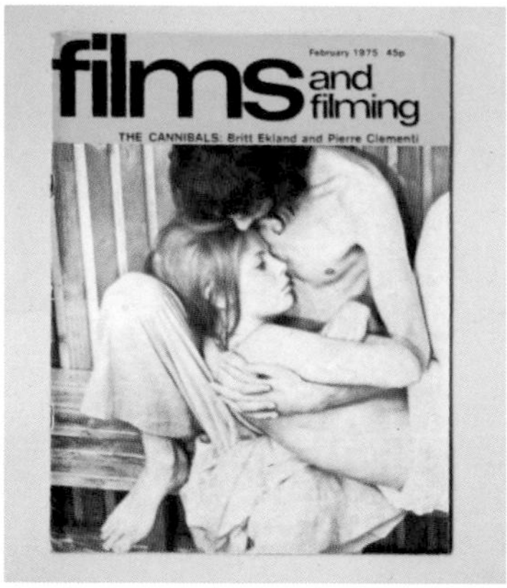

△ Films and Filming

• *February 1975*
Published by Hanson Books.
• £5 • Book & Comic

△ Interview

• *1977*
Newspaper format of Andy Warhol's magazine, *Interview*.
• £18 • Book & Comic

▽ Batman's Detective Comics

• *1977*
Batman's Detective Comics published by D.C. No.471.
• £7.50 • Gosh

▽ Music Star

• *1976*
1976 annual of teenage pop magazine, *Music Star*.
• £4 • Book & Comic

▽ Chris Riddell

• *circa 1977–78*
Cartoon of John Bull by Chris Riddell.
• £80 • Gosh

△ Second Coming

• *1974*
Issue No.3, Volume 2, of *Second Coming*, with a special feature on Charles Bukowski.
• £35 • Book & Comic

△ Rupert

• *1979*
Rupert the Daily Express Annual, published by Express Newspapers Ltd.
• £10 • 30th Century Comics

△ History of the VC

• *1980*
24 cards commemorating winners of the Victoria Cross, from Doncella cigars.
• £18 • Murray Cards

▽ Cerebus

• *1977*
Cerebus – the Aardvark Vol.I.
• £450 • Gosh

▽ Dr Who Discovers

• *1979*
Early Man issue from a spin-off non-fiction series, *Dr Who Discovers*. Booklet with colour poster.
• £4 • Book & Comic

▽ Blakes 7

• *October 1981*
Blakes 7 magazine issue No.1, published by Marvel UK.
• £8–£12 • Book & Comic

△ Abba International

• *1981*

Issue No.1 of Abba fan magazine.

• £4 • Book & Comic

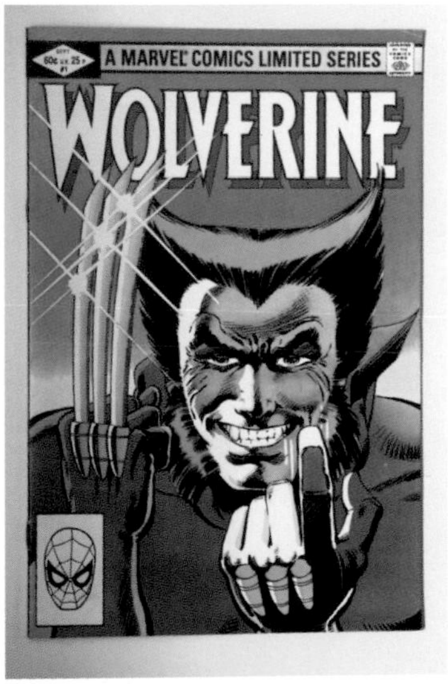

△ Wolverine

• *September 1982*

Issue No.1 by Marvel Comics.

• £7.50 • Gosh

▽ Love and Rockets

• *1982*

Love and Rockets – No.1. Published by Fantagraphics Books Inc.

• £12 • Gosh

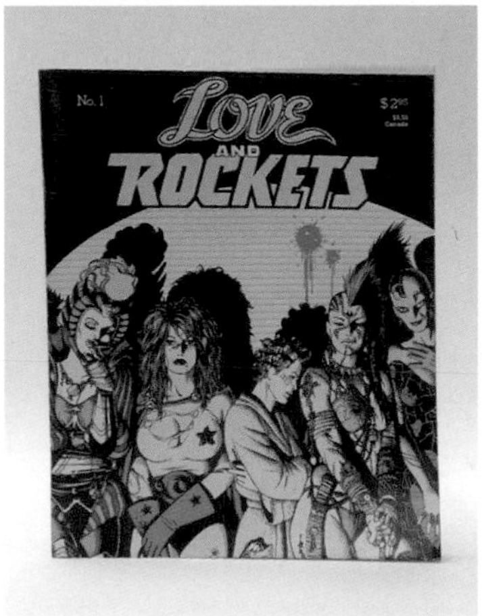

▽ i-D

• *1989*

Issue No.73 of fashion and lifestyle magazine, *i-D*.

• £3 • Book & Comic

△ London Standard Strip

• *1997*

A London *Evening Standard* strip of 'Bristow' by Frank Dickens.

• £60 • Gosh

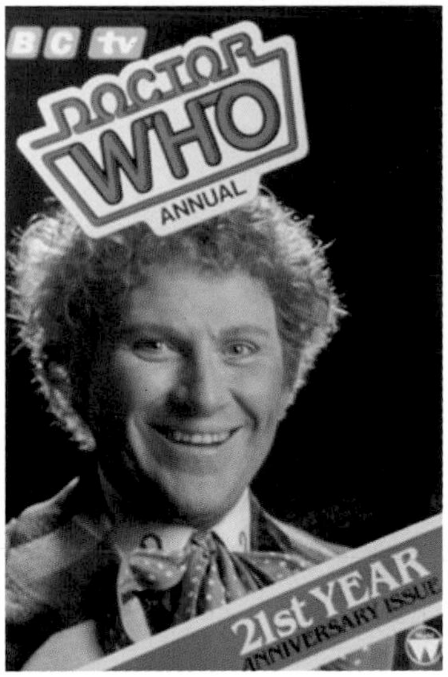

△ Dr Who Annual

• *1989*

Twenty-first anniversary annual of cult TV series, *Dr Who*.

• £3 • Book & Comic

△ Soba

• *1998*

Soba, Stories from Bosnia by Joe Sacco. Issue No.1.

• £2.95 • Gosh

▷ Radio Times Cartoon

• *1998*

A topical cartoon for *Radio Times* by Kipper Williams.

• £120 • Cartoon Gallery

▽ The Face

• *1984*

Issue No.52 of fashion and lifestyle magazine, *The Face*.

• £1 • Book & Comic

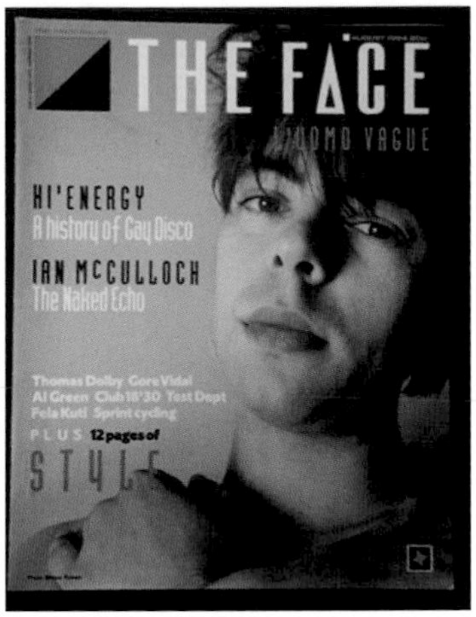

▽ V for Vendetta

• *1990*

V for Vendetta published by Vertigo/ D.C. Comics.

• £14.95 • Gosh

▽ Titanic Series

• *1999*

Set of 25 large-scale cards of the *Titanic*, produced by Rockwell Publishing at the time of James Cameron's film.

• £10 • Murray Cards

HANDBAGS

△ English Handbag

• *1831*

English leather handbag with floral design. Inside the inscription reads 'His Majesty King William the Fourth to his dutiful subject and servant John Singleton Lord Lyndhust AD 1831'.

• *width 19cm*

• £175 • Beauty

△ Black-Beaded Bag

• *1890*

Fine black-beaded Victorian bag with floral design of pink roses, blue cornflowers and daisies, with a filigree frame and paste jewels.

• *height 25cm*

• £495 • Beauty

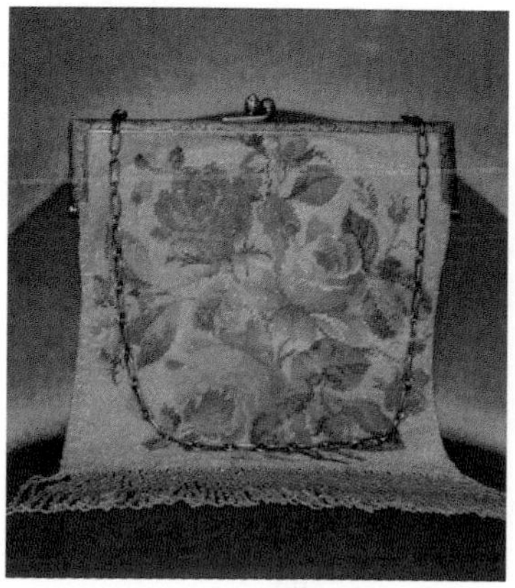

▽ Velvet Bag

• *circa 1860*

Victorian cream-velvet evening bag with a silver filigree frame, and fine cut-steel looped fringing.

• *height 23cm*

• £495 • Beauty

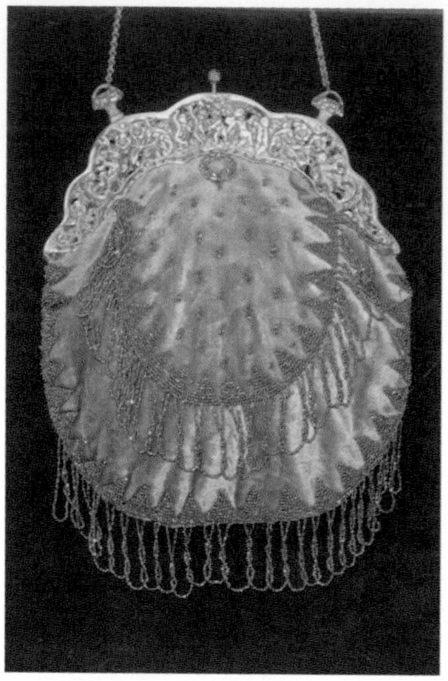

▽ Cream-Beaded Bag

• *1880*

Victorian cream-beaded bag depicting a basket of pink flowers with emerald green and pink beaded tassels, gilt clasp and chain handle.

• *height 21cm*

• £695 • Beauty

◁ Victorian Beaded Bag

• *1890*

Cream Victorian fine beaded bag with pink and yellow roses, with a silver gilt frame and pink and green glass beaded tassels.

• *height 25cm*

• £495 • Beauty

△ Velvet Bag

• *circa 1860*

Black velvet bag with cut-steel beading of a heraldic design. With metal clasp and chain.

• *height 28cm*

• £895 • Beauty

△ Victorian Bag

• *circa 1890*

Fine beaded green and gold bag with theatrical figures. Silver-gilt frame with cherubs set with semi-precious stones.

• *height 24cm*

• £695 • Beauty

▽ Art Nouveau Bag

• *1890*

Brown leather Art Nouveau chatelaine bag with irises and leaves trailing along the brass clasp.

• *height 17cm*

• £295 • Beauty

▽ Chain-Link Bag

• *1900*

Gilt chain-link bag with an Art Nouveau lady on the rim inset with sprays of berries inset with red stones and foliate design.

• *height 14cm*

• £395 • Beauty

◁ Art Nouveau Bag

• *1900*

Art Nouveau white beaded bag and frame, decorated with a floral design of poppies, wild flowers, with a gilt chain handle.

• *height 25cm*

• £295 • Beauty

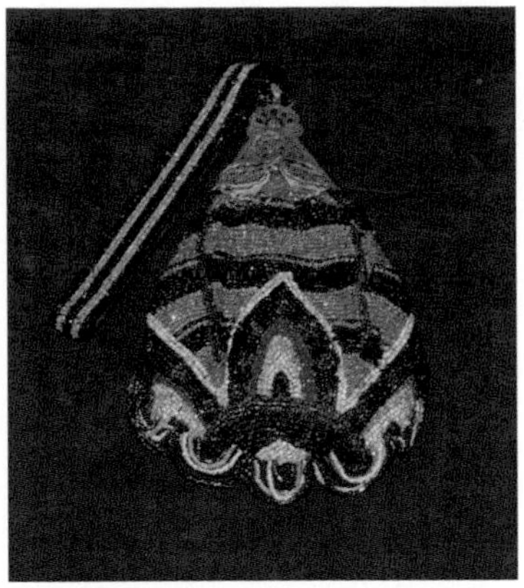

▽ Silk Evening Bag

- *circa 1920*

Black silk evening bag decorated with flowers in blue, red, and green with steel chips decoration.

- *height 18cm*
- £295 • Lynda Brine

▽ Beaded Bag

- *circa 1920*

Gold metal beaded bag with pink lotus flowers and a green and pink geometric design, with a metal clasp and gold and silver looped fringing.

- *height 20cm*
- £395 • Beauty

◁ Clochette Evening Bag

- *circa 1920*

Clochette-shaped beaded evening bag, with rows of blue and pink with a black metal filigree clasp and silver and black handle.

- *height 18cm*
- £395 • Beauty

△ Black-Beaded Bag

- *circa 1920*

Black-beaded bag with elaborate gilded frame inset with diamante.

- *height 13cm*
- £295 • Beauty

△ Metal-Beaded Bag

- *circa 1920*

Metal-beaded bag with a blue, pink and gold floral design. Gilt frame and chain.

- *height 22cm*
- £695 • Beauty

△ Leather Handbag

- *1930*

Brown leather handbag with chrome and orange bakelite clasp.

- *width 21cm*
- £295 • Beauty

△ Gold and Silver Bag

- *circa 1920*

Gold and silver beaded bag with geometric designs and gold fringing, with a metal filigree clasp.

- *height 26cm*
- £595 • Beauty

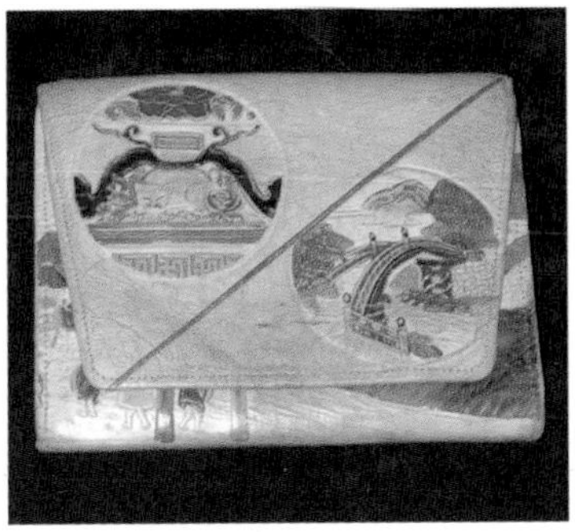

△ Leather Pochette

- *circa 1930*

Small leather pochette decorated with two cartouches; one with a sleeping cat with a peony, and the other with a red Chinese bridge over a river.

- *width 16cm*
- £125 • Beauty

▽ Sequinned Bag

- *1930*

French aubergine sequinned bag with small gold beading, a blue enamel clasp with small cornflowers, and a gilt frame.

- *width 20cm*
- £165 • Beauty

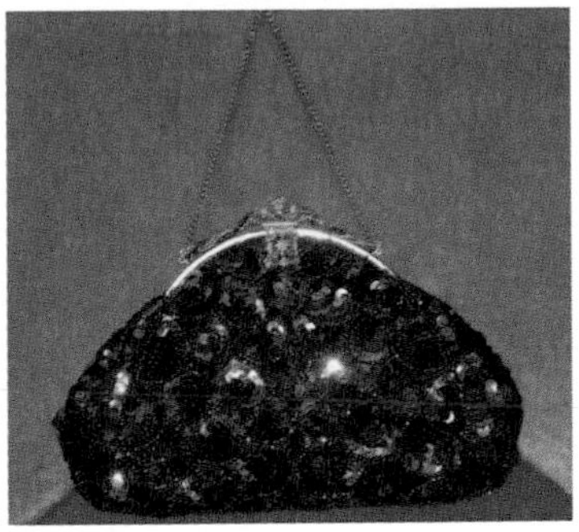

▽ Two Owls Bag

- *1930*

Brown leather bag with strap decorated with two owls with beaded glass eyes, surrounded by a foliate design.

- *width 21cm*
- £145 • Beauty

▽ Venetian Evening Bag

- *circa 1930*

Cream silk Venetian and chinoiserie design evening bag with pagoda-shaped clasp, decorated with coloured enamels and small white beads.

- *width 21cm*
- £395 • Beauty

△ Navy Shagreen Bag

- *1930*

Navy shagreen bag with unusual metal fittings and chain handle.

- *width 19cm*
- £495 • Beauty

△ Powder Compact Bag

- *1930*

Black suede French bag inset with a powder compact. A Jeannes Bernard Paris creation.

- *height 11.5cm*
- £245 • Beauty

▽ American Handbag

- *1940*

An American fabric and bamboo handbag with scrolled design.

- *24cm x 28cm*
- £150 • Linda Bee

▽ Red Snakeskin Bag

- *1940*

Red snakeskin box-shaped bag with a long carrying handle and brass fitting.

- *height 17cm*
- £295 • Beauty

▽ Crocodile Handbag

- *1940*

A 1940s classically elegant Argentinian crocodile-skin handbag with brass trim.

- *23cm x 28cm*
- £195 • Linda Bee

▽ Wicker Bag

- *1950*

Simulated wicker bag with a fabric head of palomino horse made by Atlas of Hollywood.

- *width 32cm*
- £165 • Beauty

◁ Petit Point Bag

- *circa 1940*

Petit point bag decorated with figures on horseback outside a castle, with an opaline beaded and enamel frame.

- *width 21cm*
- £395 • Beauty

◁ Blue Beaded Bag

- *circa 1940*

Blue beaded circular bag with an unusual gilt ball clasp, and generous beaded looped handle.

- *diameter 16.5cm*
- £295 • Beauty

△ American Handbag

- *circa 1950*

American clear perspex bag with geometric design on the lid.

- *height 11cm*
- £245 • Lynda Brine

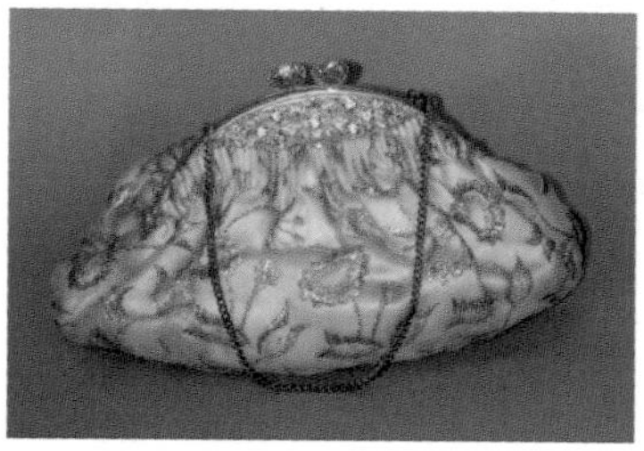

△ Evening Bag

- *circa 1950*

Cream silk evening bag with silver embroidery and beading with a chain handle.

- *height 17cm*
- £49 • Lynda Brine

△ Square Perspex Bag

- *circa 1950*

American square perspex handbag with brass design and fittings.

- *height 14cm*
- £180 • Lynda Brine

▽ Brown Bakelite Bag

- *1950*

America brown bakelite bag with lucite cover with faceted foliate design, made by Solar.

- *height 15cm*
- £395 • Beauty

▽ Plastic Tyrolean Bag

- *1950*

New York-made Tyrolean plastic bag with brass filigree foliate design, a red and black plaid pattern and a red leather handle.

- *width 20cm*
- £195 • Beauty

▽ American Handbag

- *1950*

An American 1950s handbag with a handle of pink velvet, hand-painted with pink flowers.

- *16cm x 24cm*
- £150 • Linda Bee

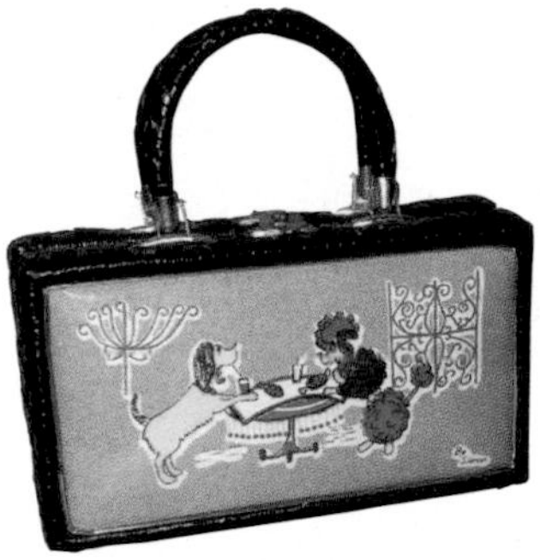

△ Poodle Handbag

- *1950*

An American fun handbag in laminated fabric with poodles on the front.

- *19cm x 28cm*
- £125 • Linda Bee

△ Bakelite Bag

- *1950*

American silver-grey bakelite bag with lucite top. With a flower and foliate design standing on ball feet.

- *height 15cm*
- £265 • Beauty

△ Bulaggi Bag

- *circa 1950*

Bulaggi plastic bag with gold metal fittings and handle, with the inscription Bulaggi on the right-hand side.

- *width 17cm*
- £85 • Lynda Brine

▽ American Felt Handbag

- *1950*

A 1950s American handbag made out of felt. Features a poodle design fashioned from sequins with a gilt chain lead.

- *28cm x 28cm*
- £220 • Linda Bee

▽ Bakelite Bag

- *circa 1950*

Bakelite tortoiseshell bag with metal clasp in the form of a flower with a pearl in the centre.

- *height 17cm*
- £290 • Lynda Brine

▽ Bakelite Bag

- *1950*

Light-brown bakelite bag with elaborate brass filigree clasp and fittings to handle.

- *width 27cm*
- £375 • Beauty

△ Pink Sequinned Bag

- *1960*

English baby-pink beaded and sequinned small evening bag.

- *width 22cm*
- £160 • Beauty

△ American Handbag

- *1960*

An American handbag made from black velvet with gold metal geometrical bands and shiny black perspex handle and lid.

- *20cm x 17cm*
- £150 • Linda Bee

△ Ken Lane Handbag

- *1960*

Ken Lane brown handbag with a dramatic coral circular diamante handle.

- *height 15cm*
- £295 • Beauty

KITCHENALIA

△ Enamel Bread Bin

- *1880*

French white-enamel bread bin decorated with a delicate painting of birds and cherry blossom and on the cover coastal landscape with mountains in the background in chinoiserie style.

- *height 33cm*
- £95 • Rookery Farm

△ Knife Sharpener

- *1880*

Knife sharpener with a brass inscription reading 'The Albert Knife Board J.& A Mc F. G.'

- *length 45cm*
- £30 • Michael Laws

▽ French Water Jug

- *1880*

Large enamel water jug with variegated blue and white base, decorated with pink flowers and green leaves.

- *height 37cm*
- £78 • Rookery Farm

▽ Enamel Storage Tin

- *1890*

French enamel storage tin with yellow and blue marbled pattern.

- *height 15cm*
- £22 • Rookery Farm

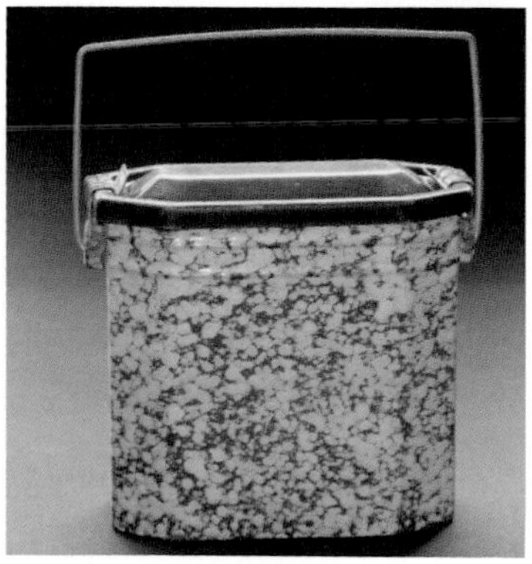

◁ Copper Pan

- *circa 1870*

Large 19th-century copper deep boiling pan, without lid. With two handles.

- *height 19cm*
- £135 • Castlegate

△ Brass Jelly Mould

- *1880*

Brass jelly mould with a hooped brass handle and fluted body.

- *height 19.5cm*
- £45 • Rookery Farm

△ Oak Cutlery Box

- *1880*

Oak cutlery tray with two compartments, divided by a central panel with a carved handle.

- *width 31cm*
- £45 • Michael Laws

△ Blue Enamel Candleholder

- *1880*

French blue enamelled candleholder with gold banding on the handle.

- *diameter 16cm*
- £20 • Rookery Farm

△ Copper Kettle

- *1860*

A Victorian copper kettle with good patination.

- *height 22cm*
- £140 • R. Conquest

△ Circular Mould

- *1880*

Ring-shaped brass jelly mould.

- *diameter 7cm*
- £24 • Magpies

△ French Water Jug

- *1880*

Large white French enamel water jug with red banding and a red pattern of squares and a central diamond with four gold bands.

- *height 29cm*
- £55 • Rookery Farm

△ Enamel Allumettes Box

- *1890*

Blue and white marbled wall hanging storage box, with the word 'Allumettes' in black writing.

- *height 20cm*
- £48 • Rookery Farm

△ French Coffee Pot

- *1890*

Orange enamel French coffee pot decorated with a bunch of cherries.

- *height 28cm*
- £85 • Rookery Farm

△ Butter Press

- *circa 1890*

Wooden butter press with a rose and leaf mould.

- *height 19cm*
- £58 • Michael Laws

▽ Larder Chest

- *1890*

French Provincial larder chest consisting of four drawers and a cupboard. The whole chest rests on ogee bracket feet. With distressed condition.

- *120cm x 90cm*
- £880 • Myriad

▽ Egg Timer

- *Victorian*

Victorian egg timer with wood-turned column and original glass reservoir.

- *height 14cm*
- £15 • Kitchen Bygones

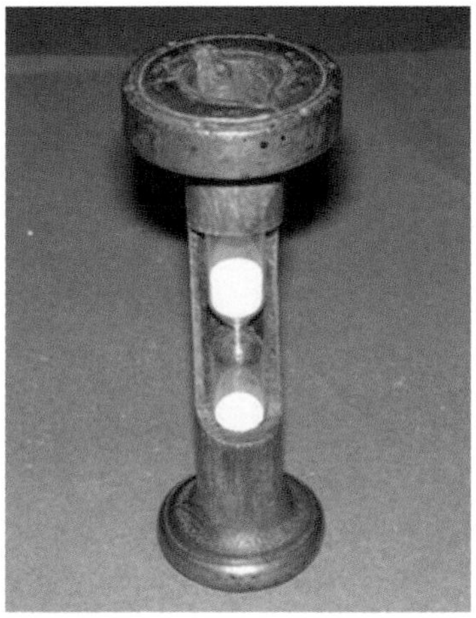

▽ Metal Weighing Scales

- *1890*

Metal kitchen weighing scales with metal base and copper scoop and weights, inscribed 'To weigh 2lbs'.

- *height 22cm*
- £98 • Rookery Farm

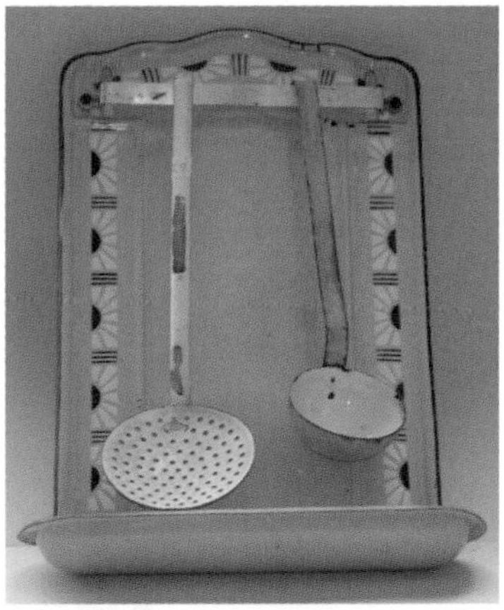

△ French Enamel Rack

- *1890*

French pale-blue enamel utensil rack with shaped top and blue and white sunshine border with two pale blue labels.

- *height 52cm*
- £70 • Rookery Farm

△ Milk Churn

- *1890*

A galvanised steel milk churn of unusual shape with floral garland and swag decoration.

- *height 65cm*
- £380 • Myriad

△ Washboard

- *1895*

Victorian washboard with a glass panel.

- *59cm x 30cm*
- £25 • Kitchen Bygones

▽ Blue and White Coffee Pot

- *1890*

A French enamel coffee pot, white with blue banding and a white scrolling pattern.

- *height 29cm*
- £78 • Rookery Farm

▽ Porcelain Jars

- *1910*

Five French cream pottery storage jars in three different sizes for farine, sucre, café, poivre and thé, each one decorated in blue with wild flowers.

- *height 22cm*
- £95 • Rookery Farm

▽ Flour Jar

- *20th century*

Glossed pottery flour jar manufactured by Hunts of Liverpool.

- *height 28cm*
- £48 • Kitchen Bygones

△ Enamel Casserole Dish

- *1910*

French enamel casserole dish with painted cornflowers and variegated blue, white and turquoise, with white handles.

- *height 18cm*
- £68 • Rookery Farm

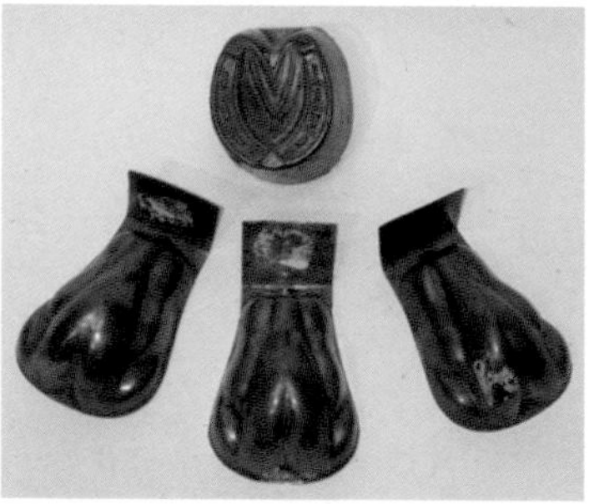

△ Brass Moulds

- *1910*

Selection of brass aspic moulds, comprising three shaped as roast chickens and one as a horseshoe. May be sold separately.

- *length 7cm*
- £60 • Magpies

△ Potato Masher

- *20th century*

Wooden potato masher with turned shaft in fruitwood on a circular wooden base.

- *height 15cm*
- £15 • Kitchen Bygones

▽ Herb Chopper

- *1910*

A Victorian double-handled herb chopping knife, with a pair of turned-wood handles.

- *length 21cm*
- £22 • Magpies

▽ Brass Weights

- *1910*

Selection of English brass weights with imperial measurements.

- £38 • Magpies

▽ French Red Pot

- *1920*

French red coffee pot with variegated panels of red and white and red handle and spout.

- *height 27cm*
- £78 • Rookery Farm

△ Brass Saucepan

- *1910*

Saucepan made of brass with iron handles and copper rivets.

- *height 6cm*
- £45 • Magpies

△ Cheese Cutter

- *circa 1910*

An Edwardian oak, brass and marble cheese cutter.

- *length 33cm*
- £295 • Castlegate

△ Art Deco Allumettes

- *1920*

Art Deco allumettes storage box decorated with a purple floral and geometric design with red spots.

- *height 13cm*
- £45 • Rookery Farm

▽ Terracotta Bread Bin

- *20th century*

Terracotta bread bin, with lid and carrying handles.

- *height 33cm*
- £65 • Kitchen Bygones

▽ Blue Coffee Pot

- *1920*

French enamel variegated blue coffee pot with noughts and crosses design.

- *height 27cm*
- £60 • Rookery Farm

▽ Shirt-Sleeve Board

- *1920*

Shirt-sleeve ironing board.

- *length 57cm*
- £25 • Kitchen Bygones

▽ Chamberstick

- *1920*

Metal chamberstick with green enamelled finish. Affixed to a fluted base and fitted with a carrying handle.

- *diameter 11cm*
- £12.50 • Magpies

▽ Sugar Sifter

- *circa 1930s*

Sugar sifter by T.G. Green, with blue and white banding, inscribed 'Sugar'

- *height 28cm*
- £58 • Magpies

▷ Brass Ladle

- *1920*

Brass ladle with long shaft.

- *length 45cm*
- £15 • Kitchen Bygones

△ Tin Opener

- *1920*

A cast-iron late Victorian tin-opener shaped like a bull's head. With steel blade and in good condition.

- *length 16cm*
- £14.50 • Magpies

△ Large Brass Kettle

- *1920*

Oversized brass English kettle.

- *height 20cm*
- £68 • Rookery Farm

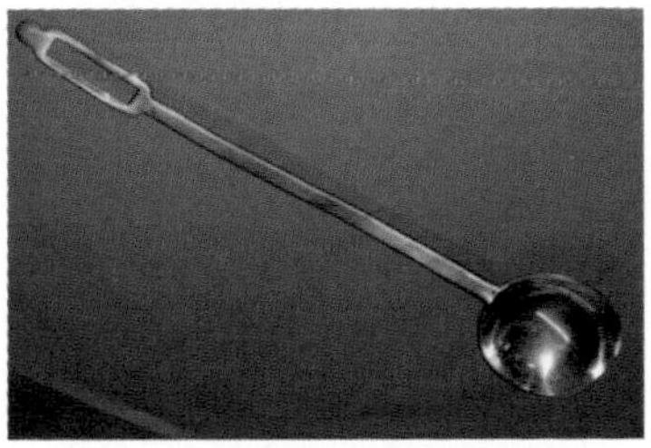

◁ Teapot

- *circa 1930*

Dartmouth Pottery teapot, with small white dots on a blue ground.

- *height 17cm*
- £38 • Magpies

△ Bakelite Thermos

- *1930*

English green bakelite thermos with metal handle.

- *height 34cm*
- £11 • Magpies

▽ Salt Jar

- *1930*

Hanging enamelled storage jar with a wooden lid and blue and white check design.

- *height 24cm*
- £38 • Rookery Farm

▽ Tea Tins

- *1920s*

Numbered and pre-painted tea tins, with oriental designs.

- £950 • North West 8

▽ Storage Jar Trio

- *1930s*

Three Cornish Ware storage jars decorated with blue and white hoops, with covers.

- *height 16cm*
- £45 • Kitchen Bygones

◁ Bread Board

- *circa 1940*

Circular wood bread board with the inscription 'Bread' and a foliate design surrounding a central flower.

- *diameter 28cm*
- £28 • Michael Laws

△ Fruitwood Flour Scoop

- *1940*

Fruitwood flour scoop carved from one piece of wood with a turned handle.

- *length 28cm*
- £20 • Michael Laws

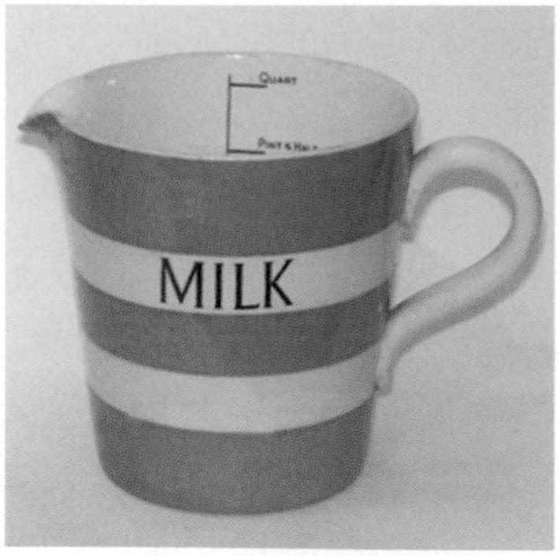

△ Measuring Jug

- *1940*

A blue and white-hooped quart measuring jug.

- *height 17cm*
- £12.50 • Magpies

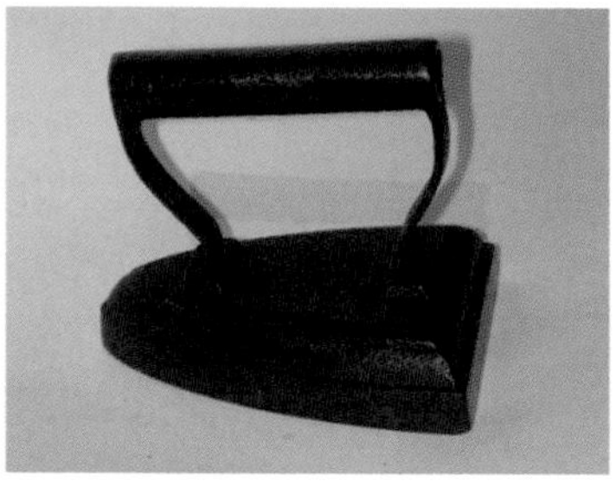

△ Household Iron

- *1940*

Small iron by J & J Siddons, West Bromwich.

- *height 8cm*
- £14.50 • Magpies

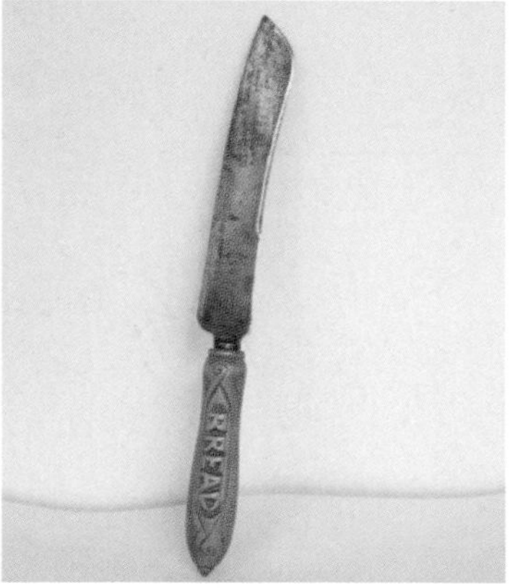

△ Bread Knife

- *1940*

Bread knife with a turned wooden handle with the inscription 'BREAD'.

- *length 31cm*
- £30 • Michael Laws

▽ Kitchen Scales

- *1940s*

Set of British-made 'Popular' kitchen scales in green enamel paint, with an accompanying set of brass weights.

- *height 45cm*
- £45 • Kitchen Bygones

▽ Flour Jar

- *1940s*

Enamelled tin flour container in flaked white and grey paint.

- *height 32cm*
- £25 • Kitchen Bygones

▽ Cornish Ware Mug

- *1940*

Cornish ware mug decorated with blue and white hoops.

- *height 8cm*
- £10.50 • Magpies

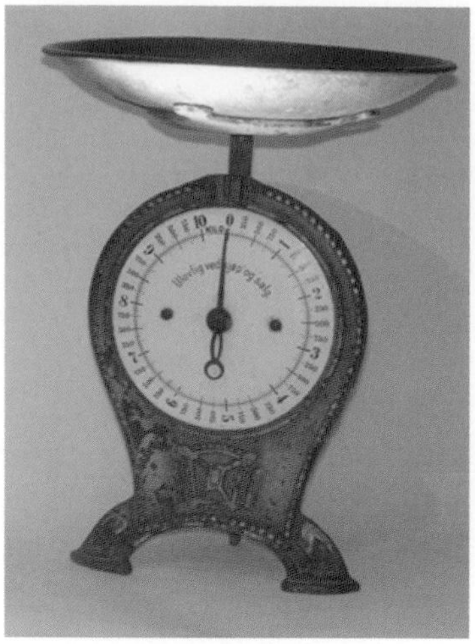

△ Weighing Scales

- *1940*

Swedish scales in bronze with enamelled dial and original weighing dish.

- *height 30cm*
- £54 • Magpies

△ Aluminium Funnel

- *1950*

An aluminium funnel manufactured by Stella.

- *height 15cm*
- £3.50 • Rookery Farm

◁ Tea-Towel Holder

- *1950*

French wall-mounted tea-towel holder made from plastic, with four metal hooks labelled in French.

- *length 34cm*
- £15 • Magpies

▽ Chicorée Tin

- *1950*

French Chicorée tin with a cream background and decorated with red flowers and a red and black geometric pattern.

- *height 21cm*
- £17 • Rookery Farm

▽ Peugeot Frères Coffee Grinder

- *1950*

Wooden coffee grinder with the makers mark in brass, Peugeot Frères, Valentigney (Doubs) with a large metal handle and wood knob.

- *height 19cm*
- £50 • Rookery Farm

◁ Pestle and Mortar

- *1940*

Pestle and mortar in white stone.

- *height 11.5cm*
- £28 • Magpies

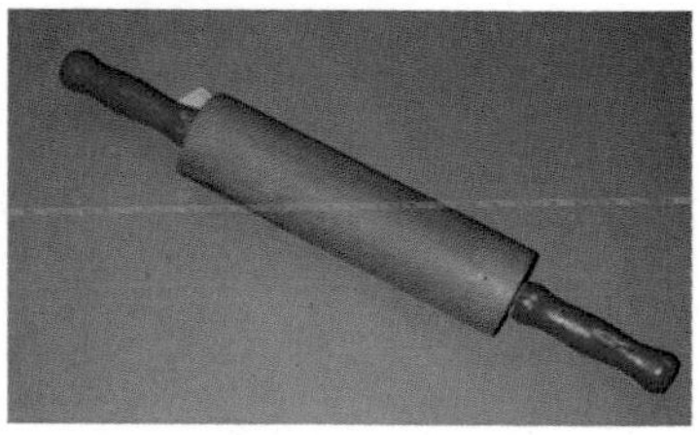

△ Rolling Pin

- *1950s*

Good quality wooden rolling pin with turned painted handles.

- *length 40cm*
- £10 • Kitchen Bygones

△ **Green Thermos**

- *1950*

Green Vacwonder metal thermos painted with a selection of sportsmen including runners, cyclists, shot putters and swimmers, made to commemorate the Olympic Games.

- *height 27cm*
- £65 • **The Manic Antique**

△ **Herb Storage Jar**

- *1950*

Herb jar and cover with red banding and the word 'Marjoram' on the body. Produced by Kleen Kitchenware.

- *height 10cm*
- £5.50 • **Magpies**

△ **Copper Kettle**

- *1950*

Copper kettle of bulbous shape with four feet and a tortoiseshell coloured glass handle.

- *height 21cm*
- £78 • **Rookery Farm**

▽ **Rocket Ice Crusher**

- *1950*

American rocket ice crusher made from aluminium with red plastic handle and container. Made by Fortuna.

- *height 32.5cm*
- £150 • **The Manic Antique**

▽ **Ceramic Rolling Pin**

- *1950*

Ceramic white rolling pin with green handles, inscribed 'Nutbrowne'.

- *length 41cm*
- £25 • **Magpies**

▽ **Devon Coffee Pot**

- *1950s*

Sandygate Devon coffee pot, with white polk dots on blue.

- *height 18cm*
- £38 • **Magpies**

▷ **Squeezer**

- *1950s*

Solid aluminium vegetable or fruit squeezer made by Atlantic.

- *height 20cm*
- £15 • **Kitchen Bygones**

△ **Coffee Pot**

- *1950*

Coffee pot by Kleen Kitchenware, with green concentric banding.

- *height 24cm*
- £28 • **Magpies**

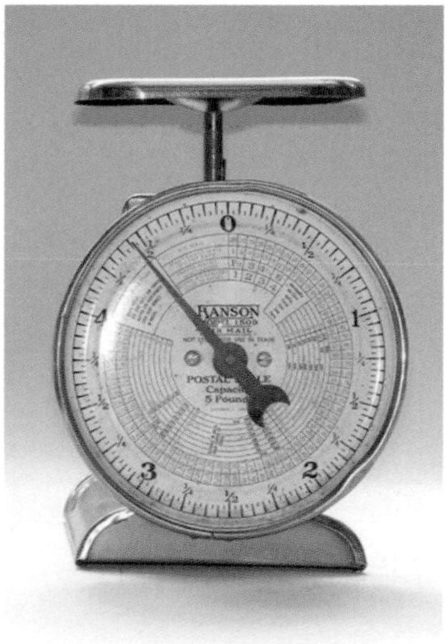

△ **Metal Weighing Scale**

- *1950*

Metal Hanson air-mail weighing scale.

- *height 25cm*
- £55 • **Rookery Farm**

▽ **Ceramic Coffee Jar**

- *1950*

Ceramic container for coffee, by Red Lamp Kitchenware.

- *height 16cm*
- £18 • **Magpies**

▽ **Pestle and Mortar**

- *1960*

Fruitwood pestle and mortar with turned decoration.

- *height 10cm*
- £12 • **Magpies**

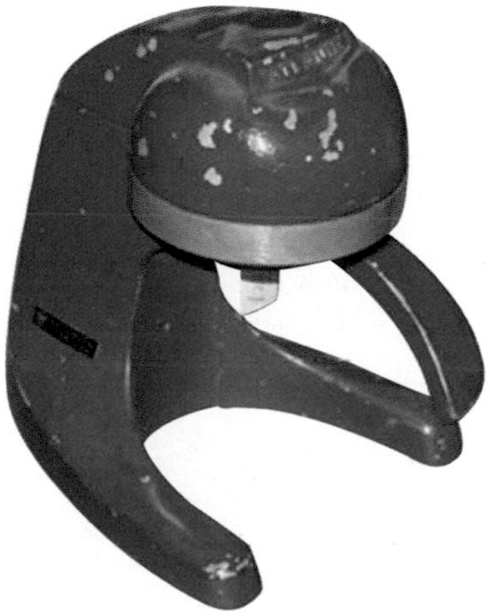

▽ **Hen-Shaped Dish**

- *1970*

Ceramic hen dish produced by Susan Williams-Ellis, Portmeirion.

- *height 13cm*
- £25 • **Magpies**

LUGGAGE

△ Travelling Trunk

- *1850*

English leather brass-studded and bound travelling trunk.

- *42cm x 91cm x 46cm*
- £400 • **Tredantiques**

▽ Top Hat and Box

- *circa 1850*

English leather box for a top hat with brass fittings and leather strap, with red velvet lining. Complete with hat.

- *38cm x 22cm 35cm*
- £290 • **Henry Gregory**

◁ Leather Gladstone Travelling Bag

- *circa 1870*

All-leather Gladstone bag with brass attachments, two straps and double handles.

- *length 69cm*
- £480 • **Henry Gregory**

△ Dispatch Satchel

- *circa 1900*

Leather dispatch satchel with a good patina, one main leather shoulder strap and three smaller straps.

- *width 61cm*
- £800 • **Bentleys**

△ Mail Bag

- *circa 1900*

Country house leather mail case with brass fixtures.

- *30cm x 25cm*
- £120 • **Henry Gregory**

△ Gun Case

- *circa 1900*

English leather gun case with brass fittings and leather handle, having leather straps with brass buckle.

- *84cm x 23cm x 9cm*
- £490 • **Henry Gregory**

▽ Collar Box

- *circa 1900*

Leather collar box in the shape of a horseshoe.

- *18cm x 17cm x 8cm*
- £48 • **Henry Gregory**

▽ Picnic Case for Two

- *circa 1910*

English Edwardian leather picnic case, fully fitted with custom-made accoutrements, including chrome-finished hip flask, food storage containers, original Thermos flask, complete bone-handled set of stainless steel cutlery and china crockery.

- *width 28cm*
- £550 • **Mia Cartwright**

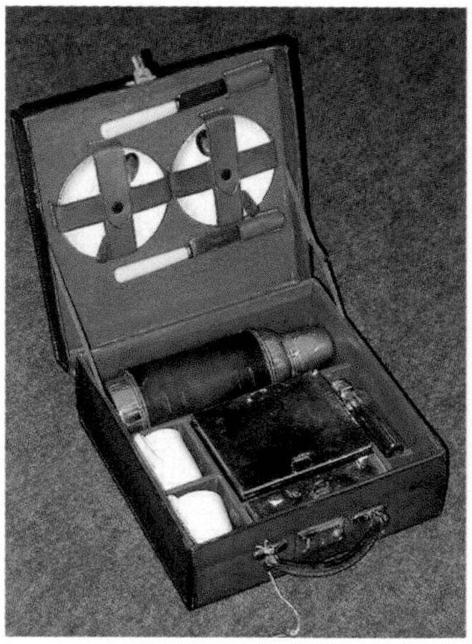

△ Hat Box

- *circa 1890*

Tan leather top hat bucket with brass fittings and leather handle.

- *height 23cm*
- £500 • **Bentleys**

▷ Leather Trunk

- *circa 1910*

With wooden base slats, reinforced corners, brass catches and locks and leather restraining straps with fitted loops. Interior is compartmentalised.

- *length 79cm*
- £70–150 • **Henry Gregory**

▽ Suitcases

- *1910*

Classic English leather suitcases with brass catches and locks and leather carrying-handles and lined interiors.

- £70 & £150 • **Henry Gregory**

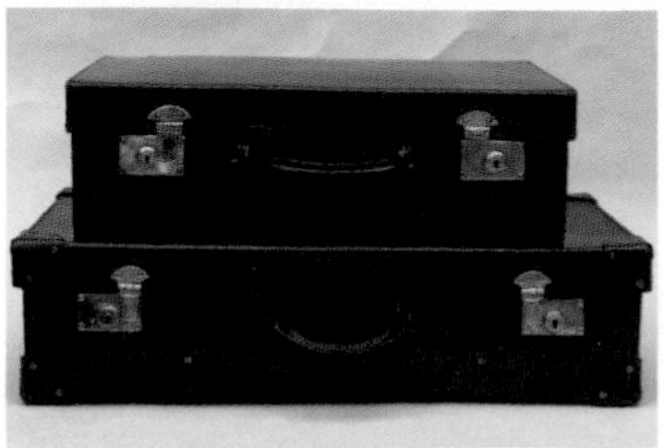

△ Leather Suitcase

• *circa 1910*
Square leather travelling case with brass fittings.
• *depth 40cm*
• £110 • **Henry Gregory**

△ Snakeskin Hat Box

• *1912*
Lady's python snakeskin hat box with snakeskin handle, made in London for a family in Brunei.
• *23cm x 33cm*
• £1,500 • **Julian Smith**

△ Goyard Hat Case

• *1920*
Goyard canvas hat case with a painted chevron pattern and a tan leather trim with small brass nails, leather handle and brass fittings.
• *25cm x 49cm*
• £1,500 • **Bentleys**

▽ Alligator-Skin Bag

• *1920*
An English stitched alligator-skin bag with leather handles.
• *55cm x 37cm*
• £175 • **John Clay**

▽ Hat Box

• *circa 1920*
Luxury leather hat box, holding several hats, with canvas lining and original travel sticker and initials 'K.C.' to front. Made in Northampton.
• *width 83cm*
• £375 • **Matthews**

▽ Leather Briefcase

• *circa 1920*
Leather brief case with circular brass fitting and leather straps and handle.
• *length 40cm*
• £500 • **Bentleys**

△ English Crocodile-Skin Bag

• *1920*
An English stitched, deep-grained, box-shaped, brown crocodile bag. The monogram initials M.A.W.P. on the top.
• *42cm x 60cm*
• £150 • **John Clay**

△ Gladstone Bag

• *1930*
Lady's gladstone leather bag with brass fittings and leather handle.
• *width 37cm*
• £75 • **Julian Smith**

△ Tan Hat Box

• *1930*
Tan leather hat box with nickel fittings and a leather handle.
• *diameter 41cm*
• £700 • **Bentleys**

◁ Louis Vuitton Case

• *1920*
Louis Vuitton case with leather trim and handle with brass fittings.
• *width 70cm*
• £1,000 • **Bentleys**

▽ Crocodile Case

• *circa 1928–29*
Crocodile case from Garrards of London, made from skin of animal shot by Captain SJ Bassett in Zanzibar in 1926. With padded satin lining.
• *37cm x 25cm*
• £1,500 • **H. & H.**

▽ Crocodile-Skin Case

• *1930*
Indian crocodile-skin case with handles each end and silver nickel locks.
• *32cm x 61cm*
• £450 • **Julian Smith**

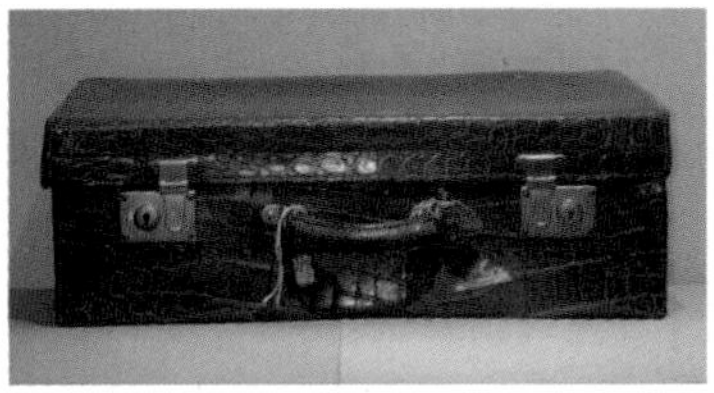

▽ Leather Suitcase

• *1930*
Brown leather suitcase with leather straps.
• *width 73cm*
• £120 • **Julian Smith**

▽ Picnic Hamper

• *circa 1940*
Made from leather, cane and canvas, with iron fittings and large rope handles at either end.
• *length 75cm*
• £480 • **Myriad Antiques**

△ Key-Wound Musical Box

• *1825*
Early key-wound musical box in plain fruitwood case with no end flap over the controls, four airs (no tune card), 19.7cm cylinder and square head comb screws.
• *9.4cm x 31.9cm*
• £2,400 • Keith Harding

△ Cylinder Piano

• *circa 1860*
Small upright domestic piano. Rosewood case with red-cloth frontal, by Hicks of London and Bristol. With 10 tunes.
• £3,300 • Keith Harding

▽ Six-Air Musical Box

• *1865*
Swiss six-air musical box in marquetry rosewood by Ducommun Girod.
• *20.5cm x 42.5cm*
• £3,300 • Keith Harding

▽ Mandoline Musical Box

• *1880*
Musical box by Nicole Frères, in marquetry rosewood. Plays twelve operatic airs, listed on original card.
• *13.75cm x 43.75cm*
• £2,900 • Keith Harding

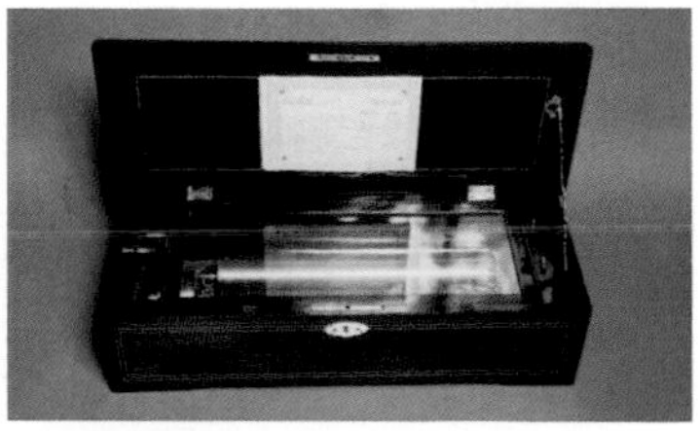

▷ Musical Box

• *circa 1895*
Nicole Frères key-wind musical box, playing eight Scottish airs. Rosewood lid with marquetry in wood and enamel.
• £3,950 • Keith Harding

△ Musical Decanter

• *circa 1835*
A very rare musical decanter of Prussian shape, with a Swiss movement. Plays two tunes.
• £1,250 • Jasmin Cameron

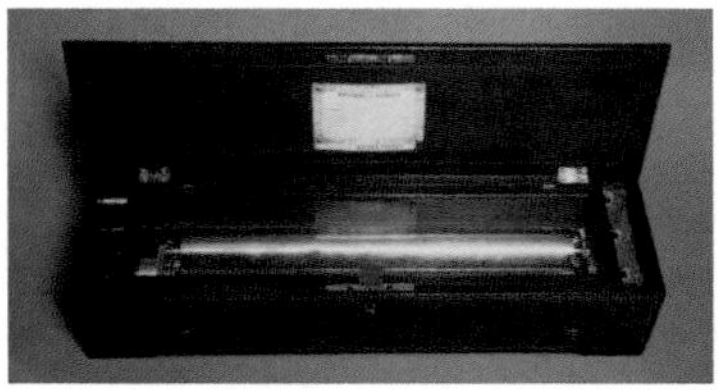

△ Musical Box

• *circa 1865*
Forte Piano by Nicole Frères of Geneva, with eight operatic airs.
• £4,995 • Keith Harding

△ Musical Box

• *1875*
Nicole Frères musical box playing eight airs, with 33cm cylinder and rosewood marquetry lid.
• *14.5cm x 56.3cm*
• £3,500 • Keith Harding

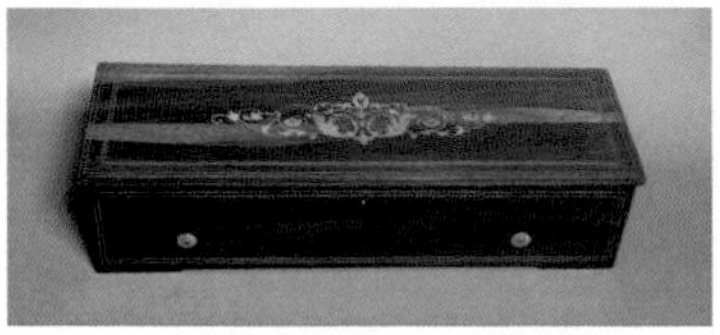

△ Swiss Musical Box

• *circa 1850*
Swiss musical box of eight tunes. Inlaid with song bird and foliage decoration.
• £3,250 • Pendulum of Mayfair

△ Victorian Cased Musical Box

• *circa 1875*
A 19th-century musical box, with marquetry designs, playing six airs.
• *length 41cm*
• £2,000 • Lesley Bragge

△ Coin-Operated Polyphon

• *circa 1880*
Polyphon in walnut case, the door centred with a brass lyre backed with red material. Supplied with ten discs.
• £5,500 • Keith Harding

▽ Musical Automaton

- *circa 1880*

With mechanically moving mill, train and ship at sea, all under a glass dome. The musical box plays two tunes.

- *height 39cm*
- £2,800 • Keith Harding

▽ Key-Wound Musical Box

- *circa 1880*

In plain fruit wood case with no end flap over the controls. Plays four airs, 22cm cylinder and square head comb screws.

- £2,400 • Keith Harding

▽ Rabbit Musical Box

- *circa 1890*

Rabbit in cabbage musical box. By Rouillet et Decamps. Rabbit first raises his head and then turns his head and disappears.

- £2,800 • Keith Harding

▷ Table Model Polyphon

- *circa 1890*

One of the most popular disc musical boxes, housed in a walnut case with floral marquetry lid. Supplied with ten discs.

- £3,500 • Keith Harding

△ Miniature Musical Box

- *circa 1890*

Two-air music box with the rare tunecard of the maker Ami Rivenc of Geneva. In fruitwood case inlaid with parquetry.

- £750 • Keith Harding

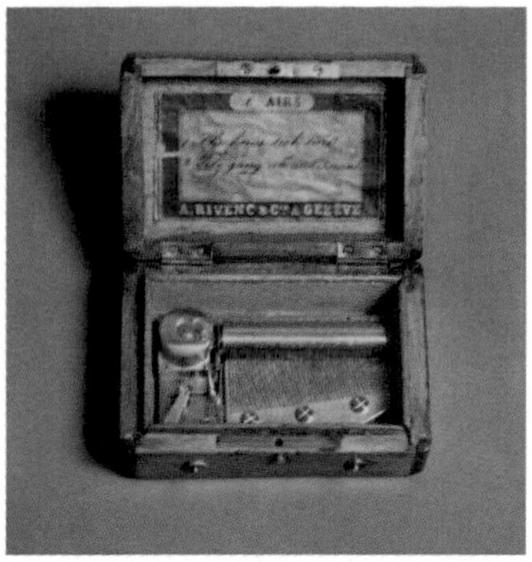

△ Musical Ballerina

- *1880*

Musical automaton ballerina, rotating and dancing arabesques. Musical movement in the red plush base by Rouillet et Decamps.

- *height 45cm*
- £4,500 • Keith Harding

▽ Swiss Musical Box

- *1888*

Swiss musical box in burr walnut with banding and six engraved bells by B. A. Bremond.

- *26.25cm x 48.75cm*
- £2,750 • Keith Harding

▽ Lecoultre Musical Box

- *circa 1890*

Musical box in a rosewood case, with original key. Plays six dance tunes, listed on original card.

- £2,400 • Keith Harding

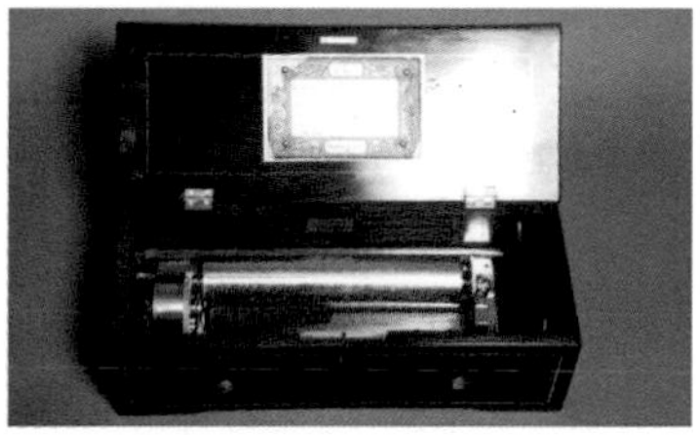

▽ Musical Banjo Player

- *1890*

French Banjo player musical automaton in orginal costume with porcelain face, by Gustave Vichy, Paris.

- *height 48cm*
- £4,900 • Keith Harding

▷ Swiss Music Box

- *circa 1890*

Unusual Swiss music box with convex glass lid by Mermod Frères.

- *27cm x 76cm*
- £4,000 • Vincent Freeman

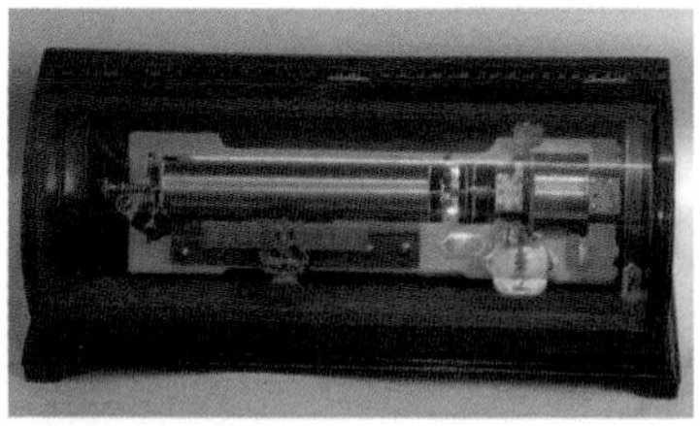

△ Bremond Mandoline Musical Box

- *circa 1890*

Cylindered musical box in a veneered rosewood case with kingwood banding.

- *cylinder 41.5cm*
- £3,950 • Keith Harding

△ Singing Bird Automaton

- *circa 1880*

Rare French singing bird automaton in a brass and gilded cage with moving chicks and singing bird. The cage with foliate design and gilded panelling.

- *58cm x 21cm*
- £6,800 • Vincent Freeman

△ Twelve-Air Musical Box

- *circa 1890*

Exceptionally good Nicole Frères 12-air, two-per-turn, forte-piano musical box, serial number 46094. Outstandingly beautiful case with exquisite marquetry on lid and front.

- £5,500 • Keith Harding

△ American Musical Box

• *1895*
Regina musical box cased in light oak with two rows of beading. On the inside of the lid is a central figure of a lady surrounded by cherubs playing instruments.
• *28cm x 55cm*
• £4,300 • Vincent Freeman

△ Phonograph

• *circa 1900*
America Edison phonograph.
• *height 42cm*
• £250 • TalkMach

▽ Phonograph

• *circa 1900*
A Columbia 'Graphophone' cylinder player.
• *height 48cm*
• £350 • Talk. Mach.

▽ Portable Street Barrel Organ

• *circa 1905*
Signed Thibouville Lamy but probably made by Marenghi of Paris. Seventeen-key action, playing six tunes – including 'Champagne Charlie' – through three ranks of pipes. With rosewood-veneered case and leather carrying strap.
• £9,500 • Keith Harding

▽ Portable Gramophone

• *circa 1920*
A Japanese portable gramophone, manufactured by Mikkephone, with unusual flattened horn speaker and carrying-case with strap.
• *width 30cm*
• £200 • TalkMach

◁ Polyphon Table Model Style 45

• *circa 1900*
Two-comb, Polyphon Sublime Harmony Piccolo, in superb carved walnut case with floral marquetry. With ten discs.
• £4,950 • Keith Harding

△ Table Polyphon

• *circa 1900*
A lockable table polyphon with a serpentine walnut case, 58-tooth comb. The polyphon is supplied with ten discs and winding handle.
• £2,600 • Keith Harding

△ Dog Model Gramophone

• *circa 1900*
By the Gramophone and Typewriter company. Model number 3. With original brass horn and concert soundbox. Completely overhauled.
• *70cm x 65cm*
• £1,950 • Keith Harding

△ HMV Gramophone

• *circa 1915*
His Master's Voice gramophone in mahogany case, with cast-iron components, straight arm and speaker below.
• *height 35cm*
• £280 • Ronan Daly

▽ Singing Bird Musical Box

• *circa 1900s*
Singing bird in brass cage with round embossed base, probably by Bontems.
• *height 28cm*
• £1,750 • Keith Harding

▽ Child's Gramophone

• *circa 1940*
A German child's gramophone, in tinplate.
• *width 17cm*
• £125 • Talk. Mach.

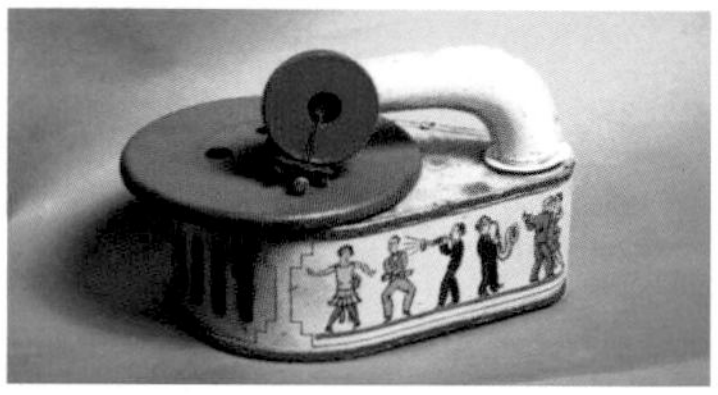

▽ Edison Phonograph

• *circa 1920*
Edison phonograph with metal swan-neck horn on a sprung support.
• *height 96cm*
• £2,900 • Keith Harding

△ Rock Ola Rocket

• *1946*
American Rock Ola Rocket juke box, type 1422, with 20 selections, in wood, chrome and bakelite, with a decorated front panel.
• *146cm x 81cm x 67cm*
• £4,000 • **Juke Box Services**

△ Rock Ola 1448

• *1955*
American Rock Ola 1448 juke box in chrome and bakelite. 120 selections.
• *141cm x 76cm*
• £5,000 • **Juke Box Services**

▽ Trashcan Juke Box

• *1948*
Trashcan juke box made from bakelite and WWII scrap airplane aluminium, the whole in a wood grain finish. With 20 selections of 78 rpms, made by Seeburg.
• *144cm x 100cm*
• £5,550 • **Juke Box Services**

▽ Ami H

• *1957*
American Ami H, one of the first of the car-influenced style of jukebox with a wrap-around glass. It holds 100 records, with orange and blue push-button electric selection, and plays both sides. Fully restored and in original condition.
• *159cm x 80cm*
• £7,000 • **Juke Box Services**

◁ Ami Continental

• *1961*
American Ami Continental juke box, which has push-button electric selection and plays both sides. In good working condition and fully restored.
• *170cm x 70cm*
• £6,500 • **Juke Box Services**

△ Rocket Juke Box

• *1952*
Rocket juke box, type 1434, in chrome, wood and bakelite, with 50 selections. This was the last 78 rpm player and the first 45 rpm player, by Rock Ola Manufacturing Company.
• *150cm x 76cm*
• £5,750 • **Juke Box Services**

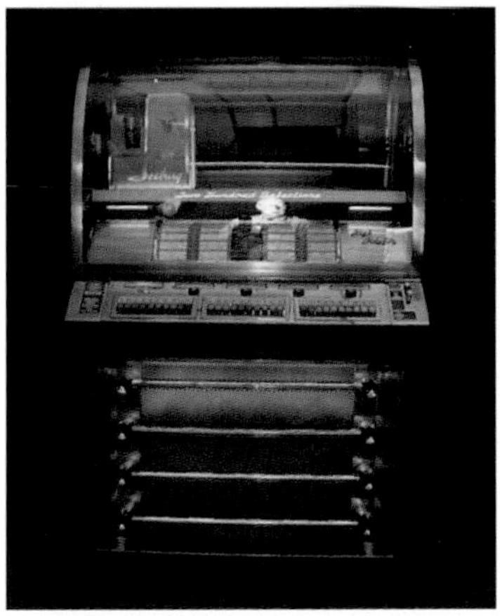

△ Seeburg V 200

• *circa 1960*
Chrome, wood and glass Seeburg V 200 in stereo, with a rotating title card drum and 200 plays.
• *height 125cm*
• £8,000 • **Juke Box Services**

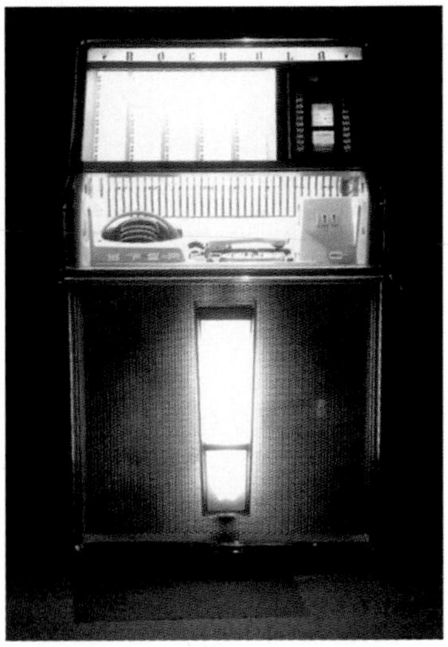

▽ Rock Ola Princess

• *1962*
Rock Ola Princess stereophonic juke-box, Model 1493. Takes 50 records. Stereo and auto mix, (plays with or without centres). In original condition. Made in the USA.
• *124cm x 76cm*
• £4,000 • **Juke Box Services**

▽ Zodiac

• *1971*
A Zodiac multi-selector model 3500 phonograph, manufactured by the Wurlitzer Company, Tonawanda, New York, USA, with the slogan 'Music for Millions'.
• *138cm x 74cm*
• £1,000 • **Juke Box Services**

◁ Mystic 478

• *1978–79*
Rock Ola Mystic 478 juke box in wood and chrome, with a digital micro-computer music system and 200 selections.
• *136cm x 104cm*
• £1,500 • **Juke Box Services**

PAPERWEIGHTS

△ French Sulphide

- *1840*

Paperweight commemorating the interment of Napoleon at Les Invalides, Paris. The sulphide with various Napoleonic emblems, inscription and date.

- *diameter 8cm*
- £250 • G.D. Coleman

△ Baccarat Blue Primose

- *circa 1850*

Baccarat glass paperweight showing a blue primrose and leaves on a clear ground with star-cut base. Good condition.

- *diameter 5.5cm*
- £1,250 • G.D. Coleman

△ St Louis Crown Weight

- *circa 1850*

St Louis Crown weight with a design of multicoloured canes.

- *diameter 5.5cm*
- £1,350 • G.D. Coleman

▽ Baccarat Millefiore

- *1847*

Closepack. Signed 'B 1847'.

- *diameter 6cm*
- £1,500 • G.D. Coleman

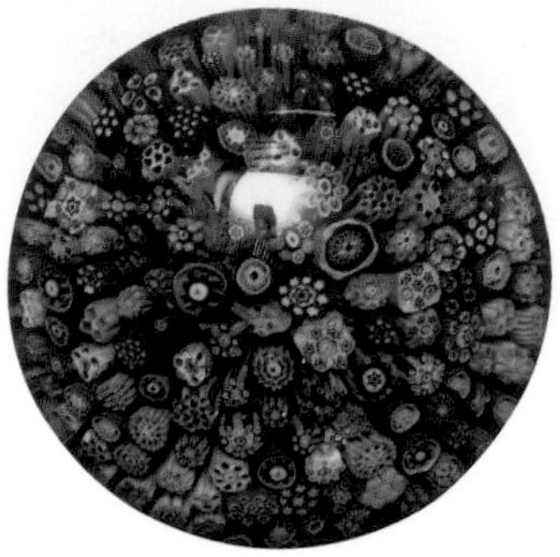

▽ Baccarat Mushroom

- *circa 1850*

Baccarat Millefiori paperweight mushroom with blue torsade and stonecut base.

- *diameter 7cm*
- £950 • G.D. Coleman

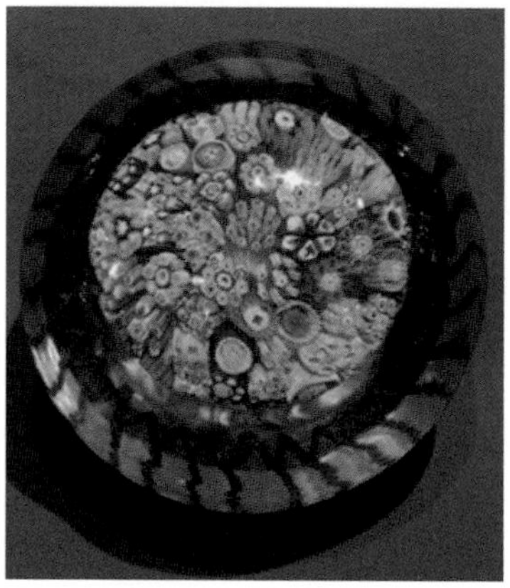

▽ Clichy Green Swirl

- *circa 1850*

Clichy paperweight with green and white swirls and central pink and white canes.

- *diameter 7cm*
- £1,350 • G.D. Coleman

△ Clichy Blue Swirl

- *1848*

A rare Clichy swirl glass paperweight in blue and white with central pink and white cones.

- *diameter 7cm*
- £1,350 • G.D. Coleman

△ Floral St Louis

- *1850*

St Louis paperweight with pink floral cone design.

- *diameter 6.5cm*
- £7,850 • G.D. Coleman

△ Baccarat Pansy

- *circa 1850*

French Baccarat paperweight, inset with a red pansy and green foliage, on stonecut base.

- *diameter 5.5cm*
- £680 • G.D. Coleman

▽ Baccarat Scrambled

- *circa 1850*

Paperweight of a type called 'End of Day', since they were made by glass workers after hours with leftovers from the floor.

- *diameter 8cm*
- £580 • G.D. Coleman

▽ Baccarat Garland Posy

- *circa 1850*

Baccarat paperweight inset with a red pansy and leaves, with stonecut base.

- *diameter 6cm*
- £1,850 • G.D. Coleman

▽ Baccarat Millefiori

- *circa 1850*

Millefiori closepack paperweight with various coloured and patterned canes.

- *diameter 6cm*
- £1,500 • G.D. Coleman

△ St Louis Sanam-Holed

- *circa 1850*

St Louis Sanam-holed, faceted paperweight with pastel jumbled cones.

- *diameter 7cm*
- £995 • G.D. Coleman

△ St Louis Miniature

- *circa 1855*

St Louis miniature paperweight with pink floral design.

- *diameter 4.5cm*
- £385 • G.D. Coleman

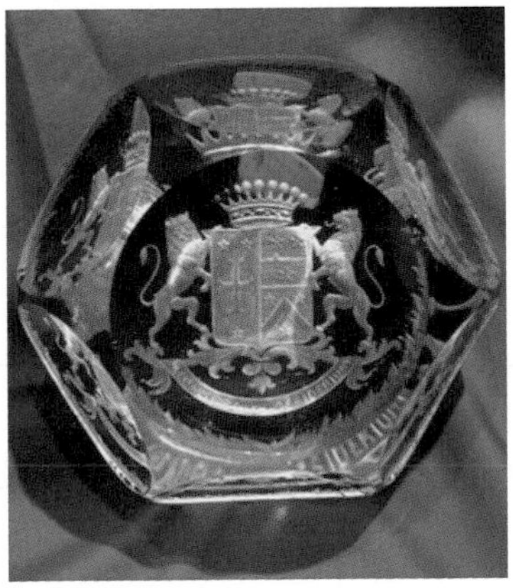

△ Bohemian Magnum

- *1890*

Glass hexagonal paperweight with an etched glass coat of arms with amber faceted flank.

- *11.5cm*
- £380 • G.D. Coleman

▽ St Louis Paperweight

- *circa 1855*

A St Louis glass paperweight with a mauve, dahlia flower pattern with green leaves.

- *diameter 8cm*
- £1,350 • G.D. Coleman

▽ Green Jasper

- *circa 1860*

Mid-19th-century St Louis paperweight with flowers on a green jasper ground.

- *diameter 6cm*
- £380 • G.D. Coleman

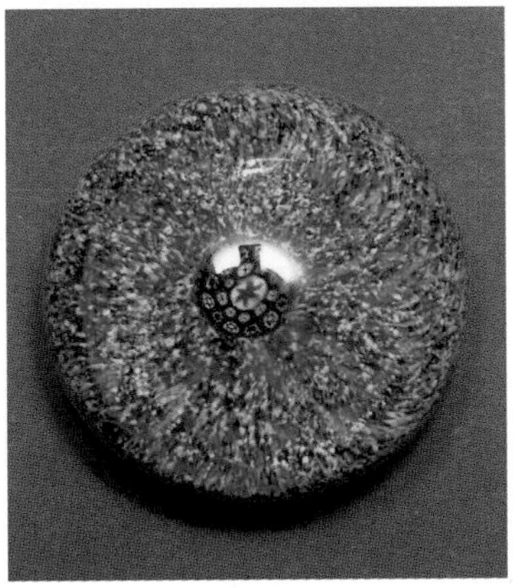

▽ American 'Cherries'

- *late 19th century*

American glass paperweight with central cherry pattern on a white latticino ground.

- *diameter 7cm*
- £620 • G.D. Coleman

△ St Louis Magnum

- *circa 1850*

Rare, magnum-sized glass paperweight, decorated with a bouquet on a cigar background. Unrecorded, so probably a one-off design and size.

- *diameter 10cm*
- £5,560 • G.D. Coleman

△ Sturbridge

- *circa 1880*

English Sturbridge Victorian concentric paperweight with multi-coloured cane design.

- *diameter 8cm*
- £380 • G.D. Coleman

△ Baccarat Millefiori

- *1960*

Millefiori closepack designed paperweight with various coloured and patterned canes.

- *diameter 7cm*
- £65 • London Antique

▽ Clichy Swirl

- *circa 1850*

Clichy swirl paperweight in green with central flower.

- *diameter 6cm*
- £1,200 • G.D. Coleman

▽ White Friars

- *circa 1880*

White Friars paperweight with concentric canes.

- *diameter 8.5cm*
- £290 • G.D. Coleman

▽ Circular Italian Paperweight

- *1960*

Circular Italian paperweight with a silver bubble effect with stylised pink and white flowers and a lime-green border.

- *diameter 7cm*
- £55 • London Antique

PHOTOGRAPHS

▽ Maynooth College

• *1858*

Maynooth College (the National College of Saint Patrick) seen through an arch. Founded in the year 1795, the college is situated in County Kildare. By the photographer William England, LSC. Black and white fibre silver gelatin 'quad' photograph, printed from original negative in Hulton Getty darkrooms. Limited edition: 300.

• *length 61cm*

• £250 • **Hulton Getty**

▽ Silver Gelatin Print

• *20th century*

'Monsieur Plitt Teaching Tupy to Jump over the Brook', Jacques-Henri Lartigue.

• *length 75cm*

• £1,850 • **Photo. Gallery**

▽ French Photograph Album

• *circa 1890*

Brass-bound album with several plates of photographs.

• *length 23cm*

• £165 • **Castlegate**

△ River Ottawa

• *1859*

Gentlemen contemplate the beauty of the Chaudière falls on the River Ottawa by photographer William England, LSC. A black and white fibre, silver gelatin photograph, printed from original negative in Hulton Getty darkrooms. Limited Edition: 300.

• *length 40.7cm*

• £185 • **Hulton Getty**

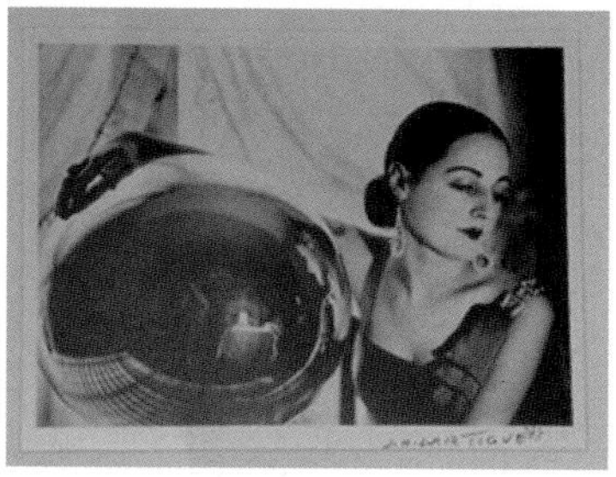

△ Silver Gelatin Print

• *1929*

'Solange David, Paris, 1929', by Jacques-Henri Lartigue. Silver gelatin print, signed recto.

• *30.5cm x 35.5cm*

• £4,600 • **Photo. Gallery**

▽ Victoria Bridge

• *1859*

Victoria Bridge – Special limited edition. A lone man sitting on the Victoria Railway Bridge over the St Lawrence River in Montreal, during its construction.

Photographer: William England/ London Stereoscopic Company. Modern platinum print made from original glass negative by Studio 31. Platinum Limited edition: 10 only.

• *paper size: 40.7cm x 30.5cm, image size: 23cm x 20.4cm*

• £500 • **Hulton Getty**

▷ Great Loss of Life

• *16th April 1912*

Newspaper boy Ned Parfett selling copies of the *Evening News* telling of the Titanic maritime disaster. Photographer: Topical Press Agency. Modern black and white, fibre silver gelatin archival photograph, printed in Hulton Getty darkrooms. Limited edition: 300.

• *length 40.7cm*

• £185 • **Hulton Getty**

△ Twin Angels

• *circa 1865*

A pair of baby twins lie sleeping while a pair of twin angels watch over them. Photographer: London Stereoscopic Co. Black and white fibre, silver gelatin photograph, printed from original negative in Hulton Getty darkrooms. Limited edition: 300.

• *length 30.5cm*

• £125 • **Hulton Getty**

▽ Children of George V

• *1st June 1902*

Autographs and photograph of the children of George V at York House, St James's Palace.

• £450 • **The Armoury**

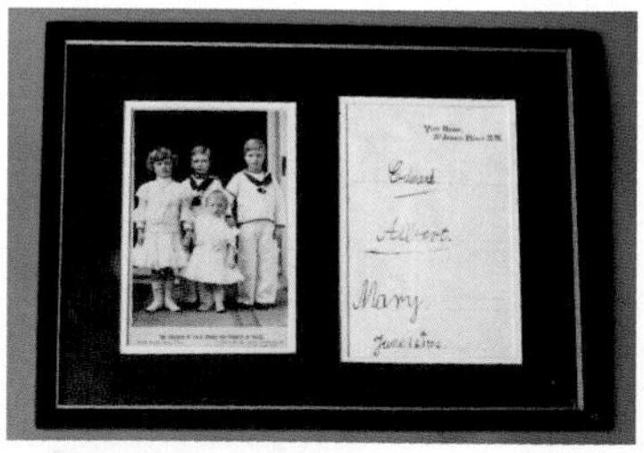

◁ Early Aircraft

• *11th April 1907*

Mr Guillon attempts to fly his Guillon and Clouzy aeroplane on the Epsom Downs, Surrey. Photographer: Topical Press Agency. Modern black and white fibre, silver gelatin archival photograph, printed in Hulton Getty darkrooms. Limited edition: 300.

• *length 40.7cm*

• £185 • **Hulton Getty**

△ Stamford Bridge

• *circa 1925*
Stamford Bridge, Chelsea Football Club's Stadium, by the photographer A.H. Robinson. Black and white fibre, silver gelatin photograph, printed from original negative in Hulton Getty Darkrooms. Limited Edition: 300.
• *61cm x pro, (panoramic format)*
• £250 • Hulton Getty

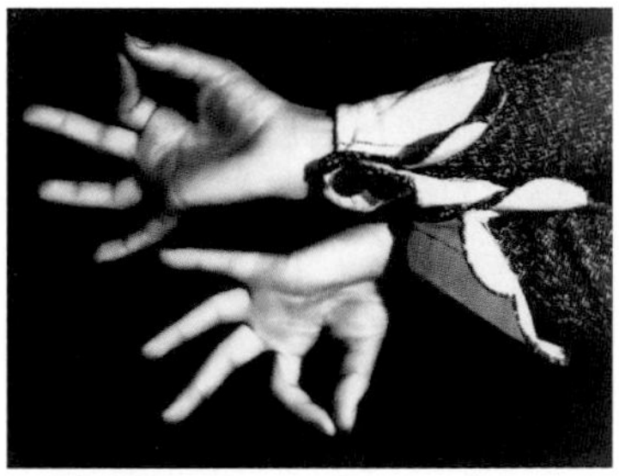

△ Jessie's Hands

• *1930*
The hands of Jessie Matthews (1907–1981), dancer and film-star, by the photographer Sasha. Black and white toned fibre, silver gelatin photograph, printed from original negative in Hulton Getty darkrooms. Limited edition: 300.
• *length 50.8cm*
• £337 • Hulton Getty

△ Signed Print

• *1931*
'El Ensueño' (The Daydreamer) taken in 1931 in Mexico, by Manuel Alvarez Bravo. Silver gelatin print, signed verso.
• *25.5cm x 20cm*
• £1,500 • Photo. Gallery

△ Signed Modern Print

• *1931*
'Renée, Paris. January 1931' by Jacques-Henri Lartigue. Signed modern silver gelatin print.
• *length 50cm*
• £3,000 • Photo. Gallery

△ Signed Modern Print

• *1938*
'Good Reputation Sleeping' by Manuel Alvarez Bravo.
• *length 20cm*
• £1,250 • Photo. Gallery

△ Racing Yacht

• *6th August 1935*
Racing Yacht 'Candida' during a race at the Cowes Regatta. Photographer: E.Dean, Topical Press Agency. Modern black and white, fibre silver gelatin archival photograph, printed in Hulton Getty darkrooms. Limited edition: 300
• *length 61cm*
• £250 • Hulton Getty

△ Bill Brandt Print

• *1930*
'Parlour Maid at Window, Kensington, 1930' by Bill Brandt. Silver gelatin print, signed recto.
• *30.5cm x 40cm*
• £1,300 • Photo. Gallery

△ SS Arctees

• *26th January 1934*
The SS *Arctees*, designed by Sir Joseph Isherwood with the 'Arcform' design of hull. This shot shows the unusual rudder design, before she was launched at Furness Shipbuilding Co's yard at Haverton-on-Tees, County Durham. Photographer: Douglas Miller, Topical Press Agency. Modern black and white, fibre silver gelatin archival photograph, printed in Hulton Getty Darkrooms. Limited edition of 300.
• *length 40.7cm*
• £185 • Hulton Getty

▽ Grand Central Light

• *circa 1930*
Beams of sunlight streaming through the windows at Grand Central Station, New York, by the photographer Hal Morey, Fox Photos. Modern black and white fibre, silver gelatin archival photograph, printed in Hulton Getty darkrooms. Limited edition: 300.
• *length 50.8cm*
• £225 • Hulton Getty

▽ Night Time, New York

• *1936*
Paramount Building in Times Square, New York, towers over Schenley's Chinese Restaurant. Photographer: Fox Photos Collection. Modern black and white, fibre silver gelatin archival photograph, printed in Hulton Getty darkrooms. Limited edition: 300.
• *length 50.8cm*
• £225 • Hulton Getty

◁ Power Station

• *circa 1935*
London's Battersea Power Station, before the chimneys increased to four. Photographer: Fox Photos Collection. Modern black and white, fibre silver gelatin archival photograph, printed in Hulton Getty darkrooms. Limited edition: 300.
• *length 40.7cm*
• £185 • Hulton Getty

△ Coronation Photograph

• *12th May 1937*
George VI coronation photograph, by Dorothy Wilding. Autographed by the King and Queen Elizabeth.
• £2,000 • The Armoury

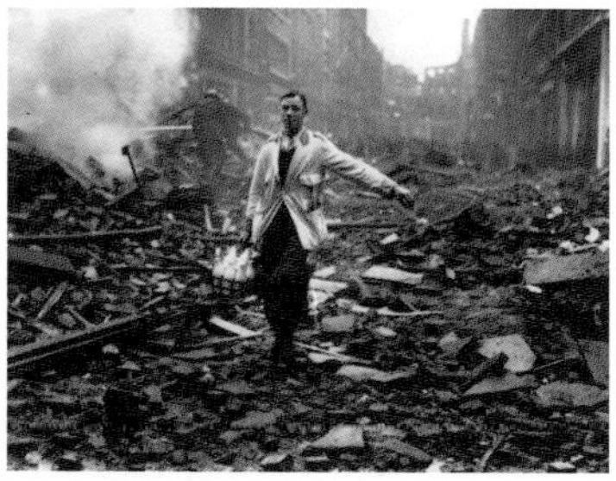

△ Delivery after Raid

• *9th October 1940*
'Delivery After Raid' – A milkman delivering milk in a London street devastated during a German bombing raid. Firemen are dampening down the ruins behind him. Photographer: Fred Morley, Fox Photos. Modern black and white, fibre silver gelatin archival photograph, printed in Hulton Getty darkrooms. Limited edition: 300.
• *length 40.7cm*
• £185 • Hulton Getty

△ Untitled Print

• *circa 1950*
Untitled silver gelatin print from the 1950s, signed recto by photographer Bert Hardy.
• *12cm x 16cm*
• £1,300 • Photo. Gallery

▽ Silver Gelatin Print

• *1937*
Signed silver gelatin print by Humphrey Spender of two small children playing on a wasteland in Bolton, Lancashire. For Mass Observation.
• *30.5cm x 40cm*
• £300 • Photo. Gallery

▽ Platinum Print

• *1949*
'Margarita de Bonampak, Mexico, 1949' by Manuel Alvarez Bravo. Platinum print, signed verso.
• *25.5cm x 20cm*
• £2,000 • Photo. Gallery

▽ Silver Gelatin Print

• *1951*
'Paris 1951' by Ed Van der Elsken. State print.
• *length 30cm*
• £650 • Photo. Gallery

▷ Signed Gelatin Print

• *1953*
'Nude, Eygalieres, France' by Bill Brandt. Signed recto.
• *length 50cm*
• £1,500 • Photo. Gallery

△ Flooded Road

• *August 1939*
A pedestrian attempts to leap across a flooded road near Hyde Park in London. Photographer: J.A. Hampton, Topical Press Agency, Hulton Getty Gallery, London. Modern black and white, fibre silver gelatin archival photograph, printed in Hulton Getty darkrooms. Limited edition: 300.
• *length 50.8cm*
• £225 • Hulton Getty

△ Paris Print

• *1951*
'Claudy and Vali in Claudy's Hotel Room' by Ed Van der Elsken.
• £2,050 • Photo. Gallery

▽ Lying on Deck

• *1st July 1939*
The crew of a 12-metre racing yacht lying on the deck to lessen windage during a big race. Photographer: Kurt Hutton, Picture Post. Modern black and white, fibre silver gelatin archival photograph, printed in Hulton Getty darkrooms. Limited edition: 300.
• *length 50.8cm*
• £225 • Hulton Getty

▽ Street Games

• *7th August 1954*
A young child wearing an Indian headdress hides in a coalhole as he takes aim under the watchful eye of a friend. By the photographer Thurston Hopkins, Picture Post collection. A black and white fibre, silver gelatin photograph, printed from original negative in Hulton Getty darkrooms. Limited edition: 300.
• *length 40.7cm*
• £185 • Hulton Getty

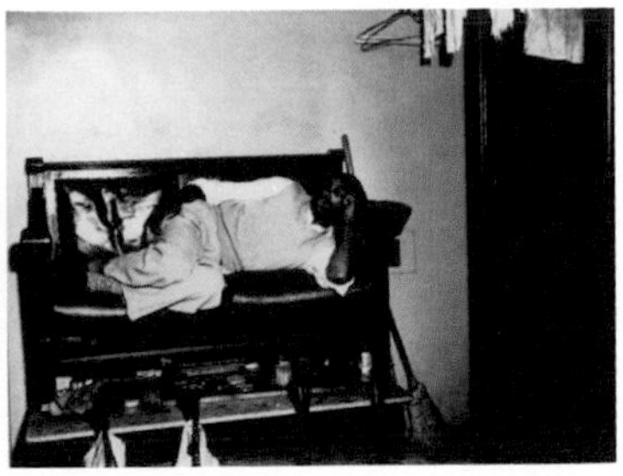

△ Estate Print

• *20th century*
'Asleep on the job' by Weegee. Silver gelatin print.
• *length 27.5cm*
• £500 • Photo. Gallery

△ Signed McBride Print

• *1957*
'Boys Romping at Jan's Place, 1957' by photographer Will McBride. Silver gelatin print, signed verso.
• *51cm x 35.5cm*
• £500 • Photo. Gallery

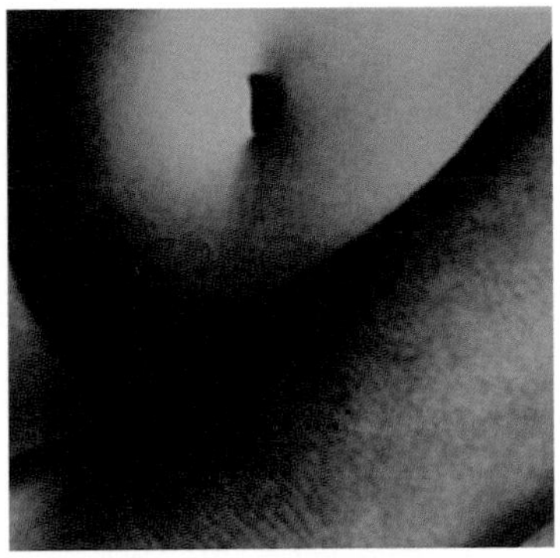

△ Signed Brandt Print

• *1956*
'Nude, London, 1956' by Bill Brandt. A silver gelatin print, signed recto.
• *30.5cm x 40cm*
• £1,800 • Photo. Gallery

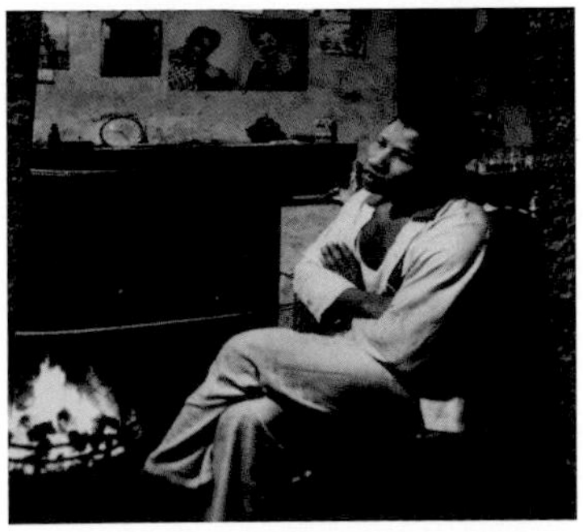

▽ Silver Gelatin Print

• *1951*
'Maidens in Waiting, Blackpool'. One of a series by Bert Hardy.
• £500 • Photo. Gallery

▽ Will McBride Print

• *1959*
'Stoffe, Magda and Em Eating Popcorn, Berlin, 1959' by Will McBride. Silver gelatin print, signed verso.
• *30.5cm x 40cm*
• £350 • Photo. Gallery

▷ Guggenheim Window

• *circa 1955*
The Guggenheim Museum of Modern and Contemporary Art in New York. Photographer: Sherman, Three Lions Collection. Black and white fibre, silver gelatin photograph, printed from original negative in Hulton Getty darkrooms. Limited edition: 300.
• *length 61cm*
• £250 • Hulton Getty

◁ Signed print

• *1955*
'Dreaming of Home' by Thurston Hopkins. Signed, modern silver-gelatin print.
• £800 • Photo. Gallery

▽ Evening Dior

• *4th September 1954*
An evening ensemble of tight-waisted jacket with long fur trimmed sleeves worn over a full, ground-length skirt. Designed by Dior in Duchess satin. Photographer: John Chillingworth, Picture Post. Black and white toned fibre, silver gelatin photograph, printed from original negative in Hulton Getty darkrooms. Limited edition: 300.
• *length 30.5cm*
• £187 • Hulton Getty

▷ Chrysler Building

• *3rd May 1957*
The Chrysler Building in New York. Photographer: Phil Burcham, Fox Photos. Modern black and white, fibre silver gelatin archival photograph, printed in Hulton Getty darkrooms. Limited edition: 300.
• *length 50.8cm*
• £225 • Hulton Getty

△ Silver Gelatin Print

• *1955*
'Locomotive 605, about to be washed, 1955' by O. Winston Link. Silver gelatin print, signed verso.
• *30.5cm x 40cm*
• £1,750 • Photo. Gallery

▽ Marilyn Monroe

- *1953*

A portrait of actress Marilyn Monroe (1926–1962) surrounded by reporters and fans outside Grauman's Chinese Theater in Hollywood, California. Photographer: Murray Garrett. A black and white fibre, silver gelatin photograph, printed from original negative in Hulton Getty Darkrooms. Signed limited edition: 75 only signed by photographer.

- *length 40.7cm*
- **From £500** • **Hulton Getty**

▽ Cary in Rain

- *1957*

British-born American actor Cary Grant (1904–1986) sheltering in a hotel porch as he waits for the rain to stop. Photographer: Express Collection. Modern black and white, fibre silver gelatin archival photograph, printed in Hulton Getty darkrooms. Limited edition: 300.

- *length 40.7cm*
- **£185** • **Hulton Getty**

△ Audrey's Funny Face

- *7th July 1956*

Actress Audrey Hepburn (1929–1993) on the set of the Paramount musical 'Funny Face'. Costumes by Givenchy. Photographer: Bert Hardy, Picture Post. Modern black and white, fibre silver gelatin archival photograph, printed in Hulton Getty darkrooms. Limited edition: 300.

- *length 50.8cm*
- **£225** • **Hulton Getty**

△ Lady Day

- *1954*

American jazz singer Billie Holiday (1915–1959) in the spotlight during a performance. Photographer Charles Hewitt, *Picture Post*. A modern black and white fibre, silver gelatin archival photograph, printed in Hulton Getty Darkrooms. Limited edition: 300.

- *length 40.7cm*
- **£185** • **Hulton Getty**

△ Duke Ellington

- *October 1958*

Modern black and white, fibre silver gelatin, archival photograph of American big band leader and legendary jazz pianist Duke Ellington (1899–1974) from the *Evening Standard* collection. Printed in Hulton Getty darkrooms. Limited edition: 300.

- *length 30.5cm*
- **£125** • **Hulton Getty**

▽ Sophia Loren

- *April 1959*

Italian film actress Sophia Loren on the phone to her mother. Photographer: Keystone Photos. Modern black and white, fibre silver gelatin archival photograph, printed in Hulton Getty darkrooms. Limited edition: 300.

- *length 40.7cm*
- **£185** • **Hulton Getty**

▽ Taylor Reclines

- *1954*

American actress Elizabeth Taylor reclining in bed by the photographer Baron. Modern black and white, fibre silver gelatin archival photograph, printed in Hulton Getty darkrooms. Limited edition: 300.

- *length 50.8cm*
- **£225** • **Hulton Getty**

◁ Hitchcock Profile

- *July 1966*

Film director Alfred Hitchcock (1889–1980) during the filming of *The Torn Curtain* by photographer Curt Gunther/BIPs Collection. Modern black and white, fibre silver gelatin archival photograph, printed in Hulton Getty Darkrooms. Limited edition: 300.

- *length 50.8cm*
- **£225** • **Hulton Getty**

△ Signed Gelatin Print

- *1965*

'Ringo' by John 'Hoppy' Hopkins. Featuring John Lennon.

- *length 30cm*
- £350 • Photo. Gallery

△ Silver Gelatin Print

- *1981*

'Flooded tree, Perwentnar, 1981' by Fay Godwin. Silver gelatin print, signed verso.

- *30.5cm x 35.5cm*
- £500 • Photo. Gallery

▽ The Rolling Stones

- *January 1967*

British rock group The Rolling Stones; from left to right, Bill Wyman, Brian Jones (1942–1969), Charlie Watts, Keith Richards and Mick Jagger. Photographer: Keystone Collection. Modern black and white, fibre silver gelatin archival photograph printed in Hulton Getty Darkrooms. Limited edition: 300.

- *length 50.8cm*
- £225 • Hulton Getty

▽ Signed Gelatin Print

- *1982*

'What she wanted and what she got, 1982' by Graham Smith. Silver gelatin print, signed verso.

- *30.5cm x 35.5cm*
- £500 • Photo. Gallery

△ Jimi Hendrix

- *August 1970*

Rock guitar virtuoso Jimi Hendrix (1942–1970) caught mid guitar-break during his performance at the Isle of Wight Festival from the *Evening Standard* collection. Modern, black and white fibre, silver gelatin archival photograph, printed in Hulton Getty darkrooms. Limited edition: 300.

- *length 50.8cm*
- £225 • Hulton Getty

△ C-Type Print

- *1999*

Untitled still life C-Type print taken in 1999 by Juliana Sohn. Signed verso.

- *30.5cm x 35.5cm*
- £450 • Photo. Gallery

◁ C-Type Print

- *20th century*

Untitled girl in hammock photograph by Nat Finkelstein.

- *length 30cm*
- £550 • Photo. Gallery

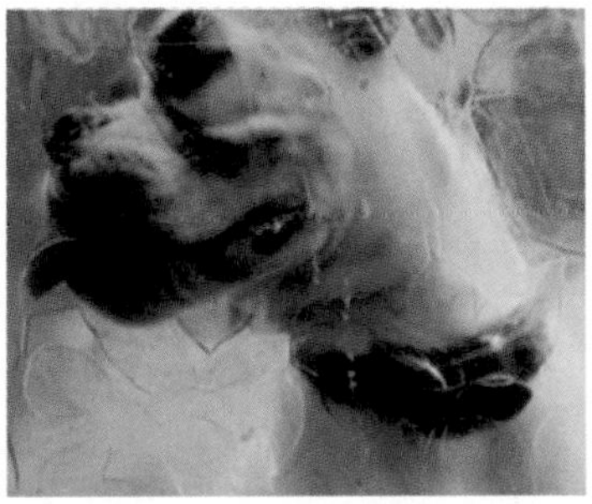

▽ Untitled Print

- *1999*

Untitled silver gelatin print taken in 1999 by Sheva Fruitman. Signed verso.

- *30.5cm x 35.5cm*
- £600 • Photo. Gallery

▽ Signed Print

- *2000*

'Snow Drops, 2000' by Delilah Dyson. C-type print, signed verso.

- *30.5cm x 40cm*
- £300 • Photo.Gallery

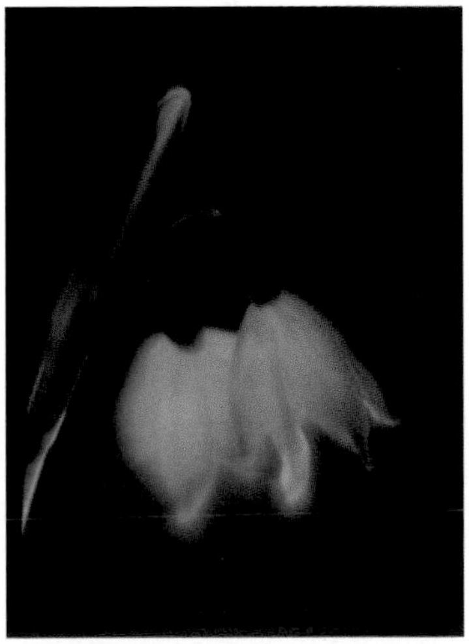

◁ C-Type Print

- *1994*

'Dog in back garden, 1994' by Matthew Murray. C-type print, signed verso.

- *30.5cm x 35.5cm*
- £200 • Photo. Gallery

POSTERS

▽ **Pseudonym Autonym**

- *circa 1890*

An Aubrey Beardsley original poster. English but printed in France.

- *length 50cm*
- £380 • Arwas

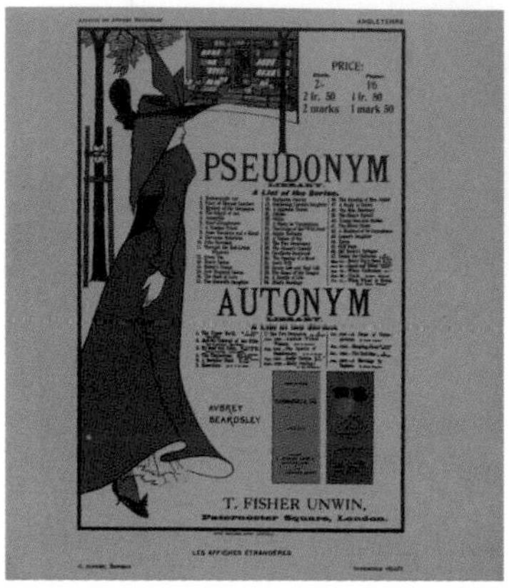

▽ **Card Sign**

- *circa 1900*

A Kenyon & Craven's card sign advertising jams and marmalade.

- *height 40cm*
- £245 • Dodo

▽ **Embossed Tin Sign**

- *circa 1910*

An embossed tin sign advertising Turnbull's Scotch Whisky.

- *height 46cm*
- £120 • Dodo

△ **'Reine de Joie' Poster**

- *circa 1890*

An original poster showing a large man with a lady in a red dress on his lap.

- *length 30cm*
- £800 • Arwas

△ **Que Viva Mexiko**

- *1932*

Original east German poster, paper backed, by Wenzer.

- *81cm x 58cm*
- £180 • Reel Poster Gallery

△ **Way Out West**

- *1937*

Way Out West with Laurel and Hardy.

- *28cm x 36cm*
- £650 • Cine Art Gallery

▽ **Embossed Tin Sign**

- *circa 1910*

An embossed tin sign showing an advertisement for alcohol.

- *height 31cm*
- £175 • Dodo

▽ **Jess Il Bandito**

- *circa 1939*

Showing actor Tyrone Power. Released by 20th Century Fox.

- *length 2m, width 1.4m*
- £1,800 • Reel Poster Gallery

▷ **Revenge of the Creature**

- *1955*

Revenge of the Creature UK Quad. John Agar and Laurie Nelson.

- *102cm x 60.5cm*
- £850 • Cine Art Gallery

△ **Monsoleil Lithograph**

- *circa 1930*

A large original lithograph for Monsoleil, Les Bons Vins Guillot.

- *height 1.54m*
- £380 • Dodo

△ **Jour de Fête**

- *1948*

Original French poster, linen-backed, for the Jacques Tati film *Jour de Fête*, featuring artwork by Eric.

- *160cm x 119cm*
- £2,500 • Reel Poster Gallery

▽ NA Vychod Od Raje/Giant

- *1955*

Original Czech poster, linen-backed, for the first Czech release of *Giant* starring James Dean.

- *84cm x 58cm*
- £750 • Reel Poster Gallery

▷ Sleeping Beauty

- *circa 1959*

A paper-backed poster of Walt Disney's *Sleeping Beauty* showing various characters from the story and the title 'Awaken to a World of Wonders!'.

- *length 76cm, width 51cm*
- £300 • Reel Poster Gallery

◁ Il Diritto di Uccidere/ In a Lonely Place

- *1950*

Original Italian poster, linen-backed, featuring artwork by Anselmo Ballester.

- *140cm x 99cm*
- £3,500 • Reel Poster Gallery

△ Moulin Rouge

- *1952*

Original Polish poster, paper-backed and unfolded, by Lucjan Jagodzinski.

- *84cm x 58cm*
- £1,800 • Reel Poster Gallery

▷ Vertigo

- *1958*

Vertigo, the international version, by Alfred Hitchcock, with Kim Novak and James Stewart.

- *83cm x 60.5cm*
- £2,500 • Cine Art Gallery

◁ High Society

- *1956*

High Society with Frank Sinatra, Gene Kelly and Bing Crosby.

- *28cm x 36cm*
- £120 • Cine Art Gallery

△ Prazoniny V Rime/ Roman Holiday

- *1953*

Original Czech poster, linen-backed, promoting the film *Roman Holiday* with Audrey Hepburn.

- *84cm x 58cm*
- £500 • Reel Poster Gallery

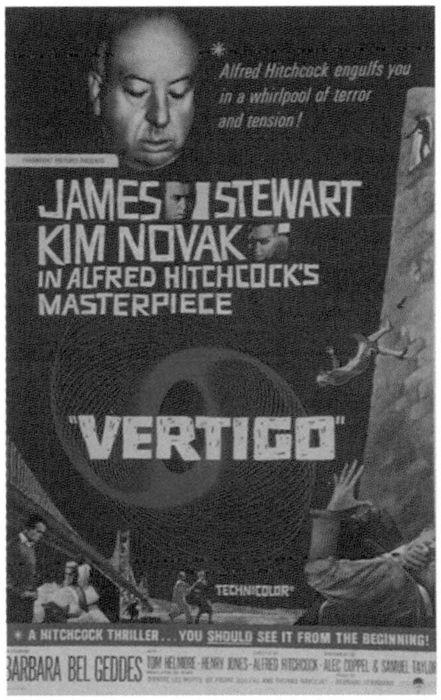

▽ The Prince and the Showgirl

- *1957*

Prince and the Showgirl. US half sheet. Starring Marilyn Monroe and Laurence Olivier.

- *22cm x 28cm*
- £850 • Cine Art Gallery

▽ Othello

- *1955*

Original Czech poster, linen-backed, for *Othello.*

- *84cm x 58cm*
- £500 • Reel Poster Gallery

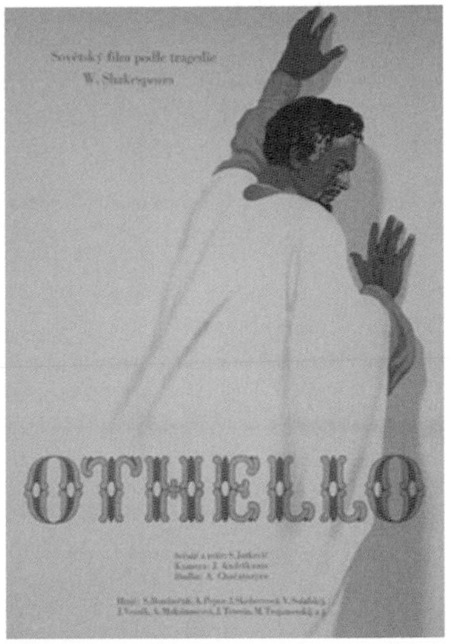

▽ Curse of Frankenstein

- *circa 1957*

Japanese, paper-backed and signed by Christopher Lee.

- *length 76cm, width 51cm*
- £950 • Reel Poster Gallery

▽ Some Like it Hot

- *1959*

Some Like it Hot, with Marilyn Monroe, Tony Curtis and Jack Lemmon.

- *28cm x 36cm*
- £450 • Cine Art Gallery

△ Przygoda L Avventura

- *1959*

Original Polish poster, paper-backed, by Jan Lenica.

- *84cm x 58cm*
- £250 • Reel Poster Gallery

△ The Apartment

- *1960*

The Apartment starring Jack Lemmon and Shirley McLaine.

- *28cm x 36cm*
- £85 • Cine Art Gallery

△ Un Homme et une Femme

- *circa 1966*

A montage of photo images from the film, in Eastman colours.

- *length 79cm, width 61cm*
- £1,250 • Reel Poster Gallery

▽ 2 Hommes Dans Manhattan

- *1959*

Original French poster, linen-backed, by Georges Kerfyser, for *2 Hommes dans Manhattan.*

- *79cm x 61cm*
- £250 • Reel Poster Gallery

▽ Psycho

- *circa 1960*

Showing Alfred Hitchcock on a blank background. Printed in England by W.E. Berry and released by Paramount Pictures. In style B.

- *length 1m, width 76cm*
- £5,000 • Reel Poster Gallery

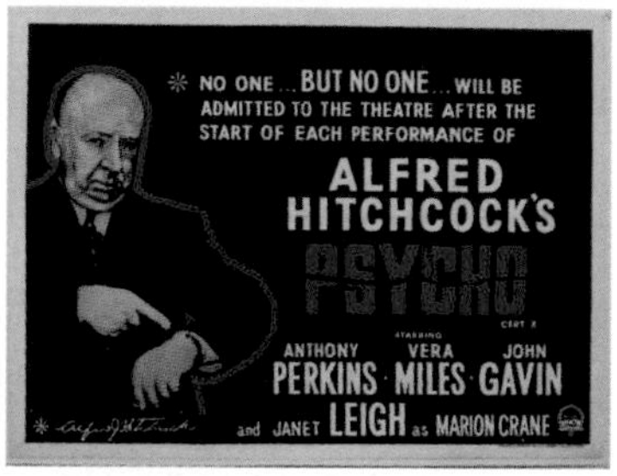

▽ Bullitt

- *1969*

Bullitt with Steve McQueen. US One sheet.

- *27cm x 21cm*
- £680 • Cine Art Gallery

△ Breakfast at Tiffany's

- *1961*

Colazione da Tiffany.

- *27.5cm x 51cm*
- £1,000 • Cine Art Gallery

△ Le Mépris

- *circa 1963*

Starring Brigitte Bardot. Linen-backed poster with artwork by George Allard.

- *length 79cm, width 61cm*
- £600 • Reel Poster Gallery

△ From Russia with Love

- *1963*

From Russia with Love, starring Sean Connery. Original UK quad.

- *76cm x 1.05m*
- £2,750 • Cine Art Gallery

▽ Casablanca

- *circa 1961*

Original Italian 1961 re-release. Art by Campejgi Silvano. Showing stars' names and the Islamic skyline.

- *length 2m, width 1.4m*
- £7,500 • Reel Poster Gallery

▽ Lawrence of Arabia

- *1963*

Lawrence of Arabia with Peter O'Toole. Re-issue 1963 of 1962 film.

- *1.02m x 56cm*
- £650 • Cine Art Gallery

▽ Midnight Cowboy

- *1969*

Midnight Cowboy with Dustin Hoffman. UK Quad.

- *76cm x 1.02m*
- £190 • Cine Art Gallery

△ Blow-Up

- *circa 1967*

Framed behind glass, in style A. Designed by Acy R. Iehman.

- *length 1m, width 76cm*
- £500 • **Reel Poster Gallery**

△ Barbarella

- *circa 1968*

Argentinian poster showing Jane Fonda. Conservation-backed.

- *height 1.07m, width 71cm*
- £500 • **Reel Poster Gallery**

△ Taxi Driver

- *1976*

Original US poster, linen-backed, featuring artwork by Guy Peelaert, Style A.

- *1.04m x 69cm*
- £500 • **Reel Poster Gallery**

▽ Le Samourai

- *1967*

Le Samourai, produced by Alain Delon, starring Nathalie Delon and François Perier.

- *height 76cm*
- £450 • **Cine Art Gallery**

▽ Rosemary's Baby

- *1968*

Original British poster designed by Steve Frankfurt.

- *1.04m x 69cm*
- £350 • **Reel Poster Gallery**

▽ The Italian Job

- *1969*

The Italian Job with Michael Caine. UK mini Quad.

- *31cm x 41cm*
- £5 • **Cine Art Gallery**

△ Rebellion/Bunt

- *1967*

Original Polish poster, paper-backed, featuring artwork by Rapnicki.

- *84cm x 58cm*
- £150 • **Reel Poster Gallery**

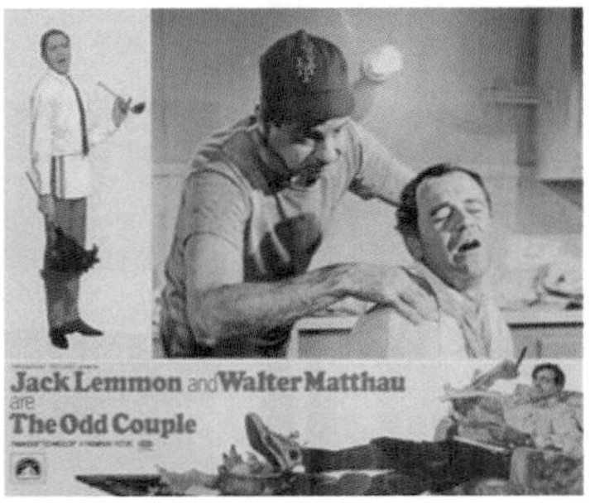

△ The Odd Couple

- *1968*

The Odd Couple, with Walter Matthau and Jack Lemmon.

- *28cm x 36cm*
- £140 • **Cine Art Gallery**

△ Star Wars Poster

- *circa 1977*

With Polish translation and paper-backed. Artwork by Jakub Enol.

- *length 97cm, width 69cm*
- £425 • **Reel Poster Gallery**

▽ Planet of the Apes

- *circa 1968*

A linen-backed, cartoon-style Romanian poster with title *Planeta Maimutelor.*

- *length 97cm, width 69cm*
- £950 • **Reel Poster Gallery**

▽ Yellow Submarine

- *1969*

Yellow Submarine with the Beatles. US. One sheet.

- *height 1.04m*
- £12,500 • **Cine Art Gallery**

▽ The Godfather Part II

- *1974*

The Godfather Part II, with Al Pacino.

- *28cm x 36cm*
- £125 • **Cine Art Gallery**

△ Crystal Set

- *circa 1910*

An English Edwardian crystal set in mahogany case with brass fittings. In good condition.

- *height 30cm*
- £585 • Talk. Mach.

△ Baird Televisol

- *circa 1930*

'The world's first television', actually a mechanical system as opposed to the later electronic tubes. Viewed through a small lens.

- *height 54cm*
- £5,000 • Vintage Wireless

△ Marconi Mastergram

- *1937*

Model 703 TV/radio/auto-radiogram. Same chassis as HMV equivalent and originally costing 120 guineas.

- *height 97.5cm*
- £3,000 • Vintage Wireless

▽ American Radio

- *circa 1930*

Designed by Harold Van Doren. Skyscraper influence, produced by AirKing. Then the largest US bakelite moulding produced.

- *height 30cm*
- £3,000 • Decodence

▽ Philips 930A

- *1931*

Philips Art Deco radio with an unusual keel-shaped shaped body, and a stars and wavy line design, standing on a square base and legs.

- *height 48cm*
- £800 • Decodence

▽ Silver Tone Bullet 6110

- *circa 1938*

Modern design push-button radio with enormous rotating turning scale. Designed by Clarence Karstacht.

- *height 17cm*
- £1,100 • Decodence

△ Wooden Radio

- *circa 1930*

Valve radio with wooden case.

- *height 30cm, width 54cm*
- £85 • Radio Days

△ Ekco RS3

- *1931*

Art Deco bakelite radio standing on metal feet. This model was one of the first bakelite radios to be manufactured in the United Kingdom.

- *height 45cm*
- £800 • Decodence

△ TV/Radio & Gramophone

- *circa 1937*

HMV model 902. Very rare set, less than five examples known to exist. Cost 120 guineas new.

- *height 1.22m*
- £3,000 • Vintage Wireless

▽ Bakelite Radio

- *1930*

Brown bakelite radio with lattice-effect front grille.

- £95 • Radio Days

▽ Philips Radio

- *circa 1931*

Hexagonal with oxidised bronze grill. Sought after for its unusual appearance.

- *height 43cm*
- £500 • Decodence

▽ TV/Radio & Gramophone

- *1938*

R.G.D. (Radio Gramophone Developments) model RG. Top of the range radiogram. Image viewed through mirror in the lid.

- *height 92.5cm*
- £3,250 • Vintage Wireless

▷ Cossor Table Model

- *1938*

Costing 23 guineas when new, the cheapest pre-war set with sound. A rare set.

- *height 44cm*
- £1,000 • Vintage Wireless

△ Murphy Console

- *circa 1938*

Model A56V. A good-quality middle of the range set costing £30, vision and TV sound only.

- *height 86cm*
- £1,000 • Vintage Wireless

△ Cossor TV/Radio

- *1939*

Cossor model 1210. When new cost 48 guineas. Top of the range of Cossor models, using the largest diameter tube.

- *height 1.21m*
- £1,000 • Vintage Wireless

▽ Ekco Table Model

- *circa 1939*

Model TA201. Original price 22 guineas. Vision only (sound was obtained by tuning a suitable radio to the TV channel).

- *height 50cm*
- £600 • Vintage Wireless

▽ Sonorette

- *1940s*

French brown radio in bakelite, with a bulbous form and grille-design speaker.

- *height 34cm*
- £500 • Decodence

▷ Grille Radio

- *circa 1945*

Chunky automobile fender grille radio. Made by Sentinel. Very desirable.

- *height 19cm*
- £1,000 • Decodence

▽ Invicta Table Model

- *1939*

Model TL5, made by Pye of Cambridge. This is the only known model of Invicta.

- *height 47.5cm*
- £800 • Vintage Wireless

▷ CKCO Model AD75

- *circa 1940*

Wartime English bakelite radio designed by Wells Coates to meet marine needs.

- *height 35cm*
- £700 • Decodence

△ Fada Streamliner

- *1940*

American onyx and amber streamlined Catalin radio, with large oval dial on the right.

- *height 19cm*
- £1,000 • Decodence

◁ 'KB' Wooden Radio

- *circa 1940*

Fully working radio. One of many produced in Great Britain during the Second World War.

- *height 46cm, width 53cm*
- £125 • Radio Days

△ HMV TV/Radio

- *circa 1938*

Model 904. Same chassis as Marconi model 706.

- *height 45cm*
- £1,800 • Vintage Wireless

▽ Console TV/Radio

- *August 1939*

HMV model 1850, cost 57 guineas new. Top of the range of four models when introduced.

- *height 1.22m*
- £1,500 • Vintage Wireless

▽ Bendix Model 526C

• *1946*
Black bakelite American radio with the inscription 'Strong Machine Age'.
• *28cm x 35cm*
• £750 • Decodence

▽ GEC Radio

• *circa 1950*
GEC radio with bakelite handles.
• *32cm x 44cm x 17cm*
• £55 • Radio Days

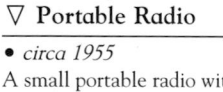

▽ Portable Radio

• *circa 1955*
A small portable radio with original leather protective case. Medium and long waves.
• *height 11cm*
• £45 • Talk. Mach.

◁ Intercom Speaker

• *1940s*
English Art Deco-style red intercom system speaker, tube-operated.
• *height 28cm*
• £100 • Decodence

△ Wooden Radio

• *circa 1940*
Fully working wooden radio from the Second World War.
• *height 30cm, width 53cm*
• £105 • Radio Days

△ HMV Record Player

• *1957*
His Master's Voice record player in a chocolate-brown case with cream interior and black handles.
• *height 27cm*
• £75 • Alfie's Antique Market

△ Mains Radio

• *circa 1950*
A very small, red-cased mains radio by Packard Bell of the USA, with large central dial and minimal controls.
• *height 14cm*
• £140 • Talk. Mach.

▷ English Radio

• *circa 1950*
Kiather Brandes BM 20, rare green bakelite radio, made of two exact halves. Made in many colours, some quite unique.
• *height 22cm*
• £500 • Decodence

△ German Radio

• *circa 1950*
A rare post-war German bakelite mains radio.
• *height 58cm*
• £175 • Talk. Mach.

◁ Bush TV

• *circa 1949*
22 Model. Most desired of all British bakelite TVs.
• *height 39cm*
• £300 • Decodence

▽ Pye Record Player

• *1955*
Pye record player in a bow-fronted teak case with cream turntable. Holds ten records on stack.
• *height 26cm*
• £100 • Alfie's Antique Market

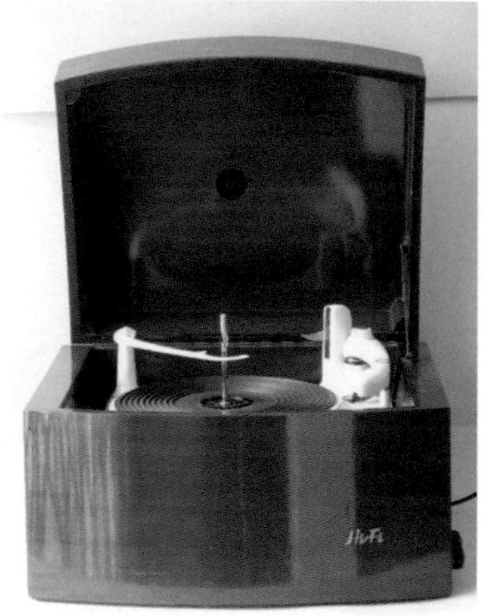

▽ Croslen Radio

• *1951*
Red American bakelite radio, styled in the shape of a speedometer.
• *height 29cm*
• N/A • Decodence

△ PYE Record Player

• *1955*
PYE record player in a grey with white polka-dot case, with unusual curved sides, white plastic carrying handles and a black and gold sparkling grill.
• *height 25cm*
• £75 • Alfie's Antique Market

△ HMV Record Player

• *1958*
His Master's Voice record player in a red and mottled grey case with red plastic carrying handles, with a Monarch deck.
• *height 25cm*
• £75 • Alfie's Antique Market

▽ Dansette Major de-luxe

• *1960*
Dansette Major de-luxe with a red and cream case, sloping front gold grill and light up Dansette badge, with cream plastic handles each side for carrying.
• *height 27cm*
• £75 • Alfie's Antique Market

▷ Dansette Conquest

• *1959*
Dansette Conquest green and cream record player, standing on four black tapered legs on circular base. Holds ten records on stack. Fully restored and re-conditioned. With cream handles each side for carrying.
• *height 67cm*
• £80 • Alfie's Antique Market

◁ Perdio Transistor

• *1962*
Perdio Super Seven Transistor radio, inscribed with 'Real Morocco leather made in England', on the back, with a dial for an aerial and phone or tape, and a large brass dial and gold writing.
• *height 12.5cm*
• £38 • Alfie's Antique Market

△ EAR Triple Four

• *1958*
EAR Triple four record player in a blue and grey Rexine case with cream piping and handles.
• *height 27cm*
• £80 • Alfie's Antique Market

◁ JVC Television

• *circa 1968*
A JVC 'Space Helmet' television of spherical form on a square plinth. Monochrome reception.
• *height 60cm*
• £200 • Talk. Mach.

▽ Wondergram Record Player

• *1959*
Very rare Wondergram record player for 45rpm and 33⅓rpm in anodised aluminium case, with folding legs. Made in England by Baird.
• *height 8.5cm*
• £350 • Alfie's Antique Market

▽ Hacker

• *1964*
Hacker record player in a black and grey case with metal fittings.
• *height 27cm*
• £50 • Alfie's Antique Market

▽ Roberts Radio

• *1970*
Roberts radio in red leather case.
• *15cm x 22cm x 8cm*
• £60 • Retro Home

◁ Red Radio

• *circa 1965*
A very Sixties round plastic red portable radio, giving medium-wave reception.
• £80 • Whitford

ROCK & POP

▽ Brenda Lee

- *1950*

Brenda Lee 'Speak to Me Pretty'.

- £27 • Music & Video

▽ Beatles Film Book

- *circa 1960*

Book based on the story and making of the Beatle's film *Help!*, illustrated with black and white photographs.

- *25cm x 14cm*
- £15 • Radio Days

▽ Bob Dylan

- *1961*

Bob Dylan's first recording, produced by John Hammond.

- £735 • Music & Video

△ 'At Home With Screamin' Jay Hawkins'

- *circa 1958*

Album by the late Jay Hawkins – known for the epic single 'I Put a Spell on You'.

- £499 • Music & Video

△ Powder Compact

- *circa 1963*

Circular powder compact featuring a Dezo Hoffman black and white shot of The Beatles.

- £475 • More Than Music

△ Official Carded Jewellery Box

- *1964*

Oval leather and brass accessories, with The Beatles' faces featured on the lid.

- £225 • More Than Music

▽ Me and My Shadows

- *1960*

Me and My Shadows Cliff Richard export copy in excellent condition.

- £70 • Music & Video

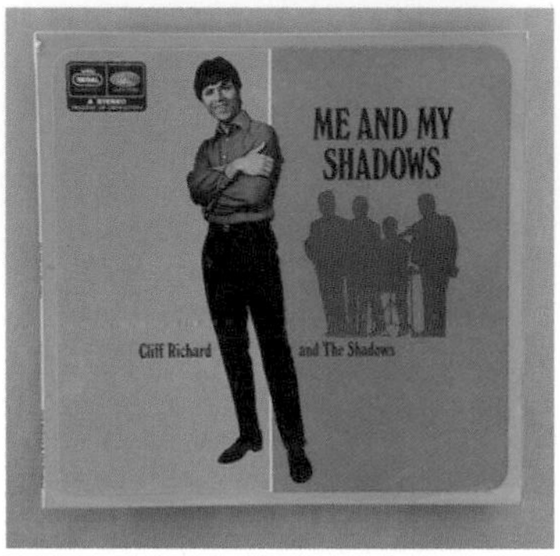

▽ The Dixie Cups

- *1962*

The Dixie Cups *Riding High*.

- £47 • Music & Video

▽ 'The Beatles'

- *circa 1964*

The JD 33rpm 'Deutscher Schallplattenclub' edition with red club label. Limited run.

- £575 • More Than Music

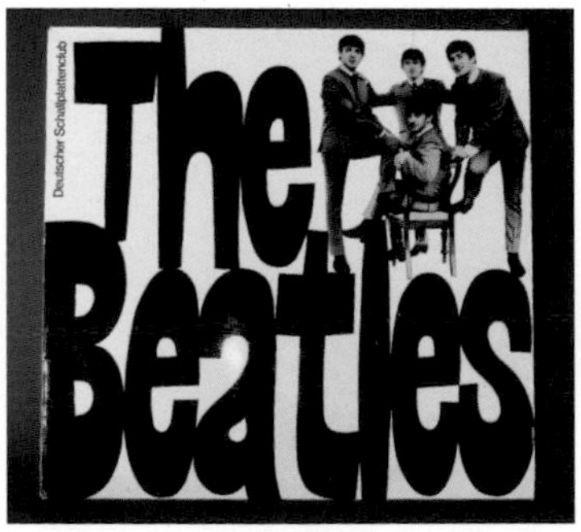

▷ Andy Warhol Magazine

- *December 1966*

Set of postcards and flip-book magazine incorporating Velvet Underground flexidisc.

- £950 • Music & Video

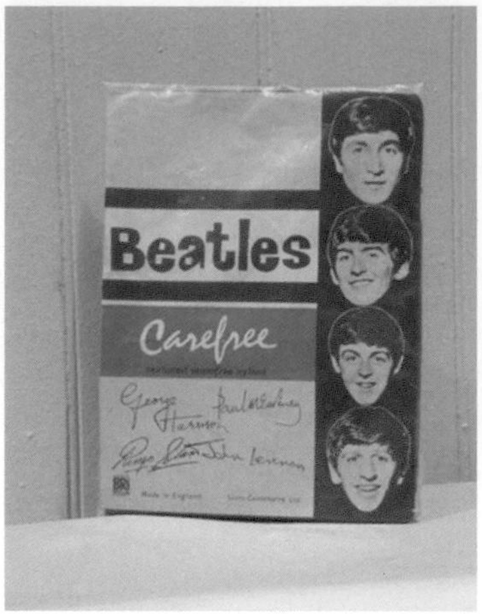

△ Pair of Beatles Stockings

- *1960*

A pair of unused Beatles stockings in original packet.

- *23cm x 17cm*
- £55 • Radio Days

△ Cliff Richard and the Shadows

- *1964*

A Forever Kind of Love by Cliff Richard and the Shadows.

- £33 • Music & Video

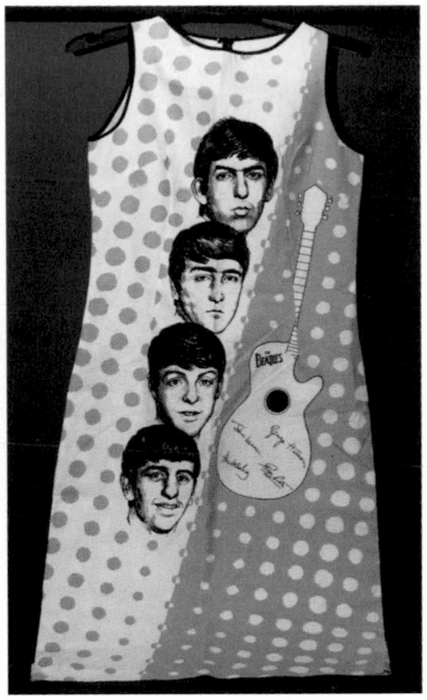

△ Beatles Dress

• *circa 1964*
Official Dutch Beatles' cotton dress in mustard with polka dots. With the makers' card tag.
• £395 • **More Than Music**

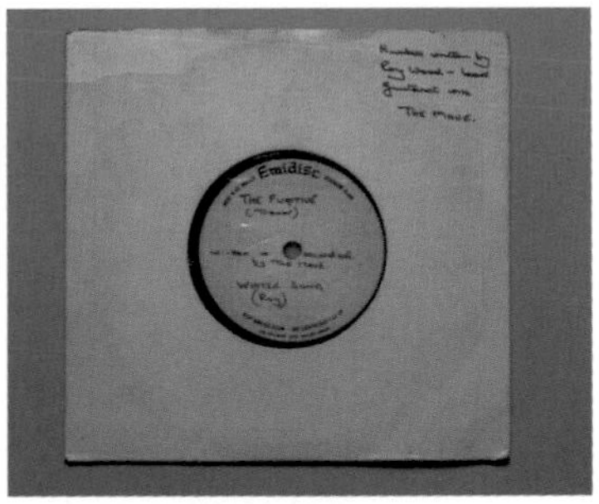

△ The Move Demo

• *1965*
The only surviving demo by The Move, with one vocal per member and featuring 'Winter Song'.
• £7,000 • **Music & Video**

△ The Who Album

• *1965*
The Who's *My Generation* album, by Brunswick, with original band line-up on cover. Poor condition.
• £40 • **Music & Video**

▽ Beatles Fan Badge

• *circa 1964*
Official Beatles' Fan Club badge, featuring faces of the Fab Four with their names beside them for identification (for true fans).
• £45 • **More Than Music**

▽ Brum Beat

• *1964*
Brum Beat including The Strangers, The Mountain Kings, The Blue Stars, The Cavern Four. Dave Lacey and The Corvettes.
• £120 • **Music & Video**

▽ Pat As I See Him

• *1966*
'Pat As I See Him', a pen and ink portrait on an envelope by Joe Meek of his lover. Annotated in verso 'Pat was Meek's boyfriend and was present at the landlady's shooting and Meek's subsequent suicide'.
• £5,250 • **Music & Video**

△ Beatles Dolls

• *1966*
Set of four NEMS/King Features syndicate inflatable cartoon dolls of the Beatles.
• *35cm x 15cm*
• £120 • **Music & Video**

△ Rubber Soul Test Press

• *circa 1965*
A Parlophone test press features side two of *Rubber Soul* with white label and track listing.
• £2,250 • **More Than Music**

△ Andy Warhol

• *1967*
Andy Warhol – *Andy Warhol's Index Box*. First hardback edition-Random House USA complete and in working order including the Velvet Underground flexi-disc. Reed's eye has not even popped!
• £1,500 • **Music & Video**

▽ Captain Beefheart

• *1965*
Captain Beefheart and his Magic Band *Mirror Man* with a broken mirror on the cover.
• £95 • **Music & Video**

▽ Yellow Submarine

• *1960s*
The Beatles – 'Yellow Submarine' and 'Eleanor Rigby'.
• £72 • **Music & Video**

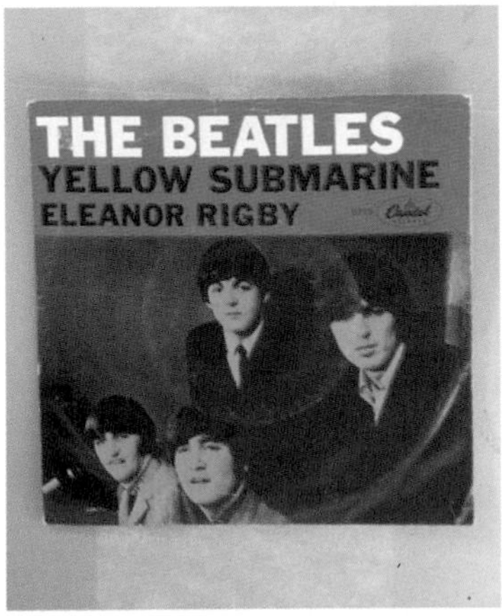

▽ 'Best of the Beach Boys'

• *circa 1966*
Special disc jockey producer copy of *The Best of the Beach Boys* LP, by EMI Records, London.
• £184 • **Music & Video**

△ Rolling Stones Hologram

• *1967*
Rolling Stones hologram 'Their Satanic Majesties Request', fully signed on front cover.
• £249 • Music & Video

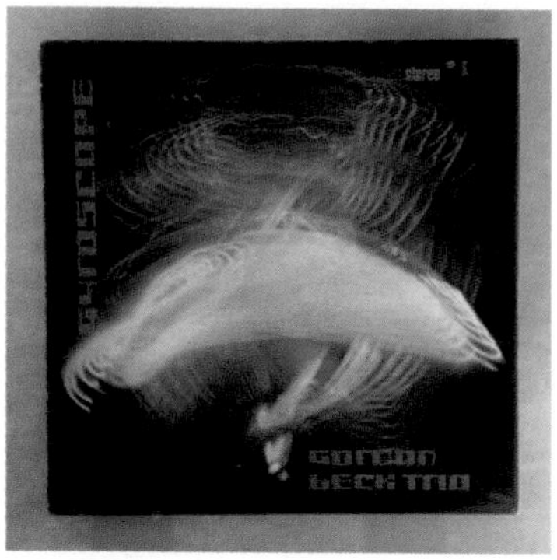

△ The Gordon Beck Trio

• *1968*
The Gordon Beck Trio Twin Stereo MJ1 Jazz series.
• £495 • Music & Video

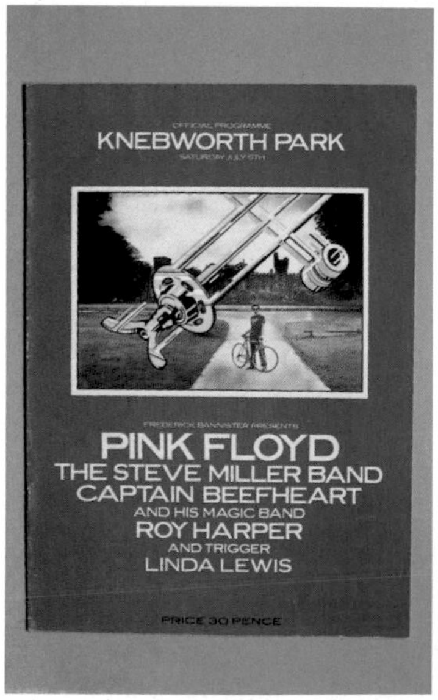

△ Knebworth Park

• *5th July 1974*
Official programme for Pink Floyd's open-air concert at Knebworth Park, in performance with other bands.
• £65 • Music & Video

▽ The Monkees

• *1968*
The Monkees' original motion picture sound-track *Head.*
• £95 • Music & Video

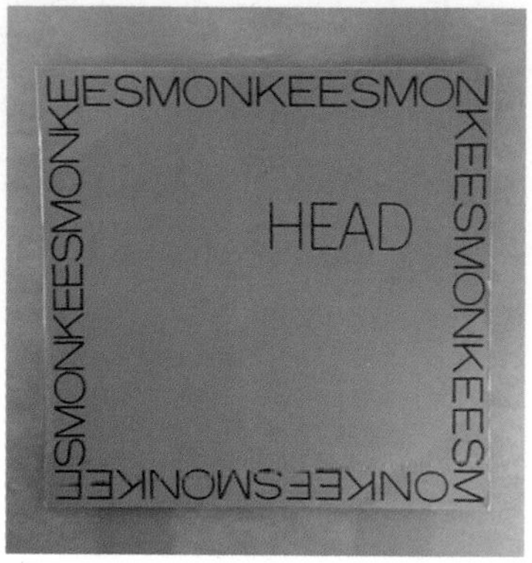

▽ John and Yoko

• *circa 1968*
Album cover for *Two Virgins* in limited mono version, available by mail order only.
• £3,250 • More Than Music

▷ John and Yoko Wedding Album

• *1969*
USA release of *Wedding Album* eight-track tape including box, slice of wedding cake, poster, photographs, postcard, bag, book, and copy of wedding certificate.
• *30cm x 30cm*
• £175 • Music & Video

△ Instant Karma Lennon

• *1971*
John and Ono Lennon *Instant Karma* produced by Phil Spector.
• £117 • Music & Video

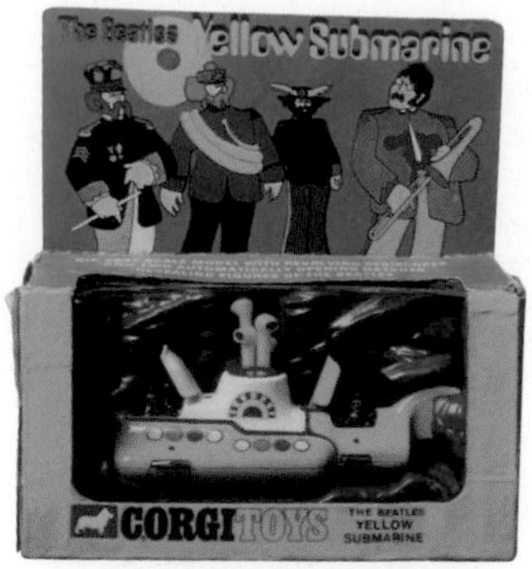

△ Official Corgi Toy

• *1968*
Die-cast metal yellow submarine with revolving periscope and one yellow and one white hatch. From the movie.
• £375 • More Than Music

△ Hollywood Blues

• *1970*
Johnny Almond Music Machine/ Hollywood Blues by Deram Records.
• £60 • Music & Video

▽ Stone Age

• *1971*
Stone Age by the Rolling Stones.
• £580 • Music & Video

▽ Lithographs

• *1970*
Packet of explicit lithographs from John Lennon's 'Bag One' exhibition. Numbered edition of 1,000.
• *30cm x 50cm*
• £500 • Music & Video

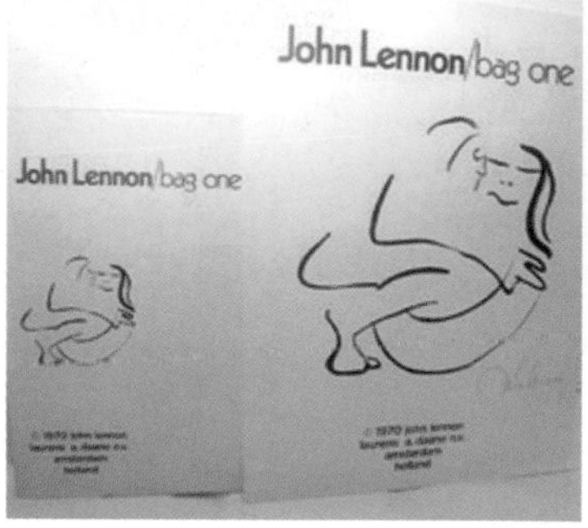

▽ 'The Beautiful Freaks'

• *circa 1969*
Oz magazine issue no. 24, with cover by Robert Crumb.
• £30 • Book & Comic

▽ Peter Wyngarde

• *circa 1970*
Cult 1960s–70s TV actor Peter Wyngarde's departure into music. Recorded at Olympic Sound Studios, Surrey.
• £120 • Music & Video

△ Oz Magazine

• *1970*

A copy of issue no. 28, the famous *School Kids* Issue.

• £80 • Book & Comic

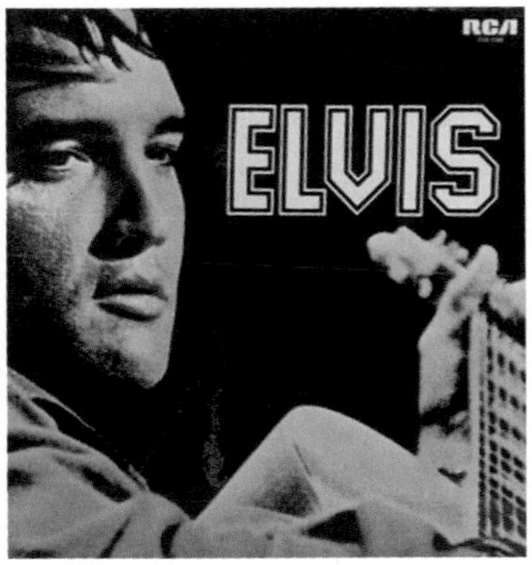

△ Elvis

• *1971*

'You'll Never Walk Alone' by Elvis. Manufactured and distributed by RCA Limited.

• £1,800 • Music & Video

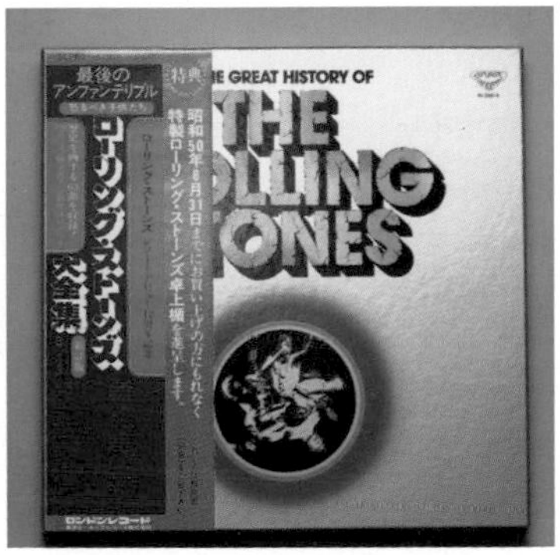

△ Rolling Stones Album

• *1975*

Japanese five-LP, 62-track promo of *The Great History of The Rolling Stones.* Box comes with large book and obi. Individually printed inner sleeves.

• £347 • Music & Video

▽ Black Sabbath Album

• *1971*

Vertigo records album *Masters of Reality*, produced by Roger Bain for Tony Hall Enterprises.

• £85 • Music & Video

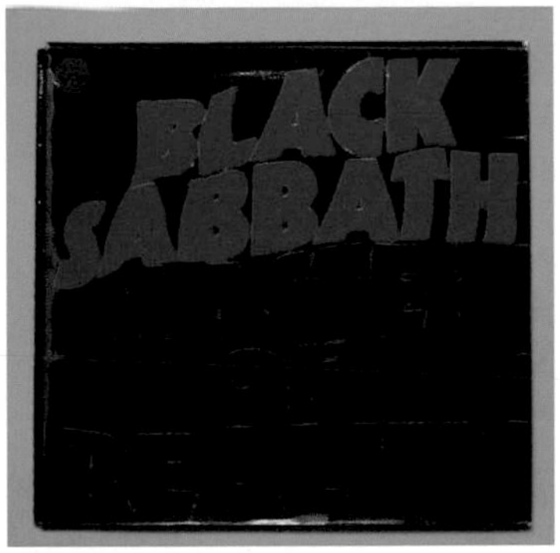

▽ Captain Beefheart

• *1975*

Trout Mask Replica Captain Beefheart and his Magic Band.

• £44 • Music & Video

▽ Mail Art

• *circa 1977*

A double-sided postcard collage by Genesis P. Orridge, featuring an industrial sea-side scene and the Queen of England.

• £300 • Music & Video

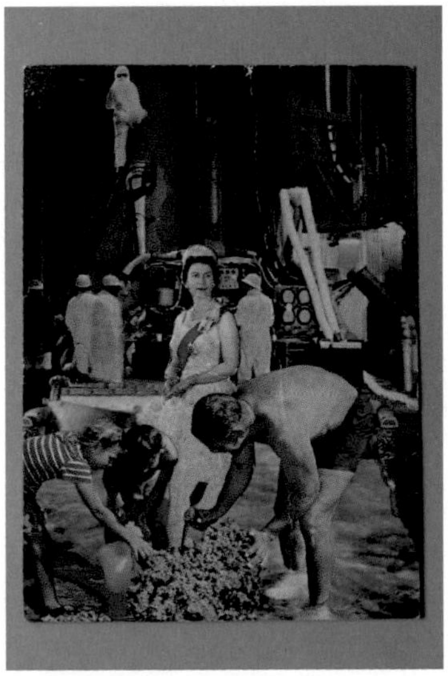

△ Brute Force Album

• *circa 1971*

Extemporaneous, recorded at Olmstead studios, with design and photography by Hal Wilson. Published by Jingle House Music.

• £499 • Music & Video

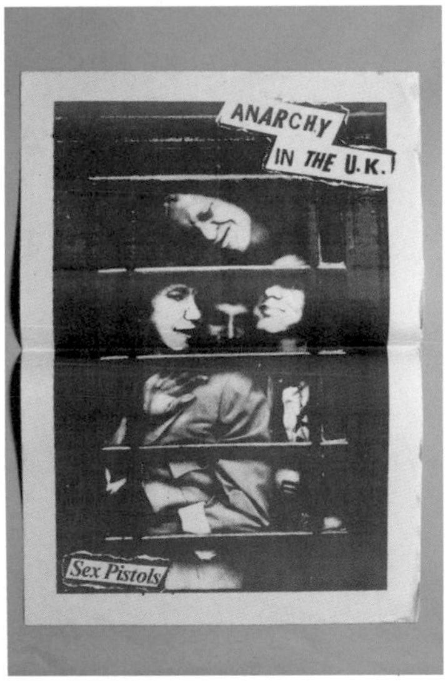

△ Sex Pistols Press Pack

• *circa 1976*

'Glitterbest' press pack for *Anarchy in the UK* album. Twenty pages on white, pink and yellow stock, hand-stamped.

• £482 • Music & Video

△ Beatles Poster with John Lennon Signature

• *1977*

Pull-out poster from American magazine *People*. Signed by band member John Lennon in 1977.

• *70cm x 45cm*

• £700 • Music & Video

▽ Rolling Stones Album

• *1971*

Export edition of Rolling Stones *Stone Age* album.

• *30cm x 30cm*

• £700 • Music & Video

▽ Heavy Metal

• *circa 1977*

Issue no. 1 of *Heavy Metal* magazine, after the cult film of the same name.

• £20 • Book & Comic

▽ No New York

• *circa 1978*

Produced by Brian Eno and recorded ar Big Apple Studio, NY. Cover by Steve Keisler.

• £65 • Music & Video

▷ U2 Single

• *1979*
U2's first single 'Three', individually numbered.
• *20cm x 30cm*
• £350 • Music & Video

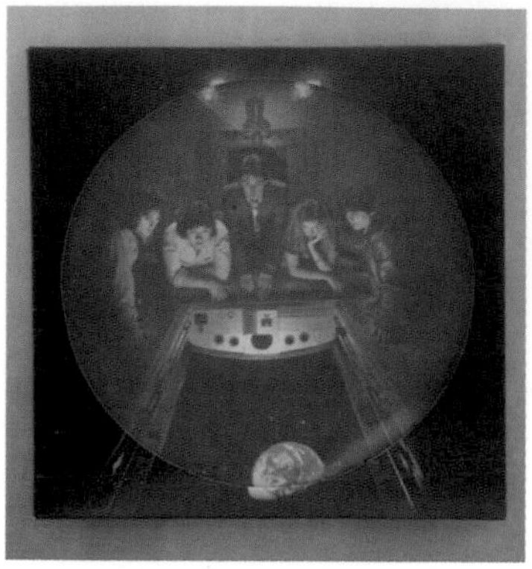

△ Wings 'Back To The Egg'

• *1979*
Wings 'Back to the Egg' promo. The only picture disc manufactured for the MPL Christmas party 1979 but delivered too late for use.
• £1,250 • Music & Video

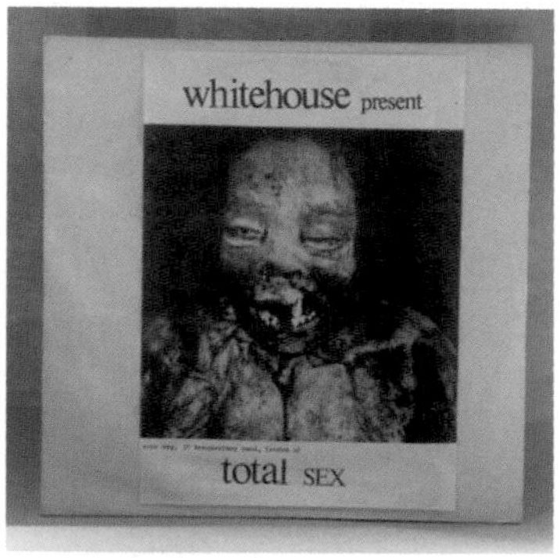

△ Whitehouse Present Total Sex

• *circa 1980*
Whitehouse present *Total Sex*.
• £125 • Music & Video

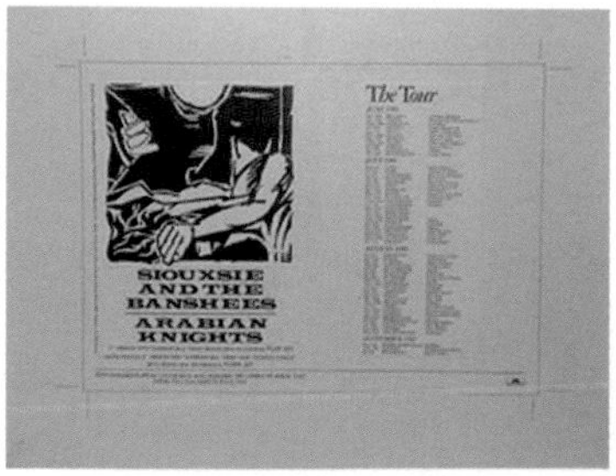

△ Siouxsie and The Banshees Memorabilia

• *1981*
Half-page artwork for promotion of the *Arabian Knights* tour by Siouxsie and the Banshees.
• *40cm x 35cm*
• £175 • Music & Video

▽ Bruce Springsteen Single

• *1981*
'Cadillac Ranch' single by Bruce Springsteen.
• *18cm x 18cm*
• £25 • Music & Video

▽ Madonna Lucky Star Single

• *1983*
Full-length version of the single 'Lucky Star' by Madonna.
• *30cm x 30cm*
• £80 • Music & Video

▽ Manic Street Preachers Single

• *1988*
Double A-side single 'Suicide Alley Tennessee' containing a letter from the band.
• *18cm x 18cm*
• £995 • Music & Video

▽ Happily Ever After

• *1980*
The Cure, *Happily Ever After*.
• £45 • Music & Video

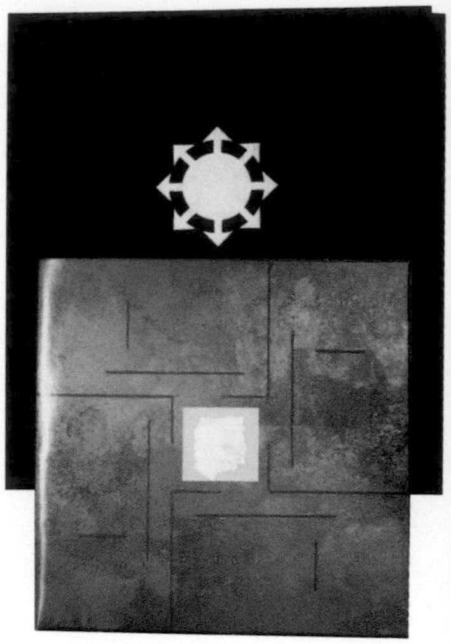

▽ Psychic TV

• *circa 1982*
A trophy cast in solid brass with an incription around the head and the base and recipient companies on shaft.
• £500 • Music & Video

△ Coil Album

• *circa 1988*
Album entitled *Gold is the Metal with the Broadest Shoulders*, by Coil. Deluxe limited edition, no. 29 of 55.
• £500 • Music & Video

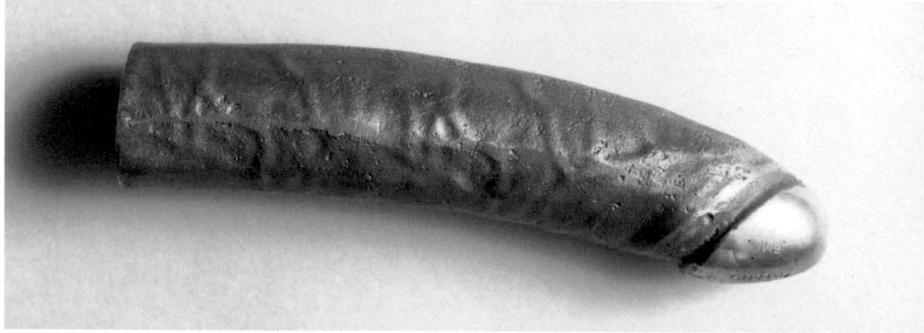

▷ Tote Bag with Five 12-inch Singles

• *1985*
Duran Duran tote bag containing five maxi 12-inch singles.
• *30cm x 35cm*
• £75 • Music & Video

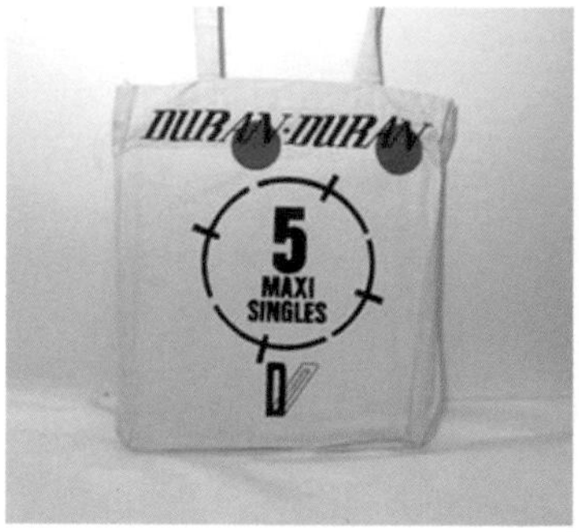

◁ John Lennon Jug

• *circa 1987*
One of a limited edition of 1,000 Royal Doulton mugs, modelled by Stanley James Taylor.
• £750 • More Than Music

▷ Straight No Chaser

• *December 1988*
Issue no.1 of the jazz magazine entitled *Straight No Chaser*, issue no. 1, dated December 1998.
• £10 • Book & Comic

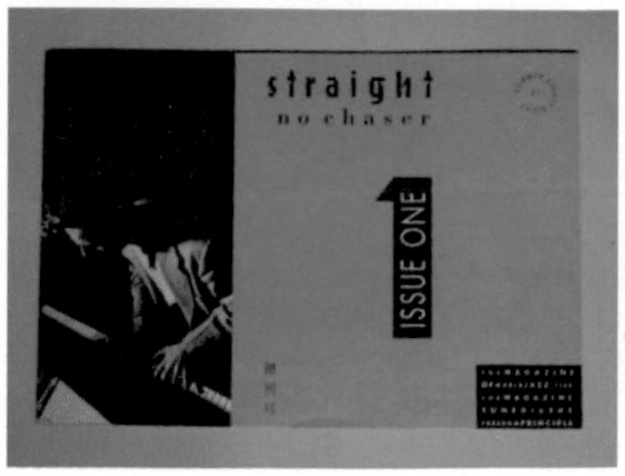

△ Iron Maiden Disc

• *circa 1983*
A picture disc of Iron Maiden's *Piece of Mind* album, illustrated on both sides.
• £40 • Music & Video

▽ Album Artwork

• *1984*
Unused album artwork for Jimmy the Hoover by Jamie Reid, with glass broken and damaged intentionally for the 'Leaving the 21st Century' series held at the Mayfair gallery.
• *50cm x 50cm*
• £200 • Music & Video

◁ The Police Singles Box

• *1990*
Embossed wooden box containing 10 gold vinyl singles together with a picture disc by The Police.
• *18cm x 18cm*
• £195 • Music & Video

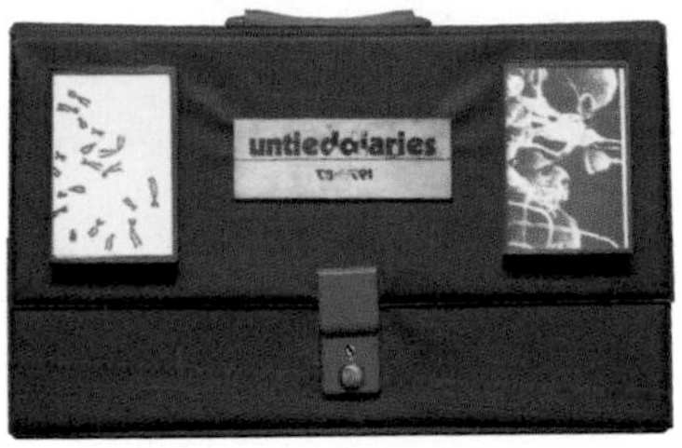

△ Untied Diaries Box Set

• *1988*
Untied Diaries edition 30, with 32 cassettes individually recorded and packaged. This is different from the vinyl version.
• £900 • Music & Video

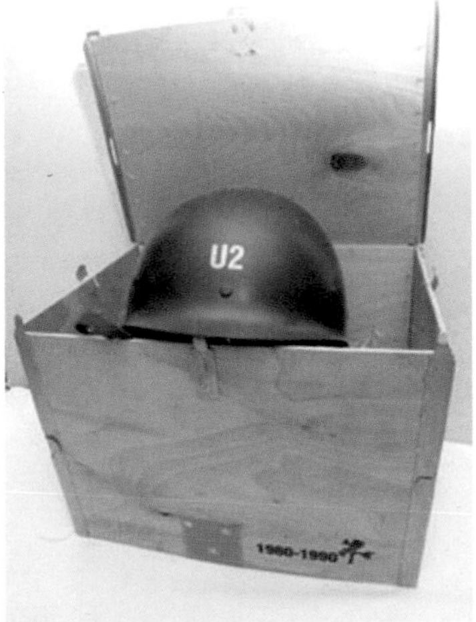

▽ Elvis 68

• *circa 1988*
A copy of the NBC TV *Comeback Special* commemorative Elvis Presley promotional album.
• £125 • Music & Video

◁ U2 Helmet

• *1998*
U2 helmet issued to promote the *Best of 1980–1990* album. Limited edition of 50 units.
• *30cm x 24cm x 23cm*
• £250 • Music & Video

◁ Manic Street Preachers Single

• *1990*
'UK Channel Boredom' flexi-disc supplied with both fanzines.
• *18cm x 18cm*
• £120 • Music & Video

▽ Mojo Magazine

• *circa 1995*
Issue no. 24 showing The Beatles. Published in three colours – this one with a red background.
• £20 • Book & Comic

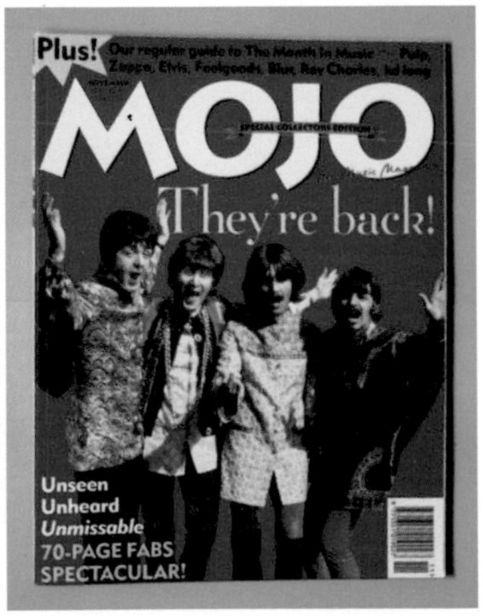

△ Kylie Promotional Handbag

• *2000*
Promotional 'Puma' handbag produced for Kylie Minogue's *Light Years* album. Contains full album and interview CDs.
• *20cm x 20cm*
• £100 • Music & Video

▽ David Bowie CD

• *circa 1996*
Sampler of *David Bowie's BBC Sessions 1969–1972*, released by Worldwide Music.
• £400 • Music & Video

△ Michael Jackson Doll

• *1995*
A singing Michael Jackson doll wearing a white shirt and black trousers in original box.
• £47 • Music & Video

SCRIPOPHILY & PAPER MONEY

△ French Revolution Note

• *31st October 1793*

A five-livre note dating from the French revolution. Extremely fine condition.

• £8.50 • C. Narbeth

△ Chinese Cash Note

• *circa 1858*

A Chinese 2,000 cash note issued during the Taiping Rebellion. In very fine condition.

• £65 • C. Narbeth

△ Railroad Shares

• *1860*

Shares note issued by the Cleveland and Toledo Railroad Company.

• £25 • C. Narbeth

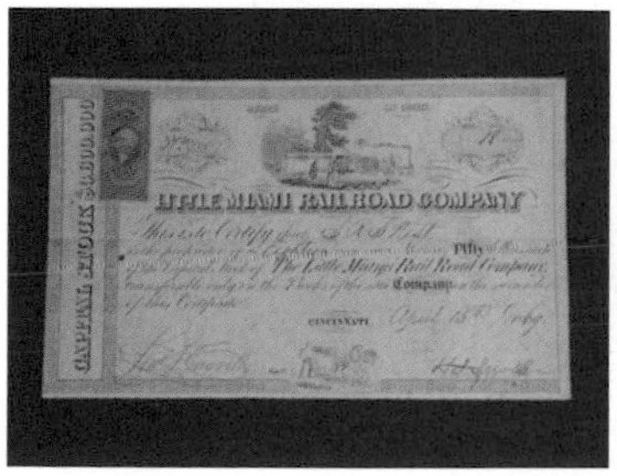

△ Railroad Shares

• *1864*

Share issued by the Little Miami Railroad Company.

• £10 • C. Narbeth

▽ Russian Note

• *1819*

Blue Russian 5-roubles note decorated with a two-headed eagle in the centre.

• £220 • Yasha Beresiner

▽ Argentian Note

• *1859*

Argentinian 500 Pesos note 'Confederacion Argentina'.

• £110 • Yasha Beresiner

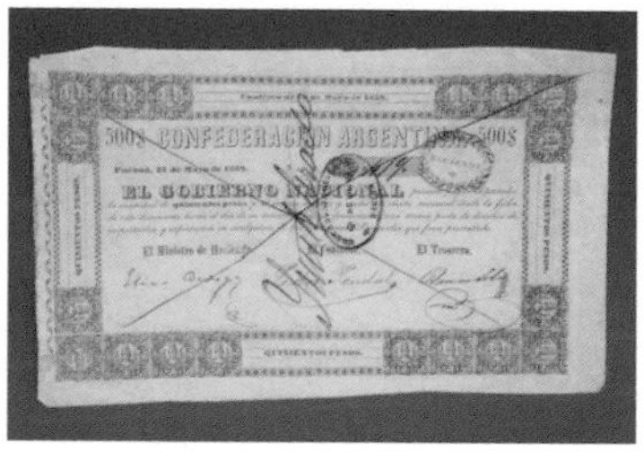

▽ Confederate States Bank Note

• *1862*

A Confederate States American Civil War bank note of $100 value with a milkmaid vignette. Fine condition.

• £25 • C. Narbeth

▽ Fijiian Treasury Note

• *12th July 1873*

Treasury note in the amount of £50, issued in Fiji.

• £495 • C. Narbeth

△ Guinea Bank Note

• *1825*

Commemorative one guinea bank note for George IV's historic state visit to Scotland. Issued by the Leith Banking Company of Edinburgh.

• £650 • C. Narbeth

△ Singapore Post Bill

• *17th August 1860*

$50 post bill used as a banknote, issued by the Chartered Bank of India, Australia and China.

• £650 • C. Narbeth

△ New Orleans Note

• *circa 1860*

New Orleans $20 note issued by Canal Bank.

• £12.50 • C. Narbeth

△ Turkey Piastres

• *1863*

Turkish Ottoman 200 Piastres 1279/1863.

• £200 • Yasha Beresiner

▽ English Banknote

• *1844*

£5 note, numbered 9374, issued by the Winchester and Hampshire Bank, England.

• £365 • C. Narbeth

▽ Oriental Bank Share

• *1850*

Share certificate issued by the Oriental Bank Corporation.

• £15 • C. Narbeth

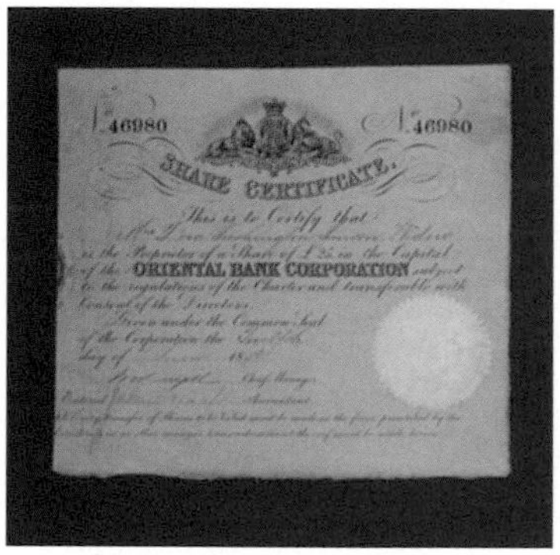

▽ Queen Victoria Letter

• *19th August 1854*

To M. le Comte de Mensdorff Pouilly. Written in German and sent from Windsor Castle.

• £600 • Jim Hanson

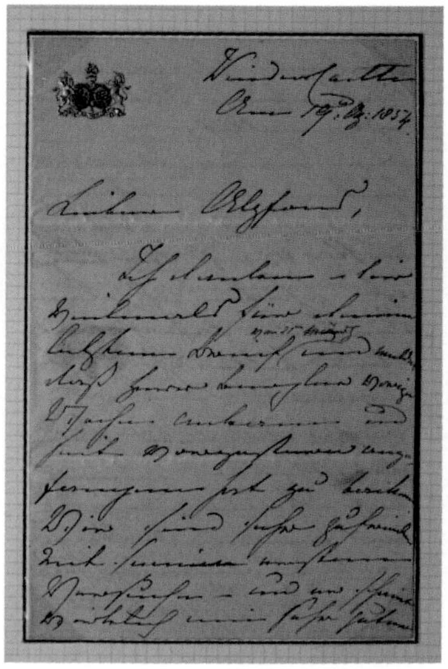

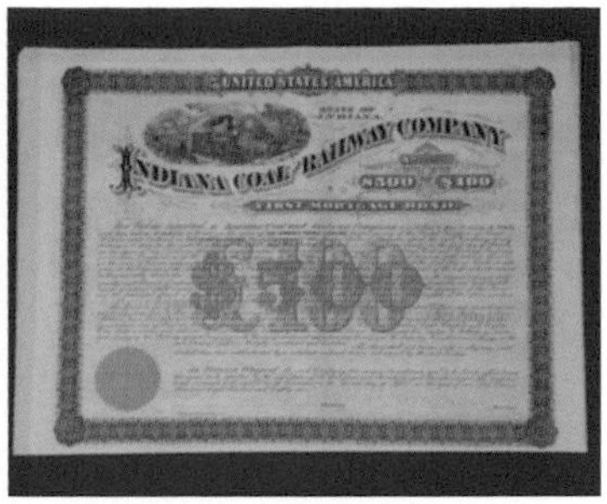

△ US Railway Bond

• *1881*
$500 dollar bond issued by the Indiana Coal and Railway Company.
• **£35** • **C. Narbeth**

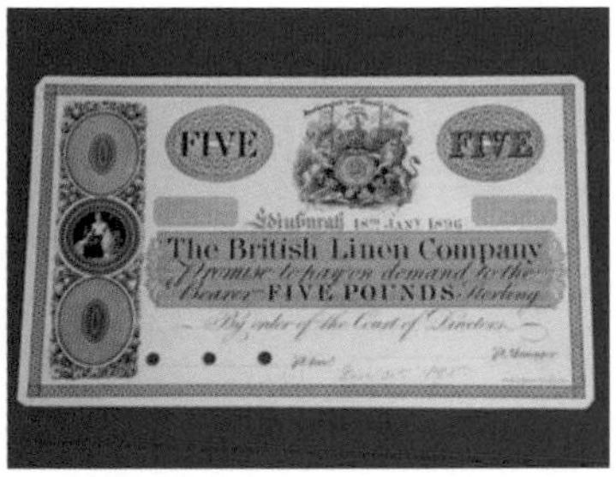

△ British Linen Co. Note

• *18th January 1896*
£5 note issued by the British Linen Company.
• **£325** • **C. Narbeth**

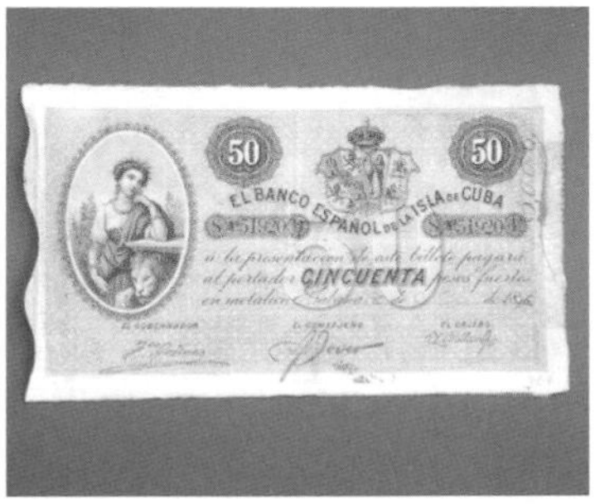

△ Cuban Note

• *1896*
Cuban 50 Pesos 'Plata' El Banco Espanol de la Isla de Cuba with a coat of arms in the centre and a lady with a lion and a lamb in a cartouche to the left.
• **£90** • **Yasha Beresiner**

△ 1,000 Marks Note

• *1910*
A German Reichsbank 1,000 mark note in very fine condition.
• **£2** • **C. Narbeth**

▽ Letter from George V

• *19th October 1873*
Written by the future king, then aged eight, from Marlborough House, to Lady Julia Lockwood.
• **£650** • **Jim Hanson**

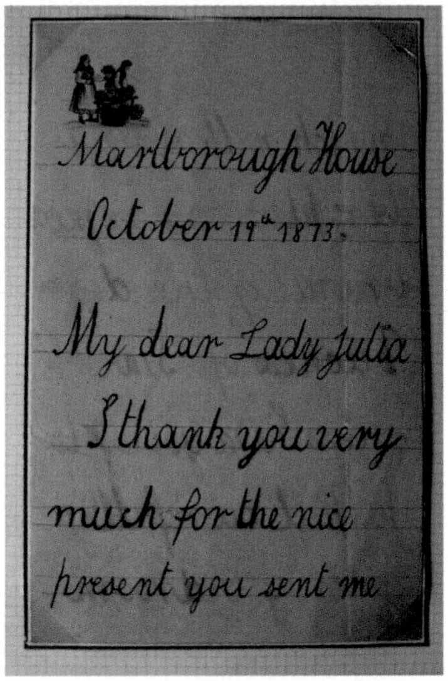
Marlborough House
October 19th 1873.
My dear Lady Julia
I thank you very
much for the nice
present you sent me

▽ Siege of Khartoum Note

• *circa 1884*
A 20 piastre note from the siege of Khartoum, Sudan. Hand-signed by General Gordon. In very fine condition.
• **£275** • **C. Narbeth**

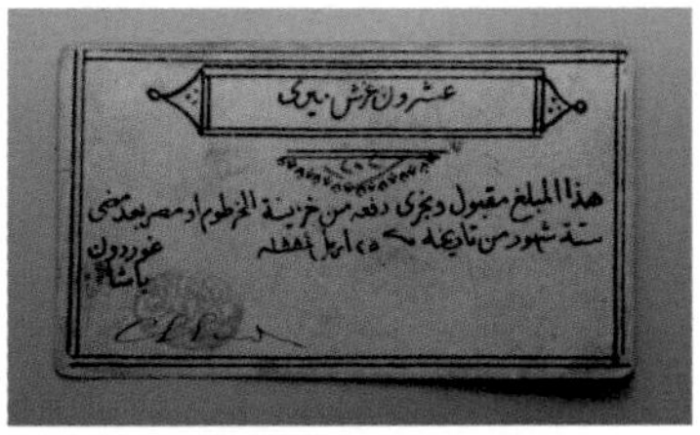

▽ Bolivian Bond

• *1887*
Bolivian note with the inscription: Compania Minera Nacional Anonima El Gallao Capital Bollivares.
• **£36** • **Yasha Beresiner**

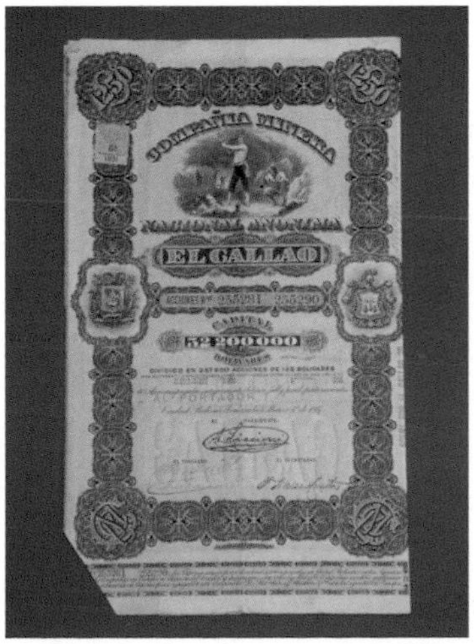

△ Russian Note

• *1884*
Russian 10 rouble note issued in the reign of Czar Alexander III.
• **£850** • **C. Narbeth**

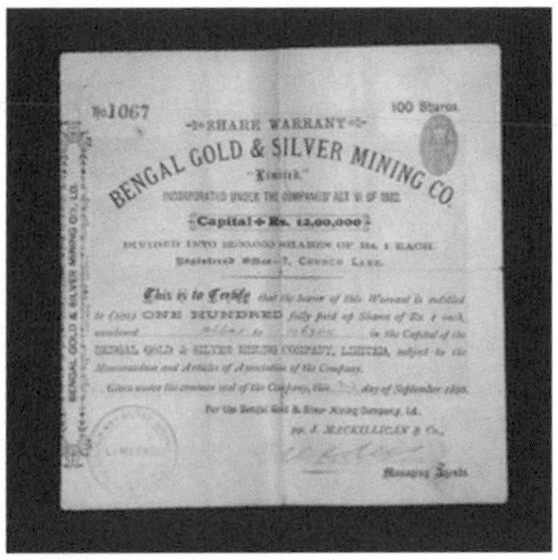

△ Share Warrant

• *1890*
Share warrant No. 1067 for one hundred shares, issued by the Bengal Gold and Silver Mining Company.
• **£7** • **C. Narbeth**

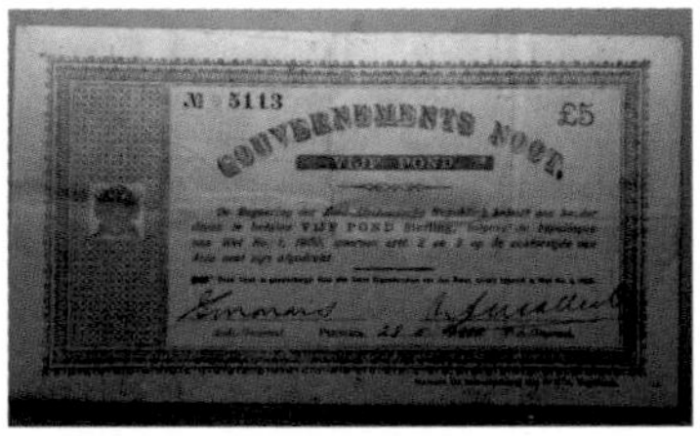

△ Boer War Note

• *1900*
A South African Boer War note of five pounds, issued from Pretoria, the Boer capital. In very fine condition.
• **£28** • **C. Narbeth**

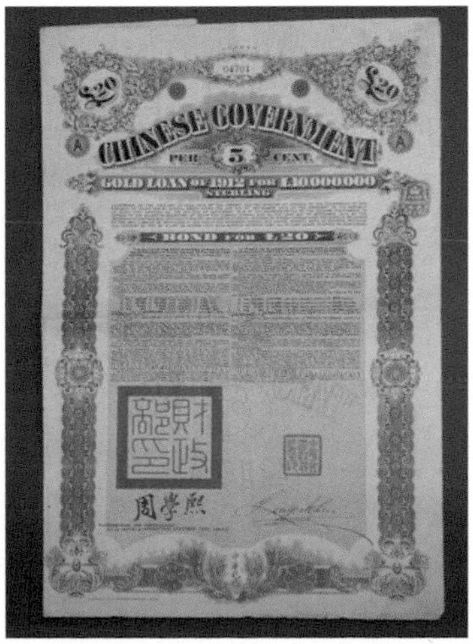

▽ Signed US Share

• *1895*
Philadelphia and Lancaster share signed "Bingham". Early US share with a vignette.
• **£795** • **C. Narbeth**

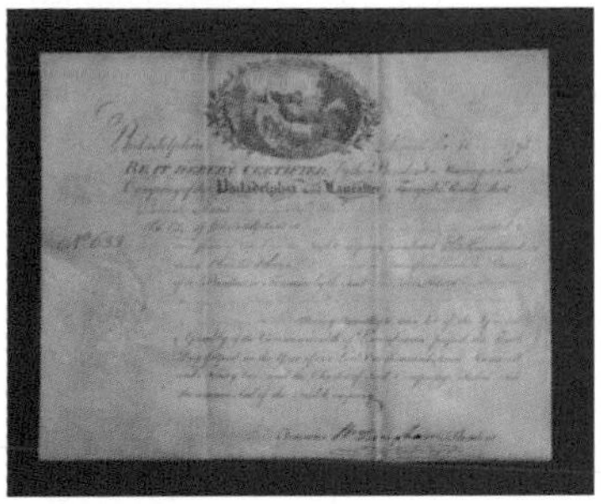

▽ Guatemala Note

• *1895*
Guatemala Banco Americano five hundred pesos written in Spanish with two seated ladies surrounded by anvil, mallet wheel, fruit and parrot with a steamship in the background.
• **£270** • **Yasha Beresiner**

▽ German Bond

• *1909*
DM 10,000 bond from Germany
• **£15** • **C. Narbeth**

◁ Chinese Gold Loan

• *1912*
Chinese Government gold loan of 1912 for L10,000,000 sterling.
• **£30** • **Yasha Beresiner**

△ 500 Rouble Note

• *1912*
A large Russian 500 rouble note, showing a portrait of Peter the Great. In extremely fine condition.
• £5 • C. Narbeth

△ Shares Note

• *1913*
Shares note issued by the Marconi Wireless Company.
• £35 • C. Narbeth

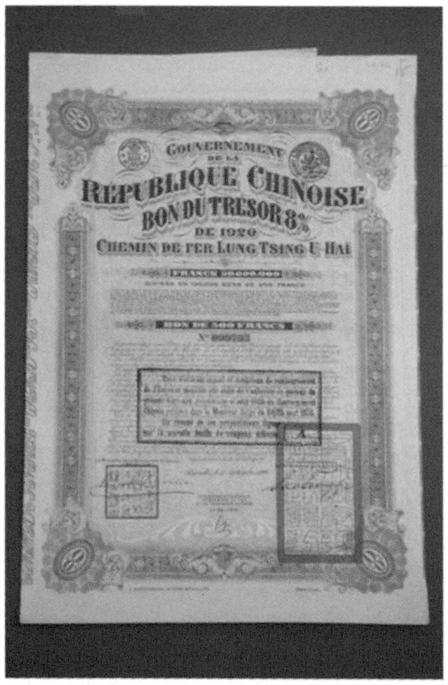

▽ Polish Bond

• *1928*
Polish Bond Banku Gospodarstwa Krajowego.
• £20 • Yasha Beresiner

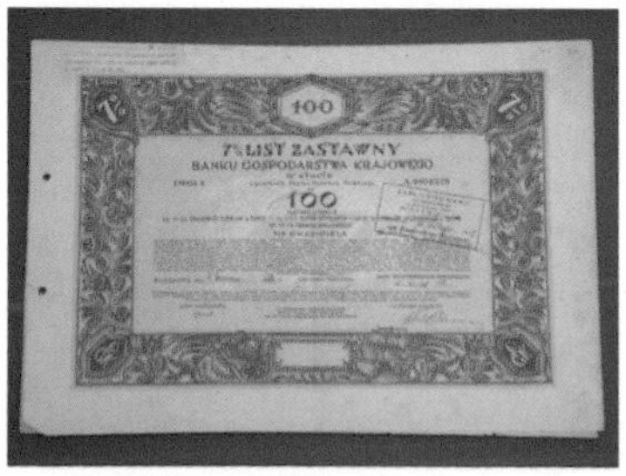

▽ Letter from Edward VII

• *18th January 1910*
A crested letter and photo regarding his private affairs. Addressed to his sister-in-law, the Duchess of Connaught, and sent from Sandringham.
• £650 • Jim Hanson

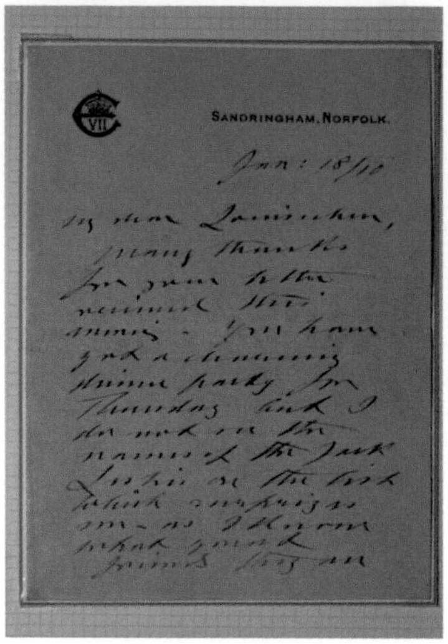

▽ Titanic Stock Certificate

• *1919*
Titanic stock certificate, with the words 'International Mercantile Marine company', which owned the White Star Line, and showing the *Titanic*.
• £50 • Yasha Beresiner

◁ Chinese Bond

• *1920*
Chinoise Bon du Trésor 8 per cent. Francs 50,000,000.
• £15 • Yasha Beresiner

△ Scottish Pound Note

• *1921*
£1 note issued by the Bank of Scotland.
• £95 • C. Narbeth

△ Chinese Bond

• *1913*
Gold bond note issued by the Chinese Government.
• £25 • C. Narbeth

△ Chinese Bond

• *1913*
'Banque Industrielle de Chine' bond decorated with a picture of China and two dogs of Fo.
• £42 • Yasha Beresiner

△ Austrian 1,000 Kronen

• *1919*
An Austrian Tausend Kronen note in mint condition.
• £3.50 • C. Narbeth

△ Ten Shilling Note

• *circa 1920*
UK ten shilling note. A third issue 'B' note, issued by John Bradbury.
• £165 • C. Narbeth

▽ English Pound Note

• *circa 1914*
Signed by John Bradbury and overprinted for the Dardenelles campaign during WW1. Very rare and in very fine condition
• £2,500 • C. Narbeth

▽ Mozambique Note

• *1919*
Mozambique 5-Libras note Banco da Beira.
• £20 • Yasha Beresiner

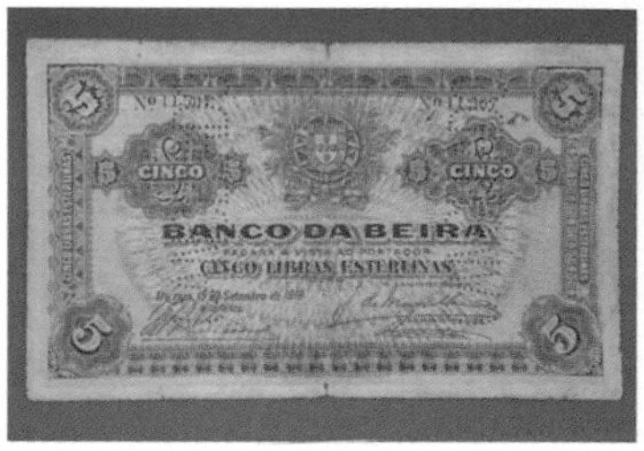

▽ Chinese Government Treasury Notes

• *1925–29*
Chinese Government 8 per cent 10 year. Treasury note for L100. Sterling.
• £50 • Yasha Beresiner

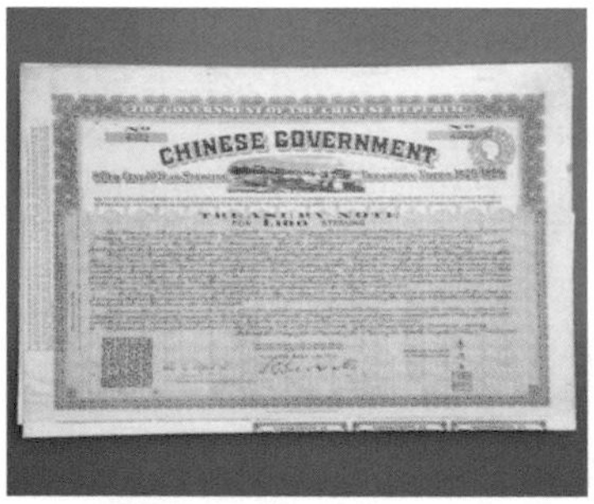

▽ Mining & Railway Co.Ltd.

• *1936*
The El Oro Mining & Railway Company, Limited.
• £52 • Yasha Beresiner

△ **Iraqi Note**

• *1931*

ID 1 banknote, numbered A 157545, from Iraq.

• £450 • C. Narbeth

△ **Five Reichsmark Note**

• *circa 1942*

Dated from the Second World War and showing a Hitler Youth in the Horst Wessel mould.

• £10 • C. Narbeth

△ **Rhodesian Pound Note**

• *1952*

Southern Rhodesian pound note, showing Queen Elizabeth II.

• £125 • Yasha Beresiner

△ **Ugandan Bank Note**

• *circa 1973*

An Idi Amin Ugandan bank note of five shillings' value. Extemely fine note.

• £4.50 • C. Narbeth

▽ **Fifty Mark Note**

• *circa 1933*

A German 50 mark note. In fine condition.

• £3.50 • C. Narbeth

▽ **Canadian Share Note**

• *1935*

Share note issued by the City of Montreal, Canada.

• £4 • C. Narbeth

▽ **Indo China Note**

• *1938*

Bank de l'Indochine 1000 Francs 'Mille Francs', painted with ladies and camels on one side and on the reverse a lady carrying a basket with the sea in the background.

• £65 • Yasha Beresiner

▽ **Hungarian Pengo Note**

• *1946*

100,000 billion pengo note – reflecting the world's highest ever inflation in post-war Hungary. In fine condition.

• £3.50 • C. Narbeth

◁ **African Republic Note**

• *circa 1974*

A 500 franc note from the Central African Republic, showing President Bokassa in a military pose. In mint condition.

• £70 • C. Narbeth

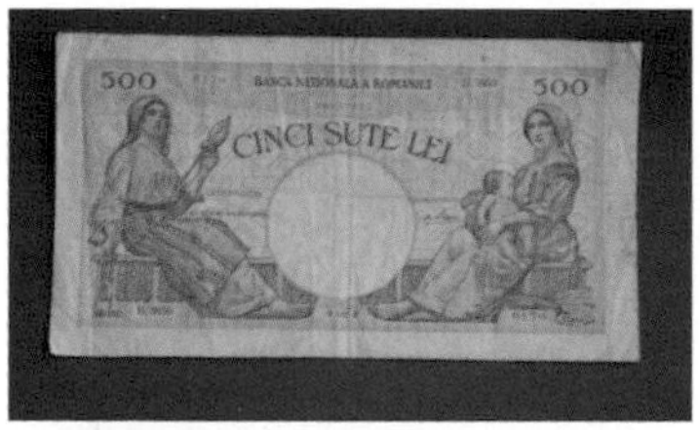

△ **Romanian Bank Note**

• *1938*

Romanian bank note 500 Lei showing two seated Romanian women, one with a baby.

• £15. • Yasha Beresiner

△ **Lebanese Bond**

• *1949*

L5,000 bond issued by the Lebanese government.

• £8 • C. Narbeth

△ **Three Pence Note**

• *circa 1960*

A British Armed Forces three pence note, mainly for use by the British Army of the Rhine in Germany.

• £12.50 • C. Narbeth

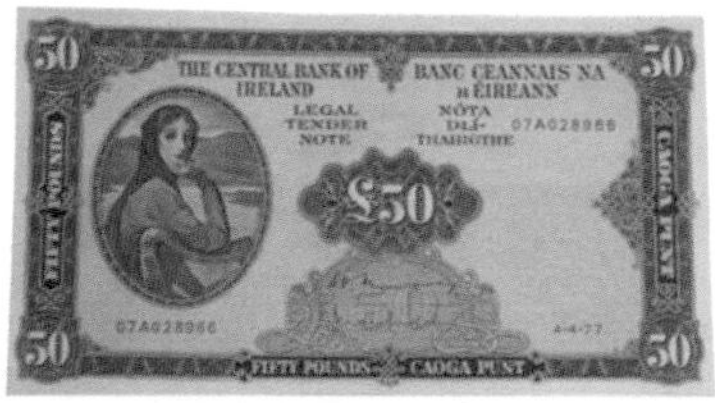

△ **Irish Banknote**

• *1977*

£50 note issued by The Central Bank of Ireland.

• £175 • C. Narbeth

▽ **Swedish Kronor**

• *1940*

A Swedish five kronor note. Extremely fine condition.

• £9.50 • C. Narbeth

▽ **Tibetan Note**

• *circa 1950*

A 100 strang denomination note from Tibet, serial numbers applied by hand by Buddhist monks. One seal represents the monetary authority and the other that of the Dalai Lama. Uncirculated.

• £22 • C. Narbeth

▽ **Columbia Pictures Note**

• *circa 1960*

Shares note issued by Columbia Pictures Corporation.

• £9 • C. Narbeth

▽ **Thailand Note**

• *1987*

Thailand 60 Baht, Government.

• £9 • Yasha Beresiner

◁ **Caribbean Note**

• *1975*

EC$100 dollar note issued by the East Caribbean Currency Authority.

• £175 • C. Narbeth

SEWING ITEMS

▽ **Quiver-Shaped Case**

• *1730*
Mother-of-pearl needle case designed in the shape of a quiver.
• *length 9cm*
• £280 • Thimble Society

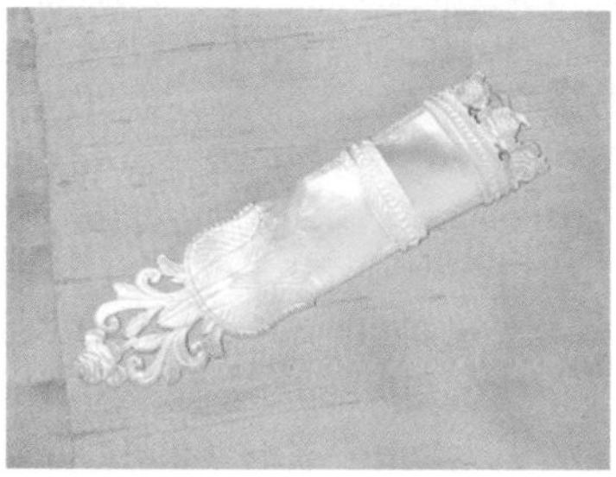

▽ **Filigree Scissor Case**

• *circa 1840*
Delicate silver-filigree scissor case with scrolling.
• *length 6.5cm*
• £480 • Arca

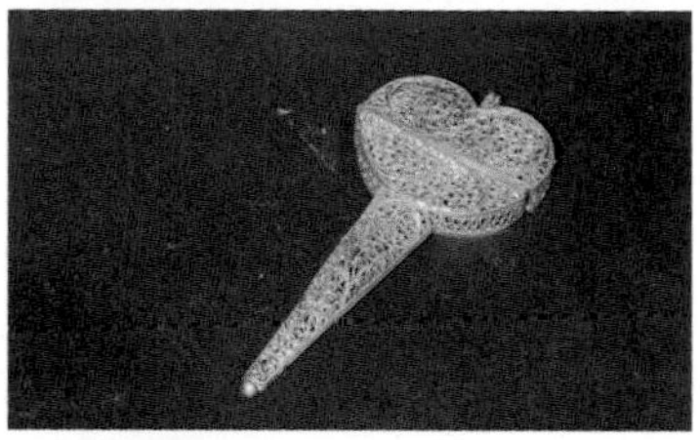

▽ **Straw-Work Sewing Box**

• *circa 1810–20*
Straw-work box made by Napoleonic prisoners-of-war, decorated with scenes of flowers, boats and houses.
• *width 27cm*
• £330 • Hygra

▷ **Sewing Table**

• *circa 1820*
Mahogany sewing table of the Regency period. Full-width cedar and pine lined drawer with original decorative brass knobs.
• *height 73cm*
• £1,850 • J. Collins

△ **Thimble Case**

• *1760*
Ormolu thimble case with hinged lid and embossed floral decoration.
• *width 3cm*
• £98 • Thimble Society

△ **English Bodkin Case**

• *circa 1780*
English lilac-enamel bodkin case in two sections with a bird cartouche.
• *length 15cm*
• £520 • Arca

▽ **Italian Scissors**

• *circa 1770*
Steel eighteenth-century Italian scissors, with handles in the shape of peacocks.
• *length 13cm*
• £230 • Thimble Society

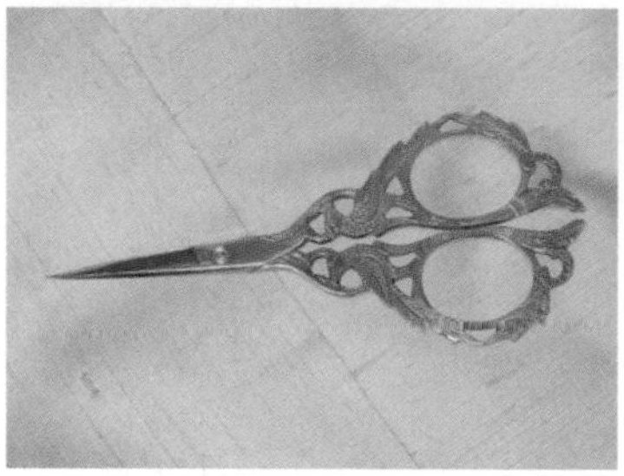

▽ **Necessaire**

• *circa 1780*
An 18th-century tortoiseshell and silver necessaire.
• *height 7.5cm*
• £1,200 • Hygra

▽ **Gold Thimbles**

• *1820–70*
Selection of continental gold thimbles, two with stone tops and one with foliate design, pearls and turquoise stones.
• *height 2.5cm*
• £325 • Thimble Society

△ **Silver-Filigree Case**

• *circa 1780*
French silver-filigree case enclosing pincushion and blue glass bottle.
• *length 5cm*
• £1,150 • Arca

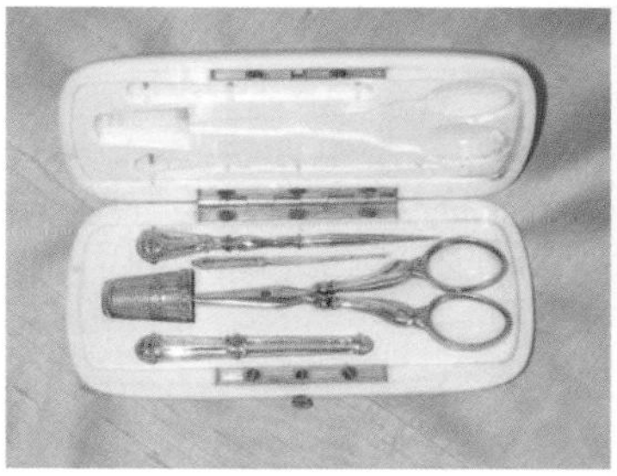

△ **Ivory Sewing Set**

• *1850*
French ivory sewing set with silver gilt tools.
• *width 10cm*
• £750 • Thimble Society

△ **Chinese Sewing Box**

• *circa 1820*
Sewing box in Chinese lacquer. The box stands on four carved wooden feet. Chinese-made for export to England.
• *width 42.5cm*
• £1,200 • Hygra

△ Rosewood Needlework Table

- *1850*

Victorian rosewood drop-leaf needlework table on six barley-twist legs, two of which pull out to support the extension flaps.

- *75cm x 85cm x 54cm*
- £1,850 • Old Cinema

△ Ivory Needle Case

- *circa 1870*

Fine ivory needle case with original needle packets and the inscription 'T.H.' on the cover.

- *height 11cm*
- £495 • Arca

△ Porcelain Thimble

- *circa 1900*

Porcelain thimble with a painted robin and roses and gold banding.

- *height 2cm*
- £210 • Arca

▽ Carpet Stitcher

- *19th century*

An American hand-powered carpet stitcher made by the Singer factory.

- *length 59cm*
- £285 • A.P. Mathews

▽ Pig Pincushion

- *circa 1880*

Ivory pig with brown-velvet pincushion on the back.

- *height 3cm*
- £360 • Arca

▽ Tortoiseshell Box

- *circa 1880*

A tortoiseshell needle case, with hinged cover.

- *height 5cm*
- £330 • Arca

▽ Small Sewing Machine

- *circa 1900*

A 'Stitchwell' hand-driven sewing machine.

- *height 14cm*
- £150 • Talk. Mach.

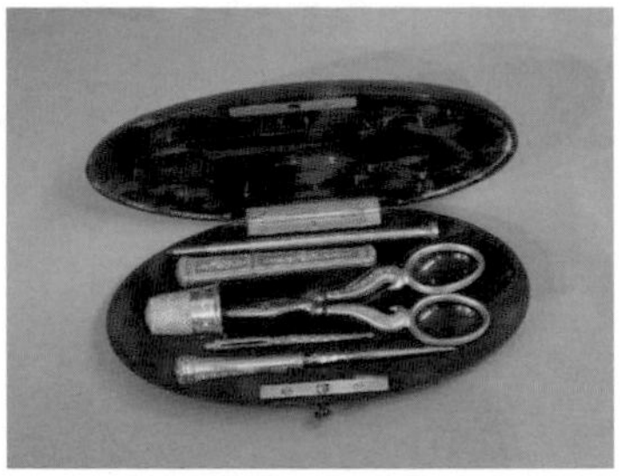

△ Oval Tortoiseshell Case

- *circa 1880*

Oval tortoiseshell sewing case, complete with gold scissors, thimble, pick, needle case and pencil.

- *length 12.5cm*
- £950 • Arca

△ Gold Egg Sewing Case

- *circa 1880*

French gold-filigree case in the shape of an egg and lined with the original red velvet. With gold thimble, scissors, needle case and pick.

- *height 8cm*
- £700 • Arca

△ Silver Bear Pincushion

- *1908*

English silver articulated bear pincushion from Birmingham.

- *height 8cm*
- £850 • Arca

▽ Sewing Box

- *circa 1875*

An exceptional Victorian straight-grain walnut sewing box, with gilded brass decoration and original blue, shot-silk interior.

- *height 34cm*
- £995 • J. & T. Stone

▽ English Thimble

- *circa 1880*

English mother-of-pearl thimble.

- *height 2cm*
- £220 • Arca

▽ Miniature Singer

- *circa 1935*

A cast-iron Singer sewing machine of the Art Deco period, hand-driven and with a raised action and bobbin board.

- *height 13cm*
- £400 • Talk. Mach.

SNUFF BOXES & SMOKING EQUIPMENT

△ Silver-Gilt Snuff Box

- *circa Louis XIV*

French silver-gilt snuff box with shell design on the top and a pastoral scene with a bird at the bottom.

- *length 8cm*
- **£980** • **Arca**

△ George II Snuff Box

- *1747*

A silver George II oval snuff box engraved with a contemporary coat of arms. Made in Dublin by Benjamin Stokes.

- *diameter 4cm*
- **£2,750** • **N. Shaw**

△ Monkey Snuff Box

- *circa 1800*

Finely carved snuffbox in the shape of a monkey.

- *height 7cm*
- **£950** • **A. & E. Foster**

▽ Gold and Tortoiseshell Snuff Box

- *1702*

Queen Anne gold and tortoiseshell snuff box made in London. The lid is inset with a gold coin commemorating Queen Anne's coronation. One of 750 that were issued at the time.

- *length 8cm*
- **£4,250** • **N. Shaw**

▽ Mother-of-Pearl Snuff Box

- *circa 1750*

Small bulbous snuff box with mother-of-pearl sections and silver banding.

- *height 5cm*
- **£750** • **Arca**

▽ Chinese Snuff box

- *1800–20*

Chinese tortoiseshell snuff box, deeply carved with figurative designs surrounded by a repetitive frieze.

- *length 8cm*
- **£225** • **Abacus Antiques**

◁ Silver Snuff Box

- *1835–36*

A silver William IV engine-turned snuff box made in Edinburgh by James Naismyth.

- *length 8cm*
- **£750** • **N. Shaw**

△ French Gold Snuff Box

- *circa 1750*

French oval snuff box with a tooled striped pattern of gold over tortoiseshell and a roped effect around the rim.

- *length 7cm*
- **£1,980** • **Arca**

△ Tortoiseshell and Silver Snuff Box

- *circa 1780*

An oval tortoiseshell snuff box with a silver floral and geometric design, with a mother-of-pearl background.

- *diameter 6.5cm*
- **£240** • **Arca**

△ Horn Snuff Mull

- *circa 1810*

Extremely rare silver-mounted horn snuff mull. Made by Robert Kaye of Perth, Scotland.

- *length 15cm*
- **£1,750** • **N. Shaw**

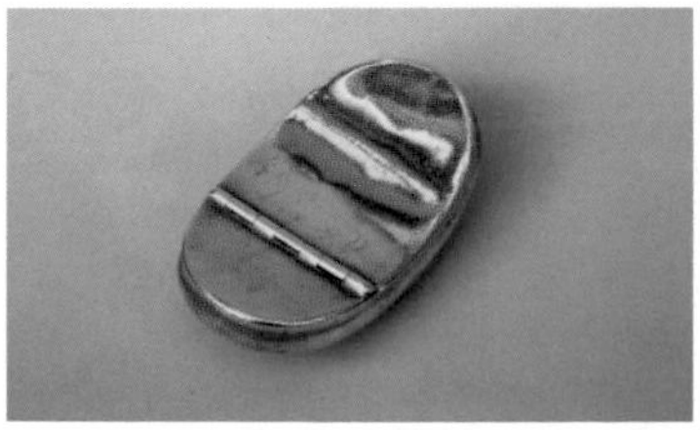

▽ George IV Snuff Box

- *1820*

An oval George IV silver tobacco box made in London by Beesley with the inscription 'Mary Annesley, Reading, 12 April'.

- *length 9cm*
- **£2,750** • **N. Shaw**

▽ Circular Painted Snuff Box

- *circa 1790*

Circular tortoiseshell painted snuff box showing a lady seated playing a harp.

- *diameter 8cm*
- **£1,750** • **Arca**

▽ George IV Snuff Box

- *1822–3*

A George IV snuff box made in Birmingham by Joseph Willmore.

- *length 4cm*
- **£450** • **N. Shaw**

◁ Miner's Snuff Box

- *mid-19th century*

Lead-lined. Half-hinged lid shaped for the back pocket.

- **£60** • **Ocean Leisure**

△ Victorian Snuff Box

- *1843–44*

A Victorian oblong silver snuff box by Charles Rawlings and William Summers.

- *width 11cm*
- £1,430 • N. Shaw

△ Goat's Head Snuff Box

- *late 19th century*

Snuff box in the shape of a goat's head. Pewter fittings. Brown and blue glaze with grey horns.

- *height 13cm*
- £1,100 • Elizabeth Bradwin

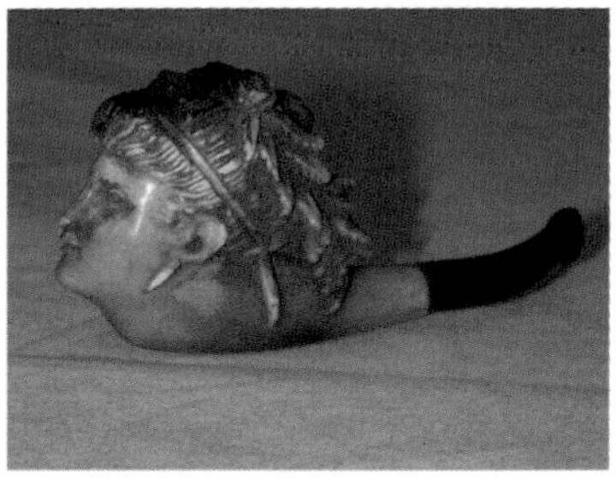

△ Lady's Pipe

- *1880*

Small carved Meerschaum lady's pipe.

- *length 4cm*
- £350 • Langfords

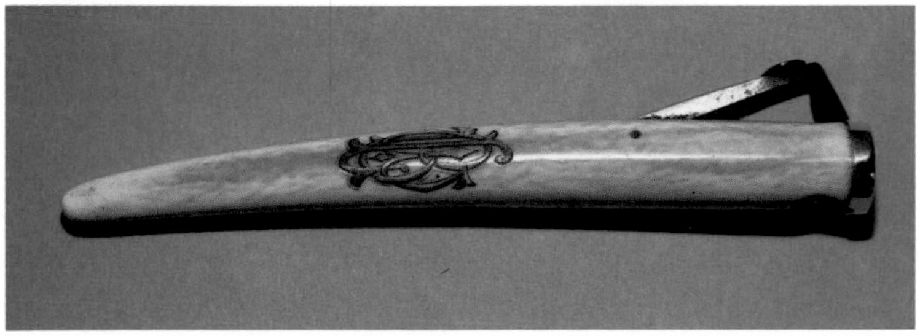

▽ Engine-Turned Snuff Box

- *1854*

Victorian engine-turned silver snuff box inscribed 'To Captain A. Droght, Indian Navy'.

- *length 4cm*
- £1,750 • N. Shaw

▽ Wooden Snuff Box

- *circa 1860*

Hand-carved Scottish snuff box.

- *length 6cm, height 6cm*
- £1,250 • Lacquer Chest

▽ Shoe-Shaped Snuff Box

- *circa 1860*

Mahogany snuff box in the shape of a shoe with brass inlay, the sole inscribed 'J.Dungey'.

- *2.5cm x 10cm*
- £375 • Bill Chapman

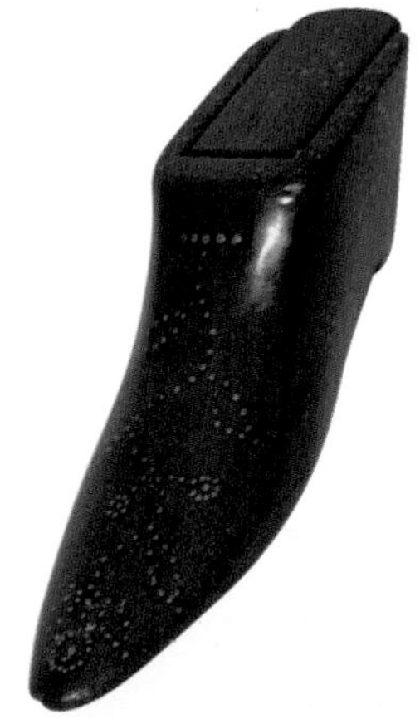

△ Silver-Gilt Snuff Box

- *1855*

A Victorian silver-gilt snuff box presented to Captain H. G. Kennedy of the ship *Parker*. Made by Edward Smith in Birmingham.

- *length 11cm*
- £2,250 • N. Shaw

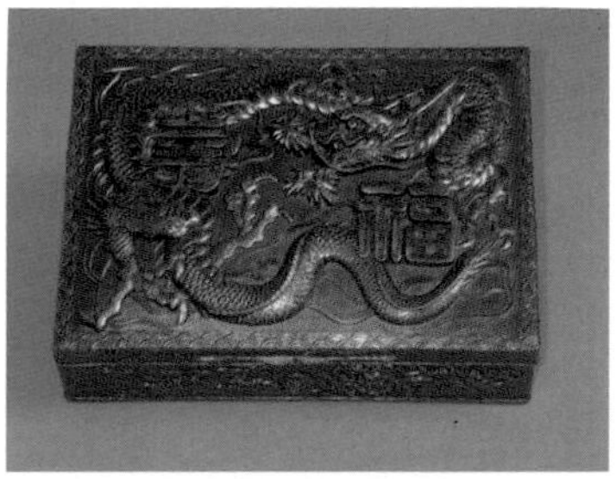

△ Japanese Cigar Box

- *circa 1880*

Japanese export cigar box with a dragon and Japanese characters on the lid characterising longevity and good fortune.

- *5cm x 18cm*
- £120 • Younger

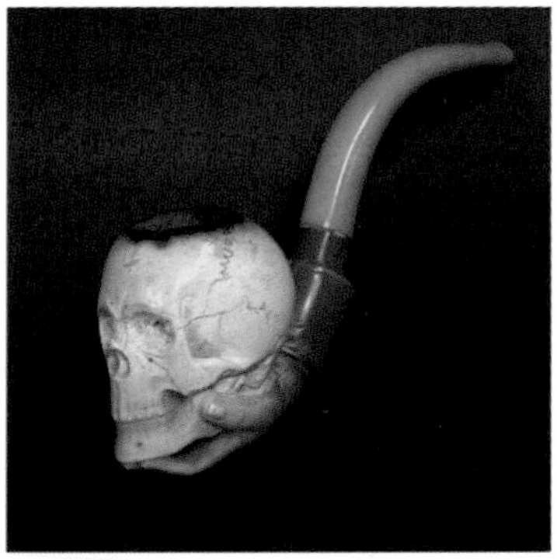

△ Skull Meerschaum

- *circa 1880*

Meerschaum pipe in the shape of a skull, with amber stem.

- *length 15cm*
- £300 • Arca

◁ Cigar Cutter

- *circa 1880*

Ivory and silver cigar cutter. Monogrammed. No marks.

- *length 15cm*
- £420 • S. & A. Thompson

▽ Mahogany Snuff Box

- *1860*

Mahogany shoe inlaid with brass design and mother-of-pearl.

- *6cm x 9cm*
- £525 • Bill Chapman

▽ Burr-Walnut Snuff Box

- *circa 1870*

Burr-walnut circular snuff box, with a painted landscape scene on the lid and gold banding.

- *diameter 6.5cm*
- £250 • Arca

▽ Ebonised Snuff Box

- *circa 1870*

Circular ebonised snuff box, painted with a portrait of a woman shown against a blue background by L. Fischer.

- *diameter 8.5cm*
- £980 • Arca

▽ Chieftain Meerschaum

- *circa 1880*

Meerschaum in the form of a chieftain with a large headdress and plume.

- *length 19cm*
- £360 • Arca

△ Novelty Vesta Case

- *1888*

A silver Victorian novelty vesta case.

- *length 6cm*
- £575 • N. Shaw

△ Match Strike

- *circa 1900*

Glass circular match strike with incised banding around outer edge for striking.

- *height 12cm*
- £98 • Magpies

△ Satinwood Humidor

- *circa 1910*

An elegant English rectangular satinwood humidor, with ivory banding and a fitted interior.

- *12.5cm x 23cm*
- £495 • A.I.G.

▽ Painted Snuff Box

- *circa 1890*

English oval papier mâché snuff box painted with the head of a young man on a red background.

- *length 7cm*
- £460 • Arca

▽ Dog Tobacco Jar

- *circa 1900*

Carved mahogany tobacco jar in the shape of a comical dog with glass eyes, wearing a hat with a tassel and a bow tie.

- *height 18cm*
- £600 • Arca

▽ Enamelled Vesta Case

- *1912*

A George V enamel-on-silver vesta case, made in Birmingham for the Royal Yacht Club.

- *length 4cm*
- £395 • N. Shaw

◁ Cigarette Box

- *1928*

A silver and enamel cigarette box.

- *width 11cm*
- £1,150 • N. Shaw

△ Victorian Vesta Case

- *1893*

A silver Victorian vesta case with central oval floral decoration made in Birmingham.

- *length 3cm*
- £375 • N. Shaw

△ Pipe Case

- *1900*

An unusual silver pipe case/tobacco box with a match box on the inside of the lid.

- *length 11.4cm*
- £750 • N. Shaw

△ Austrian Snuff Box

- *1924*

An Austrian snuff box with indigo enamel on a tooled silver base, with pierced floral cartouches in a neo-classical style.

- *length 8cm*
- £480 • Thimble Society

▽ Silver and Enamel Cigarette Case

- *circa 1896*

Silver cigarette case with an enamel picture showing a circus ring, with a lady in a pink dress astride a white horse, and a clown turning towards her.

- *length 9cm*
- £1,350 • Arca

▽ Edwardian Vesta Case

- *1909*

An Edwardian vesta case with an Edward VII relief, made in Birmingham.

- *length 4cm*
- £295 • N. Shaw

▽ Silver Vesta Case

- *1926*

A silver George V vesta case made in London by The Goldsmith and Silversmith Company Ltd.

- *length 3cm*
- £675 • N. Shaw

◁ Cigarette Box

- *circa 1940*

Silver cigarette box with 18ct gold sides. Smooth with a small lip. By Boucheron, Paris.

- £2,000 • Henry Gregory

TELEPHONES

△ Desk Telephone

- *1895*

A Dutch wooden desk phone with rotary dial.

- *height 15cm*
- £295 • Telephone Lines

△ German Telephone

- *1900*

A German-made magneto telephone with metal base and handset, and chrome earpiece and microphone.

- *30cm x 20cm*
- £285 • Telephone Lines

▷ British 'Pulpit'

- *circa 1897*

By Ericsson National Telephone Co with wood construction and outside terminal receiver.

- £1,600 • Telephone Lines

▽ Skeleton Telephone

- *circa 1895*

Highly collectable handset telephone by L.M. Ericsson and Co. Metal body with enamelling.

- £600 • Telephone Lines

▽ Desk Telephone

- *1908*

A desk phone with magneto handle, raised on a wooden base by Thomson-Houston, France.

- *33cm x 18cm*
- £385 • Telephone Lines

◁ French Wooden Telephone

- *1924*

French wooden candlestick telephone with metal dial and handset, and original wiring, by P. Jacquesson.

- *height 22.5cm*
- £475 • Telephone Lines

▽ Upright Dial Telephone

- *circa 1908*

Made from 1908 by Telefon Fabrik Automatic of Copenhagen.

- £510 • Old Telephone Co.

▽ Candlestick Telephone

- *1916*

French candlestick telephone with metal and chrome handset and wooden candlestick base by Grammont.

- *height 34cm*
- £415 • Telephone Lines

▷ Ericsson Telephone

- *circa 1905*

A Swedish-made, Ericsson, wooden wall-mounted phone with bell-ring display to top.

- *69cm x 26cm*
- £495 • Telephone Lines

△ Chrome Handset

- *1900*

A French candlestick telephone with a metal base and chrome handset by Thomson-Houston.

- *height 32cm*
- £385 • Telephone Lines

△ Candlestick Telephone

• *circa 1920*
Candlestick telephone with steel handle with black bakelite top and brass and separate wood and brass ring box.
• *44cm x 15cm*
• £395 • H. Duffield

△ Danish Telephone

• *circa 1935*
A variation on the D30, with two exchange lines coming in. Supplied with a separate bell set.
• £420 • Old Telephone Co.

△ Series 200 Telephone

• *circa 1938*
Almost the rarest colour in the 200 series. Made by Siemens Brothers of Woolwich.
• £1,100 • Old Telephone Co.

▽ Magneto Telephone

• *circa 1925*
A classic design by L.M. Ericsson, Stockholm, made from around 1896. Also known as Eiffel Tower.
• £850 • Old Telephone Co.

▽ Series 200 Telephone

• *1930s–40s*
An English acrylic cream-coloured telephone. This type of telephone did not have a bell; the bell was installed on the wall.
• *17cm x18cm*
• £420 • Decodence

▽ Belgian Telephone

• *circa 1940*
Copper-bodied telephone by the Bell Company, with pleasant ring and carrying handle.
• £89 • Telephone Lines

▷ Series 200 Telephone

• *circa 1940*
English cream telephone with original undermounted bell box. Rare in any colour but black.
• £550 • Decodence

△ Candlestick Telephone

• *circa 1927*
Type 150, in bakelite, featuring a replacement microphone. Made by Ibex Telephones.
• £460 • Old Telephone Co.

△ Danish Telephone

• *circa 1935*
A Danish magneto telephone based on an L.M. Ericsson design. Can't be used on today's system.
• £270 • Old Telephone Co.

▽ Gecophone Telephone

• *circa 1930*
Gecophone black bakelite telephone with ringing bell.
• *18cm x 24cm*
• £185 • H. Duffield

▽ Black Telephone

• *circa 1940*
Black bakelite telephone issued by GPO.
• £180 • After Noah (KR)

▽ Swiss Telephone

• *circa 1950*
A Swiss wall-mounted telephone with bell-ring displayed to top and hook connection.
• £100 • Decodence

△ Bakelite Telephone

• *circa 1955*
A British-made, green bakelite telephone, made for the GPO, model number 332. Shows original label on all-metal rotary dial, cheese-dish address drawer and gold-coloured, fabric-covered, interwoven flex. Green is a particularly rare colour.
• £500 • Telephone Lines

△ Series 300 Telephone

• *1940s–1950s*
An English acrylic golden-yellow telephone with drawer for addresses and integral bell.
• *19cm x 18cm*
• £300 • Decodence

△ Belgian Desk Telephone

• *circa 1950*
European ivory desk telephone with large numerals and clear plastic rotary dial.
• *height 12.5cm*
• £75 • Old Cinema

△ Pink Plastic Wall Telephone

• *1950*
Pink plastic wall telephone with cream and silver banding to the ear and mouthpiece.
• *7cm x 13cm x 21cm*
• £75 • Radio Days

△ Red Telephone

• *circa 1960*
Red plastic British GPO telephone.
• *13cm x 24cm*
• £45 • Geri

◁ Blue Plastic Telephone

• *1960*
Blue plastic telephone with red dial, on a cream base with red flex.
• *14cm x 14cm x 24cm*
• £55 • Radio Days

△ Series 300 Telephone

• *circa 1955*
A series 300 black bakelite office telephone with original handset, cord and draw.
• £230 • Old Telephone Co.

△ Series 300 Telephone

• *circa 1957*
A rare 328 telephone made by Plessey, Ilford, Essex. With bell-on and bell-off push buttons.
• £650 • Old Telephone Co.

▷ Lysell & Bloomberg Telephone

• *circa 1957*
The first ever one-piece telephone designed by Ralph Lysell & Hugo Bloomberg in cream with rotary dial underneath.
• *height 23.5cm*
• £100 • Old Cinema

▽ Ericsson Telephone

• *circa 1950*
Cream bakelite Ericsson telephone with original handset and cord and large rotary dial with black numerals.
• *height 14cm*
• £185 • Old Cinema

▽ Plastic Telephone

• *circa 1950*
Blue plastic telephone with cream dial and handle and silver banding.
• *14cm x 14cm x 24cm*
• £55 • Radio Days

◁ Green Plastic Telephone

• *circa 1960*
British GPO telephone in light-green plastic .
• *13cm x 24cm*
• £45 • Geri

◁ Desk Telephone

• *circa 1960*
A Belgian desk telephone in black plastic, with black rotary dial and white base on rubber feet.
• £150 • Old Telephone Co.

△ Belgian Desk Telephone

• *circa 1960*
A Belgian ivory desk telephone. Most of these were made in black, making this very collectable.
• £190 • Old Telephone Co.

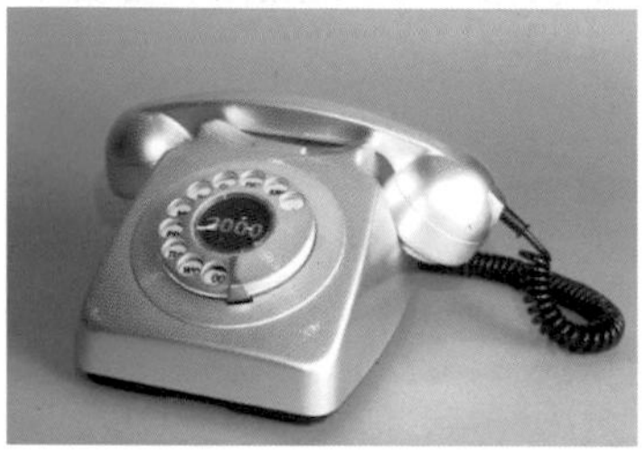

△ Series 700 Telephone

• *circa 1967*
British Telecom, acrylic with rotary dial, flexicord and handset extension. Resprayed in silver.
• £85 • After Noah

△ Trimphone

• *circa 1970*
Silver-painted British 'Trimphone' made for the GPO, with push-button dialling. With distinctive ringing tone.
• £85 • After Noah

△ Orange Plastic Telephone

• *1970*
Orange plastic telephone with cream numerals and orange flex.
• *12cm x 10cm x 21cm*
• £20 • Radio Days

▽ Belgian Wall Phone

• *circa 1960*
A Belgian wall phone repainted in red. Made in Antwerp by Bell Telephones, a subsidiary of the American Bell Telephones.
• £180 • Old Telephone Co.

▽ Pink Plastic Metallic Telephone

• *circa 1965*
Pink plastic metallic telephone with black flex.
• *14cm x 14cm x 24cm*
• £55 • Radio Days

▽ Elvis Presley Telephone

• *circa 1980*
'Jailhouse Rock' shown with guitar and period clothes. Touch tone handset.
• £99 • Telephone Lines

▷ Star Trek Telephone

• *circa 1994*
Modelled on Star Trek's 'Enterprise' with sound effects and push-button dial to base.
• £89 • Telephone Lines

△ Black Plastic Telephone

• *1960*
Black plastic telephone with white letters and numbers, and black flex.
• *13cm x 13cm x 21cm*
• £55 • Radio Days

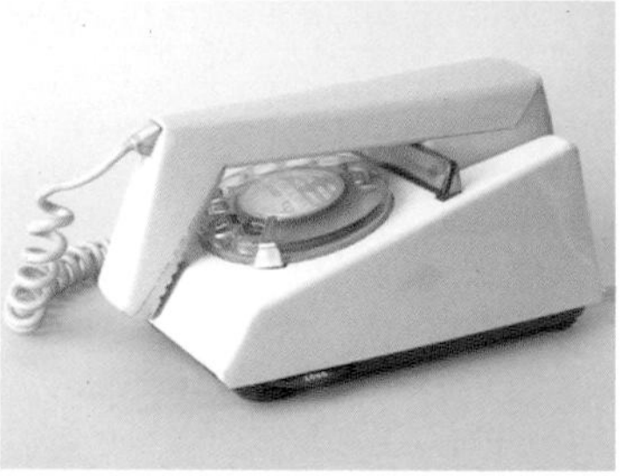

△ Two-Toned Telephone

• *circa 1970*
Two-toned adjustable-volume stone coloured British GPO telephone in plastic.
• *12cm x 10cm*
• £48 • Geri

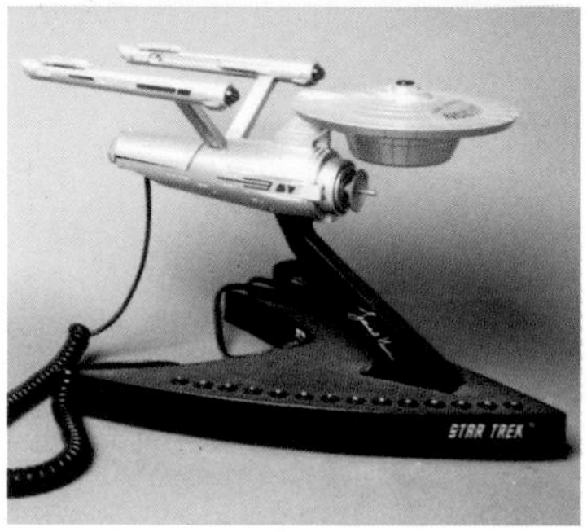

▽ Danish Telephone

• *circa 1966*
By Kristian Kirks, Telefon Fabrikka of Horsens, for the Jydsk (Jutland) telephone authority.
• £150 • Old Telephone Co.

▽ Genie Telephone

• *circa 1970*
Red 'Genie' designer telephone by A.P. Besson, manufactured by British Telecom, with push-button dial.
• *11.5cm x 22cm*
• £65 • Old Cinema

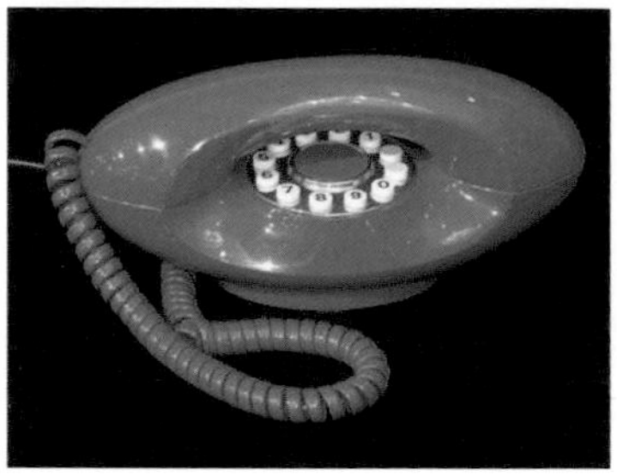

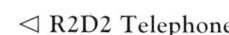

◁ R2D2 Telephone

• *circa 1980*
A telephone in the form of the character R2D2, from the 'Star Wars' films. His head moves and lifts up when the phone rings.
• £99 • Telephone Lines

△ Viscount Telephone

• *circa 1986*
A British Telecom-supplied telephone in burnt orange with cream flexcord extension.
• £20 • Retro

WALKING STICKS

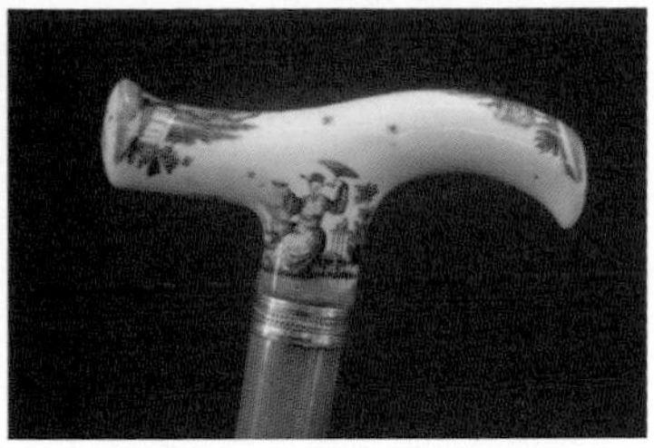

△ Porcelain Walking Cane

• *circa 1780*
Malacca cane with porcelain tau-shape Meissen handle with floral enamels.
• *length 100cm*
• £1,450 • Michael German

△ Folk-Art Cane

• *1840*
One-piece country folk-art cane with carved heads and animals along the shaft.
• £1,200 • Michael German

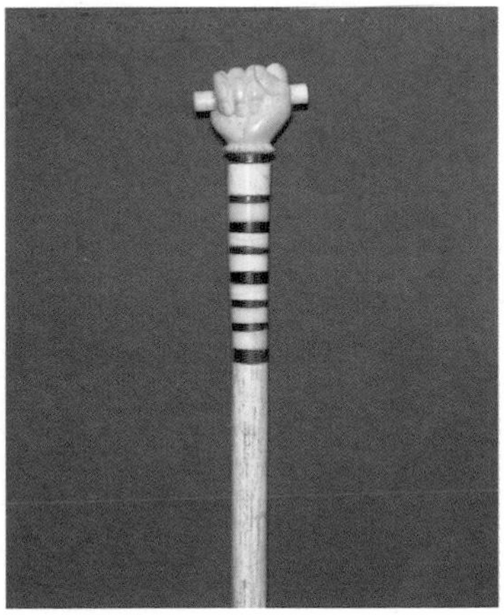

△ Whalebone Cane

• *1850*
Whalebone cane with a finely carved whale tooth handle, modelled as a hand holding a bar.
• £1,250 • Michael German

▽ Porcelain-Handled Cane

• *1820*
A fine early painted porcelain-handled stick, with a silver collar and malacca shaft.
• £1,400 • Michael German

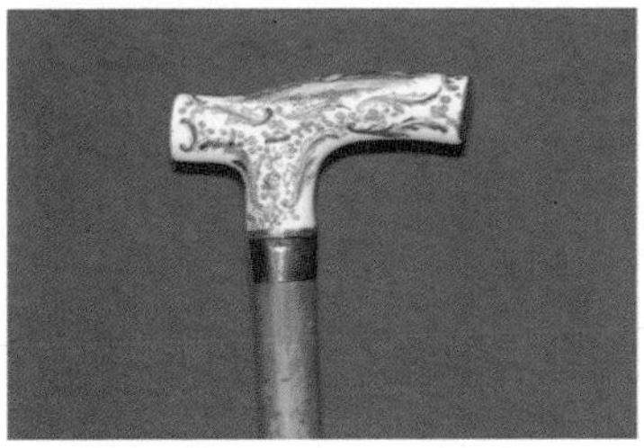

▽ Victorian Stick

• *1860*
Stick with carved handle in the shape of a grotesque dog's head. Glass eyes, open mouth with human ears. Gilt collar on a hardwood shaft.
• £400 • Michael German

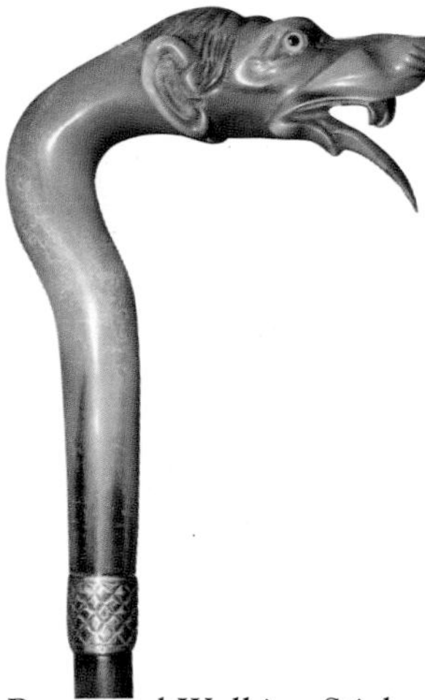

▽ Rosewood Walking Stick

• *1870*
Rare and unusual cane, with a head of a wild boar in silver and a rosewood shaft.
• £950 • Michael German

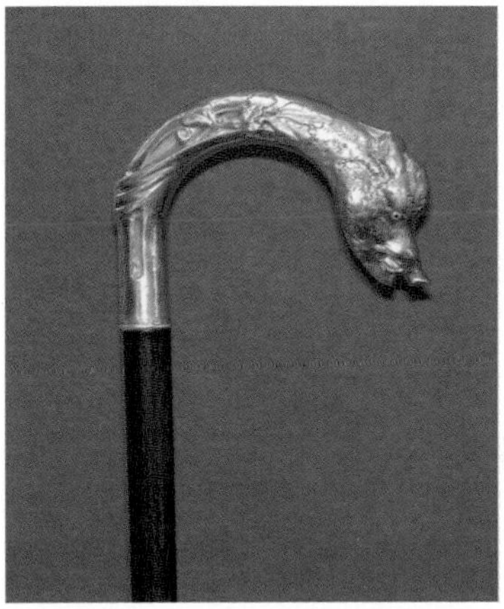

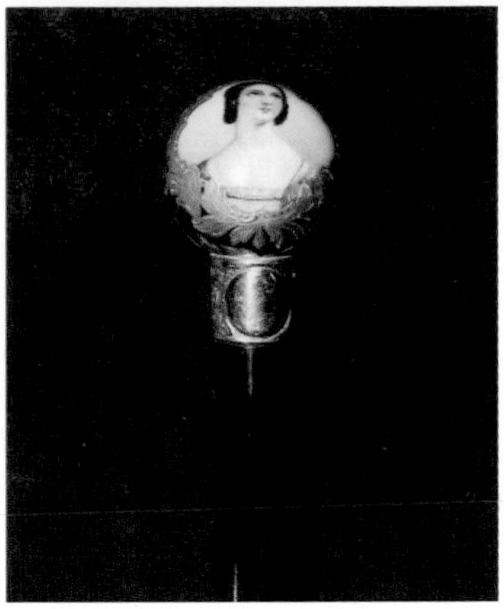

△ Rare Porcelain-Handled Stick

• *1837*
Rare porcelain cane. Handle painted with a portrait of Queen Victoria at her coronation. VR cypher and dated 1837 on reverse of handle. Gilt metal collar on ebony shaft. Painted on a gilt and blue background.
• £250 • Michael German

△ Folk Art Cane

• *1860*
Oversized folk art cane carved from one piece of wood depicting a dwarf sitting on a tree stump, laughing.
• £1,400 • Michael German

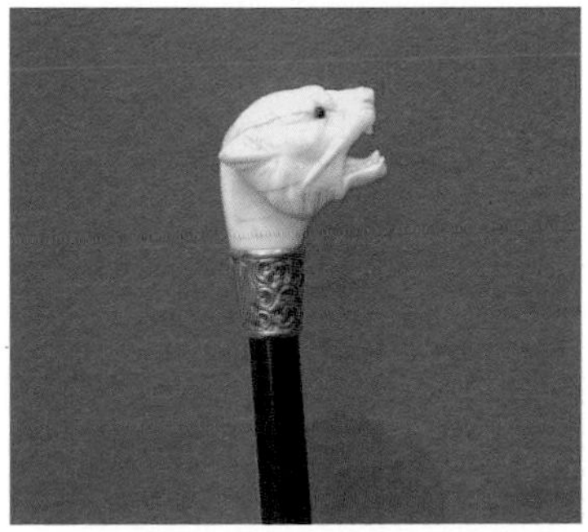

▽ Porcelain Cane

• *1840*
Porcelain painted head of a young gentleman, with a silver collar on an ebonised shaft.
• £800 • Michael German

▽ Carved Walking Stick

• *circa 1860*
Folk art cane with carved animals, trees and fruit, silver collar and rounded top.
• *length 92cm*
• £925 • Michael German

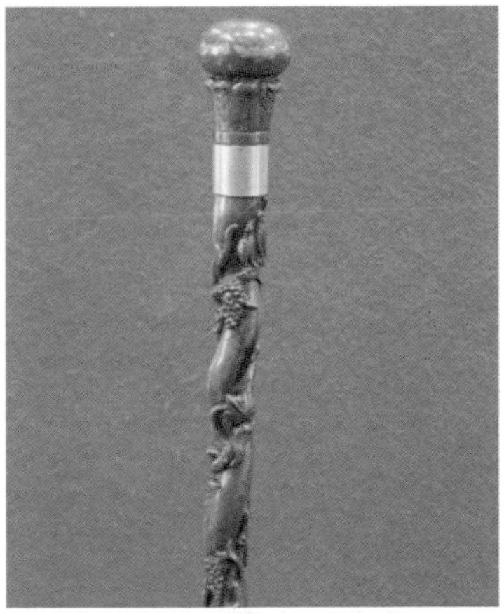

▽ Dog's Head Walking Cane

• *circa 1870*
Victorian ebonised cane with silver collar and a carved ivory dog's head with open jaw.
• *length 80cm*
• £700 • Michael German

◁ Ivory Cane

• *1870*
A carved ivory-handled cane, modelled as a tiger's head with glass eyes and and scrolled gilt collar, on an ebonised shaft.
• £1,200 • Michael German

▽ Kingfisher Walking Stick

• *1870*

Victorian stick with a well-carved and painted handle, modelled as a kingfisher mounted on an ebonised shaft.

• £380 • **Michael German**

▽ Crook-Handled Walking Stick

• *1880*

Fine crook-handled cane with a snakewood shaft surmounted by a finely moulded silver parrot's head with glass eyes.

• £1,300 • **Michael German**

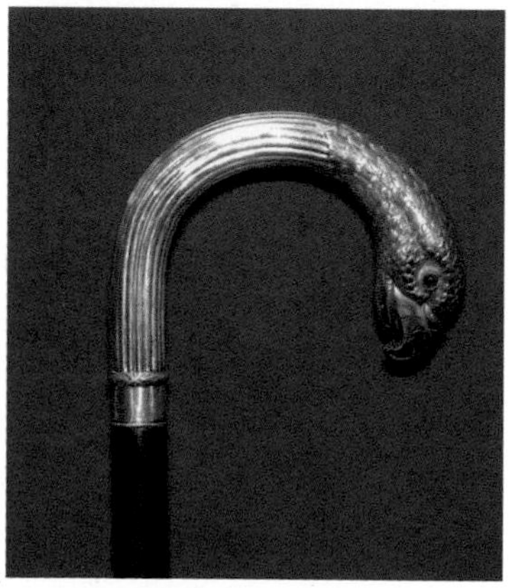

▽ Drinking Cane

• *1880*

Late 19th-century drinking cane complete with glass spirit flask, stopper and small glass goblet. Decorated with copper mounts. Has a country briar-wood shaft. Made in Austria and of good quality.

• £240 • **Michael German**

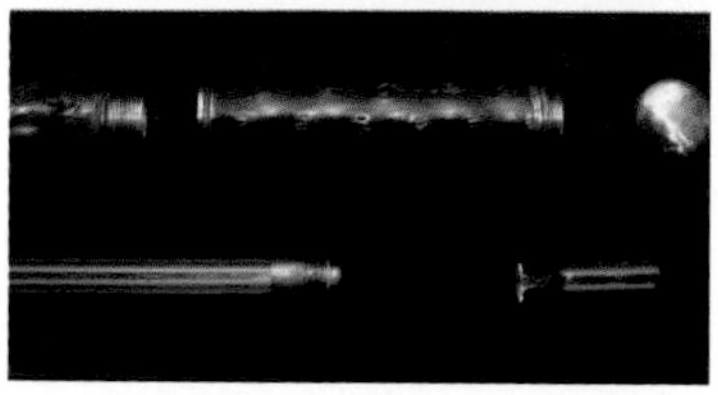

△ Cricket Ball Walking Stick

• *circa 1870*

Unusual folk-art cane with hand holding cricket ball, carved shaft.

• *length 100cm*

• £480 • **Michael German**

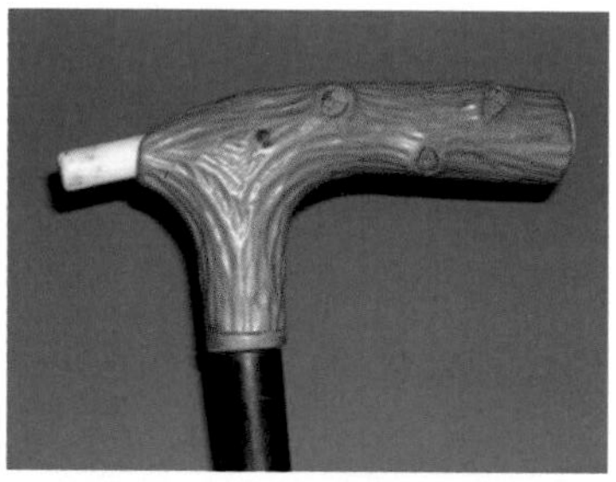

△ Cigar-Holder Walking Stick

• *circa 1880*

An unusual cane with a wood and ivory handle forming a cheroot holder mounted on an ebonised shaft.

• *length 91cm*

• £800 • **Michael German**

△ German Shepherd Cane

• *1880*

A German walking stick with the handle comically carved as a German shepherd dog with glass eyes, and ivory teeth.

• £420 • **Michael German**

▽ Victorian Porcelain Cane

• *1870*

Victorian porcelain ball-handle stick, with an enamel portrait of a young boy within a scrolled gilt border.

• £580 • **Michael German**

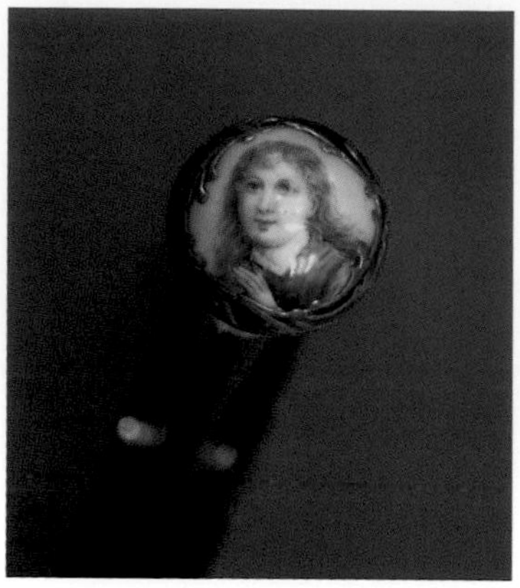

▽ Russian Cane

• *1880*

Fine Russian cane with silver niello tau-shaped handle, mounted on a hardwood shaft.

• £650 • **Michael German**

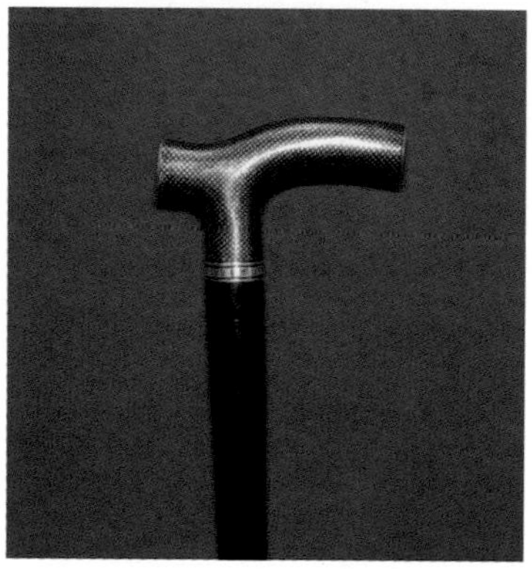

▽ German Cane

• *1880*

German Black Forest cane with the handle carved as French pug, with glass eyes and a leather collar with a bell.

• £480 • **Michael German**

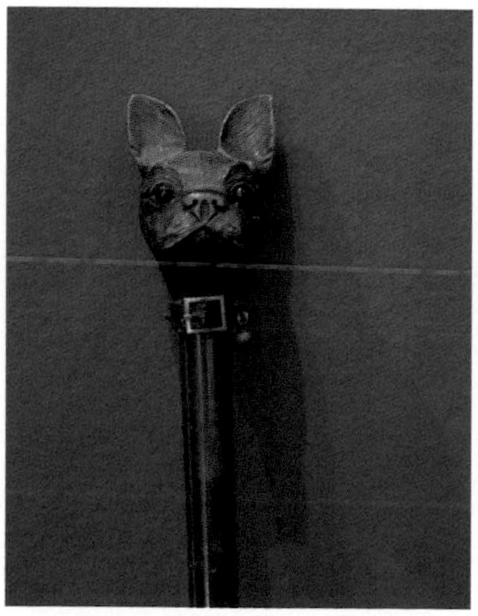

△ Brass-Headed Stick

• *1880*

Cast brass head of Mr Punch in good detail with plain brass collar and malacca shaft.

• £300 • **Michael German**

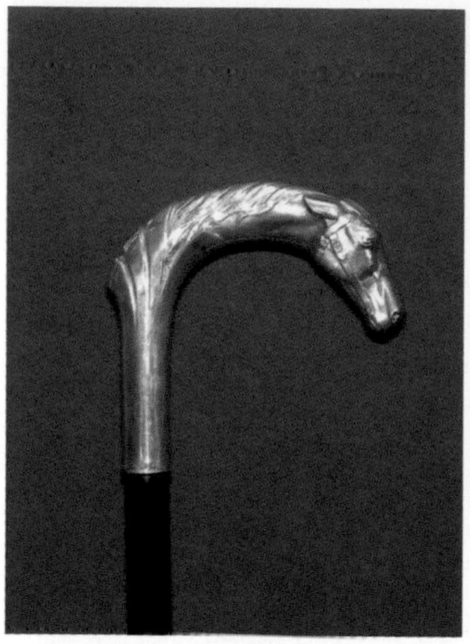

△ Silver Walking Stick

• *1880*

Russian fine crook-handled walking stick, with an ebony shaft surmounted by a silver horse's head.

• £1,000 • **Michael German**

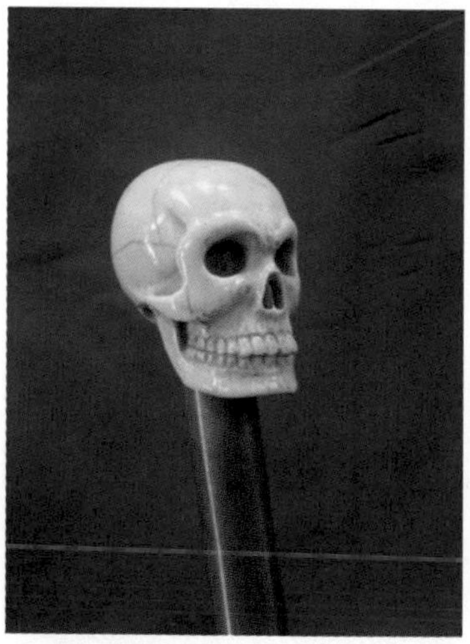

△ Skull Walking Stick

• *circa 1880*

An unusual Victorian malacca cane with an ivory skull.

• *length 91cm*

• £950 • **Michael German**

▽ Golfing Stick

• *1890*
Rare Sunday golfing stick with silver cigarette case within the handle.
• £1,150 • Michael German

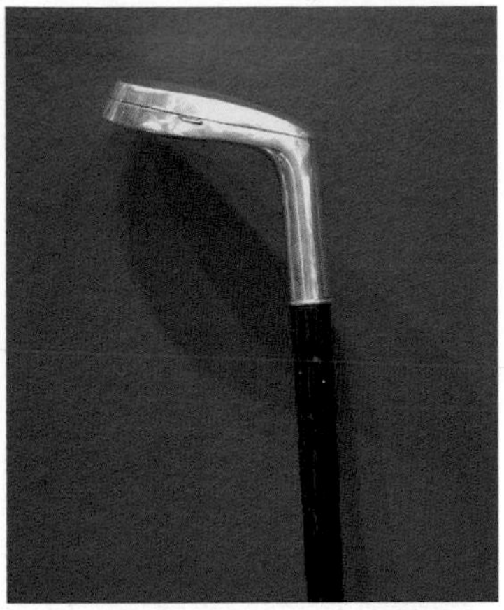

▽ Boar's Head Cane

• *1890*
Rare and unusual Austrian cane, with enamel boar's head handle on an ebonised shaft.
• £285 • Michael German

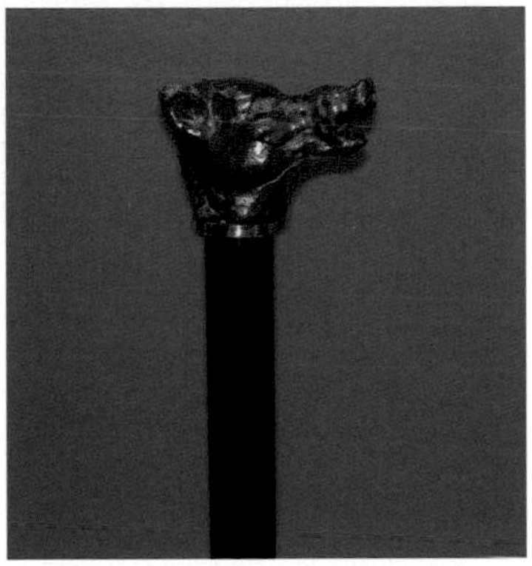

▽ Country Walking Stick

• *circa 1900*
A Scottish country walking stick with a silver-mounted snuff holder with amber inset and thistle design.
• *length 89cm*
• £550 • Michael German

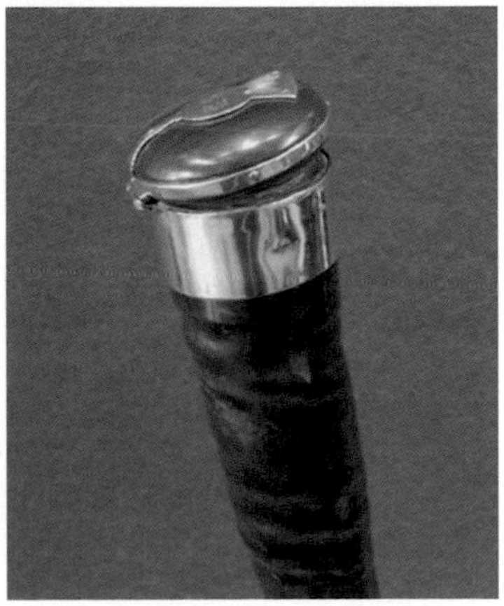

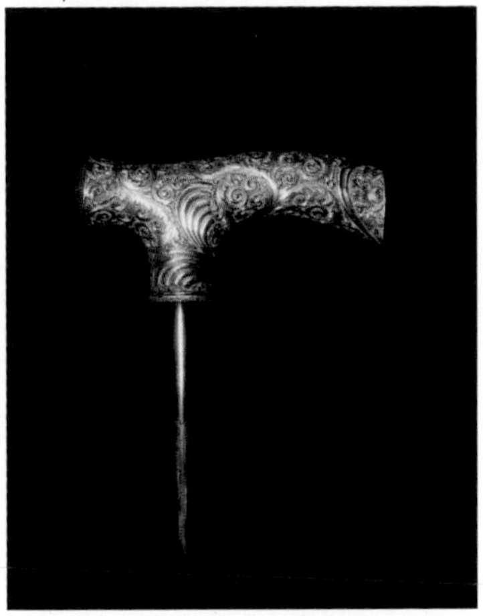

△ Gilt Metal, Hardwood Stick

• *1890*
Ebonised cane of hardwood. Large American gilt metal. Tall handle with original owner's initials and decorated with floral scrolls.
• £440 • Michael German

△ Elephant Walking Cane

• *circa 1890*
Ebonised cane with an ivory baby elephant with glass eyes, in a seated position.
• *length 78cm*
• £1,200 • Michael German

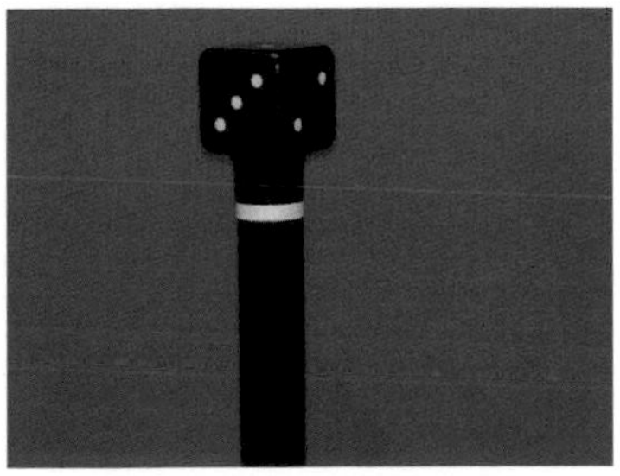

△ Dice-Handled Cane

• *1900*
Amusing wooden dice-handled cane with ivory inlay.
• £225 • Michael German

▽ Russian Walking Cane

• *circa 1890*
Russian ebonised cane with an elaborately decorated silver handle with overlaid enamel tau and Russian marks.
• *length 90cm*
• £1,400 • Michael German

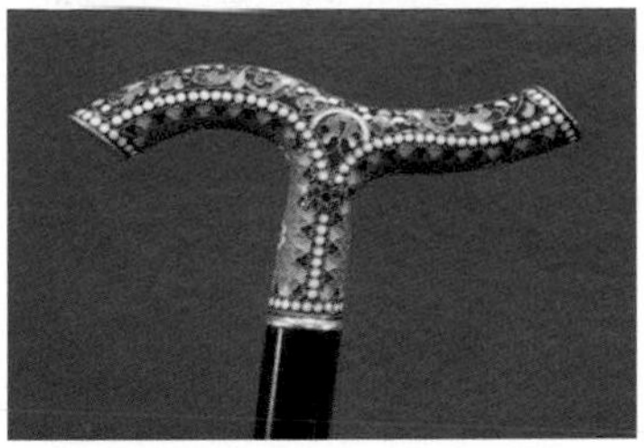

▽ Russian Walking Stick

• *1890*
Russian ebonised hardwood walking stick, with a bridled horse's head. Finely moulded, with architectural motifs.
• £1,100 • Michael German

▽ Country Walking Stick

• *1910*
Country walking stick with antler handle and silver band.
• £125 • The Reel Thing

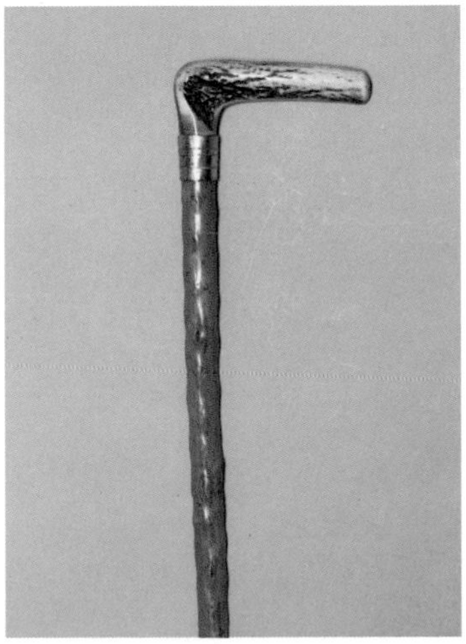

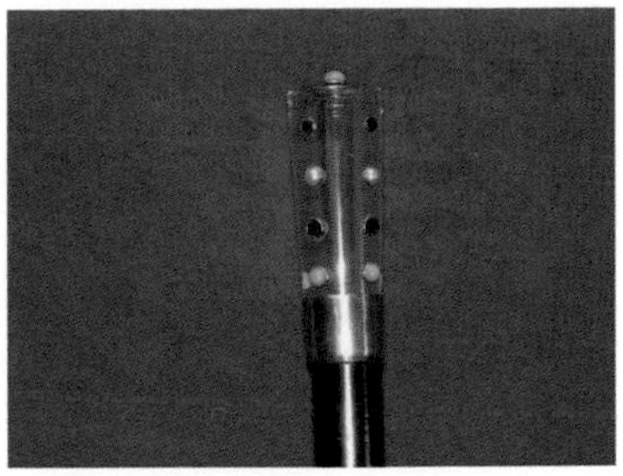

△ Rock Crystal Cane

• *1890*
Continental stick mounted with a rock crystal handle, inset with semi-precious stones, hardwood shaft and silver collar.
• £1,300 • Michael German

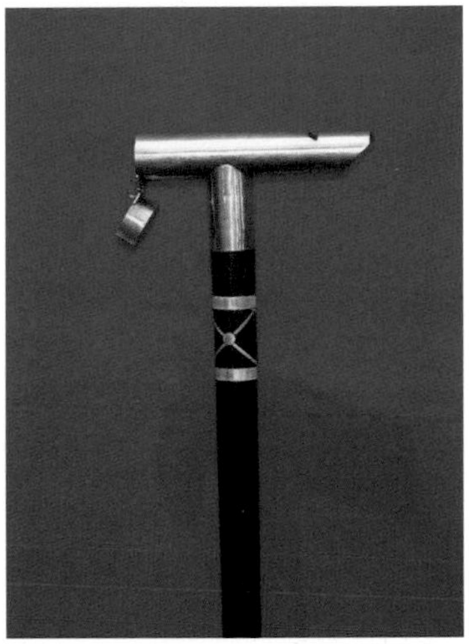

△ Vesta-Handled Cane

• *1910*
Rare vesta-handled cane with silver whistle and hinged flap, on a hardwood shaft with inlay.
• £1,400 • Michael German

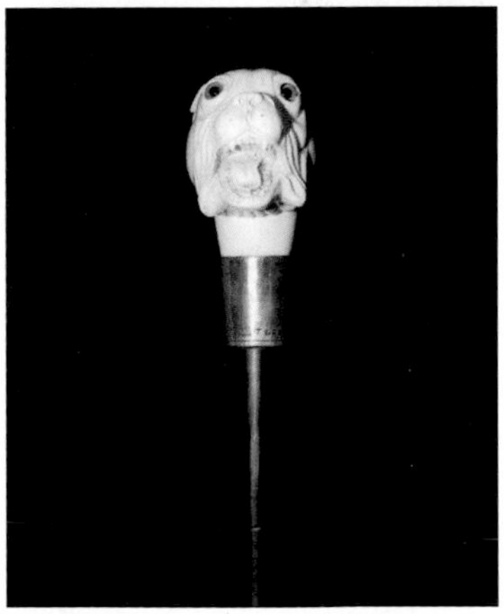

△ Large Dog's Head Stick

• *1918*
Large Victorian carved ivory dog's head handle. Carved in fine detail with snarling open mouth, drooping ears and glass eyes. Silver collar marked with Brigg, London. Shaft is made of ebony.
• £1,400 • Michael German

DECORATIVE ARTS

The term decorative arts is ambiguous and can be expressed by the modelling or carving of stone, wood and bronze. The term applies to all art that is not detailed as 'fine art', such as paintings. The idea is that there is no practical use for the item – that it is made purely for decoration, in order to enhance the surroundings and give pleasure to the beholder. The Victorian era heralded the time when decorative items became hugely popular, with the Victorians collecting and filling every nook and cranny: whether it was with a bust of a gentleman, a carving of an animal, or a stone bust of a girl, all their spaces were filled. The demand for sculptures that had been growing since the second half of the nineteenth century continued in the 1920s and 30s with an emphasis on smaller figures, either carved in ivory or cast in bronze. Today, many decorative items have enormous appeal to the interior designer and home owner. One special item may be a source of inspiration for the design of a room, an entrance hall, a public space or a garden. This is an area of collecting that is in flux – there are no rules so just focus on buying what you really like.

FIGURES & BUSTS

◁ Pair of Maidens

- *circa 1730*

One of a pair of white marble busts of maidens in the antique manner, attributed to Michael Rysbrach (1694–1770). With finely carved robes pinned at the shoulder with a brooch, the hair flowing loosely over one shoulder, supported on later Portoro marble socles.

- *76cm x 36cm*
- £33,000 • Anthony Outred

▽ Bronze Centaur

- *circa 1850*

Italian bronze of a centaur fighting a goat on marble.

- *height 17cm*
- £895 • Gavin Douglas

◁ Alabaster Wrestling Pair

- *1840*

White alabaster statue of figures wrestling.

- *52cm x 59cm*
- £4,200 • Judy Fox

▽ Marble Plaque

- *circa 1820*

Marble plaque with relief showing Hermes, Aphrodite and Paris.

- *height 1.12m*
- £19,500 • Westland & Co.

△ Maternity

• *circa 1880*
'Maternity', a fine patinated, cold painted parcel gilt bronze of a mother feeding an infant while holding a sleeping toddler, by Paul Dubois (1829–1905).
• *height 49cm*
• £3,950 • Gavin Douglas

△ Marley Horses

• *circa 1880*
A small pair of French 'Marley horses' after the model by Costeau. On black marble bases decorated with patinated friezes.
• *height 28cm*
• £1,075 • Gavin Douglas

△ Pair of Marble Statues

• *1885*
A fine pair of marble statues, signed and dated, naturalistically carved as a male and female.
• *height 83cm*
• £6,500 • Tredantiques

▽ Marble Bust

• *circa 1840*
A carved statuary marble bust of a lady in the eighteenth-century manner, the head slightly turned to her right with a full wig and two tresses of hair curling around her shoulders and swathed with drapery.
• *58.5cm x 34cm*
• £3,850 • Westland & Co.

▽ Bust of Child

• *circa 1910*
A good patinated bronze bust of a child with a rose in her hair by H. Jacobs, standing on an integral plinth inscribed 'H. Luppens & Cie, Editeurs'.
• *height 56cm*
• £2,953 • Gavin Douglas

▽ Gilt Figure of a Musician

• *1920s*
Terracotta and gold figure of a musician playing a flute, by the sculptor Vigoreux.
• *46cm x 41cm x 31cm*
• £2,800 • Bizarre

△ Augustus Caesar

• *circa 1850*
Italian marble bust of Augustus Caesar raised on a marble plinth. This is taken from the bronze full-length figure of Augustus, circa 20 BC, in the Vatican Museum. The breastplate is richly carved with mythological and historical scenes and the bust is supported on a panelled and moulded marble plinth of tapering form.
• *height 2.08m*
• £9,800 • Anthony Outred

△ Siena Marble Group

• *circa 1890*
Group of two tigers fighting, signed by Angelo Vannetti.
• *height 50.8cm*
• £25,000 • Westland & Co.

△ Terracotta Bust

• *20th century*
An Italian terracotta bust of David after Michelangelo.
• *56cm x 14cm*
• £850 • Westland & Co.

▽ Marble Bust

• *circa 1865*
An early Victorian marble bust of J.E. Boehm, statuary white, in excellent condition.
• *height 58.5cm*
• £3,850 • C. Newland

▽ Marie Antoinette

• *circa 1890*
A fine terracotta bust of Marie Antoinette, her head turned to her left and raised on a spreading square plinth.
• *65cm x 44cm*
• £950 • Westland & Co.

▽ Marble Head

• *circa 1900*
A French statuary marble head of a woman after Rodin.
• *36cm x 30cm*
• £1,250 • Westland & Co.

LIGHTING

▽ French Pricket Sticks

- *1780*

One of a pair of French pricket sticks standing on three feet.

- *height 55cm*
- £950 • Heytesbury

▽ Mongolfier Chandelier

- *circa 1800*

A fine French crystal and gilt bronze Mongolfier chandelier with four patinated bronze putti.

- *drop 1.52m*
- £12,500 • Westland & Co.

▽ Bronze Candelabra

- *1815*

Fine pair of French Empire patinated bronze ormolu candelabra.

- *height 30cm*
- £3,250 • Gavin Douglas

△ Altar Candlesticks

- *circa 1780*

Italian silvered-wood altar candlesticks, turned and profusely carved with tripod feet.

- *height 84cm*
- £3,000 • Wakelin Linfield

△ Elm Candlesticks

- *1800*

A pair of Scottish elm candlesticks of baluster form with good patina, originally from a monastery.

- *height 58cm*
- £480 • Lacquer Chest

▽ English Candlesticks

- *1815*

Pair of English patinated bronze and ormolu three-branch candelabra, with bronze figures on an oval base with gilding.

- *height 61cm*
- £5,750 • Gavin Douglas

▽ Six-Light Candelabra

- *circa 1820*

Louis XVIII bronze and gilt with a pair of angels holding the light branches. Decoration to the base.

- *height 78cm*
- £22,000 • Emanouel

◁ Pair of Candlesticks

- *early 19th century*

Pair of wooden mahogany and brass candlesticks.

- *height 37cm*
- £1,250 • P.L. James

▷ Sphinx Candelabra

- *1815*

Fine pair of three-branch sphinx candelabra with original gilding and patination.

- *height 57cm*
- £6,950 • Gavin Douglas

△ Cherub Candelabra

- *circa 1785*

Louis XVI marble, bronze and ormolu candelabra.

- *height 44cm*
- £18,000 • Norman Adams

△ Ormolu Chandelier

- *circa 1790*

A fine late 18th-century Baltic glass and ormolu chandelier, with suspended pendants and swags linking six curved branches. Converted to electricity.

- *height 1.02m*
- £40,000 • Norman Adams

▽ Pair of Candelabra

- *circa 1825*

A pair of Regency, cut glass and ormolu candelabra with two branches. The cut glass is formed in long-faceted drops. On cut-glass base and stem.

- *height 36.5cm*
- £10,000 • Norman Adams

▽ Four-Light Colza Chandelier

- *circa 1835*

A William IV-period bronze four-light colza chandelier. The foliate corona issuing four cast bronze foliate chains attached to the reservoir by applied leaf mounts, intersected by four branches in the form of duck heads supporting clear glass storm shades. The reservoir is surmounted by a bud finial and is embellished by a decorative pineapple pendant to the base.

- *diameter 61cm*
- £15,500 • Anthony Outred

▷ French Candelabra

- *1840*

A pair of Louis Philippe bronze ormolu candelabra with three arms, with floral meanderings on acanthus leaf bases.

- *height 60cm*
- £4,500 • O.F. Wilson

△ Oil Lamps

- *1825*

A pair of oil lamps with faceted glass bowls, mounted on bronze columns.

- *height 68.5cm*
- £3,250 • O.F. Wilson

△ Brass Lantern

- *circa 1835*

A fine William IV lacquered brass lantern in neo-Elizabethan style, with six etched glass panels and pierced floral decoration.

- *height 1.14m*
- £35,000 • Norman Adams

▽ Pair of Candelabra

- *circa 1825*

Pair of Regency, cut glass and ormolu, two-branch candelabra with long faceted drops.

- *height 36cm*
- £9,000 • Norman Adams

▽ French Candelabra

- *circa 1840*

One of a pair of French four-branch ormolu candelabra with a snake circling a tapered column, with scrolled acanthus leaf and shell decoration and a flame finial, the whole on a solid platform base.

- *height 60cm*
- £3,850 • O.F. Wilson

▷ 'Palmer & Co.' Lamp

- *circa 1850*

Victorian 'Palmer & Co.' lamp with original glass shade and an emerald-green column with gilt foliate design.

- *height 78cm*
- £2,200 • O.F. Wilson

△ Bronze Lamps

- *circa 1830*

Pair of bronze lamps with acanthus-leaf decoration.

- *height 51cm*
- £1,850 • Lynda Franklin

△ French Candelabra

- *circa 1840*

One of a pair of French four-light crystal candelabra in original condition.

- *height 60cm*
- £2,900 • Judy Fox

△ Ormolu Wall Sconce

- *19th century*

One of a pair of ormolu wall sconces, with decorative foliate scrolled branches.

- *height 30cm*
- £2,200 • Solaris

△ Baccarat Chandelier

- *19th century*

A French glass, 12-branch chandelier signed 'Baccarat'.

- *75cm x 62cm*
- £6,900 • M. Luther

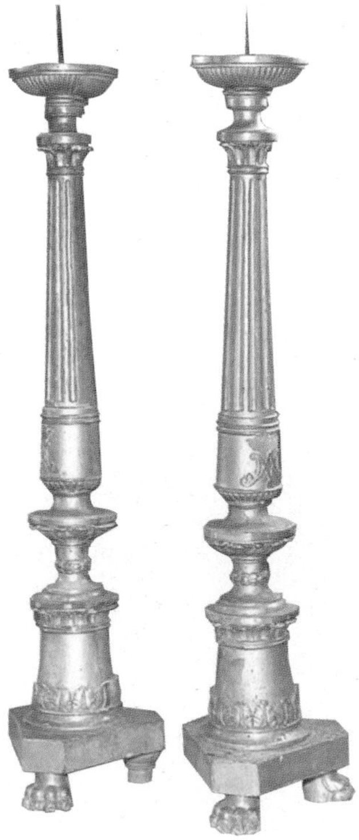

▽ Pair of Candlesticks

- *19th century*

Turned gilt-wood, single-spike candlesticks, on a triangular base with chamfered corners and carved lion's-paw feet.

- *height 90cm*
- £700 • Lynda Franklin

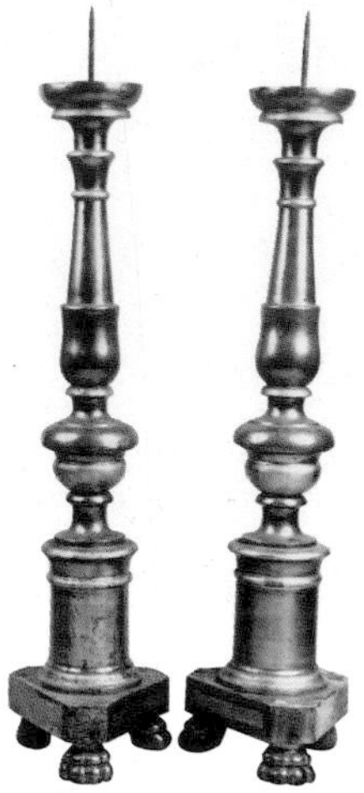

▽ Bronze Candelabra

- *1850*

A pair of bronze candelabra showing putti as caryatides holding above their heads intertwined branches with vine decoration.

- *height 54cm*
- £2,500 • C.H. Major

◁ Giltwood Prickets

- *1860*

Pair of reeded and tapered giltwood prickets, with acanthus-leaf decoration, and 'M' monogram, the whole standing on three paw feet.

- *height 83cm*
- £1,000 • Augustus Brandt

▷ Gothic Candlesticks

- *circa 1860*

A fine pair of 19th-century bronze, Gothic candlesticks with architectural and Gothic tracery with hexagonal bases on matching, white marble hexagonal plinths.

- *height 58cm*
- £1,200 • Lynda Franklin

△ Oil Lamp

- *19th century*

A Victorian oil lamp on a brass, Corinthian column, with green glass reservoir vessel and all original fittings.

- *height 81cm*
- £480 • Ranby Hall

△ Stoneware Lamps

- *circa 1850*

A pair of mid-19th-century continental stoneware, urn-shaped lamps, with double handles on square base.

- *height 75cm*
- £3,500 • Norman Adams

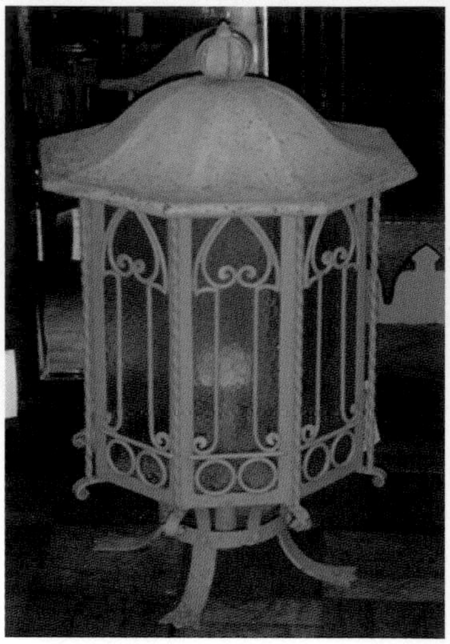

▽ Metal Lantern

- *Victorian*

One of a pair of Victorian gas lanterns, with a chinoiserie influence.

- *height 90cm*
- £3,800 • Hatchwell

▽ Candlesticks

- *1853*

A pair of Victorian figural candlesticks by Charles & George Fox, London.

- *height 87cm*
- £10,000 • N. Shaw

▽ Gilded Chandelier

- *19th century*

A decorative metal, gilded chandelier, with ornamental grapes and flowers and white ceramic roses with eight candles.

- *height 54cm*
- £475 • R. Conquest

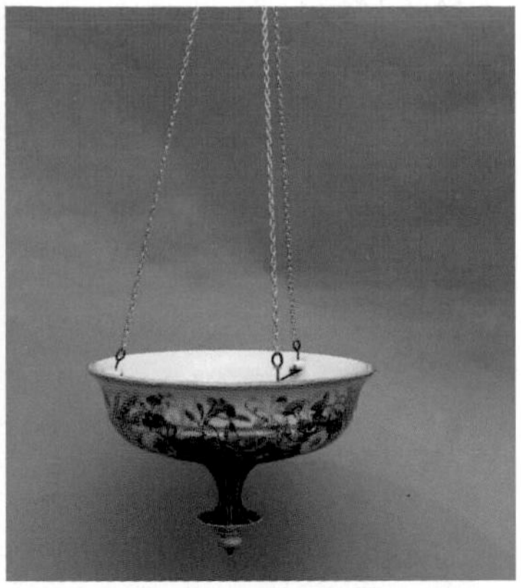

△ Paris Light Shade

• *circa 1860*
A ceramic Paris light shade with floral decoration around the body, gilding to the rim and suspended by a triple gilt chain.
• *height 53cm*
• £1,280 • P.L. James

△ Black Tôle Lamp

• *1870*
Black tôle lamp with gilt mouldings and floral swags around the base, and sprays of corn around the central column, with original patination.
• *height 74cm*
• £580 • Augustus Brandt

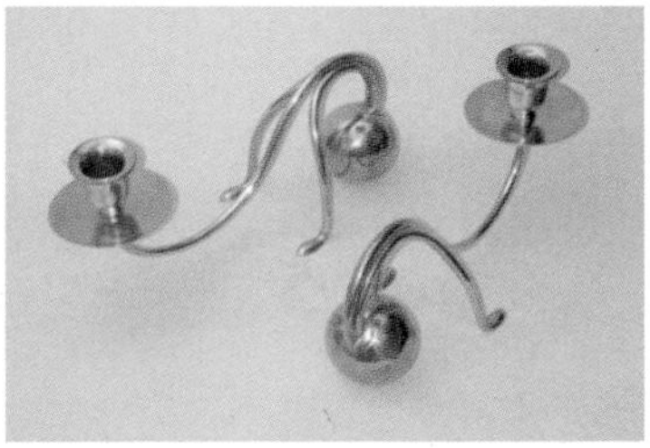

△ Copper Candlesticks

• *1880*
Copper and brass Arts and Crafts candlesticks designed by W.A.S. Benson.
• *12cm x 26cm*
• £850 • Gooday Gallery

▽ French Chandelier

• *circa 1870*
A French chandelier with twelve branches and bronze and faceted hanging crystals.
• *diameter 60cm*
• £1,250 • Rainbow

▽ English Gas Wall Lamps

• *circa 1875*
One of a pair of decorative brass wall lamps fitted with acid-etched glass shades.
• *height 33cm*
• £995 • Turn On Lighting

▽ Victorian Table Lamp

• *1880*
Victorian brass pedestal lamp with a pink and glass shade with a cherry blossom painted design.
• *height 49cm*
• £895 • Turn On Lighting

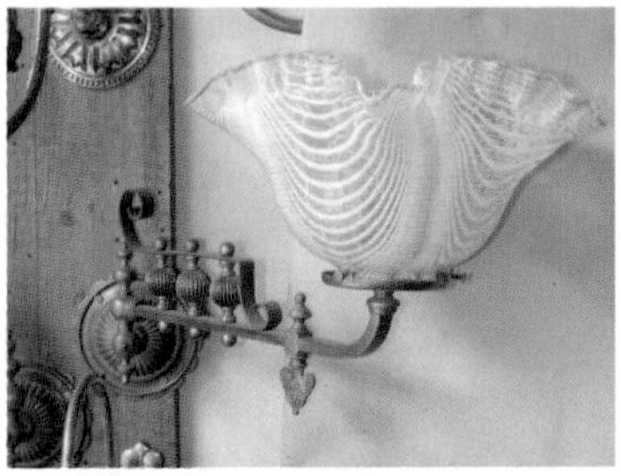

△ English Wall Lamp

• *circa 1870*
One of a pair of decorative cast-brass gas wall lamps fitted with lime-feather glass shades.
• *height 33cm*
• £1,500 • Turn On Lighting

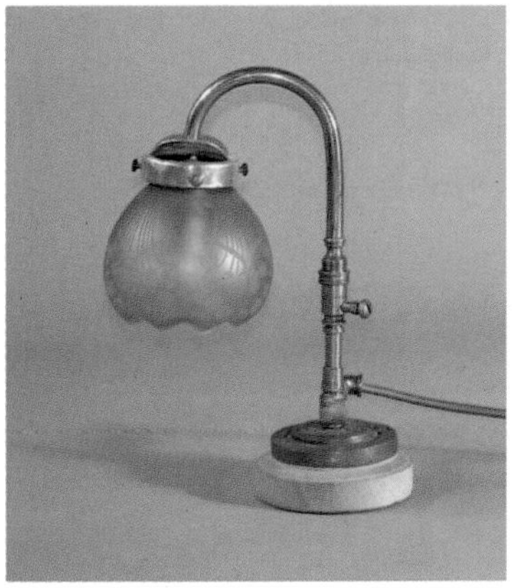

△ Victorian Bijou Lamp

• *1880*
Victorian adjustable reading lamp with a pink-glass tulip shade, metal rim and a curved brass stand, on a circular wooden base.
• *height 24cm*
• £700 • Turn On Lighting

△ Painted Lamps

• *1880*
Pair of painted tôle Boullotte lamps with pierced metal lampshades.
• *51cm x 35cm*
• £2,900 • O.F. Wilson

▽ Foliate Design Lamp

• *1870*
Green tôle lamp with 19th-century base with gilt scrolling, and dark-green shade with foliate design.
• *height 78cm*
• £580 • Augustus Brandt

▽ French Brass Lanterns

• *circa 1880*
One of a pair of large and impressive French glass and metal lanterns.
• *height 1.02m*
• £12,500 • Anthony Sharpe

▽ French Wall Lights

• *circa 1880*
A set of four French wall lights with bronze fittings and crystals.
• *height 30cm*
• £1,200 • Rainbow

△ Brass Library Lamp

• *1880*
French library brass and tôle lamp with lever movement and brass fittings, standing on an oval brass base, in original condition.
• *height 55cm*
• £550 • Augustus Brandt

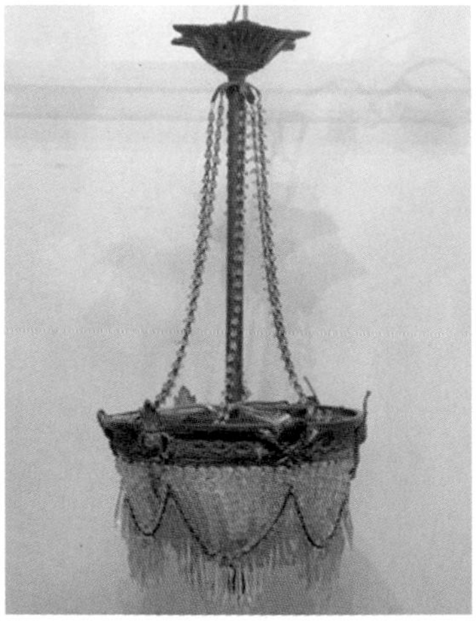

△ Italian Chandelier

• *circa 1880*
Empire-style chandelier.
• £695 • Rainbow

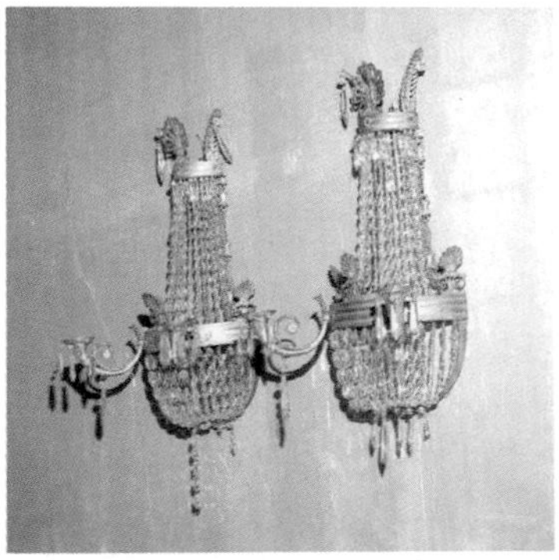

△ Wall Sconces

• *1890*
Fine quality gilt-metal wall sconces with shell decoration and crystal drops.
• *height 65cm*
• £4,250 • Augustus Brandt

▽ Elephant Oil Lamp

• *circa 1880*
Oil lamp modelled on four, outward-looking elephants, with enormous reservoir and detachable top for use as planter.
• *height 34cm*
• £790 • Elizabeth Bradwin

▽ French Candelabra

• *circa 1880*
A pair of French table candelabra with brass fittings and stand, profusely decorated in hanging, faceted crystals.
• *height 50cm*
• £750 • Rainbow

▷ Verdigris Lantern

• *circa 1890*
A copper and glass lantern with a curved quadrant chapeau.
• *height 1m*
• £1,000 • David Ford

△ French Candelabra

• *circa 1880*
French candelabra with cranberry-glass reservoir, three branches and chain link to gilded ceiling rose.
• *height 1.03m*
• £425 • R. Conquest

△ Gilt Candlesticks

• *1890*
A pair of four-branch bronze candelabra on fluted bases.
• *height 53cm*
• £1,950 • Judy Fox

▽ French Bag Chandelier

• *circa 1880*
An Empire-style French bag chandelier with eight branches and bronze and crystal chains.
• *diameter 75cm*
• £1,200 • Rainbow

▽ Cast-Brass Table Lamp

• *circa 1890*
English cast-brass table lamp fitted with a hand-painted glass lampshade decorated with a scene of birds and trailing foliage, supported by brass arms.
• *height 48cm*
• £1,100 • Turn On Lighting

▽ Wall Lamps

• *circa 1890s*
One of a pair of English bronzed electric wall lights. Fitted with cut crystal glass shades.
• *height 28cm*
• £1,800 • Turn On Lighting

△ Brass Lantern

- *circa 1895*

A late Victorian brass lantern with a tulip-shaped glass on a brass column, the whole on tripod feet.

- *height 36cm*
- £750 • Turn On Lighting

△ English Lanterns

- *circa 1895*

One of a pair of copper oxidised English lanterns fitted with blue vaseline glass shades.

- *height 26cm*
- £1,500 • Turn On Lighting

△ Victorian Lanterns

- *circa 1899*

Copper oxidised late Victorian ceiling pendants fitted with frosted-glass covers.

- *height 33cm*
- £750 • Turn On Lighting

▽ Brass Desk Lamp

- *circa 1895*

Arts and Crafts hand-beaten brass lamp with a shell-shaped shade.

- *height 42cm*
- £895 • Turn On Lighting

▽ Three-Light Ceiling Pendant

- *circa 1899*

Edwardian three-light ceiling pendant in brass, fitted with acid-etched cranberry-glass shades.

- *height 43cm*
- £1,500 • Turn On Lighting

▽ French Chandelier

- *circa 1900*

Brass-bodied French chandelier with four lights with blue crystal tear drops and heavily cut prisms.

- *height 67cm*
- £500 • R. Conquest

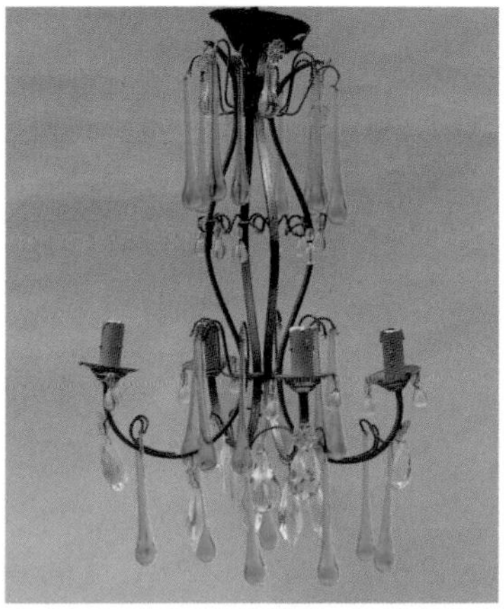

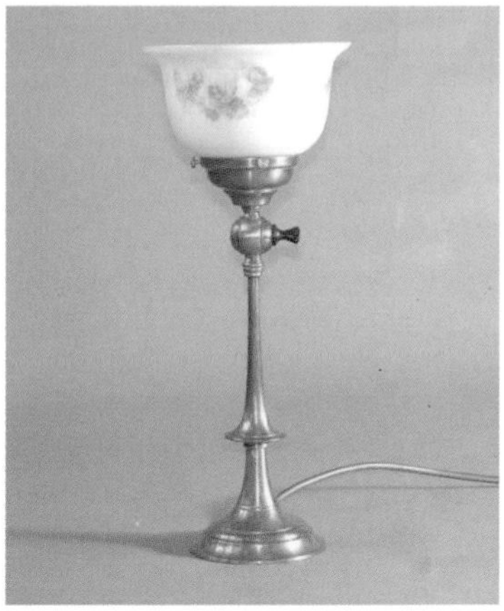

△ Farroday & Son Table Lamp

- *circa 1899*

Farroday & Son English table lamp fitted with transfer-printed lampshade. With F&S stamped on the bottom.

- *height 34cm*
- £600 • Turn On Lighting

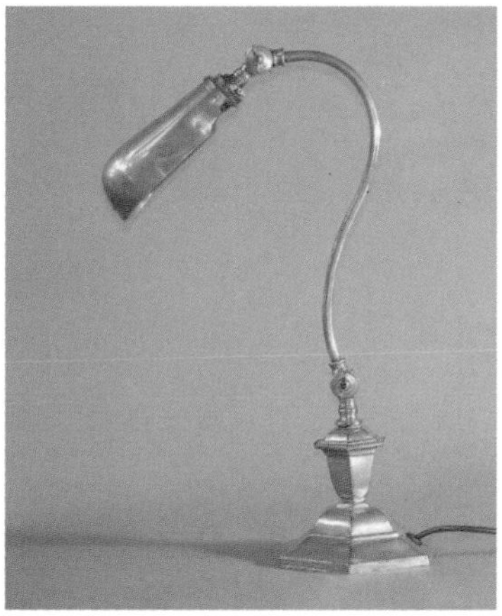

△ English Desk Lamp

- *circa 1899*

English silver plate on brass adjustable desk lamp.

- *height 43cm*
- £895 • Turn On Lighting

▽ Library Lamp

- *circa 1895*

Cast-brass library table lamp fitted with an iridescent green-glass shade. The light is adjustable for height.

- *height 33cm*
- £895 • Turn On Lighting

▽ Ecclesiastical Candelabra

- *circa 1900*

An ecclesiastical candelabra of two sections, the upper half forming a triangular section with five candle-spikes.

- *height 165cm*
- £295 • Youll's

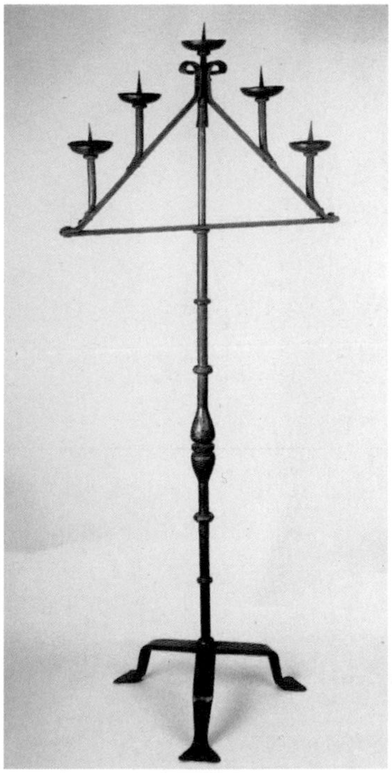

◁ Puppy Oil Lamp

- *circa 1910*

A continental oil lamp mounted on the ceramic model of a begging puppy, with glass eyes, on a moulded, circular base. New shade and frame.

- *height 32cm*
- £650 • Elizabeth Bradwin

▽ **The Reader**

- *circa 1775*

Patinated bronze, ormolu and black marble in the form of an oil lamp with a figure of a muse reading from scroll. By Boizot.

- *height 40cm*
- £6,250 • Gavin Douglas

▽ **Bronze Greyhound**

- *circa 1776-1884*

By Jean François Theodore Gechten. Greyhound with prey on a naturalistic oval base.

- *height 36cm*
- £6,650 • Ranby Hall

△ **English Candelabra**

- *circa 1790*

Pair of English George III patinated bronze, ormolu and marble figural candelabra. The marble bases in white and grey marble. The two opposing young boys are a well-known model and have their original patination. They appear to have original chains.

- *height 67cm*
- £8,950 • Gavin Douglas

△ **Lion Figure**

- *18th century*

A lead figure of a lion shown on all four legs with paw outstretched.

- *32cm x 62cm*
- £1,950 • M. Luther

◁ **Islamic Bronzes**

- *12th century*

Three Islamic bronzes from the Seljuk period. A tall-necked jar with handle, a small bottle with tear-drop design and a small pot.

- £400–600 each • Shiraz

△ **Ethiopian Cross**

- *circa 1750*

An Ethiopian processional copper cross with a presentation inscription.

- *36cm x 27cm*
- £1,850 • Iconastas

△ **Chinese Incense Burner**

- *late 18th century*

Chinese pewter incense burner of a Chinese boy holding an urn.

- *height 44cm*
- £3,500 • Brandt

▷ **Bronze Group of Mice**

- *19th century*

Bronze group with mice, grapes and pomegranate on a table, with the lid of the pomegranate lifting to reveal an incense burner. Signed by Sessei Chu.

- *height 24cm*
- £3,400 • Gregg Baker

△ **Bronze Candlestick**

- *12th–13th century*

Seljuk-period candlestick with Arabic design, standing on three legs, with some patination.

- *height 26.5cm*
- £300 • Oasis

△ **George III Candelabra**

- *circa 1800*

A fine pair of late 18th-century English George III three-branch candelabra. On white marble bases with ormolu caps, the two opposing patinated bronze children hold up the candelabra tops.

- *height 66cm*
- £5,750 • Gavin Douglas

▷ Bronze Vase

- *1800*

A fine bronze urn in the neo-classical style with foliate design around the rim and base.

- *38cm x 23cm*
- £2,950 • O.F. Wilson

△ Bronze and Ormolu Cassolettes

- *circa 1800*

Good pair of French or English patinated bronze and ormolu cassolettes. They can be used either as urns or as candleholders, with fine quality chasing.

- *height 38cm*
- £9,250 • Gavin Douglas

△ Bronze Figure

- *circa 1809–52*

Fine bronze of a man carrying a basket of fruit with his axe and his hat in his belt. Signed by Charles Camberworth.

- *height 71cm*
- £5,750 • Gavin Douglas

▽ French Empire Candlesticks

- *circa 1815*

Pair of French Empire patinated bronze, ormolu and marble figural candlesticks. The two young boys holding candle holders in the form of standards.

- *height 28cm*
- £2,450 • Gavin Douglas

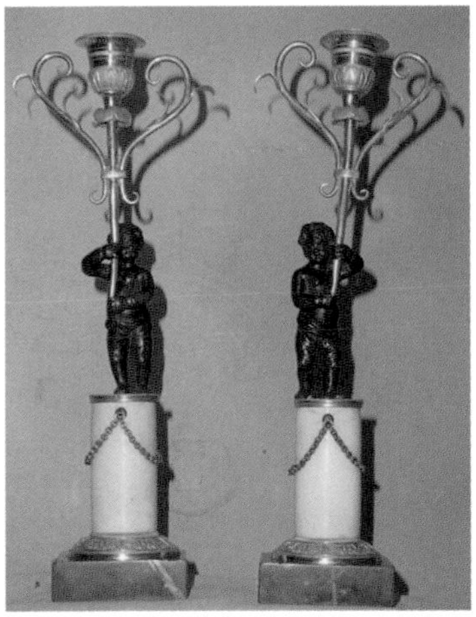

▽ Gilded Ormolu Candelabra

- *circa 1840*

A fine pair of early 19th-century mercury-gilded ormolu candelabra from a design by Pierre Gouthière. The four-branch candelabra lift out leaving a pair of candlesticks.

- *height 56cm*
- £12,000 • Gavin Douglas

▽ Silenus

- *circa 1800*

Bronze figure of Silenus and the infant Bacchus.

- *height 59cm*
- £3,750 • John Riordan

▽ Pestle and Mortar

- *1820*

A bronze Chinese apothecary's pestle with ear handles and good patination.

- *9cm x 12cm*
- £300 • Sign of the Times

▽ Steel Bucket Grate

- *circa 1840*

An English steel bucket grate with 'C' scrolling terminating in lion's-paw feet.

- *height 65cm*
- £2,800 • Riverbank

▽ Model of a Hound

- *circa 1860*

Bronze of a recumbent hound. Unsigned, probably French.

- *height 12.5cm*
- £1,200 • Elizabeth Bradwin

△ Pair of Cassolettes

- *circa 1810*

A pair of patinated bronze and ormolu campana-shaped cassolettes with scrolled handles. Bultic or Russian origin.

- *height 44cm*
- £9,750 • Gavin Douglas

△ Regency Candelabra

- *circa 1820*

A pair of Regency porcelain, ormolu and cut-glass candelabra. With triform porcelain base with gilt-enriched salmon-pink circular urns and scrolled arms cast with Amorini, terminating in hob-nail-cut drip pans, surrounded with cast foliate corona suspending cut-glass lustres.

- *34cm x 24cm*
- £5,250 • Gavin Douglas

△ Lion and Unicorn

- *circa 1840*

A fine pair of early Victorian burnished cast-iron lion and unicorn.

- *height 43cm*
- £2,500 • Westland & Co.

△ Bronze Koro

• *19th century*
Japanese koro (incense burner) in the form of a boar with a raised head.
• *height 17cm*
• £3,200 • **Gregg Baker**

△ Bronze Venus de Milo

• *19th century*
Standing on a stepped marble plinth on gilt mounted feet. With foundry stamp, Delafontaine AD.
• *height 81cm*
• £2,400 • **Ranby Hall**

▽ Bronze Sumo Wrestlers

• *19th century*
On a bronze, four-legged base with variegated motifs.
• *height 31cm*
• £1,850 • **Gregg Baker**

▽ Bronze bust

• *1860*
Bronze bust by French sculptor Albert-Ernest Carrier de Belleuse (1824–87).
• *height 30cm*
• £7,500 • **David Brower**

◁ Mounted War Lord

• *1860*
Italian fine bronze model of a Renaissance war lord on a powerful horse, based on the Colleoni monument, cast after the original by Verrocchio.
• *height 37cm*
• £3,750 • **Gavin Douglas**

△ Bronze Vase

• *19th century*
A Japanese vase of lobed form decorated with a coiled dragon.
• *height 42cm*
• £3,200 • **Gregg Baker**

△ Bronze Figures

• *19th century*
Patinated bronze of a young girl lifting a struggling child. Signed 'J. Petermann, Fondeur, Bruxelles'.
• *height 38cm*
• £5,200 • **Ranby Hall**

▽ Bronze Hawk

• *19th century*
A Japanese bronze model of a hawk on a bronze branch.
• *height 47cm*
• £2,600 • **Gregg Baker**

▽ Bronze Figure

• *19th century*
A French patinated bronze figure of a goddess, on an onyx base.
• *height 45cm*
• £2,000 • **Lynda Franklin**

◁ Chinese Priest

• *19th century*
A metal Chinese figure of a seated holy man holding an incense burner.
• *height 14cm*
• £500 • **Sign of the Times**

△ Bronze Boys

- *circa 1870*

Pair of bronze boys playing with a hoop and stick.

- *height 22cm*
- £2,300 • John Clay

△ Cloisonné Vase

- *1870*

A cloisonné vase with a polychrome enamelled design of inverted conical form, with a pair of stylised elephant trunk handles.

- *height 31cm*
- £1,400 • Sign of the Times

▽ Gamekeeper Bronze

- *circa 1870*

A signed French bronze by Dubucand. Gamekeeper carrying a dead fox with a dog by his side.

- *height 24cm*
- £1,650 • Elizabeth Bradwin

▽ French Tôle Lilies

- *circa 1880*

One of a pair of French metal tôle lilies in their own brown metal pots.

- *height 58cm*
- £2,100 • Anthony Sharpe

◁ Brass Coffee Pot and Cover

- *circa 1880*

A coffee pot from Bokhara, with elaborately swirled engraving and a pierced cover.

- *height 36cm*
- £400 • Sinai

△ Decorated Urn

- *1870*

Bronze urn with goat head and horn handles, a cherub relief and foliate design on the base, standing on a green marble plinth.

- *height 33cm*
- £1,200 • Sign of the Times

△ French Tôleware

- *circa 1880*

French tôleware painted floral wall appliqués with oak leaf decoration and candle holder.

- *height 29cm*
- £480 • Anthony Sharpe

△ English Door Knobs

- *circa 1890*

Pair of English beehive door knobs with brass mounts and turned decoration.

- *length 19cm*
- £85 • Myriad

▽ Bronze Figure

- *circa 1870s*

Bronze figure of an Egyptian girl inscribed 'Lykketer Jubileum Dagen, Arne Bastholm, Alex Conradson, F. Bohn-Willeberg. Edwing Nerving. Edgar Hansen'.

- *height 54cm*
- £2,300 • Sign of the Times

▽ Bronze Bustard

- *circa 1880*

A good bronze model of a bustard, signed by Q. Vesnal, founder, and Pascal, sculptor.

- *height 11cm*
- £900 • Elizabeth Bradwin

▽ Bronze Chinese Roe Deer

• *circa 1880*
Bronze study of a Chinese roe deer from the Chiurazzi foundry, Naples.
• *height 56cm*
• £7,800 • Wakelin Linfield

▽ Robert the Bruce

• *circa 1890*
Impressive spelter figure of Robert the Bruce wearing armour and holding a shield, standing on a square green marble base.
• *height 83cm*
• £1,500 • John Clay

◁ Coffee Pot and Cover

• *circa 1880*
Coffee pot with engraved floral and geometric designs and enamel jewel inset.
• *height 34cm*
• £400 • Sinai

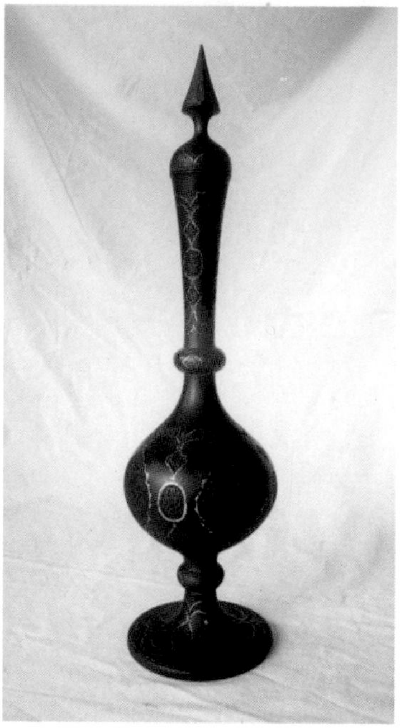

△ Persian Vase and Cover

• *circa 1880*
Bulbous body with long tapered neck, with floral cartouches and gilding.
• *height 46cms*
• £1,600 • Sinai

△ Snake-handled Coupes

• *1880*
A pair of marble and bronze coupes with snake handles.
• *height 28cm*
• £1,150 • Judy Fox

▽ Bacchante

• *circa 1880*
French bronze figure of Bacchante. Signed Clodion. Also stamped with the Barbédienne foundry stamp.
• *55cm x 54cm*
• £2,995 • John Riordan

▽ French Coat Hooks

• *circa 1880*
A pair of French coat hooks in twisted brass with acanthus-leaf mounts and ceramic knobs.
• *length 16cm*
• £116 • Myriad

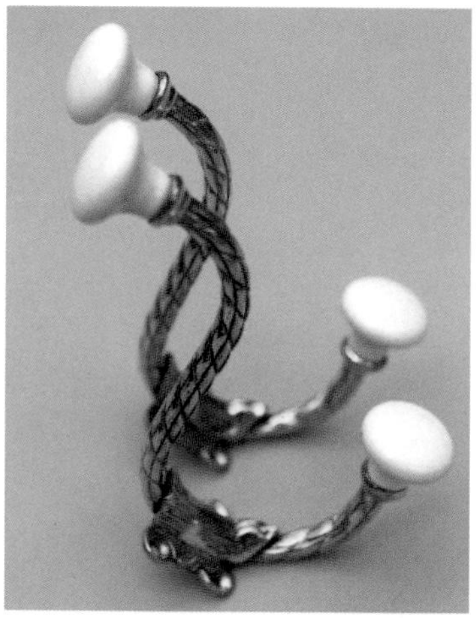

▷ Pair of Candelabra

• *circa 1886*
Patinated bronze ormolu and porphyry three-branch candelabra. Signed by Henry Dawson.
• *height 61cm*
• £10,000 • Gavin Douglas

◁ Islamic Dish

• *circa 1890*
Brass, copper and silver dish with organic designs, the rim with Islamic cursive script.
• *diameter 26cm*
• £300 • Sinai

△ Bronze Young Girl

• *circa 1880*
Bronze classical figure of a young girl semi-clad, holding her robe in one hand.
• *height 52cm*
• £1,320 • John Clay

△ Bronze Florentine Singer

• *circa 1880*
A bronze, by Paul Dubois, showing a young man in medieval costume playing a lute. From the F. Barbédienne foundry.
• *height 63cm*
• £3,750 • Gavin Douglas

▽ Brass Water Jug

- *circa 1890*

From Damascus with silver inset cursive Islamic script.

- *height 25cm*
- £450 • Sinai

▽ Live-Cast Baby Alligator

- *circa 1900*

Possibly live-cast. Cold-painted Vienna bronze from the Bergman foundary. Nickel-plated on bronze.

- *height 32cm*
- £2,200 • Elizabeth Bradwin

▽ Bronze of David

- *circa 1900*

Fine bronze by Mercie of David, stamped by F. Barbédienne, showing David replacing his sword after taking off the head of Goliath.

- *height 40cm*
- £3,750 • Gavin Douglas

△ Bronze Group

- *circa 1895*

Art Nouveau bronze of a Muse imparting her science to a blacksmith. Signed by L. Chalon.

- *height 90cm*
- £9,750 • Gavin Douglas

△ Queen Victoria

- *1901*

Metal bust of Queen Victoria by Elkington & Co, England.

- *height 22cm*
- £400 • Sign of the Times

△ Silver Figurine

- *1900*

R. Bruchmann & Sonne silver sculpture on onyx base.

- *height 50cm*
- £1,900 • Succession

▽ Leda and the Swan

- *circa 1910*

A Danish erotic bronze of Leda and the Swan by R. Tegnar. Made at the Siot foundry, numbered.

- *height 42cm*
- £3,750 • Gavin Douglas

▽ Persian Silver Beaker

- *circa 1900*

From Kirmanshah, Iran. Showing domestic and rural scenes. Profusely decorated and embossed.

- *height 10cm*
- £150 • Namdar

◁ Bronze of Young Girl

- *circa 1902*

Art Nouveau bronze with two-tone patination. Foundry stamped and signed by Rudolph Marcuse.

- *height 25cm*
- £1,550 • Gavin Douglas

△ Snake Charmer

- *circa 1925*

Gilt bronze of a snake charmer, set on a chamfered onyx base. Signed by Rudolph Marcuse.

- *height 54cm*
- £3,600 • Gavin Douglas

FURNITURE

The best way to learn about furniture is to handle it by turning the piece over, opening drawers, examining the method of construction and observing signs of wear and tear. Colour and patina also play a large part: for example, when buying a walnut table it is important that the item has not been polished in such a way that the natural grain and patina has been lost. Often a piece of furniture has been French polished to too high a finish. The quality of the wood can also be as important as style, so always go to a reputable dealer. The introduction of machine-cut veneering started a decline in quality in much nineteenth-century furniture, although the best Victorian and Edwardian furniture is highly collectable. Furniture needs taking care of and protecting from the damaging effects of damp and direct sunlight, which can cause pigments and inlays to fade. Before purchasing an item of furniture make sure you are informed about the main buying criteria including style, materials, method of construction, period and manufacturer, as these affect its value.

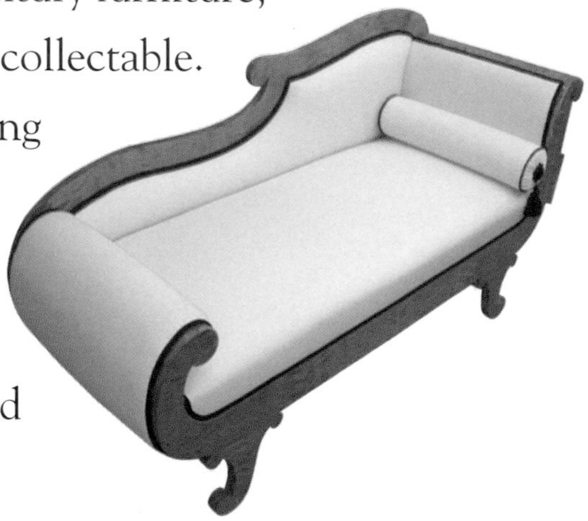

BEDS

▽ French Walnut Bedstead

- *circa 1770*

French walnut Louis XV bed with a carved head and footboard.

- *length 1.78m*
- £3,495 • Sleeping Beauty

△ Polonaise Day Bed

- *circa 18th century*

Fine Polonaise day bed with carved head and footboard, original pink-washed paintwork, with curved pillars and oval cover, with wreath and floral carving.

- *height 2.80m*
- £10,000 • Augustus Brandt

▽ Carved Throne Bed

- *18th century*

A very rare carved throne bed used by the tribal elder or chief, from the Pakistani border.

- *length 2.46m*
- £4,200 • Gordon Reece

◁ Oak Bedroom Suite

- *circa 1785*

French suite consisting of bed, bedside table, washstand, chest and much more.

- £25,000 • Sleeping Beauty

△ Chippendale-Style Bed

- *18th century*

Mahogany bed reconstructed to current size with modern cream-silk canopy.

- *width 1.82m*
- £6,500 • Mora Upham

△ Four-Poster Bed

- *18th century*

A four-poster carved bed with twisted columns.

- *height 2.16m*
- **£2,450** • **Drummonds**

△ Victorian Bedstead

- *1860*

Early Victorian brass and iron bedstead with turned, burnished decorative pillars.

- *width 1.5m*
- **£5,500** • **Sleeping Beauty**

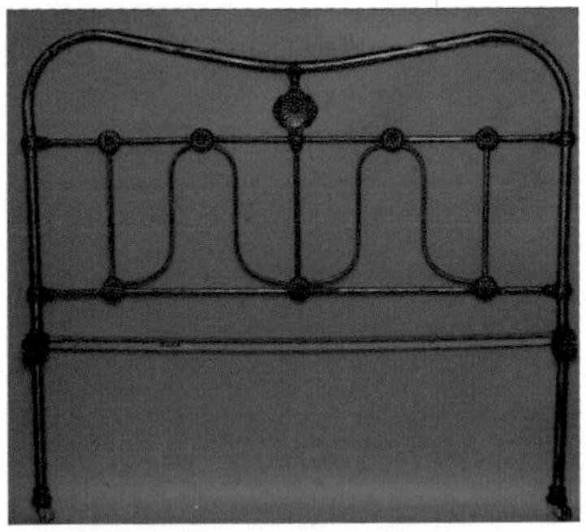

△ Mahogany French Bedstead

- *circa 1860*

Flame mahogany bedstead with highly decorative floral and ribbon ormolu mounts.

- *width 1.37m*
- **£6,000** • **Sleeping Beauty**

◁ Polished French Bedstead

- *circa 1870*

A small, double polished bedstead with floral rosettes.

- *height 1.1m*
- **£500** • **After Noah**

▽ Empire Bed

- *1860*

French Second Empire heavily-carved and ebonised four-poster bed, with scrolled broken pediment and turned posts.

- *width 1.5m*
- **£8,500** • **Sleeping Beauty**

▽ Spanish Bedstead

- *1850*

A Spanish hand-forged iron bedstead with large ornate cast brass ornamentation.

- *length 1.83m*
- **£2,600** • **Sleeping Beauty**

▽ French Renaissance-Style Bed

- *circa 1860*

Ebonised four-poster bedstead with heavily-carved and turned posts with canopy and carved footboard.

- *length 1.9m*
- **£8,500** • **Sleeping Beauty**

△ French Renaissance-Style Bed

- *circa 1860*

A heavily carved solid walnut Renaissance-style bed with finials and turned and fluted posts.

- *length 2m*
- **£4,500** • **Sleeping Beauty**

△ Bow-Fronted Bedstead

- *19th century*

Upholstered bow-fronted and padded bedstead with original green paintwork.

- *1.48m*
- **£1,295** • **Sleeping Beauty**

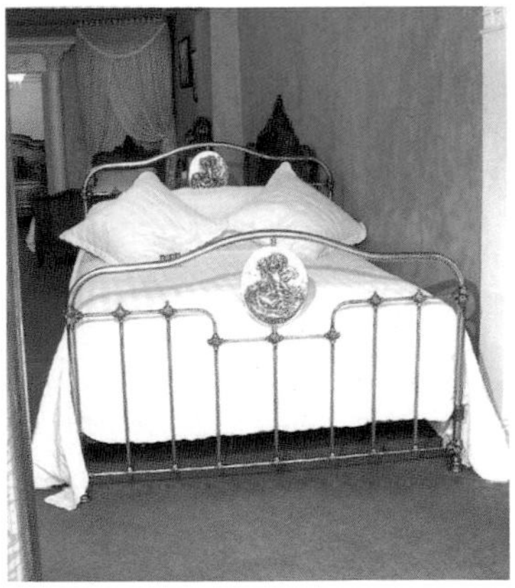

△ French Brass Bedstead

- *circa 1880*

French brass 'chapeau gendarme' with unusual oval plaques on the head and footboard with three playful cherubs and garlands of flowers.

- *length 1.79m*
- **£3,500** • **Sleeping Beauty**

△ Renaissance-Style Bedstead

• *circa 1880*
Extended Renaissance-style walnut bedstead with wreath and torchière ormolu mounts.
• *width 2.22m*
• £6,950 • Sleeping Beauty

△ Louis XV-Style Bed

• *circa 1890*
A rare six-foot-wide walnut-framed bed with heavily carved roses on footboard.
• *width 1.78m*
• £6,500 • Sleeping Beauty

△ French Mahogany Bed

• *1880–90*
A French mahogany and burr-walnut bed with carved headboard and ormulu foliate decoration, standing on tapered legs.
• *width 1.5m*
• £3,800 • Sleeping Beauty

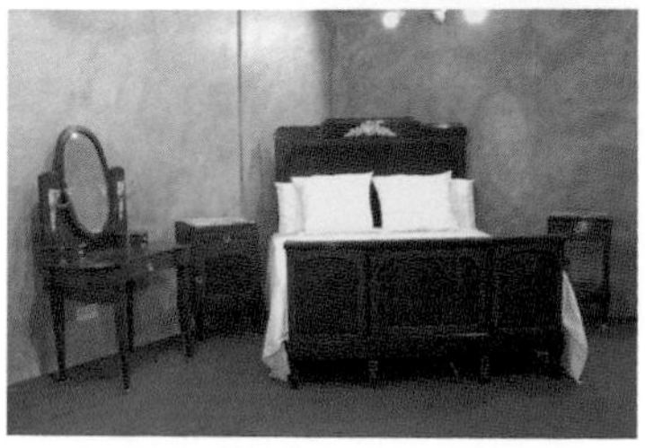

▽ Louis XV-Style Bedstead

• *1880*
Painted, padded and upholstered Louis XV-style bedstead with original gilding to headboard and base.
• *length 1.85m*
• £4,500 • Sleeping Beauty

▽ Carved Walnut Bed

• *1885*
French walnut Louis XVI-style bed, with finely carved floral swags and garlands to the bedhead and footboard.
• *width 1.6m*
• £6,500 • Sleeping Beauty

▽ Louis XV-Style Bedstead

• *19th century*
Upholstered Louis XV-style pink velvet button-backed bedstead with solid walnut frame and bow-fronted base, standing on cabriole legs.
• *length 2.22m*
• £1,495 • Sleeping Beauty

◁ French Bedroom Set

• *circa 1890*
French burr-walnut bedstead with ormolu mounts and bow front with matching bedside cabinets and dressing table.
• *width 1.53m*
• £10,500 • Sleeping Beauty

△ Walnut Bedstead

• *19th century*
Solid walnut carved Louis XV-style bedstead with a central scroll to the moulded headboard.
• *length 2.22m*
• £1,400 • Sleeping Beauty

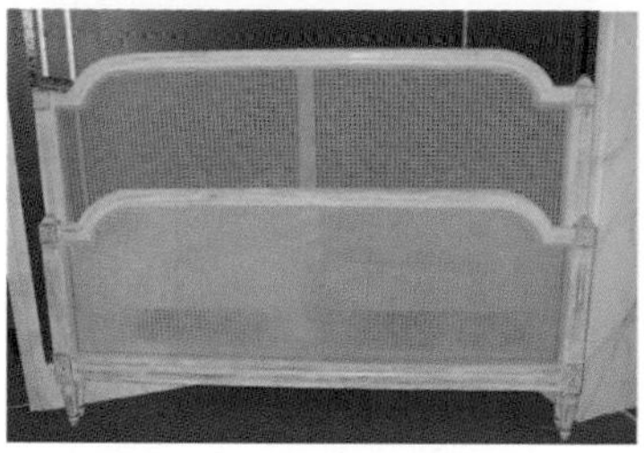

△ Bergère-Style Bed

• *1885*
French bergère Louis XVI-style bed with moulded headboard and fluted posts, standing on turned feet.
• *width 1.5m*
• £3,500 • Sleeping Beauty

△ Victorian Bedstead

• *1885*
Victorian black cast-iron bedstead with brass rail and ball finials.
• *length 2.22m*
• £1,295 • Sleeping Beauty

△ Louis XV-Style Walnut Bed

• *circa 1890*
A five-foot Louis XV-style solid walnut bed. Heavily carved with swags and roses.
• £2,250 • Sleeping Beauty

▽ French Bergère-Style Bed

• *circa 1880*
A bergère-style bow-fronted bed with carved walnut frame and central oval floral design.
• *width 1.5m*
• £6,250 • Sleeping Beauty

▽ French Mahogany Bed

• *circa 1885*
Flame-mahogany bed with moulded arch, ormolu decoration and beading, standing on turned legs.
• *width 1.5m*
• £3,800 • Sleeping Beauty

▽ Carved Bed

• *circa 1885*
A French carved padded bedhead painted in off white, standing on tapered feet.
• *width 1.5m*
• £5,000 • Sleeping Beauty

BONHEURS DU JOUR

▷ George III Mahogany Dressing Table

- *circa 1810*

An early nineteenth-century dressing table and chest of drawers with sliding mirror and pot cupboard.

- *height 90cm*
- £5,850 • Old Cinema

△ Victorian Dressing Table

- *19th century*

Victorian mahogany pedestal-style dressing table featuring two pedestals of four drawers and one central drawer, a large central mirror, two wings with scrolled pediments and fitted with the original brass handles.

- *1.3m x 1.2m*
- £1,375 • Old Cinemq

△ English Regency Bonheur du Jour

- *1815*

Outstanding and rare Regency coromandel bonheur du jour. This is a fine and elegant example of English Regency furniture.

- *1.19m x 70cm x 67cm (extended)*
- £14,500 • Freshfords

▽ Burr-Walnut Bonheur du Jour

- *circa 1860*

A Victorian burr-walnut bonheur du jour with boxwood inlay, gilt ormolu mounts and cabriole legs. The interior in rosewood with leather inset to the writing surface. Shows three mirrors.

- *height 1.42m*
- £3,800 • Judy Fox

◁ Duchess Dressing Table

- *circa 1850s*

Mid-Victorian light mahogany Duchess dressing table with swing mirror.

- *1.2m x 1.65m*
- £1,250 • Old Cinema

△ Lady's Desk

- *circa 1870*

A 19th-century English bonheur du jour in lacquered bamboo, with splayed legs on an 'H'-frame stretcher.

- *height 1.24m (to top)*
- £1,250 • North West 8

▷ Walnut Dressing Table

- *19th century*

A fine Victorian walnut dressing table with brass drop handles and tilt mirror with carved, scrolled decoration.

- *1.5m x 58cm x 1.8m*
- £2,650 • Old Cinema

▽ Rosewood Bonheur du Jour

- *circa 1820*

Regency rosewood bonheur du jour, with satinwood inlay and mirrored back panel, flanked by cupboards with oval satinwood panels, standing on straight square tapering legs.

- *1.05m x 90cm x 46cm*
- £2,995 • Harpur Deardren

△ Walnut Bonheur du Jour

- *circa 1860*

An English marquetry inlaid walnut bonheur du jour with ornately carved mounts and cabriole legs.

- *height 1.2m*
- £3,800 • Furniture Vault

BOOKCASES

▽ Secretaire Bookcase

- *circa 1780*

Faded mahogany with two glazed doors and a fitted interior.

- *height 2.29m*
- £28,500 • Wakelin Linfield

◁ George III Bureau Bookcase

- *circa 1765*

George III mahogany bureau bookcase, the astragal-glazed doors enclosing adjustable shelves with fall front and well-fitted interior of tulip wood.

- *width 109cm*
- £7,900 • Salem Antiques

△ Bureau Bookcase

- *circa 1770*

Two solid mahogany panelled doors and fitted interior with oak-lined drawers.

- *height 2.27m*
- £19,500 • J. de Haan

▷ Chinese Lacquer Bureau Bookcase

- *circa 1770*

Chinese lacquer bureau bookcase with broken arched pediment featuring an elaborate chinoiserie design, standing on bracket feet.

- *232cm x 91cm x 55cm*
- £90,000 • O.F. Wilson

◁ Gentleman's Bookcase

- *circa 1710*

Rare thuyawood and rosewood Anglo-Dutch gentleman's bookcase, with original mounts.

- *width 1.6m*
- £18,500 • M. Luther

△ George II Mahogany Bookcase

- *circa 1750*

George II mahogany bookcase, the bold swan neck pediment with foliate and rosette carving, above two astragal glazed doors opening to reveal a fitted interior. The lower section with sloping fall opening to reveal a finely fitted interior. The whole on bracket feet.

- *228cm x 100cm*
- £27,500 • Wakelin Linfield

△ Secretaire Bookcase

- *circa 1790*

George III inlaid mahogany bookcase with removable cornice.

- *height 2.75m*
- £18,500 • J. Collins

△ Satinwood Secretaire Bookcase

- *circa 1780*

Excellent secretaire bookcase of small elegant proportions. The whole veneered in satinwood heightened with cross banding in tulip wood, with shaped cornice and urn finials surmounting a corbelled frieze above two doors with moulded gothic glazing bars retaining their original glass.

- *194cm x 52cm x 23cm*
- £85,000 • Wakelin Linfield

△ Bureau Bookcase

- *circa 1790*

George III mahogany with brass fittings and a leather fitted desk.

- *height 2.27m*
- £4,800 • C. Newland

▽ Breakfronted Bookcase

- *circa 1810*

One of a pair of bookcases, with glazed doors above moulded double doors.

- *height 2.36m*
- £24,500 • Ronald G. Chambers

◁ George III Secretaire Bookcase

- *circa 1810*

George III secretaire bookcase with a well fitted interior, in excellent flame mahogany. With Gothic glazing bars to the upper section and cupboard to base.

- *221cm x 101.5cm x 58.5cm*
- £14,500 • Wakelin Linfield

▽ Regency Bookcase

- *circa 1810*

English Regency period two door chiffonier/bookcase in a mixture of pine and fruit wood with galleried and turned designs.

- *107cm x 63cm*
- £2,950 • Wakelin Linfield

▷ Rosewood Bookcase

- *circa 1830*

A late-Regency open bookcase with carved pilasters and three adjustable shelves.

- *height 1.07m*
- £2,950 • M.J. Bowdery

△ Breakfront Bookcase

- *circa 1825*

A fine Hepplewhite-period mahogany breakfront bookcase.

- *height 2.83m*
- £220,000 • Norman Adams

◁ Irish Bookcase

- *circa 1830*

Irish flame mahogany bookcase of four arched doors with brass grills standing on a square straight base, stamped Strahan Co. Dublin

- *height 168cm*
- £12,500 • Fred Anderson

▽ Breakfront Bookcase

- *circa 1830*

A 19th-century English Gothic country house burr elm and amboyna breakfront bookcase with cabinet.

- *height 1.17m*
- £9,800 • M. Luther

▽ Breakfront Bookcase

- *circa 1840*

Mahogany with boxwood styling and inlay and ebonised moulding, with three glazed doors.

- *height 2.16m*
- £7,950 • Antique Warehouse

△ **Burr Walnut Bookcase**

- *circa 1835–40*

Early Victorian open bookcase in burr walnut, with pierced gallery above a long drawer and three open shelves.

- *150cm x 105cm*
- £4,450 • Great Grooms

▽ **Mahogany Bookcase**

- *1860*

Three glazed doors above, a writing slope concealed behind sliding panels, and three panelled cupboards below.

- *190cm x 150cm*
- £3,250 • Old Cinema

◁ **Victorian Bookcase**

- *circa 1850*

A two-door glazed secretaire bookcase in mahogany with architectural pillars.

- *height 2.22m*
- £2,250 • Castlegate

△ **Ebonised Bookcase**

- *circa 1850*

Victorian ebonised bookcase of inverted breakfront outline, leading to egg and dart ormolu mounts above a central panelled frieze, with ebonised panelled back, flanked by crisp ormolu patera with a bead and flower moulding below and three adjustable ebonised shelves. Supported on inverted breakfront base.

- *117cm x 127cm*
- £7,500 • Anthony Outred

△ **Lacquered Bookcase**

- *circa 1870*

Three-tier hanging bookcase finished in black lacquer with gold banding and flower designs.

- *83cm x 70cm*
- £675 • John Clay

▽ **Victorian Bookcase**

- *circa 1880*

Flame mahogany bookcase with two glazed doors over two drawers and figured mahogany doors.

- *height 2.43m*
- £3,875 • Antique Warehouse

▽ **Victorian Bookcase**

- *circa 1890*

A late Victorian open bookcase with three shelves with carved leaf moulding to the sides, standing on a plain straight base.

- *110cm x 97cm*
- £595 • Clarke & Denny

◁ **Mahogany Bookcase**

- *circa 1880*

Mahogany bookcase with moulded pediment, pillared sides and one long single drawer at the base, standing on turned feet.

- *250cm x 125cm*
- £1,760 • John Riordan

▽ Chippendale-Style Bookcase

- *19th century*

A Chippendale-style mahogany bookcase cum display case, featuring a swan-neck pediment and Georgian-style glazing bars above panelled doors of flame mahogany. The whole standing on moulded bracket feet.

- *240cm x 150cm*
- £18,500 • Ranby Hall

▽ Victorian Bookcase

- *circa 1890s*

Victorian walnut bookcase with two glazed doors above, two drawers and cupboards below, made by Shootbird & Son. Complete with with original fittings and keys.

- *150cm x 85cm*
- £2,500 • Old Cinema

▷ Victorian Cabinet

- *circa 1910*

Mahogany bookcase with fine glazed doors, raised on slender turned feet. By Maple & Co.

- *height 98cm*
- £1,485 • Ranby Hall

▷ Biedermeier Bookcase

- *circa 1900*

Swedish birchwood bookcase in the Biedermeier style with gilt mounts, ebonised pillars and a moulded top.

- *height 1.24m*
- £4,500 • R. Cavendish

△ Edwardian Revolving Bookcase

- *1901–10*

An Edwardian mahogany revolving bookcase of small proportions, on a stand with cabriole legs and shelf.

- *84cm x 40cm*
- £1,450 • Great Grooms

▷ Mahogany Bookcase

- *circa 1900*

Fine astragal-glazed doors raised on ogee bracket feet.

- *height 99cm*
- £780 • Ranby Hall

▽ Breakfront Bookcase

- *circa 1930*

A fine neo-classical-style breakfront bookcase in elm.

- *height 2.3m*
- £9,500 • Westland & Co.

△ Tuscan Ebony Casket

• *circa 1680*
Extremely rare Tuscan ebony casket with inset marble and ivory panels, the interior lined at a later date with red silk, complete with original key.
• *26cm x 46cm*
• £6,500 • J. & T. Stone

▽ American Tea Chest

• *1730*
Rare early American eighteenth-century walnut tea chest with unusual brass decoration.
• *14.5cm x 24cm x 14cm*
• £4,950 • J. & T. Stone

▽ Knife Box

• *circa 1770*
A George III flame-mahogany knife box with satinwood inlay and brass fittings.
• *37cm x 21.7cm*
• £995 • Great Grooms

◁ Korean Lacquer Box

• *17th–18th century*
Lacquer box and cover of oval form, set with a single European engraved floral design hinge and a later European lock plate. The cover and sides decorated with a free scrolling design of flowers and leaves inlaid in mother of pearl, the stem of the vine inlaid in flat silvered wire, all on a black lacquer ground.
• *9.2cm x 37.5cm*
• £6,500 • Gerard Hawthorn

△ South German Table Cabinet

• *circa 1700*
South German cabinet in European hardwoods. The characteristic inlay style can be seen on a portative organ at the Victoria and Albert Museum in London. The shading was created using hot sand.
• *width 36cm*
• £2,400 • Hygra

△ Tortoiseshell Box

• *1760*
Anglo-Dutch box with ivory stringing and silver mounts on silver bun feet.
• *16cm x 28cm x 20cm*
• £3,000 • O.F. Wilson

△ Wig Box

• *circa 1780*
French wig box with a domed lid hand-painted with floral garlands centred by a classical folly in a heart-shaped cartouche, flanked by a lady to the right and a gentleman to the left.
• *16cm x 30cm*
• £1,050 • O.F. Wilson

▽ Satinwood Tea Caddy

• *circa 1790*
George III oval satinwood tea caddy with bat's wing pattern to the front and cover and original axe head handle.
• *height 12cm*
• £1,950 • Period Pieces

△ Georgian Tea Caddy

• *1790*
Georgian single apple fruitwood tea caddy of good shape and fine patination.
• *height 11cm*
• £5,950 • J. & T. Stone

△ Dutch Bible Box

• *18th century*
Dutch colonial Bible box, heavily carved with scrolled designs, with fine pierced and engraved mounts.
• *15.5cm x 23cm*
• £850 • Younger

△ Papier Mâché Tea Caddy

• *circa 1785*
Papier mâché tea caddy with gilt leaf decoration matched with Greek key pattern border. Probably from the factory of Henry Clay.
• *height 9cm*
• £4,950 • J. & T. Stone

▷ Tortoiseshell Tea Caddy

• *circa 1775*
Exceptional red tortoiseshell tea chest with ivory stringing, silver ball feet and top handle; the interior with three original glass canisters with silver plate lids and original key.
• *height 14cm*
• £29,500 • J. & T. Stone

△ George III Tea Caddy

- *circa 1790*

George III, decagonal ivory tea caddy with mother-of-pearl inlay. Made in England.

- *height 10cm*
- £3,950 • J. de Haan

△ Medical Box

- *circa 1790*

A fully fitted eighteenth century mahogany medical box with bottles, funnel, balance and weights.

- *width 15cm*
- £1,700 • Hygra

▽ Hexagonal Tea Caddy

- *circa 1785*

Late 18th-century, George III, hexagonal, gilded, rolled-paper single tea caddy of unusual open design.

- *height 15cm*
- £2,450 • J. & T. Stone

▽ George III Cutlery Urns

- *circa 1790*

One of a pair of George III mahogany cutlery urns, with chequered line stringing and barbers pole edging. The stepped lid with ivory finial rises to reveal the original fitted interior for twelve place settings. Standing on a platform base with barber's pole stringing.

- *height 66cm*
- £10,980 • Period Pieces

◁ Pear-Shaped Tea Caddy

- *circa 1800*

Fine pear-shaped George III tea caddy made from fruitwood, comprising two sections with brass fitting and stem.

- *height 19cm*
- £5,350 • Period Pieces

△ Cribbage Box

- *circa 1790*

Fine Anglo-Indian vizagapatnum incised ivory cribbage box.

- *width 18cm*
- £1,600 • Hygra

△ George III Tea Caddy

- *circa 1790*

George III burr-yew and parquetry-inlaid tea caddy with chamfered angles. Boxwood and chequer strung, with oval striped harewood paterae.

- *height 14cm*
- £2,950 • J. & T. Stone

△ Porcupine Box

- *circa 1800*

Unusual porcupine Georgian workbox with a hinged horn handle, standing on small bun feet.

- *height 9cm*
- £750 • Younger

▽ Ten-Sided Tea Caddy

- *1790*

Late 18th-century ten-sided, George III tea caddy. Quite unusual, blonde tortoiseshell with ivory stringing. The tea caddy has two compartments, silver top and handle with escutcheon and monogrammed initial plate and finial.

- *height 14cm*
- £5,950 • J. & T. Stone

▽ Tortoiseshell Tea Caddy

- *circa 1800*

Rare George III red tortoiseshell single tea caddy with ebony line stringing. The cover and interior lid have the original silver-plated ball handles, with original silver-plated lock and hinges.

- *height 10cm*
- £5,580 • Period Pieces

▽ Henderson Tea Caddy

• *circa 1810*
Regency tortoiseshell tea caddy by Henderson, a reputed tortoiseshell box-maker. With mother-of-pearl diamond inlay, twin compartments and a ripple serpentine front, standing on small mahogany bun feet. With maker's label.
• *height 12.5m*
• £3,500 • Period Pieces

▽ Regency Tea Caddy

• *1820*
Regency tortoiseshell, double tea caddy with pagoda top, ivory facing, silver stringing, initial plate and escutcheon.
• *15cm x 18cm x 12cm*
• £3,950 • J. & T. Stone

▽ Ivory Sewing-Box

• *circa 1830*
Magnificent early 19th-century vizagapatnum engraved and etched ivory sewing box with side drawer and sandalwood interior, in the form of a house with chimney finial and monogrammed cartouche.
• *height 14cm*
• £2,250 • J. & T. Stone

△ Tortoiseshell Tea Caddy

• *1830*
Very rare early 19th-century Regency pressed tortoiseshell two-compartment tea caddy, with ribbed and bowed front panels, domed top, silver stringing and insignia plate
• *height 18cm*
• £8,950 • J. & T. Stone

△ Circular Robe Box

• *1830*
A Japanese black lacquered robe box of circular form with gilded floral decoration to both body and lid.
• *46cm x 39cm*
• £800 • O.F. Wilson

▽ Apothecary Box

• *circa 1830*
Georgian mahogany apothecary box with an almost complete set of original bottles, some with original contents. Lower drawer has original scales, weights, mortar, pestle and key.
• *13cm x 19cm*
• £1,950 • J. & T. Stone

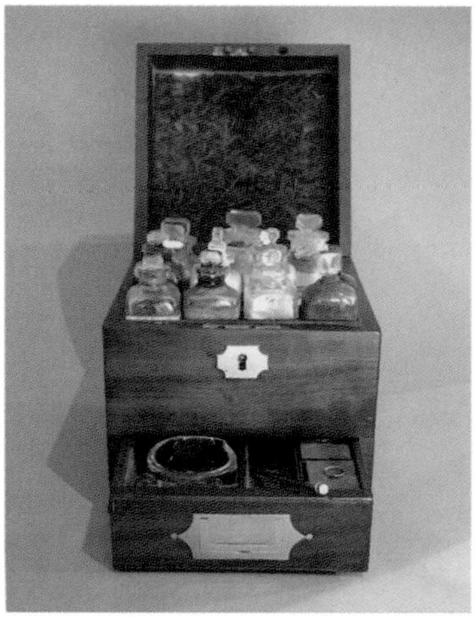

▷ Sarcophagus Tea-Caddy

• *circa 1835*
A fine quality yew-wood William IV tea caddy. Concave lid with panelled front, decorated with quarter cotton reel edging and solid rosewood ring handles. Whole is raised on a stepped cotton reel base with squat brass feet. Fine condition with original patination.
• *width 28.5cm*
• £975 • J. Collins

◁ Chinese Ivory Casket

• *18th–19th century*
A fine Canton ivory casket fitted with European carrying handle, lock plate, corner reinforcement and ball and claw feet. The red silk-lined interior fitted with three Chinese pewter-lined ivory caddies, the pierced ivory panelling of the caddies decorated with geometric diapers and floral designs within ruyi-head borders. The casket decorated with low relief panels of landscapes and flowers.
• *13.6cm x 26cm*
• £8,500 • Gerard Hawthorn

△ Sewing Box

• *1832*
Exceptional, tortoiseshell sewing-box with extensive mother-of-pearl floral inlay. With pull-out lower drawer and a note from the original owner.
• *height 14cm*
• £4,950 • J. & T. Stone

◁ Regency Tea Caddy

• *1835*
A late Regency walnut-based chevron-strung tea caddy with two compartments inside.
• *12cm x 9cm x 13cm*
• £395 • J. & T. Stone

△ Chinese Tea Caddy

- *circa 1840*

Shaped and lacquered Chinese tea caddy with gold decoration, on carved dragon feet.

- *width 21cm*
- £850 • Hygra

△ Japanese Iron Box

- *circa 19th century*

Iron kogo (box) formed as a kabuto (helmet). The top of the kogo is decorated with gilt mons (family symbol). Signed by Yoshiatsu.

- *height 6cm*
- £1,450 • Gregg Baker

△ English Tortoiseshell Tea Caddy

- *circa 1850*

Mid 19th-century English bow-front tortoiseshell tea caddy. Contains a mother-of-pearl floral inlay to the front panel. A fine quality piece.

- *height 33cm*
- £2,875 • J. de Haan

▽ Ash Tea Caddy

- *circa 1850*

Tea caddy made from Mongolian ash, with lead receptacles and an oval enamel plaque with a painted cherub. This was a wedding present in 1869.

- *height 11cm*
- £2,800 • J. & T. Stone

▽ Chinese Lacquer Tea Caddy

- *circa 1850*

Shaped Chinese lacquer tea caddy with boldly defined gold decoration and pewter lines, standing on claw feet.

- *width 19cm*
- £650 • Hygra

▽ Gold Japanese Kogo

- *19th century*

Japanese, gold lacquered 19th-century kogo (box) in the form of a very unusual piebald puppy. The box is a container for incense.

- *height 6cm*
- £1,650 • Gregg Baker

◁ Ballot Box

- *circa 1860*

Ebonised ballot box with red banding, inscribed with the words, 'For and Against' in gold letters each side of a metal postal opening.

- *height 28cm*
- £300 • Lacquer Chest

▽ Ebony Casket

- *circa 1860*

Ebony casket inlaid with ivory, mother of pearl flowers and various fruitwoods.

- *10cm x 32cm*
- £595 • A.I.G.

▽ Jewel Casket

- *circa 1860*

French lustre tortoiseshell jewel casket with bowed panels, extensive ormolu decorative mounts and original silk lined interior.

- *height 25cm*
- £9,500 • J. & T. Stone

▷ Victorian Wooden Dressing Case

- *circa 1864*

Very unusual, Victorian, wooden dressing case with 11 extensively engraved silver-topped jars and containers marked with 1864. Two secret drawers. Signed by W. H. Toole.

- £9,950 • J. & T. Stone

△ Mother-of-Pearl Tea Caddy

- *1840*

A mid 19th-century, Victorian mother-of-pearl and abalone tea caddy with two compartments and original key.

- *height 17cm*
- £995 • J. & T. Stone

△ Leather Hatbox

- *circa 1860*

Single leather Shanghai pyramid hat box cover with leaf-shaped lockplate and ruyi-form head-mounts.

- *height 30cm*
- £385 • Eastern Interiors

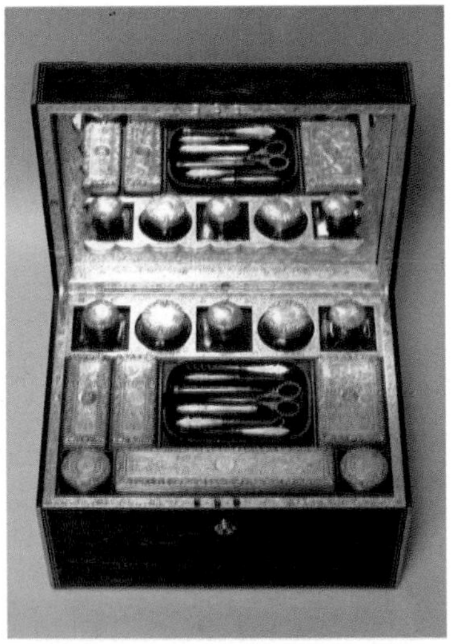

△ Box On Stand

- *circa 1870*

Leather lacquered box on stand with original brass lockplate with 'ruyi' head mounts and fittings. From Shanxi.

- *36cm x 48cm*
- £570 • Eastern Interiors

△ Document Box

- *circa 1880s*

Late Meiji period sugi wood cabinet for documents, in six sections.

- *71cm x 46cm*
- £1,395 • Gordon Reece

△ Rosewood Tea Caddy

- *late 19th century*

A simple, rosewood tea caddy comprising two compartments for different blends. Decorated with brass on the clasp and lid. This caddy incorporates a magnificent cut-glass sugar bowl.

- *width 25cm*
- £220 • Ian Spencer

▽ Jewellery Case

- *circa 1880*

Black lacquered jewellery box with a red interior and polychrome paintings of flora and fauna. Inside the lid is a folding mirror. From Fuzhou.

- *20cm x 24cm*
- £390 • Eastern Interiors

▽ Pillow Box

- *circa 1880*

Chinese pillow box made from wood with brass handles and escutcheon plate. The lid is shaped as the pillow.

- *14cm x 31cm*
- £150 • Great Grooms

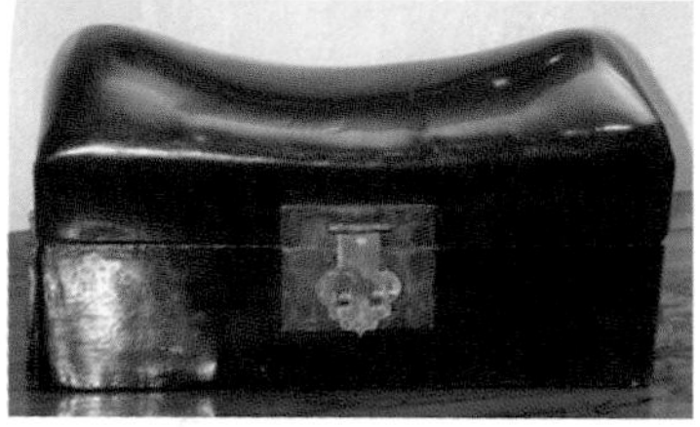

▽ Tea Tin

- *1880*

One of a set of four black metal tea tins with a central cartouche of two birds perched on a cherry blossom branch.

- *height 44cm*
- £1,500 • Goodison Paraskeva

△ Parchment Box

- *circa 1890s*

Rectangular leather red lacquered parchment box, the top and sides finely painted in gilt showing a cartouche of children playing games. From Shanghai.

- *7cm x 32cm*
- £360 • Eastern Interiors

△ Tunbridge-Ware Box

- *19th century*

Shaped Tunbridge-ware sewing box standing on turned feet. Van Dyke parquetry pattern with native and imported hardwood.

- *width 21cm*
- £900 • Hygra

△ Chinese Hat Box

- *circa 1880*

Red lacquered cylindrical Chinese hat box with original brass fittings, the interior fitted with two sandalwood plates for the storage of hats.

- *41cm x 34cm*
- £430 • Eastern Interiors

▽ Voting Box

- *circa 1880*

Victorian oak voting box inscribed with the brass letters 'Y' and 'N', with two small drawers and a central hole with emerald green satin.

- *28cm x 25cm*
- £495 • A.I.G.

▽ Black Lacquer Tea Caddy

- *circa 1880*

Victorian black lacquer papier-mâché tea caddy with ivory inlay and painted floral sprays of red roses, with floral gilt designs.

- *15.5cm x 30.5cm*
- £800 • Younger

▽ Red Merchant's Trunk

- *circa 1880*

Lacquered merchant's trunk with a moulded hinged lid, decorated with intricate brass-work of faceted and smooth rounded nails. The front lock is in the shape of a large stylised butterfly – the symbol of longevity. From Fuzhou.

- *27cm x 24cm*
- £400 • Eastern Interiors

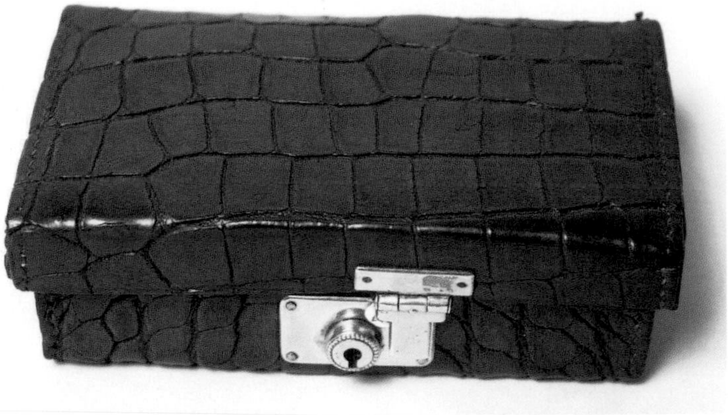

▽ Russian Hatbox

- *circa 1900*

An early 20th-century Russian hatbox made of birchwood, with a leather strap.

- *height 22.5cm, diameter 36.9cm*
- £490 • R. Cavendish

▽ Mahjong Set

- *1920*

Impressive Mahjong set of the highest quality in a solid oak case with extensive brass work decoration to the sides and top. With solid brass handle and sliding front panel revealing five similarly decorated drawers containing solid ivory tiles, game sticks and dice. Provenance: The Right Honourable The Viscount Leverhulme, K. G. of Thornton Manor.

- *29cm x 32cm*
- £5,950 • J. & T. Stone

▷ Dressing Table Set

- *circa 1930*

Art Deco turquoise shell dressing table set in original silk-lined leather box. Set comprises two wooden hair brushes with handles, two clothes brushes and bottles and pots of cut glass in various shapes and sizes, with a mirror and tray in the lid.

- £1,450 • J. & T. Stone

△ Crocodile Box

- *circa 1900*

Deep grained crocodile box with padded velvet interior and nickel mounts.

- *16cm x 9cm*
- £480 • H. & H.

△ Miniature Postbox

- *1900*

Late Victorian oak miniature postbox with original inset rate card, brass plate inscribed 'Letters', and carved leaf top.

- *height 38cm*
- £2,950 • J. & T. Stone

▷ Tortoiseshell Box

- *1930*

Small Art Deco tortoiseshell box.

- *length 10cm*
- £145 • Abacus Antiques

△ Shakespeare's House

- *circa 1920*

Whimsical novelty jewel box in the form of a model of Shakespeare's house, inset with a clock and barometer on the side. Probably a tourist item.

- *height 18cm*
- £2,950 • J. & T. Stone

▽ Tortoiseshell and Silver Perfume Box

- *circa 1918*

Original and complete. The box contains an inset of floral panel decorations. Made in England.

- *height 7.5cm*
- £1,270 • S. & A. Thompson

▽ Travelling Dressing Case

- *circa 1934*

An early 20th-century, fine-quality, Art Deco, crocodile-skin, gentleman's travelling dressing case. Made by Cartier of London. Hallmarked silver, inscribed 'Sir W. Rollo'.

- £3,995 • J. & T. Stone

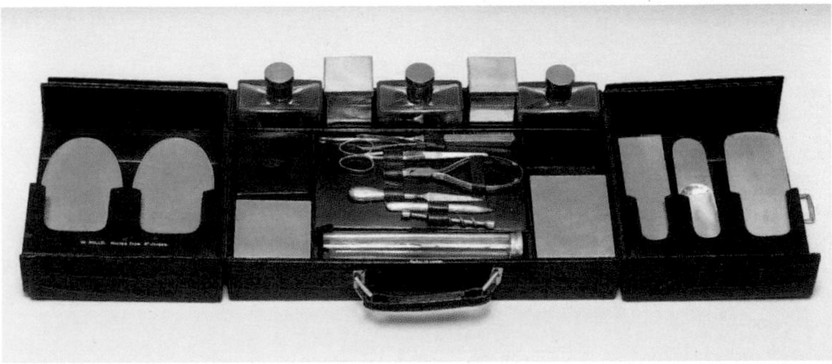

▽ Sovereign Sorter

- *early 20th century*

Originally used by shopkeepers to sort sovereigns and half sovereigns. Mahogany with brass fittings and escutcheon to the lower drawer.

- *height 27.5cm*
- £650 • Ian Spencer

▽ Sycamore Box

- *circa 1900*

A small sycamore box with oval pictures depicting Western Road, Littlehampton.

- *8.5cm x 7cm*
- £34 • John Clay

BUREAUX

▽ Oak Escritoire

- *circa 1690*

A very rare William and Mary escritoire of small size with superb colour and patina.

- *height 1.55m*
- **£11,500** • **Red Lion**

▷ Mahogany Bureau

- *circa 1780*

An 18th-century mahogany bureau without leather inlay.

- *height 1.02m*
- **£3,800** • **Mora Upham**

△ Bureau Bookcase

- *circa 1730*

George II burr oak bureau with walnut crossbanding. Fitted interior with drawers below.

- *height 2.06m*
- **£14,500** • **Red Lion**

△ William and Mary Oak Escritoire

- *circa 1690–1700*

Unusual William and Mary oak escritoire with ogee moulding, map drawer, fall front, three long drawers with drop handles, raised on turned bun feet.

- *158cm x 93cm x 54cm*
- **£11,500** • **Rod Wilson**

▽ Fall Front Bureau

- *circa 1735*

George II red walnut bureau with well-fitted breakfront interior.

- *height 1.03m*
- **£5,750** • **J. Collins**

▷ George II Escritoire

- *circa 1785*

George II kingwood and marquetry escritoire on stand.

- *height 1.21m*
- **£20,000** • **Norman Adams**

△ Walnut Bureau

- *circa 1720*

18th-century bureau with five outer drawers and typical inner compartments.

- *height 82cm*
- **£3,200** • **Antiques Pavilion**

△ Oak Bureau

- *circa 1750*

Shaped interior with drawers and pigeon holes, on bracket feet.

- *height 1.35m*
- **£2,450** • **M.J. Bowdery**

△ Mahogany Bureau

- *1740*

Mahogany bureau with well-fitted walnut interior, various pigeon holes and hidden drawers, brass ring handles and escutcheons, on moulded bracket feet.

- *92cm x 109cm*
- **£6,500** • **Pimlico**

△ Swedish Bureau

- *1780*

Swedish bureau with original paintwork and fall front with stepped interior above three long drawers, standing on original scrolled bracket feet.

- *104cm x 94cm x 54cm*
- **£6,200** • **Heytesbury**

▽ Cherrywood Secretaire

• *circa 1810*
French secretaire with griffin feet and lion brass fittings.
• *height 1.41m*
• £4,800 • Sieff

▽ Bureau Bookcase

• *circa 1820*
Mahogany with fitted interior and four drawers on bracket feet.
• *height 2.31m*
• £2,995 • Antique Warehouse

▽ George III Bureau

• *early 19th century*
Mahogany bureau with sloping lid enclosing fitted interior.
• *height 1.06m*
• £5,500 • Old Cinema

▷ French Empire Secretaire

• *circa 1800s*
A mahogany French Empire secretaire abattant with a marble top, turned columns and pierced ormolu mounts.
• *height 140cm x 80cm*
• £5,500 • C.H. Major

△ Biedermeier Secretaire

• *circa 1820*
Biedermeier-style birchwood secretaire/bureau on square feet.
• *height 1.42m*
• £9,800 • R. Cavendish

△ Empire Bureau Commode

• *circa 1820*
Swedish mahogany Empire bureau commode with fitted interior and fold down flap above three drawers.
• *94cm x 111cm x 51cm*
• £6,500 • R. Cavendish

▷ French Secretaire

• *circa 1810*
Secretaire desk with serpentine front, original paint, three long drawers with oval iron handles, brass escutcheon plates and a fall front enclosing fourteen small drawers, the whole raised on gilded feet.
• *108cm x 121cm*
• £9,000 • Augustus Brandt

◁ Oak Bureau

• *circa 1820*
Ornately carved oak bureau with original drop-handles.
• *height 82cm*
• £975 • Antiques Pavilion

△ Boulle Secretaire

• *circa 1830*
An ebonised boulle secretaire of the Louis Philippe period, with rosewood interior, ormolu mounts and decorative ivory inlay, raised on stylised bun feet.
• *136cm x 67cm*
• £2,750 • Ranby Hall

△ Secretaire/Bureau

• *circa 1825*
North European elm-wood secretaire commode. Pull-out first drawer over two other drawers.
• *height 94cm*
• £950 • M. Constantini

△ Secretaire A Abbatant

- *circa 1840*

An early nineteenth century flame mahogany secretaire à abbatant, with boxwood and ebony inlays and stringing. The fall front enclosing a well-fitted interior above two cupboard doors flanked by turned pilasters on bun feet.

- *1.54m x 1m x 52cm*
- £3,200 • Great Grooms

△ Campaign Chest

- *circa 1840*

English mahogany secretaire/campaign chest with pull-out flap, fitted compartments and brass mounts.

- *height 1.10m*
- £4,200 • Riverbank

△ Rolltop Bureau

- *circa 1860*

French with bronze mounts and authentification stamp.

- *height 1.2m*
- £15,500 • M. Mathers

▽ French Bureau Plat

- *circa 1850*

French ebony, tortoiseshell and brass-inlaid bureau plat. The antique leather top with a massive moulded gilt-bronze edge, above a large recessed central drawer flanked by two smaller drawers. Supported on four cabriole legs, mounted above the knees with a satyr's mask, and terminating in hoof feet. With chased and gilt bronze mounts. The central drawer is mounted with a large mask of Bacchus.

- *79cm x 2.02m*
- £65,000 • Anthony Outred

▽ Bureau Bookcase

- *1850*

Victorian figured walnut roll-top bureau with fitted interior below glazed doors with bookshelves.

- *231cm x 105cm x 60cm*
- £9,500 • Judy Fox

▷ Cylinder Bureau

- *circa 1880*

Victorian oak bureau with stringing and chequered inlay.

- *height 1.51m*
- £2,995 • Antique Warehouse

▽ Walnut Cabinet

- *1870*

A French walnut secretaire cabinet with arched pediment and fall front and architectural side columns, on turned bun feet.

- *1.94m x 83cm*
- £1,850 • Ranby Hall

▷ Walnut Secretaire

- *circa 1880*

Fine Swedish secretaire, heavily moulded with a burr walnut veneer. The fall front enclosing an architectural fitted interior, above three long drawers.

- *1.47m x 1.09m*
- £6,500 • Hatchwell

△ Cylinder Bureau

- *circa 1870*

Fine-quality French rosewood ormolu-mounted bureau à cylindre, with galleried top and drawers, with a well-fitted interior, standing on reeded tapered legs and brass castors.

- *52cm x 51cm x 28cm*
- £18,500 • Ranby Hall

◁ **Cylinder Bureau**

- *circa 1890*

Mahogany bureau with boxwood and satinwood crossbanding.

- *height 1.12m*
- £7,000 • Judy Fox

▷ **Druce of London Bureau**

- *circa 1880*

George III-style mahogany bureau with fall front, fitted interior and original brass fittings, standing on moulded bracket feet, with a brass plate bearing the inscription, 'Druce & Co, Baker St, London', inside the top drawer.

- *height 1.13m*
- £3,500 • Hill Farm

▽ **Pine Secretaire**

- *20th century*

A painted pine miniature secretaire with a broken pediment above the fall, with fitted interior, on shaped bracket feet.

- *height 80cm*
- £675 • Solaris

△ **Satinwood Roll-Top Bureau**

- *1890*

An early nineteenth-century-style bureau in satinwood. The gallery comprises three drawers above the roll-top desk and three drawers below, standing on square tapered legs.

- *1m x 90cm x 48cm*
- £6,000 • Judy Fox

▽ **Fiddle-Back Bureau**

- *circa 1900*

Edwardian fiddle-back mahogany roll-top bureau bookcase having three shelves, original glass, boxwood inlay, leather-top writing desk with three drawers below.

- *2.07m x 91cm x 48cm*
- £3,950 • Hatchwell

△ **French Secretaire**

- *1920*

A bombé fall-front secretaire à abattant with three small drawers, profusely decorated with foliate design, standing on splayed legs.

- *1.32m x 72cm x 40cm*
- £1,150 • Tredantiques

△ **Burr-Walnut Secretaire**

- *circa 1880*

French burr-walnut fall-front secretaire with central pillared cupboard flanked by five drawers and two below.

- *height 1.42m*
- £2,950 • The Swan

▷ **Military Chest**

- *19th century*

Campaign/military chest in camphor wood with brass handles.

- *height 1.06m*
- £3,500 • Tower Bridge

CABINETS

▷ **Cabinet from Fujian**

- *1880*

Chinese lacquer cabinet from Fujian Province, Southeast China, with a couplet on the doors stating 'The Dragon rises to the morning sun with a canopy, the phoenix breathes calligraphy into the evening air'.

- *140cm x 84m*
- £1,380 • Lotus House

▽ **Corner Cabinet**

- *1770*

Dutch black lacquer corner cupboard with chinoiserie decoration.

- *110cm x 58cm*
- £3,950 • O.F. Wilson

◁ **Double Cabinet**

- *Ming*

Fine double cabinet of the Ming dynasty with brass fittings.

- *110cm x 121cm x 44cm*
- £3,950 • Gordon Reece

◁ **George III Satinwood Cabinet**

- *circa 1775*

George III-period mahogany and satinwood cabinet designed by John Linnell. The upper doors framed in satinwood, the lower doors with a circular panel of satinwood within quartered mahogany veneers.

- *width 101cm*
- £165,000 • John Bly

△ **Lacquered Cabinet**

- *circa 1770*

A good, small English table-top cabinet with chinoiserie scenes.

- *height 69cm*
- £3,800 • P.L. James

▷ **Mahogany Chest on Chest**

- *circa 1760*

Flame mahogany chest on chest, with three small drawers at the top and four variegated drawers below, four further drawers resting on moulded bracket feet.

- *width 39cm*
- £18,500 • C. Preston

△ **Japanese Lacquer Cabinet**

- *circa 1705*

Black lacquer and gilt Japanese cabinet on base with X-stretcher, cabriole legs and pad feet.

- *135cm x 76cm*
- £8,500 • Anthony Outred

△ **Hanging Corner Cabinet**

- *circa 1740*

The cabinet has two double panelled doors with starburst marquetry inlay.

- *height 1.14m*
- £1,575 • Red Lion

▽ **George II Pot Cupboards**

- *circa 1750*

A pair of burr-walnut pot cabinets.

- *height 70cm*
- £1,675 • C. Preston

▽ **Cross-Banded Cupboard**

- *circa 1775*

An early George III oak and mahogany cross-banded hanging oak cupboard.

- *42cm x 76cm x 98cm*
- £2,450 • Great Grooms

▽ **Display Cabinet**

- *18th century*

Dutch inlaid walnut display cabinet with moulded doors.

- *77cm x 82cm x 27cm*
- £4,450 • Paul Hopwell

△ English Corner Cupboard

• *1780*

English, painted, wall-mounted corner cupboard, with carved moulded door panels and original blue paintwork

• *108cm x 81cm*

• £2,800 • **Heytesbury**

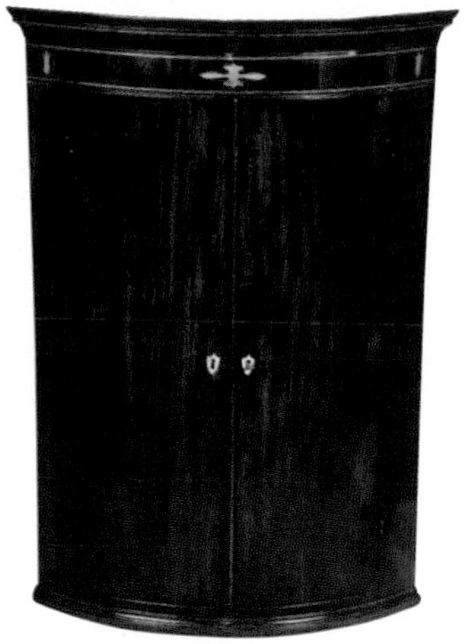

△ Hanging Corner Cabinet

• *circa 1790*

Moulded concave and sectioned cornice. Well grained doors.

• *height 1.05m*

• £2,650 • **J. Collins**

△ Pair of Low Cupboards

• *early 1800s*

One of a pair of Chinese red lacquer low cupboards with brass fittings.

• *78cm x 61cm*

• £3,100 • **Gordon Reece**

▽ Walnut Credenza

• *circa 1860*

Victorin walnut credenza with ormulo mounts and cross-banding and inlay.

• *109cm x 164cm*

• £3,950 • **The Swan**

▽ George III Demi-Lune Commode

• *circa 1790*

George III demi-lune commode decorated with fine marquetry veneers in the manner of John Linnell.

• *86cm x 73cm*

• £135,000 • **John Bly**

▽ Chinese Cabinet

• *18th century*

Chinese herbalist's cabinet with Chinese characters and painted decoration and numerous drawers.

• *118cm x 96cm*

• £2,200 • **Great Grooms**

▽ Mahogany Side Cabinet

• *circa 1790*

A cabinet of the Sheraton period, of crossbanded satinwood with ebony and boxwood stringing.

• *height 89.5cm*

• £8,500 • **J. Collins**

▽ George III Dressing Stand

• *circa 1795*

George III mahogany gentleman's dressing stand with original mirror, and brass fittings.

• *89cm x 51cm*

• £825 • **The Swan**

◁ Satinwood Cupboard

• *circa 1785*

An English, satinwood, bedside cabinet for storing the chamber pot, with inlaid detailing to the front and top, the whole on square, tapered legs.

• *height 77cm*

• £1,850 • **O.F. Wilson**

△ Walnut Chest on Chest

• *circa 1780*

A fine walnut chest on chest with unusual indented shell moulding on the bottom drawer.

• *width 101cm*

• £48,500 • **John Bly**

△ Cherrywood Armoire

• *18th century*

A provincial cherrywood armoire with moulded and arched pediment and waved apron, on squat cabriole legs with brass mounts.

• *240cm x 141cm x 56cm*

• £3,800 • **Tredantiques**

▽ Corner Cupboard

• *circa 1780*
A rare George III, chinoiserie-patterned, Japanned, standing corner cupboard.
• *height 2.03m*
• £40,000 • Norman Adams

▽ Ebonised Cabinet

• *19th century*
A fine German, nineteenth-century, ebonised cabinet with detailed Dresden porcelain plaques and figures.
• *180cm x 130cm x 52cm*
• £55,000 • Sinai

▷ Biedermeier Cabinet

• *1815–20*
Danish Biedermeier mahogany cabinet with satinwood inlay. The curvaceous shape of the door and its satinwood inlay, with griffins symbolising the 'vigilant guardian', are characteristics shared by Danish and north German Biedermeier furniture.
• *118cm x 54cm*
• £4,900 • R. Cavendish

△ Painted Sideboard

• *circa 1800*
A painted Swedish Gustavian sideboard with moulded geometric designs.
• *98cm x 107cm x 51cm*
• £4,500 • R. Cavendish

△ Regency Mahogany Side Cabinet

• *circa 1800*
A Regency flame mahogany side cabinet with oval satinwood inlay door panels, banded in satinwood. Raised on splayed bracket feet.
• *105cm x 97cm x 40cm*
• £1,650 • Ranby Hall

▷ Regency Sideboard

• *circa 1800s*
Regency mahogany and satinwood cross banded sideboard, with two drawers and cupboards, and gilt handles.
• *81cm x 121cm*
• £1,495 • Vale Antiques

▽ Two Part Kortan Cabinet

• *circa 1800*
A kortan cabinet of two parts made from elm, with four drawers above two cupboard doors with brass mounts.
• *145cm x 105cm*
• £2,950 • Wakelin Linfield

▽ Georgian Bow-Fronted Cupboard

• *circa 1810*
A Georgian glazed bow-front corner cupboard with gothic-style glazing bars.
• *100cm x 53cm*
• £1,200 • Tredantiques

▷ Red Lacquer Chinese Cabinet

• *early 1800s*
Red lacquer Chinese cabinet with long panel doors and circular brass lock.
• *92cm x 194cm*
• £11,500 • Gordon Reece

△ Indian Apothecary's Chest

• *early 1800s*
Fine antique apothecary's chest constructed in rosewood with brass handles and an ornately carved balcony.
• *38cm x 184cm*
• £3,300 • Gordon Reece

△ Neo-Classical Commode

• *circa 1800*
Semi-circular neo-classical commode decorated with flowers and brass inlay, on turned legs.
• *45cm x 117cm*
• £26,500 • Ranby Hall

△ Regency Cabinet

- *circa 1820*

Regency mahogany side cabinet, with maple amboyna veneer and one long and two small drawers above a central cupboard, flanked by two long cupboards.

- *92cm x 108cm*
- £2,750 • W. John Griffiths

△ Regency Cabinet

- *1830*

A Regency flame mahogany bedside cabinet, with black marble top, the door with moulded foliate designs on a gadrooned square plinth base.

- *79cm x 47cm*
- £2,800 • John Clay

▽ Regency Chiffonier

- *circa 1820*

Regency mahogany chiffonier with silk panel doors, a pierced gallery and one long mirror, with two Corinthian columns, lion's head ring handles and brass ormulu mounts.

- *118cm x 100cm*
- £1,650 • R. Macklin Smith

▽ Mizuya Kitchen Cabinet

- *Edo period (1830)*

A Japanese Mizuya kitchen cabinet with a lacquered hinoki frame and keyaki drawer fronts.

- *height 1.66m*
- £3,400 • Gordon Reece

▽ Biedermeier Secretaire

- *circa 1830*

Swedish Biedermeier secretaire in masur birch and birchwood.

- *116cm x 107cm*
- £6,700 • R. Cavendish

◁ Bedside Cupboard

- *1830*

Mahogany bedside cupboard with gallery and single cupboard with small turned handle, standing on slender tapering legs.

- *height 79cm*
- £550 • Salem Antiques

△ Regency Cabinet

- *circa 1825*

Regency linen press with two arched moulded panelled doors with ebony inlay and three drawers, standing on turned feet.

- *width 110cm*
- £5,800 • C. Preston

△ Italian Petite Commodes

- *circa 1830*

One of a pair of Italian walnut and boxwood inlaif commodes, with stylised swan pillars and original grey marble tops.

- *78cm x 60cm*
- £8,750 • C. Preston

▽ French Side Cabinets

- *1830*

One of a pair of French Louis Philippe flame mahogany side cabinets with figured marble tops and panelled cupboard.

- *38cm x 81cm*
- £580 • Ranby Hall

▽ Walnut Cabinet

- *circa 1840*

A Danish figured walnut cabinet with single panelled door raised on a circular plinth base.

- *142cm x 63cm*
- £4,650 • Hatchwell

◁ Rosewood Specimen Cabinet

- *circa 1850*

An unusual rosewood specimen cabinet with panelled doors fitted with wire grilles and pleated silk. Each corner fitted with canted brass cornering, with pigeonholes in the interior above a fall-front satinwood drawer leading to rosewood and satinwood panelled doors enclosing ten graduated drawers with a further fourteen of various sizes. The whole raised on a stand with barley twist supports and stretchers.

- *137cm x 78cm*
- £3,750 • Anthony Outred

▽ Victorian Credenza

- *circa 1860*

A Victorian ebonised credenza with oval painted porcelain panels with gilt mounts and banding.

- *110cm x 178cm x 37cm*
- £3,250 • Ranby Hall

▽ Oriental Lacquer Cabinets

- *1870*

One of a pair of oriental red lacquer cabinets with chinoiserie designs and gilding, above a moulded apron.

- *91cm x 59cm x 39cm*
- £1,385 • Ranby Hall

△ Side Cabinet

- *circa 1860*

A Victorian, walnut-veneered serpentine side cabinet.

- *height 1.08m*
- £1,980 • Ranby Hall

△ Gesso Side Cabinet

- *circa 1860*

A pair of Napoleon III ebonised gilt-bronze and painted gesso side cabinet. The black Porta marble tops with a panelled central door decorated in the Louis XVI style.

- *110cm x 144cm*
- £9,500 • Westland & Co.

△ Victorian Credenza

- *circa 1870*

A Victorian ebonised credenza with ormolu mounts, showing painted porcelain plaques.

- *height 1.19m*
- £3,850 • Kenneth Harvey

▷ Display Table

- *circa 1860*

Victorian marquetry display table with floral designs and brass mounts, on cabriole legs.

- *74cm x 46cm*
- £2,650 • Great Grooms

▽ Small Chinese Cabinet

- *1880*

Small Chinese cabinet from Zhejiang Province, decorated with carvings of a phoenix and lotus plants.

- *81cm x 55cm*
- £550 • Lotus House

▽ Breakfront Cabinet

- *1866*

A mahogany cabinet by Gillow, signed Thos Whiteside. With architectural and leaf decoration.

- *height 98cm*
- £6,850 • Ronald G. Chambers

◁ Pier Cabinet

- *circa 1865*

A Victorian ebonised two-door pier cabinet inlaid with amboyna.

- *height 1.06m*
- £2,600 • Judy Fox

△ Walnut Pier Cabinet

- *circa 1860*

Nineteenth-century walnut pier cabinet with a mirror-fronted door panel and gilt-metal mounts.

- *height 1.08m*
- £1,980 • Ranby Hall

▽ Mahogany Chiffonier

- *circa 1880*

Victorian flame-mahogany chiffonier with scrolled carved moulded back, a single shelf supported by pillars, one single long drawer and two enclosed cupboards.

- *93cm x 84cm*
- £1,700 • Salem Antiques

▽ Japanese Merchant Chest

- *circa 1890*

A Japanese Choba Dansu merchant chest with a lacquered hinoki and sugi frame and secret compartments with copper and iron handles

- *90cm x 95cm*
- £3,400 • Gordon Reece

◁ Continental Painted Cabinet

- *circa 1880*

Continental fruitwood display cabinet with circular moulded pediments, two glazed doors, flanked by bevelled glass, below two cupboard doors painted with ribbons and flowers, surmounted with a pierced brass rail, standing on small cabriole legs.

- *175cm x 135cm*
- £3,500 • Hill Farm

△ Display Cabinet

- *19th century*

A cabinet with waved pediment, central carved cartouche and overglazed doors. With S-shape drawers and ormolu fittings to front and sides.

- *height 2.47m*
- £6,850 • Ranby Hall

△ Japanese Lacquer Cabinet

- *circa 1880*

Japanese lacquer cabinet with two doors decorated with mother-of-pearl floral inlay, two small drawers and one long drawer inlaid with boxwood.

- *39cm x 29cm*
- £450 • Younger

▽ Victorian Cabinet

- *circa 1880*

Small bedside cabinet with brass gallery with mirror below, single cupboard with scrolled carving panel, ebony inlay and brass handles each side, standing on turned legs.

- *height 100cm*
- £875 • C. Preston

▽ Italian Walnut Cabinet

- *circa 1880*

A cabinet in the Bambocci (figural) manner, decorated with heavily carved uprights and panelled doors.

- *height 91.5cm*
- £2,400 • Westland & Co.

◁ Walnut Bedside Cabinets

- *circa 1880*

One of a pair of Louis XV-style walnut bedside cabinets with one single drawer above a carved and moulded cupboard door, raised on cabriole legs.

- *height 88cm*
- £1,650 • Hill Farm

△ Tortoiseshell Vitrine

- *circa 1880*

A miniature tortoiseshell and ormolu table top vitrine on C-scrolled cabriole legs with shell and leaf decoration

- *25cm x 38cm*
- £2,595 • Great Grooms

△ Tibetan Chest

- *circa 1890*

A red lacquered Tibetan chest with raised carved decoration depicting dragons and long-life symbols.

- *74cm x 83cm*
- £2,200 • Great Grooms

△ Victorian Cabinet

- *circa 1890*

Victorian walnut and plane-wood bedside cabinet, with moulded cupboard doors, raised on a plinth base.

- *height 85cm*
- £450 • Hill Farm

△ Dutch Display Cabinet

- *19th century*

A bombé-fronted Dutch marquetry display cabinet.

- *height 1.6m*
- £12,500 • P.L. James

△ 'Globe Wernicke' Bookcase

- *late 19th century*

An oak three-section Wernicke with three hinged glass flaps for housing books or geological specimens.

- *120cm x 95cm*
- £795 • Old Cinema

▽ Chinese Cabinet

- *1890*

Nineteenth-century Chinese cabinet in red and black lacquer with carvings of birds and foliage and Chinese characters from the Fujian Province, Southeastern China.

- *151cm x 90cm x 43cm*
- £2,500 • Lotus House

▽ Empire-Style Vitrine

- *circa 1890*

A late 19th century empire-style vitrine with gilt banding, a brass gallery and one glass door enclosing two shelves, standing on turned legs.

- *146cm x 70cm*
- £1,895 • John Riordan

◁ Chinese Lacquer Cabinet

- *circa 1900*

Lacquer cabinet from Eastern China with a couplet in Chinese characters on the doors: 'Research in the art of craft. Writing on cookery skill'.

- *height 154cm*
- £980 • Younger

▽ Display Cabinets

- *circa 1900*

One of a pair of fine mahogany Chippendale-style display cabinets of cylindrical form, with gallery cornice above glazed doors, and heavily carved and moulded bases concealing two double doors.

- *203cm x 81cm*
- £15,000 • Butchoff

▽ School Cupboard

- *1900s*

English oak school cupboard with two interior shelves and moulded panel doors with bun handles.

- *140cm x 153cm*
- £600 • Old School

◁ Biedermeier-Style Cupboard

- *circa 1899*

Danish Biedermeier-style cupboard in birchwood, with a central oval inlay in rosewood and satinwood of an urn with a spray of flowers.

- *128cm x 55cm*
- £5,600 • R. Cavendish

△ Gustavian-Style Cabinets

- *circa 1890s*

One of a pair of Swedish-Gustavian style cabinets signed: 'AFI' and 'S&E'. Made in the style of Louis XVI.

- *72cm x 42cm*
- £3,400 • R. Cavendish

△ Corner Cabinets

- *circa 1910*

One of a pair of Edwardian mahogany cabinets with glazed upper part and a cupboard base.

- *height 2.16m*
- £750 • Canonbury

▽ Demi-Lune Vitrine

- *circa 1900*

An Edwardian inlaid mahogany single-door vitrine with compartment beneath and on square tapered spade feet.

- *height 1.7m*
- £2,700 • Judy Fox

▽ Display Cabinet

- *circa 1900*

Edwardian display cabinet with ebony stringing, on swept feet.

- *height 2.2m*
- £2,750 • Ian Spencer

▷ Biedermier Cabinet

- *1920*

A Biedermier light mahogany cabinet inlaid with figurative and floral designs.

- *height 130cm*
- £3,850 • Ranby Hall

△ Collector's Cabinet

- *circa 1900*

Steel and glass collector's cabinet with brass mountings.

- *height 1.25m*
- £1,500 • David Ford

△ French Gothic Cabinet

- *1910*

A French gothic carved-oak cocktail cabinet in seventeenth-century-style with extensive gothic tracery.

- *182cm x 112cm x 58cm*
- £2,250 • Tredantiques

△ Display Cabinet

- *circa 1905*

An unusually small, English Edwardian, mahogany, inlaid, bow-fronted cabinet, well proportioned with solid wood stretcher and tapered legs on spade feet.

- *height 1.66m*
- £2,950 • S. & A. Thompson

△ Corner Cabinet

- *circa 1920*

A glazed cabinet with carved decoration, on three cabriole legs.

- *height 1.78m*
- £2,950 • Kenneth Harvey

▽ French Mahogany and Satinwood Cabinet

- *circa 1910*

A French mahogany and satinwood cabinet with marble top over a moulded frieze drawer, the panelled doors with decorative inlay in satinwood with moulded front on cabriole legs and ormolu decoration.

- *162cm x 220cm x 42cm*
- £1,400 • Tredantiques

▽ Marquetry Cabinet

- *circa 1920*

An 18th-century style Dutch marquetry vitrine on a bombé chest base and standing on paw feet.

- *height 2m*
- £2,250 • Canonbury

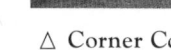

CANTERBURIES

△ **Mahogany Canterbury**

- *circa 1790*

Mahogany canterbury comprising four sections with a single side drawer with circular ring handle, raised on square tapered legs with original brass casters.

- *height 39cm*
- £1,950 • John Clay

△ **Mahogany Canterbury**

- *circa 1810*

A mahogany canterbury with two drawers, finials and turned legs with original brass castors.

- *height 52cm*
- £2,200 • Ronald G. Chambers

△ **Victorian Canterbury**

- *circa 1880*

Mahogany wood with turned supports and legs and one drawer.

- *height 56cm*
- £1,025 • Antiques Warehouse

▽ **Mahogany Canterbury**

- *circa 1815*

Mahogany canterbury with turned columns and legs with brass castors.

- *height 54cm*
- £2,800 • Tredantiques

▽ **Folio Stand**

- *1820*

Early 19th-century mahogany folio stand.

- *height 56cm*
- £4,000 • Graham Walpole

▽ **Walnut Canterbury**

- *circa 1880*

Victorian walnut canterbury with four sections with heavily carved and pierced floral designs, turned handles, and a single side drawer, the whole raised on turned legs with brass castors.

- *height 54cm*
- £1,295 • The Swan

△ **Regency Canterbury**

- *circa 1820*

A Regency mahogany canterbury with one drawer and four compartments and carved wreath decoration, on brass castors.

- *34cm x 65cm*
- £2,450 • C.H. Major

△ **Victorian Canterbury**

- *circa 1850*

Burr walnut with turned supports on original porcelain castors.

- *height 55cm*
- £1,400 • Judy Fox

▽ **Double Music Stand**

- *19th century*

English mahogany stand with lyre motif and carved triangular base.

- *adjustable height*
- £2,300 • Judy Fox

▽ **Music Stand**

- *circa 1920*

Regency-style painted, wrought-iron music canterbury with profuse floral pierced decoration and splayed legs.

- *height 68cm*
- £1,275 • Brown's

CHAIRS

▽ Turner's Chair

- *circa 1660*

A 17th-century turner's chair in ash, with profuse turning demonstrating the maker's skills.

- *height 1.28m*
- £4,500 • M.J. Bowdery

▽ Laburnum-Wood Chair

- *1700*

An extremely rare chair of laburnum wood, having a tall back with scrolled arms and bulbous turned legs.

- *116cm x 53cm x 43cm*
- £7,850 • Wakelin Linfield

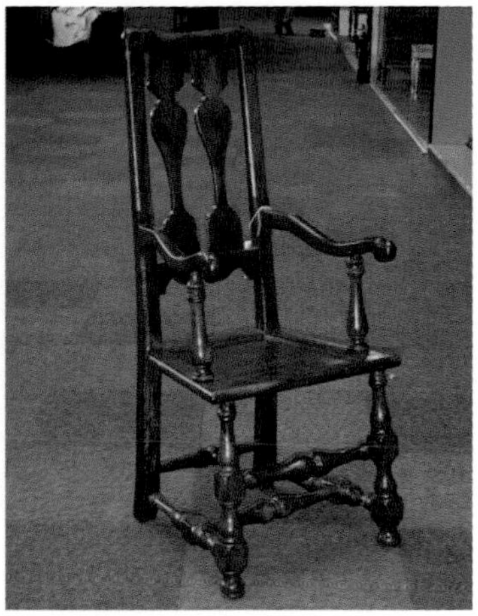

▷ Queen Anne Desk Chair

- *circa 1705*

Queen Anne walnut single desk chair with interesting and boldly shaped front legs and back splat.

- *102cm x 40cm*
- £1,750 • Wakelin Linfield

▽ Queen Anne Chair

- *circa 1700*

A very rare Queen Anne transitional chair with excellent colour and patina.

- *height 1.02m*
- £3,450 • Red Lion

◁ Oak Wainscot Chair

- *circa 1660*

An oak wainscot chair, with deep floral carved decoration, shaped arms and straight supports.

- *height 27cm*
- £3,650 • Rod Wilson

△ Tapestry Armchair

- *circa 1680*

A rare French hardwood armchair with tapestry cover.

- *height 1.21m*
- £6,500 • Raffety Walwyn

△ Queen Anne Armchair

- *circa 1710*

Very stylish and of bold proportions with repairs to frame.

- *height 83cm*
- £1,975 • Red Lion

▷ George I Oak Chairs

- *circa 1720*

A solid pair of George I oak chairs with good colour.

- *height 99cm*
- £595 • Red Lion

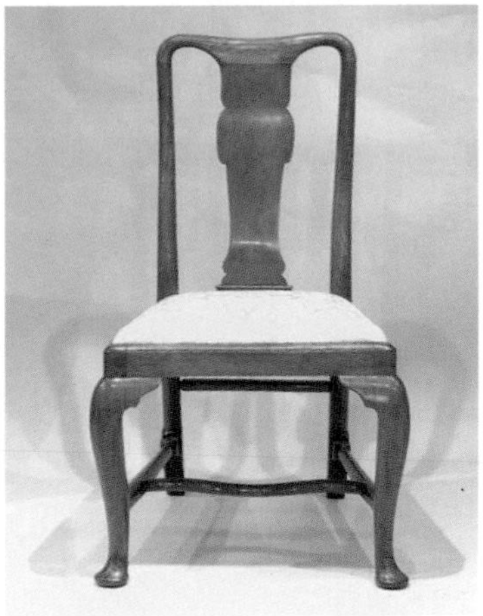

△ George I Walnut Chair

- *circa 1715*

One of a pair of George I walnut side chairs with vase-shaped splats, the front cabriole legs and back legs united by a turned wavy stretcher.

- *height 96cm*
- £6,800 • Wakelin Linfield

△ Oak-Panelled Armchair

- *1720*

George I oak-panelled chair with a recessed seat and baluster supports.

- *116cm x 63cm*
- £8,750 • Paul Hopwell

△ Ladder-Back Chair

- *circa 1730*

A single elm chair with turned legs and nipple decoration.

- *height 97cm*
- £125 • Castlegate

△ George II Irish Armchair

- *circa 1730*

A rare George II Irish mahogany armchair of outstanding quality and design, the chair is beautifully carved throughout and in exceptional condition for its age.

- *height 98cm*
- £6,500 • Freshfords

▽ Wing Chair

- *circa 1730*

George II wing chair with padded seat and back, with scrolled arms, on square legs.

- *176cm x 78cm*
- £2,750 • Rod Wilson

▷ Carved Walnut Armchairs

- *1740*

One of a pair of walnut armchairs, Louis XV, with carved apron, raised on cabriole legs.

- *106cm x 69cm x 60cm*
- £14,000 • O.F. Wilson

▽ Walnut Corner Chair

- *1740*

A walnut corner chair with shaped backrest and carved apron, standing on pad feet.

- *125cm x 76cm x 65cm*
- £1,400 • Midwinter

◁ Walnut Chairs

- *18th century*

A magnificent pair of early eighteenth century walnut chairs with original needlework and shaped apron with x-frame stretchers.

- *109cm x 71cm*
- £18,500 • Wakelin Linfield

△ Oriental Elm Chairs

- *18th century*

A pair of eighteenth century Southern Chinese elm chairs with cane seats.

- *104cm x 56cm x 48cm*
- £3,500 • Gerard Hawthorn

▽ George II Chairs

- *circa 1740*

One of a set of four oak chairs with spoon backrest and cabriole front legs.

- *height 98cm*
- £950 • Albany

▷ French Fauteuils

- *circa 1755*

One of a pair of open-arm gilt wood chairs, stamped 'Iocob'.

- *height 88cm*
- £5,500 • Michael Davidson

▽ Red Walnut Chairs

- *circa 1730*

One of a fine pair of red walnut chairs with cabriole legs.

- *height 96cm*
- £9,500 • Raffety Walwyn

△ Louis XV Fauteil

- *circa 1750*

Louis XV French giltwood fauteil, with carved floral designs raised on cabriole legs.

- £1,250 • Mora Upham

△ English Windsor Chair

- *circa 1750s*

Unusual rustic, mid-18th century, Windsor chair made from elm, with turned supports and solid seat, with good warm patina.

- *100cm x 53cm*
- £3,850 • Wakelin Linfield

△ Mahogany Chair

- *circa 1760*

A mahogany chair of the Chippendale period with carved scrolling decoration, pierced back splat and generous seat.

- *height 98cm*
- £1,650 • Riverbank

▽ Mahogany Chairs

- *circa 1755*

One of a set of six chairs with caned seats, pierced back, and sabre back legs.

- *height 82cm*
- £3,750 • Lesley Bragge

▽ Georgian Fruitwood Chairs

- *circa 1760*

Georgian fruitwood chairs of the Chippendale period, with unusual rosewood splat and square chamfered legs. Original colour and patina.

- *height 95cm*
- £485 • R.S. Antiques

▷ Chippendale Armchairs

- *circa 1760*

A pair of Chippendale-period mahogany armchairs with generously proportioned seats.

- *height 95cm*
- £26,000 • Norman Adams

◁ Fauteuils

- *circa 1760*

One of a pair of walnut and beechwood French chairs with floral tapestry.

- *height 1.15m*
- £28,000 • O.F. Wilson

△ Venetian Armchair

- *1760*

A Venetian armchair, with carved moulded back and front, scrolled padded arms and cabriole legs painted with pink foliate design.

- *108cm x 74cm x 64cm*
- £12,500 • O.F. Wilson

▽ Chippendale-Style Chairs

- *1760*

One of a pair of Chippendale-style mahogany chairs with carved back splat and straight square legs.

- *height 94cm*
- £575 • Red Lion

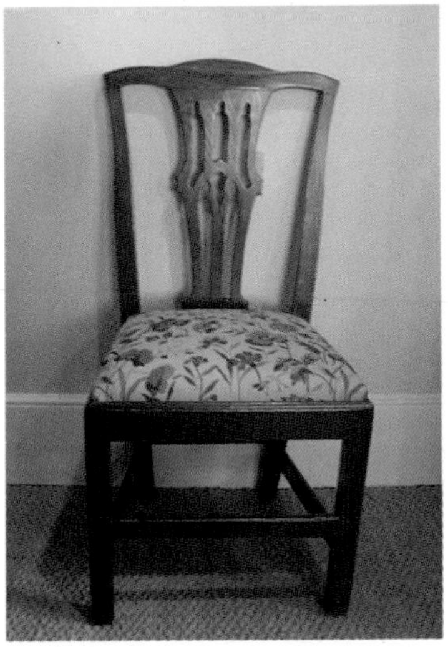

▽ Horseshoe-shaped chairs

- *circa 1850*

A pair of very low Chinese horseshoe-shaped back rail chairs.

- *82cm x 57cm*
- £1,480 • Gordon Reece

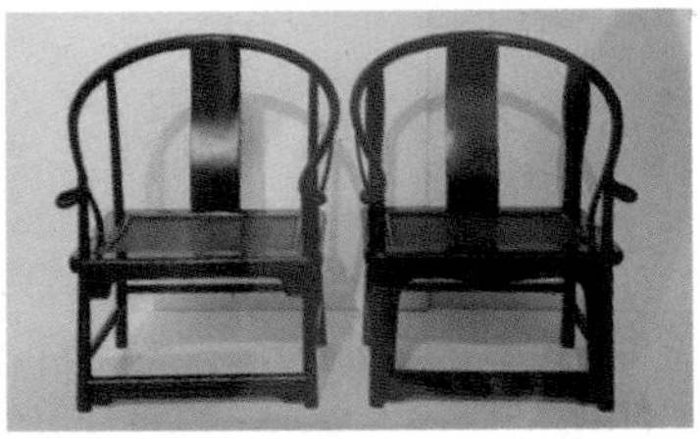

◁ Windsor Chair

- *circa 1760*

Windsor chair in ash and elm with comb back and cabriole legs.

- *height 1.08m*
- £5,800 • Raffety Walwyn

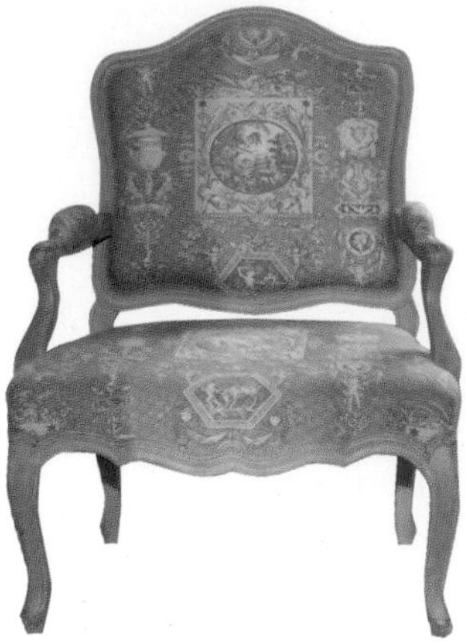

△ French Louis XV Fauteuils

• *circa 1760*
One of a pair of Louis XV fauteuils with curved top rail, inverted arm supports and serpentine front rail, raised on cabriole legs.
• *height 84cm*
• £5,250 • O.F. Wilson

△ Hepplewhite Armchairs

• *circa 1770*
One of a pair of shield-back Hepplewhite armchairs with the decoration restored as new.
• *height 83cm*
• £3,850 • P.L. James

▽ Painted Fauteuils

• *circa 1760*
One of a pair of beechwood fauteuils with oval backs and gilt foliate designs over cream paint. Stamped 'Premy'.
• *height 83cm*
• £7,800 • O.F. Wilson

▷ Louis XVI Side Chair

• *1780*
One of a set of four French giltwood dining chairs, with original cream paintwork and gilt pastel pink covers.
• *89cm x 43cm*
• £6,800 • Augustus Brandt

△ Chippendale Chair

• *circa 1780*
With a pierced vase-shaped splat, solid seat and square chamfered legs with stretchers.
• *height 95cm*
• £1,450 • M.J. Bowdery

◁ Hepplewhite Chair

• *circa 1780*
A fine single chair in mahogany with carved cabriole legs.
• *height 91cm*
• £1,950 • J. de Haan

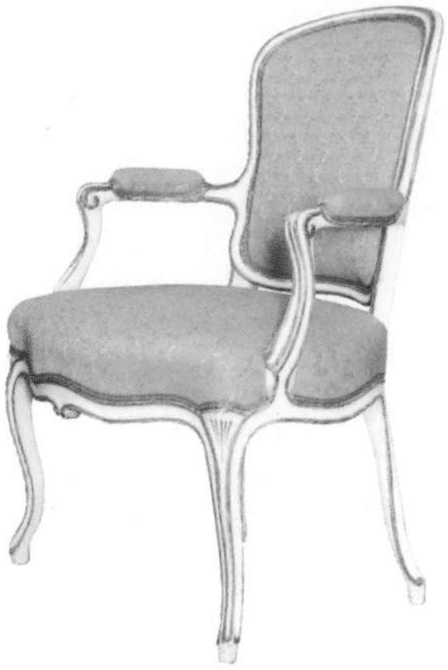

△ French Fauteuil

• *circa 1770*
With terracotta highlights, light-blue cloth and floral designs.
• *height 91cm*
• £2,200 • O.F. Wilson

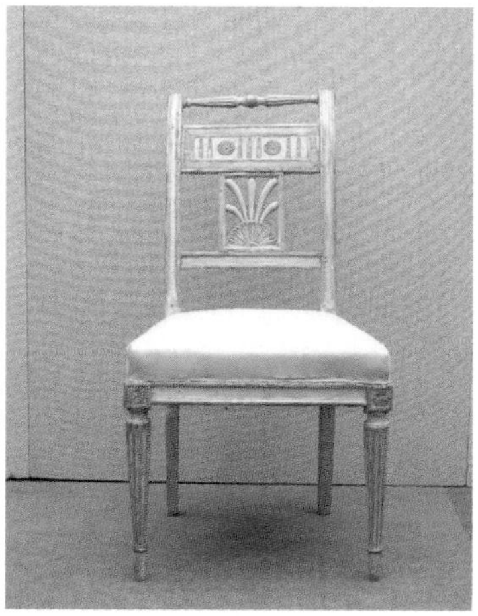

▽ Mahogany Hall Chairs

• *circa 1775*
One of a pair of English mahogany hall chairs inspired by designs from Chippendale's pattern books, the circular carved and pierced backs in the form of spoked wheels, the dished seats shaped to reflect this pattern, the turned front legs decorated with ring turning.
• *95cm x 35cm*
• £10,500 • Wakelin Linfield

▽ Windsor Chair

• *circa 1760*
Windsor chair with excellent colour and a wide seat.
• *height 1.02m*
• £1,800 • Red Lion

▽ Hepplewhite Armchair

• *circa 1780*
Ebonised hepplewhite armchair with shield back, curved arm supports and straight tapered legs with hand-painted designs of trailing foliage and ribboning.
• *height 96.5cm*
• £4,450 • O.F. Wilson

▽ Swedish High-SidedArmchairs

• *18th century*
A pair of Swedish armchairs with high backs and sides with original velvet and tapestry.
• *height 95cm*
• £3,200 • Solaris

△ Louis XVI Chairs

- *circa 1780*

One of a pair of lyre-backed, Louis XVI chairs, with a carved oval seat rail and pale green paint, raised on turned legs.

- *height 92cm*
- £8,500 • O.F. Wilson

△ Sheraton Chair

- *circa 1780*

An English green-painted chair decorated with floral designs.

- *height 90cm*
- £4,600 • O.F. Wilson

▽ Swedish Chairs

- *18th century*

Pair of late eighteenth-century Swedish open armchairs, with carved back splats on cabriole legs.

- *139cm x 63cm*
- £9,900 • Heytesbury

▽ English Hepplewhite Chair

- *circa 1780*

English Hepplewhite oval-back chair, with three Prince of Wales peacock feathers carved into the back splat, above a shaped front rail, raised on elegant cabriole legs, with floral and shell motifs.

- *height 84cm*
- £5,500 • Mora Upham

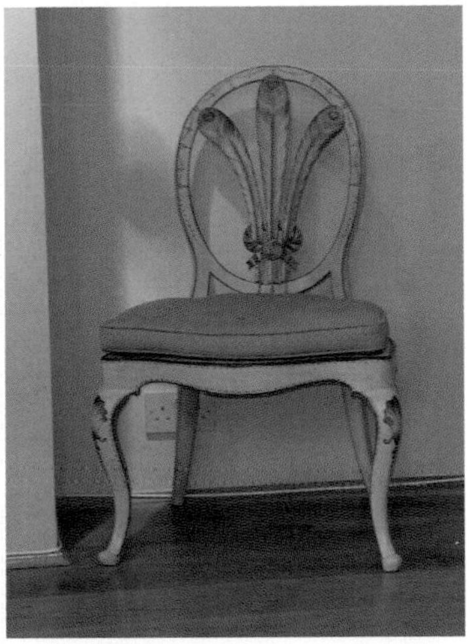

△ Hepplewhite Chairs

- *circa 1780*

Two from a set of eight mahogany shield-back dining chairs.

- *height 92.5cm*
- £60,000 • Norman Adams

▽ Flat-Back Fauteuil

- *circa 1780*

A French Louis XV flat-back fauteuil, with serpentine drop-in seat, in moulded frame, on cabriole legs.

- *height 94cm*
- £7,500 • Butchoff

△ Carved Mahogany Chair

- *1780*

Mahogany chair with ribbon carving to the back and top rail, on scrolled cabriole legs with hoofed feet.

- *101cm x 51cm*
- £1,550 • Sign of the Times

▷ East Anglian Reclining Chair

- *18th century*

Unusual back-tilting elm chair, known as an East Anglian reclining chair.

- *117cm x 68cm x 43cm*
- £3,950 • Lacquer Chest

◁ Italian Gondola Chairs

- *circa 1780*

A pair of 18th-century Venetian gondola chairs, in wood, part-covered in leather with silver damask upholstery and extravagant baroque lines.

- *width at base 94cm*
- £4,250 • French Country

△ French Walnut Chairs

- *circa 1780*

One of a pair of French walnut open bergères standing on cabriole legs.
- £3,800 • Mora Upham

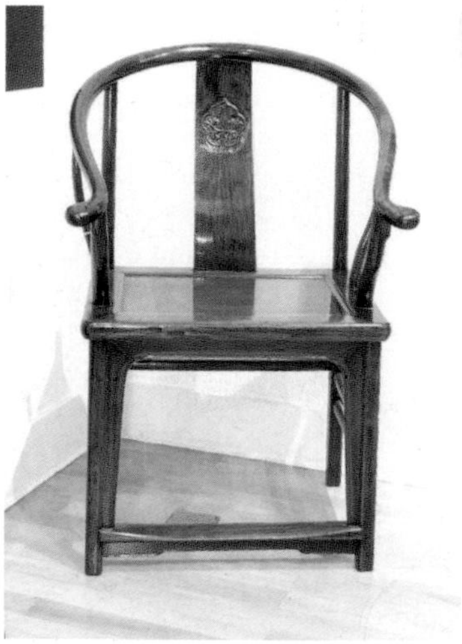

△ Horseshoe-Back Chairs

- *18th century*

One of a pair of Chinese antique horseshoe-back chairs, each bearing a moon symbol.
- *97cm x 24cm x 18cm*
- £2,680 • Gordon Reece

▽ Sheraton Chairs

- *circa 1780*

One of a set of eight singles and two carvers with Sheraton decoration.
- *height 80cm*
- £15,000 • P.L. James

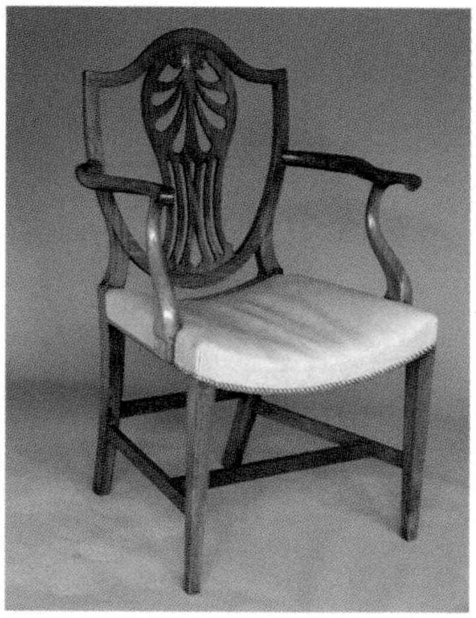

▽ Hepplewhite Armchair

- *1785*

Hepplewhite mahogany armchair, with shield back and shaped arm rests with scrolled terminals on wavy supports, the whole raised on square tapered legs.
- *98cm x 57cm*
- £26,000 • Wakelin Linfield

▷ Painted Fauteuils

- *1780*

One of four painted Louis XVI French fauteuils with scrolled back and straight arms on turned legs.
- *86cm x 60cm x 47cm*
- £9,000 • O.F. Wilson

◁ Shield-Back Chair

- *1780*

Mahogany shield-back armchair on square tapered legs.
- *height 95cm*
- £2,950 • Ashcombe House

△ Hepplewhite Chair

- *circa 1780*

Cherrywood Hepplewhite elbow-chair, with shaped arms standing on square straight tapered legs, and padded horsehair-covered seat.
- *height 92cm*
- £995 • A.I.G.

△ Hepplewhite-Period Chair

- *circa 1780*

In mahogany with pierced backrest and turned legs.
- *height 88cm*
- £520 • Castlegate

▽ Oak Chair

- *circa 1780*

A country oak chair with turned decoration on a solid seat.
- *height 91cm*
- £195 • Lacquer Chest

▽ Set of Dining Chairs

- *circa 1780*

A set of six 18th-century fruitwood dining chairs, set on turned, candlestick legs, with classical motifs throughout.
- £3,200 • Sieff

▽ George III Armchairs

- *circa 1790*

A pair of beech, shield-back armchairs with fine original painted decoration.
- *height 97.5cm*
- £30,000 • Norman Adams

▽ French Painted Chair

- *circa 1790*

A painted chair with portcullis back and octagonal, tapered legs.

- *height 92cm*
- £1,250 • Riverbank

▽ Sheraton Armchair

- *circa 1795*

A Sheraton-period painted and gilded armchair.

- *height 88.5cm*
- £8,000 • Norman Adams

▽ Rosewood Chairs

- *circa 1800*

A rare pair of French rosewood chairs with undecorated rectangular backs with square-section upright supports. The shaped arms with low relief carved decoration to the upper surface, terminating in very well carved rams heads above scrolled supports with low relief carved decoration to the front. With a straight seat rail above an apron.

- *1m x 59.5cm*
- £15,500 • Anthony Outred

△ Desk Chair

- *19th century*

Oak desk chair, with moulded back and arms and scrolled lyre-shape back.

- *84cm x 50cm*
- £295 • Old Cinema

△ George III Armchair

- *circa 1790*

Mahogany open armchair with moulded serpentine toprail, pierced, carved decoration to the back splat and a upholstered seat, the whole on bun feet.

- *height 89cm*
- £1,250 • Westland & Co.

▷ Windsor Chair

- *circa 1800*

A rare ash and elm windsor chair with crinoline stetcher.

- *height 1.01m*
- £1,795 • Red Lion

▽ Child's Rocking chair

- *circa 1790*

An 18th-century turned ash and elm child's rocking chair.

- *height 51cm*
- £265 • Castlegate

▽ Child's Highchair

- *circa 1800*

A bergère highchair with turned front and splayed rear legs. Easily converted to a table and chair, with a central screw to table base.

- *height 94cm*
- £1,350 • John Clay

◁ George III Chair

- *circa 1800*

George III mahogany ladder-back chair in a Chippendale style, standing on square-section legs.

- *93cm x 54cm*
- £1,200 • Sign of the Times

▽ Shield-Back Dining Chairs

- *circa 1800*

One of a set of eight mahogany Hepplewhite-style shield-back dining chairs, with two carvers.

- *height 80cm*
- £7,450 • Great Grooms

▽ Library Chair

- *circa 1810*

A deep button-backed library chair with original upholstery.

- *height 1.06m*
- £2,200 • Riverbank

▽ Gilt Chairs

- *1805*

A pair of gilt fauteuil chairs made for the palace of Louis Bonaparte, King of Holland, by Jacobs Desmalter.

- *100cm x 76cm*
- £85,000 • Pimlico

▽ Court Chairs

- *circa 1810*

One of a pair of Chinese court chairs of simple elegant form.

- *100cm x 61cm*
- £3,100 • Gordon Reece

▽ Regency Chairs

- *circa 1820*

One of a set of restored Regency chairs including six singles and two armchairs.

- *height 80cm*
- £12,800 • P.L. James

△ Regency Mahogany Chair

- *circa 1810*

Regency mahogany elbow chair, with curved arms and turned legs and leather seat.

- *height 89cm*
- £995 • Old Cinema

△ lst Empire Chair

- *circa 1810*

French lst Empire, giltwood chair with carved stylised floral decoration.

- £3,800 • Mora Upham

▽ Regency Giltwood Armchair

- *1810*

A Regency giltwood armchair with painted floral decoration on tapered legs.

- *82cm x 53cm*
- £2,750 • Pimlico

▷ Regency Armchair

- *circa 1820*

A Regency rosewood armchair with scrolled back and arms on cabriole legs.

- *152cm x 60cm x 50cm*
- £2,000 • John Nicholas

△ Ladder-Back Chairs

- *1820*

One of a set of six ladder-back chairs with turned decoration on hoof feet, the carvers with splayed arms.

- *99cm x 57cm*
- £375 • Red Lion

◁ Empire Bergère

- *circa 1815*

Mahogany Empire bergère, with turned top rail and curved, padded arms.

- *height 94cm*
- £2,850 • O.F. Wilson

△ Oak Country Chair

- *1810*

One of a pair of oak ladder-back chairs with a rush seat, standing on turned legs and pad feet.

- *height 104cm*
- £495 • Old Cinema

▽ Chinese Chairs

- *circa 1820*

One of a rare pair of tall-backed Chinese hardwood chairs.

- *height 82cm*
- £680 • P.L. James

△ Swedish Empire-Style Chairs

• *circa 1820*
Pair of Swedish mahogany Empire-style chairs, with gilt decoration on sabre back legs.
• *height 80cm*
• £2,700 • R. Cavendish

△ Pierced-Back Armchair

• *circa 1820*
A mahogany armchair with pierced back splat and needlepoint seat panel depicting exotic birds, standing on scrolled cabriole legs.
• *92cm x 65cm x 57cm*
• £780 • Ranby Hall

▽ Provincial Fauteuil

• *circa 1820*
An oversized French provincial walnut open armchair, with escargot feet, covered in moleskin.
• *width 1.15m*
• £1,950 • French Country

▽ Leather Library Chair

• *circa 1825*
A rosewood library chair with moulded and shaped arms reminiscent of the lyre form.
• *height 1.02m*
• £10,500 • Wakelin Linfield

▷ Mahogany Dining Chair

• *circa 1820*
One of a set of five Regency mahogany dining chairs, with carved back rest and supports, raised on tapering, turned legs, with carved decoration.
• *height 82cm*
• £2,300 • Hill Farm

◁ Venetian Chair

• *1820*
Venetian Rococo-style carved fruitwood armchair, in original condition.
• *104cm x 84cm*
• £8,000 • Augustus Brandt

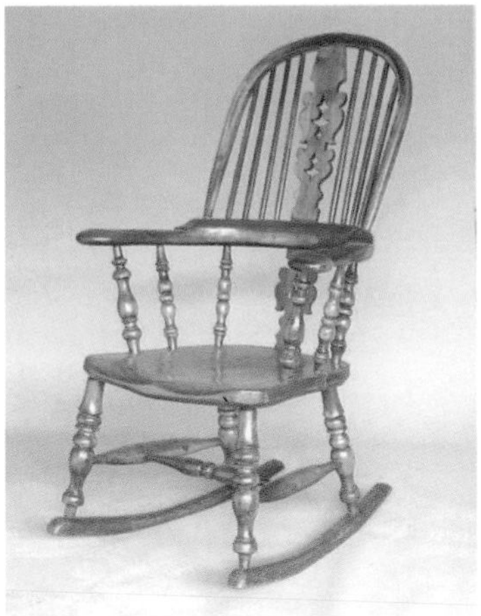

△ Yew-wood Rocking Chair

• *circa 1820s*
Yew-wood early 19th-century rocking chair, with carved and turned decoration.
• *105cm x 49cm*
• £1,750 • Wakelin Linfield

△ Child's Chair

• *circa 1820*
Provincial child's chair with good colour and patination.
• *87cm x 30cm x 31cm*
• £375 • Rod Wilson

▽ French Mahogany Chair

• *1830*
French mahogany chair featuring a carved back with scrolled top rail, on turned legs with pad feet.
• *91cm x 49cm*
• £560 • John Clay

▽ Italian Carver Chairs

• *circa 1820*
A spectacular pair of Italian walnut carver chairs with ornately carved mythological dog's heads to arms and back and heavy leaf decoration to legs.
• *153cm x 81cm x 61cm*
• £22,000 • Simon Hatchwell

▽ Pair of Fauteuils

• *circa 1820*
A pair of early 19th-century French mahogany fauteuils with original tapestry upholstery.
• £1,900 • Sieff

△ **Child's Armchair**

- *circa 1830*

Nineteenth-century ash and elm Windsor child's armchair.

- *92cm x 48cm x 42cm*
- £795 • Rod Wilson

△ **English Faux-Bamboo Chairs**

- *circa 1830*

One of a set of four English faux-bamboo chairs, with cane seats, and splayed front legs.

- *85.5cm x 44.5cm x 38cm*
- £2,750 • O.F. Wilson

▽ **Nursing Chair**

- *circa 1830*

Rosewood nursing chair with original rose-decorated upholstery, on turned legs with castors.

- *89cm x 52cm*
- £950 • John Clay

▽ **Regency Chair**

- *circa 1830*

Regency rosewood chair with scrolled top rail, splayed back legs and turned front legs.

- *84cm x 51cm*
- £980 • Lacquer Chest

▷ **Victorian Low Chair**

- *19th century*

A walnut low chair with carved decoration and turned legs terminating in castors.

- *height 76cm*
- £695 • Old Cinema

◁ **Library Chair**

- *circa 1840*

A Victorian library buttoned slipperback chair on castors.

- *height 87cm*
- £1,850 • C. Preston

△ **Chinese Horseshoe Chairs**

- *19th century*

A pair of Chinese horseshoe-backed chairs.

- *103cm x 64cm*
- £1,600 • Gordon Reece

△ **Convertible Child's Chair**

- *early 19th century*

A bergère highchair with turned front and splayed rear legs. Easily converted to a table and chair, with a central screw to table base.

- *59cm x 42cm*
- £1,356 • John Clay

▽ **Mahogany Elbow Chair**

- *circa 1835*

With scrolled arm rests, turned front legs and sabre back legs.

- *height 81cm*
- £400 • Castlegate

▽ **Rosewood Chairs**

- *circa 1840*

One of a set of four rosewood balloon-back chairs, the carved back decorated with floral swags, on cabriole legs.

- *height 85cm*
- £1,650 • Great Grooms

▽ **French Fauteuil**

- *circa 1840*

A well-proportioned French fauteuil. The carved beech frame retaining traces of original painted decoration.

- *100cm x 73cm*
- £5,500 • Wakelin Linfield

△ Gothic Hall Chairs

- *circa 1840*

One of a pair of Gothic chairs with period architectural back with the letters 'A.S.'.

- *height 92cm*
- £495 • Castlegate

△ Egyptian Armchair

- *circa 1840*

An unusual Egyptian inlaid walnut armchair.

- *depth 85cm*
- £5,800 • D. Martin-Taylor

▽ Victorian Carved Chair

- *1840*

Walnut chair with shield back, carved top rail and deeply carved cabriole c-scroll legs, and stretcher.

- *116cm x 55cm*
- £1,200 • Sign of the Times

▽ Ladder-Back Chair

- *1850*

A Lancashire elmwood ladder-back chair with an unusually high back, rush seating, and turned legs.

- *123cm x 56cm x 42cm*
- £395 • Lacquer Chest

◁ Spanish Hall Chairs

- *circa 1850*

A pair of decorative Spanish walnut hall chairs with well-carved mushroom engravings to the front panels.

- *height 80cm*
- £2,000 • Gabrielle de Giles

△ Oak Armchair

- *circa 1840*

With button back, turned fluted front legs and carved decoration.

- *height 85cm*
- £850 • John Clay

△ Grotto Harp Stool

- *circa 1850*

A grotto stool with scallop-shell seat on acanthus cabriole legs and claw feet. The whole in gilt.

- *height 65cm*
- £1,600 • Lynda Franklin

▽ Country Armchair

- *circa 1840*

An ash and elm country armchair with good patination, with turned arm supports and legs.

- *height 91cm*
- £195 • Castlegate

▽ Victorian Library Chair

- *circa 1850*

A mahogany Victorian library chair, with scrolled arms and turned front legs.

- *height 79cm*
- £1,150 • Old Cinema

◁ Hall Chair

- *circa 1850*

An English mahogany mid 19th-century hall chair, with scrolled arms and an extensively turned frame, the whole resting on bun feet. The chair is in perfect condition, and reupholstered, with a red and gold Gothic pattern.

- *height 98cm*
- £1,800 • Gabrielle de Giles

▽ Neo-Gothic Armchair

- *19th century*

Impressively carved chair, with Gothic-syle tracery, twisted and fluted decoration and solid-wood seat, the whole on turned legs.

- *height 1.31m*
- £1,750 • Old Cinema

▽ Folding Campaign Chair

- *circa 1860s*

Victorian folding campaign chair made from mahogany with cane seat.

- *70cm x 37cm*
- £395 • Old Cinema

△ French Walnut Chairs

- *19th century*

One of a pair of walnut chairs with carved leaf decoration and scrolling designs, on cabriole legs.

- *height 83cm*
- £1,450 • Lynda Franklin

△ Victorian High Chair

- *circa 1860*

Victorian ash and elm child's high chair, with turned decoration.

- *height 99cm*
- £395 • The Swan

▽ Open Armchair

- *circa 1860*

A mahogany George III-style open arm chair with padded back and seat, and s-shaped arms, standing on cabriole legs with claw-and-ball feet.

- *91cm x 70cm*
- £1,880 • Ranby Hall

▷ Balloon-Back Chair

- *1860*

Victorian mahogany balloon-back armchair with scrolled decoration to arms and legs.

- *45cm x 73cm x 87cm*
- £3,200 • Judy Fox

▽ Dutch Oak Chair

- *circa 1860*

A Dutch carved oak chair. with carved oval panels with foliate designs, standing on cabriole legs.

- *88cm x 42cm*
- £850 • Tredantiques

◁ Irish Desk Chairs

- *19th century*

A pair of mahogany chairs with carved decoration to backrest.

- *height 93cm*
- £1,125 • Old Cinema

△ Mahogany Rocking Chair

- *circa 1860*

Rocking chair with new upholstery, scrolled arms and turned legs.

- *height 1.04m*
- £725 • Castlegate

▽ Victorian Lacquered Chair

- *circa 1860*

Small Victorian black lacquered chair with mother-of-pearl inlay, wicker back and seat and elongated arms, standing on turned legs with brass castors.

- *height 75cm*
- £995 • Serendipity

△ French Mahogany Side Chairs

- *circa 1860*

One of a pair of French mahogany side chairs with brass finials on the top rail.

- *height 95cm*
- £3,250 • Serendipity

△ Victorian Rosewood Chair

- *circa 1860*

Victorian rosewood spoon-back armchair, finely carved with floral designs and raised on scrolled legs fitted with castors.

- *height 96cm*
- £1,895 • A.I.G.

▽ Painted Child's Chair

- *19th century*

A child's ash, painted chair with a high straight comb back, standing on turned tapered legs.

- *83cm x 30cm*
- £3,600 • Paul Hopwell

▽ Folding Campaign Chair

- *circa 1870*

A folding campaign chair in green upholstery.

- *height 82cm*
- £330 • Lacquer Chest

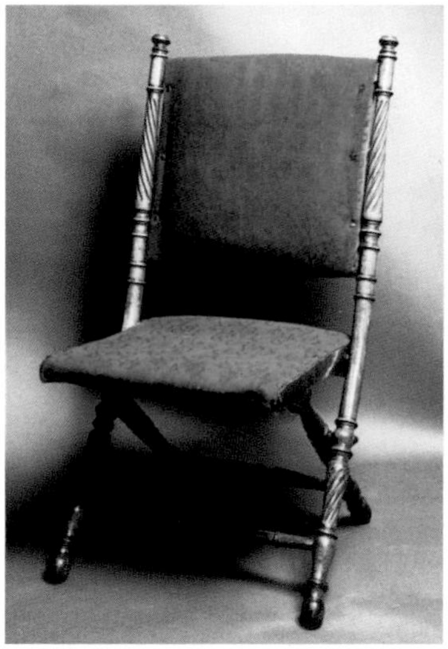

▷ Chippendale-Style Elbow Chair

- *1870*

A Chippendale-chinoiserie-style ribbon back chair with scrolled cabriole legs on claw and ball feet.

- *107cm x 64cm x 49cm*
- £1,500 • Judy Fox

◁ Victorian Tub Chair

- *1870*

A small mahogany tub chair with buttoned leather padded seat, and lyre-shaped back splat, on turned legs.

- *50cm x 72cm x 72cm*
- £1,275 • Old Cinema

△ Victorian Oak Chair

- *circa 1870*

Victorian oak country chair with shaped back and turned supports, above a solid seat, raised on turned legs, with good patina.

- *height 87cm*
- £450 • Hill Farm

△ Reclining Chair

- *1860*

Reclining chair with scrolled arms and turned legs on original brass castors with original leather upholstery.

- *101cm x 56cm x 65cm*
- £1,200 • Lacquer Chest

▽ Victorian Chairs

- *circa 1860*

One of a very attractive pair of walnut single chairs with carved and pierced backs, on cabriole legs with escargot feet.

- *height 87cm*
- £575 • M.J. Bowdery

▽ Six Mahogany Chairs

- *circa 1870*

One of a set of six mahogany and brass inlaid dining chairs in Gillows' style.

- £3,200 • Mora Upham

▽ Mahogany Dining Chairs

- *19th century*

Six chairs with moulded camel backs and good patination.

- *height 96.5cm*
- £7,500 • J. Collins

△ Venetian Chairs

- *circa 1875*

One of a set of six 19th-century Venetian chairs with interlaced backs and original silk covers.

- *height 91cm*
- £6,000 • Wakelin Linfield

△ American Rocker

- *circa 1880*

Rocking chair with profuse turned decoration and tartan upholstery.

- *height 1.03m*
- £395 • Castlegate

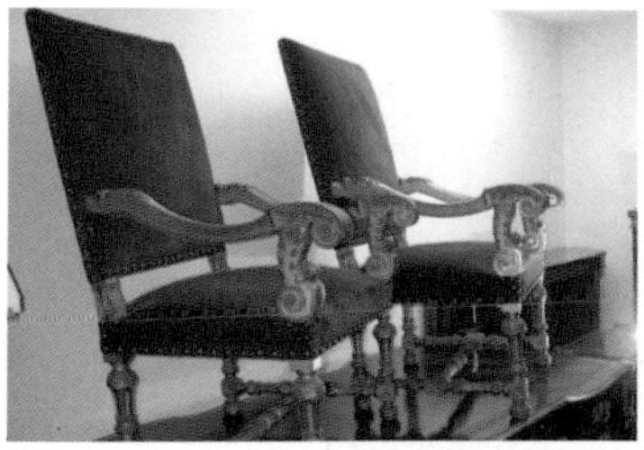

△ Gilt Walnut Chairs

- *1880*

A pair of gilt walnut French chairs, with high padded backs, scrolled arms and turned baluster legs.

- *1.58m x 68cm x 82cm*
- £4,500 • Judy Fox

▽ Victorian Nursing Chair

- *1880*

Victorian Nursing chair with a circular padded seat and a padded back.

- *height 74cm*
- £550 • Old Cinema

▽ Louis XV-Style Armchair

- *circa 1880*

French walnut armchair with carved floral decoration.

- *height 87cm*
- £1,050 • The French Room

▽ Chippendale-Style Dining Chairs

- *circa 1880*

Chippendale-style carver from a set of eight chairs with carved, pierced splats and cabriole legs on claw and ball feet.

- *height 96cm*
- £8,750 • Serendipity

△ Victorian Sofa Chairs

- *19th century*

One of a pair of Victorian sofa chairs.

- *height 40cm*
- £1,650 • Fiona McDonald

△ French Desk Chair

- *circa 1880*

French mahogany desk chair in the Louis XV style, with gilt ormolu mounts and carved front rail.

- *height 95cm*
- £1,950 • Hatchwell

△ Lancashire Spindle-Back Chairs

- *circa 1880*

One of a set of ten Harlequin Lancashire rush seat spindle-back chairs.

- *height 98cm*
- £6,750 • Gerald Brodie

▽ Hepplewhite-Style Carver

- *1880*

One of a set of eight mahogany Hepplewhite-style, dining chairs including two carvers.

- £11,000 • Butchoff

▽ French Armchair

- *circa 1880*

Brass inlaid with gilt decoration on turned and fluted legs.

- *height 1.1m*
- £1,550 • Youll's

▽ Leather Library Chair

- *1885*

Mahogany ox-blood leather upholstered library chair, with curved arms raised on sabre back legs.

- *53cm x 65cm x 57cm*
- £995 • Old Cinema

△ French Side Chairs

- *circa 1880*

One of a pair of French side chairs, with carved back and original padded seat cover, raised on cabriole legs, with escargot feet.

- *height 89cm*
- £575 • **The Swan**

△ Regency-Style Armchair

- *circa 1880*

Regency-revival armchair with mahogany frame carved with honeysuckle and harebell motifs, raised on moulded bun feet.

- *83cm x 54cm*
- £1,395 • **R. & S. Antiques**

▽ French Walnut Chairs

- *1880*

One of a pair of French bergères with walnut frames, carved with a fruit motif on cabriole legs.

- *1.5m x 70cm x 54cm*
- £2,800 • **J. Fox**

▽ Biedermeier-Style Chairs

- *circa 1885*

One of a pair of Swedish birchwood chairs covered in damask fabric.

- *height 85cm*
- £2,900 • **R. Cavendish**

▷ Leather Desk Chair

- *circa 1885*

Leather and mahogany chair with brass stud work, on tapered legs.

- *height 99cm*
- £260 • **Youll's**

◁ Elbow Chair

- *1890*

One of a pair of mahogany elbow chairs with foliate carving on slender turned legs with cane back and seat.

- *height 97cm*
- £1,450 • **Old Cinema**

△ Beechwood Child's Chair

- *1880*

A child's beechwood chair with cane seat and spindle back on turned legs.

- *42cm x 22.5cm x 20cm*
- £235 • **Lacquer Chest**

△ Swedish Armchair

- *circa 1880*

Swedish armchair, with gilded floral decoration to the back rail, carved and gilded supports to the arms and original neutral paint. Part of a set comprising a sofa, armchair and four single chairs.

- *height 1.06m*
- £18,500 set • **Wakelin Linfield**

▽ Victorian Bedroom Chair

- *1880*

A Victorian chair with cane seat, painted a soft green, decorated with red autumn leaves, standing on sabre legs

- *81cm x 46cm x 38cm*
- £340 • **Lacquer Chest**

▽ Walnut Armchair

- *circa 1890*

Walnut open armchair with carved top rail and arm supports, button upholstered back and seat, raised on cabriole legs, with original castors.

- *76cm x 70cm*
- £695 • **The Swan**

▽ French Armchairs

- *circa 1890*

A pair of ornately carved French painted armchairs with original cream paint, on cabriole legs.

- *height 92cm*
- £2,850 • **Tredantiques**

△ Oak Dining Chair

- *circa 1890*

One of a set of four late Victorian oak dining chairs, in the Chippendale style, raised on square straight legs.

- *100cm x 50cm*
- £695 • Old Cinema

△ Child's Chippendale-Style Chair

- *circa 1890*

Chippendale-style mahogany child's chair, with pierced back splat, serpentine top rail and straight tapered legs.

- *height 78cm*
- £475 • The Swan

▽ Arts & Crafts Chair

- *circa 1890*

Russian Arts & Crafts chair of triangular outline, with a tablet back, profusely inlaid with numerous wood specimens including walnut, mahogany, satinwood and harewood in geometric patterns. The shaped back splat is decorated with inlaid woods, with decorated arms issuing from tablet back, and an overstuffed shaped brown leather seat. Raised on turned legs of alternate specimen woods.

- *86.5cm x 58.5cm*
- £3,400 • Anthony Outred

▽ Arts & Crafts Chair

- *1890*

Arts and Crafts chair with curved arms and turned legs, with pressed brass inlay back.

- *height 115cm*
- £550 • Old Cinema

◁ Mahogany Curved-Back Library Chair

- *circa 1890*

A George I-style mahogany library chair with curved back and studded leather seat on cabriole legs.

- *139cm x 55cm*
- £1,875 • Harpur Deardren

△ Elm and Beech Chair

- *circa 1890*

Elm and beech kitchen chair.

- *height 97cm*
- £65 • Nicholas Mitchell

△ French Walnut Chair

- *1890*

French walnut chair with carved mask decoration, standing on a cross stretcher base.

- *height 87cm*
- £595 • Old Cinema

▽ Mahogany Child's Chair

- *circa 1890*

Unusual child's mahogany corner chair, with heavily carved floral decoration.

- *height 60cm*
- £425 • The Swan

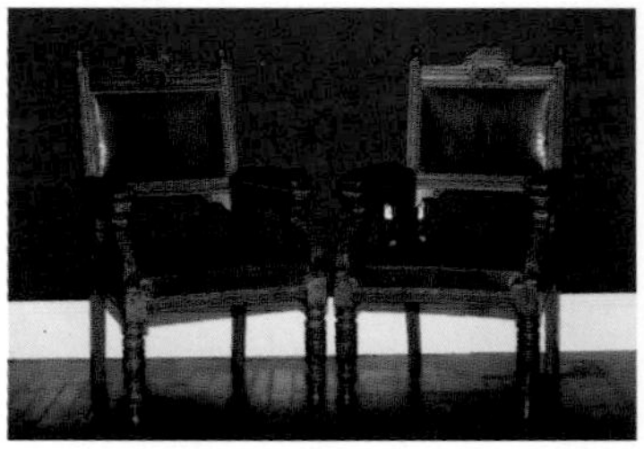

▽ Oak Armchairs

- *19th century*

A pair of 19th-century oak armchairs with leather upholstery.

- *height 1.07m*
- £2,750 • Brown's

▽ Oak Elbow Chair

- *circa 1890*

Late Victorian oak elbow chair, with padded and buttoned top rail.

- *90cm x 55cm*
- £395 • Old Cinema

◁ Elm Elbow Chair

- *circa 1890s*

One of a pair of elbow chairs in elm from southern China, of sculptural 'oxbow' form, from a merchant's house.

- *125cm x 60cm*
- £6,000 • Wakelin Linfield

△ Chinese Elmwood Chair

- *circa 1890*

One of a pair of Chinese elmwood lacquer chairs from Zhejiang Province, Eastern China.

- *height 96cm*
- £980 • Younger

△ Satinwood Cane Chair

- *circa 1900*

A Hepplewhite-style satinwood cane chair with painted decoration. Oval caned back and seat standing on turned legs.

- *143cm x 56cm x 52cm*
- £1,495 • John Nicholas

△ Officer's Chair

- *1901–10*

Edwardian officer's revolving comb-back chair on brass castors.

- *88cm x x 53cm*
- £665 • Old Cinema

▽ Wing Chair

- *circa 1899*

19th-century William and Mary-style wingchair, with generous scrolled arm rests, raised on turned legs.

- *125cm x 105cm*
- £5,950 • Wakelin Linfield

▽ Child's Rocking Chair

- *circa 1900*

A turned child's rocking chair in ash and elm.

- *height 85cm*
- £145 • Castlegate

▽ Biedermeier-Style Chairs

- *circa 1915*

One of a pair of Swedish masur birch chairs in cream ultra-suede.

- *height 93cm*
- £4,900 • R. Cavendish

△ Painted Fauteuils

- *early 20th century*

A pair of French painted fauteuils in the manner of Louis XVI.

- *87cm x 60cm x 58cm*
- £350 • Westland & Co.

△ Satinwood Chair

- *circa 1900*

A satinwood armchair with a turned spindle rail back and cane seat, standing on turned legs, with painted floral designs.

- *131cm x 52cm x 48cm*
- £1,650 • John Nicholas

△ Nursing Chair

- *1910*

An Edwardian rosewood inlaid nursing chair with lyre back, standing on square tapered legs with a spade feet.

- *height 74cm*
- £895 • Great Grooms

▽ Empire-Style Chairs

- *circa 1900*

One of a pair of Swedish, mahogany chairs with sabre back legs and gilded decoration to the backrest.

- *height 84cm*
- £2,300 • R. Cavendish

▽ Set of Chairs

- *circa 1900*

A set of four painted and gilded Northern Italian chairs with shell and mushroom motifs, on cabriole legs.

- *height 85cm*
- £1,450 • Andrew Bewick

▽ Swedish Mahogany Armchairs

- *circa 1900*

One of a pair of Empire-style Swedish mahogany armchairs with a lyre-shaped front, on scrolled legs.

- *height 83cm*
- £4,500 • R. Cavendish

CHAISES LONGUES & DAY BEDS

△ English Chaise Longue

- *circa 1820*

A Regency green watered silk, faux-rosewood chaise longue with carving.

- *length 1.88m*
- **£2,900** • **Mora Upham**

▽ Mahogany Chaise Longue

- *circa 1830*

Fine mahogany William IV covered chaise longue.

- *length 1.47m*
- **£8,500** • **Butchoff**

▽ Walnut Settee

- *circa 1860*

English, canvas with button back, standing on cabriole legs.

- *length 2.2m*
- **£4,950** • **S. & A. Thompson**

△ Victorian Chaise Longue

- *circa 1860*

Victorian mahogany chaise longue with curved button back and scrolled arm, standing on turned legs with original brass castors.

- *length 150cm*
- **£1,375** • **The Swan**

▽ Victorian Chaise Longue

- *circa 1870*

Recently upholstered. Original marble castors and brass fittings.

- *length 2.13m*
- **£1,900** • **Gabrielle de Giles**

△ Rosewood Chaise Longue

- *circa 1860*

A mid-Victorian rosewood chaise longue, with finely carved rose decoration, scrolled arms, moulded serpentine apron and original porcelain castors.

- *length 186cm*
- **£2,800** • **Drummonds**

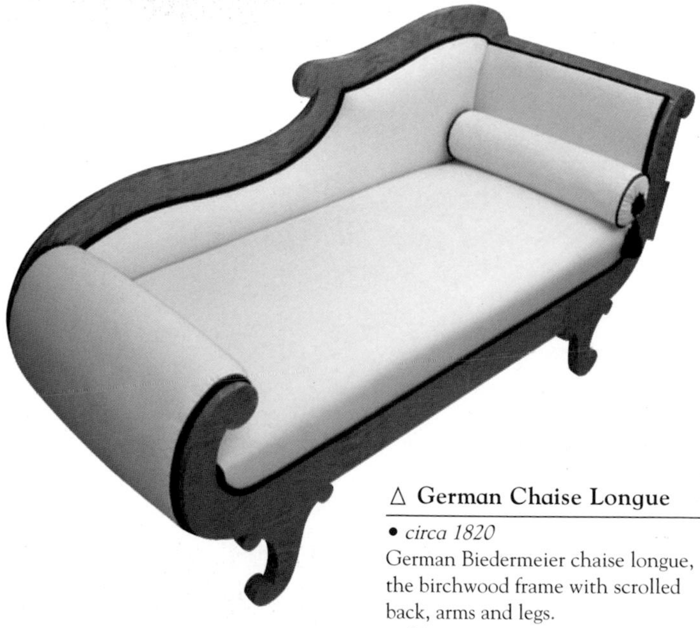

△ German Chaise Longue

- *circa 1820*

German Biedermeier chaise longue, the birchwood frame with scrolled back, arms and legs.

- *95cm x 183cm x 70cm*
- **£9,800** • **R. Cavendish**

▷ Cuban Chaise Longue

- *1880*

A Cuban mahogany bergère longue with serpentine back and padded seat, on claw feet.

- *91cm x 193cm x 94cm*
- **£5,750** • **Old Cinema**

▽ Mahogany Chaise Longue

- *circa 1840*

With feather-padded button back, gold damask upholstery and carved, turned decoration.

- *length 189cm*
- £1,650 • The Swan

▽ William IV Day Bed

- *circa 1835*

William IV rosewood daybed.

- *length 1.84m*
- £5,500 • Butchoff

▷ Mahogany Chaise Longue

- *19th century*

Victorian mahogany chaise longue with scrolled padded back and seat, raised on turned baluster legs.

- *43cm x 197cm x 76cm*
- £1,995 • Old Cinema

▽ Victorian Chaise Longue

- *circa 1880*

Mahogany frame, cabriole legs and acanthus-leaf decoration.

- *length 84cm*
- £1,550 • Castlegate

△ French Chaise Longue

- *circa 1890*

A French Third Republic chaise longue in mahogany, with brass mounts. The whole raised on turned legs with brass castors.

- *length 2.11m*
- £2,300 • Ian Spencer

▽ French Day Bed

- *circa 1890*

Painted and upholstered and adorned with circular engravings on both uprights. With decorated frieze, fluted legs and grey/cream-coloured upholstery.

- *length 1.79m*
- £2,500 • Victoria Harvey

◁ Victorian Chaise Longue

- *19th century*

With pierced and scrolling leaf decoration, on cabriole legs.

- *height 96cm*
- £1,675 • Castlegate

△ Louis XVI-Style Chaise Longue

- *circa 1890*

Double-ended chaise longue in the Louis XVI style.

- *length 1.7m*
- £2,700 • North West 8

▷ French Chaise Longue

- *circa 1900*

Mahogany walnut Louis XVI-style méridienne.

- *length 84cm*
- £1,650 • French Room

CHESTS OF DRAWERS & COMMODES

▽ **Oak Plank Chest**

• *circa 1630*
An oak plank chest of exceptionally small proportions with good original carving and original iron lock.
• *50cm x 80cm x 33cm*
• £1,850 • Rod Wilson

▽ **William & Mary Chest of Drawers**

• *1690*
William & Mary chest of two short and three long drawers on turned bun feet, the whole in oyster laburnum with broad cross banding.
• *84cm x 94cm x 26cm*
• £24,500 • Wakelin Linfield

▷ **Oak Mule Chest**

• *circa 1670*
Mule chest with panelled top and sides, long drawer and original chain lock, on bracket feet.
• *60cm x 105cm x 48cm*
• £1,450 • Rod Wilson

△ **Oak Chest of Drawers**

• *circa 1680*
A 17th-century oak chest of drawers with applied geometric moulding, the whole on stile feet.
• *height 84cm*
• £7,750 • Angel Antiques

△ **Oak Chest of Drawers**

• *circa 1670*
Walnut, sandalwood and fruitwood chest of drawers, of two-part construction, with carved and moulded decoration, raised on turned bun feet.
• *102cm x 1150cm*
• £8,750 • Wakelin Linfield

◁ **Small Carved Coffer**

• *circa 1680*
A well-carved late seventeenth-century oak coffer in good original condition.
• *53cm x 108cm x 46cm*
• £1,400 • Rod Wilson

△ **Italian Arca Chest**

• *17th century*
Bologna walnut Arca (Ark) chest of heavy construction with good colour and patination. The top, front and side panels inset with brass roundels and rosettes.
• *140cm x 190cm*
• £16,500 • Wakelin Linfield

△ **Heavily-Carved Coffer**

• *circa 1680*
Oak coffer with bold carving and superb colouring and patination.
• *195cm x 144cm x 47cm*
• £1,650 • Rod Wilson

△ **Oak Chest of Drawers**

• *circa 1680*
Oak chest of drawers, with moulded decoration and brass mounts.
• *height 90cm*
• £2,500 • Angel Antiques

△ **Oak Coffer**

• *17th century*
A 17th-century oak coffer with organic and geometric carving, on bracket feet.
• *height 99cm*
• £1,200 • Angel Antiques

▽ **William and Mary Chest of Drawers**

• *circa 1690*
Excellent and rare William and Mary chest of drawers with two short and three long drawers, the top, sides and drawer fronts decorated with reserves of floral marquetry on well-figured walnut.
• *93cm x 96cm x 59cm*
• £48,000 • Wakelin Linfield

△ Oak Coffer

• *circa 1700*
A small late seventeenth-century oak six-plank chest with iron detailing, on straight legs.
• *50cm x 100cm x 33cm*
• £1,450 • Rod Wilson

▽ Oak Coffer

• *circa 1670*
An oak coffer carved with central roses and foliate designs. Standing on straight square legs.
• *45cm x 105cm x 75cm*
• £1,295 • Rod Wilson

▽ William and Mary Chest of Drawers

• *1690*
An excellent example of William and Mary-period chest of drawers with two short and three long drawers on turned bun feet. The whole in oyster laburnum with broad cross-banding to the sides, top and drawer fronts.
• *84cm x 91cm x 56cm*
• £24,000 • Wakelin Linfield

△ Mule Chest

• *circa 1700*
Oak mule chest with original lozenge carving and two drawers.
• *length 1.04m*
• £1,650 • Red Lion

△ Chest on Stand

• *circa 1710*
A fine chest on original stand with exceptional patina.
• *height 1.32m*
• £7,000 • Raffety Walwyn

▽ Bachelor Chest

• *circa 1705*
An unusual, small Queen Anne walnut bachelor chest, with original mounts.
• *height 81cm*
• £80,000 • Norman Adams

▽ Japanese Chest

• *early 18th century*
Japanese calligraphy chest with two tiers of drawers with bun handles and iron fittings.
• *32cm x 20cm*
• £795 • Gordon Reece

△ Queen Anne Chest

• *circa 1710*
In elm, fruitwood and oak, crossbanded on bracket feet.
• *height 99cm*
• £3,200 • Angel

△ Chest of Drawers

• *circa 1725*
George I figured-walnut chest of drawers with slide and original handles on moulded bracket feet.
• *height 83cm*
• £16,000 • Norman Adams

▽ Marriage Coffer

• *circa 1724*
A Swedish coffer in pale oak with original paint and iron strapwork.
• *length 1.53m*
• £3,800 • Riverbank

▽ Dutch Marquetry Chest

- *circa 1730*

Dutch marquetry chest, inlaid with floral design, the top with shaped front and sides, the bombé front with three drawers, standing on carved paw feet.

- *70cm x 95cm x 53cm*
- £7,950 • Rod Wilson

▽ Kingwood Commode

- *circa 1740*

French kingwood commode with ormolu mounts and rouge royale serpentine marble top.

- *85cm x 118cm x 60cm*
- £22,000 • Guinevere

▽ Chest on Stand

- *circa 1750*

A walnut and feather-banded chest on stand. The stand has an arched apron on turned legs with serpentine stretcher on ball feet.

- *60cm x 40.7cm x 23.5cm*
- £4,995 • Great Grooms

△ George II Chest of Drawers

- *circa 1730*

George II chest of three drawers with original brass handles.

- *height 88cm*
- £8,750 • Paul Hopwell

△ Walnut Tallboy

- *circa 1730*

A tallboy of good colour and proportions, with engraved brass handles and cabriole legs.

- *height 1.58m*
- £9,500 • Red Lion

△ Italian Commode

- *circa 1750*

Serpentine-fronted commode with profuse painted decoration.

- *height 86cm*
- £7,500 • Lynda Franklin

△ Dutch Chest of Drawers

- *circa 1725*

An excellent early 18th-century Dutch chest of drawers of serpentine form, with four graduated long drawers. The top quarter-veneered and walnut-strung. This is an exceptionally small example of this type of furniture.

- *75cm x 79cm*
- £18,750 • Wakelin Linfield

△ Two-Part Chest

- *circa 1750*

Rare, George II, walnut, two-part chest of drawers on bracket feet.

- *height 1.02m*
- £3,975 • Red Lion

▽ Burr-Walnut Tall Boy

- *circa 1740*

A good George II-period burr-walnut tall-boy with original metalwork. The top surmounted with a canted concave cornice above three short drawers and three graduated long drawers, all drawers having herringbone inlay and cross-banded with panels of distinctively figured walnut and fitted with open brass plate handles, with fluted canted corners terminating in an ogee point. The lower section with moulded lip above three long graduated drawers flanked by canted fluted corners headed and terminating in ogee points.

- *191cm x 109cm*
- £25,500 • Anthony Outred

◁ George III Chest

- *circa 1760*

George III mahogany chest of drawers, of small proportions, with four graduated drawers and original brass handles, raised on bracket feet.

- *86cm x 77cm*
- £4,950 • Barry Cotton

▽ Swedish Pine Chest of Drawers

• *circa 1760*
Swedish painted pine chest of drawers with serpentine moulded top and four long drawers with foliate ormolu handles and lockplates, standing on short cabriole legs.
• *height 88cm*
• £8,600 • Augustus Brandt

▽ Georgian Chest of Drawers

• *circa 1760s*
Georgian chest with four graduated drawers, with original paint and turned handles, standing on moulded bracket feet.
• *90cm x 86cm*
• £1,700 • Heytesbury

△ Chest on Chest

• *circa 1760*
Mahogany chest on chest, the top with moulded cornice.
• *height 1.79m*
• £4,200 • Old Cinema

△ Dressing Chest

• *circa 1760*
A dressing chest, in mahogany, with top drawer fitted with original mirror and shaving box.
• *height 82cm*
• £3,250 • C. Preston

▷ English Oak Coffer

• *circa 1760*
An English oak chest with three carved panels.
• *75cm x 118cm x 49cm*
• £575 • Tredantiques

▽ Venetian Commode

• *circa 1760*
Superb Venetian commode with a trailing foliate painted design overall, two deep drawers with large metal handles, a painted marble top, and moulded carved apron on cabriole legs.
• *35cm x 101cm*
• £18,750 • C. Preston

▽ Chest on Stand

• *circa 1770*
Oak chest with walnut veneer, with drawers of graduated sizes, on later oak base with serpentine stretchers and turned legs.
• *height 1.5m*
• £3,900 • Angel Antiques

◁ Italian Commode

• *circa 1785*
A double bow-fronted Italian commode, made in the 18th century and painted in the early 19th, with découpage decoration. (Découpage is the art of using paper cutouts to decorate furniture and accessories such as boxes and trays, after they have been sanded and painted. The finished object which has been so decorated looks and feels, after the application of a protective sealant, like fine enamel).
• *height 78cm*
• £5,850 • Brown

▽ Tall Chest of Drawers

• *circa 1775*
A Hepplewhite-period, mahogany serpentine chest of drawers.
• *height 1.53m*
• £20,000 • Norman Adams

▽ Bombé Chest

• *circa 1780*
European bombé-fronted chest of drawers and linen press.
• *height 2.2m*
• £6,500 • L. & E. Kreckovic

△ **Directoire Commode**

- *circa 1795*

A directoire French commode.

- *height 83cm*
- £16,500 • Wakelin Linfield

△ **Georgian Chest**

- *circa 1790*

With pierced, latticed brass mounts, on bracket feet.

- *height 78cm*
- £950 • Albany

△ **China Trade Chest**

- *circa 1820*

A China trade chest of amboyna, with military-style handles.

- *height 1.01m*
- £14,500 • Wakelin Linfield

△ **Swedish Chest of Drawers**

- *circa 1790*

Swedish painted commode with four long drawers, in original condition with pillared sides.

- *107cm x 121cm*
- £5,850 • Anthony Sharpe

△ **Georgian Tallboy**

- *circa 1820*

Late Georgian mahogany, seven-drawer tallboy with oval brass handles and replacement pediment, on bracket feet.

- *height 2.09m*
- £2,850 • Old Cinema

△ **Gustavian Commode**

- *circa 1800*

Swedish Gustavian commode with three long drawers and original brass handles, standing on square legs.

- *86cm x 103cm*
- £6,700 • R. Cavendish

△ **Walnut Chest of Drawers**

- *circa 1820*

Walnut chest of five drawers standing on bracket feet, with original handles.

- *height 98cm*
- £4,800 • Denzil Grant

△ **Bow-Fronted Chest**

- *circa 1820*

Regency mahogany chest of drawers with shaped apron and brass handles on swept feet.

- *100cm x 70cm*
- £1,750 • C.H. Major

▽ **Bow-Fronted Commode**

- *circa 1800*

A lift-top commode on splayed feet with replacement mounts.

- *height 66cm*
- £420 • Albany

▽ **Regency Chest of Drawers**

- *circa 1810*

Small Regency chest of exceptional quality and patina with two small and two long drawers on a moulded apron with bracket feet.

- *height 84cm*
- £1,950 • C. Preston

▽ **German Chest**

- *circa 1825*

By Biedermeier, in birchwood, with four deep drawers with ebonised shield escutcheons.

- *height 96cm*
- £4,500 • R. Cavendish

◁ **Demi-Lune Commode**

- *circa 1810*

An English demi-lune commode in veneered satinwood, the top and side panels cross-banded in kingwood and strung in ebony and boxwood. With painted decoration to the front and four cedar-lined drawers.

- *91cm x 104cm*
- £12,950 • Wakelin Linfield

△ Step Commode

• *circa 1830*
William IV commode in the form of library steps, with hinged compartment, on four turned legs.
• *height 79cm*
• £950 • Castlegate

△ Apothecary's Chest

• *early 19th century*
An apothecary's chest with 16 small drawers and one long one, and white porcelain handles, standing on bun feet.
• *73cm x 55cm x 97cm*
• £1,350 • Gordon Reece

△ Campaign Chest

• *circa 1850*
Mahogany military chest in two parts, the whole on bun feet.
• *height 1.09m*
• £1,425 • Ranby Hall

▽ Wellington Chest

• *circa 1830*
Flame mahogany Wellington chest with original brass mounts and bracket feet.
• *height 1.4m*
• £3,800 • Castlegate

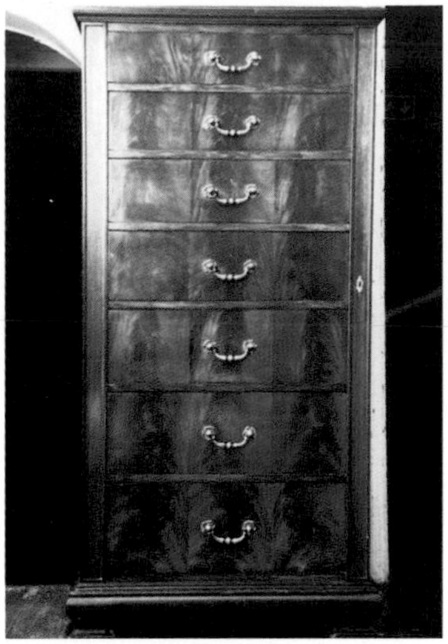

▽ Chests of Drawers

• *circa 1890*
One of a pair of burr-walnut-veneered pedestal chests of four drawers on bracket feet.
• *height 189cm*
• £1,750 • The Swan

▽ Burgundy Chest

• *circa 1870*
Chest with linen-fold side panels and Gothic-style pilasters and tracery.
• *height 72cm*
• £2,850 • Old Cinema

△ Continental Commode

• *19th century*
Mahogany and rosewood commode with ormolu mounts.
• *83cm x 112cm x 53cm*
• £2,850 • Harpur Deardren

△ Linen Press

• *circa 1860*
Victorian mahogany linen press with oval panel doors.
• *height 2.31m*
• £4,450 • Ranby Hall

△ Miniature Chest of Drawers

• *circa 1850*
A mid-19th century miniature chest of drawers in figured mahogany, with bowed top drawer above three smaller drawers and turned architectural columns, the whole on bun feet.
• *height 72cm*
• £1,150 • Graham Walpole

▽ Small Chest of Drawers

• *circa 1830*
A mahogany chest of drawers, with a rectangular breakfront top with 'B' moulded edge.
• *height 94.5cm*
• £3,200 • J. Collins

▽ Biedermeier Tallboy

• *1842–43*
Biedermeier birchwood tallboy with a gentleman's chest interior signed and dated: Carl Christian Hoff, Trondhjem, Norway.
• *140cm x 118cm*
• £8,800 • R. Cavendish

▽ Ryobaki

• *circa 1860*
High quality Ryobaki (chest on chest) with fine copper strapping and lock. The top door reveals red lacquer drawers and a similar treatment of the locking safe and batch of drawers. Kiri wood.
• *114.5 cm x114.5cm*
• £7,495 • Gordon Reece

▽ Victorian Chest

- *1870*

Victorian mahogany bedside cabinet with long drawer, standing on a straight square base.

- *height 84cm*
- **£495** • **A.I.G.**

▷ Indian Brass Chest

- *circa 1890*

An Indian repoussé and engraved, floral, banded-design brass chest with teak interior. The slightly domed lid decorated with studded bands interspersed with repoussé floral stripes, flanked by stripes decorated with diamonds. The lid with brass inscribed catch; the front panel of grid design with repoussé decorated squares within a banded frame, standing on concealed wooden wheels.

- *70cm x 97cm*
- **£3,500** • **Anthony Outred**

△ Plum Chest of Drawers

- *circa 1840*

Unusual plum chest of four deep drawers with a fan hollywood inlay to each corner, turned handles and standing on turned legs.

- *height 120cm*
- **£5,850** • **Denzil Grant**

▽ Pine Chest of Drawers

- *circa 1880*

A Victorian painted pine chest of drawers with white porcelain handles and plinth base.

- *height 98cm*
- **£395** • **Old Cinema**

▽ Japanese Chest

- *circa 1880*

Large standing Meiji-period Japanese chest, possibly for futon storage.

- *171cm x 180cm*
- **£4,995** • **Gordon Reece**

▽ Lacquer Commode

- *late 19th century*

An Italian lacquer commode with a white marble top and five painted drawers with a chinoiserie influence, on turned bun feet.

- *86cm x 113cm x 58cm*
- **£4,800** • **M. Luther**

▷ Medicine Chest

- *1880*

A Kusuri Dansa medicine herb chest made from Hinaki and sugi woods with copper and iron hardware.

- *45cm x 57cm*
- **£1,700** • **Gordon Reece**

△ Directoire-style Commode

- *circa 1880*

French directoire-style mahogany and marble-topped commode with three long drawers, square elongated handles and interesting gilt ormolu mounts.

- *87cm x 112cm*
- **£5,400** • **Anthony Sharpe**

◁ Lacquer Commode

- *circa 1860*

English bombé commode, chinoiserie painted and lacquered.

- *height 92cm*
- **£8,000** • **David Ford**

△ Victorian Chest of Drawers

- *circa 1880*

Victorian mahogany chest of drawers with two short and four long drawers with original turned mahogany handles, standing on bracket feet.

- *126cm x 86cm*
- **£1,200** • **Hill Farm**

▽ French Commode

- *1880*

French marquetry commode of small proportions, with serpentine top and fine gilt ormolu mounts.

- *79cm x 74cm*
- **£5,500** • **Butchoff**

▷ Inlaid Commode

- *circa 1890*

A late 19th-century, inlaid Louis XV-style serpentine commode with fruitwood and satinwood marquetry and ormolu mounts, on splayed legs.

- *height 85cm*
- £1,250 • Youll's

△ Miniature Chest of Drawers

- *circa 1890*

Miniature rustic oak chest, with six small drawers and original turned wooden handles.

- *30cm x 38cm*
- £160 • The Lacquer Chest

△ Victorian Mahogany Chest

- *circa 1880*

Chest with six small drawers above three long ones, with turned handles.

- *118cm x 110cm*
- £1,250 • Old Cinema

△ Oak Chest of Drawers

- *circa 1900*

An oak chest of drawers comprising two short drawers and three long drawers on a plinth base with brass handles.

- *130cm x 95cm*
- £595 • Old Cinema

▽ English Blanket Box

- *1900s*

An English well-figured pine chest in restored condition on turned bun feet.

- *51cm x 99cm x 59cm*
- £225 • Old School

▽ Mahogany Chests of Drawers

- *circa 1890*

One of a pair of small Victorian mahogany chests of four drawers.

- *height 93cm*
- £1,380 • The Swan

▷ Oak Chest of Drawers

- *circa 1895*

A Jacobean-style chest of drawers with geometric lozenge moulding to drawers and brass drop handles, all on bracket feet.

- *height 96cm*
- £1,850 • Fulham

△ Blanket Box

- *1899s*

Nineteenth-century pine chest with scrolled apron, standing on bracket feet.

- *104cm x 49cm x 52cm*
- £220 • Old School

△ Pine Chest of Drawers

- *1900s*

A pine chest having three tiers of drawers with scrolled decoration, brass fittings, standing on bun feet.

- *95cm x 58cm x 77cm*
- £400 • Old School

▽ Bombé Commode

- *circa 1890*

Swedish serpentine-fronted, walnut bombé commode, with cross-banded designs and gilt brass mounts raised on splayed legs.

- *82cm x 92cm x 20cm*
- £2,250 • Hatchwell

▽ Mahogany Chest of Drawers

- *circa 1890s*

Louis XVI-style Swedish mahogany chest of four long drawers with tapered legs and ormulu mounts and a marble top.

- *83cm x 77cm*
- £2,900 • R. Cavendish

◁ Victorian Chest of Drawers

- *1890*

Victorian mahogany chest of drawers, with pull-out writing slope, above four tiered drawers, fine painted floral decoration and brass ring handles, raised on shaped bracket feet.

- *82cm x 86cm*
- £6500 • Butchoff

DAVENPORTS

△ **Regency Davenport**

- *circa 1800*

Regency faux-rosewood davenport with pen drawer to the right-hand side and fire screen.

- *75cm x 51cm x 37cm*
- £995 • Great Grooms

△ **Burr Walnut Davenport**

- *circa 1850*

Decorated with boxwood marquetry with Wellington door-closing mechanism.

- *height 84cm*
- £5,400 • Judy Fox

▽ **George IV Davenport**

- *1830*

Camphorwood davenport with pull over the knee action, ebony knob handles and fruitwood stringing. The door concealing three drawers raised on turned bun feet.

- *88cm x 60cm*
- £3,800 • Midwinter

▽ **Victorian Walnut Davenport**

- *circa 1850*

A Victorian burr-walnut piano-top davenport with four side drawers and carved supports.

- *91cm x 55cm*
- £5,600 • Great Grooms

◁ **Light Oak Davenport**

- *1870*

A Victorian light oak davenport with unusual geometric style panelled cupboard on bracket feet, by Lamb of Manchester.

- *81cm x 56cm*
- £3,500 • New Century

△ **Walnut Davenport**

- *circa 1860*

With secret pen tray, cabriole legs, leaf decoration and brass gallery, the whole on bun feet.

- *height 84cm*
- £1,650 • Castlegate

▽ **Rosewood Davenport**

- *19th century*

Original leather insert with turned side columns.

- *height 84cm*
- £2,850 • Ranby Hall

▽ **English Regency Davenport**

- *circa 1820*

Regency rosewood davenport stamped 'Johnstone & Jeans, New Bond Street, London', with pierced gallery and leather writing slope.

- *80cm x 57cm*
- £4,500 • C.H. Major

◁ **Piano-Top Davenport**

- *1860*

A piano pop-up davenport in burr-walnut with fitted interior and sliding writing surface with red leather inlay and carved supports on bun feet.

- *height 90cm*
- £4,000 • Judy Fox

△ **Burr Elm Davenport**

- *circa 1880*

Burr elm davenport with lift top and brass gallery.

- *height 85cm*
- £8,700 • Butchoff

DESKS

△ **Oak Kneehole Desk**

• *1727–60*

A George II kneehole desk made from oak with brass handles and central cupboard, resting on bracket feet.

• *height 79cm*

• £2,650 • Great Grooms

△ **Reading Table**

• *circa 1785*

A George III satinwood reading table of simple lines, with prop-up reading and writing surface and two drawers with original ceramic handles, on tapering legs with brass castors.

• *height 74.5cm*

• £15,000 • Norman Adams

▷ **Kneehole Desk**

• *circa 1760*

An 18th-century mahogany kneehole desk with original, circular brass drop handles and central, two-door cupboard.

• *height 79cm*

• £3,500 • Mora Upham

△ **English Library Desk**

• *circa 1840*

A rare and sought-after English 19th century burr-walnut, kidney-shaped library desk in the manner of Gillow. The top with original brass gallery is fitted with three frieze drawers with a bank of four graduated drawers either side of the kneehole, with the opposing side fitted with bookshelves. This desk relates to a design by Gillows recorded in their 'Estimate Sketch Book' of 1840.

• *76.2cm x 122cm*

• £43,500 • Freshfords

▽ **Partners' Desk**

• *circa 1780*

A large, mahogany partners' desk with frieze drawers and plain curved brass handles, all raised on shaped bracket feet.

• *height 77cm*

• £2,600 • Ian Spencer

△ **Walnut Desk**

• *circa 1840*

A figured walnut pedestal desk with rounded corners and heavy mouldings. Original knob handles.

• *height 78cm*

• £5,500 • Ian Spencer

△ **Birch Desk**

• *circa 1830*

Unusual satinwood, birch and ebony line-inlaid desk with a rising lid.

• *height 95cm*

• £1,450 • M.J. Bowdery

▽ **Kneehole Desk**

• *circa 1740*

A rare kneehole desk in solid cherrywood with good patina.

• *height 89cm*

• £2,750 • Red Lion

▽ **Cylinder Bureau**

• *circa 1865*

A French Second Empire mahogany and gilt-mounted cylinder bureau.

• *height 129cm*

• £18,500 • Ranby Hall

◁ **Mahogany Partner's Desk**

• *circa 1810*

A large George III partner's desk in figured light mahogany. Provenance: the American author Sydney Sheldon.

• *162cm x 89cm*

• £20,000 • Pimlico

▷ Walnut Kneehole Desk
- *1870*

With four small drawers each side of the kneehole, and one central drawer and cupboard, with leather writing top.
- *78cm x 107cm x 66cm*
- £2,400 • Old Cinema

▽ Lady's Writing Table
- *circa 1880*

With seven drawers and ebonised stringing. Standing on tapered legs.
- *length 1.22m*
- £1,995 • Antique Warehouse

▷ Chinese Lacquered Desk
- *1870*

Red lacquer desk with three drawers above ornately carved kneehole.
- *height 95cm*
- £1,585 • Ranby Hall

△ Roll-Top Desk
- *circa 1880*

Flame mahogany roll-top kneehole desk. The fitted interior with pigeonholes, eight small drawers and leather adjustable book rest, above a kneehole flanked by eight drawers with turned wood handles.
- *121cm x 135cm*
- £5,250 • Drummonds

▷ Lacquer Kneehole Desk
- *circa 1880s*

Black lacquer and gilt kneehole desk, of colonial influence.
- *103cm x 103cm*
- £1,700 • Sign of the Times

▷ Lady's Desk
- *circa 1880*

Nineteenth-century rosewood lady's desk, with boxwood inlay, decorated with penwork to a floral design, with leather insert. The desk stands on eight tapering legs, with spade feet and castors.
- *height 94cm*
- £3,600 • Judy Fox

◁ Gothic Revival Desk
- *circa 1870*

Carved oak and burr walnut with black tooled leather and single drawers over end legs.
- *height 1.07m*
- £1,500 • M. Constantini

△ Walnut and Ormolu Writing Desk
- *circa 1860*

Walnut and ormolu-mounted writing desk in the manner of Gillows, with serpentine top above a central drawer flanked by two side drawers. The whole desk is raised on cabriole legs with fine ormolu mounts.
- *width 137cm*
- £16,500 • Butchoff

△ Chinese Writing Table
- *late 19th century*

Rosewood bombé/serpentine-shaped writing table.
- *height 1.16m*
- £1,950 • John Clay

△ Fruitwood Country Desk
- *19th century*

In fruitwood with cabriole legs and three drawers.
- *height 77cm*
- £1,835 • I. & J. L. Brown

◁ Tambour Desk

• *circa 1890*

American mahogany desk with writing slides, original handles and self-locking drawers. Stamped 'Buddha – 1012 McFarland St, Normal, Oklahoma'.

• *width 1.55m*

• £12,750 • C. Preston

▽ Satinwood Kidney-Shaped Desk

• *circa 1900*

A satinwood kidney desk having five drawers with original handles and good locks. All keys are supplied. Having a crossbanded and leather top standing on string inlaid legs with spade feet.

• *75cm x 120cm x 65cm*

• £3,500 • Hatchwell

△ Kneehole Desk

• *1880*

Small oak and mahogany kneehole desk with cupboard, one long drawer, and three drawers either side of kneehole.

• *77cm x 89cm x 44cm*

• £995 • Great Grooms

▷ Victorian Partners' Desk

• *circa 1880*

A 19th-century mahogany desk with reversible full-hide leather pedestals.

• *length 1.76m*

• £4,950 • Antique Warehouse

△ Chippendale-Style Writing Table

• *circa 1900*

A Chippendale-style writing table comprising one long drawer and two side drawers on either side of the kneehole. All drawers are fitted with drop handles. The whole is raised on architectural carved legs.

• *77cm x 126cm x 60cm*

• £4,950 • Brown

▽ Pedestal Desk

• *circa 1930*

A continental Art Deco pedestal desk made in birch with two panelled cupboards with four sliding shelves and three drawers with locks and keys.

• £1,600 • C. Newland

▽ Carlton House Desk

• *circa 1910*

Fine Sheraton-revival mahogany desk. Signed, with brass handles.

• *height 1m*

• £9,500 • Brown's

▽ Louis XV-Style Bureau Plat

• *circa 1900*

Fine French Louis XV-style mahogany bureau plat with gilt bronze mounts.

• *80cm x 145cm x 76cm*

• £9,500 • Hatchwell

△ Writing Desk

• *circa 1920*

Mahogany Hepplewhite writing desk with brass-bound and leather top on carved cabriole legs.

• *height 73cm*

• £695 • Fulham

▷ Mahogany Desk

• *circa 1920*

Early 20th-century mahogany desk in the George III manner. The top is inlaid with calf leather and decorated with gold tooling.

• *height 79cm*

• £1,500 • Westland & Co.

DINING TABLES

▽ Extending Table

- *circa 1840*

Cuban mahogany-top extending table, with tapered legs and brass tips. Comes complete with original mahogany chairs.

- *width 1.8m*
- £3,750 • Abbey Green

△ Regency Dining Table

- *1820*

A fine Regency mahogany extending dining table made by Thomas Wilkinson of London, with a scissor-action lazy tongs mechanism for extending the table.

- *height 86cm*
- £1,765 • Freshfords

△ Mahogany Extending Dining Table

- *circa 1820*

Regency mahogany extending dining table by Thomas Wilkinson of London. The scissor-action, 'lazy-tongs' mechanism for extending the table was covered by the King's patent.

- *length 379cm*
- £32,000 • Freshfords

△ Three-Pillar Table

- *circa 1795*

A Scottish mahogany three-pillar dining table from the Sheraton period. The pedestals have turned stems on splayed legs.

- *length 3.2m*
- £200,000 • Norman Adams

△ Five-Leaf Table

- *circa 1830*

A circular, figured Cuban mahogany dining table with five leaves on reeded legs, extending to seat twelve people.

- *diameter 145cm*
- £9,800 • M. Luther

▽ Drop-Leaf Table

- *circa 1825*

George IV mahogany drop-leaf dining table on six turned legs.

- *width 1.67m*
- £4,300 • L. & E. Kreckovic

△ 'D'-End Dining Table

- *circa 1810*

Mahogany 'D'-end dining table of the Regency period, to seat six persons. The table retains its original loose leaf.

- *length 1.95m (extended)*
- £8,750 • J. Collins

△ Mahogany Dining Table

- *circa 1860s*

A mid-Victorian mahogany circular dining table. The moulded top in two halves, on a large ring-turned shaft with gadrooned stem, on an X-frame base with scrolled feet and countersunk brass castors. Provenance: by repute, William Hesketh Lever, 1st Viscount Leverhulme (d.1925).

- *75cm x 274.5cm*
- £80,000 • Anthony Outred

△ Victorian Dining Table

- *1837–1901*

Victorian dining table in its original condition, with figured mahogany.

- *height 74cm*
- £3,750 • Old Cinema

▽ Extendable Dining Table

- *circa 1870*

Victorian mahogany table with baluster fluted legs, extendable to 300cm.

- *74cm x 138cm x 150cm*
- £3,500 • Tredantiques

▽ Cuban Mahogany Table

- *19th century*

Cuban mahogany three-leaf dining table of wide proportions with heavily carved and turned legs on brass castors.

- *300cm x 105cm*
- £4,950 • Old Cinema

▽ English Dining Table

- *circa 1880*

Circular dining table with finely figured mahogany tilt top, cross-banded, with a gadrooned edge above a cross-banded frieze, raised on a tri-form, panelled pedestal, with large scrolled feet.

- *height 75cm*
- £32,000 • Anthony Outred

▷ Mahogany Three-Leaved Dining Table

- *1885*

Late nineteenth-century mahogany dining table with three leaves on carved and turned legs with original castors.

- *74cm x 122cm*
- £4,250 • Old Cinema

▽ French Dining Table

- *late 19th century*

French fruitwood provincial farmhouse dining table.

- *76cm x 200cm*
- £1,950 • Old Cinema

△ Swedish Dining Table

- *circa 1920*

Swedish Biedermeier-style dining table made from birchwood, with masur birch banding on a square pedestal base.

- *136cm x 196cm*
- £10,500 • R. Cavendish

◁ Mahogany Dining Table

- *circa 1850*

Four-pillar table with royal patented wind-up mechanism and five leaves.

- *length 1.76m*
- £5,000 • John Bly

▽ French Farmhouse Table

- *circa 1890*

Large table with pine top and turned and tapered walnut legs.

- *length 2.4m*
- £2,000 • Gabrielle de Giles

△ Walnut Dining Table

- *circa 1880*

Burr-walnut oval Victorian tilt-top dining table on pillared triform base with carved feet and ceramic castors.

- *height 87cm*
- £1,750 • Fulham

▽ Extending Table

- *circa 1920*

Swedish birchwood extending table with ebonized feet.

- *length 2.63m (extended)*
- £4,900 • R. Cavendish

DOORS

▽ Carved Doors

• *17th century*
A pair of 17th-century Oriental doors with a carved geometric design, and twenty-eight panels.
• *180cm x 93cm*
• £1,980 • Gordon Reece

▽ Indian Panelled Doors

• *18th century*
Antique panelled doors with elaborate strapwork and floral decorated brass.
• *192cm x 120cm*
• £1,250 • Gordon Reece

▷ Queen Anne Doorcase

• *circa 1710*
A rare Queen Anne carved pine Baroque doorcase with a projecting canopy on scrolled brackets. The central frieze is carved with the attributes of war flanked by fluted Tuscan pilasters.
• *308cm x 189cm*
• £14,500 • Westland & Co.

△ Linen-Fold Door

• *circa 1640*
Oak door with four panels, the upper and lower sections carved with linen-fold designs.
• *177cm x 77cm*
• £820 • Drummonds

▷ Overdoor

• *circa 1890*
A fine French carved Beaux Arts overdoor with scrolls centred by a mask with wings.
• *height 59cm*
• £7,500 • Westland & Co.

▽ English Circular Doors

• *circa 1770*
Unusual pair of tall English oak curved doors, carved with asymmetric scrolled mouldings, with fine original brass locks and fittings.
• *340cm x 155cm*
• £5,800 • Drummonds

▽ George III Door Surround

• *circa 1790*
A large and imposing George III carved pine door surround. The arched top with an egg and dart cornice together with an anthemion frieze centred by a wrought-iron fanlight. The fluted pilasters with Ionic capitals with anthemion carving.
• *354cm x 221cm*
• £15,500 • Westland & Co.

△ Italian Double Doors

• *circa 1790*
A pair of gilt wood and ivory, painted double doors from an Italian palazzo. The moulded gilt wood decoration centred by a jasper panel.
• *295cm x 71cm*
• £15,000 • Westland & Co.

△ Dynastic Tribal Door

• *18th century*
Dynastic tribal door from central India. Created for the chieftain of the Gond tribe, a Dravidian group of Primitives who are animist believers.
• *145cm x 90cm*
• £1,450 • Gordon Reece

▽ Oriental Door and Frame

• *circa 1860*
With heavily carved surround and inset with a frieze incorporating interlaced dragons with scrolled, foliate tracery.
• *225cm x 124cm*
• £2,900 • **Drummonds**

▽ Pine Overdoor

• *circa 1890*
Carved pine overdoor in the George I style.
• *height 77.5cm*
• £450 • **Westland & Co.**

▽ French Doors

• *circa 1900*
Two pairs of French doors with Art Nouveau polychrome glass.
• *height 2.32m*
• £950 (pair) • **Westland & Co.**

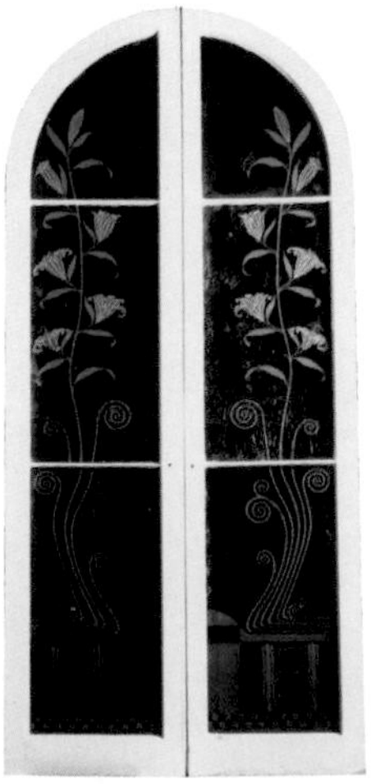

△ Gothic-Style Church Doors

• *19th century*
A pair of arched gothic-style church entrance doors with original iron fittings.
• *245cm x 150cm*
• £2,420 • **Drummonds**

△ Oak Panelled Door

• *circa 1880*
English oak door with two central panels.
• *204cm x 88cm*
• £1,190 • **Drummonds**

▽ Revolving Doors

• *circa 1900*
Revolving doors, within a cylindrical housing with moulded frames, glazed panels and brass door furniture.
• *236cm x 190cm*
• £6,625 • **Drummonds**

▽ Four Pairs of Doors

• *circa 1890*
Four pairs of carved neoclassical-style carved doors with matching frames.
• *height 2.46m*
• £5,500 • **Westland & Co.**

◁ Walnut Doorway

• *circa 1885*
Carved walnut doorway in the Renaissance manner.
• *height 2.62m*
• £18,000 • **Westland & Co.**

▷ Baroque-Style Overdoor

• *circa 1890*
A carved wood overdoor in the baroque manner.
• *height 1m*
• £1,600 • **Westland & Co.**

△ Folding Bronze Doors

• *circa 1930*
A very substantial and unusual pair of 1930s double folding bronze doors with twenty-eight raised and fielded panels. The doors show some patination.
• *height 2.64m*
• £6,500 • **Westland & Co.**

△ Double Doors

• *circa 1910*
A pair of six-panelled mahogany doors with brass furniture.
• *height 2.8m*
• £3,500 • **Ian Spencer**

DRESSERS

△ **Charles II Cupboard**

- *circa 1680*

Oak court cupboard with heraldic central panel.

- *height 1.64m*
- £3,850 • **Angel Antiques**

▷ **James II Oak Cupboard**

- *1687*

Overhanging cornice with carved frieze and 'RS' initialled.

- *height 2m*
- £7,950 • **Old Cinema**

△ **Court Cupboard**

- *1691*

A Westmorland oak court cupboard, with overhanging cornice and turned decoration with turned wood handles and good patina.

- *160cm x 133cm x 56cm*
- £7,950 • **Peter Bunting**

◁ **English Cupboard**

- *1700*

An English court cupboard with carved oak panels, and turned columns below a moulded pediment.

- *203cm x 150cm*
- £3,850 • **Red Lion**

▷ **Welsh Deuddiarw**

- *circa 1740*

An original eighteenth century Welsh deuddiarw. The upper section with cornice above panelled cupboards.

- *177cm x 104cm x 52cm*
- £5,950 • **Rod Wilson**

△ **George II Oak Dresser**

- *circa 1750*

George II oak dresser with panelled back, two shelves with three small drawers with turned handles and two cupboards below standing on straight square legs.

- *height 245cm*
- £11,750 • **Paul Hopwell**

◁ **Carved Oak Dresser**

- *late 17th century*

English oak dresser with heavily carved sides and doors, standing on straight square feet with iron fittings.

- *131cm x 172cm x 56cm*
- £2,500 • **Tredantiques**

▽ **Deuddiarw Carved Cupboard**

- *1760*

An oak deuddiarw carved dresser with good patina, with carved pediment and drop finials above two cupboards, three drawers and panel doors.

- *167cm x 143cm*
- £6,850 • **Red Lion**

△ Painted French Dresser

• *18th century*
French painted pine dresser with two glass doors, and panelled cupboards below on a square base.
• *height 183cm*
• £3,400 • Solaris

△ Cupboard/Dresser

• *circa 1800*
Oak press cupboard/dresser with two doors above three tiers of drawers.
• *height 1.95m*
• £5,750 • Red Lion

△ Oak Dresser Base

• *circa 1780*
George III oak dresser base with central panelled door flanked by two sets of three long drawers with original brass handles, and standing on bracket feet.
• *height 110cm*
• £14,750 • Paul Hopwell

▽ Buffet de Corps

• *18th century*
A rare yew wood buffet de corps with three tiers of shelves above a base with three drawers and two cupboard doors.
• *200cm x 137cm*
• £5,950 • Red Lion

▽ George III Plate Rack

• *circa 1780*
George III open oak plate rack with pierced rail and architectural side columns.
• *height 102cm*
• £3,750 • Paul Hopwell

△ English Oak Dresser

• *1780*
An English oak dresser with moulded pediment and carved apron front, having four drawers on turned legs.
• *200cm x 206cm*
• £6,950 • Red Lion

△ French Cupboard

• *18th century*
Cupboard in oak with serpentine frieze with floral carving.
• *length 1.69m*
• £1,200 • Lynda Franklin

▽ Irish Dresser

• *1780*
An Irish chestnut dresser with moulded pediment, scrolled pilasters and moulded cupboard doors.
• *200cm x 145cm*
• £3,950 • Red Lion

▽ Corner Cupboard

• *1800*
A fine George III one-piece standing corner cupboard in faded mahogany. The upper section having doors with 18 octagonal panels. The lower section with central drawer above two panelled moulded doors.
• *218cm x 110cm*
• £14,500 • Wakelin Linfield

◁ Painted Sideboard

• *18th century*
French sideboard with carved floral design and scrolled feet.
• *height 96cm*
• £2,750 • Lynda Franklin

△ Sideboard

- *circa 1820*

Mahogany sideboard with cellaret cupboard, raised on spade feet.

- *height 1.54m*
- £2,000 • Ian Spencer

▽ Bombé Cabinet

- *circa 1820*

Anglo-Indian bombé-front cabinet, carved in rosewood.

- *height 1.13m*
- £3,400 • L. & E. Kreckovic

△ French Pine Cabinet

- *circa 1830*

French country pine dresser with glazed cupboards above two cupboards below and steel fittings, all on block feet.

- *height 1.83m*
- £1,000 • Albany

▽ Chiffonier

- *circa 1830*

A late Regency, two-door mahogany chiffonier.

- *height 1.26m*
- £1,650 • Castlegate

△ Victorian Mahogany Chiffonier

- *1850*

Victorian mahogany chiffonier with long drawer above two panelled cupboards, standing on small bun feet.

- *91cm x 42cm x 104cm*
- £590 • Tredantiques

▽ French Mahogany Dresser

- *1860*

A fine figured mahogany dresser with two shelves, the back having a scallop design, with two drawers and panelled cupboards below, standing on bun feet.

- *169cm x 123cm x 46cm*
- £1,800 • Tredantiques

△ Display Case

- *19th century*

Queen Anne-style with lattice work and floral decoration.

- *height 2.06m*
- £5,850 • Ranby Hall

▽ Early Victorian Sideboard

- *19th century*

Mahogany pedestal sideboard with moulded decoration.

- *height 1.6m*
- £3,850 • Ranby Hall

▽ Mahogany Cupboard

- *circa 1870*

A figured mahogany, oval-panelled cupboard with boxwood inlay to drawers and brass handles. The whole raised on bracket feet.

- *height 1.2m*
- £1,450 • Ian Spencer

▽ Poland Oak Sideboard

- *late 19th century*

Back carved with 'Mirth Becomes A Feast' above panels.

- *length 2.3m*
- £5,000 • Old Cinema

△ Pedestal Sideboards

- *circa 1880*

Twin sideboards with mirror back and floral carving.

- *length 2.14m*
- £3,595 • **Antique Warehouse**

△ Oak Sideboard

- *19th century*

Mirror-backed dentil cornice with architectural details above.

- *height 1.96m*
- £3,495 • **Antique Warehouse**

△ Glazed Pine Dresser

- *1900s*

Pine dresser consisting of three glazed doors with shelving above a pine base, with two shallow drawers and panelled cupboard with brass fittings.

- *128cm x 98cm x 55cm*
- £700 • **Old School**

▽ Maplewood Chiffonier

- *1885*

An early Victorian maplewood chiffonier with open shelf and back board and two glazed cupboard doors flanked by turned barley-twist columns.

- *138cm x 107cm x 40cm*
- £2,950 • **S. Duggan**

▽ Mahogany Sideboard

- *circa 1900*

Mahogany sideboard with rosewood crossbanding and boxwood and ebony stringing.

- *height 93cm*
- £4,800 • **David Pickup**

▷ Ash Sideboard

- *circa 1915*

An English sideboard of substantial construction.

- *height 1.02m*
- £1,295 • **Castlegate**

▽ Pine Open Dresser

- *circa 1880*

Open-back pine dresser with four shelves. The base with three long drawers above three panelled cupboard doors, with alloy handles and fittings.

- *275cm x 170cm*
- £850 • **Drummonds**

▽ Victorian Sideboard

- *circa 1880*

Impressive sideboard with a deep central drawer, centered with a raised ivory classical plaque, flanked by two deep large cupboards, standing on two pedestals with bun feet.

- *90cm x 198cm*
- £4,850 • **Drummonds**

△ Walnut Dresser

- *circa 1890*

Aesthetic Movement dresser, with panels of birds, highlighting, amboyna back and acorn finials.

- *height 1.72m*
- £1,250 • **Travers Antiques**

△ Arts & Crafts Buffet

- *circa 1905*

English walnut buffet carved with strapwork decoration.

- *height 93cm*
- £10,000 • **David Pickup**

DUMB WAITERS & WHATNOTS

△ George II Washstand

• *circa 1750*

George II mahogany two-tier washstand with fan carving to the sides, and a small drawer standing on slender legs and pad feet.

• *height 85cm*

• £3,850 • John Bly

△ Butler's Tray

• *1850–70*

A Victorian mahogany butler's tray resting on a Georgian-style stand.

• *54cm x 65.5cm*

• £795 • Great Grooms

▽ Hanging Shelves

• *circa 1830*

Mahogany hanging shelves with turned columns.

• *height 71cm*

• £475 • Lynda Franklin

▽ Mahogany Buffet

• *circa 1850*

A mid 19th-century English three-tiered buffet or dumb waiter, in mahogany, with turned supports. Each tier has a gallery and the whole is supported on original ceramic castors with brass brackets. There are two shallow drawers to the base, with carved button handles, and carved acorn finials to the top.

• *height 1.2m*

• £1,800 • Judy Fox

▽ Satin Birch Whatnot

• *circa 1840*

English satin birchwood whatnot with three shelves, the lower section with a single drawer with barley-twist supports, stamped Mills Cabinetmakers, raised on gadrooned feet with original brass castors.

• *99cm x 53cm x 39.5cm*

• £4,250 • O.F. Wilson

▽ Wall Shelves

• *circa 1840*

A hanging wall shelf made from kingswood, with ormolu decorative mounts .

• *59cm x 39cm x 15cm*

• £1,650 • Butchoff

▷ George IV Dumbwaiters

• *1825*

One of a pair of mahogany George IV dumbwaiters with brass gallery, three well-figured shelves, raised on carved supports with bun feet.

• *117cm x 124cm*

• £16,500 • Butchoff

△ Pot Cupboard

• *William IV*

Unusual flame-mahogany pot cupboard.

• *height 82cm*

• £850 • Victoria Harvey

△ Dumb Waiter

• *18th century*

All mahogany with folding tiers. Turned column on a tripod base with drop levers.

• *height 1.08m*

• £3,850 • Ronald G. Chambers

▽ Mahogany Washstand

• *circa 1860*
Mahogany washstand inset with a circular pink marble top and two shelves, supported by pillared turned legs on a triangular base, raised on shallow bun feet.
• *85cm x 32cm*
• £980 • Lacquer Chest

▽ Bijouterie Whatnot

• *1860*
An unusual bijouterie mahogany whatnot with five shelves, standing on plain bracket feet.
• *146cm x 56cm x 47cm*
• £1,800 • Tredantiques

▷ Amboyna and Tulipwood Etagères

• *circa 1880*
One of a pair of amboyna and tulipwood bordered etagères with pierced brass gallery raised on splayed legs.
• *75cm x 48cm x 33cm*
• £5,800 • Butchoff

△ Walnut Whatnot

• *circa 1870*
Victorian walnut three-tier whatnot with carved scrolled pierced gallery, on turned supports.
• *height 132cm*
• £1,950 • The Swan

△ Rosewood Cake Stand

• *circa 1880*
Rosewood circular cake stand with a turned base.
• *height 19cm*
• £400 • Sign of the Times

△ Oriental Cake Stand

• *1880*
Oriental cake stand with three circular tiers carved with six leaf-shaped receptacles, around a central circular design, within a carved frame.
• *height 82cm*
• £110 • Poppets

▽ Cake Stand

• *1880*
Mahogany cake stand with satinwood banding, incorporating three graduated circular shelves. Surmounted by a ball finial, raised on splayed legs.
• *height 93cm*
• £280 • John Clay

▽ Brass Cake Stand

• *1890*
Victorian lacquered brass cake-stand with two circular tiers embossed with an organic repeating design, raised on scrolled legs with hoof feet.
• *height 88cm*
• £295 • A.I.G.

◁ Three-Tier Stand

• *1890*
A three-tier mahogany cake stand with fruitwood banding
• *height 89cm*
• £195 • Great Grooms

△ Four-Tier Walnut Whatnot

• *circa 1880*
Four-tier walnut corner whatnot inlaid with boxwood and burr walnut, acorn finial and turned supports.
• *height 137cm*
• £875 • The Swan

MIRRORS

▷ **William and Mary Mirror**

- *circa 1690*

Fine William and Mary cushion frame mirror, decorated with floral and bird motifs including stained ivory.

- *109cm x 92cm*
- £22,500 • **Wakelin Linfield**

△ **Venetian Mirror**

- *circa 1610*

Venetian Moorish-style mirror, flanked by two elongated narrow mirrors, within a carved wood frame with spires, finials, and a raised floral carving.

- *height 117cm*
- £5,800 • **Augustus Brandt**

△ **Toilet Mirror**

- *circa 1725*

A George I walnut toilet-mirror with one drawer.

- *height 77.5cm*
- £10,000 • **Norman Adams**

▽ **Easel Mirror**

- *circa 1725*

A rare George I, gilded, carved gesso easel mirror.

- *height 78cm*
- £16,000 • **Norman Adams**

▽ **Mercury-Plate Mirror**

- *circa 1850s*

Small mid-19th century Venetian blue oval glass mirror, etched with floral sprays, with original mercury plate mirror.

- *56cm x 43cm*
- £2,250 • **Looking Glass**

▷ **Queen Anne Mirror**

- *circa 1710*

Rare black lacquer Queen Anne table mirror of large proportions, retaining the original glass with bureau front on turned bun feet.

- *95cm x 48cm*
- £4,900 • **Ashcombe House**

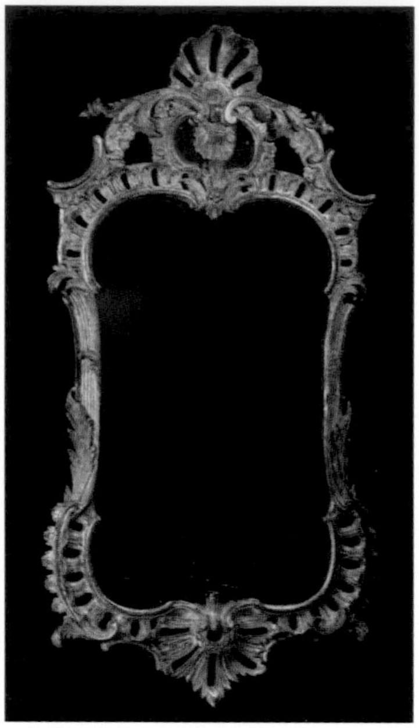

▷ **Queen Anne Mirror**

- *circa 1710*

Small Queen Anne maroon lacquered mirror with original plate.

- *60cm x 29cm*
- £1,500 • **O.F. Wilson**

▽ **Walnut Wall Mirror**

- *1750*

A mid-eighteenth century walnut mirror with carved fretwork and gilding.

- *height 70cm*
- £2,950 • **Ashcombe House**

◁ **George II Mirrors**

- *circa 1750*

One of a matched pair of George II, gilded, carved wood mirrors.

- *height 1.38m*
- £90,000 • **Norman Adams**

△ Florentine Mirror

- *circa 1750*

A Florentine silvered and giltwood mirror with a carved stylised acanthus leaf frame.

- *130cm x 75cm*
- £6,500 • Guinevere

△ Mercury Plate Mirror

- *circa 1800s*

Rectangular Austro-Hungarian water-gilt mirror with a scrolling floral border and original plate glass.

- *96.5cm x 81cm*
- £5,350 • Looking Glass

▽ Rococo Mirrors

- *circa 1760*

One of a pair of Venetian rococo giltwood shield mirrors with asymmetric carved decoration.

- *65cm x 65cm*
- £11,000 • Guinevere

▽ Chippendale Mirror

- *circa 1760*

A small, cartouche-shaped, carved wood and gilt mirror.

- *height 89cm*
- £8,000 • Norman Adams

◁ Hour-Glass Mirror

- *1800*

A giltwood hour glass-shaped mirror surmounted by an urn with trailing foliage, with two candelabra, with cut glass droplets.

- *96cm x 46cm*
- £9,500 • O.F. Wilson

△ Louis XVI Mirror

- *circa 1780*

Small giltwood Louise XVI mirror, surmounted by carvings of broken arrows and a flower, arranged at the base of a laurel wreath, in original green paintwork.

- *height 67cm*
- £1,500 • Augustus Brandt

▽ Irish Mirrors

- *circa 1800*

A pair of Irish mirrors.

- *height 70cm*
- £3,800 • P.L. James

▽ English Regency Mirror

- *circa 1810*

An English regency convex giltwood mirror, surmounted with a carved eagle.

- *112cm x 76cm*
- £5,400 • M. Luther

◁ Toilet Mirror

- *circa 1780*

A Chinese export lacquered toilet mirror.

- height 68cm
- £3,850 • P.L. James

△ Sheraton Mirror

- *circa 1800*

A gilded, carved wood and papier mâché rectangular mirror.

- *height 151cm*
- £14,500 • Norman Adams

▽ Italian Carved Mirror

- *circa 1810*

Giltwood mirror with a carved, scrolled floral border, surmounted by a scallop shell and a head of a young girl at the base.

- *99cm x 68.5cm*
- £3,600 • Looking Glass

▽ Regency Convex Mirror

- *circa 1820s*

Fine Regency giltwood convex mirror with ebonised slip and ball-encrusted frame, surmounted by an eagle suspending a ball on a columned finial.

- *99cm x 56cm*
- £3,950 • Looking Glass

▷ Rectangular Mirror

- *circa 1830*

A William IV giltwood overmantel mirror with architectural details and ebonised slip.

- *185cm x 75cm*
- £2,950 • M. Luther

△ Regency Toilet Mirror

- *circa 1810*

Regency mahogany toilet mirror with three drawers,cross-banded in satinwood with boxwood and ebony stringing.

- *height 68cm*
- £1,150 • Barry Cotton

△ Italian Giltwood Mirror

- *circa 1820s*

Italian giltwood mirror with carved and moulded frame and trailing floral designs.

- *43cm x 35.5cm*
- £475 • Looking Glass

▷ Regency Mirror

- *1820*

Regency convex gilt mirror surmounted with an eagle and decorated with carved acanthus leaf and beading.

- *117cm x 64cm*
- £3,680 • Looking Glass

△ Console and Mirror

- *circa 1830*

Scandinavian-made, with crested detail to the head of mirror.

- *height 320cm*
- £10,500 • Ranby Hall

△ Venetian Mirror

- *1850*

Venetian etched glass oval mirror, engraved with floral and leaf designs.

- *135cm x 77cm*
- £3,350 • Looking Glass

▽ Mirror and Console Table

- *1830*

A flame-mahogany console table and mirror with frieze and scrolled pilasters, on a moulded base.

- *300cm x 63cm x 35cm*
- £3,800 • Ranby Hall

▽ Venetian Mirror

- *circa 1850*

A fine etched and engraved Venetian mirror.

- *height 148cm*
- £3,300 • Paul Andrews

△ French Oval Mirror

- *circa 1850s*

Second Empire small French oval mirror with original bevelled plate.

- *56cm x 46cm*
- £785 • Looking Glass

△ Octagonal Mirror

- *circa 1850*

French cushion gilt with reverse shell base and profuse flowers.

- *height 132cm*
- £2,500 • Looking Glass

▽ Giltwood Mirror

- *mid-18th century*

An eighteenth-century English wall mirror

- *110cm x 88cm*
- £4,200 • M. Luther

▽ Seahorse Mirror

- *1860*

Circular bevelled plate mirror, within an architectural frame. The pediment gilded with a gilt lyre flanked by seahorses, with gilt ormolu butterfly mounts.

- *107cm x 87.3cm*
- £2,800 • Looking Glass

▷ English Mirror

- *circa 1870*

Giltwood mirror with Prince of Wales cartouche.

- *height 86cm*
- £1,550 • Looking Glass

◁ French Mirror

- *19th century*

A French mirror with painted panel and gilt moulded shell and scrolling decoration.

- *height 170cm*
- £2,200 • Lynda Franklin

△ French Mirror

- *circa 1860*

A fine French gilt wood and gesso looking glass in the Louis XV manner. The arched frame headed by a foliate and shell cresting.

- *194cm x 132cm*
- £1,950 • Westland & Co.

△ Oval Wall Mirror

- *19th century*

Nineteenth-century English giltwood oval wall mirror with carved floral decoration.

- *130cm x 111cm*
- £4,950 • M. Luther

▽ English Convex Mirror

- *circa 1870s*

Victorian circular convex mirror with a repeating stylised floral border and beaded rim.

- *68.5cm x 58.5cm*
- £1,750 • Looking Glass

▽ Victorian Giltwood Mirror

- *circa 1870s*

Victorian gilded oval mirror with foliate carving and flowers, with scrolling and crest above.

- *135cm x 82.5cm*
- £4,230 • Looking Glass

▽ Adam-style Mirror

- *circa 1875*

Adam-style neo-classical, urn and husks on a oval gilt mirror.

- *height 85cm*
- £1,350 • Looking Glass

△ **Silver-Gilt Mirror**
- *1880*

French silver-gilt mirror with asymmetric shell designs, with bevelled glass
- *196cm x 117cm*
- £2,880 • Looking Glass

△ **Lacquered Hall Mirror**
- *19th century*

A lacquered oak-framed hall mirror with moulded edge.
- *122cm x 48cm*
- £2,850 • M. Luther

▽ **Octagonal Mirror**
- *1880*

French octagonal mirror with a carved urn surrounded with leaf designs on a moulded and beaded edge.
- *99cm x 62cm*
- £2,100 • Looking Glass

▽ **Victorian Gilt Mirror**
- *circa 1890*

Gilt mirror with shelf, scrolls, broken pediment and heart-shaped mirror.
- *height 100cm*
- £850 • Looking Glass

▷ **Porcelain Mirror**
- *1890*

Late nineteenth-century German mirror with flower-encrusted decoration, below two cherubs joined with a floral garland.
- *height 15cm*
- £95 • A.D. Antiques

◁ **Regency Mirror**
- *circa 1890*

A simple gilt Regency mirror.
- *diameter 50cm*
- £1,100 • Looking Glass

△ **Mantel Mirror**
- *circa 1890*

A three division, over-mantel mirror with decorated frieze.
- *length 142cm, height 87.5cm*
- £2,250 • Looking Glass

△ **Italian Mirror**
- *circa 1890*

Small, rectangular giltwood and fretted Florentine mirror.
- *height 55cm*
- £850 • Looking Glass

△ **Victorian Bow Mirror**
- *circa 1890s*

Victorian oval giltwood mirror with a trailing foliate design terminating in a bow.
- *142.4cm x 94cm*
- £5,600 • Looking Glass

△ **Bevelled Glass Mirror**
- *1880*

Large French gilt, bevelled glass mirror, with ribbon-moulded designs and floral swags.
- *152cm x 145cm*
- £3,850 • Looking Glass

△ Victorian Circular Mirror

- *1880*

Victorian circular mirror with a convex glass surrounded with gilded and beaded edge.

- *diameter 49cm*
- £2,300 • Looking Glass

△ English Mirror

- *circa 1890*

An English round mirror in a rectangular gilt frame.

- *height 55cm*
- £650 • Looking Glass

△ Venetian Mirror

- *circa 1890*

A highly ornate, oval Venetian etched-crest mirror.

- *height 1.32m*
- £2,850 • Looking Glass

▽ Trumeau Mirror

- *circa 1885*

A slim, gilt continental trumeau mirror, showing pastoral scene.

- *height 123cm*
- £1,600 • Looking Glass

▽ French Mirror

- *circa 1895*

A French winged-dragon gilt, bevelled mirror.

- *height 115cm*
- £875 • Looking Glass

△ English Mirror

- *circa 1890*

An English carved giltwood mirror with mandolin and flute on top.

- *height 72.5cm*
- £650 • Looking Glass

△ German Table Mirror

- *circa 1910*

German table mirror, mounted on ivory tusks on a wooden base with convex glass.

- *44cm x 20cm*
- £3,000 • Emanouel

△ Painted Mirror

- *1910*

A carved wood mirror with unusual paint effect with C-scroll border.

- *65cm x 55cm*
- £380 • Myriad

▽ Art Nouveau Mirror

- *circa 1910*

A Louis Majorelle mirror, leather backed with glass behind door.

- *height 18cm*
- £2,800 • Cameo Gallery

▽ Walnut Wall Mirror

- *circa 1920s*

George II-style walnut and parcel-gilt wall mirror with swan-neck pediment and beaded edges.

- *112cm x 68cm*
- £1,250 • M. Luther

▽ Carved Oak Mirror

- *1940*

An Italian heavily carved oak mirror, carved with large golden apples and pears.

- *102cm x 159cm*
- £2,800 • Judy Fox

△ Library Steps

- *1770*

French library steps made from walnut consisting of four steps, with turned and carved decoration.

- *99cm*
- £4,850 • Augustus Brandt

△ George III Bucket

- *circa 1790*

A mahogany brass-bound bucket of navette shape.

- *height 33cm*
- £2,350 • J. de Haan

▽ Jardinière Stand

- *1780*

A walnut jardinière stand on a tripod base carved as cherubs, with cloven feet.

- *height 79cm*
- £1,400 • Sign of the Times

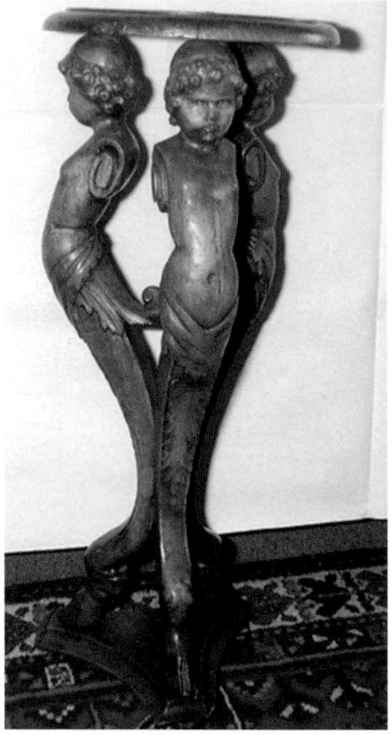

▷ Painted Jardinère

- *late 19th century*

Painted steel body with floral scrolled handles.

- *height 21cm*
- £90 • Riverbank

△ Butler's Tray

- *circa 1780*

A mahogany butler's tray with stand and hinged side flaps.

- *height 32cm*
- £1,250 • Lynda Franklin

◁ Painted Washstand

- *circa 1800*

Green buff pine with darker green coaching lines. Large cupboard, deep drawer and pull-out bidet.

- *height 102cm*
- £2,350 • John Clay

△ Umbrella and Coat Stand

- *circa 1790*

In patinated mahogany with fine shaped pegs and turned finials. With original zinc liner.

- *height 181cm*
- £2,850 • Wakelin Linfield

▽ Mahogany Cellaret

- *circa 1790*

A mahogany cellaret with boxwood stringing and chequered line inlay.

- *height 66cm*
- £3,250 • J. de Haan

▽ Indian Shrine

- *late 18th century*

An Indian Hindu shrine with pink moulded dome with pierced iron rail, ornately decorated with carved pillars painted pink and green, standing on a square base.

- *153cm x 76cm x 76cm*
- £4,700 • Gordon Reece

▽ Oval Tea Tray

- *circa 1790*

A tray of the Sheraton period, having a wavy edge with the outside inlaid with joined loops.

- *width 71cm*
- £850 • J. Collins

▽ Papier Mâché Tray

- *circa 1800*

A red lacquered papier mâché tray showing Oriental decoration.

- £2,850 • P.L. James

△ Butler's Tray

• *circa 1810*
A mahogany butler's tray and reading stand with turned and tapered legs.
• *height 32cm*
• £480 • P.L. James

△ Georgian Wash Stand

• *1820*
A George III wash stand with hinged top enclosing basin above a sliding door on tapered legs.
• *height 75cm x 40cm*
• £1,800 • C.H. Major

△ Papier Mâché Tray

• *circa 1850*
A papier mâché tray standing on a rectangular, wooden stand. In good condition.
• *height 45cm*
• £1,050 • North West 8

△ English Washstand

• *circa 1820*
In mahogany with inlay, three drawers and brass handles.
• *height 1.25m*
• £850 • Youll's

△ Victorian Bucket

• *circa 1860*
Oak bucket with brass hoops, silver wash, brass handle and name plaque.
• *height 33cm*
• £150 • Albany

▽ Music Stand

• *circa 1825*
Regency rosewood music stand with lyre-shaped design. The reeded column with turned and gadrooned decoration raised on a tripod base with bun feet.
• *height 108cm*
• £3,600 • O.F.Wilson

▽ Tôle Plant-Holder

• *1850*
One of a pair painted English tôle plant-holders decorated with hand-painted chrysanthemums and peonies. With pierced gilt foliate rail around the top, flanked by brass lion handles.
• *height 34.5cm*
• £1,250 • Goodison Paraskeva

▽ Regency Jardinière

• *circa 1820*
A Regency painted metal jardinière of octagonal form with chinoiserie designs.
• *length 41.5cm*
• £3,250 • O.F. Wilson

△ Victorian Wagonwheel

• *circa 1836–1901*
Metal-banded elm Victorian wagonwheel.
• *diameter 74cm*
• £75 • Curios

△ Pair of Jardinières

• *circa 1840*
One of a pair of walnut tripod jardinières with scrolled feet and copper lines.
• *height 107cm*
• £14,500 • Wakelin Linfield

△ Artist's Portfolio and Stand

• *1860*
An elaborately carved oak artist's portfolio with brushes and artist's palette, with foliate design in the carving, standing on a mahogany trestle base.
• *110cm x 84cm*
• £13,500 • Ranby Hall

△ Mahogany Boot Rack

• *circa 1860*
Fine English mahogany boot rack.
• *height 1.0m*
• £495 • Lacquer Chest

△ Gothic-Style Stand

• *late 19th century*
Pentagonal stand with gothic tracery.
• *height 110cm*
• £450 • Youll's

△ Victorian Washstand

• *circa 1870*
Victorian burr-walnut washstand with a grey and white marble top above three drawers and a moulded cupboard, standing on a straight moulded base.
• *85cm x 124cm*
• £850 • Hill Farm

▽ Library Steps

• *late 19th century*
Three-runged oak library steps with supporting pole to platform.
• *height 162cm*
• £450 • Riverbank

▽ Towel Rail

• *circa 1870*
Victorian satin birchwood towel rail with carved and turned decoration.
• *height 90cm*
• £220 • Nicholas Mitchell

▷ French Plant-Holder

• *1880*
Dark green French circular tôle plant-holder, standing on gilt paw feet with a laurel wreath design around the lip, and a cartouche of a hand-painted classical scene.
• *height 49cm*
• £495 • Goodison Paraskeva

▷ Gothic Hall Stand

• *late 19th century*
French hall stand with profusely carved tracery and lifting seat.
• *height 242cm*
• £1,400 • Youll's

△ Gueridon Pedestal

• *late 19th century*
A Black Forest gueridon pedestal with an intertwined, tree-like central column.
• *height 77cm*
• £880 • North West 8

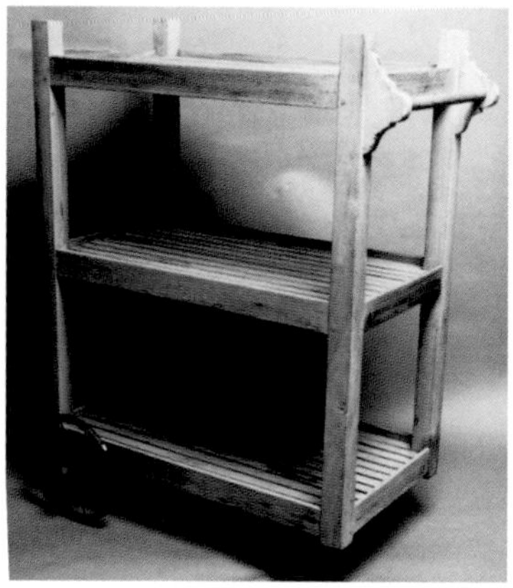

△ Teak Trolley

• *circa 1880*
A three-shelved teak trolley with two large, spoked wheels.
• *height 100cm*
• £300 • Lacquer Chest

▽ Rice Bucket

• *1880*
Chinese rice bucket with brass fittings, central carved handle and painted Chinese characters.
• *31cm x 25cm*
• £50 • Great Grooms

▽ Cast-Iron Safe

• *1880*
A solid cast-iron safe with four drawers at front and combination lock, marble-topped.
• *102cm x 54cm x 40cm*
• £285 • Tredantiques

▽ Oak Pulpit

- *circa 1890*

A fine Victorian pulpit in the Arts and Crafts manner.

- *height 143cm*
- £850 • Westland & Co.

▽ Coal Box in Sarcophagus Form

- *1890*

A nineteenth-century mahogany coal box in sarcophagus form with lid and a brass handle.

- *54cm x 33cm*
- £395 • Great Grooms

▽ Urn Stands

- *circa 1880*

A pair of Oriental stands with marble tops and pierced flower decoration.

- *height 92cm*
- £660 • Castlegate

△ Victorian Hall Stand

- *circa 1890*

Oak hall stand with ceramic tiles and marble-topped drawer.

- *height 206cm*
- £950 • Old Cinema

△ Knife Sharpener

- *circa 1900*

Pine knife sharpener, with the maker's name 'Kent's', on cast-iron support.

- *120cm x 75cm*
- £475 • Drummonds

△ Library Steps

- *circa 1900*

Oak library steps with carved decoration to the sides.

- *height 47cm*
- £500 • Lacquer Chest

▽ Umbrella Stand

- *1900*

Brass umbrella stand.

- *height 60cm*
- £950 • Mac Humble

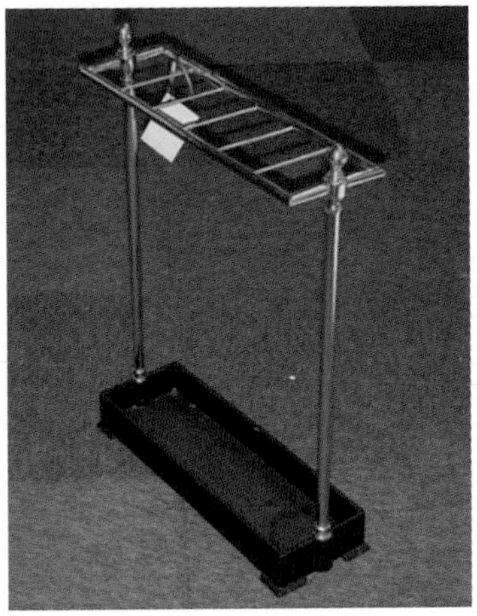

▽ Waste Paper Baskets

- *circa 1910*

Silver plated baskets with pierced rim and frieze below.

- *height 33cm*
- £880 • Lesley Bragge

▽ Plate Drainer

- *circa 1910*

A pine draining board for drying dishes, with carved ends.

- *width 64cm*
- £150 • Lacquer Chest

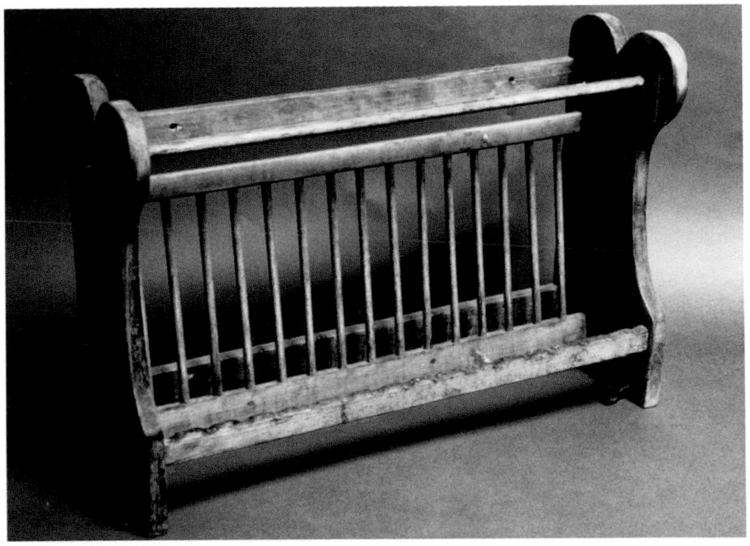

△ Marble and Gilt Stand

- *circa 1900*

A French marble stand of Doric form with fine ormolu mounts.

- *height 113cm*
- £2,500 • Wakelin Linfield

△ Edwardian Gong

- *circa 1913*

An oak and horn gong with baton and trophy plaque.

- *height 34cm*
- £165 • Castlegate

△ Six-Fold Paper Screen

- *18th century*

Ink and colour on a buff ground with clouds in gold leaf.

- *height 77cm, length 1.73m*
- £8,800 • Gregg Baker

△ Leather Dutch Screen

- *1800*

A four-panelled Dutch leather screen embossed with scrolled foliate and shell designs.

- *length 130cm*
- £1,500 • C.H. Major

△ Regency Tapestry Screen

- *circa 1810*

Mahogany with ebony inlay with a counter-balanced tapestry screen.

- *height 1.46m*
- £595 • Castlegate

△ Mahogany Pole Screen

- *circa 1770*

George III mahogany pole screen with well-drawn base and earlier needlework banner.

- *height 156cm*
- £4,250 • John Bly

△ Mahogany Screen

- *19th century*

Late Georgian with sliding side screens and turned stretchers.

- *height 1.1m*
- £695 • Old Cinema

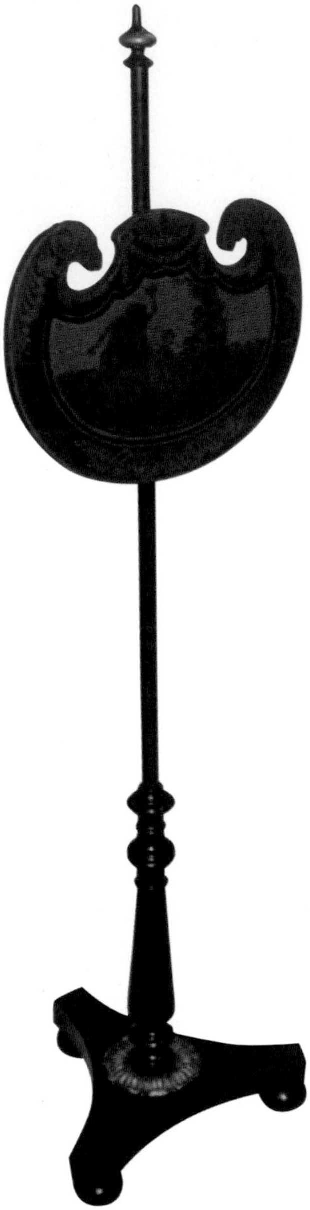

△ Ebonised Fire Screen

- *1820*

A Regency ebonised fire screen, in the shape of a shield on a tapered stand with tripod base and bun feet.

- *135cm x 38cm*
- £650 • Mac Humble

▽ Regency Fire Screen

- *circa 1830*

Walnut and needlepoint fire screen.

- *height 71cm*
- £1,450 • Ronald G. Chambers

▽ Mahogany Pole Screen

- *1830–37*

A William IV mahogany pole screen with a tapestry of golden pheasant in petit point.

- *height 153cm*
- £975 • Harpur Deardren

▽ Paper Screens

- *18th century*

One of a pair of screens of the Edo period decorated in ink, colours and gilt on a buff ground. Signed 'Raisai Dogin Show'.

- *height 69cm, length 2.69m*
- £20,000 • Gregg Baker

△ Victorian Beadwork Screens

• *circa 1840*
One of a pair of Victorian pole screens in walnut-carved frames containing fine examples of beadwork of the period.
• *height 140cm*
• £4,500 • **Wakelin Linfield**

△ Victorian Fire Screen

• *1900s*
A brass-framed fire screen with enamelled floral designs.
• *61cm x 43cm*
• £80 • **Old School**

△ Two-Fold Paper Screen

• *20th century*
Taisho-period screen in ink and colour with hydrangea, peony and poppy.
• *1.81m x 1.62m*
• £8,600 • **Gregg Baker**

▽ Chinese Fire Screen

• *circa 1860*
Chinese fire screen embroidered with peonies, chrysanthemums, butterflies and birds, in silk with gold threads. Supported by a mahogany stand.
• *78cm x 62cm*
• £385 • **Younger**

▽ Japanese Screen

• *1868–1912*
A Japanese cloisonné two-fold lacquer screen with floral decoration.
• *167.5cm x 57.5cm*
• £6,500 • **David Brower**

▽ Paper Screen

• *19th century*
A pair of two-fold paper screens painted in ink on a gold ground.
• *length 53.3cm*
• £4,800 • **Gregg Baker**

▽ Needlepoint Fire Screen

• *circa 1880*
A Victorian mahogany needlepoint fire screen with a King Charles spaniel lying on a red cushion within a turned and carved frame.
• *74cm x 65cm*
• £1,350 • **Drummonds**

▽ Silk Screen

• *20th century*
Ink and colour on a buff ground with pine trees, bamboo fences, paths and lanterns.
• *height 90cm, length 1.76m*
• £5,600 • **Gregg Baker**

△ Silk Screen

• *early 20th century*
Two-fold silk screen painted in ink with birds flying above rose mallow on which are a praying mantis and a cricket.
• *height 1.81m, length 1.17m*
• £6,800 • **Gregg Baker**

△ Chinese Screen

• *1850*
One of a pair of antique Chinese filigree screens made of cyprus wood with geometric designs .
• *109cm x 51cm*
• £1,350 • **Gordon Reece**

△ Four-Fold Paper Screen

• *20th century*
Silver and gold leaf on buff ground with imprint of three fuki (butterbur).
• *height 171m, length 2.69m*
• £8,500 • **Gregg Baker**

SETTEES & SOFAS

▽ French Restoration Sofa

- *1820*

French Restoration-period sofa with a moulded wood frame painted cream with gilt banding, on stylised bun feet, designed by Julian Chichester.

- *81cm x 202cm x 78cm*
- **£3,800** • **Ranby Hall**

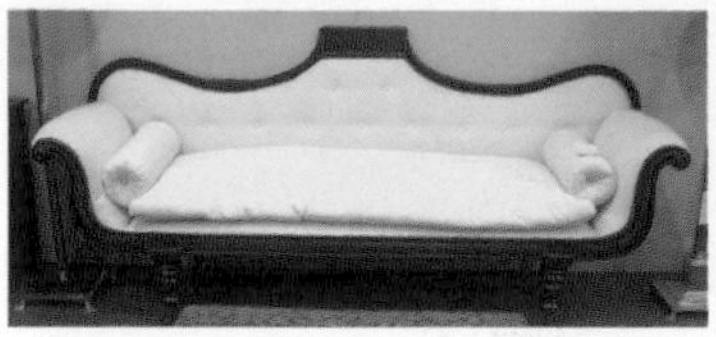

△ Regency Mahogany Sofa

- *circa 1824*

A Regency mahogany double-ended sofa raised on turned legs with original brass castors and maker's name and date on top back rail.

- *95cm x 220cm*
- **£1,950** • **Old Cinema**

△ Mahogany Hall Bench

- *circa 1800*

Mahogany hall bench with scrolled reeded back with applied reeded roundels, central oval frame and mahogany panel.

- *85cm x 105cm*
- **£5,850** • **Wakelin Linfield**

▽ Regency Sofa

- *circa 1810*

An English Regency-period green sofa on eight turned mahogany legs with original brass castors.

- *width 1.9m*
- **£3,500** • **Ian Spencer**

△ English Painted Settee

- *late 18th century*

An English painted and decorated settee with caned back and sides.

- *79cm x 170cm x 82cm*
- **£11,000** • **O.F. Wilson**

△ Country House Settee

- *circa 1810*

English painted rosewood settee in the George Smith manner. On castors with fleur-de-lys design.

- *width 2.09m*
- **£4,800** • **M. Luther**

▽ 'Dolphin' Sofa

- *circa 1820*

North German birchwood and masur birch sofa covered in calico. With noticeable tunnel armrests with dolphin designs. The whole resting on scrolled feet.

- *width 2.1m*
- **£7,500** • **R. Cavendish**

△ French Louis XVII Sofa

- *circa 1780*

French Louis XVII sofa with painted and moulded carved wooden frame, curved back and a padded seat and small arm rests, above a moulded apron and fluted legs.

- *82cm x 191cm*
- **£6,200** • **Augustus Brandt**

▽ Bouson-Covered Sofa

- *circa 1820*

A French early nineteenth-century bouson-covered sofa with gilt decoration.

- *width 1.76m*
- **£5,000** • **Mora Upham**

△ Biedermeier Sofa

- *circa 1820*

Biedermeier birchwood sofa with serpentine back and front and carved decoration to the apron.

- *95cm x 199cm*
- **£5,600** • **R. Cavendish**

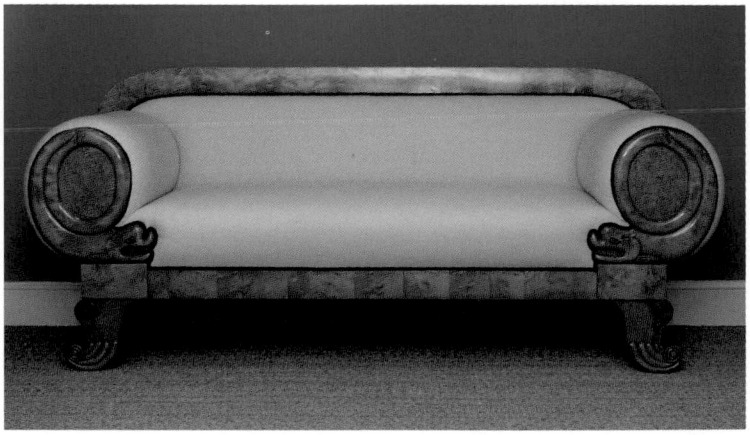

△ Mahogany Sofa

- *circa 1830*

William IV mahogany double-ended sofa raised on turned legs with original brass castors.

- *height 85cm*
- £1,650 • Castlegate

▽ Double-Ended Mahogany Sofa

- *early 19th century*

An early nineteenth-century mahogany double-ended sofa. Upholstered in selling fabric.

- *152cm x 205cm x 65cm*
- £3,995 • Harpur Deardren

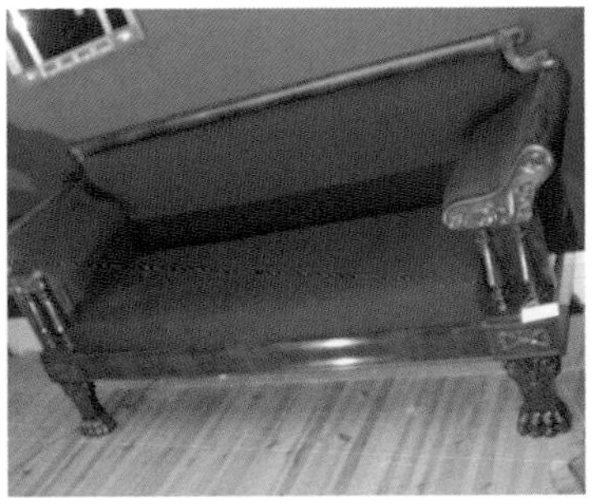

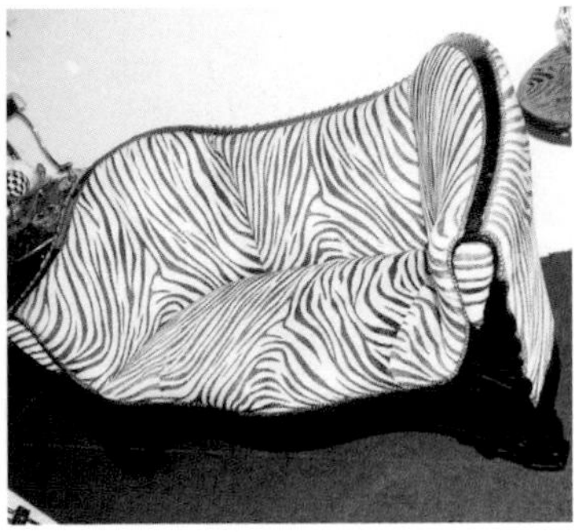

△ Zebra-Striped Sofa

- *circa 1830*

An early 19th-century cowhide sofa painted in zebra stripes with ogee mahogany feet, with double balloon back and serpentine front. A unique design with elegant covers to both back and front.

- *width 1.36m*
- £4,500 • B. & T. Antiques

▽ Victorian Sofa

- *circa 1870*

Walnut sofa on turned legs with carved arm rests.

- *width 1.53m*
- £2,900 • L. & E. Kreckovic

△ French Sofa and Chairs

- *1860*

A French Louis XVI-style sofa with curved padded back and seat with needlepoint covers, splayed arms and turned legs, together with four chairs,

- *width 125cm (settee), 65cm (chair)*
- £5,500 • Judy Fox

▽ Victorian Sofa

- *circa 1820*

Howard-style cream-coloured sofa, complete in selling fabric, raised on terracotta castors with brass fittings.

- *width 1.5m*
- £1,450 • Tredantiques

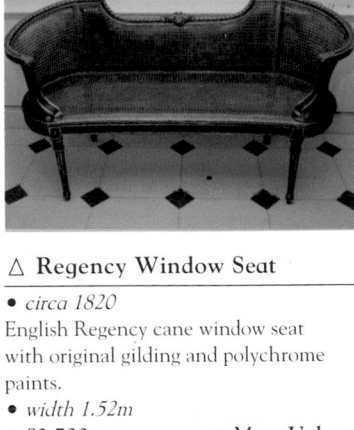

△ Regency Window Seat

- *circa 1820*

English Regency cane window seat with original gilding and polychrome paints.

- *width 1.52m*
- £3,700 • Mora Upham

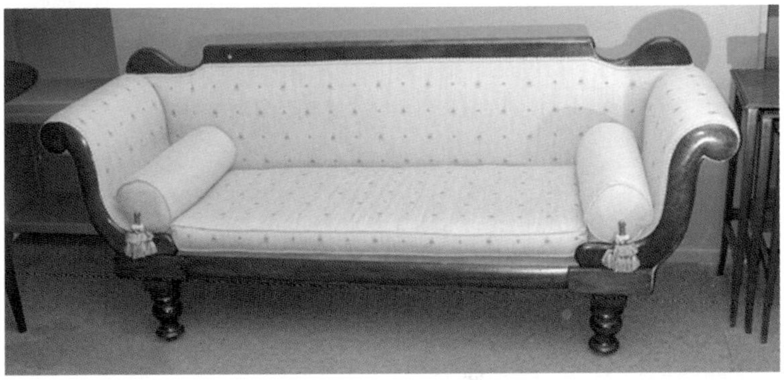

△ Lyre-Shaped Settee

- *1860*

A mahogany lyre-shaped sofa with scrolled arms on turned legs.

- *210cm x 55cm*
- £1,500 • Great Grooms

▽ Biedermeier Sofa

- *circa 1860*

A nineteenth-century Biedermeier mahogany sofa with lyre back and scrolled shaped arms with carved bun feet.

- *106cm x 274cm x 64cm*
- £5,600 • Ranby Hall

△ High-Back Oak Settee

- *circa 1840*

Oak high-back four-panelled settee with moulded arms and padded seat, standing on cabriole legs with pad feet.

- *82cm x 189cm*
- £1,875 • Drummonds

△ French Giltwood Sofa

- *circa 1860*

A giltwood French Louis XV-style canapé with curved, arched padded back and sides and a serpentine apron on cabriole legs.

- *120cm x 120cm x 69cm*
- £6,800 • Ranby Hall

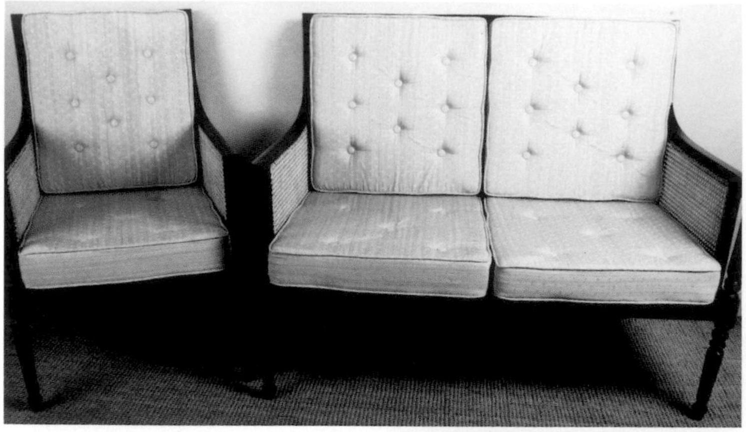

△ Cane Sofa

- *19th century*

Cane sofa and two chairs, with studded upholstery backs and turned and fluted legs.

- *width 1.4m*
- £3,400 • Lynda Franklin

△ Calico Sofa

- *circa 1880*

Sofa by Howard & Sons on square mahogany tapered legs.

- *width 1.6m*
- £3,500 • David Ford

▽ Victorian Sofa

- *circa 1880*

Small Victorian sofa with low button back, mahogany scrolled arms and escargot feet.

- *width 1.65m*
- £2,150 • Antique Warehouse

△ Chesterfield Sofa

- *circa 1860*

Victorian Chesterfield sofa upholstered in Venetian damask, with padded moulded back and seat, standing on turned legs.

- *length 197cm*
- £1,950 • The Swan

△ Day-Bed Sofa

- *circa 1870*

A mid-Victorian satinwood day-bed sofa, in the Regency style, with gilt decoration, scrolled ends and swept feet.

- *width 2.14m*
- £1,895 • Antique Warehouse

▽ Canapé Sofa

- *circa 1880*

An unusual ebonised cherrywood and canapé sofa. Bow-backed carvings and lovely scroll shape overall.

- *width 1.95m*
- £2,800 • Sieff

△ Wing Sofa

- *circa 1880*

Armchair sofa raised upon ebonised cabriole legs on pad feet.

- *height 1.3m*
- £1,850 • Ranby Hall

▽ Walnut Sofa

- *circa 1890s*

Small late Victorian sofa with arched padded button back and carved walnut frame with small scrolled arms.

- *94cm x 133cm*
- £1,200 • John Riordan

▷ Victorian Sofa

- *19th century*

Two-seater, re-upholstered sofa, the moulded frame profusely carved.

- *width 1.88m*
- £1,350 • Tower Bridge

△ Walnut Settee

- *circa 1870*

A Victorian walnut settee, with back carved into three ovals and serpentine front, all raised on cabriole legs with china castors.

- *width 2.5m*
- £3,200 • Judy Fox

△ Victorian Two-Seat Settee

- *circa 1880*

Elegant Victorian settee with a brass rose in the centre of the moulded top rail, six rail splats and moulded arms terminating with a brass rose, standing on shaped and tapered legs.

- *89cm x 99cm*
- £825 • Drummonds

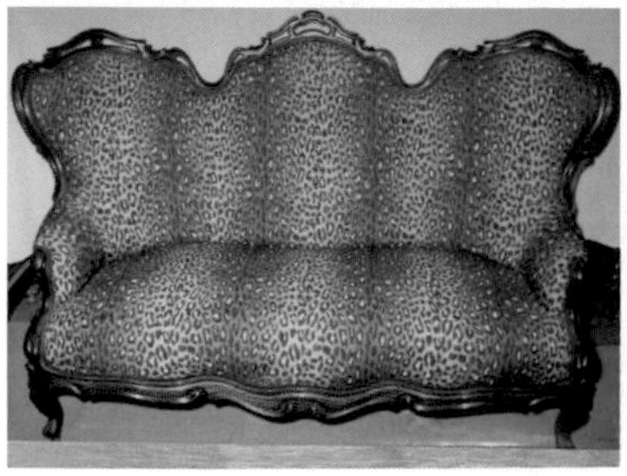

◁ Gustavian Suite

- *circa 1880*

Suite of Gustavian-style furniture including a sofa, pair of armchairs and four chairs.

- £5,600 (suite) • R. Cavendish

▽ Beechwood Canapé

- *circa 1890s*

A grey painted and carved beechwood canapé in the style of Louis XVI.

- *105cm x 173cm*
- £1,500 • Westland & Co.

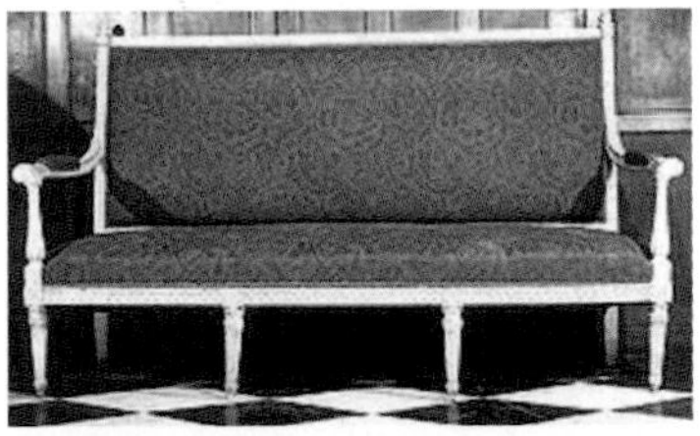

▽ George III-Style Settee

- *circa 1890*

A George III-style mahogany settee, with shaped back and scrolled arm rests on chamfered legs.

- *78cm x 175cm x 60cm*
- £1,850 • Ranby Hall

△ Victorian Three-Seater Sofa

- *19th century*

Oak sofa with two matching chairs with ornate carvings of birds at the crest of the sofa.

- *width 1.75m*
- £3,200 • Tower Bridge

▽ Birchwood Sofa

- *circa 1890*

Swedish birchwood Biedermeier-style sofa showing an architectural influence, with a central black plaque of an angel in a chariot below an arched pediment, the whole on square legs.

- *97cm x 211cm*
- £3,900 • R. Cavendish

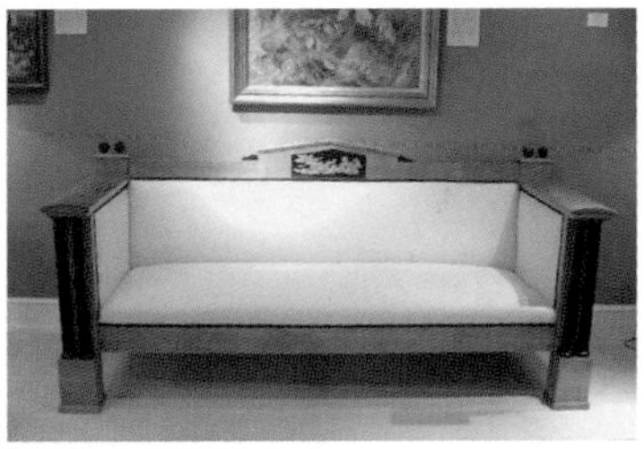

◁ Two-Seater Sofa

- *19th century*

Two-seater sofa with cushions and reeded turned legs.

- *width 1.92m*
- £1,850 • Ranby Hall

△ Gustavian Style Sofa

- *circa 1899*

Swedish Louis XVI style Gustavian style birchwood sofa, upholstered in calico with noticeable carved and scrolled arm rests and moulded back, the whole resting on carved scrolled feet.

- *135cm x 158cm*
- £3,400 • R. Cavendish

△ High-Back Settee

- *circa 1880*

Victorian mahogany high-back settee with scrolled high arched and sides, standing on cabriole legs.

- *107cm x 88cm*
- £3,200 • John Clay

△ Three-Seater Sofa

- *circa 1930*

French Art Deco walnut three-seater sofa with two matching chairs.

- *width 1.8m*
- £2,200 (the set) • Oola Boola

▽ Swedish Settee

- *circa 1940*

Brown leather settee with tapered legs.

- *width 1.95m*
- £2,500 • B. & T. Antiques

▷ Chesterfield Sofa

- *circa 1900*

A two-seater chesterfield with mahogany bun feet and brass castors, covered in hessian.

- *width 1.72m*
- £1,250 • Annette Puttnam

STOOLS

▽ **Louis XV Stool**

- *circa 1760*

A Louis XV walnut stool with a circular buttoned top, the seat rail scrolled to meet the cabriole legs, standing on a scroll foot with a scrolled stretcher.

- *height 75cm*
- £1,650 • Butchoff

▽ **Walnut Stool**

- *18th century*

Walnut stool from the William and Mary period, with 'X'-frame stretcher. Restored in 1900.

- *height 46cm*
- £1,795 • Red Lion

△ **Elm Stool**

- *circa 1710*

English elm stool on four legs.

- *height 45cm*
- £95 • Castlegate

△ **Chinese Stools**

- *18th century*

A pair of Chinese hardwood stools with caned seats, hump-back stretchers and horse's hoof feet.

- *45cm x 35cm*
- £1,600 • Gordon Reece

△ **Louis XVI Footstool**

- *circa 1780*

Giltwood footstool with carved acanthus moulding and foliate legs.

- *height 14cm*
- £2,900 • O.F. Wilson

▷ **French Stool**

- *circa 1750*

French stool in the Louis XV style with gilded wooden legs.

- *height 46cm*
- £2,000 • O.F. Wilson

▽ **George I Walnut Stool**

- *circa 1720*

George I walnut stool with cabriole legs, carved at each knee with a carved shell.

- *height 54cm*
- £22,500 • John Bly

▽ **Queen Anne Stool**

- *1710*

A rare Queen Anne-period stool in walnut, with a circular top mounted on four carved cabriole legs with turned stretcher.

- *height 47cm*
- £15,500 • Wakelin Linfield

△ **Giltwood Stool**

- *circa 1720*

An early 18th-century giltwood stool on ornate 'H' frame with reeded legs.

- *height 90cm*
- £950 • Fulham

△ **Painted Tabourets**

- *1790*

Pair of late eighteenth century tabourets with painted decoration. Fluted tapered legs and carved frieze.

- *16cm x 31cm x 25cm*
- £2,600 • O.F. Wilson

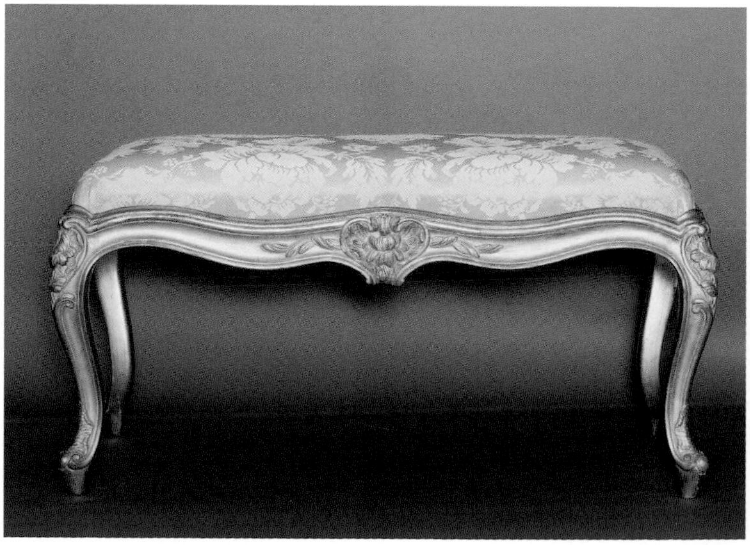

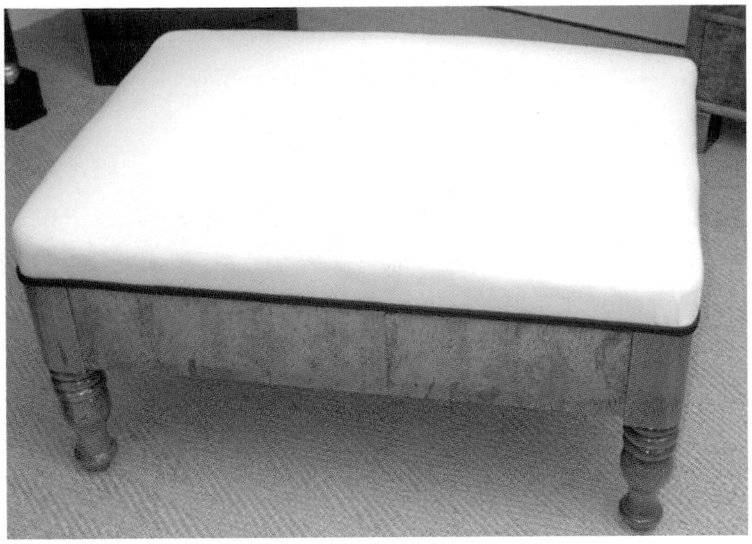

◁ Biedermeier Bench

- *circa 1820*

North German Biedermeier bench. Birchwood and masur birch.

- *50cm x 94cm x 68cm*
- £3,400 • R. Cavendish

▽ Victorian Mahogany Stool

- *19th century*

Victorian mahogany stool with brass claw and ball feet.

- *height 92cm*
- £650 • Solaris Antiques

▽ Birchwood Stools

- *1820–30*

One of a pair of Swedish Biedermeier birchwood stools raised on splayed legs.

- *39cm x 35cm*
- £3,400 • R. Cavendish

△ French Stool

- *circa 1820*

French mahogany X-frame stool with upholstered top.

- *length 52cm*
- £685 • M.J. Bowdery

△ Miniature Stool

- *circa 1820s*

Early 19th century fruit wood miniature stool with turned stretcher and legs.

- *19cm x 18cm*
- £395 • Wakelin Linfield

◁ Victorian Stool

- *circa 1840*

Early Victorian carved stool in gilt with cabriole legs and salmon-velvet upholstery.

- *height 18cm*
- £265 • Castlegate

△ Pair Of Stools

- *circa 1820*

A pair of Swedish stools designed by the architect Sundvall.

- *height 42cm*
- £2,700 • R. Cavendish

◁ French Giltwood Stool

- *circa 1840*

French giltwood stool, the legs carved with a rope twist design terminating on tassel feet.

- *height 42cm*
- £4,000 • Augustus Brand

◁ Piano Stools

- *circa 1835*

A pair of William IV rosewood revolving and adjustable stools.

- *height 58cm*
- £2,650 • J. Collins

▷ Biedermeier Stools

- *circa 1825*

One of a pair of German birchwood stools covered in horsehair.

- *height 58cm*
- £ 4,500 • R. Cavendish

▽ Piano Stool

- *circa 1830s*

William IV piano stool on adjustable reeded and carved column, on a platform base with scroll end feet and original tapestry seat.

- *height 54cm*
- £495 • The Swan

▽ Walnut Stool

- *late 19th century*

French walnut stool with button seat cover and cabriole legs.

- *height 49cm*
- £565 • Lesley Bragge

▽ Rosewood Stool

- *circa 1860*

Rectangular upholstered top on four cabuchon and leaf-carved, moulded cabriole legs, terminating in scrolled, leaf-carved toes.

- *height 42cm*
- £950 • J. Collins

△ Mahogany Stool

- *19th century*

Nineteenth-century mahogany stool with turned legs on brass castors by Gillows.

- *height 49cm*
- £400 • Old Cinema

△ Walnut Footstools

- *circa 1850*

A pair of walnut footstools. Rectangular overstuffed serpentine seats.

- *height 14cm*
- £950 • J. Collins

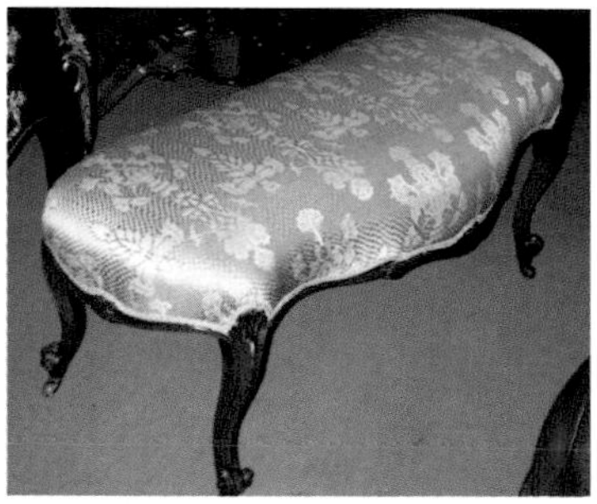

△ Victorian Walnut Stool

- *circa 1870*

A serpentine-fronted, upholstered walnut stool or window seat, seating two, with original ceramic castors. Re-covered.

- *height 44cm*
- £3,200 • Judy Fox

▽ Carved Mahogany Stool

- *1835*

A finely carved mahogany stool of good design and colour. Flowing X-frame legs with stretcher supports.

- *48cm x 69cm x 38cm*
- £2,950 • Mac Humble

◁ Carved Oak Stool

- *mid 19th century*

A Victorian oak stool with contemporary needlework to cover, cabriole legs and original ceramic castors.

- *height 42cm*
- £16,000 • Norman Adams

△ Piano Stool

- *1870*

A Victorian rosewood revolving piano stool on a carved column and scrolled feet.

- *height 59cm*
- £480 • Salem Antiques

△ French Painted Stool

- *circa 1870*

French window seat with carved frame and two arms traditionally re-upholstered in cream-striped fleur-de-lys fabric.

- *height 64cm*
- £795 • R.S. Antiques

△ Pair of Walnut Stools

- *1870*

A pair of Victorian walnut stools, on bulbous turned legs.

- *18cm x 35cm*
- £650 • Judy Fox

△ Mahogany Stools

- *1880*

A pair of Hepplewhite-style mahogany stools with scrolled arms, padded seats and standing on tapered legs.

- *73cm x 66cm*
- £2,650 • Judy Fox

▽ Chippendale-Style Stool

- *Victorian*

Late Victorian stool in the Chippendale style on ball and claw feet.

- *40cm x 47cm x 34cm*
- £425 • Fay Orton

▽ Mahogany Stool

- *circa 1880*

Mahogany oblong country oak stool standing on square straight legs, with scrolls at each corner.

- *56cm x 34cm*
- £495 • Macnaughton-Smith

▽ French Window Seat

- *circa 1890*

Seat with scrolled carving and floral decoration on turned legs with 'X' frame stretcher.

- *length 1.1m*
- £650 • North West 8

△ Walnut Footstool

- *circa 1880*

Small walnut footstool with circular re-upholstered padded top, standing on small cabriole legs.

- *width 36cm*
- £290 • Salem Antiques

△ Tapestry Stool

- *1880*

Fine walnut tapestry Queen Anne-style stool raised on cabriole legs carved with acanthus leaf designs, with claw and ball feet.

- *48cm x 51cm*
- £3,500 • Butchoff

▽ Empire-Style Window Seats

- *circa 1880*

One of a pair of mahogany Empire-style window seats with scrolled arms and gilded dolphin supports, on swept feet.

- *height 70cm*
- £2,800 • Mora Upham

▽ Wicker-Seated Stool

- *circa 1880*

Louis XVI-style stool with cane seat with turned and fluted legs, with X-frame stretcher.

- *height 49cm*
- £485 • The Swan

◁ Late-Victorian Stool

- *circa 1890*

A mahogany stool of the late 19th-century, of an X-frame construction, with bone stringing and boxwood and rosewood inlay.

- *height 54cm*
- £895 • Judy Fox

△ Sabre-Leg Stool

- *circa 1950*

Pair of Regency-style stools with turned supports in fruitwood.

- *height 95cm*
- £1,000 • L. & E. Kreckovic

△ Mahogany Stool

- *circa 1890*

Miniature mahogany stool fashioned as a small table.

- *22cm x 33cm*
- £89 • The Swan

△ Piano Stool

- *1890*

Victorian piano stool with green leather seat on carved acanthus leaf legs.

- *height 51cm*
- £400 • Judy Fox

△ Cane Stool

- *circa 1900*

An Edwardian Louis XV-style gilt and caned stool on cabriole legs with scrolled feet.

- *height 42cm*
- £295 • French Room

▽ Marquetry Table

- *circa 1690*

Good William and Mary floral marquetry table, inlaid with various woods.

- *height 80cm*
- £8,850 • P.L. James

△ Side Table

- *circa 1690*

Exceptional William and Mary marquetry side table with 'X' stretcher and original bun feet.

- *height 71cm*
- £4,400 • Walwyn Raffety

▷ Portuguese Rosewood Table

- *circa 1700*

A solid rosewood table, the top with a decorative bead-moulded edge, the frieze with chevron-pattern decoration, raised on spiral-twist legs with discs and bulbous turnings, with similar stretchers, joined at the corners with decorative pegs.

- *79cm x 112cm*
- £6.800 • Anthony Outred

▽ Serving Table

- *circa 1740*

Fine George II carved mahogany serving table with fluted frieze above six heavily carved legs with leaf decoration.

- *height 89cm*
- £130,000 • Norman Adams

▽ Oak Side Table

- *17th century*

A seventeenth-century oak side table with a single drawer on a ball-and-reel turned frame, with rich patina, on ball feet.

- *68cm x 77cm x 54cm*
- £5,600 • Peter Bunting

▽ Swedish Console Table with Griffin

- *18th century*

Swedish giltwood console table with central carved griffin on black-figured marble plinth.

- *82cm x 75cm x 47cm*
- £8,500 • Heytesbury

▽ Mahogany Card Table

- *1740*

Superb mahogany card table on cabriole legs, with a secret drawer. Exhibited at Bradford Art Gallery in 1925.

- *74cm x 84cm x 41cm*
- £8,900 • Dial Post House

△ Yew Flip-Top Table

- *circa 1750*

A fine original eighteenth-century yew-wood tripod and flip-top table with good colouring and proportions.

- *67cm x 75cm*
- £2,250 • Rod Wilson

△ Marble-Topped Table

- *circa 1740*

Eighteenth-century marble-topped table on turned legs with ball feet.

- *height 71cm*
- £1,250 • Lynda Franklin

△ Walnut Lowboy

- *1760*

Chippendale-style lowboy made of walnut, with carved apron on straight legs.

- *70cm x 78cm x 49cm*
- £3,850 • Mac Humble

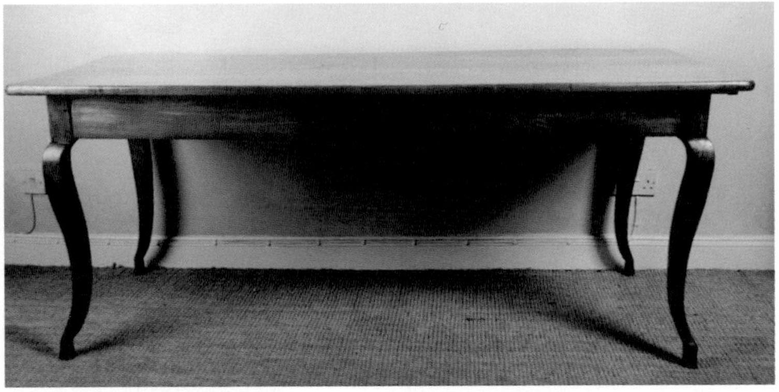

△ Cherrywood Table

- *circa 1760*

French table on cabriole legs.

- *length 180cm*
- £3,200 • Lynda Franklin

△ Mahogany Tripod Table

- *circa 1760*

Mahogany tilt-top, birdcage table with turned support raised on splayed legs.

- *height 69.5cm*
- £4,800 • O.F. Wilson

△ Spider-legged Work Table

- *1800*

Mahogany work table with unusual spider legs.

- *72cm x 53cm x 40cm*
- £4,200 • O.F. Wilson

▽ Urn Table

- *circa 1760*

An unusual Chippendale-period mahogany urn table, with fret gallery, inlaid floral side panels and turned, fluted legs.

- *height 61cm*
- £33,000 • Norman Adams

▽ Octagonal Rosewood Table

- *1800*

An octagonal rosewood table with floral satinwood inlay, on tapering cabriole legs.

- *72cm x 78cm*
- £450 • Tredantiques

▽ Pembroke Table

- *circa 1770*

English mahogany Pembroke table of typical form, veneered with satin and tulipwood, strung with ebony and boxwood. The table has drawers at either end with brass fittings, a side flap and the whole rests on four square tapering legs terminating in brass castors.

- *height 74cm*
- £4,850 • Wakelin Linfield

▽ Walnut Side Table

- *circa 1780*

Good French walnut side table with single drawer and square, tapered legs.

- *height 72cm*
- £1,100 • Lynda Franklin

▽ Rosewood Table

- *1800–30*

A Regency rosewood table, with solid trestle base on castors.

- *75cm x 153cm x 78cm*
- £3,995 • Harpur Deardren

△ Supper Table

- *circa 1780*

Georgian mahogany tambor-fronted gentleman's supper table on square legs with side flaps.

- *height 70cm*
- £4,000 • Castlegate

△ Card Table

- *circa 1790*

George III mahogany card table.

- *height 71cm*
- £3,950 • J. de Haan

△ Lady's Work Table

- *circa 1850s*

A Victorian burr- and quarter-sawn walnut serpentine-outline lady's work table with boxwood foliate inlays.

- *71cm x 58cm*
- £2,495 • Great Grooms

△ Sheraton Card Table

- *1805*

George III Sheraton mahogany card table. Beautifully inlaid with rosewood.

- *76cm x 92cm x 46cm*
- £9,750 • Freshfords

△ Writing Table

- *1810–20*

Swedish mahogany writing/console table. The top with fitted drawers and gallery, above a central drawer, raised on four turned columns, with a solid stretcher base.

- *72cm x 74cm*
- £3,700 • R. Cavendish

△ Regency Work Table

- *1820*

An octagonal Regency red lacquer work table, with gilt foliate designs on square tapered legs.

- *79cm x 49cm x 36cm*
- £3,200 • Ranby Hall

▽ Regency Pembroke Table

- *circa 1810*

Fine quality Regency period mahogany and ebony inlaid Pembroke table. Standing on a twin double C- scrolled supports joining out-swept legs, with brass caps and castors.

- *73cm x 104cm x 51cm*
- £10,950 • Wakelin Linfield

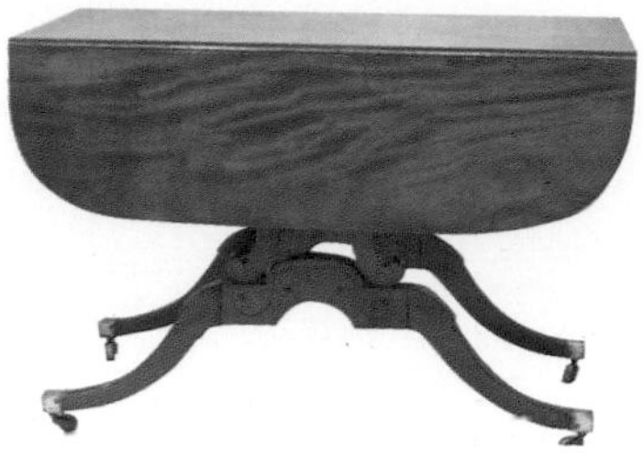

▽ Games/Sewing Table

- *circa 1810*

Miniature Pembroke sewing/games table with three-tiered drawers with ring handles in mask decoration, raised on ring-turned legs, terminating on brass castors.

- *73cm x 35cm*
- £5,250 • Wakelin Linfield

▽ Giltwood ConsoleTable

- *circa 1820*

A Louis XVI-style French carved console table with mottled green and white marble top with mythical beast supports, standing on claw feet.

- *54cm x 61cm x 48cm*
- £850 • Tredantiques

△ Occasional Table

- *circa 1810*

Regency mahogany occasional table in pristine condition.

- *height 72cm*
- £1,650 • J. Collins

△ Regency Table

- *1812–30*

Regency mahogany table on an ebonised, X-framed stretcher base.

- *71cm x 107cm*
- £3,350 • Old Cinema

△ Satinwood Table

- *1815*

Satinwood table banded in rosewood, on a single pedestal on a tripod base with scrolled feet.

- *74cm x 52cm*
- £5,900 • Dial Post House

▽ Regency Table

- *1820*

Regency rosewood worktable with oval folding top, one single drawer and small turned handles, standing on four moulded tripods and arched legs with brass castors.

- *height 48cm*
- £1,695 • A.I.G.

▽ Writing Table

- *circa 1830*

A William IV mahogany partner's library writing table with drawers each side of a tooled leather inset. The top raised on octagonal legs and original brass castors.

- *74cm x 92cm*
- £2,600 • Great Grooms

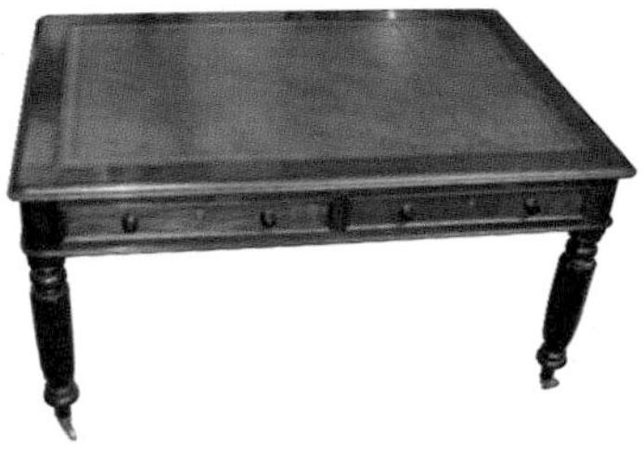

▽ Card Table

- *circa 1830*

Mahogany envelope card table with baize to inside on turned column with platform base.

- *height 71cm*
- £2,200 • John Clay

▽ Granite-Top Table

• *1830*

A Louis Philippe table with a granite top, on central pedestal, with heavily carved tripod base, and scrolled paw feet.

• *77cm x 100cm*

• £5,250 • Ranby Hall

▽ Games Table

• *circa 1835*

Mahogany, fold-over games table raised on central pedestal.

• *height 75cm*

• £1,650 • Ranby Hall

▽ Oak Table

• *circa 1840*

Oak country corner table with triangular top standing on three straight square legs, and straight stretcher.

• *85cm x 54cm*

• £1,100 • Lacquer Chest

▽ Biedermeier Tables

• *1830–40*

One of a pair of Swedish birchwood Biedermeier tables raised on baluster-turned columns with a solid, shaped base, with four scrolled feet.

• *70cm x 58cm*

• £4,900 • R. Cavendish

▽ English Writing Table

• *1840*

A fine English rosewood writing table with pierced gallery above four drawers with a moulded edge. Stretcher base and castors.

• *76cm x 83cm x 50cm*

• £2,800 • Ranby Hall

◁ William IV Table

• *circa 1830s*

William IV mahogany table with brass drop handles and single drawer, raised on turned, tapering, candy-twist legs.

• *76cm x 56cm*

• £750 • Macnaughton-Smith

△ Lady's Sewing Table

• *early 19th century*

A Regency figured-mahogany inlaid lady's sewing table with a set of four drawers with ivory escutcheons, turned handles, standing on square tapered legs, with S-shaped stretcher.

• *83cm x 48cm x 37cm*

• £1,950 • S. Duggan

△ Victorian Circular Table

• *1840*

A Victorian mahogany occasional table, with grey and cream circular marble top with central stand and tripod base with claw feet.

• *72cm x 48cm*

• £1,500 • Tredantiques

◁ Oak Library Table

• *circa 1835*

Medieval-revival library table in the manner of Richard Bridgens. The top with rounded corners and decorated with a border of an interlocking band design defined on each side by a string inlay of ebony and with stylised motifs at each corner. The whole on stepped moulded feet.

• *74cm x 150cm*

• £28,000 • Anthony Outred

△ Sutherland Table

• *circa 1835*

Walnut Sutherland table with satinwood and boxwood inlay.

• *height 72cm*

• £450 • The Swan

△ Rosewood Work Table

• *1840*

Rosewood work table raised on a U-shaped pedestal base.

• *72cm x 80cm x 40cm*

• £2,800 • Midwinter

▽ Parquetry Top Table

- *circa 1840*

Occasional table with an inlaid parquetry octagonal top table with central pedestal and standing on a tripod base on ball feet.

- *height 78cm*
- £995 • A.I.G.

▽ Demi-Lune Card Table

- *1837–1901*

Victorian burr-walnut demi-lune card table with scrolled carved legs and feet.

- *74cm x 35cm x 43cm*
- £1,995 • Old Cinema

▽ Regency Side Table

- *circa 1850*

Regency side table with straight moulded top with beading, on straight supports joined by a turned stretcher.

- *height 79cm*
- £850 • Hill Farm

△ Games Table

- *circa 1840*

Rosewood games table of exceptional quality with original ormolu paw feet.

- *height 74cm*
- £3,800 • Ranby Hall

△ Regency Table

- *circa 1820*

Adjustable Regency mahogany table, with a central tan hide top, standing on a tall central pedestal and a tripod base.

- *height 104cm*
- £1,395 • A.I.G.

△ Hall Table and Chairs

- *1850*

Oak hall suite comprising of a table on turned legs with carved back, and two hall chairs. Rijn style, marked 'SP'.

- *width 94cm (table)*
- £3,350 • Mac Humble

▷ Shearing Table

- *circa 1850*

Primitive, V-shaped wooden table for sheep-shearing.

- *height 38cm*
- £520 • Lacquer Chest

▽ Marquetry Table

- *circa 1850*

19th-century French marquetry table with floral designs and brass mounts.

- *height 71cm*
- £1,250 • Lynda Franklin

▽ Victorian Mahogany Table

- *circa 1850*

Victorian mahogany circular table on a turned baluster stand, raised on a tripod base, with splayed legs on circular ball feet.

- *height 84cm*
- £850 • Hill Farm

△ Painted Occasional Table

- *circa 1850*

A satinwood occasional table, the top with a circular painted romantic scene on square slender tapered legs with splayed feet and finial stretcher.

- *77cm x 43cm x 29cm*
- £2,500 • Butchoff

△ Walnut Work Table

- *1840–50*

An unusual walnut work table pictured open with fitted interior on a carved pedestal base.

- *74cm x 46cm x 57cm*
- £3,900 • Fay Orton

▽ Italian Table

- *circa 1850*

Italian walnut occasional table carved with figures of Bacchus, Pan and other mythological gods.

- *height 74cm*
- £8,000 • Ian Spencer

▽ Victorian Console Table

- *circa 1860*

A carved walnut console table with a shaped marble top with carved apron, raised on scrolled cabriole legs.

- *97cm x 135cm x 54cm*
- £4,450 • Browns

▽ Victorian Occasional Table

- *circa 1860s*

A Victorian rosewood and marquetry inlaid occasional table.

- *64cm x 50cm*
- £440 • Old Cinema

▷ Side Table

- *19th century*

French oval side table.

- *height 75cm*
- £650 • Youll's

△ Tray Top Work Table

- *circa 1850s*

Victorian mahogany and marquetry inlaid tray top work table.

- *69cm x 54cm*
- £995 • Old Cinema

△ Marble-Top Table

- *circa 1860*

With specimen marble top on carved stretcher base.

- *100cm x 93cm x 51cm*
- £4,800 • Fay Orton

▽ Victorian Inlaid Card Table

- *circa 1860*

Victorian figured walnut card table with moulded inlaid top raised on cabriole legs.

- *75cm x 83cm*
- £1,495 • W. John Griffiths

▽ Games Table

- *circa 1860*

Victorian mahogany games table with inlaid chess board on a circular top, pedestal column and three splat legs.

- *height 75cm*
- £1,200 • Lacquer Chest

▽ Victorian Tea Table

- *1860*

An English Victorian rosewood tea table, on cabriole legs with X-framed stretcher and carved finial.

- *24cm x 22cm*
- £1,585 • Ranby Hall

△ French Side Table

- *circa 1860*

French provincial side table with pine top, two long drawers and a serpentine apron, the whole standing on straight square legs.

- *73cm x 123cm*
- £1,250 • Anthony Sharpe

△ Mahogany Snap-Top Table

- *1860*

An English flame-mahogany snap-top table on a tripod base with claw feet.

- *72cm x 62cm x 49cm*
- £775 • Tredantiques

△ Oak Cricket Table

- *circa 1860*

Oak cricket table with circular top, single shelf, standing on three turned pillared legs.

- *70cm x 38cm*
- £780 • Lacquer Chest

△ Egyptian Inlaid Table

- *19th century*

An Egyptian table heavily inlaid with mother-of-pearl and ivory.

- *82cm x 54cm*
- £5,500 • Sinai

△ Victorian Writing Table

- *circa 1870*

Victorian writing table/workbox, standing on cabriole legs and stretcher base.

- *84cm x 70cm*
- £5.500 • The Swan

▽ Kingwood and Porcelain Work Table

- *circa 1860*

A kingwood and porcelain work table by Alphonse Giroux in Louis XV-style, the shaped, hinged, quarter-veneered top centred by a porcelain plaque with floral decoration on a bleu celeste ground, enclosing a fitted interior on cabriole legs. Leaf-cast chutes joined by a platform stretcher.

- *68cm x 43cm*
- £3,500 • Emanouel

▽ Cricket Table

- *circa 1870*

Fine rustic elm cricket table, with good original patina, raised on three turned legs.

- *height 78cm*
- £3,750 • Gerald Brodie

◁ Victorian Marquetry Table

- *1870*

Victorian mahogany and marquetry two tier table with inlaid top, and a removable tray with pierced top rail and carrying handles.

- *height 88cm*
- £995 • Old Cinema

△ Burr-Walnut Card Table

- *circa 1870*

Burr-walnut Victorian card table with marquetry inlay, serpentine basket base and scrolled legs with upturned finial.

- *height 87cm*
- £3,750 • The Swan

△ Console Table

- *circa 1870*

An ornately carved giltwood console table with heavily scrolled legs and a marble top with three green chinoiserie cupboards below.

- *99cm x 197cm x 80cm*
- £18,000 • Ranby Hall

△ Rosewood Writing Table

- *circa 1870*

A Parisian rosewood writing table with satinwood inlay on straight tapered legs with a turned stretcher base.

- *75cm x 85cm x 55cm*
- £12,500 • Harpur Deardren

▽ Victorian Tea-Poy

- *circa 1870*

Victorian burr-walnut hexagonal tea-poy with a turned pedestal and carved tripod base.

- *height 74cm*
- £1,295 • A.I.G.

▽ Light-Oak Side Table

- *circa 1870*

Victorian light-oak side table with moulded back and scrolled designs, with side drawers, standing on turned tapering legs.

- *height 110cm*
- £950 • Hill Farm

▽ Mahogany Writing Table

- *circa 1870s*

19th-century mahogany writing table with tooled leather writing surface and reeded, turned and tapered legs.

- *75cm x 110cm*
- £1,675 • Shirley Knight

▽ Table with Ormolu Mounts

• *1870*
Two-tier mahogany table with inlaid shaped top, with ormolu pierced mounts and curved legs.
• *height 88cm*
• £1,395 • Old Cinema

▽ Mahogany Side Table

• *circa 1870*
French mahogany table with pierced brass rail, pink marble top and single long drawer. With brass and gilt banding.
• *84cm x 70.5cm x 35cm*
• £4,850 • O.F. Wilson

▽ Mahogany Sofa Table

• *circa 1880s*
Empire-style mahogany Swedish sofa-table with side flaps on a cylindrical support, raised on a quatral base with lion paw feet.
• *76cm x 92cm*
• £2,900 • R. Cavendish

△ Console Table

• *circa 1870*
Empire-style console figured maple wood table with a pink marble top, central winged brass motif, on a single drawer flanked by ebonised pillars with oriental busts.
• *91cm x 92cm*
• £2,400 • Old Cinema

△ Burr-Walnut Table

• *circa 1880*
Victorian burr-walnut table with a circular top inlaid with boxwood foliate design and carved leaves around the rim, with a turned pedestal standing on a tripod base.
• *height 69cm*
• £875 • A.I.G.

△ Library Tables

• *circa 1880*
One of a pair of mahogany library tables with two side drawers raised on turned reeded legs with brass castors.
• *72cm x 122cm*
• £750 • Westland & Co.

▽ Kingwood Table

• *1880*
French kingwood two-tier oval marquetry table, cross-banded, with gilt ormolu mounts above a solid inlaid stretcher.
• *height 110cm*
• £5,800 • Butchoff

▽ Work Table

• *circa 1880*
An octagonal work table with games top on an eight-sided, fluted base, tapering to base with three legs.
• *height 79cm*
• £950 • Castlegate

▽ Victorian Table

• *circa 1870*
Walnut and marquetry table on a pedestal base with carved gadrooned decoration and carved splat legs, by Taylor & Son, Dover St, London.
• *height 137cm*
• £9,800 • Butchoff

△ Folding Card Table

• *circa 1880*
Mahogany folding card table, with hinged flap and legs.
• *height 70cm*
• £950 • John Clay

△ Italian Occasional Table

• *circa 1880*
Superb Italian giltwood occasional table with inlaid top, raised on a heavily carved support with C-scroll legs and stylised leaf carving with a drop finial.
• *height 105cm*
• £39,500 • Hatchwell

△ Victorian Dressing Table

• *circa 1885*
Victorian mahogany dressing table with an oval mirror with heavily carved decoration, above fitted drawers and turned front legs.
• *height 1.3m*
• £4,500 • Sleeping Beauty

▽ Tilt-Top Table

- *circa 1890*

Mahogany tilt-top table with turned support raised on a tripod base with splayed legs.

- *height 83cm*
- £295 • Great Grooms

▽ Mahogany Sutherland table

- *circa 1898*

A late Victorian mahogany Sutherland table with serpentine top and swing legs.

- *68cm x 68cm*
- £440 • Old Cinema

▽ Rosewood Games Table

- *1900*

A rosewood games table with roulette wheel and card table on tapered legs and brass castors.

- *74cm x 1.09m x 93cm*
- £1,200 • Judy Fox

△ Irish Side Table

- *circa 1890*

Irish mahogany side table with a gadrooned edge above a plain frieze, the decorative, shaped apron centred by a lion's-head mask within a rope twist border, flanked by stylised birds with feathered wings and foliate decoration. Raised on cabriole legs with handsome ball and claw feet decorated at the knees with low-relief carved decoration of stylised birds.

- *81cm x 1.57m*
- £12,500 • Anthony Outred

△ Inlaid Card Table

- *circa 1900*

A mahogany card table with inlaid marquetry banding and medallions, on straight tapered legs.

- *72cm x 45cm*
- £2,550 • Great Grooms

▽ Oak Side Bookstand

- *circa 1890s*

Late Victorian oak side table/bookstand with carved scrolled supports.

- *63cm x 57cm*
- £695 • Old Cinema

◁ Birchwood Oval Table

- *circa 1890s*

Swedish birchwood Biedermeier-style oval table of small proportions, cross-banded and inlaid, with central drawer, raised on square tapered legs.

- *70cm x 69cm*
- £2,450 • R. Cavendish

▽ Regency Rosewood Teapoy

- *circa 1900*

A Regency rosewood brass inlaid tea-poy, the sarcophagus top centred with brass arabesques, lifting to reveal fitted interior. With brass ring handles, on lyre support and sabre legs with brass paw cappings.

- *72cm x 27cm*
- £4,500 • Great Grooms

▷ Tilt-Top Table

- *circa 1890*

Mahogany circular tilt-top occasional table on a turned baluster support with three splayed legs.

- *85cm x 17cm*
- £485 • Vale Antiques

△ Console Table

- *circa 1890*

Late 19th-century carved walnut console table in George I style, with cabriole legs.

- *height 85cm*
- £2,450 • Brown's

△ French Giltwood Table

- *circa 1900*

A French Third Republic giltwood table, with moulded pink marble top, the fluted tapering legs joined by a beaded stretcher.

- *82cm x 85cm x 53cm*
- £1,100 • Tredantiques

△ Edwardian Occasional Tables

- *1910*

A nest of three Edwardian occasional tables with boxwood inlay and banding and tapered straight legs.

- *55cm x 50cm*
- £495 • Great Grooms

▷ Coffee Table

- *circa 1925*

Empire-style table in French mahogany, with gilt mounts and curved frame stretchers.

- *length 1m*
- £2,900 • R. Cavendish

△ Elephant Table

- *circa 1900*

Very detailed, carved table sitting on four elephants' heads, the trunks as legs, with ivory tusks.

- *height 62cm*
- £1,250 • C. Preston

◁ Satinwood Table

- *circa 1920*

Two-tier, Edwardian satinwood table on square, splayed legs.

- *height 70cm*
- £2,100 • T. Morse & Son

▽ Occasional Table

- *1910*

Small English occasional table with a large decorative cat on the surface, with one central drawer and slender legs on pad feet.

- *74cm x 87cm x 50cm*
- £1,200 • Lacquer Chest

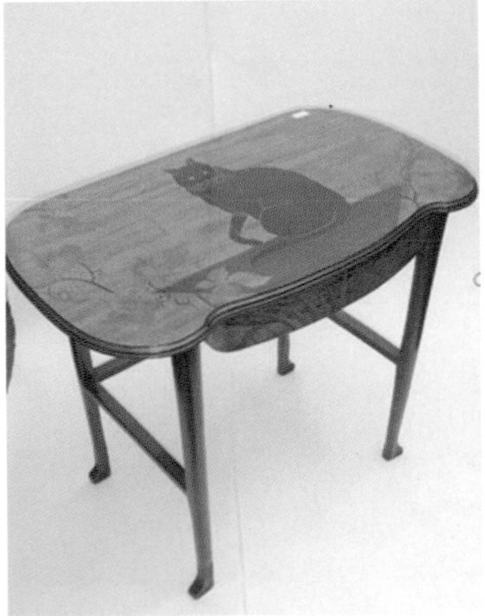

▽ Art Deco Coffee Table

- *circa 1925*

Masur birch and rosewood coffee table with inlays of satinwood and cross-banding in 'tiger' birch.

- *length 99cm*
- £2,700 • R. Cavendish

◁ Art Deco Coffee Table

- *circa 1925*

Swedish walnut table with inlays of center, burr elm and fruitwood.

- *diameter 1m*
- £2,700 • R. Cavendish

▽ Pair of Tables

- *circa 1910*

One of a pair of early 20th-century birchwood and masur birch side tables with top drawer and lower platform, the whole resting on four square tapering legs.

- *height 74cm*
- £2,900 • R. Cavendish

▽ Swedish Sofa Table

- *circa 1915*

Swedish sofa table in birchwood, with central, ebonised column, folding side flaps and a central drawer.

- *length (flaps up) 90cm*
- £3,900 • R. Cavendish

WARDROBES

▽ Oak Cupboard

- *1680*

A Charles II oak-panelled cupboard with lunette carved decoration. Standing on straight square legs. Of good rich patina.

- *182cm x 110cm x 48cm*
- **£8,950** • **Paul Hopwell**

▽ Red Lacquer Cupboard

- *late 18th century*

Chinese red lacquer hardwood cupboard with carved foliate design and two interior drawers.

- *173cm x 84cm x 43cm*
- **£9,600** • **M. Luther**

△ North Breton Armoire

- *18th century*

With primitive carving, lined with 19th-century fabric.

- *height 1.6m*
- **£2,400** • **Angel**

▽ Linen Press

- *circa 1780*

An 18th-century mahogany linen press with original fittings.

- *height 2.2m*
- **£6,800** • **Ronald G. Chambers**

▽ Venetian Armoire

- *late 17th century*

Venetian armoire with painted panel doors with dentil course and cast-bronze cherub handles.

- *height 1.95m*
- **£7,500** • **Paul Andrews**

◁ Linen Press

- *circa 1780*

18th-century mahogany linen press with oval door panels, oval brass mounts and moulded cornice, on splayed bracket feet.

- *height 1.6m*
- **£6,800** • **Ronald G. Chambers**

△ Corner Cupboard

- *circa 1790*

George III bow-fronted mahogany corner cupboard fitted with four shelves and two small drawers, with shell inlay to frieze and Greek key moulded cornice.

- *height 105cm*
- **£2,450** • **Serendipity**

△ English Cupboard

- *circa 1780*

Very fine cupboard with secret compartments, heavily cut frieze and pilaster decoration.

- *height 2.6m*
- **£12,800** • **Riverbank**

△ Oak Cupboard

- *circa 1780*

Oak cupboard with two six-panelled doors above four drawers, on bracket feet.

- *height 1.95m*
- **£4,800** • **Red Lion**

△ French Armoire

- *circa 1790*

A Provençale armoire with serpentine apron.

- *height 1.69m*
- **£1,200** • **Lynda Franklin**

△ Linen Press

- *circa 1800*

Elegant mahogany linen press in original condition, with oval panels of matching veneers and satinwood cross banded doors.

- *height 225cm*
- £8,950 • Barry Cotton

△ Pedestal Cupboard

- *circa 1810*

Swedish Gustavian cream painted pine pedestal cupboard with two doors and square moulded and painted green base.

- *147cm x 107cm*
- £2,900 • R. Cavendish

▽ Dutch Linen Press

- *early 19th century*

Mahogany with pilasters and gilt mounts on plinth feet.

- *height 2m*
- £4,500 • Old Cinema

▽ Georgian Linen Press

- *circa 1830*

A mahogany linen press with moulded and cavetto cornice, two short and two full-width mahogany and pine-lined cockbeaded drawers fitted with oval brass decorations.

- *height 2.1m*
- £3,950 • J. Collins

◁ English Linen Press

- *circa 1830*

An English light mahogany country house linen press, with panelled doors enclosing occasional slides and fittings.

- *145cm x 126cm x 54cm*
- £3,850 • Ranby Hall

△ Housekeeper's Cupboard

- *circa 1800*

An early nineteenth century housekeeper's cupboard with carved oak panelling, with four drawers below, standing on ogee bracket feet.

- *72cm x 134cm x 53cm*
- £5,750 • Rod Wilson

▽ Walnut Armoire

- *circa 1840*

With deep carvings, a simple cornice with shell motif, ornate hinges and a shaped apron.

- *height 2.2m*
- £3,750 • Town & Country

▽ Elm Press

- *circa 1820*

English linen-press cupboard on shaped bracket feet.

- *height 1.8m*
- £2,850 • Angel Antiques

◁ Breakfront Compactum

- *circa 1830*

An English George IV flame-mahogany breakfront compactum with central pediment, having panelled cupboards, and three long drawers below.

- *208cm x 226cm x 57cm*
- £3,850 • Ranby Hall

△ William IV Linen Press

- *circa 1835*

William IV mahogany linen press retaining its old trays, with two finely figured panelled doors decorated with beading. The lower section with figured drawer fronts and original handles. The whole raised on turned and gadrooned feet.

- *214cm x 120cm x 50cm*
- £8,750 • Wakelin Linfield

▽ Architectural Breakfront Wardrobes

- *circa 1850*

Pair of ebonised wardrobes designed by Anthony Salvin for Peckforton Castle. Each with ogee-moulded cornice above a central cupboard, revealing five slides, over two short and two long drawers. Flanked by hanging compartments. Each door with decorative panelling.

- *221cm x 258cm*
- £28,000 • Anthony Outred

▽ Mirrored Wardrobe

- *1860*

An Italian mirrored wardrobe with a swan-neck bonnet top and galleried pediment, with porcelain plaques either side of the mirror and gilt ormolu decoration.

- *height 240cm*
- £7,800 • Ranby Hall

△ Ash Wardrobe

- *circa 19th century*

Hungarian wardrobe with four doors above two deep drawers.

- *height 2.8m*
- £5,995 • Old Cinema

△ Victorian Compactum

- *mid-19th century*

Comprising two hanging side cabinets, drawers and shelves.

- *height 2.5m*
- £3,750 • Old Cinema

△ Triple Wardrobe

- *Victorian*

Victorian burr-walnut triple wardrobe with centre mirror. Wonderful matched grain and veneer. Unusual sliding removable hanging unit. Four sliding shelves and three drawers below.

- *203cm x 188cm x 58cm*
- £2,895 • Old Cinema

▽ Victorian Linen Press

- *circa 1860*

A fine Victorian flame-mahogany linen press, with panelled doors above two short and two long drawers, enclosing an interior with sliding drawers, standing on a plinth base.

- *149cm x 129cm x 54cm*
- £4,450 • Ranby Hall

▽ Mahogany Linen Press

- *circa 1860*

Mahogany linen press, having two arched panelled door enclosing three sliding drawers and two long and two short drawers below.

- *width 125cm*
- £2,450 • The Swan

▷ Victorian Wardrobe

- *circa 1880*

Victorian single-door wardrobe with central mirror, moulded pediment and one long deep drawer with turned handles, the whole standing on a moulded square base.

- *height 207cm*
- £995 • Old Cinema

△ Dutch Corner Cupboard

- *circa 1850*

Dutch chinoserie-painted corner cupboard with stylised butterflies, birds, and figures, with three green-painted interior shelves, original brass butterfly hinges, and a moulded base.

- *92cm x 59.5cm x 40cm*
- £5,500 • O.F. Wilson

△ Victorian Compactum

- *circa mid-19th century*

Mahogany compactum comprising two hanging cupboards, two linen presses and five tiers of drawers.

- *height 2.2m*
- £3,750 • Old Cinema

△ Breakfront Wardrobe

- *1860–80*

A Victorian breakfront mahogany wardrobe with three doors enclosing pull-out shelves.

- *210cm x 60cm x 202cm*
- £2,250 • Old Cinema

△ Flame-Mahogany Wardrobe

- *circa 1890*

Flame-mahogany Victorian wardrobe with central pediment above bow-fronted doors, with four drawers flanked by long cupboards with oval mirrors.

- *width 240cm*
- £2,650 • Drummonds

▽ Bedroom Suite

- *1875–80*

A French Second Empire-style wardrobe being part of a bedroom set including bed, wardrobe, and two side cabinets. The wardrobe with a moulded cornice, mirrored cupboards and ormolu foliate decoration, standing on bun feet.

- *height 240cm*
- £35,000 • Sleeping Beauty

▽ Pine Wardrobe

- *1900s*

A pine wardrobe, with arched pediment above three panelled doors with two shallow drawers below.

- *211cm x 142cm x 62cm*
- £800 • Old School

◁ Edwardian Wardrobe

- *circa 1901*

An Edwardian inlaid mahogany wardrobe with central mirror and side panelling, and long drawer below.

- *180cm x 138cm*
- £975 • Old Cinema

△ Chinese Cupboard

- *1930*

A Chinese red-lacquered cupboard with butterfly and floral painted decoration.

- *190cm x 103cm*
- £1,960 • Great Grooms

△ Breakfront Wardrobe

- *circa late 19th century*

Inverted mahogany breakfront wardrobe with brass mounts, on shaped bracket feet.

- *height 2m*
- £3,995 • Old Cinema

△ Arts and Crafts Wardrobe

- *circa 1910*

Art and Crafts oak wardrobe with central mirror and one long drawer, standing on bracket feet.

- *212cm x 112cm x 55cm*
- £975 • Old Cinema

◁ Victorian Wardrobe

- *circa 1890s*

A late Victorian single-door mahogany wardrobe with central mirror, flanked by circular carved panels with ribbon decoration.

- *170cm x 90cm*
- £925 • Old Cinema

GLASS

Glass has been undervalued until recently but is now highly treasured for its decorative beauty and fragility. It has myriad uses and throughout history has been shaped, coloured and moulded for a variety of purposes, from the stained glass windows in a cathedral to the ordinary drinking vessel used in the home. The Ancient Egyptians produced coloured glass, including blue, green, violet, black and red, to imitate semi-precious stones. In England, on the other hand, coloured glass was rare until the early nineteenth century with the introduction of 'Bristol' glass products ranging from luxury items such as scent bottles to tablewares that included jugs, fingerbowls and decanters. The most popular colour was blue, closely followed by deep green and amethyst. Nailsea is a generic term given to a range of nineteenth-century glass objects, for example bottles and jugs, in shades of green and often incorporating flecks of white glass. Nailsea derived from a factory near Bristol in England and was also produced in America during the nineteenth century.

△ German Beaker

- *circa 1700*

Engraved with forest, deer, pastoral subjects and Latin script.

- *height 24cm*
- £580 • Mousa

▽ Toasting Glass

- *circa 1700*

Toast master's glass with bell-shaped bowl, large circular knop stem with enclosed tear drop.

- *height 12cm*
- £1,800 • Somervale

◁ Posset Pot

- *circa 1740*

Posset pot with a trumpet bowl with a curved spout flanked by two scroll handles, on a plain conical foot.

- *height 7cm*
- £995 • Somervale

△ Newcastle Goblet

- *circa 1750*

Newcastle goblet with a finely engraved foliate design, central air-beaded and ball knops to the stem, and domed foot.

- *height 19cm*
- £1,800 • Somervale

▽ Wine Glass

- *circa 1745*

Wine glass with trumpet bowl on stem with multiple spiral air twist stem on a folded conical foot.

- *height 18cm*
- £500 • Somervale

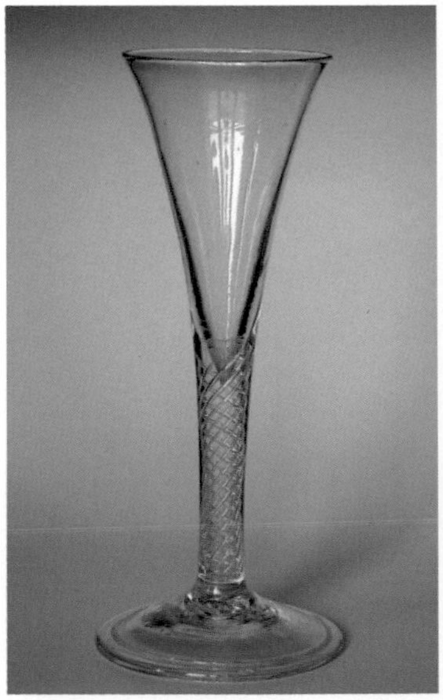

◁ Monteith or Bonnet Glasses

- *circa 1750*

Mid 18th-century glasses.

- *height 8cm*
- £220 • Jasmin Cameron

▽ Wine Glass

- *circa 1750*

An 18th-century wine glass with double spiral cables on the stem and a domed foot.

- *height 16cm*
- £450 • Jasmin Cameron

▽ Cordial Wine Glass

- *circa 1750–60*

George II cordial wine glass with an air-twist stem.

- *height 10cm*
- £460 • Jasmin Cameron

▽ Bristol Wine Glasses

- *circa 1785*

A pair of tulip-shaped glasses with a peacock-blue tint.

- *height 12cm*
- £235 (pair) • Jasmin Cameron

△ Gilded Wine Glass

- *1750*

George II wine glass, with gilded rim and hexagonal facet shank on a domed foot.

- *height 14.5cm*
- £560 • Jasmin Cameron

△ Green Wine Glass

- *1760*

Green wine glass with elegant air-twist stem.

- *height 18cm*
- £3,000 • Somervale

▽ Jacobite Wine Glasses

- *circa 1750*

Fine pair of Jacobite wine glasses with engraved bowls showing the Jacobite Rose and two buds, on double-knopped, multiple spiral air-twist stems, and domed bases.

- *height 16cm*
- £2,200 • Somervale

▽ Decanter with Geometric Cutting

- *circa 1780*

Tapered body with geometric-cut design, the body engraved with stars.

- *height 30cm*
- £400 • Somervale

▷ Ship's Glass

- *1770–90*

Exceedingly rare ship's glass with 10-ply corkscrew and opaque bands on a quarter-inch thick circular foot.

- *height 15cm*
- £1,500 • Jasmin Cameron

◁ Cordial Wine Glass

- *circa 1770*

A wine glass with red and green coloured bands. Made in Bristol.

- *height 11.7cm*
- £780 • Jasmin Cameron

△ Late Georgian Wine Glass

- *1750–70*

A late Georgian wine glass with multi-spiral opaque twist stem on a slender foot.

- *height 12cm*
- £460 • Jasmin Cameron

△ Wine Glass

- *circa 1755*

A mid-18th century bell-bowl baluster wine glass with domed, folded foot.

- *height 16.2cm*
- £270 • Jasmin Cameron

▽ Claret Decanter

- *circa 1780*

Decanter with mallet-shaped body engraved with 'Claret' within a moulded cartouche with floral and grape design, and bevelled-edge disc stopper.

- *height 30cm*
- £880 • Somervale

▽ Blue Rum Decanter

- *1790*

Bristol-blue decanter with the inscription 'Rum' in gilt lettering within a cartouche of trailing grapes and vine leaves and a gilt 'R' on the stopper.

- *height 27cm*
- £380 • Somervale

▽ Wine Goblets

- *circa 1800*

A pair of goblets of ovoid shape with a raised cut diamond pattern.

- *height 15cm*
- £445 (pair) • Jasmin Cameron

△ Wine Rinser

- *circa 1790*

An early yellow wine rinser with an extreme double lip. Originally part of a dessert set.

- *height 10cm*
- £400 • Jasmin Cameron

△ Blue Decanter

- *circa 1790*

Club-shape Bristol-blue spirit decanter with a plain lozenge-shape stopper.

- *height 32cm*
- £220 • Somervale

△ Nailsea Glass Cloche

- *circa 1800*

Clear glass bell-shaped garden cloche by Nailsea.

- *height 34cm*
- £400 • Somervale

▽ Irish Oval Fruit Dish

- *circa 1790*

Fine Irish oval fruit bowl with panels of raised diamond design, knopped stem and radial moulded dual-scalloped foot.

- *height 22cm*
- £2,600 • Somervale

▽ Engraved Goblet

- *circa 1800–15*

A late Georgian goblet, the bowl engraved with hunting scenes.

- *height 18.5cm*
- £700 • Jasmin Cameron

▽ Amethyst Cream Jug and Sugar Bowl

- *1800*

Amethyst baluster cream jug and sugar bowl, with gilt writing.

- *height 12cm*
- £600 • Somervale

△ Cream Skimmer Bowl

- *circa 1800*

Large shallow glass cream skimmer bowl with central boss and moulded rim.

- *diameter 51cm*
- £500 • Somervale

△ Baluster Cream Jug

- *circa 1800*

Blue baluster cream jug with pinched lip and barley twist design.

- *height 12cm*
- £155 • Somervale

△ Six Irish Wine Rinsers

- *circa 1810*

One of six rinsers with parallel prismatic steps, sawtooth rim, and double lip.

- *height 19cm*
- £900 (set) • Jasmin Cameron

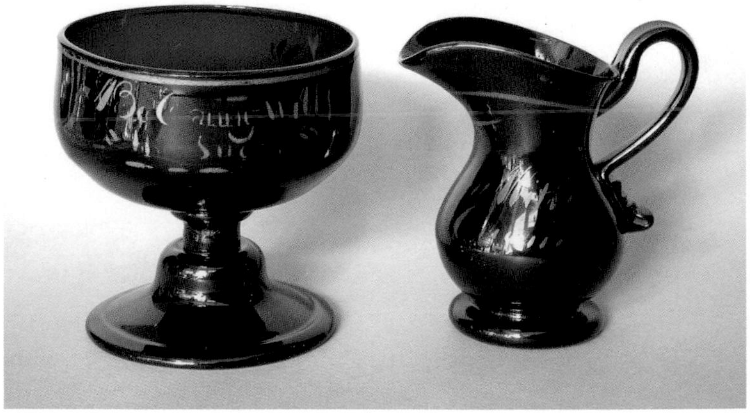

△ Georgian Rummer

- *1809*

A late Georgian rummer, the notched bowl with terracing on a square flat foot.

- *height 14cm*
- £340 • Jasmin Cameron

△ Cut Glass Goblet

- *1810*

Large goblet engraved with the words 'London to Bath' and a scene showing a horse and carriage, with knop to stem and a square heavily-cut base.

- *height 17cm*
- £1,500 • Somervale

△ Amber Glass Cane

- *circa 1810*

Amber glass barley-twist cane with knob.

- *length 100cm*
- £150 • Somervale

▽ Rummer

- *circa 1810*

A rummer, slightly waisted, with triple banding around bowl.

- *height 13cm*
- £140 • Jasmin Cameron

▽ Georgian Wine Glass

- *1810*

Late Georgian pan-topped wine glass on a domed foot.

- *height 12cm*
- £110 • Jasmin Cameron

▽ Nailsea Jug

- *circa 1810*

Dark olive-green bulbous-shape Nailsea jug with white inclusions.

- *height 18.5cm*
- £380 • Somervale

▽ Wine Carafe

- *circa 1810*

Flat panels, prismatic steps and a star base with faceting to the lip.

- *height 18cm*
- £235 • Jasmin Cameron

▽ Champagne Glasses

- *1820*

One of a set of ten Regency champagne flutes, with fluted body, knopped stem and a cylindrical base.

- *height 16.5cm*
- £780 • Jasmin Cameron

▷ Newcastle Glass Goblet

- *circa 1810*

Large bowl-shaped goblet engraved with a horse and carriage, scrolling foliate and grape design and the words 'Newcastle to York', on a domed base.

- *height 24cm*
- £800 • Somervale

△ 'J. Jacobs of Bristol' Bowl

- *circa 1810*

Bristol blue bowl and dish with gilt key pattern design around the rim of the bowl, and a gilt stag in the centre of the plate. Signed on the base of each J. Jacobs, Bristol, in gilt.

- *height of bowl 9cm*
- £1,000 • Somervale

△ Ship's Decanter

- *1810–20*

Exceedingly rare ship's decanter cut with small diamonds and flutes, with cut mushroom stopper.

- *height 23cm*
- £540 • Jasmin Cameron

△ **Scottish Gill Measure**

- *1810–50*

Scottish measure of one gill, a quantity of spirit to be dispensed.

- *height 12cm*
- £240 • Jasmin Cameron

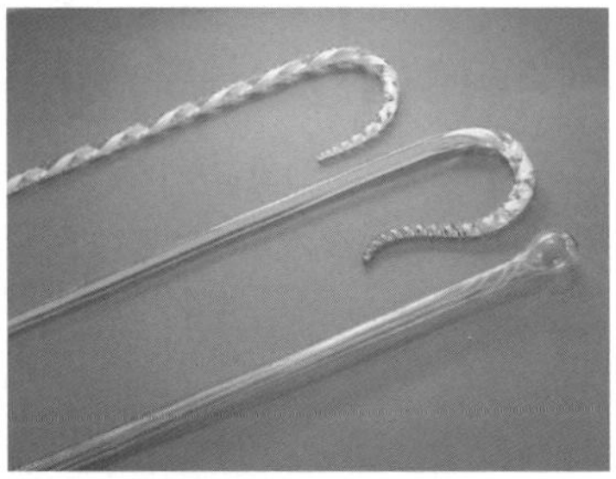

△ **Glass Twisted Canes**

- *1830*

Three assorted glass barley-twist canes.

- *length 110cm*
- £150 • Somervale

△ **Spirit Decanter**

- *1825*

An early nineteenth-century English spirit decanter, with gilded design and fluted body.

- *height 21cm*
- £1,500 • Jasmin Cameron

▽ **Celery Glass**

- *1820*

Large engraved celery glass with acid-etching around the bowl, on a pedestal base.

- *height 24cm*
- £300 • Jasmin Cameron

▽ **Green Wine Glasses**

- *1825*

Set of bowl-shaped green wine glasses with raspberry encrustation applied to the stems, raised on circular bases.

- *height 17cm*
- £600 set of three • Somervale

▽ **Spirit Decanters**

- *circa 1835*

With silver collars, linen fold panels and a star base and stopper.

- *height 25cm*
- £490 (pair) • Jasmin Cameron

△ **Amethyst Cream Jug**

- *1820*

Pear-shaped amethyst cream jug with 'Be canny with the cream' inscribed on the body, trails of gold enamelling, a loop handle, splayed lip and plain base.

- *height 14cm*
- £300 • Somervale

△ **Glass Rummer**

- *1830*

Regency Sunderland Bridge rummer, with short knopped stem, on a folded conical foot.

- *height 15cm*
- £850 • Templar

▽ **Amethyst Wine Rinser**

- *circa 1820*

One of a pair, with a double lip and bulbous shape. A rare colour.

- *height 9cm*
- £450 (pair) • Jasmin Cameron

▽ **Wine Carafe**

- *1830*

A William IV wine carafe with fluted body and faceted neck.

- *height 27cm*
- £265 • Jasmin Cameron

▽ **Port Glass**

- *circa 1840*

A nineteenth-century port glass with knop and domed base.

- *height 11cm*
- £45 • Jasmin Cameron

◁ **Bristol Wine Glass**

- *1820*

A green Bristol wine glass with a tulip bowl and baluster stem.

- *height 11cm*
- £120 • Jasmin Cameron

△ Chemist's Balls

- *circa 1840*

Early 19th-century chemist's glass balls, with engraved star patterns, on turned ebonised bases.

- *height 58cm*
- £2,800 • D. Martin-Taylor

△ Jelly Plate

- *19th century*

Clear glass ice jelly plate, with crenellated rim.

- *diameter 12cm*
- £130 • Jasmin Cameron

△ Pink Glass Bottle

- *1850*

A dark-pink glass bottle decorated with white shell scrolling around the globular base and elegant fluted neck.

- *height 19cm*
- £180 • Somervale

▽ Cylinder Spirit Decanter

- *1840*

Clear glass cylinder spirit decanter with mushroom stopper.

- *height 23cm*
- £185 • Jasmin Cameron

▽ Ale/Beer Glass

- *circa 1850*

A half-litre glass on a pedestal, by Thomas Webb & Co.

- *height 20cm*
- £180 • Jasmin Cameron

▽ Victorian Silver Tantalus

- *circa 1860*

Victorian silver-plated tantalus with three decanters.

- *height 32cm*
- £650 • Barry Cotton

△ Finger Bowl

- *1845*

An early Victorian green Bristol glass finger bowl.

- *height 9cm*
- £180 • Jasmin Cameron

△ Green Bristol Wine Glass

- *1850*

Green Bristol wine glass with scale-cut leg and domed foot.

- *height 11cm*
- £75 • Jasmin Cameron

△ Bohemian Glass

- *circa 1860*

Showing a romantic portrait of a lady with flowers on reverse. With enamel and gilding.

- *height 16cm*
- £360 • Mousa

▽ Bristol Dessert Plate

- *1850*

Amethyst Bristol glass dessert plate, part of a set of three.

- *diameter 24cm*
- £180 • Jasmin Cameron

▽ English Centrepiece

- *circa 1860*

A light green centrepiece with painted birds and flowers. Gilding to scrolled handles, lip and base.

- *height 35cm*
- £580 • Mousa

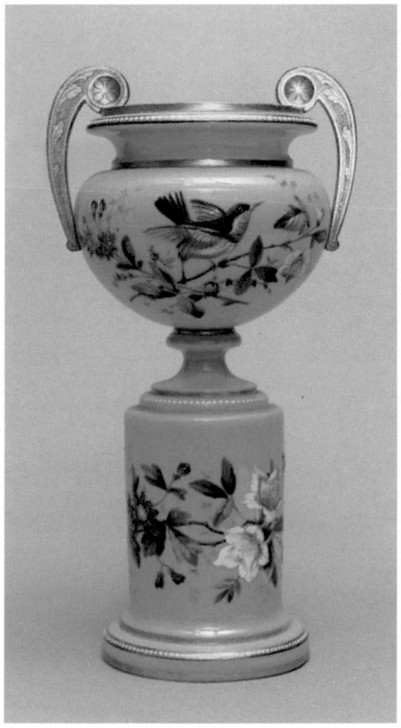

▽ Nailsea Rolling Pins

- *1860*

Two glass Nailsea rolling pins in blue and red.

- *length 41cm*
- £180 • Somervale

△ Victorian Glass Epergne

- *1860*

Victorian vaseline-glass épergne with four central trumpets and green glass twists around the stem.

- *height 44cm*
- £650 • Templar

△ Bohemian Glass

- *circa 1860*

With enamelled floral panels and ormolu mounts, with the figures of three swans.

- *height 20cm*
- £1,100 • Shahdad

△ Green Bohemian Glasses

- *circa 1860*

Green Bohemian glasses comprising five pieces in all with profuse gilt decoration.

- £10,000 • Sinai

▽ French Bottle

- *circa 1850*

A French bottle and stopper with applied brass decoration and lid, with ornate handles.

- *height 21cm*
- £370 • Mousa

▽ Lithyalin-GlassVases

- *circa 1860*

A pair of German vases with spider and cobweb design and jewellery to base and neck.

- *height 22cm*
- £480 • Mousa

△ Pair of Centrepieces

- *circa 1860*

One of a pair in green overlay with painted flower enamels and gilding.

- *height 33cm*
- £1,300 • Mousa

◁ Goblet and Cover

- *circa 1860*

Bohemian red glass with deeply engraved hunting scene.

- *height 51cm*
- £18,500 • Sinai

▽ Shot Glasses

- *circa 1868*

Set of four shot glasses with a lightly engraved rim.

- *height 3.5cm*
- £120 • Jasmin Cameron

▽ Bohemian Glass Goblet

- *19th century*

Glass goblet with cover. Showing an engraved forest scene.

- *height 52cm*
- £1,200 • Sinai

◁ German Glass Beaker

- *circa 1860*

Showing a painted pastoral scene. With a heavily cut base.

- *height 12cm*
- £280 • Mousa

△ Nailsea Glass

- *circa 1865*

A Nailsea factory door porter with tears.

- *height 12cm*
- £165 • Jasmin Cameron

△ Decanter

- *circa 1870*

A lead-crystal locking decanter, with silver-plated handle.

- *height 16cm*
- £420 • **Graham Walpole**

△ Bohemian Vases

- *circa 1870*

A pair of Bohemian cranberry glass vases with gilt leaf decoration and central cartouches showing portraits of a lady in a wedding dress and a lady in country dress.

- *height 39.5cm*
- £5,500 • **Sinai**

▽ German Ewer

- *circa 1870*

A German green glass ewer with armorial and key form design.

- *height 27.5cm*
- £160 • **Namdar**

▽ Claret Jug

- *circa 1870*

A Victorian lead-crystal claret jug with silver-plated lid and handle.

- *height 27cm*
- £275 • **Barham Antiques**

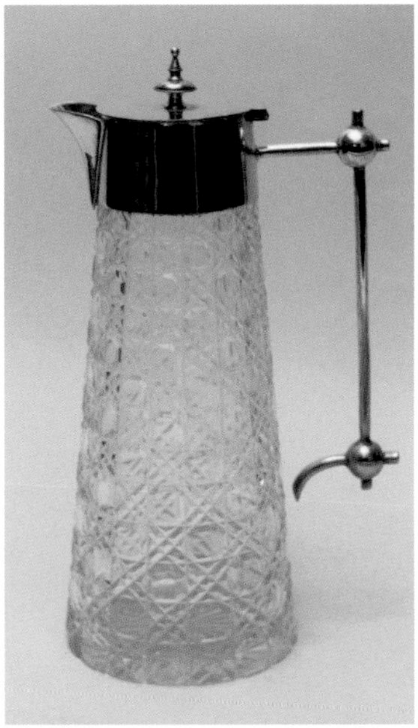

◁ Cranberry Decanter

- *1870*

A Victorian cranberry-glass decanter with pinched lip, oversized clear-glass stopper and moulded handle.

- *height 15cm*
- £165 • **Barham Antiques**

△ English Vase

- *circa 1870*

English clear cylindrical glass vase engraved with birds among foliage and geometric designs, with a star-cut base.

- *height 38cm*
- £680 • **Mousa**

△ Lamp Base

- *19th century*

A lamp base in gilded bronze and glass with stylised leaf and scrolled decoration.

- *height 55cm*
- £1,800 • **Riverbank**

▽ Bohemian Vase

- *circa 1870*

In red glass with a painted flower frieze and gilded floral decoration.

- *height 31cm*
- £380 • **Mousa**

▽ Chamber Pot

- *circa 1880*

A blue glass chamber pot with floral gilding to bowl and lip.

- *height 16cm*
- £250 • **Mousa**

▽ Venetian Vases

- *19th century*

Two millefiore double-handled vases in perfect condition.

- £400, £500 • **Shahdad**

▽ French Scent Bottle

- *circa 1880*

An opaline scent bottle with cover and gilded decoration.

- *height 11cm*
- £650 • Sinai

▽ French Opaline Bottle

- *circa 1880*

Gilded, with a moulded rim. The body decorated with trailing roses and turquoise foliate designs, raised on a circular base.

- *height 25cm*
- £300 • Mousa

▽ Scent Bottles

- *circa 1880*

A pair of Bohemian glass scent bottles with fluted necks and globular bodies.

- *height 15cm*
- £280 • Mousa

△ Bohemian Centrepiece

- *circa 1880*

Bohemian red glass centrepiece, with a circular clear glass dish supported on a red stem engraved with a trailing foliate pattern.

- *height 38cm*
- £1,400 • Mousa

△ Vase and Cover

- *19th century*

A Bohemian vase and cover in three sections of white, red and gold enamelling. With Eastern panels and flower and leaf designs.

- *height 64cm*
- £3,800 • Sinai

▽ Bohemian Bottle and Dish

- *19th century*

Heavily cut, twisted and fluted with enamelling and gilding.

- *height 26cm*
- £550 • Sinai

▽ Bohemian Red Candle Vase

- *circa 1880*

Red Bohemian chalice-shaped vase, with white overlay and a gilt band painted with a floral frieze, above a knopped stem supported on a splayed foot with gilt banding.

- *height 27cm*
- £580 • Mousa

▷ Green Bohemian Goblets

- *1880*

A pair of magnificent green hexagonal, cut and faceted Bohemian goblets with gilding.

- *height 15cm*
- £550 • Mousa

△ Green and White Bohemian Vases

- *circa 1880*

A pair of Bohemian green vases with turret-shape rim and a white diamond design within gilded arches, raised on a knopped stem with a large splayed foot.

- *height 30cm*
- £780 • Mousa

△ Amber Bohemian Beaker

- *circa 1880*

One of a set of six Bohemian amber beakers, with cut and moulded decoration and a central gilt foliate cartouche of flowers.

- *height 13cm*
- £380 • Mousa

▽ Tall Bohemian Blue Vase

• *circa 1880*
Tall slender cobalt-blue vase engraved with an interlaced stylised leaf pattern, raised on a domed foot.
• *height 42cm*
• £290 • Mousa

▽ Bohemian Glass Bowl

• *circa 1880*
Bohemian amber-coloured glass bowl.
• *height 18cm*
• £200 • Sharif

▷ Pair of Blue Ewers

• *1880*
A pair of blue glass ewers with pinched lip and ribbon handle, enamelled with foliate designs.
• *height 24cm*
• £135 • Mousa

△ Set of Vases

• *circa 1880*
A set of three green matt-glaze vases, with gilding. Centre-piece shown with white snake about stem and base.
• £1,300 • La Bohème

△ Glass Tankard

• *circa 1880*
A Bohemian tankard with an engraving of forest and birds.
• *height 17cm*
• £180 • Mousa

▽ Red Bohemian Bottles

• *1880*
A pair of enamelled Bohemian bottles with onion-top stoppers, heavily cut with eastern motifs.
• *height 18cm*
• £450 • Mousa

▽ Cup and Cover

• *19th century*
With enamelled panel of maidens and a cherub in a classical setting. Gilding and fluted decoration.
• *height 37cm*
• £3,500 • Sinai

▷ Engraved Liqueur Glass

• *circa 1880*
One of six, thumb-cut to bowl with vine and fruit decoration.
• *height 9cm*
• £190 • Jasmin Cameron

△ Bohemian Green Vase

• *circa 1880*
Bohemian castellated green vase with gilt star pattern and white overlay panels with gilt flowers, supported on a knop stem with white panels and gilding.
• *height 34cm*
• £300 • Mousa

△ Red Glass Candlesticks

• *circa 1880*
Red Bohemian glass candlesticks with a scalloped rim, tapered stem on a circular star-cut base with a shaped edge.
• *height 23cm*
• £650 • Mousa

△ Bohemian Octagonal Goblet

- *1880*

Blue Bohemian octagonal goblet with enamelled foliate designs and gilding.

- *height 19cm*
- £290 • Mousa

△ Bohemian Beaker

- *circa 1880*

Amber glass with three engraved panels showing seascapes.

- *height 11cm*
- £170 • Mousa

△ Dessert Service

- *circa 1890*

20-piece enamelled dessert service with gilded vine and fruit decoration.

- £4,200 • Sinai

▽ Scent Bottle

- *circa 1880*

A Bohemian cut-glass scent bottle with stopper and floral gilding on a blue ground.

- *height 12cm*
- £210 • Mousa

▷ Sugar Caster

- *1880*

A cranberry-glass sugar caster with fluted sides, mounted with a silver-plated top with small finial.

- *height 7cm*
- £110 • Barham Antiques

△ Bohemian Vase

- *1880*

Bohemian red glass vase of bottle shape on a pedestal base, with enamel and gilt foliate designs on the bowl, neck and base.

- *height 26cm*
- £480 • Mousa

▷ Blue Spirit Bottle

- *1890*

Blue tapering spirit bottle with flute cutting and a cut spire stopper.

- *height 34cm*
- £480 • Somervale

△ Champagne Glasses

- *1880*

One of a set of ten Victorian hollow-stemmed champagne glasses.

- *height 12cm*
- £900 • Jasmin Cameron

▽ Blue Bohemian Goblet

- *1880*

Blue Bohemian glass goblet with a waisted bowl on a pedestal foot with white foliate design and gilt banding.

- *height 18cm*
- £340 • Mousa

▽ Bohemian Vases

- *1880*

Pair of fluted Bohemian red vases with white panels, and gilding around the rim and base.

- *height 21cm*
- £450 • Templar

▽ Jug and Two Beakers

- *1890*

Green Bohemian glass jug and two beakers with white enamelling and gilding.

- *height 18m*
- £126 • Mousa

△ Bohemian Goblets

- *circa 1890*

A pair of blue glass Bohemian goblets showing running stags in a forest setting.

- *height 20cm*
- **£480 (pair)** • Mousa

△ Russian Drinking Set

- *late 19th century*

Five pieces comprising a wine carafe and four shallow dish glasses with floral enamel and gilded decoration.

- **£2,600** • Sinai

△ Blue and Gold Bohemian Bottle

- *circa 1890*

Bohemian azure-blue glass bottle with gilt floral and leaf designs, surmounted by an oversized lozenge-shaped stopper.

- *height 27cm*
- **£490** • Mousa

▽ Match Holder

- *circa 1890*

Ovoid match holder with a silver rim and etched glass body.

- *height 8cm*
- **£150** • Henry Gregory

▽ German Liquor Set

- *circa 1890*

Moser glass company hexagonal decanter and four glasses chased with gilt paisley designs round clear red-glass windows, surmounted by a spire-shaped stopper.

- *height 24cm*
- **£580** • Mousa

▽ Gallé Scent Bottle

- *circa 1890*

Metal mounts and crackled finish with flowers, praying mantis and moth finial on the stopper.

- *height 10cm*
- **£1,600** • Cameo Gallery

▽ Lemonade Jug

- *1895*

Tankard-shape lemonade jug with traces of gilding around the rim and handle.

- *height 22.5cm*
- **£185** • Jasmin Cameron

▽ Venetian Glasses

- *circa 1900*

Seventy-two pieces with profuse gilding and deep-red glass panels inset within the bowls

- **£5,500** • Sinai

◁ Red Sweet Dish

- *circa 1890*

Red Bohemian sweet dish painted with alternating panels of portraits and white diamond patterns, within gilt foliage, supported on a white overlay stem with a circular base.

- *height 34cm*
- **£1,300** • Mousa

△ French Vase

- *circa 1900*

By E. Rousseau, Paris. Showing a Japanese man with apple blossom. On a base with bun feet.

- *height 18cm*
- **£2,800** • Cameo Gallery

△ Gallé Vase

- *circa 1900*

Black, amber and orange, showing a harbour scene with lighthouse.

- *height 32cm*
- **£8,500** • Cameo Gallery

JEWELLERY

The demand for jewellery is as strong now as it has been since the time of Cleopatra. The wide range of necklaces, rings and brooches available today embraces most styles and periods from history. Victoriana is extremely popular amongst collectors, especially lockets and pendants, which were produced in vast numbers and often set in 9ct gold with garnets and pearls, or other gemstones, and usually designed with matching earrings. Art Deco jewellery is very popular and can be distinguished by its elegance and the innovative and artistic use of materials and design, which was a reaction against Edwardianism. This led to the birth of a new freedom in style and experimentation which resulted in different techniques being used, such as enamelling with silver. Horn was popular, with its light translucent colours often being coupled with softly coloured gems such as moonstones. It could be carved in fine detail and shaped into hair combs.

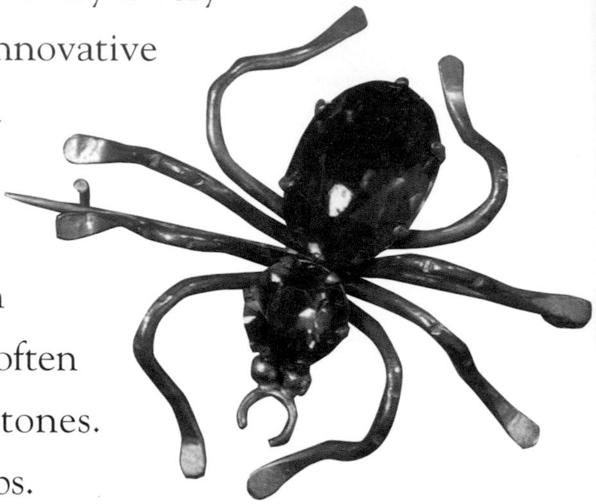

▽ Polychrome Brooch

• *circa 1630*
A very early enamelled gold brooch depicting St George doing battle with the Dragon.
• £6,500 • Sandra Cronan

▽ Italian Brooch

• *circa 1650*
Italian 17th-century enamel, emerald and gold flower-spray brooch.
• *height 7.5cm*
• £8,600 • Sandra Cronan

△ Miniature

• *1650–1760*
An enamelled oval miniature of the soldier and statesman George Monck, 1st Duke of Albemarle, who was awarded his dukedom for the part he played in the restoration of the monarchy. The miniature is mounted within a heart-shaped, diamond-set frame. The enamel is dated 1650 on the reverse, the frame is circa 1760.
• £6,800 • Sandra Cronan

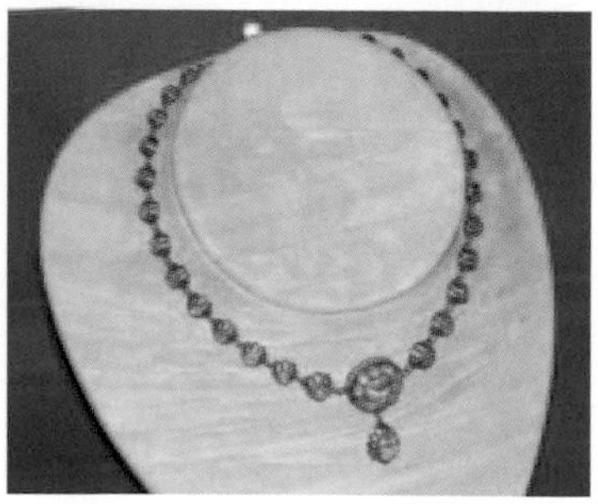

▽ Painted Enamel Ring

• *circa 1780*
Georgian oval ring with a painted head of a young lady on enamel within a gold foliate setting.
• *diameter 3cm*
• £750 • RBR Group

▷ Cameo Brooch

• *1820*
An Italian cameo of a lady's head in an English setting.
• *height 5cm*
• £750 • RBR Group

◁ Diamond Necklace

• *18th century*
French rose-cut diamond ribbon necklace.
• £4,500 • Michele Rowan

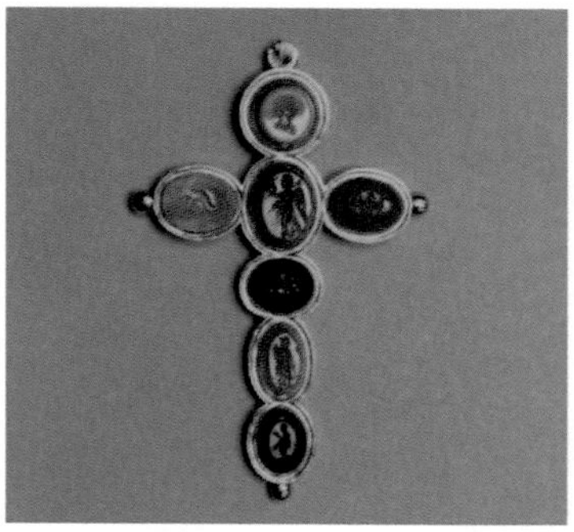

△ Gold Cross

• *circa 1810*
Georgian gold cross set with Roman intaglios – sealed gems ornamented with sunken or incised designs. Made in England.
• *length 8cm*
• £4,800 • Sandra Cronan

▽ Gold Brooch

- *1820*

Brooch in 18ct gold, encrusted with emeralds, rubies and pearls.

- *diameter 4cm*
- £950 • RBR Group

▽ William IV Brooch

- *1830*

Gold brooch with a main central diamond surrounded by three others, and a pear-shaped ruby drop.

- *length 5cm*
- £1,950 • RBR Group

▽ Fob Seals

- *1840*

Two 18ct gold English fob seals, ornately decorated with pineapples and foliage. With carved agate stones.

- *height 3.5cm*
- £300 each • Michele Rowan

▽ Enamel Earrings

- *circa 1840*

Enamel earrings with painted classical landscapes within an 18ct gold setting of seed-case design.

- *length 4cm*
- £950 • RBR Group

▽ Shell Cameo Earrings and Brooch

- *1840*

Shell cameo set with a mythological tone, in 18ct gold with scrolled borders.

- £2,500 • RBR Group

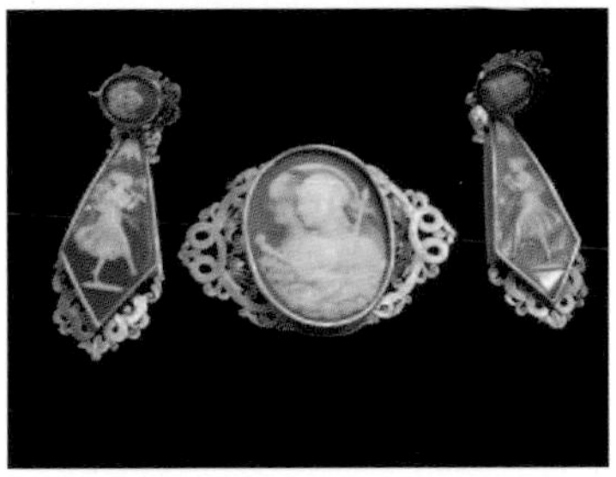

▽ Necklace

- *circa 1850*

With 18ct gold backing and silver front. Five rose-cut diamond flowers suspended from a silver and diamond chain. Three cabochon emeralds hanging delicately from many diamond strands and fringes.

- *length 41cm*
- £9,500 • Emmy Abé

▽ Swiss Enamel Brooch

- *1850*

Swiss enamel brooch of Madonna and Child within a pearl border.

- *height 6cm*
- £1,500 • RBR Group

▽ Hand-Painted Enamel Locket

- *circa 1850*

French hand-painted enamel locket of a lady with three small diamonds in her hair on an 18ct gold base.

- *height 5cm*
- £750 • RBR Group

◁ Early Victorian Diamond

- *circa 1840*

Early Victorian rock crystal and diamond earrings set in silver and gold.

- *length 3cm*
- £2,850 • Wimpole Antiques

△ Diamond and Garnet Brooch

- *1850*

Large Victorian oval gold filigree pendant with a central ruby surrounded by medium and smaller diamonds, three ruby lozenge-shaped droplets, mounted by a diamond-encrusted platinum ribbon.

- *length 9cm*
- £16,000 • N. Bloom

△ Opal Earrings

- *circa 1850*

Austro-Hungarian four-stage drop opal earings, with silver settings.

- *length 6cm*
- £750 • Emmy Abé

△ Italian Cameo Brooch

• *1860*
An Italian cameo brooch depicting a Biblical scene set in an English 15ct gold base.
• *length 3cm*
• £1,500 • **RBR Group**

△ Gold Brooch

• *circa 1860*
Victorian 18ct gold brooch with a key pattern border and a pietra dura panel of flowers.
• *height 5cm*
• £650 • **RBR Group**

△ Knot Brooch

• *circa 1860*
Victorian eagle's head knot brooch 18ct gold set with emeralds, pearls and rubies.
• *diameter 4cm*
• £1,850 • **RBR Group**

▽ Coral Necklace

• *circa 1860*
Whitby jet fossilised coral necklace. Large anchor links attached to a jet heart with applied cameo.
• *length 30cm*
• £750 • **Michele Rowan**

▽ Pearl and Diamond Brooch

• *circa 1860*
Pearl, diamond and black enamel brooch with nine large pearls set in 18ct gold with five hanging diamond drops. The whole fashioned as three domes, surrounded by 12 diamonds.
• *height 10cm*
• £9,500 • **Emmy Abé**

▷ Gold 15ct Bracelet

• *circa 1870*
Gold 15ct linked bracelet with a design of bars with chain-link borders.
• *length 15cm*
• £1,475 • **Wimpole Antiques**

△ Cameo Brooch

• *1860*
Hardstone cameo brooch of a Classical woman with a ewer and bowl, encrusted with diamonds and pearl drops.
• *height 4cm*
• £2,500 • **RBR Group**

△ Gold Earrings

• *1870*
Gold and coral Etruscan-revival hooped earrings.
• £650 • **Michele Rowan**

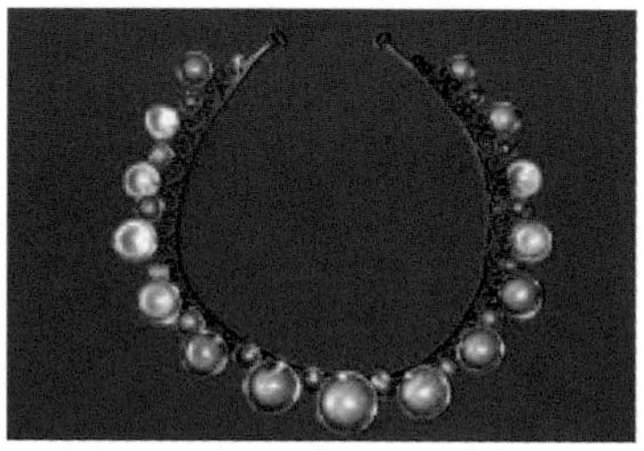

△ Rock Crystal Tiara

• *1870*
Victorian silver and rock crystal tiara in a Gothic-revival style.
• *diameter 17cm*
• £1,500 • **Michele Rowan**

▽ Shell Cameo

• *circa 1870*
Shell cameo set in 15ct gold chain mount. Subject showing George and Dragon.
• *height 8cm*
• £650 • **Michele Rowan**

▽ Art Nouveau Brooch

• *1900*
Art Nouveau 9ct gold brooch set with a turquoise and baroque pearl drop. Marked 'Liberty & Co'.
• *length 3cm*
• £480 • **Gooday Gallery**

△ Victorian Gold Earrings

• *circa 1875*
A pair of Victorian 15ct gold Etruscan-revival earrings with an applied globular design.
• *length 2cm*
• £875 • Wimpole Antiques

△ Gold Victorian Earrings

• *circa 1875*
Victorian Etruscan-revival 15ct gold earrings with a central wheel motif.
• *width 1cm*
• £875 • Wimpole Antiques

△ Victorian Star Brooch

• *1880*
Victorian diamond star brooch set with a lapis centre with a further ten stones radiating from the centre.
• *diameter 4cm*
• £1,850 • RBR Group

△ Perfume Bottle Pendant

• *1880*
Fine grey agate perfume bottle with engraved floral designs to the obverse, a hanging chain and the reverse showing a panel with three lions.
• *length 6cm*
• £820 • S. & A. Thompson

△ Scarf Clip

• *circa 1880*
Victorian brooch that can also be used as a scarf clip. Made of silver, with paste settings.
• *length 6cm*
• £65 • Sugar

◁ Butterfly Brooch

• *circa 1880*
French 19th-century diamond, emerald and ruby butterfly brooch, with large pearl mounted on the thorax. The main construction is of silver and gold, with filigree to the wings.
• *height 5cm*
• £5,800 • Sandra Cronan

▽ Victorian Gold Brooch

• *1880*
Victorian 18ct-gold brooch with pearl flowers set within delicate gold scrolling and a drop pendant from gold chains.
• *diameter 4cm*
• £1,500 • RBR Group

▽ Victorian 15ct Earrings

• *circa 1880*
15ct gold Victorian articulated lozenge-shaped earrings.
• *length 5cm*
• £1,295 • Wimpole Antiques

◁ Shell Cameo Brooch

• *1880*
Shell cameo of a lady feeding a bird, set within 15ct gold.
• *height 5cm*
• £850 • RBR Group

▷ Ethiopian Pendant

• *circa 1890*
An Ethiopian silver pendant cross.
• *height 5cm*
• £48 • Iconastas

△ Locket and Collar

• *1880*
Victorian silver locket on interlocking silver collar. Of Estruscan-revival design, with 18ct gold ribbon inlay and etching to the silver of the locket.
• *length 23cm*
• £450 • Michele Rowan

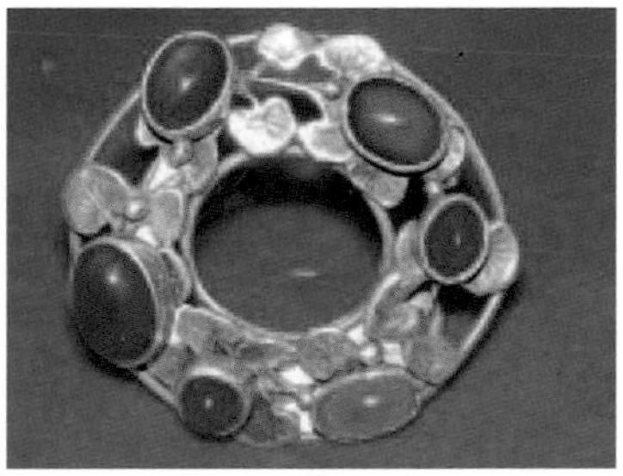

△ Cornelian Brooch

• *1890*
Arts and Crafts silver brooch of a foliate design set with cornelians, by Amy Sonheim.
• *diameter 4cm*
• £280 • Gooday Gallery

▽ Silver Brooch

- *1890*

Art and Crafts silver brooch set with Mexican fire opals and citrines.

- *diameter 3cm*
- £520 • Gooday Gallery

◁ Mythological Cameo Brooch

- *1890*

Shell cameo brooch of centaur and cupid mounted in an 18ct-gold base and set with diamonds and natural pearls.

- *length 5cm*
- £2,000 • RBR Group

▽ Amethyst Necklace

- *circa 1890*

Large lozenge-shape amethyst stones of graded size set in 15ct gold, with gold double linkages.

- *length 47cm*
- £3,550 • Wimpole Antiques

△ Emerald Pearl Pendant

- *circa 1890*

French polished emerald set in 18ct gold with floral and swag designs, with diamonds and a single pearl.

- *length 8.5cm*
- £1,975 • Wimpole Antiques

△ American Brooch

- *circa 1900*

An American natural pearl and diamond brooch in the form of a chrysanthemum, composed of Mississippi river pearls and an old brilliant-cut 1.1ct diamond set at the centre.

- £6,800 • Sandra Cronan

▽ Opal and Ruby Necklace

- *circa 1900*

Opal and ruby necklace with oval opals set in 15ct gold, hanging from a gold chain with ruby linkages.

- *length 47cm*
- £3,985 • Wimpole Antiques

▽ Art Nouveau Brooch

- *1900*

Art Nouveau 9ct-gold brooch set with a turquoise and baroque pearl drop. Marked 'Liberty & Co'.

- *length 3cm*
- £480 • Gooday Gallery

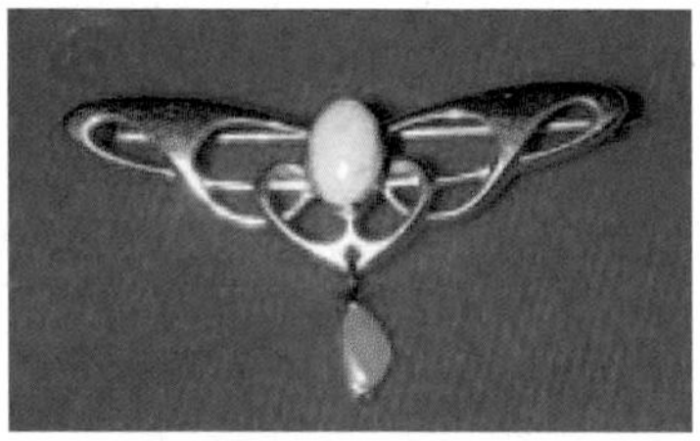

▽ Snake Brooch

- *circa 1900*

English gilt brooch modelled as a snake with stone settings.

- *6cm x 3cm*
- £150 • Linda Bee

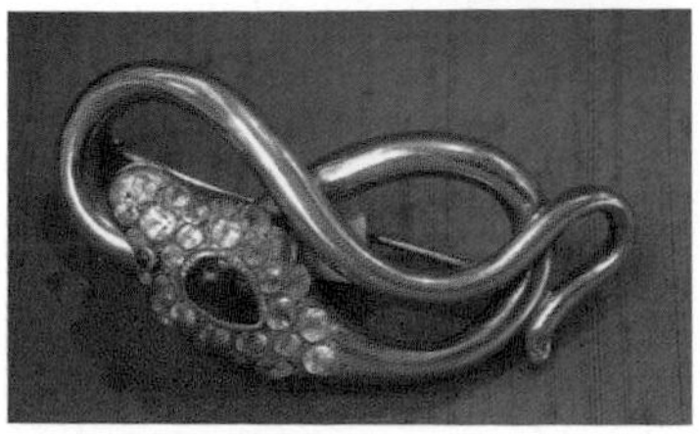

▽ Peridot and Pearl Necklace

- *circa 1900*

Peridot and pearl Edwardian necklace set in 15ct gold with graduated pearls and two lozenge-shaped peridots.

- £795 • Wimpole Antiques

◁ Diamond Brooch

- *circa 1900*

Exceptional diamond brooch with a central diamond within a ring and ribbon design, with four diamonds, within an octagonal border, encrusted with diamonds set in platinum with bow, 4.5ct of diamonds.

- *width 3.5cm*
- £9,750 • Wimpole Antiques

△ Peridot Necklace

- *circa 1900*

Peridot and pearl Edwardian necklace set in 15ct gold with lozenge and circular peridots linked by pearls.

- £1,785 • Wimpole Antiques

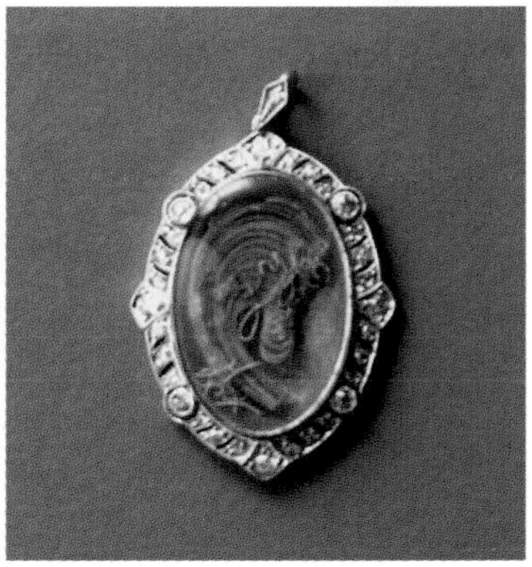

△ Mourning Pendant

- *circa 1910*

An Edwardian mourning pendant, with 18ct-gold backing and silver front surrounding glass containing a strand of hair in the form of a feather.

- *length 4cm*
- £1,250 • Emmy Abé

▽ Mixed Gemstones Earrings

- *circa 1910*

Pendulous set of earrings set in gold with mixed gemstones of garnet, sapphire, zircon, and citrine.

- *length 6.5cm*
- £985 • Wimpole Antiques

▽ Edwardian Jade Earrings

- *1910*

Edwardian circular jade earrings set in plain gold with two bands of roping.

- *width 1.5cm*
- £1,200 • N. Bloom

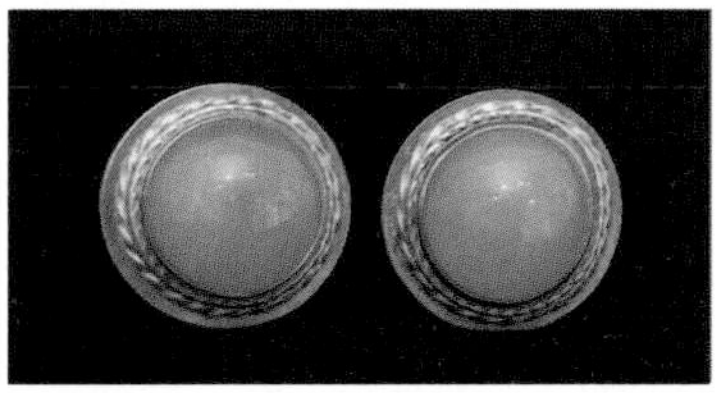

▽ Lapis and Crystal Brooch

- *1912*

Lapis and moulded panel brooch with bands of diamonds set in platinum, made in San Francisco, USA.

- *width 4.5cm*
- £3,300 • N. Bloom

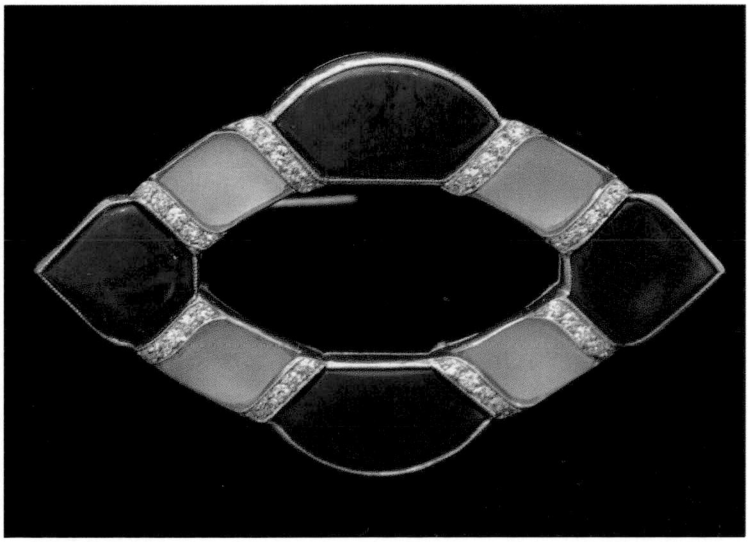

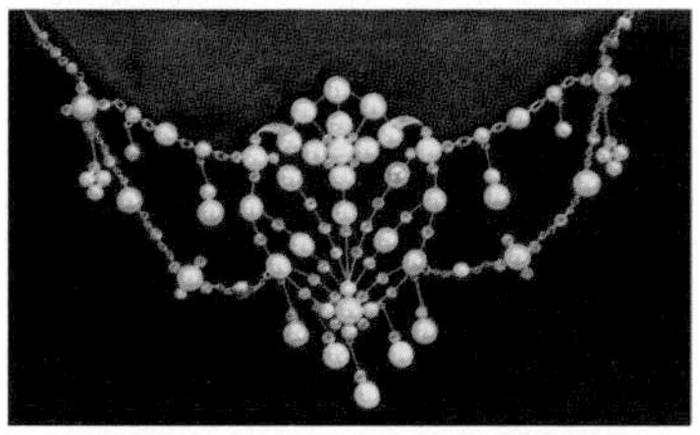

△ Pearl and Diamond Necklace

- *1905*

Edwardian pearl and diamond necklace with droplets and swag designs.

- *length 6cm*
- £3,950 • Wimpole Antiques

△ Silver Tiara

- *circa 1910*

Silver and paste Belle Epoque tiara in original box. French provenance, with Greek key pattern and wreath design.

- *length 15cm*
- £1,250 • Michele Rowan

△ Arts and Crafts Brooch

- *circa 1910*

Silver and gold Arts and Crafts brooch set with crystal and turquoise flowers.

- *diameter 3cm*
- £650 • RBR Group

▽ Turquoise Cuff

- *circa 1920s*

American Indian silver cuff set with graduated teardrop and lozenge-shaped turquoise stones in a sunburst design.

- *diameter 8cm*
- £2,300 • Wilde Ones

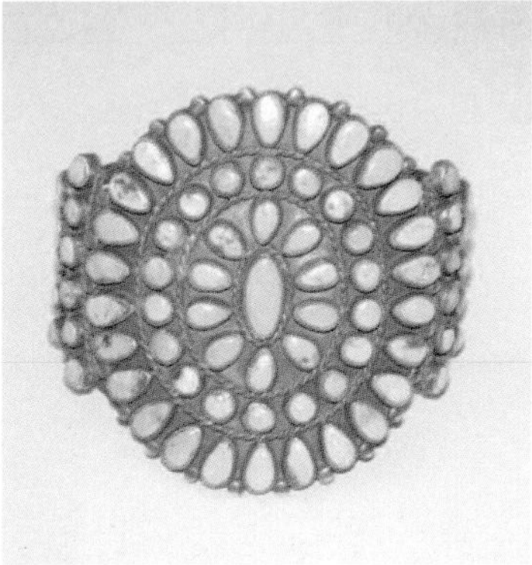

▽ Diamond Earrings

- *1920*

Pair of diamond earrings with oval, circular and rectangular diamonds within gold settings.

- *length 2.5cm*
- £4,400 • N. Bloom

▽ Zuni Pendant and Chain

- *1920*

Circular silver pendant set with 18 stones surrounded by silver scrolling, and a silver necklace.

- *diameter 6cm*
- £699 • Wilde Ones

◁ Egyptian-Style Pendant

- *1920*

An Egyptian-style octagonal-shaped pendant with silver sphinx and teardrop amber stone.

- *length 2cm*
- £120 • Linda Bee

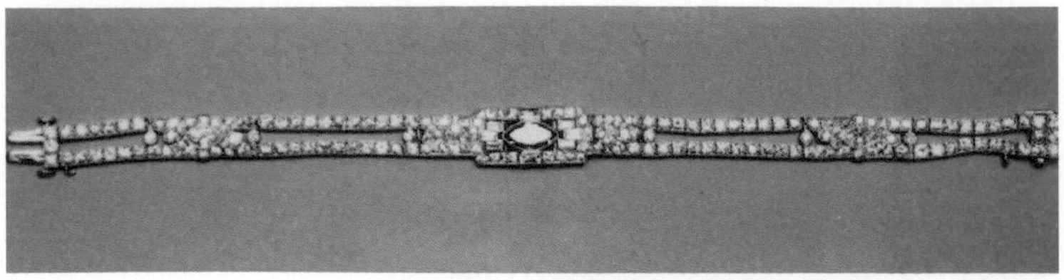

△ Diamond Bracelet

- *circa 1920*

Art Deco diamond bracelet set with a rare marquise-shaped natural fancy blue diamond, mounted in platinum.

- £155,000 • Sandra Cronan

▽ French Art Deco Bracelet

- *1920*

French sapphire and diamond bracelet by Trabert and Hoeffer/Mauboussin of Paris.

- *length 19cm*
- £44,500 • N. Bloom

△ Diamond Bracelet

- *circa 1920s*

Incorporating 6.5ct diamonds in total, with five large cushion-cut settings with interspersed links.

- *length 11cm*
- £7,900 • Emmy Abé

▽ Austrian Bracelet

- *1920*

Austrian Art Deco diamond bracelet set with a large central diamond surrounded by emeralds.

- *length 16cm*
- £15,000 • N. Bloom

▽ Blister-Pearl Heart

- *1920*

Heart-shaped blister-pearl pendant set with diamonds.

- *width 2cm*
- £2,950 • N. Bloom

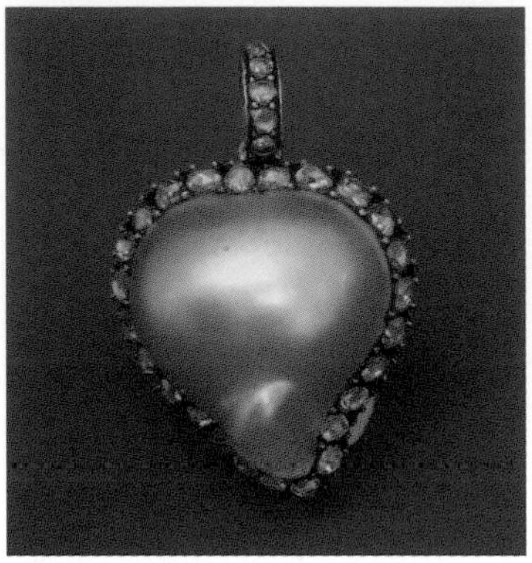

▽ Art Deco and Diamond Clasp

- *1920*

Art Deco jade and diamond clasp together with a re-strung twisted culture pearl necklace.

- *clasp 4cm*
- £3,950 • N. Bloom

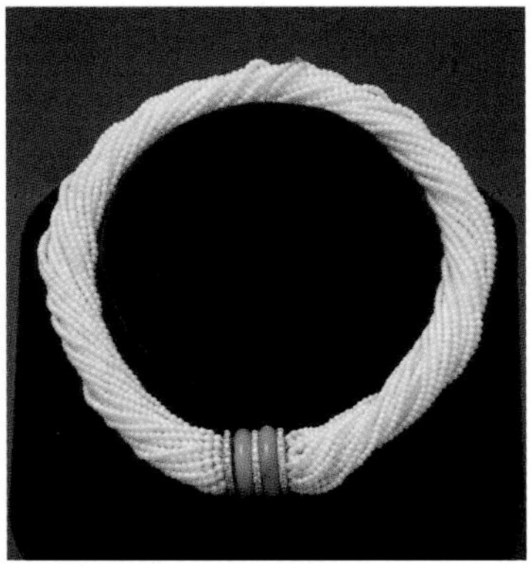

▷ Basket Brooch

- *circa 1925*

An Art Deco basket brooch by Cartier of Paris, of carved onyx with ruby flowers and cabochon emeralds and sapphires, mounted on platinum.

- £9,000 • Sandra Cronan

△ Boucheron Diamond Pin

- *1920*

Diamond-encrusted pin in the shape of a tie by Boucheron.

- *length 4cm*
- £11,500 • N. Bloom

△ Navajo Bracelet

- *1920*

Sterling silver Navajo bracelet with three main and two smaller, square turquoise panels. There is additional silver cast work between the settings. A traditional Navajo design.

- £699 • Wilde Ones

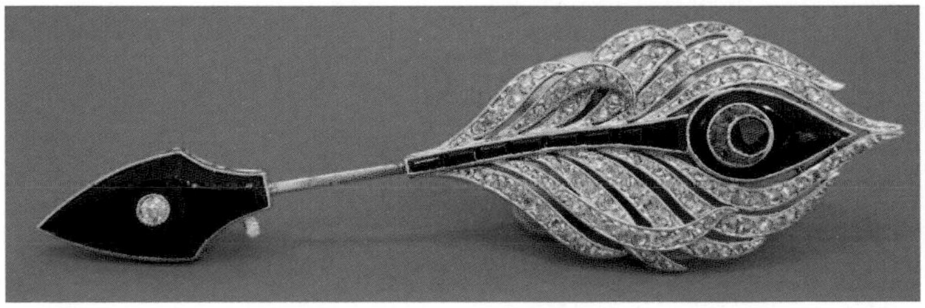

◁ Navajo Coral Bracelet

- *1920*

Navajo cast silver scrolled bracelet with a natural coral set in the centre.

- *length 16cm*
- £599 • Wilde Ones

△ Art Deco Feather Pin

- *1920*

Art Deco peacock feather pin encrusted with diamonds each side.

- *length 8cm*
- £4,500 • N. Bloom

△ Stork Brooch

- *circa 1925*

A diamond and gem-set stork brooch. His head and shirt are set with cushion-cut diamonds; his waistcoat is carved aquamarine; the cravat pin is cabochon cat's-eye; his cloak is carved garnets; his trousers are carved sapphires; his beak is amethyst and yellow topaz; his eyes are cabochon rubies; his monocle is a diamond and he has pink enamel feet. The whole is mounted on gold.

- *height 7cm*
- £32,000 • Sandra Cronan

△ Art Deco Bracelet

- *circa 1925*

An early and highly unusual French Art Deco bracelet with ruby, sapphire and emerald beads. The clasp is set with rubies and diamonds and the whole presents a twisted, interwoven appearance.

- £21,000 • Sandra Cronan

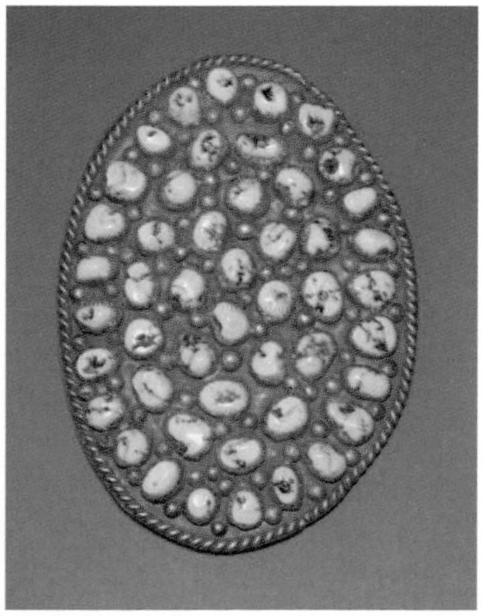

▽ Diamond Leaf Earrings

- *circa 1925*

Mille grain set in platinum diamond earrings in the form of a leaf.

- *length 2cm*
- £3,475 • Wimpole Antiques

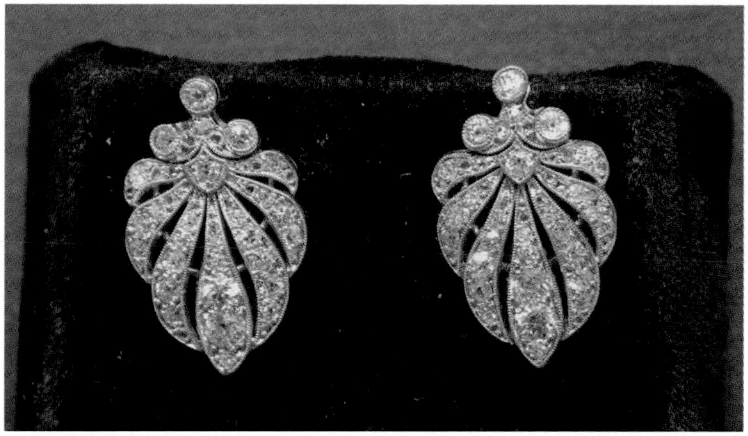

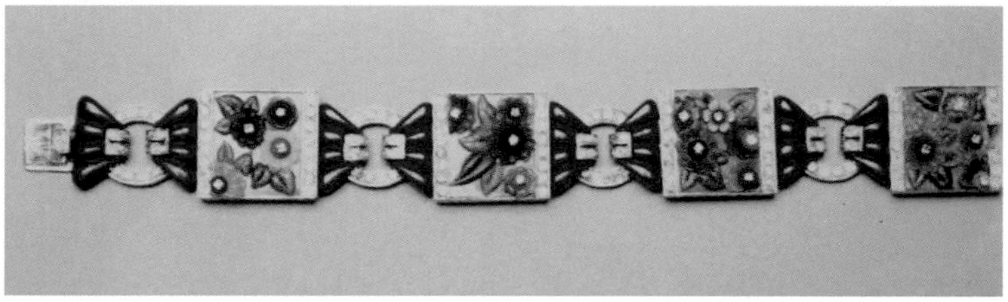

△ Art Deco Bracelet

- *circa 1925*

An Art Deco bracelet by Paulcho of Vienna, with enamel plaques, representing water, with floating flowers of carved jade and agate mounted on platinum and gold.

- *length 17cm*
- £100,000 • Sandra Cronan

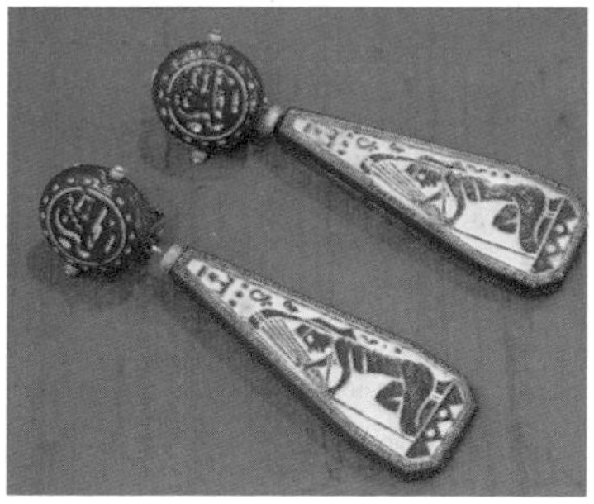

△ French Earrings

- *1930s*

A pair of French Egyptian-revival glass earrings.

- *7cm x 2cm*
- £95 • Linda Bee

◁ Zuni Belt Buckle

- *1930*

Zuni oval belt buckle with turquoise nuggets on a silver setting.

- *length 8cm*
- £699 • Wilde Ones

▷ Ball Pendant

- *circa 1925*

Lapis ball-drop pendant with diamonds within a star-shaped platinum setting.

- *diameter 5cm*
- £850 • RBR Group

▽ Pearl and Diamond Earrings

- *circa 1925*

Pendulous natural pearl and diamond earrings set in 18ct gold and platinum.

- *length 3.5cm*
- £3,785 • Wimpole Antiques

▽ Zuni Concha Belt

- *circa 1930s*

Zuni belt with alternating conchas of bow and lozenge form, set with turquoise, signed 'VMB'.

- *length 107cm*
- £1,999 • Wilde Ones

▽ Czechoslovakian Necklace

- *1930*

Czechoslovakian glass necklace made up of 18 triangular emerald glass segments.

- *length 33cm*
- £95 • Linda Bee

▽ Dress Clip

- *circa 1925*

A French silver dress clip of the Art Deco period, with a carved bakelite centre within a paste setting, showing a woman's face, swathed in elaborate silver head-dress and gathered veil.

- *height 4.5cm*
- £150 • Hilary Conqy

▽ Snail Brooch

- *1930*

A snail brooch in paste and silver.

- £65 • Linda Bee

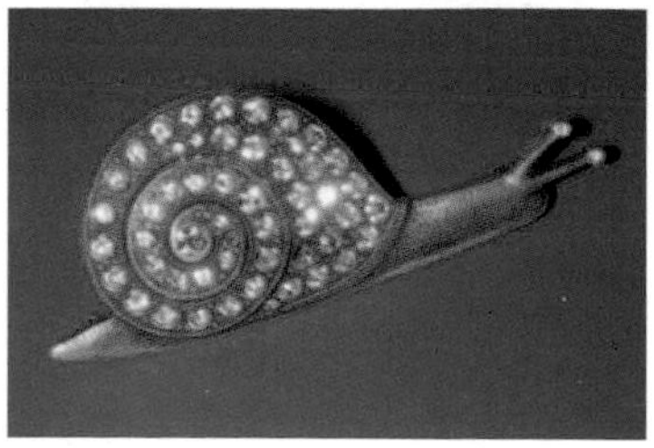

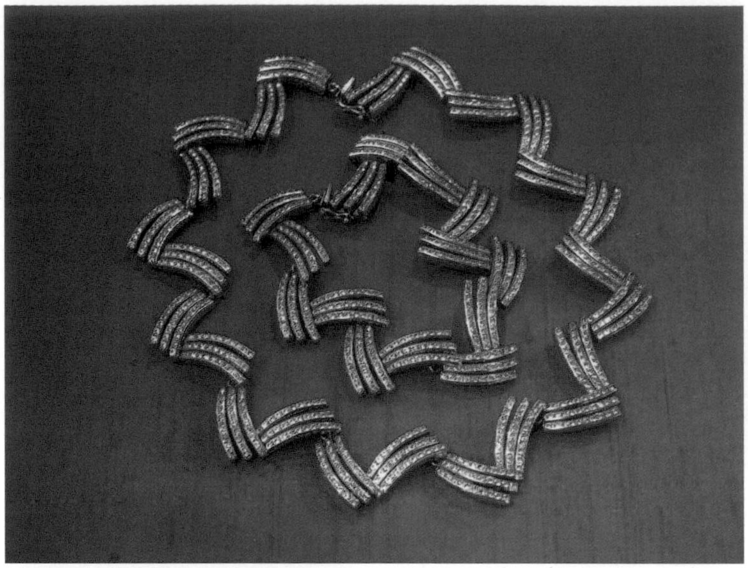

△ **Necklace and Bracelet Set**
- *1930s*

Rare interlinked diamante necklace and bracelet set by DRGM, Germany.
- *length 36cm (necklace), 18cm (bracelet)*
- £350 for the set • Linda Bee

△ **French Art Deco Necklace**
- *1930*

A French green bakelite and silver link necklace.
- *diameter 2cm*
- £120 • Linda Bee

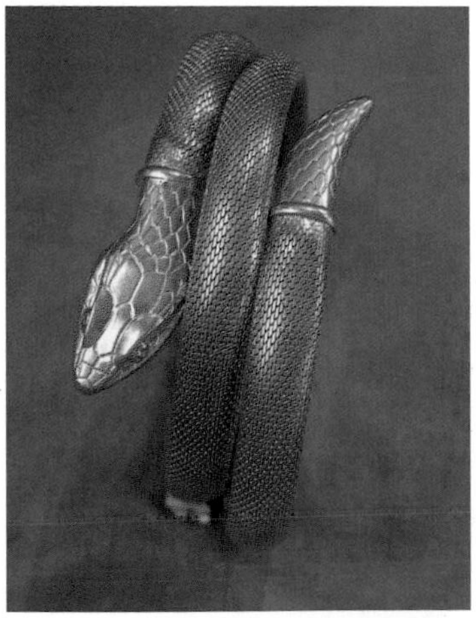

△ **Snake Bracelet**
- *1930*

Gilt bracelet styled as a coiled serpent with a spiralled chain link body and scale design to the head and tail.
- *8cm x 8cm*
- £85 • Linda Bee

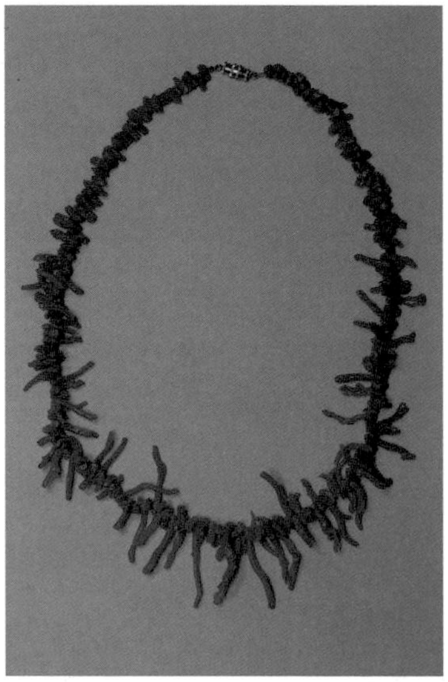

△ **Coral Necklace**
- *circa 1938*

Red coral necklace of the Zuni tribe, of natural red coral, hand-drilled and strung. Red is a sacred colour to the Zuni, bringing good luck and longevity.
- *length 44cm*
- £399 • Wilde Ones

▷ **Czechoslovakian Brooch**
- *circa 1930*

A Czechoslovakian brooch of blue glass on a plenal base. Of diamond shape with a large, central diamond-shaped stone with a clasp mount.
- *length 7.5cm*
- £40 • Sugar

▽ **Bow Brooch**
- *1930*

Rhinestone and black enamel brooch fashioned as a bow tie.
- *4cm x 12cm*
- £85 • Linda Bee

▽ **Burmese Ruby Ring**
- *1930*

Burmese Art Deco gold ring with four large rubies surrounded by diamonds.
- £2,000 • Michele Rowan

▽ **Necklace and Bracelet**
- *1930*

German DRGM metal and paste necklace and bracelet.
- £195 • Linda Bee

△ **Amazonite Ring**
- *circa 1930*

Navajo amazonite ring with traditional setting in silver, the whole of an elongated lozenge shape, with beading around the stone and moulded bezel.
- *height 5cm*
- £329 • Wilde Ones

△ **Wedding Necklace**
- *circa 1930*

Navajo squash-blossom wedding necklace with naga centrepiece, representing union, and silver, handcast beads with turquoise stones.
- *length 60cm*
- £1,499 • Wilde Ones

▽ Brooch

• *circa 1940*
Brooch of glass-encrusted flowers with blue beads.
• *length 7cm*
• £45 • Sugar

▽ Bow Brooch

• *circa 1940s*
With baguettes of faux sapphire and paste. Signed by Marcel Boucher.
• *height 6cm*
• £95 • Hilary Conqy

▽ Zuni Pendant

• *circa 1940*
Zuni pin pendant showing an eagle dancer with turquoise, spiny oyster shell, jet, and mother-of-pearl on a silver base with beading.
• *diameter 7cm*
• £950 • Wilde Ones

▽ Padlock Brooch

• *1940*
An American heart-shaped brooch in the form of a padlock connected to a key, with paste diamonds. Designed by Castlecliff and set in sterling silver.
• *diameter 2cm*
• £120 • Linda Bee

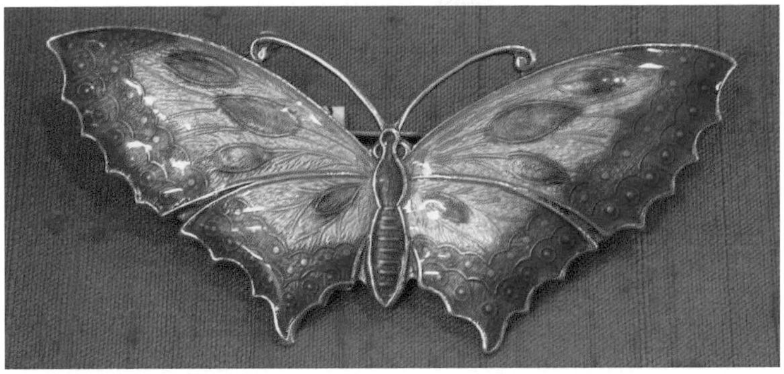

▽ Gold 18ct Bracelet

• *circa 1940*
Gold 18ct double-chain-link bracelet with light and dark gold linkages.
• *length 15cm*
• £1,350 • Wimpole Antiques

△ English Silver Brooch

• *1940s*
English silver and enamel brooch modelled as a butterfly.
• *6.5cm x 3cm*
• £125 • Linda Bee

◁ Plane Pin

• *1940s*
Unusual metal pin in the shape of a plane with a map of south-west United States.
• *diameter 5cm*
• £85 • Linda Bee

▽ Pair of Ruby Clasps

• *1940*
Pair of ruby and diamond clasps set in stylised gold leaf.
• *length 5cm*
• £2,500 • N. Bloom

▽ English Jewellery Set

• *circa 1940s*
English jewellery set with silver gilt top hat pin with faux pearl and earrings.
• *8cm x 3cm*
• £120 • Linda Bee

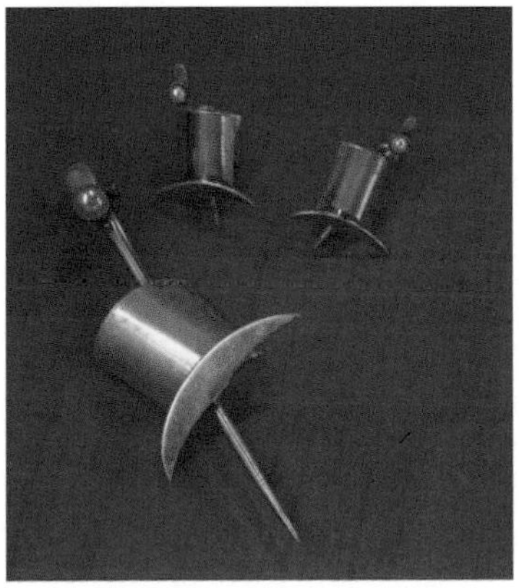

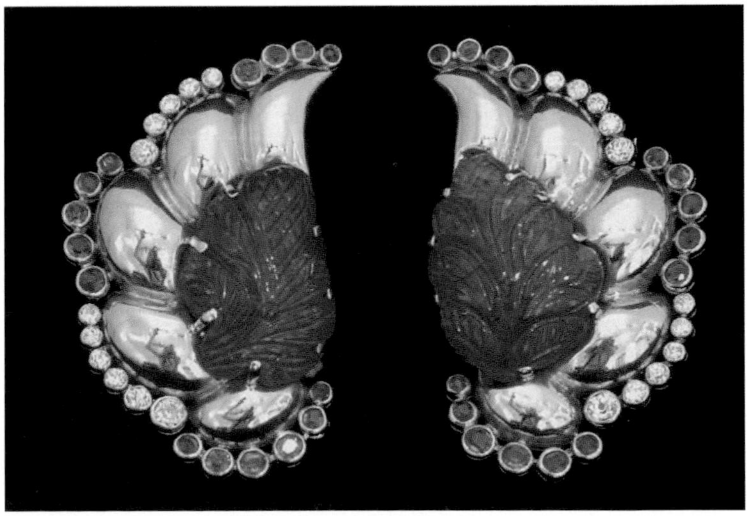

▽ Bead Necklace

• *circa 1940s*
A necklace of turquoise-blue beads with glass-encrusted flowers interwoven. The pendant is a flower cluster in pink, white, blue and yellow.
• *length 45cm*
• £35 • Sugar

▽ Coro Duet

• *circa 1940s*
Sterling silver coro duet brooch with removable fur clip, featuring green and black enamel stylised owls with green crystal eyes in paste settings.
• *height 5cm*
• £120 • Hilary Conqy

△ French Jade Brooch

- *1940*

French jade carved dragon bar brooch set in gold with gold scrolling.

- *length 9cm*
- £2,400 • N. Bloom

△ Silver Gilt Brooch

- *1940s*

American large silver gilt and cut glass sapphire floral brooch.

- *7cm x 6cm*
- £95 • Linda Bee

△ Enamel Cat Brooch

- *circa 1950*

Silver-gilt cat with turquoise enamelled eyes and an enamelled butterfly to the tail.

- *length 6cm*
- £85 • Sugar

△ Spider Brooch

- *1940s*

Gilt metal spider brooch with two cut amethysts.

- *5cm x 5cm*
- £45 • Linda Bee

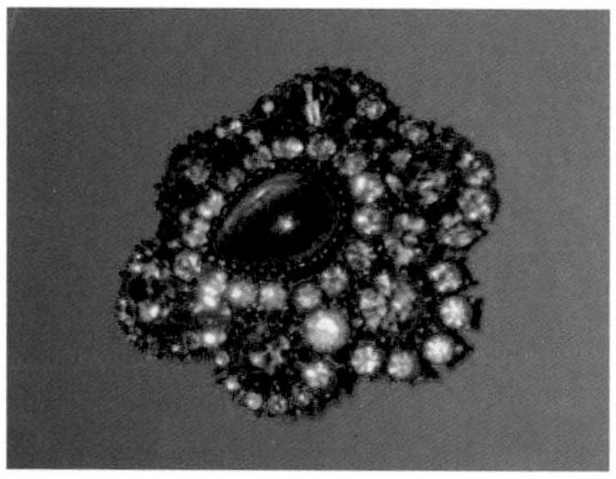

△ Green Lozenge-Shape Brooch

- *1950*

Czechoslovakian brooch set with a dark green lozenge stone surrounded by bright green, faceted stones.

- *diameter 5cm*
- £55 • Linda Bee

△ Zuni Ring

- *circa 1950*

A Zuni flower design ring consisting of a central lozenge of turquoise, surrounded by twelve smaller stones interspersed with silver globules.

- *diameter 4cm*
- £299 • Wilde Ones

▽ Corsage Brooch

- *1940*

Flower corsage brooch styled as two exotic flower heads with leaves.

- *13cm x 6cm*
- £65 • Linda Bee

▽ American Metal Bracelet

- *1940*

An American metal bracelet with bakelite plaques decorated with flowers.

- *height 2cm*
- £120 • Linda Bee

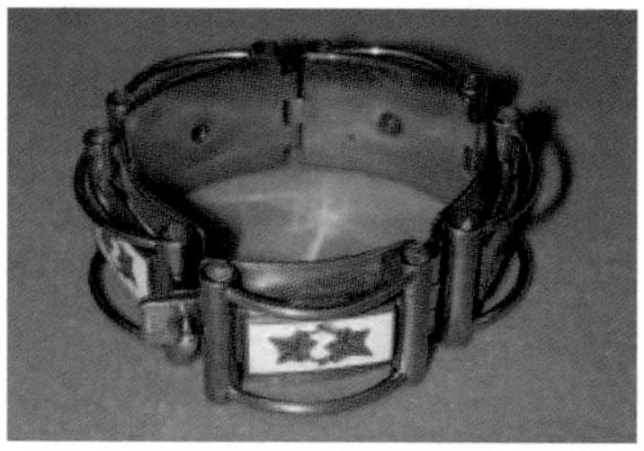

▽ Austrian Violet Brooch

- *1950*

Austrian violet brooch with diamonds and jade leaves, set in silver.

- *height 6.5cm*
- £1,650 • N. Bloom

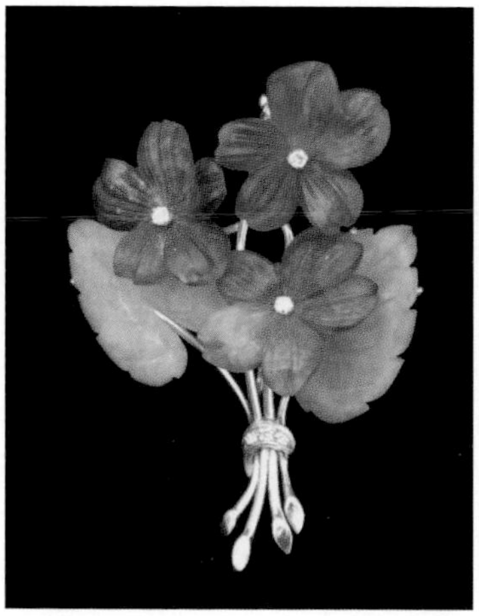

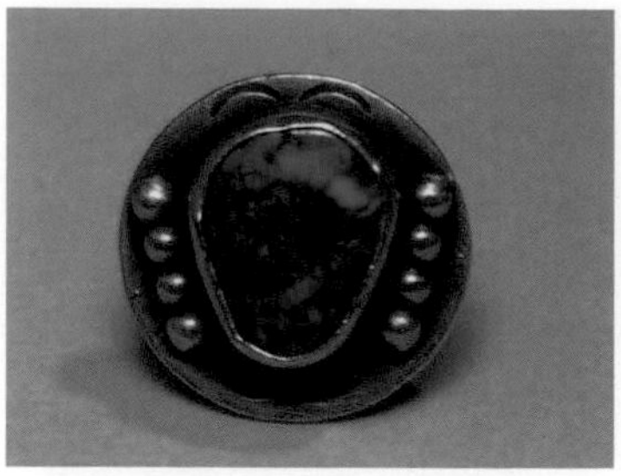

△ Navajo Ring

- *circa 1940*

Turquoise and silver ring with stones set on circular plate. Turquoise has four globules of silver to each side.

- £199 • Wilde Ones

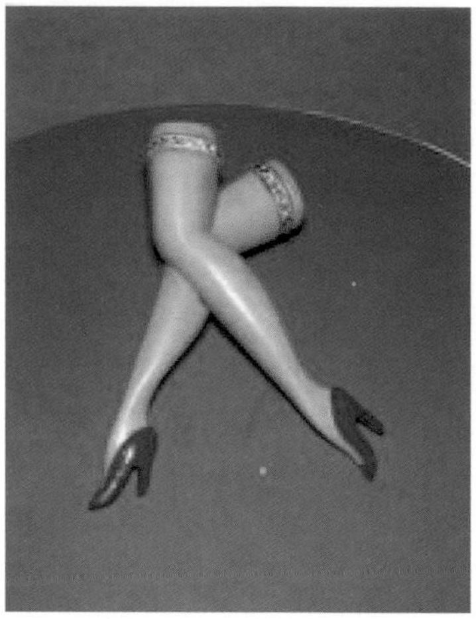

△ French Brooch

- *1950*

A French brooch styled as a pair of lady's legs with paste garters and red high-heeled shoes.

- *height 7cm*
- £85 • Linda Bee

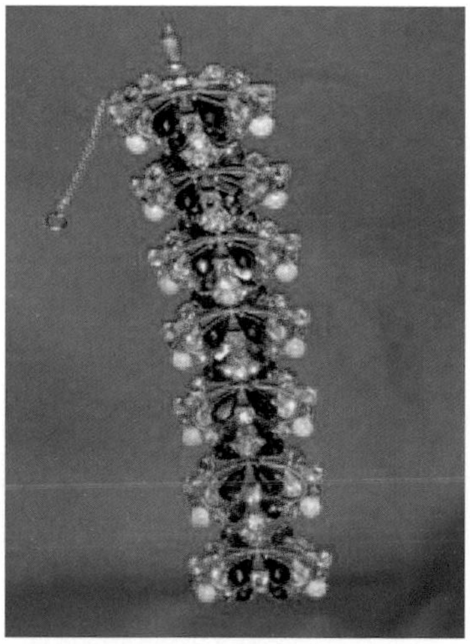

△ Schiaparelli Bracelet

- *circa 1950*

Bracelet with emerald-green and sea-green stones, designed by Schiaparelli.

- *length 12cm*
- £550 • Sue Mautner

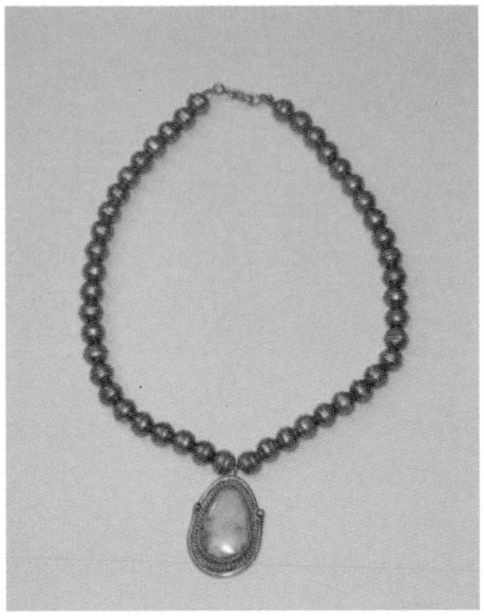

△ Silver Choker

• *circa 1950*
American Indian silver-beaded necklace with an almond-shaped turquoise pendant set in silver.
• *length 3.5cm*
• £289 • Wilde Ones

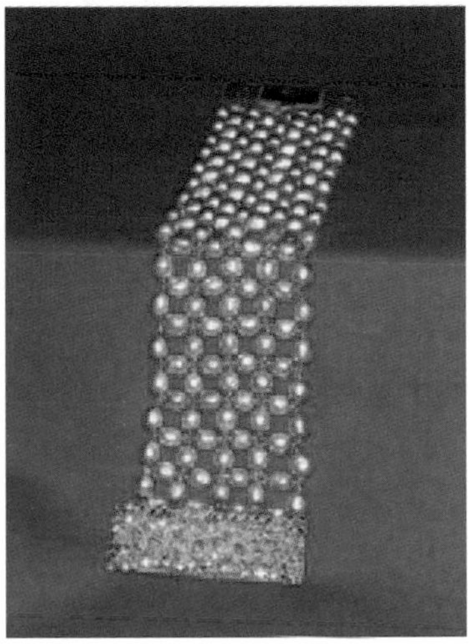

△ Linked Pearl Bracelet

• *circa 1950*
Miriam Haskell bracelet linked with flowers and set with pearls.
• *length 14cm*
• £750 • Sue Mautner

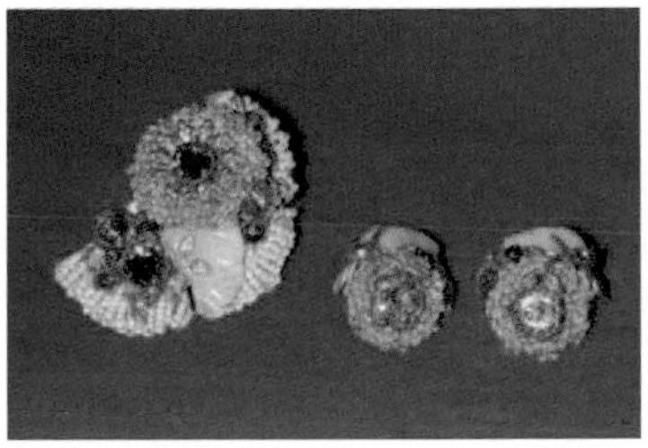

△ Brooch and Earrings

• *circa 1950s*
American jewellery set consisting of a brooch and a pair of earrings styled as flowers by Miriam Haskell.
• *length 5cm (brooch)*
• £550 • Sue Mautner

▽ Miriam Haskell Brooch

• *circa 1950*
American Miriam Haskell brooch with glass stones, set within a stylised floral arrangement.
• *length 4cm*
• £450 • Sue Mautner

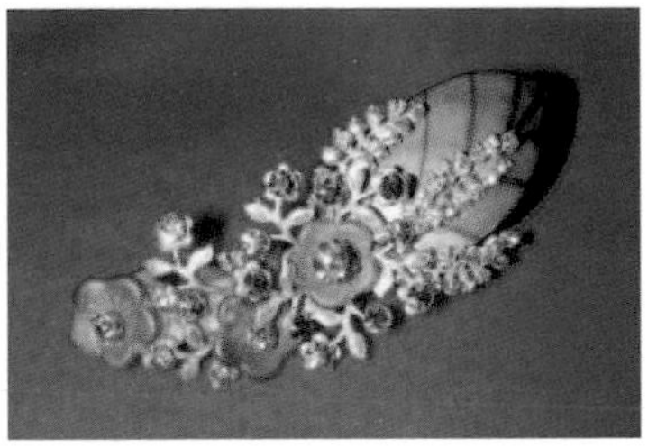

▽ Belt Buckle

• *circa 1955*
A Navajo silver belt buckle with sunburst design, of ovate shape encompassing seven turquoise stones to centre.
• *height 11cm*
• £399 • Wilde Ones

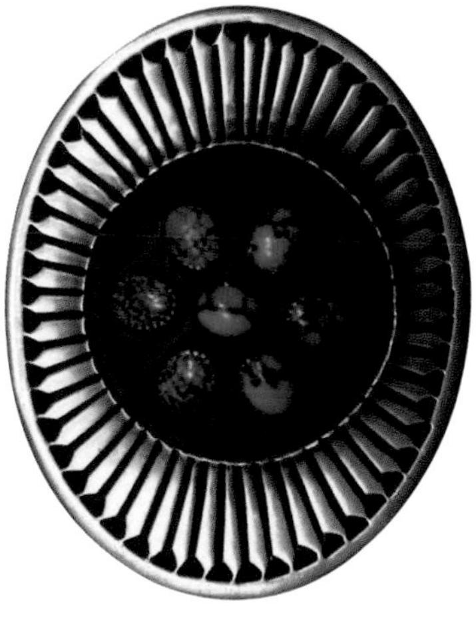

▽ Coral Zuni Earrings

• *1950*
Coral diamond-shaped Zuni earrings, with a smaller diamond shape inside.
• *length 8cm*
• £169 • Wilde Ones

△ Salvador Dali Brooch

• *1950*
18ct gold stylised leaf in the form of a hand with red-painted nails, signed Dali on the right-hand leaf.
• *length 6.5cm*
• £3,750 • N. Bloom

△ American Earrings

• *1950*
American turquoise glass earrings by Tiffany, modelled as flower petals within gold settings.
• *3.5cm x 3.5cm*
• £85 • Linda Bee

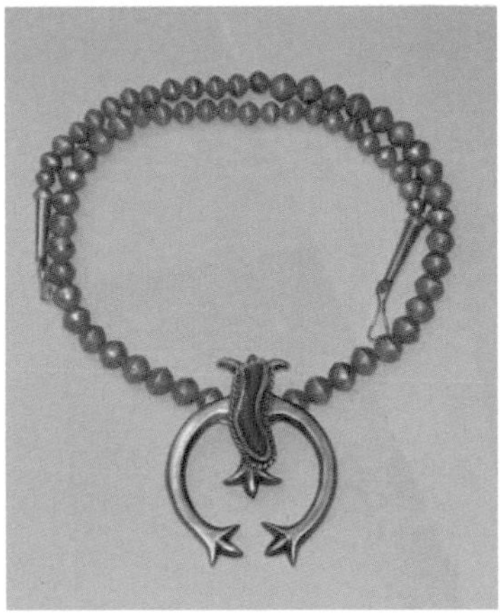

△ Silver Necklace

• *circa 1950s*
American Indian silver-beaded necklace with a silver Naga inset with coral, with fleur-de-lys terminals.
• *diameter 5.5cm*
• £699 • Wilde Ones

▽ Zuni Cuff

• *1950*
'Sleeping Beauty' Zuni cuff with 33 turquoise stones set in silver in a traditional design.
• *diameter 9cm*
• £1,200 • Wilde Ones

▽ French Ceramic Brooch

• *1950*
A green French ceramic brooch in the shape of a poodle with bronze decoration and metal clasp.
• *length 5cm*
• £45 • Linda Bee

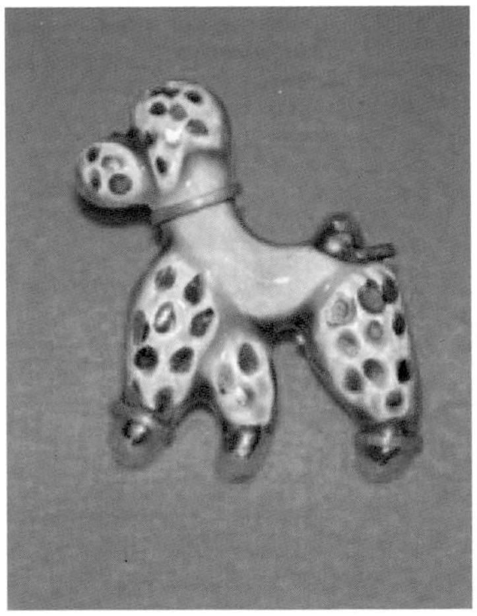

▽ Brooch and Earrings

• *circa 1950*
American brooch and earrings by Miriam Haskell.
• £850 • Sue Mautner

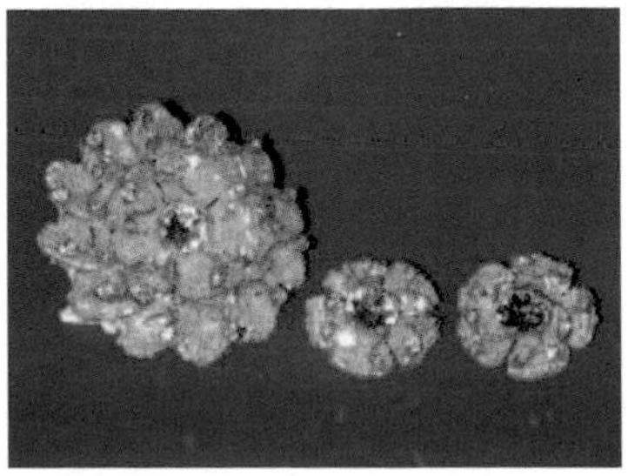

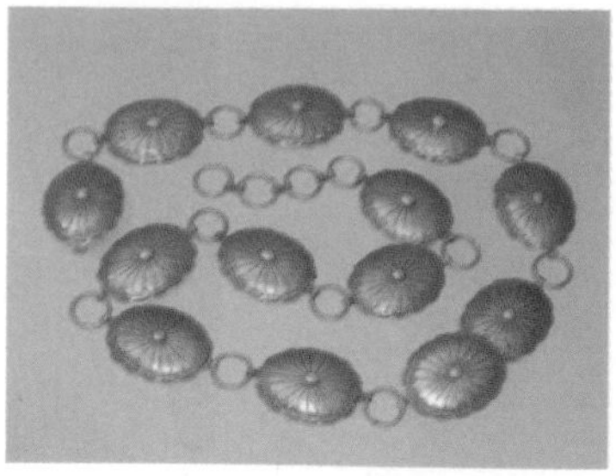

△ Navajo Concha Belt

- *circa 1960*

Navajo silver concha engraved belt set with turquoise stones.

- *length 98cm*
- £699 • Wilde Ones

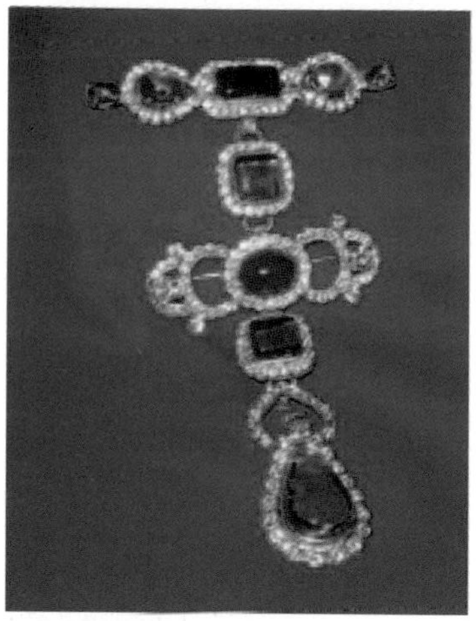

△ Chanel Linked Brooch

- *circa 1960*

Dramatic Chanel brooch encrusted with paste diamonds and blue, red and black stones.

- *length 12cm*
- £650 • Sue Mautner

△ Green Ring

- *1960*

A fun fashion green plastic and metal fun ring.

- *width 1cm*
- £45 • Linda Bee

▽ Fun Hooped Earrings

- *1960*

English green plastic hooped earrings made in London.

- *diameter 4cm*
- £25 • Linda Bee

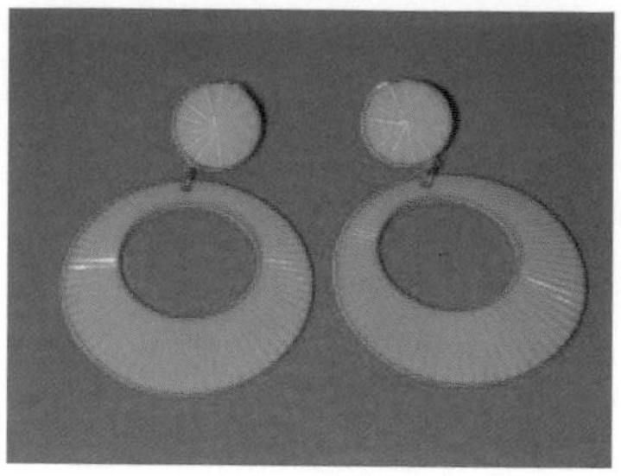

▽ Zuni Butterfly

- *1960*

Butterfly with black and mother-of-pearl head and turquoise coral and mother-of-pearl body and wings, set in silver.

- *width 6cm*
- £599 • Wilde Ones

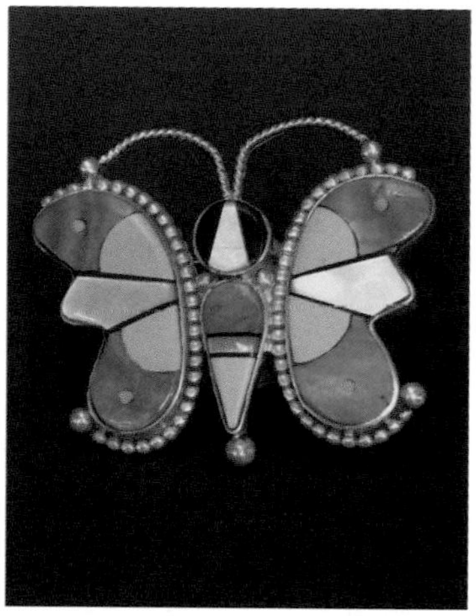

▽ Coral Earrings

- *1960*

A pair of coral earrings set in gold with gold balls.

- *height 8cm*
- £6,600 • N. Bloom

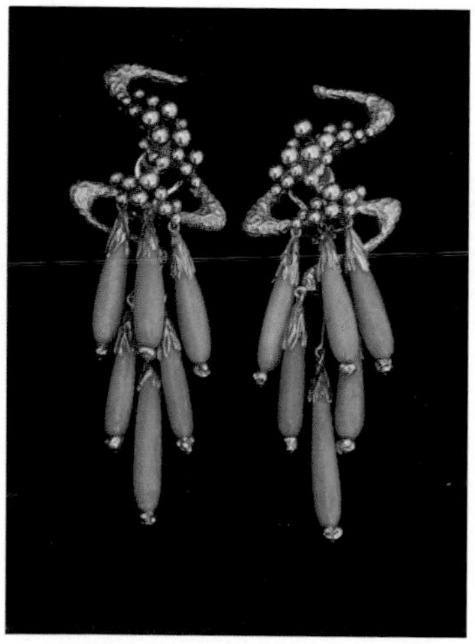

△ Fashion Ring

- *1960*

Swedish ring with large central stone surrounded by metal band.

- £95 • Linda Bee

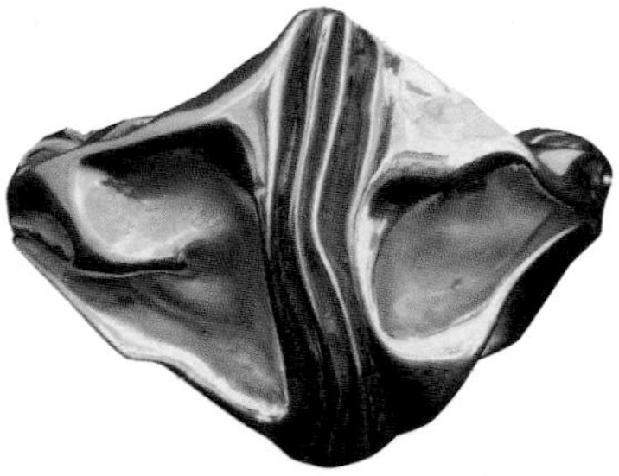

△ Swiss Balainot Bracelet

- *1960*

Swiss gold bracelet by Balainot from the 'Sheet Range'.

- *height 6cm*
- £3,950 • N. Bloom

△ Acrylic Rings

- *circa 1965*

Moulded, clear acrylic rings with panels of colour running vertically throughout. Designed by Mary Quant.

- £20 • Themes

▽ Christian Dior Brooch

- *1960*

Circus horse brooch by Christian Dior.

- £295 • Linda Bee

▽ Brooch by Andrew Grima

- *1967*

Andrew Grima asymmetric crystal brooch with three gold leaves set with diamonds.

- *diameter 5cm*
- £1,850 • N. Bloom

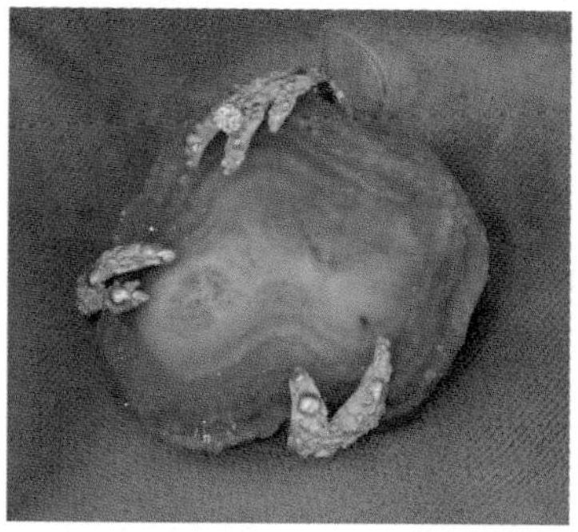

▽ Christian Dior Brooch

- *1966*

Christian Dior brooch with pearls.

- *height 8.5cm*
- £275 • Linda Bee

▽ Navajo Bear-Claw Necklace

• *1970*
Rare necklace with six bear claws set in silver with five large 'Sleeping Beauty' turquoise nuggets from Arizona.
• *length of claw 4cm*
• **£1,899** • **Wilde Ones**

▽ Zuni Pendant

• *1998*
Zuni knife wing pin pendant, showing an eagle dancer. An example of inlay jewellery using turquoise, coral, jet and abalone on a silver base. The wings, circular in form, are beaded in silver, with further silver decoration to the ears and hat. Made by D. Iahi.
• **£899** • **Wilde Ones**

▽ Italian Glass Necklace

• *circa 1990*
Italian glass necklaces, made up of blue, turquoise, lilac, indigo and clear glass beads linked by gold metal beads.
• *length 37cm*
• **£85 each** • **Francesca Martire**

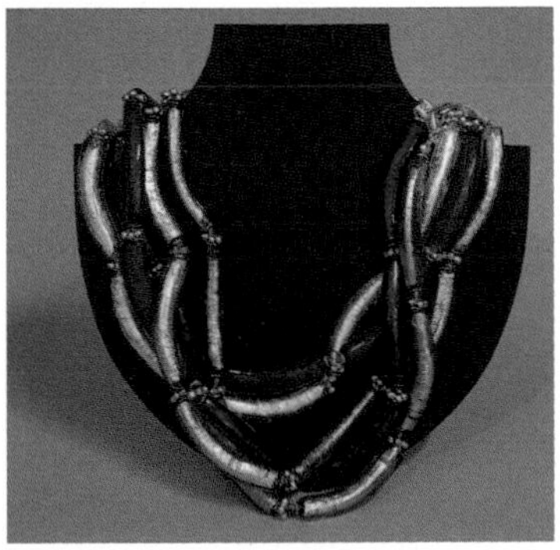

△ Kokopelli Brooch

• *circa 1970s*
An American Indian silver brooch showing the fertility god Kokopelli blowing a flute, inset with a circular turquoise stone.
• *length 5cm*
• **£129** • **Wilde Ones**

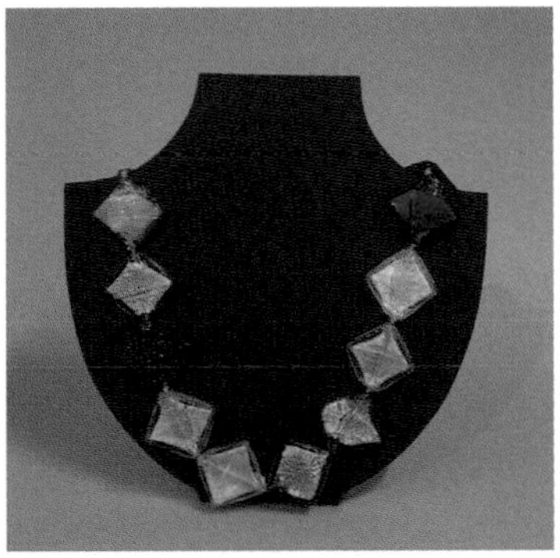

△ Glass Italian Necklace

• *circa 1990*
Hand-blown glass necklace, made from, blue, gold, red, green and clear glass squares.
• *length 37cm*
• **£135** • **Francesca Martire**

△ Zuni Silver Cuff Set

• *circa 2000*
Zuni silver cuff set with jet and turquoise stones in a geometric pattern radiating from a stylised eagle, signed 'Benji & Shirley Tzuni'.
• *diameter 6cm*
• **£899** • **Wilde Ones**

▽ Indian Ring

• *1980*
Indian blue lapis ring with large amber stone set in gold.
• *length 2cm*
• **£8,880** • **N. Bloom**

▽ Zuni Brooch

• *circa 1999*
Circular silver Zuni brooch with graduated teardrop and lozenge-shaped turquoise stones set in a radiating sunburst pattern.
• *diameter 11cm*
• **£899** • **Wilde Ones**

▽ Zuni Fetish Necklace

• *circa 2000*
Four-stranded Zuni fetish necklace with a menagerie of animals including eagles, ravens, turtles, coyotes and crows set in jet, turquoise, coral and other semi-precious stones.
• *length 89cm*
• **£699** • **Wilde Ones**

▷ Navajo Ring

• *2000*
Navajo natural coral from the 1920s, designed with a turquoise stone in a heavy silver setting with scrolling, by Rowan Horse.
• *length 4cm*
• **£399** • **Wilde Ones**

△ Navajo Ring

• *circa 1970s*
Silver Navajo ring with two oval turquoise stones set within a feather design.
• *length 4cm*
• **£169** • **Wilde Ones**

△ Zuni Bracelet

• *1998*
A Zuni bracelet with three panels of geometric design, showing the four-direction medicine wheel for the protection of the wearer. Made of jet, coral, lapus lazuli and turquoise. By H. Kaslfestewa.
• **£1,499** • **Wilde Ones**

MARINE ITEMS

Marine items have always been popular amongst collectors, with chronometers, sextants, models of boats, compasses and barometers being the most highly sought-after in today's marketplace. Hand-held telescopes were commonly used by seamen, along with the earliest refracting telescopes, and the examples one can find today are usually eighteenth-century, with vellum-covered card body tubes, often tooled in gilt with ivory and ebony mounts. The outer tubes can be covered in shagreen. A vast quantity of surveying instruments were made from brass, copper, silver and platinum and unfortunately were often consigned to the melting pot as scrap. Today, that is no longer the case, as the fine workmanship and mathematical precision of these instruments designed by engineers is now increasingly appreciated. Other marine items that are collectable include posters, ship's decanters in boxes, models of boats, globes on stands, ship's wheels, backstaffs, books and anchor lamps.

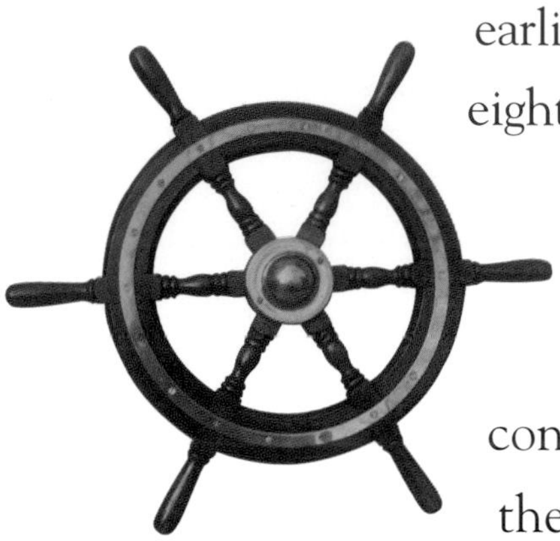

△ Backstaff

- *circa 1779*

A boxwood and lignum backstaff. The central crossbar is lignum on one side and boxwood on the other.

- £6,500 • T. Phillips

▽ Octagonal Telescope

- *circa 1780*

Fine octagonal fruitwood telescope with brass single draw and lens housing.

- *length of case 31cm*
- £800 • Langfords Marine

▽ Parallel Rule

- *circa 1800*

A 12-inch ebony parallel rule, for use in navigation. Unusual, with cut out polished brass straps.

- £49 • Ocean Leisure

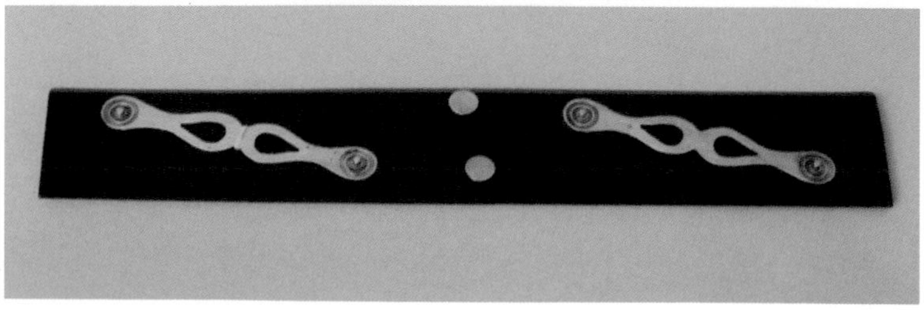

△ Pater Compass

- *circa 1800*

Dry card, Pater compass on a two-inch turned wood base. Hand-painted card. By Stockert, Bavaria, for the English market.

- £429 • Ocean Leisure

△ Dry Land Compass

- *circa 1800*

Gimballed dry land compass in brass case.

- *diameter 11.5cm*
- £1,150 • Langfords Marine

▽ Napoleonic Ship

- *circa 1800*

A Napoleonic prisoner-of-war model of a ship, made of beef bones, with fine detail to the rigging and deck.

- *42cm x 36cm*
- £3,400 • Langfords Marine

▽ Small Brass Barometer

- *circa 1800*

Barometer, *HMS Britannia* prize, by Coomes of Devonport, in original leather box.

- *diameter 5.5cm*
- £850 • Langfords Marine

▽ Georgian Coconut Cup

- *circa 1810*

Georgian coconut cup with silver mounts raised on splayed legs with paw feet.

- *height 13.5cm*
- £690 • Langfords Marine

▽ Dwarf Sextant

- *1820*

Dwarf sextant signed 'G. Whitbread, London', and housed in its original mahogany travelling case, with further pieces and accessories.

- *19cm*
- £2,500 • T. Phillips

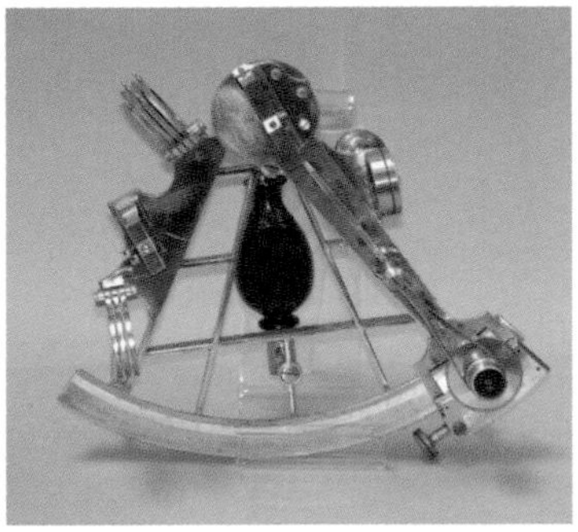

▽ Ebony Octant

- *circa 1840*

Ebony and brass octant in original oak box with label and the inscription, 'W. Hughes, Instrument Maker, 40 Fenchurch Street, London'.

- *width 28cm*
- £785 • Langfords Marine

△ Chinese Porcelain Bowl

- *circa 1817*

Chinese blue and white porcelain, from the ship *Diana*, which sank near Malacca on 4 March 1817 on the India-China route.

- *diameter 17.5cm*
- £220 • Langfords Marine

△ Sea Chest

- *circa 1830*

Antique sea chest Funa Dansu with original metalware.

- *35cm x 45cm x 39cm*
- £1,600 • Gordon Reece

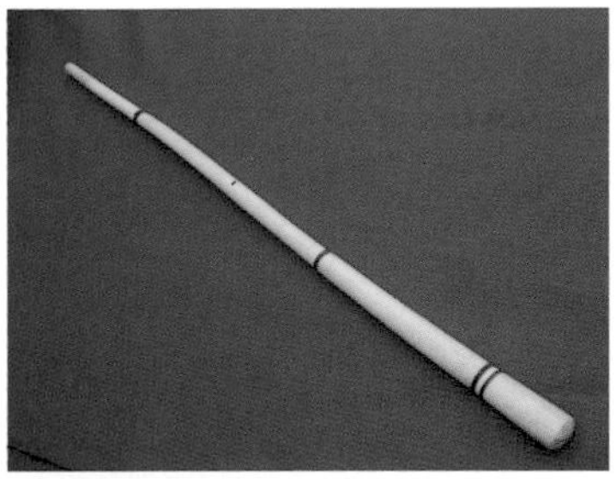

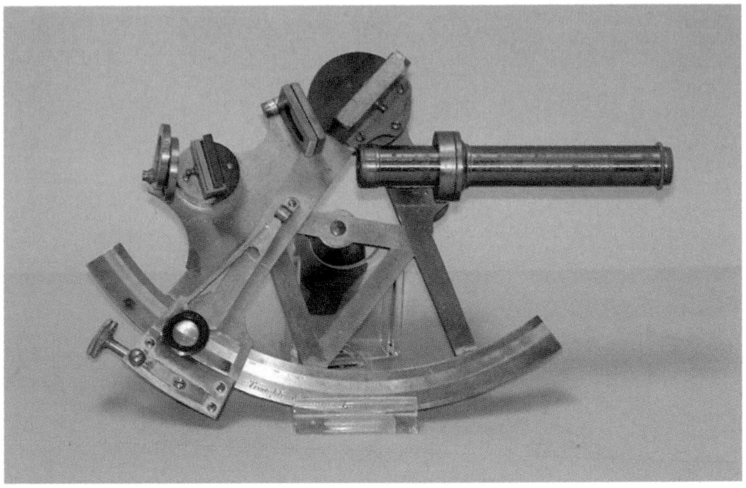

▽ Brass Candlestick Balance

- *1840*

Victorian brass candlestick or lighthouse balance. The words, 'POSTAL BALANCE' embossed with a spring scale on a circular moulded foot.

- *height 17cm*
- £299 • Langfords Marine

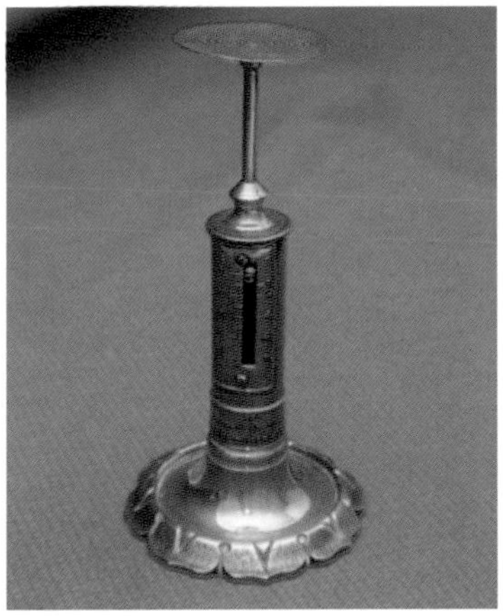

◁ Ivory Baton

- *1837–1901*

An ivory and ebony regimental baton or swagger stick.

- *length 53cm*
- £149 • Langfords Marine

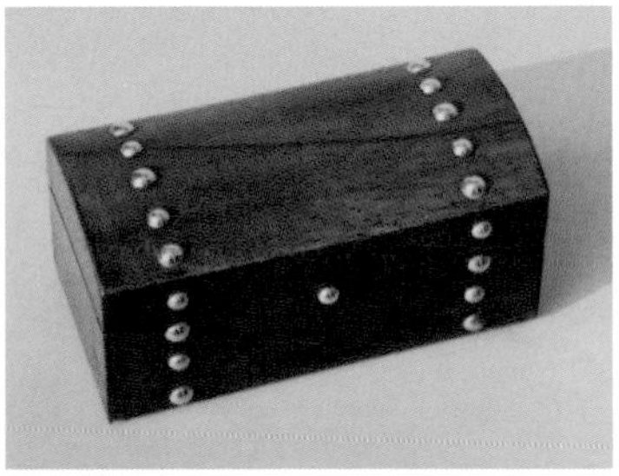

△ Ship's Box

- *circa 1870*

Brass-studded and domed-topped ship's box.

- *height 19cm*
- £99 • Ocean Leisure

△ Dwarf Sextant

- *circa 1835*

Dwarf sextant by Troughton & Simms. The instrument is housed in its original mahogany box with accessories. This would be used for navigation and surveying. Edward Troughton went into partnership with Simms in 1826.

- *height 13.5cm*
- £5,750 • T. Phillips

△ Ivory Box

- *circa 1840*

An unusual and charming ivory box, possibly originally a toothpick holder, the hinged lid with a compass inset, the base with rose-gold fastener.

- *7cm x 3cm*
- £239 • Langfords Marine

△ Chinese Bowl

- *circa 1850*

A blue and white oriental dish recovered from a wreck of the *Diana* in the China Seas.

- *diameter 14cm*
- £240 • The Deep

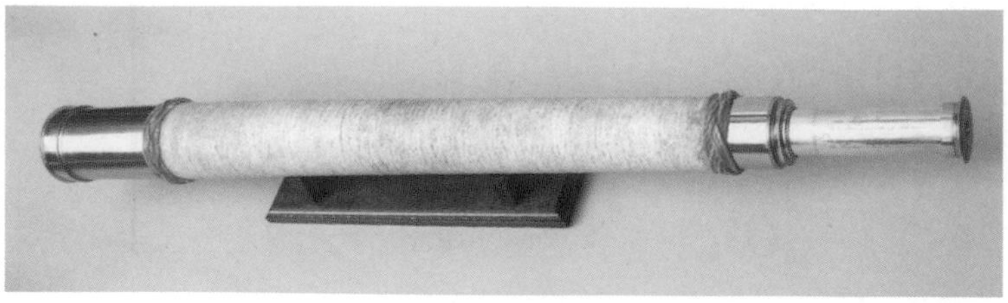

△ Naval Telescope

- *circa 1870*

Rare, single-draw naval telescope made of silver and brass. Rope bound with 'Turk's Heads' at both ends of the tunnel. By John Browning, London.

- £549 • Ocean Leisure

△ Anchor Brooch

- *late 19th century*

Silver sweetheart anchor bar brooch.

- £49 • Ocean Leisure

▽ Anchor

- *circa 1880*

Cast-iron ship's anchor.

- *height 1m*
- £80 • Curios

◁ Carved Coconut

- *1880*

Victorian coconut with carving of a ship, cat, guitar, frog and foliage. These coconuts were usually carved by sailors.

- *length 6cm*
- £85 • Langfords Marine

▽ Diorama

- *circa 1880*

Diorama of a three-masted barque with smaller sailing vessels in the foreground. Made by a sailor.

- *length 90cm, height 46cm*
- £1,450 • Langfords Marine

▽ Bone Beaker Aberdeen Schooner

- *circa 1880*

Bone beaker with the inscription 'Succefs to the Aberdeen Schoone Proto', below an engraved schooner in full sail.

- *height 9.5cm*
- £320 • Langfords Marine

▽ Brass Monocular

- *1880*

Brass monocular with six draws.

- *height 28cm*
- £580 • Langfords Marine

▽ Shipwright's Tools

- *circa 1880*

Collection of four shipwright's tools made of wood and iron.

- *68cm x 25cm*
- £180 • Langfords Marine

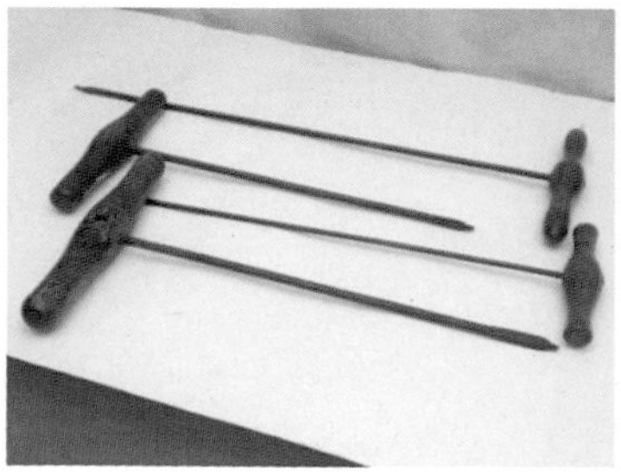

△ Half Sailing Boat

- *1880*

Victorian mahogany half sailing boat.

- *length 97cm*
- £4,400 • Langfords Marine

△ Air Meter

- *1882*

A polished and lacquered brass air meter with a silvered dial by Elliot Bros, London.

- *diameter 28cm*
- £699 • Langfords Marine

△ Aneroid Pocket Barometer

- *1890*

Victorian aneroid pocket barometer by C.W. Dixey, New Bond Street, London.

- *diameter 5cm*
- £360 • Langfords Marine

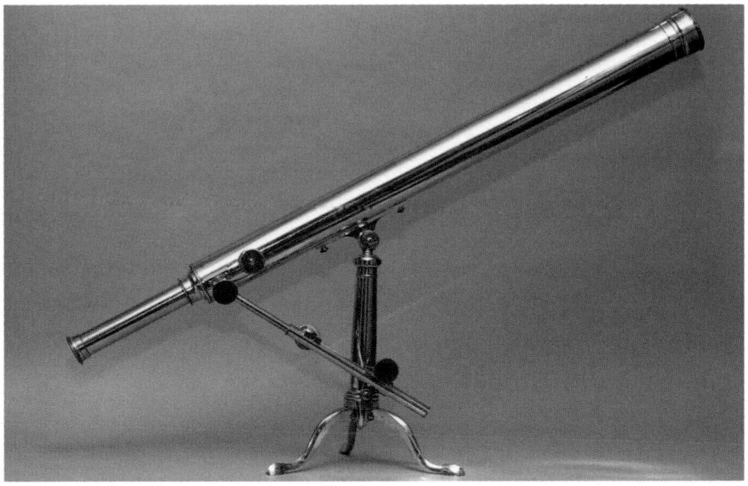

△ Brass Telescope

- *late 19th century*

Made by W. Ladd, Chancery Lane, London. In original mahogany box.

- £2,900 • **Langfords Marine**

▽ Pedestal Globe

- *1890*

A Victorian globe circled with a brass meridian and horizon circle, standing on a mahogany pedestal with a square base.

- *height 99cm*
- £625 • **Langfords Marine**

▽ Half-Boat

- *circa 1900*

Half-boat racing yacht, made from fruitwood for use as a boat-builder's model.

- *width 87cm*
- £1,600 • **Langfords Marine**

▽ Compass

- *circa 1900*

A dry-card compass in a brass drum case with pull-off cover. Knurled edge. Original condition.

- £120 • **Ocean Leisure**

▽ Model of an Anchor

- *circa 1900*

Polished brass model of an anchor, probably a paperweight.

- *height 18cm*
- £59 • **Ocean Leisure**

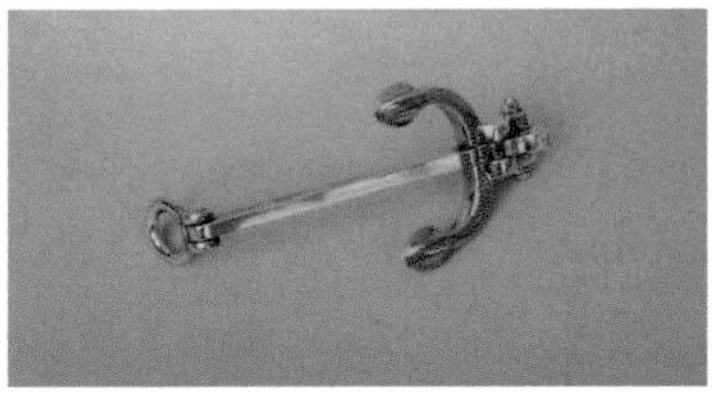

▷ Pond Yacht Model

- *circa 1900*

Pond-yacht model of an East Coast oyster smack, showing full sail including gaff topsail and staysails to the bowsprit.

- *length 1.1m, height 1.05m*
- £3,300 • **Langfords Marine**

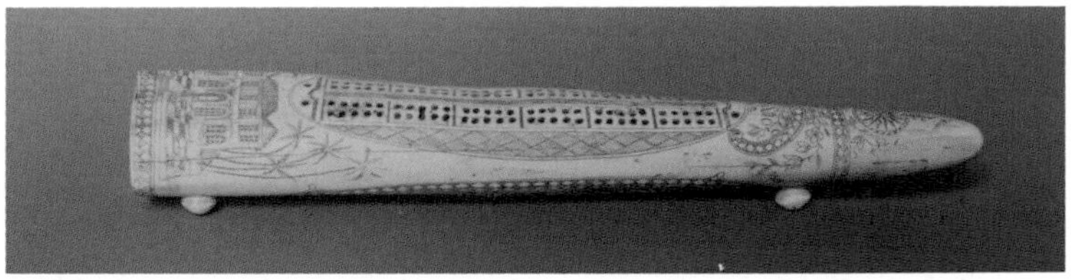

△ Carved Tusk

- *19th century*

A carved whale's tusk showing Caribbean scene, with compass mark. The initials 'J.H. J.A.' are on the reverse.

- *length 32cm*
- £40 • **Briggs**

△ Porthole

- *1901–10*

Polished seven-inch-diameter porthole made of brass with hinge and locking nut and six bevelled screw holes.

- *diameter 17cm*
- £69 • **Ocean Leisure**

△ Oak Ship's Wheel

- *circa 1910*

A six-spar oak ship's wheel, bound in brass.

- £299 • **Ocean Leisure**

▽ Scrimshaw Box

- *circa 1900*

A scrimshaw box with incised carving showing the central motif of a two-fluke anchor surrounded by breaking waves.

- *length 6cm*
- £60 • **Mark Sullivan**

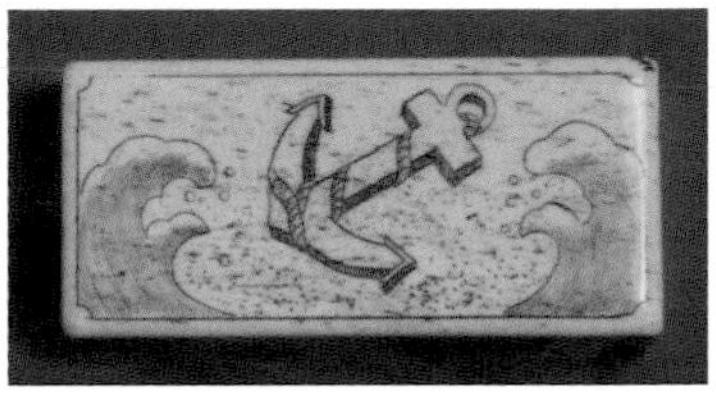

▽ Compass

- *1902*

An early Edwardian liquid boat's compass, of teak with brass fittings. Made by Dent for the Royal Navy.

- *height 37cm*
- £1,850 • **Langfords Marine**

▽ Barograph and Thermometer

- *circa 1910*

Wall barograph with thermometer, in a mahogany box with brass handle. Probably made for a yacht club.

- £1,850 • **Langfords Marine**

▽ Decanter Case

- *circa 1910*

A fine, four-bottle, brass-inlaid box with decanters and glasses, by Thornhill & Co, London.

- *height 27cm*
- £4,000 • Langfords Marine

▽ Taffrail Ship's Log

- *circa 1920*

Polished and lacquered brass Cherub III outrigger-pattern in original, specially constructed and weatherproofed box. By Thos. Walker and Son.

- £250 • Ocean Leisure

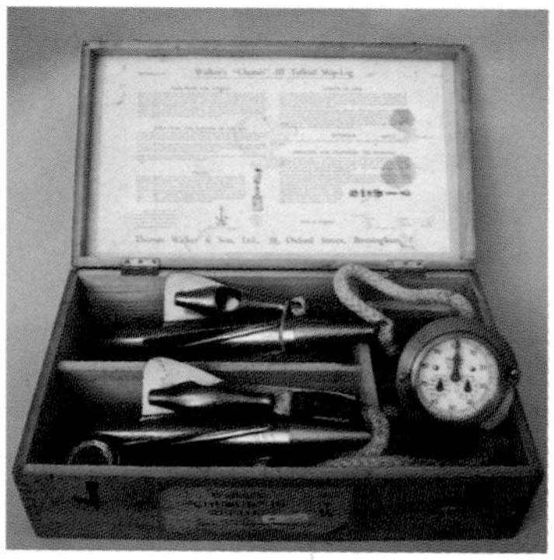

▽ Signalling Telescope

- *circa 1920*

A three-draw signalling telescope. Polished and lacquered brass on the outer barrel.

- £339 • Ocean Leisure

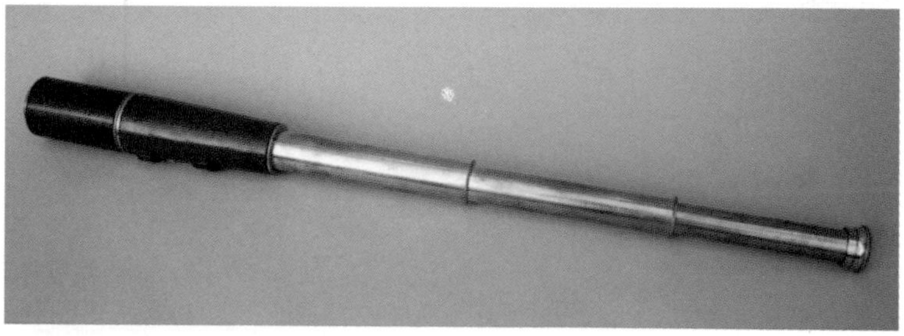

△ Cornish Skiff

- *circa 1910*

Model of *The Vengeance*, a Cornish fishing skiff.

- *height 24cm*
- £480 • Langfords Marine

△ Bulkhead Clock

- *circa 1920*

An eight-day ship's bulkhead clock marked 'Smiths Empire', with a painted enamelled dial and Arabic numerals.

- *diameter 18cm*
- £240 • Langfords Marine

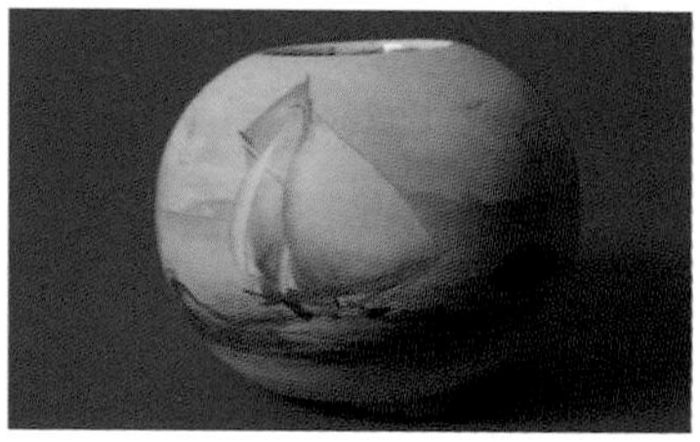

△ Nautical Match Holder

- *circa 1920*

Porcelain match holder painted with a sailing yacht in a seascape.

- *diameter 8cm*
- £365 • Langfords Marine

▽ First Aid Kit

- *1920s*

A rare and unique piece of shipping memorabilia, 'First aid outfit for lifeboats', approved by the Ministry of Transport.

- *height 30cm*
- £99 • Langfords Marine

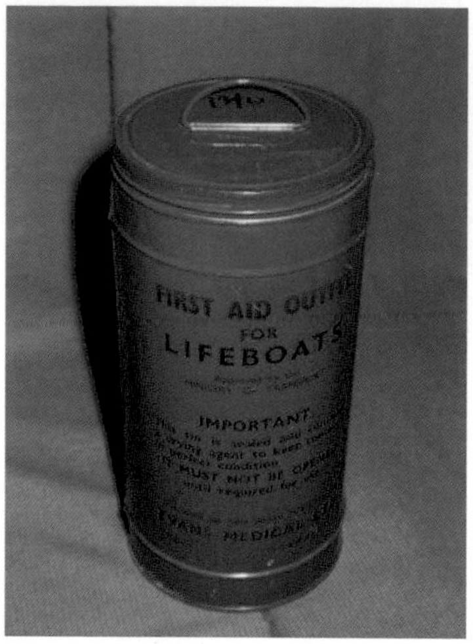

▽ Atlas Globe

- *circa 1920*

Bronze figure of Atlas supporting a globe with brass supports.

- *height 53cm*
- £1,250 • Langfords Marine

▷ Wooden Box

- *20th century*

An oval wooden box with shipping scenes painted to the sides and the top showing a running battle between an English and a French man'o' war, both with all sails set and firing cannon on a turbulent sea.

- £75 • Mark Sullivan

△ Cunard White Star Jigsaw Puzzle

- *circa 1930*

Jigsaw puzzle of RMS *Queen Elizabeth*. Made in England by Lumar. Excellent condition.

- £59 • Ocean Leisure

△ Binnacle

- *circa 1930*

A 'Faithful Freddie' brass binnacle, commonly used on submarines. This one refitted to one of the 'Little Ships' for the evacuation of Dunkirk.

- *height 48cm*
- £1,650 • Langfords Marine

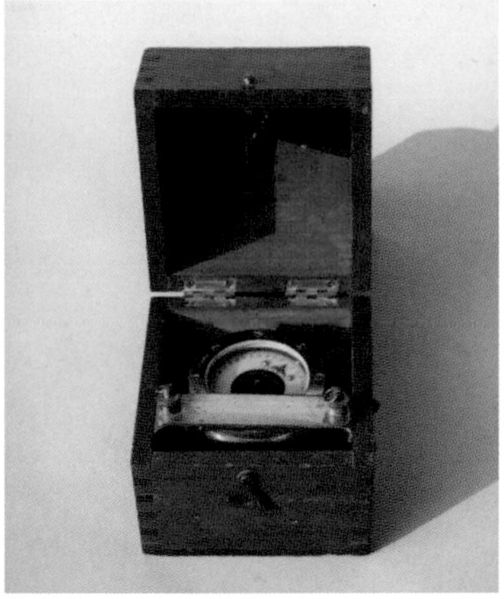

△ Hand-Bearing Compass

- *circa 1930*

An ex-Royal Navy hand-bearing compass, gimballed and contained in its original chest, stamped 'small landing compass no.124/C'.

- £189 • Ocean Leisure

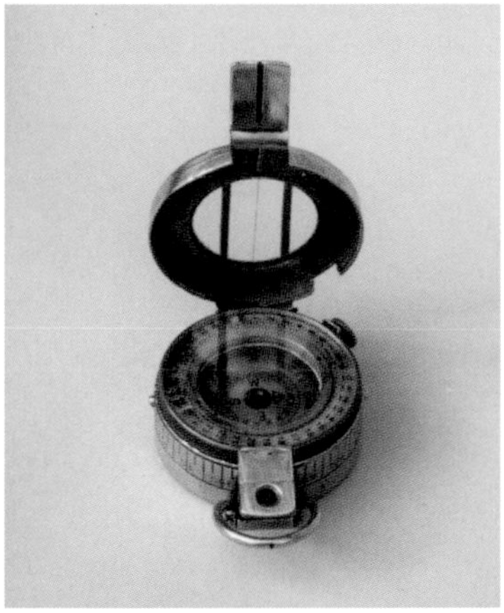

△ Prismatic Compass

- *circa 1940*

An English brass, hand-held, military compass from the Second World War.

- £99 • Ocean Leisure

△ Viking Ship Brooch

- *circa 1940*

A Scottish silver shawl brooch showing a Viking ship on a shielded base.

- £39 • Ocean Leisure

▽ Rolling Rule

- *circa 1940*

Brass polished and lacquered parallel rolling role in original box.

- *length 42cm*
- £149 • Langfords Marine

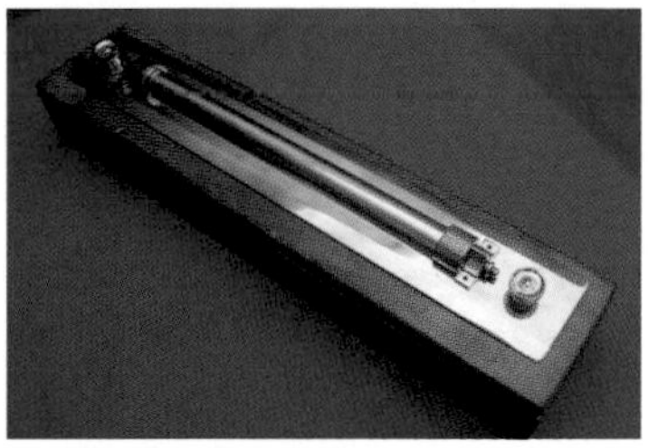

▽ Proportional Dividers

- *circa 1941*

A pair of polished brass proportional dividers with steel points, for navigation. Stamped Luco Art Metal Co Ltd.

- £129 • Ocean Leisure

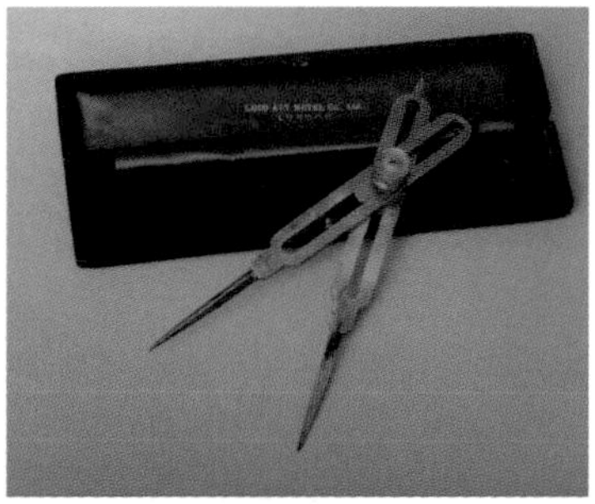

▽ Anchor Lamp

- *circa 1940*

Copper and brass anchor lamp. With 'Seahorse' trade mark.

- *height 22cm*
- £180 • Ocean Leisure

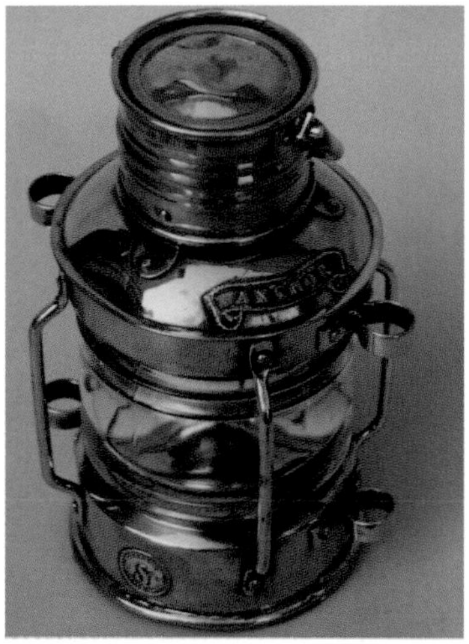

▷ Ship's Log

- *circa 1950*

A brass ship's log by Walker & Sons of Birmingham.

- *length (on mount) 60cm*
- £550 • Hatchwell

△ Bone Model of a Boat

- *circa 1940*

Bone model ship by a prisoner of war with three masts and the rigging made from hair, standing on a maple-wood stand with satinwood inlay.

- *height 36cm*
- £8,600 • Langfords Marine

△ Celestial Globe

- *circa 1950*

Celestial globe with brass fittings, and original oak box with carrying handle.

- *height 28cm*
- £1,280 • Langfords Marine

△ Ship's Linen

- *circa 1950*

Souvenir linen from the Cunard company's *RMS Mauretania*.

- £19 • Ocean Leisure

△ Cunard Ashtray

- *circa 1950*

Cunard *RMS Queen Elizabeth* bone-china ashtray, showing starboard view of ship. With scalloped gilt edge.

- £35 • Ocean Leisure

MUSICAL INSTRUMENTS

Before you begin to collect musical instruments it is worth researching the various makers, as it can be very expensive if you do not know what you are buying. Quality of materials, craftsmanship and musical quality are all very important factors to take into consideration before making your purchase. A good maker's name can also considerably enhance the value of the instrument, for example, a Steinway concert grand piano can fetch astronomical sums. The provenance of the musical instrument also plays a huge part in the value of the item, for example, a piano that was once owned by Elton John fetched a price at auction that was out of reach of most ordinary buyers. The signature of a famous player on an instrument, which they often do for charity, can also add to its value. The beauty of buying a musical instrument is that each one is individually crafted as there is no way to mass-produce good instruments. To collect musical instruments can therefore be a very joyful experience as you are buying something that can never be replicated.

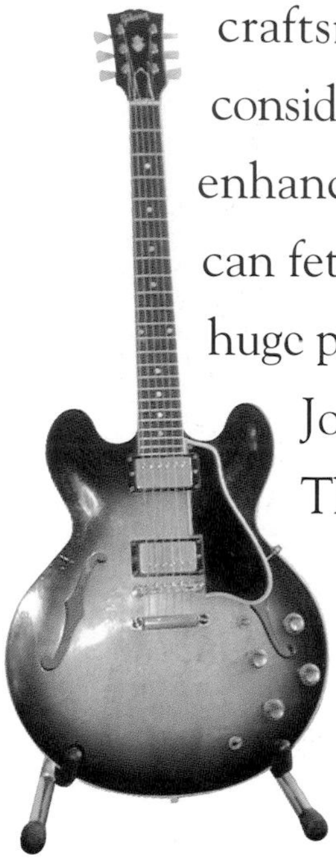

▽ **Single-Action Harp**

• *circa 1805*
Harp with ram's-head decoration to the crown and acanthus-leaf scrolling.
• £9,000 • Clive Morley

◁ **Violin**

• *circa 1815*
An early 19th-century John Baptiste Schweitzer violin, made for Amati Pestini.
• £550 • Finchley

▷ **Mahogany-Cased Organ**

• *1805*
Rare organ by Broderip & Wilkinson, London, complete with six barrels.
• *height 2.26m*
• £24,500 • Anthony Outred

▽ **Harp Lute**

• *circa 1810*
A light harp lute with a painted black case with gold work and raised detailing to the pillar.
• £2,525 • Robert Morley

△ **Grecian Harp**

• *circa 1821*
Grecian harp by S. & P. Erard of Paris, with 43 strings. Painted black with gold decoration to the pillar.
• £9,575 • Clive Morley

△ Grand Piano

• *circa 1868*

A London grand piano by John Broadwood and Sons, with rosewood case.

• *length 2.35m*

• £4,820 • **Robert Morley**

▽ Grand Piano

• *circa 1850–60*

A superb example of a burr walnut grand piano with lyre-shaped pedal-board raised on turned and carved legs.

• *95cm x 1.43m x 2.40m*

• £10,500 • **Brown**

△ Irish Harp

• *circa 1880*

Green Irish harp by Harkness with gilt edging 36 strings and 18 semitone levers.

• *1.02m x 69cm*

• £2,500 • **Clive Morley**

▽ Acoustic Guitar

• *1929*

Martin model No. 00045 with Brazilian rosewood back and sides, and pearl inlay.

• £26,000 • **Vintage Guitars**

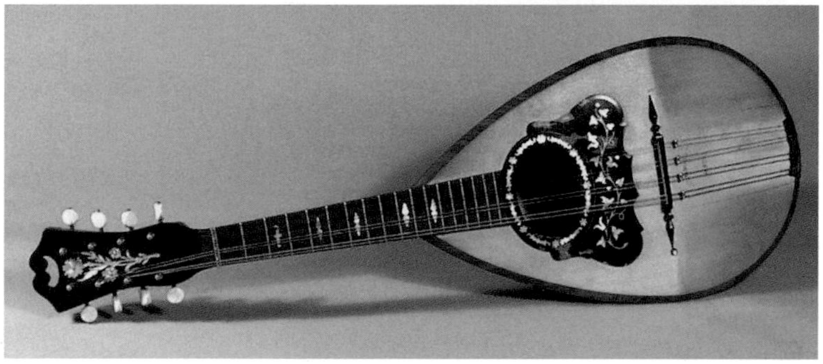

△ Concert Mandolin

• *circa 1890*

Double-soundboard concert mandolin by Umberto Ceccherine of Naples.

• £4,500 • **Hygra**

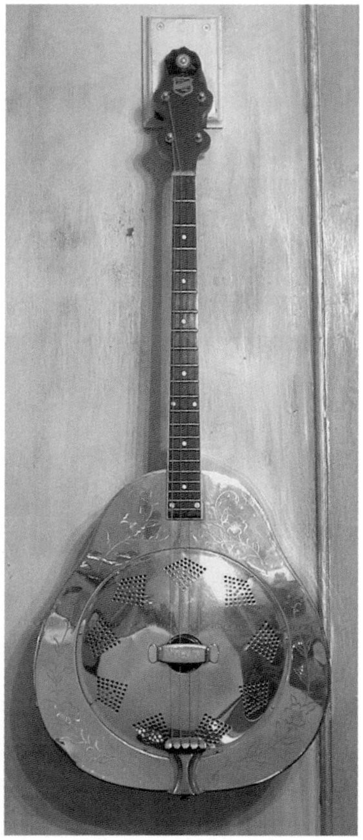

▽ French Erard Harp

• *circa 1890*

French double-pedal harp in maple and gold with decorated pillar, made in Paris by Erard.

• *1.08m x 1.83m*

• £23,000 • **Clive Morley**

◁ National Guitar

• *1929*

National Model Style 2 Irish rose tenor. Very rare. Original case. S/N 684.

• *height 89cm*

• £2,250 • **Vintage Guitars**

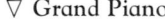

◁ Gibson L-5 Guitar

• *1935*

Gibson L-5 1935 guitar with F holes, scratch plate and mother-of-pearl inlaid fret board.

• *length 1.08m*

• £3,500 • **Vintage Guitars**

▽ Grand Piano

• *1939*

Steinway model M grand piano, fully rebuilt by Steinway, in high-polished mahogany.

• *length 1.7m*

• £27,500 • **Steinway**

▽ Fender Broadcaster

• *1950*
Fender Broadcaster with maple neck and black pick-guard and the first electric solid-body guitar. Previously owned by John Entwhistle of the rock band The Who.
• £18,000 • Vintage Guitars

▽ Flying Vee

• *circa 1958*
Gibson Flying Vee, serial no. 83161. The 'Holy Grail' of vintage, solid-body guitars.
• £55,000 • Vintage Guitars

△ Gibson Guitar

• *1953*
Gibson Model SJ200. Sunburst finish. S/N A17263.
• £5,850 • Vintage Guitars

△ Gibson Acoustic

• *1952*
Serial no. A 8760, with original case and natural colour finish. One of 89 produced in 1952.
• £7,500 • Vintage Guitars

△ Amplifier

• *circa 1958*
Tweed Fender amp with leather handle. Pre-CBS Fender.
• *height 42cm*
• £795 • Vintage Guitars

▽ Gretsch Guitar

• *1953*
Model 35 made by Gretsch with De-Armond Rhythm Chief floating pick-up.
• *1.10m x 41cm*
• £1,295 • Vintage Guitars

▽ Les Paul Guitar

• *1954*
Gibson Les Paul guitar with gold top. Provenance: Richie Sanbora of American rock band Bon Jovi.
• £7,000 • Vintage Guitars

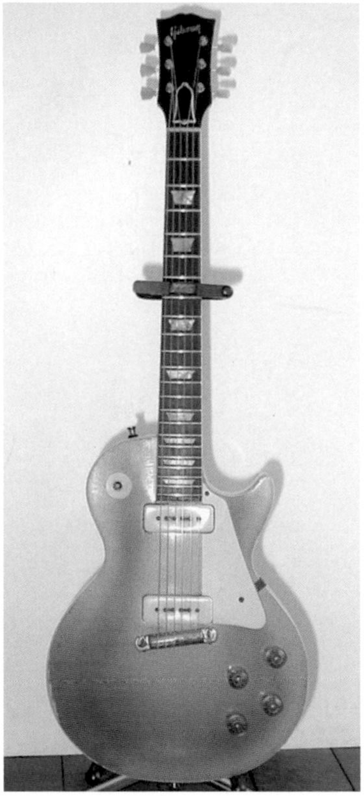

▷ Fender Esquire

• *1954*
Butterscotch Blonde, serial no. 4047. In original condition down to slot-headed screws.
• £5,000 • Vintage Guitars

△ Silverjet Gretsch

• *1955*
American Gretsch guitar in silverjet finish.
• £5,500 • Vintage Guitars

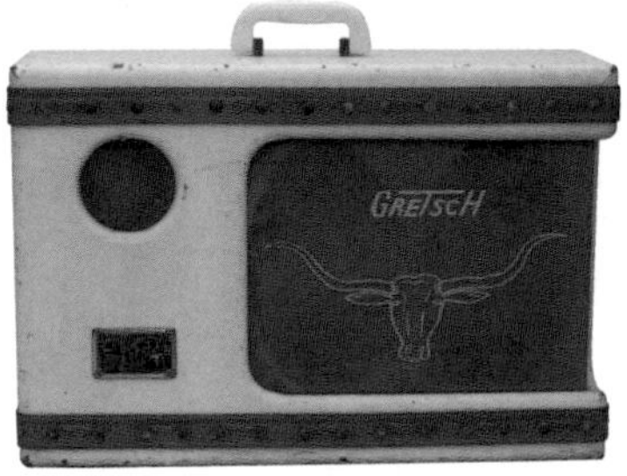

△ Valve Guitar Amp

• *October 1956*
Gretsch 'Western Roundup' amp, with leather belt and brass studs.
• *height 40cm*
• £2,000 • Vintage Guitars

▽ Gretsch Country Club

• *1959*

Chet Atkins 6119 Gretsch in western orange with single PAF filtertron pick-up.

• £2,600 • Vintage Guitars

▽ Gibson Les Paul Junior

• *1959*

Gibson Les Paul Junior in TV yellow with double cutaway.

• £4,250 • Vintage Guitars

△ Gretsch Guitar

• *1959*

Gretsch Anniversary model 6125 with F holes and cream finish.

• *1.07m x 41cm*

• £1,895 • Vintage Guitars

△ Sunburst Gibson Guitar

• *1959*

Gibson guitar in sunburst with dot neck. Serial No. ES 335.

• £7,560 • Vintage Guitars

▽ Fender Stratocaster

• *1960*

Rare custom-ordered metallic blue sparkle Stratocaster with slab rosewood fingerboard. Believed to be one of only five ever made.

• £18,500 • Vintage Guitars

▽ Avocado Gretsch

• *circa 1961*

A two-tone, smoked-green, semi-acoustic guitar with original scratch-plate and fittings.

• £2,200 • Vintage Guitars

▽ Ebonised Piano

• *1958*

Model B black ebonised piano in a high gloss, fully rebuilt by Steinway & Sons.

• *length 2.08m*

• £39,500 • Steinway

△ **Framus Starbass**

• *1960*

Cherry sunburst Framus Starbass guitar, as used by the Rolling Stones.

• £1,960 • Zoom

△ **Fender Jazz Bass**

• *1961*

Sunburst Jazz Bass, serial no. 44210. A fine example of the most sought-after vintage bass.

• £7,250 • Vintage Guitars

▽ **Gibson Guitar**

• *1962*

Gibson model: ES350TN. Blonde finish with original case.
S/N 80935.

• *height 1.05m*

• £4,250 • Vintage Guitars

▽ **Fender Jazzmaster**

• *1966*

Left-handed Fender Jazzmaster in fiesta red finish. It is very rare to find this type of left-handed custom-coloured Fender.

• *1.09m x 32cm*

• £3,000 • Vintage Guitars

▷ **Lighting Ornament**

• *circa 1965*

Drum kit light – 110 volt – with green and red flashing alternately.

• *height 32cm*

• £250 • Vintage Guitars

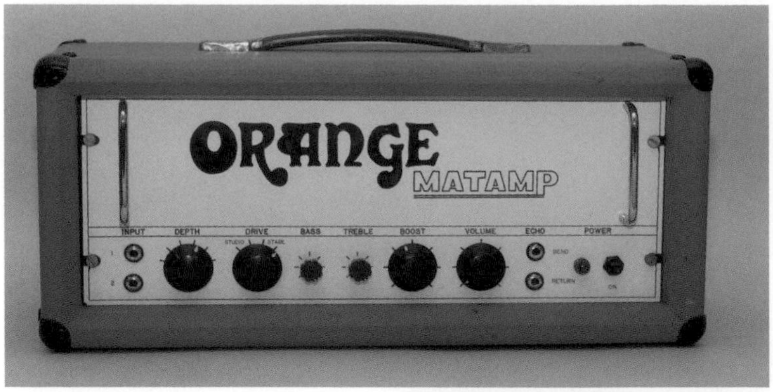

△ **Amplifier**

• *circa 1965*

A very early Orange Matamp with hand-painted Orange logo, finished in orange vinyl with single black handle.

• £995 • Vintage Guitars

△ **Cherry-Red Guitar**

• *1962*

Gibson guitar in cherry red with block markers. Serial no: ES 335.

• £4,950 • Vintage Guitars

△ **Martin Guitar**

• *1965*

Martin model D28. Brazilian rosewood. Replaced fingerboard.
S/N 201923

• *height 1.03m*

• £2,300 • Vintage Guitars

△ **Fender Vibro Champ**

• *1966*

Fender Vibro Champ with black face.

• *height 42.5cm*

• £495 • Vintage Guitars

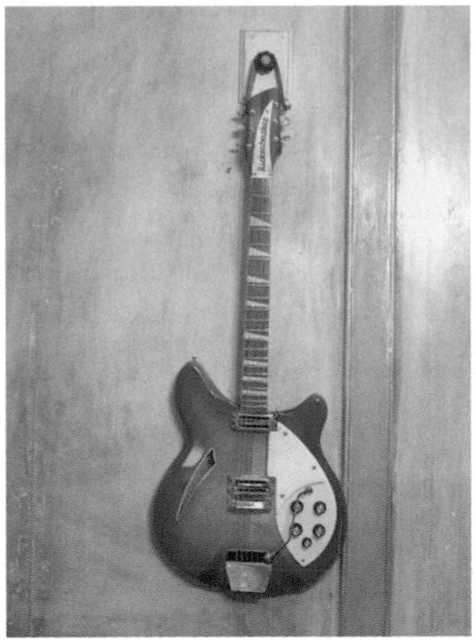

△ **Rickenbacker Guitar**

• *1967*
Rickenbacker model 365. Fireglow finish. S/N GC1415.
• *height 98cm*
• £1,895 • Vintage Guitars

△ **Fender Deluxe Amp**

• *1966*
Fender Deluxe Reverb amplifier with 12-inch speaker and black face.
• £1,500 • Vintage Guitars

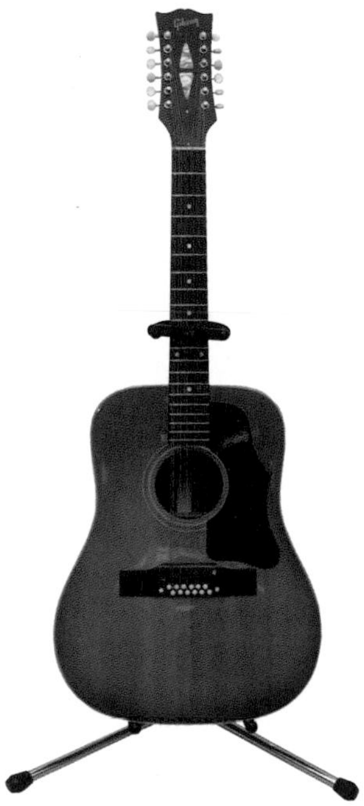

▽ **Gibson 12-String**

• *circa 1967*
Acoustic guitar in cherry sunburst, previously owned by Noel Gallagher, with authenticating letter.
• £1,495 • Vintage Guitars

▽ **Epiphone Guitar**

• *1967*
Epiphone Casino model. Long-scale model. Near mint condition. Original card case.
• *height 1.08m*
• £2,500 • Vintage Guitars

◁ **Epiphone Riviera**

• *circa 1967*
Riviera, in sunburst, with a Frequentata tailpiece, mini-humbuckers and F holes. Favoured by The Beatles.
• £1,800 • Vintage Guitars

△ **Marshall Amp**

• *1969*
A Marshall 100-watt valve amp with superlead red tolex, and small metal logo.
• *height 72.5cm*
• £1,500 • Vintage Guitars

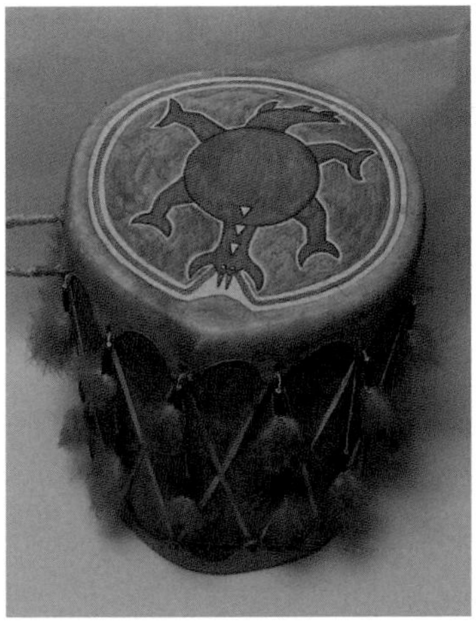

△ **Drum**

• *circa 1970*
Native American drum made of wood and skin and decorated with bone and feathers, with a green turtle on the skin.
• *height 65cm*
• £400 • Wilde Ones

△ **Thunderbird Bass**

• *1976*
Rare black model with reverse body styling, bass, treble and volume knobs.
• £1,750 • Vintage Guitars

▽ **Les Paul Deluxe**

• *circa 1972*
Gold top finish with mini-humbuckers, the pick-up surrounds stamped 'Gibson'. A great investment.
• £1,495 • Vintage Guitars

▽ **Jazz Bass**

• *1972*
Fender jazz bass with maple neck, black binding and black markers with a natural body finish.
• £1,500 • Vintage Guitars

SILVER & PEWTER

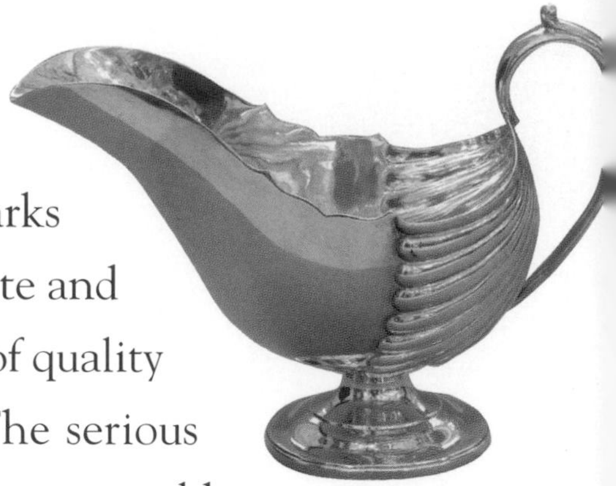

The advantage of collecting silver and pewter is that the hallmarks guarantee their quality and provide information on the maker, date and place of manufacture. A good maker's name is usually indicative of quality and can have an enormous bearing on the value of an item. The serious collector would not need to look at the marks first, as their experience would enable them to identify the maker through the style of the object. Silver from the late seventeenth century by important silversmiths such as Nelme and Pyne is highly sought after and includes practical items such as beakers, tankards, bowls and candlesticks, which are of a much simpler design than those of the eighteenth and nineteenth centuries, by makers such as Gilpin, Hemming, Wakelin, Bateman, Chawner and Schofield, which have more ornamentation. In the 19th century, weight was synonymous with quality and therefore some very heavy pieces were produced. The Victorian era heralded an upsurge in the decoration of silver pieces, with elaborate chasing becoming very popular. This can be seen in items such as silver tea services and Victorian cake baskets, with their beading, waved rims and scrolls.

▷ Jug

• *1573*
Elizabethan silver-gilt tigerware jug. Maker's mark 'CC' linked with shaped punch above a device. London.
• *height 22cm*
• £27,500 • Marks Antiques

△ Pilgrim's Badge

• *15th century*
An early pewter pilgrim's badge.
• *height 5cm*
• £20 • Jane Stewart

▷ Straining Spoon

• *1611*
James I silver straining spoon made by Edward Martin of London.
• *length 44cm*
• £27,500 • Marks Antiques

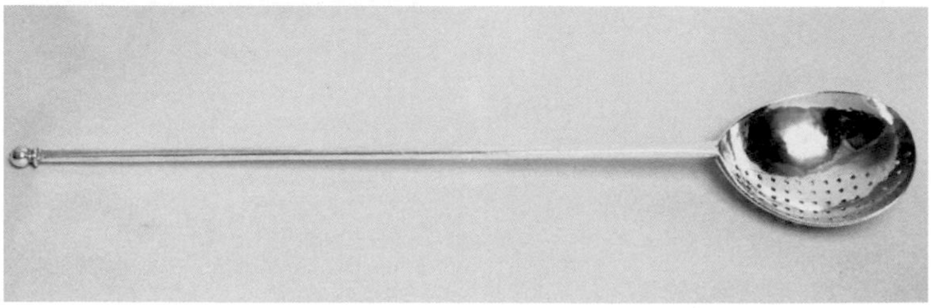

▽ Charles II Porringer

• *1676*
A Charles II silver porringer with double-scrolled handles, engraved foliate designs, and centred with an armorial cartouche.
• *16cm x 12cm*
• £6,500 • B. Silverman

△ Charles II Tankard

• *1677*
A silver Charles II tankard and cover with pierced thumb piece, floral engraving and maker's mark.
• *height 16cm*
• £12,500 • B. Silverman

△ Miniature Brazier

- *1700*

A finely detailed William III silver miniature brazier, handcrafted by George Manjoy.

- *diameter 4cm*
- £1,600 • **B. Silverman**

△ Candlesticks

- *1713*

Fine pair of Queen Anne candlesticks on octagonal bases. Made by William Twell.

- *height 19cm*
- £22,500 • **Marks Antiques**

△ Coffee Pot

- *1734*

George II coffee pot of cylindrical form and plain design. With fruitwood handle. London, by Gabriel Sleath.

- *height 23cm*
- £5,950 • **Langfords**

▽ Dutch Charger

- *1700*

A pewter charger with single reeded rim with wriggled work decoration.

- *diameter 42cm*
- £400 • **Jane Stewart**

▽ Cup and Cover

- *1714*

George I Britannia standard silver cup and cover, made in London by Anthony Nelme.

- *height 33cm, width 27cm, diameter 17cm*
- £9,500 • **Marks Antiques**

▽ Cream Jug

- *1734*

A silver George II cream jug with a sparrow beak and scrolled ribbon handle, raised on a splayed base, by Thomas Rush.

- *height 9cm*
- £2,200 • **B. Silverman**

△ Tankard

- *1706*

Queen Anne Britannia standard tankard by Robert Timbrell.

- *height 17cm*
- £9,000 • **Marks Antiques**

△ English Charger

- *circa 1726*

A William and Mary-style 'wriggle' work charger, made during the George I period. Shows ownership initials – A.K. Wriggle work, which was effected by punching with a hammer, is evident around the rim.

- *diameter 41cm*
- £275 • **Jane Stewart**

△ Continental Pewter Bowl

- *18th century*

Continental pewter deep dish, with floral engraving to the centre, with a single reeded rim.

- *diameter 23cm*
- £70 • **Jane Stewart**

▽ Tea Caddies

- *1719*

Fine pair of George I tea caddies, made in London by John Farnell.

- *height 10cm*
- £13,500 • **Marks Antiques**

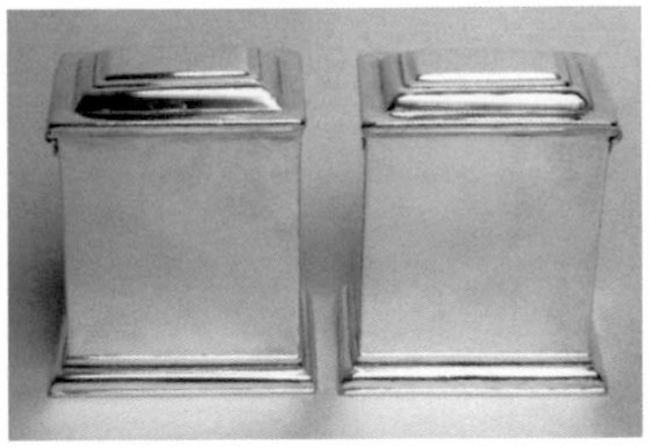

▽ Snuffer Tray

- *1734*

A fine George II silver snuffer tray, by Augustus Courtauld with moulded shaped rim and thumb piece.

- *width 17cm*
- £3,750 • **B. Silverman**

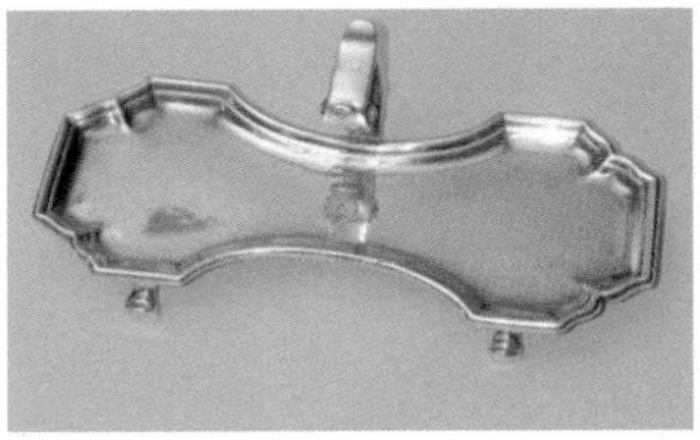

▽ Set of Four Dishes

- *1736*

An unusual set of four George II silver chalice-shaped dishes, by John Le Sage.

- *5cm x 9cm*
- £11,500 • **B. Silverman**

▽ Miniature Porringer

- *1716*

A fine George I miniature silver porringer with fluted body and scrolled double handles by John Cole.

- *diameter 5cm*
- £1,200 • **B. Silverman**

▽ Early Georgian Tankard

- *1740*

A pewter tankard of quart capacity with straight sides, banded waist and curved handle.

- *height 16cm*
- £85 • Jane Stewart

▽ English Charger

- *circa 1740*

Georgian English pewter charger, of plain design with a single reeded rim.

- *46cm*
- £350 • Jane Stewart

▽ Salvers

- *circa 1745*

Fine pair of George II armorial salvers, with gadrooned borders, by Paul de Lamerie, London.

- *diameter 20cm*
- £55,000 • Marks Antiques

▷ Tankard

- *1744*

Baluster form tankard with domed lid and banding, by Humphrey Payne of London.

- *height 18cm*
- £3,250 • Percy's Ltd

△ Inkstand

- *1745*

Very fine George III inkstand comprising inkwell, sand or pounce caster and original bell on florally engraved, serpentine tray, all on four scrolled feet. By John Swift, London.

- *length 27cm*
- £14,500 • Marks Antiques

▽ Silver Salts

- *circa 1760*

Pair of Georgian silver salts with beaded decoration and blue glass liners.

- *height 7cm*
- £675 • Barrett Towning

△ Silver Casters

- *1759*

A set of George II silver casters with decorative piercing and engraving, on a tall foot with good unrestored finial.

- *height 19cm*
- £2,900 • B. Silverman

▽ Set of Pewter Plates

- *1750*

A set of four pewter plates with plain moulded borders, made in London.

- *diameter 15cm*
- £60 • Jane Stewart

△ Cake Basket

- *1759*

George II cake basket with pierced decoration and hinged handle. Made in London by Samuel Herbert & Co.

- *length 35cm*
- £17,950 • Marks Antiques

▽ Sugar Bowl

• *1761*
Fine George III sugar bowl, made in Edinburgh by Lothian & Robertson. Engraved with initials 'CM'. Flared, serpentine rim.
• *height 12cm*
• £800 • N. Shaw

△ Cruet Frame

• *1761*
A Warwick cruet frame comprising three casters and two glass bottles all in a vase shape. By John Delmester.
• *height 22cm*
• £5,500 • Langfords

▽ Tea Caddies

• *1764*
A pair of George III tea caddies, stamped H.N., with lion's feet.
• *12cm x 9cm*
• £4,750 • Marks Antiques

▽ Stuffing Spoon

• *1769*
A large George III, Onslow-pattern, silver stuffing spoon.
• *length 33cm*
• £750 • B. Silverman

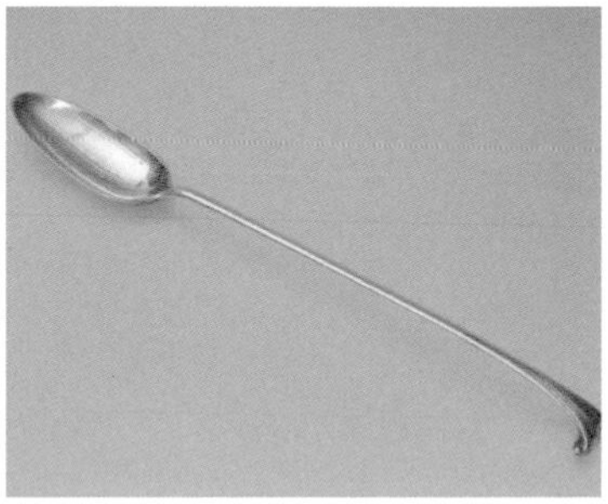

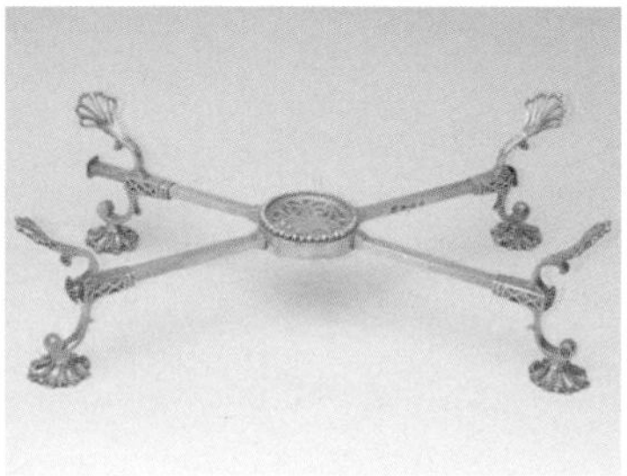

△ English Dish Cross

• *1767*
A finely detailed adjustable dish cross manufactured by Samuel Herbert of London.
• *length 29cm*
• £2,475 • Percy's Ltd

▽ Late Georgian Basket

• *1763*
A fine silver circular cake basket with pierced floral decoration, with a hinged handle and chased designs, on a circular splayed base, made by Richard Aldridge of London.
• *10cm x 42cm x 33cm*
• £4,350 • Percy's Ltd

▽ Candlesticks

• *1768*
Pair of George III cast silver candlesticks, on square beaded bases, made in London by Ebenezer Coker.
• *height 26cm*
• £6,750 • Marks Antiques

▽ Georgian Inkwell

• *1767*
Georgian inkwell set in a pierced tray standing on small ball and claw feet, made in London.
• *8cm x 18cm*
• £1,950 • Stephen Kalms

▽ Sheffield Plate Candlesticks

• *1765*
Pair of Sheffield plate candlesticks in the classical style, the column stem with floral and mask decoration, on a shaped base.
• *height 34cm*
• £1,150 • Ashcombe House

▽ George III Tankard

• *1764*
A fine silver George III tankard, made by Francis Crump with lobed cover, scrolled handle and shaped thumb piece.
• *height 21cm*
• £3,500 • B. Silverman

▽ Engraved Coffee Pot

• *1765*
A silver coffee pot with engraved scroll designs, C-scroll handle and ornate finial, made by William Cripps of London.
• *height 25cm*
• £1,765 • Percy's Ltd

△ George III Candlesticks

• *1770*
A pair of English silver candlesticks of classical design with Corinthian columns, standing on a raised plinth base with beading and floral designs, by Richard Rugg, London.
• *height 34cm*
• £3,850 • Percy's Ltd

▽ Silver Bed Pan

• *circa 1780*
Rare English late Georgian silver bed pan of looking glass form, with a wide border and handle with banded decoration.
• *length 45cm*
• £2,240 • Jane Stewart

△ Cream Pail and Sugar Basket

• *circa 1770*
Pierced silver with blue glass liners and pierced lattice handles, the pail on a pedestal. London.
• £1,625 (or separately) • Percy's Ltd

▽ Candelabra

• *1773*
Pair of cast silver, George III candelabra, with 'C' scroll detachable branches on gadroon base. By John Carter, London.
• *height 36cm*
• £25,000 • Langfords

▽ Continental Pewter Plate

• *circa 1780s*
Continental pewter plate with single reeded rim.
• *diameter 25cm*
• £70 • Jane Stewart

▽ Irish Card Tray

• *1779*
A fine Irish silver card tray, raised on three small feet with asymmetric gadrooned borders, made in Dublin.
• *diameter 15cm*
• £1,400 • B. Silverman

▽ George III Argyle

• *1783*
A fine George III Argyle with finial lid, thumb piece, reeded side handle and gadrooned base, made in London.
• *height 11cm*
• £6,250 • Stephen Kalms

▽ Salt Cellars

• *1783*
French Louis XVI salts with pierced trophy decoration and finial handle.
• *height 10cm*
• £550 • Vivienne Carroll

▽ Horn Beaker

- *circa 1783*

A horn beaker with silver rim and maker's mark repeated three times. Made by John Ollivant of Manchester.

- *height 13cm*
- £590 • B. Silverman

▽ Silver Corkscrew

- *1789*

A very fine George III silver corkscrew inlaid with mother-of-pearl.

- *length 8cm*
- £1,400 • B. Silverman

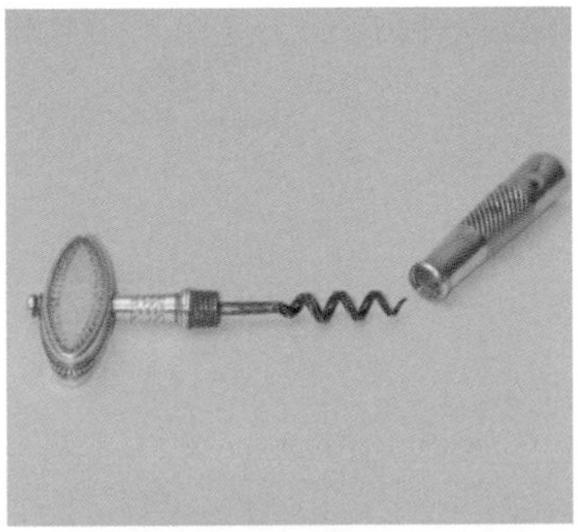

△ Beaker

- *circa 1785*

Swedish pewter beaker of fluted design with splayed foot.

- *height 14cm*
- £85 • Jane Stewart

△ Silver Fruit Basket

- *circa 1790*

Silver fruit basket of oval form with a plain hinged handle, pierced with geometric designs, and raised on an oval moulded base.

- *height 11cm*
- £550 • B. Silverman

▽ Brandy Saucepan

- *1788*

Splay-lipped brandy saucepan with turned wooden handle. Made by Samuel Meriton.

- *height 8cm*
- £1,250 • Percy's Ltd

▽ Continental Pewter Dish

- *circa 1790*

Continental dish with single reeded rim and the owner's initials I.F.B. ort the front and rear.

- *diameter 35cm*
- £200 • Jane Stewart

▽ Salt Boats

- *1794*

A pair of George III silver salts with ribbon handles, handcrafted by Henry Chawner.

- *width 12cm*
- £975 • B. Silverman

◁ Georgian Silver Salt

- *circa 1794*

Elegant silver Georgian salt with a fluted body, scrolled handles, standing on a square base.

- *height 8cm*
- £210 • Barrett Towning

△ Silver Argyle

- *1788*

A fine silver Argyle with scrolled horn handle, made by Benjamin Cartwright of Sheffield.

- *height 21cm*
- £4,650 • Percy's Ltd

△ Sugar Basket

- *1790*

George III sugar basket of octagonal form, bright cut with gold-wash interior. London.

- *height 16cm*
- £875 • Percy's Ltd

△ Tea Caddy

- *1793*

George III tea caddy of oval form with lock and key. Bands of engraving and floral finial. By John Swift, London.

- *height 12cm*
- £3,500 • Langfords

△ English Sugar Basket

- *1796*

A silver sugar basket with hinged handle, raised on a central pedestal foot on a moulded oval base, made by Thomas Wallis of London.

- *height 10cm*
- £750 • Percy's Ltd

▽ Wine Funnel

- *1798*

A silver wine funnel made by Robert and David Hennell of London.

- *height 15cm*
- £2,250 • Percy's Ltd

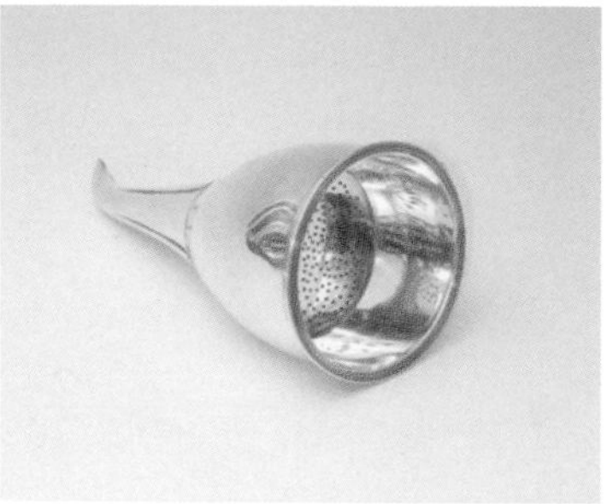

△ English Beaker

- *circa 1800*

An English, half-pint pewter beaker, with owner's initials – J.H.C. – and banded decoration to circular foot.

- *height 10cm*
- £50 • Jane Stewart

▽ Gilded Silver Salts

- *1799*

A pair of elegant silver salts with gilded interior and shaped end grips, made by William Adby of London.

- *height 7cm*
- £765 • Percy's Ltd

△ Georgian Silver Basket

- *circa 1799*

Oval Georgian sweetmeat basket, with a swing handle, pierced foliate designs and apron support.

- *11cm x 38cm*
- £4,000 • Barrett Towning

▽ Late Georgian Jug

- *1800*

A baluster-shaped pewter measuring jug with excise marks, splayed lip and curved handle, on a moulded base.

- *height 10cm*
- £40 • Jane Stewart

△ Dutch Urn

- *circa 1800*

A Dutch urn and cover with an embossed floral leaf design and a wood knob finial.

- *13cm x 10cm*
- £65 • Jane Stewart

▽ Armenian Cross

- *circa 1800*

A silver Armenian reliquary cross with a lozenge-shaped river pearl and coral stones.

- £350 • Iconastas

▽ Chamber Candlestick

- *1800*

George III chamber stick with gadrooned border and fluted capital. By R. Crossley, London.

- *height 9.5cm*
- £1,250 • Langfords

◁ Pair of Candlesticks

- *circa 1800*

One of a pair of English pewter candlesticks with baluster knop and push-up ejectors, bases gadrooned at the edge.

- *height 19cm*
- £225 • Jane Stewart

▷ Pewter Syringe

• *1800*
A late Georgian pewter syringe.
• *length 19cm*
• £60 • Jane Stewart

△ Armorial Dish

• *circa 1800*
German armorial pewter dish with ownership mark – F.A.K. Central panel engraved with armorial crest, surrounded by gadrooned border; floral engraved decoration to rim; the whole showing original patina.
• *diameter 33cm*
• £150 • Jane Stewart

▷ Butter Tubs

• *1806*
An excellent pair of silver-gilt butter tubs with glass liners, made by Digby Scott and Benjamin Smith. The arms are of Montgomerie, Earl of Eglington.
• *length 19cm, height 15cm*
• £110,000 • Marks Antiques

△ Wine Coaster

• *1809*
George III wine coaster with pierced, fluted and gadrooned body, with egg and dart border and wooden base. By Richard Crossley of London.
• *height 5cm*
• £1,050 • Langfords

▽ Bronze Cauldron

• *1800*
A solid bronze cauldron of typical West Country form, raised on three moulded feet.
• *height 18cm*
• £150 • Jane Stewart

△ Silver Chamber Stick

• *1800*
A fine George III silver chamber stick with snuffer, by Samuel Whitford.
• *diameter 11cm*
• £1,650 • B. Silverman

△ Coasters

• *1807*
Set of four George III wine coasters, with pierced vine and fruit decoration and beading to rim and base.
• *diameter 14cm*
• £9,500 • Marks Antiques

▽ Entrée Dishes

• *1807*
One of a set of four George III silver entrée dishes, from the Rutland Marine Service, made in London by Benjamin Smith. The arms are those of John Henry Manners, 5th Duke of Rutland (1757–1844). Decorated with gadrooning, beading and fluting, with domed cover and highly ornate finial.
• *height 23cm, width 23cm, length 30cm*
• £175,000 • Marks Antiques

△ Sauce Tureens

• *1808*
Pair of English Regency sauce tureens. With acorn finial, standing on four ball feet. Made by Henry Nutting and Robert Hennel, London.
• *height 13cm*
• £1,900 • J. First

△ Entrée Dishes

• *circa 1810*
Pair of old Sheffield silver entrée dishes, designed by Matthew Bolton.
• *width 29cm*
• £1,200 • B. Silverman

▽ Georgian Candelabra

• *1801*
A late Georgian pair of three-branch candelabra with interlaced branches on a shaped square base.
• *height 36cm*
• £9,350 • Percy's Ltd

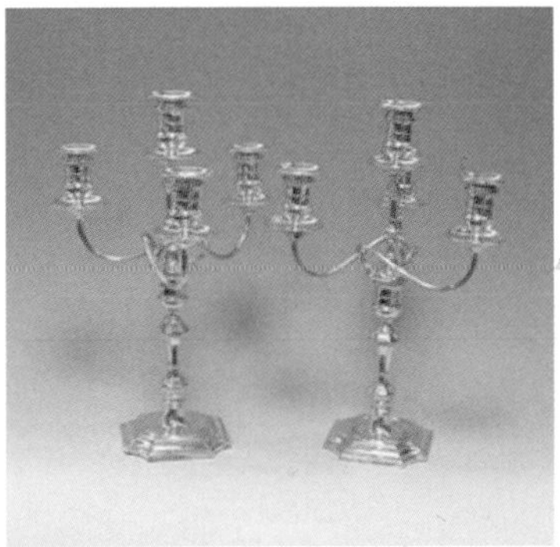

▽ French Pewter Plate

• *early 19th century*
French pewter plate with an embossed central design depicting Joan of Arc, with cartouche moulded border.
• *diameter 24cm*
• £65 • Jane Stewart

▽ Regency Candlesticks

• *1816*
A pair of silver candlesticks with a French influence, made by John and Thomas Settle of Sheffield.
• *height 30cm*
• £5,250 • Percy's Ltd

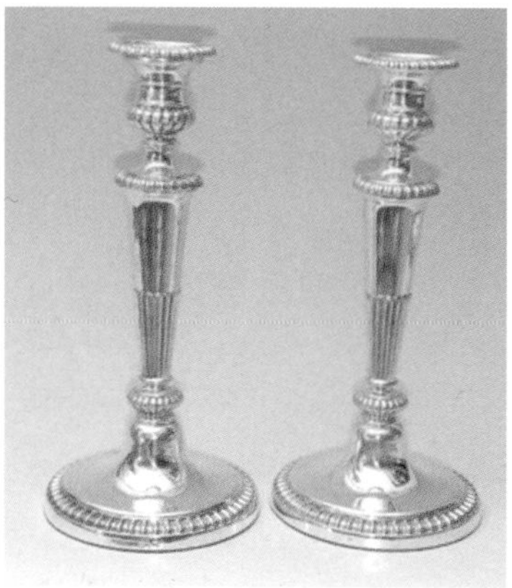

▽ Teapot

• *1822*
By royal silversmith Paul Storr, circular half fluted and compressed body with leaf shell and gadrooned borders.
• *height 10cm*
• £6,500 • Langfords

◁ Magnifying Glass

• *1813*
Silver magnifying glass with ornate handle and original lens. Birmingham.
• *length 19cm*
• £68 • Vivienne Carroll

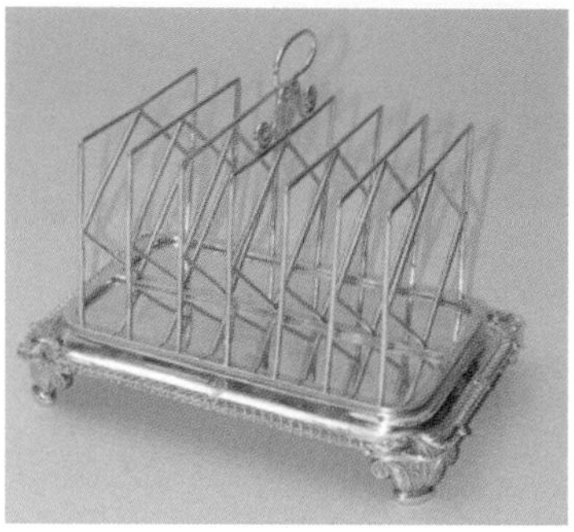

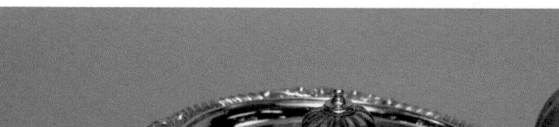

△ Silver Toast Rack

• *1815*
A silver George III toast rack with six bays and shaped handle, raised on scrolled feet, by Paul Storr.
• *height 12cm, width 19cm*
• £5,550 • B. Silverman

▽ Candlesticks

• *1811*
Set of four George III silver-gilt candlesticks, made in London by Paul Storr for William, 1st Earl of Lonsdale, with crest.
• *height 23cm*
• £120,000 • Marks Antiques

◁ Cruet

• *1817*
A fine George III Regency silver cruet, with two miniature claret jugs on a base with a heart-shaped handle. Made in London by Paul Storr.
• *height 29cm*
• £9,500 • Marks Antiques

△ Japanese Silver Mirror

• *19th century*
Japanese silver mirror centred with a jade panel carved with apple blossom, within a silver embossed border with natural cut jade and amethysts, and a carved jade handle.
• *length 22cm*
• £500 • Barrett Towning

▽ Entrée Dishes

• *1825*
Pair of entrée dishes in old Sheffield plate, with acanthus and fluted design and serpentine scrolled borders.
• *height 30cm*
• £3,250 • Percy's Ltd

▷ Snuff Box

• *1817*
George III silver, reeded snuff box with an enclosed painting on ivory of a hunter with dogs. Rubbed maker's mark, Birmingham.
• *length 8cm*
• £2,100 • S. & A. Thompson

△ **Regency Cruet Set**

- *1820*

A silver cruet set consisting of four cut glass bottles held within a frame by a central handle on a tray with gadrooned borders and scrolled feet. London.

- *height 15cm*
- £1,200 • Stephen Kalms

△ **Wager Cup**

- *1831*

A silver gilt wager cup, in the style of a Turkish King holding an embossed cup above his head, by Reilly and Storer.

- *height 22cm*
- £12,000 • B. Silverman

▽ **English Pewter Ladle**

- *1820*

English pewter ladle with a wide circular bowl.

- *length 33cm*
- £50 • Jane Stewart

▽ **Silver Vinaigrette**

- *1830*

A fine small William IV silver vinaigrette.

- *width 3.5cm*
- £750 • B. Silverman

▽ **Tea and Coffee Set**

- *1835*

William IV tea and coffee set of four pieces, compressed melon design, each piece on four feet, silver-gilt lining. Made in London by J.A. Savory.

- £4,250 • Langfords

△ **Georgian Silver Tureen**

- *circa 1825*

Georgian oval entrée dish of plain design with banded decoration, surmounted by a handle in the form of a coiled snake.

- *length 28cm*
- £895 • Barrett Towning

▽ **Silver Cake Basket**

- *circa 1839*

A pierced cake basket of unusual design with chased acanthus decoration, and double handles, raised on a pedestal foot.

- *9cm x 4cm*
- £1,675 • Percy's Ltd

△ **William IV Coasters**

- *1835*

A set of four coasters made by Barnards of London with heavily scrolled borders and sides.

- *diameter 18cm*
- £6,750 • Percy's Ltd

▽ **Sugar Vase**

- *1839*

Sugar vase with floral piercing with rose-tinted glass reservoir and acanthus finial. By J. & G. Angel, London.

- *height 26cm*
- £1,575 • Percy's Ltd

△ **Mug**

- *1839*

Solid-silver mug with gold wash interior, fluted and waisted body with scrolled handle with thumb piece. Made in London.

- *height 11cm*
- £400 • Stephen Kalms

△ **Sheffield Teapot**

- *1840*

A pewter teapot of circular form with finial decoration by Shaw & Fisher of Sheffield.

- *height 13cm*
- £60 • Jane Stewart

△ **Centrepiece**

- *circa 1843*

A magnificent, solid-silver, finely cast, figural centrepiece of leaf and foliage design, surmounted by original cut-glass dish, the whole on acanthus-scroll feet. By J. & J.F. Hunt, London.

- *height 53cm*
- £16,750 • Percy's Ltd

▷ **Tea and Coffee Service**

- *1842*

Tea and coffee service comprising coffee and tea pots, sugar bowl with tongs and cream/milk jug, with fine, flat-chased, melon-fluted pattern. By Emes & Barnard, London.

- £5,750 • Percy's Ltd

△ **Silver Cutlery Set**

- *1840*

A magnificent silver cutlery set incorporating a rare design. It comprises 12 table spoons, table forks, dessert spoons, dessert forks, teaspoons, two sauce ladles, one soup ladle, one sugar sifter spoon, and one butter spreader.

- £18,500 • B. Silverman

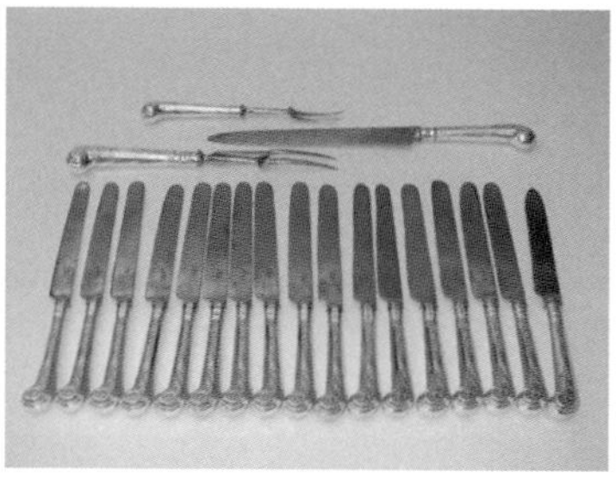

△ **Knife Set**

- *1843–47*

Sixteen table knives with pistol grip handles with foliate designs, and additional four-piece carving set, by Robert Garrard of London.

- *length 17cm*
- £3,500 • B. Silverman

▷ **Glass-Lined Sugar Basket**

- *1845*

A fine silver sugar basket made by John Foligno of London, with pierced floral designs and with a hinged handle and a shaped clear blue glass liner.

- *height 10cm*
- £875 • Percy's Ltd

△ **Ethiopian Cross**

- *circa 1850*

Silver Ethiopian processional cross with presentation inscription.

- *49cm x 35cm*
- £2,500 • Iconastas

▽ **Half-Pint Tankard**

- *1840*

A half-pint tankard with scroll thumb piece and banding on a splayed base.

- *height 10cm*
- £45 • Jane Stewart

◁ **Dish Cover**

- *circa 1850*

Oval dish cover in polished pewter, by James Dickson of Sheffield, with beading around the base and handle, which has moulded, floral decoration.

- *height 20cm*
- £75 • Jane Stewart

△ **Scrolled Silver Box**

- *1840*

Oblong silver box with embossed scrolling and floral designs and a cartouche inscribed with the name 'Hilda'.

- *length 13cm*
- £175 • Barrett Towning

△ Christening Cup

- *1856*

A silver christening cup of baluster form with scrolled handle, floral engraving and gilded interior, made in London.

- *height 12cm*
- £425 • Stephen Kalms

△ Victorian Cruet Set

- *1860*

A fine silver cruet with original glass bottles made by Emmes and Barnard of London.

- *height 22cm*
- £2,650 • Percy's Ltd

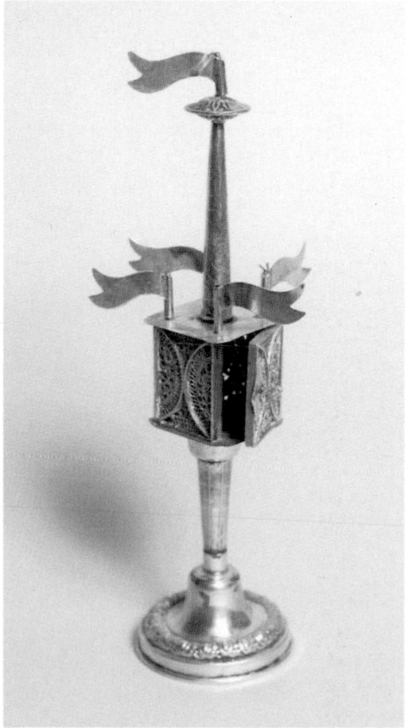

▽ Tankard

- *circa 1850*

English straight-sided, handled tankard of quart capacity, with banded decoration, the whole in polished pewter.

- *height 15cm*
- £85 • Jane Stewart

▽ Ewer

- *1860*

Kashmiri silver ewer with intricate floral designs and snake handle terminating in snake's head thumbpiece on lid.

- *height 29cm*
- £350 • Namdar

▷ Silver Centrepiece

- *1865*

A silver centrepiece with finely chased figures of 'romantic' children by the Barnards. Fully hallmarked.

- *height 33cm*
- £5,750 • Percy's Ltd

◁ Spice Tower

- *19th century*

Austrian silver filigree spice tower with pennants.

- *height 20cm*
- £650 • John Clay

△ Victorian Cream Jug

- *1860*

A Victorian pewter jug with scrolled handle.

- *height 7cm*
- £15 • Jane Stewart

△ Lattice-Work Sugar Bowl

- *1863*

A silver sugar bowl with pierced lattice decoration and hinged handle with clear blue glass liner. Made in Birmingham.

- *10cm x 11cm*
- £650 • Stephen Kalms

▷ Claret Jug

- *1866*

Silver-mounted claret jug with etched glass and scrolled handle. By W. & G. Sissons, Sheffield.

- *height 28cm*
- £3,850 • Percy's Ltd

△ Processional Cross

- *circa 1860*

Silver Ethiopian processional cross with presentation inscription.

- *42cm x 24cm*
- £1,850 • Iconastas

▽ Victorian Silver Salver

- *1869*

A silver salver with shell gadrooned borders on paw feet, made in Sheffield.

- *diameter 22cm*
- £600 • Stephen Kalms

◁ Victorian Pewter Cup

- *circa 1870*

Victorian engraved pewter cup with floral engraving, scrolled handle and banded decoration, inscribed with the name Maude.

- *7.5cm x 10cm*
- £50 • **Jane Stewart**

△ Bachelor Tea Set

- *1870*

Boxed bachelor set comprising three melon-shaped pieces with gold-washed interior, the teapot with ivory handle. By H. Wilkinson, London.

- £1,950 • **Stephen Kalms**

▽ Silver-Inlaid Comb

- *1870*

Tortoiseshell comb with silver inlay grip, in original fitted box.

- *length 15cm*
- £250 • **Tagor**

▽ Card Case

- *1872*

Victorian silver card case, profusely decorated with maple leaf and scrolled designs. By Frederick Marson, Birmingham.

- *height 10cm*
- £440 • **Linden & Co.**

△ Centrepiece on Stand

- *1873*

Mirrored stand and matching figural centrepiece by Stephen Smith, London.

- *height 48cm*
- £4,750 • **J. First**

▽ Tea and Coffee Set

- *1871*

Four pieces, with engraved floral design, made in Birmingham by Elkington & Co.

- £5,250 • **Marks Antiques**

◁ Viennese Silver Jardinières

- *1875*

Solid silver Austrian jardinière, one of a pair, the body finely chased, handles with cast figures. Made in Vienna by Klincosch.

- *width 40cm*
- £8,750 the set • **Percy's Ltd**

◁ Silver Shovel

- *1872*

Miniature engraved silver shovel with bone handle, made in Birmingham.

- *length 12cm*
- £375 • **S. Kalms**

△ Richard Hood Candlesticks

- *1875*

Four candlesticks on gadrooned square bases, by Richard Hood of London.

- *height 12cm*
- £2,450 • **Percy's Ltd**

△ Silver Goblet

- *1874*

A single silver engraved goblet with gilded interior and knop stem raised on a splayed base, made by Mappin and Webb of London.

- *height 13cm*
- £300 • Stephen Kalms

△ Victorian Silver Urn

- *1874*

Victorian silver urn, of ovoid shape, on a pedestal base with two handles, and foliate chasing, by Robert Hannell III.

- *27cm x 16cm*
- £1,400 • B. Silverman

▽ Dutch Nautilus Cup

- *circa 1875*

A rare Dutch nautilus cup in the 17th century style. The shell is finely engraved with classical scenes.

- *height 25cm*
- £5,250 • Percy's Ltd

▽ Tazzas

- *1880*

One of a pair of silver-gilt tazzas with engraved glass dishes and moulded, serpentine bases. Made by Tiffany.

- *height 15cm*
- £9,500 • Marks Antiques

◁ French Candlesticks

- *1880*

Pair of French candlesticks with asymetric wave forms to the base, made to 950 standard.

- *height 21cm*
- £750 • J. First

▽ Chinese Box

- *1880*

Rectangular, pierced box with dragon decoration with clouds. Standing on stylised tiger feet. By Wang Hinge.

- *height 9cm*
- £650 • J. First

◁ French Liquor Set

- *1880*

French liquor set of twelve silver cups with foliate scrolling and matching tray, engraved with the initials J. C.

- *height of cup 5cm*
- £575 • Tagor

▽ Silver Vesta Box

- *circa 1880*

Ladies' silver vesta box with floral engraving and a plain shield panel, ring to the side.

- *length 5cm*
- £70 • H. Gregory

△ Swan Centrepiece

- *circa 1880*

Victorian centrepiece by Elkington of England, with elaborate foliate chased designs. The stand supporting an opaque glass dish, flanked by two silver swans on a moulded base standing on silver scrolled supports.

- *34cm x 51cm*
- £6,500 • Stephen Kalms

△ Claret Jug

- *1880*

Late nineteenth-century claret jug, with silver mounts and domed lid with finial and scrolled handle.

- *height 24cm*
- £250 • North West 8

△ Silver Cruet Set

- *circa 1880*

Silver cruet set with salt, mustard and pepper pot with lobed lower bodies and gadrooned borders.

- *height 11cm*
- £190 • Henry Gregory

△ Palm Centrepiece

- *circa 1880*

Silver palm centrepiece supporting a glass oval dish. Part of a set of three, by Bradbury of England.

- *height 34cm*
- £6,000 • Stephen Kalms

▽ Cymric Dish

- *1880*

Liberty-marked Cymric dish with two enamelled ears with blue/green organic-shape enamel.

- *diameter 14cm*
- £800 • Kieron

△ Claret Jugs

- *1880*

Hand-cut crystal, by G. Keller, Paris.

- *height 23cm*
- £5,950 • Marks Antiques

▽ Claret Jug Boxed Set

- *circa 1880*

Fluted glass and silver-mounted claret jug with twelve pierced silver and etched glass beakers, the whole in original case. European silver.

- £9,500 • Stephen Kalms

▷ Claret Jug

- *1881*

Claret jug with naturalistically styled silver mounts showing lily pad; double woven handle and glass engraved with fish and aquatic scenes. By E.H. Stockwell, London.

- *height 19cm*
- £7,500 • Langfords

△ Candelabra

- *1885*

Pair of Victorian candelabra, made in London by Edward Barnard & Sons. Scrolled branches and gadrooned base.

- *height 45cm*
- £9,750 • Marks Antiques

△ Vesta Box

- *circa 1880*

Plain silver vesta box with hinged lid and striker on the base.

- *length 5.5cm*
- £72 • Henry Gregory

◁ Christening Cup

- *1882*

Christening cup with engraved floral designs and trellis borders. Made in London.

- *height 9cm*
- £220 • Vivienne Carroll

▽ Set of Four Salts

- *1883*

Set of four silver salts embossed with bird and floral designs, four silver spoons with gilt bowls, in original box finished in velvet and silk.

- *width of box 21cm*
- £675 • Barrett Towning

▽ Pilgrim Bottle

- *1884*

Silver pilgrim bottle of pineapple form, made in London, with lion mask handles linked with a silver chain.

- *height 32cm*
- £4,740 • Stephen Kalms

▽ Hip Flask by George Unite

- *circa 1890*

Faceted glass flask with silver mounts, hinged stopper and base by George Unite of Birmingham.

- *height 16cm*
- £275 • Barrett Towning

▷ Galleon Decanter

- *1890*

Silver galleon, standing on wheels decorated with fruit and foliate designs, with small figures drinking and climbing the rigging, made by Bernard Muller.

- *66cm x 60cm*
- £45,000 • Stephen Kalms

△ Glass Claret Jug

- *1886*

A silver and glass claret jug with foliate etchings, made by J. Gilbert & Sons of Birmingham.

- *height 22cm*
- £900 • Linden & Co.

▽ Silver Fish Servers

- *circa 1886*

Silver serving fish knife and fork in a presentation box from Frazer and Haws, Garrards, London.

- *length 28cm*
- £595 • Barrett Towning

◁ Mug

- *1887*

Embossed with woodland scenes of children playing by gate. By Bradbury & Henderson, London.

- *height 9cm*
- £1,200 • Stephen Kalms

△ Claret Jug

- *1886*

A claret jug with heavy vine and leaf decoration and twig handle. London.

- *height 31cm*
- £5,250 • Percy's Ltd

△ Scent Bottle

- *1890*

Late Victorian scent bottle, deeply cut glass body with a silver stopper.

- *height 15cm*
- £250 • Evonne Antiques

△ Candelabra

- *circa 1890*

Pair of silver and glass candelabra. Designed by Farnham for Tiffany.

- *19cm x 34cm*
- £13,500 • Marks Antiques

△ Victorian Sauce Boat

- *circa 1891*

Victorian silver sauce boat with vacant panel within embossed decoration raised on a splayed foot.

- *height 9.5cm*
- £240 • **Barrett Towning**

△ Silver Mustard Pot

- *circa 1896*

Silver mustard pot with hinged lid and blue liner with a circular scrolling pattern about the body.

- *height 6cm*
- £225 • **Barrett Towning**

△ Victorian Silver Goblet

- *1896*

A fine silver goblet of conical form on a pedestal base made in Sheffield.

- *height 19cm*
- £225 • **Stephen Kalms**

▽ Hand Mirror

- *1892*

Silver hand mirror with swirl fluted back and twist fluted handle. Made in Birmingham.

- *length 29cm*
- £350 • **Linden & Co.**

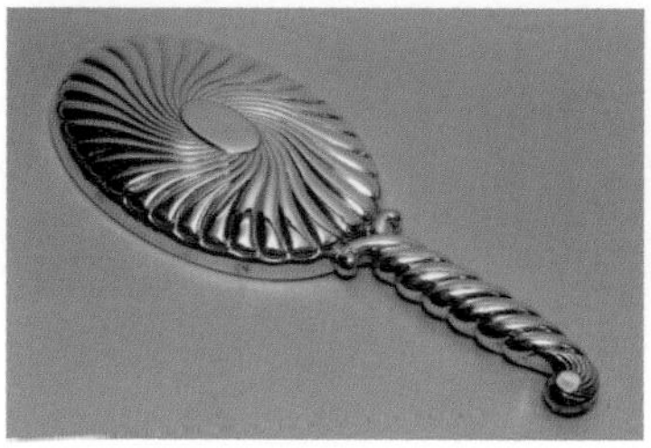

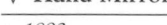

◁ Regimental Statuette

- *1894*

A barometer and clock set in marching drum of a military figure of the Prince of Wales regiment, standing on a silver and slate plinth. Made by Mappin & Webb, London.

- *height 26cm*
- £6,500 • **Langfords**

▷ Silver Frame

- *1899*

William Commings heart-shaped silver frame with pierced decoration, cherubs, scrolling and mask designs.

- *height 18cm*
- £450 • **Alfie's Antique Market**

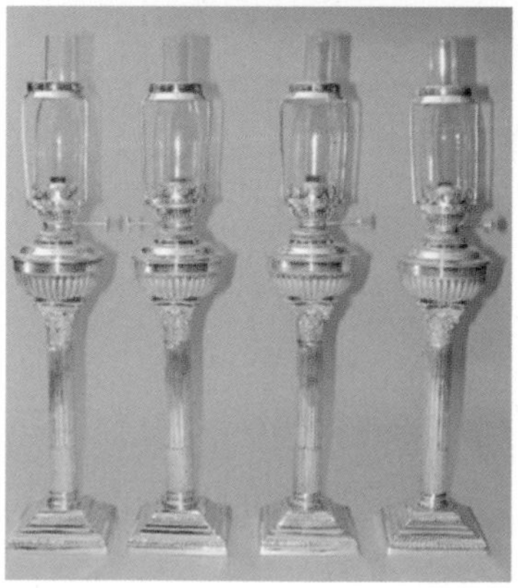

▷ Tulip Vase

- *circa 1900*

Silver Art Nouveau Tudric tulip vase with foliate style handles on a circular base.

- *height 21cm*
- £680 • **Arwas**

◁ Four Lamps

- *circa 1900*

A set of four electro-plated lamps with original glass on square plain bases.

- *height 47cm*
- £2,500 • **B. Silverman**

△ Birmingham Match Striker

- *1899*

Small glass match striker with silver rim, made in Birmingham.

- *height 7cm*
- £180 • **Alfie's Antique Market**

◁ Horse Hooves Ink Well

- *circa 1900*

Silver writing set made of two horse hooves, set in silver with two ink wells with silver covers, standing on a silver base on ball feet.

- *width 46cm*
- £900 • **Stephen Kalms**

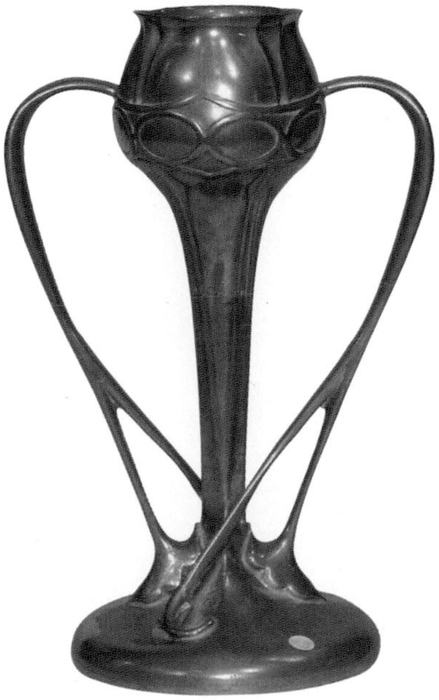

▽ Art Nouveau Pewter Tray

- *1900*

Art Nouveau pewter and mahogany tray designed by Orivit.

- *length 45cm*
- £650 • Gooday Gallery

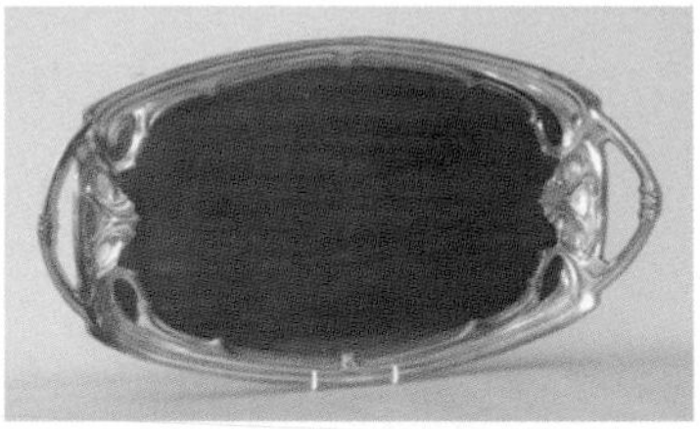

◁ Art Nouveau Butter Dish

- *circa 1900*

Silver Art Nouveau butter dish with cut glass liner and lid with tulip design, standing on bracket tulip feet, by W. M. F.

- *12cm x 7cm*
- £500 • Arwas

▽ German Candlesticks

- *circa 1900*

Silver, cannon-shaped candlesticks, with a musketeer and a foot soldier.

- *height 21cm*
- £1,500 • J. First

▷ Centaur

- *1900*

Silver statue of a centaur. Signed on back left leg R. de Luca.

- *height 29cm*
- £2,400 • Stephen Kalms

△ Pot by Kayserzinn

- *circa 1900*

German pewter Art Nouveau butter dish on raised feet, with foliate and tulip designs, by Kayserzinn.

- *height 13cm*
- £300 • Arwas

△ Beaker

- *circa 1900*

Persian beaker from Kirmanshah. Profusely decorated and embossed with rural and domestic scenes.

- *height 10cm*
- £150 • Namdar

△ French Pewter Dish

- *circa 1900*

A French pewter plate depicting Leda and the Swan, signed by Jules Desbois.

- *diameter 27.5cm*
- £2,000 • Arwas

◁ Dutch Spoon

- *circa 1900*

Water-carrier motif on engraved handle. Tavern scenes and pierced floral decoration.

- *length 23cm*
- £90 • Namdar

△ Silver Teapot with Bee

- *circa 1900*

Silver teapot with unusual foliate and insect design with a bee finial, and stylised bamboo spout and handle.

- *height 16cm*
- £1,500 • Alfie's Antique Market

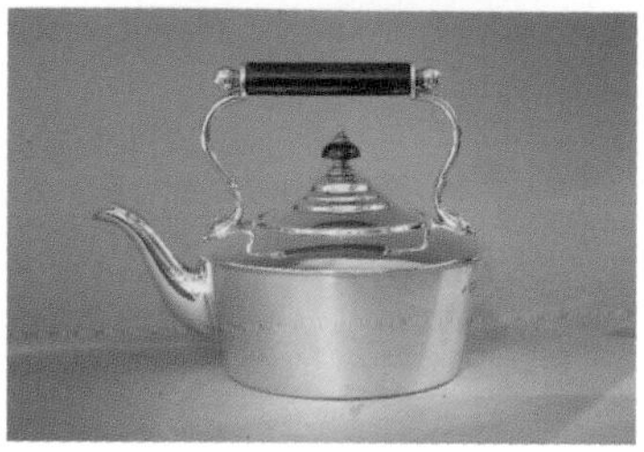

△ Small Silver Teapot

- *circa 1904*

Small Edwardian silver teapot with bone handle and finial lid.

- *height 15cm*
- £240 • **Alfie's Antique Market**

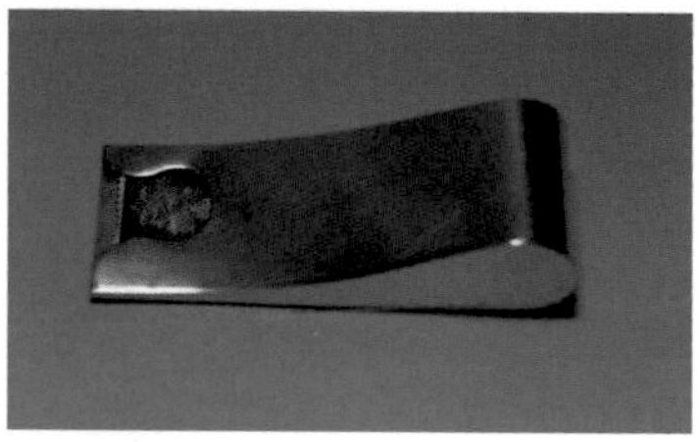

△ Stamp Dispenser

- *1904*

Rare English piece made in Birmingham by Gray & Co.

- *length 8cm*
- £1,250 • **S. & A. Thompson**

△ Knox Pewter Dish

- *1903*

Art Nouveau pewter fruit bowl with green glass liner raised on three legs reserved on a circular base, designed by Archibald Knox for Liberty & Co.

- *13cm x 13cm*
- £650 • **Gooday Gallery**

▽ Art Nouveau Pewter Vase

- *1903*

Art Nouveau pewter vase with green glass liner designed by Archibald Knox for Liberty & Co.

- *height 18cm*
- £950 • **Gooday Gallery**

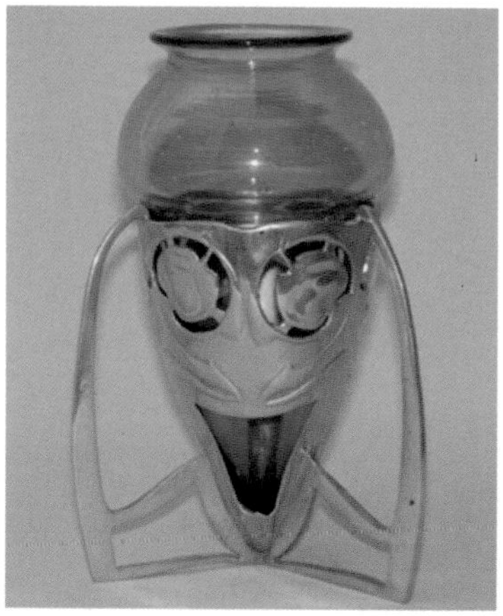

▽ Pewter Dish

- *1905*

Art Nouveau pewter dish with three lobed sections decorated with stylised leaves by Gallia.

- *20cm x 31cm*
- £250 • **Gooday Gallery**

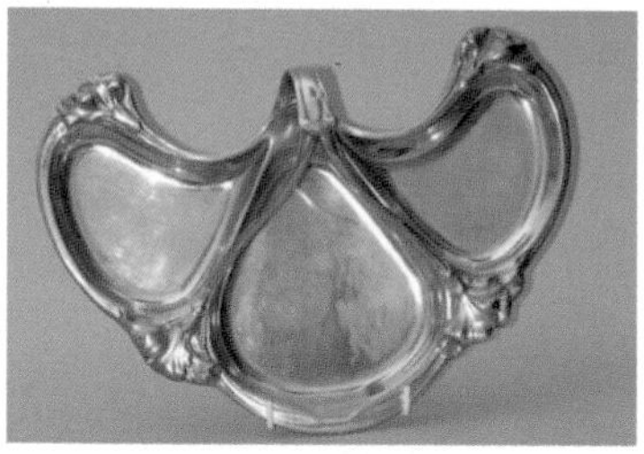

▽ Osiris Fruit Basket

- *1905*

Art Nouveau pewter fruit basket, with a handle engraved with cherries, by Osiris.

- *34cm x 18cm*
- £250 • **Gooday Gallery**

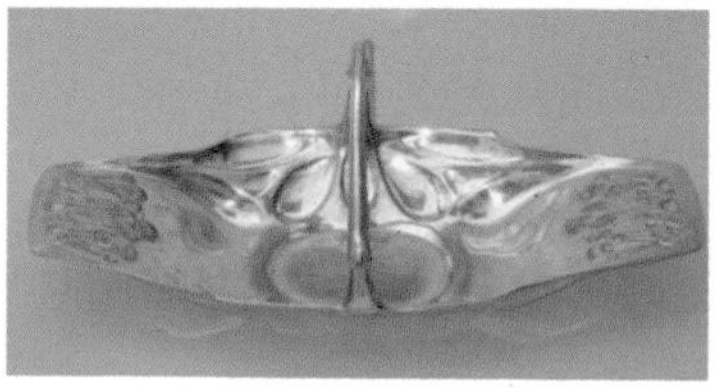

◁ Pair of Cockerels

- *circa 1900*

Pair of continental silver cockerels, finely and naturalistically detailed, in fighting stance.

- *height 23cm approx.*
- £1,200 • **Stephen Kalms**

▽ Tudric Rose Bowl

- *circa 1903*

Liberty & Co Tudric rose bowl signed by Archibald Knox. Previously attributed to Rex Silver.

- *23cm x 19cm*
- £2,250 • **Liberty plc**

▽ Rattles

- *1887–1909*

Group of rattles with bells and whistles, red coral handles. One in form of sea monster. By Hilliard & Thompson.

- £500–1,000 • **Jack Simons**

▽ Wine Coolers

- *1905*

A pair of silver urn-shaped wine coolers raised on pedestal feet on a plain square base, by Walker and Hall of Sheffield.

- *27cm x 25cm*
- £12,750 • **Percy's Ltd**

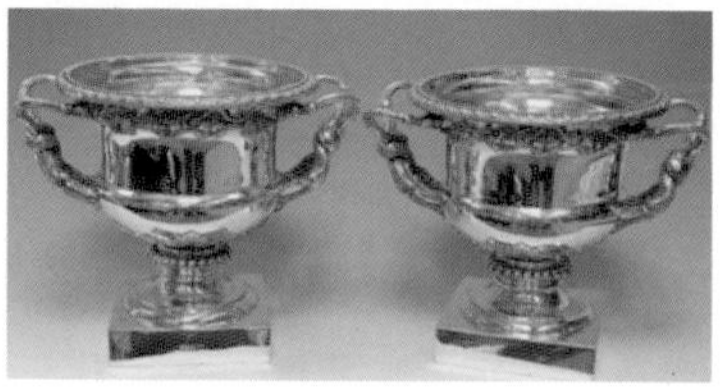

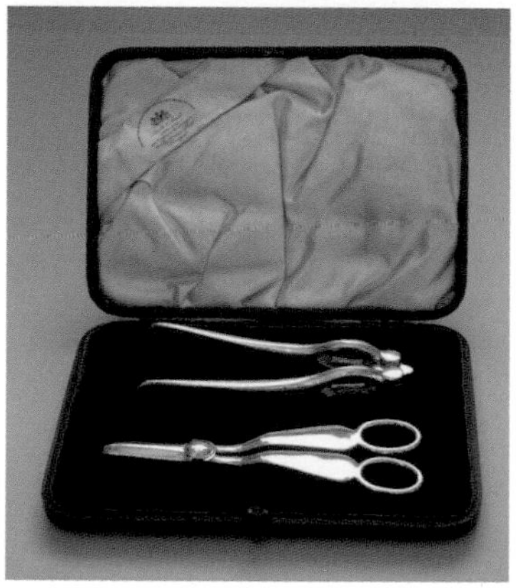

△ Nut Cracker and Grape Peeler

- *circa 1904*

Silver nut cracker and grape peeler, made in Sheffield, in original silk lined and blue velvet box.

- *length 14cm*
- £675 • **Barrett Towning**

△ Pewter Fruit Bowl

- *1905*

Art Nouveau pewter fruit bowl with green glass liner and pewter mounts incorporating organic designs, by Orivit.

- *11cm x 16.5cm*
- £380 • **Gooday Gallery**

△ Double-Handled Dish

- *1905*

A silver double-handled chalice-shaped dish, raised on a pedestal foot, made in London.

- *23cm x 38cm*
- £2,750 • Stephen Kalms

△ Silver Postal Weighing Scale

- *1909*

Rare silver postal weighing scale with blue enamel, made in Birmingham.

- *height 7cm*
- £750 • Alfie's Antique Market

△ Goblet

- *1909*

With beaded base and knop stem; the bowl has fluting. By Walker & Hall, Sheffield.

- *height 20cm*
- £400 • Stephen Kalms

▽ Glass Sugar Shaker

- *circa 1906*

Glass sugar caster of baluster form, with a pierced silver cover, engraved floral designs and ball finial.

- *height 16.5cm*
- £225 • Barrett Towning

▽ Epergne

- *1908*

Epergne with three flower-form flutes on a moulded base. By Martin Hall, Sheffield.

- *height 47cm*
- £2,950 • Stephen Kalms

▽ Cigarette Case

- *circa 1910*

With enamelled plaque of a robust Cleopatra with asp at her breast. European 900 mark.

- *length 9.5cm*
- £1,400 • S. & A. Thompson

△ Pepperpot

- *1908*

Rare monkey pepperpot, seated with one arm tucked under the other. By H. Heywood.

- *height 7cm*
- £2,300 • S. & A. Thompson

△ Liberty Pitcher

- *circa 1910*

Liberty green glass pitcher with a pewter lid, handle and base.

- *height 21cm*
- £1,200 • Arwas

▽ Stamp and Cigarette Case

- *circa 1910*

Silver stamp and cigarette case with blue enamel lid.

- *width 9cm*
- £275 • Barrett Towning

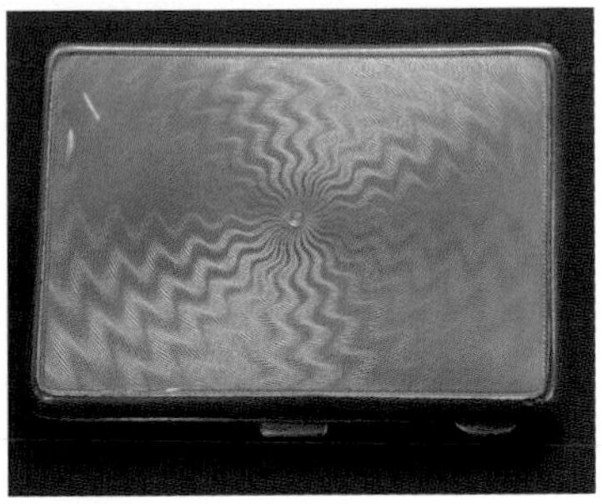

▽ Punch Bowl

- *1911*

Punch bowl with fluted body with inverted beading, pedestal foot and serpentine rim with moulded edge. Made in London.

- *diameter 29cm, height 22cm*
- £2,475 • Langfords

▽ Fabergé Bowl and Ladle

- *circa 1917*

Imperial Russian silver bowl and ladle, made by Fabergé in St Petersburg immediately prior to the revolution.

- £24,750 • Marks Antiques

◁ Sovereign Case

- *1912*

Heart-shaped silver sovereign case, engraved with floral designs. By E.J. Houlston, Birmingham.

- *length 5cm*
- £250 • Linden & Co.

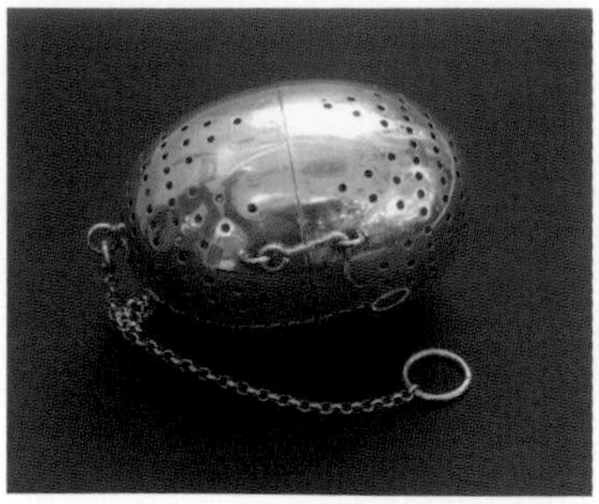

△ **Silver Tea Infuser**

- *circa 1919*

Rare silver tea infuser in the form of an egg, of two sections with silver chain.

- *length 9.5cm*
- £485 • **Barrett Towning**

△ **Silver Cream Jug**

- *circa 1920*

Silver cream jug with scallop shell design and scrolled handle, supported on a raised circular foot.

- *height 11.5cm*
- £317 • **Barrett Towning**

△ **Conical Silver Vases**

- *circa 1930*

Two tall conical vases with chased scrolling and cartouches of cherubs, musicians, dancers and revellers, surrounded by foliage, birds and flowers, standing on a circular base, made in Germany.

- *height 61cm*
- £5,500 • **Stephen Kalms**

▽ **Candlesticks**

- *1920*

A pair of neo-classical candlesticks, with trumpet-style stems on circular bases. By L.A. Crichton of London.

- *height 29cm*
- £2,650 • **Langfords**

▽ **Silver Blotter**

- *1921*

Silver blotter of plain design with chalice-shaped thumb piece.

- *length 17cm*
- £280 • **Alfie's Antique Market**

▽ **Silver Salt and Pepper Pot**

- *circa 1923*

Matching silver salt and pepper pot, of octagonal baluster form with finial lid, from E. Johnson & Son Ltd., Derby.

- *height 9cm*
- £240 • **Barrett Towning**

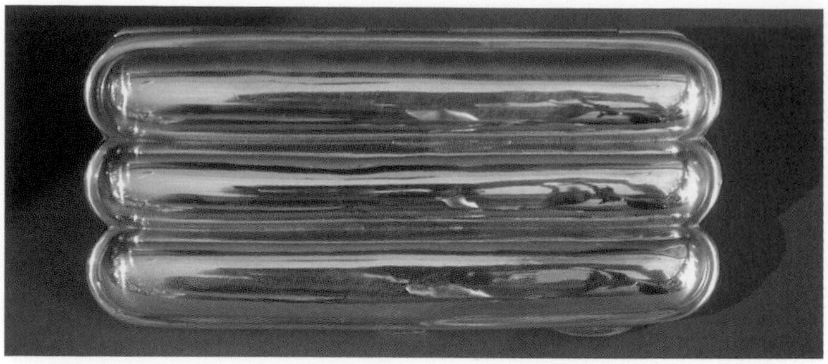

△ **Cigar Case**

- *circa 1920*

Silver cigar case with three compartments allowing for half caronas.

- *length 12cm*
- £160 • **Henry Gregory**

▽ **Pewter Ice Bucket**

- *circa 1920*

Pewter ice bucket with tulip pattern, designed by Orivit.

- *20cm x 21cm*
- £700 • **Arwas**

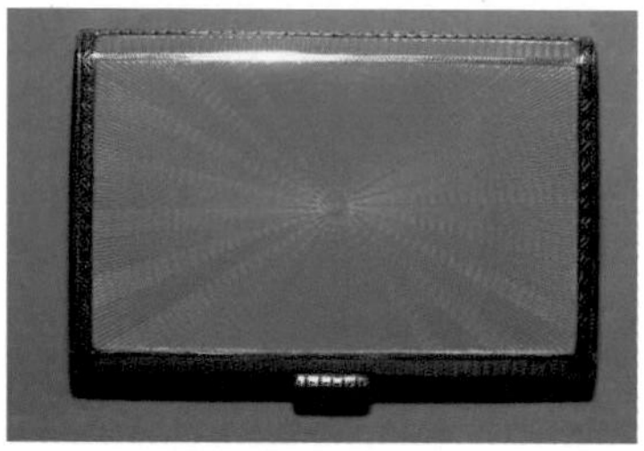

△ **Cigarette Case**

- *1928*

Silver, turquoise and black enamel cigarette case with silver gilt interior. European with London import mark.

- *length 8cm*
- £950 • **S. & A. Thompson**

▽ **English Sauce Boats**

- *1928*

A pair of George III-style sauce boats made by Thomas Bradbury of London.

- *height 6cm*
- £6,775 • **Percy's Ltd**

△ **Circular Mustard Pot**

- *circa 1929*

Mustard pot of drum design with blue glass liner, hinged lid, scrolled handle and scalloped thumb piece.

- *height 5.5cm*
- £248 • **Barrett Towning**

▽ **Silver Cruet Set**

- *circa 1930*

Silver Art Deco cruet set consisting of mustard, salt and pepper in the style of tankards.

- *height 5cm*
- £360 • **Henry Gregory**

▽ Water Jug

- *1930*

A pewter water jug of bulbous proportions with unusual splayed lip and curved handle.

- *height 24cm*
- £60 • Jane Stewart

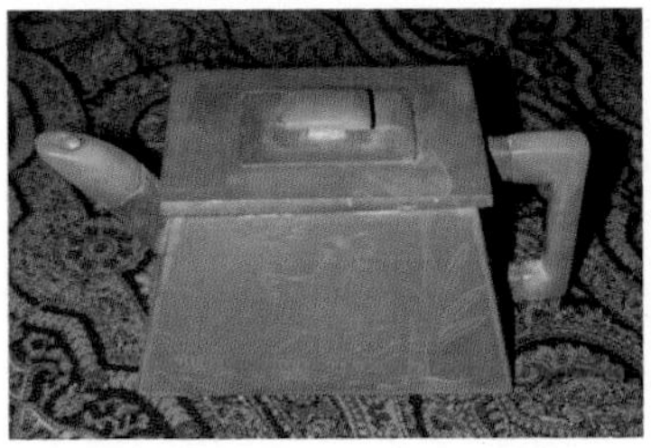

△ Tea Pot

- *1930*

A pewter Chinese tea pot with jadeite spout, handle and finial.

- *height 15cm*
- £85 • Jane Stewart

◁ Silver Snuff Box

- *circa 1939*

Small silver snuff box made in Sheffield, England.

- *6cm x 6cm*
- £110 • Barrett Towning

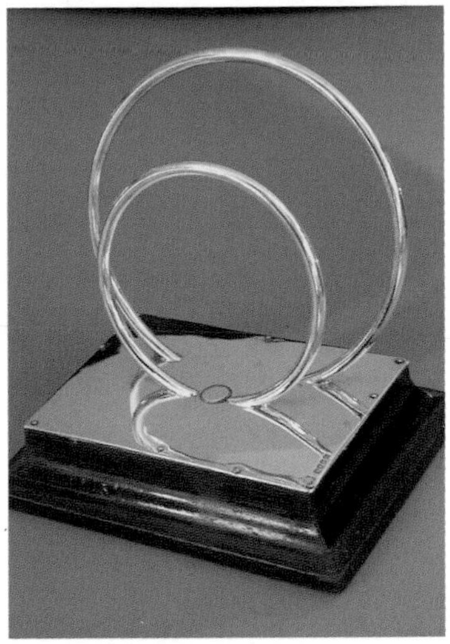

△ Letter Rack

- *1937*

Silver letter rack, of double circle design, mounted on a mahogany base.

- *height 17cm*
- £350 • Alfie's Antique Market

▽ Sheffield Silver Dish

- *1937*

Octagonal silver dish with double handles of ivory, made in Sheffield, England.

- £180 • Alfie's Antique Market

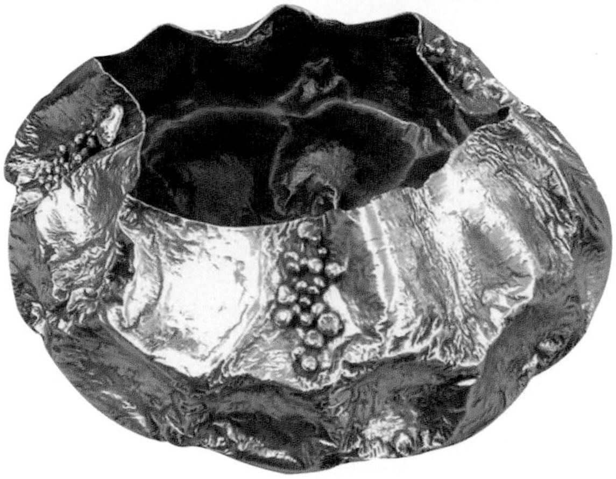

△ Silver Bowl

- *1930*

Silver 'Crumpled Paper' bowl with fruit decoration.

- *height 16cm*
- £1,100 • Stephen Kalms

△ Silver Tea Strainer

- *1942*

Silver double-handled tea strainer made in London with pierced and chased decoration.

- *length 16cm*
- £250 • Stephen Kalms

△ Dressing Table Set

- *1966*

Three-piece enamel and silver set consisting of hairbrush, clothes brush and mirror with red rose design. By Barker, Ellis Silver Co., Birmingham.

- £360 • Linden & Co.

▷ Silver Goblets

- *1970*

Four silver goblets with silver gilt interiors, by Christopher Lawrence.

- *height 15cm*
- £1,000 • Themes

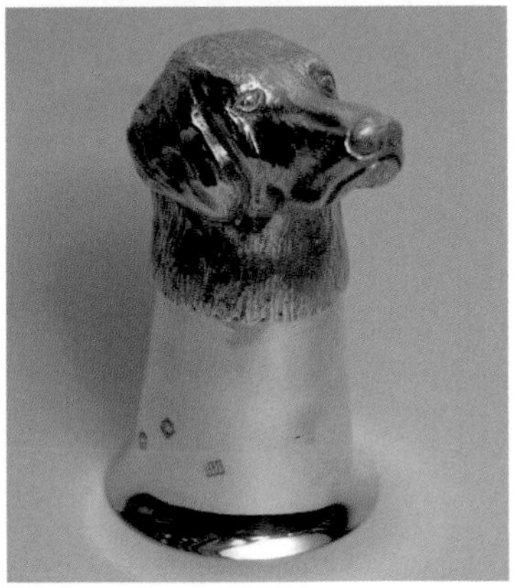

△ Stirrup Cup

- *1974*

Sheffield stirrup cup with excellently formed etched hound base. Heavy quality silver.

- *height 11.5cm*
- £575 • Linden & Co.

SPORTING ITEMS

Nostalgia plays an important part in purchasing sporting-related items, which have an extensive and world-wide appeal. From the avid collector seeking out his favourite sporting hero's football, to the interior designer furnishing a speciality sports restaurant, all contribute to the ever increasing demand for sporting memorabilia. The relatively new interest in football (soccer) memorabilia and the huge sponsorship given to sport has also helped to expand the market for sporting-related items. A football clubhouse may spend vast amounts of money adorning their walls with football memorabilia, for example shirts, caps and trophies of famous sporting heroes. This trend has pushed up the prices world-wide, and this has been further exacerbated by the proliferation of sport-themed restaurants, especially in the United States. Vintage guns are highly sought-after and, if they have the original case and maker's mark, this can increase their value. Cricket, tennis and golf have a wide appeal and fishing provides ample scope for the collector because of the wide range of large and smaller items available, such as canes, fishing rods, leather wallets and coarse fishing reels. These items have an enormous following internationally.

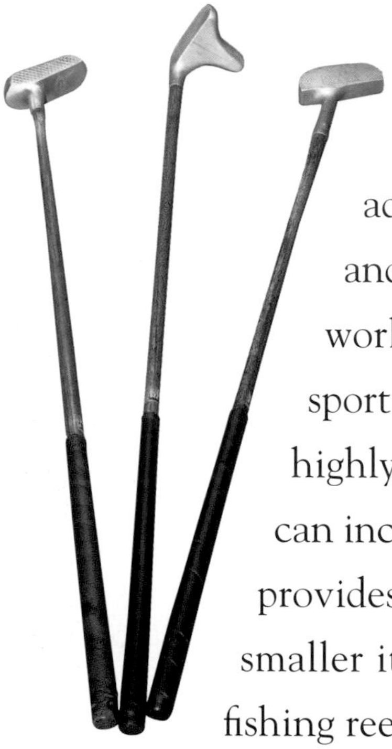

GENERAL

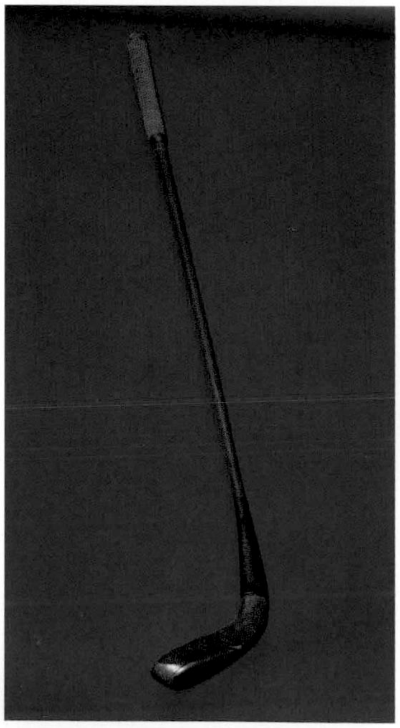

▽ Lawn Tennis Racquet

- *circa 1860*

Mid-19th-century lawn tennis racquet. Racquet has original thick gut strings. Shown with mahogany multipress with brass butterfly screws and mounts. Used to maintain racquet shape.

- **£1,850, £495 resp.** • **Sean Arnold**

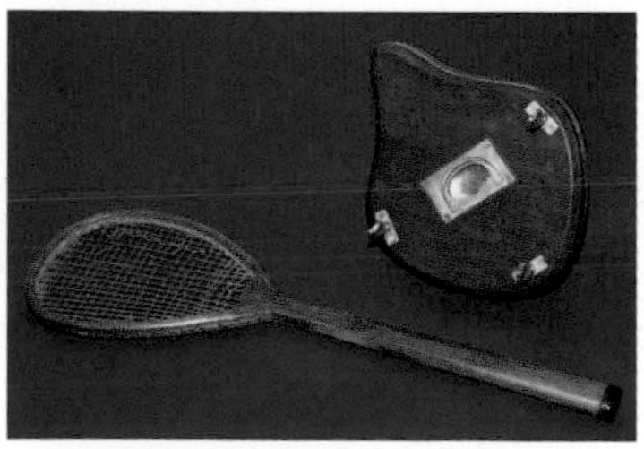

◁ Long-Nose Driver

- *circa 1850*

A beech head long-nose driver. Made by McEwan of Scotland.

- **£1,850** • **Sean Arnold**

△ Pottery Stick Stand

- *1870*

A pottery stick stand in the form of riding boots by Dimmock & Co.

- **£3,000** • **Pimlico**

▽ Crocodile-Skin Hip Flask

- *1880*

A large crocodile-skin, silver-plated hip flask, with the inscription 'F.M.P.M'.

- *height 16cm*
- **£445** • **The Reel Thing**

△ **Child's Riding Seat**

- *1880*

A child's saddle made from wicker, with curved base and leather fasteners, to fit on a pony.

- *height 57cm*
- £275 • Sporting Times

▽ **Hand-Stitched Football**

- *circa 1890*

Original hand-stitched leather football with laces and unusual panelling.

- *diameter 25cm*
- £680 • Sean Arnold

◁ **One of a Pair of Water Buffalo Horn Oil Lamps**

- *circa 1880*

Lamps are brass-mounted and are decorated with a heavy leaf design.

- *height 77cm*
- £950 for pair • H. & H.

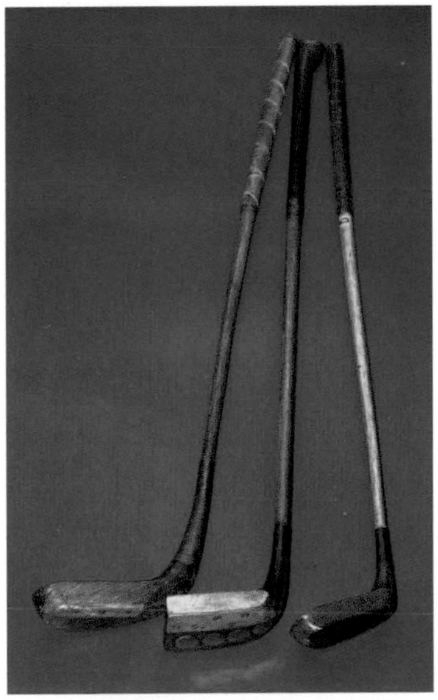

△ **Wooden-Headed Putters**

- *circa 1880*

Hickory-shafted wooden-headed golf putters. From left to right are a rare longnose putter by McEwan, a gassiat putter and a socket-head putter.

- £1650, £950, £380 • Sean Arnold

▽ **Original Racquets**

- *circa 1880*

Original racquet for playing the game of racquets with original stringing and leather press.

- *height 58cm*
- £475 • Sean Arnold

◁ **Plates and Tea Strainer**

- *circa 1885*

Pair of terracotta tennis plates and a silver tea strainer.

- *length 15cm, diameter 15cm*
- £485, £440 • Sean Arnold

△ **Tennis Jelly Mould**

- *circa 1885*

Tennis jelly mould by Copeland. Crossed tennis racquets appear in the centre of the mould.

- *length 15cm*
- £380 • Sean Arnold

△ **Victorian Cricket Bat**

- *circa 1890*

Late 19th-century Victorian cricket bat. Styled with rounded back and crafted from willow. Shows good patina and bound handle.

- £220 • Sean Arnold

△ **Leather Fencing Mask**

- *circa 1890*

Leather Kendo fencing mask with metal mesh and leather-padded interior.

- *diameter 18cm*
- £95 • Sporting Times

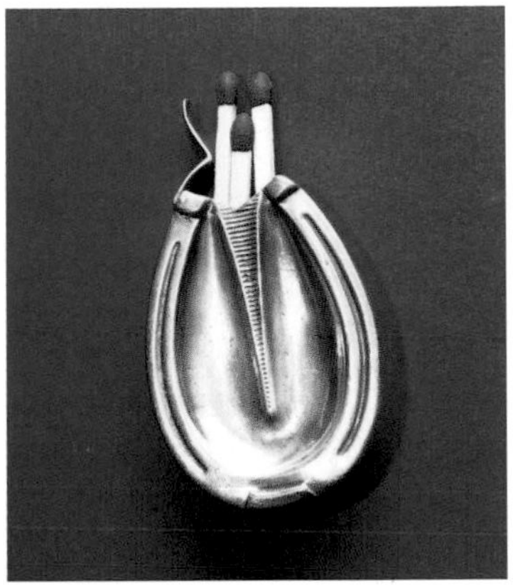

△ **Horseshoe Vesta Case**

- *circa 1890*

Vesta case in form of horseshoe. Brass with enamelling.

- *length 5cm*
- £145 • Sean Arnold

△ **Rugby Player**

- *circa 1890*

English bronze figure of a rugby player holding a ball.

- *height 46cm*
- £1,750 • Sean Arnold

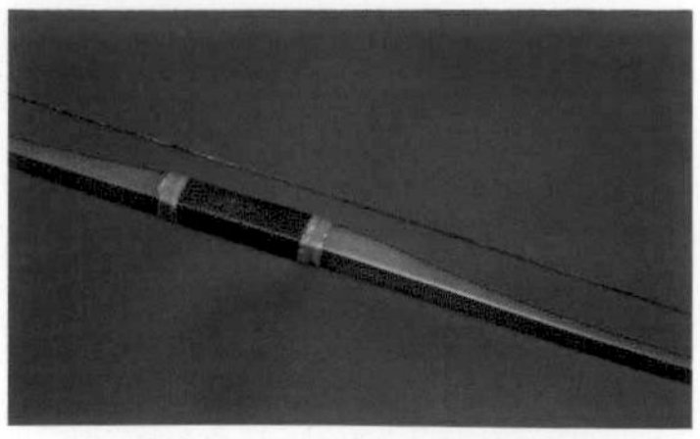

△ English Longbow

- *circa 1900*

Early 20th-century 'Old English' longbow. The bow is yew-wood and has a leather grip. Includes the bow string.

- *length 1.20m*
- £165 • Sean Arnold

△ Willow Cricket Bat

- *1900*

Leather cricket bag with leather handle and straps, and willow cricket bat.

- *length 75cm*
- £120 • Sean Arnold

△ Football Trophy

- *1900*

Silver-plated football trophy in the form of early football with a silver foliate tripod stand on a circular base.

- *height 45cm*
- £775 • Sean Arnold

▽ Telescope & Binoculars

- *circa 1900*

Telescope and binoculars made from leather and brass. By F. Davidson.

- £345, £95 • Sean Arnold

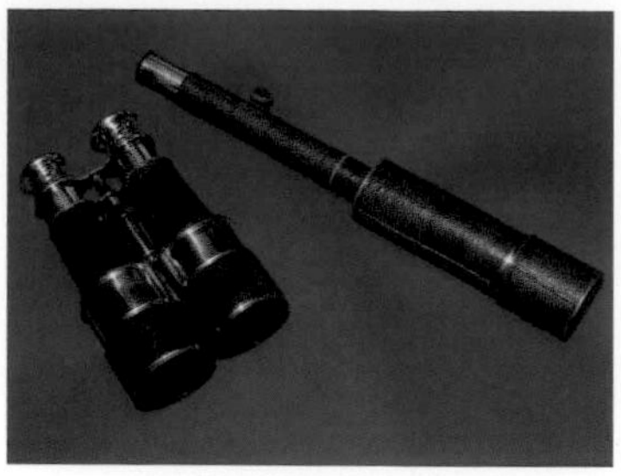

▽ Golf Club Ballot Box

- *circa 1900*

Authentic golf-club ballot box from Muirfield Golf Club. Made of mahogany. Of very fine quality.

- *height 34cm*
- £6,500 • Sean Arnold

▽ Golf Putters

- *circa 1905*

Hickory-shafted patent aluminium putters. Made by, from left: Schenectady, Fred Saunders and Mallet putter.

- £460, £840, £480 resp.
- Sean Arnold

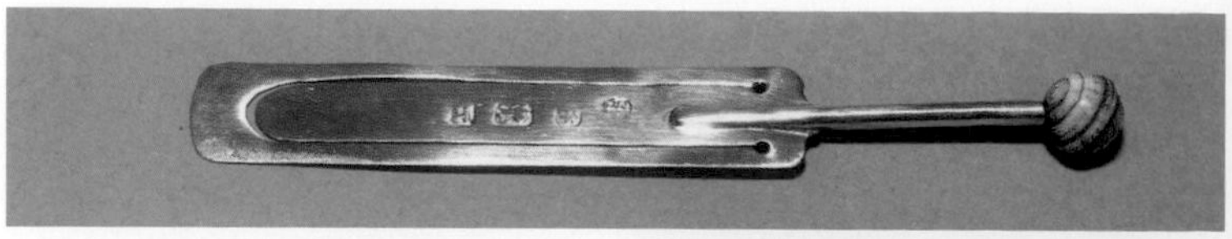

△ Cricket Bat Bookmark

- *1907*

Early 20th-century bookmark in the form of a cricket bat. The top of the bat shows an ivory ball. Made by A. & J. Zimmerman of Birmingham.

- *length 9.5cm*
- £425 • S. & A. Thompson

△ Sporting Books

- *circa 1910*

Sporting books on golf, tennis, fishing, and cricket, including a morocco-bound limited edition book *British Sports and Sportsmen.*

- £65–280 • Sean Arnold

△ Golf Ball Vesta

- *circa 1907*

Golf ball vesta in the form of a golf ball. Shows incised patterns. Made by Henry Williamson Ltd, Birmingham.

- *length 5cm*
- £745 • S. & A. Thompson

▽ Squash Racquets

- *circa 1910*

Pair of squash racquets. Shown with heavy gut stringing. Racquets bound with leather grips. In good condition.

- *length 68cm*
- £125 each • Sean Arnold

△ Lawn Bowls

- *circa 1910*

Set of four lignum vitae lawn bowls. Ivorine inserts with owner's initials and numbers. Pictured with white porcelain jack.

- £38, £26 each • Sean Arnold

△ Model of Thames Barge

• *circa 1910*
Well-constructed 20th-century model of a Thames barge. Gaff rig, metal keel and rudder. In good condition.
• *height 1.05m, width 80cm*
• £695 • Sean Arnold

▽ Hickory Golf Clubs

• *circa 1910*
Hickory shafts, leather grips and makers' names. Persimmon-headed wood, hand-forged.
• **£75, £45, £55** • Sean Arnold

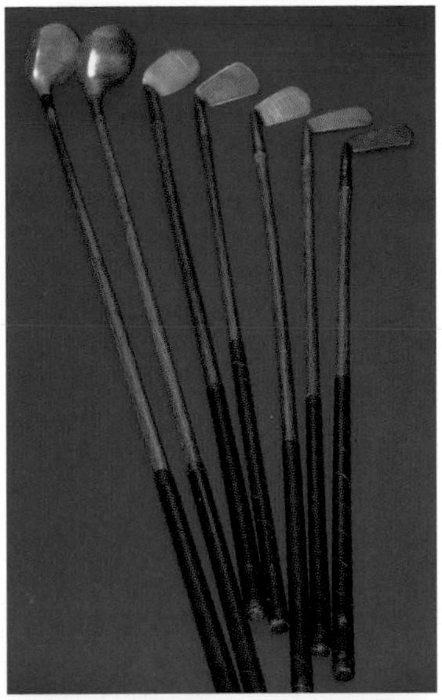

△ Football Medals

• *circa 1920*
A collection of football medals. Enamelled silver.
• **£80, £120, £120 resp.**
• Sean Arnold

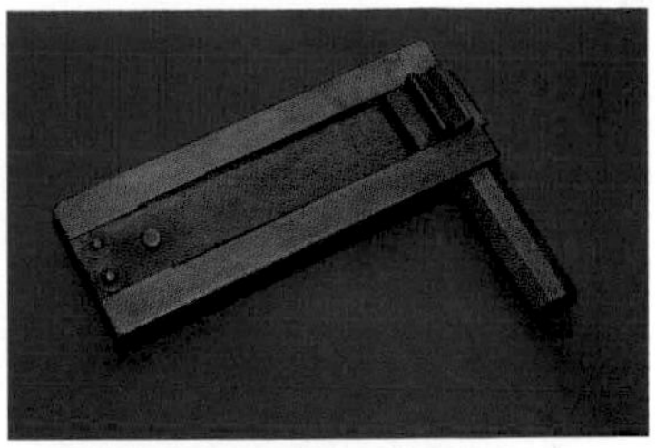

△ Football Rattle

• *circa 1920*
Early 20th-century football rattle. Made from wood and used by football supporters. In good condition.
• £75 • Sean Arnold

△ Football Caps

• *circa 1898–1930*
Velvet sporting caps. Metallic tassels representing various sports.
• £180–360 • Sean Arnold

△ Badminton Racquets

• *circa 1920*
Wooden with presses. Gut strings. Feather shuttlecocks.
• £65 racquet, £7 cock • Sean Arnold

△ Football Items

• *circa 1920*
Football items from early 20th century. From left: boots, shin pads and Hotspur boots. All items are handmade from leather. Made in England.
• **£165, £65, £225 resp.**
• Sean Arnold

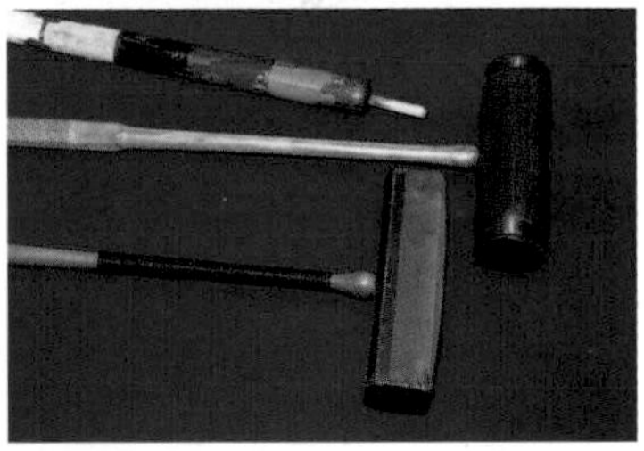

△ Croquet Mallets

• *circa 1920*
From top, brass-bound croquet mallet by Jacques of London, and square mallet by Slazenger of London. Boxwood.
• *height 95cm*
• £65, £110 • Sean Arnold

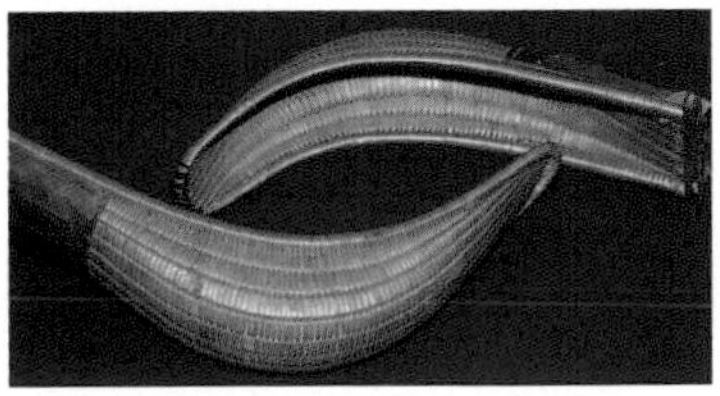

△ Wicker and Leather Pelota Cradles

• *circa 1910*
Early 20th-century pelota cradles. Made from wicker with leather gloves. Used for high-speed ball game of Spanish origin.
• *length 50cm*
• £110 each • Sean Arnold

◁ Polished Pewter Figure

• *circa 1920*
Naturalistically styled polished pewter golfing figure mounted on a pewter rectangular base. Signed by Zwick.
• *height 34cm*
• £1,075 • Sean Arnold

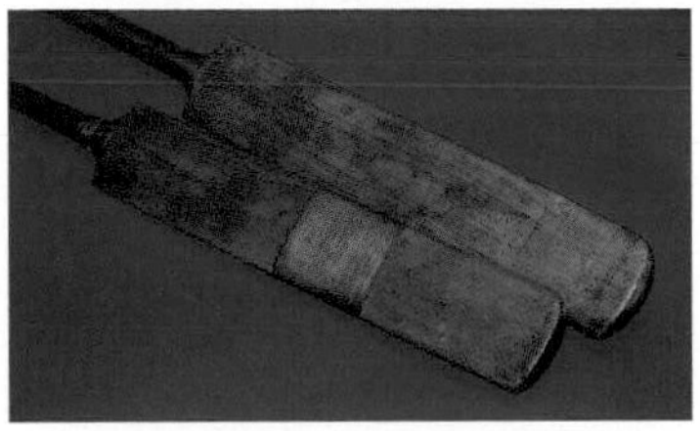

◁ Cricket Bats

• *circa 1920*
'Autographed' cricket bats – incised with names of famous players. Quality willow, English.
• £85 • Sean Arnold

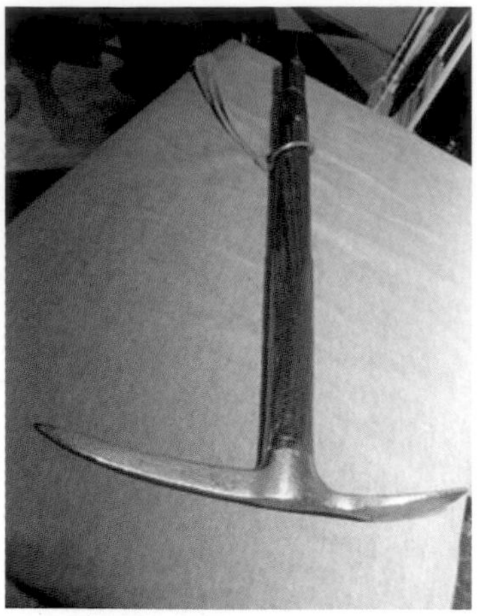

△ Steel Ice Axe

- *circa 1920*

A steel ice axe with a mahogany handle and leather strap.

- *length 58cm*
- £68 • Henry Gregory

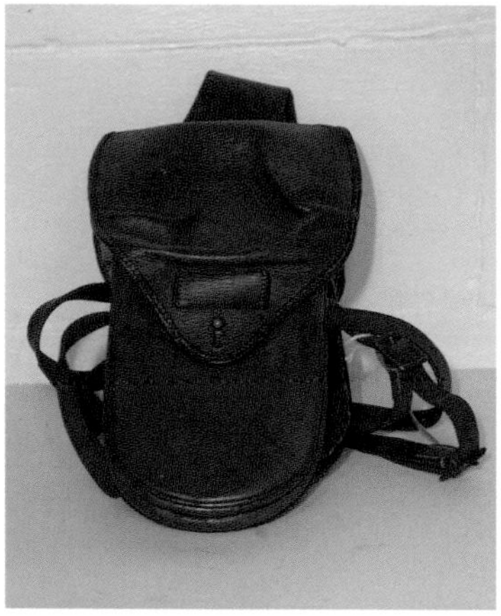

△ Saddle Bags

- *circa 1930*

Leather saddle bags in fine condition with leather straps and brass buckles.

- *length 18cm*
- £155 • Sporting Times

▽ Leather Gaitors

- *circa 1920*

Pair of leather gaitors with leather straps and metal buckles.

- *length 29cm*
- £28 • Sporting Times

▽ Selection of Boxing Items including Boots, Gloves and Bag

- *circa 1920*

Group of sporting items showing leather boxing boots, leather boxing gloves and a leather punch bag. Made by various English sporting manufacturers.

- **£165, £60, £125 resp.**
- **Sean Arnold**

▽ Cigar Polo Mallets

- *circa 1925*

Pair of Salters cigar polo mallets with bamboo shafts, sycamore or ash heads.

- *length 1.30m*
- £48 • Sean Arnold

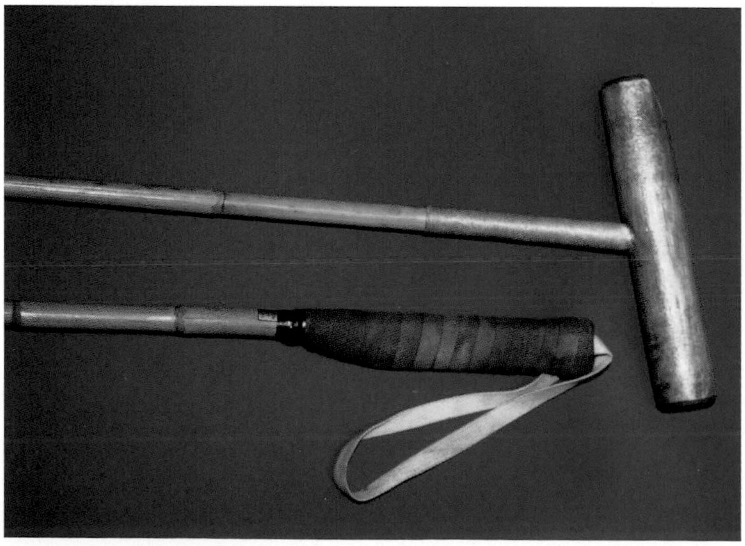

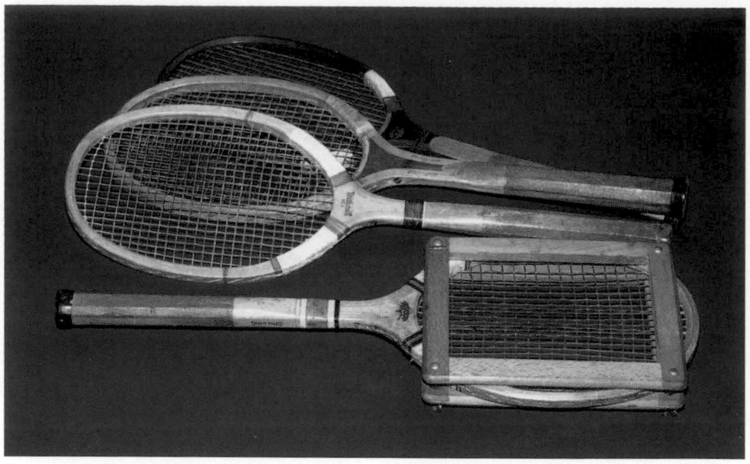

▽ Hazell Tennis Racquet

- *1934*

Hazell Streamline tennis racquet of first aerodynamic design. Blue star.

- *length 68cm*
- £425 • Sean Arnold

△ 1920s Tennis Racquets

- *circa 1920*

Tennis racquets with wooden handles and presses.

- £38 each • Sean Arnold

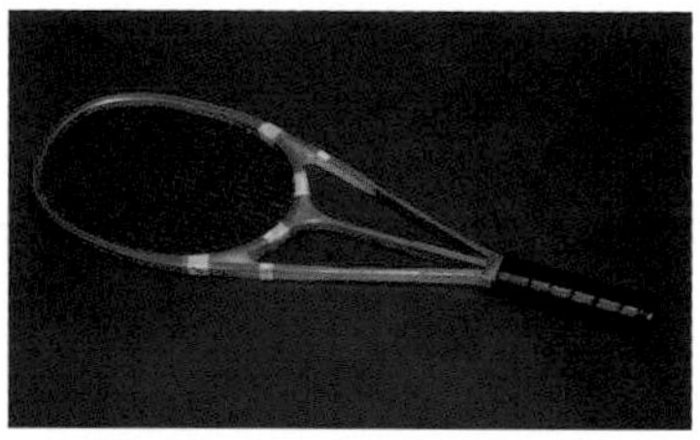

▽ Ice Axes

- *1930*

Continental ice axes with wood handles and metal axe head, of various sizes. Hickory-shafted.

- *length 84cm*
- £60 • Sean Arnold

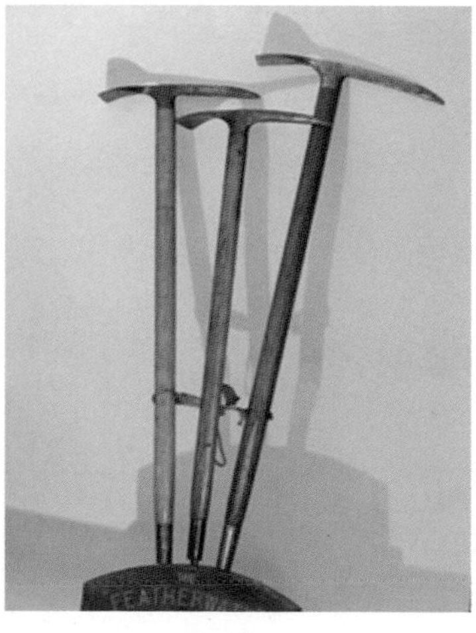

△ Croquet Set

- *1930*

Portable croquet set on mahogany stand with brass handle and feet, containing four mallets, hoops and colour balls.

- £495 • Sean Arnold

▷ Lizard-Skin Flask

- *circa 1930*

Early 20th-century large silver lizard-skin flask. Flask is hallmarked with inscription 'Death to Filias'. Shows a silver hinged screw to the stopper. Has a glass reservoir inside. Flask is in very good condition.

- £435 • H. & H.

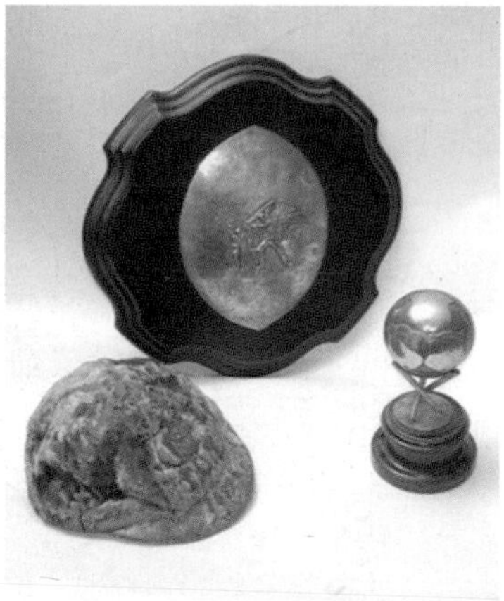

△ **Cricket Cap, Shield and Trophy**

• *1895–1931*
Silver-plated cricket shield on a mahogany base depicting an early cricketer. Blue velvet cricket cap with metallic embroidery. I.C.C. Cricket trophy decorated with a cricket ball and bearing three engraved silver shields and details of 'Hat Trick' base in the form of cricket stumps.
• **shield £375, cap £135, trophy £225**
• **Sean Arnold**

▽ **Child's Football Boots**

• *1930*
Child's leather football boots in original condition.
• *length 18cm*
• **£125** • **Sporting Times**

▷ **Nickel-Plated Binoculars**

• *circa 1930*
Nickel-plated binoculars with leather grips.
• *length 6cm*
• **£125** • **The Reel Thing**

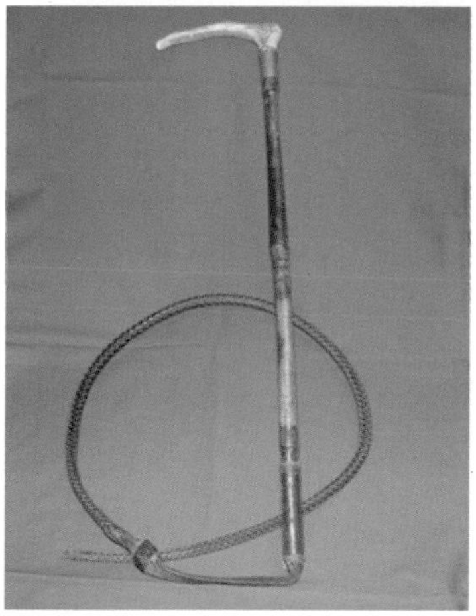

△ **Hunting Crop**

• *1940*
Hunting whip with braided leather strap, ivory handle and brass collar.
• *length 120cm*
• **£145** • **The Reel Thing**

△ **Polo Helmet and Knee Pads**

• *circa 1930*
White polo helmet with red ribbon trim, and leather knee pads.
• *diameter 28cm*
• **helmet £65, knee pads £35**
• **Sean Arnold**

▽ **Photograph and Tennis Racquet**

• *1932*
Photograph of Bunny Austin, who popularised the racquet, and a Hazell Streamline Blue Star tennis racquet.
• **£795** • **Sean Arnold**

△ **Leather Riding Boots**

• *1930*
Pair of gentleman's brown leather polo boots with laces, three straps with brass buckles and wooden shoe trees.
• *height 61cm*
• **£170** • **Sporting Times**

▷ **Golfing Figure**

• *circa 1930*
Donald Duck plaster figure.
• *height 23cm*
• **£850** • **Sean Arnold**

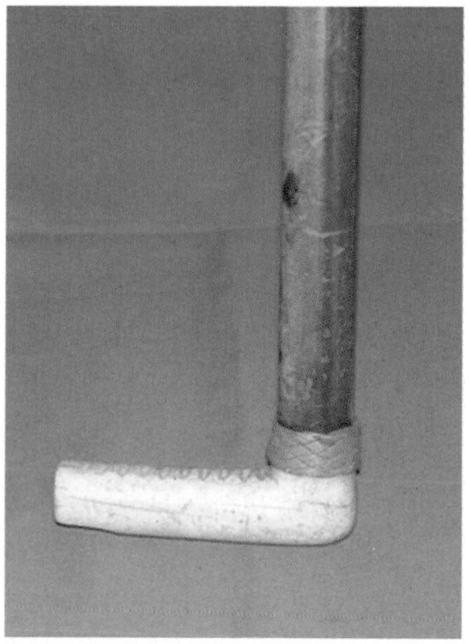

△ **Riding Crop**

• *1930*
A leather riding crop with notched ivory handle and silver collar.
• *length 55cm*
• **£85** • **The Reel Thing**

▽ **Brass Dinner Gong**

• *circa 1930*
Brass dinner gong flanked by two brass tennis racquets, supported on an oval mahogany stand.
• *30cm x 24cm*
• **£695** • **Sean Arnold**

△ **Bottle Opener**

- *circa 1940*

Metal bottle opener in the form of a jockey's riding cap, decorated with red and white enamel.

- *diameter 7cm*
- £45 • Sporting Times

△ **Football Trophy**

- *1956*

Football trophy presented to Mr and Mrs Clarke of Berkhamsted Football Club 1956.

- *height 17cm*
- £45 • Sporting Times

▽ **Football Collectables**

- *circa 1940*

Leather-covered trinket box in shape of a football. Marble ashtray. Football tankard.

- £125, £135, £95 • Sean Arnold

▽ **Mounted Car Mascot**

- *circa 1950*

A horse-racing figure with an enamelled rider. On marble.

- *height 16cm*
- £225 • Sean Arnold

◁ **York Rowing Cap**

- *1940s*

Rowing cap with the braid and cap badge of York City Rowing Club.

- *29cm x 18cm*
- £50 • Henry Gregory

△ **Hunting Tankards**

- *circa 1940*

A set of 3 pottery tankards with hunting motifs. Made by Arthur Wood. Shows a treacle glaze.

- *height 12cm*
- £130 set • Sean Arnold

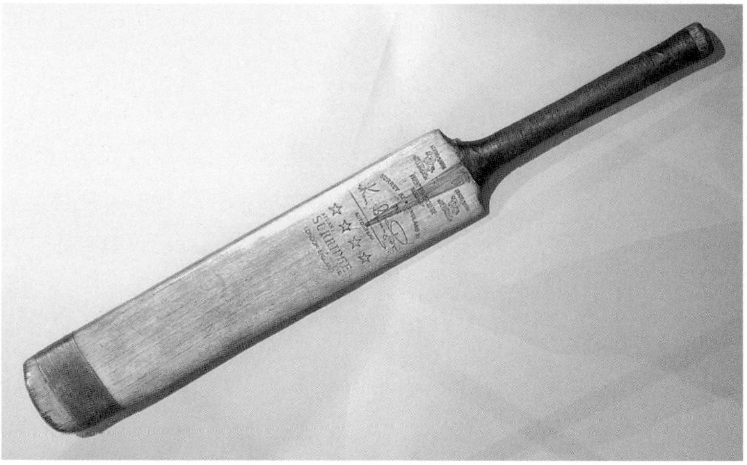

△ **Stuart Surridge Bat**

- *1940s*

Stuart Surridge cricket bat autographed by Ken Barrington .

- *78cm*
- £72 • Henry Gregory

△ **Croquet Set**

- *circa 1950*

Boxed croquet set by John Jacques, London. Pine box.

- *1.10m x 25cm x 30cm*
- £225 • Sean Arnold

▷ **Tartan Shooting Stick**

- *1950s*

Chrome shooting stick with hinged seat and tartan liner.

- *83cm*
- £48 • Henry Gregory

▽ **Football**

- *1950s*

Brown leather football in original condition.

- *25cm*
- £70 • Henry Gregory

△ **Polo Player on Pony**

- *1970*

Bronze figure of a polo player on a galloping pony, one of a limited edition of ten, signed the artist.

- *height 40cm*
- £4,950 • Sean Arnold

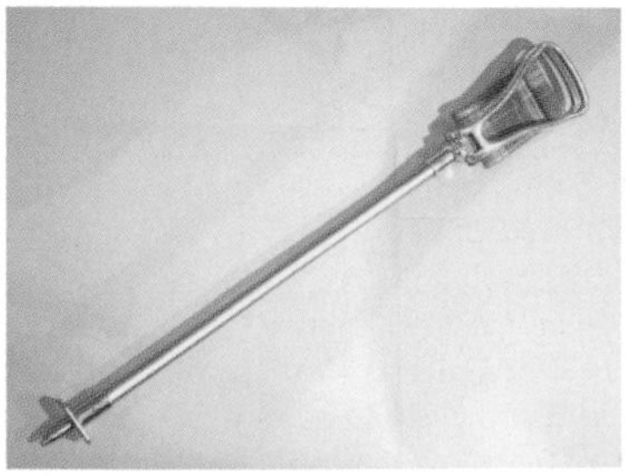

△ Marine Navigation Instruments Book

• *circa 1980*

Rare copy of *Marine Navigation Instruments* by Jean Randier.

• £149 • Ocean Leisure

△ Signed World Cup Football

• *1990*

Football signed by the English team from the Italian World Cup of 1990. The signatures include those of Gazza, Lineker and Platt.

• £850 • Sean Arnold

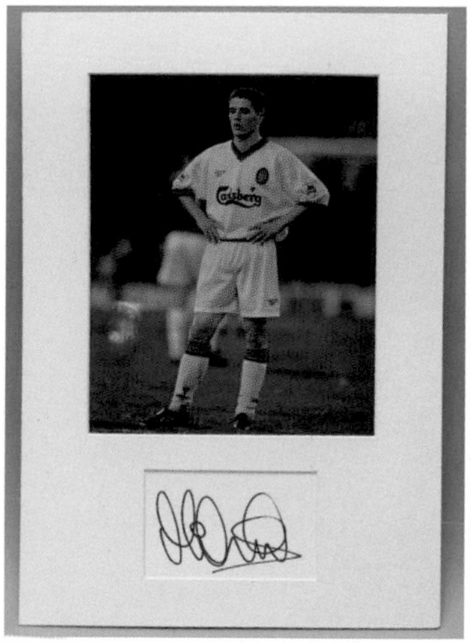

△ Framed Photograph of Michael Owen

• *1998–99*

Recently photographed single-mounted photograph of footballer Michael Owen, one of Britain's rising stars. Matted with Owen's signature. Photograph shows the Liverpool team's yellow strip.

• £50 • Star Signings

▽ Gianfranco Zola Photograph

• *1998*

Signature with photographs of Gianfranco Zola scoring the winning goal in the Cup Winners Cup Final, Stockholm, 1998.

• £200 • Star Signings

▽ Signed Liverpool Team Shirt

• *circa 1999–2000*

Football jersey from the Liverpool team, 2000 season. With all the team signatures including football greats such as Owen, Fowler, Hyppia and Camara.

• £350 • Star Signings

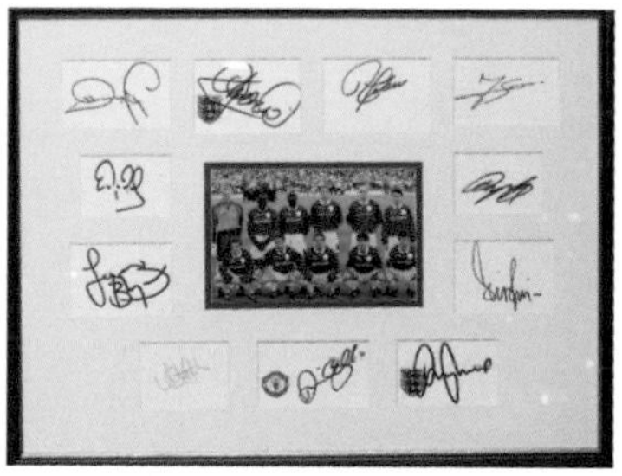

△ European Cup Photograph

• *1998–99*

Manchester United squad photo taken in the 1998–99 season at a European Cup match. Photo and signatures include Beckham, Cole and Schmeichel.

• £350 • Star Signings

△ Team Barcelona Photograph

• *1999–2000*

Photograph of the 1999–2000 Barcelona squad. Signed at Wembley stadium, in the match against Arsenal. Includes Rivaldo, Kluivert and Figo.

• £350 • Star Signings

△ Signed Arsenal Shirt

• *2000*

Signed Arsenal shirt from the 2000 season. Signatures include popular football players such as Bergkamp, Overmars and Kanu.

• £350 • Star Signings

▽ 1999 European Cup Final Programme

• *1999*

Programme signed by the Manchester United squad. Game between Manchester United and Bayern Munich.

• £600 • Star Signings

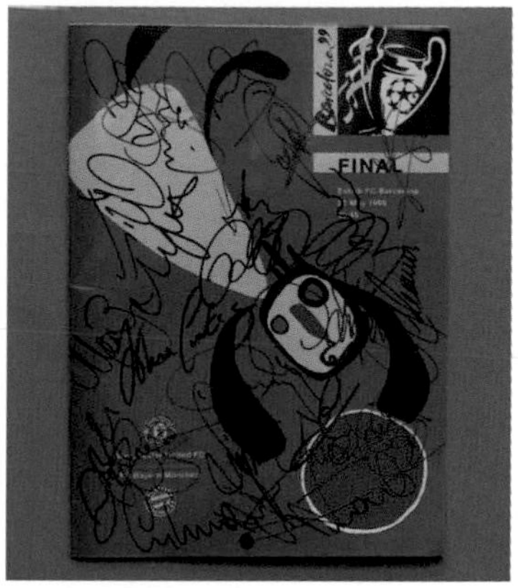

▽ Manchester United Football Shirt

• *1998–99*

Signed Manchester United football shirt of treble winners. Showing 21 signatures from the 1998–99 season squad. Signatures include Beckham, Sheringham, Schmeichel and Keane.

• £1,750 • Star Signings

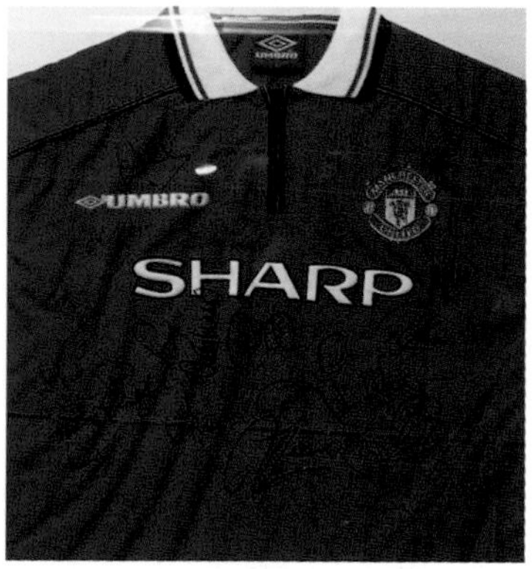

▽ Signed Chelsea Team Photograph

• *1999–2000*

Chelsea team photograph including signatures of the players. Taken prior to playing AC Milan in Champions League.

• £350 • Star Signings

FISHING

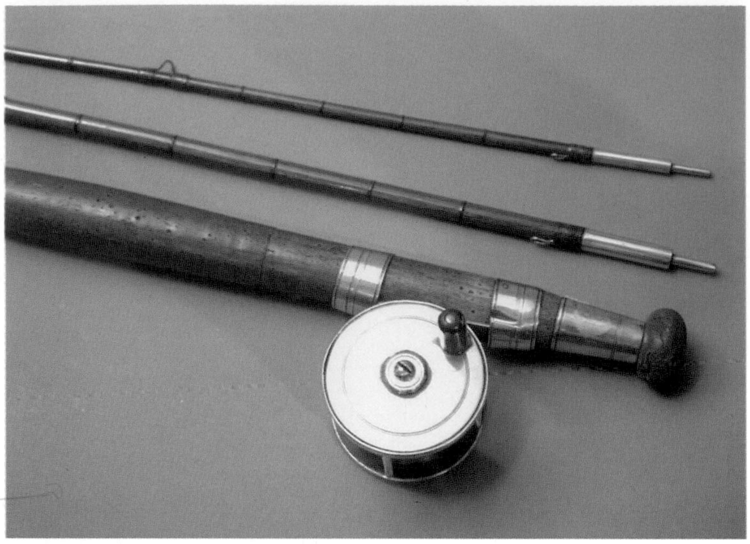

◁ Fly Rod

- *circa 1880*

Green-heart fly rod of three sections with machine reels.

- *300cm*
- £150 • **Henry Gregory**

△ Salmon Fly

- *1895*

Well kept 'gut-tied' fly used for salmon fishing.

- £95 • **The Reel Thing**

△ Every Star Salmon Fly

- *circa 19th century*

Particularly bright and alluring replica of star fly used for salmon fishing.

- £45 • **The Reel Thing**

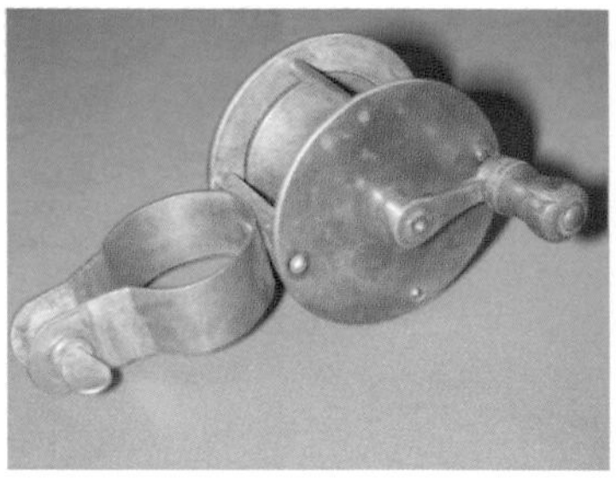

△ Winch Reel

- *circa 1880*

Solid brass winch reel, with turned wooden handle.

- *diameter 10cm*
- £200 • **The Reel Thing**

△ Hardy 2¼-Inch Reel

- *circa 1890*

Hardy 2¼-inch 'Red' reel. Brass body with ivory handle. Made in Birmingham. Very good example.

- £445 • **The Reel Thing**

▽ Hardy Perfect 4-Inch

- *1896*

Late 19th-century 'Perfect 4-inch' ivory-handled brass-faced reel with brass and steel components. Very rare and in excellent condition.

- £595 • **The Reel Thing**

▽ Reel by Hardy

- *circa 1900*

Hardy fishing reel,with a unique Duplication Mark II inscription.

- *diameter 10cm*
- £245 • **The Reel Thing**

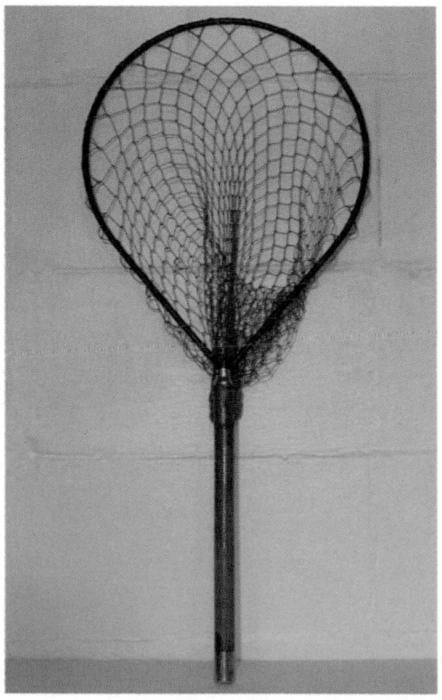

◁ Landing Net

- *circa 1900*

Landing net with tooled brass fittings and a wood handle.

- *length 78cm*
- £120 • **Sporting Times**

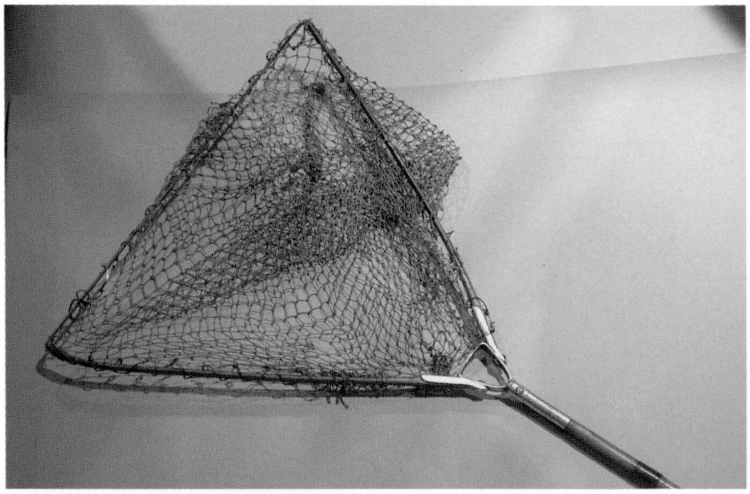

△ Hardy Landing Net

- *circa 1890*

Hardy's triangular folding landing net with brass fittings.

- *115cm x 48cm*
- £230 • **Henry Gregory**

◁ Willow Creel

- *circa 1900*

Small willow fishing creel with leather strap handle.

- *25cm x 19cm*
- £90 • **Henry Gregory**

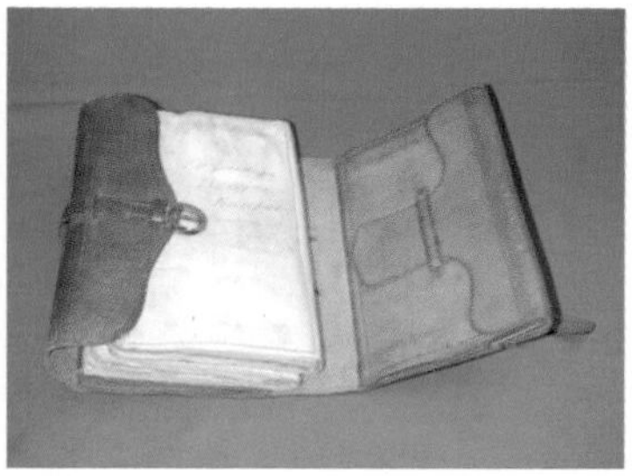

△ Fly Wallet

- *circa 1900*

Pigskin fly wallet with various compartments made by Hardy Bros.

- *length 20cm*
- £250 • The Reel Thing

△ Bakelite Powder Case

- *circa 1900*

Dusting powder case made of bakelite.

- *height 8cm*
- £30 • The Reel Thing

▽ Japanned Fly Box

- *circa 1910*

Tortoiseshell bakelite fly box with ten ranks of fly hooks, containing assorted flies.

- *21cm x 12cm*
- £95 • Henry Gregory

▽ Victorian Trout Rod

- *circa 1900*

Victorian split cane trout rod with silver banding, by Hardy Bros.

- *length 250cm*
- £600 • The Reel Thing

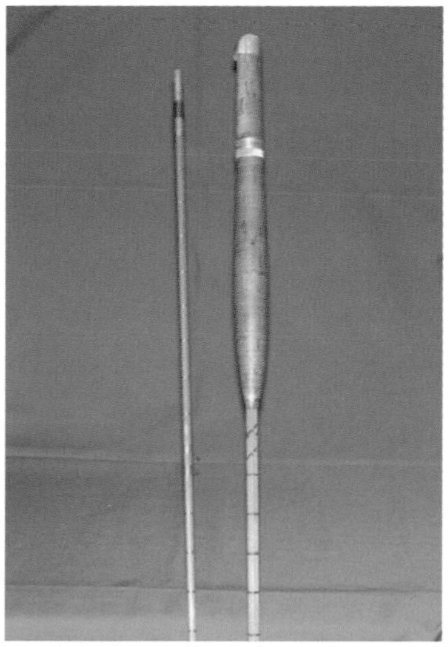

◁ Hardy Creel

- *early 20th century*

With webbing strap and netting.

- £650 • The Reel Thing

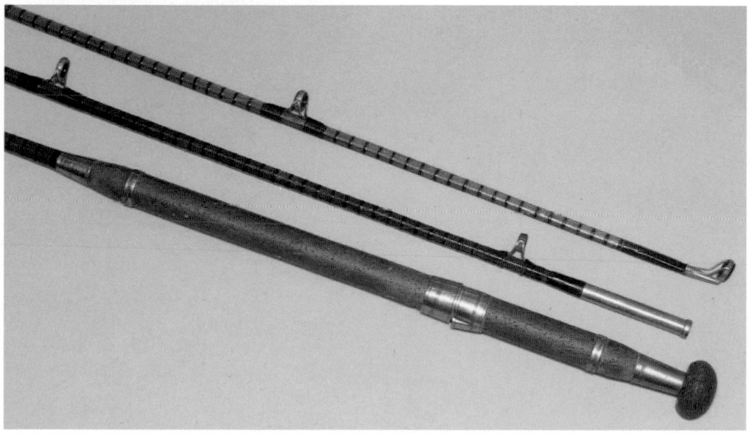

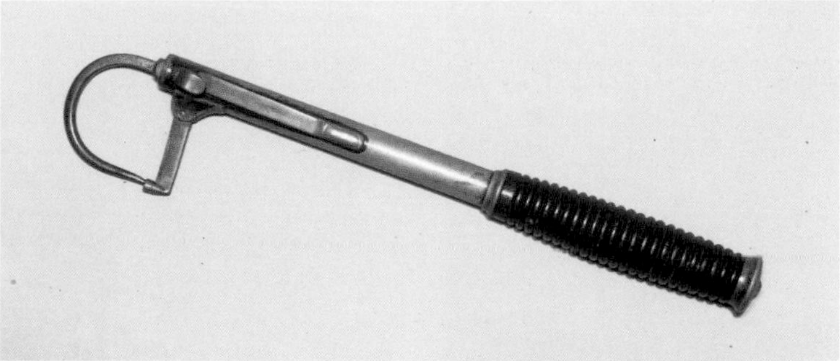

△ Hardy Telescopic Gaff

- *early 20th century*

Deep-sea telescopic gaff, for big game fishing. With belt clip. Brass with rosewood handle and spring safety clip.

- £250 • The Reel Thing

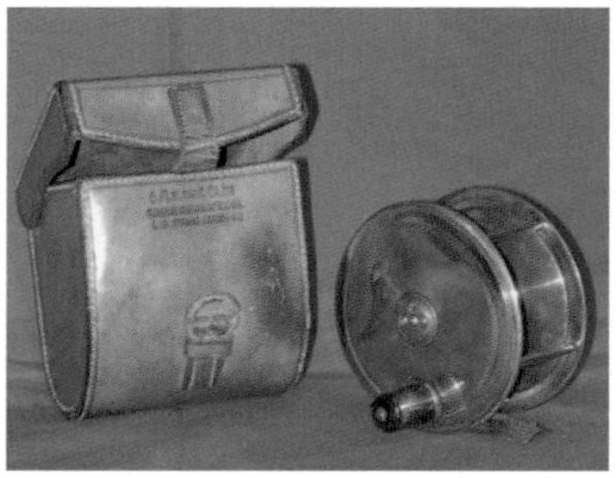

△ Brass Salmon Reel

- *circa 1910*

Solid brass salmon fly fishing reel with bone handle and original leather case, by C. Farlow.

- *diameter 11cm*
- £450 • The Reel Thing

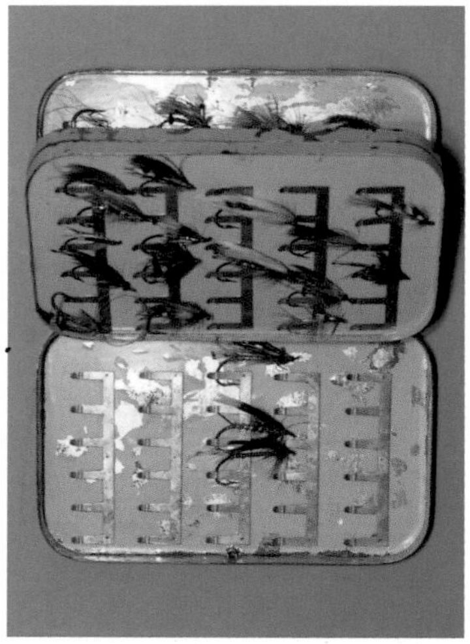

△ Salmon Fly Box

- *circa 1910*

Japanned box with four compartments including various gut-tied flies.

- £245 • The Reel Thing

◁ Boat Rod

- *circa 1910*

Split-cane boat rod. 7 feet.Two sections.

- £125 • The Reel Thing

△ Brass Reels

- *circa 1910*

Three brass fly-fishing reels

- *7cm (left), 5.5cm (centre), 5cm (right)*
- £35–50 • Henry Gregory

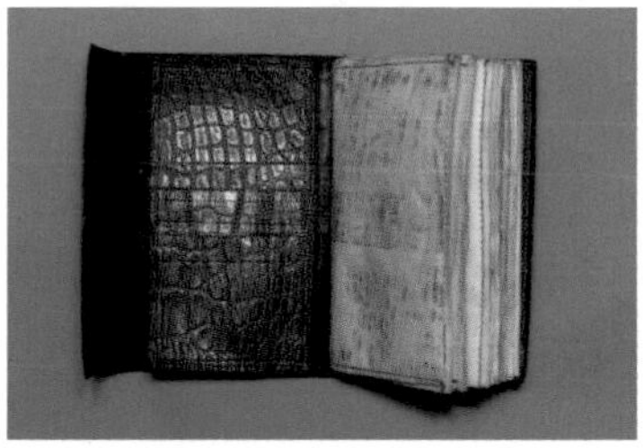

△ Crocodile-Skin Fly Wallet

- *circa 1910*

Made by G. Little & Co., Haymarket. The wallet contains various compartments.

- £225 • The Reel Thing

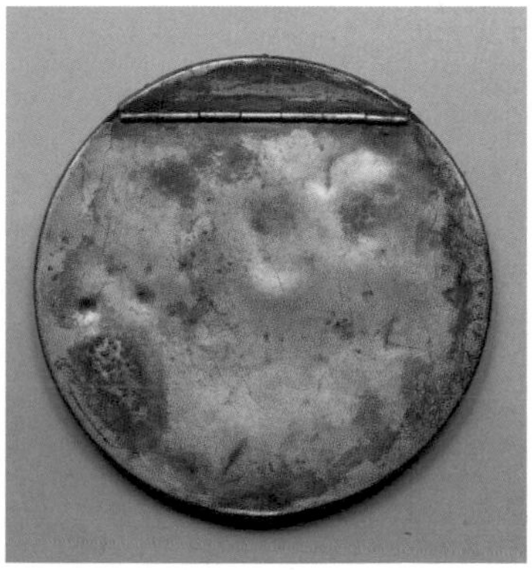

△ Brass Fly Case

- *1910*

Circular brass fly case with hinge. Three cloths.

- *diameter 10cm*
- £75 • The Reel Thing

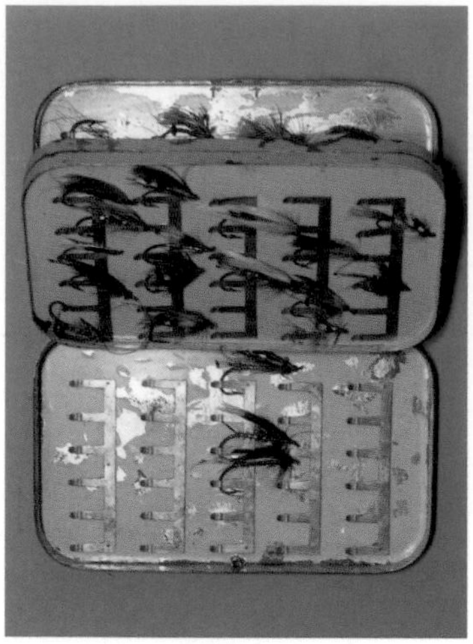

△ Salmon Fly Box

• *circa 1910*
Japanned box with four compartments including various gut-tied flies.
• £245 • The Reel Thing

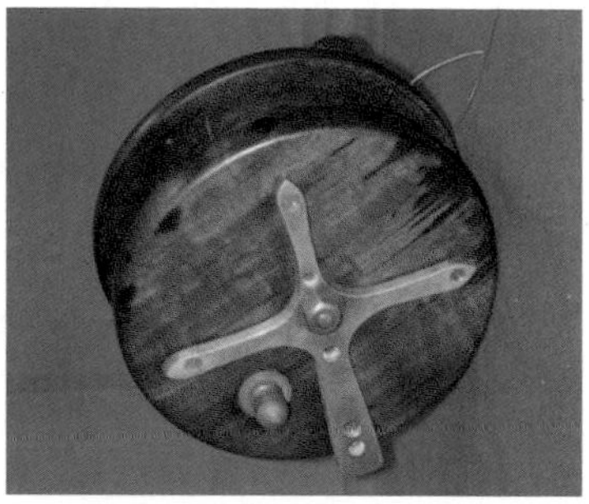

△ Starback Reel

• *1910*
Starback wooden sea-fishing reel, with star-shaped brass mounts.
• *diameter 10cm*
• £115 • The Reel Thing

△ Creel

• *circa 1910*
Fine French weave wicker split-reed pot-bellied creel with sloping lid and fish slot.
• £145 • Sean Arnold

▽ Murdoch Rod

• *circa 1920*
The Murdoch split-cane fishing rod made by Hardy.
• *length 3.95m*
• £295 • The Reel Thing

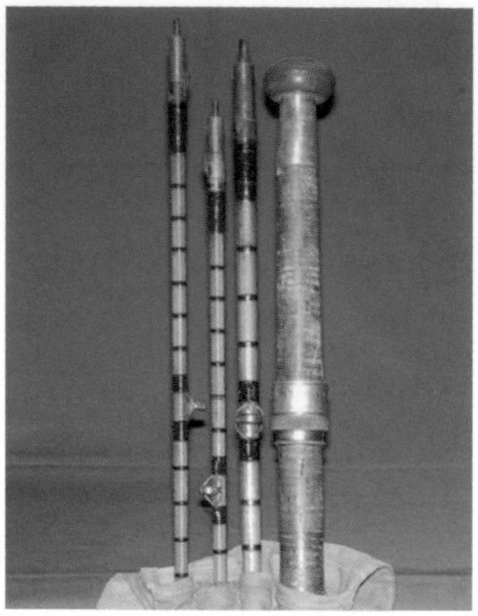

▽ Hardy Neroda Dry Fly Box

• *circa 1920*
Hardy Neroda case with nickel-plated fittings, in tortoiseshell and bakelite. Six sections with trout flies.
• £245 • The Reel Thing

▷ Leather Reel Case – 3⅛ Inch

• *circa 1920s*
Early 20th-century reel case. The case is made from leather and has red velvet lining.
• £145 • The Reel Thing

△ Brown Hunting Hat

• *circa 1920*
Brown linen hunting hat with a leather lining and the maker's inscription in gold lettering 'by S. H. Batcha & Sons, Moore Market, Madras'.
• *width 34cm*
• £60 • Sporting Times

△ Farlows Spring Balance

• *circa 1920*
Farlows spring balance. Metric and imperial scales up to 100lbs and measuring 9 inches. Made in London.
• £95 • The Reel Thing

▽ Hardy Neroda Case

• *circa 1925*
Large. Brass fittings. Metal liner with hooks to hang flies. Tortoiseshell and bakelite.
• £195 • The Reel Thing

▽ Hardy Allinone

• *1925*
An early 20th-century fisherman's companion from Hardy Neroda, containing a brass weighing measure. The item incorporates various pouches.
• £495 • The Reel Thing

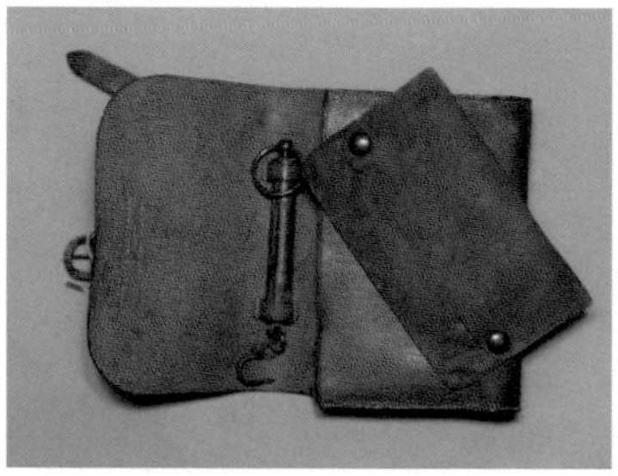

▽ Starback Fishing Reel

• *circa 1920–40*
Starback wood fishing reel with turned decoration and brass fittings.
• *diameter 12cm*
• £55 • Sporting Times

◁ Wooden Reels

• *circa 1920*
Two wooden fly-fishing reels with brass cross backs.
• *9cm (left), 9cm (right)*
• £45–90 • Henry Gregory

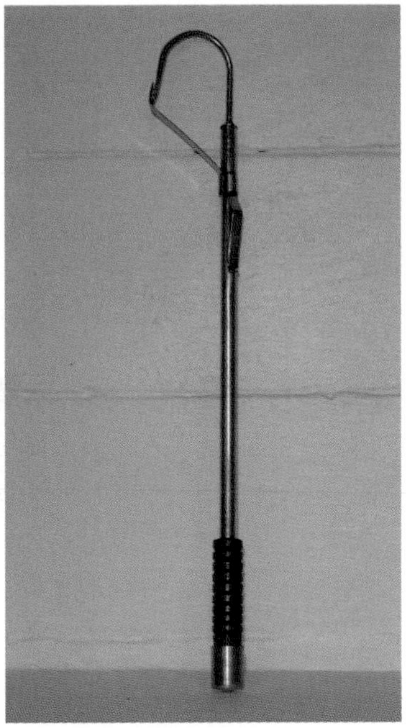

△ Brass Telescopic Gaff

- *circa 1920*

Brass telescopic gaff with turned wooden handle.

- *length 61cm*
- £120 • Sporting Times

△ John Macpherson Reel

- *1930*

John Macpherson bakelite reel with original box, by Allcock & Co.

- *diameter 9cm*
- £95 • The Reel Thing

▷ Hardy 'St George'

- *circa 1932*

Hardy 'St George' 3⅜ inch. Brass and metal components. A gate line guard.

- £295 • The Reel Thing

△ Fly Wallet

- *1930*

Pigskin fly wallet with leather strap, in excellent original condition.

- *length 18cm*
- £280 • The Reel Thing

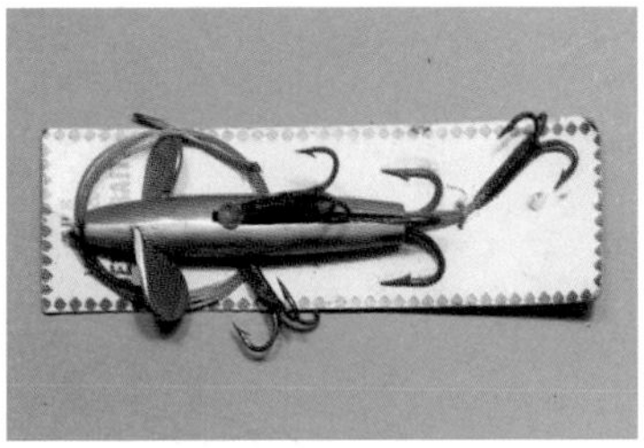

△ Devon Bait Lure

- *circa 1930*

Artificial bait lure, with four triple hooks, manufactured by Devon. With original case.

- £40 • The Reel Thing

△ Fishing Basket

- *circa 1940*

Fine split-reed fishing basket with leather carrying strap and buckle fasteners, on circular legs with a canvas strap.

- *35cm x 42cm*
- £65 • Old School

◁ English Line Dry

- *1990*

An English mahogany Line Dry with bone handle.

- *height 32cm*
- £288 • The Reel Thing

▽ The Dry Fly Dresser

- *circa 1930*

Used as a line dryer. Made by Hardy Brothers Ltd.

- £75 • The Reel Thing

▽ Hardy Fishing Lure

- *circa 1940*

An unused 'Jock Scott' lure, manufactured by Hardy for sea angling.

- £60 • The Reel Thing

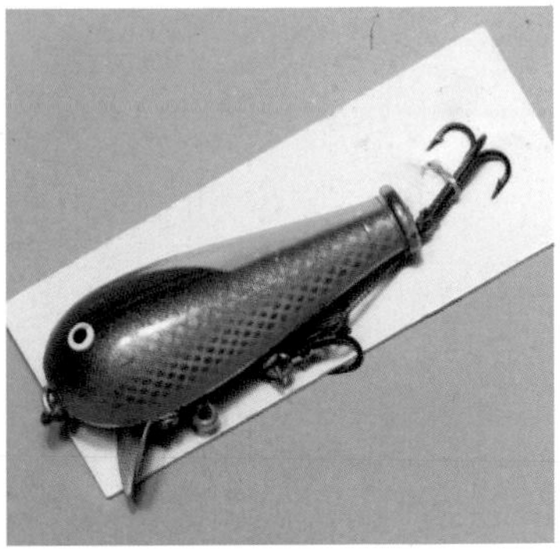

▽ Angler's Knife

- *mid-20th century*

Unnamed angler's knife with six attachments including scissors in steel and brass. Sideplates marked with imperial scale 1–3 inches.

- £245 • The Reel Thing

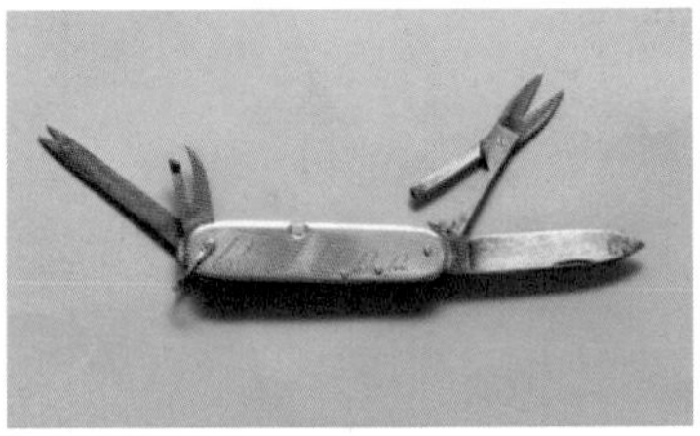

△ Fishing Priest

- *circa 1940*

A fishing priest of antler horn, with leather strap.

- £85 • The Reel Thing

▽ Fly Rod

- *1975*

Hardy 'Palakona' fly fishing rod. Split-cane, 7 feet 2 inches with canvas sleeve.

- £500 • The Reel Thing

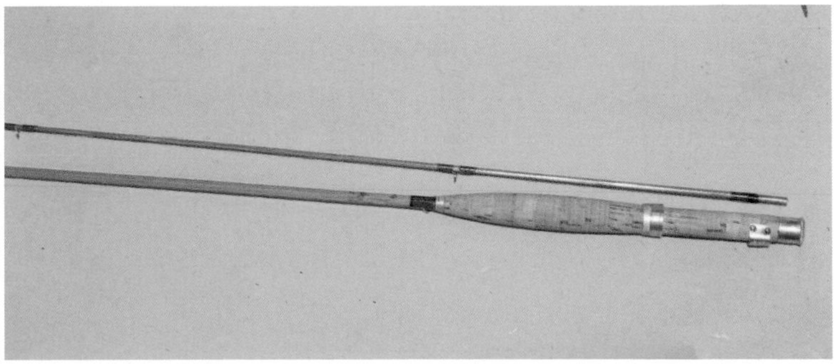

SHOOTING

▽ Pistol

• *circa 1840*

Flintlock percussion double-barrel pistol with back-action locks, engraved lockplates and trigger guards.

• *25cm x 10cm*

• £430 • H. & H.

▽ Magazine Box

• *circa 1890*

Leather magazine box with strap, buckle and a lock, by James MacNaughton, Gun and Rifle Maker, Edinburgh.

• *23cm x 24cm*

• £650 • H. & H.

▽ Spoon Warmer

• *circa 1880*

A Victorian Scottish Britannia metal spoon warmer, with a removable brass screw handle resting on a stylised rock base.

• *29cm x 14cm*

• £510 • H. & H.

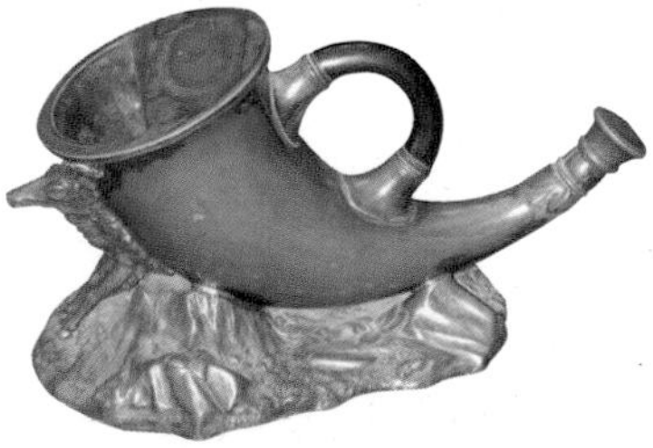

▷ Hunting Items

• *circa 1920*

Canvas game bag, silver-topped flask in leather case, deer-hoof walking stick, and game carrier.

• £95 game bag

• £245 flask

• £65 deer stick

• £130 carrier • Sean Arnold

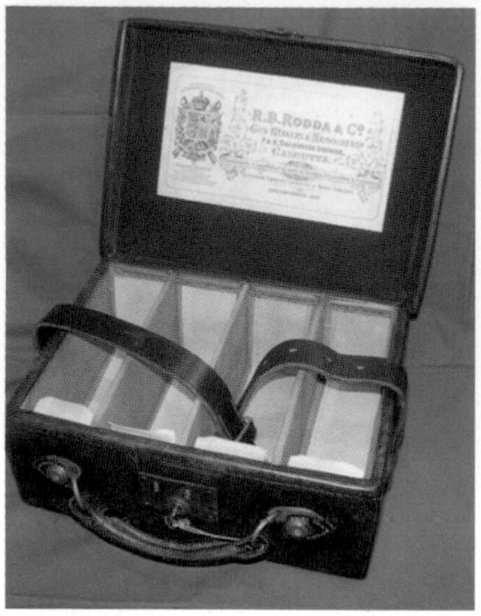

△ Cartridge Case

• *circa 1880*

Leather cartridge case for 250 cartridges with strap and key. R. B. Rodda & Co., Gun Makers and Armourers, 7–8 Dalhousie Square, Calcutta.

• £795 • The Reel Thing

△ Crocodile-Skin Rifle Case

• *circa 1925*

Crocodile-skin rifle case with leather straps and handle. By Manton and Co., Delhi & Calcutta, India.

• *76cm x 18cm*

• £1,200 • H. & H.

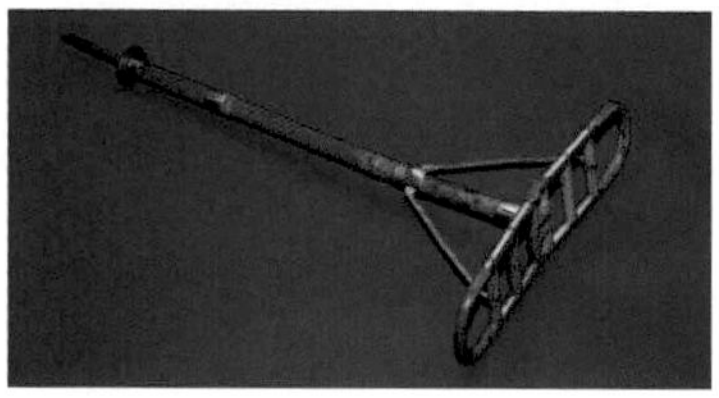

△ Shooting Stick

• *circa 1900*

Gentleman's shooting stick with malacca cane and bamboo seat. Folding seat with handsome brass mounts.

• *height 68cm*

• £215 • Sean Arnold

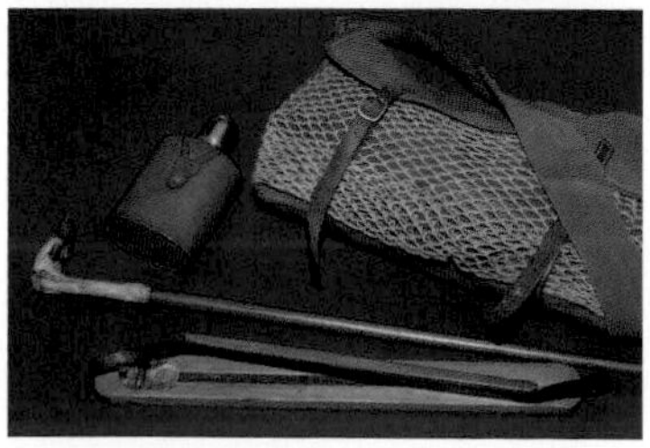

▽ Leather Gun Case

• *circa 1860*

A leg-of-mutton leather gun case, with brass fittings and a leather shoulder strap.

• *80cm x 26cm x 6cm*

• £260 • Henry Gregory

▽ Duck Decoy

• *circa 1890*

Vintage duck decoy. Painted in natural colourings.

• £295 • The Reel Thing

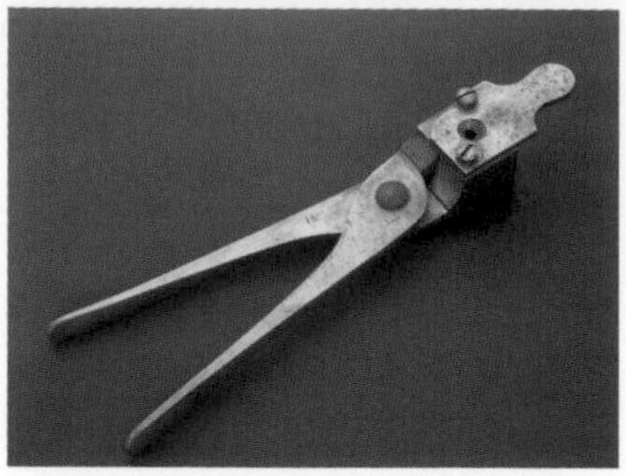

△ Bullet Mould

• *circa 1895*

16-bore brass bullet mould. Paradox stock.

• *27cm x 8cm*

• £550 • H. & H.

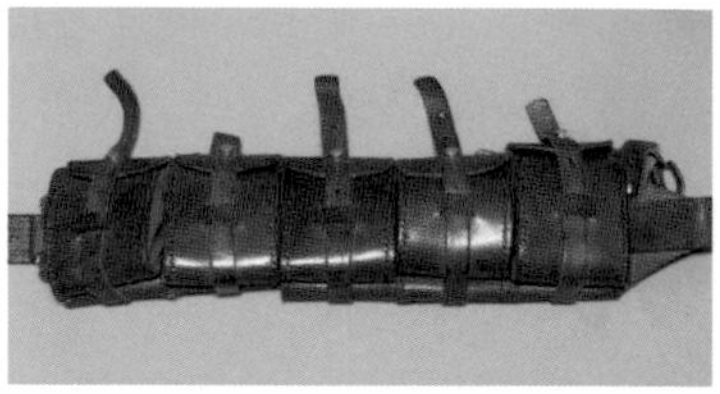

△ Ammunition Pouch

• *circa 1920*

Leather ammunition ten-pouch belt with well-preserved and polished leather pouches and straps and brass mounts. In good condition.

• £75 • The Reel Thing

▽ Rifle of .240 Calibre

• *1927*

Gun of .240 calibre with a 22.5-inch barrel and mahogany stock and telescopic sight. Of best quality.

• £5,000 • H. & H.

△ Rifle of .375 Calibre

• *1926*

Original Mauser bolt action, 24-inch barrel. With Q/D mounts and peep sight to bolt head.

• £5,250 • H. & H.

△ Leather Gun Case

• *circa 1930*
Single oak and leather gun case, with red base interior and leather straps. Brass mounts with carrying handle. Various compartments.
• £1,250 • H. & H.

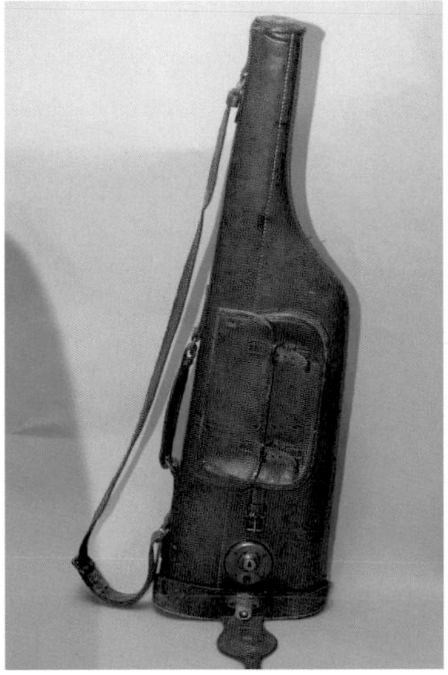

△ Gun Case

• *circa 1930*
Leg-of-mutton gun case. Brass fittings. Cogswell and Harrison. Six compartments with leather pull straps.
• £375–425 • The Reel Thing

△ Decoy Duck

• *1940s–50s*
Mid-20th-century vintage duck decoy. Made from applewood. With painted highlights and realistic colouring.
• £225 • The Reel Thing

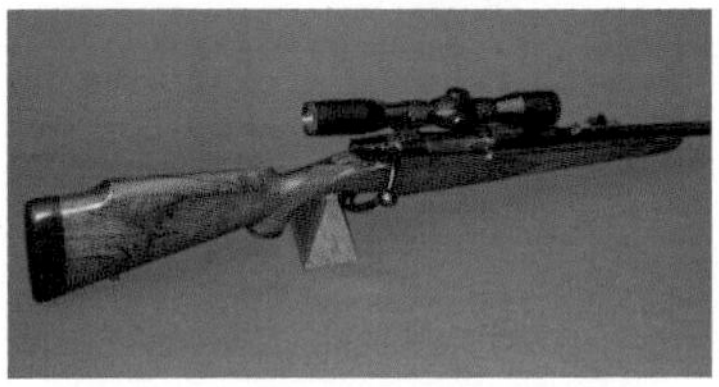

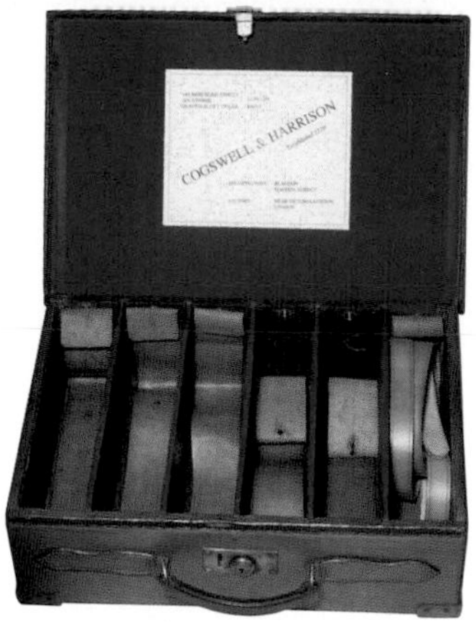

△ Magazine Case

• *circa 1930*
Leather magazine case with brass fittings. Cogswell and Harrison. Six compartments with leather pull straps.
• £750 • The Reel Thing

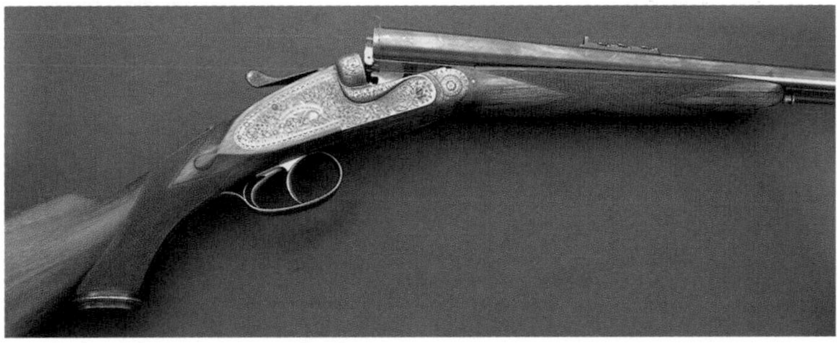

▽ Shooting Bag

• *circa 1950*
Canocs leather and net shooting bag with leather strap.
• £175 • The Reel Thing

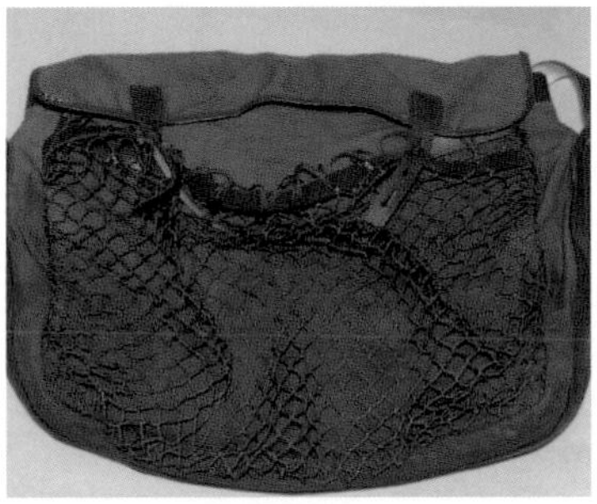

◁ Magazine Rifle

• *1975*
Excellent quality Holland & Holland 7mm-calibre magazine rifle, with telescopic sight.
• *length 64cm*
• £7,000 • H. & H.

△ Canochy Cartridge Loader

• *1930*
Canochy cartridge loader encased in leather with a leather strap.
• *diameter 15cm*
• £1,500 • H. & H.

△ Double-Barrel Hunting Rifle

• *1949*
A 300-calibre Flanged Dominion double-barrel hunting rifle, by Holland and Holland.
• *length 71cm*
• £19,750 • H. & H.

△ Royal Rifle

• *1945*
Model 300 back-action double rifle.
• *length 1.14m*
• £32,000 • H. & H.

▽ 20-Bore Shotgun

• *2001*
Holland & Holland sporting over and under 20-bore single-trigger shotgun.
• *length 115cm*
• £25,000 • H. & H.

▽ Dominion .300 Rifle

• *1935*
Dominion .300 gun, back action double rifle. Rubber pad, shoulder strap fittings and 25-inch barrels.
• £19,000 • H. & H.

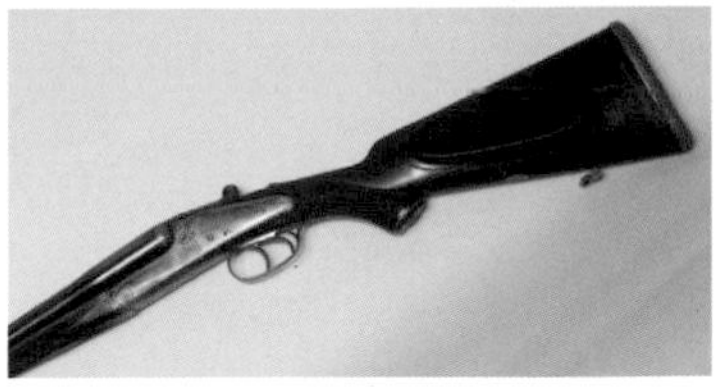

▽ Badminton Shotgun

• *1937*
Holland & Holland Badminton model 12-bore side-by-side shotgun.
• *length 71cm*
• £14,000 • H. & H.

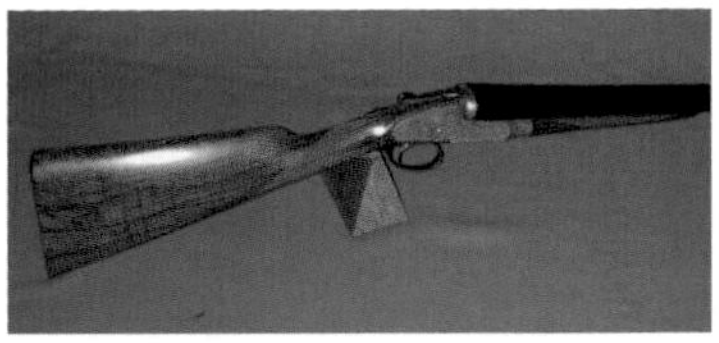

▽ 12-bore Self Opener

• *1960*
12-bore Royal self opener with 26.5-inch barrel with double trigger. Stock and fore. Superb walnut finish.
• £18,000 • H. & H.

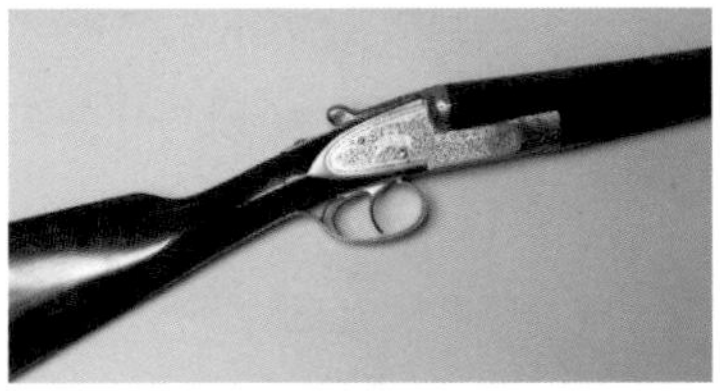

▽ Pair of 12-bore Guns

• *1978*
One of a pair of Royal Deluxe guns with acanthus-leaf and game scene engraving. Single trigger.
• £54,000 • H. & H.

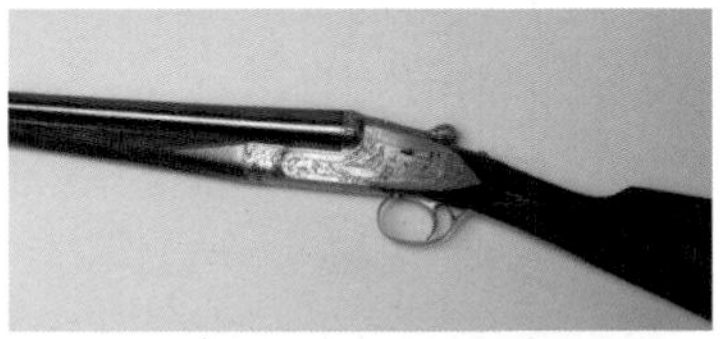

TAXIDERMY

The art of taxidermy as a technique for keeping animals, birds, insects and fish in a preserved state is of great importance to the scientist, academic researcher and sportsman alike. Taxidermy has always been a popular and desirable way of preserving a trophy, especially at the turn of the century when big game was hunted in Africa and India. Nowadays, however, it is more usual to find a smaller stuffed animal, such as your Aunt Betty's favourite dog, than to find a large stuffed lion in someone's house. These wilder and more exotic animals can now be found decorating a film set or photo shoot, where they are being used more and more, not only because they don't move, but also because it is a lot safer and cheaper than working with the real thing. In the past, before the advent of photography and television, most people would not have known what a polar bear, tiger or chameleon looked like, except from drawings or paintings. Taxidermy is also an important way to preserve examples of species that are heading for extinction. For most people in the past, travel was very limited, if not impossible, so the work of the taxidermist became an important means for people to view the natural world around them at museums, where these creatures would be displayed.

△ **Bird Collection**

- *circa 1880*

Victorian oval glass dome with a display of ten South American birds, perched on branches.

- *height 53cm*
- £375 • Get Stuffed

▽ **Zebra**

- *circa 1900*

A mounted zebra head with a fine expression, preserved in England.

- *height 1.2m*
- £475 • Tredantiques

▽ **Polar Bear Skin Rug**

- *circa 1920*

A Canadian polar bear skin rug, well preserved, with a fearsome expression.

- *2.85m*
- £2,500 • John Clay

▷ **Peacock**

- *20th century*

A peacock, shown with tail closed, set on a square base.

- *height 1.8m*
- £395 • Get Stuffed

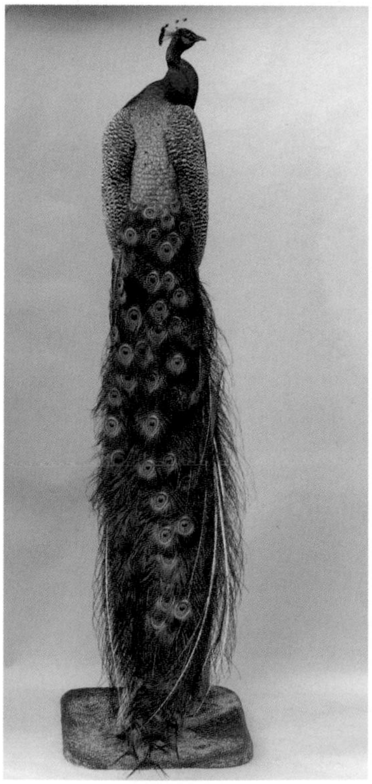

△ Lizard

• *20th century*
Egyptian monitor lizard modelled in an alert posture.
• *length 1.0m*
• **£375** • **Get Stuffed**

△ Sparrow Hawk

• *20th century*
Sparrow hawk with wings spread, mounted on a branch set on a polished wood base.
• *height 61cm*
• **£195** • **Get Stuffed**

△ Rabbit

• *20th century*
White rabbit modelled on the theme of *Alice in Wonderland*.
• *height 48cm*
• **£190** • **Get Stuffed**

▽ Butterfly Collection

• *20th century*
A collection of nine South American butterflies, mounted in a display case.
• *height 31cm*
• **£65** • **Get Stuffed**

▽ Blackbird

• *20th century*
Blackbird traditionally perched upon a branch, with oval wood base.
• *height 27cm*
• **£95** • **Get Stuffed**

▽ Mallard

• *20th century*
Two male mallards, one shown standing and the other recumbent.
• *40cm x 64cm*
• **£295** • **Get Stuffed**

▽ Hedgehog

• *20th century*
Adult hedgehog on all fours, mounted on wooden base.
• *height 15cm*
• **£125** • **Get Stuffed**

▽ Red Fox

• *20th century*
Adult European Red Fox standing naturalistically on all fours, without a base.
• *height 51cm*
• **£200** • **Get Stuffed**

▽ Roach

• *1996*
Roach in a bow-fronted case with natural grasses and weeds, with gilt lettering documenting the catch.
• *32cm x 50cm*
• **£385** • **Get Stuffed**

▷ Crowned Crane

• *20th century*
African crowned crane shown on an oval base.
• *height 1.03m*
• **£295** • **Get Stuffed**

△ Mongrel Dog

• *20th century*
Naturalistically seated mongrel dog shown in an alert pose.
• *height 62cm*
• **£295** • **Get Stuffed**

▷ Display Case

• *20th century*
A South American spider and insect, mounted in display case.
• *length 40cm*
• £75 • Get Stuffed

△ Albino Cobra

• *20th century*
An albino cobra shown in an aggressive pose.
• *60cm x 28cm*
• £195 • Get Stuffed

△ Ginger Cat

• *20th century*
Naturalistically posed ginger cat shown curled up and asleep.
• *width 33cm*
• £295 • Get Stuffed

▽ Chameleon

• *20th century*
Chameleon with a curious expression shown with branch.
• *23cm x 38cm*
• £175 • Get Stuffed

▽ Barn Owl

• *20th century*
Barn owl with outstretched wings shown posed on a branch on a polished wood base.
• *height 68cm*
• £390 • Get Stuffed

◁ Bush Baby

• *20th century*
Bush baby in good condition, naturalistically posed within the branches of a tree.
• *60cm x 54cm*
• £195 • Get Stuffed

▽ Bullfrog

• *20th century*
Bullfrog skeleton in sections with documentation.
• *30cm x 40cm*
• £140 • Get Stuffed

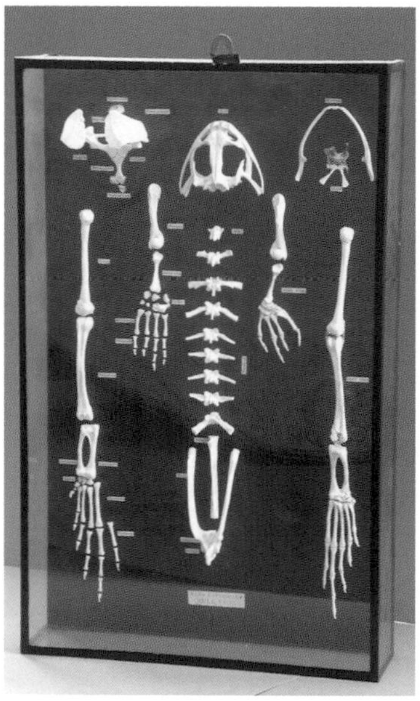

▽ Mouse

• *20th century*
Mouse shown on hind legs with forearms raised, posed on a red apple.
• *height 13cm*
• £75 • Get Stuffed

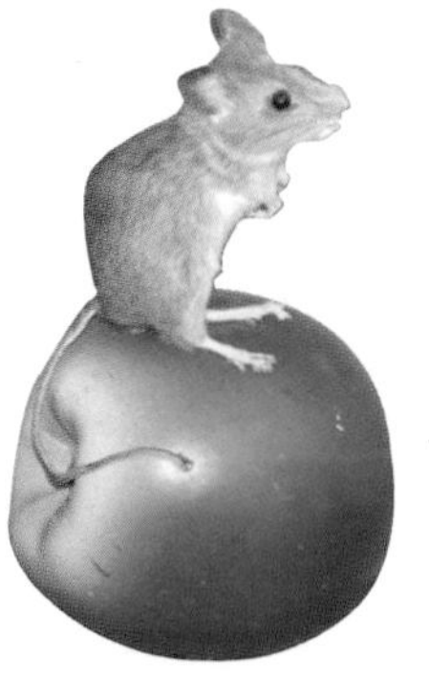

▽ Doves

• *20th century*
Pair of doves naturalistically posed, on a mahogany base with foliate decoration. (With glass dome supplied).
• *height 43cm*
• £350 • Get Stuffed

▽ Eagle Owl

• *20th century*
Eagle owl mounted on a tree stump on an oval wood base.
• *height 59cm*
• £260 • Get Stuffed

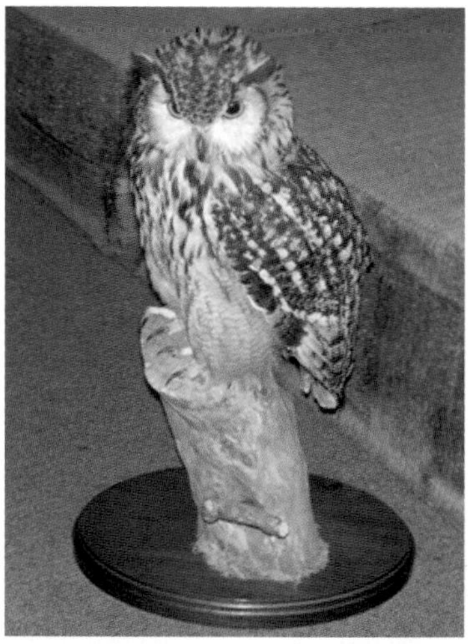

▽ Pelican

• *20th century*
Pelican shown standing with open beak.
• *95cm x 63cm*
• £75 • Get Stuffed

▽ Rooster

- *20th century*

Magnificent rooster naturalistically posed in crowing position, without a base.

- *height 57cm*
- £245 • Get Stuffed

▽ Rudd

- *20th century*

A rudd displayed in a bow-fronted case decorated with vegetation.

- *length 48cm*
- £475 • Get Stuffed

▽ Hooded Crow

- *20th century*

Hooded crow shown perched on a branch and mounted on a plinth base.

- *57cm x 28cm*
- £125 • Get Stuffed

▷ Tortoise

- *20th century*

An adult leopard tortoise with finely preserved shell.

- *height 16cm*
- £185 • Get Stuffed

△ Mallard Drake

- *20th century*

Mallard drake shown with wings outstretched, mounted on a base.

- *height 45cm*
- £195 • Get Stuffed

△ Dog

- *20th century*

Lhasa Apso Tibetan dog on all fours, with attentive expression.

- *height 36cm*
- £425 • Get Stuffed

△ Grey Rabbit

- *20th century*

Adult grey rabbit with white tail, shown in an alert pose.

- *height 25cm*
- £125 • Get Stuffed

▽ Rat

- *20th century*

A rat shown on hind legs with forearms raised.

- *length 20cm*
- £95 • Get Stuffed

▽ Chameleon

- *20th century*

African chameleon shown with its tail coiled around a branch, on an oval wood base.

- *height 33cm*
- £175 • Get Stuffed

▽ Armadillo

- *20th century*

Adult armadillo on all fours.

- *length 65cm*
- £240 • Get Stuffed

△ Amazon Parrots

- *20th century*

Two Amazon parrots, theatrically mounted on a branch.

- *55cm x 32cm*
- £195 • Get Stuffed

△ Magpie

- *20th century*

Magpie perched on a wooden branch and mounted on a mahogany base.

- *52cm x 32cm*
- £95 • Get Stuffed

△ Yorkshire Terrier

- *20th century*

Yorkshire terrier seated with a curious expression and a red ribbon.

- *30cm x 20cm*
- £245 • Get Stuffed

TEXTILES & FANS

The interest in textiles has increased considerably in the past few years. They are not only popular because of their decorative appeal, they also give us an insight into history and the lives of the women who created them, from those who sewed for necessity, for example making clothes and bed covers, to those ladies of leisure who occupied their days at embroidery or needlepoint for cushion covers, fire screens and wall tapestries. Samplers were originally used as a reference for stitch patterns, which could then be copied. Later they were used to record a child's name and age, houses, gardens, animals or plants. The earliest English sampler known dates back to 1598, and is on display in the Victoria and Albert Museum in London, among a large selection of textiles and tapestries. Patchwork quilts have a traditional quality, some come with geometric designs, while others have highly elaborate patterns. Costumes from the eighteenth century have always been highly collectable and popular items include jackets, hats, dresses and gloves. The market for vintage costumes has greatly expanded recently as modern designers dip into the past to create the fashion of today. Some vintage 1950s' dresses by top designers are having a renaissance and this is further enhanced by their popularity amongst Hollywood film stars at award ceremonies.

△ **Bird Tapestry**

- *16th century*

Feuilles de Choux tapestry panel with a broad design of a bird among foliage.

- *2.26m x 35cm*
- £4,800 • Marilyn Garrow

▽ **Hanging Fragment**

- *17th century*

A fragment of a hanging – Portuguese or Italian – with canvas work on silk, showing oversized birds and flowers.

- £4,000 • Marilyn Garrow

◁ **Beauvais Tapestry**

- *17th century*

Beauvais tapestry with a broad design of white and red flowers, with green foliage on a cream background.

- *36cm x 49cm*
- £2,200 • Marilyn Garrow

▽ **Armorial Tapestry**

- *17th century*

An Italian bishop's armorial tapestry, embroidered with gold on a crimson background.

- *40cm x 42cm*
- £1,500 • Marilyn Garrow

◁ **Hunting Scene Tapestry**

- *17th century*

Tapestry portraying a hunting scene in a wood, showing a horseman with footman and a dog in the foreground.

- *width 75cm*
- £3,800 • Marilyn Garrow

▽ Cromwellian Needlework Panel

- *circa 1650*

Cromwellian-period needlework panel depicting King Solomon and the Queen of Sheba with attendants.

- *32cm x 28cm*
- £8,500 • Midwinter

▽ French Louis XIV Needlepoint

- *circa 1670*

French Louis XIV needlepoint panel showing a mythological scene with Neptune, romantic figures and animals in an Arcadian setting.

- *32cm x 30cm*
- £4,000 • Marilyn Garrow

▷ Embroidered Panel

- *circa 1725*

A canvas-work embroidered panel showing classical vase with flowers on a red ground.

- *height 72cm*
- £4,500 • Marilyn Garrow

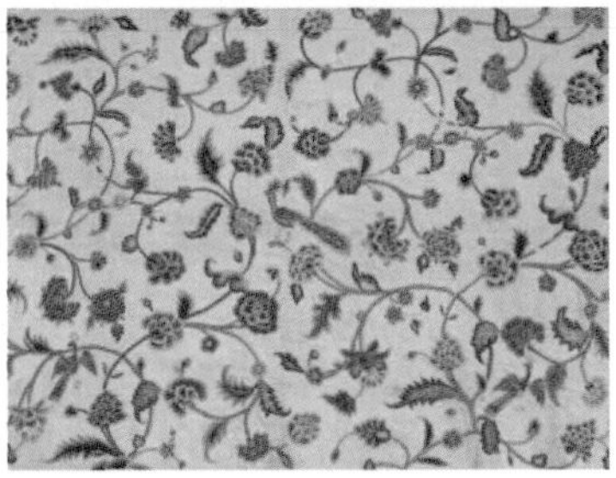

△ Georgian Pillow Case

- *circa 1720*

Exquisite Georgian pillow case with foliate design from eighteenth century.

- *60cm x 40cm*
- £9,500 • Marilyn Garrow

△ English Cushions

- *circa 1750*

One of a pair of English, 18th-century crewelwork cushions, with stylised floral decoration on a white ground. With generous fringe.

- £350 • Marilyn Garrow

◁ Crewelwork Hanging

- *circa 1680*

A pair of 'Tree of Life' wall hangings showing animals, birds and exotic flowers.

- *height 1.75m*
- £10,000 • Marilyn Garrow

▽ European Embroideries

- *circa 1690–1720*

A pair of embroideries – European, probably German – in chinoiserie style.

- *height 1.85m*
- £7,000 • Marilyn Garrow

▽ Part of Bed Hanging

- *circa 1775*

Strong, polychrome silks and gold thread with swirled floral design and frieze.

- *length 1.3m*
- £4,500 • Marilyn Garrow

△ Italian Frontpiece

- *17th century*

Framed Italian tabernacle frontpiece with religious scenes of Catholic origin.

- £900 • Marilyn Garrow

△ Embroidered Purse

- *circa 1740*

Small lady's Georgian silk purse with red flowers and green foliage.

- *width 12cm*
- £450 • Marilyn Garrow

△ Georgian Silk Purse

- *1740*

Georgian silk purse embroidered with gold silk ribboning and foliate designs.

- *width 15cm*
- £450 • Marilyn Garrow

△ French Cushion

• *18th century*
A French cushion, filled with down and fine feather, with silver and gold thread interlacing among floral designs of pink and blue, with roses.
• £1,200 • **Marilyn Garrow**

◁ Silkwork Picture

• *1785*
A late 18th-century silkwork picture, worked by ten-year-old Mary Philcox, showing roses, bluebells and honeysuckle. Oval in form and gilt-framed.
• *height 55cm*
• £1,200 • **Marilyn Garrow**

△ Four Panels

• *18th century*
Four panels in blue, pink, green and yellow silk, rectangular in shape, with sloping shoulders, showing geometric maze patterns.
• *height 1.64m*
• £10,000 • **Marilyn Garrow**

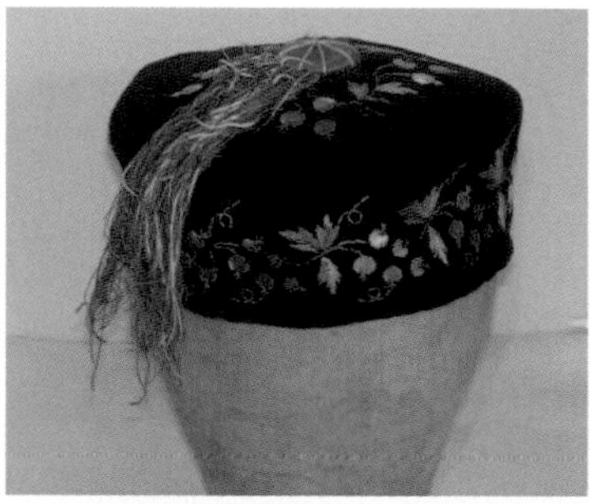

▷ Gentleman's Smoking Hat

• *circa 1880*
Black velvet gentleman's smoking hat with trailing foliate designs of pink and blue flowers, surmounted by a red satin-covered button on the top with a trailing green, white and red tassel.
• *size 6*
• £110 • **Sheila Cook**

△ Slipper Pattern

• *circa 1850*
Unused beaded slipper 'cut out' pattern, with turquoise background, pink and yellow flowers and two deer by a river.
• *length 22cm*
• £225 • **Sheila Cook**

△ Mandarin Fan

• *circa 1820*
An ivory and sandalwood fan with silver-gilt, enamel and mother-of-pearl sticks.
• *length 53cm*
• £2,000 • **Brandt**

▽ Mandarin Fan

• *circa 1830*
A Chinese fan with ivory sticks in natural and red and showing a mandarin in silk robes, with parallel panels of river views.
• *length 50cm*
• £1,000 • **Brandt**

△ Ivory Fan

• *circa 1820*
Chinese ivory filigree fan, for export to Europe, with armorial crest and pierced decoration.
• *length 41cm*
• £1,200 • **Brandt**

▷ Silk Smoking Hat

• *circa 1870*
Brown silk smoking hat with trailing foliate embroidery of small white flowers.
• *size 6*
• £125 • **Sheila Cook**

△ Cream Child's Dress

• *circa 1880*
Cream cotton child's dress with lace trim and navy-blue ribboning on the hips and collar.
• *small*
• £265 • Sheila Cook

△ Textile Block

• *20th century*
Carved wooden textile printing block in pseudo-Japanese script pattern design.
• *30cm x 26cm*
• £250 • Zakheim

△ Straw Hat

• *circa 1935*
Black straw hat by Wooland Brothers, trimmed with two large beige flowers. Crown decorated with top-stitching.
• £48 • Sheila Cook

▽ Beaded Armorial Design

• *1880*
Beaded armorial design on a turquoise background with a stylised fleur-de-lys surrounded by gold thistles, within a floral border.
• *75cm x 55cm*
• £750 • Sheila Cook

▽ Gold Bolero

• *circa 1900*
A fine, handmade golden-braided Greek bolero, of circular design, set on red satin and lined with cream satin.
• *UK size 12*
• £145 • Sheila Cook

▽ Ivory Fan

• *circa 1904*
Cream silk fan with a trailing design of pink and yellow apple blossom mounted on carved ivory spines.
• *length 35cm*
• £125 • Sheila Cook

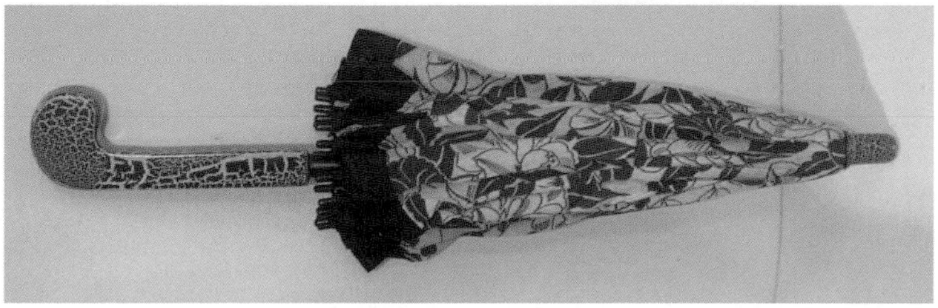

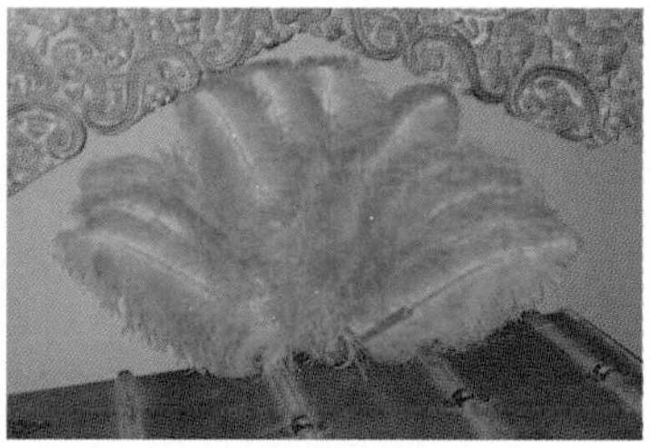

△ Pink Ostrich Fan

• *circa 1900*
A bright pink ostrich feather fan with tortoiseshell sticks. Provenance: Princess Marie Maximilianova of Lichtenberg (1841–1911).
• £750 • Zakheim

△ Cushion

• *circa 1930*
Cushion with stylised prince and princess, of embroidered canvas on satin.
• £65 • Tin Tin

◁ Lady's Parasol

• *circa 1920*
Lady's parasol with a black floral design and a handle with a black and beige geometric pattern.
• *length 53cm*
• £95 • Sheila Cook

▽ Royal Feather Fan

• *circa 1900*
Feather fan with tortoiseshell sticks applied with the gold Royal cypher of Princess Marie Maximilianova of Lichtenberg (1841–1911).
• £850 • Zakheim

▽ Japanese Fan

• *circa 1900*
Japanese ivory fan with a finely handpainted watercolour of water and mountains.
• *width 28cm*
• £555 • Japanese Gallery

◁ Georgette

• *circa 1935*
A black, floral-patterned, silk georgette with stitched bust with square collar at the back and matching silk scarf.
• *size 10*
• £295 • Sheila Cook

△ Patchwork Quilt

• *circa 1950*
Patchwork quilt with a bold, multi-coloured and patterned, geometric design.
• *1.6m x 1.56m*
• £195 • Sheila Cook

TOOLS

A good starting point for those interested in building a collection is tools, as their prices are reasonable, and in the future these items will prove to be of great historical importance. In recent years there has been a marked interest in early blacksmith tools such as hammers and anvils, along with early scientific tools. Increasingly we see lawnmowers, sprayers, garden edgers and agricultural tools coming into this expanding and popular market. Carts, wheelbarrows, and wheelwright's tools are also finding collectors. The most popular tools tend to be connected with the cabinet-making or joinery trades, good examples being box planes and chisels. It is the skill of the historical craftsman's hand that makes these simple, yet effective tools so desirable. In fact, this interest in tools of the past is currently being energised by the onslaught of petrol-powered lawn mowers, electric hedge clippers and other powered gadgets that now cover the shelves in our local DIY stores.

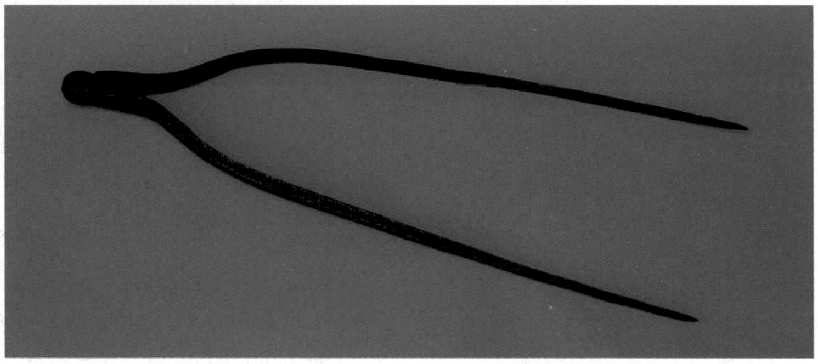

△ Dividers

- *17th century*

Large pair of English dividers for transferring measurements to substantial items of furniture.

- *length 62cm*
- £280 • Old Tool Chest

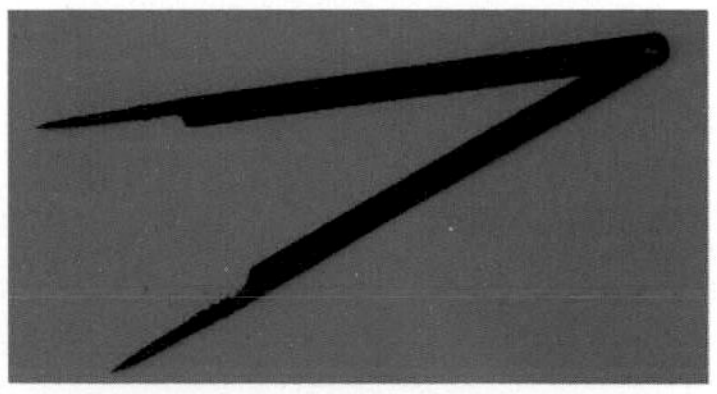

▽ Dividers

- *circa early 18th century*

Set of French cabinet-maker's dividers used for transferring measurement from plans to the workbench.

- *length 37cm*
- £350 • Old Tool Chest

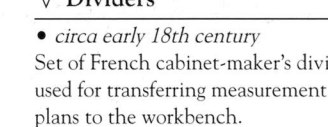

◁ Cooper's Anvil

- *circa 1680*

A very fine French late 17th-century anvil, fashioned in cast iron and used in the manufacture of hammered iron bandings for barrels.

- *height 94cm*
- £950 • Old Tool Chest

▽ Oak Router

- *circa 1760*

Oak router with rosewood wedge, carved in the form of three turrets with beautiful patina.

- *width 17.5cm*
- £480 • Tool Shop Auctions

▽ Brace

- *circa 1780*

Late 18th-century brace, made by John Green, with brass chuck.

- *length 36cm*
- £140 • The Old Tool Chest

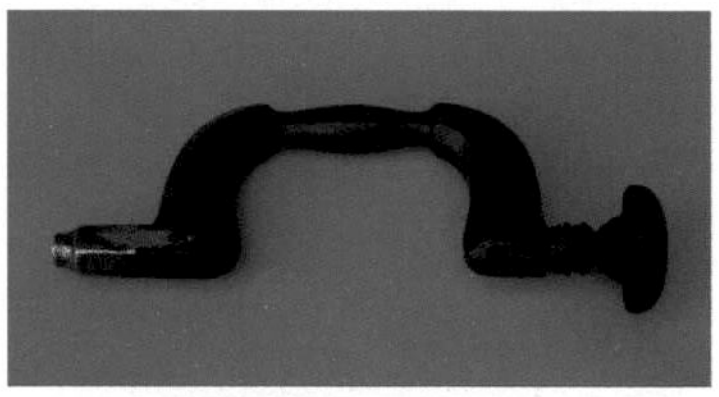

▽ Mortise Chisel

- *circa 1780*

A stonemason's mortise chisel for use in precision recessing.

- *length 33.5cm*
- £40 • Old Tool Chest

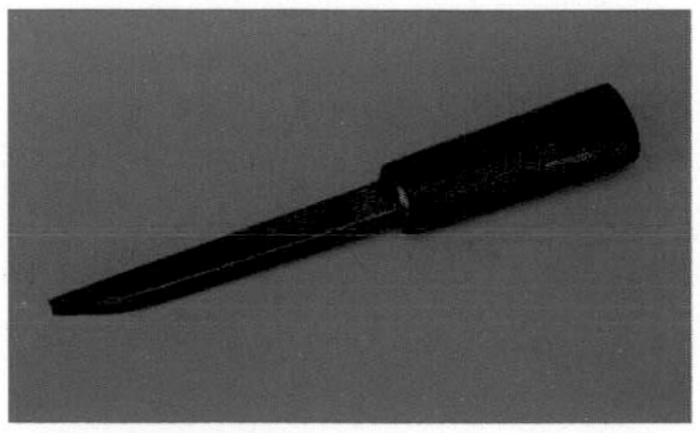

◁ Sliding Bevel

- *1777*

Brass and mahogany sliding bevel dated 1777.

- *length 17.5cm*
- £160 • Tool Shop Auctions

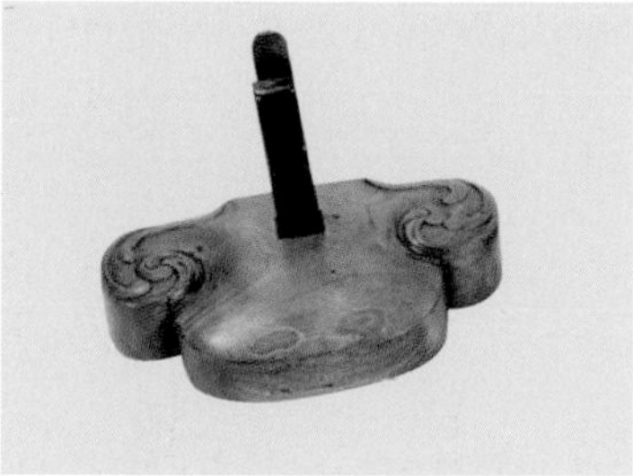

△ Carved Router

- *1780*

European fruitwood carved router with figured rosewood wedge.

- *width 15cm*
- £50 • **Tool Shop Auctions**

△ Dado Plane

- *circa 1780*

An 18th-century English dado plane, by the celebrated manufacturer John Green.

- *length 24cm*
- £24 • **Old Tool Chest**

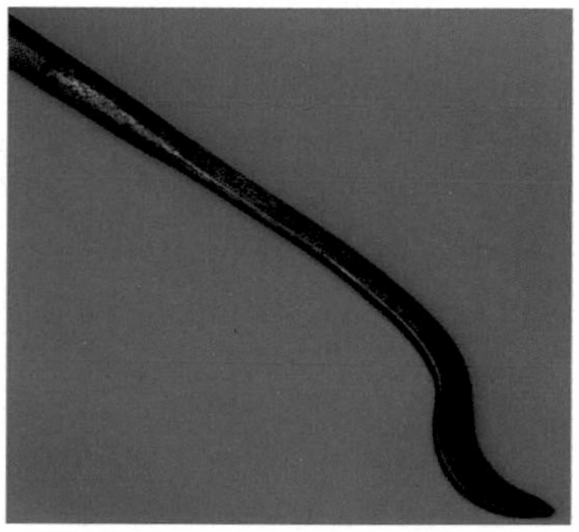

△ Swan-Neck Mortise Chisel

- *circa 1840*

A 19th-century, swan-necked mortise chisel for use in precision cutting of slots or recesses in wood for the receipt of the tenon in a mortise and tenon joint.

- *length 55cm*
- £38 • **Old Tool Chest**

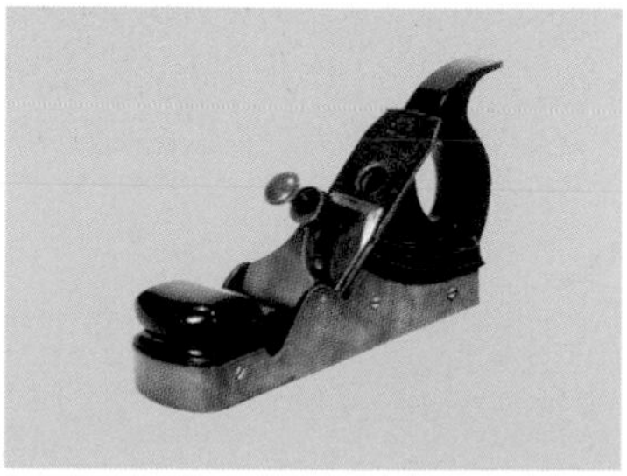

▽ Badger Plane

- *circa 1790*

Large wooden 'badger' plane, for planing into corners by John Green, a famous tool-maker of the late 18th/early 19th century.

- *length 33cm*
- £250 • **Old Tool Chest**

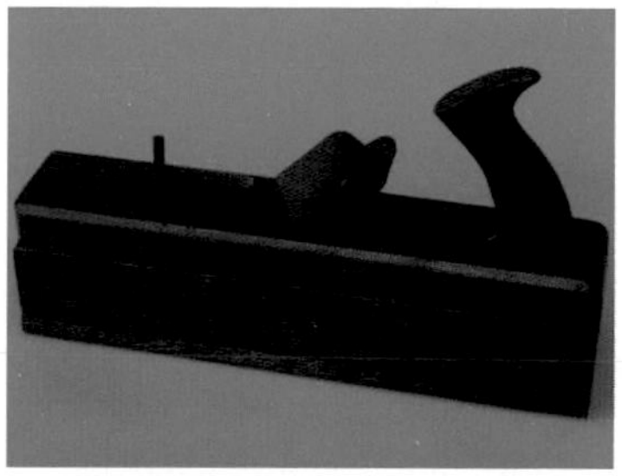

▽ Boot Scraper

- *circa 1800*

Dual-purpose boot scraper which can either be used in the hand to remove mud from boots, or dug into the ground for scraping soles.

- *length 53cm*
- £75 • **Old Tool Chest**

▽ Lady's Brace

- *1860*

A beech lady's brace with cocobolo head.

- *length 27.5cm*
- £75 • **Tool Shop Auctions**

◁ Scottish Smoothing Plane

- *1860*

Stylish Scottish iron smoothing plane with walnut overstuffing, cove front and moulded infill at the rear.

- *length 22cm*
- £280 • **Tool Shop Auctions**

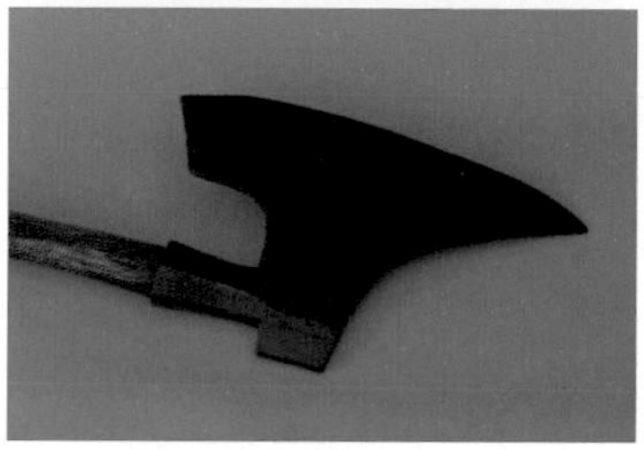

△ Austrian Sideaxe

- *circa 1820*

An early 19th-century Austrian sideaxe, cast in iron with a beechwood haft, used for forestry and related occupations.

- *length 65cm*
- £475 • **Old Tool Chest**

△ Rounding Plane

- *circa 1850*

A rounding plane with original locking plates. Curved both ways, for use by a cooper or coach-maker.

- *length 28cm*
- £130 • **Old Tool Chest**

△ Tinsmith's Shears

- *circa 1800*

Cast-iron shears.

- *length 61cm*
- £38 • **Old Tool Chest**

▽ Brace

- *circa 1830*

An ebony brace with steel chuck with the bit as a permanent feature, dating from the early 19th century, for use in the coopering trade.

- *length 40cm*
- £85 • **Old Tool Chest**

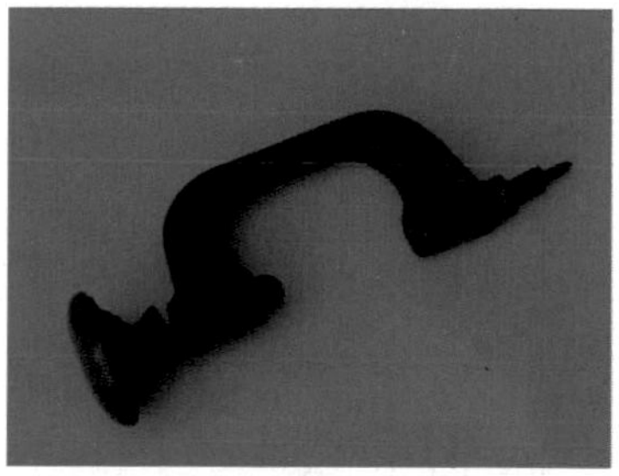

▽ Mandrel Lathe

- *circa 19th century*

Hand-driven, for making pocket-watch parts. Comprising cross slide, T-rest and centre. Of brass, steel and wood.

- *height 27cm*
- £1,000 • **Aubrey Brocklehurst**

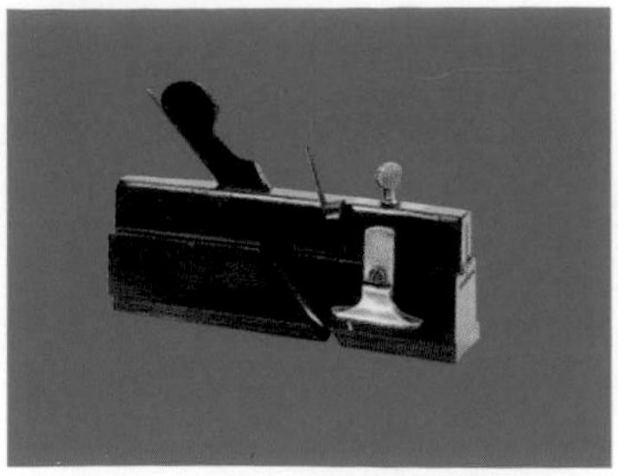

△ Moving Fillister

- *1870*

A moving fillister plane in solid Brazilian rosewood with brass fittings and boxwood stem wedges.

- *length 25cm*
- £180 • Tool Shop Auctions

△ Sash Fillister

- *1870*

Rare Victorian beautifully crafted sash fillister in solid Brazilian rosewood with brass fittings and boxwood stem wedges.

- *length 25cm*
- £400 • Tool Shop Auctions

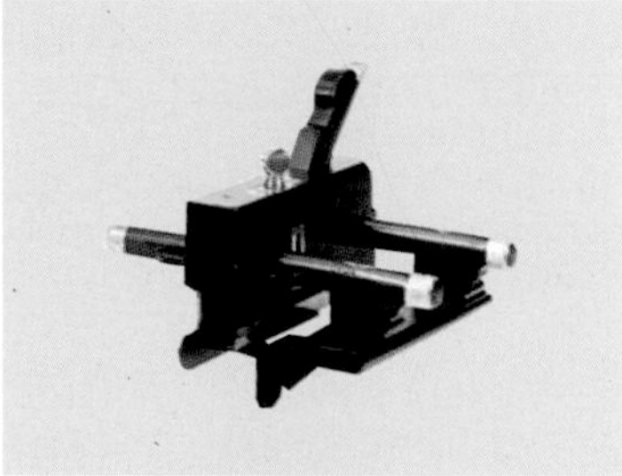

△ Plough Plane

- *1880*

A fine quality rosewood plough plane by Mathieson with rosewood stem wedges and brass fittings and skate front.

- *length 25cm*
- £590 • Tool Shop Auctions

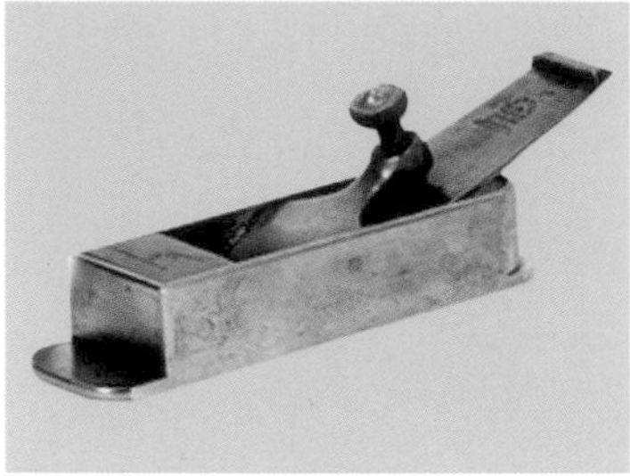

▽ Mitre Plane

- *1870*

An 8-inch dovetailed mitre plane with rosewood infill by Mathieson with super fine mouth.

- *length 21.3cm*
- £510 • Tool Shop Auctions

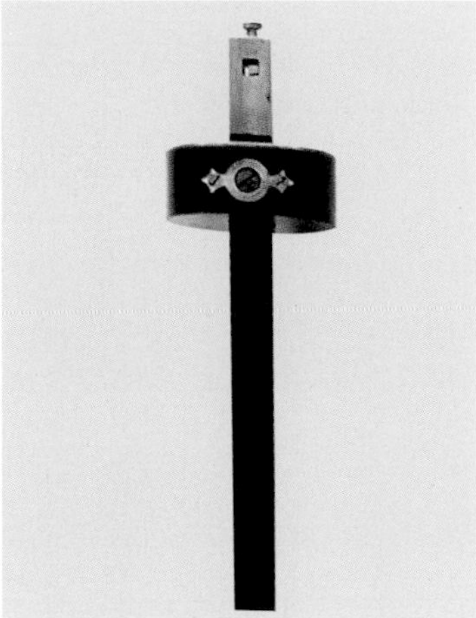

▽ Cutting Gauge

- *1895*

A Victorian fine quality ebony and brass cutting gauge by Frost.

- *length 25cm*
- £110 • Tool Shop Auctions

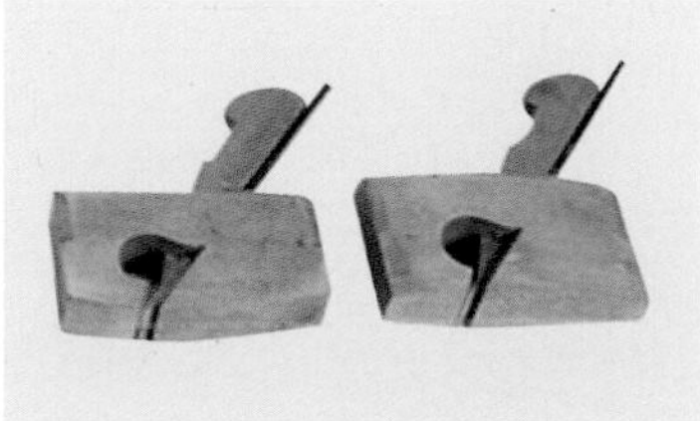

▽ Boxwood Planes

- *1880*

A pair of rare, miniature boxwood planes by Preston, with a radiused rebate and a compassed rebate.

- *length 7.5cm*
- £210 • Tool Shop Auctions

◁ Garden Sprinkler

- *circa 1900*

Brass and cast-iron sprinkler with two arms with brass nozzles which rotate under the pressure of water from an attached hosepipe. Of very good weight and in full working order.

- £85 • S. Brunswick

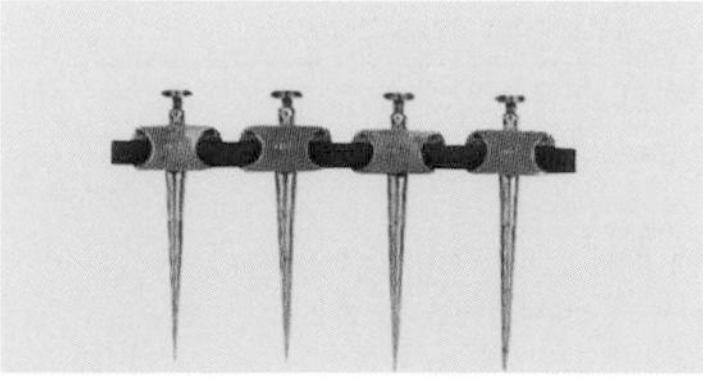

△ Trammels

- *1870*

A rare set of four trammels with brass and steel tips, seven inch.

- £140 • Tool Shop Auctions

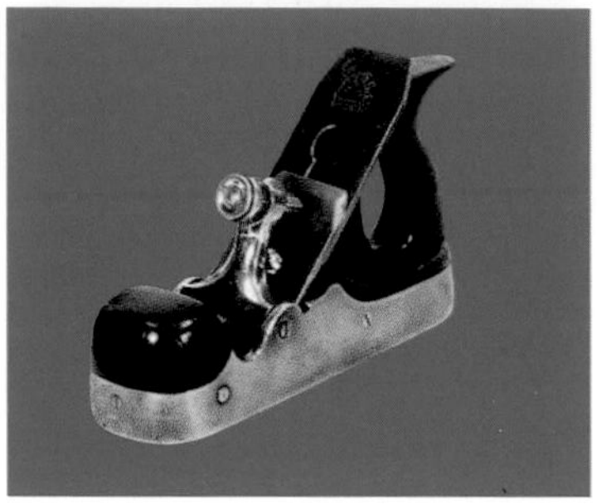

△ Scottish Plane

- *1870*

Victorian gunmetal Scottish smoothing plane with overstuffed rosewood infill.

- *length 23cm*
- £220 • Tool Shop Auctions

△ Shoulder Plane

- *1880*

Victorian one-inch Mathieson dovetailed shoulder plane with rosewood infill and Marples cutter.

- *length 23cm*
- £120 • Tool Shop Auctions

▽ Sheffield-Plated Brace

- *1875*

Victorian beech Sheffield-plated brace, unnamed.

- *length 37cm*
- £65 • Tool Shop Auctions

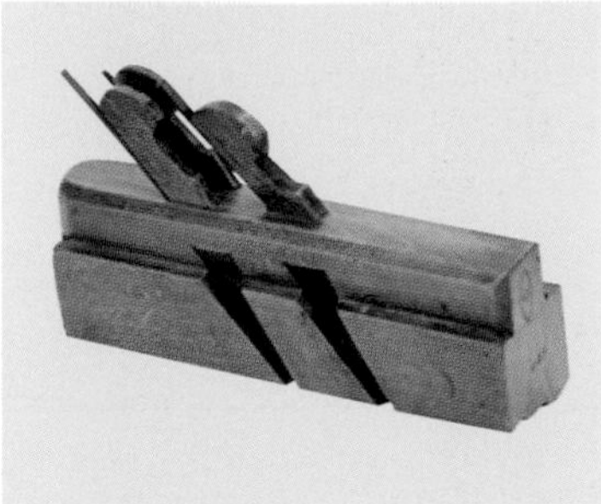

▽ Moulding Plane

- *1880*

A rare, complex two-inch, triple iron moulding plane by Mathieson.

- *length 23.8cm*
- £240 • Tool Shop Auctions

▽ Bulb Planter

- *circa 1900*

A Kentish bulb-planting tool with turned ash handle and cross-piece for exerting foot pressure. For use in planting bulbs in lawns and replacing turf plug.

- £75 • S. Brunswick

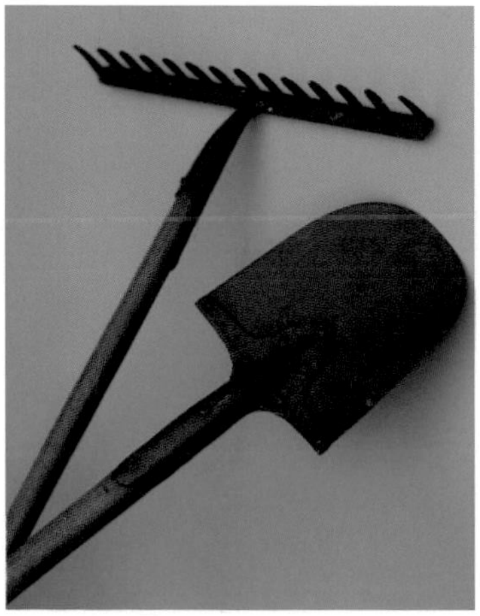

◁ Set of Gardening Tools

- *early 20th century*

A set of assorted garden tools, all with hornbeam wood shafts, including a 14-tine garden rake and a three-quarter spit trenching shovel. Mostly of steel construction.

- £48 each • Myriad

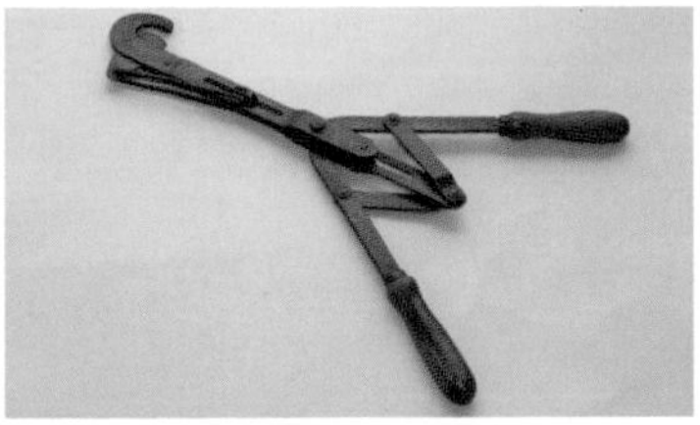

△ Pruner

- *1920*

Trademarked 'Mighty Cutter' pruner, with patented action for use with lever arms or worked by wire on pole. Made in England for fruit tree pruning.

- £48 • **S. Brunswick**

△ Soil Sifter

- *circa 1940*

Made of bentwood, cut and steamed to be moulded into shape, with a steel grill for catching stones when sifting.

- *diameter 45cm*
- £20 • **Curios**

△ Watering Can

- *circa 1940*

Galvanised steel watering can with a large, detachable nozzle rose and handle of a tubular construction. Possibly a converted milk-churn.

- *height 42cm*
- £38 • **Myriad**

▽ Mathieson Plane

- *circa 1920s*

A Mathieson dovetailed parallel-sided smoothing plane with rosewood infill made as a special order for a man with large hands.

- *length 26.3cm*
- £575 • **Tool Shop Auctions**

▽ Garden Sprayer

- *circa 1930*

Pressurised sprayer with copper and brass components, with copper cylinder and brass pump with turned wooden handle. Webbing carrying straps. All original materials.

- *height 77cm*
- £140 • **S. Brunswick**

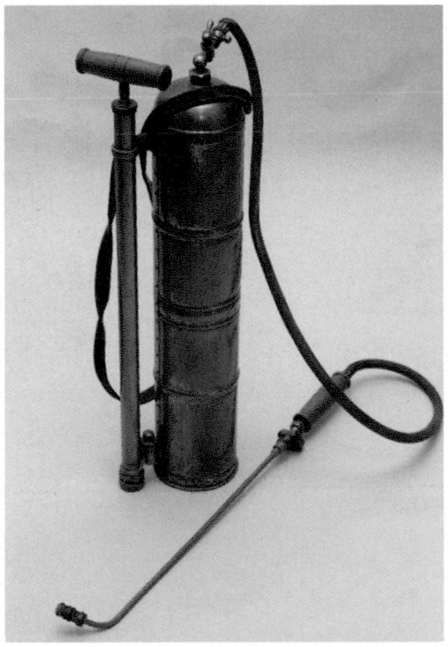

▽ Norris Smoothing Plane

- *1920*

A Norris 20R gunmetal smoothing plane in its original box.

- *length 22cm*
- £700 • **Tool Shop Auctions**

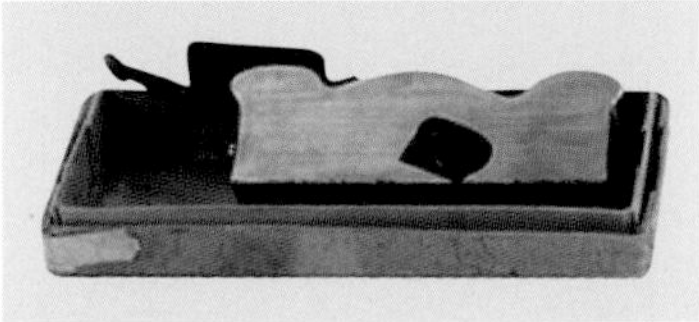

▽ Lawn Edger

- *circa 1950*

Steel and cast-iron lawn edger with aluminium handle and rubber grips.

- £55 • **S. Brunswick**

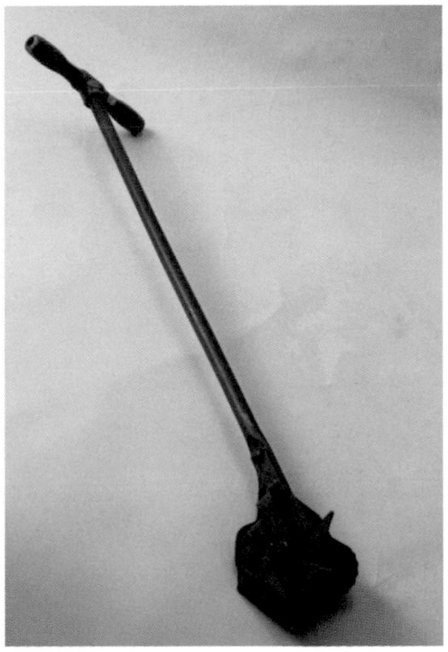

△ Garden Fork

- *circa 1940*

An English classic four-tine garden fork. Steel with turned wooden shaft and half-turned, all wooden handle.

- *height 94cm*
- £15 • **Curios**

△ Lawn Aerator

- *circa 1950*

A lawn aerator with a turned, polished wood shaft and handle. The mechanism is a rotating cylinder with flat spikes driven by the forward motion of the front rollers. English-made, in full working order.

- £65 • **S. Brunswick**

◁ Shovel

- *circa 1940*

A classic English shovel of steel and wood construction with a turned shaft and a partly turned, all-wooden handle.

- *height 94cm*
- £15 • **Curios**

▷ Webb Lawnmower

- *circa 1955*

A Webb's push mower with cross-over handles and rubber grips. With grass box, adjustable cutter bar and cutter base-plate and adjustable height nuts on the front roller.

- £40 • **Curios**

TOYS, GAMES & DOLLS

The international market for antique toys is extremely strong. Toy cars are very popular and include those manufactured by the early French C.I.J. Company in the late 1920s, commemorating the Grand Prix, along with British Dinky and Matchbox cars, and the German Orober vans. German tinplate toys by Carette, Gunthermann and Lehmann, made between 1900 and 1930, are fetching premium prices. These companies also produced ships, aeroplanes and figures, all of which were pieces of remarkable engineering. British manufacturers such as Wells, Brimtoy and Chad Valley began to compete with the Continental market in the 1930s and 1940s, producing cars, aeroplanes and trains on a cheaper basis. At this time Tri-Ang began to produce small tinplate commercial vehicles with clockwork mechanisms known as Mimic Toys, which are now highly collectable. Dolls and teddy bears remain hugely popular to the toy collector, along with finely made eighteenth-century French porcelain jointed dolls.

▷ Hubert the Cottage Youth

- *1812*

Hubert the cottage youth by S. & J. Fuller. In original slip case.

- *height 13cm*
- £400 • **Judith Lassalle**

△ Walnut Carved Doll

- *17th century*

English walnut doll wearing a dress.

- *length 19cm*
- £500 • **Judith Lassalle**

▷ Comic Girl

- *1830*

The comic girl by Faber, comprising three heads, a rabbit, a chicken and two hats. With stand and jacket complete with original box. German.

- *height 29cm*
- £665 • **Judith Lassalle**

▽ Spooner's Transformation

- *1820*

Spooner's Transformation No. 3. Print of woman and cat transform when lit from behind, eyes open and cat turns tortoiseshell, with eyes open.

- *height 29cm*
- £175 • **Judith Lassalle**

△ Papier Mâché Doll

- *circa 1850*

German boy doll, attired in original costume of frock coat, silk waistcoat, white stock and brown trousers and shoes, and equipped with penknife and fob watch.

- *height 54cm*
- £895 • Big Baby Little Baby

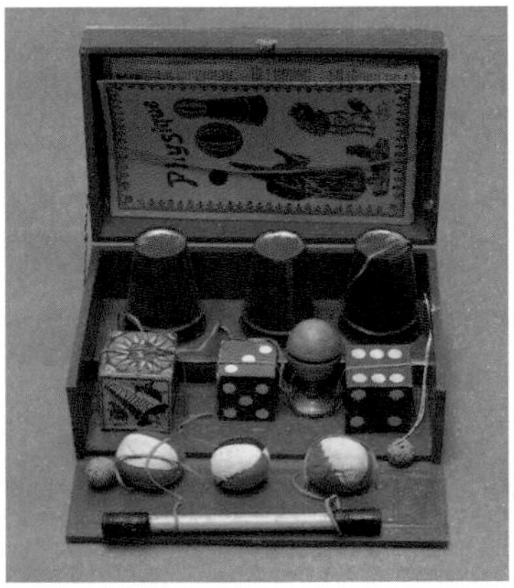

△ Magic Set

- *circa 1860*

French boxed magic set, complete with three cups, two dice, balls, magic wand and other tricks with original instruction book.

- *length 38cm*
- £500 • G.D. Coleman

▷ Bagatelle

- *circa 1860*

German bagatelle board showing a sylvan scene on half-moon surface. Complete with original balls, six holes and in working order. With floral decoration.

- *height 46cm*
- £200 • Judith Lassalle

▽ Jigsaw

- *1853*

Jigsaw of the Spithead Review 1853. Comprises key picture, taken from a contemporary painting, the original box and the complete jigsaw.

- *length 20cm*
- £37 • Judith Lassalle

▽ German Squeak Toy

- *circa 1860*

Painted German squeak toy of papier mâché in the shape of a dog's head with two faces. Sound produced by leather diaphragm.

- *height 10cm*
- £350 • Judith Lassalle

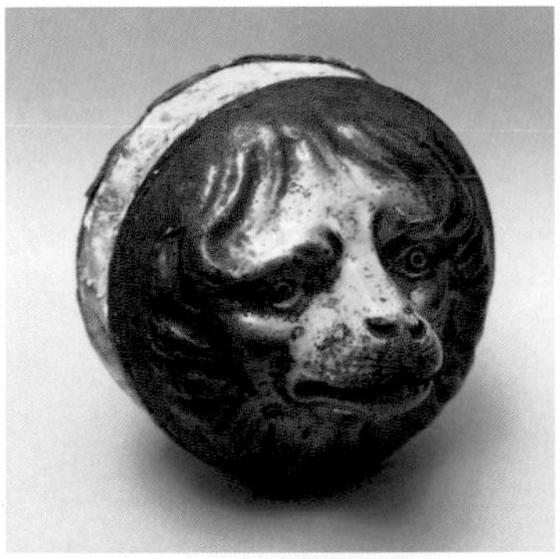

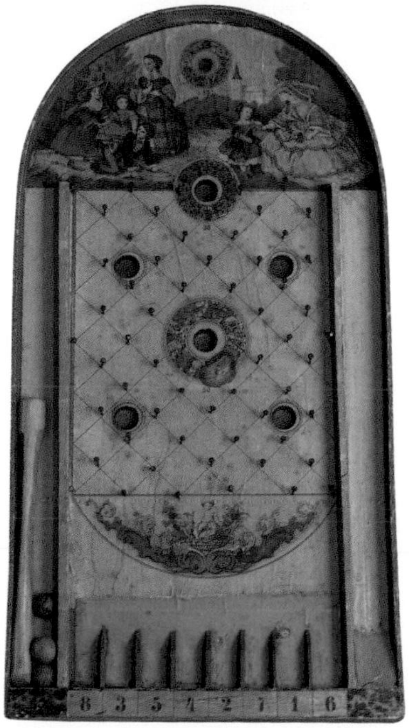

△ Noah's Ark

- *1860*

Comprising 53 carved wooden pieces: three people and fifty animals, all hand-painted, with a hand-painted wooden ark with a hinged roof.

- *height 20cm*
- £750 • Judith Lassalle

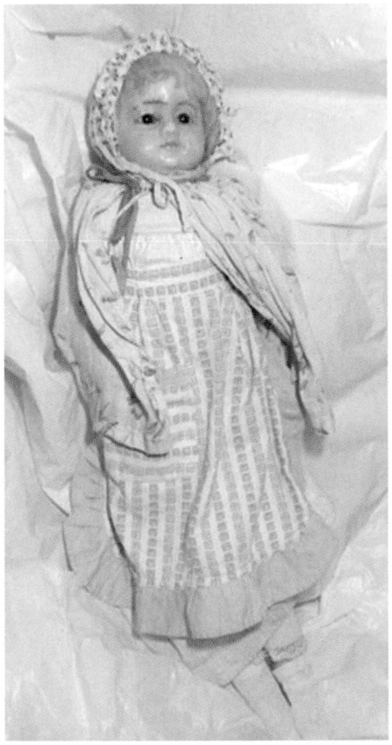

△ Wax Doll

- *1870*

Victorian hand-painted wax doll with blue eyes and blonde hair, wearing cape embroidered with pink roses and a blue and white dress and bonnet.

- *height 65cm*
- £150 • Dolly Land

▷ Acrobat on Trapeze

- *1880*

French somersaulting acrobat on trapeze wearing blue conical hat and red tunic with painted face. Made from wood and paper.

- *height 23cm*
- £350 • Judith Lassalle

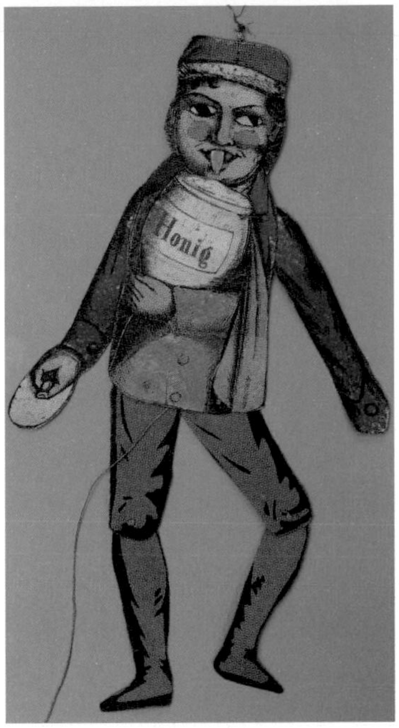

△ Paper Puppet

- *1870*

A German dancing paper puppet. A man holding a honey pot with tongue intermittantly protruding to lick it during dancing. Activated by drawstring.

- £195 • Judith Lassalle

△ Bru Walker Doll

- *circa 1880*

Bru 'Kiss throwing walker doll' with long auburn hair and brown glass eyes, wearing a cream cotton and lace dress, a bonnet with lilac bows and brown leather shoes.

- *height 62cm*
- £3,750 • Glenda Dolls

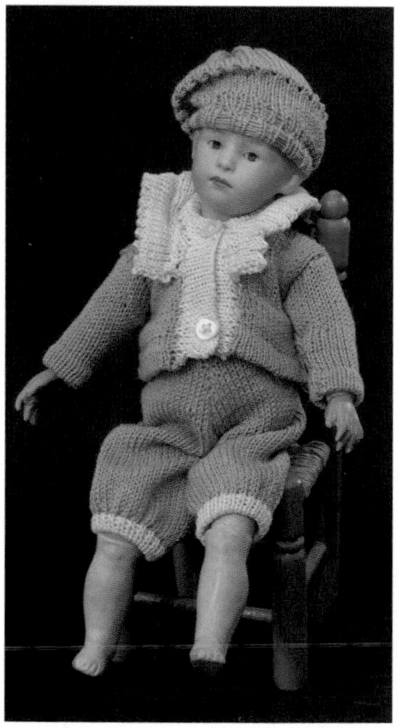

△ Heubach Boy Doll

- *circa 1890*

Heubach jointed porcelain boy doll with a painted face, wearing a matching beige and cream outfit with hat.

- *height 25cm*
- £395 • Glenda Dolls

▽ Norah Wellings Admiral

- *circa 1880*

Soft toy of an admiral by Norah Wellings, wearing a brown velvet uniform with silver metal buttons, and a blue hat with gold trimmings.

- *height 28cm*
- £90 • Glenda Dolls

▽ Porcelain Doll

- *circa 1894*

Porcelain hand-painted German doll, wearing a red and blue tartan dress with lace pantaloons and black boots.

- *height 57cm*
- £450 • Dolly Land

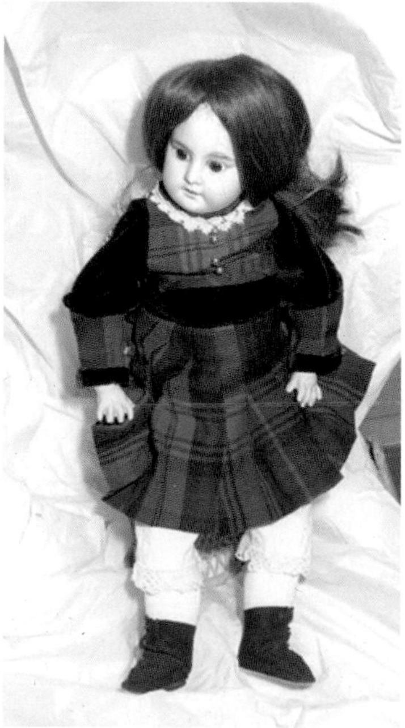

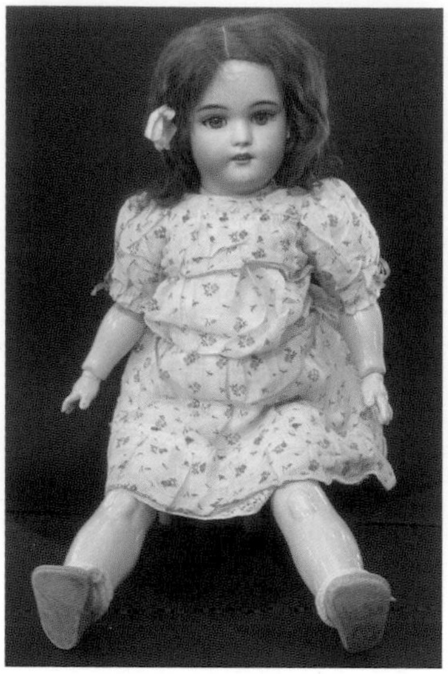

△ Simon & Halbig Doll

- *circa 1880*

Jointed porcelain girl doll with blue eyes, long dark hair and a painted face, wearing a floral dress and green leather shoes, by Simon & Halbig.

- *height 52cm*
- £648 • Glenda Dolls

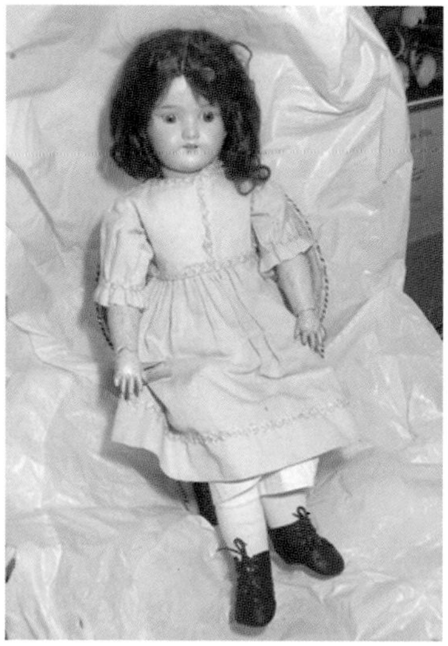

△ Armand Marceau Porcelain Doll

- *circa 1890*

Porcelain hand-painted Armand Marceau doll with original blue dress and black lace-up boots.

- *height 59cm*
- £250 • Dolly Land

▽ Konig & Wernig

- *circa 1890*

Konig & Wernig character baby doll with blonde curly hair, brown glass eyes and jointed porcelain body, wearing a lilac dress with small red spots and a pink velvet hat with lace and satin bows.

- *height 24cm*
- £525 • Glenda Dolls

▽ Pintel & Godchaux Doll

- *circa 1900*

French porcelain jointed doll with blonde hair, blue eyes and painted face, wearing a lace dress, with a pink satin bow and lace socks, made by Pintel & Godchaux.

- *height 43cm*
- £595 • Glenda Dolls

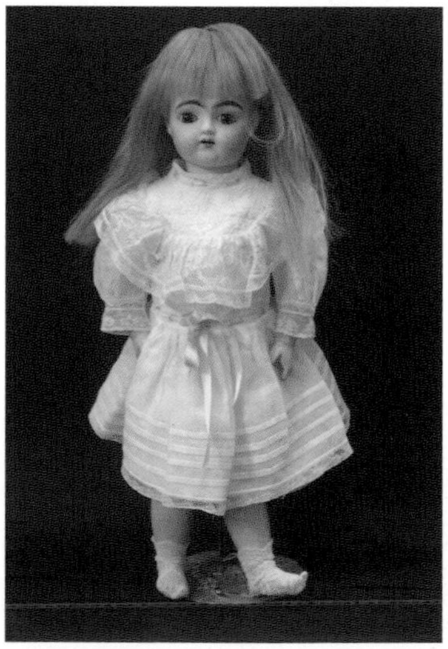

◁ Tin Beetle

- *circa 1895*

Crawling beetle with green and gold wings, red eyes, black body and six legs. A superb example of an early lithographic tin toy. Made by Lehmann. No 431.

- *length 11cm*
- £185 • P. McAskie

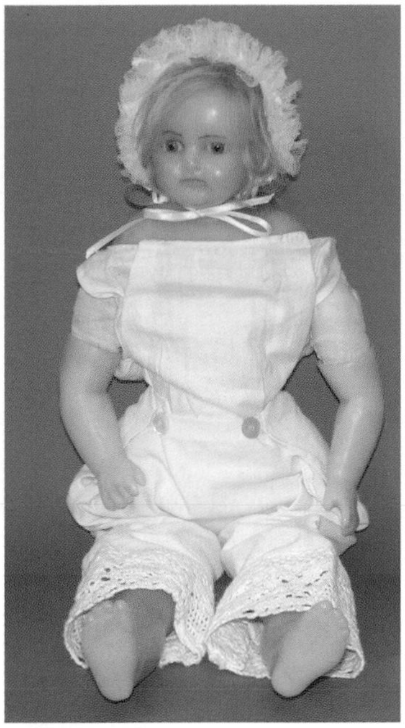

△ Wax Doll

• *circa 1900*
Wax girl doll with blonde hair, blue eyes and a painted face, wearing a linen top and pantaloons with lace embroidery, and a lace cap.
• *height 48cm*
• £475 • Glenda Dolls

△ Transitional Green Car

• *circa 1900*
Electric tin-plate green car, 'Penny Toy', made in Germany.
• *height 6cm*
• £275 • P. McAskie

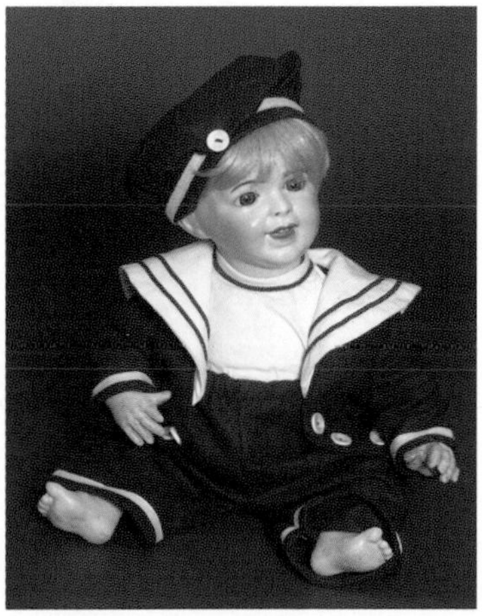

▽ Kestner Doll

• *circa 1900*
Porcelain jointed doll by Kestner with blue glass eyes and long auburn hair, wearing linen and lace dress and brown leather shoes.
• *height 38cm*
• £595 • Glenda Dolls

▽ Tailless Donkey Game

• *circa 1905*
'Pin the tail on the donkey' game, complete with donkey poster and tails and a curious snake.
• *49cm x 27cm*
• £55 • Stephen Long

▽ Rule Britannia Box

• *circa 1910*
A box with 'Britannia Rules the Waves' comprising many carved pieces for building men o' war, cruisers, torpedoes, boats and forts. All in original box.
• *length 45cm*
• £300 • Judith Lassalle

◁ Sailor Doll

• *1910*
A doll representing a boy in original sailor costume. Small firing crack in forehead, otherwise perfect.
• *height 39cm*
• £450 • Big Baby Little Baby

△ Ei des Colombus

• *circa 1900*
Puzzle game, comprising several pieces which make up different shapes and instructions. Made in Germany.
• *10cm x 8cm*
• £80 • Stephen Long

△ Le Loto Comique

• *circa 1905*
Lotto/Bingo style game. Contains games pieces with numbers, pictures and boards with pictorial montages.
• *43cm x 35cm*
• £118 • Stephen Long

▽ Simon & Halbig Doll

• *1910*
Simon & Halbig 1078 doll with perfect bisque head. Contains glass flirty eyes and moveable joints.
• *height 69cm*
• £795 • Big Baby Little Baby

△ Heinrich Doll

• *1905*
Pretty doll made by Heinrich. Hand-worked head with perfect open and shut eyes. Body in good condition.
• *height 57cm*
• £450 • Big Baby Little Baby

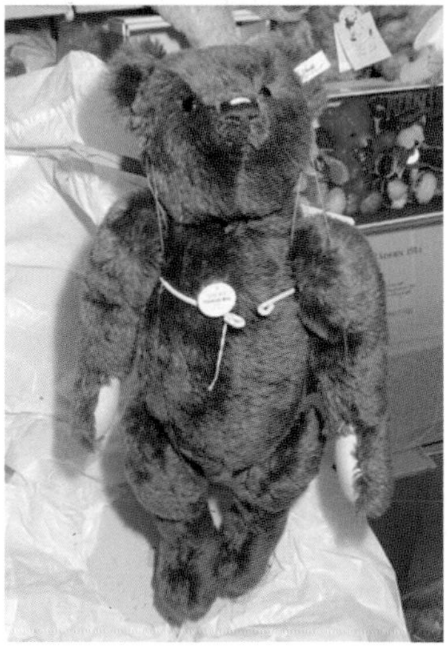

△ Phantom Brown Bear

• *circa 1910*
Brown Bear made by Phantom, limited edition of 4,000.
• *height 61cm*
• £380 • Dolly Land

△ Fischer Car

- *circa 1910*

Stylish version of Fischer car cabriolet with driver. Predominantly white with brown canopy. Was featured in *American Motor Toys* by Lillian Gottschalk.

- *length 19cm*
- **£1,780** • **P. McAskie**

△ Hessmobil Car

- *1910*

German blue motor car with yellow wheels and yellow trim around the doors, made by Hessmobil.

- *length 24cm*
- **£1,250** • **Dolly Land**

▽ Bucking Bronco

- *1910*

Bucking bronco horse with rider. Made in Germany by Lehmann, serial no. 625. Tinplate clockwork and base. Man is in red shirt and brown trousers.

- *height 19cm*
- **£585** • **P. McAskie**

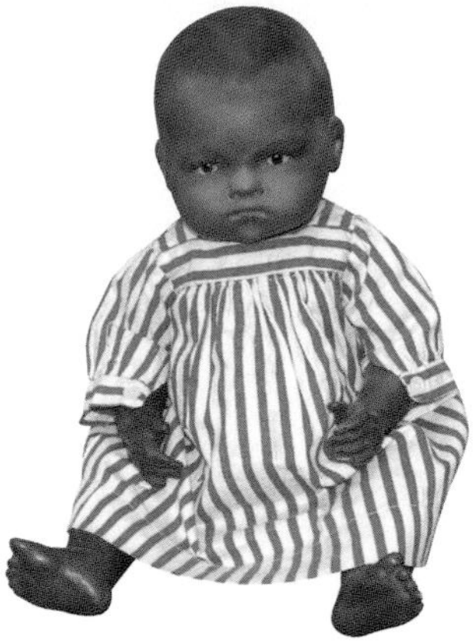

△ Spanish Racing Car

- *circa 1920*

Blue and yellow racing car with driver and passenger, and the number 7 on the side. Manufactured by Paya in Spain.

- *length 27cm*
- **£225** • **P. McAskie**

▽ American Fastback

- *1920*

American fastback orange car with black running boards and red enamel wheels, by Mano IL.

- *length 8cm*
- **£75** • **Dr Colin B. Baddiel**

◁ Dream Baby

- *circa 1920*

Porcelain jointed black 'Dream Baby', in perfect condition.

- *height 28cm*
- **£398** • **Glenda Dolls**

△ Doll

- *circa 1920s*

A German character doll from the 1920s, in original woollen romper suit with open and shut eyes and a china head.

- *height 25cm*
- **£265** • **Big Baby Little Baby**

▽ Tin Metal Boxers

- *1920*

Tin metal boxers on wheeled base made by Einfeilt, Germany.

- *13cm x 19cm*
- **£275** • **P. McAskie**

▽ Toy Pheasant

- *1920*

German clockwork toy pheasant.

- *4cm x 6cm*
- **£125** • **Dr Colin B. Baddiel**

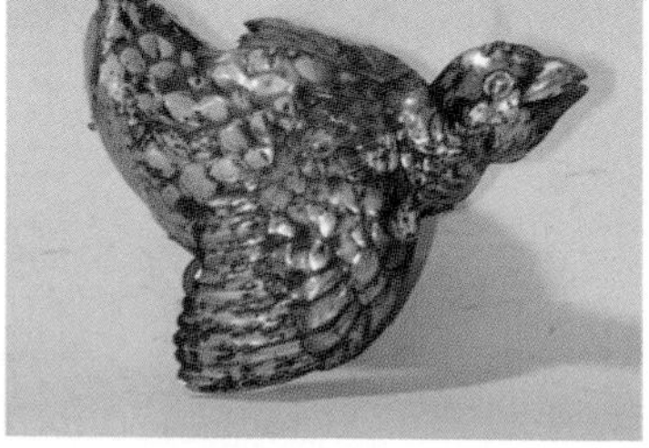

△ Hornby 4-4-4 Train

- *circa 1920s*

Clockwork Hornby model of L.M.S. 4-4-4 locomotive, with original burgundy and black paint and brass fittings.

- *length 26.5cm*
- **£195** • **Wheels of Steel**

▷ Dream Baby

- *1920*

Dream Baby doll in excellent condition with open and close eyes, original white apparel and painted features.

- *length 34cm*
- **£325** • **Big Baby Little Baby**

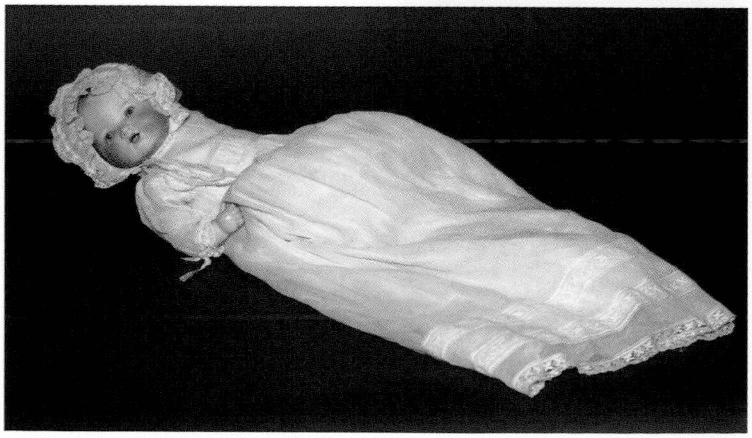

△ Cloth Doll

• *1920*
All original and good condition, with red hair, a red hair ribbon and flirting eyes.
• *height 59cm*
• £298 • **Big Baby Little Baby**

△ American Tootsie Car

• *1930*
American brown Tootsie car, by La Salle.
• *length 12 cm*
• £120 • **Dr Colin B. Baddiel**

△ Snow White

• *circa 1930*
French padded doll of Snow White with composition face and hands.
• *height 44cm*
• £368 • **Glenda Dolls**

▽ Snap

• *1920*
Pack of Snap cards, complete and in good condition with original box, depicting characters from the pantomime and nursery rhymes. British.
• £55 • **Judith Lassalle**

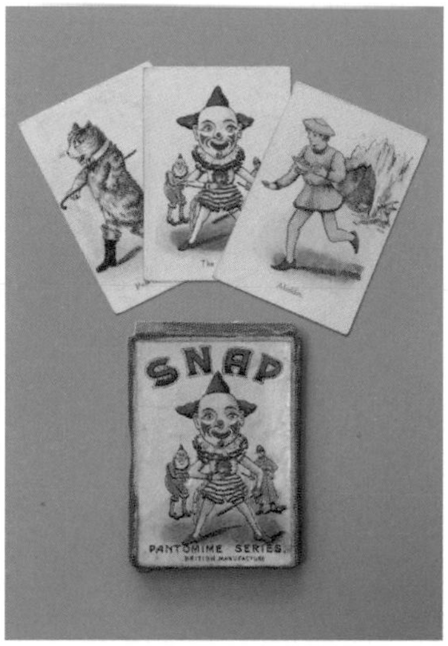

▽ Hornby Train

• *circa 1930*
Brown Hornby train with yellow trim around the windows and black wheels. O-gauge.
• *length 32cm*
• £120 • **Jeff Williams**

▽ Smiley of the Seven Dwarfs

• *circa 1930*
Padded soft toy of 'Smiley', one of the dwards from the children's story, 'Snow White and the Seven Dwarfs'.
• *height 27cm*
• £160 • **Glenda Dolls**

▽ Motorbike and Sidecar

• *circa 1930*
Composition elastolin model of German army motorbike and sidecar with driver and passenger. Made in Germany.
• *height 10cm*
• £150 • **Stephen Naegel**

▽ Bluebird Car

• *1930*
Blue Bluebird racing car, by Kosuge & Co.
• *length 21cm*
• £425 • **Lennox Gallery**

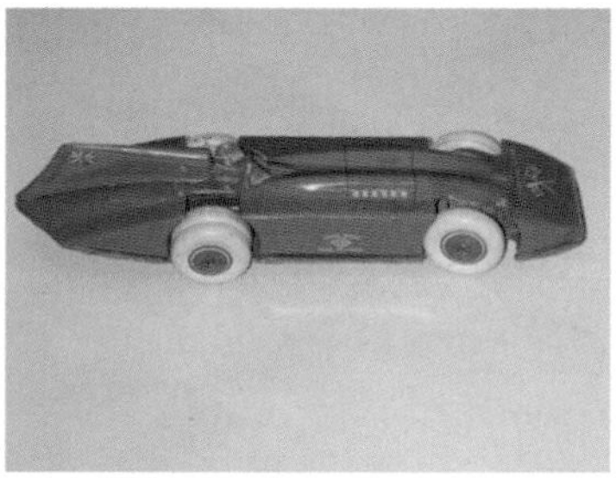

▽ Hornby Pullman Coach

• *circa 1930s*
Hornby series, 'O' gauge Pullman coach with a beige roof and a dark-brown body. Windows with the original cellophane panes. Interior has lamps and curtains. Doors open and have keys.
• *length 33cm*
• £120 • **Wheels of Steel**

◁ American Ford

• *1920*
Tan American Ford with black wheels and brass radiator, made by Tootsie.
• *length 10cm*
• £27 • **Dr Colin B. Baddiel**

△ Clockwork Circus Clown

• *1930*
Clockwork Shiuko circus clown with a drum.
• *height 6cm*
• £145 • **Dr Colin B. Baddiel**

△ Celluloid Doll

• *circa 1930*
A French celluloid doll in a green velvet suit and white blouse – both original. A 'bent limb boy'.
• *height 45cm*
• £145 • **Dolly Land**

∇ Merrythought Mohair Bear

- *1930s*

Merrythought mohair bear. A limited edition of 50 was produced in white brown and black.

- *height 38cm*
- £55 • **Dolly Land**

∇ Clockwork Whoopee Car

- *circa 1930*

American clockwork tin plate orange Whoopee car. Graffiti on bonnet, for example 'squeak easy'. Makes crazy erratic movements. Illustrated on Maxime Pinksy volume 2. Made by Louis Marx toys. Clown shown driving.

- *length 19cm*
- £245 • **P. McAskie**

∇ Racing Car

- *1930*

Clockwork metal, blue and red French racing car with driver, by Charles Rossignol, Paris.

- *length 40cm*
- £485 • **Lennox Gallery**

△ Shirley Temple Doll

- *1934*

Shirley Temple porcelain doll with blonde hair, wearing suede dungarees with silver studs and a red check shirt.

- *height 325cm*
- £325 • **Dolly Land**

△ Dummer Boy

- *1930*

Drummer boy with a tin-plate body, legs and arms, and a celluloid head, with the maker's name 'Fecuda', Japan.

- *height 24cm*
- £275 • **P. McAskie**

∇ Peugeot Fire Engine

- *circa 1930*

Peugeot 601 fire engine in painted bright red tin-plate. Made by Charles Rossignol, Paris. Three firemen inside and a swivelling ladder on the top.

- *height 37cm*
- £485 • **P. McAskie**

∇ Hornby Nord Loco

- *circa 1930*

Hornby Nord Loco and Tender. Clockwork mechanism. Brown tin plate and black Hornby front.

- *length 43cm, including tender*
- £295 • **Wheels of Steel**

∇ German Doll

- *1930*

With hand-painted porcelain face, blue eyes and blonde hair, wearing a red hat, jacket and dress, with white lace trim.

- *height 57cm*
- £325 • **Dolly Land**

◁ Police Van

- *1930s*

Black police van, made by Wells.

- *length 11cm*
- £75 • **Dr Colin B. Baddiel**

△ Oriental Baby Doll

- *circa 1930*

Small Oriental porcelain jointed baby doll with brown glass eyes and a painted face.

- *height 18cm*
- £300 • **Glenda Dolls**

△ Welsh Doll

- *circa 1930*

A Welsh Moa 200 porcelain hand-painted doll, wearing an emerald-green velvet dress with a large ribboned belt with diamante clasp, bonnet and black shoes.

- *height 61cm*
- £395 • **Dolly Land**

▽ Royal Scot Train

- *1935*

Red English Royal Scot metal train with black trim and wheels.

- *length 26cm*
- £425 • **Jeff Williams**

△ Trix Twin Train

- *circa 1937*

Train of four coaches, loco and tender. L.M.S OO-gauge. Maroon with dark green roofs. Each coach has four wheels.

- *length 50cm per coach*
- £110 • **Wheels of Steel**

△ Sailorboy and Girl Doll

- *circa 1930*

A Schuco sailor and girl doll, made in Germany, both made of tinplate and celluloid, with felt clothes. Clockwork mechanism in full working order.

- *height 7cm*
- £250 • **Dolly Land**

▽ Motorbike with Rider

- *1930*

Grey motorbike with rider made by Arnold, Germany, Reg A643.

- *length 25cm*
- £230 • **P. McAskie**

△ Snow White

- *1938*

Snow White and the Seven Dwarfs, in painted lead. Part of Britains Civilian Series.

- *height 4cm–6.5cm*
- £225 • **Stephen Naegel**

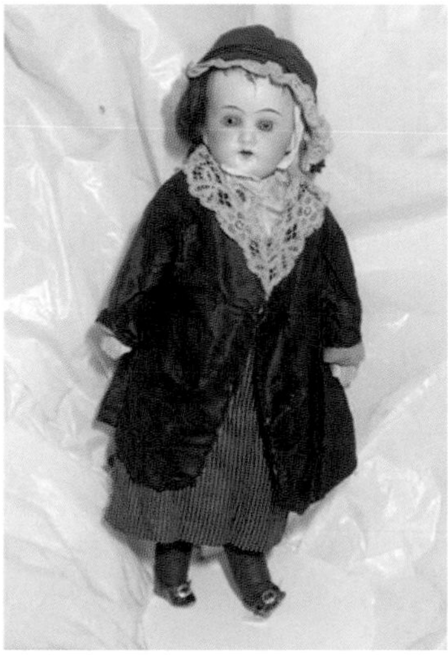

△ German Doll

- *1930*

Original porcelain and hand-painted German doll, wearing original black coat with lace collar, red dress and hat with lace trim, and black laced boots.

- *height 37cm*
- £175 • **Dolly Land**

△ Steiff Pekinese

- *1940*

Velvet padded pekinese by Steiff, with glass eyes.

- *height 10cm*
- £48 • **Glenda Dolls**

▽ Austin 7

- *circa 1940*

Cornflower-blue Austin 7, 35 series with pneumatic tyres.

- *height 3cm*
- £38 • **P. McAskie**

▽ Frazer Nash Sports Car

- *1940*

Frazer Nash sports car made by Dinky, with a blue body and wheels, and a grey interior.

- *length 8cm*
- £48 • **Dr Colin B. Baddiel**

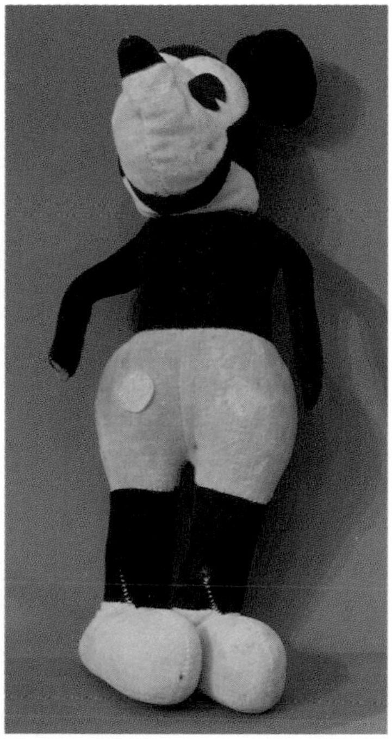

△ Mickey Mouse

- *circa 1930*

Velvet padded Mickey Mouse with a large smiling expression.

- *height 33cm*
- £110 • **Glenda Dolls**

◁ Petrol Tanker

- *1930*

Red lead petrol tanker by Taylor and Barrett.

- *length 10cm*
- £85 • **P. McAskie**

△ Mussolini Figure

- *circa 1940*

Hand-painted, lead figure of Il Duce in typically aggressive, arms akimbo, pose.

- *height 25cm*
- £150 • **Stephen Naegel**

△ Circus Elephant

- *1950*

Clockwork grey circus elephant with blue eyes and red decorative trimmings.

- *height 14cm*
- £88 • **Dr Colin B. Baddiel**

▷ Horse Roller

- *1940*

Farm roller with farm hand and horse, from Britains Home Farm series, set of nine. Patriotic wartime toy in original strong cardboard box.

- £80 • **Stephen Naegel**

▷ Model Pandas

- *1949*

Set 9011 in Britains Zoo series. Giant panda standing on all fours and two baby pandas (one on two legs and the other on all fours). With original box.

- £35 • **Stephen Naegel**

▽ Elephant See-Saw

- *1950*

Two elephants on a toyland see-saw, with key winder playing drums, made by M.S. Toys, Japan.

- *18cm*
- £335 • **P. McAskie**

◁ Light Goods Van

- *1948*

Van from Britains Motor and Road Series set 2024, with driver. All original paintwork with 'Britains Ltd' signwritten on side panels. Original box.

- £350 • **Stephen Naegel**

◁ Rope Swinging Cowboy

- *circa 1950*

Rodeo cowboy made of tinplate and celluloid. Dressed in cotton trousers and printed shirt. Also equipped with felt hat, tin feet, tin arms and tin gloves. Contains clockwork mechanism that swings the lasso and moves his hips. Original box. Japan.

- *height 22cm*
- £165 • **P. McAskie**

△ Cottage Doll

- *circa 1950*

Small padded 'Cottage Doll' made by Glenda O'Connor, with blonde plaits, blue eyes and a pleasant expression, wearing a pink gingham dress, green hat, top and shoes.

- *height 21cm*
- £58 • **Glenda Dolls**

▽ American Footballer

- *1950*

American footballer with red and white helmet.

- *height 9cm*
- £85 • **Dr Colin B. Baddiel**

▽ Daimler Ambulance

- *circa 1950*

Primrose-yellow Dinky Daimler ambulance, no. 253, with a red cross on the side and red hub plates, and original box.

- *height 4cm*
- £45 • **P. McAskie**

▽ Chad Valley Train

- *1950*

An English brown bakelite toy train with two carriages with black wheels on the train, and ivory on the carriages. Maker's name: Chad Valley.

- *length 58cm*
- £700 • **Decodence**

▽ Chad Valley Teddy

- *1950*

Chad Valley padded teddy with glass eyes and a pleasant expression.

- *height 44cm*
- £250 • Glenda Dolls

▷ Britains' Zoo Series

- *1950*

Set 908 Indian rhinoceros, grey with cream-coloured horn. With original box and paint.

- *height 5cm*
- £50 • Stephen Naegel

△ Japanese Motor Launch

- *circa 1950*

Japanese red, yellow, orange and blue motor launch with driver in a helmet, and hand crank.

- *length 21cm*
- £73 • P. McAskie

△ Blue and Silver Metal Dalek

- *1950s*

Unusual blue and silver metal dalek from the 1950s.

- *height 12cm*
- £225 • Dr Colin B. Baddiel

△ Tri-ang Red Racing Car

- *1950*

Red Tri-ang Mimic racing car with driver, the car bearing the number 3.

- *length 15cm*
- £45 • P. McAskie

▽ Oriental Doll Family

- *20th century*

Japanese family of dolls wearing traditional costumes, the girls having black wigs and hand-painted faces.

- *height 36cm (girl)*
- £250 • Dolly Land

▷ Hornby Garage

- *1950s*

French Hornby O-gauge model representing the main station at Bordeaux. White and orange hand-painted wood, decorated with small posters of Normandy and a painted clock.

- *length 53cm*
- £125 • Wheels of Steel

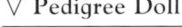

△ Metal Soldiers

- *1950*

Set of lead, hand-painted, model British soldiers and horses.

- *height 4cm (soldier)*
- £1,500 • Stephen Naegel

△ Horse and Milk Float

- *1950*

Matchbox horse-drawn red milk float with driver.

- *height 3cm*
- £18 • P. McAskie

△ Green Flying Scotsman

- *1950*

Green Flying Scotsman by Bassett, coke O-gauge.

- *length 28cm*
- £1,950 • Jeff Williams

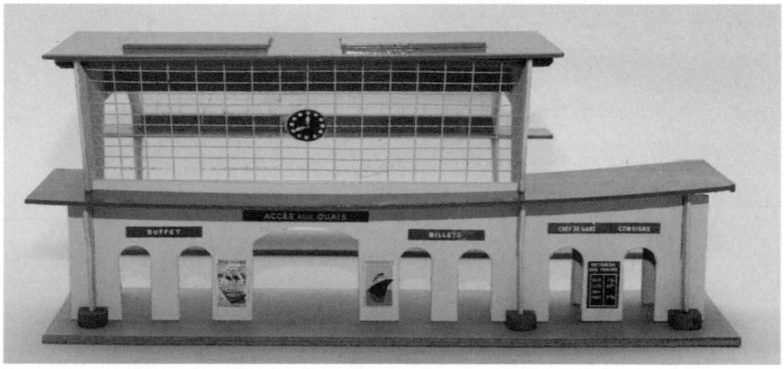

▽ Pedigree Doll

- *1950*

Pedigree doll in original dress. Walking doll with flirting eyes, naturalistic hair and red hair-ribbon.

- *height 56cm*
- £110 • Big Baby Little Baby

▽ Round the World Space Toy

- *circa 1950*

Round the World space toy made by Technofix, Germany.

- *length 60cm*
- £265 • P. McAskie

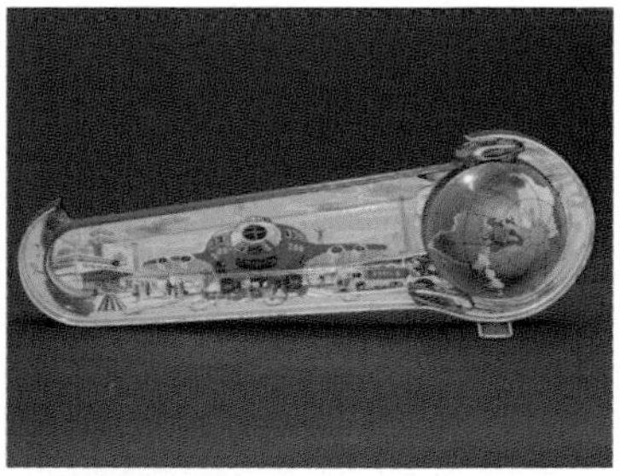

△ Black Seal

- *circa 1950*

Black seal balancing a striped ball, manufactured in Japan.

- *height 16cm*
- £90 • P. McAskie

△ Steiff Owl

- *circa 1950*

Steiff owl with large glass eyes and a menacing expression.

- *height 14cm*
- £49 • Glenda Dolls

△ Union Pacific Train by Lionel & Co.

- *1957*

Plastic orange Union Pacific train with black wheels, by Lionel & Co.

- *length 28cm*
- £85 • Jeff Williams

▽ Robot Money Bank

- *1960*

Silver robot with large round eyes, designed with a silver scoop for the money, sitting on a circular brown container.

- *height 14cm*
- £25 • Dr Colin B. Baddiel

▷ Pedigree Doll

- *circa 1950*

Early 1950s pedigree doll with stylised hair, moving limbs and open and shut eyes. Figure shown in grass skirt.

- *height 34cm*
- £120 • Big Baby Little Baby

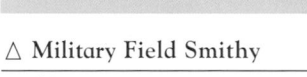

△ Military Field Smithy

- *1950*

Field smithy drawn by four horses with two outriders on original plinth. Modelled in lead by Lucotte Mignot.

- £250 • Stephen Naegel

△ Red London Bus

- *1950s*

Red London double-decker bus, by Triang toys.

- *length 17cm*
- £170 • Dr Colin B. Baddiel

△ Hornby Train

- *circa 1930*

Brown Hornby train with yellow trim on windows and black wheels. O-gauge.

- *length 32cm*
- £120 • Jeff Williams

△ Fleischmann Train

- *1955*

Fleischmann train with rails, in original box. HO-gauge.

- *width 38cm/box*
- £85 • Jeff Williams

▽ Ford Sedan

- *1950s*

Marusan Ford Sedan toy car. A lovely bright yellow with lithographed seat and crosshatched floor. Chrome bumper, lights and trim.

- *length 25.5cm*
- £250 • P. McAskie

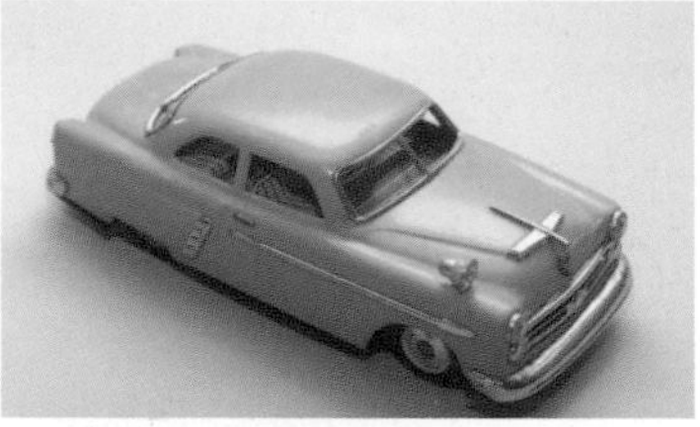

▽ Wooden Garage

- *circa 1950*

Wooden Esso garage with forecourt and petrol pumps. Original white paint with blue details. Includes hand-operated lift.

- *height 26cm*
- £85 • After Noah

▽ Merrythought Golly

- *1960*

Merrythought golly, limited edition of 100.

- *height 32cm*
- £40 • Dolly Land

◁ Yeomen Guard Models

- *1950*

Britains set 1257 Yeomen of the Guard from their 'Original Historical Series', complete with box displaying the nine figures.

- £140 • Stephen Naegel

▽ Black Clockwork Robot

- *1960*

American black clockwork robot with red boots, with original cardboard box.

- *height 125cm*
- £168 • Dr Colin B. Baddiel

▽ Rocking Horse

- *circa 1960*

Pressed steel arm with seat and painted head with leather ears. Simulated rocking action caused by spring and lever movement.

- *length 52cm*
- £54 • After Noah

▽ Fred Flintstone

- *1960*

Tin-plate 'Fred Flintstone' sitting astride his dinosaur 'Dino', made by Louis Marks in Japan.

- *length 12cm*
- £265 • P. McAskie

△ Telstar Kaleidoscope

- *1960*

Telstar kaleidoscope with a rocket, stars and satellite and a blue background, made by Green Monk of England.

- *height 17cm*
- £20 • P. McAskie

△ Vespa and Driver

- *1960*

Green Vespa with a driver wearing red, made in England by Benbros.

- *height 5cm*
- £22 • P. McAskie

▽ Austin Healey

- *1960*

Cream Austin Healey sports car with red wheels and interior, with driver and the number '23' on the side.

- *length 8cm*
- £113 • Dr Colin B. Baddiel

△ Velam Bubble Car

- *1960*

French cream Velam bubble car with grey roof, made by Quiralu, with original box.

- *height 4cm*
- £78 • P. McAskie

△ Animated Santa Bank

- *circa 1960s*

Deluxe animated Santa piggy bank with original box. Battery- and coin-operated. Eyes flash, head moves and bell rings. Santa has a vinyl face and sits on a tinplate house. Japan.

- *height 30cm*
- £285 • P. McAskie

△ Wild West Models

- *1960*

A set of Britains Swoppets Wild West plastic models, hand-painted and all complete with the original box shaped to accommodate the ten scale models.

- £150 • Stephen Naegel

△ Yellow Ferrari

- *1960*

Yellow Ferrari with original box, made by Dinky.

- *length 10cm*
- £40 • Dr Colin B. Baddiel

△ Red Fire Engine

- *1960s*

Red fire engine operated by battery with a box snorkel.

- *34cm x 20cm*
- £85 • Dr Colin B. Baddiel

△ Batmobile Car

• *1960*
American black Batmobile, with red interior.
• *length 10cm*
• £48 • **Dr Colin B. Baddiel**

△ Robot

• *circa 1970*
A tin robot spaceman, made in Japan, with walking mechanism. Silver-painted with yellow and blue design.
• *height 14cm*
• £75 • **Dolly Land**

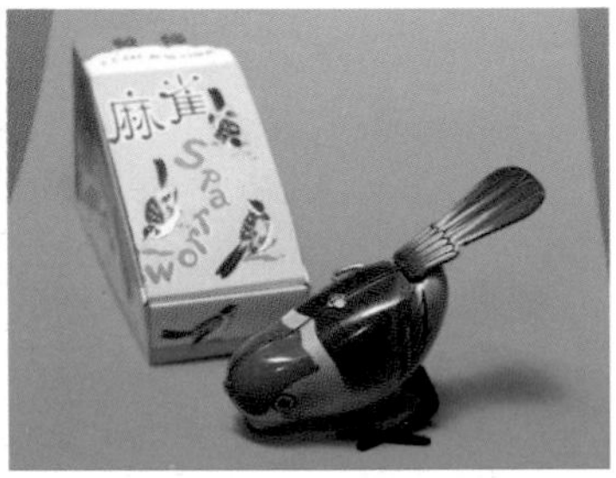

△ Clockwork Sparrow

• *1976*
Chinese clockwork sparrow in full working order and complete with original box. Sparrow is vividly painted and pecks the ground when activated.
• *height 8.5cm*
• £13 • **Retro Exchange**

▽ German Crocodile Train

• *circa 1960*
Green German crocodile train by Marklin. HO-gauge.
• *length 23cm*
• £445 • **Jeff Williams**

▽ Kiddy Computer

• *late 1970s*
Kiddy computer, with original box, which features addition, subtraction, multiplication and division, but looks as if it does rather more.
• *height 19cm*
• £18 • **Retro Exchange**

▽ Green Racing Car

• *1980*
Dinky green Connaught racing car with driver, with its original box.
• *length 16cm*
• £80 • **Dr Colin B. Baddiel**

◁ Robot

• *1985*
Battery-operated robot named 'Crackpot'. By Tomy, made in Singapore, with animated preset moves, moving arms, head and flashing lights.
• *height 17cm*
• £55 • **Retro Exchange**

△ UFO Jigsaw

• *1970*
A complete UFO jigsaw puzzle comprising 320 pieces by Anow Games Ltd., after a TV series. Shows a scene with 'Shadows' space engineers – one of a series of three designs.
• *18cm x 18cm*
• £10 • **Retro Exchange**

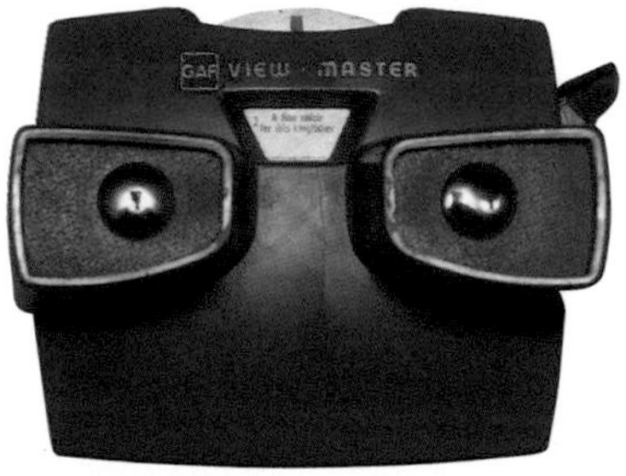

△ View Master

• *1980*
A GAF View Master and one ornithological slide. In working order. Circular slides contain several transparencies which are selected by lever on side of viewer.
• *width 15cm*
• £8 • **Retro Exchange**

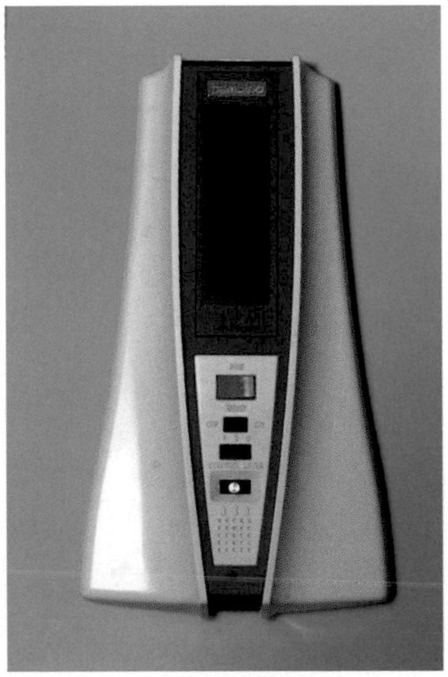

△ Master Blaster Station

• *1981*
UFO Master Blaster Station battery operated by Bambino, made in Japan.
• *length 21cm*
• £15 • **Retro Exchange**

▽ Skedoodle

• *1979*
A Skedoodle etching game with stencils made in Brevete, France, by Estanger. Complete with all original attributes.
• £16 • **Retro Exchange**

▽ Noddy

• *1980*
Noddy wearing a red shirt, yellow spotted scarf and blue hat with a yellow pom-pom, in his yellow rubber car with red fenders.
• *19cm x 27cm*
• £30 • **P. McAskie**

▽ Rubik's Cube

• *1980*
Rubik's cube in box shown in complete form with sticker 'Toy of the Year 1980'. From the Ideal Toy Corporation. Made in Hungary.
• *8cm square*
• £20 • **Retro Exchange**

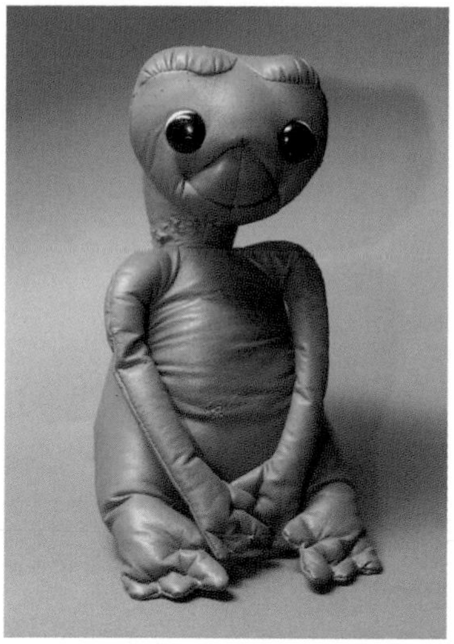

△ ET Doll

- *1982*

Plastic stuffed doll from the feature film *ET* by Stephen Spielberg.

- *height 24cm*
- £18 • Retro Exchange

△ Replica Bear

- *1991*

A replica of a Steiff 35PB teddy bear of 1904, with string mechanism and sealing-wax nose.

- *height 50cm*
- £450 • Dolly Land

△ VW Beetle Model

- *1998*

A gold Beetle of 1:1/18 scale modelled after 1955 car, 1,000,000 off the production line. In die-cast aluminium, with opening doors, boot and bonnet.

- £20 • Retro Exchange

▽ Somersault Bear

- *circa 1990*

A replica of a 1909 Somersault bear with clockwork mechanism that makes him lift his arma and do his trick. In old gold mohair. Edition limited to 5,000.

- *height 29cm*
- £375 • Dolly Land

▽ GI Soldier

- *1987*

US soldier in combat uniform with helmet and rifle. Battery-operated sequence where soldier crawls and fires weapon.

- *length 34cm*
- £40 • Retro Exchange

▽ Steiff Bear and Golly

- *1996*

Jolly Golly and Steiff Bear set, part of a limited edition of 1,500.

- *height 45cm*
- £295 • Dolly Land

▷ Jousting Knights

- *circa 2000*

Hand-made and painted pewter 15th-century Jousting Knight (right) and Crusader Knight. 90mm scale.

- *height 17cm*
- **£1,000 (jouster), £850 (crusader)**
- **The Armoury**

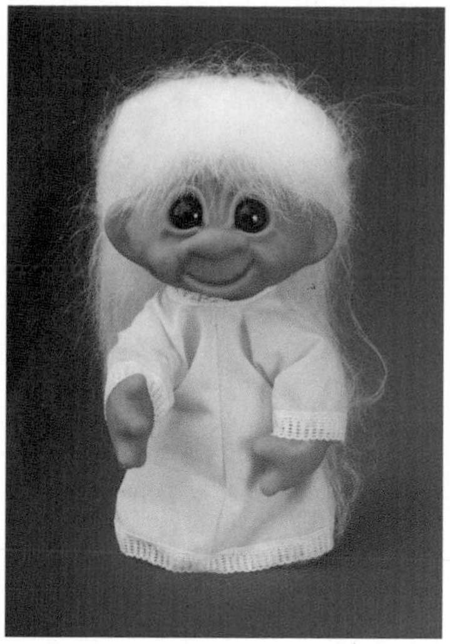

△ Troll

- *circa 1990*

One of the celebrated Troll family, made in Denmark. This particular effort has long white hair and is wearing a yellow dress with white trim.

- *height 26cm*
- £18 • Dolly Land

△ Teddy Bears

- *circa 1993*

A replica of a 1907 Steiff bear, one of the largest made. The materials used are all as the original. The bear is in the sitting position, wearing a red bow.

- *height 70cm*
- £750 • Dolly Land

▽ Wellington Bear

- *1992*

Limited edition of Merrythought Wellington Bear.

- *height 54cm*
- £125 • Dolly Land

▽ Mounted Drummer

- *circa 2000*

Hand-made and painted pewter mounted French drummer, with plumes to rider and mount, on a modelled painted base and a wooden plinth.

- *height 17cm*
- £850 • The Armoury

TREEN

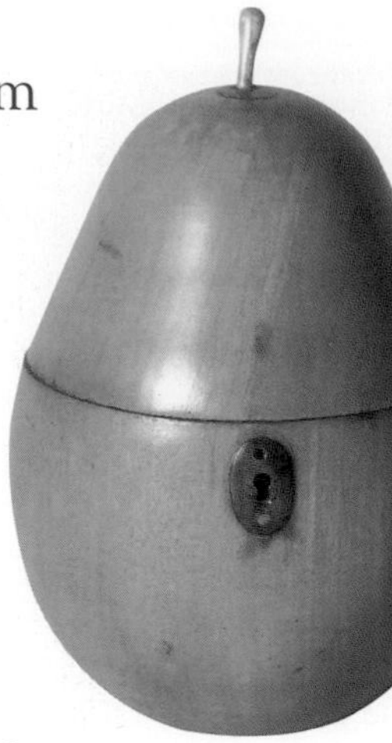

Treen applies to those items which are carved from wood and encompasses a wide range of items, from the simple napkin ring to the highly decorative and heavily carved oak plaque. The word treen actually means 'made from trees' and therefore the beauty of collecting treen lies in the variety of artefacts that are available. Occasionally, objects dating back to the seventeenth century arrive on the market, with the workaday items, such as cups and other vessels being fashioned from hardwoods such as sycamore and holly, while the more important were carved from lignum vitae, which had to be imported into England. If you are about to embark on your first journey to collect treen it is worth noting that boxes and love tokens are among the most desirable types. Look out for burr walnut or rosewood snuff boxes, which attract the collector with their sleek lines and simple design. Treen is a good area for the beginning collector as some of the items are still relatively inexpensive.

△ Virgin and Child

- *circa 1500*

German/Flemish group with extensive original polychrome.

- *height 39cm*
- £2,200 • A. & E. Foster

△ English Carved Oak Panel

- *circa 1500*

With early representations of an elephant and a leopard.

- *length 39cm*
- £850 • A. & E. Foster

▷ Religious Carvings

- *17th century*

Italian walnut carvings of St Theresa and St Filipo, bought in Florence in 1877, by J.D. Irven.

- *height 51cm*
- £650 • Castlegate

◁ Coffer Frontpiece

- *circa 1600*

English oak coffer frontpiece with carved double spiral and oak leaf spandrels.

- *length 1.12m*
- £3,200 • A. & E. Foster

▽ Carved Panel

- *circa 1600*

A very fine English carved oak caryatid of exceptionally large size, probably from a bedhead.

- *height 1.2m*
- £2,800 • A. & E. Foster

△ Oak Carvings

- *1600*

Pair of oak carvings showing winged mythical creatures, possibly from an overmantel.

- *height 55cm*
- £1,780 • Dial Post House

△ Powder Flask

- *17th century*

German powder flask with iron mounts and turned decoration.

- *diameter 17cm*
- £850 • A. & E. Foster

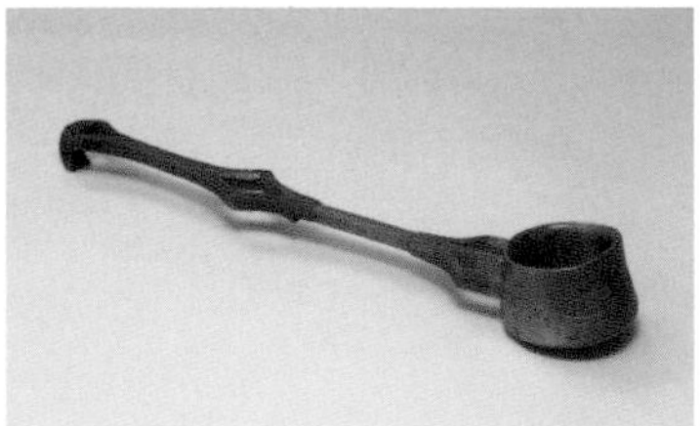

△ Scottish Ladle

- *circa 1720*

A Scottish ladle with chip carving to handle and fish carved on the bowl.

- *length 31cm*
- £395 • A. & E. Foster

▽ Oak Panel

- *circa 1620*

Carved Dutch panel depicting the conversion of St Paul, retaining original polychrome.

- *height 62cm*
- £2,200 • A. & E. Foster

▽ Gilt Wall Sconces

- *late 17th century*

One of a pair of gilt wall sconces with candlesticks.

- £6,000 • Dial Post House

▽ Nutcracker

- *circa 1720*

A good boxwood nutcracker with the carving of a bearded man with teeth. English.

- *length 16cm*
- £1,650 • A. & E. Foster

◁ Burr-Walnut Snuff box

- *circa 1770*

Burr-walnut snuff box with a blank silver plaque on the lid.

- *length 8.5cm*
- £380 • Rupert Gentle

△ Cornucopia

- *circa 1680*

A pair of carved oak 17th-century, Flemish cornucopias.

- *height 55cm*
- £2,600 • A. & E. Foster

△ Carving of Bacchus

- *17th century*

A rare English seventeenth-century limewood carved figure of the Greek god Bacchus seated on a barrel pouring wine into a goblet.

- *height 25cm*
- £1,600 • Dial Post House

△ Pipe Tamper

- *18th century*

Boxwood pipe tamper with handle in shape of a greyhound devouring its prey.

- *height 10cm*
- £695 • A. & E. Foster

▽ Ethiopian Cross

- *17th century*

Wooden Ethiopian hand blessing cross.

- *length 16cm*
- £350 • Iconastas

▽ Oak Plaque

- *17th century*

A heavily carved oak seventeenth-century plaque showing scrolling geometric patterns around a central rose motif.

- *height 20cm*
- £1,150 • Dial Post House

▽ Pipe Tamper

- *18th century*

A silver mounted pipe tamper, carved in the shape of a head, inscribed to Francis Stone.

- *length 10cm*
- £695 • A. & E. Foster

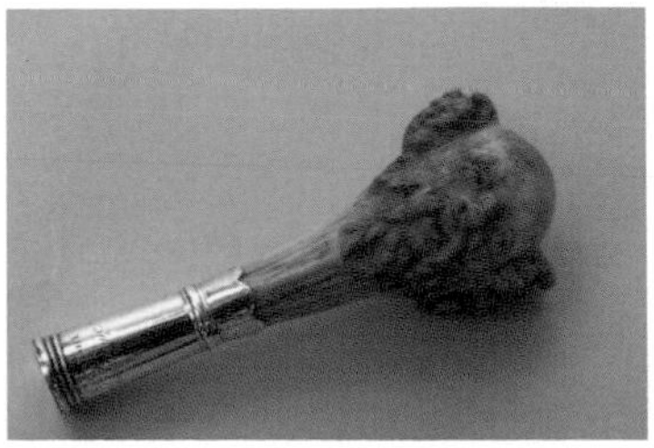

△ Cribbage Board

- *circa 1780*

A chip-carved maple board from Friesland, with additional carving to front forming a cribbage board.

- *length 83cm*
- £490 • A. & E. Foster

△ Tea Caddy

- *circa 1790*

George III fruitwood single tea caddy, comprising six sections of stained and natural woods.

- *height 14cm*
- £4,950 • J. & T. Stone

△ Tea Caddy

- *circa 1790*

Fine 18th-century fruitwood apple tea caddy with traces of original colour.

- *height 14cm*
- £4,950 • J. & T. Stone

▽ French Carved Flowers

- *1780*

One of a pair of French carved stands, with scrolled foliate designs and seven giltwood flowers on a moulded serpentine base.

- *height 93cm*
- £1,450 • Heytesbury

▽ Yew-Wood Coaster

- *circa 1840*

Yew-wood coaster with a raised diamond flower in the centre and a linked border, with maker's name, M. Scott.

- *diameter 17cm*
- £650 • Rupert Gentle

△ Toolbox

- *circa 1780*

Wooden, possible elm, toolbox with locking mechanism to front.

- *length 56cm*
- £150 • Curios

▽ Rosewood Snuff Box

- *circa 1780*

Circular snuff box with the inscription 'A. C. B. to J. G. B. 1821'.

- *diameter 9cm*
- £380 • Rupert Gentle

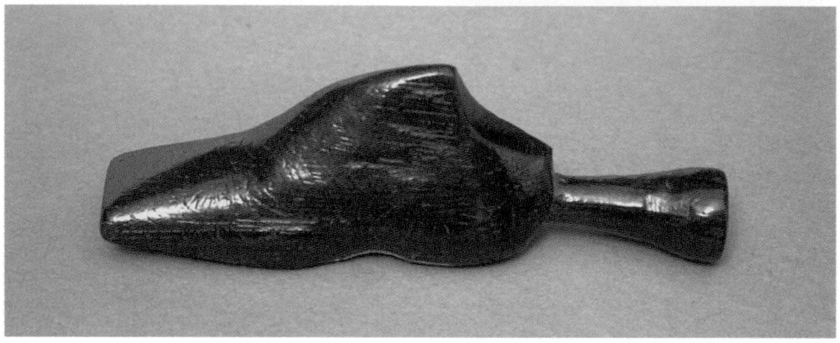

△ Pipe Tamper with Royal Charter

- *circa 1780*

Pipe tamper with a 'Royal Charter' label on the base.

- *length 7.5cm*
- £350 • Rupert Gentle

△ Tea Caddy

- *circa 1790*

Late 18th-century fruitwood tea caddy, fashioned in the shape of a pear, with stalk finial and keyplate to the front.

- *height 15cm*
- £4,950 • J. & T. Stone

◁ Capitals

- *19th century*

Large carvings, one of a large Corinthian capital, the other in a swirling, organic form. Both carved from walnut.

- £165, £100 resp. • Castlegate

▽ Toad

- *19th century*

Japanese carving of a toad, with inlaid eyes, naturalistically carved and polished. Signed Ryukei.

- *length 6cm*
- £5,800 • Gregg Baker

▽ Shoe Lasts

- *19th century*

Pair of English wooden shoe lasts.

- *length 28cm*
- £75 • John Clay

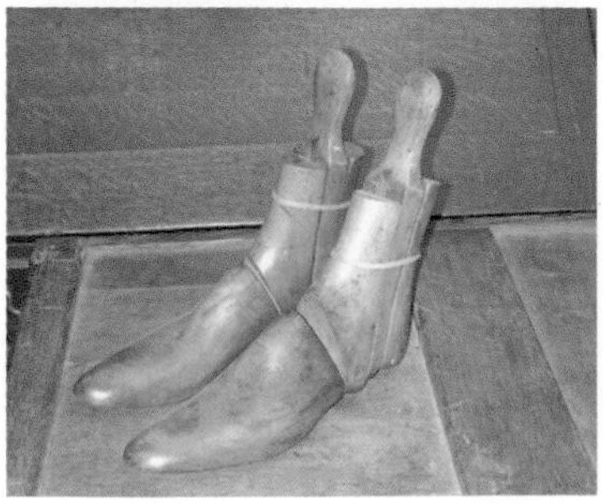

△ Four Egg Cups
- *circa 1840*

A set of four turned mahogany egg cups.
- *height 9cm*
- £375 • Rupert Gentle

▽ Paintbox
- *circa 1890*

An English mahogany paintbox with colours, porcelain mixing dishes and glass water pot.
- *length 19cm*
- £150 • Judith Lasalle

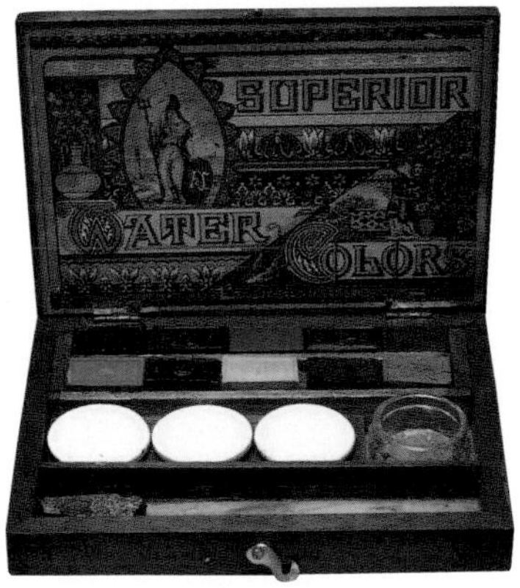

△ Carved Cherubs
- *19th century*

Carved walnut figures of adolescent cherubic girls.
- *height 45cm*
- £395 • Castlegate

▽ Sycamore Container
- *1900*

Sycamore cylindrical container with a view of the Windsor Castle round tower.
- *height 9cm*
- £45 • John Clay

△ Amboyna and Maplewood Dish
- *circa 1910*

Dish fashioned from amboyna and maplewood with turned decoration. The dish rests on four maple balls.
- *diameter 32cm*
- £145 • John Clay

▽ Pill Box
- *circa 1900s*

Austrian bullet-shaped pill box inscribed with the words: 'Apotheke Zum Heil Agidius. J. Brady Wien VL, Gumpendorferst 105'.
- *height 7cm*
- £38 • John Clay

▽ Sycamore Beaker
- *circa 1900*

A sycamore beaker with a view of the Linn of Dee.
- *height 7cm*
- £48 • John Clay

▽ Dutch Carved Vases
- *1920*

A pair of Dutch carved vases with the figures of two women in a forest setting.
- *height 38cm*
- £375 • John Clay

△ Austrian Stamp Box
- *1860*

Small Austrian stamp box with carved relief of oak leaves.
- *1.5cm x 5cm*
- £35 • Jasmin Cameron

△ Napkin Rings
- *circa 1900*

Three sycamore Mauchlin-ware napkin rings showing various British scenes.
- *height 2cm*
- £18 • John Clay

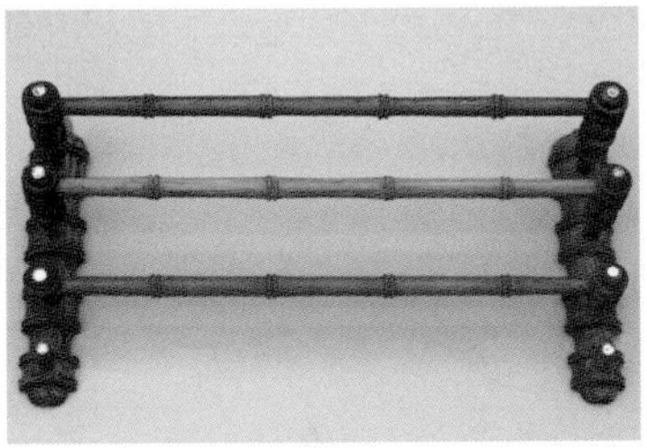

△ Towel Rack
- *circa 1900*

French faux bamboo towel rack with turned decoration.
- *height 50cm*
- £78 • Myriad

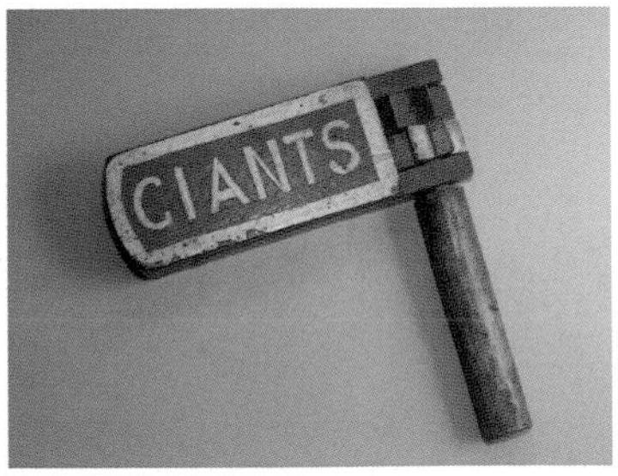

△ American Handclapper
- *circa 1940*

All wood American football rattle with 'Giants' painted on one side. Solid wooden handle.
- *height 30cm*
- £34 • After Noah

TRIBAL ART

As the world becomes smaller with the rise in travel, and the onset of mass globalisation begins to turn us into a global village, tribal art has become an important way for countries to preserve and promote their cultural heritage and present their unique identity to the world. Obviously travel has also opened up the world and it is because of people's hunger to find new and isolated destinations that more tribal art is finding its way onto the market place, as even twenty years ago some of these countries would have been far too remote to reach. Tribal art was created to mark rites and watersheds in a person's life: from the birth of a child to going into battle, all were recorded with these works of art and sculpture. Some of the tribal artefacts on the collector's market today, such as the wrought-iron stick men figures used on the Cameroon borders in the late nineteenth century, were originally created as currency, but we now consider them to be works of art, collected to be displayed.

△ **Currency**

- *ancient*

Large, wrought-iron mahonia leaf-form currency. Excavation piece from the Cameroon.

- *height 62cm*
- £200 • Gordon Reece

▽ **Dance Sceptre**

- *ancient*

A rare ceremonial dance sceptre, excavated in Chad and thought to belong to Dogon tribe of Mali.

- *height 61cm*
- £1,200 • Gordon Reece

▷ **Yarli Lions**

- *1700s*

Pair of mythical beasts called Yarli Lions from Kanataka province in south-western India. Originally they were brackets that featured on a chariot or juggernaut.

- *46cm x 18cm*
- £1,420 • Gordon Reece

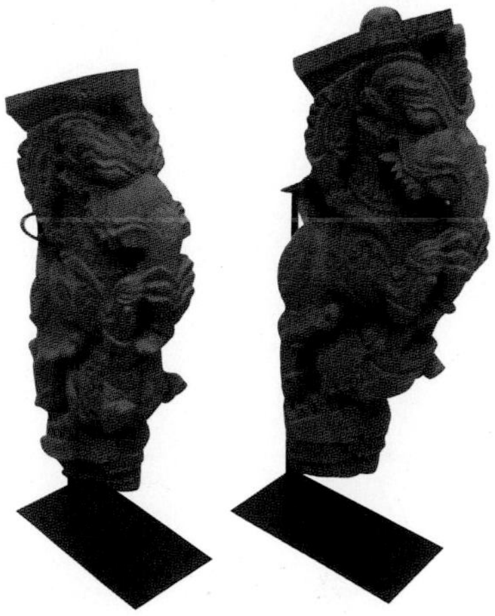

◁ **Tamil Nadu Wall Carvings**

- *mid 18th century*

Erotic carvings from a temple cart.

- *71cm x 26cm*
- £1,800 • Gordon Reece

△ **Himalayan Mask**

- *circa 1700*

An ancient Himalayan mask in the form of a snow lion. A most unusual broad form by Nepalese standards. Possibly 200–300 years old. Much valued and cared for judging from sympathetic repairs (code HYM96100).

- *24cm x 28cm*
- £795 • Gordon Reece

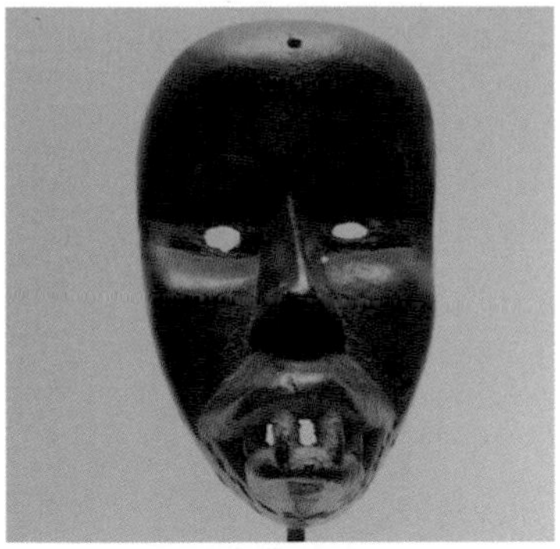

△ Kulu Mask

• *circa 1800*
A mask of the Himalayan Indian Gaddei tribe of the Kulu Valley. Flat and simple in form with two bars representing teeth.
• *height 25cm*
• £770 • Gordon Reece

△ Mask with Birds

• *circa 1820*
A fine early Ivory Coast mask with the crest of two birds and facial fringe. In intact condition. From a London collection.
• *height 42cm*
• £1,250 • Gordon Reece

△ African Stool

• *19th century*
An African stool, made of bush wood.
• *27cm x 46cm*
• £225 • Tredantiques

▽ Pair of Naga Sculptures

• *late 1800s*
Pair of standing Naga figures.
• *64cm x 14cm*
• £1,900 • Gordon Reece

▽ Carved African Stools

• *early 19th century*
Four unusual carved African stools with handles.
• *4cm x 12cm x 13cm*
• £360 • Gordon Reece

▽ Anchor Currency

• *circa 1880*
A heavily patinated, excavated anchor-shaped piece of currency, from the Congo.
• *height 51cm*
• £210 • Gordon Reece

△ Himachal Pradesh Mask

• *early 1900s*
A most unusual form with the upper features on a dome-like area, with exaggerated slit eyes and a stylised mouth, with signs of applied silver and other applications. From the Himachal Pradesh region of India.
• *26cm x 40cm*
• £1,300 • Gordon Reece

△ Round Box

• *circa 1880*
A cylindrical wooden box with carved lid and elaborately carved finial, the body with three individually carved figures, attached with rafiawork. From Sarawak, North Borneo.
• *height 16cm*
• £120 • Gordon Reece

▽ Bronze Cobra

• *circa 1840*
Cast-bronze cobra from the Khond tribe of central India.
• *height 30cm*
• £339 • Gordon Reece

▽ Mythical Guardians

• *circa 1880*
A pair of statues from Orissa, Eastern India, repesenting male human forms with bovine heads, in carved and painted wood.
• *height 83cm*
• £1,750 • Gordon Reece

◁ Grassland Cameroon Stool

• *1890*
An African grassland Cameroon stool in anthropomorphic form.
• *height 35cm*
• £340 • Gordon Reece

△ Indian Naga Mask

- *19th century*

Naga wooden mask from India carved with headdress and teeth.

- *30cm x 18cm*
- £550 • Zakheim

△ Wild Bronze Boar

- *circa 1890*

Cast bronze wild boar of strong form with raised spine from the Khond tribe in middle India.

- *13cm x 19cm*
- £280 • Gordon Reece

△ Yoruban Mask

- *circa 1900*

Nigerian Yoruban helmet mask.

- *50cm x 24cm*
- £400 • Gooday Gallery

▽ Naga Tribal Pendant

- *circa 1890*

Double-headed Naga tribal pendant with original blue beaded necklace.

- *width 9.5cm*
- £140 • Gordon Reece

▽ African Wooden Sculptures

- *early 1900s*

Three African tribal carved wood sculptures.

- *11cm x 70cm*
- £360 • Gordon Reece

▽ Kulia Valley Mask

- *circa 1900*

Very old mask from the Kulia valley area. The heavy wear and patination suggests a very early date or continued heavy usage (code PR9822).

- *26cm x 38cm*
- £1,450 • Gordon Reece

△ Chieftain's Stool

- *circa 1890*

Ashanti Abzma Owa chieftain's stool, carved from one piece of wood and into interlocking, semicircular symmetrical design. Once used by Queen Elizabeth, the Queen Mother.

- *height 31cm*
- £480 • Gordon Reece

△ Tshokwe-Mbuna Mask

- *early 1900s*

A striking mask with natural patination fibre additions, from Tshokwe-Mbuna.

- *28cm x 40cm*
- £400 • Gordon Reece

△ African Mask

- *early 1900s*

A finely drawn mask with a good patination from the Incangala Tshokwe.

- £800 • Gordon Reece

▽ Figure used by Trance Diviners

- *circa 1890*

Magnificent example of a seated male figure showing scarification and detailed coiffeur. Used by trance diviners and kept in their private shrines. From the Ivory Coast.

- *height 34cm*
- £15,000 • Gordon Reece

▽ Ivory Coast Figures

- *circa 1890*

Bete carved figures.

- *height 19cm*
- £490 • Gordon Reece

▽ Yoruba Crown

- *20th century*

Yoruban crown decorated with coconut hair and a face created from cowrie shells.

- *height 35cm*
- £650 • Zakheim

▽ Wrought-Iron Sculpture

• *early 1900s*
Three wrought-iron currency forms.
• *18cm x 48cm*
• £380 • Gordon Reece

▽ Yoruban Iron Staff

• *early 1900s*
Ancient ceremonial wrought-iron staff, from Yoruba, Nigeria.
• *64cm x 24cm*
• £720 • Gordon Reece

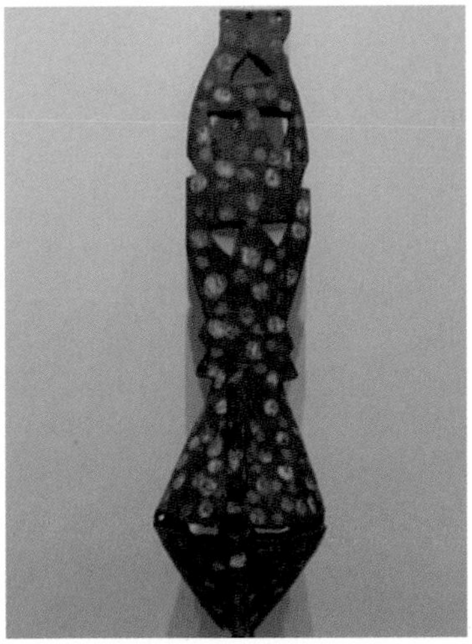

▽ African Tribal Masks

• *circa 1900*
Two African tribal masks.
• *16cm x 25cm*
• £3,600 • Gordon Reece

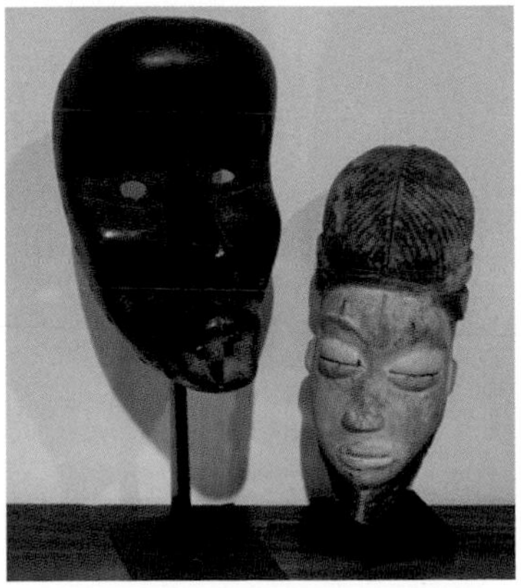

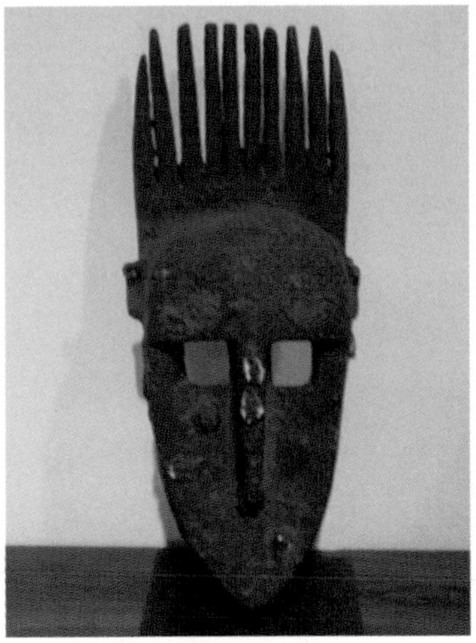

△ Bambra Mask

• *early 1900s*
Mask from the Bambara tribe but with a strong influence from the Dogon.
• *66cm x 18cm*
• £3,400 • Gordon Reece

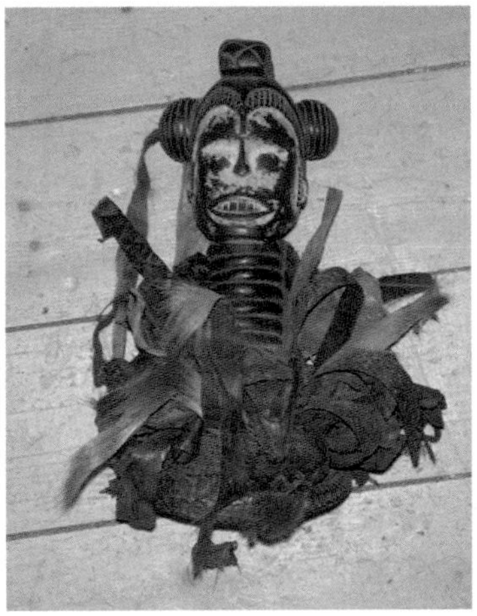

△ Kongo Figure

• *early 20th century*
Kongo wooden fetish with snake skin strands and monkey hair, with traces of gesso decoration.
• *height 35cm*
• £650 • Zakheim

▽ Iron Lamp

• *early 1900s*
Ancient wrought-iron lamp decorated with birds.
• £820 • Gordon Reece

▽ Bakot Figure

• *circa 1900*
Bakot reliquary figure.
• *40cm x 15cm*
• £480 • Gooday Gallery

◁ Mask

• *circa 1900*
A Dan-Khan mask showing some Guere influence.
• *height 25cm*
• £3,600 • Gordon Reece

▷ Weapon

• *circa 1900*
A Manjbetu, Mambele tribe or Trumbafit cleaver weapon, with wooden handle. From Zaire, formerly the Belgian Congo.
• *length 40cm*
• £220 • Gordon Reece

△ Tribal Mask

• *early 1900s*
Heavily patinated tribal mask (code 9427).
• *22cm x 15cm*
• £740 • Gordon Reece

△ Javanese Mask

• *early 1900s*
Javanese mask of a Mahabarata/ Ramayana character.
• *19cm x 14cm*
• £550 • Gordon Reece

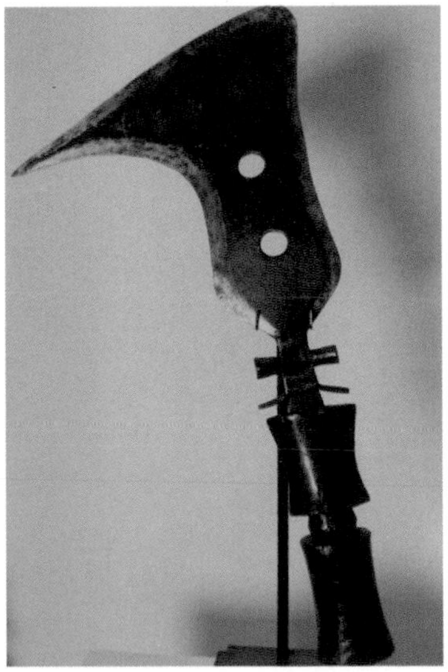

▽ Burmese Statue

- *circa 1900*

Statue of the squatting figure of a man, in a relaxed, fluid style. From the Burmese Naga tribe.

- *height 54cm*
- £1,750 • Gordon Reece

▽ Suku Fetish

- *circa 1900*

Suku finely carved figure used as a fetish with additional fibre, beads and feathers, from Northern Zaire.

- *height 43cm*
- £950 • Gordon Reece

▷ Yonba Maternity Figure

- *circa 1910*

Yonba carved wood maternity figure of a seated woman with a child at her breast.

- *height 59cm*
- £1,700 • Gordon Reece

△ African Mask

- *circa 1900*

A Songye Kifwebe mask from Zaire.

- *30cm x 29cm*
- £450 • Gooday Gallery

△ Nigerian Delta Region

- *circa 1910*

Spirit mask from the Nigerian Delta region, the head crowned by four men and a boat, with classical red pigmentation. The figures, originally white, have been overpainted black.

- *height 53cm*
- £1,100 • Gordon Reece

▽ Mask

- *circa 1910*

A fine Borneo mask, complete with original paintwork and applied skin and fibre.

- *height 34cm*
- £3,200 • Gordon Reece

▽ Igbo Tribe Figures

- *circa 1910*

One of a pair of figures from the Igbo tribe of terracotta seated ancestoral types, displaying crested headdress and multiple anklets, bracelets and necklaces symbolising wealth.

- *height 54cm*
- £6,500 • Gordon Reece

▽ Himalayan Chest

- *20th century*

A chest in Himalayan pine, with three panels to the front showing profuse chip carving and curved apron.

- *height 83cm*
- £770 • Gordon Reece

△ Chieftain's Stool

- *circa 1915*

An excellent chieftain's stool carved from one piece of wood. From Tanzania, East Africa.

- *height 35cm*
- £790 • Gordon Reece

△ Elephant Stool

- *circa 1930*

A small, hardwood stool, carved from one piece of hardwood, showing an African bull elephant on pedestal as support.

- *height 28cm*
- £15 • Something Different

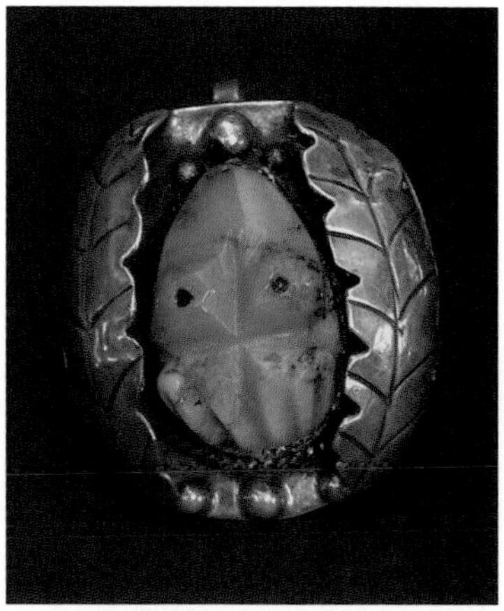

△ Zuni Fetish Frog

- *1930*

Large Zuni fetish circular gold-coloured pendant with a central turquoise styled as a frog flanked by gold-coloured leaves.

- *length 4.5cm*
- £59 • Wilde Ones

▽ Gable Mask

- *early 20th century*

A gable mask from Papua New Guinea with cowrie shells.

- *height 90cm*
- £550 • Gooday Gallery

▽ Naga Mask

- *20th century*

Naga wooden mask.

- *30cm x 18cm*
- £550 • Zakheim

▽ Mahogany Stool

- *circa 1970*

A red mahogany stool, carved from one piece of wood, showing an elephant. From the Shona or Matabele tribe of Zimbabwe.

- *height 51cm*
- £230 • Something Different

△ Bapende Mask

- *20th century*

Bapende tribal mask decorated with shells and coconut hair.

- *40cm x 17cm*
- £490 • Zakheim

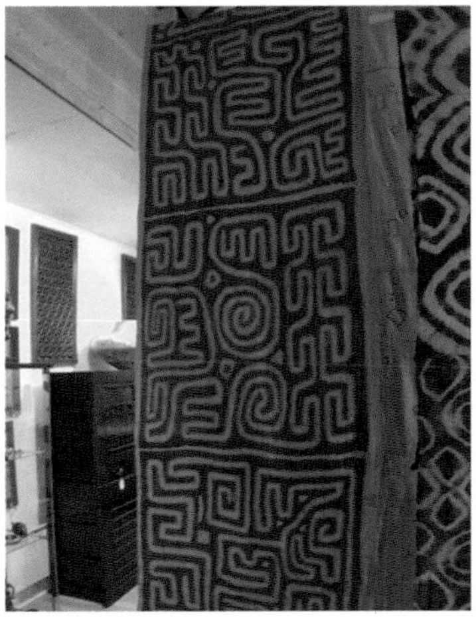

△ Kuba Dance Skirt

- *mid-20th century*

Zairean Neongo tribe Kuba dance skirt. Dyed raffia appliquéd.

- *76cm x 4m*
- £1,900 • Gordon Reece

▽ Kota Figure

- *early 20th century*

Kota wooden figure decorated with brass and copper plaques.

- *71cm x 33cm*
- £850 • Zakheim

▽ Apache Bag

- *1950*

Apache suede pipe bag with a long strap and fringing and a central glass bead work of a red and black frog.

- *length 50cm*
- £169 • Wilde Ones

◁ Zuni Fetish Pot

- *circa 2000*

Zuni fetish pot shaped as an owl with its owlet.

- *height 8cm*
- £89.99 • Wilde Ones

△ Dan Mask

- *early 20th century*

Dan mask from Liberia.

- *25cm x 16cm*
- £400 • Gooday Gallery

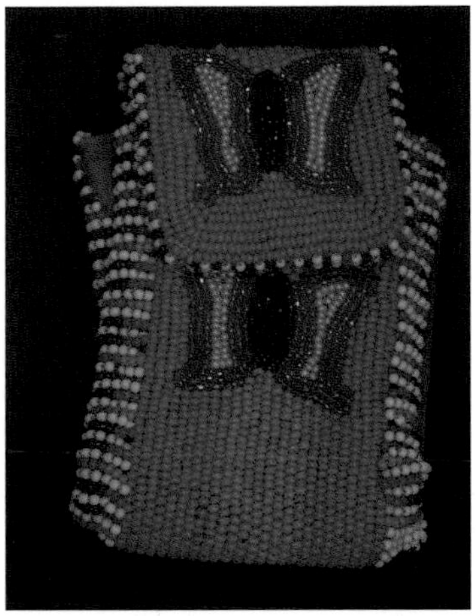

△ Apache Smoking Pouch

- *1950*

Apache Indian smoking pouch with a red, white and black butterfly on an orange background, made from glass beads sewn on leather.

- *12cm x 7cm*
- £160 • Wilde Ones

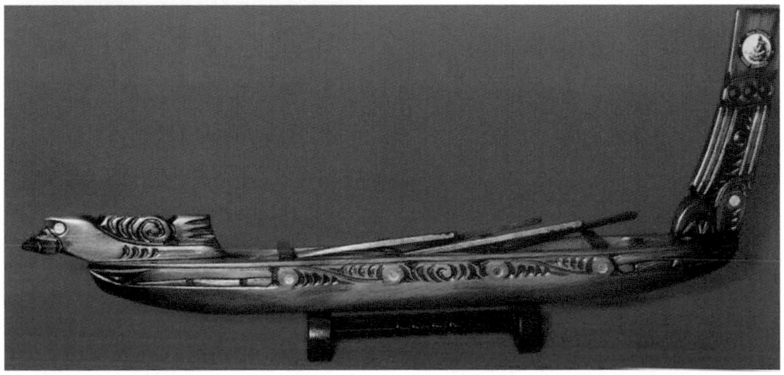

△ Maori Canoe

- *circa 1992*

Model of a Maori war canoe, with space for four oarsmen.

- *length 50cm*
- £80 • Pacifica

TWENTIETH-CENTURY DESIGN

From the 1900s the design of furniture and ceramics took on an exciting futuristic vibrancy, with designers experimenting with moulded plywood, fibreglass, plastic and leather. The famous Eames chair, successfully manufactured from the 1950s by the Herman Miller Company, with its moulded rosewood veneer and steel base, exemplifies this. These new materials completely changed the way furniture design was viewed, and the moulded organic shape became popular, with the innovators Eames and Saarinen winning prizes for their prototype chairs at the Organic Design in Home Furnishings Exhibition held at the Museum of Modern Art in New York in 1940. This exhibition was to have a profound effect on post-war ceramic design. Roy Midwinter designed two startling ranges of ceramics known as 'Stylecraft' and 'Fashion' in the new curving shapes and commissioned innovative new ranges of patterns from the resident designers Jessie Tait and Terence Conran. In Italy numerous designers and workshops produced highly individualistic and original work, with one of the most influential of these designers being Carlo Mollino (1905–73), who used aircraft manufacturing technology to produce complex, curved forms.

CERAMICS

◁ Clarice Cliff Plate

- *circa 1900*

Clarice Cliff palette-shaped 'Cruise Ware', decorated with a parasol and a pair of lady's legs on the left side, and a funnel of a ship above, made by Wilkinson Ltd.

- *diameter 24cm*
- £400 • Arwas

▷ Lambeth Vase

- *1900*

Lambeth vase decorated with a green foliate design and pale blue flowers on a dark grey background. Made by Francis Pope.

- *height 30cm*
- £1,900 • Richard Dennis

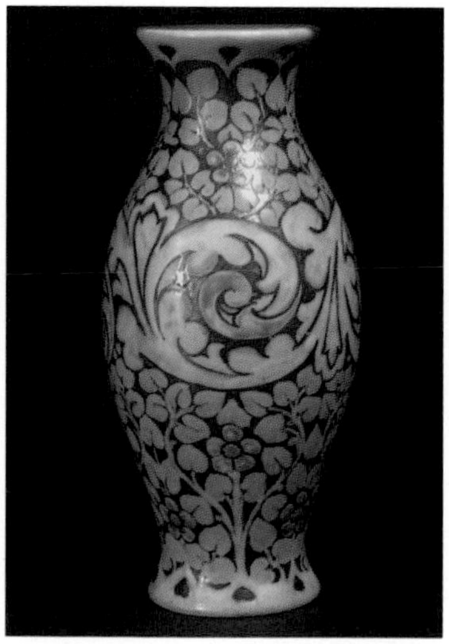

△ Belgian Budgerigars

- *circa 1900*

A pair of white budgerigars in biscuit porcelain, the characteristic unglazed modelling allowing for excellent detail in the plumage. Each bird mirrors the other and they are set on square plinths incorporating the tail feathers.

- *height 15cm*
- £250 • P. Oosthuizen

△ Enamelled Daum Vase

- *1900*

Daum vase showing a winter scene with enamelled silver birch and sunset.

- *height 9cm*
- **£1,500** • **French Glasshouse**

△ Nude by M. Guevara

- *circa 1900*

Painted clay figure of a nude girl in a hat by Brazilian artist Monica Guevara.

- *height 28cm*
- **£450** • **Arwas**

△ Large Gouda Vase

- *1910*

Zuid-Holland factory. Gouda two-handled large vase.

- *height 43cm*
- **£2,050** • **P. Oosthuizen**

▽ Cruise Ware Plate

- *circa 1900*

'Cruise Ware' Clarice Cliff plate by Wilkinson, with a young lady leaping beside a net holding a ring, and a funnel above her.

- *diameter 24cm*
- **£400** • **Arwas**

▽ Dunmore Vase

- *early 20th century*

Scottish Dunmore ovoid vase in a turquoise glaze with a splayed neck with moulded rim.

- *height 29cm*
- **£80** • **A.D. Antiques**

▽ Glazed Inkwell

- *1915*

Zuid-Holland factory. Gouda. Glazed inkwell with two lids. By A.M. Rijp.

- *length 22cm*
- **£250** • **P. Oosthuizen**

△ Royal Doulton Vase

- *circa 1900*

Lambeth ware vase by Royal Doulton with a border of yellow and green petals with a dark blue centre, and a lilac body.

- *height 28cm*
- **£350** • **Arwas**

△ Porcelain Cup and Saucer

- *1903*

Eggshell porcelain cup and saucer, with orchid and parrot decoration, by Rudolph Sterken From Rozenburg company, The Hague.

- *height 8cm*
- **£1,100** • **P. Oosthuizen**

△ Morris Ware Vases

- *circa 1910*

Pair of Morris ware vases in thistle pattern by George Cartridge.

- *height 32cm*
- **£1,360** • **A.D. Antiques**

▽ Flambé Vase

- *1905–15*

Flambé vase of bottle shape with a deep red glaze, made by Bernard Moore.

- *height 15cm*
- **£195** • **A.D. Antiques**

▽ Amsterdam Tiles

- *1900*

Panel of six 'Distel' Amsterdam tiles, mounted in the original wooden frame with gilded inset.

- *62cm x 47cm*
- **£700** • **P. Oosthuizen**

▽ Lustre Vase

- *1910*

Pilkington Royal Lancaster lustre vase with floral decoration on a rich flambé ground by Annie Burton.

- *height 20cm*
- **£665** • **A.D. Antiques**

△ Flambé Pot

• *1912*

Red and bronze flambé glazed pot of conical form, tapering to the foot with a small finial lid, by Howsons.

• *height 22cm*

• £265 • A.D. Antiques

△ Art Nouveau Set

• *1920*

Art Nouveau-style jug and bowl set, comprising five pieces.

• £195 • A.D. Antiques

△ Two-Handled Vase

• *April 1920*

Large two-handled baluster vase by Zuid-Holland factory. Gouda design 'Crocus'.

• *height 44cm*

• £1,100 • P. Oosthuizen

▽ Arnhem Factory Vase

• *1916*

'Lindus' design two-handled, bottle-shaped vase with stylised flowers from the Arnhem factory.

• *height 27cm*

• £325 • P. Oosthuizen

▽ Zuid-Holland Candlesticks

• *1923*

Gouda pair of candlesticks in the 'Rio' design, with extra-large, moulded drip-pans and globular bases tapering upwards.

• *height 30cm*

• £360 (pair) • P. Oosthuizen

▽ Tea Service

• *circa 1920s*

Belleek Irish porcelain tea service with shamrock pattern and a basketweave design with twig handle. Stamped with black mark. Made in Fermanagh.

• £1,500 • R.A. Barnes

△ Gouda Night Light

• *1915*

Zuid-Holland factory. Design 'A Jour'. Made for La Marquise de Sevigné Rouzand'.

• *height 17.5cm*

• £300 • P. Oosthuizen

△ Solitary Polar Bear

• *1920s*

Royal Copenhagen solitary polar bear walking on all fours, all feet on the ground. Dated and signed.

• *height 10.5cm*

• £280 • Cameo Gallery

△ Elephant Bookends

• *circa 1920s*

Pair of pink French elephant bookends in working pose, on octagonal plinths.

• *height 15cm*

• £150 • P. Ooosthuizen

▽ Royal Bonn Vase

• *1916*

'Old Dutch' design vase of bulbous form, with disproportionately narrow, baluster-shaped neck. By Frank Anton Mehlem.

• *height 21cm*

• £350 • P. Oosthuizen

▽ Doulton Flambé Vase

• *1920s*

Royal Doulton flambé vase showing shepherd in landscape. Vermilion with a lustre finish.

• *height 19cm*

• £600 • Cameo Gallery

◁ Dessert Service

• *circa 1920*

Wedgwood porcelain dessert service, set of twelve. Borders of vines and grapes edged with gold. Decorated with centre medallion of putti taking part in various activities. Made by Holland and Hedgekiss.

• £1,500 • R.A. Barnes

△ **Gouda Baluster Vase**

- *1920*

From Regina factory, Zuid-Holland. A baluster vase in the 'D'Arla' design, with repeated design of stylised bird, swirls and floral decoration, with matt gilding, rich blues and black.

- *height 43cm*
- £300 • P. Oosthuizen

△ **Polar Bears**

- *circa 1920s*

Royal Copenhagen model of two adult polar bears fighting. The whole design is circular in form, giving it momentum. Signed.

- *height 15.5cm*
- £475 • Cameo Gallery

△ **Moon & Mountain**

- *1928*

'Moon and Mountain' plate with a hand-painted abstract design by Susie Cooper.

- *length 26cm*
- £325 • Susie Cooper

▽ **Eagle and Pine Tree Vase**

- *1924*

Unusually large Royal Copenhagen vase, signed and dated. Baluster form vase with eagle and pine tree decoration.

- *height 49cm*
- £7,500 • Cameo Gallery

▽ **Vienna Baluster Vase**

- *circa 1925*

Ernst Wahliss 'Pergamon' Vienna baluster vase. Abstract floral pattern with lustre finish.

- *height 32cm*
- £300 • P. Oosthuizen

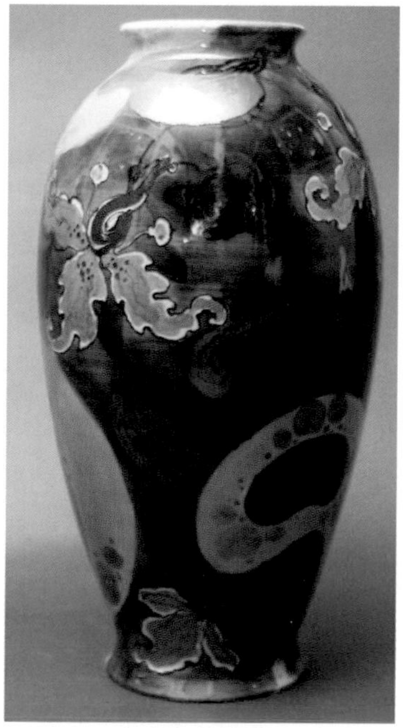

▷ **Gouda Wall Plate**

- *1928*

Zuid-Holland factory. Gouda wall plate. 'Corona' design by W.P. Hartsring.

- *height 31.5cm*
- £380 • P. Oosthuizen

△ **Gouda Tile**

- *1923–30*

Zuid-Holland factory. Gouda tile, with stork motif, designed by Jan Schonk.

- *11cm x 19cm*
- £350 • P. Oosthuizen

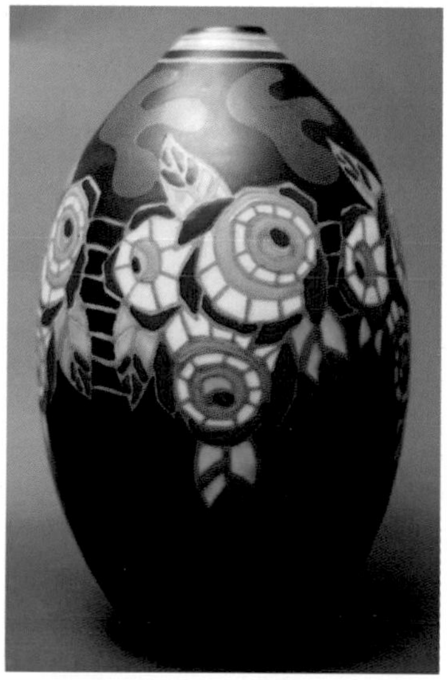

△ **Boch & Frères Vase**

- *1925*

Early 20th-century Keramis baluster vase by Charles Catteau.

- *height 31cm*
- £500 • P. Oosthuizen

▽ **Art Deco Figure**

- *1926*

Art Deco ceramic figure by Stanley Nicholson Babb.

- *height 25cm*
- £600 • Gooday Gallery

▽ **Shelley Tea Plate**

- *1927*

Shelley tea plate with orange border, black trees and green woodland border.

- *diameter 16cm*
- £20 • Susie Cooper

▽ **Floral Poole Vase**

- *circa 1929–34*

Smaller Poole Pottery vase with a highly coloured floral decoration. There is a chain-link pattern to the neck of the vase and a floral frieze about the waist.

- *height 17cm*
- £220 • Richard Dennis

△ Baluster Vase

• *1929*
Zuid-Holland factory. Gouda vase. Design 'Unique' by G.P. Van der Akker.
• *height 67.5cm*
• £2,250 • P. Oosthuizen

△ Poole Pottery Vase

• *circa 1930*
Poole pottery vase with stylised yellow and purple flowers and a purple, green and lilac design around the rim.
• *height 20cm*
• £200 • Richard Dennis

△ Albino Rabbit

• *circa 1930*
Japanese model of a comical, albino rabbit, with pink highlights, painted red eyes, disproportionately small feet and large, caricatured ears.
• *height 22cm*
• £780 • Gregg Baker

▽ Ross's Lime Juice Cordial

• *1929*
Small bowl by Susie Cooper inscribed with the advertisement for Ross's Lime Juice Cordial of Belfast.
• *diameter 14cm*
• £250 • Susie Cooper

▽ Royal Worcester

• *circa 1930*
Royal Worcester turquoise bulb vase with dark blue butterflies and birds.
• *height 27cm*
• £850 • Arwas

▽ Rosenthal Butterfly

• *circa 1930*
Rosenthal butterfly with green, black and blue enamels on a circular base.
• *height 5.5cm*
• £400 • Arwas

△ Bauhaus Jug

• *circa 1930*
Bauhaus pink and orange moulded jug by Leuchtenburg.
• *height 19cm*
• £450 • Arwas

△ Whieldon Ware Vase

• *circa 1930*
Whieldon Ware bulbous blue and orange floral design vase with gold leaves by F. Winkle & Co. Ltd, England. Orient design.
• *height 11cm*
• £160 • Arwas

△ Susie Cooper Sugar Pot

• *1929*
Sugar pot by Susie Cooper with a black, orange, yellow, brown and green geometric pattern.
• *height 9cm*
• £275 • Susie Cooper

△ Picasso Plate

• *1930s*
Ovate form, raised decoration of face. Hand-painted and glazed. Foundry stamped and numbered 22/100.
• *height 31cm*
• £6,000 • Cameo Gallery

△ Poole Pottery Vase

• *circa 1930*
Poole pottery bulbous vase with stylised yellow lilac flowers and green folia.
• *height 13cm*
• £75 • Richard Dennis

△ Paysage Vase
- *circa 1930*

Zuid-Holland factory. Gouda 'Paysage' vase. Realistically painted farmer with horse ploughing, with sunset sky in background.
- *height 47cm*
- £950 • P. Oosthuizen

△ Poole Ware Jug
- *1932*

Small Poole ware bulbous jug with a yellow, black and grey abstract design on a chalk white ground.
- *height 13cm*
- £350 • Arwas

△ Clarice Cliff Pot
- *1934*

With 'tulip' pattern on the lid, a stylised acorn finial and blue and green body.
- *height 5cm*
- £160 • Susie Cooper

▽ Monart Vase
- *1930*

Unusual vase of bulbous proportions with bubble inclusions within a deep red glaze, by Monart.
- *height 22cm*
- £595 • A.D. Antiques

▽ Clarice Cliff Pot
- *1934*

Pot by Clarice Cliff with blue lid with off-set finial, painted pattern on body and set on four feet.
- *height 9cm*
- £750 • Susie Cooper

▽ Teapot by Clarice Cliff
- *1936*

'Blue Chintz' collection teapot with pink crocus by Clarice Cliff.
- *height 15cm*
- £450 • Susie Cooper

△ Poole Vase
- *circa 1930*

Poole vase of ovoid form with yellow, blue and green design.
- *height 26cm*
- £400 • Richard Dennis

△ Vase Tulip Pattern
- *1934*

Vase of baluster form, hand-painted by Clarice Cliff with a 'tulip' pattern and green and red banding on a blue ground.
- *height 12cm*
- £650 • Susie Cooper

△ Carlton Ware Service
- *20th century*

Carlton Ware five-piece teaset consisting of two cups and saucers, a sugar pot and teapot, milk jug and two saucers with a pistachio glaze and gilded decoration.
- £450 • Bizarre

▽ Gouda Bowl
- *1931*

Zuid-Holland factory Gouda bowl. Design 'Floro'.
- *height 12cm*
- £225 • P. Oosthuizen

▽ Dessert Plates
- *1935*

Part of set of Royal Worcester plates in silver form with beaded gilt edge. Fruit Worcester design of apples, peaches and grapes painted by Smith.
- *diameter 24cm*
- £200 each • R.A. Barnes

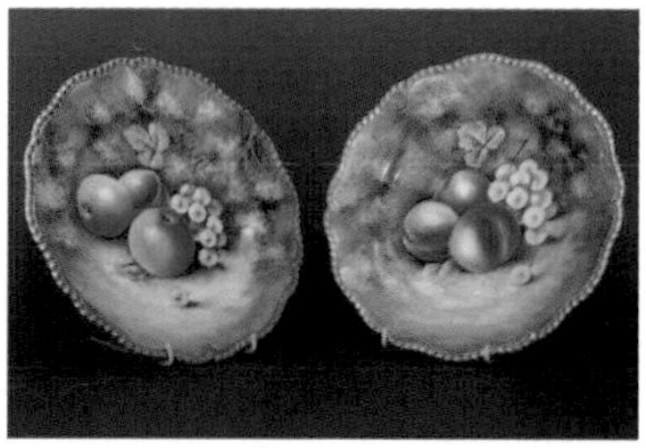

▽ Royal Worcester Bird
- *1936*

Limited edition American bluebird perched on apple-blossom branch. Shown to life size and depicting a spring scene, the whole standing on a wooden plinth.
- *height 30cm*
- £900 • R.A. Barnes

▽ Torso by Zaccagnini

- *circa 1940*

Ceramic torso of a nude lady by Zaccagnini.

- *height 61cm*
- £1,050 • Vincenzo Caffarella

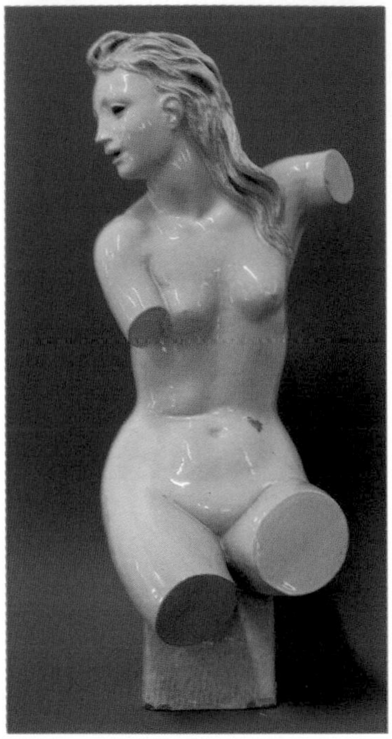

▽ French Grey Vase

- *1950*

Small French vase of conical form with a textured finish and a black geometric design with a large red dot.

- *height 16cm*
- £55 • Goya

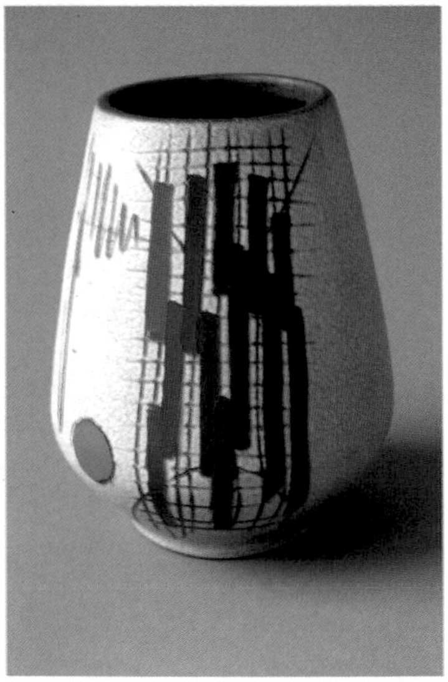

▷ Italian Ribbed Vase

- *1950*

Italian elegant bottle-shaped vase with long neck, ribbed body and a matt black finish.

- *height 33cm*
- £65 • Ventesimo

△ Butter Container

- *circa 1940*

Cream cheese dish and cover with a floral design and moulded rim.

- *14cm x 20cm*
- £30 • Old School

△ Bird on Pine Cone

- *circa 1950*

Poole pottery. Bluetit on a pine cone. Heavily modelled naturalistic representation, with pine-cone design reflected in the plumage.

- *height 12.5cm*
- £70 • P. Oosthuizen

△ Painted Poole Vase

- *circa 1950s*

Poole pottery vase showing the printed dolphin mark. Paint has been applied directly to the pot, unlike the ealier pre-war models which were terracotta with a tin glaze. Decoration shows an asymetrical serpentine pattern with yellow and black detailing.

- *height 29cm*
- £500 • Richard Dennis

△ Rosenthal Pottery

- *circa 1950*

Peynet vase designed by Rosenthal Pottery entitled 'The Marriage'.

- *height 29cm*
- £300 • Richard Dennis

▽ Poole Vase

- *circa 1950s*

Organic shape with blue, grey and green abstract vertical banners, interlacing circles. Stamped with dolphin mark.

- *height 20cm*
- £450 • Richard Dennis

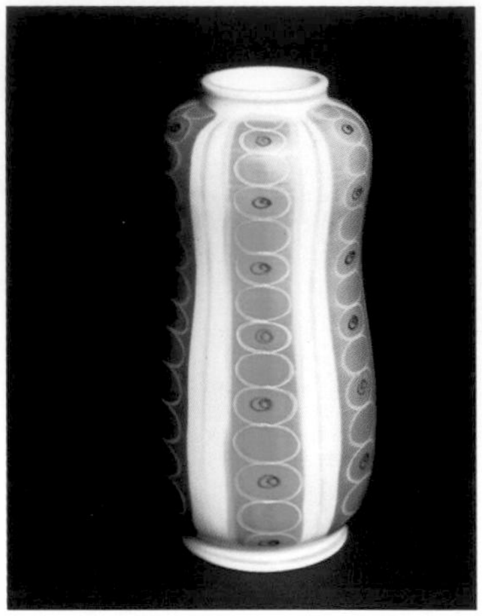

▽ Italian Ceramic Jug

- *1950*

Matt-brown Italian jug of ovoid form with stylised black and white enamel horses and strap handle.

- *height 22cm*
- £75 • Ventesimo

▽ Royal Dux Sculpture

- *circa 1950*

Royal Dux abstract wall sculpture by Cernoch.

- *height 41cm*
- £600 • Arwas

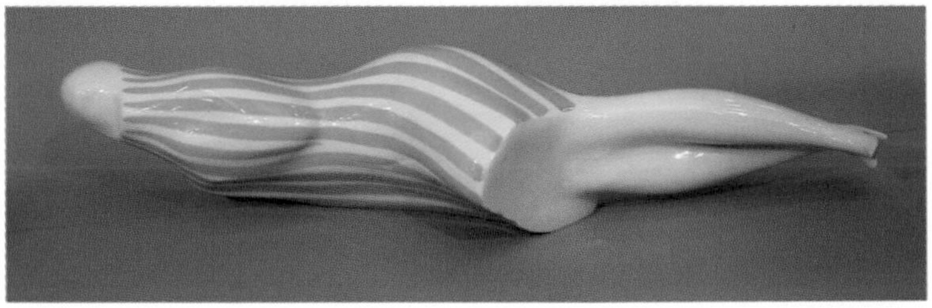

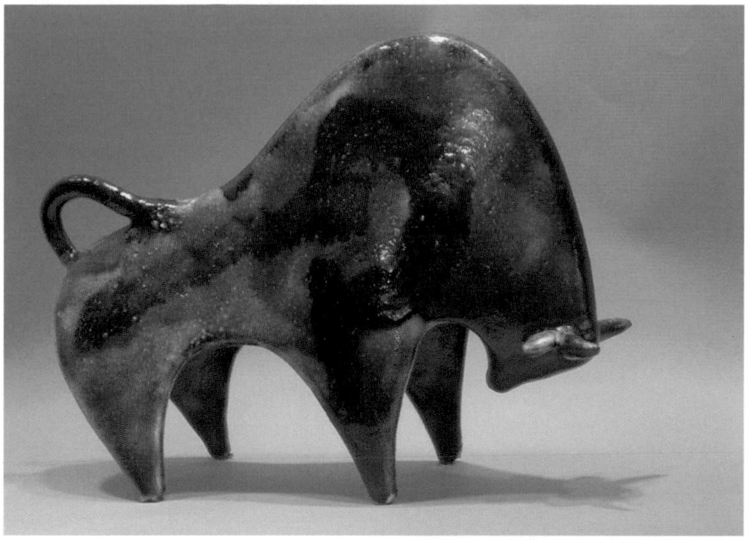

▽ Enamel Vase

- *1960*

Enamel vase of conical form with a gilded neck and lip.

- *height 20cm*
- £45 • Ventesimo

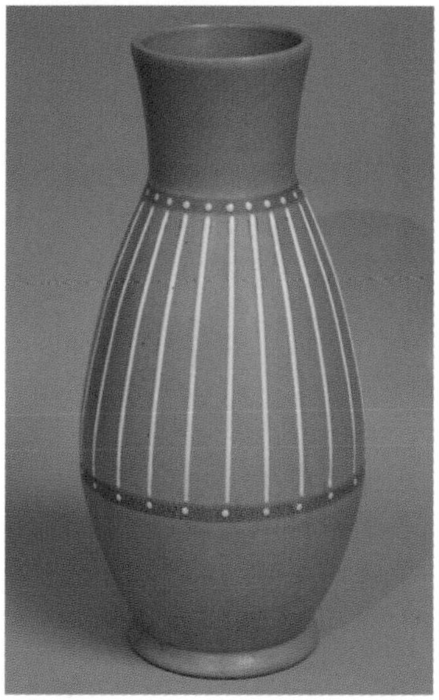

△ Denby Vase

- *circa 1960s*

Bourne Denby vase of conical form with white vertical stripes within a border of variegated dots.

- *height 30cm*
- £45 • Francesca Martire

△ Two Bluetits

- *1961*

A pair of Royal Worcester bluetits, male and female, made by Dorothy Doughty. Made to lifesize, showing a spring scene with pussy willow, each mounted on a wooden plinth.

- £750 • R.A. Barnes

◁ Taurus

- *1950*

Blue stylised bull 'Taurus' with head bowed and tail up by Gambone.

- *height 25cm*
- £2,000 • Themes

▽ German Red Vase

- *1950*

Red vase of double conical form with a raised black and white abstract design around the middle.

- *height 22cm*
- £30 • Goya

▽ Vase by John Criswick

- *1960*

John Criswick vase of double conical form, dated and signed on the base 10.11.1960.

- *height 44cm*
- £380 • Francesca Martire

▷ Troika

- *circa 1965*

Troika vase with cream and turquoise geometric design from St Ives.

- *36cm x 17cm*
- £895 • The Country Seat

△ Poole Planter

- *circa 1960s*

Poole planter printed with the Poole mark of a dolphin. The pot is incised with a scratched pattern and glazed with burnt orange, yellow and blue.

- *height 22cm*
- £200 • Richard Dennis

△ Cornish Moon Troika

- *circa 1960*

Pottery blue vase of conical form by Troika St Ives with cream circles on a textured brown and green ground.

- *height 26cm*
- £285 • The Country Seat

▽ Plate by Geramim

- *1970*

Circular plate with a floral design in red, black and yellow enamels by Geramim S. Rocco, Torrita de Sirvo.

- *diameter 38cm*
- **£145** • **Ventesimo**

▽ Stamped Poole Vase

- *circa 1980s*

A bulbous vase with short neck stamped with the Poole pottery mark. The detailing shows a bracelet pattern of bands around the base, middle and neck. Banding also around base and rim.

- *height 20cm*
- **£500** • **Richard Dennis**

▽ Dinanderie Plate

- *20th century*

Red and black glazed Dinanderie dish signed by Linossier.

- *diameter 19cm*
- **£2,400** • **Bizarre**

△ Italian Fishbone Vase

- *1970*

Grey Italian flask-shaped vase with a raised grey fishbone design on a burnt orange ground.

- *height 33cm*
- **£95** • **Goya**

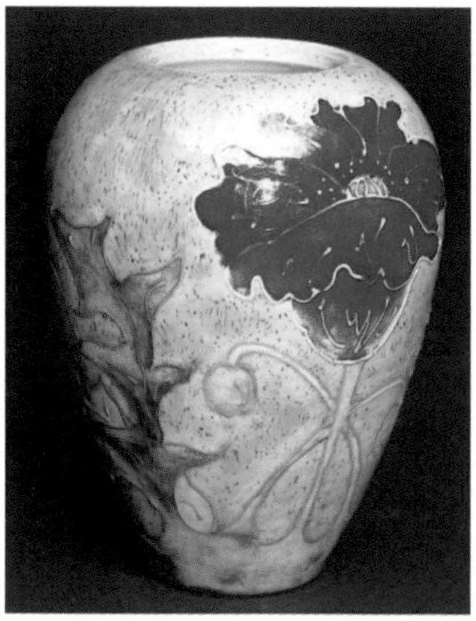

△ Moorcroft Vase

- *1994*

Lisa Moorcroft vase of oriental shape, with poppy flower and leaf design in red and green, on a green base.

- *height 14cm*
- **£105** • **Richard Dennis**

△ Dinonderie Tray

- *20th century*

Dinonderie tray with a red glaze and gilded decoration, signed by Linossier.

- *21cm x 12cm*
- **£1,200** • **Bizarre**

▽ Ceramic Plate

- *1973*

Large ceramic plate with six-eye design, on a grey base, by Salvatori Meli.

- *diameter 59cm*
- **£3,000** • **Themes**

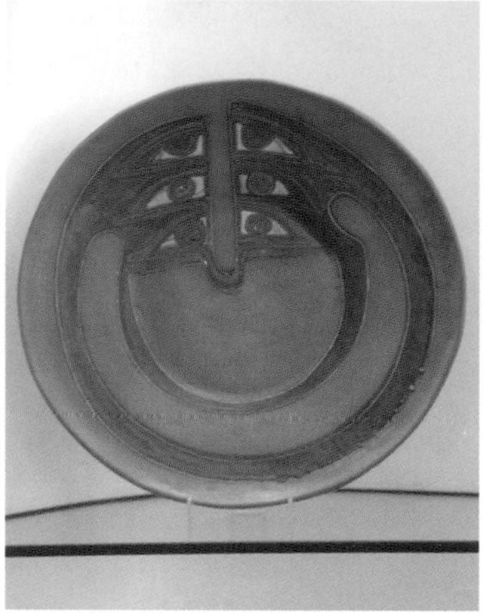

▽ Poole Studio Vase

- *1997*

Signed and dated. The design shows peacocks and floral decorations on a blue background with a painted green rim.

- *height 21cm*
- **£100** • **Richard Dennis**

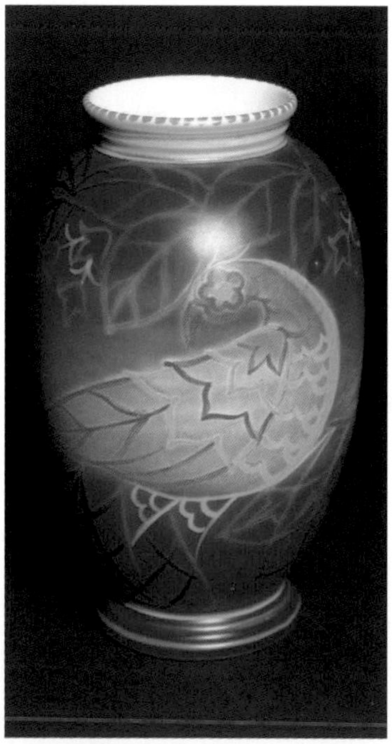

▷ D. Bernam Smith Pot

- *1998*

A small pot and cover decorated with an architectural repeated pattern on a blue ground. The lid is also similarly decorated and signed by David Burnham Smith.

- *height 11cm*
- **£150** • **Richard Dennis**

△ Plate by Capron

- *1970*

Plate by Roger Capron for Valaurido with a red and orange design within borders of matt grey.

- *diameter 22cm*
- **£85** • **Goya**

△ Ceramic Model of a Tower

- *1998*

A tower, inspired by scenes from the Bayeux tapestry, by David Burnham Smith. Demonstrates highly intricate technique in painting and craft. The painting is internal as well as external.

- *height 30cm*
- **£1,100** • **Richard Dennis**

▽ Gagnier Vase

- *circa 1998*

Double cone form with spherical centre around which are four nodules. Olivier Gagnier, Italy.

- *height 49cm*
- £250 • Themes

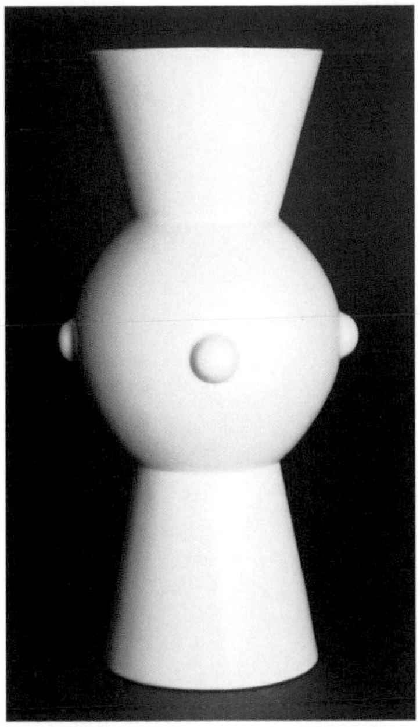

▽ Dennis Vase

- *1999*

Dennis Chinaworks vase in Indian shape. The vase shows a tiger on a tiger-print ground. Charcoal glaze on inside with red bands.

- height 46cm
- £750 • Richard Dennis

▷ Moorland Vase

- *1999*

A Moorland thistle vase. Cast and turned on a lathe with hand-painted metallic glaze. Signed and dated.

- *height 26cm*
- £95 • Richard Dennis

△ Unusual Teapot

- *1998*

David Burnham Smith teapot is of unusual shape with a fish-like quality. Intricately painted with architectural scrolling pattern. It is signed and dated.

- *height 10cm*
- £700 • Richard Dennis

△ Lotus Pattern Poole Plate

- *1999*

A contemporary and highly collectable Poole studio plate, printed with dolphin mark and signed N. Massarella. Painted with a lotus pattern with orange glaze. Black glaze on the reverse.

- *diameter 40cm*
- £300 • Richard Dennis

▽ Dennis Bowl

- *1998*

Dennis Chinaworks bowl of oriental shape with blue and pink glaze. Two dragonflies are imprinted on the inside of the dish. Bowl rests on a small base.

- *diameter 18cm*
- £100 • Richard Dennis

▽ Lion's Head Vase

- *1999*

Dennis Chinaworks vase of bulbous form, showing three resplendent lion heads on an interlacing background of burnt orange and yellow glaze.

- *height 21cm*
- £300 • Richard Dennis

▽ Spiral Poole Plate

- *1999*

A Poole pottery plate showing a spiral pattern in red glaze with blue overglaze and black overglaze on the reverse. Signed by Janice Tchelenko.

- *diameter 40cm*
- £375 • Richard Dennis

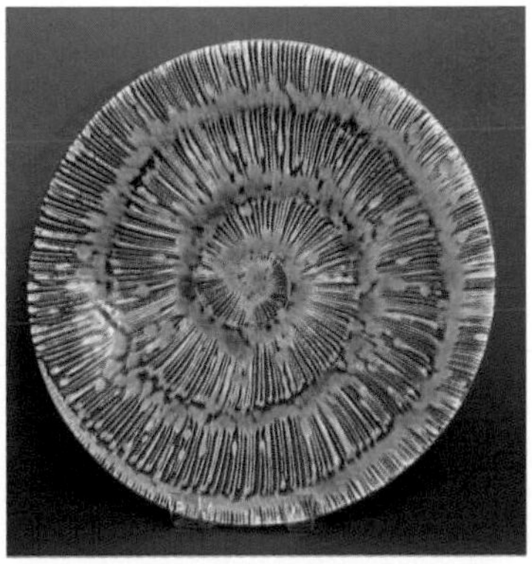

△ Dennis Iris Vase

- *late 1990s*

English ceramic vase decorated with irises by Dennis China Works.

- *height 36.25cm*
- £940 • Richard Dennis

△ Dennis Plate

- *1999*

A Dennis Chinaworks plate showing a cockerel with head turned and tail feathers on display. Brightly painted on a beige base, with a green glaze to the reverse.

- *diameter 36cm*
- £423 • Richard Dennis

△ Baxter Mug

- *1999*

A Glen Baxter mug created for Poole pottery with a cartoon representation. Signature and motif is on reverse.

- *height 9cm*
- £8 • Richard Dennis

△ Mission Chair

- *circa 1900*

An American oak rocking chair with slatted back and sides and tanned leather seat, possibly by Stickley Bros.

- *height 85cm*
- £950 • After Noah

△ Ebonised Music Stool

- *circa 1900*

Ebonised Arts and Crafts music stool with curved seat with scrolled terminals, on a shaped stretcher with turned legs, by Liberty & Co.

- *57.5cm x 32.5cm*
- £750 • Liberty plc

▽ Revolving Bookcase

- *circa 1900*

Rare Art Nouveau revolving mahogany bookcase, with fruitwood inlays on each of the four panelled doors, on swept legs.

- *1.92m x 60cm*
- £2,500 • Liberty plc

▽ Rocking Chair

- *circa 1900*

Rocking chair with rush seat and slat back on turned legs with a rocker base, by Liberty & Co.

- *height 87.5cm*
- £495 • Liberty plc

◁ Rosewood Chair

- *circa 1904*

Rare Art Nouveau rosewood chair on turned legs with pad feet. Designed by Walter Cave for Liberty & Co.

- *92.5cm x 62.5cm*
- £3,500 • Liberty plc

▷ Orkney Chair

- *circa 1905*

Child's stained oak Orkney chair with carved arms and legs. Original Liberty & Co London enamel label on underside of chair.

- *height 82.5cm*
- £475 • Liberty plc

△ Reclining Armchair

- *circa 1900*

One of a pair of oak reclining armchairs of solid design with slatted side panels, raised on square tapered legs.

- *90cm x 70cm*
- £900 • Old Cinema

△ Umbrella Stand

- *circa 1900*

Oak umbrella stand with tapered plank ends with a pierced inverted heart motif, above three zinc trays within the base, by Liberty & Co.

- *72.5cm x 82.75cm*
- £695 • Liberty plc

▽ Oak Hall Cupboard

- *circa 1900*

Art Nouveau oak hall cupboard with mirror panelled door and carved decoration.

- *2m x 1.03m*
- £495 • Old Cinema

▽ Arts and Crafts Chair

- *circa 1905*

One of three Arts and Crafts single chairs with moulded top rail and curved splat with fruitwood inlay standing on straight square legs.

- *88cm x 44cm*
- £2,250 • Liberty plc

▽ Revolving Bookcase

• *circa 1905*
An Edwardian mahogany revolving bookcase with pierced side panels raised on four splayed legs.
• *80cm x 43cm*
• £795 • Old Cinema

▽ Art Nouveau Bureau

• *circa 1905*
Art Nouveau oak bureau with folding writing slope above a single drawer with organically designed copper metalwork.
• *1.2m x 90cm*
• £565 • Old Cinema

▽ Hathaway Table

• *circa 1905*
Extendable oak draw table with panelled top, X-shaped cross-stretcher and tapered legs, by Liberty & Co.
• *height 1.37m*
• £2,350 • Liberty plc

△ Edwardian Three-Tier Stand

• *circa 1905*
An unusual wrought-iron and copper Edwardian three-tier stand with scrolled decoration.
• *95cm x 25cm*
• £135 • Old Cinema

△ Edwardian Occasional Table

• *circa 1905*
A very good quality Edwardian satinwood and inlaid octagonal occasional table.
• *72cm x 54cm*
• £495 • Old Cinema

▽ Arts and Crafts Dining Chairs

• *circa 1905*
One of a pair of oak Arts and Crafts carvers with scrolled arms and turned supports.
• *1.05m x 58cm*
• £550 • Liberty plc

▽ Walnut Side Table

• *circa 1905*
Walnut Arts and Crafts table. The design and quality of this table suggests the work of C. R. Ashbee and the Guild of Handicraft.
• *52cm x 40cm*
• £650 • Liberty plc

▷ Art Nouveau Chair

• *circa 1910*
One of six Art Nouveau oak chairs consisting of two carvers and four single chairs, with slatted back splat and curved top rail above square tapered legs.
• *1.4m x 53cm*
• £825 • Old Cinema

◁ Arts and Crafts Table

• *circa 1910*
Arts and Crafts oak table of solid construction with straight supports and circular stretcher.
• *52cm x 69cm*
• £280 • Old Cinema

△ Arts and Crafts Lamp Table

• *circa 1905*
Arts and Crafts mahogany occasional table with three supports and carved and pierced decoration.
• *69cm x 43cm*
• £220 • Old Cinema

△ Edwardian Bookcase

• *circa 1905*
A good quality Edwardian bookcase with moulded decoration above three shelves.
• *1.18m x 1.25m*
• £995 • Old Cinema

△ Oak Bookcase

- *circa 1910*

Glazed oak bookcase with arched pediment and double-glazed doors.

- *1.9m x 80cm*
- £890 • Old Cinema

△ Swedish Art Deco Birch Desk

- *circa 1920*

A rare example of a Swedish Art Deco desk. It is unique and is veneered in a particularly beautiful masur birch.

- *76cm x 1.2m x 60cm*
- £4,500 • R. Cavendish

△ Mirrored Dressing Table

- *1920*

Art Deco dressing table, made of mirrors with elegant sabred legs and a fixed mirror with glass handle to drawer.

- *70cm x 86cm x 45cm*
- £800 • Myriad

▽ Oak Hall Seat

- *circa 1910*

Unusual carved oak hall seat with side table and umbrella stand.

- *height 79cm*
- £995 • Old Cinema

▽ Art Nouveau Music Cabinet

- *circa 1910*

Mahogany Art Nouveau music cabinet with boxwood and ebony inlays, lined shelves and a leaded glass door decorated with floral motifs. With carved top and side columns, by Liberty & Co.

- *height 1.2m*
- £4,500 • Liberty plc

▷ Hardwood Dining Table

- *circa 1920*

Oak dining table from a West Country cricket club, with pull-out leaves above square chamfered legs on bun feet.

- *76cm x 91cm*
- £975 • Old Cinema

△ Art Nouveau Table

- *circa 1918*

Art Nouveau table with organic inlay designs on four pierced legs.

- *height 81cm*
- £420 • Castlegate

△ Walnut Coffee Table

- *circa 1920s*

Walnut reproduction coffee table with scalloped decoration and cabriole legs with acanthus-leaf carving.

- *52cm x 1m*
- £275 • Old Cinema

△ Walnut Sofa

- *circa 1920*

A fine walnut three-piece suite with caned back rest and side panels and turned decoration, raised on circular bun feet.

- *91cm x 1.82m*
- £3,900 • Old Cinema

▽ Parisian Café Table

- *circa 1920*

A small Parisian wrought-iron café table, on a heavy moulded cast-iron tripod base.

- *height 70cm*
- £320 • Myriad

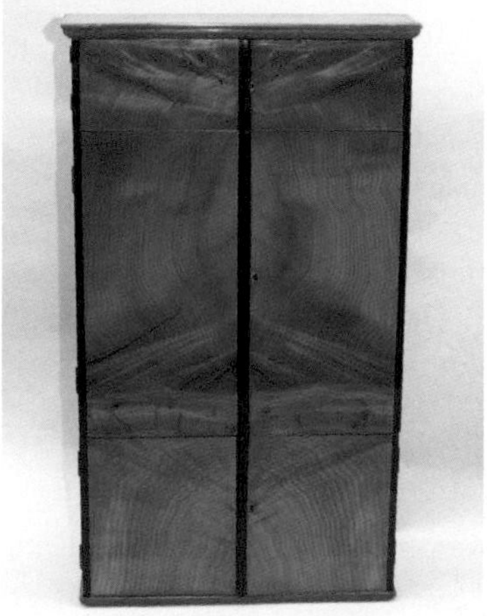

▽ Wall Cabinet

- *circa 1920*

French figured-beechwood wall cabinet with ebonised mouldings, with two large panelled doors above two smaller ones.

- *height 84cm*
- £1,550 • North West 8

▽ Gout Stool

- *circa 1920*

An adjustable stool for the gout-sufferer, made of oak and metal, on roller castors.

- *height 33cm*
- £150 • North West 8

▽ Mahogany Desk

- *1925*

Fine mahogany partners' desk with embossed and gilded leather top. Two cupboards at front and rear, standing on bun feet.

- *79cm x 1.75m x 84cm*
- £12,500 • Hatchwell

▽ Dining Set

- *circa 1930*

Sixteen-sided rosewood and mahogany dining table, with six chairs covered in raw silk.

- £20,000 • Bizarre

▽ Oak Sideboard by Richter

- *circa 1930*

Oak sideboard with central stepped cupboard flanked by two short and two long drawers with bun handles, standing on square straight legs. Made in Bath, England, and illustrated in *Modern British Furniture.*

- *height 1.12m*
- £1,490 • Country Seat

▷ Art Deco Table

- *circa 1940s*

An oak two-tier Art Deco side table with square tapered supports.

- *70cm x 53cm*
- £225 • Old Cinema

△ French Art Deco Brown Leather Chairs

- *1925*

One of a pair of brown leather French Art Deco chairs with a curved padded back, scrolled arms and turned feet.

- *height 1.2m*
- £3,500 • Bizarre

△ Nursery Chest

- *circa 1930*

Heal's oak nursery chest with double and single panelled doors, three short drawers and two long drawers.

- *1.5m x 1.15m*
- £1,850 • Old Cinema

▽ French Art Deco Armchairs

- *circa 1925*

One of a pair of armchairs inlaid with exotic woods and with mock tiger fabric.

- *height 80cm*
- £5,900 • R. Cavendish

▽ Diner Stools

- *circa 1940*

A set of four round American diner stools with chromed steel base and red leather-covered seats. Very typical of the Art Deco, American café style.

- *height 51cm*
- £350 • After Noah

▽ French Cast-Iron Chairs

- *1940*

One of a pair of French cast-iron chairs with intertwined lattice back and yellow leather seats, on cabriole legs.

- *height 95cm*
- £1,400 • Solaris

△ Modernist Table

- *circa 1930*

Modernist table for use as a library table or cocktail cabinet, made from oak with crossbanded decoration raised on moulded bracket feet.

- *51cm x 60cm*
- £185 • Old Cinema

△ Cocktail Cabinet

- *circa 1930*

A modernist, Art Deco British cocktail cabinet.

- *height 80cm*
- £2,900 • Libra Designs

△ Factory Stool

- *circa 1940*

Factory worker's stool. Originally painted mild steel, adjustable elm seat on three legs. English made.

- *height 56cm*
- £145 • After Noah

△ Harry Bertoia Wire Chair

- *circa 1950*

Wire chair and stool by Harry Bertoia, who was born in Italy and later worked with Charles and Ray Eames at Evans, and also with his ground-breaking wire chairs at Knoll International.

- *height 1.04m*
- £1,800 • Country Seat

△ Occasional Tables

- *1950*

German wood occasional tables inlaid with gilt porcelain plaques, by Rosenthal.

- *42.5cm x 42.5cm x 60cm (largest)*
- £1,400 • Themes

△ Italian Dining Table

- *circa 1950s*

Italian interlocking sycamore dining table by Ico Parisi.

- *2.52m x 77.5cm*
- £8,500 • Themes

▽ Mahogany Dining Chairs

- *circa 1950s*

One of a set of six mahogany dining chairs with pierced backsplat, drop-in seat cushion and cabriole legs.

- *1m x 48cm*
- £1,250 • Old Cinema

▽ Auditorium Chair

- *circa 1950*

Italian, by Carlo Mollino, for the Auditorium in Turin. Velvet upholstery with brass fittings and flip-up seat.

- *height 85cm*
- £2,500 • Themes

▽ Lounge Chair

- *circa 1950*

Aluminium and bent rosewood ply lounge chair, covered in natural leather.

- *height 1.05m*
- £3,950 • Country Seat

△ Eames Chair

- *circa 1950*

Leather lounge chair designed in 1946 by Ray Eames and manufactured by Herman Miller. Sold with a stool.

- *height 83cm*
- £3,950 • Country Seat

△ Chair by Carl Jacobs

- *circa 1950*

One of a set of six red chairs by Carl Jacobs for Kandya Ltd., with teak legs.

- *72cm x 51cm*
- £485 • Country Seat

▽ Nursing Chair

- *circa 1950*

A mid-20th century nursing chair with a metal frame and wooden slatted seat.

- *height 58cm*
- £30 • Curios

▽ Mahogany Armchair

- *circa 1950s*

Mahogany elbow chair with pierced back splat, curved arm rests and cabriole legs.

- *1.1m x 62cm*
- £250 • Old Cinema

◁ 'Medea' Chairs

- *circa 1955*

One of a pair of moulded beechwood 'Medea' chairs by Vittoria Nobli, with an oblong hole in the seat and straight black metal legs.

- *height 82cm*
- £450 • Francesca Martire

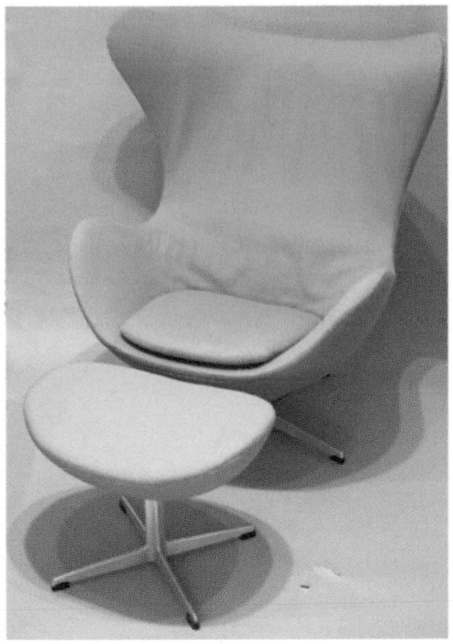

△ Arne Jacobsen Egg Chair

- *1958*

Padded wool turquoise 'Egg Chair' by Arne Jacobsen, together with ottoman.

- *height 1.3m*
- **£2,850** • **Country Seat**

△ Danish Sideboard

- *1960*

Danish sideboard Jacaranda, by Korod Larsenfor Faarup Mobel Fabarik.

- *78cm x 2.3m x 50cm*
- **£3,500** • **Themes**

△ 'Red Object'

- *1961*

'Red Object' by Michael Kidner, sculpture in perspex.

- *height 1.1m*
- **£1,750** • **Whitford**

▽ Teak Armchairs

- *circa 1960*

Pair of teak and black leather armchairs by Hans Wegner for Carl Hanse.

- *height 70cm*
- **£2,800** • **Themes**

▽ Red Leather Chair

- *circa 1960*

One of a pair of Italian chairs, one red and the other black leather, with teak legs and back rest.

- *height 98cm*
- **£800** • **Vincenzo Caffarella**

▽ Dieter Rams Armchairs

- *1962*

Armchairs by Dieter Rams, for Vitsoe, made from green leather on a white fibreglass base.

- *69cm x 86cm*
- **£2,900** • **Themes**

◁ 'Amphys' Red Sofa

- *1968*

Designed by Pierre Paulin for Mobilier International.

- *length 2.14m*
- **£2,800** • **Whitford**

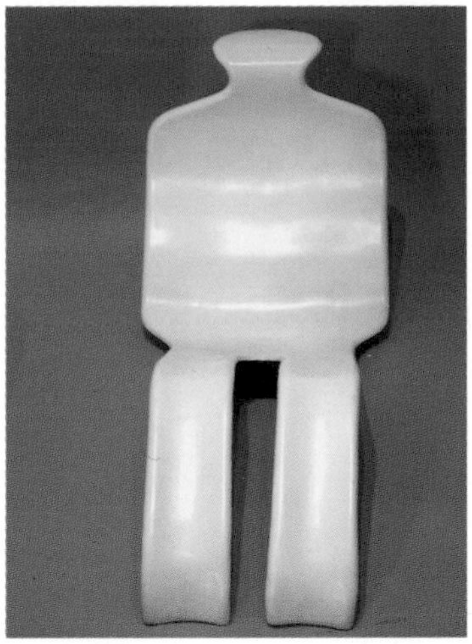

△ White Fibreglass Lounger

- *circa 1960*

Moulded fibreglass lounger with oval headrest, square body and raised leg rests, by French designer Olivier Mourgue.

- *length 1.64m*
- **£500** • **Country Seat**

△ Stool by Verner Panton

- *circa 1960*

Wire stool with original circular suede padded cover, by Verner Panton, Danish.

- *height 43cm*
- **£745** • **Country Seat**

△ Set of Four Chairs

- *circa 1965*

One of a set of four single chairs with detachable squab seats. Designed by Harry Bertoia.

- *height 31.5cm*
- **£865 (four)** • **Country Seat**

▽ Wicker Chair

- *circa 1960*

An Eero Aarnio wicker chair of circular form.

- *height 65cm*
- **£675** • **Libra Designs**

▽ Spiral Umbrella Stands

- *1960*

Italian Pluvium interlocking spiral umbrella stands in red and white plastic, designed by Giancarle Piretti for Castelli.

- *height 62.5cm*
- **£125** • **Zoom**

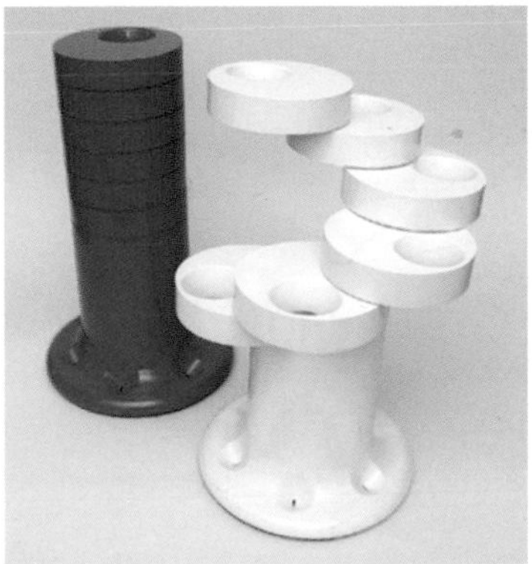

▽ Universe Chair

- *circa 1967*

'Universe' design black plastic stacking chair by Joe Columbo.

- *70cm x 43cm*
- **£220** • **Country Seat**

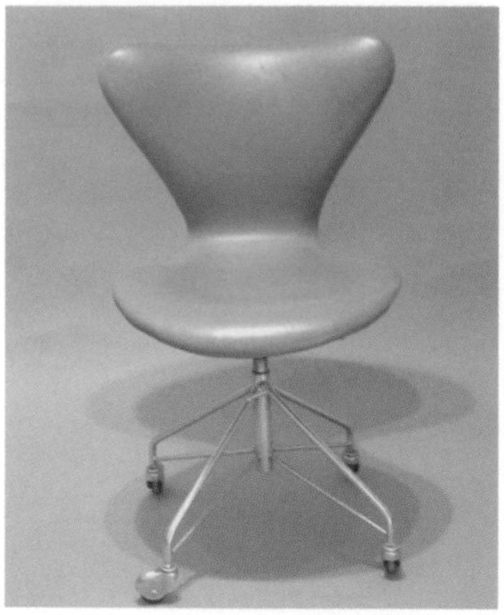

△ Leather Rotating Chair

- *1970*

Tan leather rotating and adjustable desk chair with padded seat and back, and metal legs on wheels.

- *height 74cm*
- £495 • Country Seat

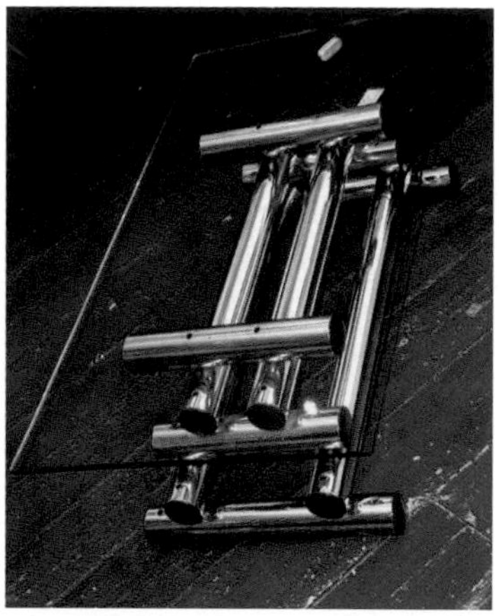

△ Coffee Table

- *circa 1970*

A unique chrome and glass crossbar coffee table. Of rectangular form.

- *height 32cm*
- £265 • Planet Bazaar

▽ Orange Chair

- *circa 1970*

Thermoplastic, injection-moulded chair by Verner Panton from his 'series 2' series.

- *height 78cm*
- £450 • Whitford

▽ Car Radiator Chair

- *circa 1970*

French-commissioned green fibreglass chair with square vinyl cushions, in the style of a car radiator and wings with headlights in working order.

- *82cm x 1.2m x 75cm*
- £2,200 • Country Seat

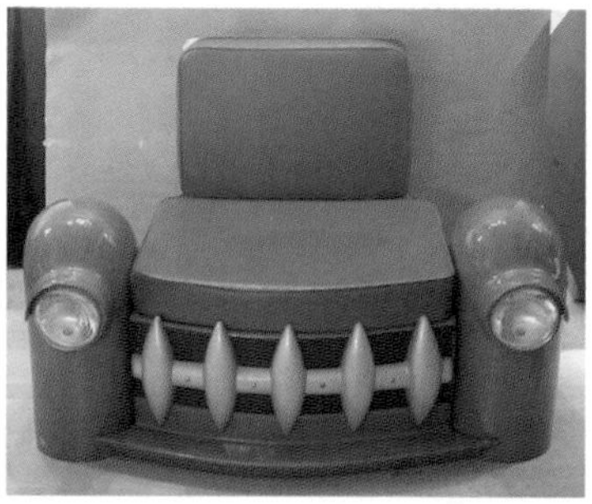

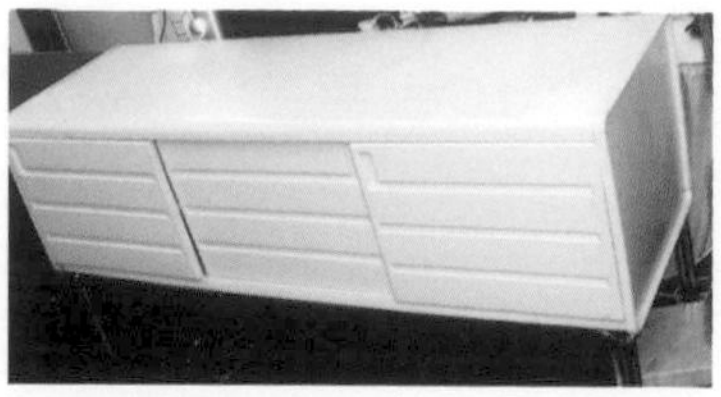

▽ Cone Chair

- *circa 1970*

A DanishVerner Panton cone chair, with wool upholstery.

- *height 84.5cm*
- £1,200 • Themes

▽ Coffee Table

- *circa 1970*

Chrome and ceramic tile-topped coffee table by Belanti, Italy. Glazed in avant-garde style.

- *height 38cm*
- £345 • Planet Bazaar

◁ Finnish Armchair and Footstool

- *circa 1970*

Armchair and footstool in brown padded leather and aluminium by Ilmari Lappalainen, Finland.

- *height 77cm*
- £1,600 • Themes

◁ Plastic Sideboard

- *circa 1970*

Cream-coloured moulded plastic sideboard designed by Anow, France. With two sliding doors.

- *length 1.47m*
- £295 • Planet Bazaar

△ 'Spring' Lamp

- *circa 1970*

French chrome 'spring' lamp with coiled innovative design and spherical, light bulb holder.

- *height 36cm*
- £145 • Planet Bazaar

△ Swivel Office Chair

- *1970*

Charles Eames, high-back office swivel and tilt chair, with black wool upholstery and aluminium stand on castors.

- *height 82cm*
- £600 • Zoom

△ Harlow Chairs

• *1971*
Set of four 'Harlow' chairs with red wool-padded seats and backs, standing on aluminium bases and stands, by Ettore Sottsass for Poltronova.
• *height 82cm*
• £3,500 • Themes

△ Red Onyx Desk

• *1973*
Moulded compartments with adjustable chrome metal lamp.
• *width 1.02m*
• £1,350 • Whitford

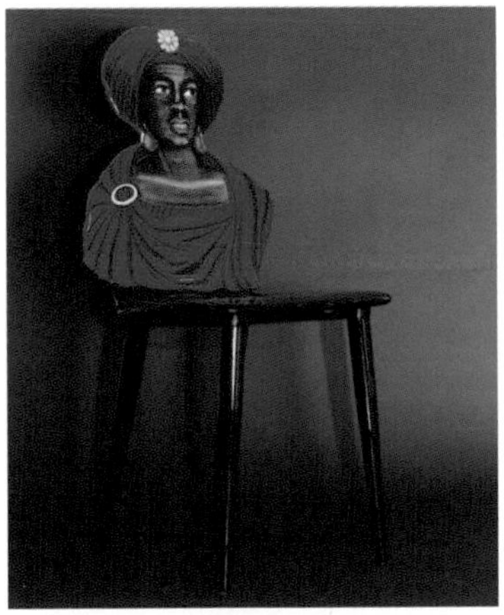

△ Figure-Backed Chair

• *circa 1980*
Fornasetti, Italian design. With a printed and lacquered figure in red dress above a black seat.
• *height 96cm*
• £1,600 • Themes

▷ Club Chair

• *20th century*
Leather and rattan club chair, with lion's paw feet. By Maitland-Smith.
• *height 80cm*
• £1,850 • Butchoff Interiors

▷ 'Safari' Seating Booth

• *circa 1975*
Glass-fibre reinforced-polyester frame with leather upholstery, designed by Poltronova for Archiroom Associati.
• £18,000 • Whitford

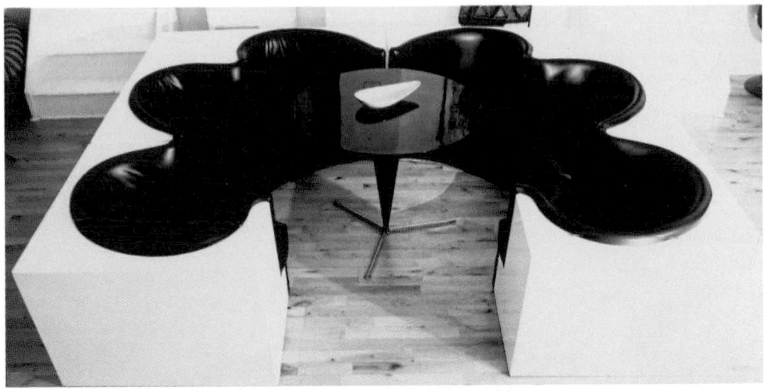

△ Chrome Dining Chairs

• *1975*
One of a set of four chairs with grey leather and chrome, by Prebenfabricus & Dorgen Kastholm for Alfred Kill.
• *height 70cm*
• £2,200 • Themes

△ Corner Suite

• *circa 1980*
An upholstered corner seating suite, covered in vermilion cloth, with all-moveable components.
• *height 1.2m*
• £650 • Spencer

▽ French Chairs

• *20th century*
Four provincial chairs in fruitwood, with asymmetric backs and rush seats.
• *height 89cm*
• £680 • Myriad

▽ End Table

• *20th century*
A mahogany end table with carved swan heads. Made by Maitland-Smith.
• *height 68cm*
• £1,750 • Butchoff Interiors

▷ 'Airborne' Armchairs

• *20th century*
A pair of 'Airborne' armchairs, in black leather.
• *height 70cm*
• £1,500 • Libra Designs

△ French Leather Chairs

• *1977*
Pair of chairs by Michel Cadestin and George Laurent for the Library of the Centre Pompidou Beaubourg, made from wire with leather seat and back. Illus: *Les Années 70*, by Anne Bony.
• *74.5cm*
• £1,200 • Themes

△ Silk-Covered Chair

• *20th century*
With striped silk upholstery and silver arm ends.
• *height 78cm*
• £1,800 • Butchoff Interiors

GLASS

▽ Gallé Vase

- *circa 1900*

A Gallé vase of tapered form, acid-etched with wisteria flower and leaf decoration.

- *height 12cm*
- **£2,600** • **French Glasshouse**

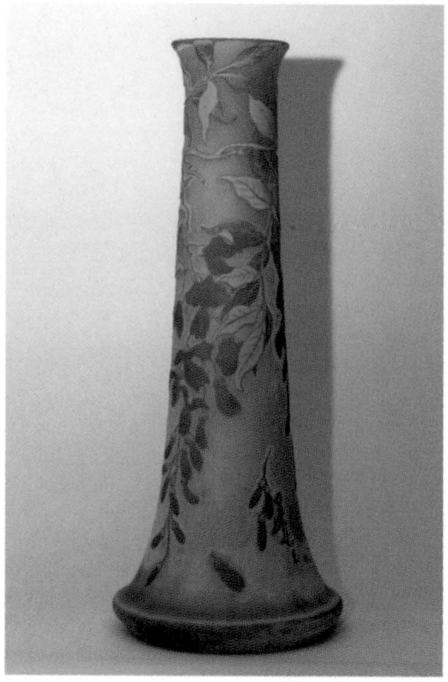

▽ Daum Bluebell Vase

- *circa 1900*

A Daum vase with a cut and pulled lip, showing Cross of Lorraine with background of blue sky and a green grass ground.

- *height 12cm*
- **£6,400** • **French Glasshouse**

▷ Daum Enamelled Vase

- *1900*

French Daum vase with splayed lip, showing a summer scene with enamelled trees.

- *height 21cm*
- **£3,500** • **French Glasshouse**

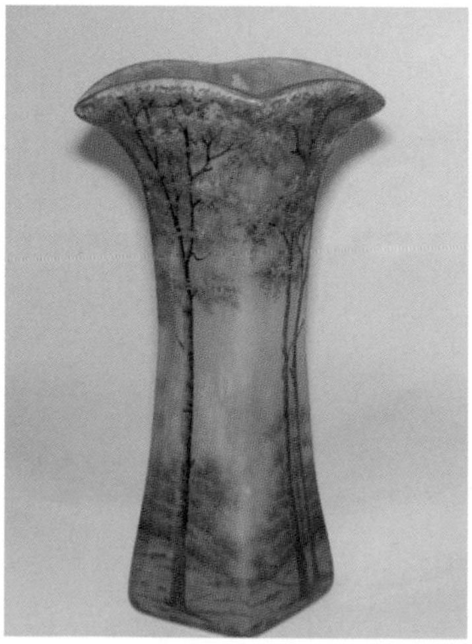

△ Daum Vase

- *circa 1900*

A larger than average, double-handled Daum vase with pastoral setting and hand work to foreground toadstools.

- *height 15.5cm*
- **£8,500** • **French Glasshouse**

△ Small Square Daum Vase

- *circa 1900*

A Daum vase showing winter scene of trees and snow ground against a pink-tinged sky.

- *height 9cm*
- **£1,500** • **French Glasshouse**

▽ Gallé Vase

- *circa 1900*

A Gallé vase showing scenes of mountain, lake and forest in a desirable purple-blue colour, fading to yellow.

- *height 20cm*
- **£2,000** • **French Glasshouse**

▽ Cranberry Glass Vases

- *circa 1900*

A pair of Bohemian cranberry glass vases with engraved decoration depicting castles and a forest setting with a leaping deer, on a faceted and moulded base.

- *height 44cm*
- **£4,200** • **Sinai**

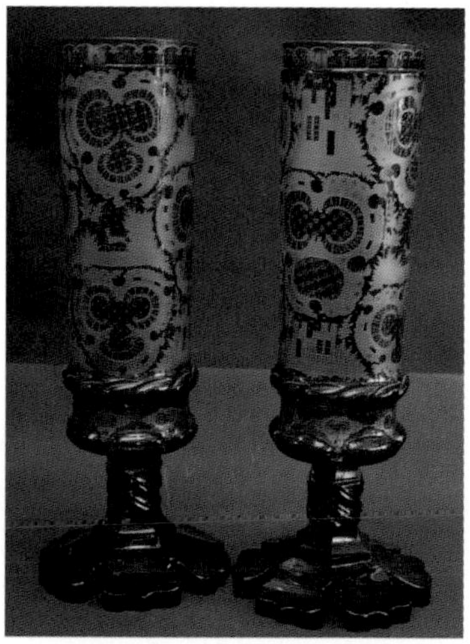

▷ Daum Conical Vase

- *circa 1900*

A Daum vase with splayed foot, showing orchid and spider web. Acid-etched decoration.

- *height 25cm*
- **£2,700** • **French Glasshouse**

△ Tube-Shaped Vase

- *circa 1900*

An Emile Gallé, tube-shaped vase with popular design of red roses on red overlay.

- *height 43cm*
- **£2,800** • **French Glasshouse**

△ Daum Rain Vase

- *circa 1900*

Vase showing acid-etched rain on the surface, with wind-blown trees in winter landscape of watermelon colour.

- *height 8cm*
- £3,400 • French Glasshouse

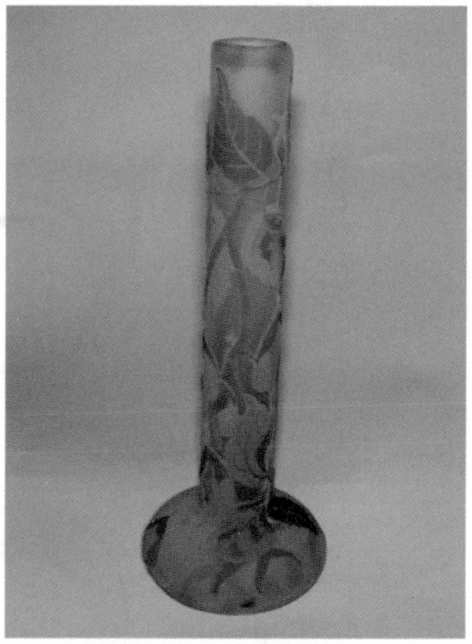

△ Overlay Cameo Vase

- *circa 1900*

Gallé Art Nouveau overlay cameo glass vase, decorated with pink orchids and foliate design.

- *height 17cm*
- £600 • French Glasshouse

△ Gallé Glass Box

- *circa 1900*

A Japanese-inspired box and cover of circular shape in purple, blue and yellow colourings with blue flowerheads.

- *height 9.5cm*
- £2,700 • French Glasshouse

▽ Daum Vase

- *1900*

Daum vase with pink poppies and green foliage with dragonflies.

- *height 12cm*
- £2,400 • French Glasshouse

▽ Muller Circular Box

- *circa 1900*

Muller circular box and cover with overlay of red poppies and folia.

- *height 8cm*
- £1,300 • French Glasshouse

▽ Small Gallé Vase

- *1900*

A small Gallé vase with purple foliate design on a graduated blue and yellow ground.

- *height 15cm*
- £1,900 • French Glasshouse

△ Gallé Ovoid Vase

- *circa 1900*

An Emile Gallé vase of ovoid form, with foliate decoration in purple, blue and yellow.

- *height 12cm*
- £1,800 • French Glasshouse

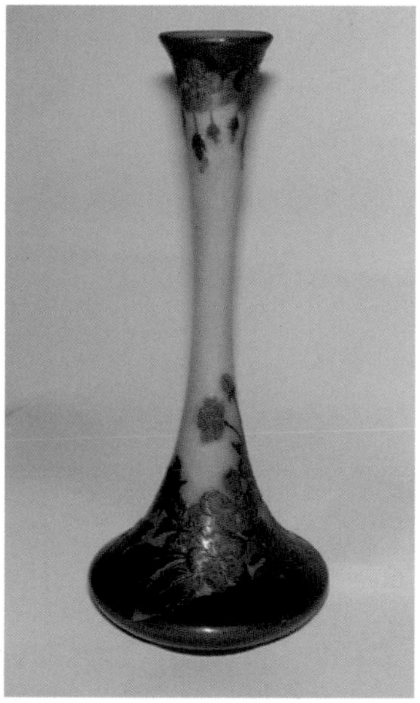

△ Tinted Cameo Vase

- *1900*

French Gallé tinted cameo glass vase, decorated with purple flowers around the base and neck.

- *height 22cm*
- £950 • French Glasshouse

△ Loetz Bowl

- *circa 1905*

A Loetz bowl with blue Papillon oxide finish. The bowl rests on three lemon iridescent feet.

- *height 10.5cm*
- £950 • French Glasshouse

▽ Daum Tumbler-Shaped Vase

- *circa 1900*

A Daum vase showing floral and leaf decoration.

- *height 12.5cm*
- £1,400 • French Glasshouse

▽ Daum Conical Vase

- *circa 1900*

A conical Daum vase showing deep winter village scene with windmill, snow within the glass and acid-etched trees to the outside.

- *height 30cm*
- £7,500 • French Glasshouse

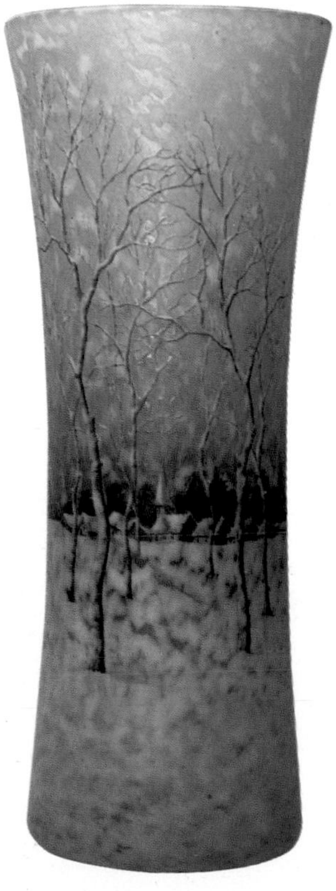

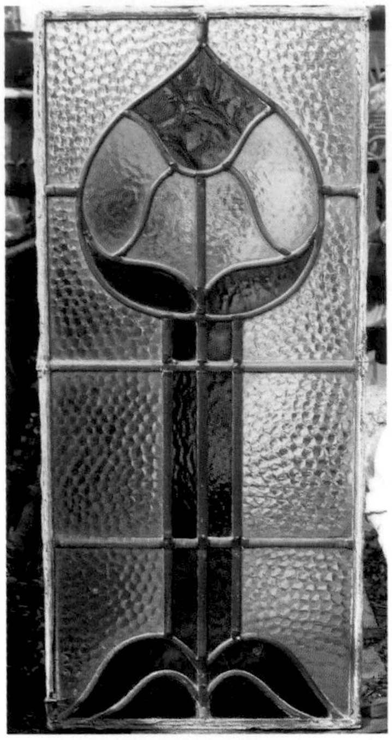

△ Stained Glass Panel

- *circa 1910*

Decorative panel showing tulip-shaped floral image of nineteen, geometric leaded sections.

- *height 58cm*
- £45 • Curios

△ Lalique Vase

- *1920*

'Estoril'-pattern Lalique glass vase of conical design with concentric leaf pattern in relief.

- *height 13cm*
- £1,000 • Susie Cooper

▽ Loetz Glass Bowl

- *circa 1910*

A Loetz bowl of ovoid form, with pinched lip, in rose amber with gold-lustre finish.

- *height 13cm*
- £1,900 • Kieron

▽ Fern by Lalique

- *1920*

Lalique vase of ovoid form with narrow circular neck and a raised 'Fern' pattern.

- *height 19cm*
- £1,400 • Susie Cooper

▽ Lalique Bird

- *1920*

Lalique naturalistically formed glass finch.

- *length 13cm*
- £280 • Susie Cooper

◁ Art Nouveau Inkwell

- *circa 1920*

A German glass inkwell, by Loetz, with brass top. Stamped with design registration mark.

- *height 6cm*
- £265 • Barham Antiques

△ Loetz Vase

- *circa 1910*

A Loetz vase with silver overlay with organic patterns applied to the surface. Iridescent oxides.

- *height 19cm*
- £5,500 • French Glasshouse

△ Scrolled Pattern Lalique

- *1920*

Lalique glass vase with raised interlaced scrolled design.

- *height 14cm*
- £1,400 • Susie Cooper

△ Lalique Bowl

- *circa 1920*

Lalique bowl with frosted finish and four lilies terminating in fan legs. With acid-etched signature.

- *height 12.5cm*
- £950 • Kieron

▽ Chrysanthemum Bowl

- *1910*

A green bowl with domed lid by Gallé, decorated with chrysanthemums.

- *height 14cm*
- £2,400 • French Glasshouse

▽ Vase with Poppy Design

- *1920*

Glass vase by Lalique with raised poppy-head border and tapering stems with blue patina.

- *height 14cm*
- £950 • Susie Cooper

▽ Poppy Vase

- *circa 1920*

Argy-Rousseau pâte de verre vase, of coloured glass with repetitive poppy design.

- *height 7.5cm*
- £4,200 • French Glasshouse

△ **Whitefriars Powell Vase**
- *circa 1930*

An English vase of baluster form in cloudy French blue colour.
- *height 25cm*
- **£345** • **Circa**

△ **Rostrato**
- *circa 1939*

A Rostrato vase, by Ferro, Barovier and Toso, in Murano glass.
- *height 16cm*
- **£3,500** • **Themes**

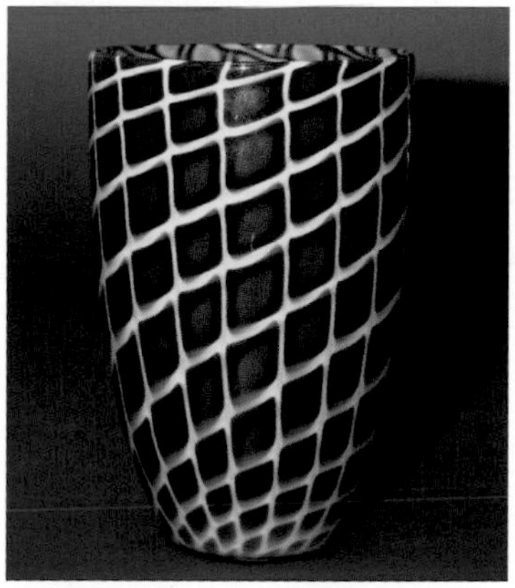

△ **Italian Glass Vase**
- *circa 1950*

A glass vase by Archimede Seguso, decorated with a spiralling pattern in white, dark purple and mauve.
- *height 29cm*
- **£1,500** • **Themes**

▷ **Tiffany Centrepiece**
- *circa 1930*

Tiffany gold iridescent centrepiece with organic designs.
- *diameter 25cm*
- **£4,000** • **Arwas**

△ **Monart Bowl**
- *circa 1930*

A Scottish, aqua-green bowl, by Monart, with single-folded rim.
- *height 8cm*
- **£90** • **Circa**

△ **Green Glass Vase**
- *circa 1939*

Green glass vase, by Barovier & Toso, with pinched handles and lustre finish.
- *height 30cm*
- **£600** • **Vincenzo Caffarella**

△ **Cenedese Deep Bowl**
- *circa 1950*

A deep, Cenedese bowl with aquatic scenes of fish, jellyfish and organic forms.
- *height 25cm*
- **£850** • **Vincenzo Caffarella**

▽ **Three Ruby Vases**
- *circa 1948*

Collection of three ruby wave-rubbed vases by Whitefriars.
- *height 30cm (left), 15cm (middle), 21cm (right)*
- **£130, £34, £44 resp** • **Circa**

▽ **Venini Bottle**
- *circa 1950*

Italian emerald-green bottle with large stopper by Venini.
- *height 36cm*
- **£800** • **Arwas**

▽ **Scandinavian Green Glass Vase**
- *1950*

Scandinavian green glass vase of conical form with blue abstract inclusions.
- *height 29cm*
- **£180** • **Francesca Martire**

▽ **Group of Three Items**
- *circa 1950*

Ashtray, vesta and other receptacle, of globular design with gold and bronze inclusion, by Barovier, Italy.
- **£570** • **Alfie's Antique Market**

▽ Blue Cactus Vase

- *circa 1950*

Blue glass 'Cactus' vase by Riccardo Licata for Murano.

- *height 44cm*
- £1,200 • Francesca Martire

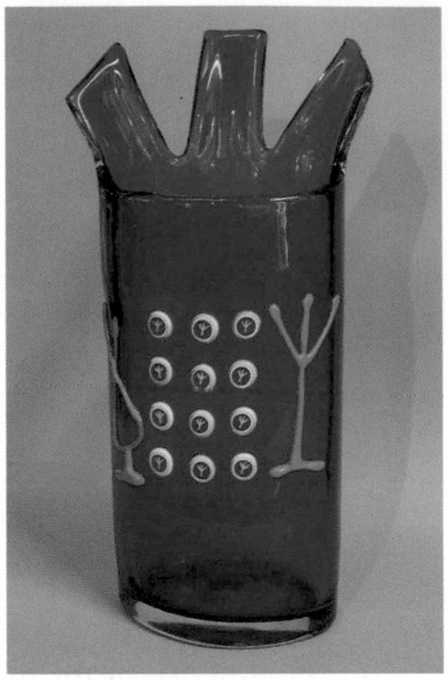

▽ Pair of Glass Candlesticks

- *circa 1950*

A pair of glass-pedestalled candlesticks with metal liners.

- *height 21cm*
- £480 • Kieron

▽ Cenedese Vase

- *circa 1950*

Of ovoid form with small reservoir and red and blue spiral with tears.

- *height 26cm*
- £1,350 • Vincenzo Caffarella

△ Archimede Seguso Vases

- *circa 1950*

Italian Murano green and orange dimple vases of globular form, with a gold leaf border and a crumpled moulded design.

- *height 30cm*
- £800 • Vincenzo Caffarella

△ Cenedese Glass Vase

- *circa 1950*

A Cenedese glass vase with orange centre fading to many bubbles within ovoid form.

- *height 24cm*
- £1,350 • Vincenzo Caffarella

▽ Timo Sarpaneva Vase

- *circa 1950*

A vase, designed by the Finnish designer Timo Sarpaneva for Iittala.

- *height 22cm*
- £50 • Circa

▽ Swedish Vase

- *circa 1950*

A Skruf Talaha Swedish vase, with engraved base.

- *height 20cm*
- £3,800 • Themes

◁ Perfume Bottle

- *circa 1955*

A Cenedese perfume bottle with an oversized stopper and yellow and amber centres.

- *height 44cm*
- £800 • Vincenzo Caffarella

▷ Guitar Mirror

- *1950*

Guitar-shaped metal mirror.

- *length 83cm*
- £120 • Goya

△ Murano Glass Vase

- *circa 1950*

A Murano Flavio Pozzi glass vase, showing elliptical design and colour graduation.

- *height 25cm*
- £650 • Vincenzo Caffarella

△ Decanter

- *circa 1950*

An amber-tinted circular-form decanter with pinched lip and splayed base. Signed by Venini.

- *height 23.5cm*
- £180 • Circa

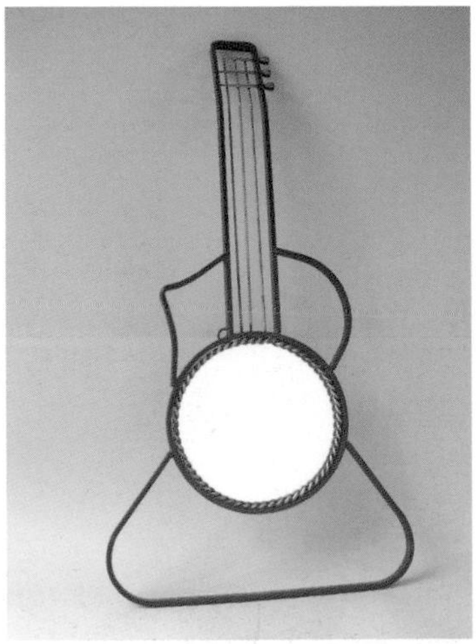

△ Murano Glass Ashtray

- *1950*

Fish-shaped Venetian Murano glass ashtray decorated with gold splashes.

- *2cm x 8.5cm*
- **£45** • **Paolo Bonino**

△ Glass Paperweight Abstract Sculpture

- *circa 1960*

Italian orange, red, black and white abstract glass sculpture.

- *height 16cm*
- **£125** • **Francesca Martire**

△ Whitefriars Kingfisher Blue Set

- *1960–70*

Ashtray and vase set in bark-textured kingfisher-blue glass.

- **£20, £34 resp** • **Circa**

▽ Venetian Glass Vase

- *circa 1950s*

Venetian glass vase with applied white, green and black spun and dripped decoration.

- *50cm x 28cm*
- **£3,750** • **Zakheim**

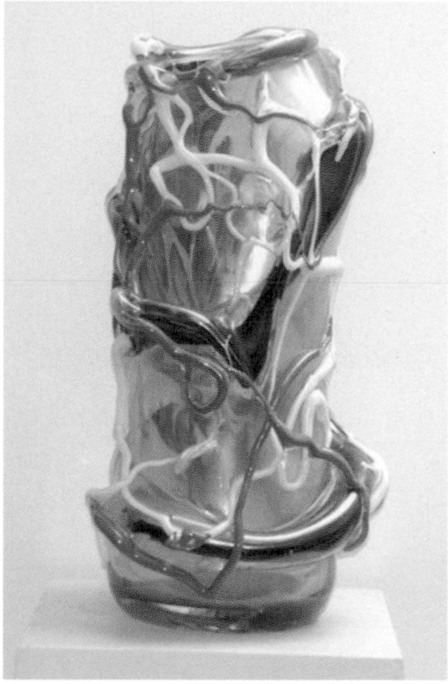

▽ Italian Murano Glasses

- *circa 1960s*

A pair of Murano glasses of globular form on a circular base, by Barovier & Toso.

- *height 13.5cm*
- **£200** • **Vincenzo Caffarella**

▽ Pair of Whitefriars Candle Holders

- *circa 1960–70*

A pair of ruby-coloured, bark-textured candle-holders.

- *height 6cm*
- **£22** • **Circa**

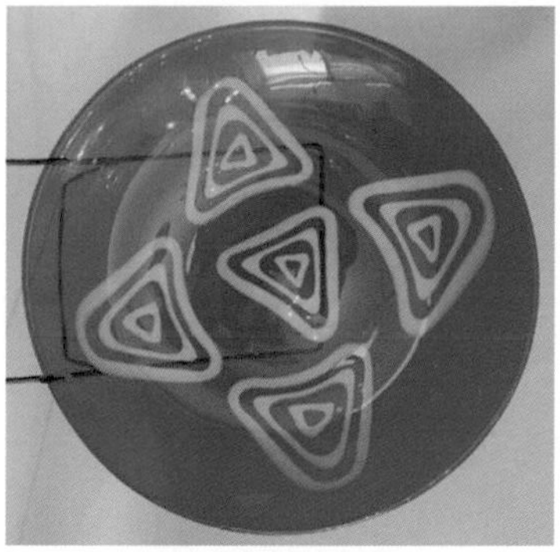

△ Venetian Plate

- *circa 1958*

A circular Venetian plate with white abstract design on a scarlet ground.

- *diameter 18cm*
- **£235** • **Paolo Bonino**

△ Murano Paperweight

- *circa 1960*

Murano paperweight of compressed globular form with an abstract pattern of blue, white, lime green, pink and gold.

- *diameter 23cm*
- **£325** • **Francesca Martire**

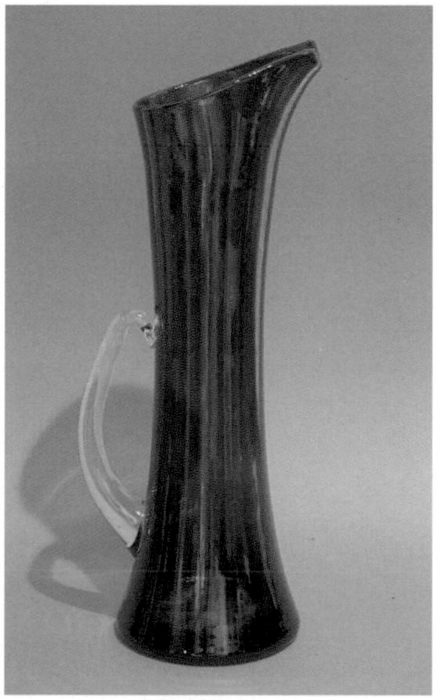

△ Martini Jug

- *circa 1962*

Whitefriars kingfisher-blue Martini jug with a clear handle. A 'Whitefriars Studio' range by Peter Wheeler.

- *height 36cm*
- **£95** • **Country Seat**

▽ Jug and Glass Set

- *circa 1950s*

Rare French glass water jug with two glasses from a set of eight, with gold banding and black geometric patterns.

- **£165** • **Goya**

▽ Vistosi Polychrome Glass

- *circa 1960*

Made from polychromatic glass, with red soda predominant.

- *height 46cm*
- **£4,000** • **Themes**

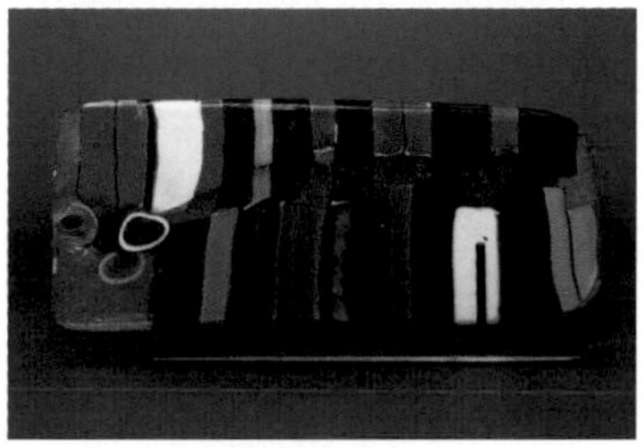

▽ Coffin Vase

- *circa 1960–70*

Clear-cased coffin-shaped vase, bark-textured finish in ruby.

- *height 13cm*
- **£22** • **Circa**

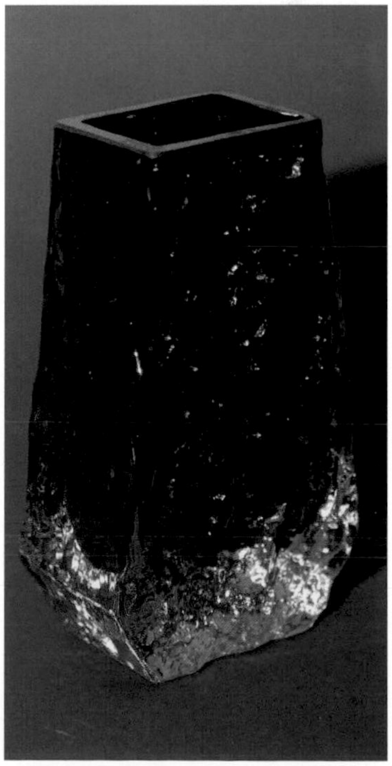

△ Venetian Glass Bowl

- *circa 1960s*

Venetian glass bowl with a red spiral design within the glass, with white enamel on the reverse.

- *9cm x 16cm*
- £58 • Paolo Bonino

△ Vase by Baxter

- *circa 1969*

Whitefriars kingfisher-blue vase by Baxter with an abstract design and textured finish.

- *height 29cm*
- £235 • Country Seat

▽ Cucumber Vase

- *1967*

Whitefriars red 'Cucumber' vase, with a frosted textured finish, by Baxter.

- *height 30cm*
- £185 • Country Seat

▽ Whitefriars Vase

- *circa 1969*

Rare Whitefriars ovoid brown and orange vase. 'Studio range' by Peter Wheeler.

- *height 22.5cm*
- £245 • Country Seat

△ Tangerine Vase by Baxter

- *circa 1969*

Large tangerine dimpled vase with an amorphic globular design by Baxter.

- *height 30cm*
- £245 • Country Seat

△ Tangerine Vase

- *1969*

Tangerine vase with concentric circular design and a textured finish by Baxter.

- *18cm x 17cm*
- £140 • Country Seat

△ Patterned Glass Bowl

- *early 1970s*

Italian glass bowl with a blue and yellow swirling pattern within the glass.

- *9cm x 11.5cm*
- £58 • Paolo Bonino

▽ Tangerine Log Vase

- *1969*

Tangerine Whitefriars 'Log Vase' of cylindrical form with a bark-textured finish, by Baxter.

- *height 23cm*
- £140 • Country Seat

▽ Toni Zuccheri for Venini

- *circa 1970*

Fine glass and bronze stork by Toni Zuccheri for Venini.

- *height 33cm*
- £550 • Vincenzo Caffarella

▽ Mila Schon for Arte Vetro Murano

- *circa 1970*

Large Murano purple-glass plate with circular vortex design, by Mila Schon for Arte Vetro. It has the option of being wall-mounted.

- *width 63cm*
- £450 • Vincenzo Caffarella

△ Bubbled Vase

- *circa 1970*

An English, lobed vase of tapered form, by Whitefriars, in blue bubbled glass.

- *height 23cm*
- £60 • Circa

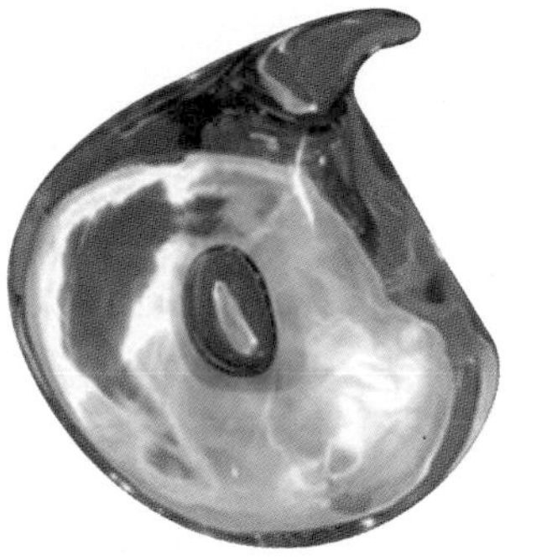

△ Cenedese Glass Vase

- *circa 1980s*

An amorphous Cenedese glass vase sculpture, with blue and amber designs within the glass.

- *height 31cm*
- £850 • Vincenzo Caffarella

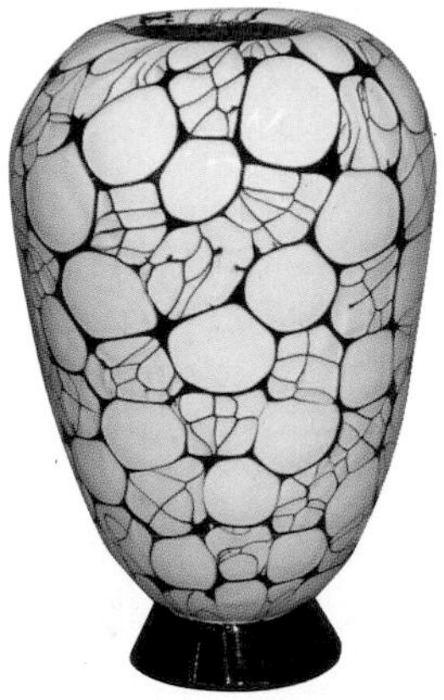

△ V. Ferro for Murano

- *1998*

Yellow vase of bulbous proportions with black cobweb effect, raised on a splayed circular foot.

- *height 28cm*
- £1,500 • Francesca Martire

▽ Aubergine Vase

- *circa 1972*

A textured, Whitefriars vase in aubergine colour, designed by Geoffrey Baxter.

- *height 14cm*
- £48 • Circa

▽ Oriental-Style Vase

- *circa 1980*

A blue and white vase, by Michael Bang for Holmegaard, from his Atlantis series.

- *height 16cm*
- £72 • Circa

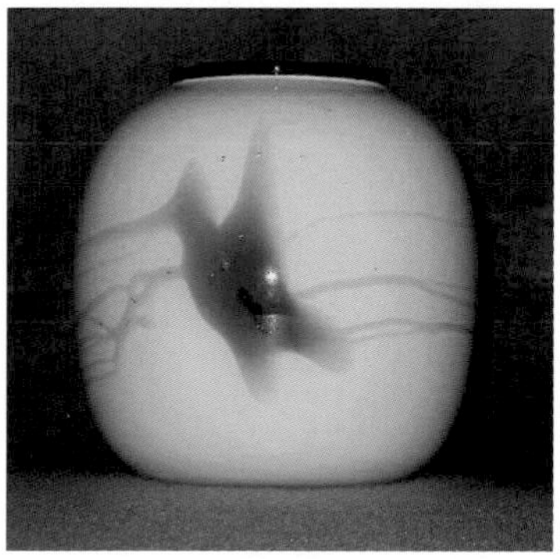

▽ Mosaic Vase by Ferro

- *1998*

Mosaic Murano glass vase by Ferro, for the Venice Biennale 1998.

- *height 29cm*
- £1,200 • Francesca Martire

△ Italian Glass Sculpture

- *1970*

Glass sculpture with red, yellow, green and turquoise free-form shapes within the glass, by Livio Seguso.

- *height 25cm*
- £4,000 • Themes

△ Abstract Glass Structure

- *circa 1990*

Orange and black abstract glass vase of cylindrical form with gold flaked inclusions, by Nichetti for Murano.

- *height 27cm*
- £380 • Francesca Martire

△ Glass Sculpture

- *1999*

Glass sculpture by Sir Terry Frost, entitled Millennium Disc and made from Murano glass.

- £3,800 • Whitford

▽ The Wave

- *circa 1980s*

'The Wave', a clear glass sculpture by Colin Reid with internal colouring of blues, grey and rust.

- *42cm x 39cm*
- £5,750 • Zakheim

▽ Incalmo Glass Vase

- *1990–91*

'Incalmo' glass vase with a vermilion red cane design neck, and a white glass globular shape base, by Laura Diaz de Santillana.

- *height 41cm*
- £2,400 • Themes

▽ Silvio Vigliaturo Sculpture

- *1999*

Glass 'Ikomos' series sculpture by Silvio Vigliaturo, signed and dated.

- *height 40cm*
- £1,200 • Francesca Martire

LIGHTING

△ Table Lamp

- *circa 1900*

Silver-plated brass table lamp on a tripod base and fitted with a cut-crystal glass shade.

- *height 44cm*
- £995 • Turn On Lighting

△ Brass Library Lamp

- *circa 1900*

A brass library lamp with two branches, green glass shades, a finial top and base.

- *height 45cm*
- £350 • Castlegate

▽ Beaded Chandelier

- *1900*

Small chandelier with beaded frame and faceted pendant drops.

- *height 38cm*
- £275 • R. Conquest

▽ Brass Lantern

- *circa 1900*

An Arts and Crafts brass lantern, of square form, with textured glass and organic decoration to the frame.

- *height 36cm*
- £750 • Turn On Lighting

◁ Crystal Chandelier

- *circa 1900*

An Italian copperleaf chandelier with six branches and faceted, drop crystals.

- *height 80cm*
- £850 • Rainbow

△ Bronze Chandelier

- *circa 1900*

Italian Flemish-style bronze chandelier with eight branches.

- *height 90cm*
- £1,300 • Rainbow

△ Austrian Loetz Lamp

- *1900*

Austrian Art Nouveau Loetz lamp with iridescent lampshade, the base by Gerchner.

- *height 46cm*
- £7,500 • Succession

▽ Cherub Wall Sconce

- *1900*

Two-branch gilded wall sconce with scrolling leaves and carved wooden cherub.

- *height 72 cm*
- £550 • R. Conquest

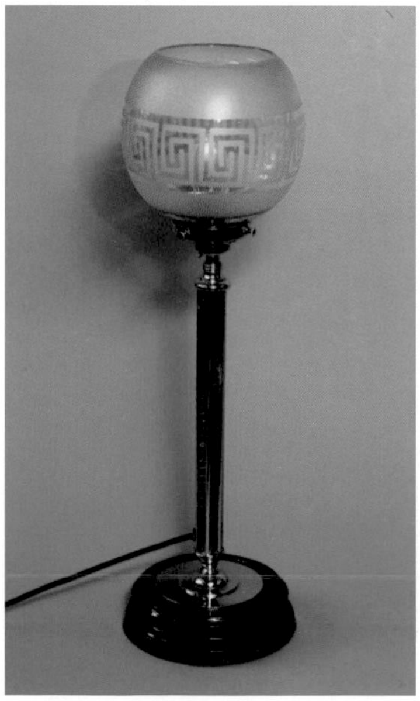

▽ Edwardian Table Lamp

- *circa 1905*

Chrome and porcelain lamp with globe, both decorated with Greek key pattern.

- *height 58cm*
- £895 • Turn On Lighting

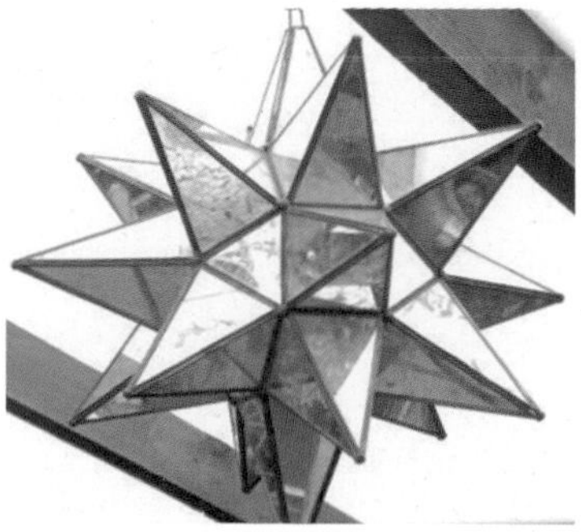

◁ Ceiling Star Light

- *1900*

Moroccan star ceiling light of mirrored glass.

- *diameter 62cm*
- £240 • Myriad

△ Glass and Bronze Lamp

• *circa 1900*
French bronze horse chestnut Art Nouveau lamp, with an Austrian-made glass shade by Loetz.
• *height 64cm*
• £2,200 • **Succession**

△ Bronze Table Lamp

• *1905*
Very rare bronze table lamp by Pete Tereszczuk in cire perdu, with an owl at the base. The turquoise and indigo shade is by Loetz.
• *height 38cm*
• £7,000 • **Succession**

△ Giltwood Chandeliers

• *early 20th century*
One of a pair of giltwood seven-branch chandeliers in 18th-century style.
• *70cm x 69cm*
• £2,800 • **M. Luther**

▽ Austrian Lamp

• *circa 1900*
Austrian hanging lamp, with a moss-green shade with gilt thread decoration, designed by by Loetz.
• *height 25cm*
• £850 • **Succession**

▽ Daum Lamp and Shade

• *1902*
French Art Nouveau lamp with glass lamp and shade, signed by Daum.
• *height 36cm*
• £6,000 • **Succession**

▽ Table Lamp

• *circa 1918*
A cast-brass table lamp fitted with a flakestone glass shade decorated with leaf motifs.
• *height 46cm*
• £450 • **Turn On Lighting**

△ Pewter Candlestick

• *circa 1900*
French pewter Art Nouveau candlestick with a moulded figure within the base, signed 'H Siburd'.
• *length 15cm*
• £340 • **Succession**

△ Art Nouveau Lamp

• *1910*
American Art Nouveau lamp with green shade on a metal stand.
• *height 45cm*
• £600 • **Succession**

▽ Table Lamp

• *circa 1910*
A silver-plated brass table lamp decorated with a floral transfer-printed glass shade.
• *height 37cm*
• £600 • **Turn On Lighting**

▽ Table Lamp

• *circa 1920*
A cast-brass lamp fitted with a flakestone glass shade, and decorated with Roman motifs.
• *height 51cm*
• £575 • **Turn On Lighting**

◁ Wedgwood Desk Lamp

• *circa 1920*
Porcelain and chrome adjustable desk lamp. Signed Wedgwood.
• *height 56cm*
• £1,300 • **Turn On Lighting**

△ Painted Lamp Stand

- *1920*

Naturalistically modelled and painted metal lamp stand showing a floral arrangement of daisies, poppies and wheatsheafs.

- *height 1.1m*
- £420 • Myriad

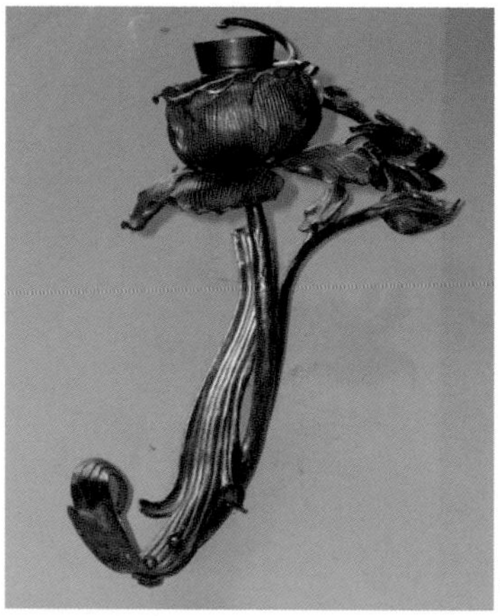

△ Art Nouveau Wall Lights

- *circa 1920s*

One of a pair of bronze Art Nouveau wall lights with leaf design.

- *height 30cm*
- £380 • Solaris

△ Empire-Style Chandelier

- *circa 1920*

French Empire-style crystal and ormolu chandelier, with anthemion decoration to the rim and crystal tiers below.

- *30cm x 55cm*
- £4,850 • Hatchwell

▽ Hand-Painted Chandelier

- *1920*

Green tôle chandelier with hand-painted porcelain roses.

- *height 54cm*
- £320 • R. Conquest

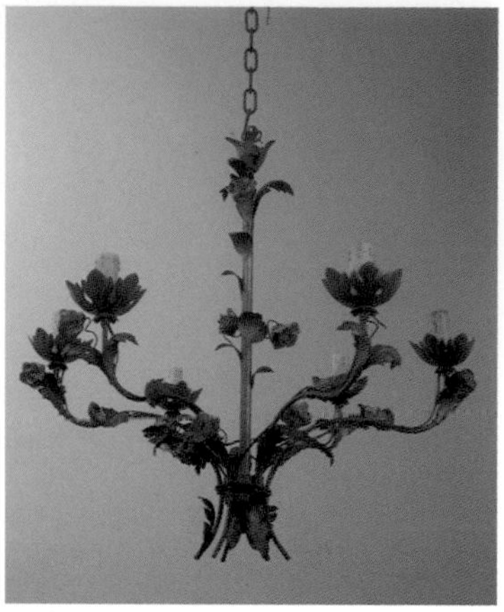

▽ Italian Wall Light

- *circa 1920*

A pair of Italian wall lights with hanging crystals.

- *height 45cm*
- £480 • Rainbow

▽ Brass Chandelier

- *1920*

Chandelier with brass frame and faceted clear and green crystal pendant drops.

- *height 70cm*
- £380 • R. Conquest

△ Oak Candelabra

- *1920*

Pair of German, carved Black Forest oak candelabra in castellated style.

- *height 48cm*
- £1,950 • Lacquer Chest

△ Italian Chandelier

- *circa 1920*

Chandelier with floral motifs, coloured crystal and bronze.

- *height 60cm*
- £750 • Rainbow

△ Wooden Chandelier

- *circa 1920*

An ornate Italian, gilded, wooden, sixteen-branch chandelier with filigree.

- *height 1.1m*
- £750 • Rainbow

▽ French Chandelier

- *1920*

Delicate French chandelier with a metal hour-glass base, with wire and coloured drops.

- *height 66cm*
- £325 • R. Conquest

▽ Italian Wall Light

- *circa 1920*

A single Italian gilt-metal wall light with cut-glass crystals hanging from three branches and central wall-plate.

- *height 70cm*
- £450 • Rainbow

▽ Alabaster Lamps

- *20th century*

One of a pair of alabaster lamps with gilt wrought-iron appliqués.

- *width 45cm*
- £1,200 • Bizarre

△ Gilded Foliage Chandelier

• *1920*
French chandelier with gilded frame of flowing leaves, each bearing a blue opaline glass pendant drop.
• *height 65cm*
• £1,100 • R. Conquest

▽ Louis XVI-Style Chandelier

• *circa 1920*
Two-tiered Louis XVI-style, fine quality cut-crystal chandelier, with four light sconces at the top, and eight below.
• *height 1.2m*
• £6,000 • Hatchwell

▽ Anglepoise Lamp

• *circa 1930*
Polished aluminium and chrome, designed by Cawardine, based on the constant tensioning principles of the human arm, and made by Terry & Sons.
• *height 92cm*
• £175 • After Noah

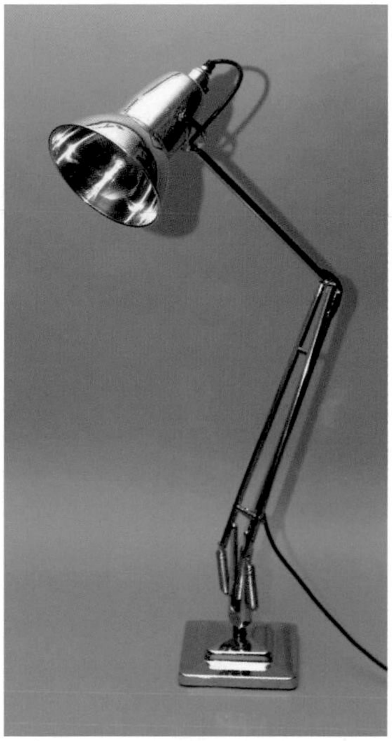

◁ Three-Branched Chandelier

• *1920*
Chandelier with three branches, with rose opaline glass drip-pans and clear faceted crystals.
• *height 75cm*
• £420 • R. Conquest

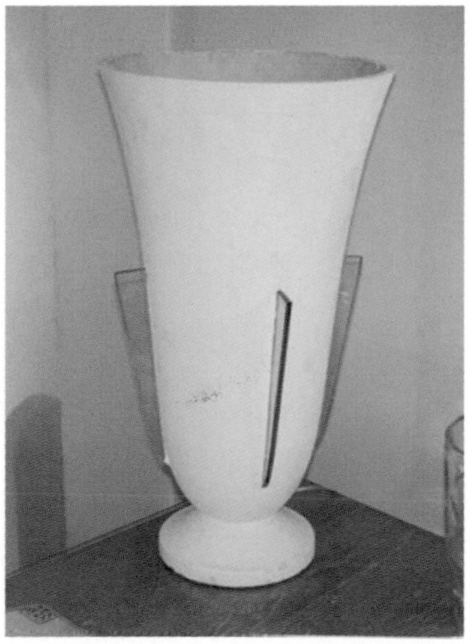

△ Art Deco Lamp

• *20th century*
Art Deco white ceramic vase-shaped lamp, with elongated slats for effective lighting.
• *height 32cm*
• £350 • Bizarre

△ Bronze Hanging Lantern

• *circa 1920s*
Cylindrical bronze hanging lantern in the style of Lutyens.
• *80cm x 38cm*
• £4,900 • M. Luther

△ Tôle Chandelier

• *1920*
A French tôle chandelier with painted flowers.
• *height 50cm*
• £200 • R. Conquest

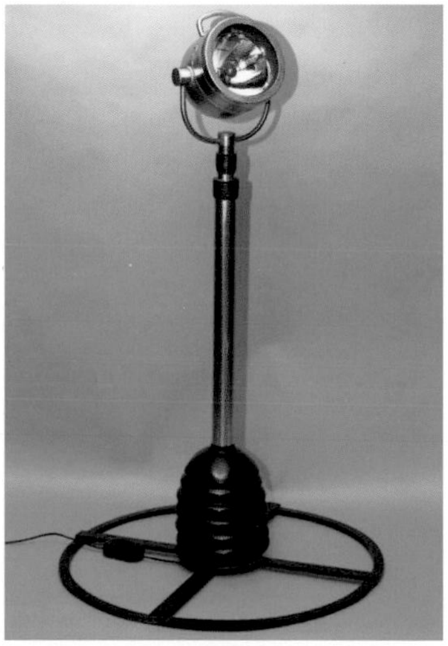

▽ Art Deco Uplighter

• *circa 1920*
An Art Deco chromium-plated table lamp.
• *height 70cm*
• £450 • Turn On Lighting

▽ Hand-Painted Table Lamp

• *circa 1920*
A copper-oxidised table lamp with hand-painted shade showing an Egyptian landscape.
• *height 44cm*
• £450 • Turn On Lighting

◁ Hospital Lamp

• *circa 1930*
With ball joint for lateral adjustment and telescopic shaft.
• *height 1.78m*
• £350 • After Noah

△ Iron Wall Lights

• *circa 1930*
A pair of Italian painted iron wall lights with floral motifs.
• *height 36cm*
• £100 • Rainbow

△ Brass Chandelier

• *1930s*
Italian brass chandelier of foliate design, with turquoise teardrop glass pendants.
• *50cm x 40cm*
• £375 • Rainbow

△ Art Deco Lamp

• *1930*
French Art Deco chrome table lamp with a domed shade, curved stand and circular base.
• *height 32cm*
• £250 • Ventesimo

▽ Laboratory Lamp

• *circa 1930*
By Chas Hearson & Co Ltd, London. Brass stand on wooden base with maker's plaque.
• *height 45cm*
• £145 • After Noah

▽ Etling Lamp

• *1930*
French black lamp with red chinoisiere influence, designed by Etling.
• *47cm x 30cm*
• £1,200 • Bizarre

▽ Hutschenreuther Candelabra

• *20th century*
Candelabra with two branches of leaves supporting candleholders, with a central cherub standing on a gold circular ball, with a round white base, by Hutschenreuther.
• *height 22cm*
• £1,400 • Bizarre

△ Italian Lanterns

• *circa 1930*
One of a pair of brass Italian lanterns holding four lights.
• *height 70cm*
• £650 • Rainbow

△ Table Lamp

• *circa 1930*
Chrome and plastic table lamp with a glass shade.
• *height 41cm*
• £98 • Henry Hay

▽ Chrome Desk Lamp

• *circa 1930*
A chrome anglepoise desk reading lamp with heavy, stepped, square base.
• *height 90cm*
• £125 • Henry Hay

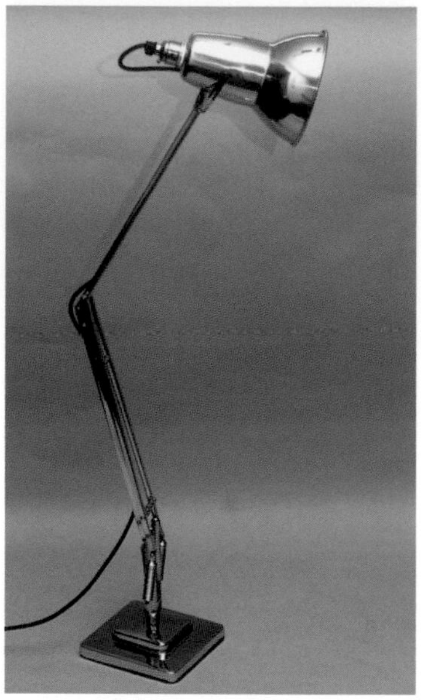

▽ Art Deco Verdigris Lantern

• *circa 1930*
Art Deco bronze lantern of tapered form, each side centred by a moulded oval motif below a stepped fan cresting, fitted with replaced glass, the sides at the base of the lantern centred by scrolls issuing palmettes, with S-scroll brackets leading to a lower suspended bracket.
• *94cm x 41.5cm sq*
• £6,500 • Anthony Outred

◁ Birdcage Frame Chandelier

• *circa 1930*
French silvered bronze birdcage-frame chandelier with plaquette glass drops.
• *130cm x 85cm*
• £6,000 • Guinevere

△ Italian Chandelier

- *circa 1930*

An Italian chandelier with six branches and beaded frame with crystal teardrops.

- *height 85cm*
- £850 • Rainbow

△ American Silver Candlesticks

- *1930s*

Unusual American horseshoe-shaped candelabra and two small circular candleholders on clear glass, designed by Chase.

- *height 25cm*
- £270 • Bizarre

▽ Bovolone-Style Chandelier

- *circa 1930*

Bovolone-style Italian chandelier with six branches and a beaded frame, with turquoise teardrops.

- *height 90cm*
- £975 • Rainbow

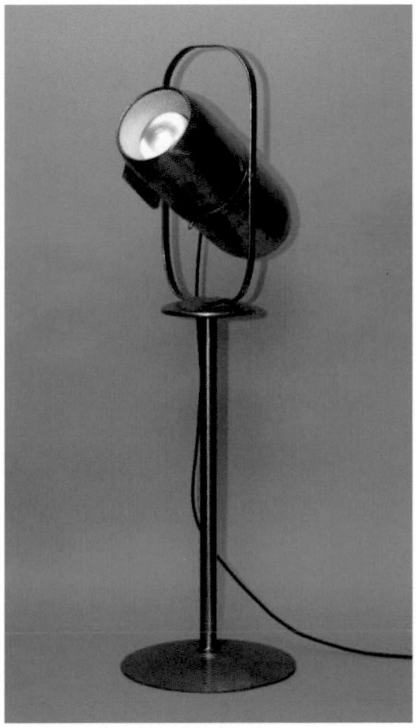

▽ American Lamp

- *circa 1940*

Polished steel adjustable lamp on a steel stand. Probably originally for medical use with heat-bulb. By Westinghouse.

- *height 106cm*
- £275 • After Noah

◁ Cast-Iron Lamp

- *circa 1940*

An American industrial, adjustable lamp (ex-factory) with cast aluminium fittings, standing on a cast-steel base.

- *height 58cm*
- £250 • After Noah

△ Gilded Chandelier

- *1930*

Chandelier with gilded foliate frame, crystal drops and ceramic roses.

- *height 64cm*
- £1,500 • R. Conquest

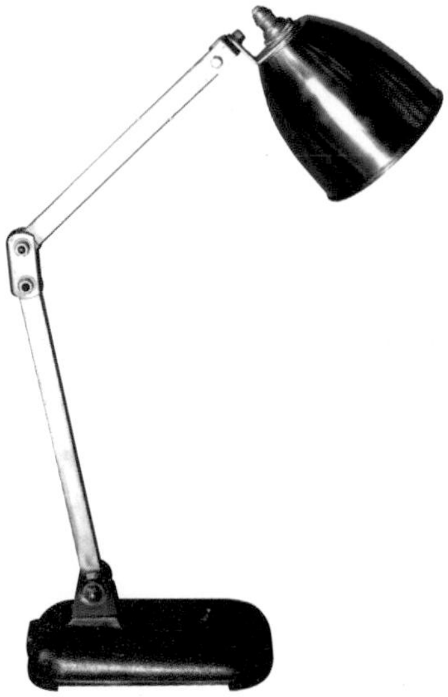

△ Steel Desk Lamp

- *circa 1930*

A steel desk lamp fitted with a spun-metal shade.

- *height 38cm*
- £450 • Turn On Lighting

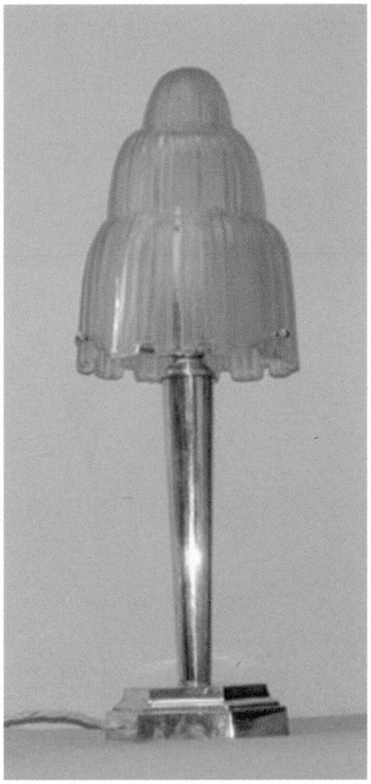

▽ French Table Lamp

- *1930*

French Art Deco table lamp with sandblasted glass shade and silvered bronze stand, signed by Sabino.

- *height 64cm*
- £2,200 • Succession

▽ Italian Gold Mesh Lamp

- *circa 1940*

Table lamp with mesh lampshade supported on a black and white marble base.

- *height 49cm*
- £900 • Vincenzo Caffarella

◁ English Ceiling Lamp

- *1952*

Lantern-style ceiling lamp designed by George Nelson for Howard Miller.

- *width 46cm*
- £350 • Zoom

▽ Coloured Shade Lamp

- *circa 1950*

With three shades of different colours, on a circular base. By Gino Safatti for Arteluce.

- *height 60cm*
- £550 • Vincenzo Caffarella

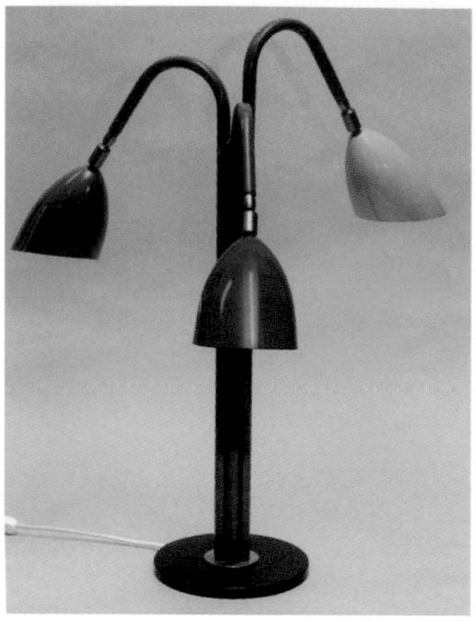

▽ Italian Glass Lamp

- *circa 1950s*

Italian white glass bowl-shaped lamp on a chrome stand by Guzzi.

- *height 2m*
- £750 • Zoom

▽ English Wall Lamps

- *1950s*

Pair of English blue metal wall lamps with brass wall fittings.

- *height 25cm*
- £90 • Zoom

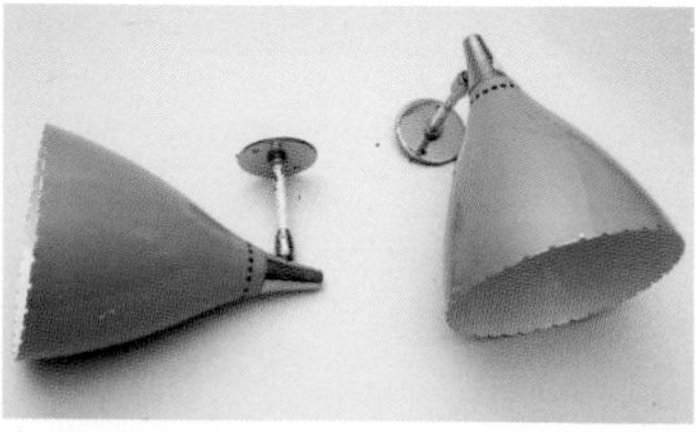

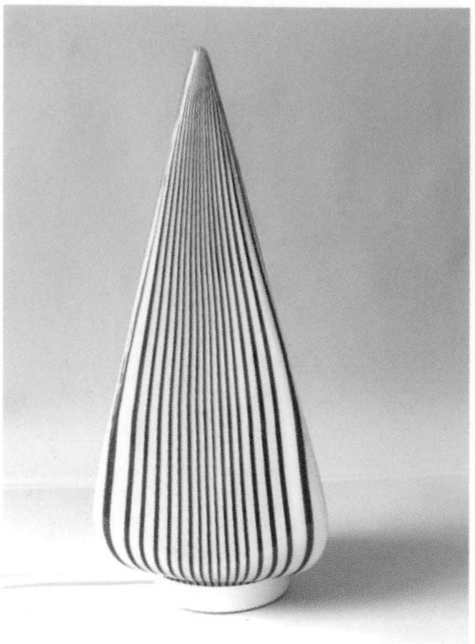

△ Italian Striped Lamp

- *1950*

One of a pair of tear-shaped, brown-and-white striped Italian table lamps.

- *height 23cm*
- £250 • Ventesimo

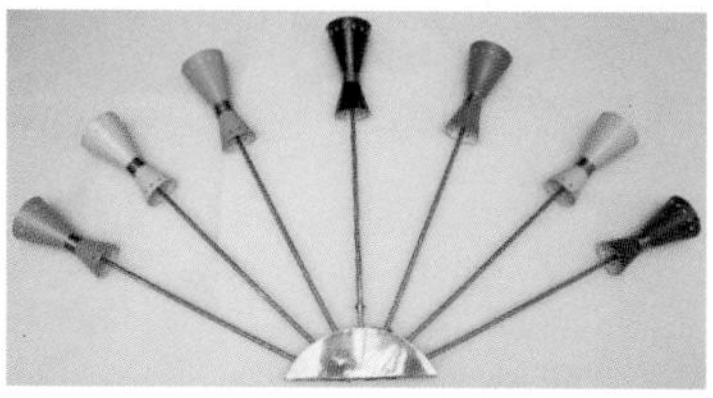

△ Safatti Fan Lamp

- *1950s*

Aluminium and glass fan-shaped lamp by Gino Safatti, Italy.

- *height 1.6m*
- £900 • Zoom

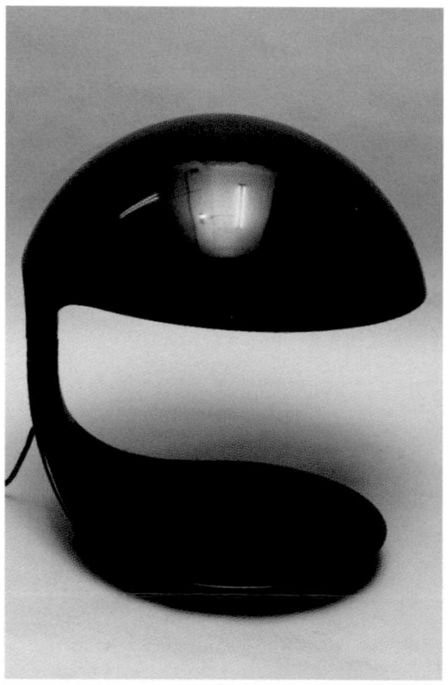

△ Italian Table Lamp

- *circa 1950*

Moulded plastic lamp, incorporating base and shade, designed by Flio Martinelli.

- *height 37cm*
- £750 • Alfie's Antique Market

▽ Venetian Lamp Base

- *circa 1950*

Cenedese Murano glass with three fish on dark green.

- *height 36cm*
- £500 • Vincenzo Caffarella

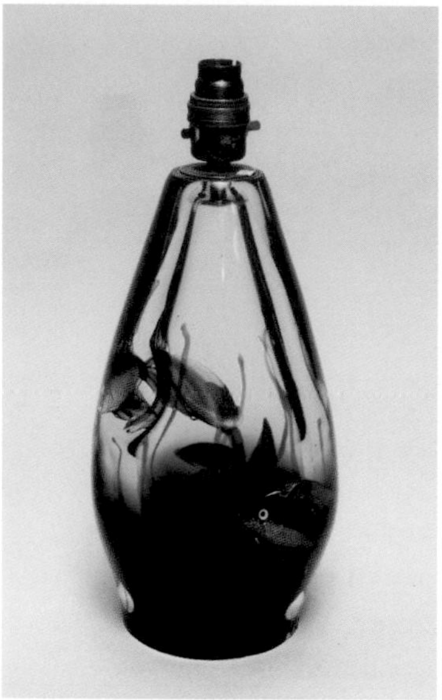

▽ Adjustable Lamp

- *circa 1950s*

Metal, brass and aluminium adjustable lamp by Gino Safatti for Arteluce, Italy.

- *height 1.87m*
- £1,600 • Zoom

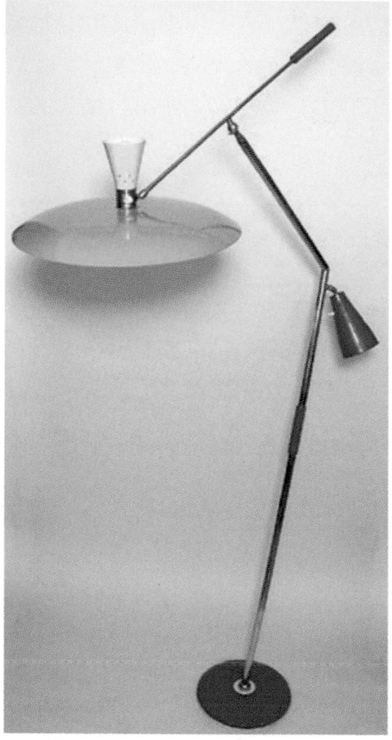

▷ Italian Table Lamp

- *1950*

Black Italian table lamp of baluster form with blue, yellow and red dots, within a white graffiti-patterned border.

- *height 15cm*
- £50 • Alfie's Antique Market

△ Tubular Lamp

- *1950*

Italian chrome graduated tubular lamp with coiled decoration.

- *height 44cm*
- £250 • Ventesimo

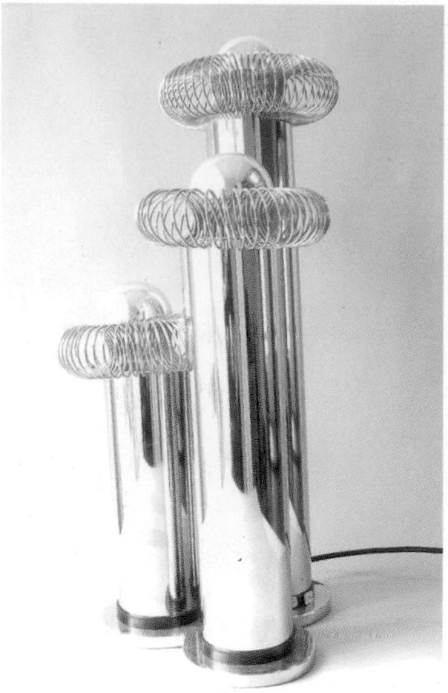

△ Fibre-Optic Lamp

- *1950*

Plastic fibre-optic lamp with plastic flowers within the base.

- *height 75cm*
- £200 • Zoom

▽ Mazzega Table Lamp

- *circa 1960*

Italian Murano glass wave-effect table lamp by Mazzega.

- *54cm x 43cm*
- £1,150 • Vincenzo Caffarella

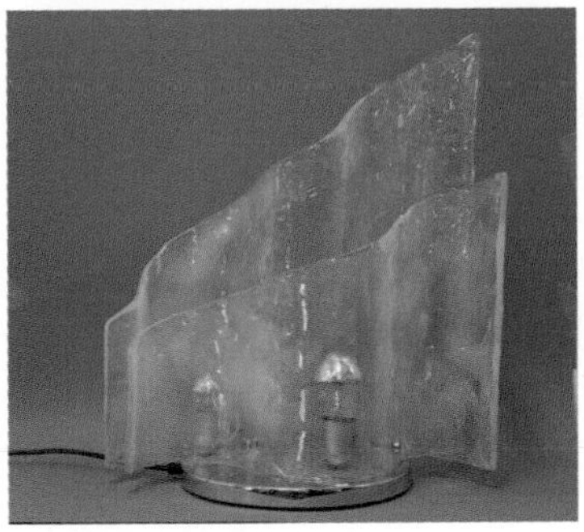

▽ Colomba Lamp

- *1960*

Italian metal and glass, four globe, white Colomba lamp.

- *height 60cm*
- £350 • Zoom

▽ Italian Glass Lamp

- *circa 1960*

By Mazzega in Murano glass with yellow and grey swirls.

- *height 57cm*
- £850 • Alfie's Antique Market

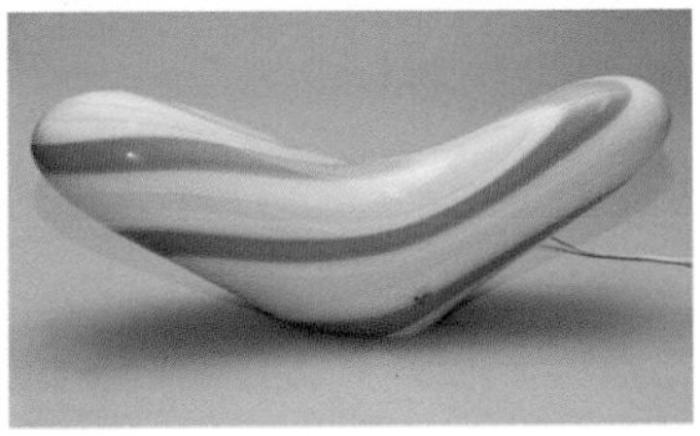

▷ Plastic Ceiling Lamp

- *1960*

Italian oval-shaped ceiling lamp in amber and yellow plastic.

- *diameter 42.5cm*
- £350 • Zoom

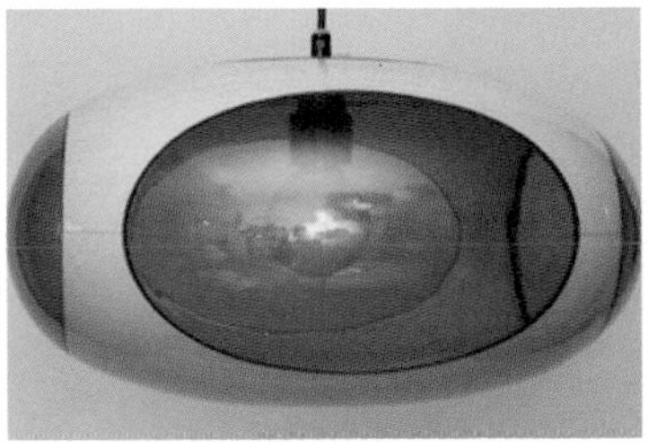

△ Cube Table Lamp

- *circa 1960*

A glass cube table lamp with amber-coloured swirls on an aluminium base.

- *height 47cm*
- £1,000 • Vincenzo Caffarella

△ Italian Hat Lamp

- *circa 1960*

Large Italian table lamp in the form of a large striped sunhat with red flowers on one side and a large black ribbon.

- *diameter 44cm*
- £290 • Alfie's Antique Market

▽ Italian Globe Lamps

- *circa 1960*

One of a pair of clear and ripple effect globe table lamps with a white band running through the body.

- *height 54cm*
- £300 • Vincenzo Caffarella

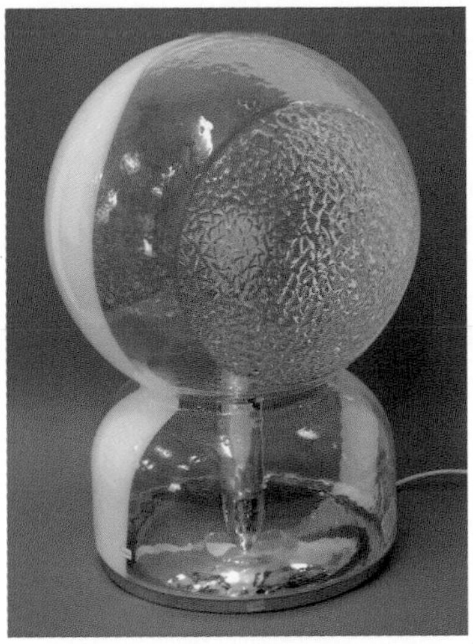

▽ Yellow Sunhat Lamp

- *circa 1960*

Large yellow Italian sunhat lamp with a green ribbon and assorted floral design.

- *diameter 44cm*
- £290 • Alfie's Antique Market

▽ Chrome Ceiling Lamp

- *circa 1960s*

Chrome ceiling lamp with a series of interlocking metal tubes.

- *diameter 60cm*
- £750 • Zoom

△ Tulip Lamp

- *circa 1960*

Gio Ponti tulip, chrome, triple lamp from the workshop of Arredo Luce.

- *height 60cm–1.2m*
- £600 • Vincenzo Caffarella

△ Murano Glass Lamps

- *circa 1960*

Murano Italian glass lamp with yellow and orange ribbed body. The metal covers are ashtrays.

- *height 32cm*
- £450 • Vincenzo Caffarella

△ Amber Glass Lamp

- *1960*

Amber glass ceiling lamp with a metal top to flex.

- *height 26cm*
- £55 • Retro Home

▽ Italian Table Lamp

- *1960*

Italian white table lamp with black base and rubber mobile arm.

- *height 40cm*
- £45 • Retro Home

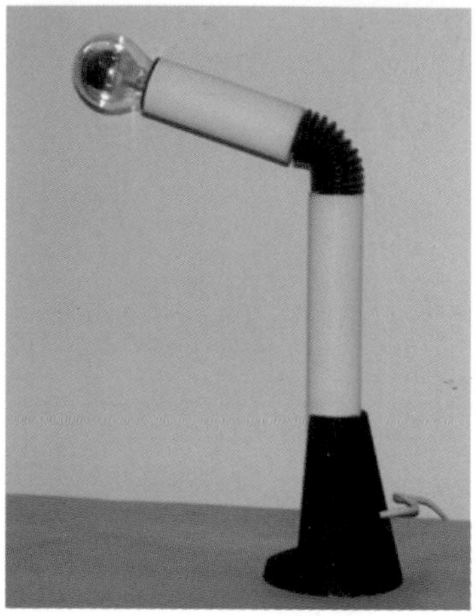

▽ Metal and Chrome Lamp

- *1970*

Italian table lamp with painted black metal shade and chrome base.

- *height 56cm*
- £350 • Zoom

▽ Dome-Shaped Lamp

- *circa 1970s*

Italian dome-shaped glass lamp, with the light lit from within the glass base, by Mazzega.

- *height 52.5cm*
- £650 • Themes

△ English Lamp

- *1960*

English lamp with wood base and plastic shade in brown and white check pattern.

- *height 52cm*
- £10 • Retro Home

△ Fruit-Shaped Lamp

- *circa 1970s*

Italian plastic ceiling lamp in the shape of a peeled orange.

- *diameter 32.5cm*
- £60 • Zoom

△ Kodak Lampshade

- *1970*

Plastic lampshade with the lettering Kodak in red on a deep yellow background.

- *height 25cm*
- £149 • Jessop Classic

▽ White Lamp

- *1960*

White ceiling lamp, with rubber flex and stainless steel collar.

- *height 35cm*
- £50 • Retro Home

▽ Albini Chrome Lamp

- *1969*

Italian ceiling lamp by Franco Albini.

- *height 45cm*
- £350 • Zoom

▽ Chrome Lamp

- *circa 1970*

Of conical form with a chrome metal finish, in three sections.

- *height 50cm*
- £300 • Vincenzo Caffarella

▷ Panthella Lamps

- *1970*

Panthella lamps designed for Louis Poulson by Vernen Paton, Denmark.

- £550 • Zoom

△ Snowflake Chandelier

- *1960–70*

Atomic metal chandelier of a snowflake design.

- *diameter 40cm*
- £850 • Zoom

△ Italian Angled Lamp

- *1970s*

Italian fully adjustable angled lamp.

- *height 37.5cm*
- £175 • Zoom

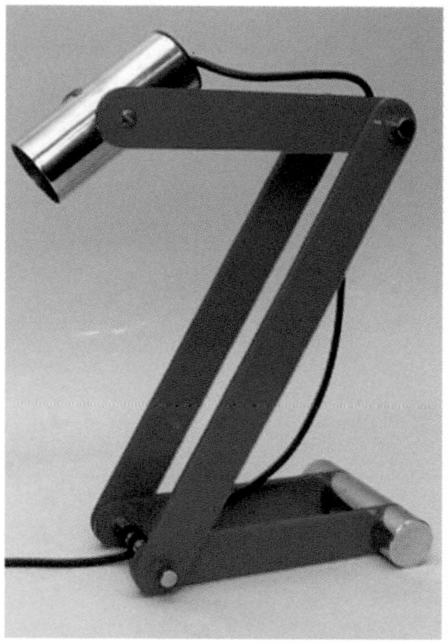

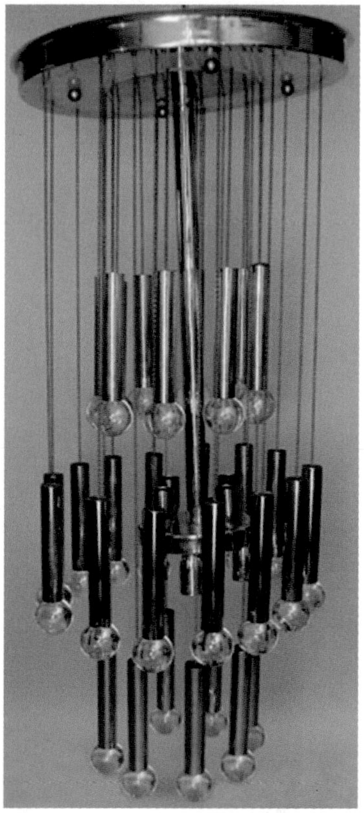

△ Wind Chime Lamp

- *1970*

Wind chime ceiling lamp with crystal glass balls on chrome drops.

- *100cm x 40cm*
- £1,700 • Zoom

△ Gaku Light

- *circa 1990*

Gaku light by Ingo Maurer made from Japanese paper on an aluminium stand.

- *height 95cm*
- £560 • Themes

▽ Selenova Lamps

- *circa 1970*

A pair of Selenova lamps, with glass enclosing four coloured lights, on a circular splayed chrome base.

- *height 52cm*
- £1,400 • Vincenzo Caffarella

▽ Vistosi Lamp

- *1978*

Italian Murano white glass lamp of ovoid form by Vistosi.

- *height 57cm*
- £1,200 • Themes

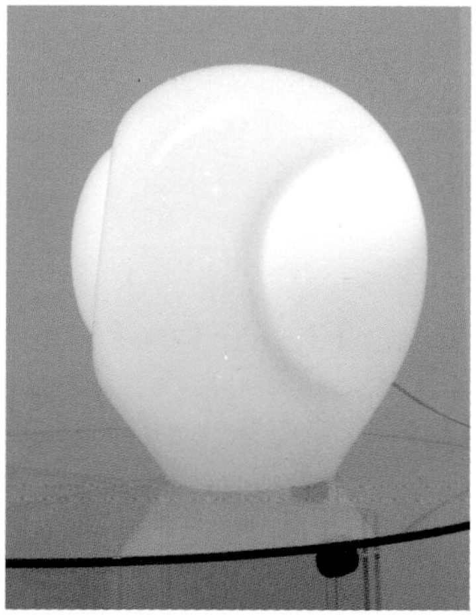

▽ Star Light

- *circa 1990s*

Star-shaped light made from paper and reinforced with metal, by Tom Dixon.

- *height 47.5cm*
- £280 • Themes

△ Pistillo Wall Lamp

- *1970*

Italian silverised wall lamp in a Pistillo design by Studio Tetrarch.

- *diameter 60cm*
- £250 • Zoom

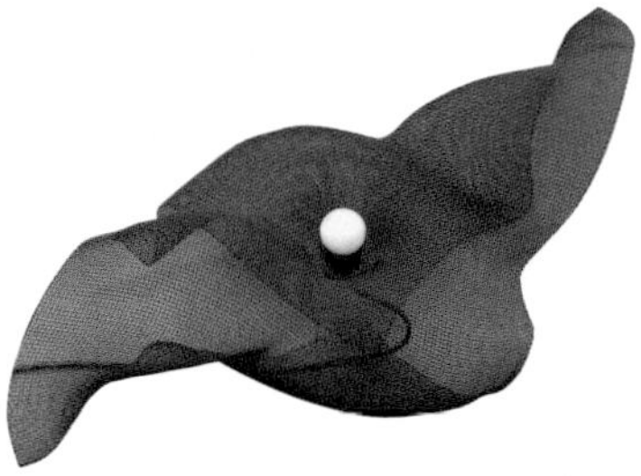

△ Pagani Mesh Lamp

- *circa 1970*

Italian black metal mesh lamp stylised as a flower by Luciano Pagani.

- *width 76cm*
- £385 • Vincenzo Caffarella

△ British Spiral Lamp

- *early 1990s*

Gold-coloured leaf spiral lamp on a circular base by Tom Dixon.

- *height 150cm*
- £980 • Themes

▽ Italian Tube Lamp

- *circa 1970s*

Murano glass lamp with tubes carrying a white abstract design within the glass, on a chrome cylindrical base.

- *height 40cm*
- £1,200 • Zoom

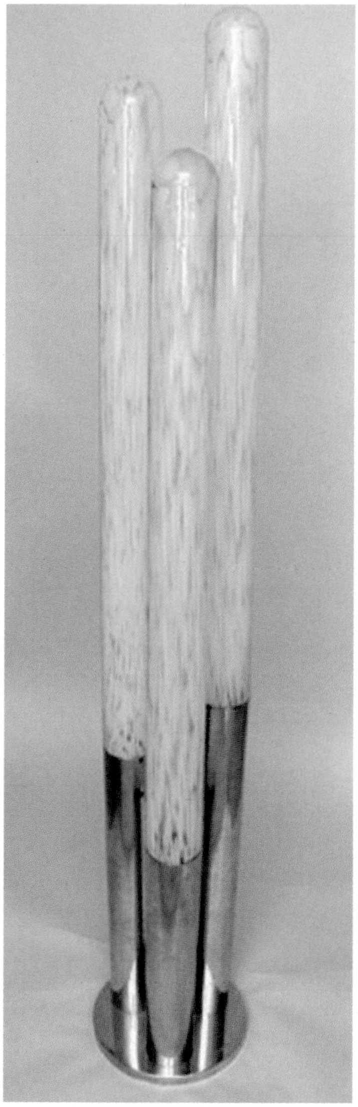

▽ 'The Samurai'

- *20th century*

By German designer Ingo Maurer for the Ma-Mo-Nouchies collection. Made in Japanese pleated paper, stainless steel, silicone and glass.

- *height 80cm*
- £620 • Themes

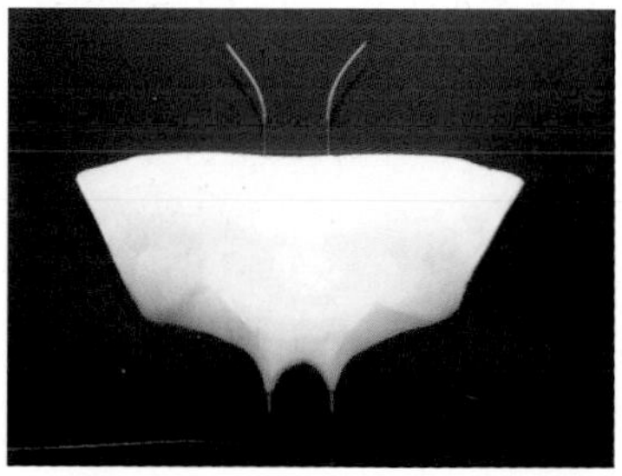

METALWARE

△ Gilt Bronze Lady

- *1900*

Gilt patinated bronze figure of a lady by H. Varenne, signed and dated 1905, with bronze founder's mark of Susse Frères.

- *18.5cm*
- £2,500 • Arwas

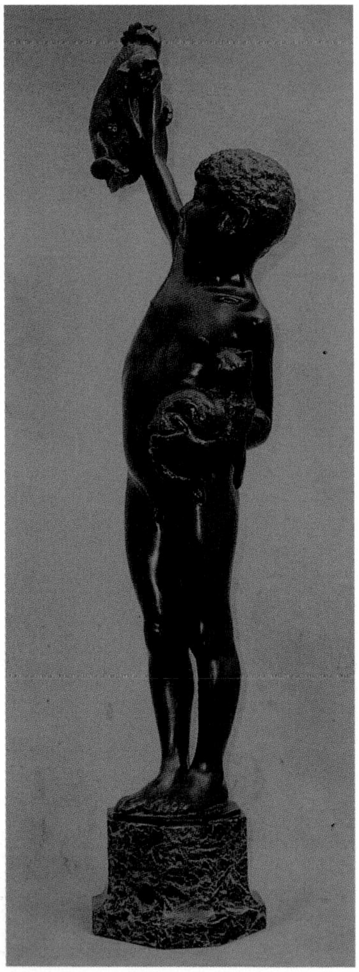

▷ Benson Tea Set

- *circa 1900*

A copper and brass tea set designed and made by W.A.S Benson. Stamped 'Benson'.

- *42cm x 18cm*
- £895 • Liberty plc

△ French Bon-Bon Dish

- *circa 1900*

French gilt bronze bon-bon dish with a young girl on the lid, by A. Charpentiers.

- *16cm x 29cm*
- £3,500 • Arwas

◁ Italian Bronze Boy

- *1904*

A fine Italian bronze of a naked young boy playing with kittens. He holds one up while cuddling the other. The bronze is signed Marcuse, Roma. On a chamfered marble base.

- *height 75cm*
- £5,950 • Gavin Douglas

△ World War I Frame

- *circa 1914*

Iron sculpture of a winged angel of Mercy and a soldier with a lion, fashioned as a picture frame.

- *height 47cm*
- £285 • Hayman

▽ Copper Charger

- *circa 1910*

Gilded, hand-crafted circular charger, exquisitely worked in a continuous band of flowerheads on a punched background.

- *height 30cm*
- £475 • David Pickup

▽ German Silver Tray

- *1905*

German silver Art Nouveau tray decorated with red poppies and head of a girl with long red hair.

- *32cm x 40cm*
- £7,000 • Succession

▽ Dalou Bronze

- *circa 1905*

Bronze figure of a man digging, by Aimé Joule Dalou. Pupil of Carpeaux and Duret his debut was at the Salon in Paris in 1867, signed with the Swiss French Foundry mark.

- *height 9cm*
- £1,650 • Gavin Douglas

△ La Musicienne

- *1912*

French gilt bronze of a lady with a sistrum, by Muller.

- *18.5cm*
- £2,500 • Arwas

△ Ivory Figure

- *1925*

Very fine painted bronze and ivory and gold figure, by F. Preiss.

- *height 18cm*
- £3,950 • Gavin Douglas

▽ Figure by H. Varenne

- *1912*

Figure of a lady with a large hat by H. Varenne, founder's mark Susse Frères.

- *19cm*
- £2,500 • Arwas

▽ Art Deco Figure

- *circa 1925*

Art Deco bronze of a young man holding a lariat, on a marble plinth.

- *height 30cm*
- £1,275 • Gavin Douglas

◁ Bronze Cow

- *circa 1925*

Bronze reclining calf, signed by Richard Garve.

- *7cm x 14cm*
- £2,500 • Arwas

△ Bronze and Ivory Figure

- *circa 1920*

A lovely bronze and ivory figure of a child playing the accordion with original gilding and marble base.

- *height 25cm*
- £4,900 • Gavin Douglas

△ Chrome & Bakelite Candlestick

- *circa 1926*

Art Deco candlestick featuring a two-dimensional woman, arms outstretched, holding a candle in each hand.

- *height 21cm*
- £65 • Beverley

▽ Lorenzl Bronze

- *circa 1920*

Gold enamelled figure of a girl in pyjamas holding a parrot.

- *height 30cm*
- £2,300 • Kieron

▽ Hussman Bronze Figure

- *circa 1920*

Erotic bronze of a nude man on horseback, Signed 'Hussman'.

- *height 35.5cm*
- £2,750 • Gavin Douglas

▽ Art Deco Figure

- *1930*

French Art Deco silvered bronze figure of a dancer, by Henri Molins.

- *height 47cm*
- £1,400 • Succession

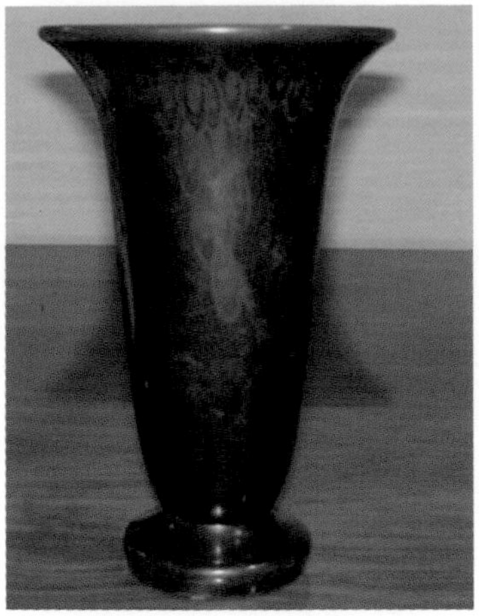

△ Bronze Vase

- *1930s*

Dinanderie bronze vase designed by Grange.

- *height 27cm*
- £1,500 • Bizarre

△ Pair of Candlesticks

- *circa 1930*

A pair of Art Deco chrome and decorative green plastic candlesticks with clear holders and conical sconces.

- *height 9cm*
- £42 • Henry Hay

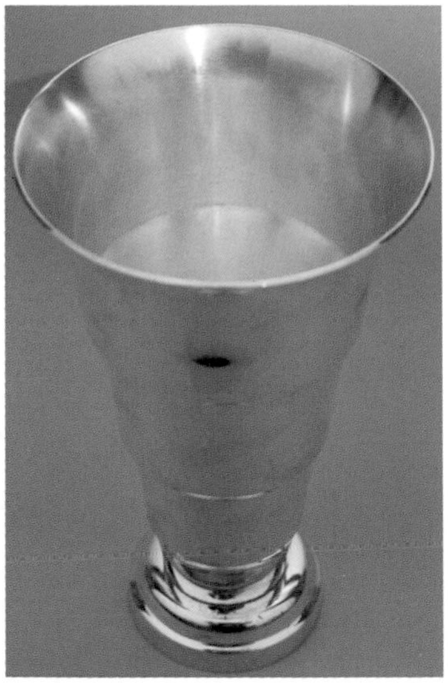

△ Silver-Plate Vase

- *circa 1930*

A conical, stepped, silver-plated vase on a stepped, circular base.

- *height 31cm*
- £200 • Beverley

▽ Tudric Jug

- *1930*

Tudric jug of ovoid proportions made for Liberty of London.

- *height 25cm*
- £85 • Jane Stewart

▽ Pair of Ball Candlesticks

- *circa 1930*

A pair of hollowed, decorative chromium-plated balls on a square base. American.

- *height 6.5cm*
- £120 • Bizarre

▽ Silverplate Bowl

- *circa 1935*

Bowl with green bakelite base.

- *diameter 22.5cm*
- £175 • Beverley

▽ Chrome Bath-Rack

- *circa 1930*

An early compartmentalised chromium bath-rack with adjustable shaving mirror.

- *height 23cm*
- £98 • Henry Hay

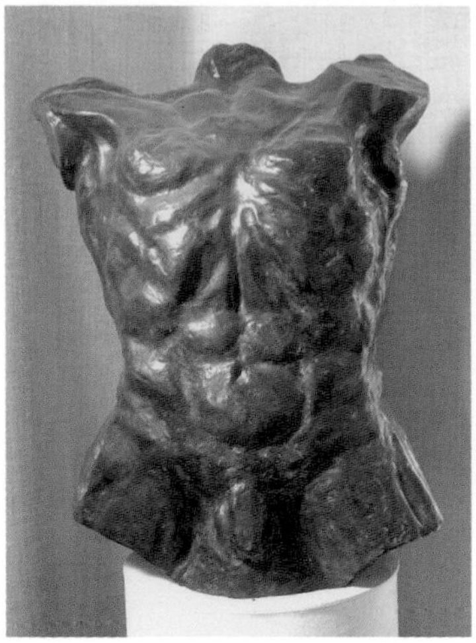

△ Lifesize Bronze Torso

- *circa 1930*

Emotive life-size bronze torso by Hubert Yenge from the foundry of Alexis Rudier, Paris, founder to Rodin.

- *71cm x 55cm*
- £8,750 • Country Seat

△ Five-Piece Tea Service

- *circa 1930*

Tea service in EPNS, consisting of teapot, coffeepot, milk jug, sugar bowl and tray, with bakelite handles. By Art Krupp.

- *length 43cm (tray)*
- £750 • Bizarre

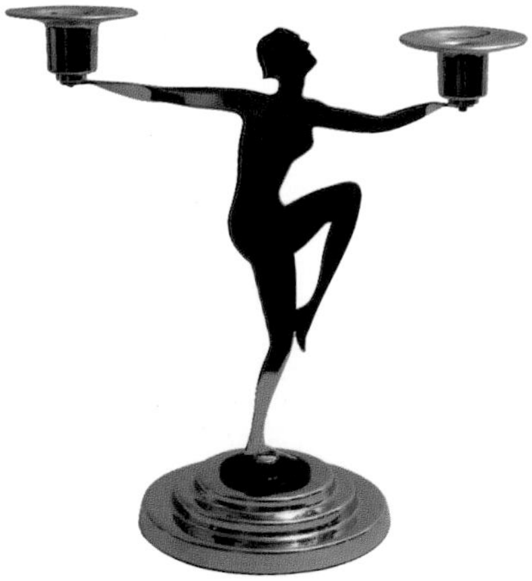

△ Pair of Candlesticks

- *circa 1930*

A pair of chrome, two-branch candlesticks on a circular base, holding a sconce in each hand.

- *height 21cm*
- £78 • Henry Hay

▽ Polychrome Figure

- *circa 1930*

Etched steel model of a Greek Koure princess. French.

- *height 1.9m, width 60cm*
- £3,500 • Westland & Co.

▽ Classical Figure

- *20th century*

Bronze and ivory figure from a model by Varnier, showing a classical maiden holding a flower aloft. On an onyx and marble base.

- *height 26.7cm*
- £785 • London Antique

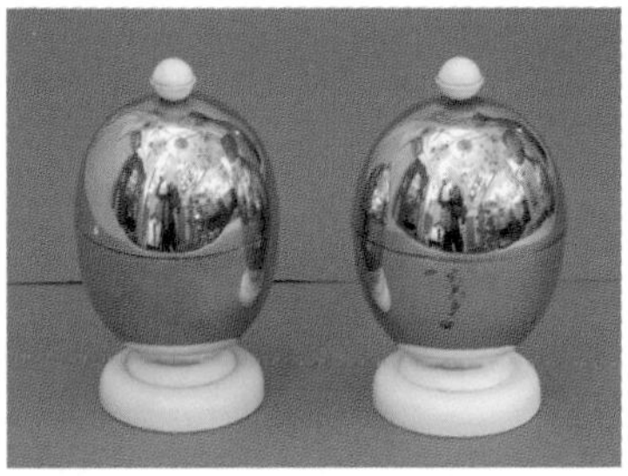

△ Chrome Egg Cups

- *circa 1950*

Pair of Italian chrome egg cups with covers.

- *height 11cm*
- £50 • Alfie's Antique Market

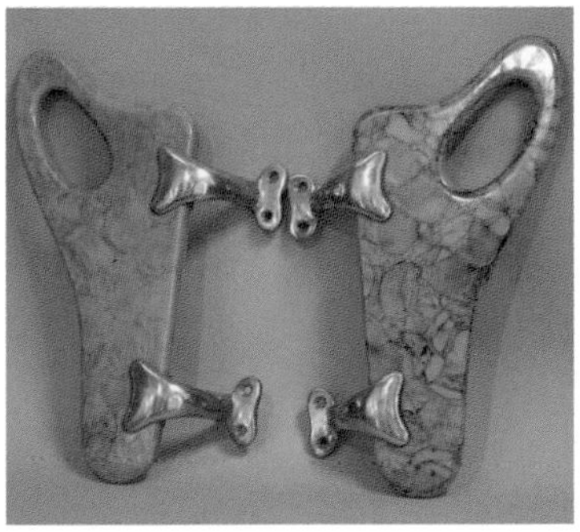

△ Turquoise Door Handles

- *circa 1960*

Italian stylised palette-shape metal door handles with turquoise marbleised enamel overlay and large brass mounts.

- *length 33cm*
- £320 • Francesca Martire

△ Mexican Horse

- *20th century*

A naively-modelled tin horse, with saddle and four straight legs, the whole on a square, tin base.

- *height 1m, width 1.2m*
- £200 • Curios

▽ Tall Bronze Bottle

- *circa 1950*

A Japanese Tsuro flower vessel of Kubi form. Vessel is signed by Roku IV.

- *height 40cm*
- £1,600 • Gregg Baker

▽ American Chrome Lighter

- *1960*

Ball-shaped chrome lighter by Ronson of Newark, New Jersey, USA.

- *height 7.5cm*
- £45 • Zoom

▷ Lenoir Bronze

- *20th century*

Patinated French bronze figurine of a nude lady with an outstretched cloak, by Pierre Lenoir.

- *height 32cm*
- £950 • Bizarre

◁ Warrior Figure in Bronze

- *20th century*

Bronze figure of an African warrior holding a gilt shield and throwing a spear, by Rena Rosenthal.

- *height 20cm*
- £300 • Bizarre

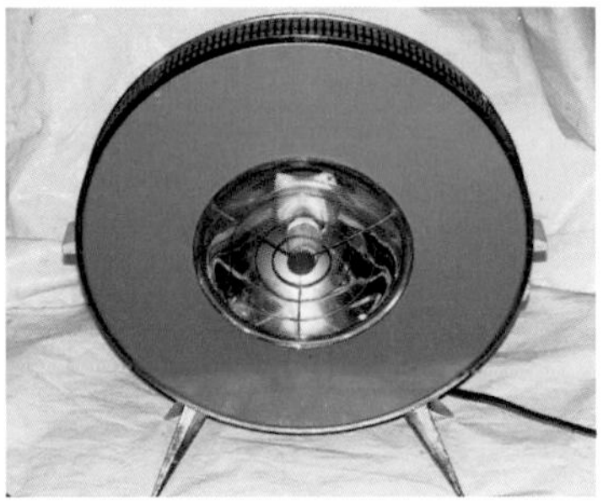

△ Radiator/Convector Heater

- *circa 1950*

Made of sheet metal with chrome legs, bakelite switches and knobs. By Soforo.

- £250 • Zoom

△ Rosenthal Bronze

- *20th century*

Bronze figure of a dancer in a straw skirt in a stylised form, by Rena Rosenthal.

- *height 20cm*
- £300 • Bizarre

△ Chrome Clocks

- *1970*

Scottish-made chrome clocks with red, purple and blue dials, by Westclox.

- *height 18.75cm*
- £50 • Zoom

▽ Chrome Syphon

- *1960*

British-made chrome siphon and ice bucket.

- *height 40cm*
- £240 • Zoom

▽ Bronze Dancer

- *20th century*

Bronze figure of a female dancer by Rena Rosenthal.

- *height 20cm*
- £300 • Bizarre

▽ Spelter Figure

- *20th century*

Bronze spelter bust of the dancer Isadora Duncan, of a phantasmagorical theme.

- *height 42cm*
- £4,500 • Bizarre

WINE-RELATED ITEMS

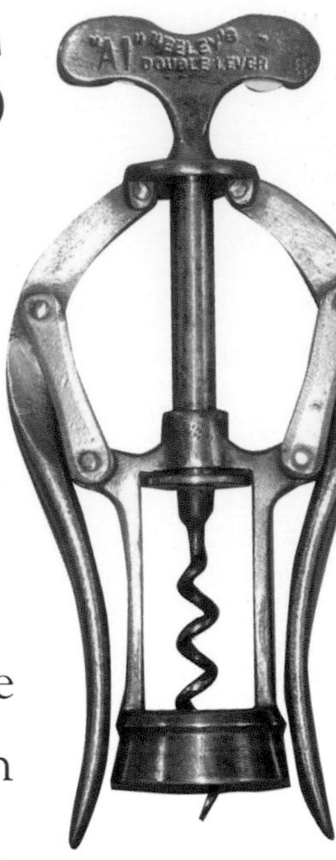

There is a tremendous interest in wine-related items covering a wide range of styles and periods. From George III silver punch ladles to champagne taps, all have their place in the collector's market. The humble corkscrew has been elevated to a work of art and comes in a huge range of different styles, from the staghorn corkscrew made by McBindes in the 1900s, to rosewood corkscrews with grip shanks and brushes to remove the dust off bottles from the cellars. Decanters are also hugely popular. The first decanters, made in the seventeenth century, were of heavy blown moulded glass with indentations in the base. These early decanters were used to serve wine but not to store it. They often have imitation labels bearing the name in gilt lettering of the wine or spirit for which they were intended. Some were made in sets of three with labels for brandy, rum and gin. Bottle trolleys and tantaluses are highly collectable and were especially popular in the Victorian period. Keep a look out for rare three-bottle trolleys.

△ Wine Taster

- *circa 1660*

A silver wine taster made in Norwich by Arthur Haselwood, of shallow oval form, pinched and embossed with bead decoration.

- *length 9cm*
- £6,500 • N. Shaw

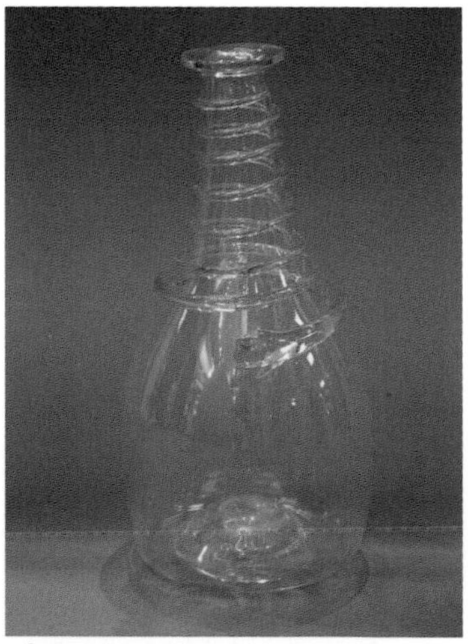

▽ Glass Flask

- *circa 1720*

Glass flask in the fashion of Venice moulding.

- *height 15.5cm*
- £180 • Jasmin Cameron

◁ Wine Funnel

- *1780*

A silver wine funnel with filter insert and beaded borders, made by John Carmen of London.

- *height 13cm*
- £1,050 • Langfords

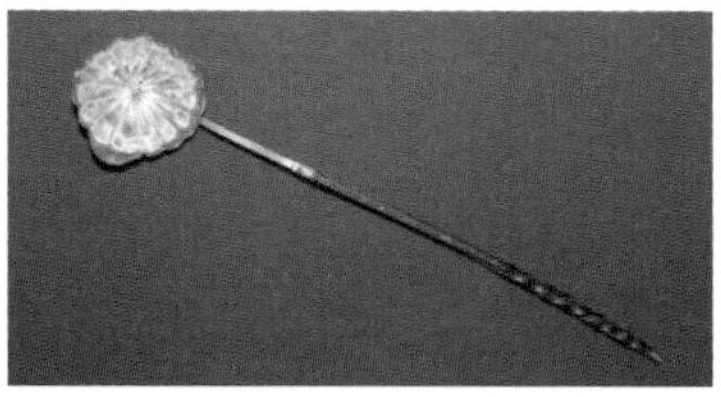

△ Toddy Ladle

- *1745*

An English George II toddy ladle with a silver, lobed bowl and lip and twisted, whalebone handle with a silver finial.

- *length 45cm*
- £690 • Jasmin Cameron

△ Chinese Wine Cooler

- *circa 1770*

Chinese export wine cooler with handles of European silver, decorated with flowers within elaborate borders.

- *height 29cm*
- £3,100 • Cohen & Cohen

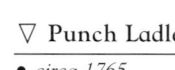

▽ Punch Ladle

- *circa 1765*

George III silver punch ladle with feathered stem and whalebone handle.

- *length 38cm*
- £150 • Jasmin Cameron

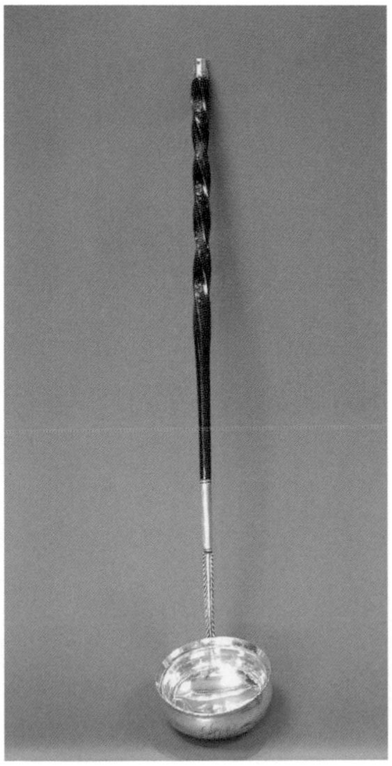

▽ Wine Cooler

- *circa 1790*

Octagonal mahogany cooler with original brass binding and lion-mask handles, on tapered legs.

- *height 58cm*
- £4,450 • Ronald G. Chambers

▷ Regency Wine Cooler

- *circa 1820*

English mahogany wine cooler of sarcophagus form, the rectangular ebony-strung edged top with canted corners above a cavetto moulding and cross-banded frieze with an ebonised upper and lower strung edge. Each side of the body decorated with an ebonised string inlay, the sides fitted with finely cast lions' heads, the base finished with a triple-reeded moulding above finely cast brass hairy paw feet.

- *61cm x 71cm*
- £11,500 • Anthony Outred

△ Silver Wine Coaster

- *1811*

George III silver wine coaster with gadroon edge, on a wooden base by Rebecca Eames and Edward Barnard of London, England.

- *diameter 9cm*
- £900 • Linden & Co.

△ Decanter Labels

- *1798*

Thread design silver labels with the pierced letters 'Sherry', and 'W Wine', by Joseph Taylor of Birmingham.

- *7cm x 4cm*
- £250 • Linden & Co.

▽ Liqueur Funnel

- *circa 1820*

An early 19th-century fluted glass liqueur funnel of twisted shape.

- *height 13cm*
- £55 • Jasmin Cameron

▽ Leather Vessel

- *circa 1800*

Small leather hand-cut and stretched drinking vessel.

- *height 18cm*
- £250 • H. & H.

▽ Silver-Plated Wine Strainer

- *circa 1820*

Silver-plated wine strainer.

- *height 14cm*
- £220 • Jasmin Cameron

▽ Silver Wine Coaster

- *circa 1820*

One of a pair of silver wine coasters.

- *diameter 15cm*
- £320 • Jasmin Cameron

△ Oak Travelling Case

- *circa 1810*

Travelling case with six spirit decanters, two smaller decanters, three trumpet glasses and four flutes.

- *height 30cm*
- £2,850 • Ranby Hall

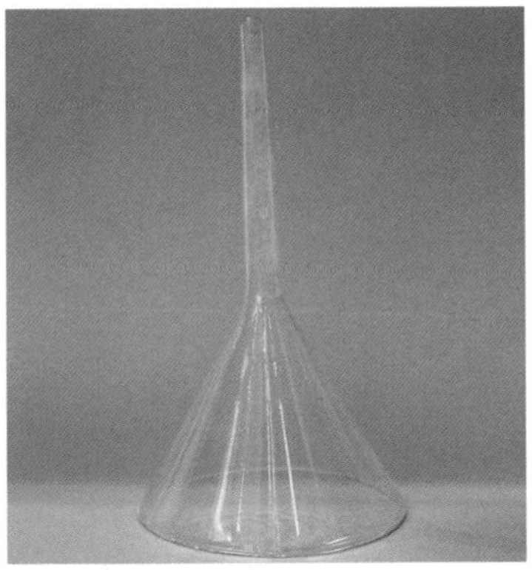

△ Wine Funnel

- *circa 1820*

Clear glass wine funnel.

- *diameter 10cm*
- £75 • Jasmin Cameron

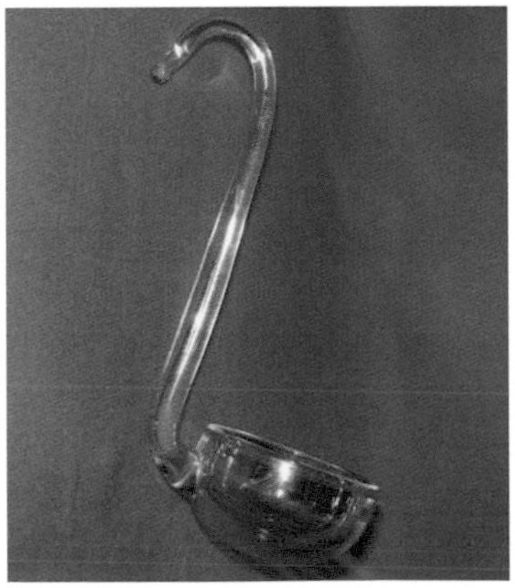

△ Punch Ladle

- *1820*

Regency glass punch ladle.

- *length 22cm*
- £220 • Jasmin Cameron

△ Rum Label

- *1830*

Silver rum label, made in London.

- *length 5cm*
- £68 • Henry Gregory

△ Wine Cooler

- *circa 1840*

A 19th-century mahogany wine cooler with beaded top edge.

- *height 50cm*
- £2,450 • Ronald G. Chambers

△ Kluk Kluk

- *1850*

Spirit decanter with a moulded body known as a Kluk Kluk.

- *height 27cm*
- £275 • Jasmin Cameron

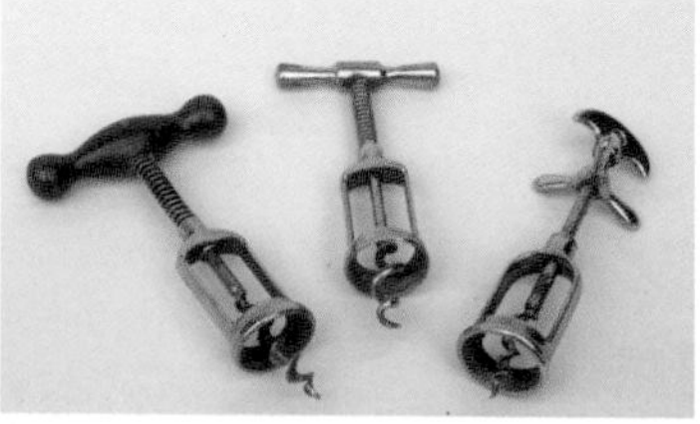

▽ Dutch Decanter

- *1830*

Dutch oblong decanter with flash gilding flowers.

- *height 25cm*
- £175 • Jasmin Cameron

▽ Corkscrew

- *circa 1850*

Lignum vitae corkscrew by R. Burrow. With bristle brush to remove residue from bottle rim.

- £145 • Jasmin Cameron

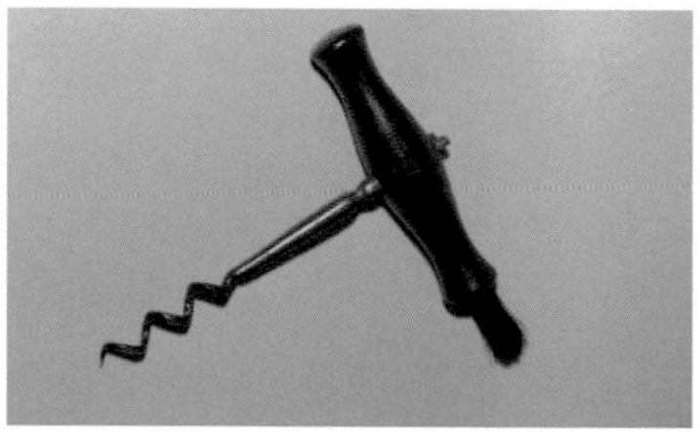

▽ Claret Jug

- *1850*

Deeply faceted claret jug, electroplated lip and cover, twisted rope handle and an acorn finial.

- *height 20cm*
- £440 • Jasmin Cameron

◁ Corkscrews

- *circa 1850*

Three steel corkscrews, with varying double-action mechanisms and variously shaped handles in wood and steel.

- £18–22 • Henry Gregory

△ Pair of Spirit Decanters

- *1840*

One of a pair of fine oblong spirit decanters with faceted shoulders and lid.

- *height 28cm*
- £540 • Jasmin Cameron

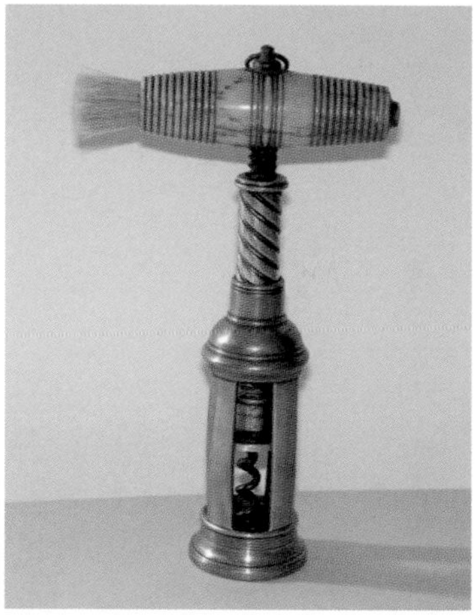

△ Four-Pillar Corkscrew

- *1850*

Four-pillar English corkscrew, made by Thomson, with a brass base and bone-handled brush.

- *height 18cm*
- £450 • Emerson

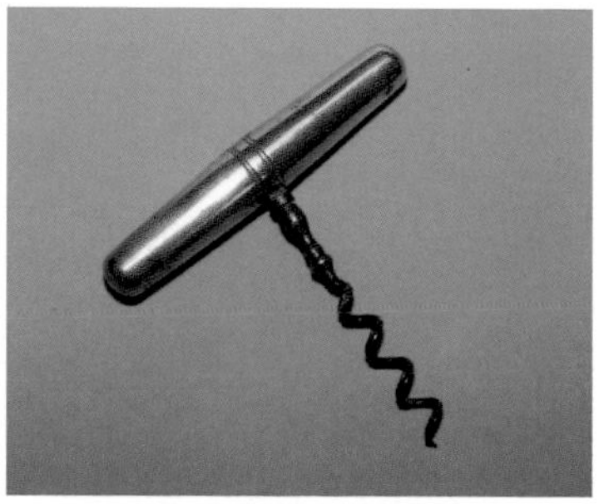

△ Travelling Corkscrew

- *circa 1873*

Travelling corkscrew in heavy white metal. Shank retreats into one half of casing.

- £130 • Jasmin Cameron

▽ Thomson Corkscrew

- *circa 1850*

Thomson brass corkscrew, with brush and a patent badge.

- *height 17.5cm*
- £490 • Emerson

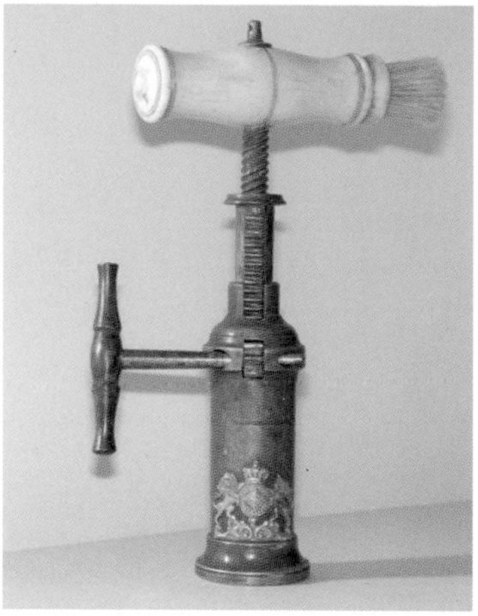

▽ Silver Wine Goblet

- *1870*

Silver wine goblet made by Cooke & Kelvey of Calcutta, India.

- *height 16cm*
- £275 • Linden & Co.

▽ Rosewood Corkscrew

- *1870*

Corkscrew with rosewood handle, and steel screw, by W. Higgs & Son.

- *height 13cm*
- £120 • Emerson

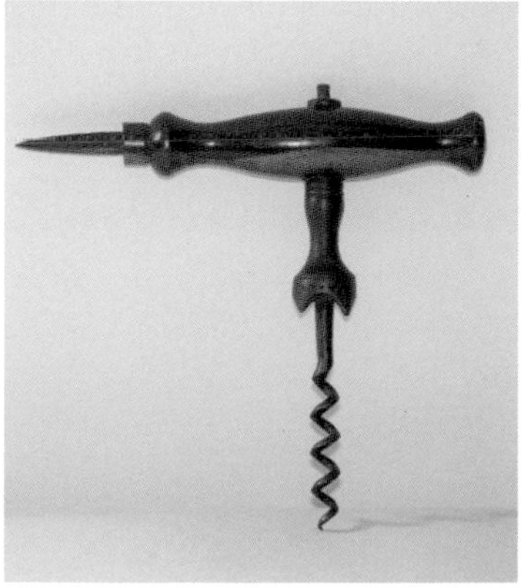

△ Magnum Claret Jug

• *1872*
An extremely rare Victorian magnum claret jug with beautiful engraving, the cast silver mount with dragon handle, by Stephen Smith, London.
• *height 40cm*
• £8,750 • Percy's Ltd

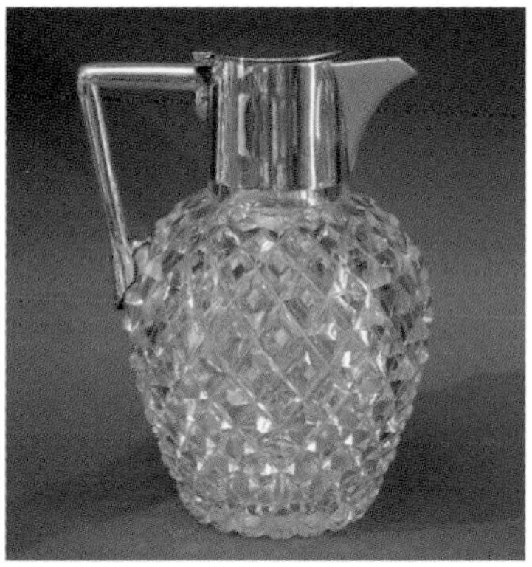

△ Claret Jug

• *1880*
Victorian claret jug with diamond faceted body and silver handle and lid.
• *height 21cm*
• £270 • Henry Gregory

▽ Corkscrews

• *circa 1880*
A selection of three 19th-century corkscrews made of steel and wood with brushes made from pig's hair bristle.
• £40–£60 • Henry Gregory

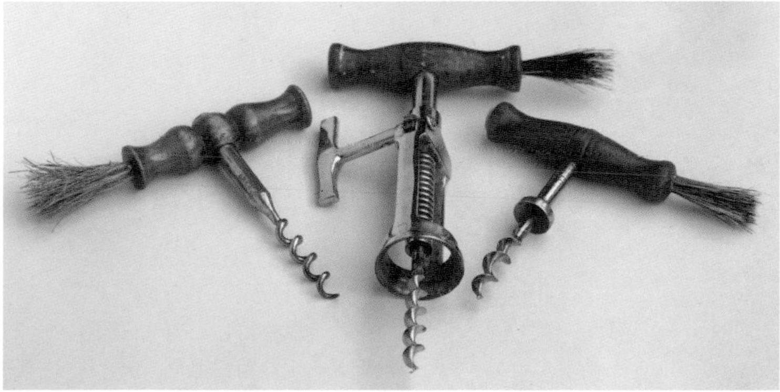

▽ Cut-Glass Claret Jug

• *1875*
Victorian cut-glass claret jug, the silver mount chased with Bacchus mask spout. By C.B., London.
• *height 35cm*
• £3,750 • Percy's Ltd

▽ English Kingscrew

• *circa 1880*
A classic English kingscrew, with a bronze barrel, steel sidewinder and bone handle.
• *height 18.5cm*
• £400 • Emerson

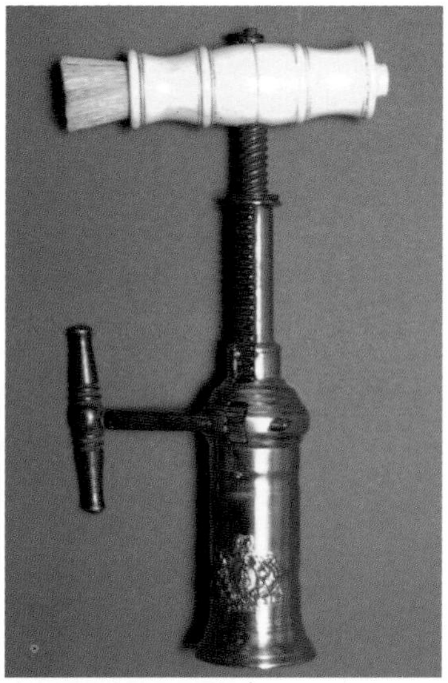

△ Oak-Handled Corkscrew

• *circa 1880*
Oak-handled corkscrew with a metal screw and brush.
• *length 13cm*
• £96 • Henry Gregory

△ Bee Hive Spirit Decanter

• *1880*
Bee hive spirit decanter with spout.
• *height 24cm*
• £165 • Jasmin Cameron

▽ Ivory-Handled Corkscrew

• *circa 1880*
Ivory-handled corkscrew with metal screw and brush.
• *length 14cm*
• £120 • Henry Gregory

▽ Games Tantalus

• *circa 1880*
A late Victorian boxed games tantalus with three lead crystal cut decanters, the tantalus with silver-plated pierced mounts in the Scottish baronial style.
• *height 33cm*
• £690 • Barham Antiques

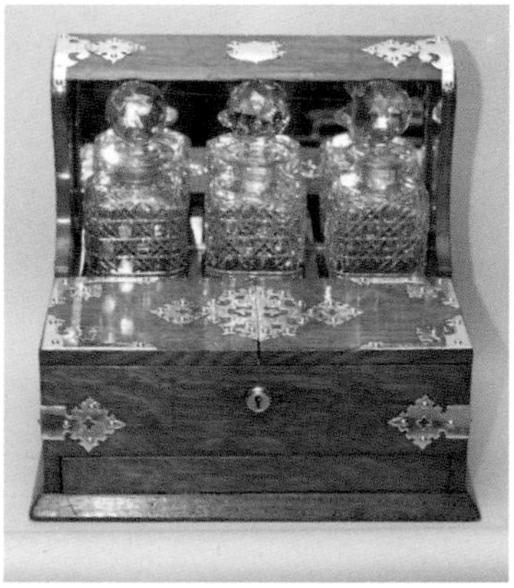

▽ Silver Ladle

• *19th century*
A good Danish silver ladle with a turned bone handle.
• *length 45cm*
• £680 • A. & E. Foster

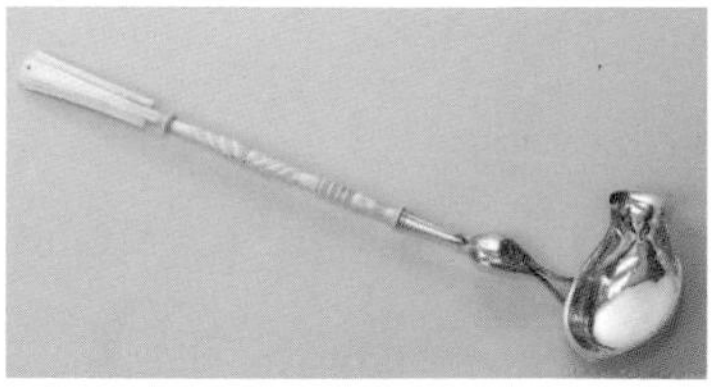

◁ Italian Corkscrew

• *circa 1880*
Italian boxwood corkscrew with an Archemedian worm.
• *height 19.5cm*
• £340 • Emerson

△ Claret Jug

• *circa 1880*

Continental elegant claret jug with fine engraving around the body and a silver geometric band around the neck, standing on a plain silver circular base.

• *height 29cm*

• £335 • Henry Gregory

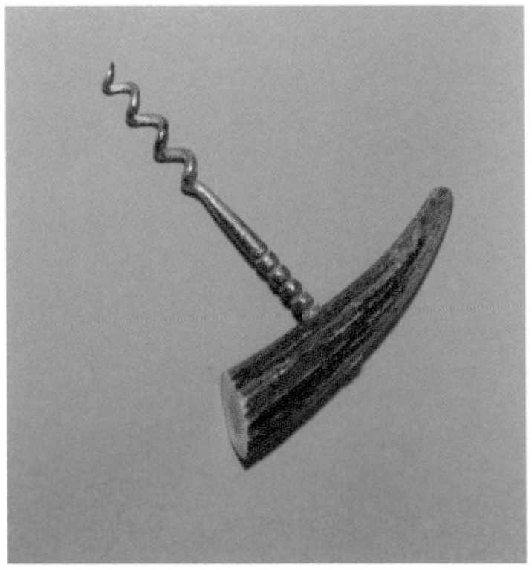

△ Corkscrew

• *circa 1880*

A 19th-century crossbar corkscrew, with the handle fashioned from a stag's horn. Probably from Scotland.

• £55 • Jasmin Cameron

▽ Lead Crystal Decanter

• *circa 1880*

A cylindrical Victorian lead crystal diamond-cut decanter.

• *height 32cm*

• £95 • Barham Antiques

▽ Champagne Corkscrew

• *1880*

Holborn champagne nickel-plated corkscrew with wood handle.

• *height 17cm*

• £260 • Emerson

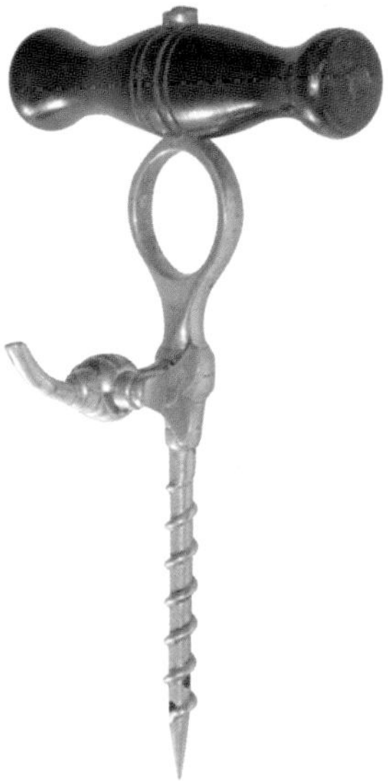

◁ Victorian Claret Jug

• *1888*

A rare claret jug, the body cut with an unusual design, by Barnards, London.

• *height 40cm*

• £4,750 • Percy's Ltd

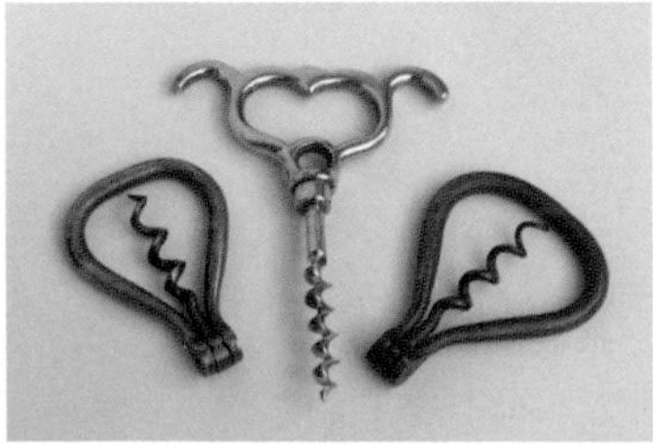

△ Beer Tankards

• *circa 1880*

Pair of English beer tankards made of oak, with silver banding and shields.

• *height 18cm*

• £280 • Henry Gregory

△ Oak Water Jug

• *circa 1880*

Oak cordial jug with silver lid, ball finial and spout with a shield below, standing on three ball feet.

• *height 29cm*

• £330 • Henry Gregory

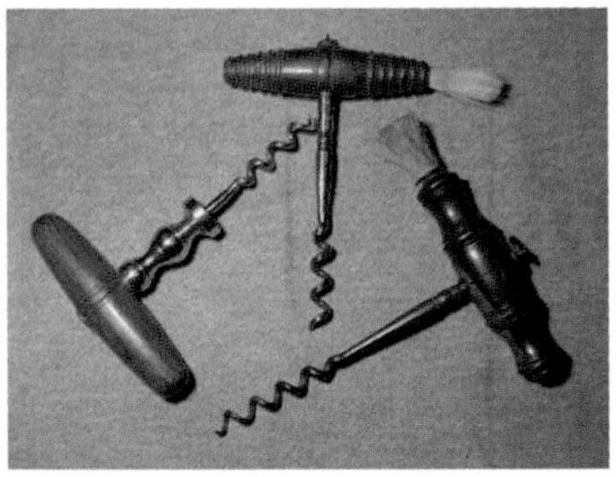

△ Victorian Corkscrews

• *1890*

Selection of Victorian corkscrews with mahogany handles and steel screws. Two have brushes.

• *length 10cm*

• £60 • Henry Gregory

◁ Steel Corkscrews

• *circa 1880*

Three steel corkscrews, two of them identical with folding handles and one with a handgrip doubling as bottle opener.

• £18–£22 each • Henry Gregory

▽ Oak Ice Bucket

• *1880–1900*

Oak barrel ice bucket with silver plate banding and lid.

• *15cm x 13cm x 16cm*

• £75 • Henry Gregory

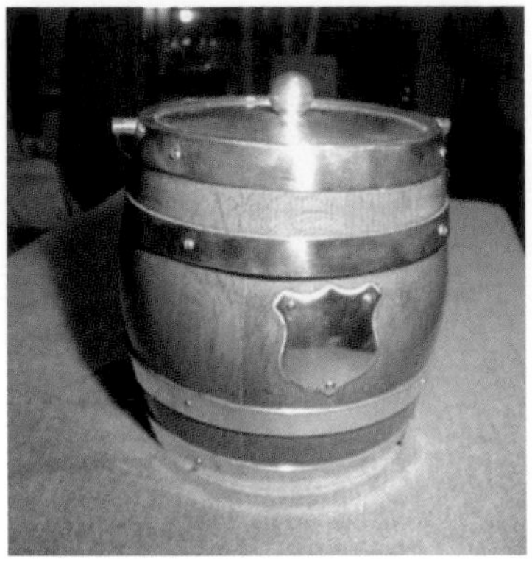

▽ Spire Stopper Decanter

• *circa 1880*

Victorian spire stopper decanter.

• *height 33cm*

• £78 • Henry Gregory

▽ Lady's Legs Corkscrew

• *circa 1894*

A German, folding corkscrew with enamelled lady's legs that open to form the crossbar.

• *height 6.5cm*

• £310 • Emerson

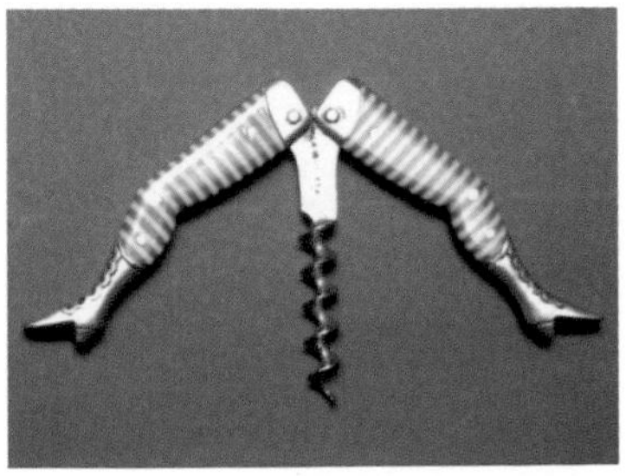

▽ Spirit Decanter

- *1890*

Spirit decanter with moulded body, fluted silver neck and four spouts, known as a Kluk Kluk.

- *height 27cm*
- £420 • Jasmin Cameron

▽ Victorian Port Decanter

- *circa 1890*

Victorian circular port decanter with faceted design on the body.

- *height 30cm*
- £55 • Henry Gregory

▽ Metal Corkscrew

- *circa 1890*

Victorian metal corkscrew.

- *20cm x 9cm*
- £160 • Henry Gregory

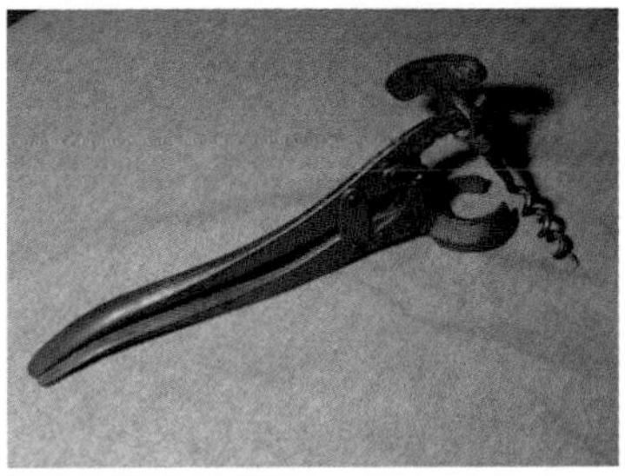

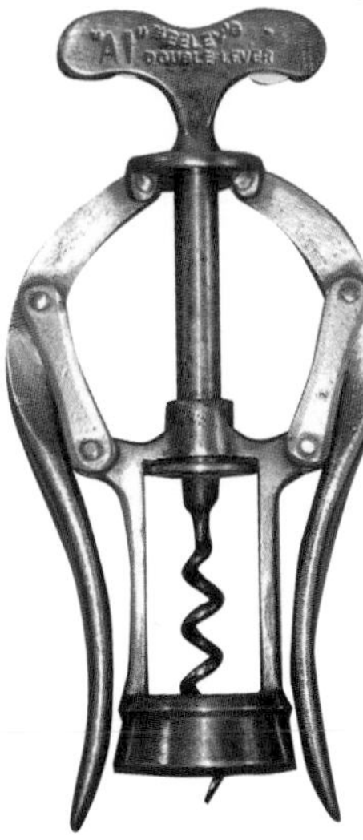

△ Heeley Corkscrew

- *circa 1890*

Steel corkscrew made by Heeley.

- *height 16cm*
- £180 • Henry Gregory

△ Claret Jug

- *1890*

English claret jug with floral engraving and a silver handle and lid.

- *height 30cm*
- £620 • Jasmin Cameron

▽ Wine Cradle

- *1890*

Brass wine cradle with circular ebonised base.

- *height 31cm*
- £950 • Emerson

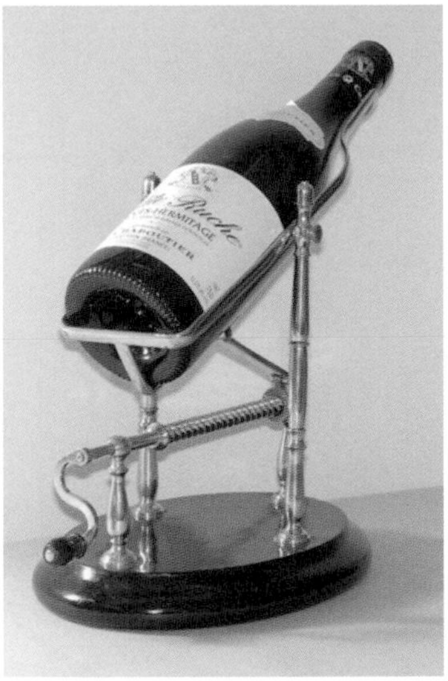

▽ Clamp Wine Opener

- *circa 1890*

Gaskell & Chambers clamp wine opener with extensive moulding.

- *height 24cm*
- £200 • Henry Gregory

▷ Pair of Glass Decanters

- *circa 1890*

Pair of glass decanters with diamond pattern on the body and stopper.

- *height 27cm*
- £150 • Henry Gregory

◁ Brass Bar Screw

- *1890*

Brass bar screw made by Merritt.

- *length 46cm*
- £450 • Emerson

△ Grape Hod

- *1890*

Grape harvesting container with leather straps for carrying bearing the Saint-Emilion Chateau Gironde emblem.

- *height 65cm*
- £420 • R. Conquest

△ Brandy Flagon

- *circa 1895*

Miniature silver brandy flagon by H. Thornhill, London, with handle and screw top.

- *height 13cm*
- £590 • S. & A. Thompson

△ Champagne Corkscrew

- *circa 1900*

Rare and unusual boxwood champagne corkscrew made by McBindes.

- *length 11cm*
- £295 • **Jasmin Cameron**

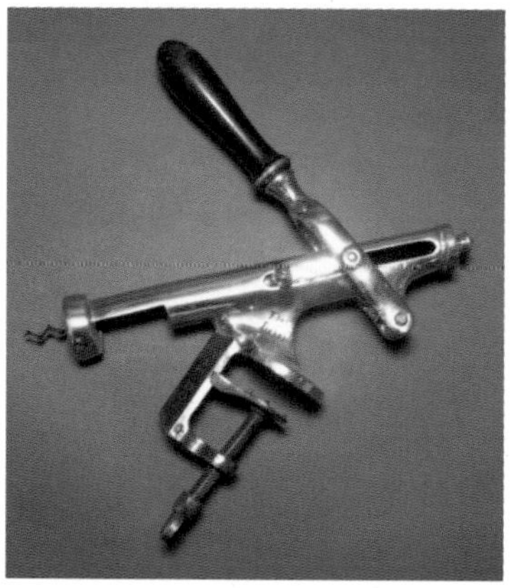

△ English Corkscrew

- *circa 1900*

An English bar corkscrew with steel clamp in polished brass with an ebonised handle.

- *height 33cm*
- £320 • **Emerson**

▽ Bohemian Decanter

- *circa 1900*

Bohemian diamond-cut, tapered decanter with applied, green overlay to body and lip.

- *height 41cm*
- £195 • **Barham Antiques**

▽ Picnic Flasks

- *circa 1900*

Unusual green glass flask with silver and enamel top. Original travelling leather case. English.

- *height 26cm*
- £1,250 • **S. & A. Thompson**

▽ Spirit Labels

- *1910*

Spirit labels on chains for port, shrub and madeira.

- *length 5cm*
- £45 • **Henry Gregory**

▽ Wine Coaster

- *circa 1900*

A silver-plate wine coaster with scrolled handles and pierced floral and geometric design.

- *height 57cm*
- £72 • **Henry Gregory**

▽ Silver Hip Flask

- *1904*

Edwardian silver hip flask in excellent condition with silver hinged lid made in London.

- *height 16cm*
- £550 • **Stephen Kalms**

△ Oak Tantalus

- *circa 1900*

An oak tantalus with three original decanters, shown with secret drawer open.

- *height 34cm*
- £695 • **Finchley**

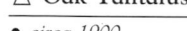

△ Wine Labels

- *circa 1900*

A late-Victorian set of six wine labels, enamelled by Thomas Goode & Co, South Audley Street, London, and in their original velvet-lined case with leather exterior.

- £385 • **Lesley Bragge**

△ Lion-Mask Coaster

- *circa 1900*

Silver circular coaster with scrolling to the rim and lion ring handles.

- *height 16cm*
- £70 • **Henry Gregory**

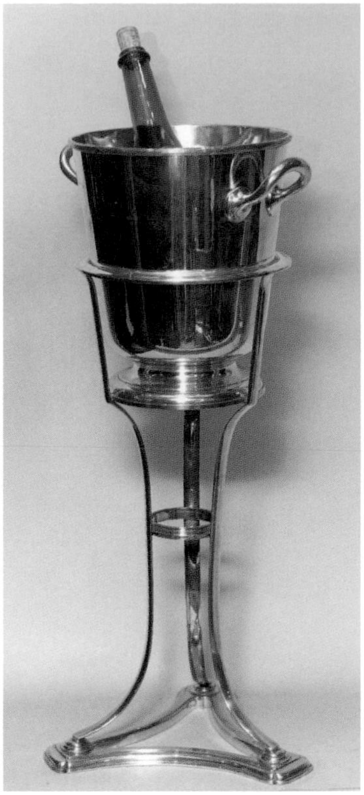

△ Champagne Bucket

- *circa 1910*

A silver-plated Edwardian champagne bucket on open tripod stand. Made by Mappin & Webb, Sheffield.

- *height 61cm*
- £350 • Barham Antiques

△ Wooden Barman

- *circa 1930*

An American barman carved from wood, with cocktail shaker.

- *height 20cm*
- £140 • Emerson

▽ Metal Corkscrew

- *circa 1910*

Expanding polished metal corkscrew.

- *length 14cm*
- £50 • Henry Gregory

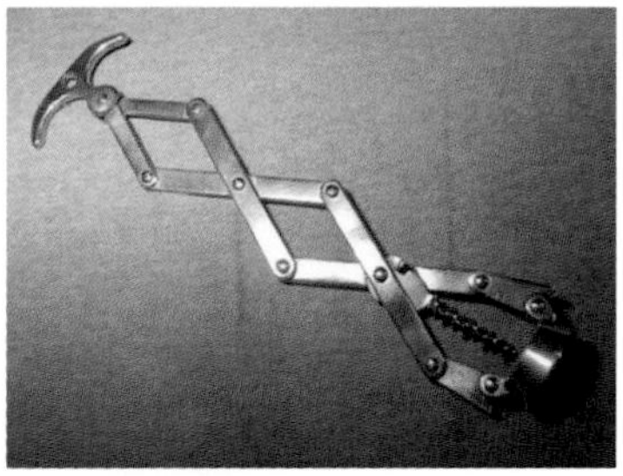

▽ Bottle Stopper

- *early 20th century*

A silver-plated bottle stopper, probably continental.

- £33 • Lesley Bragge

▽ Ice Bucket

- *circa 1930*

Silver-plated ice bucket with bun handles each side and two sets of ring patterns.

- *height 21cm*
- £130 • Henry Gregory

▷ Silver Beer Mugs

- *circa 1940*

Silver beer mugs with glass bottoms and bamboo decoration.

- *height 13cm*
- £130 the pair • Henry Gregory

△ Silver Coaster

- *circa 1920*

Silver-plated circular coaster, one of a pair with scrolled rim and a teak base.

- *diameter 17cm*
- £160 • Henry Gregory

△ Crocodile-Skin Hip Flask

- *1920*

Glass hip flask with crocodile-skin cover, silver mounts and silver cup.

- *height 18cm*
- £595 • Stephen Kalms

△ Silver Wine Taster

- *1939*

Silver wine taster engraved 'Souvenir of Schroder and Schyler & Co., Bordeaux 1739–1939'.

- *diameter 8cm*
- £145 • Jasmin Cameron

▽ Cocktail Shaker

- *1920*

Silver-plate cocktail shaker.

- *height 20cm*
- £68 • Henry Gregory

▽ Wine Cooler

- *circa 1935*

An oak, lead-lined wine cooler with fruit, leaf and lion-mask carved decoration.

- *height 57cm*
- £1,250 • Lesley Bragge

▽ Dachshund Corkscrew

- *1930*

Dachshund novelty corkscrew, with brass corkscrew tail.

- *length 8cm*
- £45 • Emerson

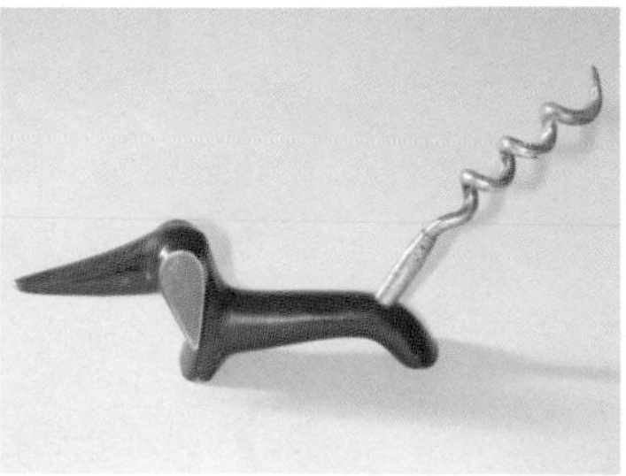

WORKS OF ART & SCULPTURE

Works of art and sculpture covers a broad spectrum of antiques and we have therefore focused in this book on the works of art of four areas, which include Asian/Oriental, European, Middle Eastern and Russian. Each section covers a wide range of periods, with emphasis placed on figurative and unusual items. It is interesting to note how the market place is affected by the political climate of the time. For example, during the mid-1990s there was a sudden influx of Russian art due to the fall of the Communist regime. This in turn has led to the rise in popularity of Soviet works of art and sculpture, which now have great historical value as they depict a way of life that no longer exists. There is currently a huge rise of interest in Middle Eastern works of art, reflecting the current political climate. It is therefore worth being up to date on world affairs when you go to seek out works of art. This is a huge area, so make sure you do your research before you embark on your journey. When purchasing overseas, make sure you have the correct exportation and importation documentation in place, particularly with expensive items, as dealing with customs authorities can be an exasperating and lengthy procedure.

ASIAN/ORIENTAL

△ **Chinese Neolithic Jar**

- *4th–2nd millennium BC*

A painted pottery jar from Gansu province, with red and black pigments.

- *height 30cm*
- £1,200 • **Little River**

▽ **Machang-type Jar**

- *late 3rd or early 2nd millennium BC*

Machang-type jar of painted pottery, Gansu or Qinghai province of China, with an unusual circular design and geometric pattern.

- *height 32cm*
- £650 • **Ormonde**

◁ **Chinese Malachite Axe Head**

- *1600–1000 BC*

Bronze axe head encrusted with malachite from the Shang Dynasty.

- *length 20cm*
- £750 • **Ormonde**

△ **Bronze Heads**

- *1600–1100 BC*

Two bronze halberd heads 'ge' showing a tiger and owl with good patination.

- *height 20cm*
- £1,100 • **Malcolm Rushton**

▽ **Food Vessel**

- *1650–1027 BC*

Bronze Chinese food vessel 'ding' with 'thread relief' frieze of animal masks to the body and similar decoration to the legs, from the Shang Dynasty.

- *46cm x 34cm*
- £9,000 • **Malcolm Rushton**

▽ Chinese Bronze Wine Vessel

• *circa 1100–771 BC*
Western Chow Dynasty bronze wine vessel with a 'hu' lid.
• *height 18cm*
• £2,800 • Malcolm Rushton

▽ Stick Figure

• *206 BC–220 AD*
Stick figure of a man standing, from the Han Dynasty of China.
• *height 60cm*
• £1,200 • Ormonde

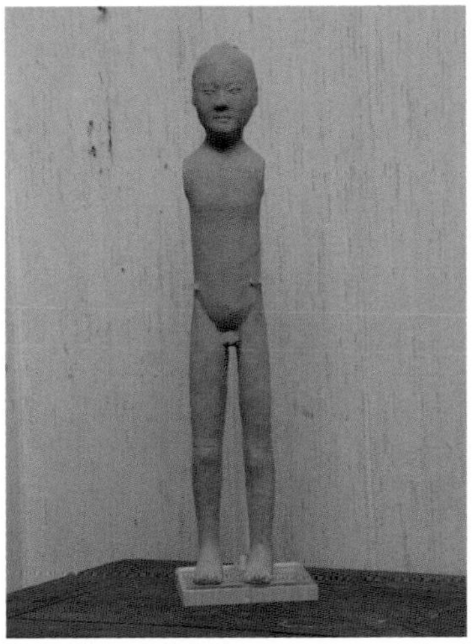

▽ Chinese Han Vase

• *206 BC–220 AD*
Unusual garlic-headed bottle-shaped vase with original pigment of pink, white and crimson. Han Dynasty.
• *height 34cm*
• £750 • Ormonde

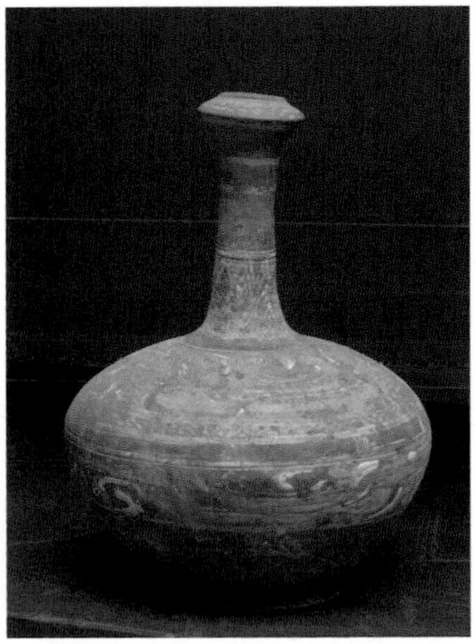

△ Bronze Sword

• *481–221 BC*
Bronze sword with blade coated in silver, with the silver showing through heavy green patination in some areas.
• *length 48cm*
• £1,400 • Malcolm Rushton

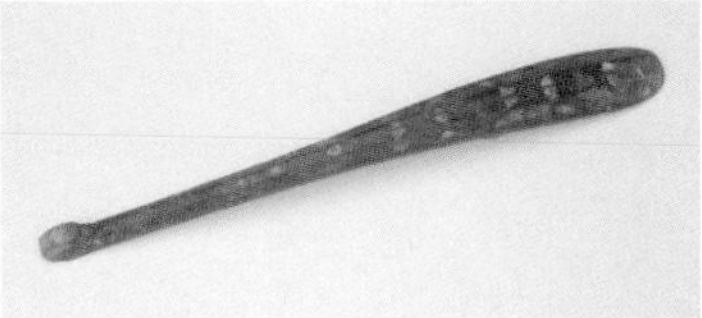

△ Bronze Belt Hook

• *4th–3rd century BC*
Bronze belt hook.
• *length 15cm*
• £150 • Ormonde

△ Wine Jar

• *206 BC–220 AD*
Large Chinese pottery wine jar with cover after a bronze original. The jar and cover are from the Han Dynasty.
• *45cm x 32cm*
• £2,200 • Nicholas S. Pitcher

△ Chinese Pottery Duck

• *206 BC–220 AD*
Chinese slipware, white pottery duck of good form from the Han Dynasty. Includes test certificate.
• *length 35cm*
• £4,200 • Nicholas S. Pitcher

▽ Chinese Lifan Amphora

• *481–221 BC*
A Lifan culture burnished black pottery amphora, from the Sichuan Province.
• *33cm x 32cm*
• £2,500 • Little River

▽ Witch Doctor

• *Han Dynasty 206 BC–220 AD*
Chinese Han Dynasty witch doctor with large ears and a ferocious face.
• *height 1.1m*
• £2,800 • Ormonde

▽ Head of Horse

• *206 BC–220 AD*
A Chinese terracotta model of a horse's head naturalistically styled, with pigmentation, from the Han Dynasty.
• *height 24cm*
• £550 • Ormonde

△ Chinese Shaman Beads

• *206 BC–220 AD*
Cream jade beads that once belonged to a shaman, from the Han Dynasty.
• *length 2cm*
• £2,000 • Ormonde

△ Incense Burner

• *Han Dynasty 206 BC–220 AD*
Incense burner in the shape of a mountain (representing the Isles of the Blessed), the abode of the mortals. The incense burner rests on a tall tray with a solid foot hollowed out beneath the stem.
• *height 21cm*
• £300 • Ormonde

△ Hill Jar

• *200 BC–200 AD*
In dark green glaze showing creatures from Chinese mythology.
• *height 28cm*
• £850 • J.A.N. Fine Art

△ Green Glazed Horse

- *206 BC–220 AD*

A Chinese green-glazed pottery horse from the Han dynasty.

- *height 110cm*
- £12,000 • Malcolm Rushton

△ Chinese Bronze Bottle

- *206 BC–220 AD*

A Chinese bronze Han dynasty bottle in original patination with a garlic neck.

- *height 37cm*
- £1,000 • Nicholas S. Pitcher

△ Chinese Fish Man

- *280–589*

Two very different pottery fish man images. This combination of images seems to have denoted protection for deceased scholars.

- *28cm x 19cm*
- £600 • Malcolm Rushton

▽ Jade Bi Disc

- *206 BC–220 AD*

Jade disc with raised spirals, dating from the Han dynasty.

- *diameter 19cm*
- £3,000 • Malcolm Rushton

▽ Painted Snake

- *536–581 AD*

Painted Chinese pottery snake with a human head at each end 'fuxi and Nuwa' with traces of red and white pigment remaining. Has been Oxford TL tested.

- *length 30cm*
- £900 • Malcolm Rushton

▽ Funeral Jar

- *265–317 AD*

An intricately modelled pottery Daoist funeral jar showing a pagoda-roofed celestial city, presided over by six Daoist immortals. Of the Jin dynasty, from western China.

- *height 31cm*
- £3,200 • Malcolm Rushton

△ Ear Cup

- *200 BC–200 AD*

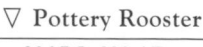

A Han-dynasty ear cup of ovate shape and double handles with a green glaze. A tomb find.

- *height 11cm*
- £280 • J.A.N. Fine Art

△ Pottery Horse

- *618–907 AD*

Tang Dynasty glazed equestrienne of an unusual apple-green colour. Provenance: Eskenazis inaugural exhibition in London 1972.

- *49cm x 35cm*
- £5,500 • Malcolm Rushton

△ Glazed Horse

- *386–535 AD*

One of a pair of rare amber and brown glazed horses from the Wei dynasty of northern China. Both have Oxford TL certificate.

- *height 31cm*
- £38,000 • Malcolm Rushton

▽ Pottery Rooster

- *206 BC–220 AD*

A Chinese Han-dynasty tomb figure of a rooster, with traces of green, lead glaze.

- *height 12cm*
- £350 • David Baker

▽ Sichuan Pottery Boar

- *206–220 AD*

A Sichuan pottery boar naturalistically poised on all four legs from the Han Dynasty of China.

- *length 57cm*
- £4,800 • Nicholas S. Pitcher

▽ Terracotta Head

- *200–300 AD*

Head of a secular youth with an elaborate curled hairstyle. From Gandhara, Pakistan, and showing a blend of Greek and eastern styles.

- *height 23cm*
- £4,500 • Malcolm Rushton

△ Pottery Horsemen

- *534–549 AD*

Pair of Chinese painted pottery horsemen. The figures retain much of their original pigment with horses leather armour clearly delineated, from the Eastern Wei Dynasty.

- *36cm x 29cm*
- £8,000 • Malcolm Rushton

△ Zodiac Animals

- *7th–9th century AD*

Rare group of pottery Zodiac animals from the Chinese T'ang Dynasty.

- *height 28cm*
- £550 • Ormonde

△ Chinese Amphora

- *618–907 AD*

Green glazed dragon handled pottery amphora – inscription reads 'Li Man Shu' – almost certainly belonged to a minor member of the T'ang royal family.

- *55cm x 28cm*
- £3,500 • Malcolm Rushton

▽ Mongolian Pottery Figure

- *550–581 AD*

Painted pottery figure in animal skin cloak with elaborate head dress, from the Mongolian border, with traces of red and white paint.

- *31cm x 20cm*
- £2,000 • Malcolm Rushton

▽ Pottery Horse

- *618–907 AD*

Small red Chinese pottery horse decorated with black, yellow and white pigments, from the T'ang Dynasty in the Henan Province.

- *20cm x 18cm*
- £450 • Little River

▽ Cups and Tray

- *618–907 AD*

T'ang San-Sai glazed cups and tray in green, brown and yellow glaze.

- *diameter 24cm*
- £1,250 • J.A.N. Fine Art

△ Chinese Stoneware Jar

- *618–906 AD*

Chinese cream-glazed stoneware jar from the T'ang Dynasty.

- *19cm x 22cm*
- £1,500 • Nicholas S. Pitcher

△ Pottery Court Ladies

- *618–907 AD*

Pair of painted pottery court ladies, one with painted leaves in her hair. Both have Oxford TL certificates.

- *height 48cm*
- £20,000 • Malcolm Rushton

△ Glazed Pottery Vase

- *983 AD*

A glazed pottery vase with four handles with the inscription 'made in the 8th year of the Emperor Tai Ping Hing Ko'.

- *24cm x 19cm*
- £7,000 • Malcolm Rushton

▽ Pottery Camel

- *618–907AD*

A Chinese unglazed pottery model of a Bactrian camel. The tomb-figure still has traces of paint on the surface. From the T'ang dynasty.

- *height 30cm*
- £1,400 • David Baker

▽ Chinese Painted Figure

- *circa 618–906 AD*

Chinese painted figure of a groom from the T'ang dynasty. The figure is rare due to the gilding.

- *height 35cm*
- £3,300 • Nicholas S. Pitcher

▽ Sealed Pottery Vessel

- *960–1279 AD*

Sealed brown glazed pottery vessel containing remains of original wine used for ritual purposes.

- *19cm x 15cm*
- £2,500 • Malcolm Rushton

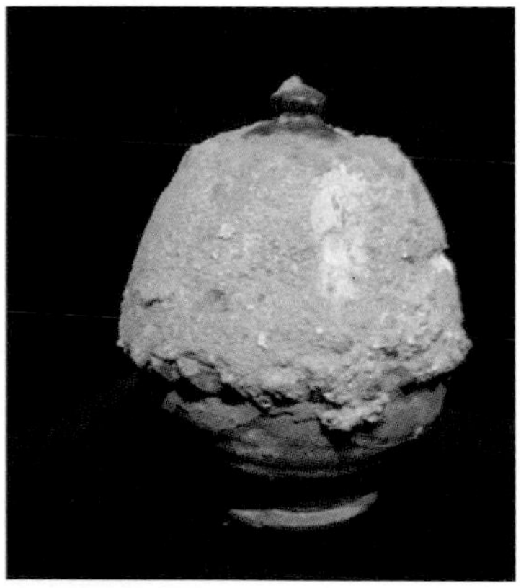

◁ Cambodian Figure

- *9th–10th century AD*

Figure of the bronze deity Avalokitesvara from Angkor-wat, Cambodia.

- *height 16.5cm*
- **£900** • **David Baker**

▽ South Indian Sandstone

- *10th–11th century AD*

Part of a frieze, showing three elephants and two women.

- *height 34cm*
- **£6,000** • **Shahdad**

△ Cambodian Bronze Figure

- *12th century AD*

Bronze Boddisatva figure from Angkor-wat, Cambodia. Shows figure wearing dhoti and holding religious objects.

- *height 18cm*
- **£850** • **David Baker**

▽ Amida Buddha

- *circa 1600 AD*

A giltwood figure depicting Amida Buddha on a lotus base.

- *height 58cm*
- **£6,500** • **Brandt**

▽ Jade Lion

- *17th century AD*

Jade lion group shown with its jaws clamped around its captured prey. Ming Dynasty.

- *length 15cm*
- **£650** • **Ormonde**

▽ Chinese Henan Jar

- *12th–13th century AD*

Chinese Henan glazed pottery jar from the Jin Dynasty.

- *18cm x 19cm*
- **£1,350** • **Nicholas S. Pitcher**

▽ Chinese Enamel Censer

- *17th century AD*

A cloisonné enamel censer of archaic Fang Ding form, supported on four curved legs of monster mask and bird design. The underside decorated with four flowers amid scrolling foliage, the body divided by vertical gilded flanges

- *height 35cm*
- **£14,000** • **Gerard Hawthorn**

△ Indian Bronze Casket

- *16th century AD*

A beautiful bronze casket, with panels of engraved deer and geometric borders. Excellent provenance as it once belonged to the Sultan of Delhi.

- *14cm x 20cm x 14cm*
- **£5,000** • **Ghaznavid**

△ Chinese Ming Ewer

- *14th–17th century AD*

Chinese Ming ewer made for export to Iran, featuring an allegorical figure to the neck and with green and blue openwork to the body.

- *height 30cm*
- **£6,000** • **Yazdani**

△ Chinese Box

- *17th century AD*

A Chinese intricately carved box with black, red and dark green lacquer,with designs of peaches and blossom, from the Ming Dynasty.

- *8.5cm x 12cm x 12cm*
- **£1,800** • **Gerard Hawthorn**

△ Chinese Cloisonné Box

- *1736–95 AD*

Small Chinese cloisonné and gilt metal incense box.

- *diameter 11cm*
- **£2,500** • **Brandt**

△ **Indian Brass Surahi**

- *18th century AD*

Brass bottle-shaped surahi with an inscised spiral decoration around body.

- *24cm x 18cm*
- £325 • Arthur Millner

△ **Brass Finial**

- *18th century AD*

Brass palanquin finial in the form of a stylised leopard head.

- *26cm x 14cm*
- £750 • Arthur Millner

△ **Japanese Dog**

- *circa 1880 AD*

A study of a small Japanese long-haired dog lying on a fan on a padouk wood stand.

- *11cm x 7cm*
- £985 • Japanese Gallery

▽ **Three-Tiered Chinese Box**

- *18th century AD*

A three-tiered box, inlaid with mother-of-pearl and hard stones.

- *11cm x 21cm x 13cm*
- £2,750 • Gerard Hawthorn

▽ **Bishop's Staff**

- *circa 1800 AD*

An Indian bishop's staff in iron in the Byzantine style.

- *length 59cm*
- £1,250 • Iconastas

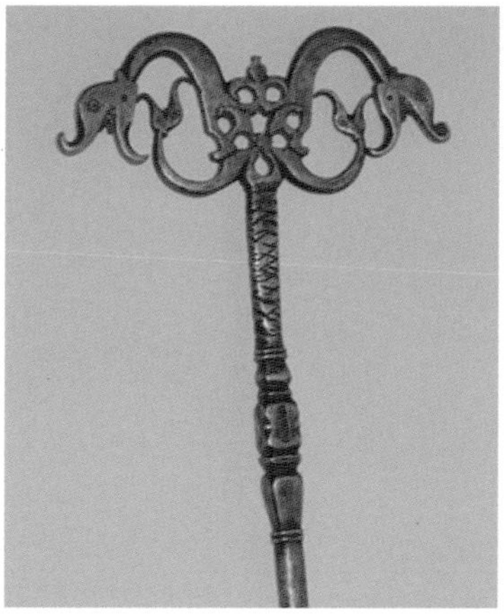

▽ **Netsuki of Two Rats**

- *circa 1880 AD*

Japanese carved wood okimono-style netsuki of two rats, signed 'Ittantu'.

- *height 3cm*
- £1,950 • Japanese Gallery

▷ **Japanese Water Dropper**

- *19th century AD*

Japanese bronze and silver artist's water dropper in the form of a lotus leaf.

- *diameter 20cm*
- £2,500 • Brandt

△ **Hand Warmer**

- *18th century AD*

Chinese Canton enamel hand warmer, from the Ch'ing Dynasty, decorated with a scrolling floral design with brass handle.

- *9cm x 18cm x 13cm*
- £4,500 • Gerard Hawthorn

△ **Japanese Bronze Hare**

- *1868–1912 AD*

Japanese bronze model of a crouching hare, from the Meiji period.

- *height 25cm*
- £3,800 • Brandt

△ **Japanese Plaque**

- *circa 1880 AD*

A Japanese circular hardwood plaque pierced with interlaced foliate designs.

- *diameter 67cm*
- £980 • Westland & Co.

▽ **Chinese Kendi**

- *18th century AD*

Chinese kendi and cover with Chinese silver mounts.

- *height 28cm*
- £1,650 • Nicholas S. Pitcher

▽ **Bronze Vase**

- *1868–1912 AD*

A bronze Japanese vase of the Meiji period, of ovoid form with a silver overlaid crane and stylised clouds.

- *height 39cm*
- £2,200 • Brandt

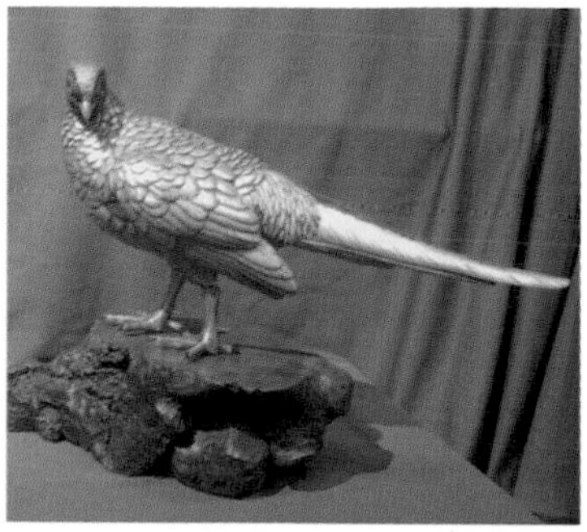

▽ **Model of a Pheasant**

- *1868–1912 AD*

Japanese silver and mixed metal model of a pheasant, standing on a rock modelled out of wood.

- *height 29cm*
- £5,500 • Brandt

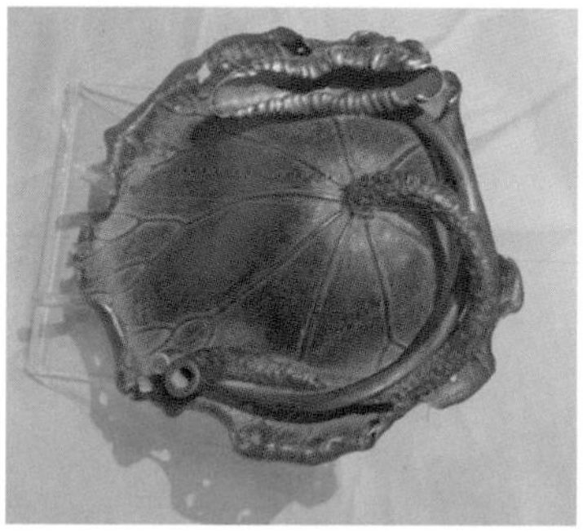

EUROPEAN

△ Glass Panel

• *15th century*
Fragmentary stained and leaded glass panel. Probably English.
• *length 86cm*
• £3,000 • Shahdad

△ Lead Cockerel

• *18th century*
A rare eighteenth century lead cockerel. Provenance: ex Drakelow Hall, Burton on Trent.
• *72cm x 48cm*
• £10,500 • Crowthers

▽ Carved Wood Figure

• *early 18th century*
Bohemian fine carved wood and polychrome figure of St John Nepomuk.
• *height 1.63m*
• £8,500 • Westland & Co.

▽ Marble Bust

• *circa 1790*
Fine marble bust of an unknown gentleman shown *a l'antica* with a toga about his shoulders.
• *height 56cm*
• £7,500 • Crowthers

◁ Overdoor

• *circa 1820*
French carved oak beaux arts overdoor. With central cartouche and cherub and floral swags.
• *height 59cm*
• £7,500 • Westland & Co.

△ Molière Head

• *early 18th century*
An Louis XIV carved stone head of the French dramatist Molière looking to dexter.
• *63.5cm x 55cm*
• £3,500 • Westland & Co.

△ Faustina

• *late 18th–early 19th century*
An Italian plaster bust of Faustina, attributed to Bartolomeo Caveceppi.
• *60cm x 38cm*
• £2,200 • Crowthers

▽ European Glass Panel

• *circa 1788*
Central European stained and leaded glass, probably Swiss. Depicting armorial devices.
• *length 58.5cm*
• £4,250 • Shahdad

▽ The Sleeping Shepherd Boy

• *circa 1817–18*
Italian marble figure of 'The Sleeping Shepherd Boy', by John Gibson, made for the Lord George Cavendish, the nephew of the 6th Duke of Devonshire.
• *height 1.05m*
• £100,000 • Crowthers

◁ Bust of Niobe

• *circa 18th century*
Larger than life-size statuary marble classical bust of Niobe, attributed to the 18th-century sculptor F. Harwood.
• *height 96cm*
• £15,000 • Crowthers

△ Stone Lion

- *19th century*

Carved statuary stone lion, in Portland stone, on stone base.

- *height 1m*
- £11,750 • Drummonds

△ Stone Ionic Columns

- *circa 1840*

One of a pair of columns in the form of male figures with arms raised above head supporting the capital.

- *height 2.06m*
- £24,000 • Westland & Co.

▽ Statue

- *circa 1825*

An original statue of Sir Walter Raleigh from the Palace of Westminster.

- *height 3.3m*
- £28,000 • Drummonds

▽ Stained-Glass Windows

- *circa 1860*

Set of twelve windows. The arch centred by a cross with a heart.

- *height 2.72m*
- £12,000 • Westland & Co.

◁ Dresden Schneeballen Vase

- *circa 1870*

Dresden *schneeballen* vase and cover after the Meissen original, applied all over with blue mayflowers and songbirds perched among white snowballs and other encrusted flowers growing from rustic twig handles, the finial in the form of a parrot on a fruiting branch.

- *height 79cm*
- £3,500 • Emanouel

△ Neo-classical Statue

- *circa 1840*

French terracotta neo-classical statue of a muse.

- *height 1.45m*
- £8,500 • Westland & Co.

△ Carved Figure

- *circa 1860*

Finely carved pine figure of a Medieval knight. In the Gothic revival manner.

- *height 1.93cm*
- £4,500 • Westland & Co.

▽ Pair of Sèvres Vases

- *19th century*

A pair of Sèvres gilt metal mounted fuchsia vases and covers, with an inner design depicting Romantic couples in a pastoral setting.

- *height 98cm*
- £22,000 • Emanouel

▽ Young Bacchus

- *circa 1860*

Marble figure of the young Bacchus clad in only a crumpled tunic and carrying a bunch of grapes in his left hand, while clutching another bunch in the crook of his elbow.

- *height 1.02m*
- £15,700 • Crowthers

◁ Cruet Set

- *circa 1870*

A fine Viennese cruet set carved from rock crystal, with silver gilt and enamelling.

- *height 25cm*
- £10,000 • Bazaart

△ Walter Scott

- *circa 19th century*

Marble bust of Sir Walter Scott on original socle, signed by the sculptor James Fillans, born in Paisley, Scotland.

- *height 81cm*
- £5,750 • Crowthers

△ Torso of a General

- *circa 1890*

Torso of a French general.

- *height 60cm*
- £1,000 • Drummonds

▽ Statue of Boy

- *circa 1880*

Statue of Boy with Windmill, by Butti of Milan. Finely carved in white marble on a four-foot, green marble rotating base.

- *height 1m*
- £11,750 • Drummonds

▽ Stained-Glass Window

- *circa 1890*

English Victorian Gothic-arched stained-glass window showing Jesus preaching. In Arts and Crafts style and colouring.

- *height 1.5m*
- £1,500 • Westland & Co.

◁ Three Graces

- *circa 1880*

Signed French marble clock with movement in black enamel, marble signed 'Falconet'.

- *height 67cm*
- £18,500 • Emanouel

△ Sèvres Vases

- *circa 1880*

Pair of large gilt metal mounted vases with covers. Painted with figures in 18th-century costume, with birds to reverse.

- *height 32cm*
- £13,000 • Emanouel

△ Figure by Pocchini

- *circa 1890*

Italian white marble figure of a young woman by V. Pocchini, the girl in rustic costume and clasping a flower. Signed V. Pocchini.

- *height 94cm*
- £14,500 • Crowthers

▽ Corneille van Cleeve

- *circa 1880*

Fine French Rococo marble bust of the 17th-century sculptor Corneille van Cleeve, looking dexter, after the original by Jean Jacques Caffieri. The original is to be found in the Musée de Louvre, Paris.

- *height 71cm*
- £9,800 • Crowthers

▽ Earthenware Vase

- *circa 1880*

Massive earthenware vase with gilt decoration and pastoral scenes.

- *height 1.1m*
- £25,000 • Emanouel

◁ Wolf and Lamb

- *circa 1880*

Val d' Orse wolf and lamb on oval stone base.

- *height 1.5m*
- £28,700 • Drummonds

△ Marble Figure

- *circa 1890*

An Italian marble figure of virtue after Tino di Camaino. Possibly work of Alceo Dossena.

- *height 1.05m*
- £4,500 • Westland & Co.

△ Bronze Group

- *circa 1930s*

Bronze group of a mother clutching her child astride a horse, executed in a richly patinated bronze. Signed by E. de Valeriola.

- *56cm x 23cm*
- £4,250 • Zakheim

▽ Esmeralda and her Goat

- *1881*

Italian statuary marble figure of Esmeralda, the gypsy-girl heroine from Victor Hugo's *The Hunchback of Notre Dame*, and her goat. Signed Prof. P. Romanelli.

- *height 1.02m*
- £21,000 • Crowthers

▽ Proserpine and Mercury

- *mid-20th century*

Composition stone group of Proserpine and Mercury. Mercury with winged helmet, standing contraposto with drapery drawn across his torso and playing a pipe. The figure of Proserpine kneels at his side.

- *height 1.96m*
- £28,000 • Crowthers

◁ Limestone Maquette

- *circa 1930*

Limestone maquette of two seated and embracing figures, after Henry Moore.

- *23cm x 24cm*
- £12,500 • Zakheim

△ Torso

- *circa 1920*

Modernist Jiri Strada torso of a woman cropped at top of head and thighs.

- *height 1.5m*
- £5,300 • Drummonds

△ Sculpted Head

- *1970*

English carved limestone head of a female with her hair in a chignon, on a square wooden base, by Mike Grevatte.

- *height 70cm*
- £2,850 • Zakheim

▽ Bronze Plaque

- *circa 1930*

Art Deco plaque depicting Hermes, the Greek messenger of the gods.

- *26cm x 28cm*
- £750 • Zakheim

▽ Danish Sculpture

- *1960*

An abstract wooden sculpture designed by Simon of Denmark.

- *height 37.5cm*
- £800 • Zoom

▽ Bronze Sculpture

- *20th century*

Amorphous French polished bronze sculpture after Jean Arp.

- *width 23cm*
- £4,450 • Zakheim

◁ Limestone Head

- *circa 1970*

English head of a girl carved from limestone, by Mike Grevatte.

- *height 70cm*
- £2,850 • Zakheim

MIDDLE EASTERN

△ Bronze Dish

• *2nd–3rd century AD*
A Sassanian broad shallow bronze dish with a lamb's head design to the handle and good patina.
• *length 45cm*
• £1,200 • Yazdani

△ Stone Cat

• *10th century AD*
Stone carving of a cat with turquoise glaze eyes. From Samanid, Iran.
• *height 16cm*
• £1,500 • Samiramis

▽ Incense Burner

• *2nd–3rd century AD*
Bronze tripod incense burner decorated with three gazelle head terminals
• *height 11cm*
• £1,400 • Yazdani

▽ Persian Glass Bottle

• *11th century AD*
A fire-blown cobalt-blue glass bottle with a fluted body and a long tapered neck with splayed lip with iridescence. The bottle is in excellent condition.
• *height 25cm*
• £800 • Pars

◁ Bronze Vase and Stand

• *12th–13th century AD*
With pierced decoration to splayed lip and plinth base, on a tripod stand.
• *height 95cm*
• £5,000 • Hadji Baba

▷ Fish Incense Burner

• *17th century AD*
A bronze incense burner in the form of a fish with stylised fins and inlaid with gold scales.
• *length 30cm*
• £950 • Yazdani

△ Early Christian Limestone

• *5th century AD*
Limestone carved relief with dedicatory inscription from Byzantine Egypt.
• *31cm x 20cm*
• £3,000 • Axia

△ Oil Lamp

• *12th century AD*
Oil lamp in brass with copper inlay, with ovoid body on a high foot and an arabesque cartouche. From Afghanistan.
• *height 24cm*
• £1,500 • Samiramis

▽ Cut-Glass Bottle

• *circa 500–600 AD*
Sassanian Persian cut-glass bottle with circular relief decoration.
• *height 10cm*
• £4,000 • Hadji Baba

▽ Bronze Oil Lamp

• *13th century AD*
A bronze oil lamp on a splayed base with a large arm, ornate thumbpiece with bird decoration and decorated lid.
• *height 17cm*
• £1,400 • Samiramis

▽ Seljuk Stem Cup

• *13th century AD*
A bronze cup with engraved designs of birds, trees and floral cartouches, with birds and fish to the centre, all on a splayed base.
• *height 13cm*
• £1,500 • Samiramis

△ Koran Stand

- *circa 1800 AD*

Ottoman Koran stand composed of two folding panels, with a geometrical design and inlaid with mother-of-pearl.

- *43cm x 63cm*
- £1,750 • **Arthur Millner**

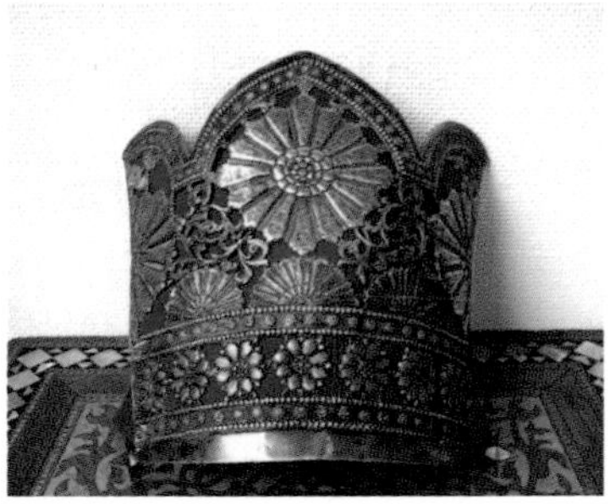

△ Persian Silver Crown

- *circa 1900 AD*

Three-point open-work element composed of floral and scrolling foliate designs and mounted on a later suede backing.

- *height 21cm*
- £700 • **Samiramis**

△ Turkish Table

- *circa 1920 AD*

Turkish table with mother-of-pearl and bone inlay on architecturally carved legs.

- *64cm x 44cm*
- £400 • **Sharif**

▽ Ink Holder

- *circa 1870 AD*

Persian ink holder decorated with bronze medallions along the shaft, from the Quarshar Dynasty.

- *height 25cm*
- £120 • **Sharif**

▽ Mirror and Stand

- *circa 1900 AD*

Elaborate mother-of-pearl and ivory oblong inlay mirror with scrolled carving, and chest with one long drawer and two smaller, with carved moulded top, and feet, from Damascus.

- *height 2.1m*
- £6,000 • **Sharif**

▽ Syrian Box

- *1910 AD*

Wooden box with mother-of-pearl inlay and red satin interior from Damascus.

- *25cm x 16.25cm*
- £120 • **Sharif**

△ Persian Box

- *19th century AD*

A Persian painted box with bone and ivory inlay in geometric patterns on moulded bracket feet.

- *14cm x 35cm x 28cm*
- £850 • **John Clay**

△ Architectural Table

- *circa 1910 AD*

Mother-of-pearl hexagonal table with geometric patterns and architectural legs.

- *55cm x 43cm*
- £200 • **Sharif**

△ Damascus Table

- *circa 1920 AD*

Side table from Damascus with mother-of-pearl and bone inlay, single small drawer with brass handle, standing on cabriole legs.

- *43cm x 36cm*
- £150 • **Sharif**

▽ Teak Octagonal Table

- *circa 1880 AD*

Table with bone and ivory inlay in geometric patterns and Islamic, architecturally carved legs.

- *height 62cm*
- £450 • **Sharif**

▽ Persian Beaker

- *circa 1910 AD*

Persian silver beaker with embossed foliate designs within shaped borders.

- *height 11.25cm*
- £50 • **Sharif**

▽ Islamic Tray

- *circa 1920 AD*

Persian circular brass tray with engraved Islamic lettering and geometric patterns to centre.

- *diameter 58.75cm*
- £110 • **Sharif**

RUSSIAN

▽ Saint John

- *circa 1450*

Saint John in the Wilderness. Painted in Constantinople by an artist of the circle of Angelos.

- *33.5cm x 25cm*
- £120,000 • Temple Gallery

▽ Brass and Blue Enamel Cross

- *circa 1800*

Brass and blue enamel cross with Christ on the crucifix at the centre, surrounded by depictions of festivals and surmounted by seraphim.

- *height 28cm*
- £750 • Iconastas

▷ Blue Russian Vases

- *1855–81*

A pair of amphora-shaped Alexander II porcelain vases, with ormolu mounts from the Imperial porcelain factory, profusely moulded with scrolling strawberries, wild flowers, birds and butterflies against a pale lilac ground, enclosing two painted reserves of varying spring bouquets, resting on an elaborate gilt foliate base, by M. Morozov.

- *height 1.07m*
- £65,000 • Emanouel

△ Three Saints

- *17th century*

Carved decoration with three saints (only two shown). Balkan.

- *23.6cm x 56.2cm*
- £5,500 • Temple Gallery

△ Porcelain Dessert Plate

- *1825–55*

A rare St Petersburg porcelain dessert plate from the coronation service of Tzar Nicolas I 1825. Ex-Romanoff Collection, Winter Palace.

- *diameter 22cm*
- £1,200 • P. Boyd-Carpenter

△ Icon of Sts John, Nicholas and Ulita

- *18th century*

Octagonal icon depicting the Saints John, Nicholas and Ulita, with her son Kyric, covered with a silver-gilt riza.

- *9.5cm x 10.5cm*
- £1,850 • Iconastas

△ Dormition of the Virgin

- *early 19th century*

Image from the Palekh school, in gesso on wood panel, with gold. Based on the Katyed Cami, from Istanbul.

- *37.4cm x 10.5cm*
- £2,500 • Temple Gallery

▽ Miniature Tankard

- *circa 1787*

Miniature 'Charka', or silver tankard, engraved with two eagles above two flowers connected by a ribbon.

- *height 4cm*
- £625 • Iconastas

▽ Quadratych

- *circa 1840*

A brass and enamel folding quadratych depicting festivals and venerations of icons of the Virgin and Child.

- *17cm x 40cm*
- £290 • Iconastas

▽ St Sergei Pendant

- *circa 1840*

Enamel painted pendant of St Sergei set in an oval frame with paste diamonds, on a silver chain.

- *6cm x 4cm*
- £690 • Iconastas

◁ Brass Cross with Enamel Inlay

- *circa 1830*

Large brass Russian cross showing Christ on the crucifix, with enamel inlay.

- *41cm x 20.5cm*
- £390 • Iconastas

△ Silver Bowl

- *mid-19th century*

Silver-marked Russian silver bowl from Georgia, showing six panels of beasts and forestry scenes, with central roundel.

- *diameter 20cm*
- £1,200 • Shahdad

△ Black Lacquer Box

- *circa 1870*

Circular Russian black lacquer box with a painting of a landscape in a Dutch style by the Lukutin factory.

- *diameter 9cm*
- £1,350 • Iconastas

△ Painted Laquered Box

- *circa 1890s*

Russian painted lacquered box depicting a courting couple in a countryside setting, by the Vishniakov factory.

- *12cm x 8cm*
- £590 • Iconastas

▽ Oval Lacquer Box

- *1870*

Oval red lacquer painted box showing a Russian peasant girl wearing a Kokoshnik, by the Lukutin factory.

- *length 7cm*
- £1,250 • Iconastas

▽ St George and the Dragon

- *circa 1880*

Balkan icon of St George on horseback slaying the dragon with enamelled face and hands, covered with a silver riza.

- *10cm x 12cm*
- £690 • Iconastas

▽ Fabergé Picture Frame

- *circa 1890*

Fabergé satinwood picture frame with silver beading, the gold initial 'A', and four silver roses at each corner. The photo shows Tsarina Alexandra.

- *14cm x 11cm*
- £4,500 • Iconastas

△ Dancing Scene

- *1860*

Russian painted lacquer box depicting dancers in colourful costumes linking hands in a woodland setting.

- *15cm x 8cm*
- £1,250 • Iconastas

△ Moscow Yacht Tankard

- *circa 1871*

Miniature silver tankard with arms of the Moscow Yacht Club.

- *height 6cm*
- £750 • Iconastas

▽ Set of Salts

- *circa 1877*

Set of six circular silver salts on three ball feet with silver spoons by Gachen in original oak box.

- *diameter 18cm*
- £750 • Iconastas

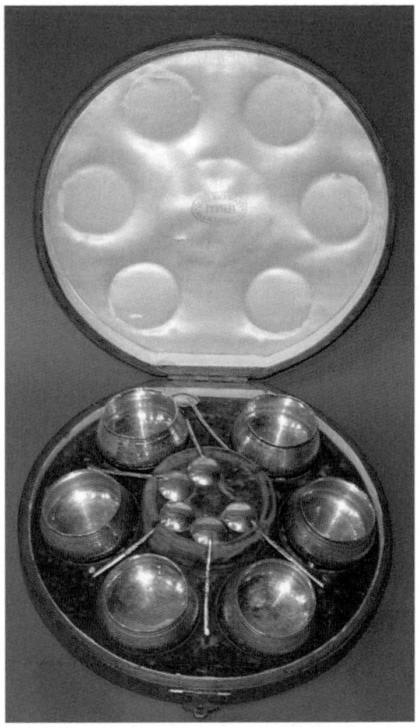

▽ Drinking Goblet

- *19th century*

Russian drinking goblet with a geometric and swirling design enamelled in blue, turquoise and white gold. Made for Tiffany.

- *height 12cm*
- £1,450 • Iconastas

◁ Silver Gilt and Enamel Beaker

- *circa 1885*

Silver gilt beaker with blue scrolling and white flowers.

- *height 11.5cm*
- £1,850 • Iconastas

△ Virgin of Vladimir

- *19th century*

Orthodox iconic depiction of the Virgin of Vladimir, showing Virgin Mary with Child.

- *34.5cm x 30cm*
- £860 • Temple Gallery

△ Archangel Michael

- *19th century*

Archangel Michael Voyevoda (warrior) in iconic form, shown on wood panel and depicted on horseback.

- *34.8cm x 30.4cm*
- £1,650 • Temple Gallery

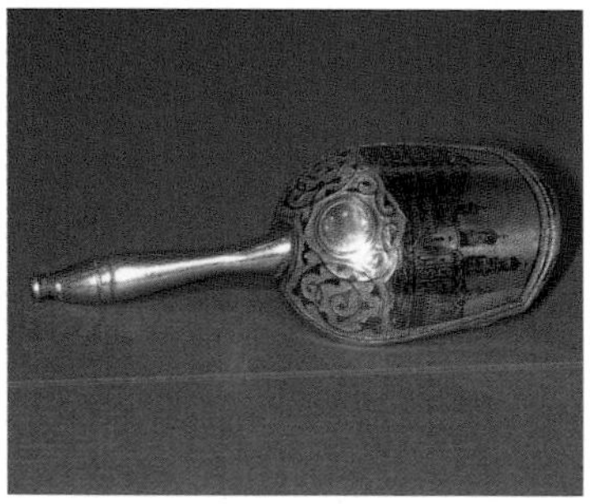

△ Tea Caddy Spoon

- *circa 1900*

Silver gilt tea caddy spoon showing an Imperial Russian scene and a foliate design.

- *length 8cm*
- £180 • Iconastas

▽ Virgin of Kazan

- *circa 1895*

Virgin of Kazan covered with an engine-turned silver riza.

- *15cm x 11.5cm*
- £1,250 • Iconastas

▽ Prophet Elijah

- *19th century*

Iconic representation of the Prophet Elijah. The prophet is in his cave in the wilderness, with raven. God is depicted in a chariot carried by a red cloud.

- *31.5cm x 26cm*
- £1,500 • Temple Gallery

▽ Enamel Blotter

- *circa 1900*

Enamel blue and pink floral design blotter with gold borders by Semonova.

- *length 14cm*
- £900 • Iconastas

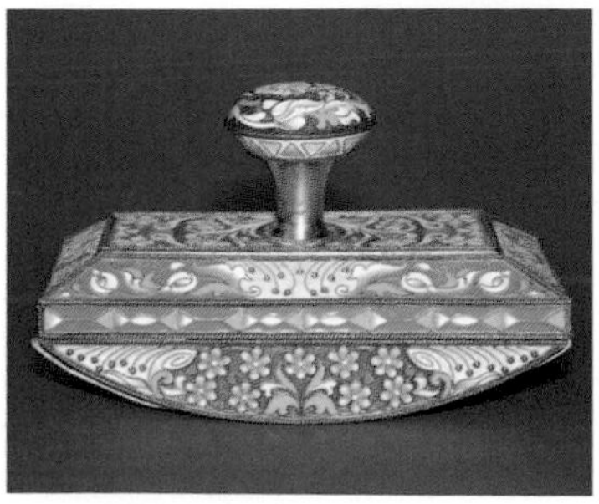

△ Virgin of Kazan

- *19th century*

Icon of the Virgin of Kazan, capital of Tartarstan.

- *37.7cm x 31.5cm*
- £650 • Temple Gallery

△ Christ Pantocrator

- *circa 1900*

Russian icon depicting Christ Pantrocrator painted on a wooden panel shown holding a bible, covered with a silver riza with an enamel halo and enamel letters on the bible.

- *34cm x 28cm*
- £1,250 • Iconastas

▽ Archangel Michael

- *19th century*

Iconic representation of Archangel Michael of Voyevoda.

- *33.5 x 28.8cm*
- £1,450 • Temple Gallery

▽ Icon of Sts Samon, Gury and Aviv

- *1900*

Russian icon showing the Saints Samon, Gury and Aviv, covered with a silver and turquoise blue enamel riza, by Michelson, Moscow, 1900.

- *7cm x 6cm*
- £1,250 • Iconastas

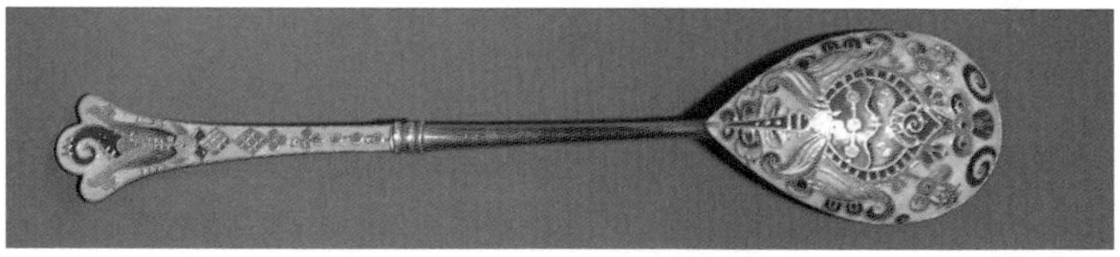

▽ Fabergé Spoon

- *circa 1900*

A silver spoon with a gilt bowl, produced by Fabergé.

- *length 16cm*
- £425 • Iconastas

△ Enamelled Spoon

- *circa 1900*

Silver spoon enamelled with a dark blue, green and pink foliate design.

- *length 15cm*
- £1,300 • Iconastas

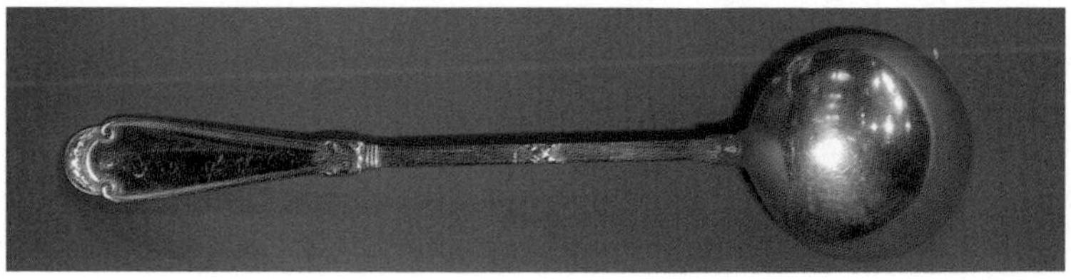

△ Opalin Glass Sweet Jars

- *circa 1905*

Opalin glass sweet jars modelled as busts of the Tsar and Tsarina Nicholas and Alexandra, made for the Imperial visit to France.

- *height 35cm*
- £500 the pair • Iconastas

△ Russian Kovsh

- *circa 1900*

Russian enamel kovsh, decorated with blue turquoise foliate design by Lubwin.

- *length 19cm*
- £1,200 • Iconastas

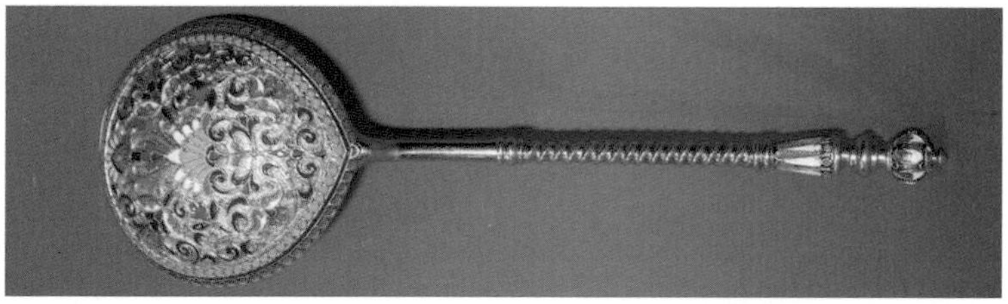

▽ Musicians by Yakovlevich

- *circa 1910*

Pair of terracotta musicians by Golovin Alexander Yakovlevich.

- *height 28cm*
- £5,500 the pair • Iconastas

▷ Russian Gilt Enamel Spoon

- *circa 1900*

Silver gilt spoon with pink, blue, red and yellow foliate design.

- *length 18cm*
- £1,000 • Iconastas

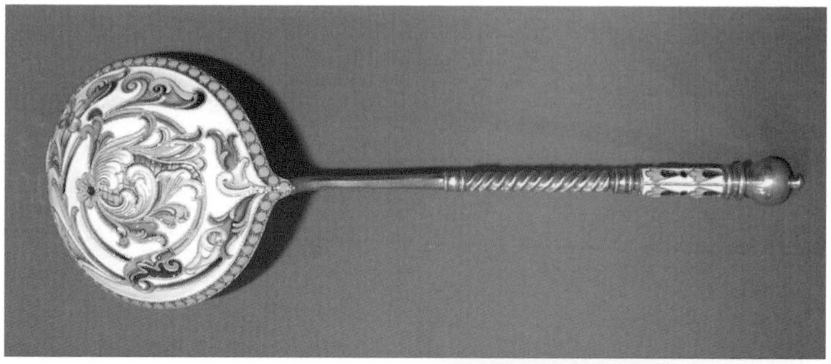

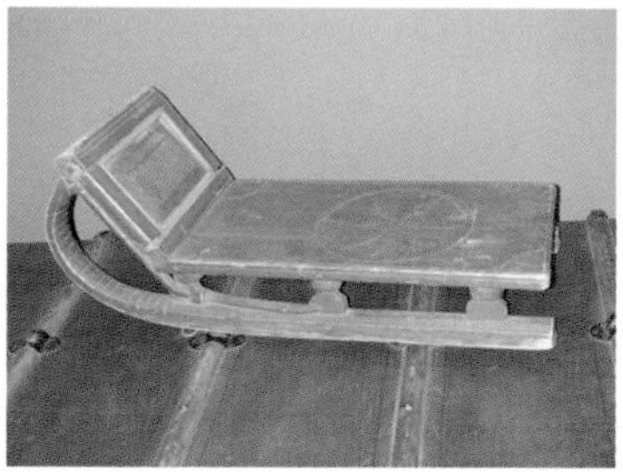

△ Wooden Toboggan

- *1901*

Russian painted red wooden toboggan from the Volodga region.

- *length 65cm*
- £120 • Zakheim

▽ Silver Gilt and Gold Enamel

- *circa 1900*

Silver gilt spoon with turquoise, white, green and dark blue, foliate design with an emerald-green border.

- *length 11cm*
- £400 • Iconastas

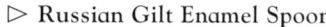

▽ Cigarette Case

- *circa 1900*

Russian cigarette champlevé case with a repeating floral pattern in blue, red and white enamel.

- *10cm x 6cm*
- £890 • Iconastas

▽ Silver Tankard

- *circa 1900*

A Russian silver tankard made for political propaganda, with engraved cartouches showing a bountiful harvest.

- *height 8cm*
- £1,900 • Iconastas

△ Fabergé Kovsh

- *1910*

Fabergé ceramic and silver kovsh set with cut amethysts. Provenance: Princess of Baden, from the Baden collection.

- *height 15cm*
- £5,000 • Iconastas

△ Fabergé Hand Mirror

- *1910*

Silver hand mirror by Fabergé, with raised engraved crest.

- *length 21cm*
- £1,400 • Iconastas

△ Stalin

- *circa 1920*

Soviet white-glazed porcelain figure of Stalin shown in his youthful revolutionary 'Hero' style. Signed.

- *height 36cm*
- £2,450 • Iconastas

△ Soviet Porcelain Plate

- *circa 1920*

Russian, Soviet porcelain plate with floral design and stylised 'CCCP' by Natalya Girshfeld.

- *diameter 23cm*
- £1,650 • Iconastas

▽ Lenin

- *circa 1920*

Rare plaster figure of Lenin by Mauetta.

- *height 34cm*
- £2,450 • Iconastas

▽ Soviet Bowl

- *circa 1921*

Soviet bowl painted with strong brush-strokes in vibrant colours by Rudolf Vilde (1868–1942).

- *diameter 26cm*
- £2,200 • Iconastas

▽ Arctic Rescue Tea Set

- *circa 1925*

Tea set commemorating rescue of the Swedish Arctic Expedition, led by Nobel, by the Soviet icebreaker *Krasin*.

- *diameter of plate 24cm*
- £2,500 • Iconastas

△ Ceramic Platter

- *circa 1920*

Commemorative ceramic platter, only one other recorded. Showing Lenin in centre with various faces of revolutionary Russia in red and grey charcoal glaze.

- *diameter 42cm*
- £5,500 • Zakheim

△ Lenin Inkwell

- *circa 1924*

The Lenin inkwell, with facsimile signatures and inscription 'Proletariat of the World Unite' and anniversary inscription on the cover. By Natalia Danko (1892–1942) from the Lomonosov factory.

- *height 17cm*
- £1,250 • Iconastas

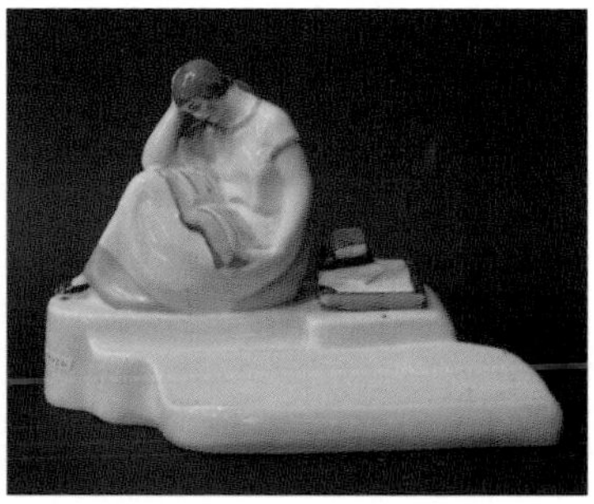

△ Soviet Inkwell

- *circa 1929*

Soviet pottery inkwell, surmounted by a young lady with a red headscarf reading a book, the lid modelled as books and pamphlets. After Danko.

- *height 16cm*
- £1,250 • Iconastas

▽ Russian Frame

- *circa 1920*

Russian rosewood picture frame with brass borders and crest of two eagles with Tsar Nicholas II of Russia.

- *28cm x 21cm*
- £1,300 • Iconastas

▽ Constructivist Plate

- *1928*

Constructivist plate painted with female skiers in linear form with strong colours. Signed and dated 1928.

- *diameter 24cm*
- £1,650 • Iconastas

▽ Soviet Pen Tray

- *circa 1930*

Soviet pottery pen tray with a reclining Uzbek reading *Pravda*, after Natalia Danko.

- *width 19cm*
- £650 • Iconastas

△ Baboushka

- *circa 1930*

Soviet white-glazed porcelain figure of a baboushka with impressed hammer and sickle mark and initials of Boris Kustodiev (1878–1927) from the Lomonosov factory.

- *height 27cm*
- £1,250 • Iconastas

△ Cast Bronze Figure

- *circa 1940*

Cast bronze of Russian Hero. Copy of a famous, full-size bronze.

- *height 35cm*
- £350 • Zakheim

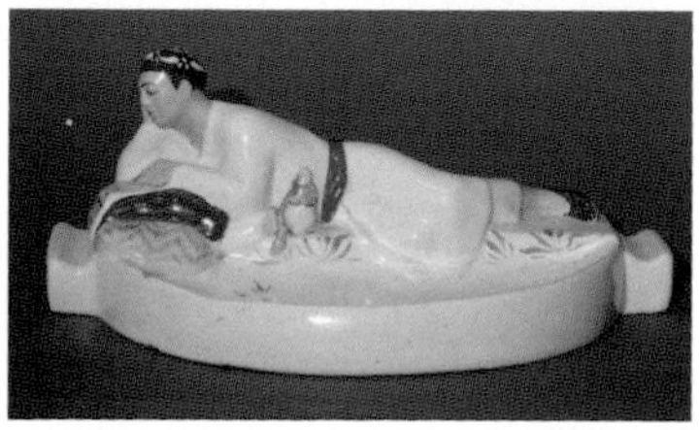

▽ Puss in Boots

- *circa 1930*

A brightly coloured Soviet figure of Puss in Boots, unmarked, probably by Boris Kustodiev.

- *height 23cm*
- £450 • Iconastas

▽ Commemorative Vase

- *circa 1940*

Baluster-shaped vase, showing Lenin, in red glaze with gilded lettering and floral decoration.

- *height 37cm*
- £750 • Zakheim

◁ Reclining Man Reading Newspaper

- *circa 1930*

Reclining figure of a man reading a newspaper dressed in white with a black and white hat.

- *length 21cm*
- £580 • Iconastas

△ Grey Horses with Riders

- *circa 1930*

Pair of grey horses with riders, one pointing, on a foliate square base.

- *26cm x 18cm*
- £2,650 • Iconastas

△ Paperweight

- *circa 1940*

Obsidian and onyx paperweight with intaglio of Lenin in profile, looking to sinister.

- *height 15cm*
- £490 • Zakheim

△ Weightlifter

- *circa 1950*

Alloy model of a weightlifter in black enamel. In the act of final lift. On an oval base.

- *height 52cm*
- £890 • Zakheim

▽ Accordion Player

- *circa 1930*

Soviet white glazed figure of an accordion player by Boris Kustodiev.

- *height 23cm*
- £490 • Iconastas

▽ Painted Lacquer Box

- *1947*

Rare wartime allegorical lacquered painted box showing the invasion of Russia by Germany, and the German army's defeat. The box is painted in icon form with the moon on the left hidden by the burning buildings, by F. Kolosov.

- *21cm x 17cm*
- £1,650 • Iconastas

▽ Commemorative Tea Holder

- *1970*

Soviet silver tea holder with a cartouche showing Lenin's head, an industrial scene and the dates 1920–1970, surrounded by a foliate design.

- *height 10cm*
- £80 • Iconastas

WRITING EQUIPMENT

The vast range of collectable writing equipment is overwhelmingly Victorian. The Victorians were fervent writers and, as a result, an abundance of writing-related items were created in this period. Victorian ink trays were often inlaid with mother-of-pearl and are highly decorative. Some were made of enamel and decorated in a chinoiserie style, which was a very fashionable decorative effect at the time. If you are a first-time collector, the field of writing equipment is a great place to start with as there is huge scope for the collector and the items can be very affordable and also usuable. They can make a bold and striking statement on any desk or in a study as they are not only decorative, but are also a great talking point. Pens are always collectable with the leading brands such as Parker, Mont Blanc and Waterman continuing to attract the highest prices because of their timeless workmanship and superior quality. The Art Nouveau period produced some intricate and innovative items of writing equipment and these pieces are currently gaining in value and desirability.

△ Writing Slope

- *circa 1760*

Extremely rare writing slope with English raised and coloured chinoiserie decoration.

- *width 41cm*
- £1,300 • Hygra

▽ Penwork Box

- *circa 1810*

Sarcophagus box with floral decoration to sides with top panel depicting Chinaman.

- *length 31cm*
- £850 • John Clay

◁ Tunbridge Ware Writing Slope

- *circa 1800*

Very rare, early Tunbridge ware parquetry writing box/slope/lap desk.

- *width 42cm*
- £950 • Hygra

△ Fruitwood Pen Tray

- *18th century*

Pen tray with inkstand and turned carrying handle and drawer. It has twin screw-closed inkwells and a pounce shaker.

- *length 30cm*
- £650 • Hygra

▽ Slope/Lap Writing Desk

- *circa 1790*

Rosewood and penwork writing slope/lap desk with original baize writing surface.

- *length 24cm*
- £750 • Hygra

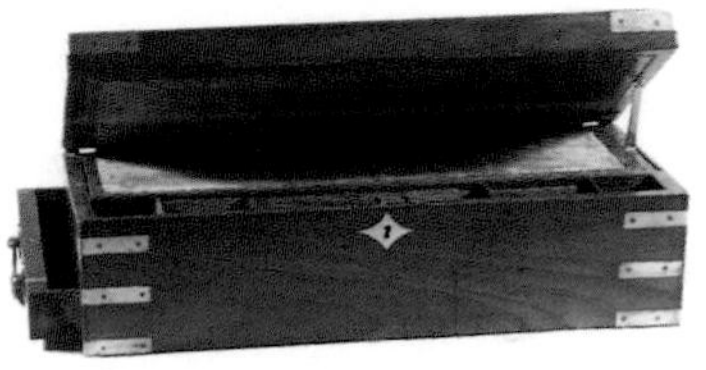

◁ Writing Box/Lap Desk

- *circa 1800*

Brass-bound mahogany box in military style with brass drop handles, a side document drawer, and brass corners, nameplate and escutcheon. Opens to reveal sloping, velvet writing surface and space for writing implements.

- *length 50cm*
- £440 • Hygra

△ Marble Rule

- *19th century*

Polished black, pink, green, grey and yellow marble rule.

- *length 25.5cm*
- £150 • Jasmin Cameron

△ Writing Box

- *circa 1820*

An Anglo-Indian writing box inlaid with ivory, opening down to reveal a writing surface and space for writing implements.

- £24 • Hygra

△ Papier Mâché Slope

- *circa 1820*

Writing slope with chinoiserie decoration opening to reveal a surface for writing.

- *length 29cm*
- £850 • Hygra

▽ Georgian Inkwells

- *1810*

Late Georgian set of glass inkwells with lobed silver covers.

- *heights from 5cm*
- £180 • Jasmin Cameron

▽ Letter/Pen Rack

- *circa 1820*

Unusual letter/pen rack.

- *height 28cm*
- £980 • P.L. James

▽ Faceted Glass Inkpot

- *circa 1830*

Faceted glass inkpot with brass hinge.

- *height 9cm*
- £85 • Jasmin Cameron

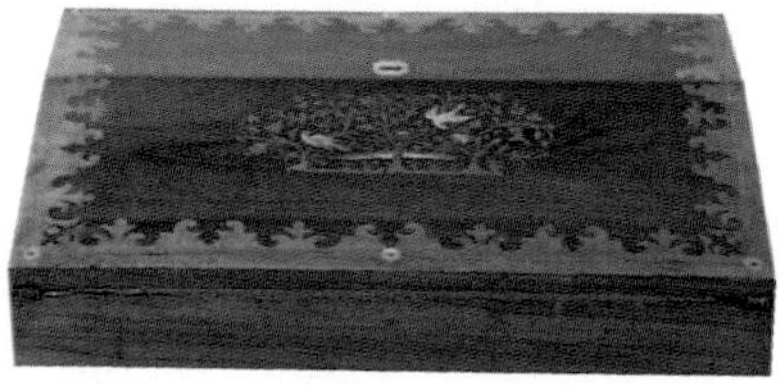

◁ Rosewood Writing Slope

- *circa 1835*

Fine inlaid rosewood and bird's eye maple writing slope/lap desk with fine mother-of-pearl inlay.

- *width 26cm*
- £750 • Hygra

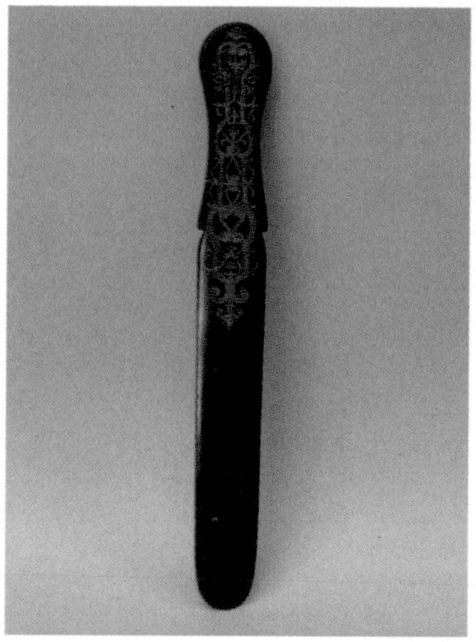

△ Rosewood Paper Knife

- *circa 1810*

Rosewood paper knife with brass filigree decoration.

- *length 29cm*
- £78 • Hayman

△ Regency Writing Slope

- *circa 1820*

Rosewood desk inlaid with cut-brass decoration, fitted with lock.

- *length 50cm*
- £850 • J. Collins

△ Glass Ink Pot

- *circa 1830*

Faceted clear glass ink pot with star-cut stopper.

- *height 9cm*
- £85 • Jasmin Cameron

▽ Vesta Box

- *1820*

English bronze vesta box with greyhound on the top, from the late Edward and Alison Gibbons collection, Elm Hill, Worcestershire.

- *height 7cm*
- £320 • Jasmin Cameron

▽ Ebony Ink Tray

- *circa 1820*

Ebony ink tray with two square inkwells with brass lids, and central stamp compartment.

- *width 34cm*
- £195 • Hayman

▽ Victorian Ink Pot

- *circa 1830*

Victorian ink pot of ovoid form with ball stopper.

- *height 7cm*
- £85 • Jasmin Cameron

△ Regency Inkstand

• *1830*
Regency gilt bronze inkstand with cut crystal glass inkwells centred with a reclining stag.
• *width 35cm*
• £1,700 • Pimlico

△ Papier Mâché Inkstand

• *circa 1850*
Papier mâché inkstand with original inkwells and pen-trays, mother-of-pearl decoration stamped on underside 'Jennens & Bettridge, Makers to the Queen 97'.
• *width 31cm*
• £340 • Hygra

△ Rococo Inkstand

• *1860*
Silver-bronze rococo inkstand in chinoiserie style.
• *28cm x 48cm*
• £1,200 • Sign of the Times

△ Writing Box

• *1860*
Victorian coromandel stationery/writing box with clear glass bottles.
• *28cm x 34cm*
• £580 • Barham Antiques

▽ Travelling Inkwell

• *circa 1830*
Travelling carved wood inkwell, painted with castellated screw top, with original glass liner.
• *height 8cm*
• £375 • Bill Chapman

▽ Silver Inkstand

• *1857*
Silver inkstand depicting a desert scene incorporating two glass ink bottles, hand crafted by Hayne & Cater of London.
• *25cm x 35cm*
• £5,250 • Stephen Kalms

▽ Bronze Stag

• *mid-19th century*
Lifting cup on a black marble base. Pens rest on antlers.
• *height 11cm*
• £690 • Elizabeth Bradwin

△ Victorian Inkstand

• *1840*
Victorian electroplate inkstand with glass inkwell, pounce pot, and holder for candle in centre. The whole on a silver stand with foliate design on the feet and rim.
• *length 25cm*
• £575 • Jasmin Cameron

△ Pewter Ink Pot

• *1850*
English Court House pewter ink pot inscribed 'Stationery Office' on the base.
• *height 10cm*
• £155 • Jasmin Cameron

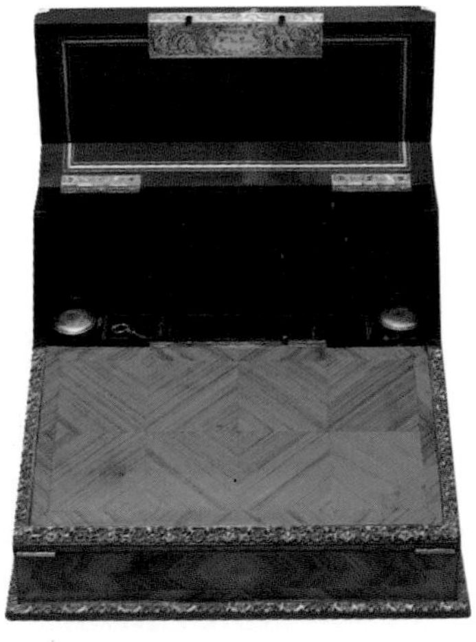

△ Stationery Cabinet

• *circa 1860*
A burr-walnut stationery cabinet with satinwood interior. Interior has writing slate, calendar, pen tilt and crown top inkwells.
• *height 33cm*
• £900 • Gerald Mathias

▽ Brass Letter Clip

• *1843*
Victorian brass letter clip inscribed 'Reg 3.10. 1843. Perry', by Pripson & Parker.
• *length 12cm*
• £175 • Jasmin Cameron

▽ Travelling Inkwell

• *circa 1860s*
Victorian travelling inkwell in original leather case.
• *height 6cm*
• £45 • Barham Antiques

▽ Lady's Writing Slope

• *1865*
Royal French kingwood writing slope with engraved hinges and lock plate. Signed Tahan of Paris.
• *length 25cm*
• £1,995 • J. & T. Stone

▽ Guttapercha Writing Set

• *circa 1860*
Ink tray made from guttapercha with two inkwells set on a scrolled base.
• *width 27cm*
• £125 • Hayman

△ Novelty Pencil

- *1870*

Victorian walnut and silver novelty pencil.

- *height 2cm*
- **£225** • **Jasmin Cameron**

▽ Writing Box

- *circa 1870*

A leather-faced writing box, by Halstaff and Hannaford, with ivory rules, letter-opener, pen and drop-forward letter rack with original key.

- *height 33cm*
- **£1,600** • **Gerald Mathias**

△ Ink Tray and Bottles

- *1877*

Fine silver ink tray comprising two cut-glass ink bottles on a shaped base with leafy shell and scroll border, made in Sheffield.

- *width 33cm*
- **£2,900** • **Stephen Kalms**

▽ Coromandel Writing Box

- *circa 1870*

A coromandel writing box with domed lid and gilt and chased fittings, crown-topped inkwells and original velvet lining.

- *height 18cm*
- **£1,475** • **Gerald Mathias**

△ Letter Rack

- *circa 1880*

Victorian pierced brass foliate designed letter rack, with a porcelain inkstand and a dark blue glass ink bottle, resting on a brass shield base with bracket feet.

- *25cm x 20cm*
- **£295** • **Barham Antiques**

▽ Brass Pen Rack

- *1880*

Victorian six-tier brass pen rack on a square base with pierced foliate design.

- *height 13cm*
- **£165** • **Jasmin Cameron**

△ Writing Box

- *circa 1875*

Victorian papier mâché lady's writing slope with extensive gilded mother-of-pearl decoration and original silver-topped inkwell.

- *length 40cm*
- **£1,575** • **J. & T. Stone**

△ Austrian Inkwell

- *circa 1890*

Austrian green and purple glass ink pot with a stylised leaf design and a hinged brass lid.

- *diameter 15cm*
- **£460** • **Jasmin Cameron**

▽ Ink Reservoir

- *late 19th century*

Silver bronzed cat and mouse with gilt highlights which opens to ink reservoir.

- *height 7cm*
- **£1,170** • **Elizabeth Bradwin**

△ Square Ink Pot

- *1880*

Victorian heavy square faceted ink pot standing on a brass tray with indentations for pens.

- *18cm x 18cm*
- **£125** • **Hayman**

△ Large Baccarat Inkwell

- *1880*

Large bulbous glass inkpot with a textured wave relief and an American moulded silver lid, by Baccarat. Fully marked.

- *height 15cm*
- **£740** • **Jasmin Cameron**

◁ Ram-Horn Writing Set

- *late 19th century*

Oak-based writing set with silver mounts and ram-horn centre piece.

- *height 21cm*
- **£1,700** • **H. & H.**

▽ Owl Pen Holder

• *circa 1890*
Owl inkwell standing on a circular base with a scrolled handles for holding pens.
• *height 21cm*
• £280 • Henry Gregory

▽ Rifle Pencil

• *1890*
Fruitwood bolt-action rifle pencil with tin barrel and brass banding.
• *length 6cm*
• £165 • Jasmin Cameron

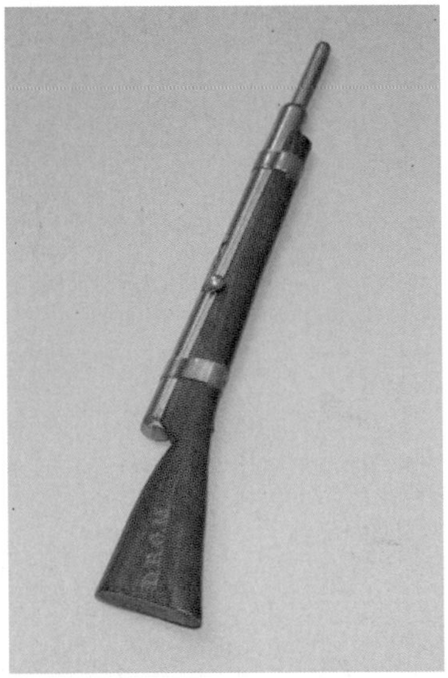

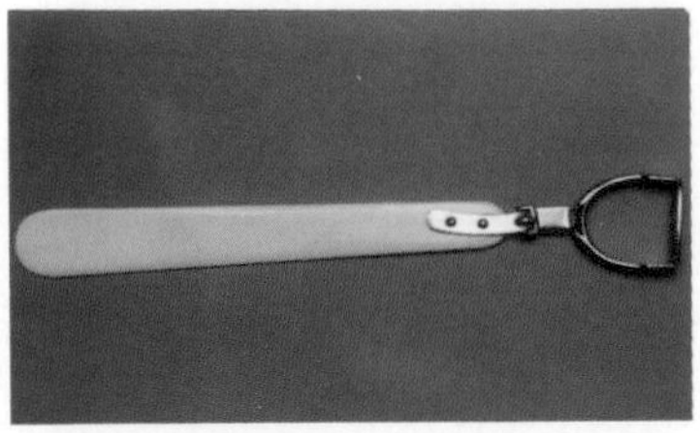

△ Letter Opener

• *1896*
Silver and ivory letter opener by Sheppard and Saunders.
• *length 20cm*
• £1,600 • Sandra Cronan

△ Circular Glass Inkwell

• *circa 1890*
Circular inkwell with a brass hinged lid.
• *height 9cm*
• £270 • Henry Gregory

△ Silver Basket Ink Pot

• *circa 1896*
Silver basket on fluted legs, with a faceted square glass ink pot with a silver lid and a silver base.
• *height 8cm*
• £325 • Barrett Towning

▽ Artist's Paintbox

• *circa 1890*
Victorian rosewood box with various paints and liftout tray.
• *length 31cm*
• £2,950 • J. & T. Stone

▽ Slide-Action Dip Pens

• *1890*
Slide-action travelling dip pen in 'Gothic design' with rolled gold nib.
• *length 14cm*
• £125 • Jasmin Cameron

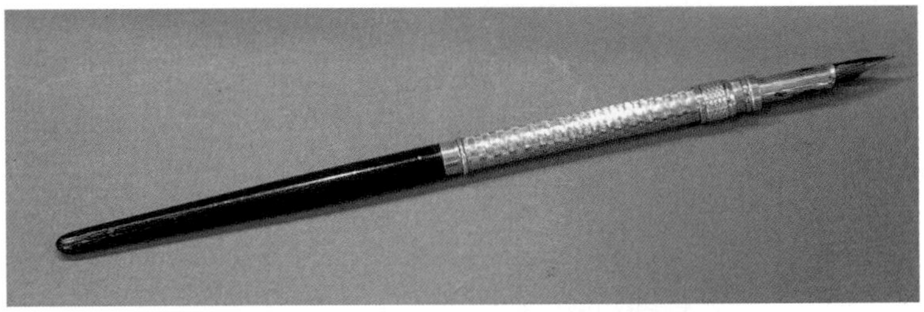

△ Inkwell

• *late 19th century*
Bronzed alligator with concealed inkwell. The back opens to reveal two reservoirs.
• *length 25cm*
• £735 • Elizabeth Bradwin

△ Ivory Boat Blotter

• *circa 1890*
Ivory boat blotter with knob handle.
• *length 11cm*
• £175 • Jasmin Cameron

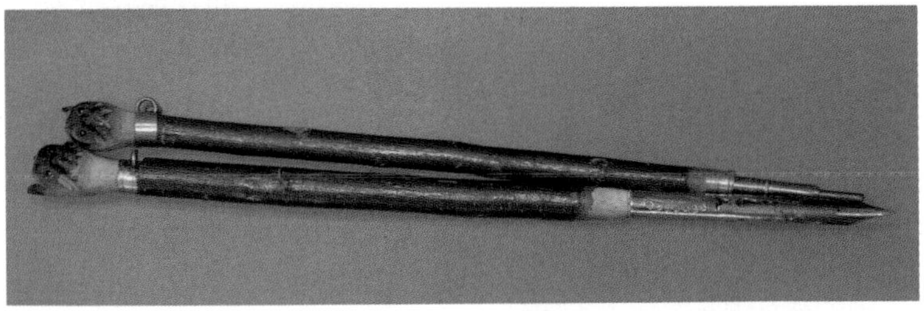

△ Dip Pen and Pencil

• *circa 1890*
A dip pen and pencil, with pugs' heads with ringed brass collars.
• *length 20cm*
• £160 • Jasmin Cameron

▷ Butterfly Letter Rack

• *circa 1890*
Brass butterfly letter rack standing on a rustic base.
• *height 10cm*
• £238 • Hayman

△ French Inkwell

- *circa 1900*

French art nouveau inkwell of a lady reclining on large flowers with a lid concealed on the top of her long hair.

- *height 16cm*
- £1,200 • Arwas

△ Beehive Ink Pot

- *circa 1905*

Silver ink pot with hinged lid. Made in London by Mappin & Webb.

- *height 6.5cm*
- £350 • Barrett Towning

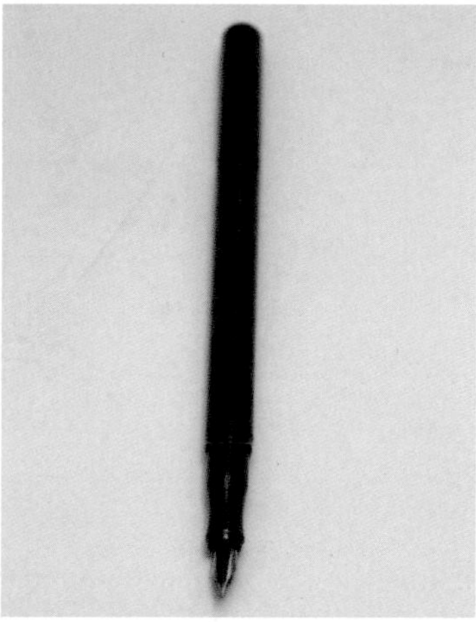

△ De La Rue Pen

- *circa 1900*

De la Rue of London 'Onoto' pen, piston filled with 18-carat gold nib.

- *length 15cm*
- £100 • Sugar

▽ 'Lovers' Ink Pot

- *circa 1900*

French sculpture of two lovers embracing on a moulded base, by Bernard.

- *width 17cm*
- £3,000 • Arwas

▽ Cut-Glass Inkwell

- *circa 1900*

A cut-glass inkwell with a hinged silver cover.

- *height 10cm*
- £260 • Henry Gregory

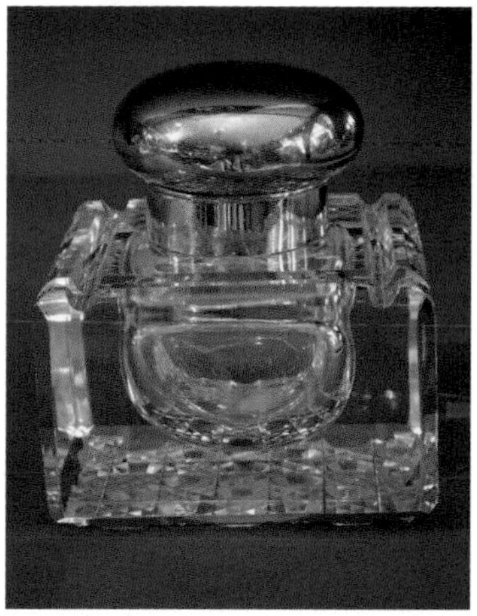

▽ Silver Tray with Inkwell

- *circa 1901*

Silver moulded tray on raised feet, with a pen holder and faceted glass inkpot with scrolled silver lid.

- *height 11cm*
- £375 • Barrett Towning

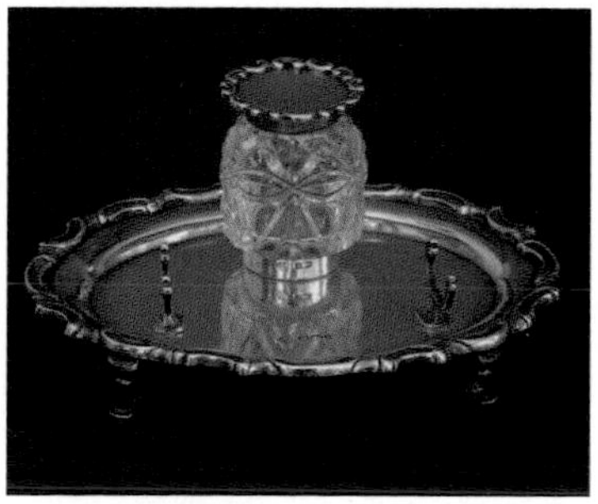

▷ Brass Blotter

- *circa 1912*

Arts and Crafts brass boat blotter. Marked GESCi 9121.

- *length 15cm*
- £260 • Jasmin Cameron

△ Non-Spill Ink Pot

- *circa 1900*

Non-spill vaseline glass ink pot of ovoid form with a central tear drop reservoir.

- *height 6cm*
- £24 • Hayman

△ Ormolu Inkstand

- *circa 1901*

Elkington ormolu inkstand decorated with blue and turquoise enamel, with two cherubs holding a monogrammed plaque, standing on bracket feet, with two clear cut glass bottles with brass and enamelled lids.

- *length 32cm*
- £850 • Barham Antiques

△ Edwardian Inkstand

- *1904*

Highly decorative inkstand with pierced gallery, two crystal glass reservoirs, and moulded apron raised on shaped feet. Made in London.

- *26cm x 15cm*
- £2,350 • Stephen Kalms

▽ Telescopic Pencil

- *1902*

Silver telescopic pencil in sheath with stirrup loop by Alfred Deeley, Birmingham, 1902.

- *length 3.75cm*
- £220 • Jasmin Cameron

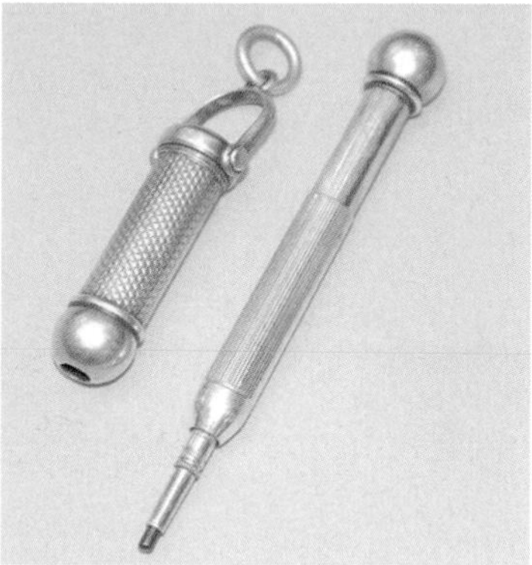

▽ Art Nouveau Inkwell

- *circa 1900*

French art nouveau pewter inkwell of a lady with long hair.

- *width 12cm*
- £1,200 • Arwas

▽ Silver Capstan

- *1912*

Inkwell made in Birmingham with porcelain bowl.

- *height 7cm*
- £285 • Jasmin Cameron

△ Double Glass Inkwell

• *circa 1910*
Double glass inkwell with silver rims around the lids, in an oblong container.
• *width 11cm*
• £96 • **Henry Gregory**

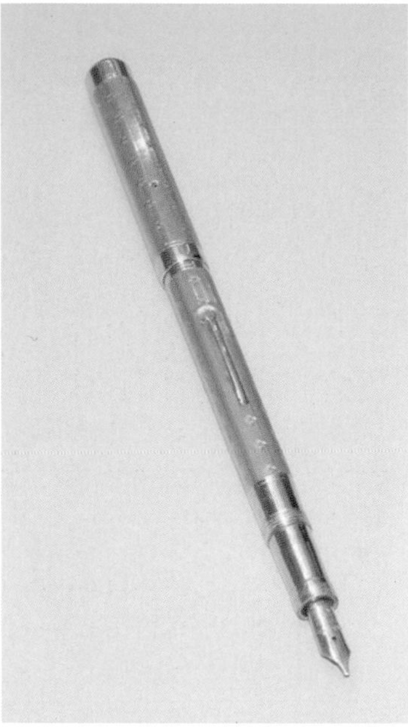

△ Gold-Plated Fountain Pen

• *1920*
Mabie Todd & Co gold-plated fountain pen with a rosette design.
• *length 13cm*
• £800 • **Jasmin Cameron**

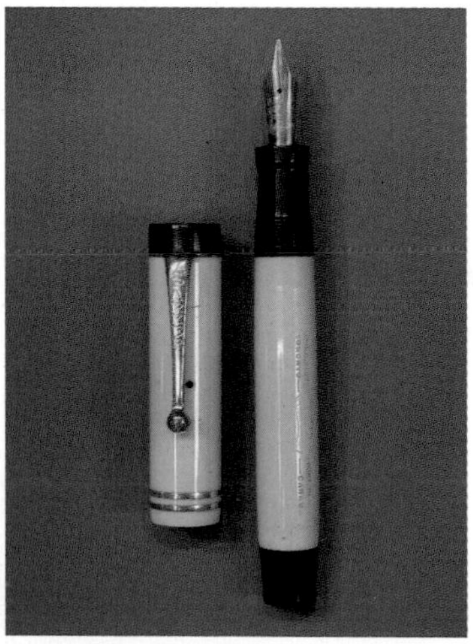

▽ Ivory-Handled Pen

• *1912*
English pen with ivory handle and silver nib, made in London, 1912.
• *length 26cm*
• £145 • **Jasmin Cameron**

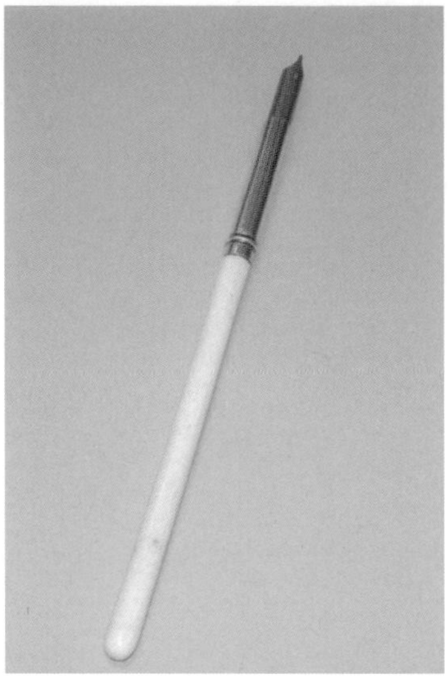

▽ Dinkie 540J

• *circa 1920*
Conway Stuart Dinkie 540J. Rare lady's pen with 14-carat gold nib and multicoloured body.
• *length 15cm*
• £220 • **Jasmin Cameron**

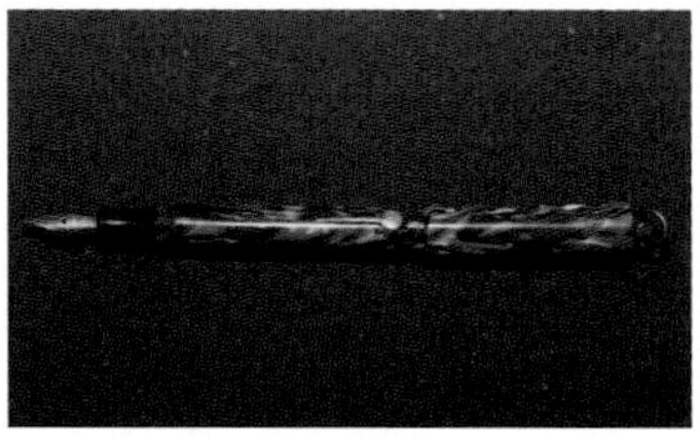

▽ Waterman Ideal 0552½

• *1924*
Lady's pen with gold-plated gothic pattern and level fill.
• *length 14cm*
• £450 • **Jasmin Cameron**

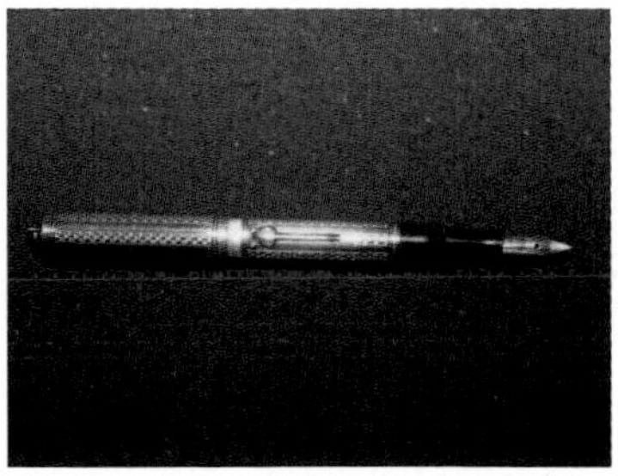

◁ 'Lucky Cup' Pen

• *circa 1928*
Canadian duofold junior, mandarin yellow Parker pen.
• *length 14cm*
• £640 • **Jasmin Cameron**

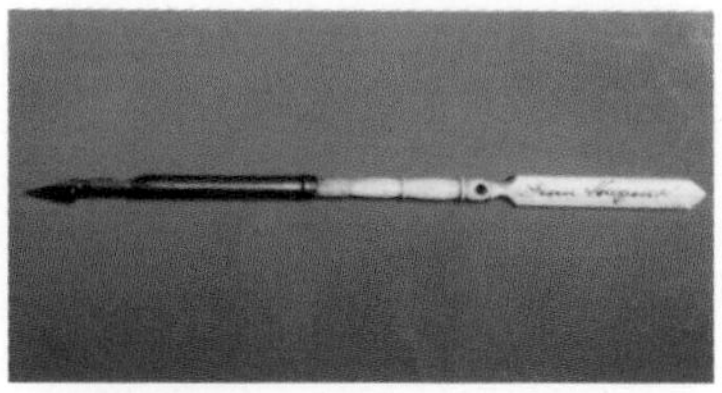

△ Bone-Handle Pen

• *circa 1910*
A souvenir, bone handle with steel nib inscribed 'A Present from Skegness'.
• *length 18cm*
• £28 • **Mark Sullivan**

△ Waterman Ideal 0552½

• *1920*
Lady's pen with lever-fill action and gold-plated nib.
• *length 14cm*
• £750 • **Jasmin Cameron**

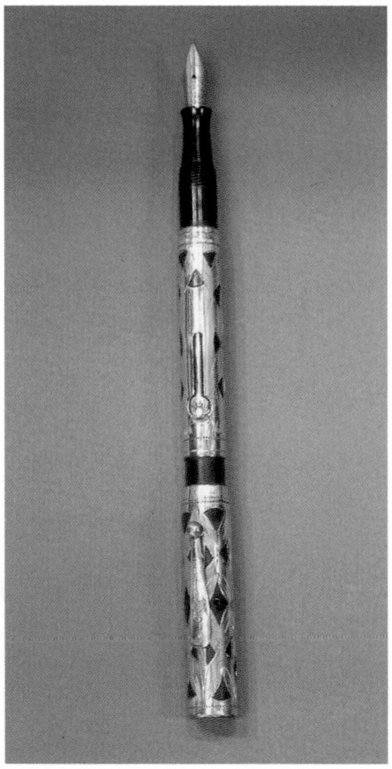

△ Waterman Fountain Pen

• *circa 1920*
Waterman 0552 gold-plated basket-weave fountain pen with half G.P.
• *length 14cm*
• £900 • **Jasmin Cameron**

▽ Ball Inkwell

• *1914*
Brass inkwell consisting of four brass balls resting on each other, one of which contains the ink, with a metal and wood base.
• *diameter 17cm*
• £78 • **Hayman**

▽ Gold Waterman Pen

• *1920*
Gold Waterman fountain pen with basketweave pattern, No.5552½, with original glass ink dropper.
• *length 14cm*
• £600 • **Jasmin Cameron**

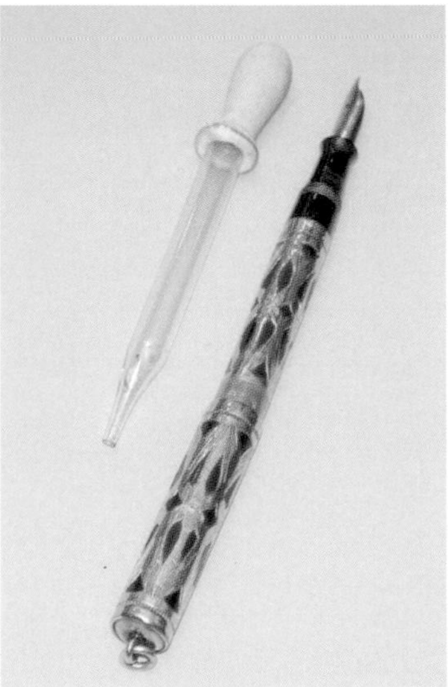

▽ Waterman Gothic

• *1924*
A Waterman 452 gothic design in sterling silver with American lever fill and 12-carat gold nib.
• *length 15cm*
• £1,000 • **Jasmin Cameron**

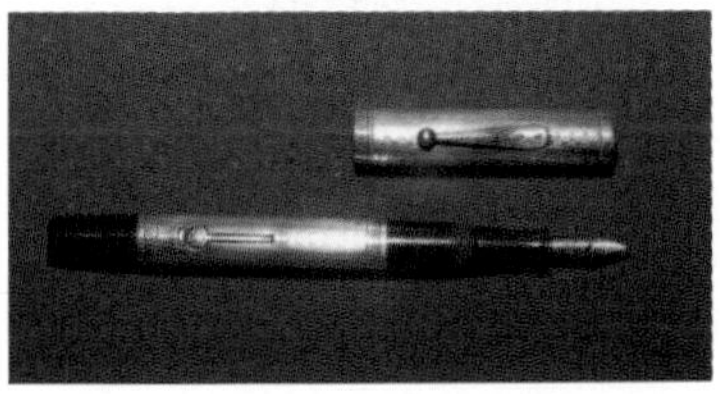

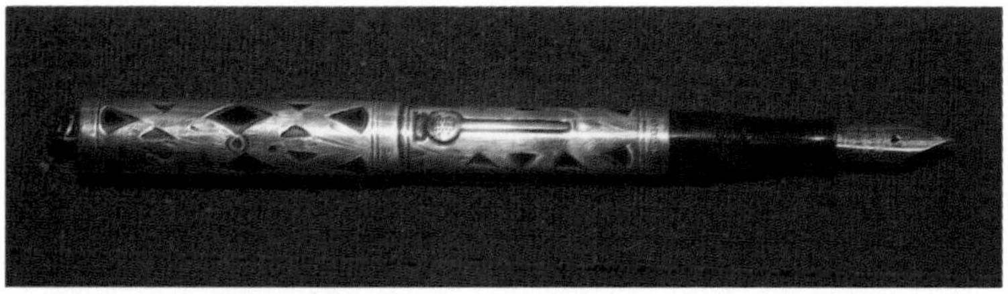

△ Waterman Ideal 452½

- *circa 1925*

Lady's pen with basketweave design in sterling silver and American lever fill.

- *length 14cm*
- £750 • Jasmin Cameron

▽ Conway Stewart Dinkie Pen

- *circa 1935*

Conway Stewart dinkie pen with a blue and amber marbling effect.

- *length 12cm*
- £220 • Jasmin Cameron

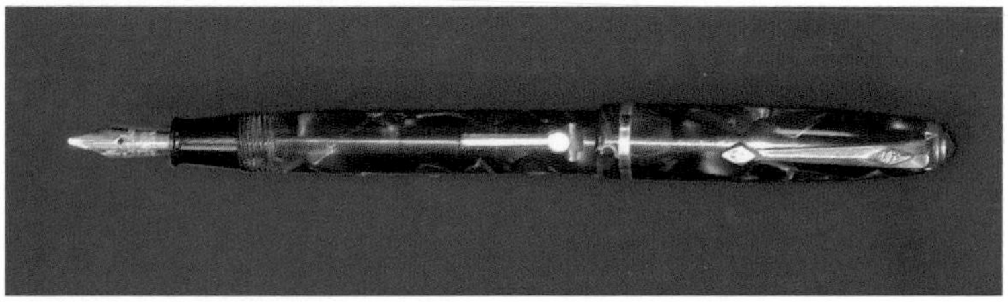

▽ Salter Letter Balance

- *1930*

Small metal letter balance with a brass dial, with the manufacturer's mark Salter and 'Made in England' on the dial.

- *height 22cm*
- £48 • Rookery Farm

▽ Limoges Inkwell

- *1930*

Limoges enamel inkwell with red flowers on a white ground and brass banding.

- *height 5.5cm*
- £115 • Hayman

▽ Silver Ink Pot

- *circa 1937*

Silver ink pot with hinged lid within a glass moulded base, and pen holder. Made in Birmingham.

- *length 14.5cm*
- £295 • Barrett Towning

▽ English Writing Desk Set

- *circa 1940*

20th-century English Phendic desk set with blotter sponge holder, double inkwell, and paper holder.

- £250 • Decodence

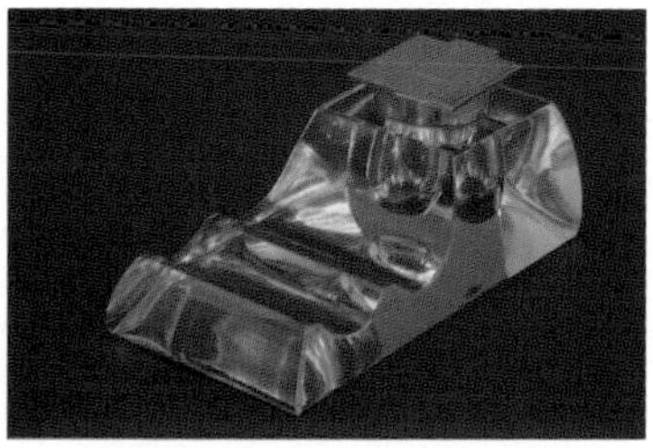

▽ Silver Pencil

- *circa 1930*

Silver-plated propelling pencil of the Art Deco period.

- *length 15cm*
- £15 • Mark Sullivan

△ Parker 51

- *1950*

Aeromatic filling system with teal-blue body, solid gold cap and medium nib.

- *length 16cm*
- £180 • Jasmin Cameron

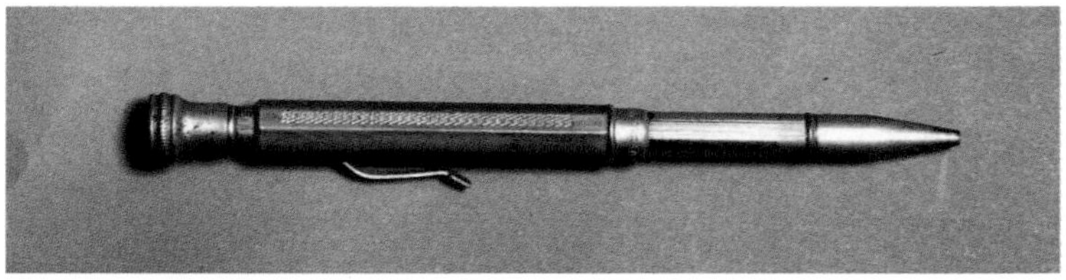

△ Glass Ink Pot

- *circa 1930*

Multi-sided glass amethyst colour American ink pot with sliding glass lid.

- £260 • Jasmin Cameron

▽ Parker Pencil

- *1934–35*

Mottled green Parker pencil.

- *length 11cm*
- £175 • Jasmin Cameron

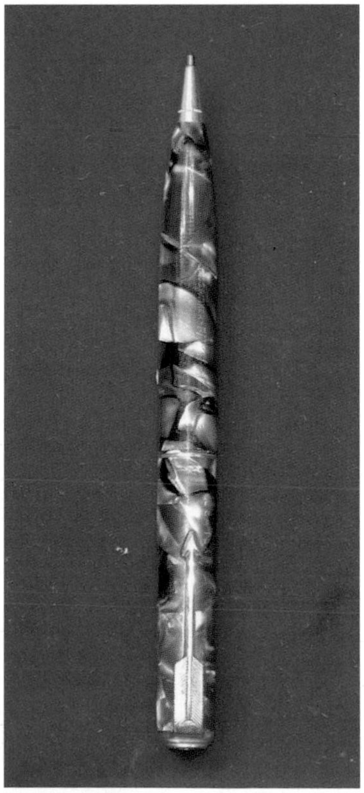

△ Curling Stone Inkwell

- *circa 1950*

Inkwell in the shape of a curling stone with a brass lid and handle.

- *diameter 6cm*
- £45 • Sporting Times

PERIOD REFERENCE

MAIN CHINESE PERIODS

Shang Dynasty	c. 1523 – 1027 BC
Chow Dynasty	1027 – 221 BC
Warring States Period	481 – 221 BC
Ch'in Dynasty	221 – 206 BC
Han Dynasty	206 BC – 220 AD
Three Kingdoms	220 – 280
Six Dynasties	280 – 589
Northern Wei	385 – 535
Eastern Wei	535 – 550
Western Wei	535 – 557
Northern Ch'i	550 – 577
Northern Chow	557 – 581
Liu Sung (South)	420 – 478
Southern Ch'i	479 – 501
Liang	502 – 557
Ch'en	557 – 588
Sui Dynasty	589 – 618
T'ang	618 – 906
Five Dynasties	907 – 959
Sung Dynasties	960 – 1280
Yuan Dynasties	1280 – 1368
Ming Dynasties	1368 – 1643
Ch'ing Dynasties	1644 – 1912

MING PERIOD

Hung Wy	1368 – 1398
Chien Wien	1399 – 1402
Yung Lo	1403 – 1424
Hung Hsi	1425 – 1425
Hsuan Te	1426 – 1435
Cheng T'ung	1436 – 1449
Ching T'ai	1450 – 1457
T'ien Shun	1457 – 1464
Ch'eng Hua	1465 – 1487
Hung-Chih	1488 – 1505
Cheng Te	1506 – 1521
Chia Ching	1522 – 1566
Lung Ch'ing	1567 – 1572
Wan Li	1573 – 1619

KOREAN PERIODS

Lo Lang	106 BC – 313 AD
Paekche	18 BC – 663 AD
Koguryo	37 BC – 668 AD
Silla	57 BC – 668 AD
Great Silla	668 – 936
Koryo	918 – 1392
Yi	1392 – 1910

CH'ING PERIOD

Shung Chih	1644 – 1661
K'ang Hsi	1662 – 1722
Yung Cheng	1723 – 1735
Ch'ieng Lung	1736 – 1795
Chia Ch'ing	1796 – 1820
Tao Kuang	1821 – 1850
Hsien Feng	1851 – 1861
T'ung Chih	1862 – 1873
Kuang Hsu	1874 – 1908
Hsuan T'ung	1909 – 1912

JAPANESE PERIODS

Jomon Period	1000 BC – 200 BC
Yayoi Period	200 BC – 500 AD
Tumulus Period	300 – 700
Asuka Period	552 – 645
Early Nara Period	645 – 710
Nara Period	710 – 794
Early Heian Period	794 – 897
Heian or Fujiwara Period	897 – 1185
Kamakura Period	1185 – 1392
Ashikaga Period	1392 – 1573
Momoyama Period	1573 – 1615
Tokugawa Period	1615 – 1868

FRENCH GENERAL PERIODS

François-Premier	1515 – 1547	Reign of Francis I
Henri-Deux	1547 – 1559 1559 – 1560 1560 – 1574 1574 – 1589	Reign of Henri II Reign of Francis II Reign of Charles IX Reign of Henri III
Henri-Quatre	1589 – 1610	Reign of Henri IV
Louis-Treize	1610 – 1643	Reign of Louis XIII
Louis-Quatorze	1643 – 1715	Reign of Louis XIV
Louis-Quinze	1715 – 1774	Reign of Louis XV
Louis-Seize	1774 – 1793	Reign of Louis XVI
Directoire	1795 – 1799	Rule of the Directorate
Empire	1704 – 1814	Reign of Napoleon
Louis XVIII	1814 – 1824	
Charles X	1824 – 1830	
Louis-Philippe	1830 – 1848	
Second Empire	1852 – 1870	Reign of Napoleon III

ENGLISH GENERAL PERIODS

Tudor	1485 – 1558	Reigns of Henry VII Henry VIII Edward VI Mary
Elizabethan	1558 – 1603	Reign of Elizabeth I
Jacobean	1603 – 1649	Reigns of James I Charles I
Commonwealth	1649 – 1660	Protectorship of Cromwell
Carolean / Late Stuart	1660 – 1689	Reigns of Charles II James II
William and Mary	1689 – 1702	Reign of William and Mary
Queen Anne	1702 – 1727	Reigns of Anne George I
Georgian	1727 – 1820	Reigns of George II George III
Regency	1800 – 1830	Reigns of George III George IV
William IV	1830 – 1837	Reign of William IV
Victorian	1837 – 1901	Reign of Victoria
Edwardian	1901 – 1910	Reign of Edward VII

ENGLISH MONARCHS SINCE 1066

William I	1066 – 1087
William II	1087 – 1100
Henry I	1100 – 1135
Stephen	1135 – 1154
Henry II	1154 – 1189
Richard I	1189 – 1199
John	1199 – 1216
Henry III	1216 – 1272
Edward I	1272 – 1307
Edward II	1307 – 1327
Edward III	1327 – 1377
Richard II	1377 – 1399
Henry IV	1399 – 1413
Henry V	1413 – 1422
Henry VI	1422 – 1461
Edward IV	1461 – 1470
Henry VI	1470 – 1471
Edward IV	1471 – 1483
Edward V	1483 – 1483
Richard III	1484 – 1485
Henry VII	1485 – 1509
Henry VIII	1509 – 1547
Edward VI	1547 – 1553
Mary	1553 – 1558
Elizabeth	1558 – 1603
James I	1603 – 1625
Charles I	1625 – 1649
Commonwealth	1649 – 1660
Charles II	1660 – 1685
James II	1685 – 1688
William and Mary	1688 – 1694
William III	1694 – 1702
Anne	1702 – 1714
George I	1714 – 1727
George II	1727 – 1760
George III	1760 – 1820
George IV	1820 – 1830
William IV	1830 – 1837
Victoria	1837 – 1901
Edward VII	1901 – 1910
George V	1910 – 1936
Edward VIII	1936 – 1936
George VI	1936 – 1952
Elizabeth II	1952 –

GLOSSARY

abadeh Highly-coloured Persian rug.

acacia Dull yellow hardwood with darker markings used for inlay and bandings towards the end of the eighteenth century.

acanthus A leaf motif used in carved and inlaid decoration.

Act of Parliament clock Eighteenth-century English clock, wall-mounted and driven by weights, with a large, unglazed dial and a trunk for weights. They often hung in taverns and public places and were relied on by the populace after the Act of Parliament of 1797, which introduced taxation on timepieces.

air-beaded Glass with air bubbles resembling beads.

air-twist Spiral pattern enclosed in a glass stem with air bubbles.

albarello Waisted ceramic drug jar.

alder Wood used for country-style furniture in the eighteenth century.

ale glass Eighteenth-century glass drinking vessel with long stem and tall, thin bowl.

amboyna West Indian wood used for veneers, marquetry and inlays. Light brown with speckled grain.

anchor escapement Late seventeenth-century English-invented clock movement, named after the anchor shape of the linkage that moves the escape wheel.

andiron Iron support for burning logs.

angle barometer Also known as signpost barometers. Barometers where the movement of mercury is shown almost on the horizontal.

annulated Ringed (of glass).

apostle spoon Spoon with the figure of an apostle as the finial.

applied Attached or added, rather than modelled or carved as part of the body.

apron The decorative panel of wood between the front legs of a chair or cabinet.

arbor The axle on which the wheel of a clock's mechanism is mounted.

arch (clockmaking) The arch above the dial of a post-1700 longcase clock.

argyle Double-skinned metal pouring jugs and tea and coffee pots.

armoire French wardrobe, linen press or large cupboard.

ash Hardwood used for making country furniture and for its white veneer.

astragal Small semi-circular moulding, particularly used as glazing bar in furniture.

automaton clock A clock where the strike is performed by mechanically operated figures.

backboard The unseen back of wall furniture.

backplate The rear plate supporting the movement of a clock, often the repository of engraved information relating to its manufacture.

baff Knot in rug-making.

balance Device counteracting the force of the mainspring in a clock's movement.

balloon-back chair Popular, rounded-backed Victorian dining or salon chair.

baluster (adj.) Having a dominant convex swell at the base, culminating in a smaller, concave one at the neck. (noun) One of a set of upright posts supporting a balustrade.

banjo barometer Wheel barometer dating from circa 1775–1900, with shape resembling a banjo.

barley-sugar twist Spiral-turned legs and rails popular in the seventeenth century. Colloquial.

bat printed Transfer printed (of ceramics).

beech Hardwood used in the manufacture of country furniture and, when stained, as a substitute for mahogany.

bellarmine Stoneware flagon made in Germany from the sixteenth century.

bergère French for an armchair, used in English to describe a chair with caned back and sides.

bevel Decorative, shaved edge of glass, e.g. mirror.

bezel The metal rim of a glass cover or jewel.

birch Hardwood used principally for carcassing; occasionally for low-quality veneer.

bird-cage Support mechanism at the top of the pedestal of some eighteenth-century tilt-top tables.

bird's eye maple Wood of the sugar maple with distinctive figure caused by aborted buds. Used in veneering.

biscuit (bisque) Ceramics fired but unglazed, originating in France in the eighteenth century.

blind fretwork Fretwork carving on a solid background.

block front Front shaped from thick boards allowing for a recessed centre section.

blue-dash Blue dabs around the rim of a delftware plate.

bob The weight at the bottom of a pendulum.

bobbin Turned furniture element, resembling a row of connected spheres.

bocage Foliage, bushes and shrubs supporting, surrounding or standing behind porcelain or pottery figures.

bombé Having an outswelling front.

bone china Clay with bone ash in the formula, almost entirely porcellanous. First produced at the end of the eighteenth century.

bonheur du jour Small, lady's writing desk with a cabinet and drawers above. Originally French, from the mid-eighteenth century.

bottle glass Low quality coloured glass for bottles, jars etc.

boulle An eighteenth-century marquetry style employing brass and tortoiseshell.

boxlock Flintlock gun with the mechanism enclosed in the breech.

boxwood Pale yellow, close-grained hardwood used for carving and turning and for inlay and pattern veneers.

bow front Convex curve on the front of chests of drawers.

bracket clock Domestic clock so called because of the necessity of standing it on a bracket to allow its weights to hang down, the term later applied to domestic clocks of the eighteenth and nineteenth centuries regardless of their motive force.

bracket foot Plain foot carved into the rail or stretcher to form an ornamental bracket.

brandy saucepan Miniature, bulbous or baluster-shaped saucepan with long handle at right angles to the spout.

breakfront Describing a piece of furniture with a central section that projects forward.

breech Rear end of the barrel of a gun.

breech-loading Gun loaded through an opening in the breech.

bright cut Late eighteenth-century silver engraving technique, making the design brilliant in relief.

Bristol glass Eighteenth-century coloured (often blue) glass produced in Bristol.

Britannia metal Form of refined pewter used as a silver substitute in the early nineteenth century.

British plate Silver substitute from the nineteenth century, preceding the introduction of EPNS.

broken arch Arch above the dial of a long-case clock which is less than a semi-circle, indicating an early Georgian date.

broken pediment Pediment with a symmetrical break in the centre, often accommodating an urn or some such motif.

bun foot Flattened spherical foot often found on later seventeenth-century furniture.

bureau Desk with a fall front enclosing a fitted interior, with drawers below.

bureau bookcase Bureau with glazed bookcase above.

burr Veneer used in furniture making, with a decorative pattern caused by some abnormality of growth or knotting in the tree.

cabriole leg S-shaped leg of a piece of furniture that curves out at the foot and in at the top. Introduced in the seventeenth century.

caddy Tea caddy.

caddy spoon Short-handled, large bowled spoon for extracting tea from the caddy.

calendar/date aperture Window in the dial of a clock displaying day, month or date.

canted corner Decoratively angled corner.

canterbury An eighteenth-century container for sheet music.

carcase/carcass The inner frame of a piece of furniture, usually made of inferior wood for veneering.

card case Case for visiting cards, usually silver, nineteenth century.

carriage clock Portable timepiece, invented in nineteenth-century France, with handle above.

cartel clock Eighteenth-century French wall clock with profusely decorated case.

case furniture Furniture intended as a receptacle, e.g. chest of drawers.

caster/castor 1. Sprinkling vessel for e.g. sugar. 2. Pivoted wheel attached to foot.

Castleford ware Shiny white stoneware made in Castleford and elsewhere from circa 1790.

caudle cup Covered cup, often in silver.

cellaret A wine cooler or container, usually eighteenth century.

centrepiece Ornament designed to sit in the centre of a dining table. Often in silver.

chafing dish Serving dish, often in silver, with stand incorporating a spirit lamp to retain heat.

chain fusee The fusee of a clock from which a chain unwinds on to the barrel of the mainspring.

chamfer A flattened angle; a corner that has been bevelled or planed.

chapter ring The ring on a clock dial on which the numbers of the hours are inscribed.

Chesterfield Deep-buttoned, upholstered settee from the nineteenth century.

chest on chest Tallboy having two chests fitting together, the lower with bracket feet, the upper with pediment. From seventeenth and eighteenth centuries.

chest on stand Known as a tallboy or highboy, a chest of drawers on a stand.

cheval mirror Tall mirror supported by two uprights on swivels.

chiffonnier Side cupboard, originally, in the eighteenth century, with solid doors, but latterly with latticed or glazed doors.

chinoiserie Oriental-style decoration on lacquered furniture or artefacts.

chronometer Precision timepiece, often for navigation.

circular movement Clock movement of circular plates.

cistern Chamber containing mercury at the base of the tube of a barometer.

claw-and-ball foot Foot modelled as a ball clutched in a claw, frequently used to terminate a cabriole leg.

clock garniture Mantelpiece ornamentation with a clock as centrepiece.

close helmet Helmet covering the whole head and neck.

coaster Small, circular tray, often in silver, for holding a bottle.

cockbeading Bead moulding applied to the edges of drawers.

cock bracket Bracket supporting a watch mainspring.

coin glass Early eighteenth-century English drinking glass with a coin moulded into the knop of the stem.

commode High quality, highly decorated chest of drawers or cabinet, with applied mounts.

compensated pendulum Pendulum with mercury reservoir, the mercury rising and falling to compensate for the effects on the pendulum of changes of temperature.

composition Putty-like substance for moulding and applying to e.g. mirror frames, for gilding.

console table Often semi-circular table intended to stand against a wall on the pier between two windows (hence also pier table).

cordial glass Glass originating in the seventeenth century, with a small bowl for strong drinks.

corner chair Chair with back splats on two sides and a bowed top rail, designed to fit into a corner.

cornice Horizontal top part of a piece of furniture; a decorative band of metal or wood used to conceal curtain fixtures.

coromandel Wood from India's Coromandel coast, used for banding and inlay.

counter-well The small oval wooden dishes inset into early Georgian card tables for holding chips or cash, hence also guinea-well.

country furniture Functional furniture made outside the principal cities. Also provincial furniture.

countwheel strike Clock mechanism determining the number of strikes per hour.

cow creamer Silver or china cream jug modelled as a cow.

crazing Fine cracks in glaze.

creamware Earthenware glazed in a cream colour giving a porcelain effect, in a widely used technique originally devised by Wedgwood in the 1760s.

credence table Late seventeenth-century oak or walnut table with folding top.

credenza Long Victorian side cabinet with glazed or solid doors.

crenellated Crinkly, wavy.

crested china Ware decorated with heraldic crests; originally by Goss, but subsequently by many Staffordshire and German potteries.

crinoline stretcher Crescent-shaped stretcher supporting the legs of some Windsor chairs.

cross-banding Decorative edging with cross-grained veneer.

cruet Frame for holding condiment containers.

crutch The arm connecting a clock's pendulum to the pallet arbor.

cuirass Breastplate (of armour).

cup and cover Round turning with a distinctly separate top, common on legs until circa 1650.

damascene Inlay of precious metal onto a body of other metal for decorative purposes.

davenport Small English desk, reputedly originally produced by Gillow for a Captain Davenport in 1834.

deadbeat escapement Version of the anchor escapement that eliminates recoil and improves accuracy.

deal Sawn pine wood.

delftware Seventeenth- and eighteenth-century tin-glazed earthenware, often decorated in the style of Chinese blue and white porcelain or after Dutch seventeenth-century painting, after the style pioneered by the Delft pottery.

Delft ware Items of delftware that actually emanate from Delft.

dentil Small, block-shaped moulding found under a furniture cornice.

dialplate Frontplate of a clock.

diamond cut (of glass) Cut in diamond shape.

dinanderie Fifteenth-century brass artefact from the factories of Dinant, Belgium.

dished table top Hollowed-out, solid top, particularly of a pie-crust, tripod table.

distressed Artificially aged.

dovetails Interlocking joints used in drawers.

double-action A gun that may be cocked or self-cocking.

douter Scissor-like implement for extinguishing a candle.

dowel Peg holding together wooden joint.

dram glass Small, short-stemmed glass with rounded bowl.

drop handle Pear-shaped brass furniture handle of the late seventeenth and early eighteenth centuries.

drop-in seat Framed, upholstered seat that sits in the framework of a chair.

drop-leaf table Table with a fixed central section and hinged flaps.

drum table Circular writing table on a central pedestal with frieze drawers.

dry-edge With unglazed edges.

dummy drawer False drawer with handle.

Dutch strike Clock chime which strikes the next hour on the half hour.

ebonise To stain a wood to the dark colour of ebony.

ebony Much imitated exotic black hardwood, used as veneer in Europe from the seventeenth century, generally for very high quality pieces.

écuelle Two-handled French soup bowl with cover and stand, often Sèvres.

electroplate The technique of covering one metal with a thin layer of another.

elm Hardwood used in the manufacture of chair seats, country furniture and coffins.

embossing Relief decoration.

enamel Second, coloured glaze fired over first glaze.

endstone In a clock mechanism, jewel on which an arbor pivots.

English dial Nineteenth-century English wall clock with large painted dial, previously a fixture in railway stations.

Engshalskrüge Large German tin-glaze jug with cylindrical neck.

épergne Centrepiece of one central bowl surrounded by smaller ones.

escritoire Cabinet with a fall-front which forms a writing surface. With a fitted interior.

escutcheon Brass plate surrounding the edges of a keyhole.

étui Small, metal oddments box.

everted Outward turned, flaring (e.g. of a lip).

facet-cut (of glass) Cut criss-cross into straight-edged planes.

faience Tin-glazed earthenware.

fairings Porcelain figures, especially German, made in the nineteenth and twentieth centuries in moulds. Usually comical and carrying descriptive captions.

fall front Flap of a bureau or secretaire that pulls out to provide a writing surface.

famille rose Predominantly pink-coloured Oriental porcelain.

famille verte Predominantly green-coloured Oriental porcelain.

fauteuil Open-sided, upholstered armchair with padded elbows.

feather banding Two bands of veneer laid at opposite diagonals.

field Area of a carpet within its decorated borders.

fielded panel Raised panel with chamfered edge fitting into a framework.

figure Natural pattern created by the grain through the wood.

finial Decorative, turned knob.

flamed veneer Veneer cut at an angle to enhance the figuring.

flatware Plates, knives and forks.

flintlock Gun mechanism whereby the priming in the pan is ignited by a spark created by a flint.

flute glass Glass with tall, slender bowl.

fluting Decorative parallel grooving.

foliate carving Carved flower and leaf motifs.

foliot Primitive form of balance for clock mechanisms.

fretwork Fine pierced decoration.

frieze Long ornamental strip.

frit The flux from which glass is made. An ingredient of soft-paste porcelain.

frizzen The metal which a flint strikes to create a spark in a flintlock mechanism.

fruitwood Generally the wood of apple, cherry and pear trees, used for ebonising and gilding, commonly in picture frames.

fusee The conical, grooved spool from which a line or chain unwinds as it is pulled by the mainspring of a clock movement.

gadroon Carved edge or moulded decoration consisting of a series of grooves, ending in a curved lip, with ridges between them.

Gainsborough chair A deep, upholstered armchair with padded, open arms and carved decoration.

galleried Having a wood or metal border around the top edge.

garniture Set of ornamental pieces of porcelain.

gateleg Leg that pivots to support a drop leaf.

gesso Plaster-like substance applied to carved furniture before gilding or moulded and applied as a substitute for carving.

gilt-tooled decoration Gold leaf impressed into the edges of leather on desk-tops.

gimbal Mounting which keeps a ship's barometer level at all times.

girandole Wall-mounted candle holder with a mirrored back.

gorget Item of armour for protecting the throat.

Goss china Range of porcelain, particularly heraldic, produced in Stoke-on-Trent from 1858.

greave Armour protecting lower leg.

Greek key Ancient key-shaped decoration often repeated in fretwork on furniture.

gridiron pendulum Clock pendulum consisting of rods of a mix of metals positioned in such a way that the dynamics of their behaviour when subjected to heat or cold keep the pendulum swing uniform.

halberd Double-headed axe weapon with projecting spike.

half hunter Watch with an opening front cover with glass to the centre and a chapter ring, giving protection to the glass over the dial.

hallmark The mark by which silver can be identified by standard, place of assay and date.

hard-paste porcelain Porcelain made with kaolin and petuntse in the Chinese fashion, pioneered in Europe at Meissen in the early eighteenth century.

hinoki A Japanese timber of the cypress family.

hunter Watch with a hinged, opening front cover in solid metal.

husk Formalised leaf motif.

ice glass Glass with uneven, rippling surface.

Imari Japanese porcelain made in and around Arita from the early eighteenth century and shipped to Europe from Imari. Blue, red and gold coloured.

improved A pejorative term implying that a piece has been altered in order dishonestly to enhance its value.

inlay The decorative setting of one material into a contrasting one.

intaglio Incised design.

ironstone Stoneware patented by Mason in 1813, in which slag from iron furnaces was mixed with the clay to toughen the ware.

istoriato Of some Italian majolica, meaning 'with a story on it'.

japanned Painted and varnished in imitation of Oriental style lacquer work.

jardinière An ornamental pot or vase for plants.

jasper ware Variety of coloured stoneware developed by the Wedgwood factory.

joined Manufactured with the use of mortice and tenon joints and dowels, but without glue.

kabuto Japanese Samurai helmet.

kingwood Exotic, purplish hardwood used in veneer.

kneehole desk Desk with a recessed cupboard beneath the frieze drawer.

knop Rounded projection or bulge in the stem of a glass.

koro An incesnse-burner.

lacquer Resinous substance which, when coloured, provides a ground for chinoiserie and gilding.

ladder-back Chair with a series of horizontal back rails.

lantern clock Clocks made in England from the sixteenth century, driven entirely by weights and marking only the hours. Similar in appearance to a lantern.

lappit Carved flap at the top of a leg with a pad foot.

latten Archaic term for brass.

lead crystal Particularly clear, brilliant glass including lead in the process.

lead-glazed The earliest glaze for Western pottery, derived from glass making.

lever escapement Modification of the anchor escapement for carriage clocks and, particularly, watches.

lion's paw foot Foot carved as a lion's paw. Commonly eighteenth century and Regency.

lock Firing mechanism of a gun.

lockplate Base holding firing mechanism on a gun barrel.

loo table Large Victorian card or games table.

longcase clock The 'grandfather' clock, housed in a tall wooden case containing the weights and pendulum.

loper Pull-out arm that supports the hinged fall of a bureau.

lowboy Small side table with cabriole legs, from the seventeenth century.

lustre ware Ceramic ware decorated with a metallic coating which changes colour when fired.

mahogany The hardwood most used in the production of furniture in England in the eighteenth and nineteenth centuries. Used as a solid wood until the nineteenth century, when its rarity led to its being used for veneer.

maidate A mythical horned beast with long rays emanating from it.

majolica Originally tin-glazed earthenware produced in Renaissance Italy, subsequently all nineteenth-century wares using the same technique.

mantel clock Clock with feet designed to stand on a mantelpiece.

maple North American hardwood used for its variety of veneers.

marine chronometer Precision clock for use in navigation at sea.

marquetry The use of wooden and other inlays to form decorative patterns.

married Pejorative term applied to a piece of furniture which is made up of more than one piece of the same period.

matchlock Firing mechanism of a gun achieved by lowering a slow match into the priming pan.

mazarine Metal strainer fitting over a dish.

mempo Japanese face mask.

mendak The ring between the blade and sheath of a dagger.

mercury twist Air-twist in glass of a silver colour.

millefiori Multi-coloured or mosaic glass.

moonwork Clock mechanism which computes and displays the phases of the moon.

moquette Heavy imitation velvet used for upholstery.

morion Helmet with upturned front peak.

mortice Slot element of a mortice and tenon joint.

moulding Decorative, shaped band around an object or a panel.

mount Invariably metal mounting fitted to a piece of furniture.

mule chest Coffer with a single row of drawers to the base.

musical clock Clock with a cylinder which strikes bells to play a tune.

Nailsea Late eighteenth-century, boldly coloured, opaque glass from Nailsea, near Bristol.

nashiji 'Pearskin' lacquer, an effect achieved with sprinkled powdered gold.

nest of tables Set of three or four occasional tables which slot into each other when not in use.

oak Hardwood which darkens with age, predominant in English furniture manufacture until the middle of the seventeenth century.

obverse The front side of a coin or medal.

ogee An S-shaped curve.

ogee arch Two S-shaped curves coming together to form an arch.

oignon Onion-shaped French watch of the eighteenth century.

ormolu From French *dorure d'or moulu*: 'gilding with gold paste', gold-coloured alloy of copper, zinc, and sometimes tin, in various proportions but usually containing at least 50% copper. Ormolu is used in mounts (ornaments on borders, edges and as angle guards) for furniture, especially eighteenth-century furniture.

orrery Astronomical clock which shows the position of heavenly bodies. Named after Charles Boyle, fourth Earl of Orrery.

overglaze *See* enamel.

overmantel mirror Mirror designed to hang over a mantelpiece.

ovolo A rounded, convex moulding, making an outward curve across a right angle.

oyster veneer Veneer resembling an open oyster shell, an effect achieved by slanting the cut across the grain of a branch.

pad foot Rounded foot on a circular base, used as termination for cabriole legs.

pair-case A double case for a watch, the inner for protection of the movement, the outer for decoration.

pallet Lever that engages in a clock's escapement wheel in order to arrest it.

papier mâché Moulded and lacquered pulped paper used to make small items of furniture and other artefacts.

parian Typically uncoloured, biscuit-style porcelain developed in the nineteenth century by Copeland and named after Parian white marble.

parquetry Veneered pattern using small pieces of veneer, often from different woods, in a geometrical design.

patera Circular ornament made of wood, metal or composition.

patina The layers of polish, dirt, grease and general handling marks that build up on a wooden piece of furniture over the years and give it its individual signs of age, varying from wood to wood.

pearlware White, shiny earthenware, often print decorated.

pedestal desk A flat desk with a leathered top standing on two banks of drawers.

pediment Architectural, triangular gable crowning a piece of furniture or a classical building.

pegged furniture Early furniture constructed with the use of mortice and tenon joints and pegged together with dowels.

pembroke table Small, two-flapped table standing on four legs or a pedestal.

pepperette Vessel, often in silver, for sprinkling pepper.

petuntse Chinese name for the feldspathic rock, an essential element of porcelain, which produces a glaze.

pewter Alloy of tin, lead and often other metals.

pie-crust Expression used to describe the decorative edge of a dished-top tripod table.

pier glass Tall mirror for hanging on a pier between windows.

pietra dura Composition of semi-precious stones applied to panels of – usually Italian – furniture.

pillar (watchmaking) A rod connecting the dial-plate and backplate of a movement.

pillar rug Chinese rug made to be arranged around a pillar.

pine Softwood used for carcassing furniture.

platform base Flat base supporting a central pedestal and table-top above and standing on three or four scrolled or paw feet.

plinth base Solid base not raised on feet.

pole screen Adjustable fire screen.

pommel Knob at the end of the handle of a dagger.

pontil mark Mark made by the pontil, or blowpipe, on the base of hand-blown glass.

porcellanous Having most of the ingredients or characteristics of porcelain.

porringer Large, two-handled cup with cover.

potboard Bottom shelf of a dresser.

pounce box A sprinkler for pounce, a powder for drying ink.

Prattware Staffordshire earthenware of the late eighteenth and early nineteenth centuries, decorated in distinctive colours on a buff ground.

print decoration Mass-produced decoration. Not hand painting.

provincial furniture *See* country furniture.

punch bowl Large bowl for the retention and dispensation of punch.

quartered top Flat surface covered with four pieces of matching veneer.

quartetto tables Nest of four occasional tables.

quillon Cross-piece of a sword.

rail A horizontal member running between the outer uprights of a piece of furniture.

rating nut Nut under the bob of a clock's pendulum by which the rate of swing may be adjusted.

redware Primitive eighteenth-century American ware made from a clay which turns red when fired.

reeding Parallel strips of convex fluting.

re-entrant corner Shaped indentation at each corner of a table.

register plate Plate on a barometer with inscriptions to be read against the level of mercury.

regulator Precision timepiece of the eighteenth century.

relief Proud of the surface.

repeating work Mechanism by which the pull of a cord or the press of a button operates the striking mechanism of a clock or watch to the last hour.

repoussé An embossed design which has been refined by chasing.

riza A covering for a Russian icon that fitted over all the pictorial field except for the figures.

rosewood Named after its smell when newly cut, rather than its flower or colour, a dark-brown hardwood with an attractive stripe or ripple, used for veneering.

rule joint Hinge on furniture which fits so well that, when open, no join can be detected between two hinged parts.

runners Strips of wood, fitted to furniture, on which drawers slide.

sabre leg Chair leg in the shape of a sabre, typical of the Regency period.

saltglaze Stoneware in which salt is added to the recipe creating a porcellanous, glassy surface. Dates back to the early eighteenth century.

salver A large metal dish or tray for transporting smaller dishes.

satinwood A light golden-coloured, close-grained hardwood used for veneer, panelling and turning from the mid-eighteenth century onwards.

scagiola Composite material resembling marble.

scalloped Having a series of circular edges in the shape of a scallop shell.

scalloped leaf Serpentine flap on some pembroke tables.

sconce 1. Cup-shaped candle holder. 2. Metal plate fixed to the wall, supporting candle holder or light.

scratch blue Eighteenth-century saltglaze decoration where the body is incised and the incisions painted blue.

scroll, scrolling Carving or moulding of a curled design.

seat rail Horizontal framework below the chair seat uniting the legs.

secretaire Writing desk with false drawer front that lets down to reveal a writing surface and fitted interior.

secretaire bookcase Secretaire with bookcase fitted above.

serpent The arm holding the match or flint by which the priming of a gun was ignited.

serpentine Of undulating shape.

settee Upholstered settle.

settle Hard bench seat with back. The earliest form of seating for two or more people.

Sheffield plate Rolled sheet silver placed either side of a layer of copper and fused. Recognised by the Sheffield assay office in 1784, but made elsewhere, notably Birmingham, as well.

shikoro In Japanese armour, a lamellar neck-guard.

shoe piece Projection on the back rail of a chair into which the splat fits.

side chair Chair without arms designed to stand against the wall.

side table Any table designed to stand against the wall.

skeleton clock Clock with the workings exposed.

slipware Earthenware to which mixed clay and water has been added as decoration.

sofa Well-upholstered chair providing seating for two or more people.

sofa table Rectangular table with hinged flaps designed to stand behind a sofa.

soft-paste porcelain Porcelain using frit or soapstone instead of the petuntse of hard-paste porcelain. English, from the eighteenth century.

spade foot Square, tapered foot.

spandrel Pierced, decorative corner bracket found at the tops of legs.

sparrow-beak jug Jug with a triangular spout.

spill vase Container for lighting-tapers.

spindle Thoroughly turned piece of wood. The upright bars of a spindle-back chair.

splat The central upright of a chair back.

sprig Applied or relief ornamentation of any kind on a ceramic artefact.

squab Detachable cushion or upholstered seat of a chair or bench.

standish Inkstand, often in silver.

stick barometer Barometer with a straight, vertical register plate running alongside the mercury tube.

stiles Term for the vertical parts of the framework of a piece of furniture.

stoneware Earthenware that is not porous after firing.

stretcher Rail joining the legs of a table or chair.

strike/silent ring Dial to disengage or re-engage the striking of a clock.

stringing Fine inlaid lines around a piece of furniture.

stirrup cup Cup used for alcoholic refreshment prior to hunting, usually shaped in the head of a fox or, less usually, a hound.

stuff-over seat Chair that is upholstered over the seat rail.

subsidiary dial Small dial, usually showing seconds, within the main dial of a clock or watch. Hence, subsidiary seconds.

sugi A Japanese timber of the cedar family.

swagged With applied strips formed in a mould (of metal).

swan-neck pediment Pediment with two broken curves.

swan-neck handle Curved handle typical of the eighteenth century.

sycamore Hardwood of the maple family, light yellow in colour, used for veneering.

tachi The original sword of the samurai warrior. The first sword to feature a long curved blade.

tang The end of the blade of a sword, covered by the hilt.

tankard Large beer-mug with a hinged lid and thumb-piece.

tazza Italian plate, cup, basin or wide-bowled glass.

teapoy Small piece of furniture designed for holding tea leaves. Usually Anglo-Indian.

tenons The tongues in mortice and tenon joints.

thumb moulding Decorative concave moulding.

thumb-piece Projection attached to a hinged lid which will open the lid when pressure is applied by the thumb.

tine Prong of a fork.

tin-glazed Lead-glazed earthenware to which tin is added, e.g. majolica.

toilet mirror Small dressing mirror with a box base and drawers.

touch mark Individual mark of the maker of a piece of early English pewter.

transfer Ceramic print decoration using colours held in oil.

trefid spoon A seventeenth-century spoon with the handle terminating in the shape of a bud, usually cleft or grooved into two lobes.

trefoil Having three lobes.

trembleuse Cup-stand with feet.

tripod table Small, round-topped table on three-legged base.

tulipwood Pinkish, naturally patterned hardwood used in veneer.

turnery Any wood turned on a lathe.

tureen Large bowl in porcelain or metal, usually with a lid and two handles.

turret clock Clock of any size driven by a weight suspended by a rope wrapped round a drum.

underglaze Colour or design painted below the glaze of a ceramic artefact.

uniface Medal or coin with modelling on one side only.

urn table Eighteenth-century table designed to hold an urn.

veneer A thin sheet of wood laid across a cheaper carcase or used as inlay decoration.

verge escapement A mechanism for regulating a clock movement before the anchor escapement.

Vesta case Match box for Vesta matches, often in silver, from circa 1850.

vinaigrette Small, eighteenth-century box, often silver, to hold a sponge soaked in vinegar to ward off germs and the unpleasant odours of the day.

wainscot chair Joined chair with open arms and a panelled back.

walnut The hardwood used in England for the manufacture of furniture from the Restoration, originally in solid form but mostly as veneer, particularly burr walnut, after the beginning of the eighteenth century.

well Interior of a plate or bowl.

Wemyss ware Late nineteenth-century lead-glazed earthenware originally from Fife, Scotland.

whatnot Mobile stand with open shelves.

wheel-back chair Originally late eighteenth-century chair with circular back with radiating spokes.

windsor chair Wooden chair with spindle back.

yew Tough, close-grained hardwood used for turning, particularly in chair legs, and in veneer.

DIRECTORY OF DEALERS

Aaron Gallery
(ref: Aaron)
34 Bruton Street,
London W1X 7DD
Tel: 020 7499 9434
Fax: 020 7499 0072
www.AaronGallery.com
Islamic and ancient art; New Eastern, Greek, Roman and Egyptian antiquities.

Abacus Antiques
Grays Antiques Market,
58 Davies Street,
London W1Y 2LP
Tel: 020 7629 9681
Antiques.

Abbey Green Antiques
(ref: Abbey Green)
Mariaplatts 45,
Utrecht 3511 LL
The Netherlands
Tel: 030 232 8065

Emmy Abé
Stand 33, Bond Street Antiques Centre,
124 New Bond Street,
London W1X 9AE
Tel: 020 7629 1826
Fax: 020 7491 9400
Exclusively selected antique and modern jewellery.

Aberg Antiques
(ref: Aberg)
42 The Little Boltons,
London SW10 9LN
Tel: 020 7370 7253
Fax: 020 7370 7253
Furniture.

Arthur Ackermann & Peter Johnson Ltd
27 Lowndes Street,
London SW1X 9HY
Tel: 020 7235 6464
Fax: 020 7823 1057
Paintings, drawings and watercolours.

Norman Adams Ltd
(ref: Norman Adams)
8–10 Hans Road,
London SW3 1RX
Tel: 020 7589 5266
Fax: 020 7589 1968
www.normanadams.com
18th-century fine English furniture, works of art, mirrors, paintings and chandeliers.

A.D. Antiques
The Swan at Tetsworth,
High Street,
Tetsworth, Thame,
Oxfordshire OX9 7AB
Tel: 07939 508171
www.adantiques.com
Decorative arts.

A.D.C. Heritage Ltd
95A Charlwood Street,
London SW1V 4PB
Tel: 020 7976 5271
Fax: 020 7976 5898
Silver and old Sheffield plate; valuations.

Aesthetics
Stand V2, Antiquarius,
131–141 Kings Road,
London SW3 4PW
Tel: 020 7352 0395
Fax: 020 7376 4057
Silver; ceramics and decorative art; particularly the Aesthetic and Arts and Crafts movements; antiquarian books.

After Noah
121 Upper Street,
London N1 8ED
Tel: 020 7359 4281
Fax: 020 7359 4281
www.afternoah.com
Antique furniture, linen and postcards.

After Noah (Kings Road)
(ref: After Noah (KR))
261 Kings Road,
London SW3 5EL
Tel: 020 7351 2610
Fax: 020 7351 2610
www.afternoah.com
Antique furniture, linen and postcards.

W. Agnew & Company Ltd
58 Englefield Road,
London N1 4HA
Tel: 020 7254 7429
Fax: 020 7254 7429
Mob: 0973 188272
Sculpture; works of art; majolica and pottery.

Agnew's
43 Old Bond Street,
London W1X 4BA
Tel: 020 7629 6176
Fax: 020 7629 4359
Old Master paintings and drawings; English paintings and watercolours; prints, sculpture and works of art; valuations.

Adrian Alan
66/67 South Audley Street,
London W1Y 5FE
Tel: 020 7495 2324
Fax: 020 7495 0204
and
219 Kensington Church St,
London W8 7LX
Tel: 020 7727 4783
Fax: 020 7727 7353
18th- and 19th-century continental furniture; clocks and barometers; European ceramics; decorations.

Albany Antiques
(ref: Albany)
8–10 London Road,
Hindhead,
Surrey GU26 6AF
Tel: 01428 605 528
Fax: 01428 605 528
Georgian furniture, 18th-century brass, Victorian antiques, porcelain and statuary.

Alfie's Antique Market
13–25 Church Street,
London NW8 8DT
Tel: 020 7723 6066
www.ealfies.com
Art Deco, silver, decorative, furniture, paintings, jewellery, ceramics and more.

AM-PM
V35 Antiquarias Antiques Market,
135 Kings Road,
London SW3
Tel: 020 7351 5654
Antique and modern watches.

Fred Anderson Antiques
(ref: Fred Anderson)
5/6 High Street,
Welshpool,
Powys SY2 1JF
Tel: 01938 553340
Mob: 07773 795931
Fine antique furniture.

Philip Andrade
White Oxen Manor,
Rattery, South Brent,
Devon TQ10 9JX
Tel: 01364 72454
Fax: 01364 73061
17th-,18th- and early 19th-century furniture, porcelain and pottery, interesting objects.

Paul Andrews Antiques
(ref: Paul Andrews)
The Furniture Court,
553 Kings Road,
London SW10 0TZ
Tel: 020 7352 4584
Fax: 020 7351 7815
www.paulandrewsantiques.co.uk
Eclectic furniture, sculpture, tapestries, paintings and works of art.

Angel Antiques
Church Street, Petworth,
West Sussex GU28 0AD
Tel: 01798 343 306
Fax: 01798 342 665
Oak, country furniture.

Anno Domini Antiques
66 Pimlico Road,
London SW1W 8LS
Tel: 020 7730 5496
or 020 7352 3084 when closed
17th-, 18th- and early 19th-century furniture.

Antique and Interiors Group Ltd, The
(ref: A.I.G.)
The Old Cinema,
160 Chiswick High Road,
London W4 1PR
Tel: 020 8742 8080
Fax: 020 8878 0184
Antiques in general.

Antiques Pavilion
175 Bermondsey Street,
London SE1 3LW
Tel: 020 7394 7856
Furniture from the Georgian period to the 1930s; also restorations.

Antique Warehouse
9–14 Dentford Broadway,
London SE8 4PA
Tel: 020 8691 3062
Fax: 020 8691 3062
www.antiquewarehouse.co.uk
Decorative antiques.

Arca
R & E Innocenti,
Stand 351, Grays Antique Centre,
Davies Street,
London W1 2LP
Tel: 020 7692 729
Innocenti@arcaantiques.freeserve co.uk
Sewing and smoking items.

Architectural Emporium, The
55 St. John's Road,
Tunbridge Wells,
Kent TN4 9TP
Tel: 01892 540368
Antique fireplaces, period lighting and garden statuary furniture.

Armoury of St James, The (ref: The Armoury)
17 Piccadilly Arcade,
London SW1Y 6NH
Tel: 020 7493 5083
Fax: 020 7499 4422
www.armoury.co.uk/home
Royal memorabilia and model soldiers.

Armstrong
10 & 11 Montpellier Parade,
Harrogate,
North Yorkshire HG1 2TJ
Tel: 01423 506843
www.harrogateantiques.com
18th- and early 19th-century English furniture and works of art; valuations.

Sean Arnold Sporting Antiques (ref: Sean Arnold)
1 Pembridge Villas,
London W2 4XE
Tel: 020 7221 2267
Fax: 020 7221 5464
Sporting antiques.

Art Nouveau Originals c.1900
11 Camden Passage,
London N1
Tel: 020 7359 4127
Mob: 0374 718096
anoc1900@compuserve.com
Eclectic mix from Art Nouveau period.

Victor Arwas Gallery (ref: Arwas)
3 Clifford Street,
London W1X 1RA
Tel: 020 7734 3944
Fax: 020 7437 1859
www.victorarwas.com
Art Nouveau and Art Deco, glass, ceramics, bronzes, sculpture, furniture, jewellery, silver, pewter, books and posters, from 1880–1940. Paintings, watercolours and drawings, 1880 to date. Original graphics, lithographs, etchings and woodcuts from 1890 to date.

Ashcombe House
Ashcombe Coach House,
Brighton Road, Lewes,
East Sussex BN7 3JR
Tel: 01273 474794
Fax: 01273 705959
18th and 19th-century furniture and decorative objects.

Ash Rare Books (ref: Ash Books)
153 Fenchurch Street,
London EC3M 6BB
Tel: 020 7626 2665
Fax: 020 7626 2665
www.ashrare.com
Books, maps and prints

Garry Atkins
107 Kensington Church Street,
London W8 7LN
Tel: 020 7727 8737
Fax: 020 7792 9010
www.englishpottery.com
English and continental pottery from the 18th century and earlier.

Atlantic Bay Gallery
5 Sedley Place,
London W1R 1HH
Tel: 020 7355 3301
Fax: 020 7355 3760
Antique Oriental and European carpets and textiles.

Aurum
Grays Antiques Market,
58 Davies Street,
London W1K 5LP
Tel: 020 7409 0215
www.aurum.uk.com
Antique and period jewellery, and Shelly china.

Axia Art Consultants Ltd (ref: Axia)
21 Ledbury Road,
London W11 2AQ
Tel: 020 7727 9724
Fax: 020 7229 1272
Islamic and Byzantine works of art, textiles, metalwork, woodwork, ceramics and icons.

Dr Colin B. Baddiel
B24 Grays Antiques Market,
Davies Mews,
London W1
Tel: 020 7408 1239
Fax: 020 74939344
Die-cast and tin toys.

Baggott Church Street Ltd
Church Street,
Stow-on-the-Wold,
Gloucestershire GL54 1BB
Tel: 01451 830370
Fax: 01451 832174
17th- to 19th-century English furniture; portrait paintings; metalwork; treen.

David Baker
Grays Mews Antique Market,
1–7 Davies Mews,
London W1Y 2LP
Tel: 020 8346 1387
Fax: 020 8346 1387
Oriental art.

Gregg Baker Oriental Art (ref: Gregg Baker)
132 Kensington Church Street,
London W8 4BH
Tel: 020 7221 3533
Fax: 020 7221 4410
www.greggbaker.com
Japanese and Chinese works of art.

B. & T. Antiques
79–81 Ledbury Road,
London W11 2AG
Tel: 020 7229 7001
Fax: 020 7229 2033
18th-century Art Deco English and continental furniture, and objets d'art.

Christopher Bangs
PO Box 6077,
London SW6 7XS
Tel: 020 7381 3532
Fax: 020 7381 2192
Mob: 0836 333 532
Works of art; domestic metalwork and metalware; valuations.

Eddy Bardawil Antiques
106 Kensington Church St,
London W8 4BH
Tel: 020 7221 3967
Fax: 020 7221 5124
18th- and early 19th-century English furniture; glass pictures; metalwork; paintings, drawings and prints.

Barham Antiques
83 Portobello Road,
London W11 2QB
Tel: 020 7727 3845
Fax: 020 7727 3845
Victorian walnut and inlaid continental furniture, writing boxes, tea caddies, inkwells and inkstands, glass épergnes, silver plate, clocks and paintings.

R.A. Barnes Antiques (ref: R.A. Barnes)
26 Lower Richmond Road,
London SW15 1JP
Tel: 020 8789 3371
Fax: 020 8780 3195
Continental glass, English and continental porcelain, Art Nouveau, small furniture, paintings, English metalware, 18th and 19th-century brass, Belleek and Wedgwood.

Barnet Antiques
79 Kensington Church St,
London W8 4BG
Tel: 020 7376 2817
18th- and early 19th-century English furniture.

Les Barrett & Ian Towning (ref: Barrett Towning)
Bourbon-Hanby Antiques Centre,
151 Sydney Street,
London SW3 6NT
Tel: 020 7352 2106
Fax: 020 7565 0003
www.antiques-u.co.uk/bourbon-hanby
English ceramics, silver, writing equipment and antique jewellery.

Nigel Bartlett
67 St Thomas Street,
London SE1 3QX
Tel: 020 7378 7895
Fax: 020 7378 0388
Architectural antiques, mainly English chimneypieces.

Baskeville Antiques
Saddlers House,
Saddlers Row, Petworth,
West Sussex GU28 0AN
Tel: 01798 342067
Fax: 01798 343956
Antique clocks and barometers.

H.C. Baxter & Sons
40 Drewstead Road,
London SW16 1AB
Tel: 020 8769 5869/5969
Fax: 020 8769 0898
18th-century furniture; valuations.

Don Bayney
Grays Mews Antiques Market,
1–7 Davies Mews,
London W1Y 2LP
Tel: 020 7629 3644
Fax: 020 8578 4701
Japanese works of art.

Bazaart 51 Antiques (ref: Bazaart)
51 Ledbury Road,
London W11 2AA
Tel: 020 7615 3472
Fax: 020 7615 472
Italian ceramics and Venetian glass from 1500–1900.

J. & A. Beare Ltd
7 Broadwick Street,
London W1V 1FJ
Tel: 020 7437 1449
Fax: 020 7439 4520
Musical instruments of the violin family; valuations.

Beauty and the Beasts (ref: Beauty)
Antiquarius Antique Centre Q9–10,
141 Kings Road,
London SW3 4PW
Tel: 020 7351 5149
Antique handbags.

Frederick Beck Ltd
(ref: F. Beck)
22–26 Camden Passage,
Islington, London N1 8ED
Tel: 020 7226 3403
Fax: 020 7288 1305
General antiques.

Linda Bee
Grays in the Mews Antiques Market,
1–7 Davies Mews,
London W1Y 1AR
Tel: 020 7629 5921
Fax: 020 7629 5921
Vintage costume jewellery and fashion accessories.

Jan Van Beers
34 Davies Street,
London W1Y 1LG
Tel: 020 7408 0434
Fax: 020 7355 1397
Oriental ceramics and works of art; porcelain, pottery and enamels; valuations.

Bellum Antiques
(ref: Bellum)
Bourbon-Hanby Antiques Centre,
151 Sydney Street,
London SW3 6NT
Tel: 020 7352 2106
Fax: 020 7565 0003
www.antiques-uk.co.uk/bourbon-hanby
English ceramics.

Julia Bennet (Antiques)
Flemings Hill Farm,
Great Easton, Dunmow,
Essex CM6 2ER
Tel: 01279 850279
18th- and early 19th-century furniture.

Bentleys
204 Walton Street,
London SW3 2JL
Tel: 020 7584 7770
Fax: 020 7584 8182
lf@bentleyslondon.com
www.bentleyslondon.com
Antique luggage and gentlemen's accessories.

Bent Ply
Unit 58 downstairs at Alfie's,
13 Church St,
London NW8
Tel: 020 8346 1387
Fax: 020 8346 1387
Mob: 07711 940931
bruna@bentply.com
20th-century avant garde furniture and design, mainly '30s and '50s.

Yasha Beresiner
Gallery at 114 Islington,
High Street (inside Camden Passage),
London N1 8EG
Tel: 020 7354 2599
Fax: 020 8346 9539
Mob: 07468 292 066
www.intercol.co.uk
Scripophily and paper money.

Berwald Oriental Art
101 Kensington Church St,
London W8 7LN
Tel: 020 7229 0800
Fax: 020 7229 1101
www.berwald-oriental.com
Chinese pottery, porcelain; works of art; valuations.

Beverley
30 Church Street,
Marylebone,
London NW8 8EP
Tel: 020 7262 1576
Fax: 020 7262 1576
English ceramics, glass, metal, wood, pottery, collectables and decorative items from 1850–1950.

Andrew Bewick Antiques
(ref: Andrew Bewick)
287 Lillie Road,
London SW6 7LL
Tel: 020 7385 9025
Fax: 020 7385 9025
Decorative antiques.

Big Baby &
Little Baby Antiques
(ref: Big Baby Little Baby)
Grays Antiques Market,
Davies Mews,
London W1
Tel: 020 8367 2441
Fax: 020 8366 5811
Dolls, teddies, prams and related collectables.

Bike Park
63 New Kings Road,
London SW3
Tel: 020 7565 0777
Bikes, rentals, repairs and clothing.

Bizarre
24 Church Street,
London NW8 8EP
Tel: 020 7724 1305
Fax: 020 7724 1316
www.antiques-uk/bazarre
Art Deco, continental furniture, wrought iron, glass, and ceramics.

Laurence Black Ltd
60 Thistle Street,
Edinburgh EH2 1EN
Tel: 0131 220 3387
Scottish furniture; pottery; glass; treen; paintings.

Oonagh Black Antiques
(ref: Oonagh Black)
Lower Farm House,
Coln Rogers,
Gloucestershire GL54 3LA
Tel: 01285 720717
Fax: 01285 720910
French and English furniture and French science and textiles.

David Black Oriental Carpets
(ref: David Black)
96 Portland Road,
London W11 4LN
Tel: 020 7727 2566
Fax: 020 7229 4599
Antique carpets and rugs.

H. Blairman & Sons Ltd
119 Mount Street,
London W1Y 5HB
Tel: 020 7493 0444
Fax: 020 7495 0766
Furniture; later 19th- and early 20th-century western applied arts; glass pictures.

N. Bloom & Son Ltd
(ref: N. Bloom)
Antique Jewellery,
124 Bond Street Antique Centre,
124 New Bond Street,
London WI8 IDX
Tel: 020 7629 5060
Fax: 020 7493 2528
nbloom@nbloom.com
www.nbloom.com
Antique jewellery.

A. & B. Bloomstein Ltd
Bond Street Galleries,
111/112 New Bond Street,
London W1Y 0BQ
Tel: 020 7493 6180
Fax: 020 7495 3493
Silver and old Sheffield plate.

Bluthners Pianos Centre
(ref: Bluthners)
8 Berkeley Square,
London W1 5HF
Tel: 020 7753 0533
Fax: 020 7753 0535
whelpdle@globalnet.co.uk
Highly decorated pianos.

John Bly
27 Bury Street,
London SW1Y 6AL
Tel: 020 7930 1292
Fax: 020 7839 4775
www.johnbly.com
18th and 19th-century English furniture, works of art, paintings, silver, glass, porcelain and tapestries.

Bobinet Ltd
PO Box 2730,
London NW8 9PL
Tel: 020 7266 0783
Fax: 020 7289 5119
Clocks and watches; scientific instruments; valuations.

Paolo Bonino
Stand S001, Alfie's Antique Market,
13–25 Church Street,
London NW8 8DT
Tel: 020 7723 6066
European 20th-century glass and ceramics.

Book and Comic Exchange
(ref: Book & Comic)
14 Pembridge Road,
London W11 3HL
Tel: 020 7229 8420
www.buy-sell-trade.co.uk
Modern first editions, cult books and comics.

Malcolm Bord
Gold Coin Exchange
(ref: Malcolm Bord)
16 Charing Cross Road,
London WC2 0HR
Tel: 020 7836 0631, 020 7240 0479 and 020 7240 1920
Dealing in all types of coin, medal and bank note.

Julia Boston
2 Michael Road,
London SW6 2AD
Tel: 020 7610 6783
Fax: 020 7610 6784
www.juliaboston.co.uk
Tapestry cartoons, engravings and 18th- and 19th-century decorative antiques.

M.J. Bowdery
12 London Road, Hindhead,
Surrey, GU26 6AF
Tel: 01428 606376
18th and 19th-century furniture.

Robert Bowman
PO Box 13393,
London SW3 4RP
Tel: 020 7730 8057
Fax: 020 7259 9195
www.icollector.com
19th- and early 20th-century sculpture in bronze and marble.

Patrick Boyd-Carpenter
(ref: P. Boyd-Carpenter)
Unit 331–332, Grays Antiques Market,
58 Davies Street,
London W1Y 2LP
Tel: 020 7491 7623
Fax: 020 7491 7623
Wide range of antiques, 16th and 18th-century sculpture, paintings and prints.

Elizabeth Bradwin
75 Portobello Road,
London W11 2QB
Tel: 020 7221 1121
Fax: 020 8947 2629
www.elizabethbradwin.com
Animal subjects.

Lesley Bragge
Fairfield House,
High Street,
Petworth,
West Sussex
Tel: 01798 342324
Wine-related items.

Brand Inglis
4th Floor, 5 Vigo Street,
London W1X 1AH
Tel: 020 7439 6604
Fax: 020 7439 6605
Silver.

Augustus Brandt
Middle Street, Petworth,
West Sussex GU28 OBE
Tel: 01798 344722
Fax: 01798 344772
brandt@easynet.co.uk
www.augustus-brandt-antiques.co.uk
Scandinavian, French, Italian and English 18th-century furniture, mirrors and lighting and unusual decorative furnishing and objets d'art.

Brandt Oriental Art
(ref: Brandt)
First Floor, 29 New Bond Street,
London W1Y 9HD
Tel: 020 7499 8835
Fax: 020 7409 1882
Chinese and Japanese works of art.

Arthur Brett & Sons Ltd
42 St Giles Street,
Norwich,
Norfolk NR2 1LW
Tel: 01603 628171
Fax: 01603 630245
Furniture; European sculpture and works of art; metalwork.

Simon Brett
Creswyke House,
High Street,
Moreton-in-Marsh,
Gloucestershire GL56 0LH
Tel: 01608 650751
Fax: 01608 651791
Fishing-related items; portrait miniatures.

Bridge Bikes
137 Putney Bridge,
London SW15 2PA
Tel: 020 8870 3934
Bikes.

Christine Bridge Antiques
78 Castelnau,
London SW13 9EX
Tel: 020 8741 5501
Fax: 020 8755 0172
Open by appointment only. Fine 18th-century collector's glass and 19th-century coloured glass.

F.E.A. Briggs Ltd
(ref: Briggs)
5 Plaza Parade,
Winchester Road,
Romsey, Hampshire SO51 8JA
Tel: 01794 510061
Victorian and Edwardian furniture and textiles.

Lynda Brine Antiques
(ref: Lynda Brine)
The Assembly Antiques Centre,
Saville Row,
Bath BAI 2QP
Tel: 01225 448488
Fax: 01225 429661
lyndabrine@yahoo.co.uk
www.scentbottlesandsmalls.co.uk
Scent bottles and bags.

Aubrey Brocklehurst
124 Cromwell Road,
London SW7 4ET
Tel: 020 7373 0319
Fax: 020 73737612
English clocks and barometers.

Gerald Brodie
Great Grooms Antique Centre,
Hungerford,
Berks RG 17 OEP
Fine furniture from the 18th century.

David Brower Antiques
(ref: David Brower)
113 Kensington Church Street,
London W8 7LN
Tel: 020 7221 4155
Fax: 020 7721 6211
www.davidbrower-antique.com
Porcelain, European bronzes, and Japanese works of art.

Brown
First Floor, 533 Kings Road,
London SW10 0TZ
Tel: 020 7352 2046
Furniture.

I. and J. L. Brown Ltd
(ref: I. & J. L. Brown)
632–636 Kings Road,
London SW6 2DU
Tel: 020 7736 4141
Fax: 020 7736 9164
www.brownantiques.com
English country and French provincial antique and reproduction furniture.

Brown's Antique Furniture
(ref: Brown's)
First Floor, The Furniture Cave,
533 Kings Road,
London SW10 0TZ
Tel: 020 7352 2046
Fax: 020 7352 6354
www.thecave.co.uk
Library and dining, and decorative objects from the early 18th century.

S. Brunswick
Alfie's Antiques Market,
13–25 Church Street,
London NW8 8DT
Tel: 020 7724 9097
Fax: 020 8902 5656
Functional and decorative furnishings for house, garden and conservatory.

Peter Bunting Antiques
(ref: Peter Bunting)
Harthill Hall,
Alport, Bakewell,
Derbyshire DE45 1LH
Tel: 01629 636203
Fax: 01629 636190
Early oak and country furniture, portraits and tapestries.

W.G.T. Burne
(Antique Glass) Ltd
PO Box 9465,
London SW20 9ZD
Fax: 0208 543 6319
Mob: 0374 725834
English and Irish glass; chandeliers; valuations.

Burns & Graham
27 St Thomas Street,
Winchester,
Hampshire SO23 9HJ
Tel: 01962 853779
Furniture up to 1850 and related objects.

Butchoff Antiques
(ref: Butchoff)
220 Westbourne Grove,
London W11 2RH
Tel: 020 7221 8174
Fax: 020 7792 8923
English and continental furniture, decorative items, porcelain and mirrors.

Butchoff Interiors
229 Westbourne Grove,
London W11 2SE
Tel: 020 7221 8163
Fax: 020 7792 8923
One-off items, textiles, collectables, dining tables, chairs, consoles and accessories.

Vincenzo Caffarella
Alfie's Antique Market,
13–25 Church Street,
London NW8 8DT
Tel: 020 7723 1513
Fax: 020 8731 8615
www.vinca.co.uk
20th-century decorative arts and antiques.

Cameo Gallery
151 Sydney Street,
London SW3 6NT
Tel: 020 7352 0909
Fax: 020 735 20066
Art Nouveau to Art Deco.

Jasmin Cameron
Antiquarias Antiques Market,
135 Kings Road,
London SW3 4PW
Tel: 020 7351 4154
Fax: 020 7351 4154
Drinking glasses and decanters 1750–1910, vintage fountain pens and writing materials.

Malcolm Cameron
The Antique Galleries,
Watling Street,
Paulerspury, nr. Towcester,
Northamptonshire NN12 6LQ
Tel: 01327 811238
17th-, 18th- and early 19th-century English furniture and barometers.

Gerard Campbell
Maple House, Market Place,
Lechlade-on-Thames,
Gloucestershire GL7 3AB
Tel: 01367 252267
Clocks; speciality: early Viennese Biedermeier-period regulators.

Canonbury Antiques Ltd
(ref: Canonbury)
174 Westbourne Grove,
London W11 2RW
Tel: 020 7229 2786
Fax: 020 7229 5840
www.canonbury-antiques.co.uk
18th and 19th-century furniture, reproduction furniture and accessories.

Patric Capon
350 Upper Street,
Islington, London N1 0PD
Tel: 020 7354 0487
or 020 8467 5722 anytime
Fax: 020 8295 1475
Clocks, marine chronometers, barometers; valuations.

Carlton Hobbs Ltd
46a Pimlico Road,
London SW1W 8LP
Tel: 020 7730 3640 / 3517
Fax: 020 7730 6080
18th-century and early 19th-century English and continental furniture and works of art.

John Carlton-Smith
17 Ryder Street,
London SW1Y 6PY
Tel: 020 7930 6622
Fax: 020 7930 9719
Clocks and barometers; valuations.

Vivienne Carroll
Stand N1, Antiquarius
135–141 Kings Road,
London SW3 4PW
Tel: 020 7352 8882
Fax: 020 7352 8734
Silver, jewellery, porcelain and ivory.

C.A.R.S. of Brighton
(ref: C.A.R.S.)
4–4a Chapel Terrace Mews,
Kemp Town,
Brighton BN2 1HU
Tel: 01273 622 722
Fax: 01273 601 960
www.carsofbrighton.co.uk
Classic automobilia and regalia specialists, and children's pedal cars.

Cartoon Gallery, The
(ref: Cartoon Gallery)
39 Great Russell Street,
London WC1 3PH
Tel: 020 7636 1011
Fax: 020 7436 5053
Comics.

Mia Cartwright Antiques
(ref: Mia Cartwright)
20th C. Theatre Arcade,
291 Westbourne Grove (Sats),
London W11
Tel: 01273 579700

Castlegate Antiques
(ref: Castlegate)
1–3 Castlegate,
Newark,
Notts NG24 1AZ
Tel: 01636 701877
18th and 19th-century furniture and decorative objects.

Manuel Castilho Antiques
53 Ledbury Road,
London W11 2AA
Tel: 020 7221 4928

R.G. Cave & Sons Ltd
Walcote House,
17 Broad Street,
Ludlow,
Shropshire SY8 1NG
Tel: 01584 873568
Fax: 01584 875050
Furniture; clocks; metalware; bijouterie; paintings and drawings; valuations.

Rupert Cavendish Antiques
(ref: R. Cavendish)
610 Kings Road,
London SW6 2DX
Tel: 020 7731 7041
Fax: 020 7731 8302
www.rupertcavendish.co.uk
European 20th-century paintings.

Cekay
Stand 172, Grays Antique Market,
58 Davies Street,
London W1Y 2LP
Tel: 020 7629 5130
Fax: 020 7730 3014
Antiques.

Ronald G. Chambers
Fine Antiques
(ref: Ronald G. Chambers)
Market Square,
Petworth,
West Sussex GU28 0AH
Tel: 01798 342305
Fax: 01798 342724
www.ronaldchambers.com
18th and 19th-century furniture, paintings, objets d'art, clocks and jewellery.

Paul Champkins
41 Dover Street,
London W1X 3RB
Tel: 020 7495 4600
Fax: 01235 751658
Oriental art, specialising in Chinese, Korean and Japanese.

Bill Chapman
Shop No. 11,
Bourbon/Hanby Antique Centre,
151 Sydney Street,
London SW3 6NT
Tel: 020 7351 5387
Collectables.

Chelsea Gallery and Il Libro
(ref: Chelsea Gallery)
The Plaza, 535 Kings Road,
London SW10 0SZ
Tel: 020 7823 3248
Fax: 020 7352 1579
Antique illustrated books, literature, prints, maps, specialising in natural history, travel, architecture and history.

Chelsea Military Antiques
(ref: Chelsea (OMRS))
Stands N13–14, Antiquarius,
131–141 Kings Road,
London SW3 4PW
Tel: 020 7352 0308
Fax: 020 7352 0308
www.chelseamilitaria.co.uk
Pre-1945 militaria, edge weapons, medals including British and foreign campaign/gallantry medals.

Antoine Cheneviere
Fine Arts Ltd
27 Bruton Street,
London W1X 7DB
Tel: 020 7491 1007
Fax: 020 7495 6173
18th- and 19th-century Russian, Austrian, German, and Italian furniture and objets d'art.

Cine Art Gallery
759 Fulham Road,
London SW6 5UU
Tel: 020 7384 0728
Fax: 020 7384 0727
www.cineartgallery.com
Vintage film posters.

Circa
L43, Grays Mews Antique Market,
1–7 Davies Mews,
London W1Y 2LP
Tel: 01279 466260
Fax: 01279 466 260
Decorative and collectable glass.

Clarke and Denny Antiques
Ref: Clarke & Denny
Great Grooms Antiques Centre,
Billingshurst,
West Sussex RH14 9EU
Antique furniture.

Classic Fabrics with
Robin Haydock
(ref: Classic Fabrics)
Unit 18,
Bourbon Hanby Antiques Centre,
151 Sydney Street,
London SW3 6NY
Tel: 020 7349 9100
Mob: 07770 931240
Antique textiles and fabrics.

Classic Library
1st Floor, The Furniture Cave,
533 Kings Road,
London SW10 0TZ
Tel: 020 7376 7653
Fax: 020 7259 0323
Antiquarian books and period library furniture.

John Clay Antiques
(ref: John Clay)
263 New Kings Road,
London SW6 4RB
Tel: 020 7731 5677
Furniture, objets d'art, silver and clocks from the 18th and 19th centuries.

Clock Clinic Ltd, The
(ref: Clock Clinic)
85 Lower Richmond Road,
Putney, London SW15 1EW
Tel: 020 8788 1407
Fax: 020 8780 2838
www.clockclinic.co.uk
Antique clocks and barometers, all overhauled and guaranteed.

Clock Workshop, The
(ref: Clock Workshop)
17 Prospect Street,
Caversham, Reading,
Berkshire RG4 8JB
Tel: 0118 947 0741
www.lapada.co.uk
English clocks and French carriage clocks.

Close Antiques
Alresford, Hampshire
Tel: 01962 732189
17th- and 18th-century country furniture; metalwork; English delftware; pottery; samplers and needlework pictures.

Cobwebs
73 Avery Hill Road,
New Eltham, London SE9 2BJ
Tel: 020 8850 5611
Furniture, general antiques and collectables.

Cohen & Cohen
101b Kensington Church Street,
London W8 7LN
Tel: 020 7727 7677
Fax: 020 7229 9653
www.artnet.com
Chinese export porcelain works of art.

Garrick D. Coleman
(ref: G.D. Coleman)
75 Portobello Road,
London W11 2QB
Tel: 020 7937 5524
Fax: 020 7937 5530
www.antiquechess.co.uk
Antiques, fine chess sets and glass paperweights.

Collectiques
44 Arundel Close,
New Milton, Hampshire BH25 5UH
Tel: 014256 20794
Fax: 07989 775891
www.antiquebottles.com
robkayrobkay@globalnet.co.uk
Antique collectable bottles.

J. Collins & Son
(ref: J. Collins)
28 High Street, Bideford,
Devon EX39 2AN
Tel: 01237 473103
Fax: 01237 475658
Georgian and Regency furniture, Victorian oil paintings and watercolours.

Colnaghi
15 Old Bond Street,
London W1X 4JL
Tel: 020 7491 7408
Fax: 020 7491 8851
www.art-on-line.com/colnaghi/colnaghi/
Old Master paintings and drawings from the 14th to the 19th centuries; English paintings.

Rosemary Conquest (ref: R. Conquest)
4 Charlton Place,
London N1 8AJ
Tel: 020 7359 0616
Continental and Dutch lighting, copper, brass and decorative items.

Hilary Conqy
Antiquarias Antiques Market,
135 Kings Road,
London SW3 4PW
Tel: 020 7352 2099
Jewellery.

Marc Constantini Antiques (ref: M. Constantini)
313 Lillie Road,
London SW6 7LL

Sheila Cook Textiles (ref: Sheila Cook)
184 Westbourne Grove,
London W11 2RH
Tel: 020 7792 8001
Fax: 020 7229 3855
www.sheilacook.co.uk
European costume, textiles from the mid-18th century to the 1970s.

Jonathan Cooper
Park Walk Gallery,
20 Park Walk,
London SW10 0AQ
Tel: 020 7351 0410
Fax: 020 7351 0410
19th- and 20th-century British and continental paintings.

Susie Cooper Ceramics Gallery 1930 (ref: Susie Cooper)
18 Church Street,
Marylebone, London NW8 8EP
20th-century ceramics.

Barry Cotton Antiques (ref: Barry Cotton)
By appointment only
Tel: 020 8563 9899
Mob: 07831 354324
barrycottonantiques@tinyonline.co.uk
www.barrycottonantiques.fsnet.co.uk
Fine-quality 18th- and 19th-century period furniture.

Thomas Coulborn & Sons
Vesey Manor,
64 Birmingham Road,
Sutton Coldfield,
West Midlands B72 1QP
Tel: 0121 354 3974
Fax: 0121 354 4614
18th-century furniture and works of art; valuations.

Country Antiques (Wales)
Castle Mill,
Kidwelly,
Carmarthenshire SA17 4UU
Tel: 01554 890534
17th- to 19th-century furniture; pottery, treen and folk art with emphasis on items of Welsh interest; valuations.

Country Seat, The
Huntercome Manor Barn,
nr Henley on Thames,
Oxon RG9 5RY
Tel: 01491 6431349
Fax: 01491 641533
fery&clegg@thecountryseat.com
www.thecountryseat.com
www.whitefriarsflass.com
20th-century furniture, ceramics and glass.

County Antiques
Burlton Hall,
Burlton,
Shrewsbury SY4 5SX
Tel: 01939 270819
17th- and 18th-century oak and walnut country house furniture – contact Mr & Mrs Michael Bailey.

Polly de Courcy-Ireland
PO Box 29,
Alresford,
Hampshire SO24 9WP
Tel: 01962 733131
17th- to early 19th-century treen and unusual objects.

Richard Courtney Ltd
112–114 Fulham Road,
South Kensington, London SW3 6HU
Tel: 020 7370 4020
Fax: 020 7370 4020
18th-century English furniture.

Crawley and Asquith Ltd
20 Upper Phillimore Gardens,
London W8 7HA
Tel: 020 7937 9523
Fax: 020 7937 2159
17th-, 18th- and 19th-century oils and watercolours; original engravings and lithographs (topographical, architectural and natural history); rare books.

Peter A. Crofts
Briar Patch,
117 High Road,
Elm, Wisbech,
Cambridgeshire PE14 0DN
Tel: 01945 584614
18th-century furniture; jewellery, bijouterie and snuff boxes; porcelain, pottery and enamels; silver and old Sheffield plate; valuations.

Sandra Cronan Ltd (ref: Sandra Cronan)
18 Burlington Arcade,
London W1V 9AB
Tel: 020 7491 4851
Fax: 020 7493 2758
Art Deco jewellery.

Crowthers of Syon Lodge (ref: Crowthers)
Architectural Antiques
for Interior and Exteriors,
77/79 Pimlico Road,
London SW1 W8PH
Tel: 020 7730 8668
Architectural antiques and sculpture.

Curios Gardens & Interiors (ref: Curios)
130c Junction Road,
Tufnell Park, London N19 5LB
Tel: 020 7272 5603
Fax: 020 7272 5603
Garden furniture, statuary, reclaimed pine furniture and antique furniture.

Ronan Daly Antiques (ref: Ronan Daly)
Alfie's Antiques Market,
13–25 Church Street,
London NW8 8DT
Tel: 020 7723 0429

Andrew Dando (ref: Dando)
4 Wood Street,
Queen Square,
Bath BA1 1JQ
Tel: 01225 422702
Fax: 012255 31017
andrew@andrewdando.uk
www.andrewdando/co.uk
English ceramics.

Michael Davidson
54 Ledbury Road,
London W11 2AJ
Tel: 020 7229 6088
Fax: 020 7792 0450
18th-century furniture, Regency furniture, objects and objets d'art.

Barry Davies Oriental Art
1 Davies Street,
London W1Y 1LL
Tel: 020 7408 0207
Fax: 020 7493 3422
Japanese works of art.

Jesse Davis Antiques (ref: Jesse Davis)
Stands A9–11, Antiquarius,
131–141 Kings Road,
London SW3 4PW
Tel: 020 7352 4314
19th-century pottery, majolica, Staffordshire and other collectable factories, and decorative objects.

Reginald Davis (Oxford) Ltd
34 High Street,
Oxford,
Oxfordshire OX1 4AN
Tel: 01865 248347
Fax: 01865 200915
Jewellery; silver and old Sheffield plate; valuations.

Decodence
21 The Mall, 359 Upper Street,
London N1 0PD
Tel: 020 7354 4473
Fax: 020 7689 0680
Classic plastics such as bakelite, celluloid and catalin; vintage radios, lighting, telephones and toys.

Deep, The
The Plaza, 535 Kings Road,
London SW10 0SZ
Tel: 020 7351 4881
Fax: 020 7352 0763
Recovered shipwrecked items.

Richard Dennis Gallery (ref: Richard Dennis)
144 Kensington Church Street,
London W8 4BH
Tel: 020 7727 2061
Fax: 020 7221 1283
Antique and modern studio ceramics.

Dial Post House
Dial Post, near Horsham,
West Sussex RH13 8NQ
Tel: 01403 713388
Fax: 01403 713388
Furniture.

Dodo
Stand Fo73, Alfie's Antiques Market,
13–25 Church Street,
London NW8 8DT
Tel: 020 7706 1545
Fax: 020 7724 0999
Posters, tins and advertising signs, 1890–1940.

Dolly Land
864 Green Lanes,
Winchmore Hill,
London N21 2RS
Tel: 020 8360 1053
Fax: 020 8364 1370
www.dollyland.com
Dolls.

Dolly Land (Steiff Club)
864 Green Lanes,
Winchmore Hill,
London N21 2RS
Tel: 020 8360 1053
Fax: 020 8364 1370
www.dollyland.com
Dolls, Steiff bears, Scalectrix, trains and die-cast toys.

Anthony Green Antiques
ref: Anthony Green
Unit 39, Bond Street Antiques Centre,
124 New Bond Street,
London W1S 1DX
Tel: 020 7409 2854
Fax: 020 7409 2854
www.anthonygreen.com
Vintage wristwatches and antique pocket watches.

Richard Green
33 New Bond Street,
London, W1Y 9HD
Tel: 020 7499 5553
Fax: 020 7499 8509
paintings@richard-green.com
www.richard-green.com
Fine Old Master paintings.

Richard Green
39 Dover Street,
London W1X 3RB
Tel: 020 7499 4738
Fax: 020 7499 3318
paintings@richard-green.com
www.richard-green.com
Victorian and Dutch romantic paintings.

Richard Green
147 New Bond Street,
London W1Y 9FE
Tel: 020 7493 3939
Fax: 020 7629 2609
paintings@richard-green.com
www.richard-green.com
British, sporting and marine paintings; French Impressionist and modern British paintings.

Henry Gregory
82 Portobello Road,
London W11 2QD
Tel: 020 7792 9221
Fax: 020 7792 9221
Silver-plate, silver, sporting goods and decorative antiques.

W. John Griffiths
Great Grooms Antique Centre,
Hungerford,
Berkshire RG17 OEP
Antique furniture.

Nicholas Grindley
13 Old Burlington Street,
London W1X 1LA
Tel: 020 7437 5449
Fax: 020 7494 2446
Chinese furniture and works of art.

Grosvenor Antiques Ltd
27 Holland Street,
London W8 4NA
Tel: 020 7937 8649
Fax: 020 7937 7179
Porcelain, enamels, works of art and 18th- and 19th-century bronzes.

Guest & Gray
Grays Mews Antique Market,
1–7 Davies Mews,
London W1Y 2LP
Tel: 020 7408 1252
Fax: 020 7499 1445
www.guest-gray.demon.co.uk
Oriental and European ceramics and works of art, and reference books.

Guinevere Antiques Limited
(ref: Guinevere)
574–580 Kings Road,
London SW6 2DY
Tel: 020 7736 2917
Fax: 020 7736 8267
Mirrors, cabinets, lights and chandeliers.

Gurr and Sprake Antiques
(ref: Gurr & Sprake)
283 Lillie Road,
London SW6 7LL
Tel: 020 7381 3209
Fax: 020 7381 9502
18th and 19th-century English and French furniture, lighting and unusual architectural pieces.

Gütlin Clocks and Antiques
(ref: Gütlin Clocks)
616 Kings Road,
London SW6
Tel: 020 7384 2439
Fax: 020 7384 2439
www.gutlin.com
Longcase clocks, mantel clocks, furniture and lighting, all 18th and 19th century.

G Whizz
17 Jerdan Place,
London SW6 1BE
Tel: 020 7386 5020
Fax: 020 8741 0062
www.metrocycle.co.uk
Bikes.

J. de Haan & Son
(ref: J. de Haan)
PO Box 95, Newmarket,
Suffolk CB8 8ZG
Tel: 01440 821388
Fax: 01440 820410
Old English furniture, barometers, gilt mirrors and fine tea caddies.

Hadji Baba Ancient Art
(ref: Hadji Baba)
34a Davies Street,
London W1Y 1LG
Tel: 020 7499 9363
Fax: 020 7493 5504
Near and Middle East antiquities.

Robert Hales Antiques
(ref: Robert Hales)
131 Kensington Church Street,
London W8 7LP
Tel: 020 7229 3887
Fax: 020 7229 3887
Oriental and Islamic arms, armour, from medieval to 19th century.

Ross Hamilton Antiques Ltd
95 Pimlico Road,
London SW1W 8PH
Tel: 020 7730 3015
Fax: 020 7730 3015
www.lapada.uk/rosshamilton/
17th to 19th-century fine English and continental furniture, 16th- to 20th-century paintings, oriental porcelain, objets d'art and bronzes.

Hancocks & Co. (Jewellers) Ltd
52–53 Burlington Arcade,
London W1X 2HP
Tel: 020 7493 8904
Fax: 020 7493 8905
Antique.Collectors-online.com
/dealers/hancocks
Antique jewellery; antique silver; objects; valuations.

Jim Hanson & Argyll Etkin Ltd
(ref: Jim Hanson)
18 Claremont Field,
Ottery St Mary,
Devon EX11 1NP
Tel: 01404 815010
Fax: 01404 815224
Philatelist and postal historian.

Keith Harding's
World of Mechanical Music
(ref: Keith Harding)
The Oak House,
High Street, Northleach,
Gloucestershire GL54 3ET
Tel: 01451 860181
Fax: 01451 861133
www.mechanicalmusic.co.uk

Robert Harman Antiques
The Red House,
Church Street, Ampthill,
Bedfordshire MK45 2EH
Tel: 01525 402322
Fax: 01525 756177
Furniture; works of art; valuations.

Harpur Deardren
First Floor, 533 Kings Road,
London SW10 0TZ
Tel: 020 7352 2046
Furniture.

Adrian Harrington
Antiquarian Bookseller
(ref: Adrian Harrington)
64a Kensington Church Street,
London W8 4DB
Tel: 020 7937 1465
Fax: 020 7368 0912
www.harringtonbooks.co.uk
Antiquarian, rare and secondhand books on literature, children's illustrated and travel.

Peter Harrington
Antiquarian Bookseller
100 Fulham Road,
London SW3 6HS
Tel: 020 7591 02220
Fax: 020 7225 7054
www.peter-harrington-book.com
Antique books and maps.

Jonathan Harris
9 Lower Addison Gardens,
London W14 8BG
Tel: 020 7602 6255
Fax: 020 7602 0488
English, continental and Oriental furniture and works of art; later 19th- and early 20th-century western applied arts; valuations.

Nicholas Harris Gallery
PO Box 14430,
London SW6 2WG
Tel: 020 7371 9711
Fax: 020 7371 9537
English and American 19th- and 20th-century silver and art silversmiths; metalwork.

Harvey & Gore
41 Duke Street,
St James's,
London SW1Y 6DF
Tel: 020 7839 4033
Fax: 020 7839 3313
Jewellery, bijouterie and snuff boxes; silver and old Sheffield plate; miniatures; valuations.

Kenneth Harvey Antiques
(ref: Kenneth Harvey)
Furniture Cave, 533 Kings Road,
London SW10 0TZ
Tel: 020 7352 8645
Fax: 020 7352 3759
www.kennethharvey.com
English and French furniture, chandeliers and mirrors from the late 17th to 20th centuries, and leather armchairs.

W.R. Harvey & Co. Ltd
86 Corn Street,
Witney,
Oxfordshire OX8 7BU
Tel: 01993 706501
Fax: 01993 706601
www.wrharvey.co.uk
Important stock of English furniture, clocks, pictures, mirrors and works of art from 1680–1830.

Victoria Harvey at Deuxieme (ref: Victoria Harvey)
44 Church Street,
London NW8 8EP
Tel: 020 7724 0738
Fax: 020 7724 0738
General decorative antiques.

Hatchwell Antiques (ref: Hatchwell)
533 Kings Road,
London SW10 OTZ
Tel: 020 7351 2344
Fax: 020 7351 3520
hatchwell@callnetuk.com
Period furniture, fine furniture and bronzes.

Gerard Hawthorn Ltd (ref: Gerard Hawthorn)
104 Mount Street,
London W1Y 5HE
Tel: 020 7409 2888
Fax: 020 7409 2777
Chinese, Japanese and Korean ceramics and works of art.

Henry Hay
Unit 5054, 2nd floor, Alfie's Market,
13–25 Church Street,
London NW8
Tel: 020 7723 2548
Art Deco and 20th-century chrome and brass lamps and bakelite telephones.

Jeanette Hayhurst Fine Glass
32a Kensington Church St,
London W8 4HA
Tel: 020 7938 1539
British glass from 17th to 20th centuries.

Hayman and Hayman (ref: Hayman)
Stand K3 Antiquarius,
135 Kings Road,
London SW3 4PW
Tel: 020 7351 6568
Fax: 020 8741 0959
hayman@wahlgren.demon.co.uk
Art deco and brass photograph frames, scent bottles and writing equipment.

Hempson
c/o 20 Rutland Gate,
London SW7 1BD
Tel: 020 7584 8058
Continental furniture and works of art.

M. Heskia
c/o CFASS Ltd,
42 Ponton Road,
London SW8 5BA
Tel: 020 7373 4489
Mainly 19th-century Oriental carpets and rugs; European tapestries; valuations.

Heytesbury Antiques (ref: Heytesbury)
PO Box 222, Farnham,
Surrey GU10 5HN
Tel: 01252 850893
Antiques.

Highgate Antiques
PO Box 10060,
London N6 5JH
Tel: 020 8340 9872
Tel: 020 8348 3016
Fax: 020 8340 1621
18th- and early 19th-century English and Welsh porcelain and glass.

W.E. Hill
PO Box 4, Aylesbury,
Buckinghamshire HP17 9UB
Tel: 01844 274 584
Fax: 01844 274 585
Open by appointment only. Musical instruments of the violin family, valuations.

Hill Farm Antiques (ref: Hill Farm)
The Old Cinema,
160 Chiswick High Road,
London W4 IPR
Tel: 020 8994 2998
and 01488 638 541 / 361
beesley@hillfarmantiques.demon.co.uk
Antique furniture.

Robert E. Hirschhorn
83 Camberwell Grove,
London SE5 8JE
Tel: 020 7703 7443
Mob: 0831 405937
English and continental furniture, particularly oak, elm, walnut and fruitwood, and works of art, 18th century and earlier; European ceramics; textiles; metalwork.

Milton J. Holgate
36 Gracious Street,
Knaresborough,
North Yorkshire HG5 8DS
Tel: 01423 865219
Pre-1830 English furniture and accessories.

Holland & Holland (ref: H. & H.)
31–33 Bruton Street,
London W1X 8JS
Tel: 020 7499 4411
Fax: 020 7409 3283
Guns.

Holmes (Jewellers) Ltd
24 Burlington Arcade,
London W1V 9AD
Tel: 020 7629 8380
Silver and jewellery; old Sheffield plate; valuations.

Hope & Glory
131a Kensington Church Street
(entrance in Peel Street),
London W8 7LP
Tel: 020 7727 8424
Commemorative ceramics including royal and political subjects.

Paul Hopwell Antiques (ref: Paul Hopwell)
30 High Street,Westhaddon,
Northamptonshire NN6 7AP
Tel: 01788 510636
Fax: 01788 510044
paulhopwell@antiqueoak.co.uk
www.antiqueoak.co.uk
17th and 18th-century English oak furniture.

Jonathan Horne
66c Kensington Church Street,
London W8 4BY
Tel: 020 7221 5658
Fax: 020 7792 3090
www.jonathanhorne.co.uk
Early English pottery, medieval to 1820.

Hotspur Ltd
14 Lowndes Street,
London SW1X 9EX
Tel: 020 7235 1918
Fax: 020 7235 4371
hotspurltd@msn.com
18th-century English furniture and works of art.

Howard & Hamilton (ref: H. & H.)
151 Sydney Street,
London SW3 6NT
Tel: 020 7352 0909
Fax: 020 7352 0066
Scientific instruments.

Christopher Howe Antiques (ref: Howe)
93 Pimlico Road,
London SW1W 8PH
Tel: 020 7730 7987
Fax: 020 7730 0157
c.howe@easynet.co.uk
Furniture and lighting from the 17th to 20th century.

Hulton Getty Picture Gallery (ref: Hulton Getty)
3 Jubilee Place,
London SW3 3TD
Tel: 020 7376 4525
Fax: 0207 376 4524
www.getty-images.com
Photographs from late 19th–20th centuries.

Huxtable's Old Advertising (ref: Huxtable's)
Alfie's Market,
13–25 Church Street,
London NW8 8DT
Tel: 020 7724 2200
Advertising, collectables, tins, signs, bottles, commemoratives and old packaging from late Victorian.

Hygra, Sign of the (ref: Hygra)
2 Middleton Road,
London E8 4BL
Tel: 020 7254 7074
Fax: 0870 125 669
boxes@hygra.com
www.hygra.com

Iconastas
5 Piccadilly Arcade,
London SW1
Tel: 020 7629 1433
Fax: 020 7408 2015
Russian fine art.

In Vogue Antiques Martin Lister
The Swan Antiques Centre,
High Street, Tetsworth, Thame
Oxfordshire OX9 7AB
Tel: 01844 281777
Fax: 01844 281770
Mob: 0773 786 103
invogueantiques@aol.com
www.theswan.co.uk
Antique furniture.

Iona Antiques
PO Box 285,
London W8 6HZ
Tel: 020 7602 1193
Fax: 020 7371 2843
www.art-on-line.com/iona
Paintings – speciality: 19th-century English paintings of animals.

Jonathan James
52/53 Camden Passage,
Islington, London
Tel: 020 7704 8266
Antique furniture and decorative objects.

P.L. James
590 Fulham Road,
London SW6 5NT
Tel: 020 7736 0183
Gilded mirrors, English and oriental lacquer, period objects and furniture.

J.A.N. Fine Art
134 Kensington Church Street,
London W8 4BH
Tel: 020 7792 0736
Fax: 020 7221 1380
Japanese, Chinese and Korean ceramics, bronzes and works of art.

Japanese Gallery Ltd (ref: Japanese Gallery)
66d Kensington Church Street,
London W8 4BY
Tel: 020 7729 2934
Fax: 020 7229 2934
Japanese woodcut prints, Japanese ceramics, swords, armour and Japanese dolls.

Tobias Jellinek Antiques
20 Park Road, East Twickenham,
Middlesex TW1 2PX
Tel: 020 8892 6892
Fax: 020 8744 9298
toby@jellinek.com
www.jellinek.com/oak
Early English furniture; European ceramics; European sculpture and works of art; early metalwork; treen and bygones; valuations.

Jessop Classic Photographica (ref: Jessop Classic)
67 Great Russell Street,
London WC1
Tel: 020 7831 3640
Fax: 020 7831 3956
Classic photographic equipment, cameras and optical toys.

C. John (Rare Rugs) Ltd
70 South Audley Street,
London W1Y 5FE
Tel: 020 7493 5288
Fax: 020 7409 7030
Carpets and rugs; tapestry, needlework and fabrics.

Lucy Johnson
2 Chester Street,
London SW1X 7BB
Tel: 020 7235 2088
Fax: 020 7235 2088
Fine English furniture; Delftware and period interiors.

Johnson, Walker & Tolhurst Ltd
64 Burlington Arcade,
London W1V 9AF
Tel: 020 7629 2615/6
Fax: 020 7409 0709
Jewellery and bijouterie; valuations.

Juke Box Services
15 Lion Road,
Twickenham TW1 4JH
Tel: 020 8288 1700
www.jbs-ltd.co.uk
Juke boxes.

Alexander Juran & Co
74 New Bond Street,
London W1Y 9DD
Tel: 020 7629 2550 and 020 7493 4484
Fax: 020 7493 4484
Carpets and rugs; tapestry, needlework and textiles; valuations.

Stephen Kalms Antiques (ref: Stephen Kalms)
The London Silver Vaults,
Chancery Lane,
London WC2A 1QS
Tel: 020 7430 1254
Fax: 020 7405 6206
Victorian and Edwardian silver, silver plate and decorative items.

K6
Antiquarius Antiques Market,
135 Kings Rd, London SW3 4PW
Tel: 020 7352 2099
1880–1960 antiques.

John Keil Ltd
154 Brompton Road,
London SW3 1HX
Tel: 020 7589 6454
Fax: 020 7823 8235
17th-, 18th and early 19th-century English furniture and works of art.

Kenworthy's Ltd
226 Stamford Street,
Ashton-under-Lyne,
Manchester OL6 7LW
Tel: 0161-330 3043
Jewellery, bijouterie and snuff boxes; silver and old Sheffield plate; valuations.

Keshishian
73 Pimlico Road,
London SW1W 8NE
Tel: 020 7730 8810
Fax: 020 7730 8803
Antique carpets, tapestries and Aubussons; Arts and Crafts and Art Deco carpet specialists.

Roger Keverne
120 Mount Street,
London W1Y 5HB
Tel: 020 7355 1711
Fax: 020 7409 7717
Chinese, Japanese and Oriental works of art.

Kieron
K6 Antiquarias Antiques Market,
135 Kings Rd,
London SW3 4PW
Tel: 020 7352 2099
Decorative arts.

John King
74 Pimlico Road,
London SW1W 8LS
Tel: 020 7730 0427
Fax: 020 7730 2515
john.king21@virigin.net
Fine and unusual antiques.

John King
Raynalds Mansion,
High Street, Much Wenlock,
Shropshire TF13 6AE
Tel: 01952 727456
john.king21@virgin.net
Fine and unusual antiques.

Kitchen Bygones
13–15 Church Street,
Marylebone, London NW8 8DT
Tel: 020 7258 3405
Fax: 020 7724 0999
Kitchenalia.

Robert Kleiner & Co. Ltd
30 Old Bond Street,
London W1X 4HN
Tel: 020 7629 1814 and 020 7622 5462
Fax: 020 7629 1239
Chinese works of art, jades, porcelains and snuff bottles.

Shirly Knight
Antiques and Decorative Furnishing,
Great Grooms Antique Centre,
Hungerford,
Berkshire RG17 0RP
Tel: 01488 6823114
Fax: 01487 8233130
Antique furniture.

L. & E. Kreckovic
559 Kings Road,
London SW6 2EB
Tel: 020 7736 0753
Fax: 020 7731 5904
Early 18th- to 19th-century furniture.

La Boheme
c21 Grays Mews,
1–7 Davies Mews,
London W1Y 2LP
Tel: 020 7493 0675
Glass.

Lacquer Chest, The (ref: Lacquer Chest)
75 Kensington Church Street,
London W8 4BG
Tel: 020 7937 1306
Fax: 020 7376 0223
Military chests, china, clocks, samplers and lamps.

Lamberty
The Furniture Cave, 533 Kings Road,
London SW10 0TZ
Tel: 020 7352 3775
Fax: 020 7352 3759
www.lamberty.co.uk

Langfords
Vault 8–10, London Silver Vaults,
Chancery Lane,
London WC2A 1QS
Tel: 020 7242 5506
Fax: 020 7405 0431
www.langfords.com
Antique and modern silver and silver plate.

Langfords Marine Antiques (ref: Langfords Marine)
The Plaza, 535 Kings Road,
London SW10 0SZ
Tel: 020 7351 4881
Fax: 020 7352 0763
www.langfords.co.uk
Nautical artefacts.

Judith Lassalle
7 Pierrepont Arcade,
Camden Passage,
London N1 8EF
Tel: 020 7607 7121
Optical toys, books and games.

LASSCO
St. Michael's, Mark St,
London EC2A 4ER
Tel: 020 7739 0448
Fax: 020 7729 6853
www.lassco.co.uk
Architectural antiques including panelled rooms, garden ornaments, stained glass and stonework.

D.S. Lavender Antiques Ltd
26 Conduit Street,
London W1R 9TA
Tel: 020 7629 1782
Fax: 020 7629 3106
Miniatures, jewellery and objets d'art; valuations.

Michael Laws
Bartlett Street Antiques Centre,
Bath BA1 2QZ
Tel: 01225 446322
Fax: 01249 658366
Antique fishing tackle and curios.

Lennox Gallery Ltd (ref: Lennox Gallery)
4 Davies Mews,
London W1Y 1LP
Tel: 020 7491 0091
Fax: 020 7491 0657
Antiquities and numismatics.

Michael Lewis
6/7 Peabody Yard,
Greenman Street,
London N1 8SB
Tel: 020 7359 7733
Fax: same
Pine and country furniture, British and Irish, 18th and 19th century.

Lewis & Lloyd
65 Kensington Church St,
London W8 4BA
Tel: 020 7938 3323
Fax: 020 7361 0086
18th- and 19th-century English furniture.

Liberty plc
210–220 Regent Street,
London W1R 6AH
Tel: 020 7734 1234
Fax: 020 7578 9876
www.liberty.co.uk
20th-century furniture, jewellery, ceramics, clothes and kitchenware.

Libra Antiques
(ref: Libra)
131D Kensington Church Street,
London W8 7PT
Tel: 020 7727 2990
English ceramics.

Libra Designs
34 Church Street,
London NW8 8EP
Tel: 020 7723 0542
Fax: 020 7286 8518
www.libradeco.com

Lida Lavender
39–51 Highgate Road,
London NW5 1RS
Tel: 020 7424 0600
Fax: 020 7424 0404
lida@lavenders.co.uk
Antique carpets and textiles for design and decoration.

Linden & Co. (Antiques) Ltd
(ref: Linden & Co.)
Vault 7, London Silver Vaults,
Chancery Lane,
London WC2A 1QS
Tel: 020 7242 4863
Fax: 020 7405 9946
Silver plate and works of art.

Lindfield Galleries
62 High Street, Lindfield,
West Sussex RH16 2HL
Tel: 01444 483817
Fax: 01444 484682
Carpets and rugs; valuations.

Andrew Lineham Fine Glass
The Mall,
Camden Passage,
London N1 8ED
Tel: 020 7704 0195 or 01243 576241
Rare and unusual 19th- and 20th-century coloured glass and European porcelain.

P. Lipitch
120 and 124 Fulham Road,
London SW3 6HU
Tel: 020 7373 3328
Fax: 020 7373 8888
General antiques.

Little River Oriental Antiques
(ref: Little River)
135 Kings Road,
London SW3 4PW
Tel: 020 7349 9080
Chinese antiquities and domestic ceramics.

London Antique Gallery
(ref: London Antique)
66e Kensington Church Street,
London W8 4BY
Tel: 020 7229 2934
Fax: 020 7229 2934
Meissen, Dresden, Worcester, Minton, Shelley, Sèvres, Lalique and bisque dolls.

Stephen Long
348 Fulham Road,
London SW10 9UH
Tel: 020 7352 8226
Painted furniture, small decorative items and English pottery, from 1780–1850.

Lotus House
Great Grooms, Hungerford,
Berkshire RG17 0EP
Tel: 01488 6823114
Oriental antiques.

Clive Loveless
54 St Quintin Avenue,
London W10 6PA
Tel: 020 8969 5831
Fax: 020 8969 5292
18th- and 19th-century Oriental tribal rugs; 17th- to 19th-century Ottoman, central Asian, African and Pre-Columbian textiles; valuations.

M. Luther Antiques
(ref: M. Luther)
590 Kings Road,
London SW6 2DX
Tel: 020 7371 8492
Fax: 020 7371 8492
18th and 19th-century English and continental furniture, tables, chairs, mirrors and lighting.

William MacAdam
86 Pilrig Street,
Edinburgh EH6 5AS
Tel: 0131 553 1364
Specialist in 18th-century collectors' drinking glasses, also later glass; valuations.

Pete McAskie Toys
(ref: P. McAskie)
Stand A12–13, Basement,
1–7 Davies Mews,
London W1Y 2LP
Tel: 020 7629 2813
Fax: 020 7493 9344
Tin toys from 1895–1980, die-cast toys, robots, battery-operated toys and lead figures.

Nicholas E. McAuliffe
(ref: N.E. McAuliffe)
First Floor, 533 Kings Road,
London SW10 0TZ
Tel: 020 7352 2046
Furniture.

Fiona McDonald
57 Galveston Road,
London SW15 2RZ
Tel: 020 2270 5559
Mirrors, decorative furniture and lighting.

Mac Humble Antiques
(ref: Mac Humble)
7–9 Woolley Street,
Bradford on Avon,
Wiltshire BA15 1AD
Tel: 01225 866329
Fax: 01225 866329
www.machumbleantiques.co.uk
18th and 19th-century furniture, needlework, samplers, metalware and decorative items.

Joyce Macnaughton-Smith
(ref: Macnaughton-Smith)
The Swan Antique Centre,
Tetsworth, Thame,
Oxfordshire OX9 7AB
Tel: 01884 281777
Antique furniture.

Mac's Cameras
262 King Street,
Hammersmith, London W6 0SJ
Tel: 020 8846 9853
Antique camera equipment.

Maggs Bros Ltd
50 Berkeley Square,
London W1X 6EL
Tel: 020 7493 7160
Fax: 020 7499 2007
Rare books, autographs, manuscripts and miniatures.

Magus Antiques
4 Church Street,
London NW8 8ED
Tel: 020 7724 1278
Fax: 020 7724 1278
Mob: 0374 271214
Antique rugs, furniture, lighting and mirrors.

Magpies
152 Wandsworth Bridge Road,
London SW6 2UH
Tel: 020 7736 3738
Small furniture, kitchenware, door furniture, cutlery, lighting, silver and silver-plate.

C.H. Major
154 Kensington Church Street,
London W8 4BH
Tel: 020 7229 1162
Fax: 020 7221 9676
18th and 19th-century English furniture.

Mallett & Son (Antiques) Ltd
141 New Bond Street,
London W1Y 0BS
Tel: 020 7499 7411
Fax: 020 7495 3179
18th-century English furniture; works of art; glass; paintings and watercolours.

Mallett Gallery, The
141 New Bond Street,
London W1Y 0BS
Tel: 020 7499 7411
Fax: 020 7495 3179
Fine paintings, watercolours, drawings; sculpture and works of art; valuations.

D.M. & P. Manheim
(Peter Manheim) Ltd
PO Box 1259,
London N6 4TR
Tel: 020 8340 9211
18th- and early 19th-century English porcelain, pottery and enamels.

E. & H. Manners
66a Kensington Church Street,
London W8 4BY
Tel: 020 7229 5516
Fax: 020 7229 5516
www.europeanporcelain.com
18th-century European porcelain and pottery.

Map House, The
54 Beauchamp Place,
London SW3 1NY
Tel: 020 7584 8559
Fax: 020 7589 1041
www.themaphouse.com
Antique maps from 15th to 19th centuries, decorative engravings from 16th to 19th centuries.

Marks Antiques
49 Curzon Street,
London W1Y 7RE
Tel: 020 7499 1788
Fax: 020 7409 3183
www.marksantiques.com
Antique silver.

G.E. Marsh
(Antique Clocks) Ltd
(ref: G.E. Marsh)
32a The Square,
Winchester,
Hampshire SO23 9EX
Tel: 01962 844443
Clocks, watches and barometers; valuations.
and
Jericho House,
North Aston, nr Bicester,
Oxfordshire OX6 4HX
Tel: 01869 340087
Fax: 01869 340087
Open by appointment only. Clocks, watches and barometers; valuations.

David Martin-Taylor Antiques
(ref: D. Martin-Taylor)
558 Kings Road,
London SW6 2DZ
Tel: 020 7731 4135
Fax: 020 7371 0029
www.davidmartintaylor.com
18th- and 19th-century continental and English furniture, objets d'art, decorative art, from the eccentric to the unusual.

Francesca Martire
Alfie's Antique Market,
13–25 Church Street,
London NW8 8DT
Tel: 020 7723 6066
www.@alfies.com
Open Tues–Sat 10–6 20th-century lighting, glass, furniture and jewellery.

Paul Mason Gallery
149e Sloane Street,
London SW1X 9BZ
Tel: 020 7730 3683 / 7359
Fax: 020 7581 9084
www.art-on-line.com/pmason
18th- and 19th-century marine, sporting and decorative paintings and prints; ship models; portfolio stands and picture easels; glass pictures; valuations.

Megan Mathers Antiques
(ref: M. Mathers)
571 Kings Road,
London SW6 2EB
Tel: 020 7371 7837
Fax: 020 7371 7895
19th-century continental and English furniture, porcelain, lighting and objets d'art.

A.P. Mathews
283 Westbourne Grove,
London W11
Tel: 01622 812590
Antique luggage.

Gerald Mathias
Stands 3–6, Antiquarius,
131–141 Kings Road,
London SW3 4PW
Tel: 020 7351 1484
Fax: 020 7351 0484
www.geraldmathias.com
Antique wooden boxes, tea caddies and stationery cabinets.

Sue Mautner Costume Jewellery
(ref: Sue Mautner)
Stand P13, Antiquarius,
131–141 Kings Road,
London SW3 4PW
Tel: 020 7376 4419
Costume jewellery from the 1940s and 1950s, including Christian Dior, Miriam Haskell, Schiaparelli and Coppolo Toppo.

David Messum
8 Cork Street,
London W1X 1PB
Tel: 020 7437 5545
Fax: 020 7734 7018
British Impressionism and contemporary art.

Metro Retro
1 White Conduit Street,
London N1 9EL
Tel: 020 7278 4884 / 01245 442047
www.metroretro.co.uk
Industrial-style furniture, lighting and home accessories.

Midwinter Antiques
(ref: Midwinter)
31 Bridge Street,
Newcastle under Lyme,
Staffordshire ST5 2RY
Tel: 01782 712483
Fax: 01630 672289
17th- and 18th-century town and country furniture, clocks and textiles.

Arthur Millner
180 New Bond Street,
London W1S 4RL
Tel: 020 7499 4484
www.arthurmillner.com
Indian and Islamic art and related European material.

Nicholas Mitchell
The Swan Antique Centre,
Tetsworth, Thame,
Oxfordshire OX9 7AB
Tel: 01844 281777
Fax: 01844 281770
www/theswan.co.uk
English and continental furniture.

Mora & Upham Antiques
(ref: Mora Upham)
584 King's Road,
London SW6 2DX
Tel: 020 7331 444
Fax: 020 7736 0440
mora.upham@talk21.com
Fine English and continental furniture, mirrors and lighting.

More Than Music Collectables
(ref: More Than Music)
C24–25 Grays Mews Antiques Market,
1–7 Davies Mews,
London W1Y 2LP
Tel: 020 7629 7703
Fax: 01519 565510
www.mtmglobal.com
Rock and popular music memorabilia, specialising in The Beatles.

Robert Morley and Company Limited
(ref: Robert Morley)
34 Engate Street,
Lewisham, London SE13 7HA
Tel: 020 8318 5838
Fax: 020 8297 0720
Pianoforte and harpsichord workshop.

Clive Morley Harps Ltd
(ref: Clive Morley)
Unit 121, Grays Antiques Market,
58 Davies Street,
London W1 5LP
Tel: 020 7495 4495
Fax: 01367 860 659
www.morleyharps.com
Harps.

Maureen Morris
Folly Cottage,
Littlebury, Saffron Walden,
Essex CB11 4TA
Tel: 01799 521338
Fax: 01799 522802
Quality samplers; early needlework; late 18th-century and early 19th-century quilts; small country furniture.

Terence Morse & Son
(ref: T. Morse & Son)
237 Westbourne Gove,
London W11 2SE
Tel: 020 7229 4059
Fax: 020 7792 3284
18th- and 19th-century fine English and continental furniture, linen presses and library furniture.

Sydney L. Moss Ltd
51 Brook Street,
London W1Y 1AU
Tel: 020 7629 4670 and 020 7493 7374
Fax: 020 7491 9278
Chinese and Japanese works of art.

Motor Books
(ref: Motor)
33 St Martin's Court,
London WC2N 4AN
Tel: 020 7836 3800
Fax: 020 7497 2539
Motoring books.

Mousa Antiques
(ref: Mousa)
B20 Grays Mews Antiques Market,
1–7 Davies Mews,
London W1Y 1AR
Tel: 020 7499 8273
Fax: 020 7629 2526
Bohemian glass specialists.

Murray Cards (International) Ltd
(ref: Murray Cards)
51 Watford Way,
London NW4 3JH
Tel: 020 8202 5688
Fax: 020 8203 7878
www.murraycards.com
Cigarette and trade cards.

Music & Video Exchange
(ref: Music & Video)
38 Notting Hill Gate,
London W11 3HX
Tel: 020 7243 8574
www.mveshops.co.uk
CDs, memorabilia, vinyl – deletions and rarities.

Myriad Antiques
(ref: Myriad)
131 Portland Road,
London W11 4LW
Tel: 020 7229 1709
Fax: 020 7221 3882
French painted furniture, garden furniture, bamboo, Victorian and Edwardian upholstered chairs, mirrors and objets d'art.

Stephen Naegel
Grays Antiques Market,
1–7 Davies Mews,
London W1Y 2LP
Tel: 020 7491 3066
Fax: 01737 845147
www.btinternet.com/~naegel
Toys.

Namdar Antiques
(ref: Namdar)
B22, Grays Mews Antiques Market,
1–7 Davies Mews,
London W1Y 2LP
Tel: 020 7629 1183
Fax: 020 7493 9344
Metalware, Oriental and Islamic ceramics, glassware and silver.

Colin Narbeth and Son
(ref: C. Narbeth)
20 Cecil Court,
London WC2N 4HE
Tel: 020 7379 6975
Fax: 0172 811244
www.colin-narbeth.com
Banknotes, bonds and shares of all countries and periods.

Gillian Neale Antiques
PO Box 247,
Aylesbury,
Buckinghamshire HP20 1JZ
Tel: 01296 23754
Mob: 0860 638700
Fax: 01296 23754
English blue and white transfer-printed pottery 1780–1850.

New Century
69 Kensington Church Street,
London W8 8BG
Tel: 020 7937 2410
Fax: 020 7937 2410
Design from 1860–1910.

New Kings Road Vintage Guitar Emporium (ref: Vintage Guitar)
65a New Kings Road,
London SW6 4SG
Tel: 020 7371 0100
Fax: 020 7371 0460
www.newkingsroadguitars.co.uk
Vintage guitars.

Chris Newland Antiques (ref: C. Newland)
30–31 Islington Green,
Lower Level, Georgian Village,
London N1 8DU
Tel: 020 7359 9805
Fax: 020 7359 9805
Furniture.

John Nicholas Antiques (ref: John Nicholas)
First Floor, 533 Kings Road,
London SW10 0TZ
Tel: 020 7352 2046
www.thecave.co.uk
18th- to 20th-century furniture, accessories, chandeliers, lighting and tapestries.

North West Eight (ref: North West 8)
36 Church Street,
London NW8 8EP
Tel: 020 7723 9337
Decorative antiques.

Edward Nowell & Sons
12 Market Place,
Wells, Somerset BA5 2RB
Tel: 01749 672415 and 01749 678738
Fax: 01749 673519
Mid-18th-century English furniture; Chinese blue and white porcelain; silver and jewellery; valuations.

Oasis Ancient and Islamic Arts (ref: Oasis)
Stand E14,
Grays Mews Antiques Market,
1–7 Davies Mews,
London W1Y 1AR
Tel: 020 7493 1202
Fax: 020 8551 4487
Ancient and Islamic art from 2000BC to 18th century.

Ocean Leisure
11–14 Northumberland Avenue,
London WC2N 5AQ
Tel: 020 7930 5050
Fax: 020 7930 3032
www.oceanleisure.co.uk

Glenda O'Connor
Grays Antique Market,
Davies Mews,
London W1
Tel: 020 8367 2441
Fax: 020 8366 5811
Dolls, teddies, prams and related collectables.

Richard Ogden Ltd
28–29 Burlington Arcade,
London W1V 0NX
Tel: 020 7493 9136 / 7
Fax: 020 7355 1508
Jewellery, specialising in rings.

Old Advertising
Keith Gretton,
26 Honeywell Road,
London SW11 6EG
Tel: 020 7228 0741
Advertising items.

Old Cinema, The
160 Chiswick High Road,
London W4 1PR
Tel: 020 8995 8801
Mob: 0777 5945482
Antique furniture from the 18th and 19th centuries.

Old Cinema Antiques Warehouse, The (ref: Old Cinema)
157 Tower Bridge Road,
London SE1 3LW
Tel: 020 7407 5371
Fax: 020 7403 0359
www.antiques-uk.co.uk
Victorian, Edwardian, reproduction furniture, babies' chairs, telephone boxes, and reproduction leather Chesterfields.

Old Father Time Clock Centre (ref: Old Father Time)
101 Portobello Road,
London W11 2QB
Tel: 020 8546 6299
Fax: 020 8546 6299
www.oldfathertime.net
Unusual and quirky clocks.

Old School
130c Junction Road,
Tufnell Park, London N19
Tel: 020 7272 5603
Gardens and interiors.

Old Telephone Company, The (ref: Old Telephone Co.)
The Battlesbridge Antiques Centre,
The Old Granary, Battlesbridge,
Essex SS11 7RE
Tel: 01245 400 601
www.theoldtelephone.co.uk
Antique and collectable telephones.

Old Tool Chest, The (ref: Old Tool Chest)
41 Cross Street,
London N1 0PG
Tel: 020 7359 9313
Ancient and modern tools of all trades, woodworking, dentistry, veterinary, mason's, and books.

Old World Trading Co (ref: Old World)
565 Kings Road,
London SW6 2EB
Tel: 020 7731 4708
Fax: 020 7731 1291
18th- and 19th-century English and French chimney places, fire dogs and grates.

Oliver-Sutton Antiques
34c Kensington Church St,
London W8 4HA
Tel: 020 7937 0633
Staffordshire pottery figures.

Oola Boola Antiques London (ref: Oola Boola)
166 Tower Bridge Road,
London SE1 3LS
Tel: 020 7403 0794
Fax: 020 7403 8405
Victorian, Edwardian, Art Nouveau, Art Deco, and Arts and Crafts furniture.

Jacqueline Oosthuizen Antiques (ref: J. Oosthuizen)
23 Cale Street,
Chelsea, London SW3 3QR
Tel: 020 7352 6071
Fax: 020 7376 3852
Staffordshire pottery and jewellery.

Pieter Oosthuizen (ref: P. Oosthuizen)
Unit 4,
Bourbon Hanby Antiques Centre,
151 Sydney Street,
London SW3
Tel: 020 7460 3078
Fax: 020 7376 3852
Dutch and European Art Nouveau pottery and Boer War memorabilia.

Oriental Bronzes Ltd
96 Mount Street,
London W1Y 5HF
Tel: 020 7493 0309
Fax: 020 7629 2665
Chinese archaeology.

Oriental Rug Gallery Ltd (ref: Oriental Rug)
Eton Group Office,
115–116 High Street, Eton,
Berkshire SL4 6AN
Tel: 01753 623000
rug@orientalruggallery.com
Antique carpets, rugs and cushions.

Ormonde Gallery (ref: Ormonde)
156 Portobello Road,
London W11 2EB
Tel: 020 7229 9800
frankormondegallery.com
Oriental ceramics, furniture, sculpture and works of art.

Paul Orssich
2 St Stephens Terrace,
London SW8 1DH
Tel: 020 7787 0030
Fax: 020 7735 9612
www.orssich.com
Maps and 20,000 rare secondhand books.

Fay Orton Antiques (ref: Fay Orton)
First Floor, 533 Kings Road,
London SW10 0TZ
Tel: 020 7352 2046
Furniture.

Anthony Outred Antiques Ltd (ref: Anthony Outred)
46 Pimlico Road,
London SW1 8LP
Tel: 020 7730 4782
Fax: 020 7730 5643 fax
antiques@outred.co.uk
www.outred.co.uk
English and continental antiques.

John Owen (ref: John Owen)
Great Grooms Antiques Centre,
Hungerford,
Berkshire RG17 OEP
Furniture from the 18th century.

Pacifica
Block 7, 479 Park West Place,
Edgware Road,
London W2
Tel: 020 7402 6717
Tribal art.

Parker Gallery
28 Pimlico Road,
London SW1W 8LJ
Tel: 020 7730 6768
Fax: 020 7259 9180
www.art-on-line.com/parker
Prints, paintings, watercolours; maps; ship models.

Pars Antiques (ref: Pars)
35 St George Street,
London W1R 9FA
Tel: 020 7491 9889
Fax: 020 7493 9344
Antiquities.

Payne & Son (Goldsmiths) Ltd
131 High Street,
Oxford,
Oxfordshire OX1 4DH
Tel: 01865 243787
Fax: 01865 793241
Jewellery, bijouterie and snuff boxes; silver.

John A. Pearson
Horton Lodge,
Horton Road,
Horton, nr. Slough,
Berkshire SL3 9NU
Tel: 01753 682136
Antiquities and works of art; furniture; porcelain, pottery and enamels; valuations.

Pelham Galleries Ltd
24 & 25 Mount Street,
London W1Y 5RB
Tel: 020 7629 0905
Fax: 020 7495 4511
Furniture; antiques and works of art; clocks and barometers; musical instruments; tapestries, needlework and fabrics; Oriental works of art.

Pendulum of Mayfair
King House, 51 Maddox Street,
London W1R 9LA
Tel: 020 7629 6606
Fax: 020 7629 6616
Clocks: including longcase, bracket and wall, and Georgian period furniture.

Percy's Ltd
16 The London Silver Vaults,
Chancery Lane,
London WC2A 1QS
Tel: 020 7242 3618
Fax: 020 7831 6541
18th- and 19th-century decorative silver and plate.

Period Pieces
Solihull,
West Midlands
Tel: 0121 709 1205
Mob: 07778 452539
susanshaw50@hotmail.com
Antique boxes.

David Pettifer Ltd
73 Glebe Place,
London SW3 4JB
Tel: 020 7352 3088
Fax: 020 7352 4088
Furniture; works of art; glass pictures; bygones.

Phelp
59 Ledbury Road,
London W11 2AA
Tel: 020 7727 7915
Old master drawings – 16th- and 17th-century European figures and busts.

Ronald Phillips Ltd
26 Bruton Street,
London W1X 8LH
Tel: 020 7493 2341
Fax: 020 7495 0843
18th- and early 19th-century English furniture; clocks and barometers; works of art.

Trevor Phillips & Son Ltd (ref: T. Phillips)
75a Jermyn Street,
London SW1Y 6NP
Tel: 020 7930 2954
Fax: 020 7321 0212
www.trevorphilip.demon.co.uk
Early scientific instruments, and 17th- to 19th-century globes.

Photographer's Gallery, The (ref: Photo. Gallery)
5 Great Newport Street,
London WC2H 7HY
Tel: 020 7831 1772
Fax: 020 7836 9704
www.photonet.org.uk

David Pickup Antiques (ref: David Pickup)
115 High Street, Burford,
Oxfordshire OX18 4RG
Tel: 01993 822555
Fine English furniture, emphasis on the Cotswold Arts and Crafts movement and early 20th century.

Pieces of Time
Units 17–19, 1–7 Davies Mews,
London W1Y 2LP
info@antique-watch.com
Antique and precision pocket watches; Judaica.

Pillows of Bond Street (ref: Pillows)
Bond Street,
London W11
Tel: 0468 947265
Pillows.

Pimlico Antiques (ref: Pimlico)
Moreton Street,
London SW1
Tel: 020 7821 8448
Furniture, works of art and paintings.

W.A. Pinn & Sons
124 Swan Street,
Sible, Hedingham,
Essex CO9 3HP
Tel: 01787 461127
Furniture, clocks and barometers, antique lighting.

A. Piotrowski
Bourbon-Hanby Antiques Centre,
151 Sydney Street,
London SW3 6NT
Tel: 020 7352 2106
Fax: 020 7565 0003
www.antiques-uk.co.uk/bourbon-hanby
English ceramics.

Nicholas S. Pitcher Oriental Art (ref: Nicholas S. Pitcher)
1st Floor, 29 New Bond Street,
London W1Y 9HD
Tel: 020 7499 6621
Fax: 020 7499 6621
Early Chinese ceramics and works of art.

Planet Bazaar
151 Drummond Street,
London NW1 2PB
Tel: 020 7387 8326
Fax: 020 7387 8326
www.planetbazaar.co.uk
Designer furniture, art, glass, lighting, ceramics, books and eccentricities from the 1950s to 1980s.

Poppets Antiques (ref: Poppets)
Bourbon Hanby Antiques Centre,
151 Sydney Street,
London SW3 6NT
Tel: 020 7352 2108
19th-century furniture.

Jonathan Potter Ltd
1st Floor, 125 New Bond St,
London W1Y 9AF
Tel: 020 7491 3520
Fax: 020 7491 9754;
jpmaps@ibm.net
Maps and atlases; books and manuscripts; valuations.

Christopher Preston Ltd (ref: C. Preston)
The Furniture Cave, 533 Kings Road,
London SW10 0TZ
Tel: 020 7352 4229
Antique furniture and decorative objects.

Pritchard Antiques at Christopher Preston Ltd
Furniture Cave, 533 Kings Road,
London SW10 0TZ
Tel: 020 7352 8587
Fax: 020 7376 3627
18th- and 19th-century furniture.

Annette Puttnam
Norton House,
Nr. Lewes, Iford,
Sussex BN7 3EJ
Tel: 01273 483366
Fax: 01273 483366

Bernard Quaritch Ltd
5–8 Lower John Street,
Golden Square,
London W1R 4AU
Tel: 020 7734 2983
Fax: 020 7437 0967
rarebooks@quaritch.com;
www.quaritch.com
Rare books and manuscripts.

Radio Days
87 Lower Marsh,
London SE1 7AB
Tel: 020 7928 0800
Fax: 020 7928 0800
Lighting, telephones, radios, clothing, magazines and cocktail bars from the 1930s–1970s.

Raffety Walwyn
79 Kensington Church Street,
London W8 4BG
Tel: 020 7938 1100
Fax: 020 7938 2519
www.raffetyantiqueclocks.com
Fine antique clocks.

Rainbow Antiques (ref: Rainbow)
329 Lillie Road,
London SW6 7NR
Tel: 020 7385 1323
Fax: 0870 052 1693
Italian and French period lighting from 1880–1940, chandeliers, lamps and lanterns.

Ranby Hall Antiques (ref: Ranby Hall)
Barnby Moor, Retford,
Nottingham DN22 8JQ
Tel: 01777 860696
Fax: 01777 701317
www.ranbyhall.antiques-gb.com
Antiques, decorative items and contemporary objects.

R. & S. Antiques
Bourbon Hanby Antiques Centre,
151 Sydney Street, Chelsea,
London SW3 6NT
Tel: 020 73522106
Fax: 020 7565 0003

Mark Ransom Ltd (ref: Mark Ransom)
62 and 105 Pimlico Road,
London SW1W 8LS
Tel: 020 7259 0220
Fax: 020 7259 0323
Decorative Empire and French furniture.

Rasoul Gallery
South Asian Antiques,,
K34/35 Grays Antiques
1–7 Davies Mews,
London W1Y 2LP
Tel: 020 7495 7422
Mob: 07956 809760
rasoulgallerya@hotmail.com
Islamic ceramics and antiquities.

Derek and Tina Rayment Antiques
Orchard House, Barton Road,
Barton, nr. Farndon,
Cheshire SY14 7HT
Tel: 01829 270429
Open by appointment. Specialists in 18th- and 19th-century English and continental barometers; valuation.

RBR Group at Grays (ref: RBR Group)
Stand 175, Grays Antiques Market,
58 Davies Street,
London W1Y 2LP
Tel: 020 7629 4769
Jewellery and objects.

William Redford
PO Box 17770,
London W8 5ZB
Tel: 020 7376 1825
Fax: 020 7376 1825
Continental furniture; works of art.

Red Lion Antiques (ref: Red Lion)
New Street,
Petworth,
West Sussex GU28 0AS
Tel: 01798 344485
Fax: 01798 342367
www.redlion-antiques.com
17th- to 19th-century furniture.

Gordon Reece Gallery (ref: Gordon Reece)
16 Clifford Street,
London W1X 1RG
Tel: 020 7439 0007
Fax: 020 7437 5715
www.gordonreecegalleries.com
Flat woven rugs and nomadic carpets, tribal sculpture, jewellery, furniture, decorative and non-European folk art especially ethnic and oriental ceramics.

Reel Poster Gallery
72 Westbourne Grove,
London W2 5SH
Tel: 020 7727 4488
Fax: 020 7727 4499
www.reelposter.com
Original vintage film posters.

Reel Thing, The
17 Royal Opera Arcade,
Pall Mall,
London SW1Y 4UY
Tel: 020 7976 1830
Fax: 020 7976 1850
www.reelthing.co.uk
Purveyors of vintage sporting memorabilia.

Paul Reeves
32b Kensington Church St,
London W8 4HA
Tel: 020 7937 1594
Fax: 020 7938 2163
Furniture and artefacts 1860–1960.

Resners
124 New Bond Street,
London W1Y 9AE
Tel: 020 7629 1413
Fax: 020 7629 1413
Jewellery, bijouterie and snuff boxes; valuations.

Retro Exchange
20 Pembridge Road,
London W11
Tel: 020 7221 2055
Fax: 020 7727 4185
www.l/fel.trade.co.uk
Space age-style furniture and 1950s kitsch.

Retro Home
20 Pembridge Road,
London W11
Tel: 020 7221 2055
Fax: 020 7727 4185
www.l/fel.trade.co.uk
Bric-a-brac, antique furniture and objects of desire.

A. Rezai Persian Carpets (ref: A. Rezai Persian)
123 Portobello Road,
London W11 2DY
Tel: 020 7221 5012
Fax: 020 7229 6690
Antique oriental carpets, kilims, tribal rugs and silk embroideries.

John Riordan
Great Grooms Antique Centre,
Charnham Street,
Hungerford,
Berkshire RG17 0EP
Tel: 01235 527698
Mob: 0780 8741823
mrjohnriordan@hotmail.com
www.bronzegriffin.com
Bronzes and antique furniture.

Riverbank Gallery Ltd (ref: Riverbank)
High Street, Petworth,
West Sussex GU28 0AU
Tel: 01798 344401
Fax: 01798 343135
Large English 18th- and 19th-century furniture, decorative items, garden furniture and decorative paintings.

Robyn Robb
43 Napier Avenue,
London SW6 3PS
Tel: 020 7731 2878
Fax: 020 7731 2878
18th-century English porcelain.

Derek Roberts Antiques
25 Shipbourne Road,
Tonbridge,
Kent TN10 3DN
Tel: 01732 358986
Fax: 01732 771842
Clocks and barometers; music boxes; some furniture.

J. Roger (Antiques) Ltd
London W14 0RR
Tel: 020 7381 2884
Tel: 020 7603 7627
18th- and early 19th-century furniture, especially small elegant pieces; prints; porcelain; decorative items.

Brian Rolleston (Antiques) Ltd
104a Kensington Church St,
London W8 4BU
Tel: 020 7229 5892
Fax: same
18th-century English furniture.

Rookery Farm Antiques and Sara Lemkow (ref: Rookery Farm)
12 Camden Passage,
London N1 8ED
Tel: 020 7359 0190
Fax: 020 7704 2095
Mob: 07798 920060
Rachel.lemko@btinternet.com
www.antique-kitchenalia.co.uk
Kitchenalia and pine furniture.

Michele Rowan
V38 Antiquarias Antiques Market,
135 Kings Road,
London SW3 4PW
Tel: 020 7352 8744
Fax: 020 7352 8744
Antique jewellery.

Malcolm Rushton
Studio 3, 13 Belsize Grove,
London NW3 4UX
Tel: 020 7722 1989
Early oriental art.

Russell Rare Books
81 Grosvenor Street,
London W1X 9DE
Tel: 020 7629 0532
Fax: 020 7499 2983
www.folios.co.uk
Rare books.

Georgina Ryder & Piers Pisani
The Music House,
The Green, Sherborne,
Dorset DT9 3HX
Tel: 01935 815209
Fax: 01935 815209
Mob: 07785 391710
antiques@pierspisani@sarghost.co.uk
Country house antiques from England and France.

Frank T. Sabin Ltd
13 The Royal Arcade,
Old Bond Street,
London W1X 3HB
Tel: 020 7493 3288
Fax: 020 7499 3593
18th- and 19th-century English sporting and decorative engravings.

Salem Antiques
Great Grooms Antiques Centre,
Hungerford,
Berkshire RG17 0EP
Tel: 01488 682314
Furniture from the 18th century.

Samiramis
M14–16 Grays Mews Antiques Market,
1–7 Davies Mews,
London W1Y 1FJ
Tel: 020 7629 1161
Fax: 020 7493 5106
Islamic pottery, silver, Eastern items and calligraphy.

Alistair Sampson Antiques Ltd
120 Mount Street,
London W1Y 5HB
Tel: 020 7409 1799
Fax: 020 7409 7717
17th- and 18th-century English furniture; metalwork and English brass; primitive paintings; 17th- and 18th-century English pottery and Delftware; Chinese porcelain and works of art; needlework

Patrick Sandberg Antiques
140–142 and 150–152 Kensington,
Church Street,
London W8 4BN
Tel: 020 7229 0373
Fax: 020 7792 3467
18th- and early 19th-century English furniture

A.V. Santos
1 Camden Street,
London W8 7EP
Tel: 020 7727 4872
Fax: 020 7229 4801
Chinese export porcelain.

Seago
22 Pimlico Road,
London SW1W 8LJ
Tel: 020 7730 7502
Fax: 020 7730 9179
17th-, 18th- and 19th-century garden ornament and sculpture; works of art; valuations.

Christopher F. Seidler (ref: C.F. Seidler)
G13 Grays Mews Antiques Market,
1–7 Davies Mews,
London W1Y 2LP
Tel: 020 7629 2851
Medals, arms and militaria.

M. & D. Seligmann
37 Kensington Church Street,
London W8 4LL
Tel: 020 7937 0400
Fax: 020 7722 4315
English country furniture; works of art and unusual items; early English pottery.

Serendipity
Rosemary Ford, The Tythings,
Preston Court, nr Ledbury,
Herefordshire HR8 2LL
Tel: 01531 660245
Mob: 07836 7222411
Traditional antiques, fine English and continental furniture from the 18th and 19th centuries.

Jean Sewell (Antiques) Ltd
3 & 4 Campden Street,
London W8 7EP
Tel: 020 7727 3122
Fax: 020 7229 1053
English, Continental and Oriental porcelain, pottery and enamels.

Shahdad Antiques (ref: Shahdad)
A16–17 Grays-in-Mews,
1–7 Davies Mews,
London W1Y 2LP
Tel: 020 7499 0572
Fax: 020 7629 2176
Islamic and ancient works of art.

Mark Shanks
The Royal Oak,
High Street, Watlington,
Oxfordshire OX9 5QB
Tel: 01491 613 317
Fax: 01491 613 318
Open Monday–Saturday 10–5; at other times by appointment. 17th-, 18th- and 19th-century furniture and barometers.

Bernard J. Shapero Rare Books (ref: Bernard Shapero)
32 George Street,
London W1R 0EA
Tel: 020 7493 0876
Fax: 020 7229 7860
www.shapero.com
Guide books from the 16th to the 20th centuries, antiquarian and rare books, English and continental literature, specialising in travel, natural history and colour plate.

Sharif
27 Chepstow Corner,
London W2 4XE
Tel: 020 7792 1861
Fax: 020 7792 1861
Oriental rugs, kilims, textiles and furniture.

Anthony Sharpe
16 Craven Hill Mews,
London W2 3DY
Tel: 020 7706 2118
s@anthonysharpe.com
19th-century lighting, bronzes, screens and tôle lighting. By appt. only.

Nicholas Shaw Antiques (ref: N. Shaw)
Great Grooms Antique Centre,
Parbrook, Billinghurst,
West Sussex RH14 9EU
Tel: 01403 786 656
Fax: 01403 786 656
www.nicholas-shaw.com
Scottish and Irish fine silver, small silver and collector's items.

Shiraz Antiques (ref: Shiraz)
1 Davies Mews,
London W1Y 1AR
Tel: 020 7495 0635
Fax: 020 7495 0635
Asian art, antiquities, glass, marble and pottery.

S.J. Shrubsole Ltd
43 Museum Street,
London WC1A 1LY
Tel: 020 7405 2712
Antique silver of the Georgian and early periods; also a large collection of interesting old Sheffield plate.

Sieff
49 Long Street,
Tetbury,
Gloucestershire, GL8 8AA
Tel: 01666 504477
Fax: 01666 504478
18th- and 19th-century French provincial fruitwood, and some 20th-century furniture.

Sign of the Times
St Oswalds Mews,
London N6 2UT
Tel: 020 7584 3842
www.antiquesline.com
Furniture, decorative metalware and glass.

B. Silverman
26 London Silver Vaults,
Chancery Lane,
London WC2A 1QS
Tel: 020 7242 3269
Fax: 020 7430 7949
www.silverman-london.com
17th- to 19th-century fine English silverware and silver flatware.

Jack Simons Antiques Ltd (ref: Jack Simons)
37 The London Silver Vaults,
Chancery Lane,
London WC2A 1QS
Tel: 020 7242 3221
Fax: 020 7831 6541
Fine antique English and continental silver and objets d'art.

Oswald Simpson
Hall Street,
Long Melford,
Suffolk CO10 9JL
Tel: 01787 377523
17th- to 19th-century oak and country furniture; samplers; Staffordshire pottery; metalwork.

Sinai Antiques (ref: Sinai)
219–221 Kensington Church Street,
London W8 7LX
Tel: 020 7229 6190
Antiques and works of art.

Gloria Sinclair
Stand F023, Alfie's Antique Market,
25 Church Street,
London NW8 8DT
Tel: 020 7724 7118
European ceramics.

Sladmore Sculpture Gallery Ltd
32 Bruton Place,
Berkeley Square,
London W1X 7AA
Tel: 020 7499 0365
Fax: 020 7409 1381
Fine 19th- and 20th-century sporting and animal bronze sculpture.

Sleeping Beauty
579–581 Kings Road,
London SW6 2DY
Tel: 020 7471 4711
Fax: 020 7471 4795
www.antiquebeds.com
Antique beds.

Ruth Macklin Smith (ref: R. Macklin Smith)
Great Grooms Antiques Centre,
Hungerford,
Berkshire RG17 OEP
Antique furniture.

Julian Smith Antiques (ref: Julian Smith)
Bartlett Street Antique Centre,
Bath
and
The Lodge, Wheelwrights Close,
Sixpenny Handley,
Dorset SP5 5SA
Tel: 01725 552 820
Mob: 07879 624734
Luggage and gentlemen's accessories.

Solamani Gallery
Gray's Antiques Centre, Stand A20,
1–7 Davies Mews,
London W1Y 2LP
Tel: 020 7491 2562
Mob: 07956 546468
Islamic ceramics.

Solaris Antiques (ref: Solaris)
170 Westbourne Grove,
London W11 2RW
Tel: 020 7229 8100
Fax: 020 7229 8300
Decorative antiques from France and Sweden, from all periods up to 1970s.

Somervale Antiques (ref: Somervale)
6 Radstock Road,
Midsomer Norton,
Bath BA3 2AJ
Tel: 01761 4122686
ronthomas@
somervaleantiquesglass.co.uk
www.somervaleantiquesglass.co.uk
English, Bristol and Nailsea glass. Shop open by appt. only, 24-hour telephone service.

Something Different
254 Holloway Road,
London N7 6NE
Tel: 020 7697 8538
Fax: 020 7697 8538
Individually made African wood and stone sculptures.

Somlo Antiques Ltd (ref: Somlo)
7 Piccadilly Arcade,
London SW1Y 6NH
Tel: 020 7499 6526
Fax: 020 7499 0603
www.somloantiques.com
Vintage wristwatches and antique pocket watches.

David L.H. Southwick
Beacon Lodge, Beacon Lane,
Kingswear, Devon TQ6 0BU
Tel: 01803 752533
Fax: 01803 752535
Oriental ceramics and works of art.

A. & J. Speelman Ltd
Oriental Art
129 Mount Street,
London W1Y 5HA
Tel: 020 7499 5126
Fax: 020 7355 3391
Oriental ceramics and works of art; valuations.

Ian Spencer
17 Godfrey Street,
London SW3 3TA
Large desks, sets of chairs and dining tables.

Spink
21 King Street,
St James's, London SW1Y 6QY
Tel: 020 7930 5500
Fax: 020 7930 5501
lengtan@spinkandson.com
Indian, Himalayan, south-east Asian and Islamic art; textiles; valuations.

Spink & Son Ltd
69 Southampton Row,
Bloomsbury, London WC1B 4ET
Tel: 020 7563 4000
Fax: 020 7563 4066
info@spinkandson.com
www.spink-online.com
Coins and banknotes; stamps; orders, decorations, campaign medals and militaria; numismatic; war medals and related books; valuations.

Sporting Times
Unit C 2A, Fitzaarland Road,
Arundel, West Sussex BN18 9JS
Tel: 01903 885656
Mob: 07976 9422059
MartinQ.Sportingtimes.isnet.co.uk
www.sportingtimes.co.uk
Antique sporting items.

Stair & Company Ltd
14 Mount Street,
London W1Y 5RA
Tel: 020 7499 1784
Fax: 020 7629 1050
18th-century English furniture and works of art.

Louis Stanton
299–301 Westbourne Grove,
London W11 2QA
Tel: 020 7727 9336
Fax: 020 7727 5424
16th- to 19th-century furniture, specialising in early oak; medieval sculpture and works of art; curiosities; metalwork and pewter; valuations.

Star Signings
Unit A18–A19 Grays Mews
Antiques Market,
1–7 Davies Mews,
London W1Y 2LP
Tel: 020 7491 1010
Fax: 020 7491 1070
Sporting autographs and memorabilia.

Steinway & Sons
(ref: Steinway)
44 Marylebone Lane,
London W1M 6EN
Tel: 020 7487 3391
Fax: 020 7935 0466
New and refurbished pianos.

Steppes Hill Farm Antiques
Steppes Hill Farm,
Stockbury, Sittingbourne,
Kent ME9 7RB
Tel: 01795 842205
Porcelain, pottery and enamels; silver and old Sheffield plate; valuations.

Jane Stewart
C 26–27, Grays Mews Antiques Market,
1–7 Davies Mews,
London W1Y 2LP
Early 17th- to 19th-century pewter, oak and writing slopes.

Constance Stobo
31 Holland Street,
London W8 4HA
Tel: 020 7937 6282
18th- and 19th-century pottery, English lustre ware, and Staffordshire animals.

Colin Stock
8 Mossborough Road,
Rainford, St Helens,
Merseyside WA11 8QN
Tel: 0174 488 2246
18th- and early 19th-century furniture.

Stockspring Antiques
(ref: Stockspring)
114 Kensington Church Street,
London W8 4BH
Tel: 020 7727 7995
stockspring@porcelain.co.uk
www.antique-porcelain.co.uk
Antique English and continental porcelain.

Jacob Stodel
Brook Street Mansion, Flat 4,
41 Davies Street,
London W1Y 1FJ
Tel: 020 7491 7717
Fax: 020 7491 9813
18th-century English and continental furniture; Oriental and European ceramics and works of art.

June & Tony Stone
(ref: J. & T. Stone)
75 Portobello Road,
London W11 2QB
Tel: 020 7221 1121
Fine antique boxes.

Strike One (Islington) Ltd
48A Highbury Hill,
London N5 1AP
Tel: 020 7354 2790
Fax: 020 7354 2790
Clocks and barometers; music boxes; valuations.

Studio 2000
4 Pierrepont Row Arcade,
Camden Passage,
London N1 8EF
Tel: 020 7359 4127 or 01733 244717
Pottery.

Succession
18 Richmond Hill,
Richmond, Surrey TW10 6QX
Tel: 020 8940 6774
Art Nouveau, Art Deco, furniture, bronzes, glass and pictures.

Sugar Antiques
(ref: Sugar)
8–9 Pierrepont Arcade,
Camden Passage,
London N1 8EF
Tel: 020 7354 9896
Fax: 020 8931 5642
www.sugarantiques.com
Wristwatches, pocketwatches, costume jewellery, lighters, fountain pens and small collectables.

Mark Sullivan
14 Cecil Court,
London WC2N 4EZ
Tel: 020 7836 7056
Fax: 020 8287 8492
Antiques and decorative items.

Sultani Antiques Ltd
(ref: Sultani)
Unit K29, Gray's Antique Centre,
1–7 Davies Mews,
London W1Y 1AR
Tel: 020 7491 3842
Mob: 07956 814 541
Islamic ceramics and antiquities.

Summers Davis Antiques Ltd
Calleva House,
6 High Street,
Wallingford,
Oxfordshire OX10 0BP
Tel: 01491 836284
Fax: 01491 833443
English and continental furniture of the 17th to 19th centuries.

Swan at Tetsworth, The
(ref: The Swan)
High Street,
Tetsworth, Thame,
Oxfordshire OX9 7AB
Tel: 01844 281777
Fax: 01844 281770
www.theswan.co.uk
Seventy dealers in historic Elizabethan coaching inn.

Sweerts de Landas
Dunsborough Park,
Ripley,
Surrey GU23 6AL
Tel: 01483 225366
Fax: 01483 224525
Antique.Collectors-on-line.com
/dealers/sweerts
Antique garden ornament.

Tadema Gallery
10 Charlton Place,
Camden Passage,
London N1 8AJ
Tel: 020 7359 1055
Fax: 020 7359 1055
Jewellery: Art Nouveau, Arts and Crafts and Art Deco.

Talbot
65 Portobello Road,
London W11 2QB
Tel: 020 8969 7011
Fine scientific instruments.

Talking Machine, The
(ref: Talk. Mach.)
30 Watford Way,
London NW4 3AL
Tel: 020 8202 3473
www.gramophones.endirect.co.uk
Mechanical antiques: typewriters, radios, music boxes, photographs, sewing machines, juke boxes, calculators and televisions.

Taurus Antiques Ltd
(ref: Taurus)
The Forge, rear of 39 Chancery Lane,
Beckenham,
Kent BR3 2NR
Tel: 020 8650 9179
Mob: 04689 48421
Furniture.

Telephone Lines Ltd
(ref: Telephone Lines)
304 High Street,
Cheltenham,
Gloucestershire GL50 3JF
Tel: 01242 583699
Fax: 01242 690033
Telephones.

Templar Antiques
(ref: Templar)
28 The Hall Antiques Centre,
359 Upper Street,
London N1 0PD
Tel: 020 7704 9448
Fax: 01621 819737
www.templar-antiques.co.uk
18th- and 19th-century glass, English, Irish and Bohemian.

Temple Gallery
6 Clarendon Cross,
Holland Park, London W11 4AP
Tel: 020 7727 3809
Fax: 020 7727 1546
www.templegallery.com
Russian and Greek icons, from 12th to 16th centuries.

Tessiers Ltd
26 New Bond Street,
London W1Y 0JY
Tel: 020 7629 0458
Fax: 020 7629 1857
Jewellery, silver and boxes; valuations.

Themes & Variations
(ref: Themes)
231 Westbourne Grove,
London W11 2SE
Tel: 020 7727 5531
Post-War design.

Thimble Society, The
(ref: Thimble Society)
Geoffrey van Arcade,
107 Portobello Road,
London W11 2QB
Tel: 020 7419 9562
Thimbles, sewing items, snuff boxes and lady's accessories.

30th Century Comics
17 Lower Richmond Road,
London SW15 1JP
Tel: 020 8788 2052
rob@thirtiethcentury.free-online.co.uk
www.thirtiethcentury.free-online.co.uk

Thompson Antiques
Tel: 01306 711970
Fax: same
Mob: 07770 882746
By appointment only. Tortoiseshell, ivory, silver, enamels and papier mâché.

Sue & Alan Thompson
(ref: S. & A. Thompson)
Highland Cottage,
Broomne Hall Road,
Cold Harbout RH5 6HH
Tel: 01306 711970
Fax: 01306 711970
Objects of vertu, antique tortoiseshell items, period furniture and unusual collector's items.

Through the Looking Glass
(ref: Looking Glass)
563 Kings Road,
London SW6 2EB
Tel: 020 7736 7799
Fax: 020 7602 3678
19th-century mirrors.

Through the Looking Glass
(ref: Looking Glass)
137 Kensington Church Street,
London W8 7LP
Tel: 020 7221 4026
Fax: 020 7602 3678
19th-century mirrors.

William Tillman Ltd
30 St James's Street,
London SW1A 1HB
Tel: 020 7839 2500
Fax: 020 7930 8106
18th- and early 19th-century English furniture and works of art.

S. & S. Timms Antiques Ltd
2/4 High Street,
Shefford,
Beds SG17 5DG
Tel: 01462 851051
Fax: 01462 817047
Mob: 07860 482995
Sstimms@tesco.net
Antique furniture.

Tin Tin Collectables
(ref: Tin Tin)
Ground Units 38–42, Antiques Market,
13–25 Church Street,
London NW8 8DT
Tel: 020 7258 1305
www.tintincollectables.com
Handbags, from Victorian to present day, decorative evening bags and luggage.

Jacqueline Toffler Pruskin
32 Ledbury Road,
London W11 2AB
Tel: 020 7221 2306
Fax: 020 7221 2306
Mob: 07971818776
Decorative arts of the 19th and 20th centuries.

Tool Shop, The
(ref: Tool Shop)
High Street,
Needham Market,
Suffolk IP6 8AW
Tel: 01449 722992
Fax: 01449 722683
www.toolshop.demon.co.uk
Antique and usable carpenter's and joiner's tools.

Tool Shop Auctions
78 High Street,
Needham Market,
Suffolk IP6 8AW
Tel: 01449 722992
www.uktoolshop.com
Auctioneers and dealers of antique woodworking tools and new Japanese, French and American tools.

Tower Bridge Antiques
(ref: Tower Bridge)
159–161 Tower Bridge Road,
London SE1 3LW
Tel: 020 7403 3660
Fax: 020 7403 6058

Town & Country Antiques
(ref: Town & Country)
88 Fulham Road,
London SW3 1HR
Tel: 020 7589 0660
Fax: 020 7823 7618
www.anthony-james.com
English furniture.

Travers Antiques
71 Bell Street,
London NW1 6SX
Tel: 020 7723 4376
Furniture and decorative items from 1820 to 1920.

Tredantiques
77 Hill Barton Road,
Whipton,
Exeter EX1 3PW
Tel: 01392 447082
Fax: 01392 462200
Furniture.

Trio/Teresa Clayton
(ref: Trio)
L24 Grays Mews Antiques Market,
1–7 Davies Mews,
London W1Y 2LP
Tel: 020 7493 2736
Fax: 020 7493 9344
Perfume bottles and Bohemian glass.

Turn On Lighting
116–118 Islington High Street,
Camden Passage,
London N1 8EG
Tel: 020 7359 7616
Fax: 020 7359 7616
Antique lighting specialists.

Vale Antiques
Great Grooms Antiques Centre,
Hungerford,
Berkshire RG 17 OEP
Tel: 01488 682314
Antique furniture.

Earle D. Vandekar of Knightsbridge
305 East 61st Street,
New York, NY 10021, USA
Tel: 001 212 308 2022
Fax: 001 212 308 2105
Fine 18th- and 19th-century ceramics; furniture; portrait miniatures and works of art.

James Vanstone
Unit 66 Admiral Vernan Arcade,
147 Portobello Road,
London W11 2QB
Tel: 020 8541 4707
Mob: 07050 153018
Specialist in coins and medals.

Ventesimo
Unit S001, Alfie's Antique Market,
13–25 Church Street,
London NW8 8DT
Mob: 07767 498766
20th-century ceramics, glass and lighting.

Vintage and Rare Guitars
(ref: Vintage Guitars)
68 Kenway Road,
London SW5 ORA
Tel: 020 7370 7834 / 6828
Fax: 020 7240 7500
Vintage and rare guitars.

Vintage Wireless Shop
(ref: Vintage Wireless)
The Hewarths Sandiacre,
Nottingham NG10 5NQ
Tel: 0115 939 3139
Radios.

Michael Wakelin
& Helen Linfield
(ref: Wakelin Linfield)
PO Box 48, Billingshurst,
West Sussex RH14 0YZ
Tel: 01403 700004
Fax: 01403 700004
Metalware, pottery, treen, lighting, textiles and mirrors.

Alan Walker
Halfway Manor,
Halfway, Newbury,
Berkshire, RG20 8NR
Tel: 01488 657 670
Fax: 01488 657 670
Mob: 0370 728 397
Fine antique barometers.

Walker Galleries Ltd
6 Montpellier Gardens,
Harrogate,
North Yorkshire HG1 2TF
Tel: 01423 567933
Fax: 01423 536664
www.harrogateantiques.com
English and continental oil paintings, watercolours and drawings; valuations.

Graham Walpole
The Coach House,
189 Westbourne Grove,
London W11 2SB
Tel: 020 7229 0267
Fax: 020 7727 7584
Small furniture, 18th- and 19th-century dolls' houses, equestrian items, bronzes, pictures and decorative items.

William Walter Antiques Ltd
London Silver Vaults,
Chancery Lane,
London WC2A 1QS
Tel: 020 7242 3248
Fax: 020 7404 1280
Antique silver and old Sheffield plate; valuations.

Wartski Ltd
14 Grafton Street,
London W1X 4DE
Tel: 020 7493 1141
Fax: 020 7409 7448
18th- and 19th-century jewellery; Russian works of art; 18th-century gold boxes; silver.

S.J. Webster-Speakman
52 Halesworth Road,
Reydon, Southwold,
Suffolk IP18 6NR
Tel: 01502 722252
18th- and early 19th-century English furniture; clocks and barometers; valuations.

A.W. Welling
Broadway Barn,
High Street, Ripley,
Surrey GU23 6AQ
Tel: 01483 225384
17th- and 18th-century oak and country furniture.

Mark J. West
Cobb Antiques Ltd,
39B High Street,
Wimbledon Village,
London SW19 5BY
Tel: 020 8946 2811
Fax: 020 8946 2811
Antique.Collectors-on-line.com
/dealers/mjwest
18th- and 19th-century English and continental glass.

Westland & Company
(ref: Westland & Co.)
St. Michael's Church,
The Clergy House,
Mark Street,
London EC2A 4ER
Tel: 020 7739 8094
Fax: 020 7729 3620
www.westland.co.uk
Period fireplaces, architectural elements and panelling.

Westminster Group
Antique Jewellery
(ref: Westminster)
Stand 150, Grays Antiques Market,
58 Davies Street,
London W1Y 2LP
Tel: 020 7493 8672
Fax: 020 7493 8672
Victorian and Edwardian secondhand jewellery and watches.

Wheels of Steel
B10–11 Grays Mews Antiques Market,
1–7 Davies Mews,
London W1Y 2LP
Tel: 020 8505 0450
Fax: 020 7629 2813
Trains and toys.

Whitford Fine Art
(ref: Whitford)
6 Duke Street,
St. James's, London SW1Y 6BN
Tel: 020 7930 9332
Fax: 020 7930 5577
Oil paintings and sculpture, from late 19th century to 20th century; post-War abstract and pop art.

Wilde Ones
283 Kings Road,
Chelsea, London SW3 5EW
Tel: 020 7352 9531
Fax: 020 7349 0828
Jewellery.

Jeff Williams
Grays Antiques Market,
58 Davies Street,
London W1K 5LP
Tel: 020 7629 7034
Toy trains.

Willow Gallery
75 Queens Road,
Weybridge,
Surrey KT13 9UQ
Tel: 01932 846095
British and European Victorian oil paintings.

Peter Wills
Room 4, The Swan Antique Centre,
High Street, Tetsworth, Thame,
Oxfordshire OX9 7AB
Tel: 01844 281 777
Fax: 01844 281 770
Antique furniture.

Rod Wilson
Red Lion,
New Street, Petworth,
West Sussex, GU28 0AS
Tel: 01798 344485
Fax: 01798 342367
Furniture.

O.F. Wilson Ltd
(ref: O.F. Wilson)
Queen's Elm Parade,
Old Church Street,
London SW3 6EJ
Tel: 020 7352 9554
Fax: 020 7351 0765
Continental furniture, French chimney pieces, English painted decorative furniture and mirrors.

Wimpole Antiques
Lynn Lindsay,
Stand 349, Grays Antique Market,
5–8 Davies Street,
London W1K 5LP
Tel: 020 7499 2889
1430@compuserve.com
Antique jewellery.

Witney Antiques
96–100 Corn Street,
Witney,
Oxfordshire OX8 7BU
Tel: 01993 703902
Fax: 01993 779852
17th- and 18th-century English furniture; clocks; works of art; textiles; pewter.

Christopher Wood
20 Georgian House,
10 Bury Street,
St James's, London SW1Y 6AA
Tel: 020 7839 3963
Fax: 020 7839 3963
Victorian, Pre-Raphaelite and European 19th-century paintings, watercolours and drawings; Gothic furniture and Arts and Crafts movement; valuations.

Clifford Wright Antiques Ltd
104–106 Fulham Road,
London SW3 6HS
Tel: 020 7589 0986
Fax: 020 7589 3565
18th- and early 19th-century English furniture and giltwood looking glasses; glass pictures; prints.

Yacobs
Grays Mews Antiques Market,
1–7 Davies Mews,
London W1Y 2LP
Tel: 020 7629 7034
Fax: 020 7493 9344
Islamic art.

D.A. & V.A. Yates
Hewarths,
Sandiacre,
Nottingham NG10 5NQ
Tel: 0115 939 3139
Fax: 0115 949 0180
Mob: 0973 958039

Yazdani Mayfair Gallery
(ref: Yazdani)
128 Mount Street,
Mayfair, London W1Y 5HA
Tel: 020 7491 2789
Fax: 020 7491 3437
Ancient and Islamic art, Islamic ceramics, sculpture and antiquities.

Youll's Antiques
(ref: Youll's)
27–28 Charnham Street,
Hungerford, Berkshire RG17 0EJ
Tel: 01488 682046
Fax: 01488 684335
www.youll.com
English/French furniture from 17th to 20th centuries, porcelain, silver and decorative items.

Robert Young Antiques
68 Battersea Bridge Road,
London SW11 3AG
Tel: 020 7228 7847
Early country furniture, folk art, naïve paintings and treen.

Younger Antiques
(ref: Younger)
Bourbon Hanby Antiques Centre,
151 Sydney Street,
London SW3 6NT
Tel: 020 7352 2106
Antique furniture.

Zakheim
52 Ledbury Road,
London W11
Tel: 020 7221 4977
Russian art from icons to Soviet, architectural, and decorator's items.

Nina Zborowska
Damsels Mill, Paradise, Painswick,
Gloucestershire GL6 6UD
Tel: 01452 812460
Fax: 01452 812912
nina@zborowska.co.uk
Late 19th- and early 20th-century British paintings and drawings, including the St Ives and Bloomsbury Group.

Rainer Zietz Ltd
1a Prairie Street,
London SW8 3PX
Tel: 020 7498 2355
Home: 020 7352 0848
Fax: 020 7720 7745
European works of art and sculpture.

Zoom
Arch 65, Cambridge Grove,
Hammersmith, London W6 OLD
Tel: 0958 372 975
Tel: 07000 966620
Fax: 020 8846 9779
www.retrozoom.com
20th-century furniture, lighting, telephones and works of art.

DIRECTORY OF ANTIQUES CENTRES & MARKETS

BEDFORDSHIRE, BUCKINGHAMSHIRE & HERTFORDSHIRE

Antiques at Wendover Antiques Centre
The Old Post Office,
25 High Street,
Wendover HP22 6DU
Tel: 01296 625335
Dealers: 30

Barkham Antiques Centre
Barkham Street,
Barkham RG40 4PJ
Tel: 0118 9761 355
Fax: 0118 9764 355

Buck House Antiques Centre
47 Wycombe End,
Old Town,
Beaconsfield HP9 1LZ
Tel: 01494 670714

Luton Antiques Centre
Auction House,
Crescent Road,
Luton LU1 2NA
Tel: 01582 405281
Fax: 01582 454080

Woburn Abbey Antiques Centre
Woburn Abbey,
Bedfordshire MK17 9WA
Tel: 01525 290350
Fax: 01525 290271
Dealers: 50

BRISTOL, BATH & SOMERSET

Bartlett Street Antiques Centre
5–10 Bartlett Street,
Bath BA1 2QZ
Tel: 01225 466689
Fax: 01225 444146
Dealers: 50+

Bath Saturday Antiques Market
Walcot Street,
Bath BA1 5BD
Tel: 01225 448263
Fax: 01225.317154
Mob: 083653 4893
Dealers: 70+

CAMBRIDGESHIRE

Fitzwilliam Antique Centre
Fitzwilliam Street,
Peterborough
PE1 2RX
Tel: 01733 565415

Gwydir Street Antiques Centre
Untis 1&2 Dales Brewery,
Gwydir St,
Cambridge CB1 2LJ
Tel: 01223 356391

Hive Antiques Market, The
Unit 3, Dales Brewery,
Gwydir St,
Cambridge CB1 2LG
Tel: 01223 300269

Old Bishop's, The Palace Antique Centre
Tower Road,
Little Downham, Nr Ely,
Cambridgeshire CB6 2TD
Tel: 01353 699177

CHESHIRE

Antique Furniture Warehouse
Unit 3–4 , Royal Oak Buildings,
Cooper Street,
Stockport,
Cheshire SK1 3QJ
Tel: 0161 429 8590
Fax: 0161 480 5375

Knutsford Antiques Centre
113 King Street,
Knutsford WA16 6EH
Tel: 01565 654092

CORNWALL

Chapel Street Antiques Market
61/62 Chapel Street,
Penzance TR18 4AE
Tel: 01736 363267
Dealers: 30–40

Waterfront Antiques Complex
4 Quay Street,
Falmouth,
Cornwall TR11 3HH
Tel: 01326 311491
Dealers: 20–25

THE COTSWOLDS

Antique and Interior Centre, The
51A Long Street,
Malmesbury
GL8 8AA
Tel: 01666 505083
Dealers: 10

CUMBRIA & LANCASHIRE

Carlisle Antiques Centre
Cecil Hall,
46A Cecil Street,
Carlisle CA1 1NT
Tel: 01228 536910
Fax: 01228 536910
carlsle-antiques.co.uk

Cockermouth Antiques Market
Courthouse,
Main Street,
Cockermouth CA15 5XM
Tel: 01900 826746

DERBYSHIRE & NOTTINGHAMSHIRE

Alfreton Antiques Centre
11 King Street,
Alfreton DE55 7AF
Tel: 01773 520781
alfretonantiques@supanet.com

Castle Gate Antiques Centre
55 Castle Gate,
Newark NG24 1BE
Tel: 01636 700076
Fax: 01636 700144
Dealers: 10

Chappells and the Antiques Centre, Bakewell
King Street, DE45 1DZ
Tel: 01629 812 496
Fax: 01629 814 531
bacc@chappells-antiques.co.uk
Dealers: 30

Memory Lane Antiques Centre
Nottingham Road,
Ripley DE5 3AS
Tel: 01773 570184
Dealers: 40–50

Portland Street Antiques Centre
Portland Street,
Newark NG24 4XF
Tel: 01636 674397
Fax: 01636 674397

Top Hat Antiques Centre
70–72 Derby Road,
Nottingham NG1 5DF
Tel: 0115 9419 143
sylvia@artdeco-fairs.co.uk

DEVONSHIRE

Abingdon House
136 High Street,
Honiton EX14 8JP
Tel: 01404 42108
Dealers: 20

Antique Centre on the Quay, The
The Quay,
Exeter EX2 4AP
Tel: 01392 493501
home free.emailamail.co.uk

Barbican Antiques Centre
82–84 Vauxhall Street,
Barbican,
Plymouth PL4 0EX
Tel: 01752 201752
Dealers: 40+

Honiton Antique Centre McBains Antiques
Exeter Airport, Industrial Est.,
Exeter EX5 2BA
Tel: 01392 366261
Fax: 01392 365572
mcbains@netcomuk.co.uk
Dealers:10

Newton Abbot Antiques Centre
55 East Street,
Newton Abbot TQ12 2JP
Tel: 01626 354074
Dealers: 40

Sidmouth Antiques and Collectors Centre
All Saints Road,
Sidmouth EX10 8ES
Tel: 01395 512 588

DORSET

Bridport Antique Centre
5 West Allington,
Bridport DT6 5BJ
Tel: 01308 425885

Colliton Antique Centre
Colliton Street,
Dorchester DT1 1XH
Tel: 01305 269398 / 01305 260115

Emporium Antiques Centre
908 Christchurch Road,
Boscombe,
Bournemouth,
Dorset BH7 6DL
Tel: 01202 422380
Fax: 01202 433348
Dealers: 8

Mattar Antique Centre
Mattar Arcade,
17 Newlands
Sherborne DT9 3JG
Tel: 01935 813464
Fax: 01935 813464

ESSEX

Baddow Antique Centre
The Bringey,
Church Street,
Great Baddow,
Chelmsford,
Essex CM2 7JW
Tel: 01245 476159

Finchingfield Antiques Centre
The Green,
Finchingfield,
Braintree,
Essex CM7 4JX
Tel: 01371 810258
Fax: 01371 810258
Dealers: 45

Harwich Antique Centre
19 King's Quay Street, Harwich, Essex
Tel: 01255 554719
Fax: 01255 554719
harwich@worldwideantiques.co.uk
Dealers: 50

Saffron Walden Antiques Centre
1 Market Row,
Saffron Walden,
Essex CB10 1HA
Tel: 01799 524534
Fax: 01799 524703

HAMPSHIRE & ISLE OF WIGHT

Antique Centre, The
Britannia Road,
Southampton,
Hampshire SO14 0QL
Tel: 0238 0221 022
Dealers: 46

Antique Quarter, The
'Old' Northam Road,
Southampton,
Hampshire SO14 0QL
Tel: 0238 0233 393
Dealers: 15

Dolphin Quay Antique Centre
Queen Street,
Emsworth,
Hampshire PO10 7BU
Tel: 01243 379994
Fax: 01243 379251
enquiriesnancy@netscapeonline.co.uk

Eversley Antique Centre Ltd
Church Lane,
Eversley,
Hook,
Hampshire RG27 0PX
Tel: 0118 932 8518
Dealers: 11

Lyndhurst Antique Centre
19–21 High Street,
Lyndhurst,
Hampshire SO43 7BB
Tel: 0238 0284 000
Dealers: 50

GLOUCESTERSHIRE

Struwwelpeter
The Old School House,
175 London Road,
Charlton Kings,
Cheltenham,
Gloucester GL52 6HN
Tel: 01242 230088
Dealers: 7

HEREFORD & WORCESTERSHIRE

Antique Centre, The
5–8 Lion Street,
Kidderminster,
Worcestershire DY10 1PT
Tel: 01562 740389
Fax: 01562 740389
Dealers: 12

Hereford Antique Centre
128 Widemarsh Street,
Hereford HR4 9HN
Tel: 01432 266242
Dealers: 35

Leominster Antique Centre
34 Broad Street,
Leominster HR6 8BS
Tel: 01568 615505
Dealers: 22

Leominster Antique Market
14 Broad Street,
Leominster HR6 8BS
Tel: 01568 612 189
Dealers: 15+

Linden House Antiques
3 Silver Street,
Stansted CM24 8HA
Tel: 01279 812 373

Malvern Link Antique Centre
154 Worcester Road,
Malvern Link,
Worcestershire WR14 1AA
Tel: 01684 575750
Dealers: 10

Ross on Wye Antique Gallery
Gloucester Road,
Ross on Wye,
Herefordshire HR9 5BU
Tel: 01989 762290
Fax: 01989 762291
Dealers: 91

Worcester Antiques Centre
15 Reindeer Court,
Mealcheapen Street,
Worcester WR1 4DF
Tel: 01905 610680/1
Fax: 01905 610681
Dealers: 45

KENT

Antiques Centre, The
120 London Road,
Tubs Hill TN13 1BA
Tel: 01732 452104

Coach House Antique Centre
2a Duck Lane,
Northgate,
Canterbury,
Kent CT1 2AE
Tel: 01227 463117
Dealers: 7

Copperfield Antique & Craft Centre
Unit 4, Copperfield's Walkway,
Spital Street,
Dartford,
Kent DA1 2DE
Tel: 01322 281445
Dealers: 35

Corn Exchange Antiques Centre
64 The Pantiles,
Tunbridge Wells,
Kent TN2 5TN
Tel: 01892 539652
Fax: 01892 538454
Dealers: 11

Tenterden Antiques Centre
66 High Street
Tunbridge Wells TN30 6AU
Tel: 01580 765885
Fax: 01580 765655
Dealers: 20+

Tunbridge Wells Antique Centre
12 Union Square,
The Pantiles,
Tunbridge Wells TN4 8HE
Tel: 01892 533708
twantique@aol.com

Village Antique Centre
4 High Street, Brasted,
Kent TN16 1RF
Tel: 01959 564545
Dealers: 15

LEICESTERSHIRE, RUTLAND & NORTHAMPTONSHIRE

Finedon Antique (Centre)
11–25 Bell Hill,
Finedon NN9 5NB
Tel: 01933 681260
Fax: 01933 681779
sales@finedonantiques.com

Village Antique Market, The
62 High Street,
Weedon NN7 4QD
Tel: 01327 342 015
Dealers: 40

LINCOLSHIRE

Astra House Antique Centre
Old RAF Helswell,
Nr Caenby Corner,
Gainsborough,
Lincolshire DN21 5TL
Tel: 01427 668312
Dealers: 50

Guardroom Antiques
RAF Station Henswell,
Gainsborough DN21 5TL
Tel: 01427 667113
Dealers: 50

Henswell Antiques Centre
Caenby Corner Estate,
Henswell Cliff,
Gainsborough DN21 5TL
Tel: 01427 668 389
Fax: 01427 668 935
info@Hemswell-antiques.com
Dealers: 270

St. Martin's Antique Centre
23a High Street,
St Martin's,
Stamford PE9 2LF
Tel: 01780 481158
Fax: 01780 766598

Stamford Antiques Centre
The Exchange Hall,
Broad Street,
Stamford PE1 9PX
Tel: 01780 762 605
Fax: 01733 244 717
anoc1900@compuserve.com
Dealers: 40

LONDON

Alfie's Antique Market
13–25 Church Street NW8 8DT
Tel: 020 7723 6066
Fax: 020 7724 0999
alfies@clara.net

Antiquarius
131–41 Kings Road SW3 4PW
Tel: 020 7351 5353
Fax: 020 7351 5350
antique@dial.pipex.com

Bermondsey
corner of Long Lane &
Bermondsey Street, SE1 3UN
Tel: 020 7351 5353

Camden Passage
Upper Street,
Islington N1
Tel: 020 7359 9969
www.camdenpassage.com

Grays Mews Antique Markets
58 Davis Street
and 1–7 Davis Mews WIY 2LP
Tel: 020 7629 7034
Dealers: 300

Hampstead Antique and Craft Market
12 Heath Street NW3 6TE
Tel: 020 7431 0240
Fax: 020 7794 4620
Dealers: 20

Jubilee Market Hall
1 Tavistock Court,
The Piazza,
Covent Garden WC2 E8BD
Tel: 020 7836 2139

Lillie Road
237 Lillie Road SW6
Tel: 020 7381 2500
Fax: 020 7381 8320

Portobello Road
In Notting Hill Gate W10 and W11
Tel: 020 7727 7684
Fax: 020 7727 7684
Dealers: 280

Spitalfields
65 Brushfield Street E1 6AA
Tel: 020 8983 3779
Fax: 020 7377 1783

NORFOLK

Fakenham Antique Centre,
The Old Congregational Church,
14 Norwich Road,
Fakenham,
Norfolk NR21 8AZ
Tel: 01328 862941
Dealers: 20

NORTHUMBERLAND & DURHAM

Village Antique Market, The
62 High Street,
Weedon NN7 4QD
Tel: 01327 342015
Dealers: 40

OXFORDSHIRE

Antique on High Ltd
85 High Street,
Oxford OX1 4BG
Tel: 01865 251075
Fax: 0129 665 5580
Dealers: 38

Country Markets Antiques and Collectables
Country Garden Centre,
Newbury Road,
Chilton,
nr. Didcot OX11 0QN
Tel: 01235 835125
Fax: 01235 833068
countrymarketsantiquesandcollectables
@breathnet.com
Dealers: 35

Old George Inn Antique Galleries
104 High Street,
Burford,
Oxfordshire OX18 4QJ
Tel: 01993 823319
Dealers: 22

Station Mill Antique Centre
Station Yard Industrial Estate,
Chipping Norton,
Oxfordshire OX7 5HX
Tel: 01608 644563
Fax: 01608 644563
Dealers: 73

Swan at Tetsworth
High Street,
Tetsworth,
Oxfordshire OX9 7AB
Tel: 01844 281777
Fax: 01844 281770
antiques@theswan.co.uk
Dealers: 80

SHROPSHIRE

Bridgnorth Antique Centre
Whitburn Street,
Bridgnorth,
Shropshire WV16 4QP
Tel: 01746 768055
Dealers: 19

Old Mill Antique Centre
Mill Street,
Shropshire WV15 5AG
Tel: 01746 768778
Fax: 01746 768944
Dealers: 90

Princess Antique Centre
14a The Square,
Shrewsbury SY1 1LH
Tel: 01743 343701
Dealers: 100 stallholders

Shrewsbury Antique Centre
15 Princess House,
The Square,
Shrewsbury SY1 1UT
Tel: 01743 247 704

Shrewsbury Antique Market
Frankwell Quay Warehouse,
Shrewsbury SY3 8LG
Tel: 01743 350619
Dealers: 30

Stretton Antiques Market
36 Sandford Avenue,
Stretton SY6 6BH
Tel: 01694 723718
Fax: 01694 723718
Dealers: 60

K.W. Swift
56 Mill Street,
Ludlow SY8 1BB
Tel: 01584 878571
Fax: 01746 714407
Dealers: 20, book market.

STAFFORDSHIRE

Lion Antique Centre
8 Market Place,
Uttoxeter,
Staffordshire ST14 8HP
Tel: 01889 567717
Dealers: 28

SUFFOLK

Church Street Centre
6e Church Street,
Woodbridge,
Suffolk IP12 1DH
Tel: 01394 388887
Dealers: 10

Long Melford Antiques Centre
Chapel Maltings, CO10 9HX
Tel: 01787 379287
Fax: 01787 379287
Dealers: 40

Woodbridge Gallery
23 Market Hill,
Woodbridge,
Suffolk IP12 4OX
Tel: 01394 386500
Fax: 01394 386500
Dealers: 35

SURREY

Antiques Centre, The
22 Haydon Place,
Corner of Martyr Road,
Guildford GU1 4LL
Tel: 01483 567817
Dealers: 6

Antiques Warehouse, The
Badshot Farm,
St George's Road,
Runfold GU9 9HY
Tel: 01252 317590
Fax: 01252 879751
Dealers: 40

Enterprise Collectors Market
Station Parade,
Eastbourne,
East Sussex BN21 1BD
Tel: 01323 732690
Dealers: 15

Hampton Court Emporium, The
52–54 Bridge Road,
East Molesey,
Surrey KT8 9HA
Tel: 020 8941 8876
Dealers: 16

Kingston Antiques Market, The
29–31 London Road,
Kingston-upon-Thames,
Surrey KT2 6ND
Tel: 020 8549 2004
Fax: 020 8549 3839
webmaster@antiquesmarket.co.uk
Dealers: 90

Packhouse Antique Centre
Hewetts Kilns,
Tongham Road,
Runfold,
Farnham,
Surrey GU10 1PQ
Tel: 01252 781010
Fax: 01252 783876
hewett@cix.co.uk
Dealers: 80

Victoria and Edward Antique Centre
61 West Street,
Dorking,
Surrey RH4 1BS
Tel: 01306 889645
Dealers: 26

SUSSEX

Almshouses Arcade
19 The Hornet
Chichester PO19 4JL
Tel: 01243 771994

Brighton Flea Market
31A Upper Street,
James's Street BN2 1JN
Tel: 01273 624006
Fax: 01273 328665
arwilkinson@aol.com

Eastbourne Antiques Market
80 Seaside,
Eastbourne BN22 7QP
Tel: 01323 642233
Dealers: 25

Lewes Antique Centre
20 Cliff High Street,
Lewes BN7 2AH
Tel: 01273 476 148 / 01273 472 173
Dealers: 60

Old Town Antiques Centre, The
52 Ocklynge Road,
Eastbourne,
East Sussex BN21 1PR
Tel: 01323 416016
Dealers: 16

Olinda House Antiques
South Street,
Rotherfield,
Crowborough,
East Sussex TN6 3LL,
Tel: 01892 852609

Petworth Antiques Market
East Street,
Petworth GU28 0AB
Tel: 01798 342073
Fax: 01798 344566

WARWICKSHIRE

Barn Antique Centre
Long Marston Ground,
Station Road,
Long Marsdon,
Stratford-upon-Avon CV37 8RB
Tel: 01789 721399
Fax: 01789 721390
barnantiques@aol.com
Dealers: 50

Bidford Antique Centre
Warwick House,
94–96 High Street,
Bidford on Avon,
Alcester,
Warwickshire B50 4AF
Tel: 01789 773680
Dealers: 7

Dunchurch Antique Centre
16a Daventry Road,
Dunchurch,
Rugby CV22 6NS
Tel: 01788 522450
Dealers: 10

Malthouse Antique Centre
4 Market Place,
Alcester,
Warwickshire B49 5AE
Tel: 01789 764032
Dealers: 20

Stables Antique Centre, The
Hatton Country World,
Dark Lane CV35 8XA
Tel: 01926 842405
Dealers: 25

Stratford Antiques and Interiors Centre Ltd
Dodwell Trading Estate,
Evesham Road CV37 9SY
Tel: 01789 297729
Fax: 01789 297710
info@stratfordantiques.co.uk
Dealers: 20

Vintage Antiques Centre
36 Market Place,
Warwick CV34 4SH
Tel: 01926 491527
vintage@globalnet.co.uk
Dealers: 20

Warwick Antiques Centre
22 High Street,
Warwick CV34 4AP
Tel: 01926 491382 / 01926 495704
Dealers: 32

WILTSHIRE

Brocante Antiques Centre
6 London Road,
Marlborough SN8 1PH
Tel: 01672 516512
Fax: 01672 516512
brocante@brocanteantiquescentre.co.uk
Dealers: 20

Marlborough Parade Antique Centre, The
The Parade,
Marlborough SN8 1NE
Tel: 01672 515331
Dealers: 70

YORKSHIRE

Arcadia Antiques Centre
12–14 The Arcade,
Goole,
East Yorkshire DN14 5PY
Tel: 01405 720549
Dealers: 20

Banners Collectables
Banners Business Centre,
Attercliffe Road,
Sheffield,
South Yorkshire S9 3QS
Tel: 0114 244 0742
Dealers: 50

Barmouth Road Antique Centre
Barmouth Court,
off Abbeydale, Sheffield,
South Yorkshire S7 2DH
Tel: 0114 255 2711
Fax: 0114 258 2672
Dealers: 60

Cavendish Antique & Collectors Centre
44 Stonegate,
York YO1 8AS
Tel: 01904 621666
Fax: 01904 644400
Dealers: 60

Halifax Antique Centre
Queens Road,
Halifax,
West Yorkshire HX1 4OR
Tel: 01422 366 657
Fax: 01422 369 293
antiques@halifaxac.u-net.com
Dealers: 30

Harrogate Antiques Centre, The
The Ginnel,
off Parliament Street HG1 2RB
Tel: 01423 508857
Fax: 01423 508857
Dealers: 50

Malton Antique Market
2 Old Maltongate,
Malton YO17 0EG
Tel: 01653 692 732

Pickering Antique Centre
Southgate,
Pickering,
North Yorkshire YO18 8BN
Tel: 01751 477210
Fax: 01751 477210
Dealers: 35

Stonegate Antique Centre
41 Stonegate,
York,
North Yorkshire YO1 8AW
Tel: 01904 613888
Fax: 01904 644400
Dealers: 120

York Antiques Centre
2a Lendal,
York YO1 8AA
Tel: 01904 641445 / 641582
Dealers: 16+

SCOTLAND

Clola Antiques Centre
Shannas School House,
Clola by Mintlaw AB42 8AE
Tel: 01771 624584
Fax: 01771 624584
Dealers: 10

Scottish Antique & Arts Centre
Abernyte PH14 9SJ
Tel: 01828 686401
Fax: 01828 686199

WALES

Antique Market
6 Market Street,
Hay-on-Wye HR3 5AD
Tel: 01497 820175

Cardiff Antiques Centre
10–12 Royal Arcade CF10 2AE
Tel: 01222 398891
Dealers: 13

Chapel Antiques
Methodist Chapel,
Holyhead Road,
Froncysyllte,
Denbighshire,
Llangollen LL20 7RA
Tel: 01691 777624
Fax: 01691 777624
Dealers: 20

Jacobs Antique Centre
West Canal Wharf,
Cardiff C51 5DB
Tel: 01222 390939
Dealers: 50

INDEX

C

D

E

T

WOODS ARECA NUT
6d
TOOTH PASTE
For removing Tartar
and whitening the Teeth
without injuring the Enamel
PROPRIETOR
W. WOODS
CHEMIST
PLYMOUTH
ARTHUR DUKE OF WELLINGTON
SINGER